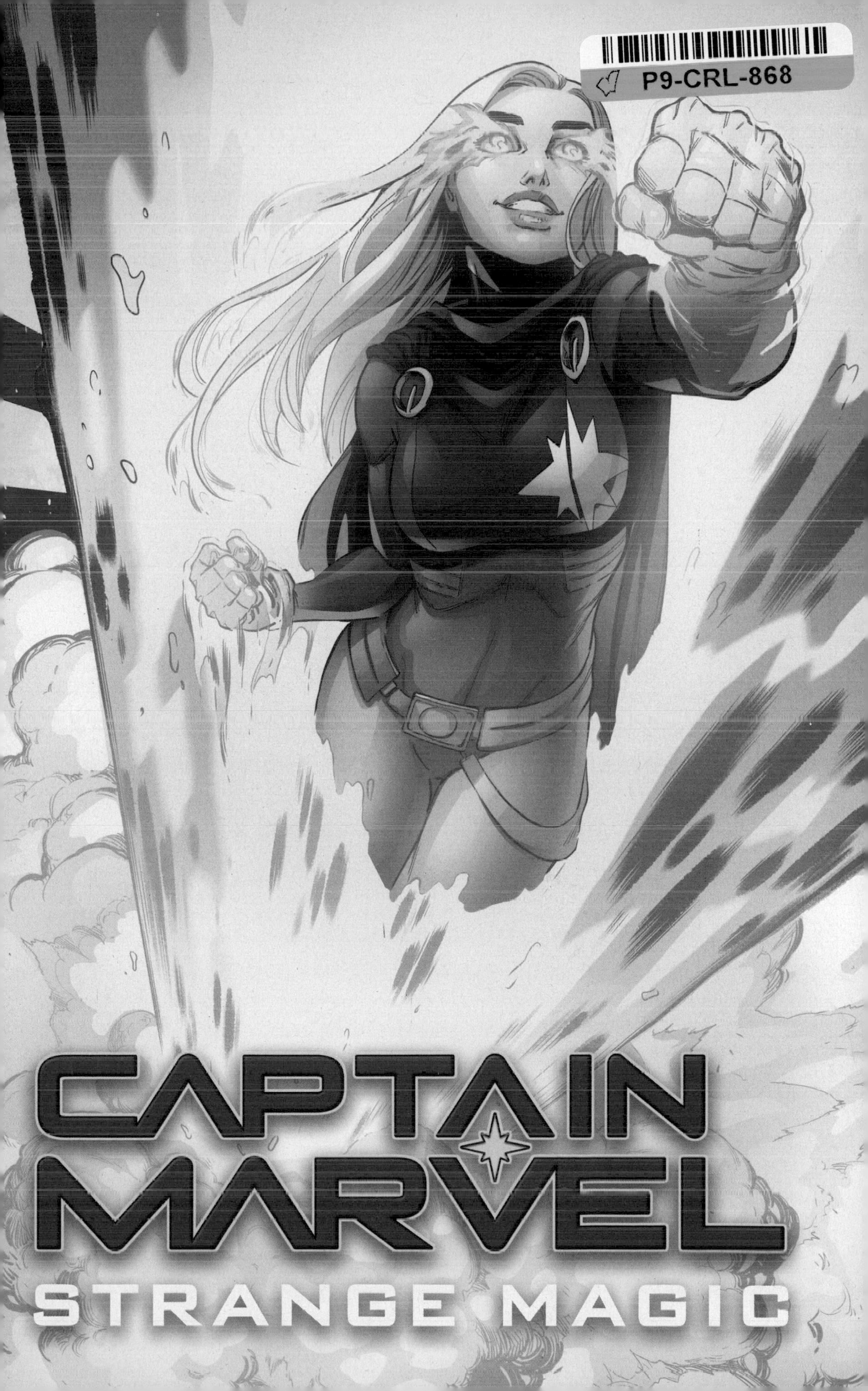
CAPTAIN MARVEL
STRANGE MAGIC

In the middle of a mission, Captain Marvel was magicked away to the apocalyptic world of the year 2052, where the child of Namor and the Enchantress ruled with an iron fist. Carol defeated Ove and his mother, but she is haunted by all those she could not save...

...and one she could. After fighting alongside his future daughter, Carol broke up with Rhodey [a.k.a. War Machine], even though she's still in love with him.

Now back in her own time and newly single, Carol is dealing with the emotional trauma that comes with seeing the end of the world, watching her friends die and losing a love she thought would last forever.

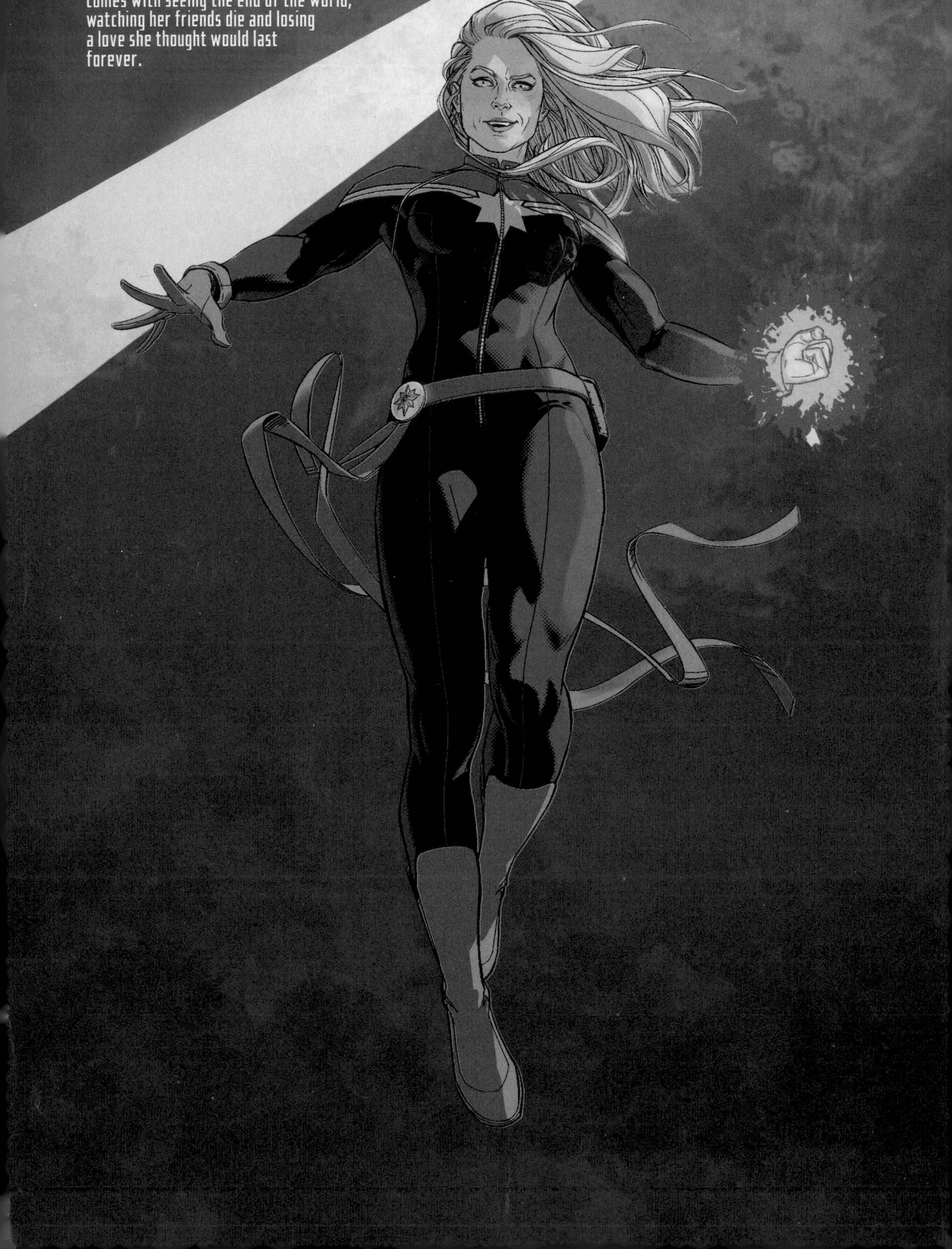

Born to a Kree mother and human father, former U.S. Air Force pilot **CAROL DANVERS** became a super hero when a Kree device activated her latent powers. Now she's an Avenger and Earth's Mightiest Hero.

CAPTAIN MARVEL
STRANGE MAGIC

KELLY THOMPSON
Writer

DAVID LOPEZ [#27] &
JACOPO CAMAGNI [#28-30]
Artists

TRÍONA FARRELL [#27] &
ESPEN GRUNDETJERN [#28-30]
Color Artists

"Ripples"
JAMIE McKELVIE
Writer/Artist/Colors

VC's CLAYTON COWLES
Letterer

MARCO CHECCHETTO
Cover Art

KAT GREGOROWICZ
Assistant Editor

SARAH BRUNSTAD
Editor

WIL MOSS
Senior Editor

Collection Editor: **JENNIFER GRÜNWALD**
Assistant Editor: **DANIEL KIRCHHOFFER**
Assistant Managing Editor: **MAIA LOY**
Assistant Managing Editor: **LISA MONTALBANO**

VP Production & Special Projects: **JEFF YOUNGQUIST**
Book Designers: **ADAM DEL RE** with **CLAYTON COWLES** & **NICK RUSSELL**
SVP Print, Sales & Marketing: **DAVID GABRIEL**
Editor in Chief: **C.B. CEBULSKI**

CAPTAIN MARVEL VOL. 6: STRANGE MAGIC. Contains material originally published in magazine form as CAPTAIN MARVEL (2019) #27-30. First printing 2021. ISBN 978-1-302-92596-3. Published by MARVEL WORLDWIDE, INC., a subsidiary of MARVEL ENTERTAINMENT, LLC. OFFICE OF PUBLICATION: 1290 Avenue of the Americas, New York, NY 10104. © 2021 MARVEL No similarity between any of the names, characters, persons, and/or institutions in this magazine with those of any living or dead person or institution is intended, and any such similarity which may exist is purely coincidental. **Printed in Canada.** KEVIN FEIGE, Chief Creative Officer; DAN BUCKLEY, President, Marvel Entertainment; JOE QUESADA, EVP & Creative Director; DAVID BOGART, Associate Publisher & SVP of Talent Affairs; TOM BREVOORT, VP, Executive Editor; NICK LOWE, Executive Editor, VP of Content, Digital Publishing; DAVID GABRIEL, VP of Print & Digital Publishing; JEFF YOUNGQUIST, VP of Production & Special Projects; ALEX MORALES, Director of Publishing Operations; DAN EDINGTON, Managing Editor; RICKEY PURDIN, Director of Talent Relations; JENNIFER GRÜNWALD, Senior Editor, Special Projects; SUSAN CRESPI, Production Manager; STAN LEE, Chairman Emeritus. For information regarding advertising in Marvel Comics or on Marvel.com, please contact Vit DeBellis, Custom Solutions & Integrated Advertising Manager, at vdebellis@marvel.com. For Marvel subscription inquiries, please call 888-511-5480. **Manufactured between** 8/6/2021 and 9/7/2021 by SOLISCO PRINTERS, SCOTT, QC, CANADA.

10 9 8 7 6 5 4 3 2 1

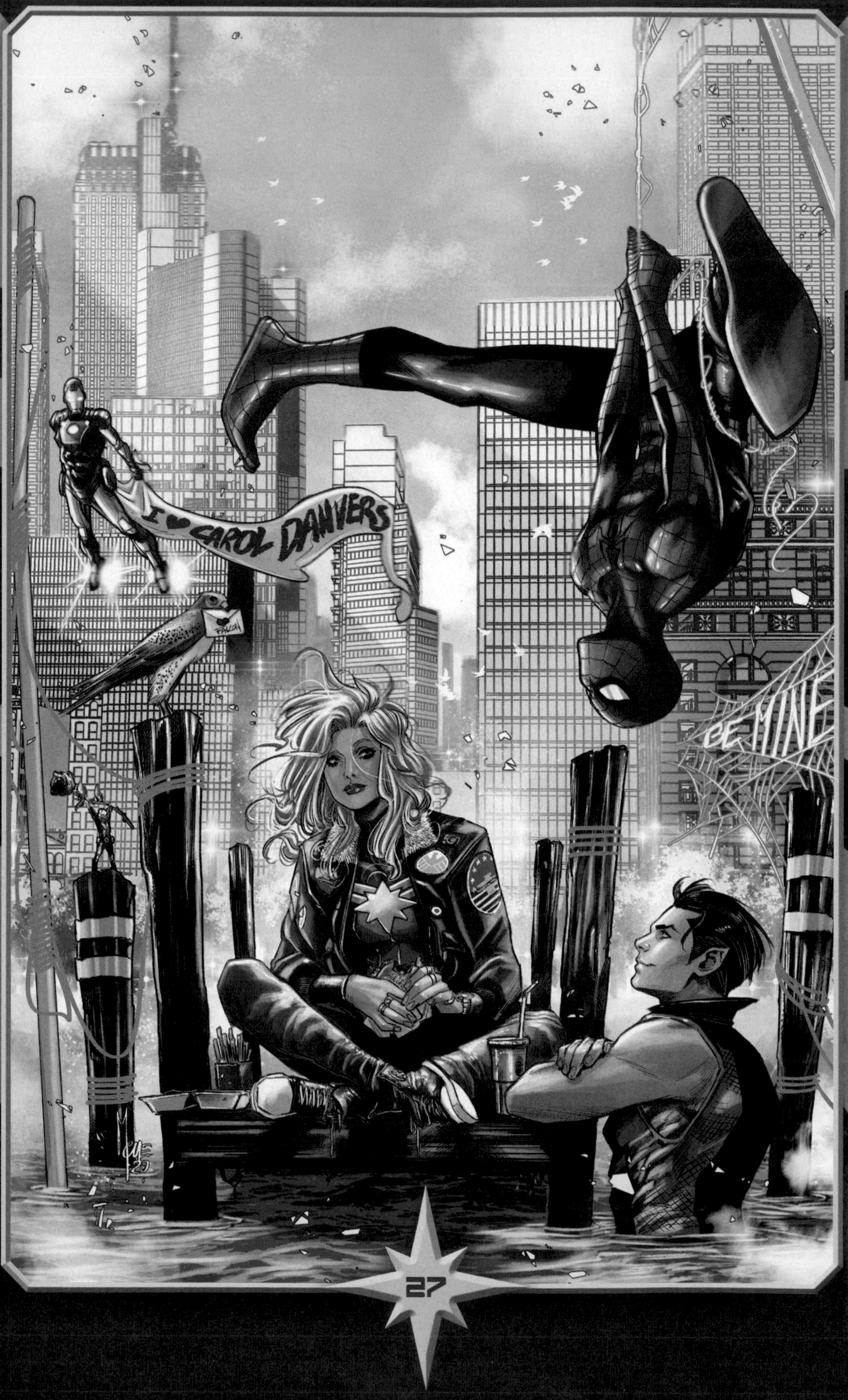
I ♥ CAROL DANVERS
BE MINE
27

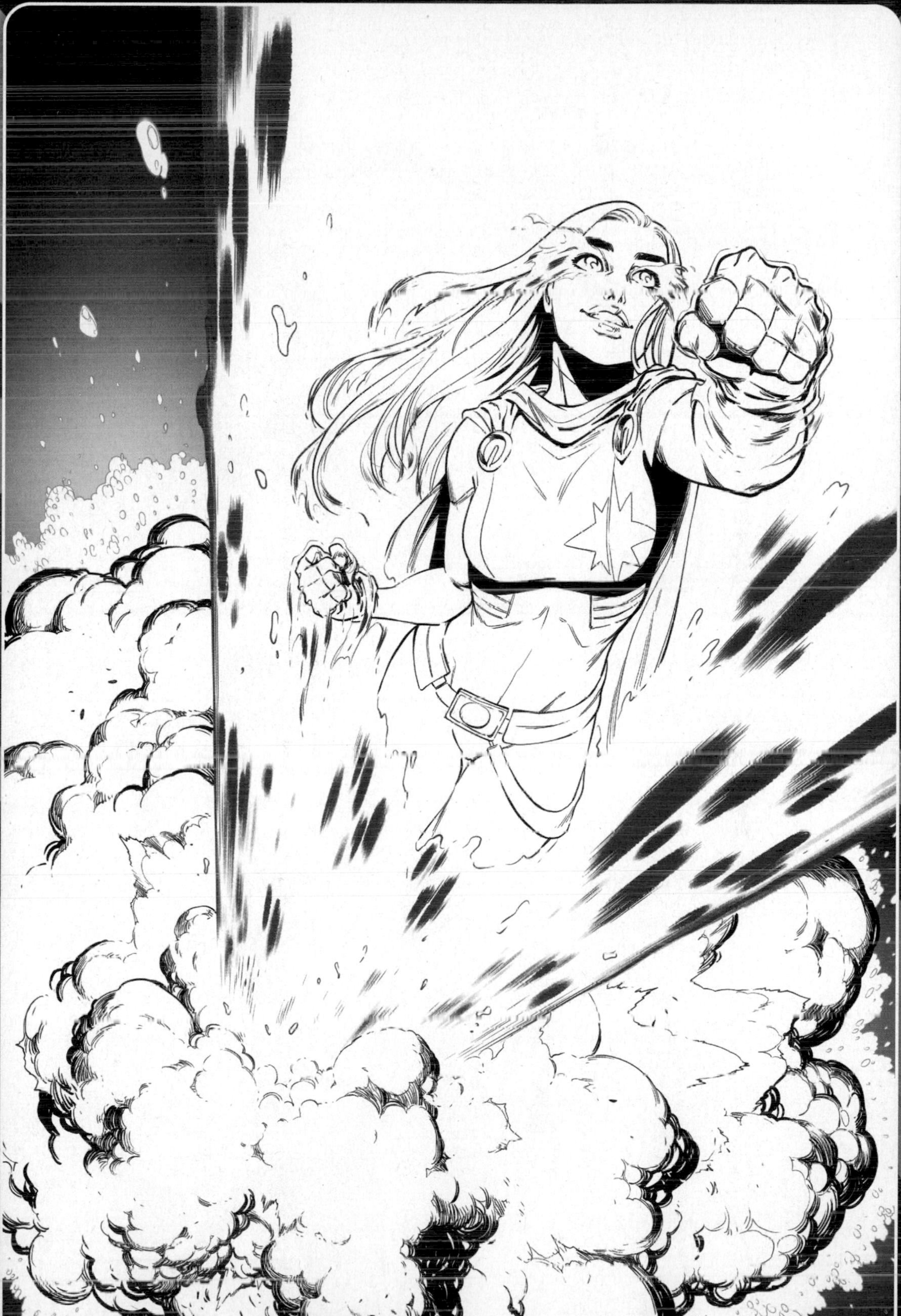

JACOPO CAMAGNI
29, PAGE 20 ART

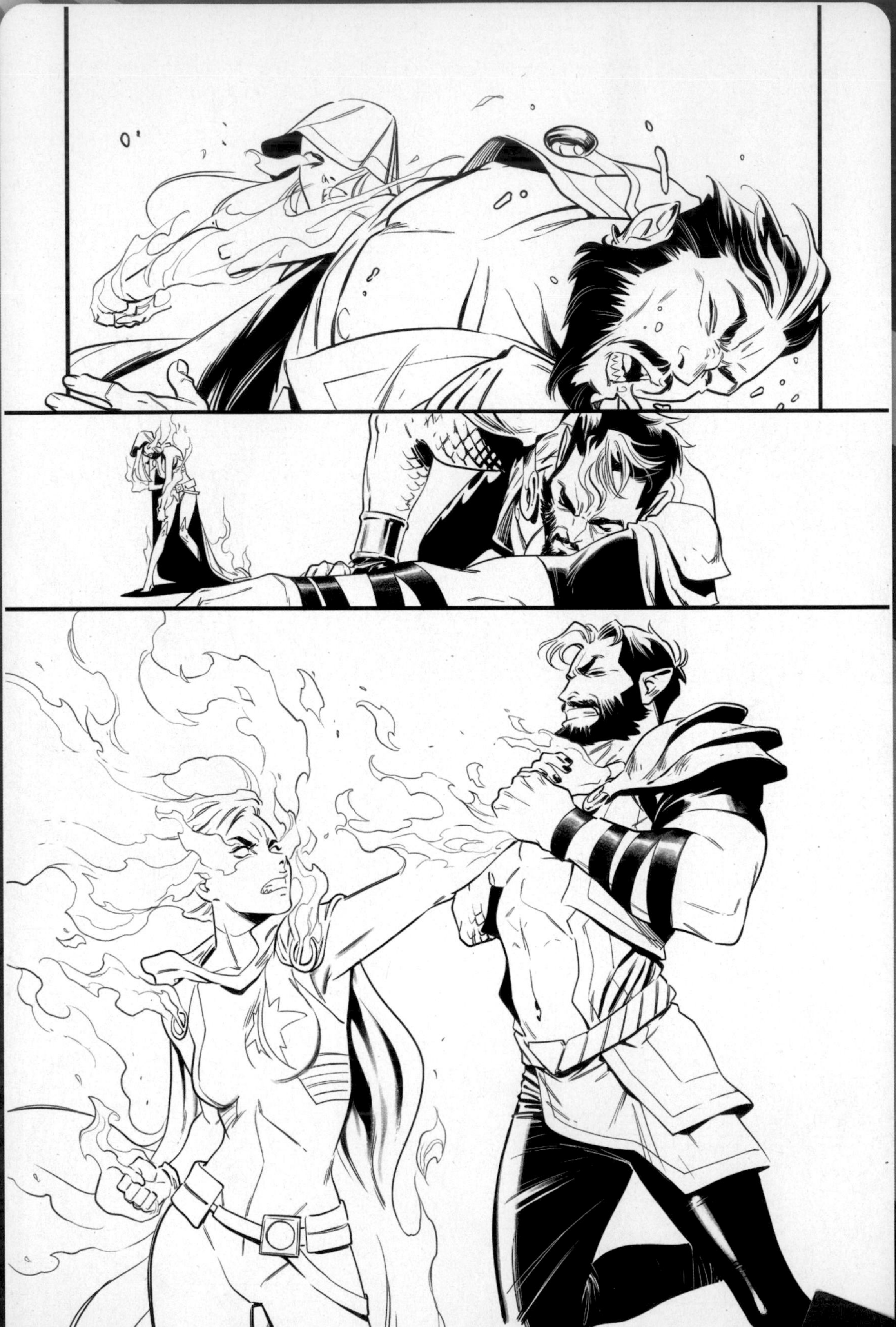

JACOPO CAMAGNI
28, PAGE 16 ART

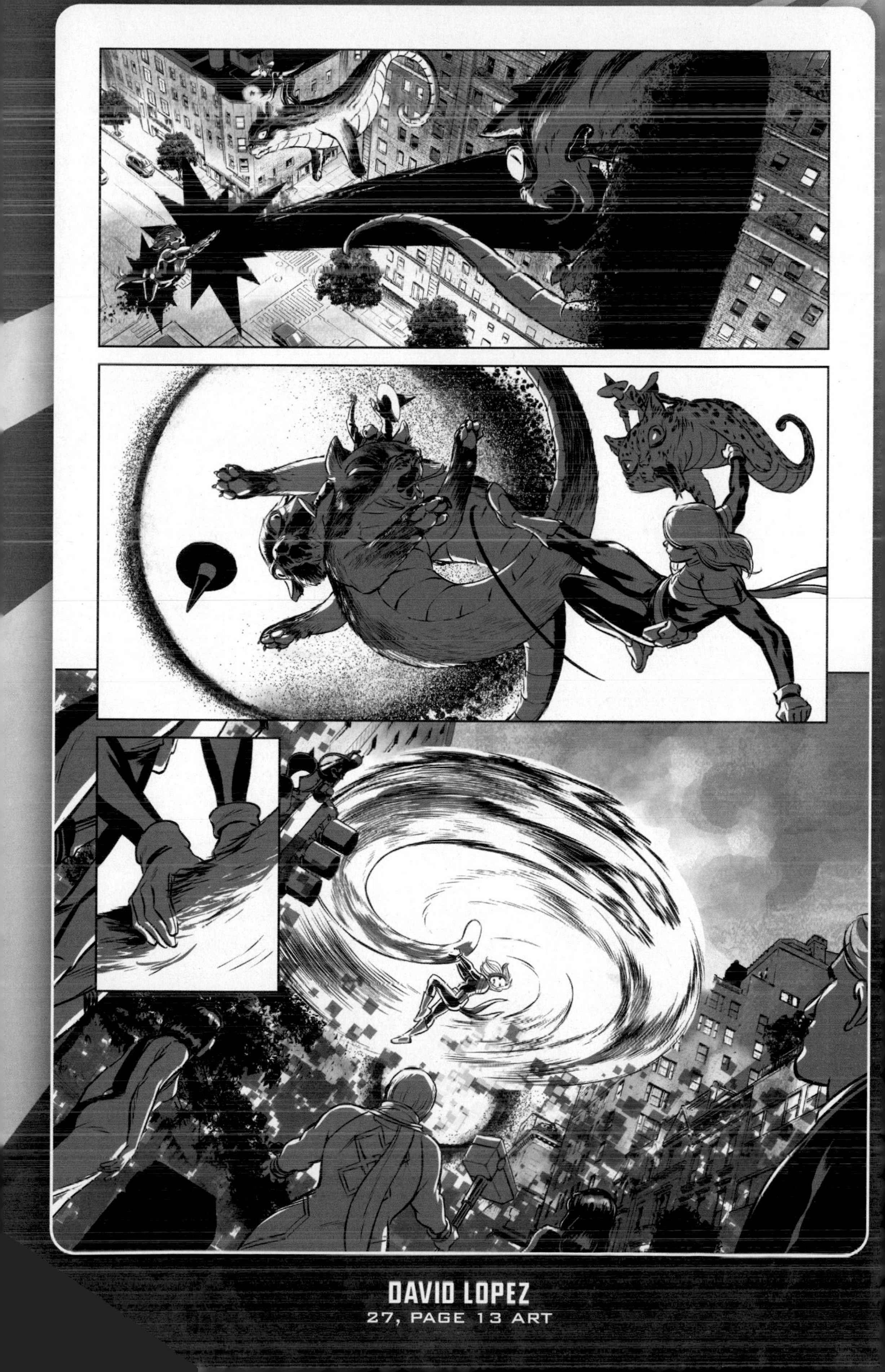

DAVID LOPEZ
27, PAGE 13 ART

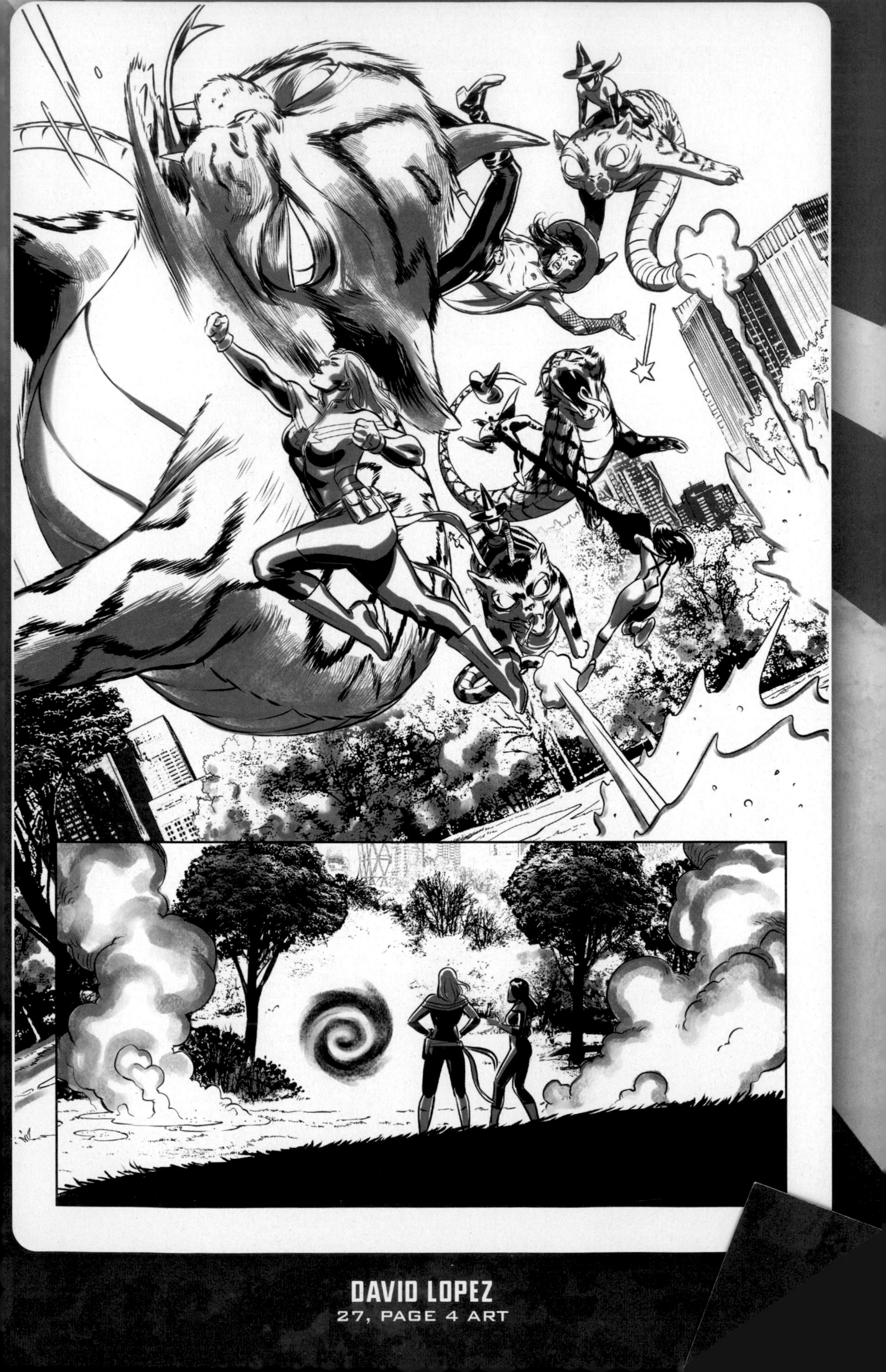

DAVID LOPEZ
27, PAGE 4 ART

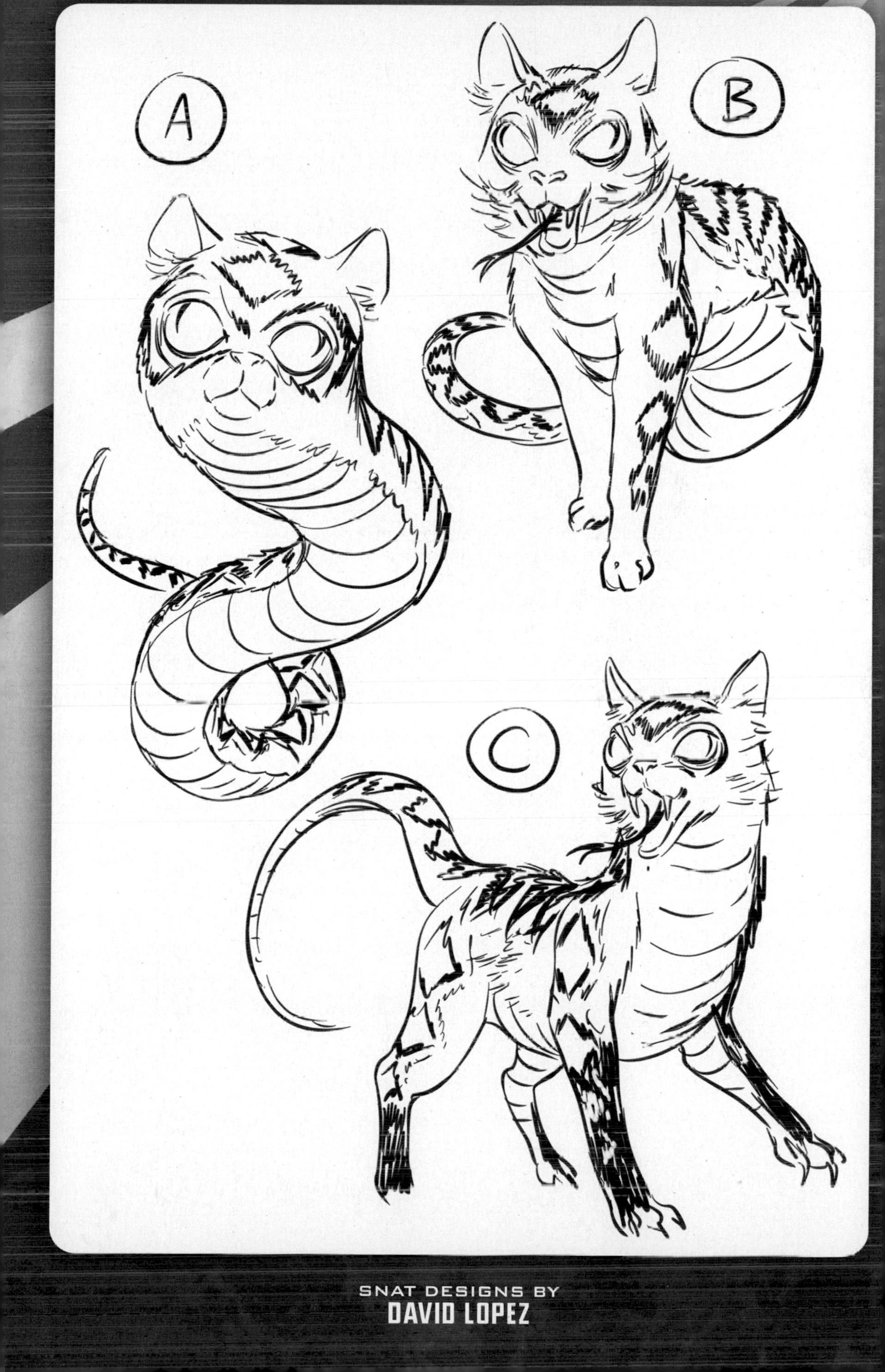
A
B
C

SNAT DESIGNS BY
DAVID LOPEZ

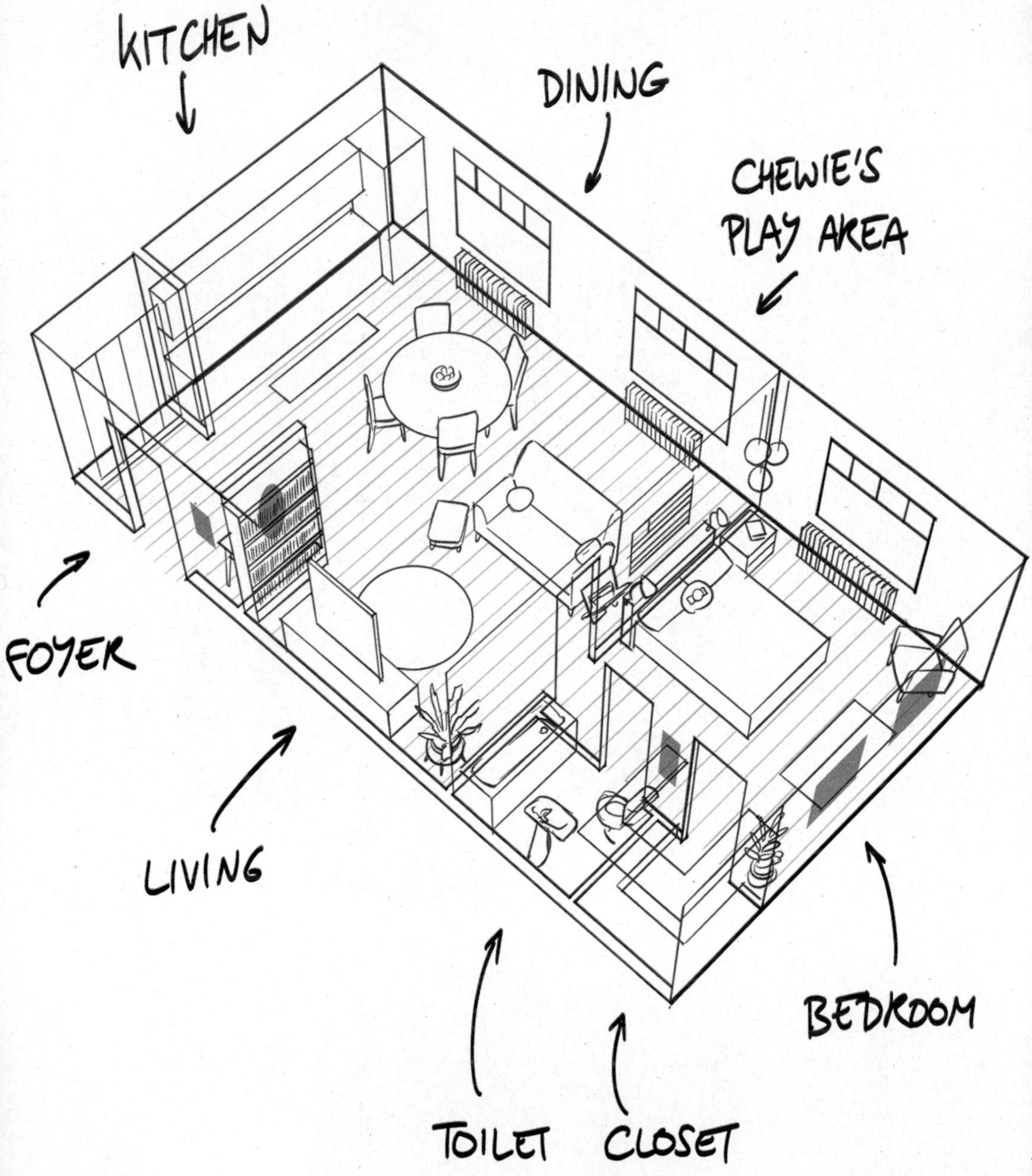
KITCHEN
DINING
CHEWIE'S PLAY AREA
FOYER
LIVING
TOILET
CLOSET
BEDROOM

CAROL'S APARTMENT DESIGN BY
DAVID LOPEZ

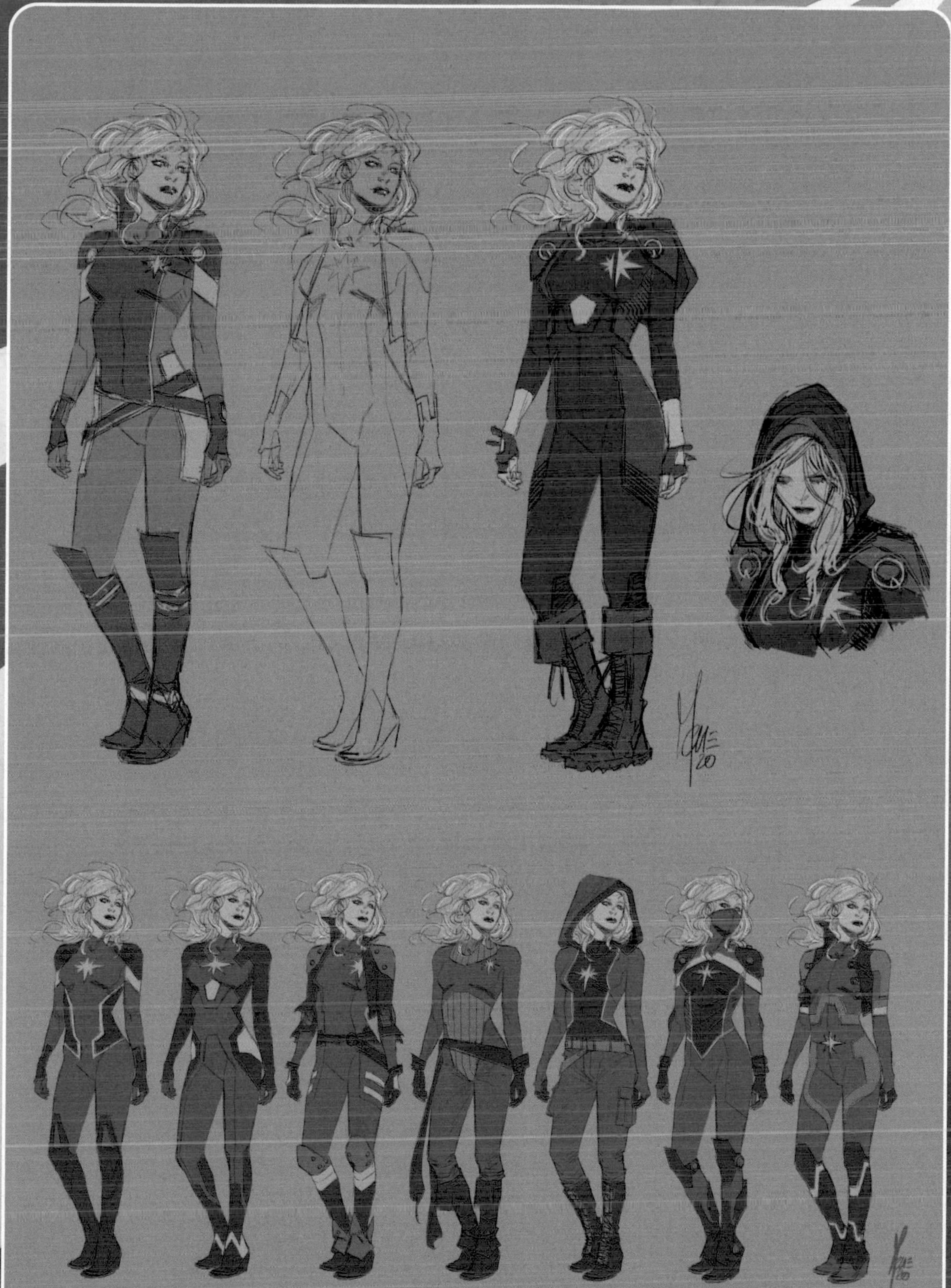

CHARACTER DESIGNS BY
MARCO CHECCHETTO

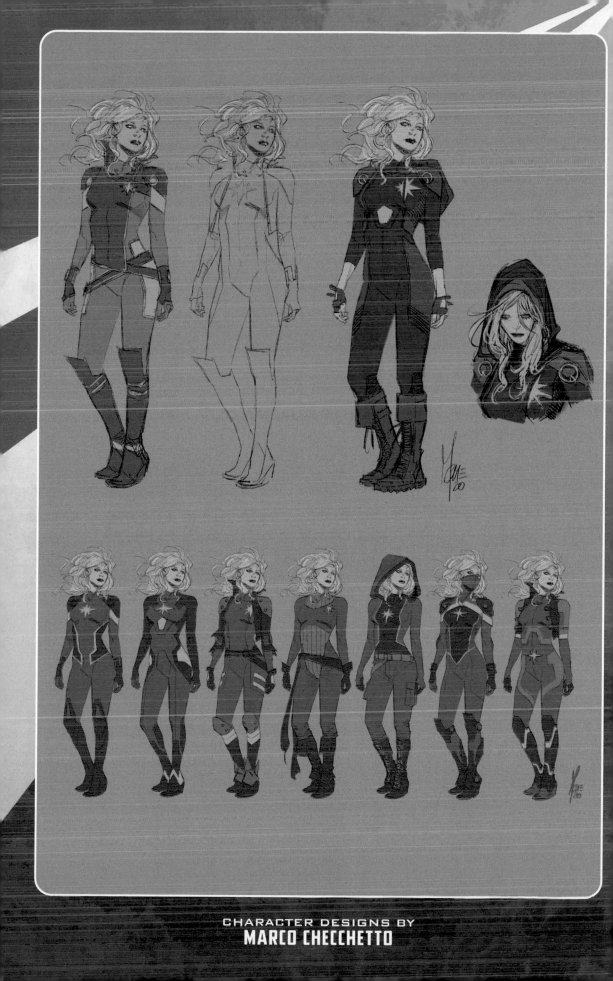

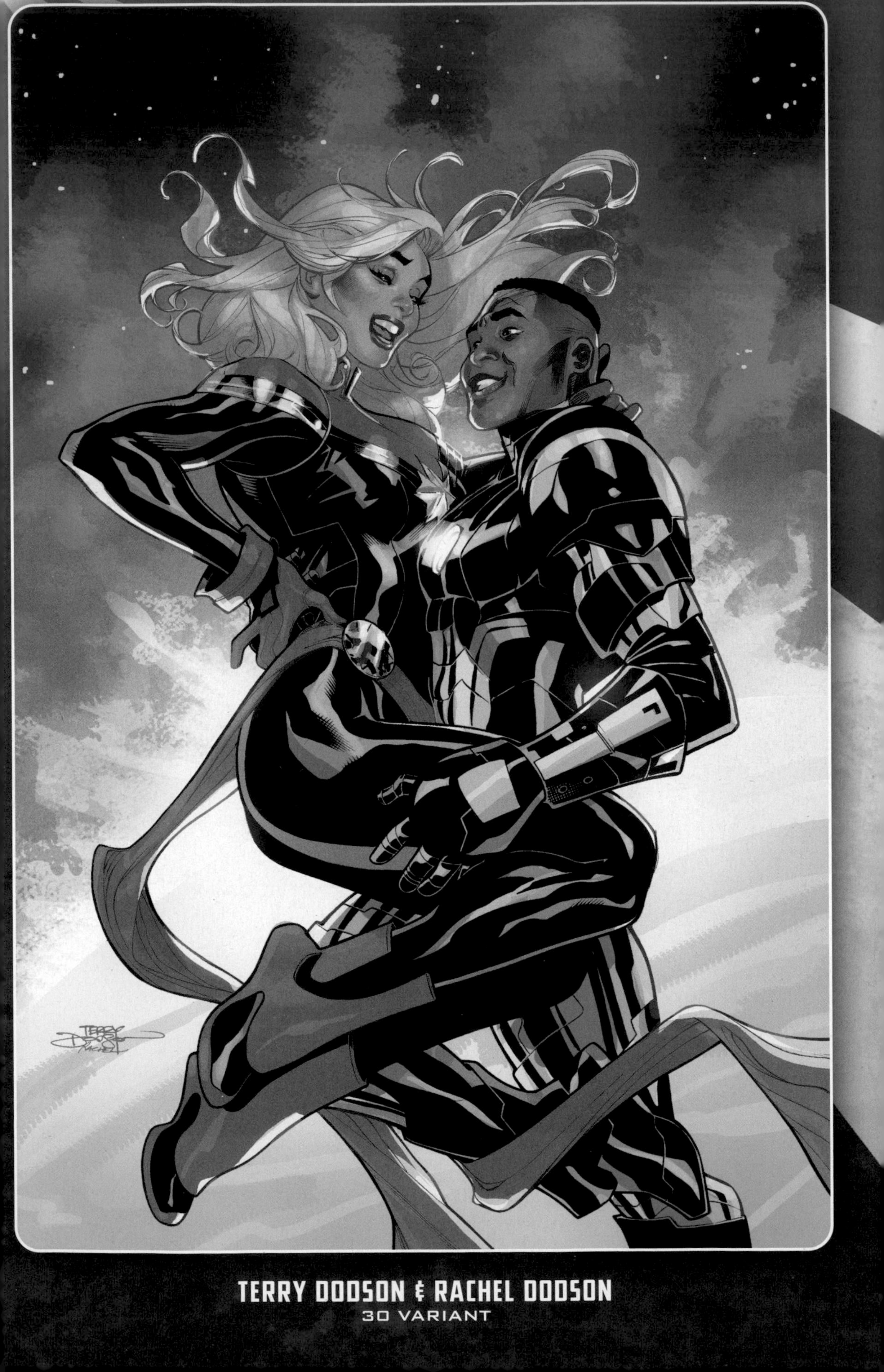

TERRY DODSON & RACHEL DODSON
30 VARIANT

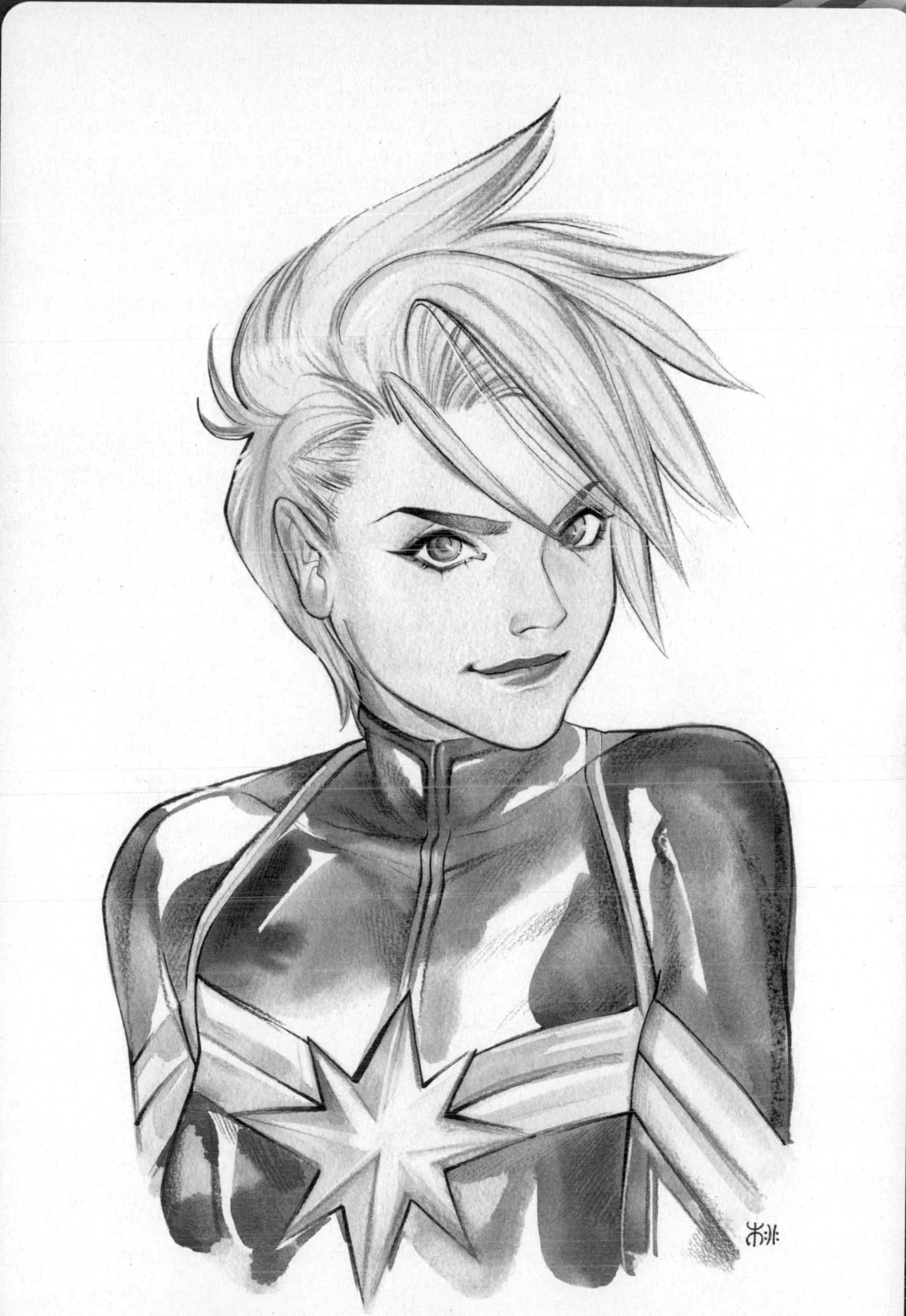

PEACH MOMOKO
30 MARVEL ANIME VARIANT

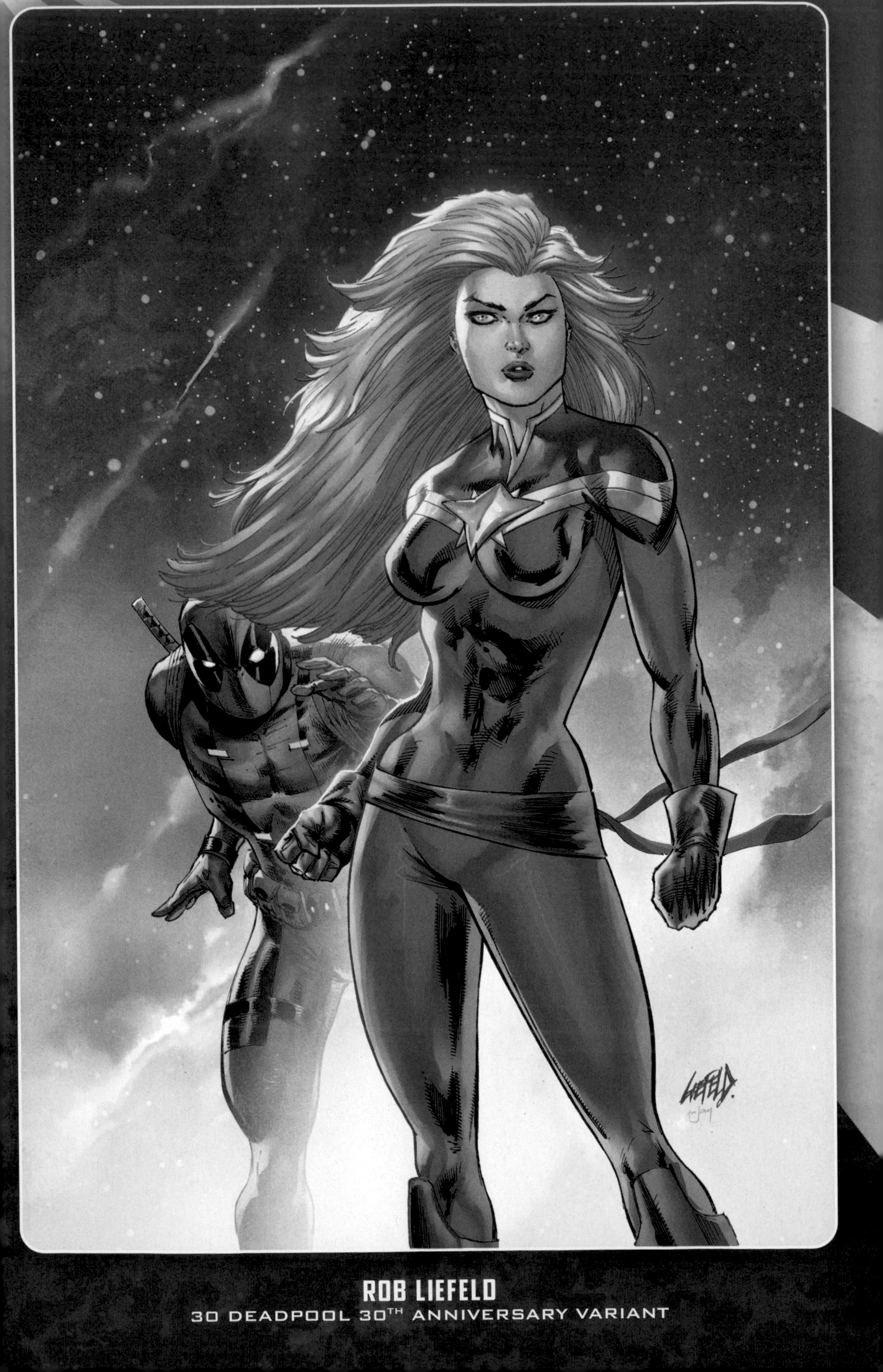
LIEFELD

ROB LIEFELD

30 DEADPOOL 30TH ANNIVERSARY VARIANT

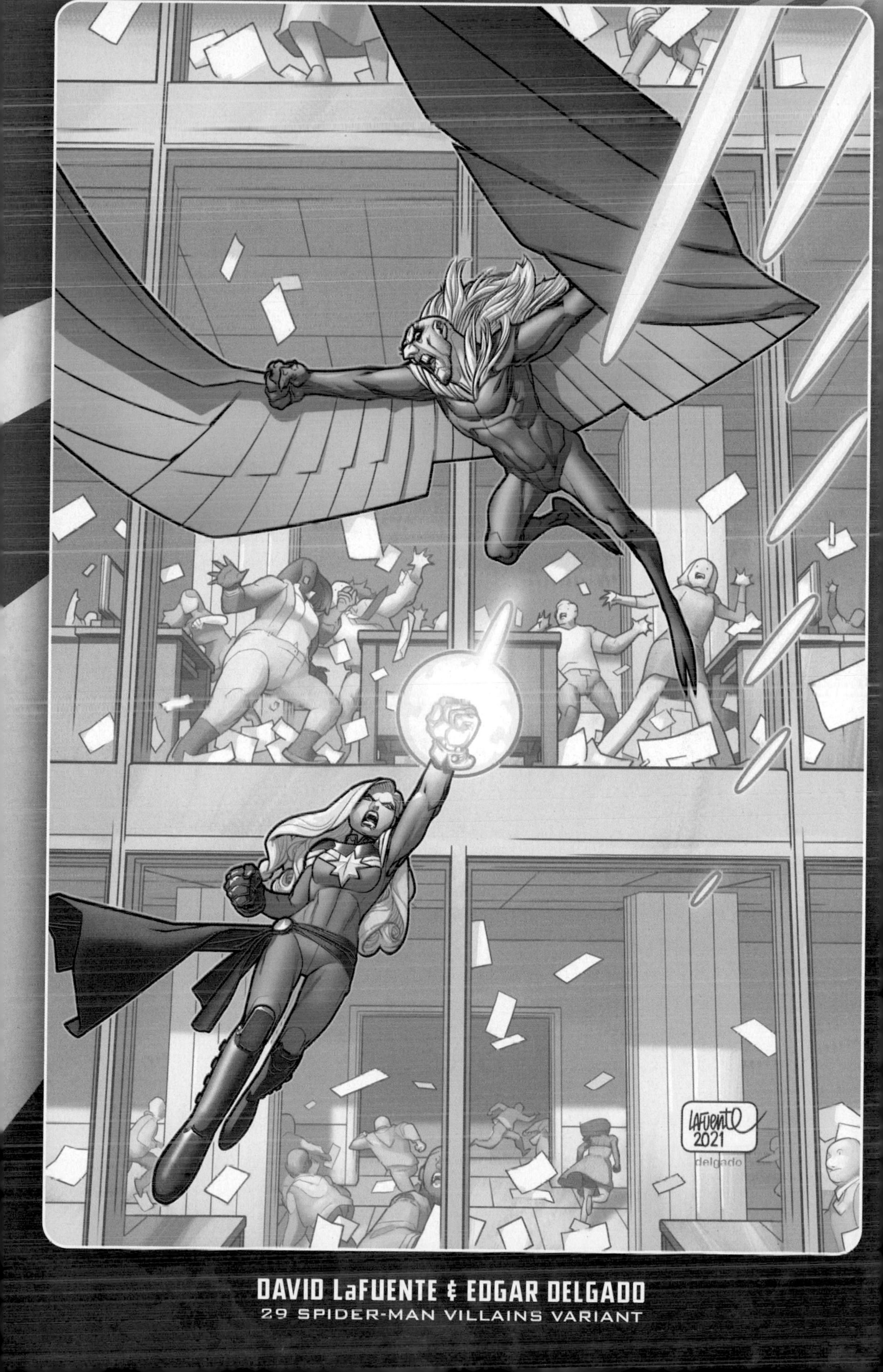
LAFUENTE
2021
delgado

DAVID LaFUENTE & EDGAR DELGADO
29 SPIDER-MAN VILLAINS VARIANT

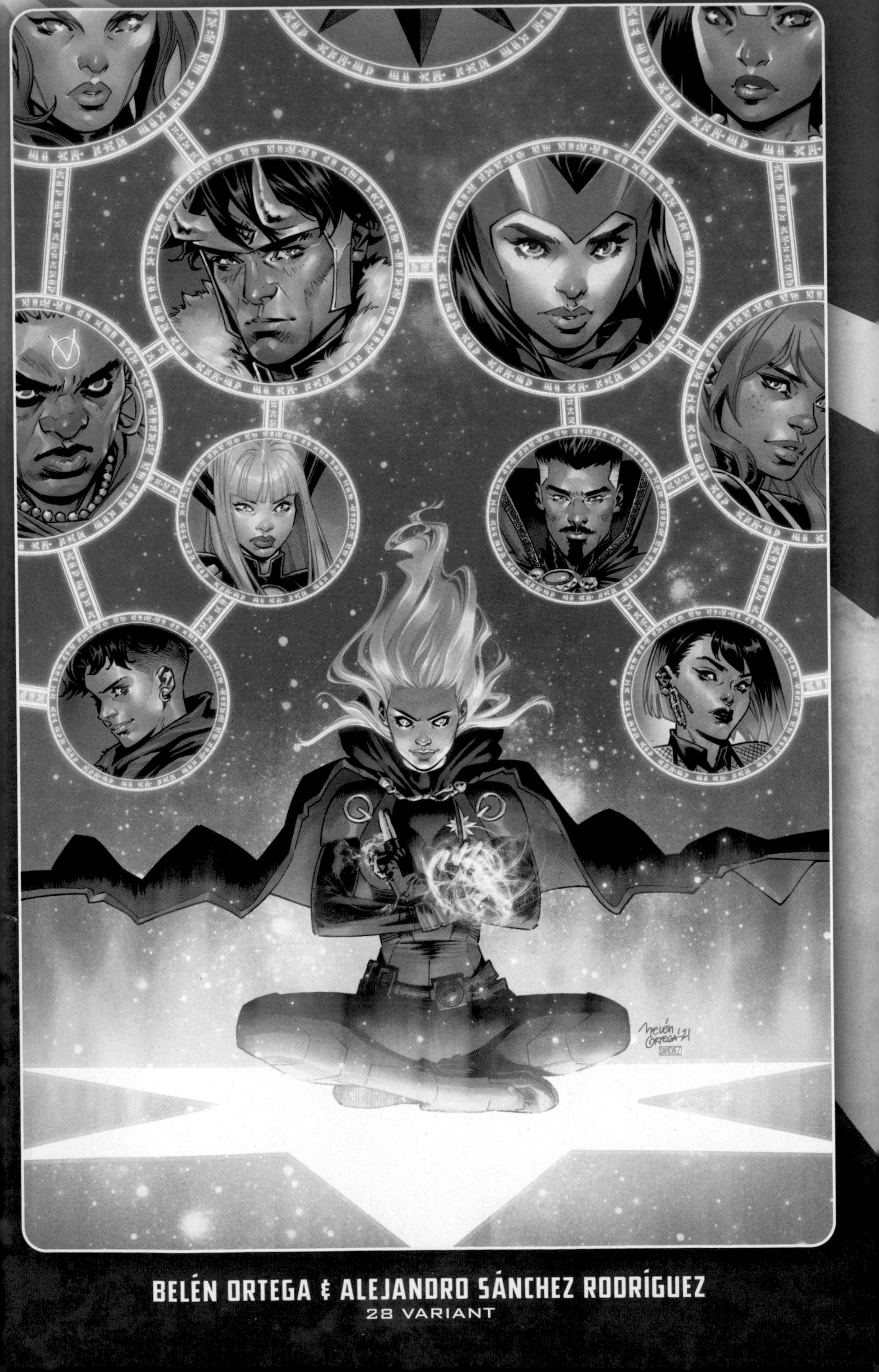

BELÉN ORTEGA & ALEJANDRO SÁNCHEZ RODRÍGUEZ
28 VARIANT

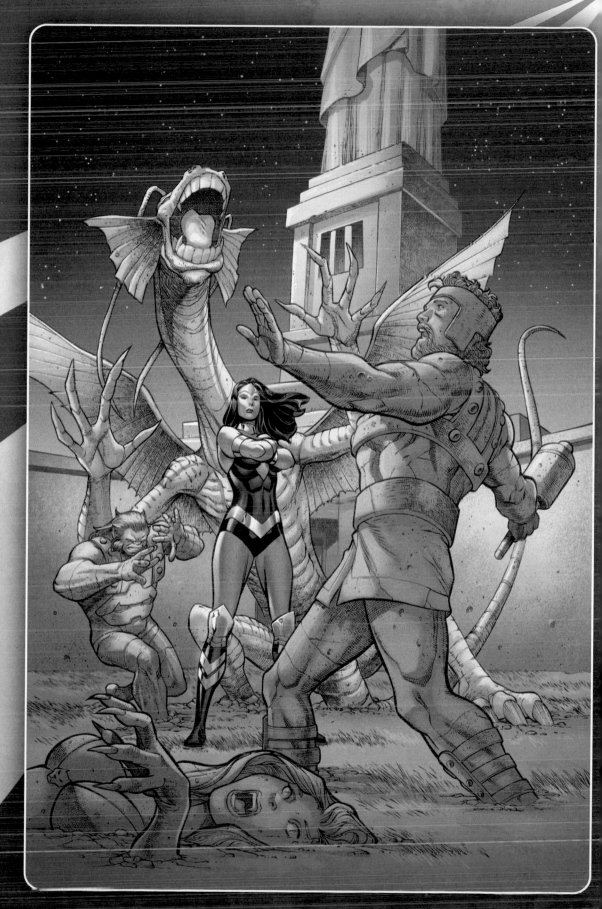

CARLOS PACHECO, RAFAEL FONTERIZ & RACHELLE ROSENBERG
28 HEROES REBORN VARIANT

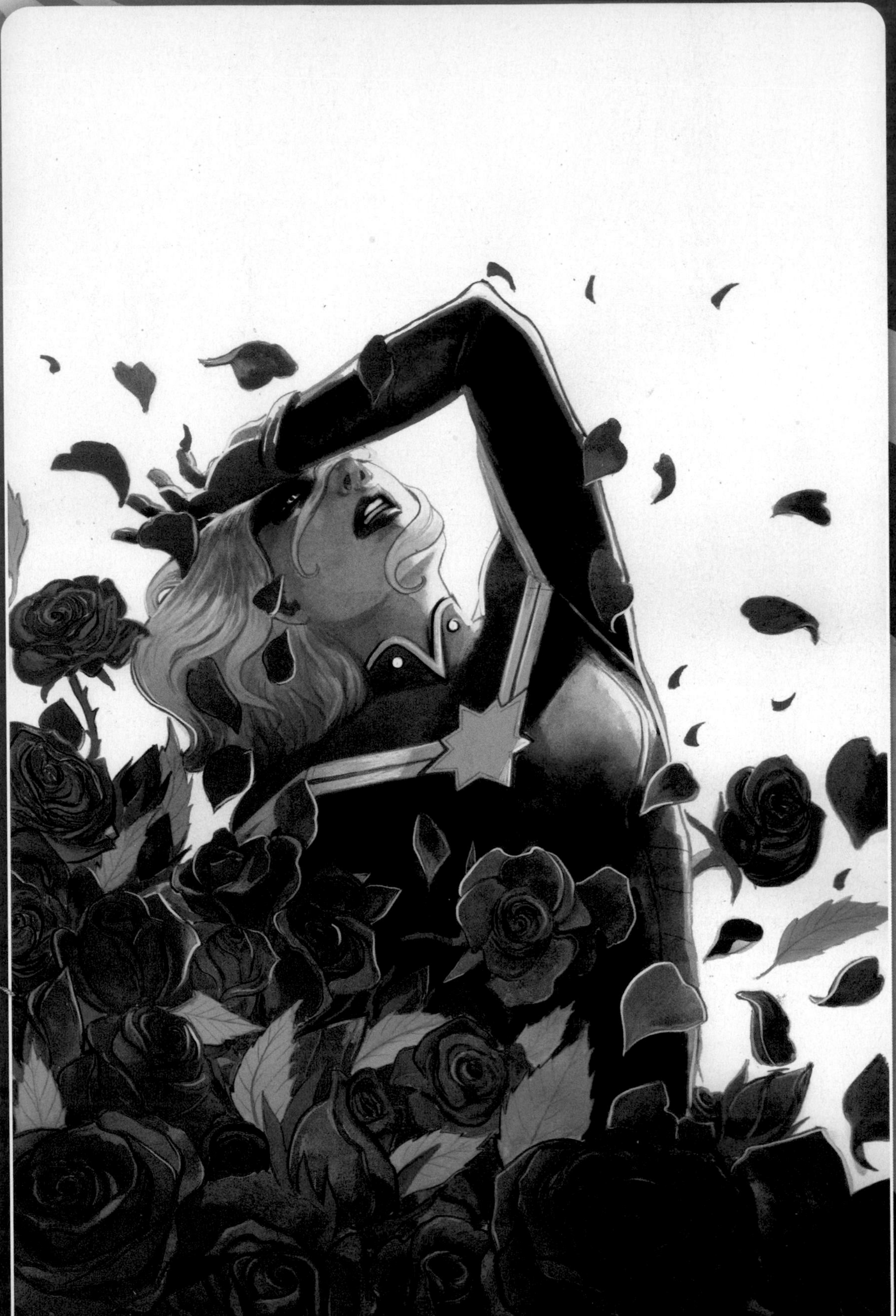

STEPHANIE HANS
27 VARIANT

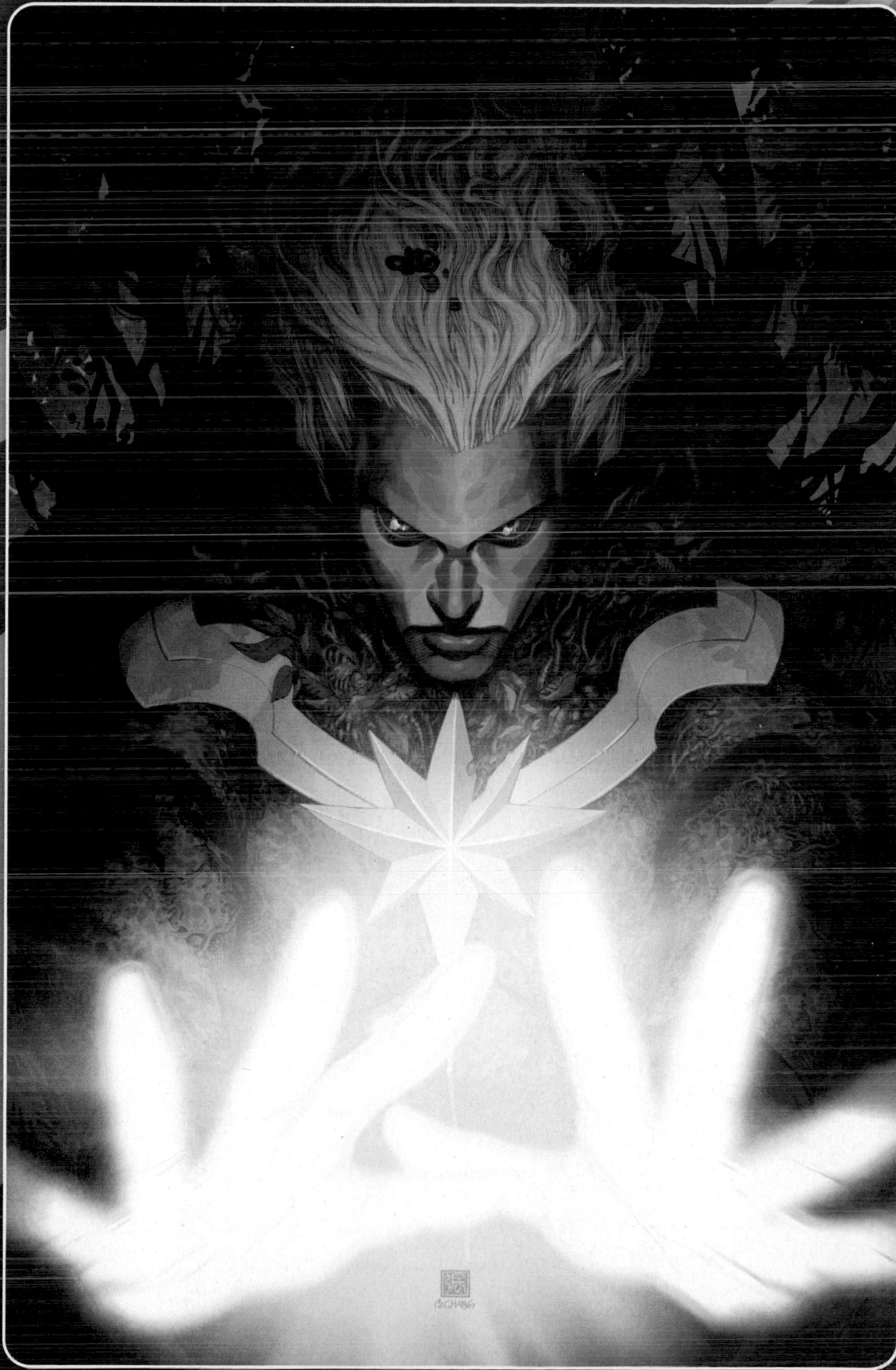
B.CHANG

BERNARD CHANG
27 MAN-THING ANNIVERSARY VARIANT

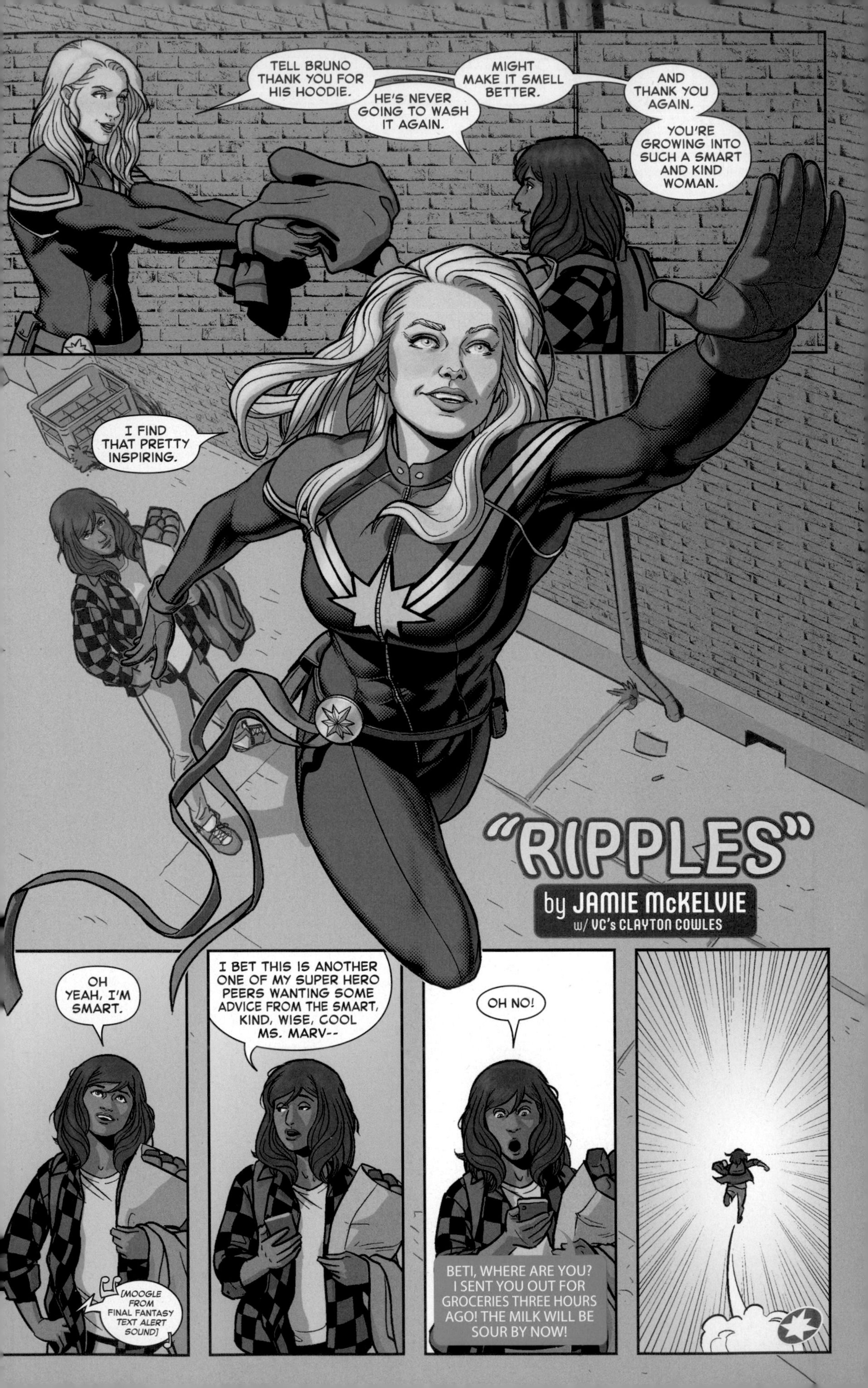
TELL BRUNO THANK YOU FOR HIS HOODIE.
HE'S NEVER GOING TO WASH IT AGAIN.
MIGHT MAKE IT SMELL BETTER.
AND THANK YOU AGAIN.
YOU'RE GROWING INTO SUCH A SMART AND KIND WOMAN.
I FIND THAT PRETTY INSPIRING.
"RIPPLES"
by JAMIE McKELVIE
w/ VC's CLAYTON COWLES
OH YEAH, I'M SMART.
[MOOGLE FROM FINAL FANTASY TEXT ALERT SOUND]
I BET THIS IS ANOTHER ONE OF MY SUPER HERO PEERS WANTING SOME ADVICE FROM THE SMART, KIND, WISE, COOL MS. MARV--
OH NO!
BETI, WHERE ARE YOU? I SENT YOU OUT FOR GROCERIES THREE HOURS AGO! THE MILK WILL BE SOUR BY NOW!

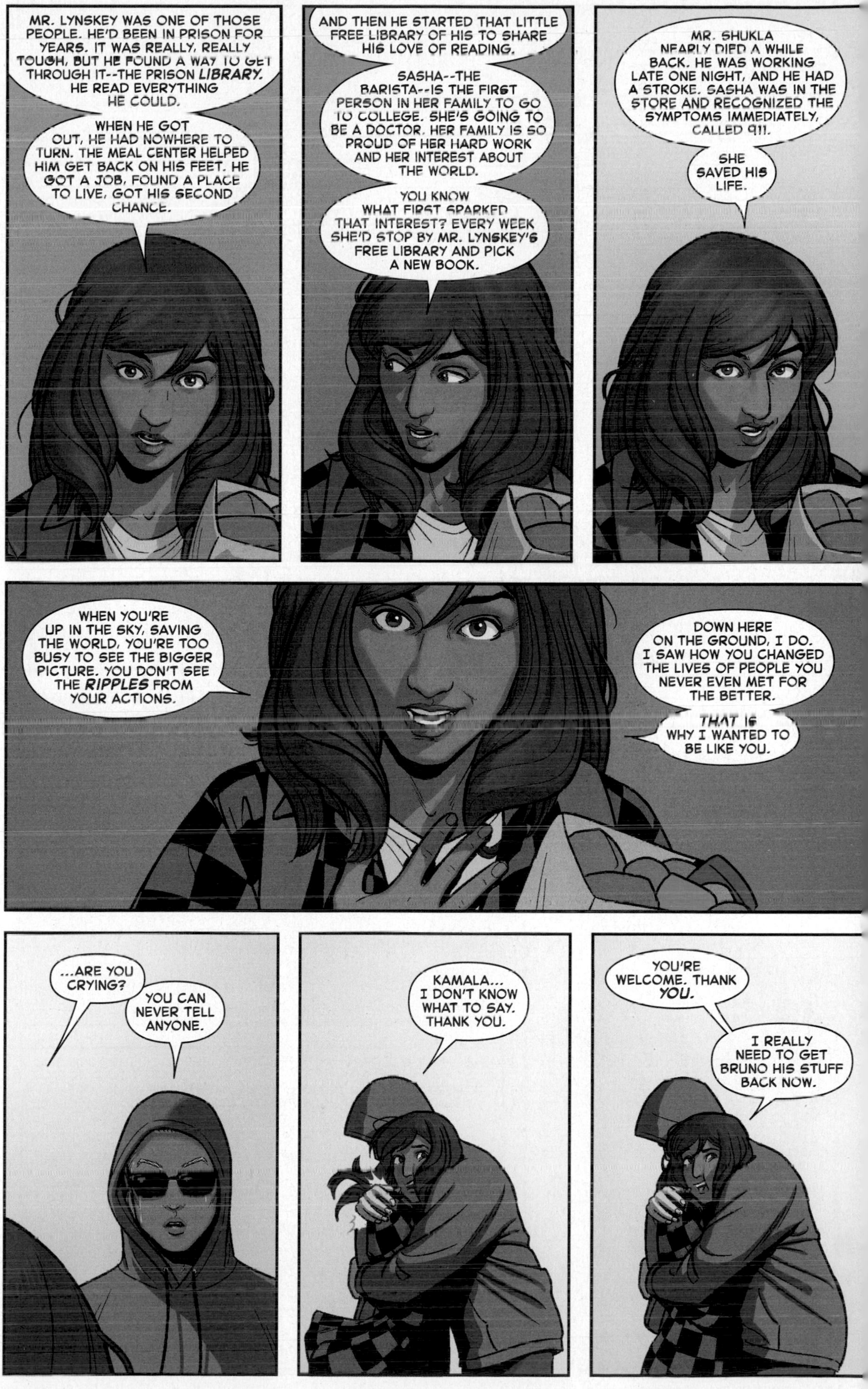
MR. LYNSKEY WAS ONE OF THOSE PEOPLE. HE'D BEEN IN PRISON FOR YEARS. IT WAS REALLY, REALLY TOUGH, BUT HE FOUND A WAY TO GET THROUGH IT--THE PRISON *LIBRARY.* HE READ EVERYTHING HE COULD.
WHEN HE GOT OUT, HE HAD NOWHERE TO TURN. THE MEAL CENTER HELPED HIM GET BACK ON HIS FEET. HE GOT A JOB, FOUND A PLACE TO LIVE, GOT HIS SECOND CHANCE.
AND THEN HE STARTED THAT LITTLE FREE LIBRARY OF HIS TO SHARE HIS LOVE OF READING.
SASHA--THE BARISTA--IS THE FIRST PERSON IN HER FAMILY TO GO TO COLLEGE. SHE'S GOING TO BE A DOCTOR. HER FAMILY IS SO PROUD OF HER HARD WORK AND HER INTEREST ABOUT THE WORLD.
YOU KNOW WHAT FIRST SPARKED THAT INTEREST? EVERY WEEK SHE'D STOP BY MR. LYNSKEY'S FREE LIBRARY AND PICK A NEW BOOK.
MR. SHUKLA NEARLY DIED A WHILE BACK. HE WAS WORKING LATE ONE NIGHT, AND HE HAD A STROKE. SASHA WAS IN THE STORE AND RECOGNIZED THE SYMPTOMS IMMEDIATELY, CALLED 911.
SHE SAVED HIS LIFE.
WHEN YOU'RE UP IN THE SKY, SAVING THE WORLD, YOU'RE TOO BUSY TO SEE THE BIGGER PICTURE. YOU DON'T SEE THE *RIPPLES* FROM YOUR ACTIONS.
DOWN HERE ON THE GROUND, I DO. I SAW HOW YOU CHANGED THE LIVES OF PEOPLE YOU NEVER EVEN MET FOR THE BETTER.
THAT IS WHY I WANTED TO BE LIKE YOU.
...ARE YOU CRYING?
YOU CAN NEVER TELL ANYONE.
KAMALA... I DON'T KNOW WHAT TO SAY. THANK YOU.
YOU'RE WELCOME. THANK *YOU.*
I REALLY NEED TO GET BRUNO HIS STUFF BACK NOW.

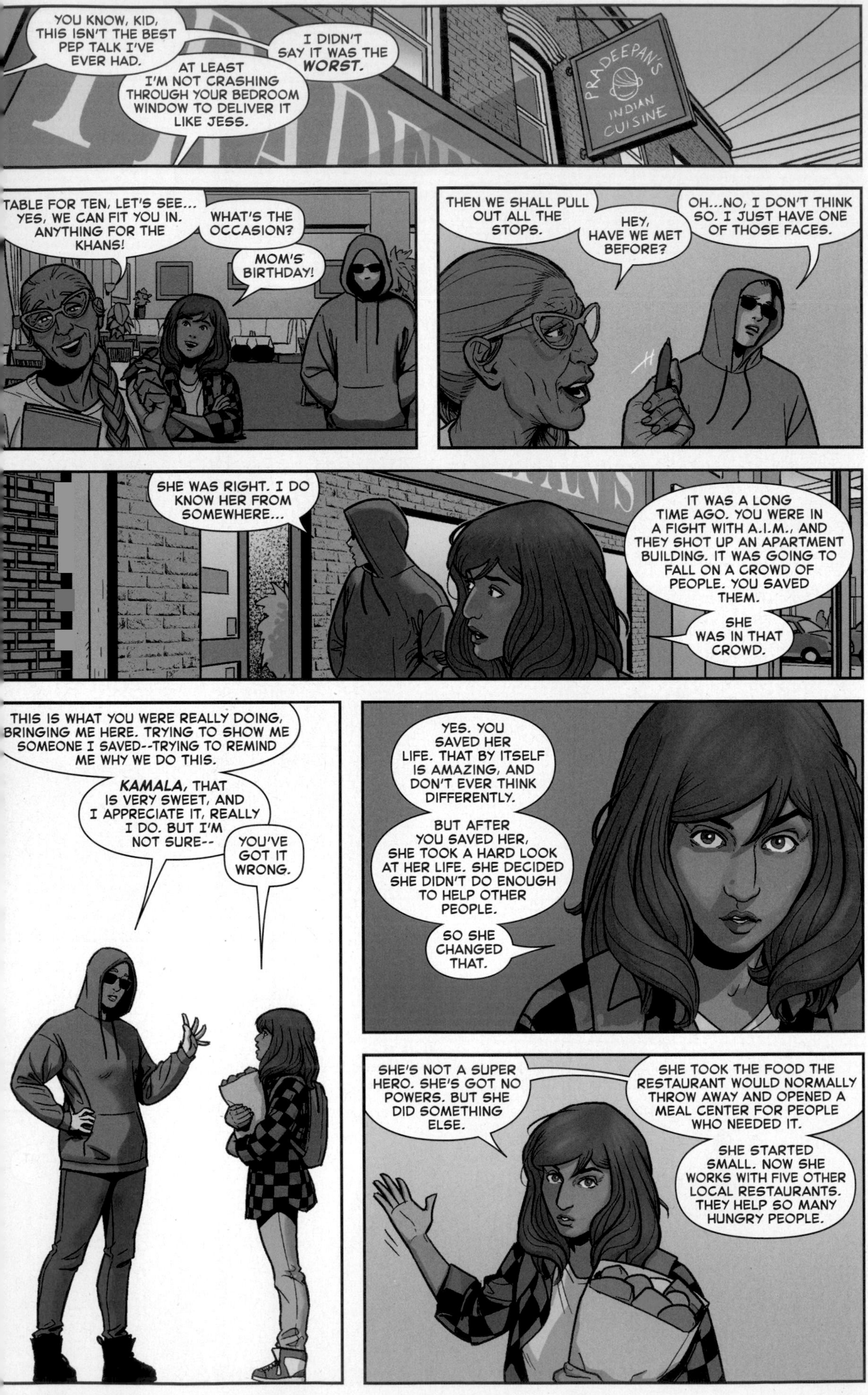
YOU KNOW, KID, THIS ISN'T THE BEST PEP TALK I'VE EVER HAD.
I DIDN'T SAY IT WAS THE WORST.
AT LEAST I'M NOT CRASHING THROUGH YOUR BEDROOM WINDOW TO DELIVER IT LIKE JESS.
PRADEEPAN'S INDIAN CUISINE
TABLE FOR TEN, LET'S SEE... YES, WE CAN FIT YOU IN. ANYTHING FOR THE KHANS!
WHAT'S THE OCCASION?
MOM'S BIRTHDAY!
THEN WE SHALL PULL OUT ALL THE STOPS.
HEY, HAVE WE MET BEFORE?
OH...NO, I DON'T THINK SO. I JUST HAVE ONE OF THOSE FACES.
SHE WAS RIGHT. I DO KNOW HER FROM SOMEWHERE...
IT WAS A LONG TIME AGO. YOU WERE IN A FIGHT WITH A.I.M., AND THEY SHOT UP AN APARTMENT BUILDING. IT WAS GOING TO FALL ON A CROWD OF PEOPLE. YOU SAVED THEM.
SHE WAS IN THAT CROWD.
THIS IS WHAT YOU WERE REALLY DOING, BRINGING ME HERE. TRYING TO SHOW ME SOMEONE I SAVED--TRYING TO REMIND ME WHY WE DO THIS.
KAMALA, THAT IS VERY SWEET, AND I APPRECIATE IT, REALLY I DO. BUT I'M NOT SURE--
YOU'VE GOT IT WRONG.
YES. YOU SAVED HER LIFE. THAT BY ITSELF IS AMAZING, AND DON'T EVER THINK DIFFERENTLY.
BUT AFTER YOU SAVED HER, SHE TOOK A HARD LOOK AT HER LIFE. SHE DECIDED SHE DIDN'T DO ENOUGH TO HELP OTHER PEOPLE.
SO SHE CHANGED THAT.
SHE'S NOT A SUPER HERO. SHE'S GOT NO POWERS. BUT SHE DID SOMETHING ELSE.
SHE TOOK THE FOOD THE RESTAURANT WOULD NORMALLY THROW AWAY AND OPENED A MEAL CENTER FOR PEOPLE WHO NEEDED IT.
SHE STARTED SMALL. NOW SHE WORKS WITH FIVE OTHER LOCAL RESTAURANTS. THEY HELP SO MANY HUNGRY PEOPLE.

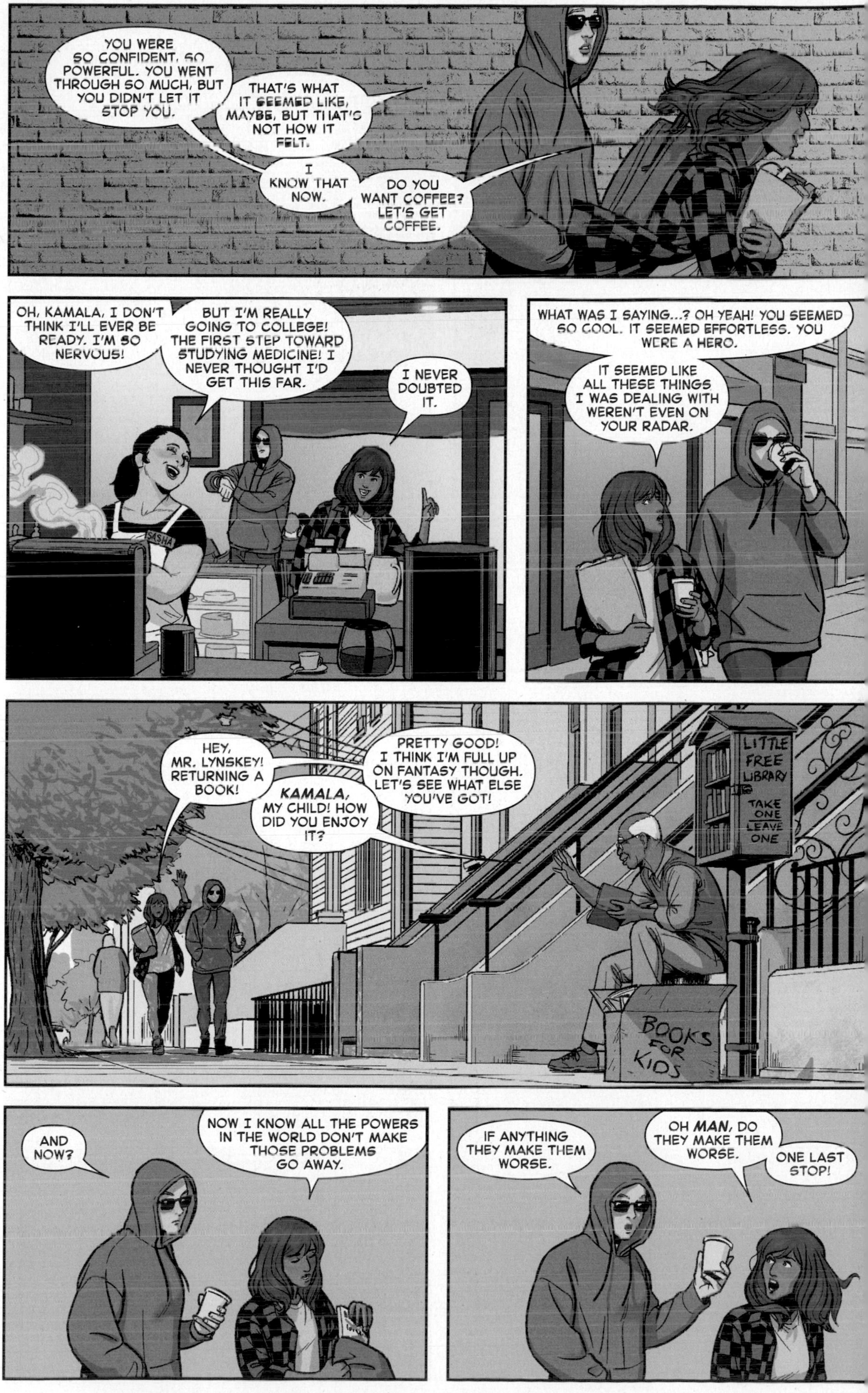
YOU WERE SO CONFIDENT, SO POWERFUL. YOU WENT THROUGH SO MUCH, BUT YOU DIDN'T LET IT STOP YOU.
THAT'S WHAT IT SEEMED LIKE, MAYBE, BUT THAT'S NOT HOW IT FELT.
I KNOW THAT NOW.
DO YOU WANT COFFEE? LET'S GET COFFEE.
OH, KAMALA, I DON'T THINK I'LL EVER BE READY. I'M SO NERVOUS!
BUT I'M REALLY GOING TO COLLEGE! THE FIRST STEP TOWARD STUDYING MEDICINE! I NEVER THOUGHT I'D GET THIS FAR.
I NEVER DOUBTED IT.
SASHA
WHAT WAS I SAYING...? OH YEAH! YOU SEEMED SO COOL. IT SEEMED EFFORTLESS. YOU WERE A HERO.
IT SEEMED LIKE ALL THESE THINGS I WAS DEALING WITH WEREN'T EVEN ON YOUR RADAR.
HEY, MR. LYNSKEY! RETURNING A BOOK!
KAMALA, MY CHILD! HOW DID YOU ENJOY IT?
PRETTY GOOD! I THINK I'M FULL UP ON FANTASY THOUGH. LET'S SEE WHAT ELSE YOU'VE GOT!
LITTLE FREE LIBRARY
TAKE ONE LEAVE ONE
BOOKS FOR KIDS
AND NOW?
NOW I KNOW ALL THE POWERS IN THE WORLD DON'T MAKE THOSE PROBLEMS GO AWAY.
IF ANYTHING THEY MAKE THEM WORSE.
OH MAN, DO THEY MAKE THEM WORSE.
ONE LAST STOP!

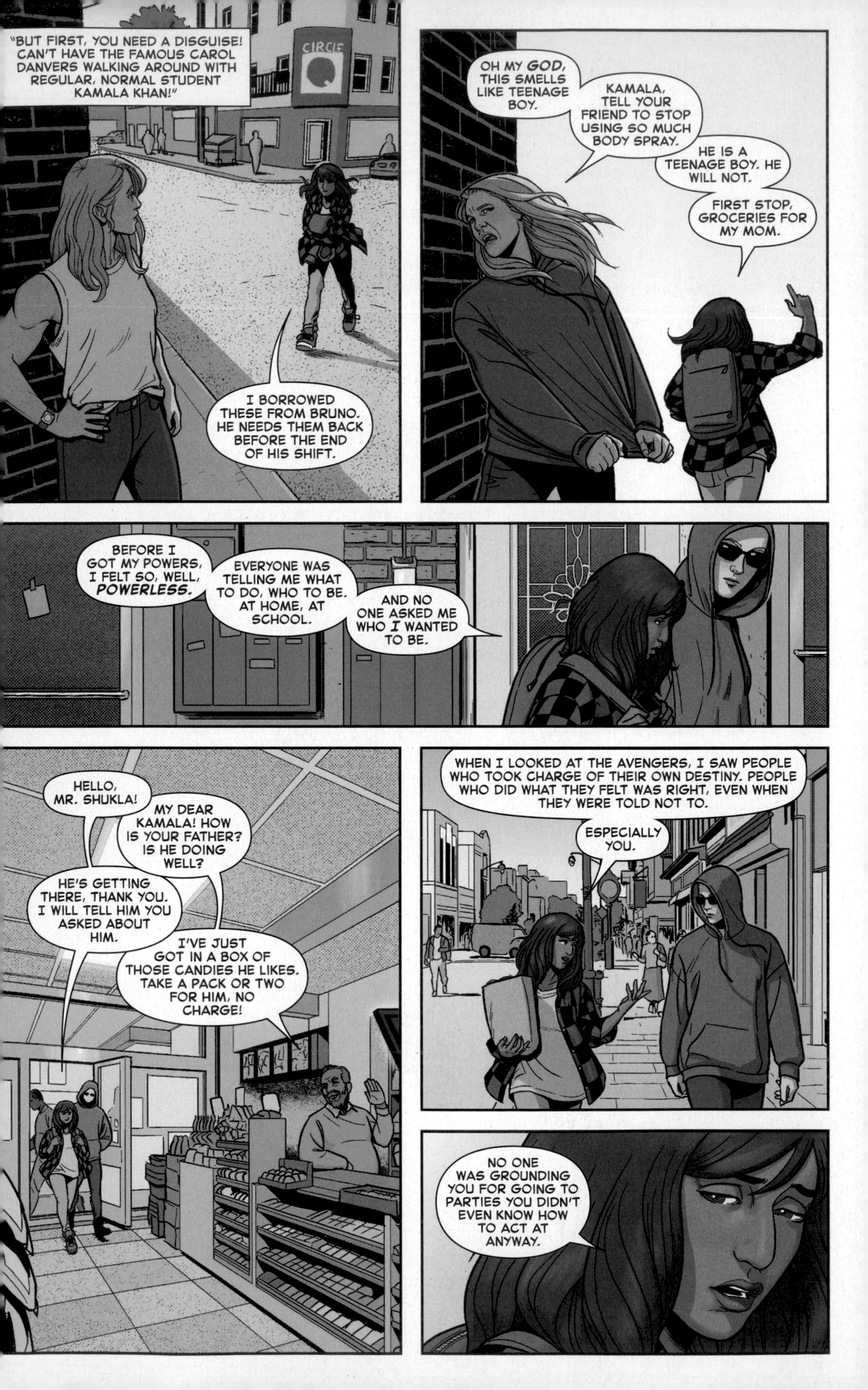
"BUT FIRST, YOU NEED A DISGUISE! CAN'T HAVE THE FAMOUS CAROL DANVERS WALKING AROUND WITH REGULAR, NORMAL STUDENT KAMALA KHAN!"
CIRCLE
I BORROWED THESE FROM BRUNO. HE NEEDS THEM BACK BEFORE THE END OF HIS SHIFT.
OH MY GOD, THIS SMELLS LIKE TEENAGE BOY.
KAMALA, TELL YOUR FRIEND TO STOP USING SO MUCH BODY SPRAY.
HE IS A TEENAGE BOY. HE WILL NOT.
FIRST STOP, GROCERIES FOR MY MOM.
BEFORE I GOT MY POWERS, I FELT SO, WELL, POWERLESS.
EVERYONE WAS TELLING ME WHAT TO DO, WHO TO BE. AT HOME, AT SCHOOL.
AND NO ONE ASKED ME WHO I WANTED TO BE.
HELLO, MR. SHUKLA!
MY DEAR KAMALA! HOW IS YOUR FATHER? IS HE DOING WELL?
HE'S GETTING THERE, THANK YOU. I WILL TELL HIM YOU ASKED ABOUT HIM.
I'VE JUST GOT IN A BOX OF THOSE CANDIES HE LIKES. TAKE A PACK OR TWO FOR HIM, NO CHARGE!
WHEN I LOOKED AT THE AVENGERS, I SAW PEOPLE WHO TOOK CHARGE OF THEIR OWN DESTINY. PEOPLE WHO DID WHAT THEY FELT WAS RIGHT, EVEN WHEN THEY WERE TOLD NOT TO.
ESPECIALLY YOU.
NO ONE WAS GROUNDING YOU FOR GOING TO PARTIES YOU DIDN'T EVEN KNOW HOW TO ACT AT ANYWAY.

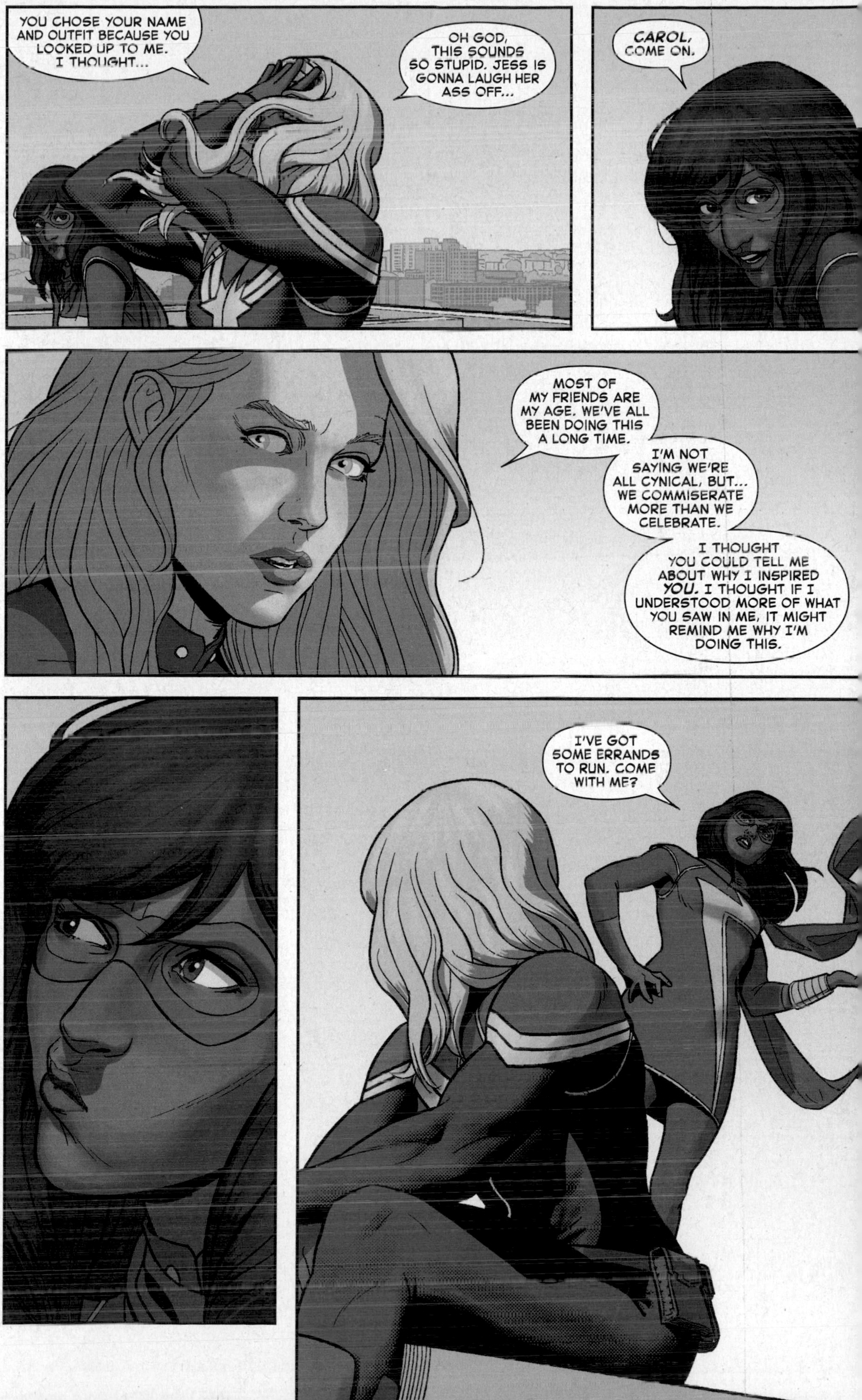
YOU CHOSE YOUR NAME AND OUTFIT BECAUSE YOU LOOKED UP TO ME. I THOUGHT...
OH GOD, THIS SOUNDS SO STUPID. JESS IS GONNA LAUGH HER ASS OFF...
CAROL, COME ON.
MOST OF MY FRIENDS ARE MY AGE. WE'VE ALL BEEN DOING THIS A LONG TIME.
I'M NOT SAYING WE'RE ALL CYNICAL, BUT... WE COMMISERATE MORE THAN WE CELEBRATE.
I THOUGHT YOU COULD TELL ME ABOUT WHY I INSPIRED YOU. I THOUGHT IF I UNDERSTOOD MORE OF WHAT YOU SAW IN ME, IT MIGHT REMIND ME WHY I'M DOING THIS.
I'VE GOT SOME ERRANDS TO RUN. COME WITH ME?

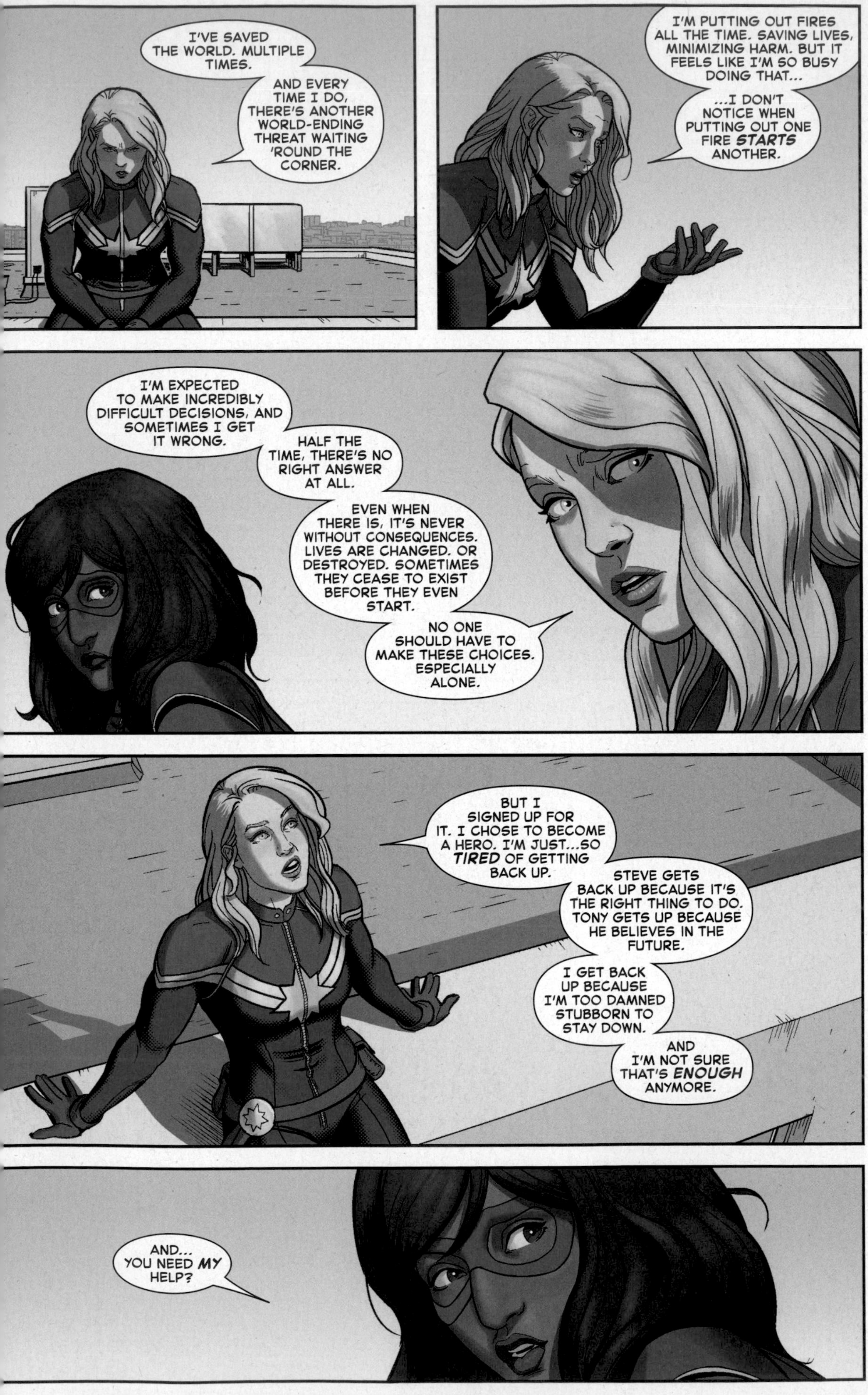
I'VE SAVED THE WORLD. MULTIPLE TIMES.
AND EVERY TIME I DO, THERE'S ANOTHER WORLD-ENDING THREAT WAITING 'ROUND THE CORNER.
I'M PUTTING OUT FIRES ALL THE TIME. SAVING LIVES, MINIMIZING HARM. BUT IT FEELS LIKE I'M SO BUSY DOING THAT...
...I DON'T NOTICE WHEN PUTTING OUT ONE FIRE *STARTS* ANOTHER.
I'M EXPECTED TO MAKE INCREDIBLY DIFFICULT DECISIONS, AND SOMETIMES I GET IT WRONG.
HALF THE TIME, THERE'S NO RIGHT ANSWER AT ALL.
EVEN WHEN THERE IS, IT'S NEVER WITHOUT CONSEQUENCES. LIVES ARE CHANGED. OR DESTROYED. SOMETIMES THEY CEASE TO EXIST BEFORE THEY EVEN START.
NO ONE SHOULD HAVE TO MAKE THESE CHOICES. ESPECIALLY ALONE.
BUT I SIGNED UP FOR IT. I CHOSE TO BECOME A HERO. I'M JUST...SO *TIRED* OF GETTING BACK UP.
STEVE GETS BACK UP BECAUSE IT'S THE RIGHT THING TO DO. TONY GETS UP BECAUSE HE BELIEVES IN THE FUTURE.
I GET BACK UP BECAUSE I'M TOO DAMNED STUBBORN TO STAY DOWN.
AND I'M NOT SURE THAT'S *ENOUGH* ANYMORE.
AND... YOU NEED *MY* HELP?

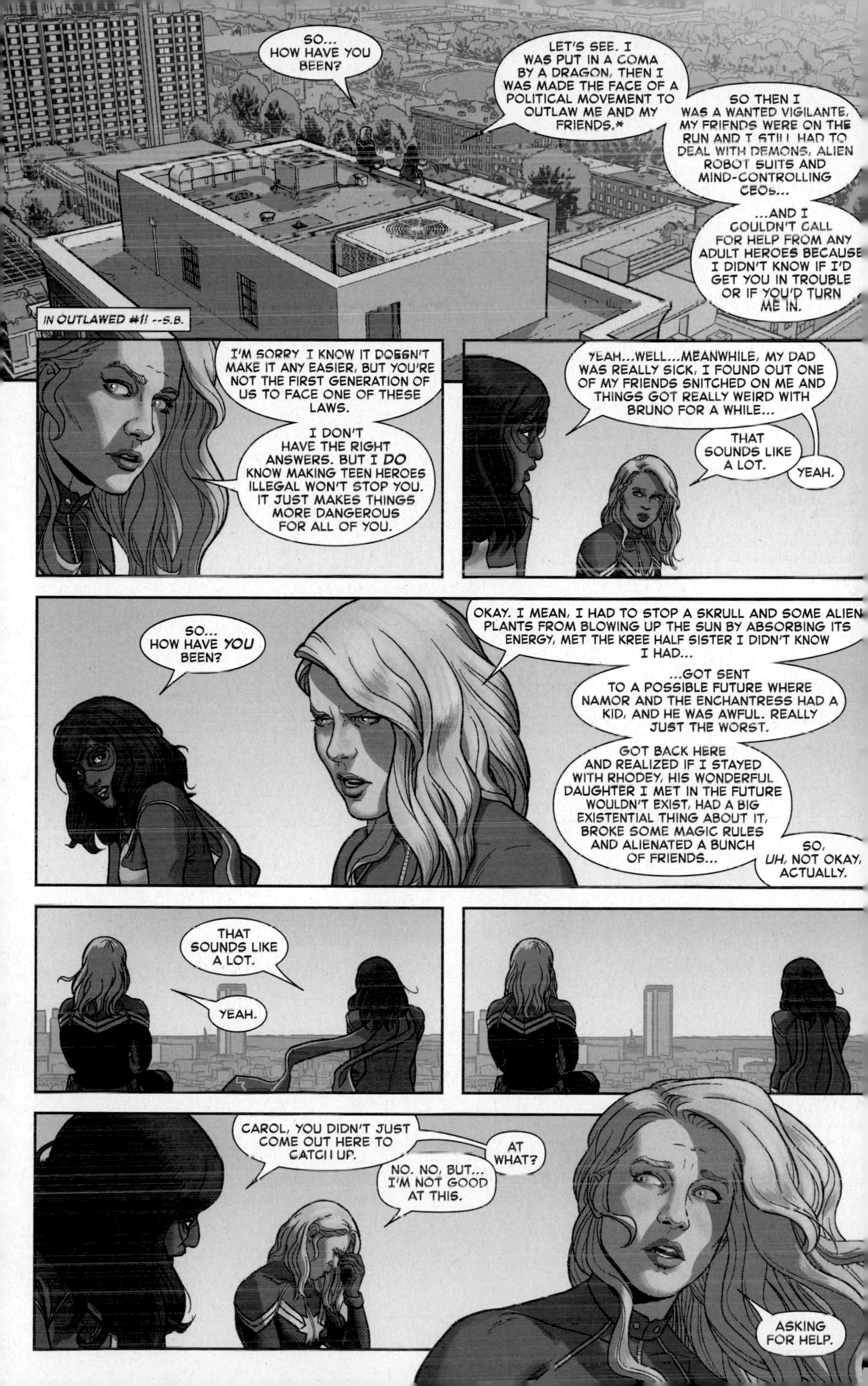
SO... HOW HAVE YOU BEEN?
LET'S SEE. I WAS PUT IN A COMA BY A DRAGON, THEN I WAS MADE THE FACE OF A POLITICAL MOVEMENT TO OUTLAW ME AND MY FRIENDS.*
SO THEN I WAS A WANTED VIGILANTE, MY FRIENDS WERE ON THE RUN AND I STILL HAD TO DEAL WITH DEMONS, ALIEN ROBOT SUITS AND MIND-CONTROLLING CEOs...
...AND I COULDN'T CALL FOR HELP FROM ANY ADULT HEROES BECAUSE I DIDN'T KNOW IF I'D GET YOU IN TROUBLE OR IF YOU'D TURN ME IN.
IN OUTLAWED #1! --S.B.
I'M SORRY. I KNOW IT DOESN'T MAKE IT ANY EASIER, BUT YOU'RE NOT THE FIRST GENERATION OF US TO FACE ONE OF THESE LAWS.
I DON'T HAVE THE RIGHT ANSWERS. BUT I DO KNOW MAKING TEEN HEROES ILLEGAL WON'T STOP YOU. IT JUST MAKES THINGS MORE DANGEROUS FOR ALL OF YOU.
YEAH...WELL...MEANWHILE, MY DAD WAS REALLY SICK, I FOUND OUT ONE OF MY FRIENDS SNITCHED ON ME AND THINGS GOT REALLY WEIRD WITH BRUNO FOR A WHILE...
THAT SOUNDS LIKE A LOT.
YEAH.
SO... HOW HAVE YOU BEEN?
OKAY. I MEAN, I HAD TO STOP A SKRULL AND SOME ALIEN PLANTS FROM BLOWING UP THE SUN BY ABSORBING ITS ENERGY, MET THE KREE HALF SISTER I DIDN'T KNOW I HAD...
...GOT SENT TO A POSSIBLE FUTURE WHERE NAMOR AND THE ENCHANTRESS HAD A KID, AND HE WAS AWFUL. REALLY JUST THE WORST.
GOT BACK HERE AND REALIZED IF I STAYED WITH RHODEY, HIS WONDERFUL DAUGHTER I MET IN THE FUTURE WOULDN'T EXIST, HAD A BIG EXISTENTIAL THING ABOUT IT, BROKE SOME MAGIC RULES AND ALIENATED A BUNCH OF FRIENDS...
SO, UH, NOT OKAY, ACTUALLY.
THAT SOUNDS LIKE A LOT.
YEAH.
CAROL, YOU DIDN'T JUST COME OUT HERE TO CATCH UP.
NO. NO, BUT... I'M NOT GOOD AT THIS.
AT WHAT?
ASKING FOR HELP.

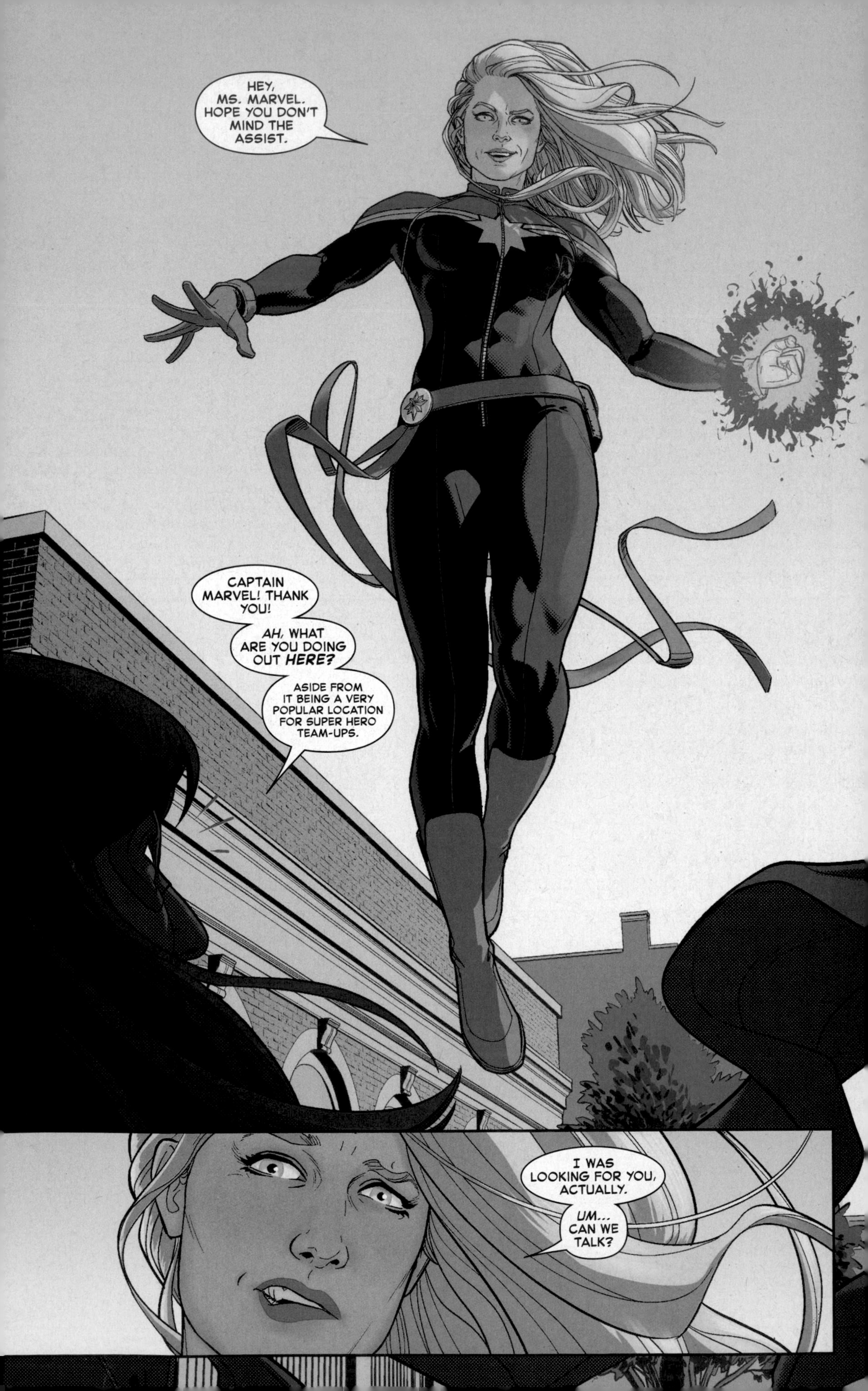
HEY, MS. MARVEL. HOPE YOU DON'T MIND THE ASSIST.
CAPTAIN MARVEL! THANK YOU!
AH, WHAT ARE YOU DOING OUT ***HERE?***
ASIDE FROM IT BEING A VERY POPULAR LOCATION FOR SUPER HERO TEAM-UPS.
I WAS LOOKING FOR YOU, ACTUALLY.
UM... CAN WE TALK?

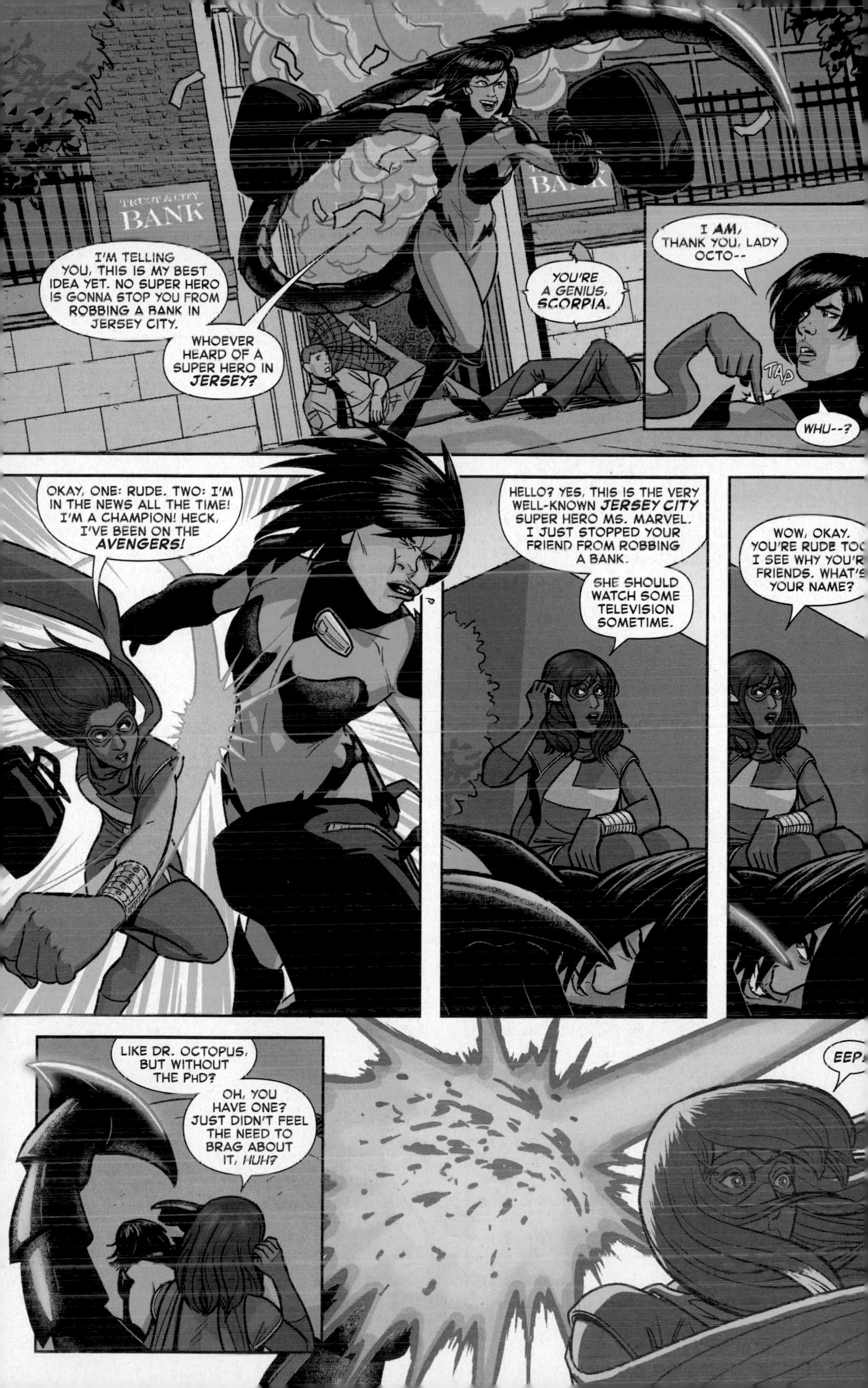

TRUST & CITY BANK
BANK
I'M TELLING YOU, THIS IS MY BEST IDEA YET. NO SUPER HERO IS GONNA STOP YOU FROM ROBBING A BANK IN JERSEY CITY.
WHOEVER HEARD OF A SUPER HERO IN JERSEY?
YOU'RE A GENIUS, SCORPIA.
I AM, THANK YOU, LADY OCTO--
TAP
WHU--?
OKAY, ONE: RUDE. TWO: I'M IN THE NEWS ALL THE TIME! I'M A CHAMPION! HECK, I'VE BEEN ON THE AVENGERS!
HELLO? YES, THIS IS THE VERY WELL-KNOWN JERSEY CITY SUPER HERO MS. MARVEL. I JUST STOPPED YOUR FRIEND FROM ROBBING A BANK.
SHE SHOULD WATCH SOME TELEVISION SOMETIME.
LIKE DR. OCTOPUS, BUT WITHOUT THE PhD?
OH, YOU HAVE ONE? JUST DIDN'T FEEL THE NEED TO BRAG ABOUT IT, HUH?

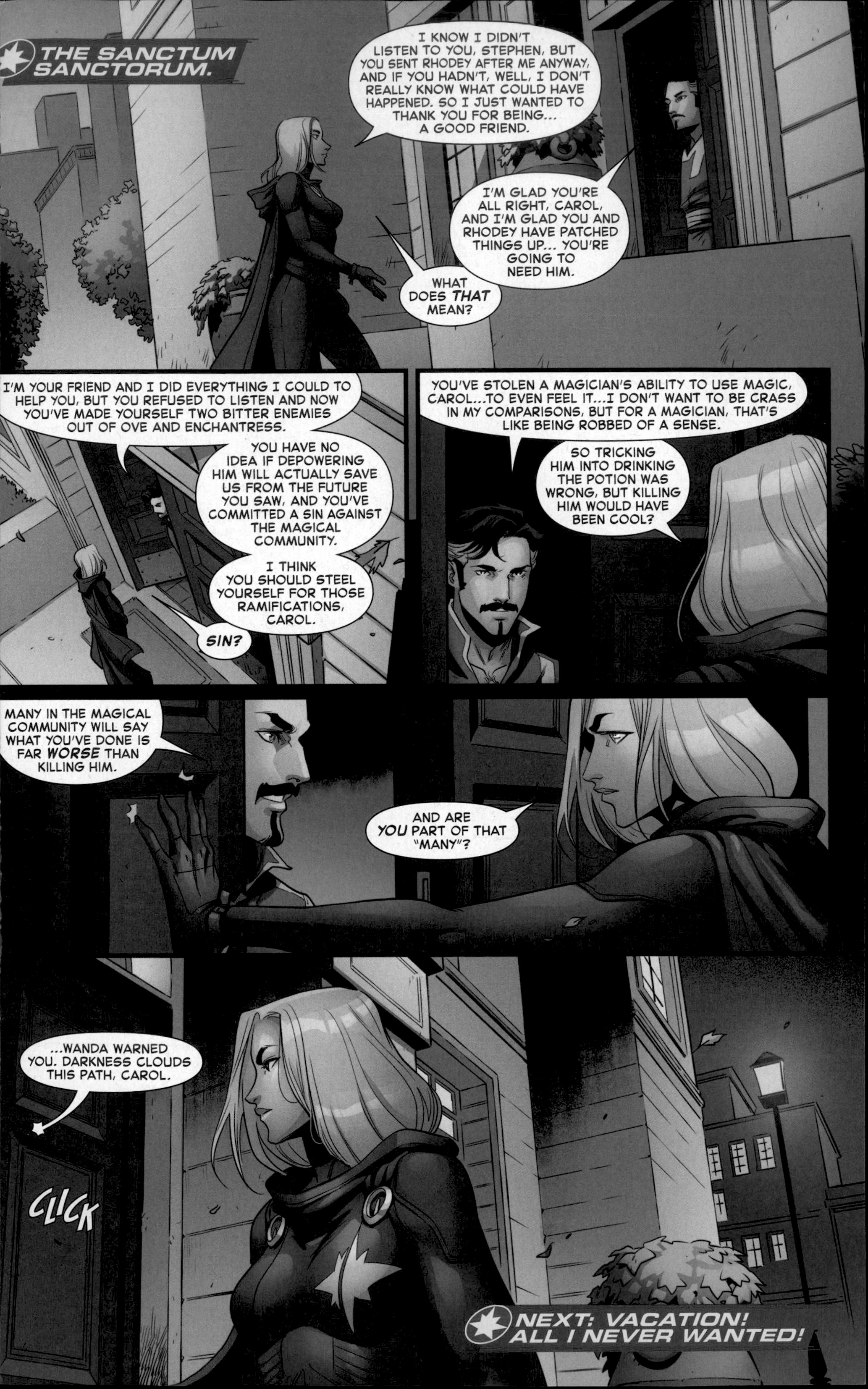
THE SANCTUM SANCTORUM.
I KNOW I DIDN'T LISTEN TO YOU, STEPHEN, BUT YOU SENT RHODEY AFTER ME ANYWAY, AND IF YOU HADN'T, WELL, I DON'T REALLY KNOW WHAT COULD HAVE HAPPENED. SO I JUST WANTED TO THANK YOU FOR BEING... A GOOD FRIEND.
I'M GLAD YOU'RE ALL RIGHT, CAROL, AND I'M GLAD YOU AND RHODEY HAVE PATCHED THINGS UP... YOU'RE GOING TO NEED HIM.
WHAT DOES THAT MEAN?
I'M YOUR FRIEND AND I DID EVERYTHING I COULD TO HELP YOU, BUT YOU REFUSED TO LISTEN AND NOW YOU'VE MADE YOURSELF TWO BITTER ENEMIES OUT OF OVE AND ENCHANTRESS.
YOU HAVE NO IDEA IF DEPOWERING HIM WILL ACTUALLY SAVE US FROM THE FUTURE YOU SAW, AND YOU'VE COMMITTED A SIN AGAINST THE MAGICAL COMMUNITY.
I THINK YOU SHOULD STEEL YOURSELF FOR THOSE RAMIFICATIONS, CAROL.
SIN?
YOU'VE STOLEN A MAGICIAN'S ABILITY TO USE MAGIC, CAROL...TO EVEN FEEL IT...I DON'T WANT TO BE CRASS IN MY COMPARISONS, BUT FOR A MAGICIAN, THAT'S LIKE BEING ROBBED OF A SENSE.
SO TRICKING HIM INTO DRINKING THE POTION WAS WRONG, BUT KILLING HIM WOULD HAVE BEEN COOL?
MANY IN THE MAGICAL COMMUNITY WILL SAY WHAT YOU'VE DONE IS FAR WORSE THAN KILLING HIM.
AND ARE YOU PART OF THAT "MANY"?
...WANDA WARNED YOU. DARKNESS CLOUDS THIS PATH, CAROL.
CLICK
NEXT: VACATION! ALL I NEVER WANTED!

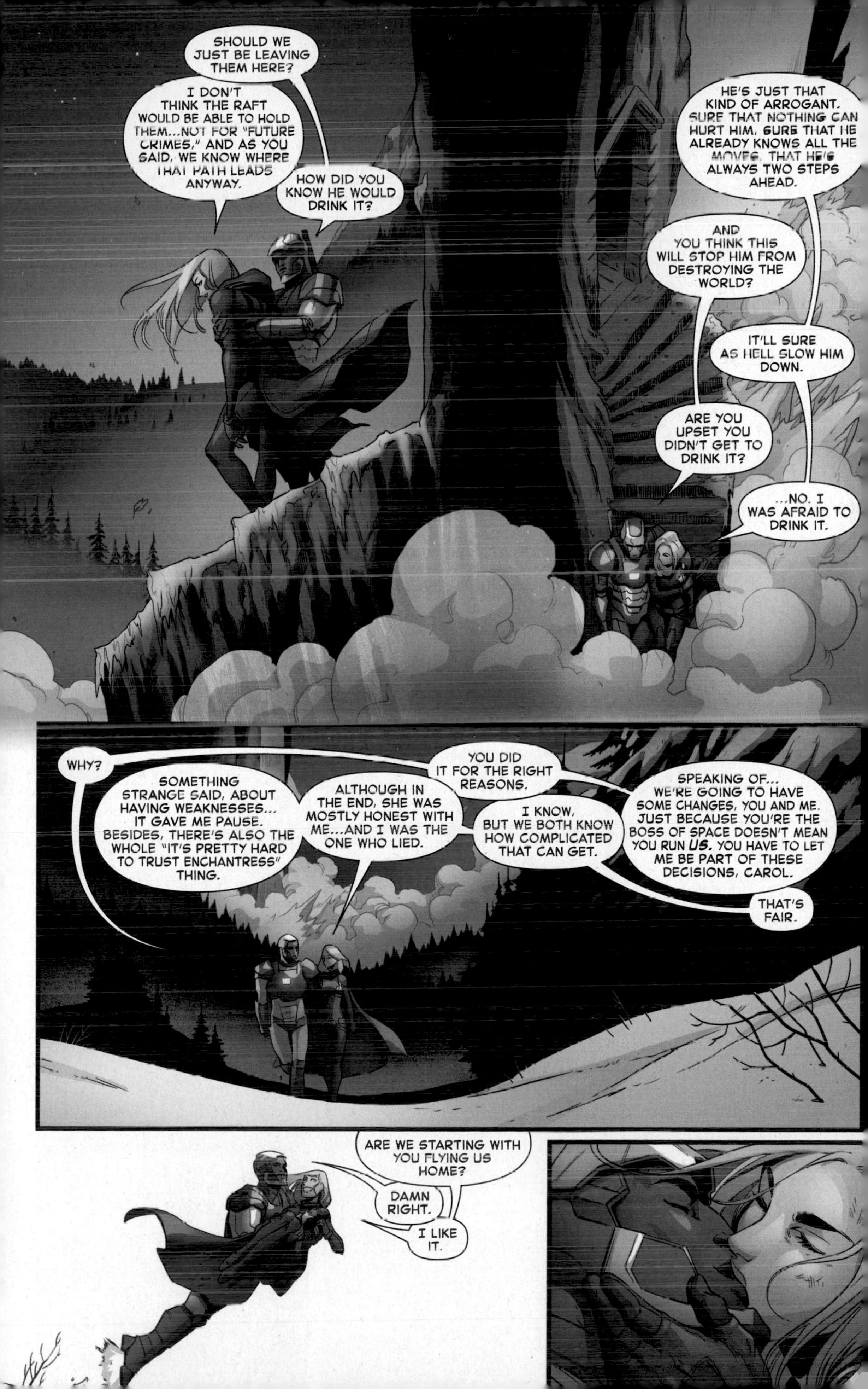
SHOULD WE JUST BE LEAVING THEM HERE?
I DON'T THINK THE RAFT WOULD BE ABLE TO HOLD THEM...NOT FOR "FUTURE CRIMES," AND AS YOU SAID, WE KNOW WHERE THAT PATH LEADS ANYWAY.
HOW DID YOU KNOW HE WOULD DRINK IT?
HE'S JUST THAT KIND OF ARROGANT. SURE THAT NOTHING CAN HURT HIM, SURE THAT HE ALREADY KNOWS ALL THE MOVES, THAT HE'S ALWAYS TWO STEPS AHEAD.
AND YOU THINK THIS WILL STOP HIM FROM DESTROYING THE WORLD?
IT'LL SURE AS HELL SLOW HIM DOWN.
ARE YOU UPSET YOU DIDN'T GET TO DRINK IT?
...NO. I WAS AFRAID TO DRINK IT.
WHY?
SOMETHING STRANGE SAID, ABOUT HAVING WEAKNESSES... IT GAVE ME PAUSE. BESIDES, THERE'S ALSO THE WHOLE "IT'S PRETTY HARD TO TRUST ENCHANTRESS" THING.
ALTHOUGH IN THE END, SHE WAS MOSTLY HONEST WITH ME...AND I WAS THE ONE WHO LIED.
YOU DID IT FOR THE RIGHT REASONS.
I KNOW, BUT WE BOTH KNOW HOW COMPLICATED THAT CAN GET.
SPEAKING OF... WE'RE GOING TO HAVE SOME CHANGES, YOU AND ME. JUST BECAUSE YOU'RE THE BOSS OF SPACE DOESN'T MEAN YOU RUN US. YOU HAVE TO LET ME BE PART OF THESE DECISIONS, CAROL.
THAT'S FAIR.
ARE WE STARTING WITH YOU FLYING US HOME?
DAMN RIGHT.
I LIKE IT.

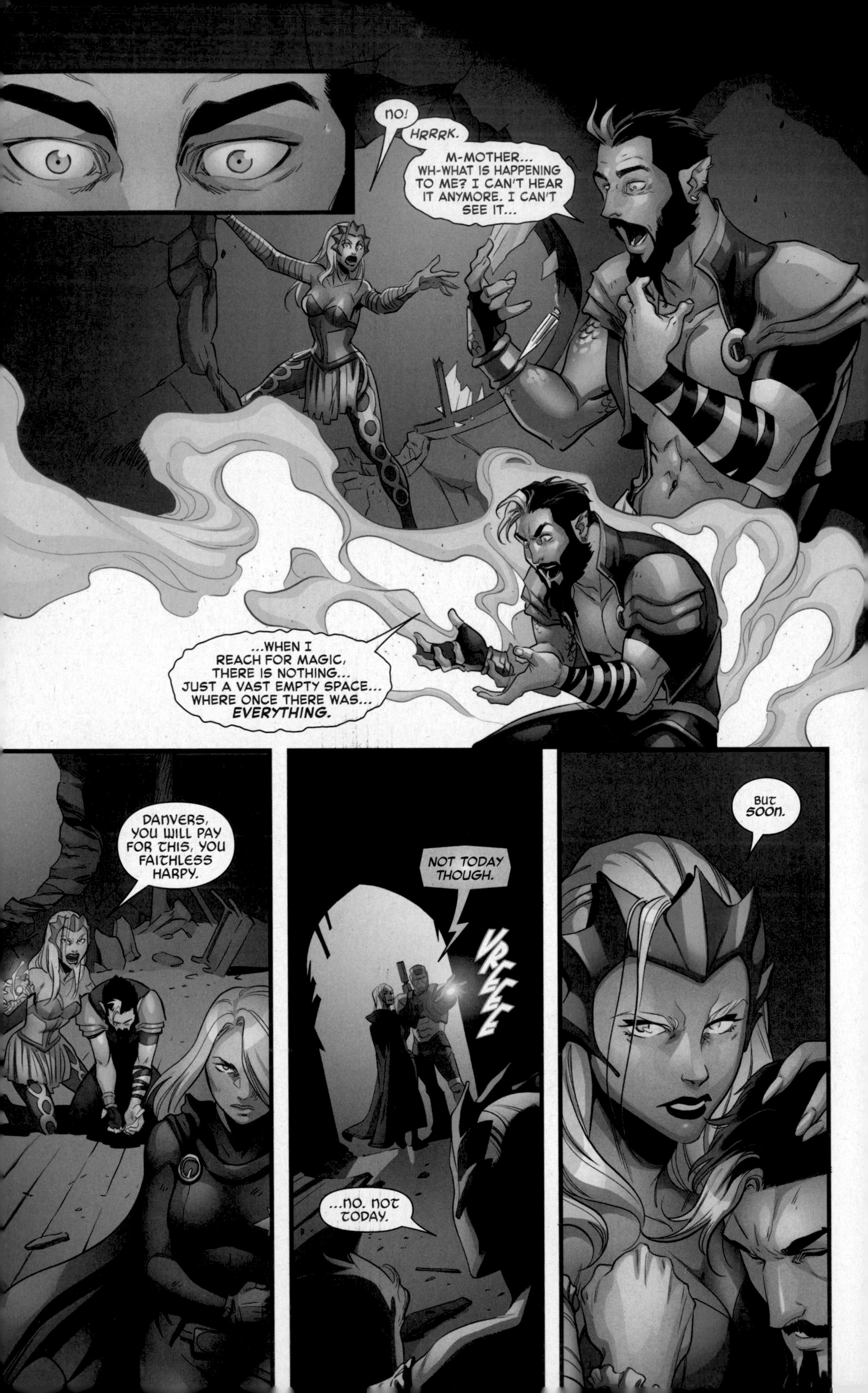
NO!
HRRRK.
M-MOTHER... WH-WHAT IS HAPPENING TO ME? I CAN'T HEAR IT ANYMORE. I CAN'T SEE IT...
...WHEN I REACH FOR MAGIC, THERE IS NOTHING... JUST A VAST EMPTY SPACE... WHERE ONCE THERE WAS... EVERYTHING.
DANVERS, YOU WILL PAY FOR THIS, YOU FAITHLESS HARPY.
NOT TODAY THOUGH.
VREEE
...NO. NOT TODAY.
BUT SOON.

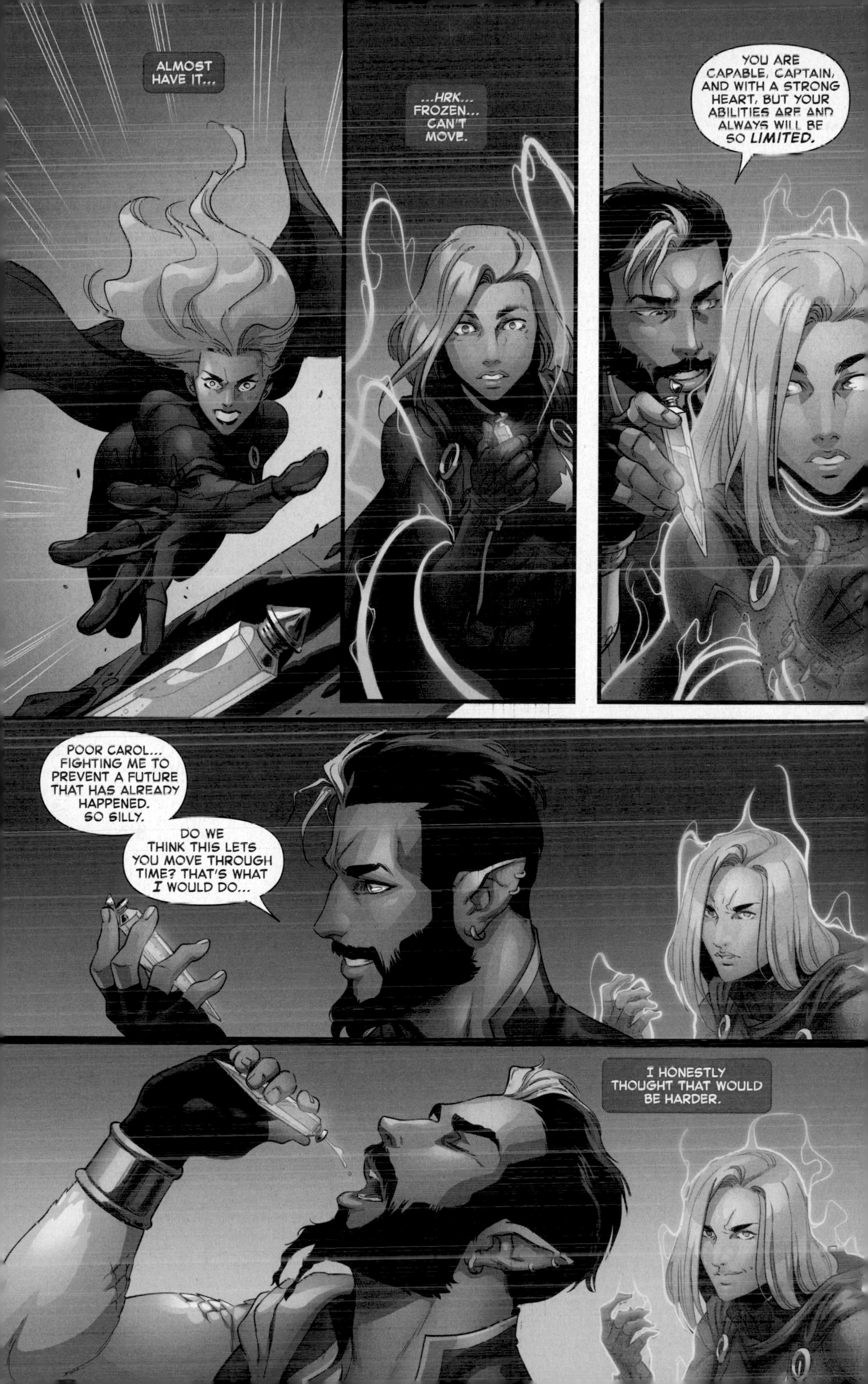
ALMOST HAVE IT...
...HRK... FROZEN... CAN'T MOVE.
YOU ARE CAPABLE, CAPTAIN, AND WITH A STRONG HEART, BUT YOUR ABILITIES ARE AND ALWAYS WILL BE SO LIMITED.
POOR CAROL... FIGHTING ME TO PREVENT A FUTURE THAT HAS ALREADY HAPPENED. SO SILLY.
DO WE THINK THIS LETS YOU MOVE THROUGH TIME? THAT'S WHAT I WOULD DO...
I HONESTLY THOUGHT THAT WOULD BE HARDER.

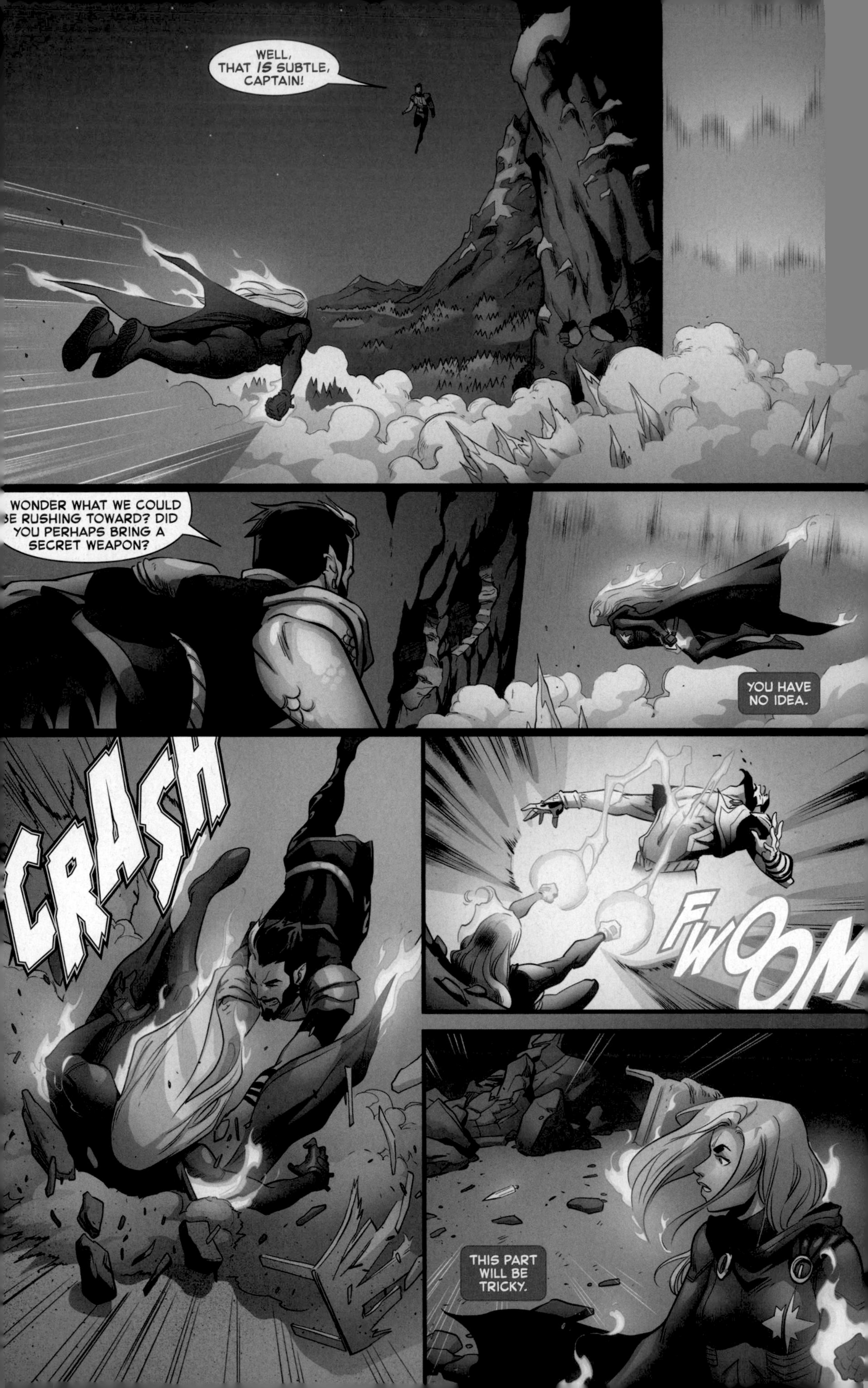

WELL, THAT IS SUBTLE, CAPTAIN!
WONDER WHAT WE COULD BE RUSHING TOWARD? DID YOU PERHAPS BRING A SECRET WEAPON?
YOU HAVE NO IDEA.
CRASH
FWOOM
THIS PART WILL BE TRICKY.

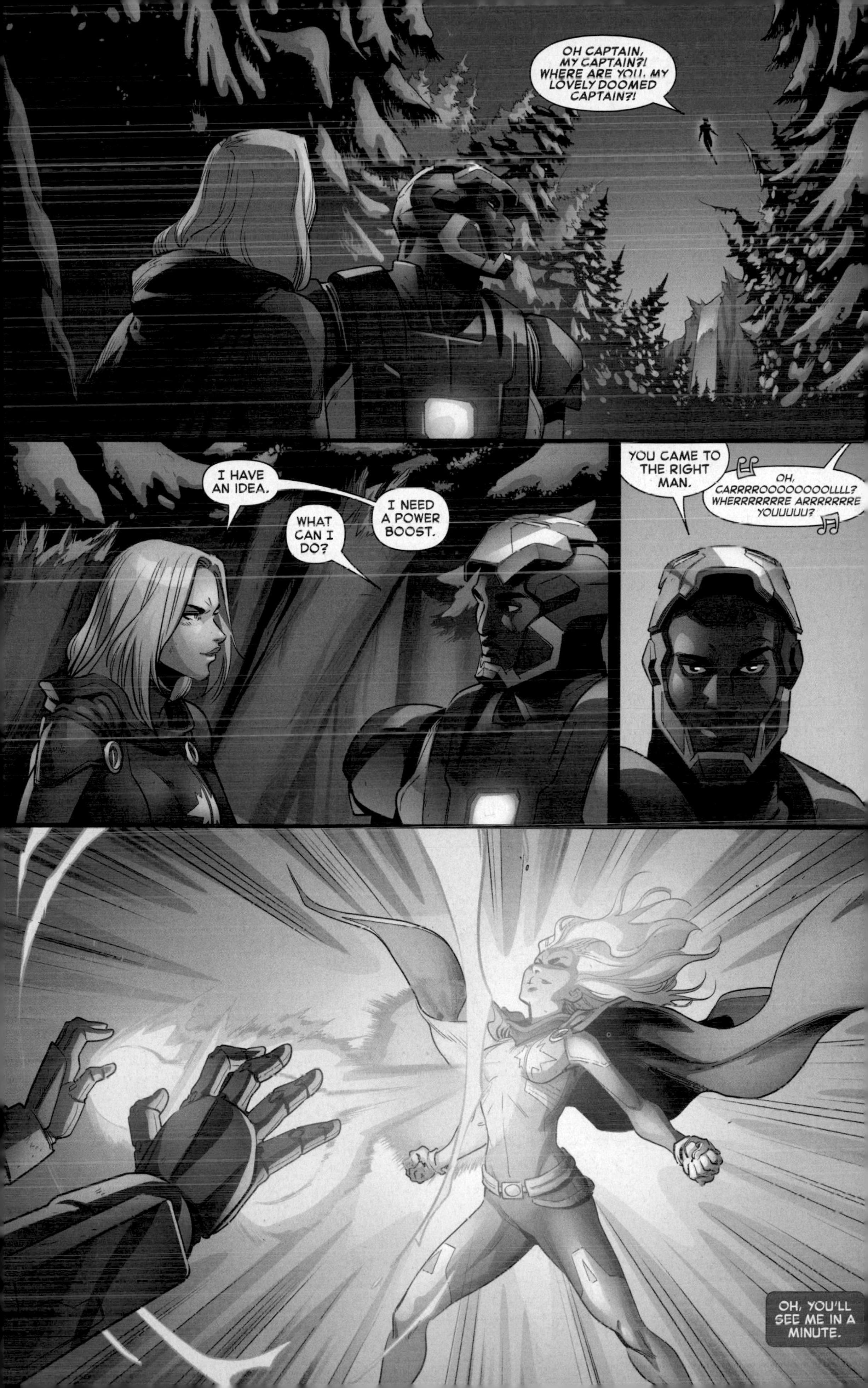
OH CAPTAIN, MY CAPTAIN?! WHERE ARE YOU, MY LOVELY DOOMED CAPTAIN?!
I HAVE AN IDEA.
I NEED A POWER BOOST.
WHAT CAN I DO?
YOU CAME TO THE RIGHT MAN.
OH, CARRRROOOOOOOOLLLL? WHERRRRRRE ARRRRRRRE YOUUUUU?
OH, YOU'LL SEE ME IN A MINUTE.

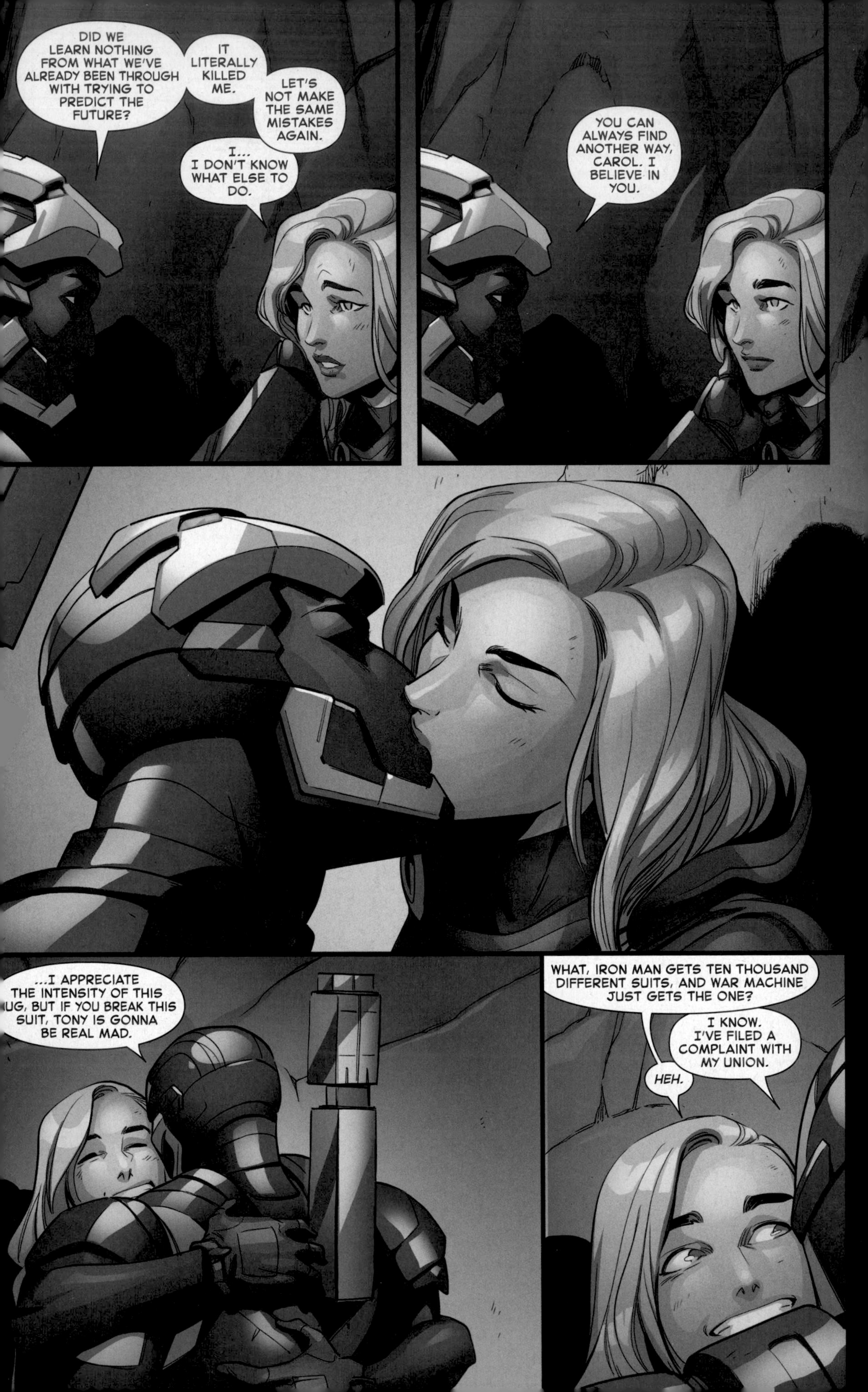
DID WE LEARN NOTHING FROM WHAT WE'VE ALREADY BEEN THROUGH WITH TRYING TO PREDICT THE FUTURE?
IT LITERALLY KILLED ME.
LET'S NOT MAKE THE SAME MISTAKES AGAIN.
I... I DON'T KNOW WHAT ELSE TO DO.
YOU CAN ALWAYS FIND ANOTHER WAY, CAROL. I BELIEVE IN YOU.
...I APPRECIATE THE INTENSITY OF THIS HUG, BUT IF YOU BREAK THIS SUIT, TONY IS GONNA BE REAL MAD.
WHAT, IRON MAN GETS TEN THOUSAND DIFFERENT SUITS, AND WAR MACHINE JUST GETS THE ONE?
HEH.
I KNOW. I'VE FILED A COMPLAINT WITH MY UNION.

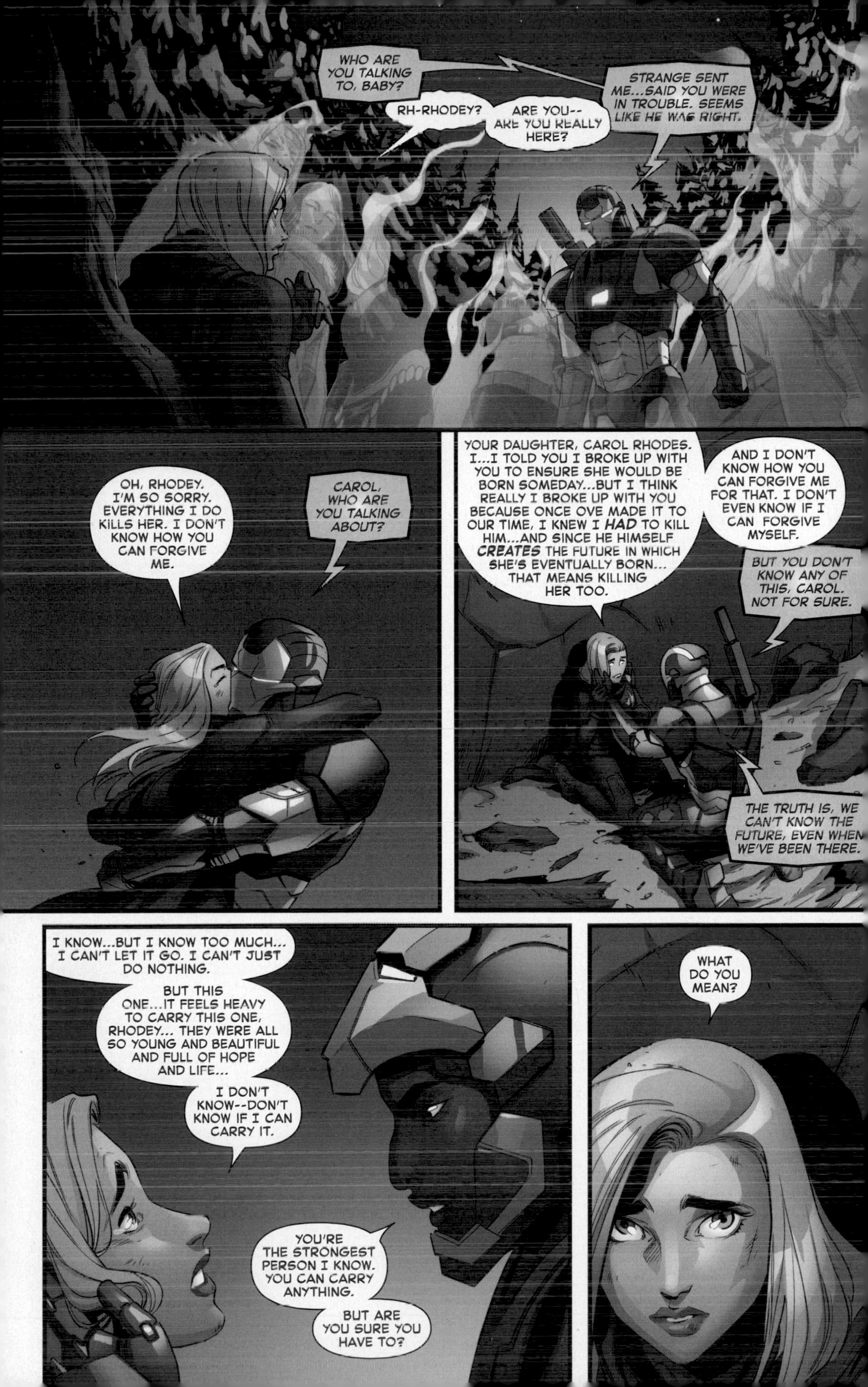
WHO ARE YOU TALKING TO, BABY?
RH-RHODEY?
ARE YOU-- ARE YOU REALLY HERE?
STRANGE SENT ME...SAID YOU WERE IN TROUBLE. SEEMS LIKE HE WAS RIGHT.
OH, RHODEY. I'M SO SORRY. EVERYTHING I DO KILLS HER. I DON'T KNOW HOW YOU CAN FORGIVE ME.
CAROL, WHO ARE YOU TALKING ABOUT?
YOUR DAUGHTER, CAROL RHODES. I...I TOLD YOU I BROKE UP WITH YOU TO ENSURE SHE WOULD BE BORN SOMEDAY...BUT I THINK REALLY I BROKE UP WITH YOU BECAUSE ONCE OVE MADE IT TO OUR TIME, I KNEW I HAD TO KILL HIM...AND SINCE HE HIMSELF CREATES THE FUTURE IN WHICH SHE'S EVENTUALLY BORN... THAT MEANS KILLING HER TOO.
AND I DON'T KNOW HOW YOU CAN FORGIVE ME FOR THAT. I DON'T EVEN KNOW IF I CAN FORGIVE MYSELF.
BUT YOU DON'T KNOW ANY OF THIS, CAROL. NOT FOR SURE.
THE TRUTH IS, WE CAN'T KNOW THE FUTURE, EVEN WHEN WE'VE BEEN THERE.
I KNOW...BUT I KNOW TOO MUCH... I CAN'T LET IT GO. I CAN'T JUST DO NOTHING.
BUT THIS ONE...IT FEELS HEAVY TO CARRY THIS ONE, RHODEY... THEY WERE ALL SO YOUNG AND BEAUTIFUL AND FULL OF HOPE AND LIFE...
I DON'T KNOW--DON'T KNOW IF I CAN CARRY IT.
YOU'RE THE STRONGEST PERSON I KNOW. YOU CAN CARRY ANYTHING.
BUT ARE YOU SURE YOU HAVE TO?
WHAT DO YOU MEAN?

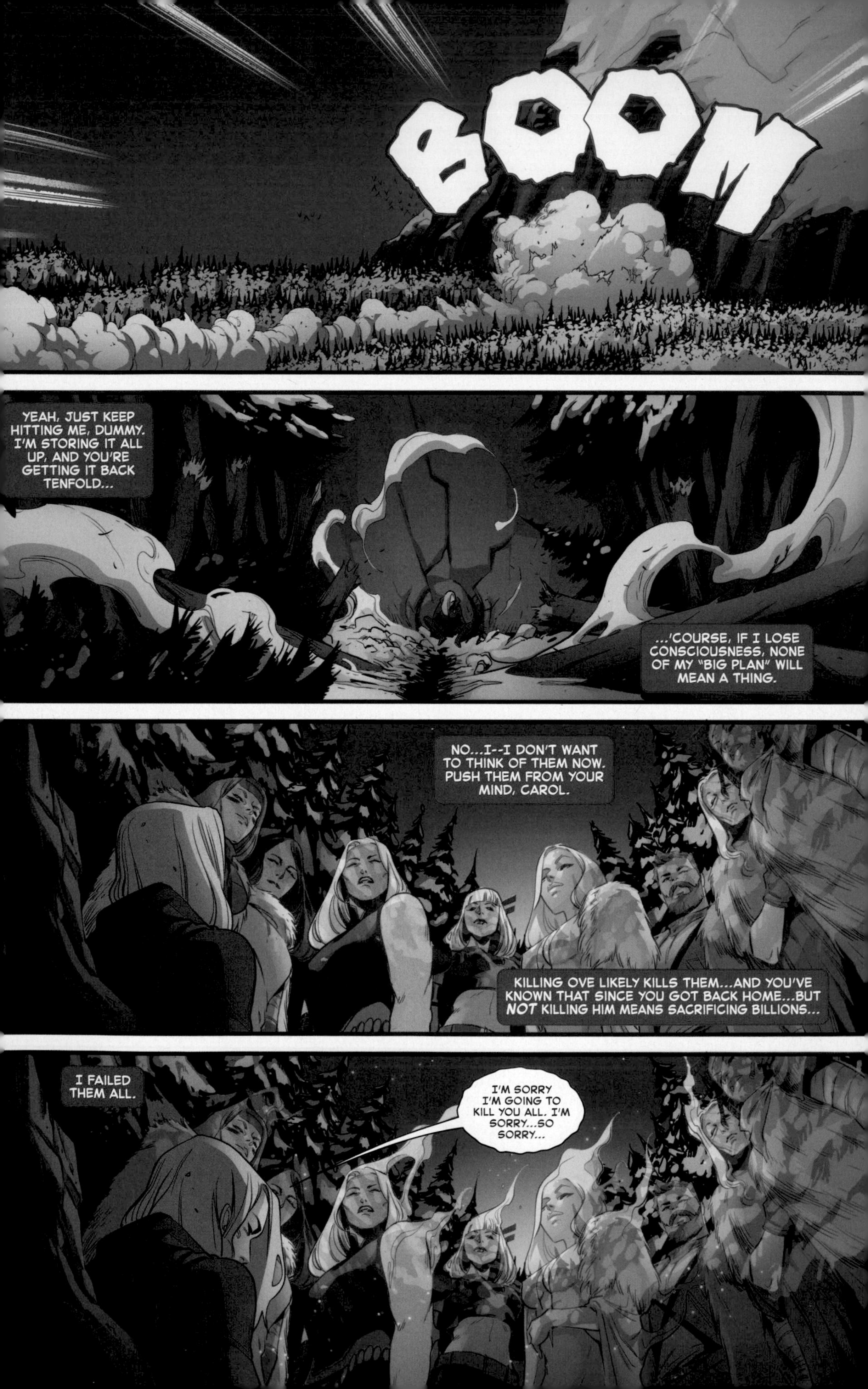
BOOM
YEAH, JUST KEEP HITTING ME, DUMMY. I'M STORING IT ALL UP, AND YOU'RE GETTING IT BACK TENFOLD...
...'COURSE, IF I LOSE CONSCIOUSNESS, NONE OF MY "BIG PLAN" WILL MEAN A THING.
NO...I--I DON'T WANT TO THINK OF THEM NOW. PUSH THEM FROM YOUR MIND, CAROL.
KILLING OVE LIKELY KILLS THEM...AND YOU'VE KNOWN THAT SINCE YOU GOT BACK HOME...BUT NOT KILLING HIM MEANS SACRIFICING BILLIONS...
I FAILED THEM ALL.
I'M SORRY I'M GOING TO KILL YOU ALL. I'M SORRY...SO SORRY...

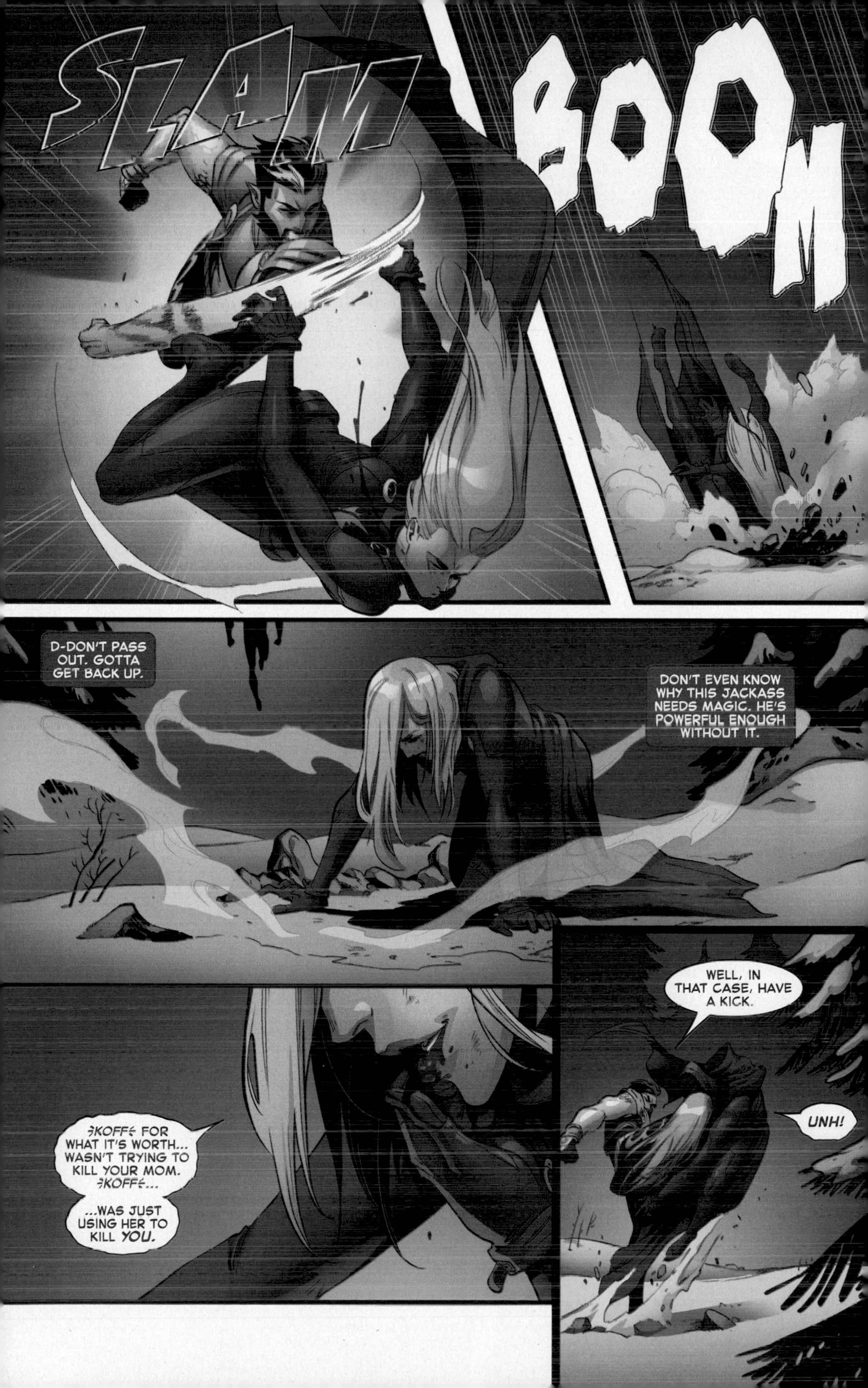
SLAM
BOOM
D-DON'T PASS OUT. GOTTA GET BACK UP.
DON'T EVEN KNOW WHY THIS JACKASS NEEDS MAGIC. HE'S POWERFUL ENOUGH WITHOUT IT.
KOFF FOR WHAT IT'S WORTH... WASN'T TRYING TO KILL YOUR MOM. *KOFF*...
...WAS JUST USING HER TO KILL YOU.
WELL, IN THAT CASE, HAVE A KICK.
UNH!

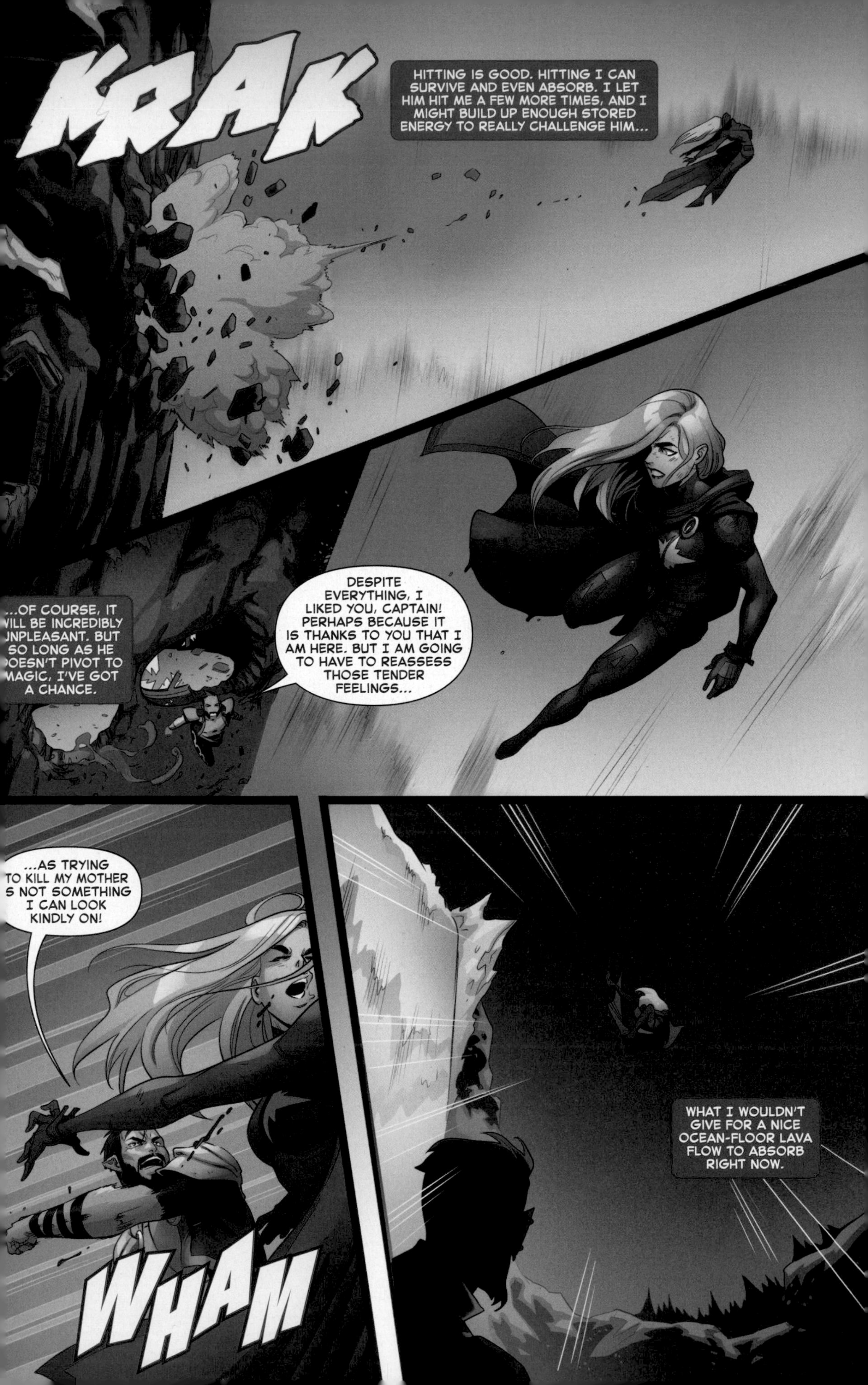
KRAK
HITTING IS GOOD. HITTING I CAN SURVIVE AND EVEN ABSORB. I LET HIM HIT ME A FEW MORE TIMES, AND I MIGHT BUILD UP ENOUGH STORED ENERGY TO REALLY CHALLENGE HIM...
...OF COURSE, IT WILL BE INCREDIBLY UNPLEASANT. BUT SO LONG AS HE DOESN'T PIVOT TO MAGIC, I'VE GOT A CHANCE.
DESPITE EVERYTHING, I LIKED YOU, CAPTAIN! PERHAPS BECAUSE IT IS THANKS TO YOU THAT I AM HERE. BUT I AM GOING TO HAVE TO REASSESS THOSE TENDER FEELINGS...
...AS TRYING TO KILL MY MOTHER IS NOT SOMETHING I CAN LOOK KINDLY ON!
WHAM
WHAT I WOULDN'T GIVE FOR A NICE OCEAN-FLOOR LAVA FLOW TO ABSORB RIGHT NOW.

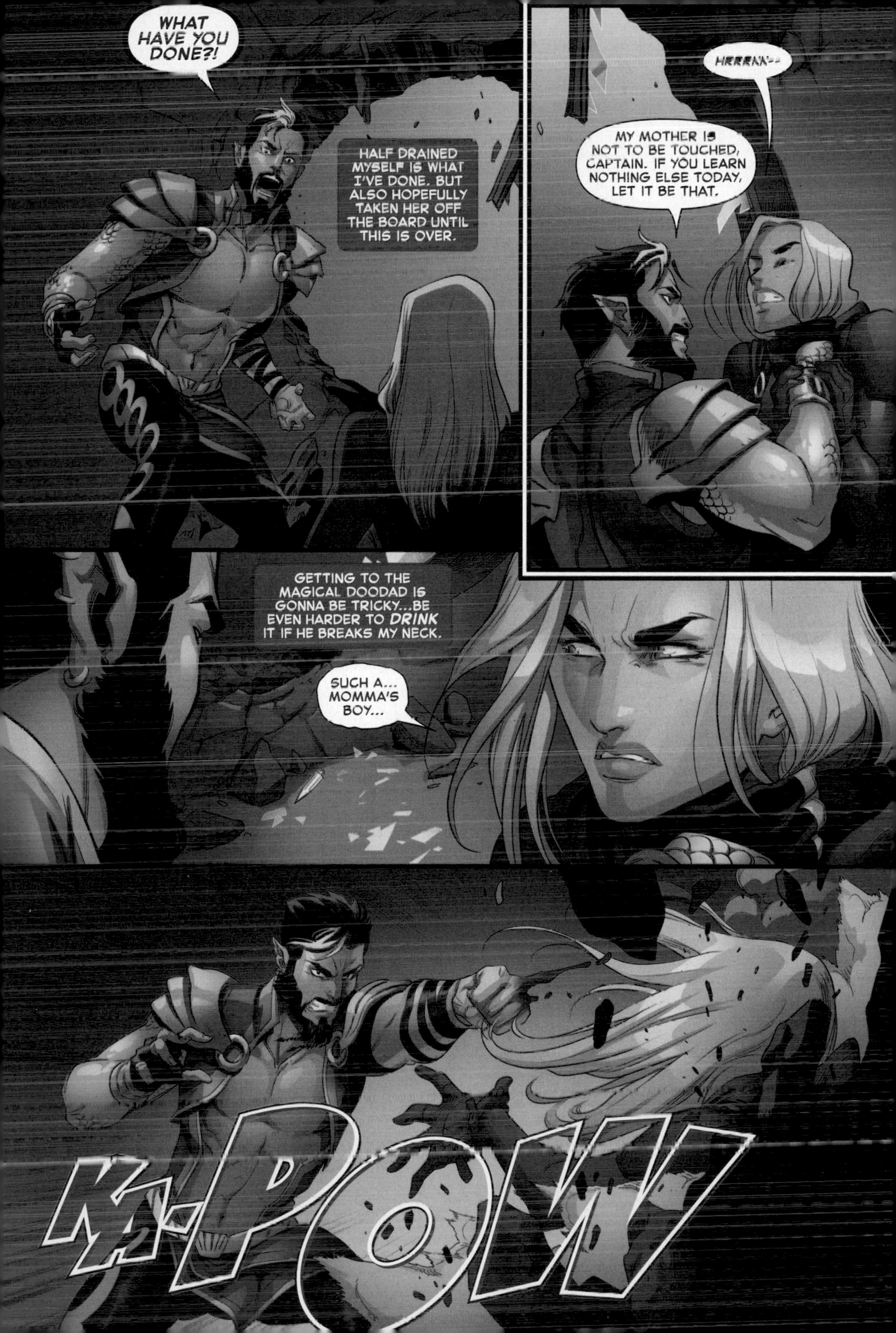

WHAT HAVE YOU DONE?!
HALF DRAINED MYSELF IS WHAT I'VE DONE. BUT ALSO HOPEFULLY TAKEN HER OFF THE BOARD UNTIL THIS IS OVER.
HRRRKK--
MY MOTHER IS NOT TO BE TOUCHED, CAPTAIN. IF YOU LEARN NOTHING ELSE TODAY, LET IT BE THAT.
GETTING TO THE MAGICAL DOODAD IS GONNA BE TRICKY...BE EVEN HARDER TO DRINK IT IF HE BREAKS MY NECK.
SUCH A... MOMMA'S BOY...
K-POW

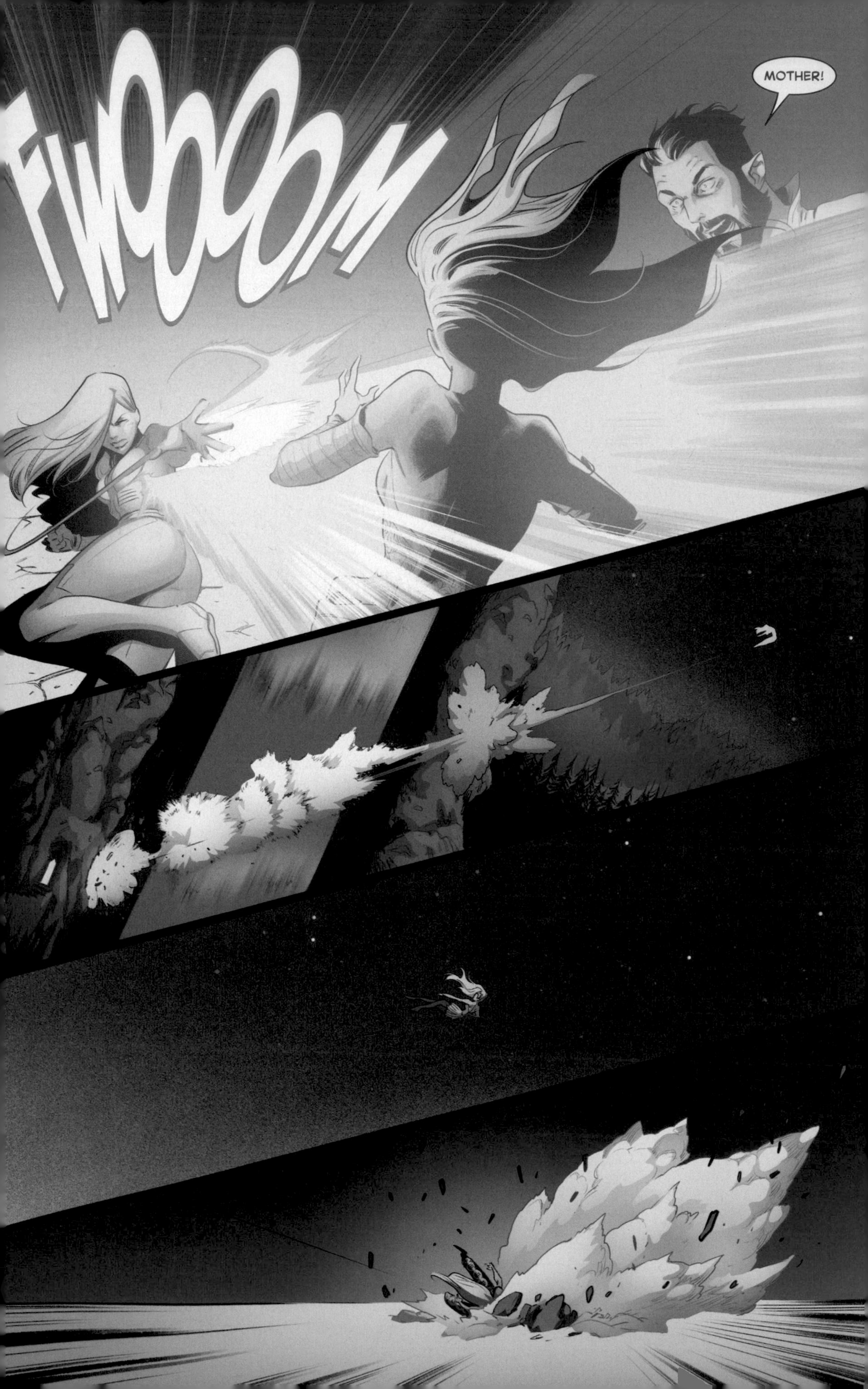
FWOOOM
MOTHER!

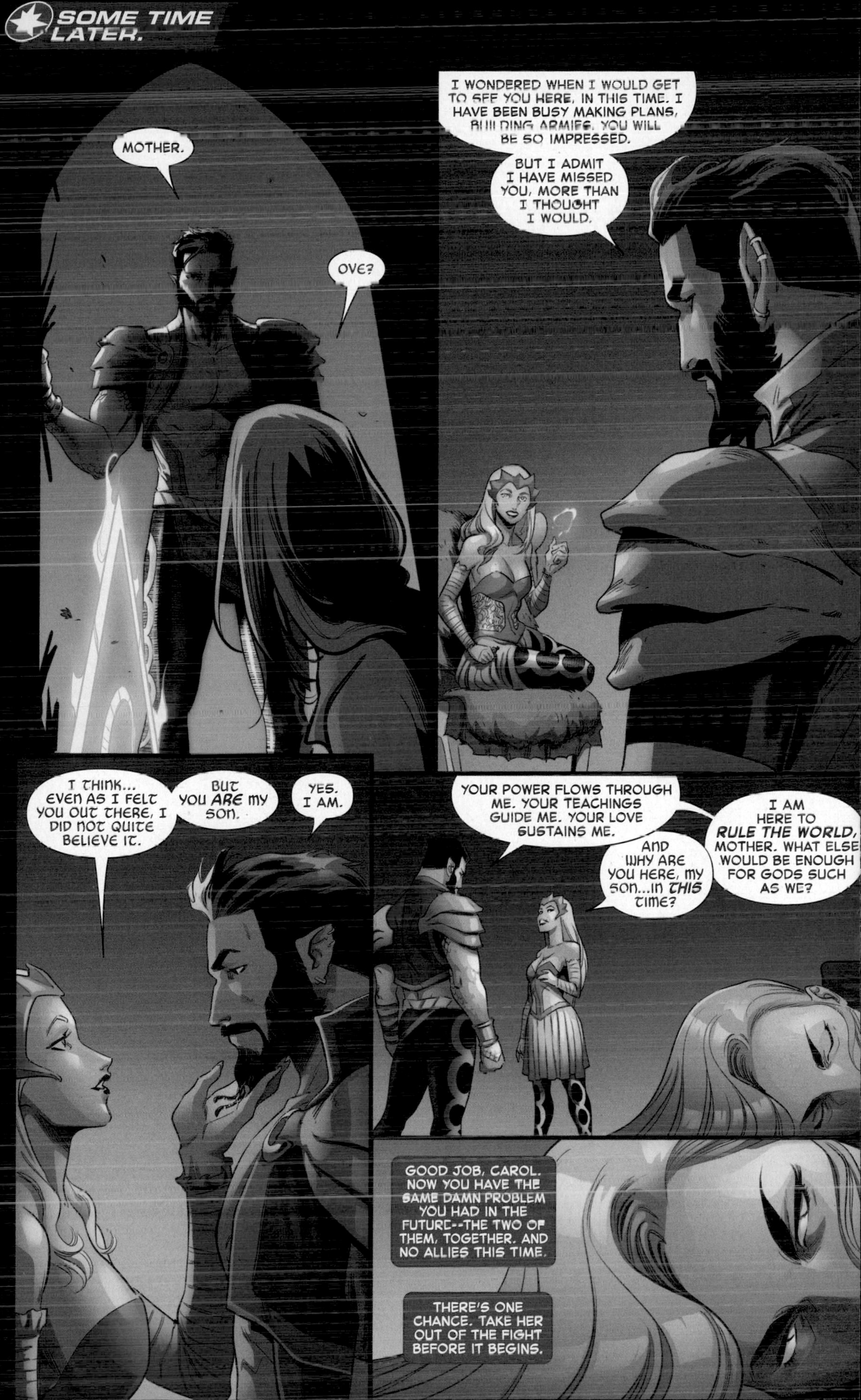
SOME TIME LATER.
MOTHER.
OVE?
I WONDERED WHEN I WOULD GET TO SEE YOU HERE, IN THIS TIME. I HAVE BEEN BUSY MAKING PLANS, BUILDING ARMIES. YOU WILL BE SO IMPRESSED.
BUT I ADMIT I HAVE MISSED YOU, MORE THAN I THOUGHT I WOULD.
I THINK... EVEN AS I FELT YOU OUT THERE, I DID NOT QUITE BELIEVE IT.
BUT YOU ARE MY SON.
YES. I AM.
YOUR POWER FLOWS THROUGH ME. YOUR TEACHINGS GUIDE ME. YOUR LOVE SUSTAINS ME.
AND WHY ARE YOU HERE, MY SON...IN THIS TIME?
I AM HERE TO RULE THE WORLD, MOTHER. WHAT ELSE WOULD BE ENOUGH FOR GODS SUCH AS WE?
GOOD JOB, CAROL. NOW YOU HAVE THE SAME DAMN PROBLEM YOU HAD IN THE FUTURE--THE TWO OF THEM, TOGETHER. AND NO ALLIES THIS TIME.
THERE'S ONE CHANCE. TAKE HER OUT OF THE FIGHT BEFORE IT BEGINS.

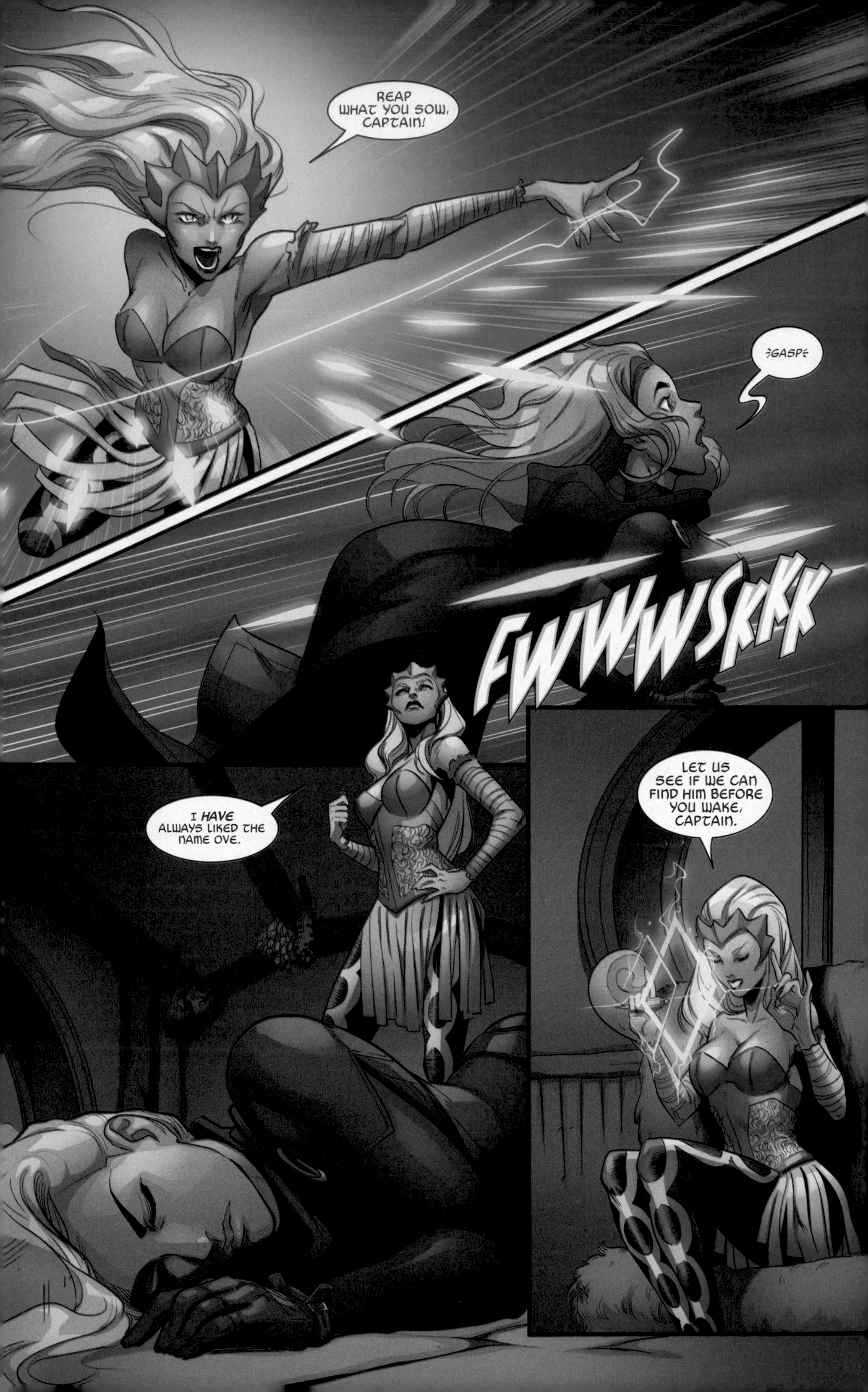
REAP WHAT YOU SOW, CAPTAIN!
GASP
FWWWSKKK
I HAVE ALWAYS LIKED THE NAME OVE.
LET US SEE IF WE CAN FIND HIM BEFORE YOU WAKE, CAPTAIN.

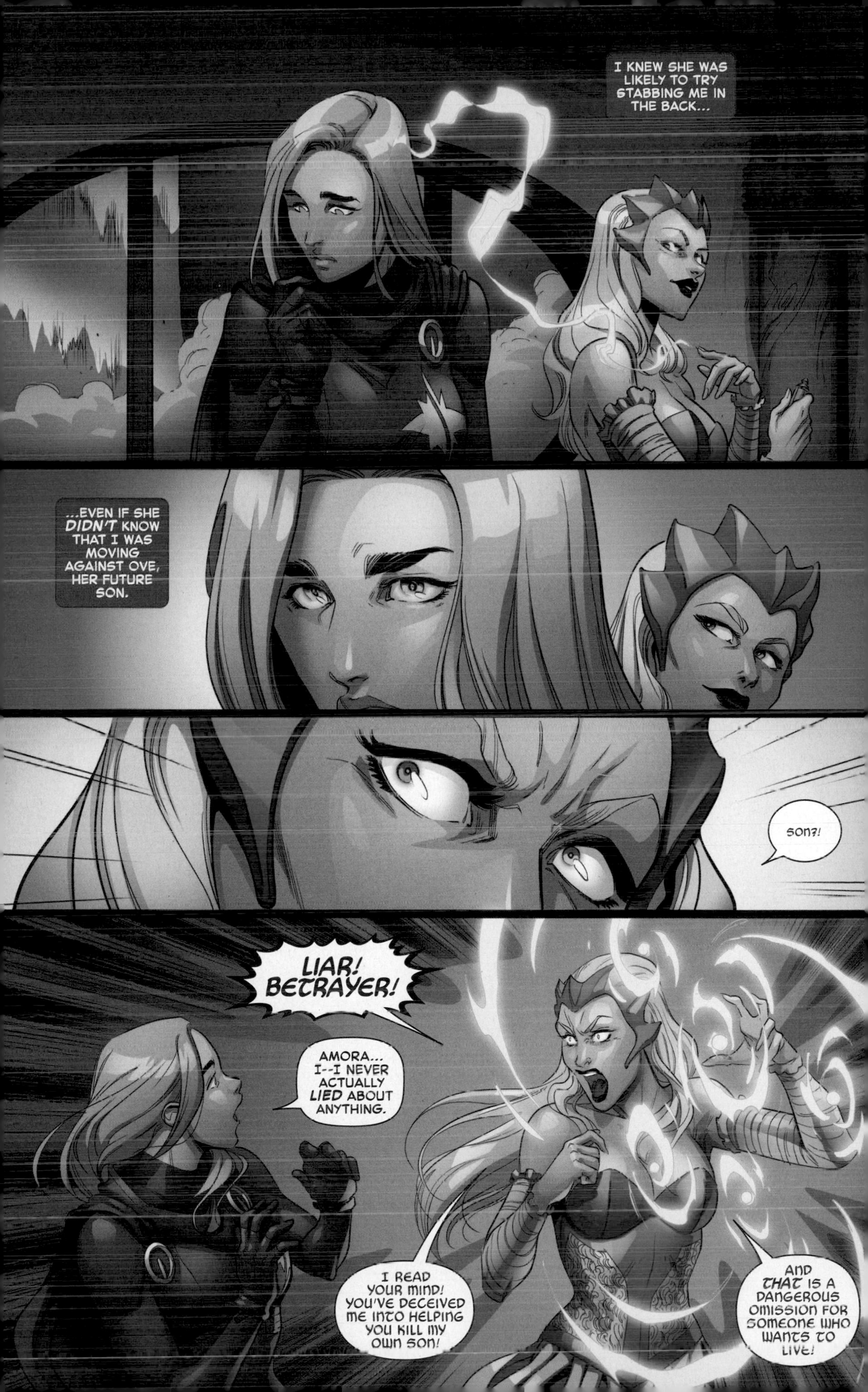

I KNEW SHE WAS LIKELY TO TRY STABBING ME IN THE BACK...
...EVEN IF SHE *DIDN'T* KNOW THAT I WAS MOVING AGAINST OVE, HER FUTURE SON.
SON?!
LIAR! BETRAYER!
AMORA... I--I NEVER ACTUALLY *LIED* ABOUT ANYTHING.
I READ YOUR MIND! YOU'VE DECEIVED ME INTO HELPING YOU KILL MY OWN SON!
AND *THAT* IS A DANGEROUS OMISSION FOR SOMEONE WHO WANTS TO LIVE!

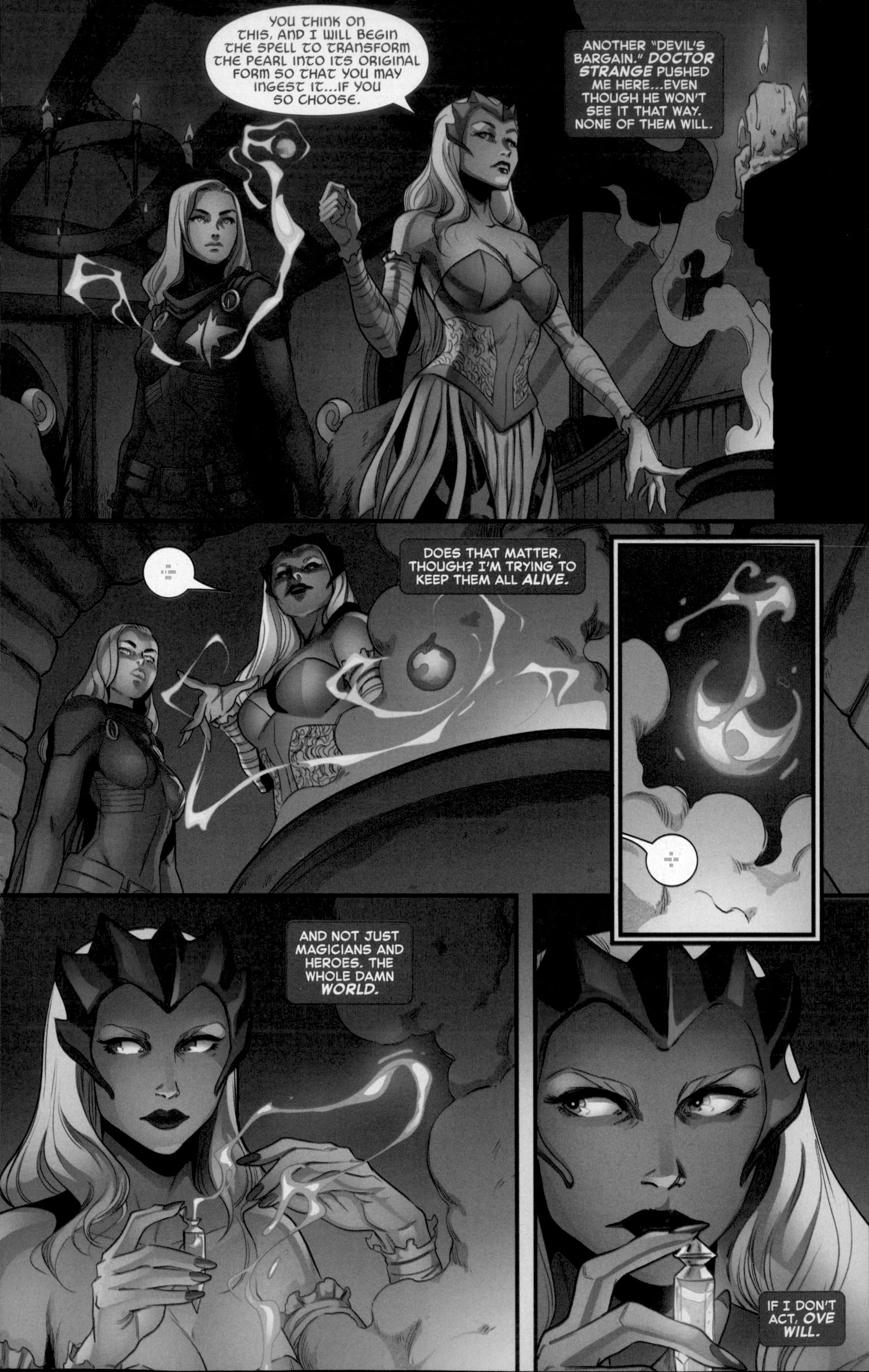
YOU THINK ON THIS, AND I WILL BEGIN THE SPELL TO TRANSFORM THE PEARL INTO ITS ORIGINAL FORM SO THAT YOU MAY INGEST IT...IF YOU SO CHOOSE.
ANOTHER "DEVIL'S BARGAIN." DOCTOR STRANGE PUSHED ME HERE...EVEN THOUGH HE WON'T SEE IT THAT WAY. NONE OF THEM WILL.
DOES THAT MATTER, THOUGH? I'M TRYING TO KEEP THEM ALL ALIVE.
AND NOT JUST MAGICIANS AND HEROES. THE WHOLE DAMN WORLD.
IF I DON'T ACT, OVE WILL.

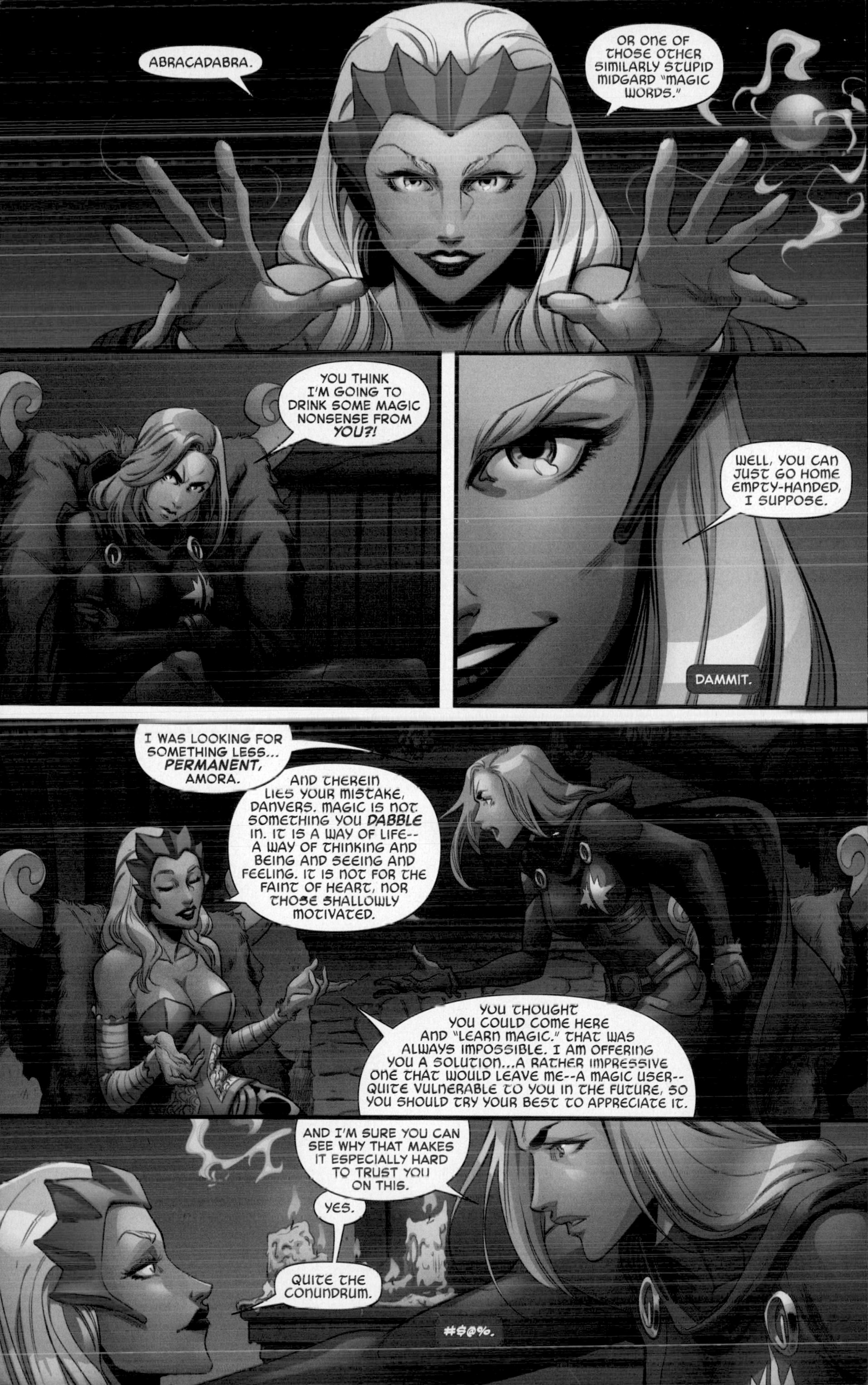
ABRACADABRA.
OR ONE OF THOSE OTHER SIMILARLY STUPID MIDGARD "MAGIC WORDS."
YOU THINK I'M GOING TO DRINK SOME MAGIC NONSENSE FROM YOU?!
WELL, YOU CAN JUST GO HOME EMPTY-HANDED, I SUPPOSE.
DAMMIT.
I WAS LOOKING FOR SOMETHING LESS... PERMANENT, AMORA.
AND THEREIN LIES YOUR MISTAKE, DANVERS. MAGIC IS NOT SOMETHING YOU DABBLE IN. IT IS A WAY OF LIFE-- A WAY OF THINKING AND BEING AND SEEING AND FEELING. IT IS NOT FOR THE FAINT OF HEART, NOR THOSE SHALLOWLY MOTIVATED.
YOU THOUGHT YOU COULD COME HERE AND "LEARN MAGIC." THAT WAS ALWAYS IMPOSSIBLE. I AM OFFERING YOU A SOLUTION...A RATHER IMPRESSIVE ONE THAT WOULD LEAVE ME--A MAGIC USER-- QUITE VULNERABLE TO YOU IN THE FUTURE, SO YOU SHOULD TRY YOUR BEST TO APPRECIATE IT.
AND I'M SURE YOU CAN SEE WHY THAT MAKES IT ESPECIALLY HARD TO TRUST YOU ON THIS.
YES.
QUITE THE CONUNDRUM.
#$@%.

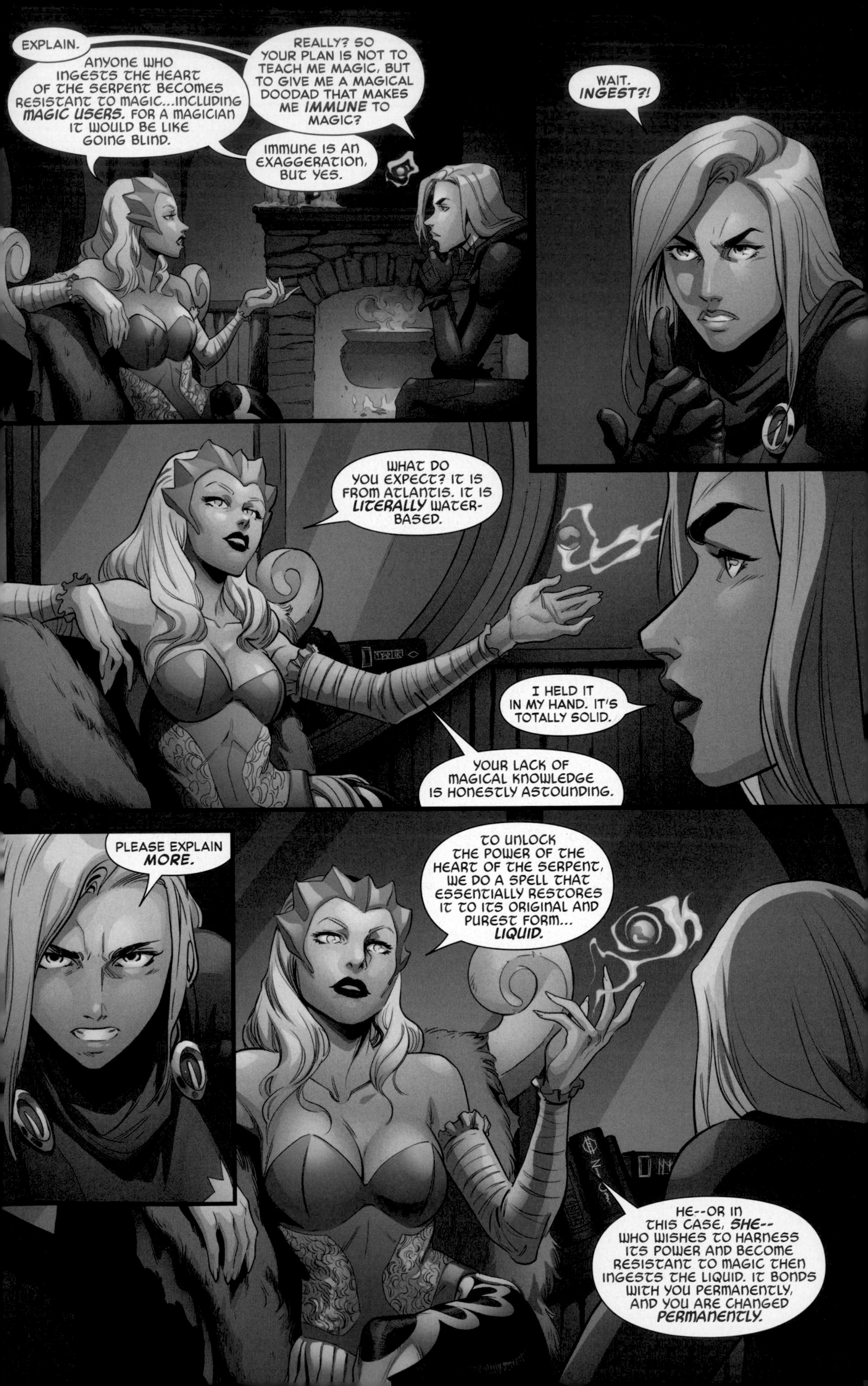
EXPLAIN.
REALLY? SO YOUR PLAN IS NOT TO TEACH ME MAGIC, BUT TO GIVE ME A MAGICAL DOODAD THAT MAKES ME IMMUNE TO MAGIC?
ANYONE WHO INGESTS THE HEART OF THE SERPENT BECOMES RESISTANT TO MAGIC...INCLUDING MAGIC USERS. FOR A MAGICIAN IT WOULD BE LIKE GOING BLIND.
IMMUNE IS AN EXAGGERATION, BUT YES.
WAIT. INGEST?!
WHAT DO YOU EXPECT? IT IS FROM ATLANTIS. IT IS LITERALLY WATER-BASED.
I HELD IT IN MY HAND. IT'S TOTALLY SOLID.
YOUR LACK OF MAGICAL KNOWLEDGE IS HONESTLY ASTOUNDING.
PLEASE EXPLAIN MORE.
TO UNLOCK THE POWER OF THE HEART OF THE SERPENT, WE DO A SPELL THAT ESSENTIALLY RESTORES IT TO ITS ORIGINAL AND PUREST FORM... LIQUID.
HE--OR IN THIS CASE, SHE-- WHO WISHES TO HARNESS ITS POWER AND BECOME RESISTANT TO MAGIC THEN INGESTS THE LIQUID. IT BONDS WITH YOU PERMANENTLY, AND YOU ARE CHANGED PERMANENTLY.

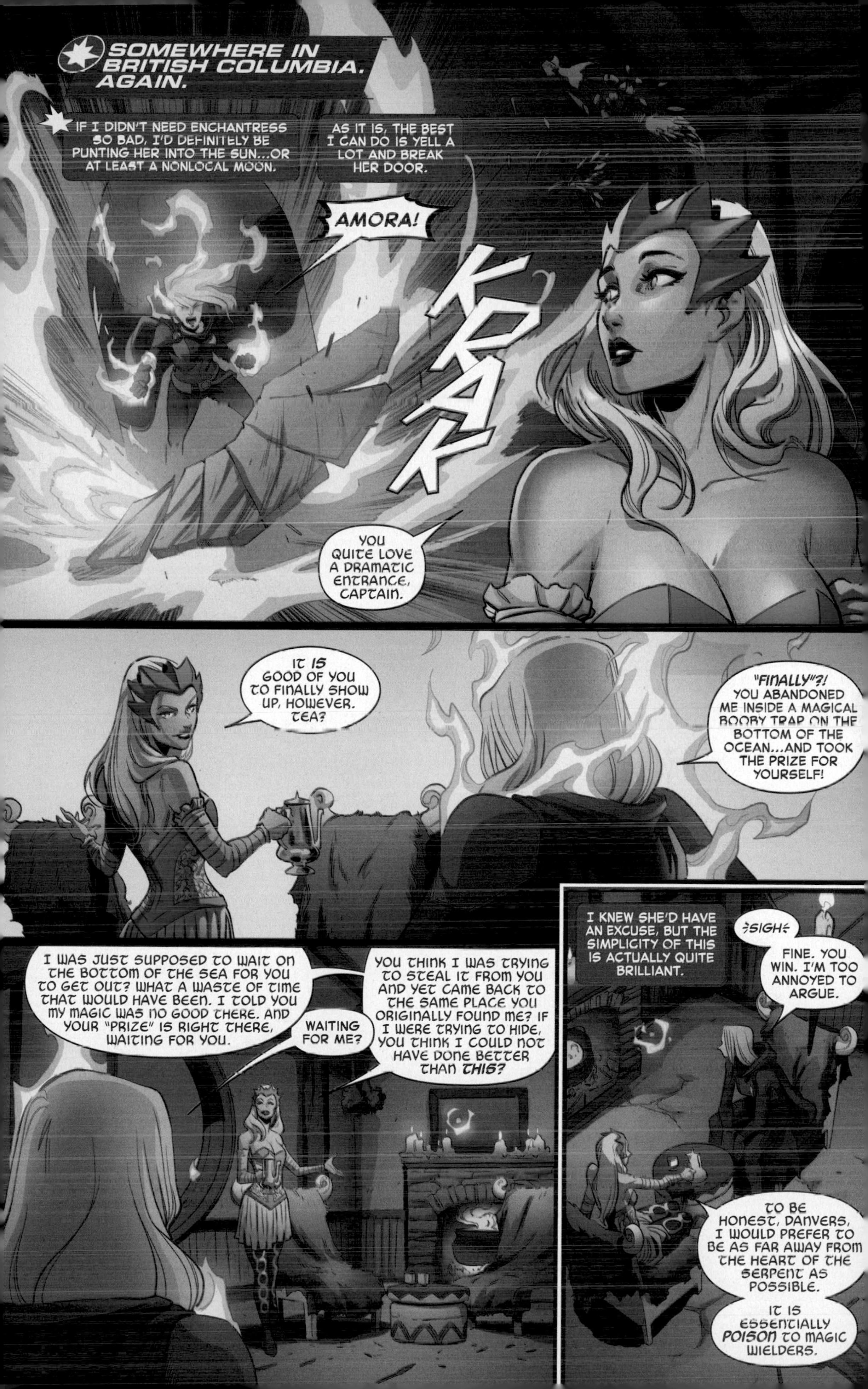
SOMEWHERE IN BRITISH COLUMBIA. AGAIN.
IF I DIDN'T NEED ENCHANTRESS SO BAD, I'D DEFINITELY BE PUNTING HER INTO THE SUN...OR AT LEAST A NONLOCAL MOON.
AS IT IS, THE BEST I CAN DO IS YELL A LOT AND BREAK HER DOOR.
AMORA!
KRAK
YOU QUITE LOVE A DRAMATIC ENTRANCE, CAPTAIN.
IT IS GOOD OF YOU TO FINALLY SHOW UP, HOWEVER. TEA?
"FINALLY"?! YOU ABANDONED ME INSIDE A MAGICAL BOOBY TRAP ON THE BOTTOM OF THE OCEAN...AND TOOK THE PRIZE FOR YOURSELF!
I WAS JUST SUPPOSED TO WAIT ON THE BOTTOM OF THE SEA FOR YOU TO GET OUT? WHAT A WASTE OF TIME THAT WOULD HAVE BEEN. I TOLD YOU MY MAGIC WAS NO GOOD THERE. AND YOUR "PRIZE" IS RIGHT THERE, WAITING FOR YOU.
WAITING FOR ME?
YOU THINK I WAS TRYING TO STEAL IT FROM YOU AND YET CAME BACK TO THE SAME PLACE YOU ORIGINALLY FOUND ME? IF I WERE TRYING TO HIDE, YOU THINK I COULD NOT HAVE DONE BETTER THAN THIS?
I KNEW SHE'D HAVE AN EXCUSE, BUT THE SIMPLICITY OF THIS IS ACTUALLY QUITE BRILLIANT.
SIGH
FINE. YOU WIN. I'M TOO ANNOYED TO ARGUE.
TO BE HONEST, DANVERS, I WOULD PREFER TO BE AS FAR AWAY FROM THE HEART OF THE SERPENT AS POSSIBLE.
IT IS ESSENTIALLY POISON TO MAGIC WIELDERS.

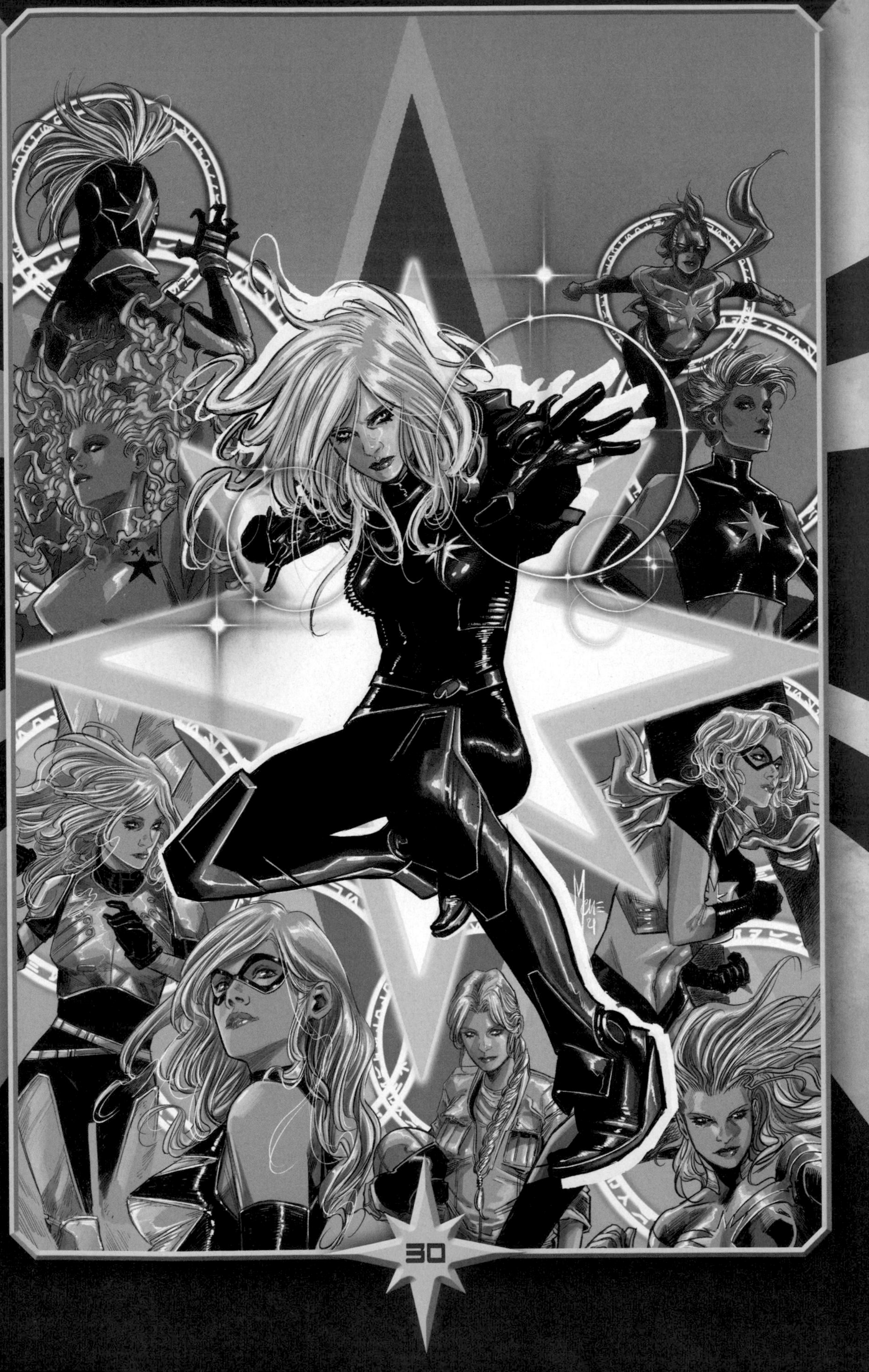
30

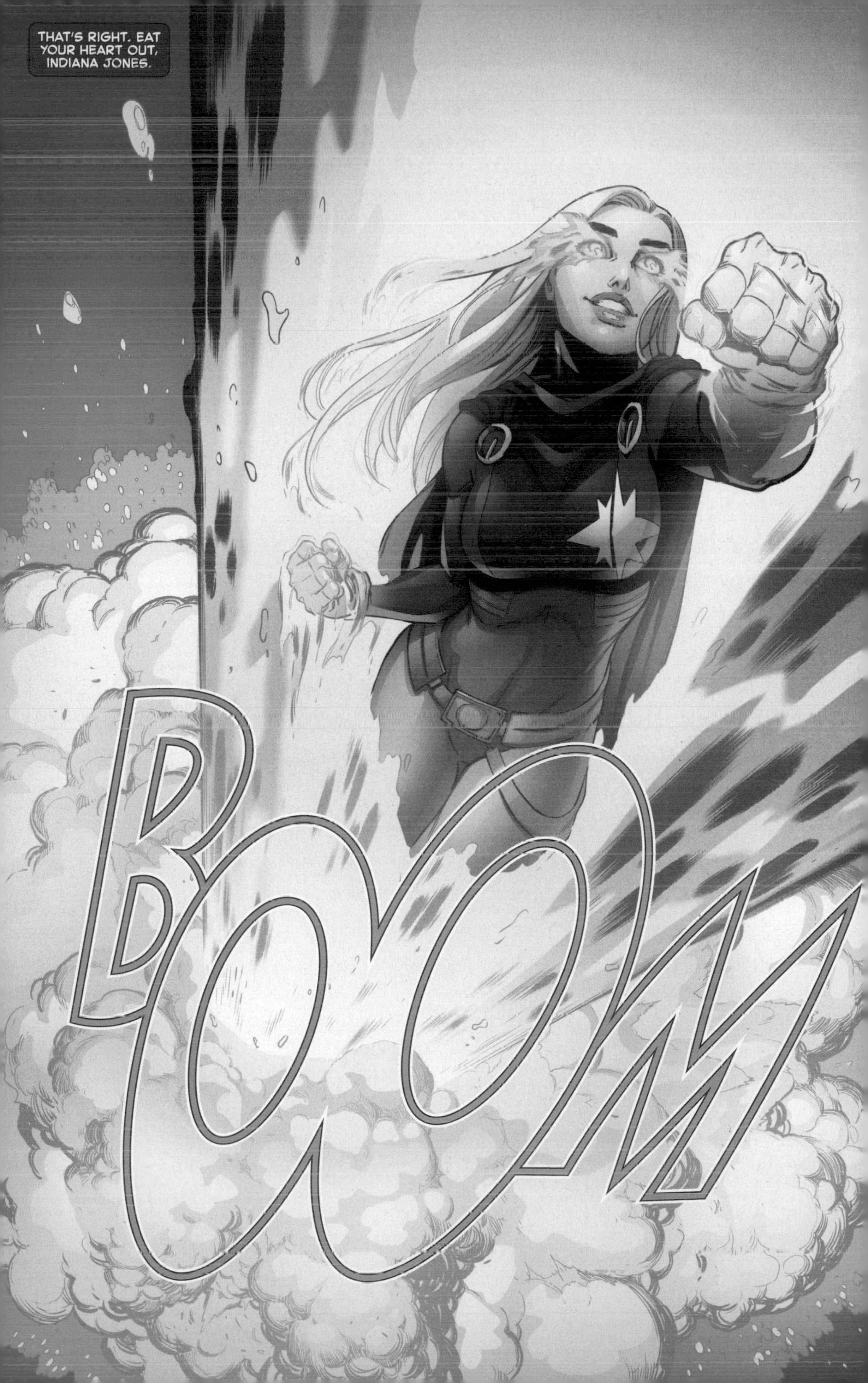
THAT'S RIGHT. EAT YOUR HEART OUT, INDIANA JONES.
BOOM

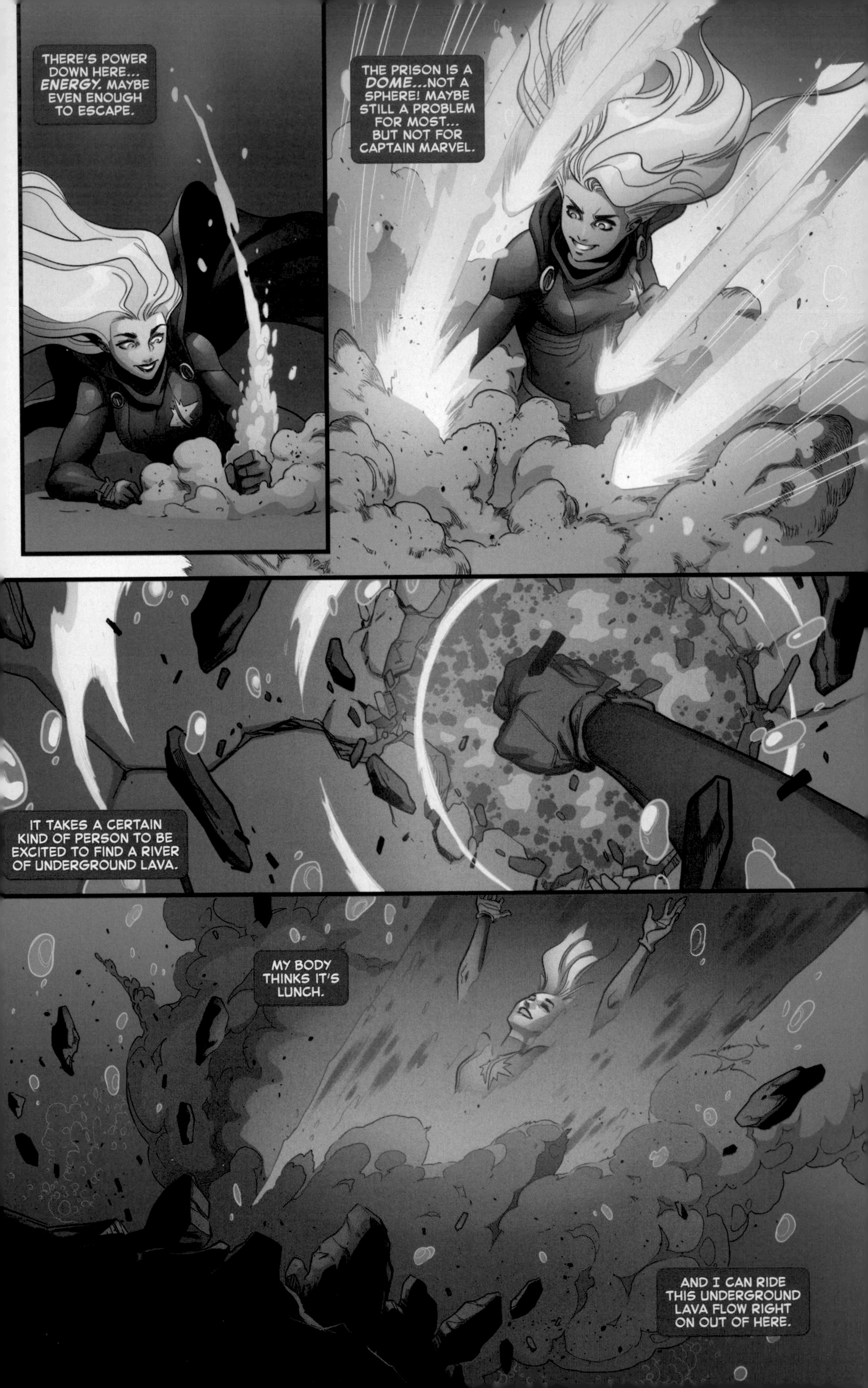
THERE'S POWER DOWN HERE... ENERGY. MAYBE EVEN ENOUGH TO ESCAPE.
THE PRISON IS A DOME...NOT A SPHERE! MAYBE STILL A PROBLEM FOR MOST... BUT NOT FOR CAPTAIN MARVEL.
IT TAKES A CERTAIN KIND OF PERSON TO BE EXCITED TO FIND A RIVER OF UNDERGROUND LAVA.
MY BODY THINKS IT'S LUNCH.
AND I CAN RIDE THIS UNDERGROUND LAVA FLOW RIGHT ON OUT OF HERE.

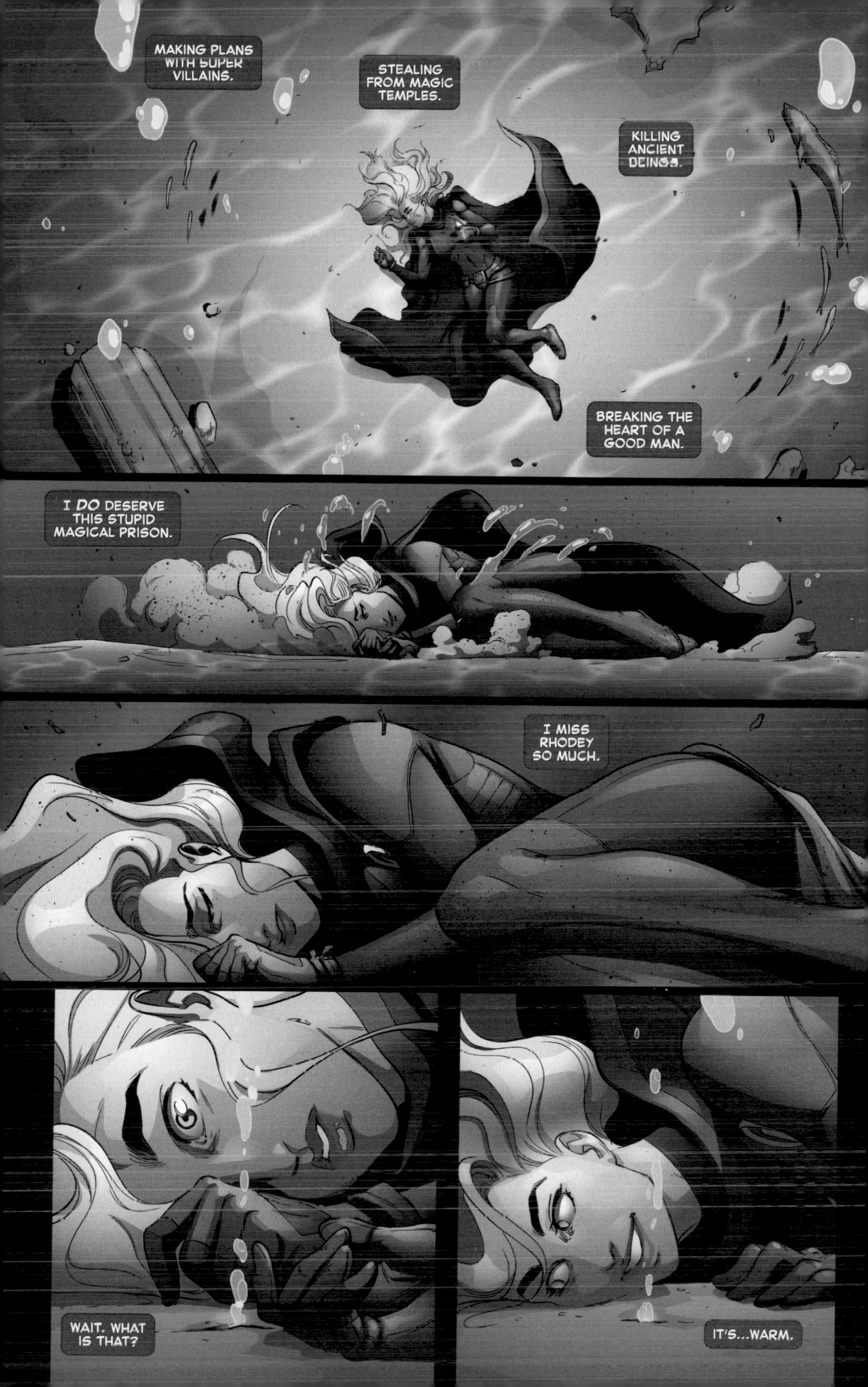
MAKING PLANS WITH SUPER VILLAINS.
STEALING FROM MAGIC TEMPLES.
KILLING ANCIENT BEINGS.
BREAKING THE HEART OF A GOOD MAN.
I *DO* DESERVE THIS STUPID MAGICAL PRISON.
I MISS RHODEY SO MUCH.
WAIT. WHAT IS THAT?
IT'S...WARM.

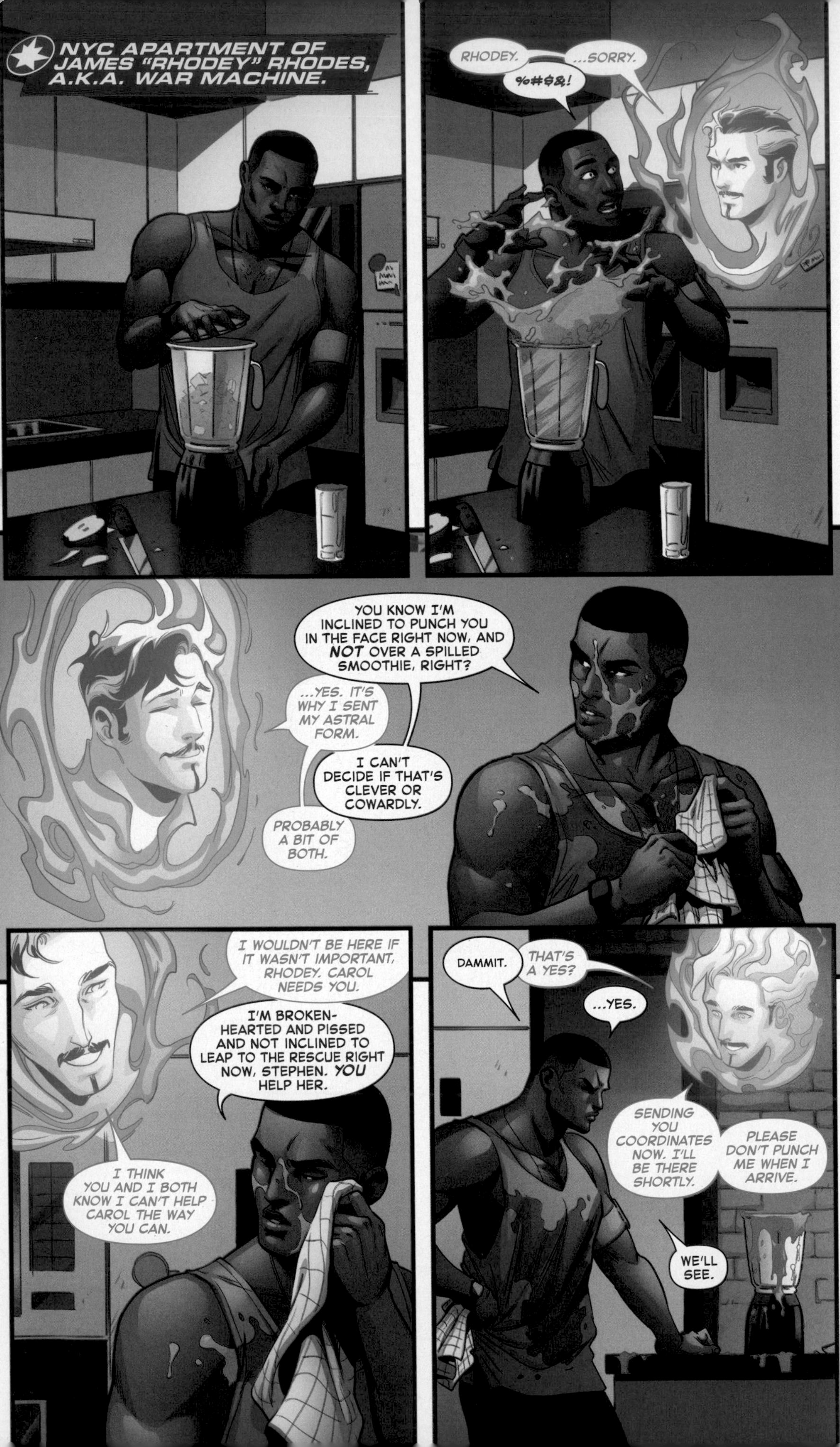
NYC APARTMENT OF JAMES "RHODEY" RHODES, A.K.A. WAR MACHINE.
RHODEY.
%#$&!
...SORRY.
YOU KNOW I'M INCLINED TO PUNCH YOU IN THE FACE RIGHT NOW, AND NOT OVER A SPILLED SMOOTHIE, RIGHT?
...YES. IT'S WHY I SENT MY ASTRAL FORM.
I CAN'T DECIDE IF THAT'S CLEVER OR COWARDLY.
PROBABLY A BIT OF BOTH.
I WOULDN'T BE HERE IF IT WASN'T IMPORTANT, RHODEY. CAROL NEEDS YOU.
I'M BROKEN-HEARTED AND PISSED AND NOT INCLINED TO LEAP TO THE RESCUE RIGHT NOW, STEPHEN. YOU HELP HER.
I THINK YOU AND I BOTH KNOW I CAN'T HELP CAROL THE WAY YOU CAN.
DAMMIT.
THAT'S A YES?
...YES.
SENDING YOU COORDINATES NOW. I'LL BE THERE SHORTLY.
PLEASE DON'T PUNCH ME WHEN I ARRIVE.
WE'LL SEE.

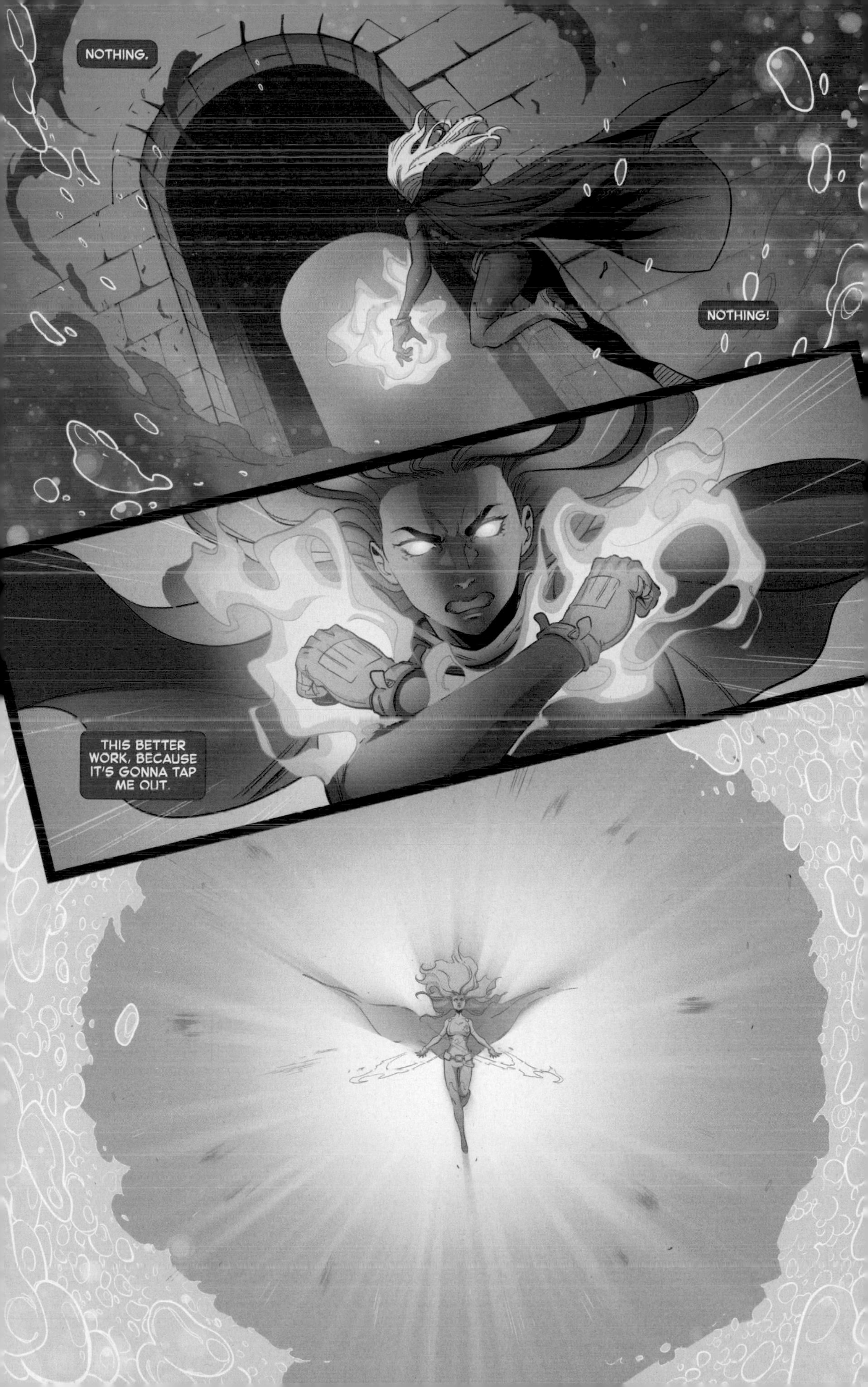
NOTHING.
NOTHING!
THIS BETTER WORK, BECAUSE IT'S GONNA TAP ME OUT.

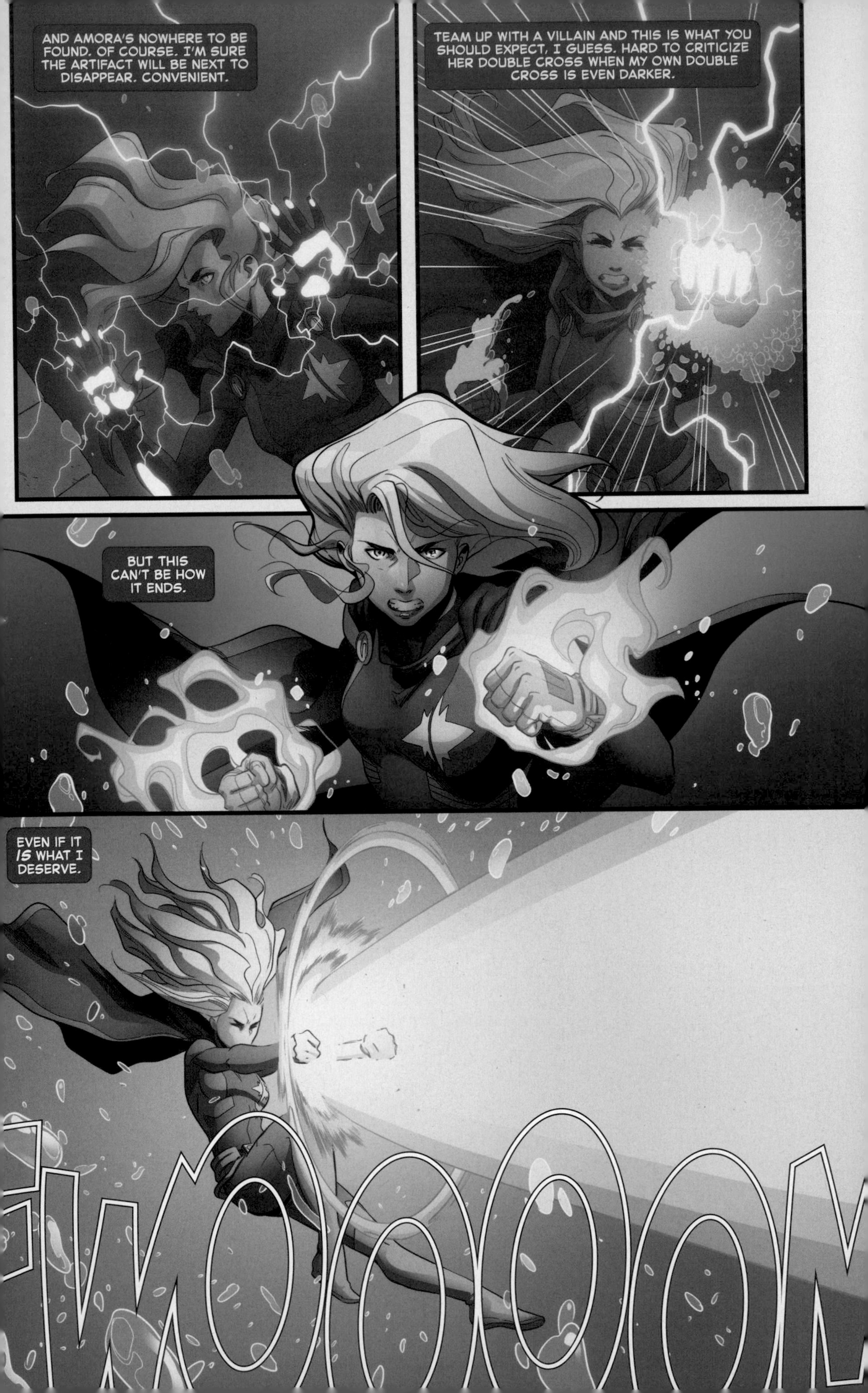
AND AMORA'S NOWHERE TO BE FOUND. OF COURSE. I'M SURE THE ARTIFACT WILL BE NEXT TO DISAPPEAR. CONVENIENT.
TEAM UP WITH A VILLAIN AND THIS IS WHAT YOU SHOULD EXPECT, I GUESS. HARD TO CRITICIZE HER DOUBLE CROSS WHEN MY OWN DOUBLE CROSS IS EVEN DARKER.
BUT THIS CAN'T BE HOW IT ENDS.
EVEN IF IT *IS* WHAT I DESERVE.
FWOOOOOM

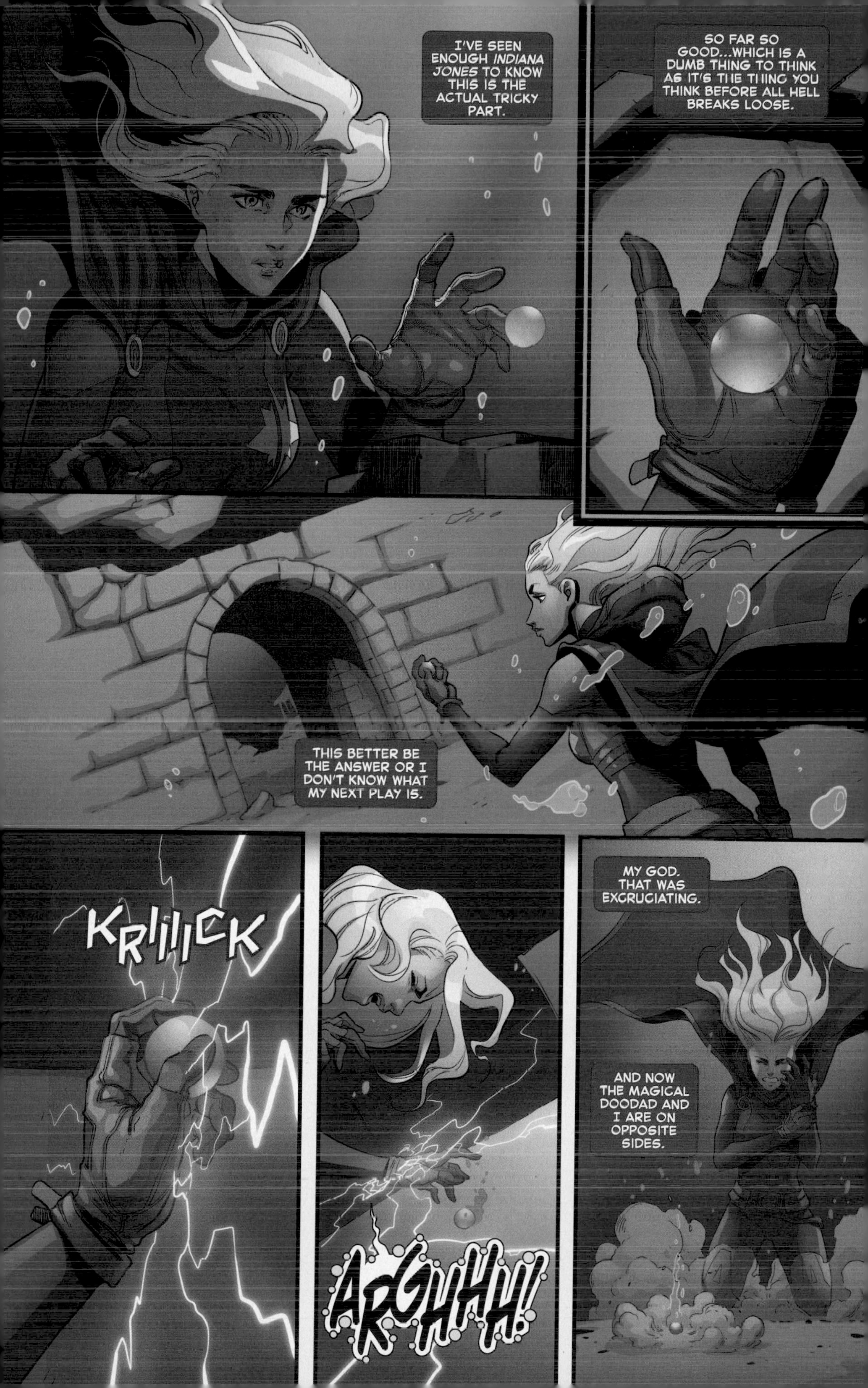
I'VE SEEN ENOUGH *INDIANA JONES* TO KNOW THIS IS THE ACTUAL TRICKY PART.
SO FAR SO GOOD...WHICH IS A DUMB THING TO THINK AS IT'S THE THING YOU THINK BEFORE ALL HELL BREAKS LOOSE.
THIS BETTER BE THE ANSWER OR I DON'T KNOW WHAT MY NEXT PLAY IS.
KRIIIICK
ARGHHH!
MY GOD. THAT WAS EXCRUCIATING.
AND NOW THE MAGICAL DOODAD AND I ARE ON OPPOSITE SIDES.

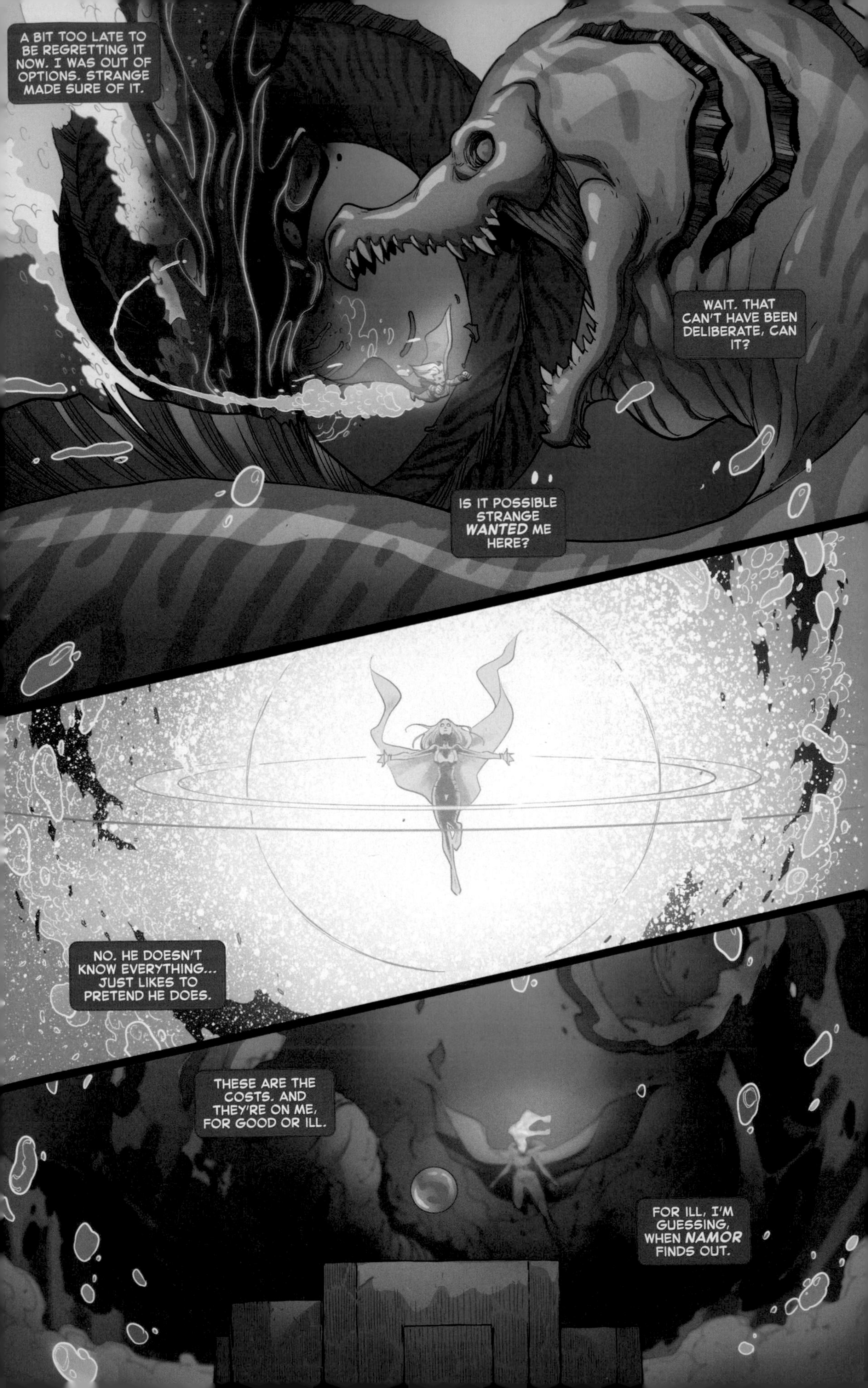
A BIT TOO LATE TO BE REGRETTING IT NOW. I WAS OUT OF OPTIONS. STRANGE MADE SURE OF IT.
WAIT. THAT CAN'T HAVE BEEN DELIBERATE, CAN IT?
IS IT POSSIBLE STRANGE *WANTED* ME HERE?
NO. HE DOESN'T KNOW EVERYTHING... JUST LIKES TO PRETEND HE DOES.
THESE ARE THE COSTS. AND THEY'RE ON ME, FOR GOOD OR ILL.
FOR ILL, I'M GUESSING, WHEN *NAMOR* FINDS OUT.

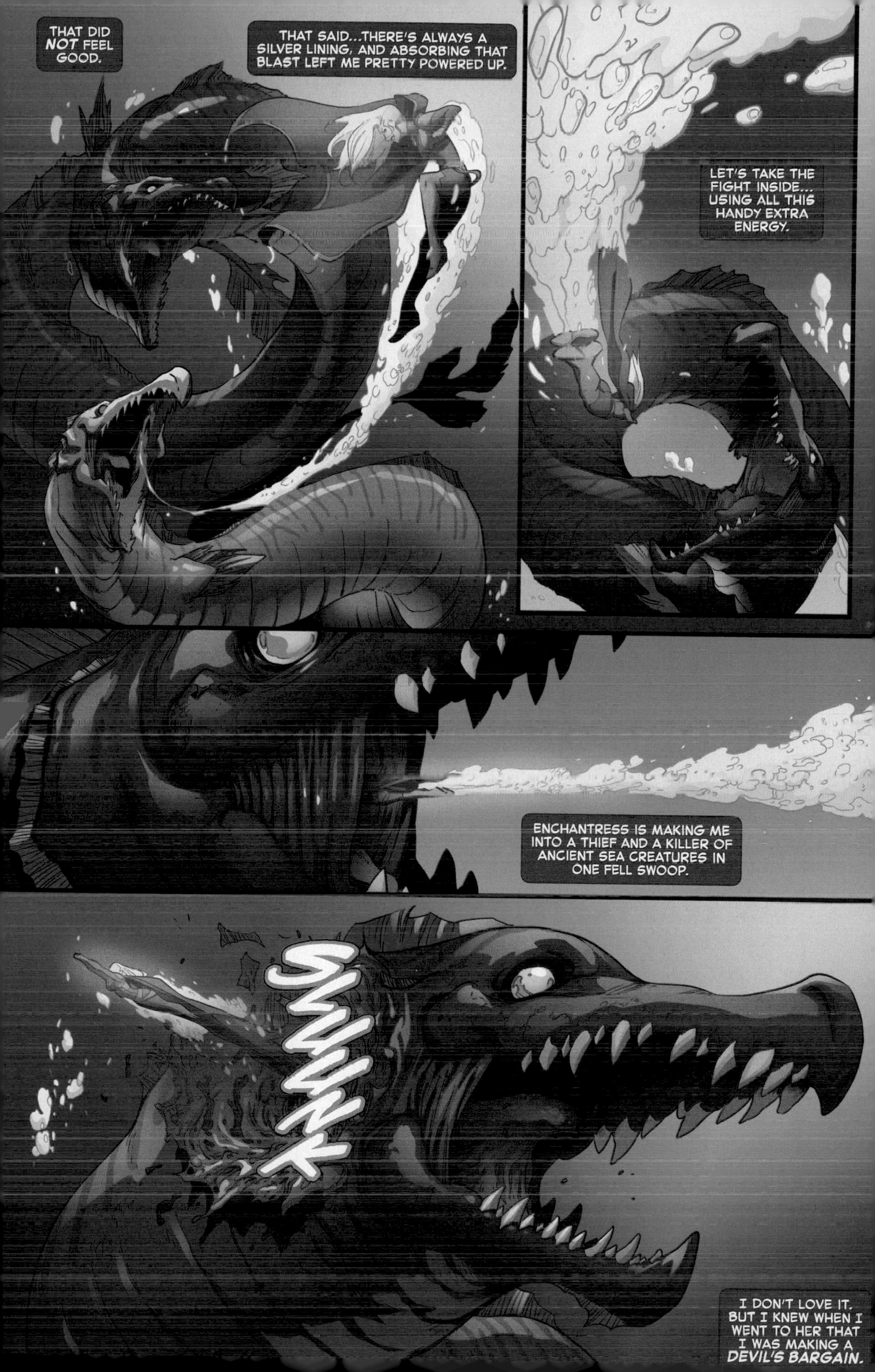
THAT DID NOT FEEL GOOD.
THAT SAID...THERE'S ALWAYS A SILVER LINING, AND ABSORBING THAT BLAST LEFT ME PRETTY POWERED UP.
LET'S TAKE THE FIGHT INSIDE... USING ALL THIS HANDY EXTRA ENERGY.
ENCHANTRESS IS MAKING ME INTO A THIEF AND A KILLER OF ANCIENT SEA CREATURES IN ONE FELL SWOOP.
SHUNK
I DON'T LOVE IT. BUT I KNEW WHEN I WENT TO HER THAT I WAS MAKING A DEVIL'S BARGAIN.

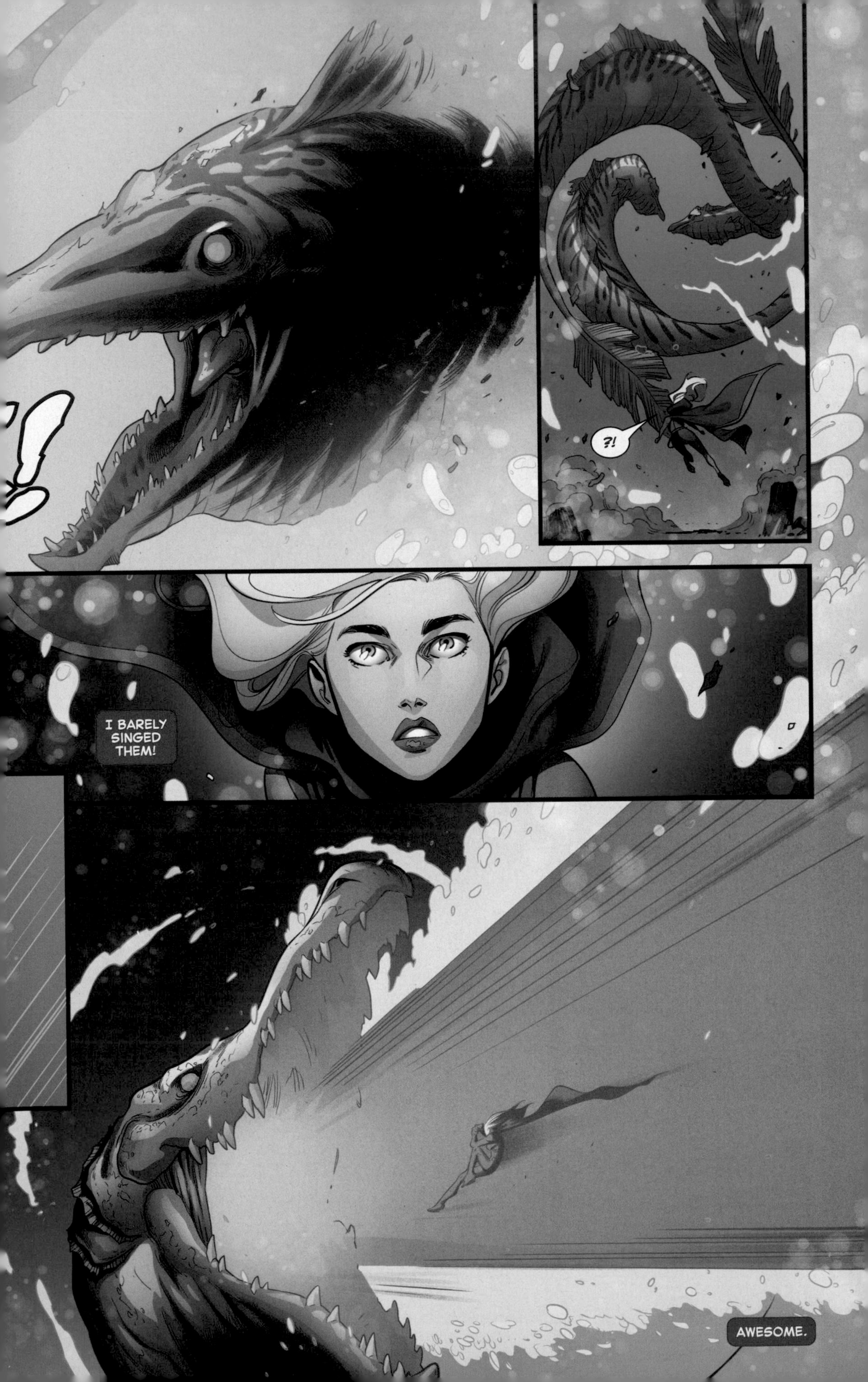
!
?!
I BARELY SINGED THEM!
AWESOME.

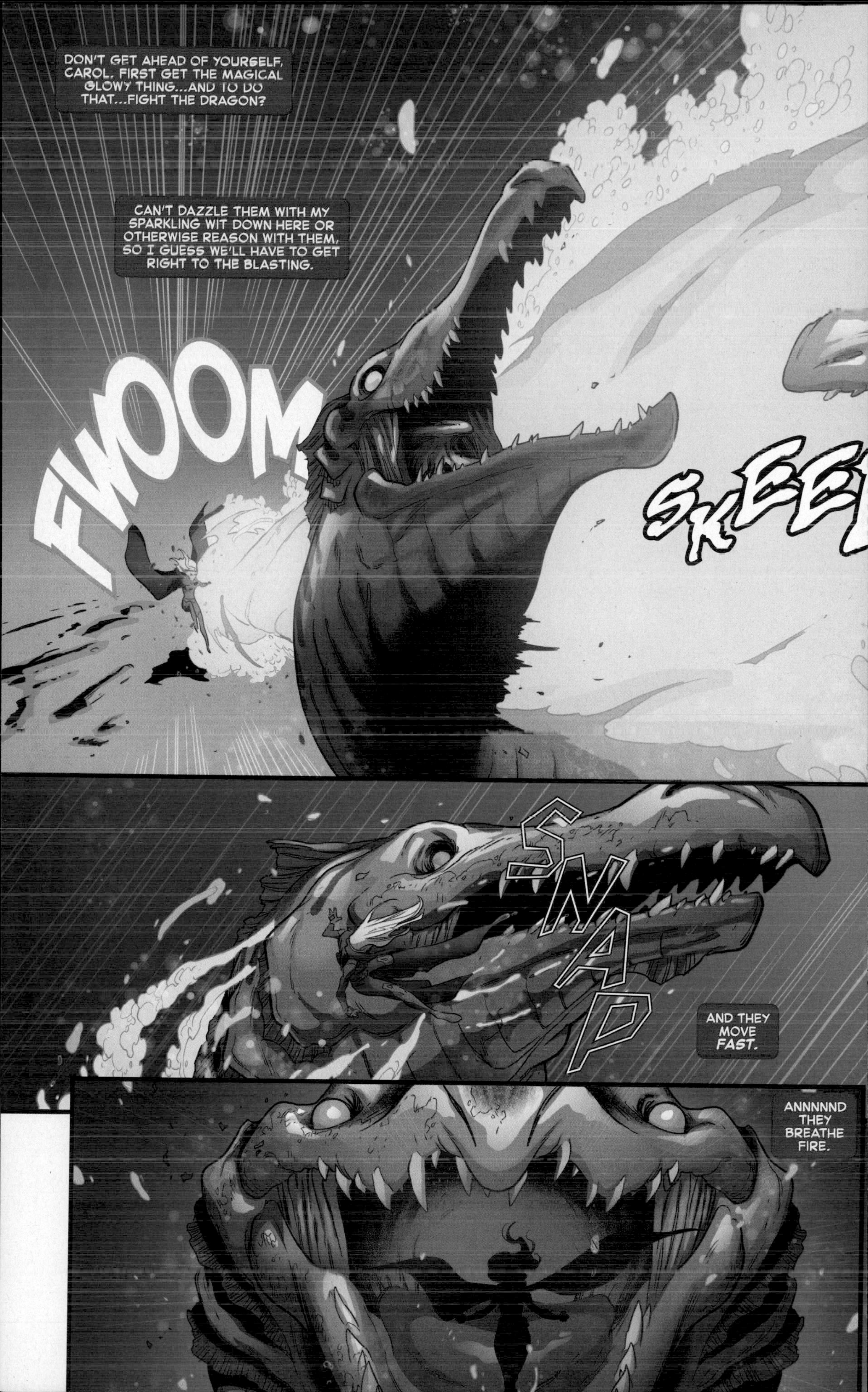
DON'T GET AHEAD OF YOURSELF, CAROL. FIRST GET THE MAGICAL GLOWY THING...AND TO DO THAT...FIGHT THE DRAGON?
CAN'T DAZZLE THEM WITH MY SPARKLING WIT DOWN HERE OR OTHERWISE REASON WITH THEM, SO I GUESS WE'LL HAVE TO GET RIGHT TO THE BLASTING.
FWOOM!
SNAP
AND THEY MOVE FAST.
ANNNNND THEY BREATHE FIRE.

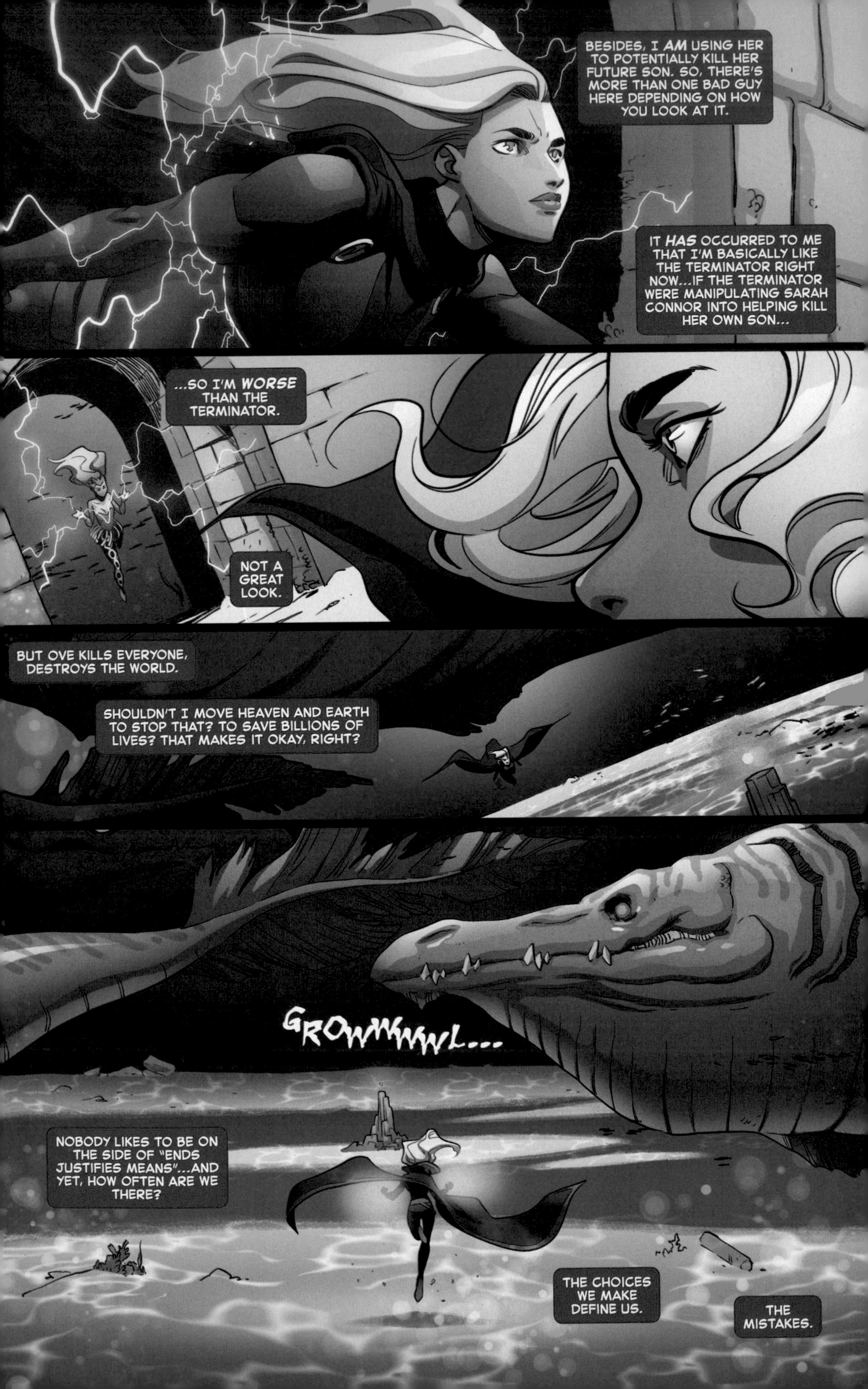
BESIDES, I AM USING HER TO POTENTIALLY KILL HER FUTURE SON. SO, THERE'S MORE THAN ONE BAD GUY HERE DEPENDING ON HOW YOU LOOK AT IT.
IT HAS OCCURRED TO ME THAT I'M BASICALLY LIKE THE TERMINATOR RIGHT NOW...IF THE TERMINATOR WERE MANIPULATING SARAH CONNOR INTO HELPING KILL HER OWN SON...
...SO I'M WORSE THAN THE TERMINATOR.
NOT A GREAT LOOK.
BUT OVE KILLS EVERYONE, DESTROYS THE WORLD.
SHOULDN'T I MOVE HEAVEN AND EARTH TO STOP THAT? TO SAVE BILLIONS OF LIVES? THAT MAKES IT OKAY, RIGHT?
GROWWWWL...
NOBODY LIKES TO BE ON THE SIDE OF "ENDS JUSTIFIES MEANS"...AND YET, HOW OFTEN ARE WE THERE?
THE CHOICES WE MAKE DEFINE US.
THE MISTAKES.

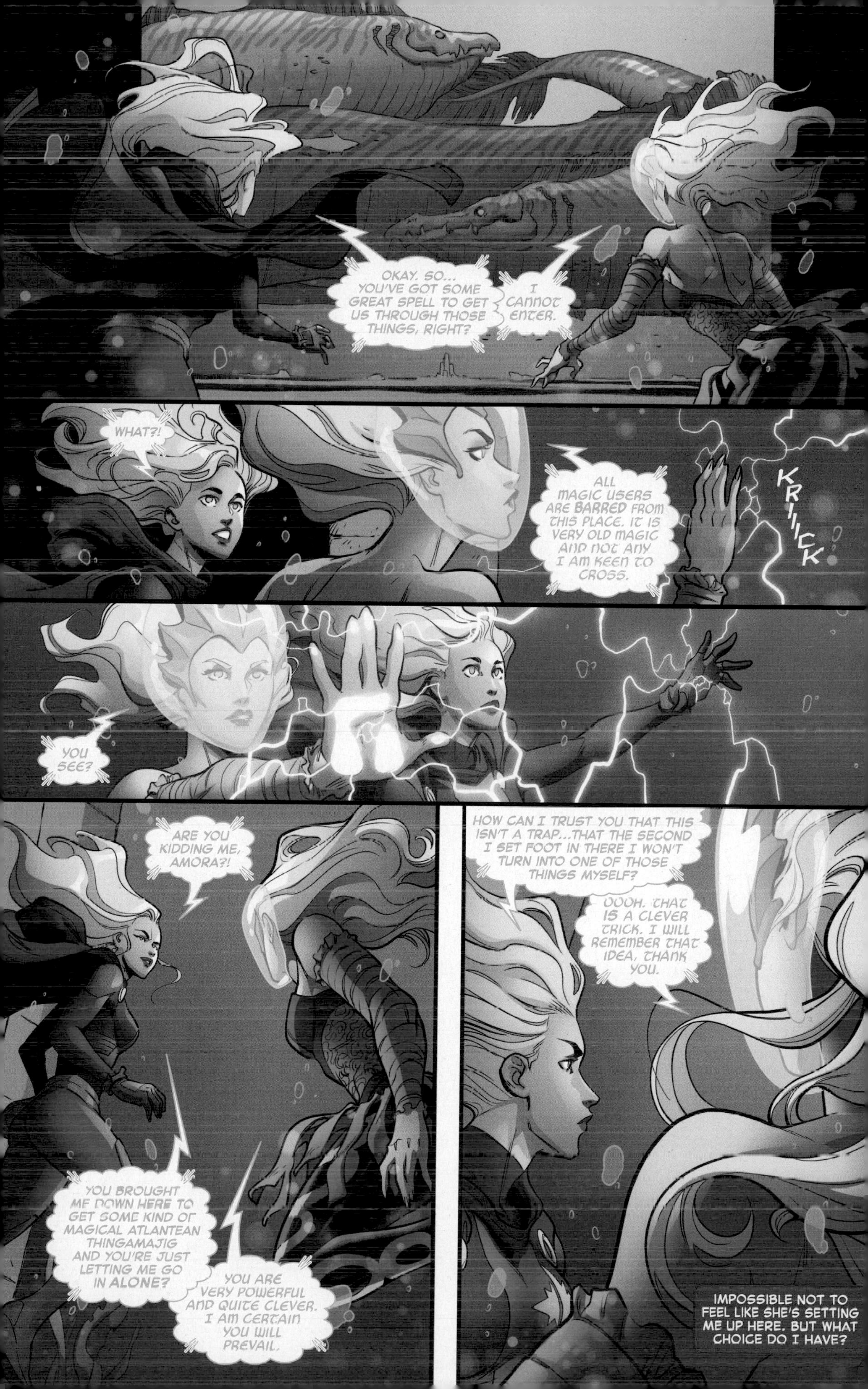
OKAY. SO... YOU'VE GOT SOME GREAT SPELL TO GET US THROUGH THOSE THINGS, RIGHT?
I CANNOT ENTER.
WHAT?!
ALL MAGIC USERS ARE BARRED FROM THIS PLACE. IT IS VERY OLD MAGIC AND NOT ANY I AM KEEN TO CROSS.
KRIIICK
YOU SEE?
ARE YOU KIDDING ME, AMORA?!
YOU BROUGHT ME DOWN HERE TO GET SOME KIND OF MAGICAL ATLANTEAN THINGAMAJIG AND YOU'RE JUST LETTING ME GO IN ALONE?
YOU ARE VERY POWERFUL AND QUITE CLEVER. I AM CERTAIN YOU WILL PREVAIL.
HOW CAN I TRUST YOU THAT THIS ISN'T A TRAP...THAT THE SECOND I SET FOOT IN THERE I WON'T TURN INTO ONE OF THOSE THINGS MYSELF?
OOOH. THAT IS A CLEVER TRICK. I WILL REMEMBER THAT IDEA, THANK YOU.
IMPOSSIBLE NOT TO FEEL LIKE SHE'S SETTING ME UP HERE. BUT WHAT CHOICE DO I HAVE?

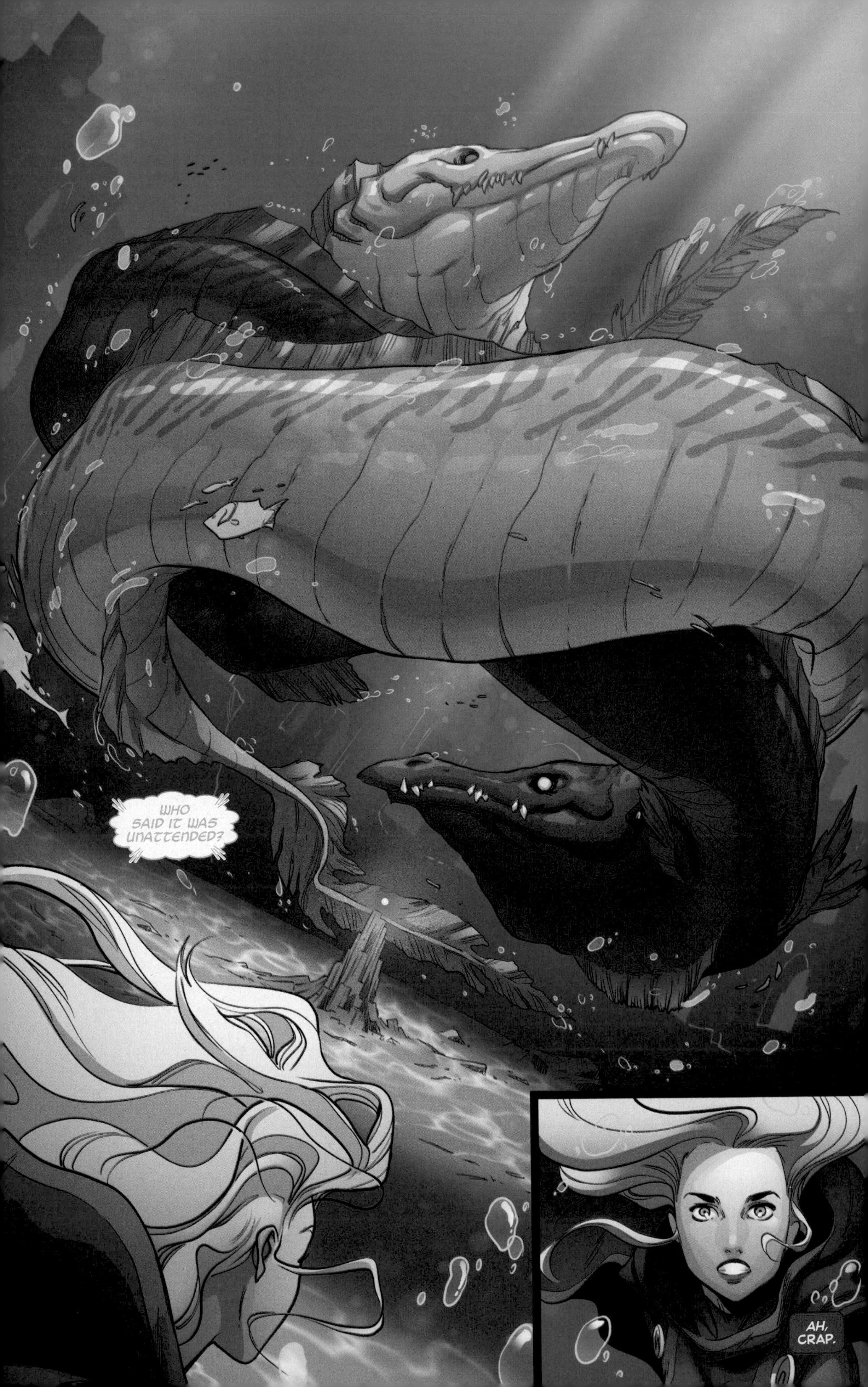
WHO SAID IT WAS UNATTENDED?
AH, CRAP.

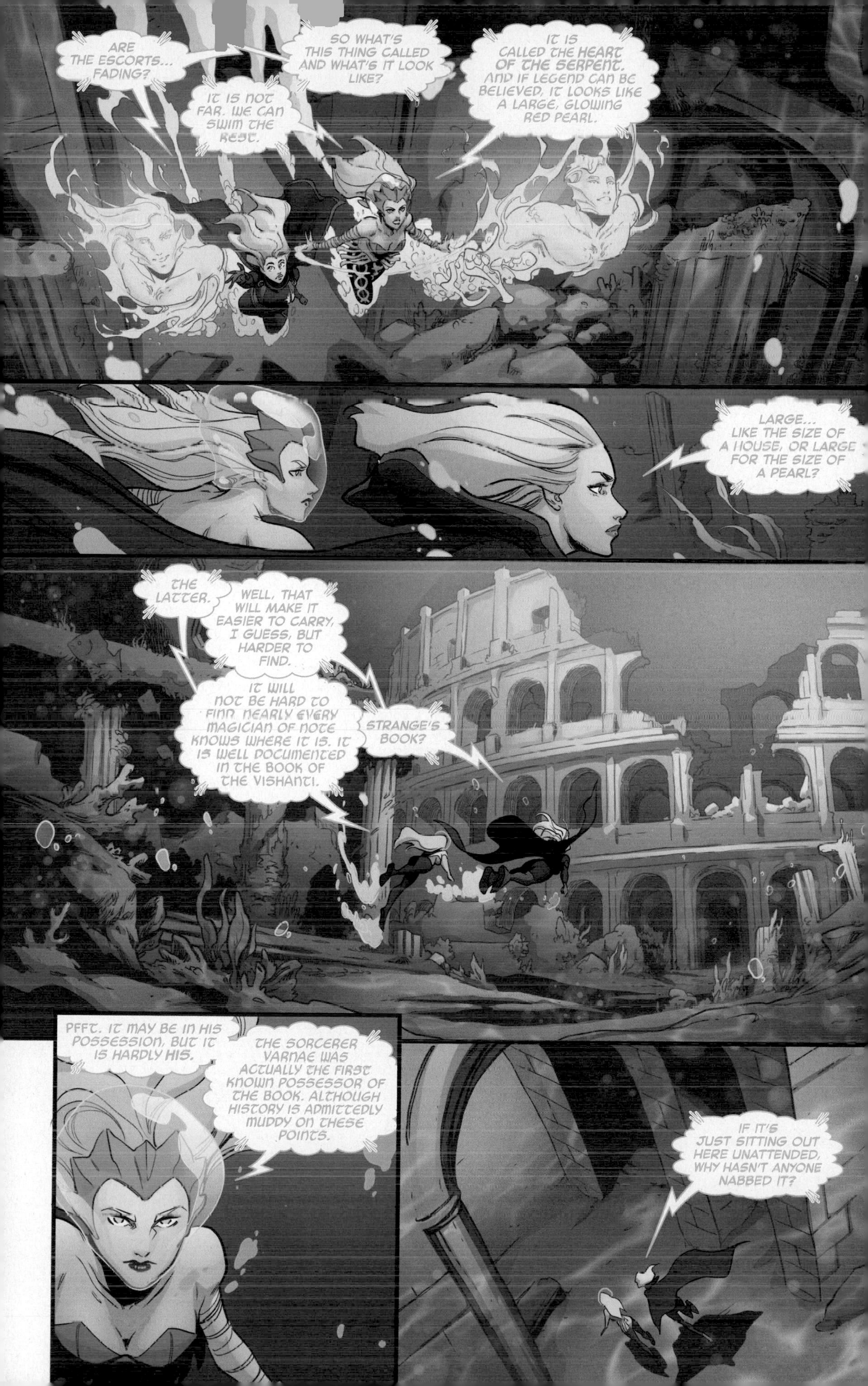
ARE THE ESCORTS... FADING?
SO WHAT'S THIS THING CALLED AND WHAT'S IT LOOK LIKE?
IT IS NOT FAR. WE CAN SWIM THE REST.
IT IS CALLED THE HEART OF THE SERPENT. AND IF LEGEND CAN BE BELIEVED, IT LOOKS LIKE A LARGE, GLOWING RED PEARL.
LARGE... LIKE THE SIZE OF A HOUSE, OR LARGE FOR THE SIZE OF A PEARL?
THE LATTER.
WELL, THAT WILL MAKE IT EASIER TO CARRY, I GUESS, BUT HARDER TO FIND.
IT WILL NOT BE HARD TO FIND. NEARLY EVERY MAGICIAN OF NOTE KNOWS WHERE IT IS. IT IS WELL DOCUMENTED IN THE BOOK OF THE VISHANTI.
STRANGE'S BOOK?
PFFT. IT MAY BE IN HIS POSSESSION, BUT IT IS HARDLY HIS.
THE SORCERER VARNAE WAS ACTUALLY THE FIRST KNOWN POSSESSOR OF THE BOOK. ALTHOUGH HISTORY IS ADMITTEDLY MUDDY ON THESE POINTS.
IF IT'S JUST SITTING OUT HERE UNATTENDED, WHY HASN'T ANYONE NABBED IT?

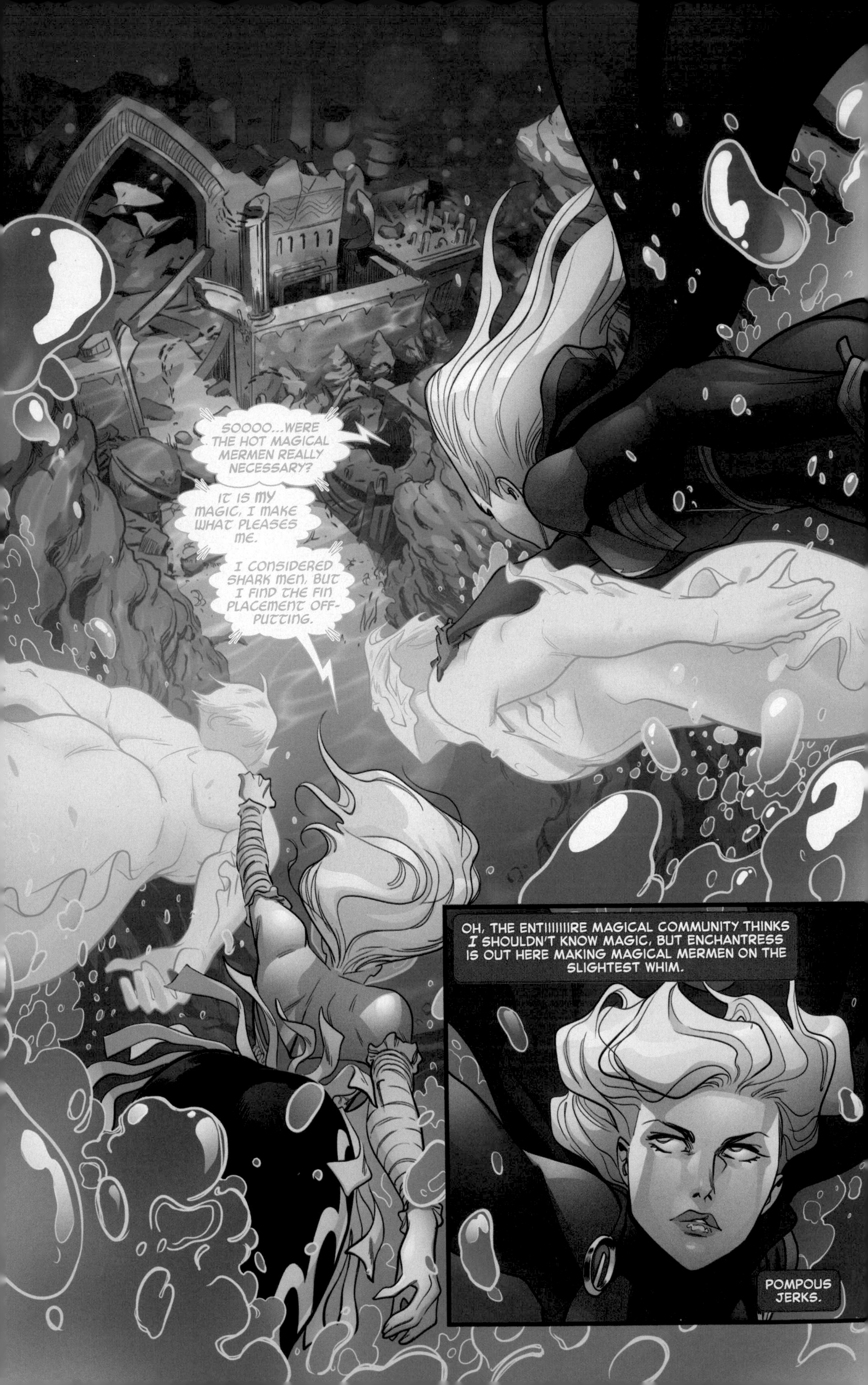

SOOOO...WERE THE HOT MAGICAL MERMEN REALLY NECESSARY?
IT IS MY MAGIC, I MAKE WHAT PLEASES ME.
I CONSIDERED SHARK MEN, BUT I FIND THE FIN PLACEMENT OFF-PUTTING.
OH, THE ENTIIIIIIIRE MAGICAL COMMUNITY THINKS *I* SHOULDN'T KNOW MAGIC, BUT ENCHANTRESS IS OUT HERE MAKING MAGICAL MERMEN ON THE SLIGHTEST WHIM.
POMPOUS JERKS.

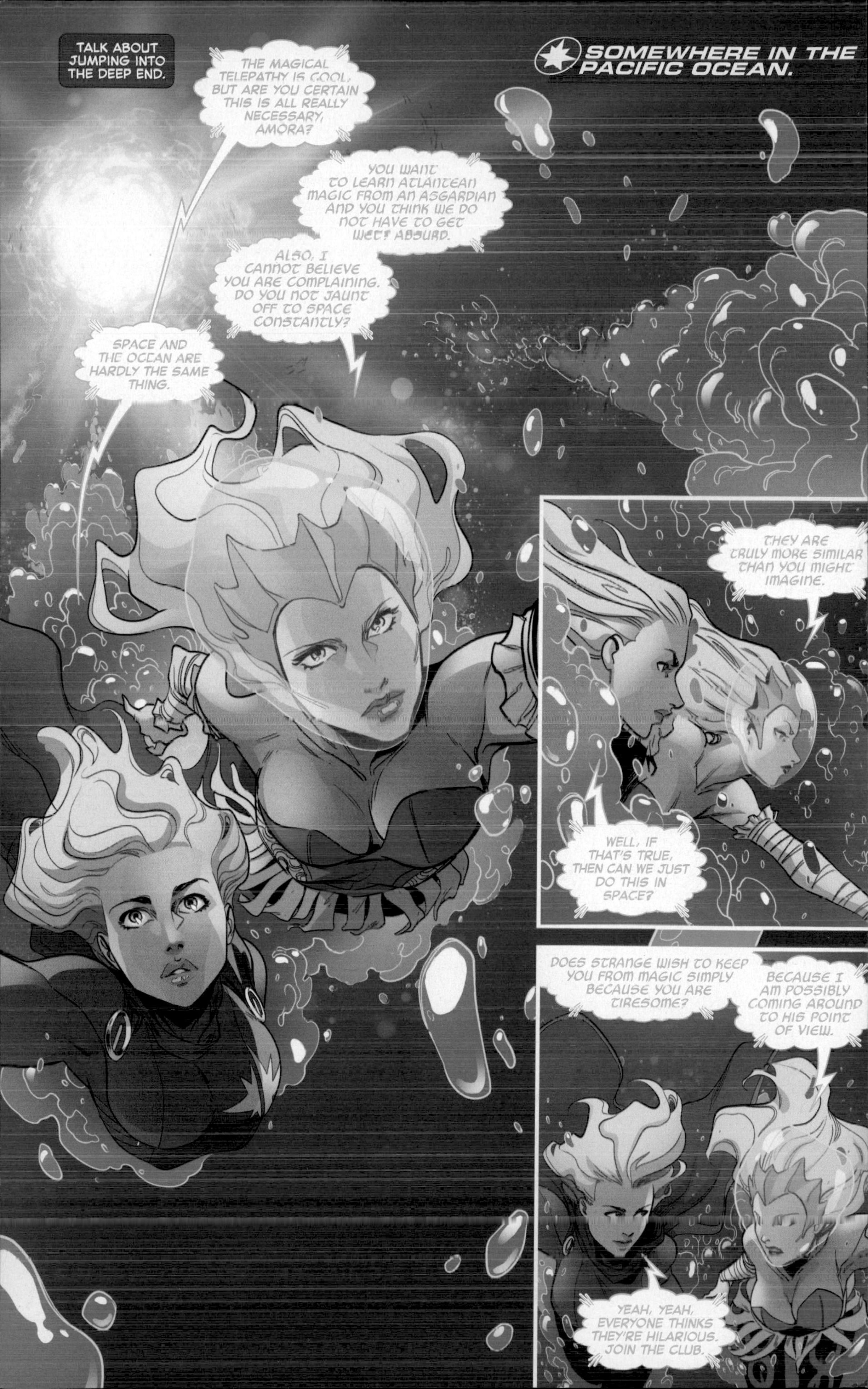
TALK ABOUT JUMPING INTO THE DEEP END.
SOMEWHERE IN THE PACIFIC OCEAN.
THE MAGICAL TELEPATHY IS COOL, BUT ARE YOU CERTAIN THIS IS ALL REALLY NECESSARY, AMORA?
YOU WANT TO LEARN ATLANTEAN MAGIC FROM AN ASGARDIAN AND YOU THINK WE DO NOT HAVE TO GET WET? ABSURD.
ALSO, I CANNOT BELIEVE YOU ARE COMPLAINING. DO YOU NOT JAUNT OFF TO SPACE CONSTANTLY?
SPACE AND THE OCEAN ARE HARDLY THE SAME THING.
THEY ARE TRULY MORE SIMILAR THAN YOU MIGHT IMAGINE.
WELL, IF THAT'S TRUE, THEN CAN WE JUST DO THIS IN SPACE?
DOES STRANGE WISH TO KEEP YOU FROM MAGIC SIMPLY BECAUSE YOU ARE TIRESOME?
BECAUSE I AM POSSIBLY COMING AROUND TO HIS POINT OF VIEW.
YEAH, YEAH, EVERYONE THINKS THEY'RE HILARIOUS. JOIN THE CLUB.

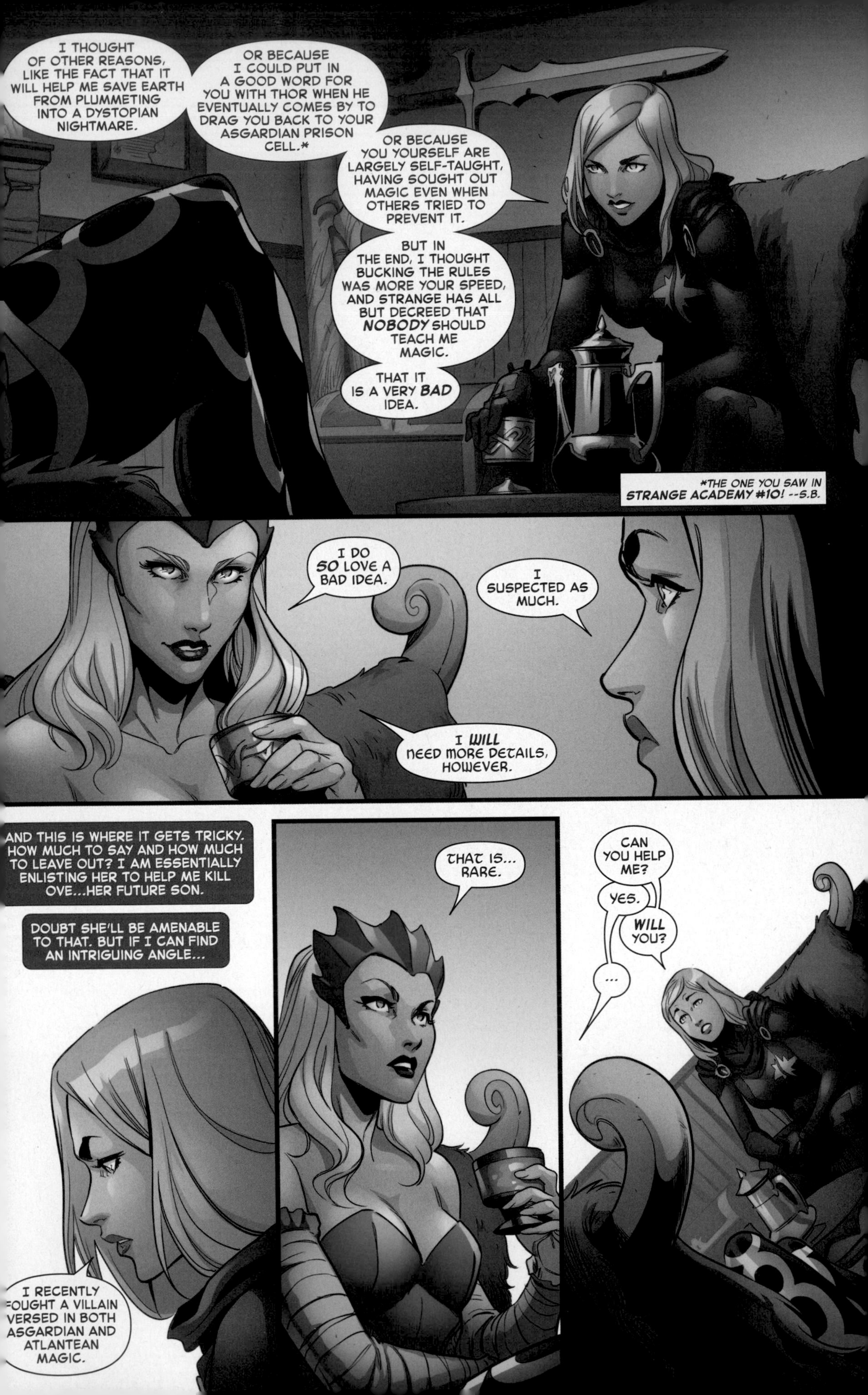
I THOUGHT OF OTHER REASONS, LIKE THE FACT THAT IT WILL HELP ME SAVE EARTH FROM PLUMMETING INTO A DYSTOPIAN NIGHTMARE.
OR BECAUSE I COULD PUT IN A GOOD WORD FOR YOU WITH THOR WHEN HE EVENTUALLY COMES BY TO DRAG YOU BACK TO YOUR ASGARDIAN PRISON CELL.*
OR BECAUSE YOU YOURSELF ARE LARGELY SELF-TAUGHT, HAVING SOUGHT OUT MAGIC EVEN WHEN OTHERS TRIED TO PREVENT IT.
BUT IN THE END, I THOUGHT BUCKING THE RULES WAS MORE YOUR SPEED, AND STRANGE HAS ALL BUT DECREED THAT NOBODY SHOULD TEACH ME MAGIC.
THAT IT IS A VERY BAD IDEA.
*THE ONE YOU SAW IN STRANGE ACADEMY #10! --S.B.
I DO SO LOVE A BAD IDEA.
I SUSPECTED AS MUCH.
I WILL NEED MORE DETAILS, HOWEVER.
AND THIS IS WHERE IT GETS TRICKY. HOW MUCH TO SAY AND HOW MUCH TO LEAVE OUT? I AM ESSENTIALLY ENLISTING HER TO HELP ME KILL OVE...HER FUTURE SON.
DOUBT SHE'LL BE AMENABLE TO THAT. BUT IF I CAN FIND AN INTRIGUING ANGLE...
I RECENTLY FOUGHT A VILLAIN VERSED IN BOTH ASGARDIAN AND ATLANTEAN MAGIC.
THAT IS... RARE.
CAN YOU HELP ME?
YES.
WILL YOU?
...

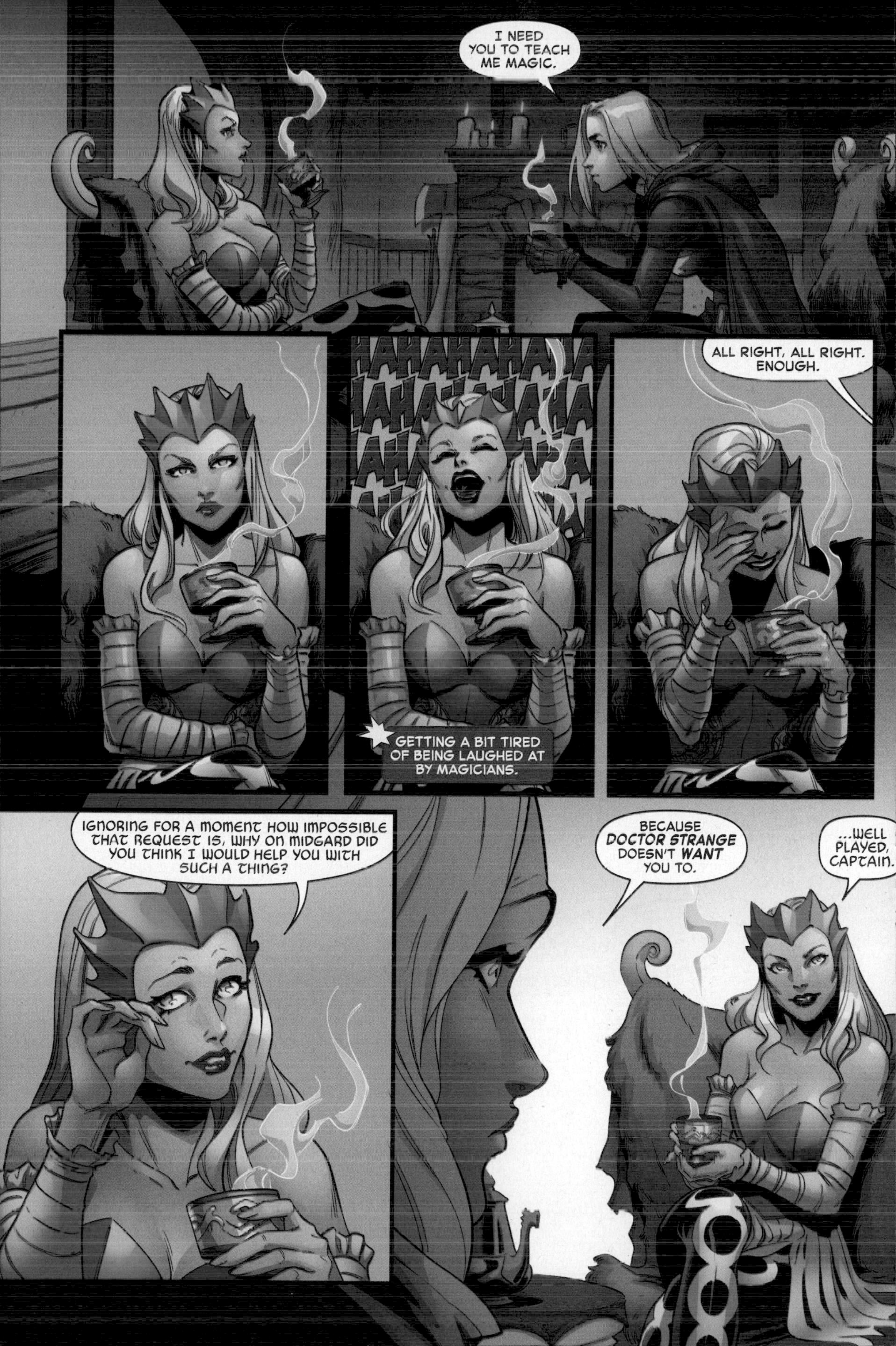
I NEED YOU TO TEACH ME MAGIC.
HAHAHAHAHAHAHAHAHAHAHAHA
GETTING A BIT TIRED OF BEING LAUGHED AT BY MAGICIANS.
ALL RIGHT, ALL RIGHT. ENOUGH.
IGNORING FOR A MOMENT HOW IMPOSSIBLE THAT REQUEST IS, WHY ON MIDGARD DID YOU THINK I WOULD HELP YOU WITH SUCH A THING?
BECAUSE DOCTOR STRANGE DOESN'T WANT YOU TO.
...WELL PLAYED, CAPTAIN.

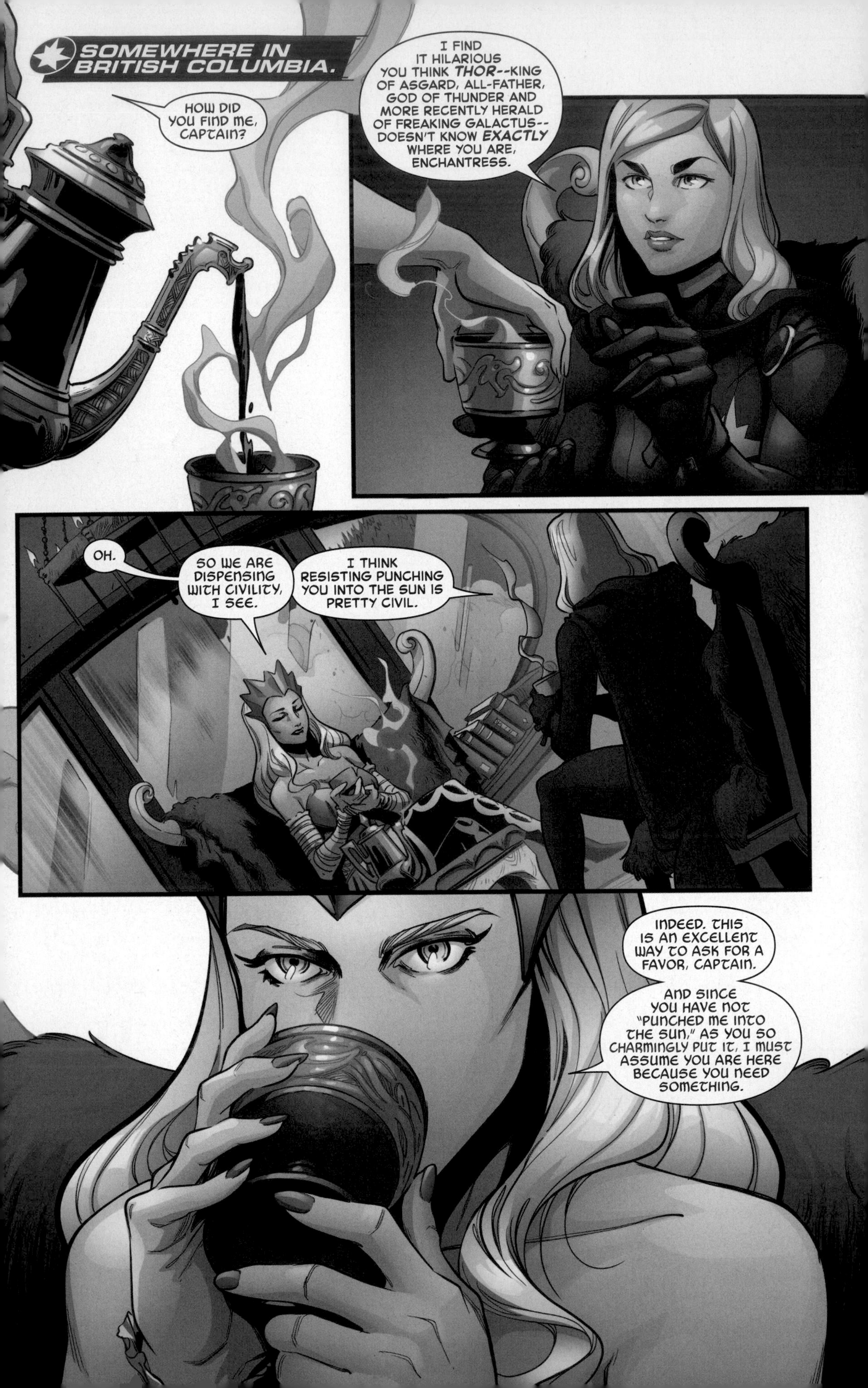
SOMEWHERE IN BRITISH COLUMBIA.
HOW DID YOU FIND ME, CAPTAIN?
I FIND IT HILARIOUS YOU THINK THOR--KING OF ASGARD, ALL-FATHER, GOD OF THUNDER AND MORE RECENTLY HERALD OF FREAKING GALACTUS--DOESN'T KNOW EXACTLY WHERE YOU ARE, ENCHANTRESS.
OH.
SO WE ARE DISPENSING WITH CIVILITY, I SEE.
I THINK RESISTING PUNCHING YOU INTO THE SUN IS PRETTY CIVIL.
INDEED. THIS IS AN EXCELLENT WAY TO ASK FOR A FAVOR, CAPTAIN.
AND SINCE YOU HAVE NOT "PUNCHED ME INTO THE SUN," AS YOU SO CHARMINGLY PUT IT, I MUST ASSUME YOU ARE HERE BECAUSE YOU NEED SOMETHING.

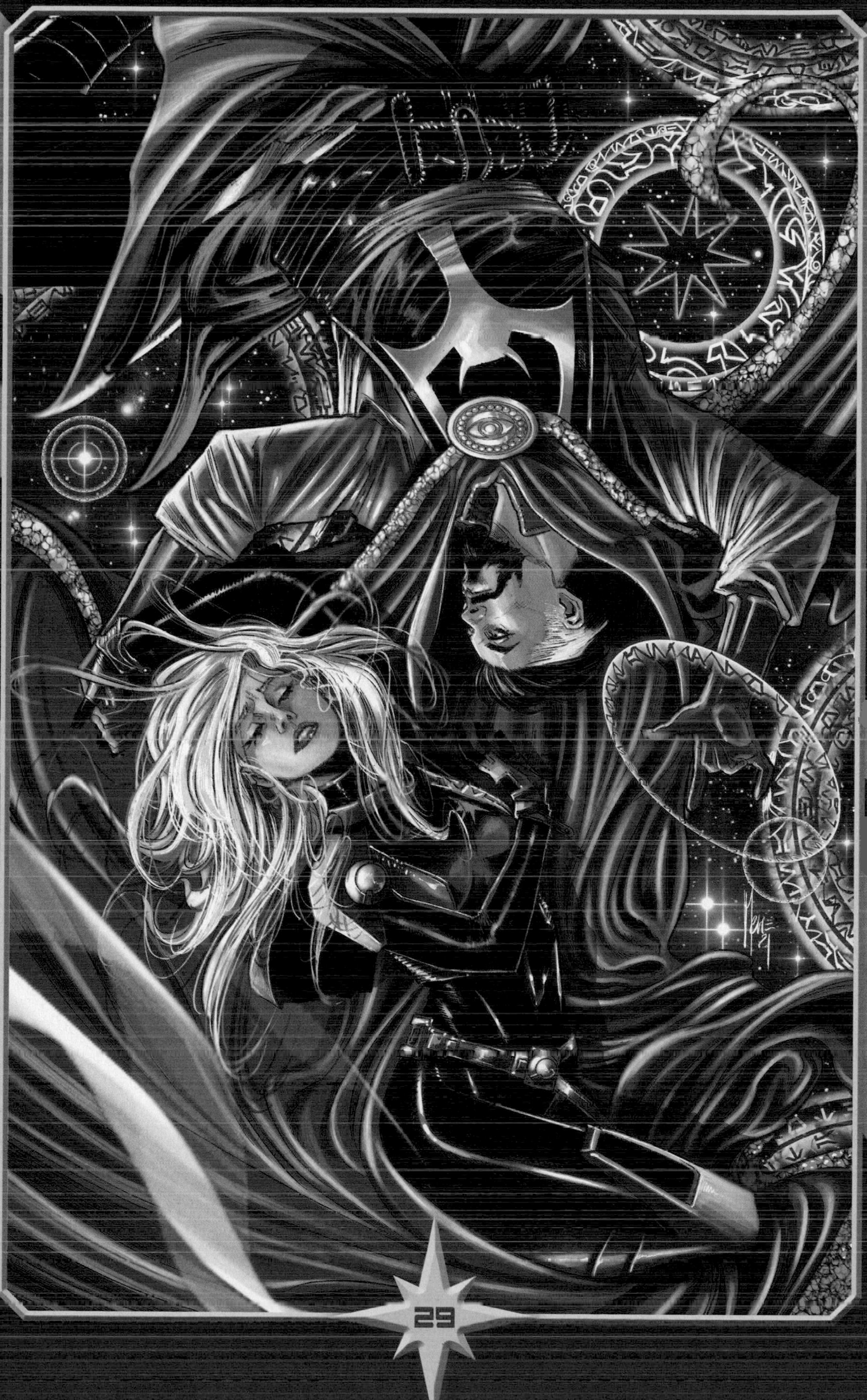
29

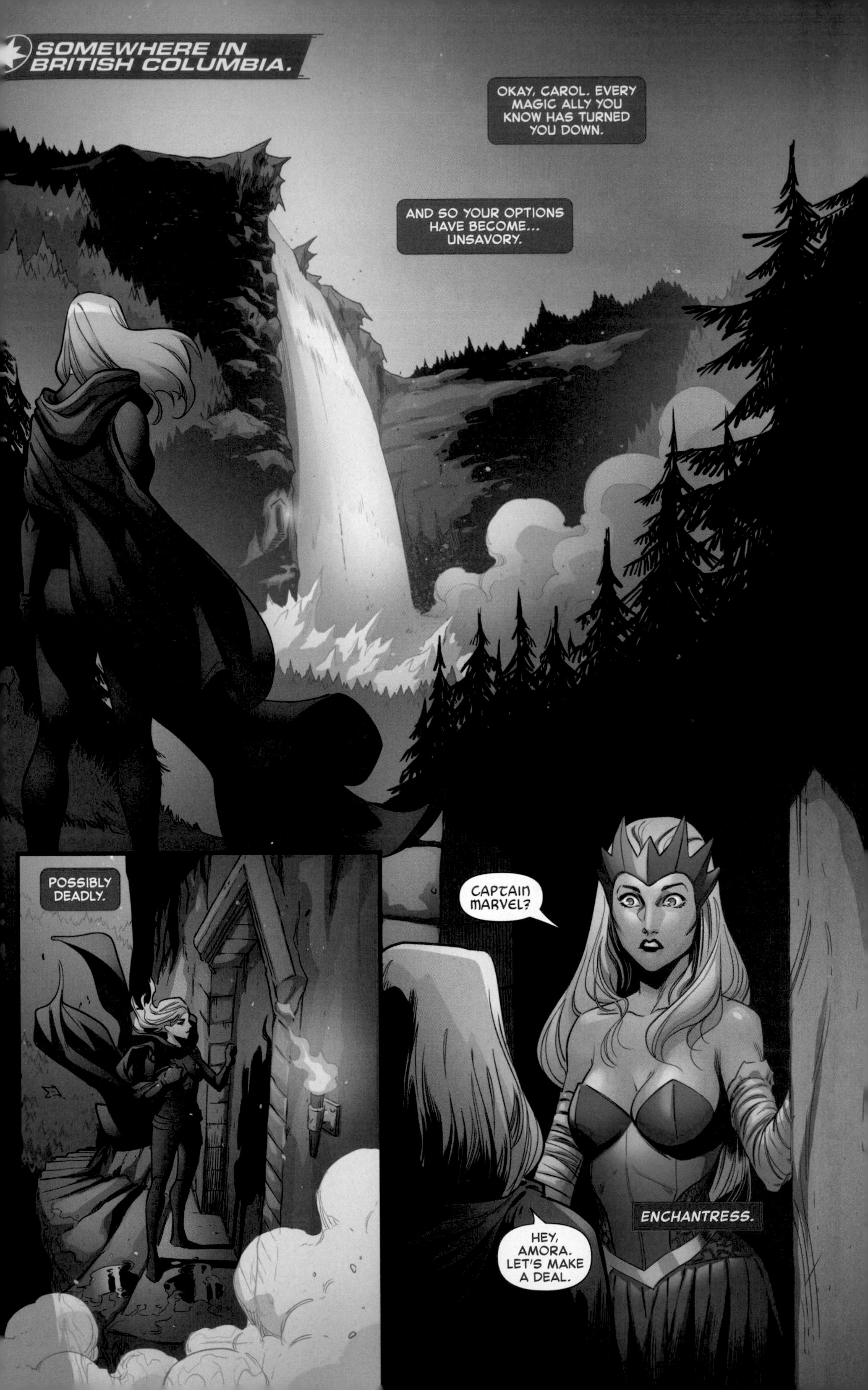
SOMEWHERE IN BRITISH COLUMBIA.
OKAY, CAROL. EVERY MAGIC ALLY YOU KNOW HAS TURNED YOU DOWN.
AND SO YOUR OPTIONS HAVE BECOME... UNSAVORY.
POSSIBLY DEADLY.
CAPTAIN MARVEL?
ENCHANTRESS.
HEY, AMORA. LET'S MAKE A DEAL.

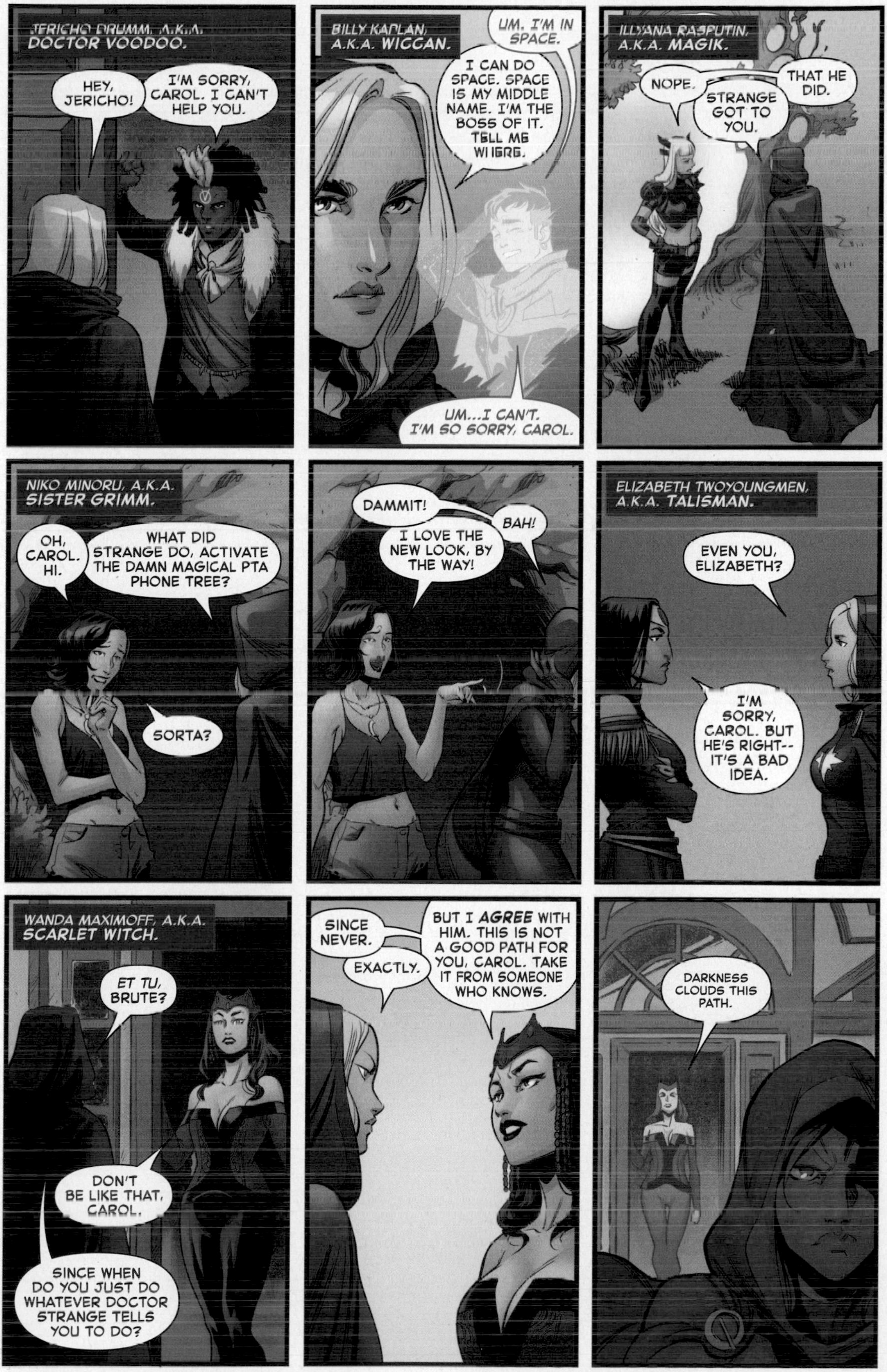
JERICHO DRUMM, A.K.A. DOCTOR VOODOO.
HEY, JERICHO!
I'M SORRY, CAROL. I CAN'T HELP YOU.
BILLY KAPLAN, A.K.A. WICCAN.
UM. I'M IN SPACE.
I CAN DO SPACE. SPACE IS MY MIDDLE NAME. I'M THE BOSS OF IT. TELL ME WHERE.
UM...I CAN'T. I'M SO SORRY, CAROL.
ILLYANA RASPUTIN, A.K.A. MAGIK.
NOPE.
STRANGE GOT TO YOU.
THAT HE DID.
NIKO MINORU, A.K.A. SISTER GRIMM.
OH, CAROL. HI.
WHAT DID STRANGE DO, ACTIVATE THE DAMN MAGICAL PTA PHONE TREE?
SORTA?
DAMMIT!
BAH!
I LOVE THE NEW LOOK, BY THE WAY!
ELIZABETH TWOYOUNGMEN, A.K.A. TALISMAN.
EVEN YOU, ELIZABETH?
I'M SORRY, CAROL. BUT HE'S RIGHT-- IT'S A BAD IDEA.
WANDA MAXIMOFF, A.K.A. SCARLET WITCH.
ET TU, BRUTE?
DON'T BE LIKE THAT, CAROL.
SINCE WHEN DO YOU JUST DO WHATEVER DOCTOR STRANGE TELLS YOU TO DO?
SINCE NEVER.
BUT I AGREE WITH HIM. THIS IS NOT A GOOD PATH FOR YOU, CAROL. TAKE IT FROM SOMEONE WHO KNOWS.
EXACTLY.
DARKNESS CLOUDS THIS PATH.

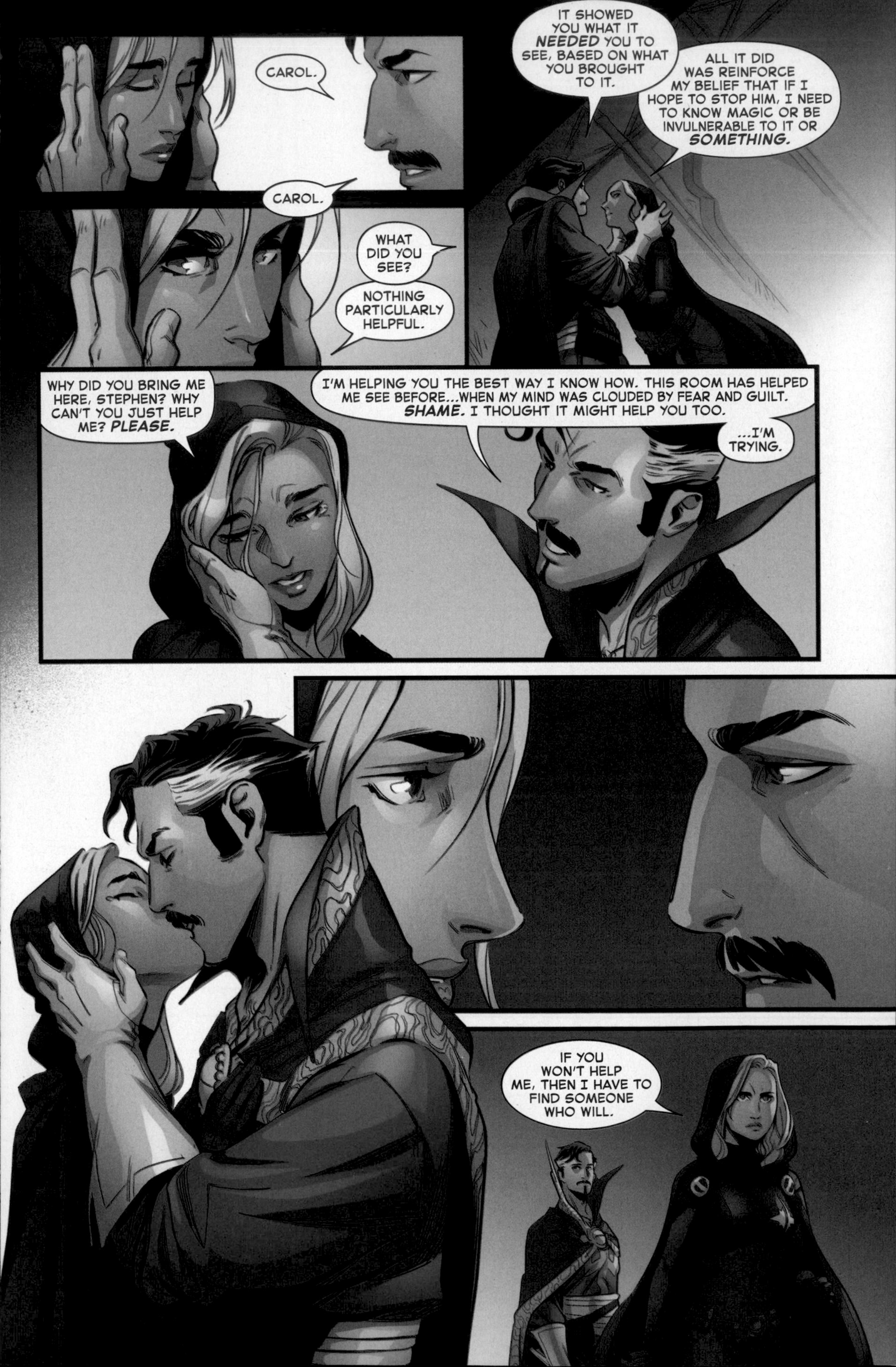
CAROL.
CAROL.
WHAT DID YOU SEE?
NOTHING PARTICULARLY HELPFUL.
IT SHOWED YOU WHAT IT *NEEDED* YOU TO SEE, BASED ON WHAT YOU BROUGHT TO IT.
ALL IT DID WAS REINFORCE MY BELIEF THAT IF I HOPE TO STOP HIM, I NEED TO KNOW MAGIC OR BE INVULNERABLE TO IT OR *SOMETHING.*
WHY DID YOU BRING ME HERE, STEPHEN? WHY CAN'T YOU JUST HELP ME? *PLEASE.*
I'M HELPING YOU THE BEST WAY I KNOW HOW. THIS ROOM HAS HELPED ME SEE BEFORE...WHEN MY MIND WAS CLOUDED BY FEAR AND GUILT. *SHAME.* I THOUGHT IT MIGHT HELP YOU TOO.
...I'M TRYING.
IF YOU WON'T HELP ME, THEN I HAVE TO FIND SOMEONE WHO WILL.

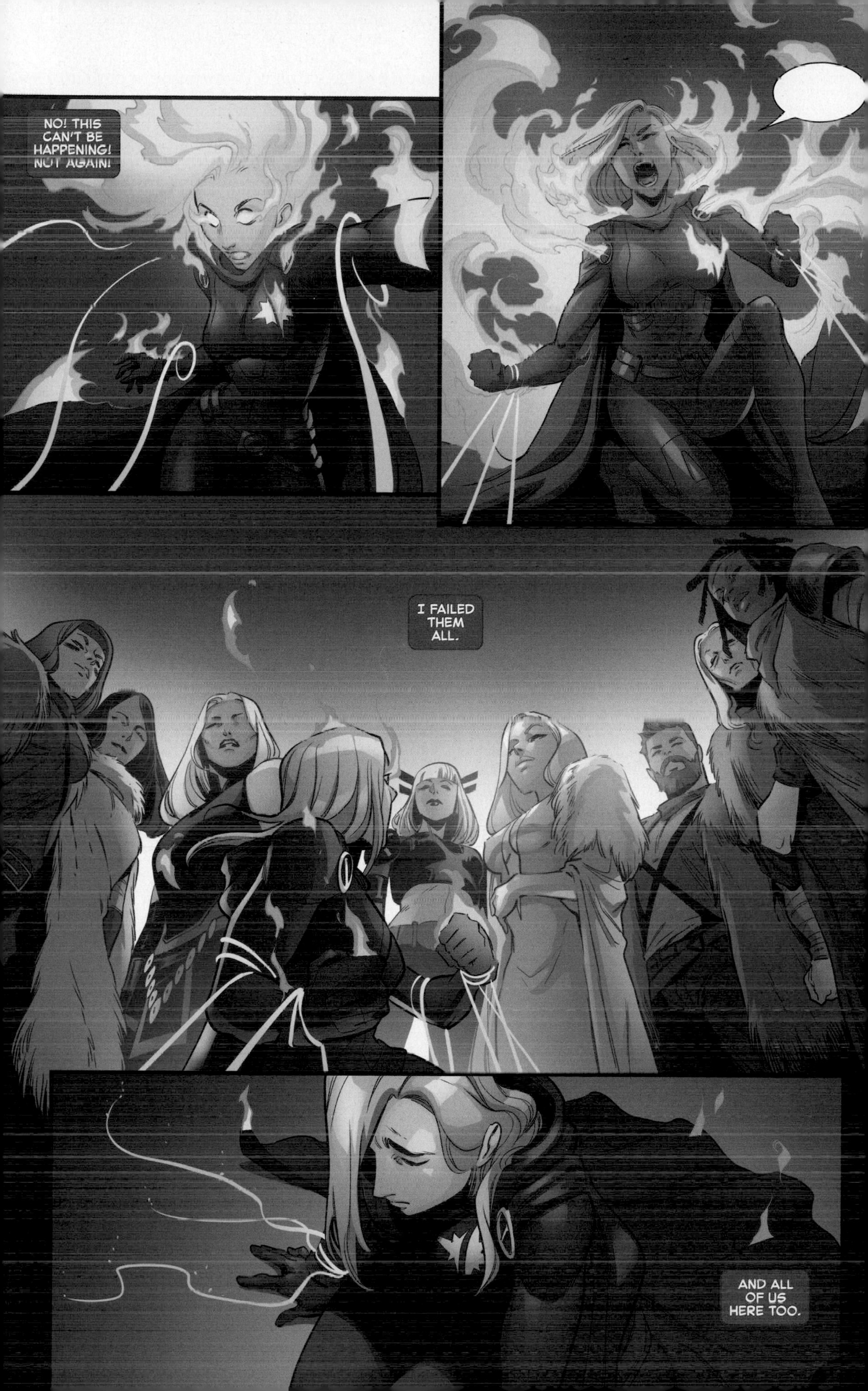
NO! THIS CAN'T BE HAPPENING! NOT AGAIN!
I FAILED THEM ALL.
AND ALL OF US HERE TOO.

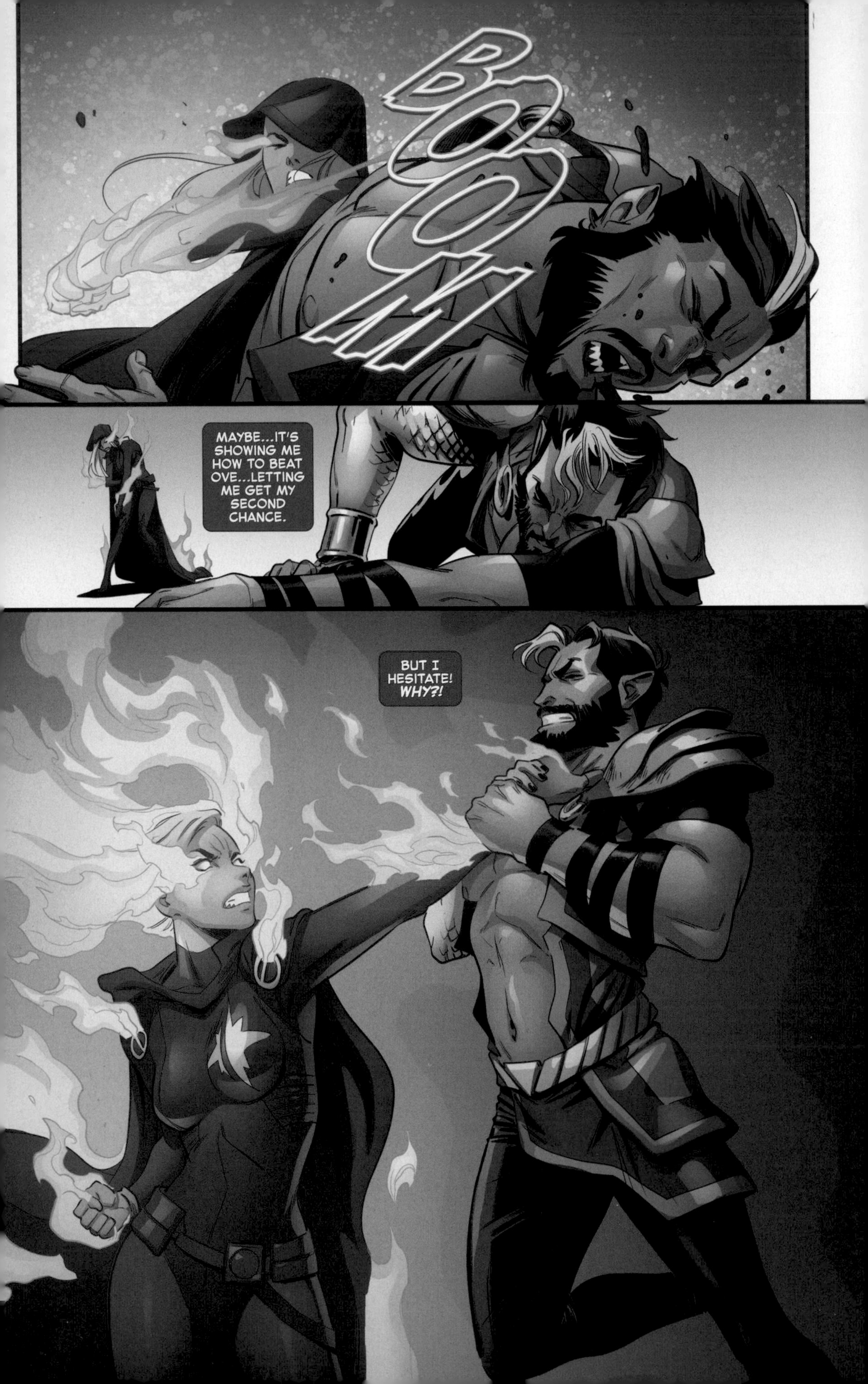
BOOM
MAYBE...IT'S SHOWING ME HOW TO BEAT OVE...LETTING ME GET MY SECOND CHANCE.
BUT I HESITATE! *WHY?!*

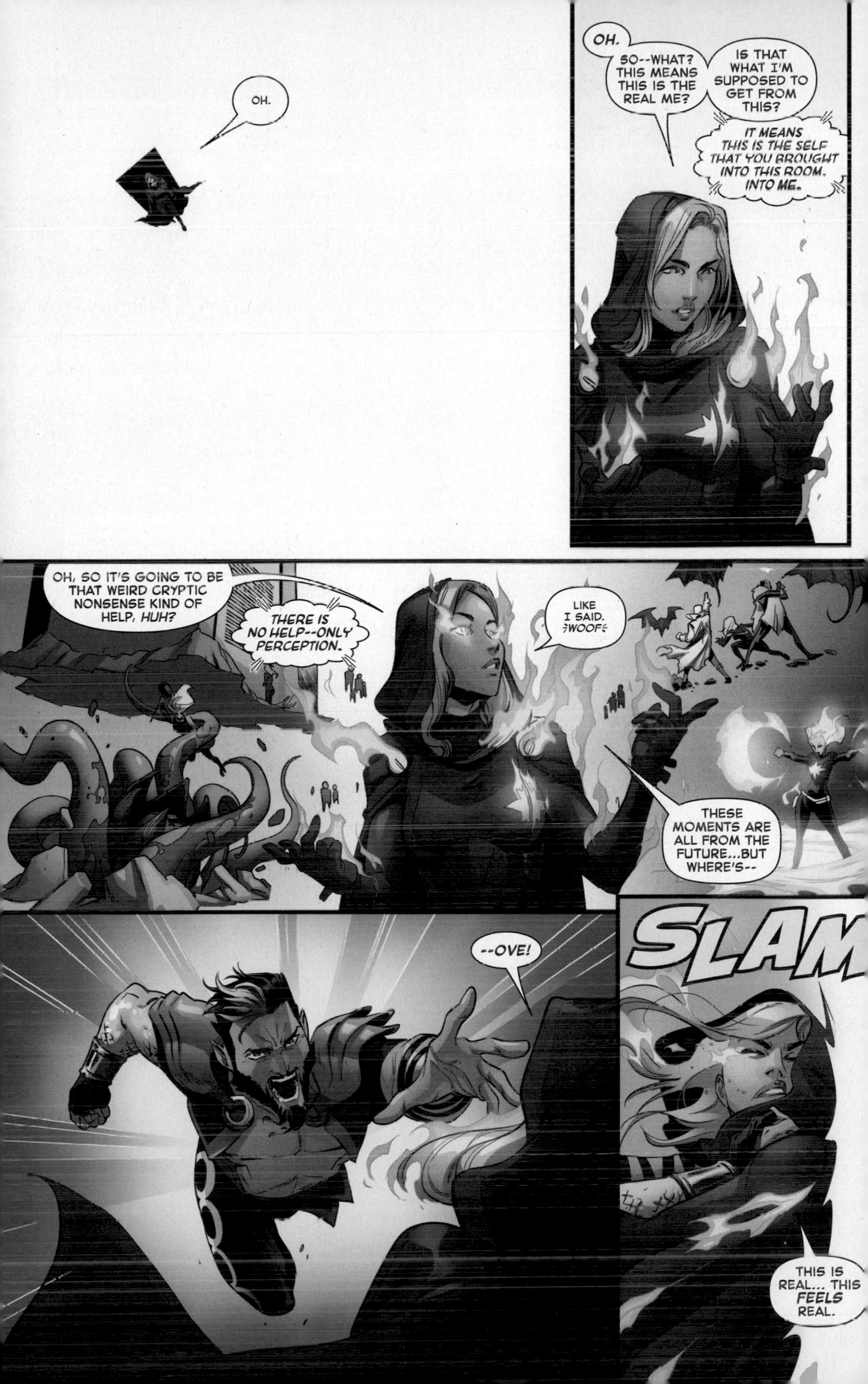
OH.
OH.
SO--WHAT? THIS MEANS THIS IS THE REAL ME?
IS THAT WHAT I'M SUPPOSED TO GET FROM THIS?
IT MEANS THIS IS THE SELF THAT YOU BROUGHT INTO THIS ROOM. INTO ME.
OH, SO IT'S GOING TO BE THAT WEIRD CRYPTIC NONSENSE KIND OF HELP, HUH?
THERE IS NO HELP--ONLY PERCEPTION.
LIKE I SAID. WOOF
THESE MOMENTS ARE ALL FROM THE FUTURE...BUT WHERE'S--
--OVE!
SLAM
THIS IS REAL... THIS FEELS REAL.

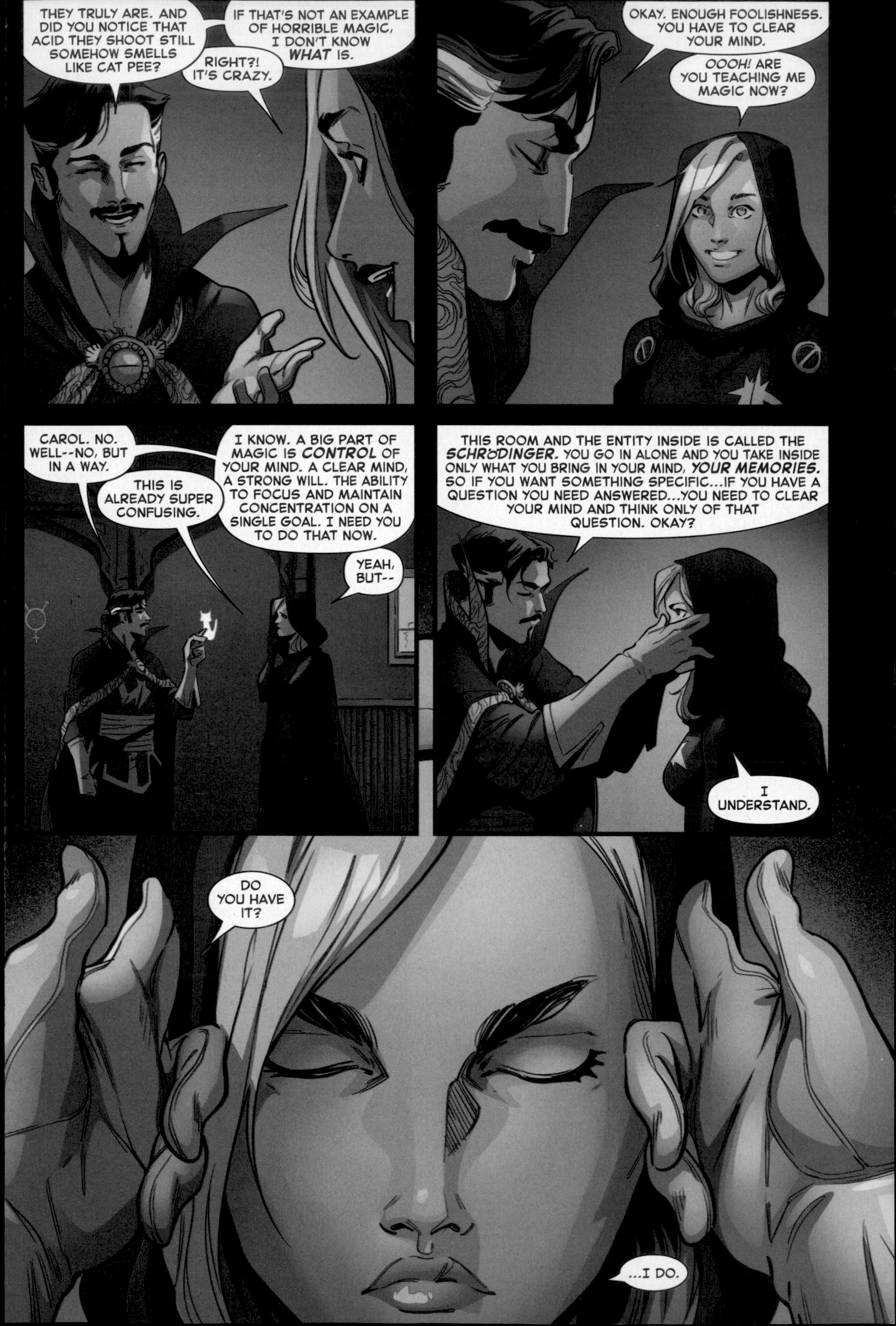

THEY TRULY ARE. AND DID YOU NOTICE THAT ACID THEY SHOOT STILL SOMEHOW SMELLS LIKE CAT PEE?
RIGHT?! IT'S CRAZY.
IF THAT'S NOT AN EXAMPLE OF HORRIBLE MAGIC, I DON'T KNOW WHAT IS.
OKAY. ENOUGH FOOLISHNESS. YOU HAVE TO CLEAR YOUR MIND.
OOOH! ARE YOU TEACHING ME MAGIC NOW?
CAROL. NO. WELL--NO, BUT IN A WAY.
THIS IS ALREADY SUPER CONFUSING.
I KNOW. A BIG PART OF MAGIC IS CONTROL OF YOUR MIND. A CLEAR MIND, A STRONG WILL. THE ABILITY TO FOCUS AND MAINTAIN CONCENTRATION ON A SINGLE GOAL. I NEED YOU TO DO THAT NOW.
YEAH, BUT--
THIS ROOM AND THE ENTITY INSIDE IS CALLED THE SCHRÖDINGER. YOU GO IN ALONE AND YOU TAKE INSIDE ONLY WHAT YOU BRING IN YOUR MIND, YOUR MEMORIES. SO IF YOU WANT SOMETHING SPECIFIC...IF YOU HAVE A QUESTION YOU NEED ANSWERED...YOU NEED TO CLEAR YOUR MIND AND THINK ONLY OF THAT QUESTION. OKAY?
I UNDERSTAND.
DO YOU HAVE IT?
...I DO.

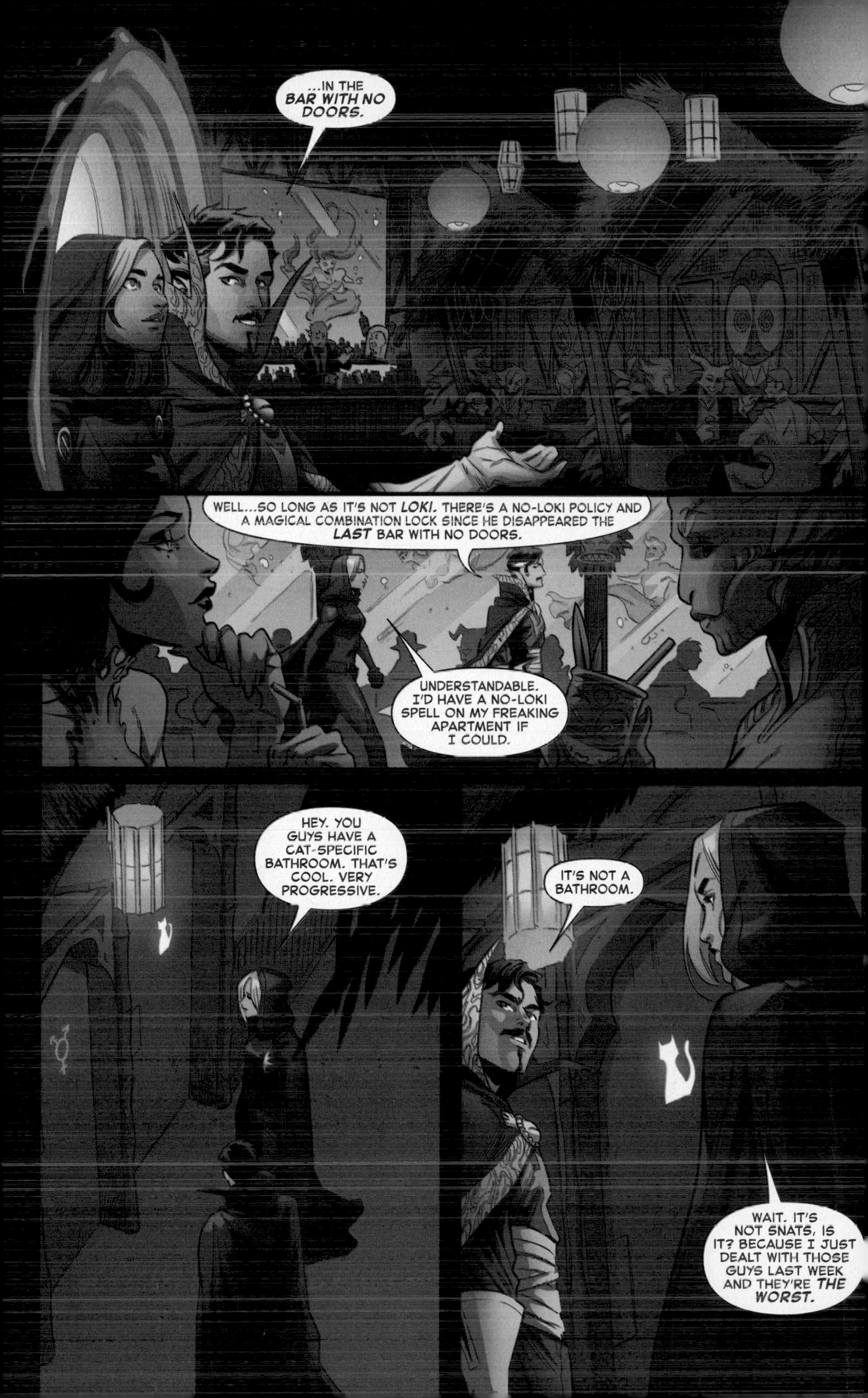
...IN THE BAR WITH NO DOORS.
WELL...SO LONG AS IT'S NOT LOKI. THERE'S A NO-LOKI POLICY AND A MAGICAL COMBINATION LOCK SINCE HE DISAPPEARED THE LAST BAR WITH NO DOORS.
UNDERSTANDABLE. I'D HAVE A NO-LOKI SPELL ON MY FREAKING APARTMENT IF I COULD.
HEY. YOU GUYS HAVE A CAT-SPECIFIC BATHROOM. THAT'S COOL. VERY PROGRESSIVE.
IT'S NOT A BATHROOM.
WAIT. IT'S NOT SNATS, IS IT? BECAUSE I JUST DEALT WITH THOSE GUYS LAST WEEK AND THEY'RE THE WORST.

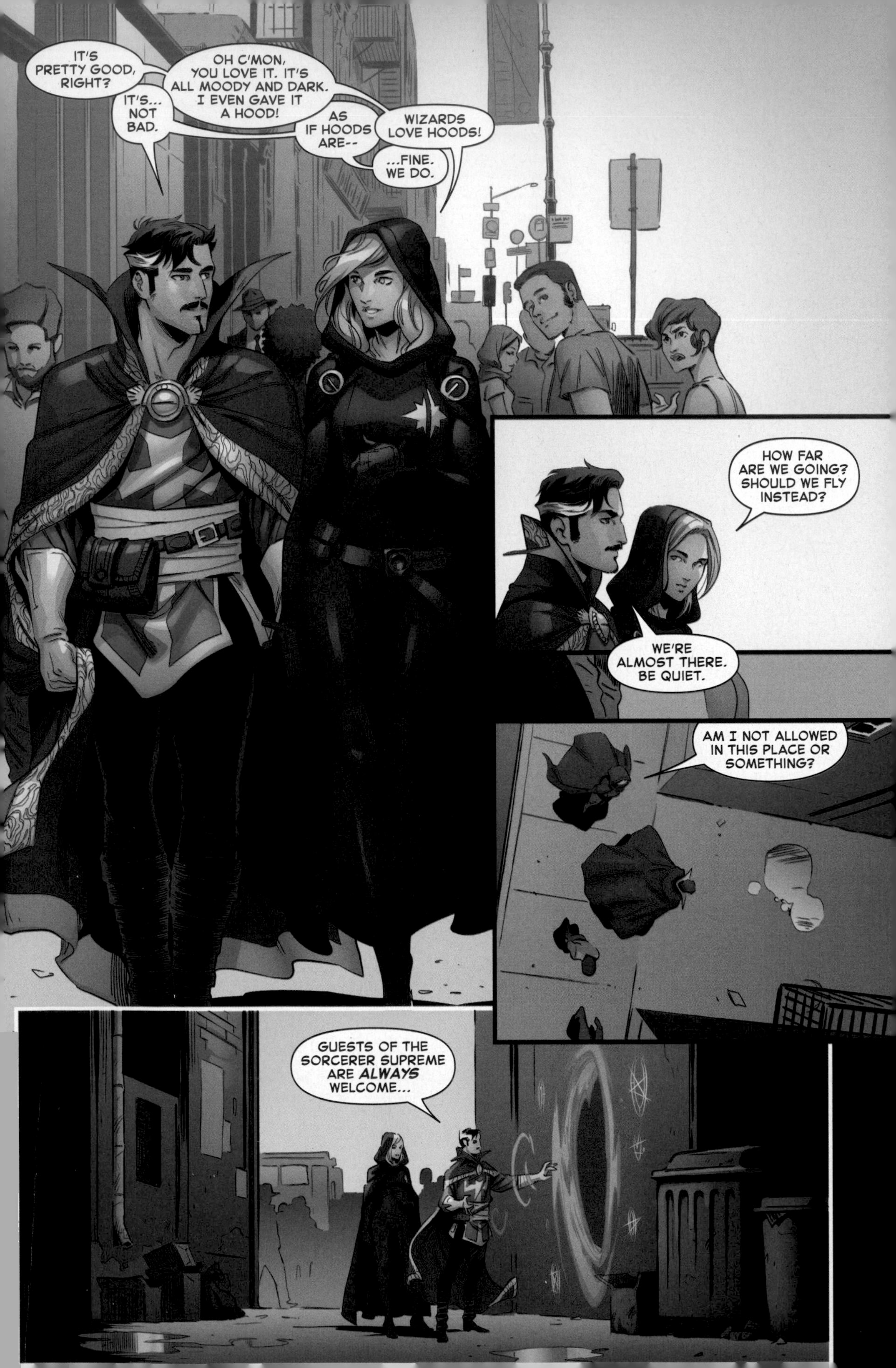
IT'S PRETTY GOOD, RIGHT?
IT'S... NOT BAD.
OH C'MON, YOU LOVE IT. IT'S ALL MOODY AND DARK. I EVEN GAVE IT A HOOD!
AS IF HOODS ARE--
WIZARDS LOVE HOODS!
...FINE. WE DO.
HOW FAR ARE WE GOING? SHOULD WE FLY INSTEAD?
WE'RE ALMOST THERE. BE QUIET.
AM I NOT ALLOWED IN THIS PLACE OR SOMETHING?
GUESTS OF THE SORCERER SUPREME ARE *ALWAYS* WELCOME...

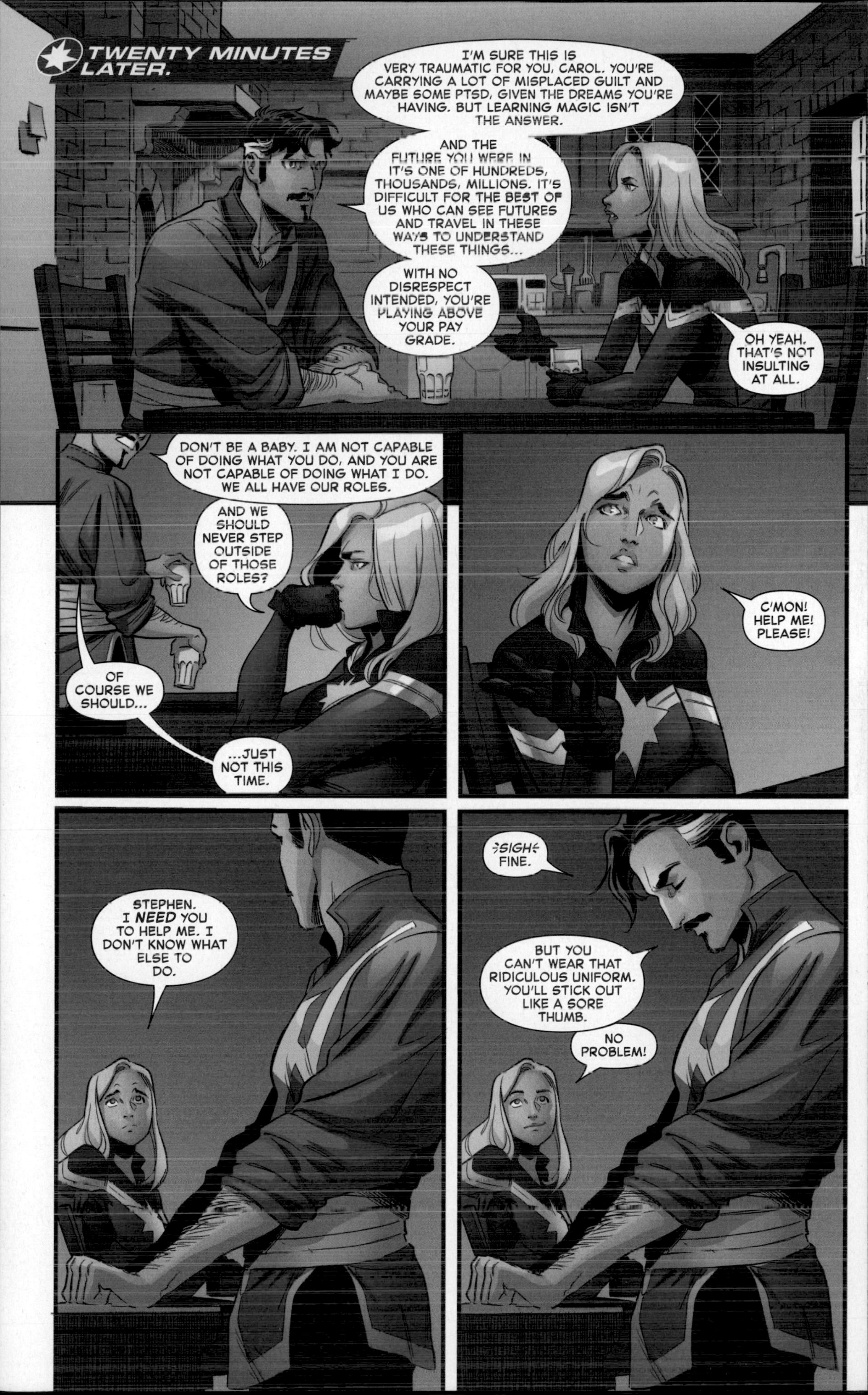
TWENTY MINUTES LATER.
I'M SURE THIS IS VERY TRAUMATIC FOR YOU, CAROL. YOU'RE CARRYING A LOT OF MISPLACED GUILT AND MAYBE SOME PTSD, GIVEN THE DREAMS YOU'RE HAVING. BUT LEARNING MAGIC ISN'T THE ANSWER.
AND THE FUTURE YOU WERE IN IT'S ONE OF HUNDREDS, THOUSANDS, MILLIONS. IT'S DIFFICULT FOR THE BEST OF US WHO CAN SEE FUTURES AND TRAVEL IN THESE WAYS TO UNDERSTAND THESE THINGS...
WITH NO DISRESPECT INTENDED, YOU'RE PLAYING ABOVE YOUR PAY GRADE.
OH YEAH, THAT'S NOT INSULTING AT ALL.
DON'T BE A BABY. I AM NOT CAPABLE OF DOING WHAT YOU DO, AND YOU ARE NOT CAPABLE OF DOING WHAT I DO. WE ALL HAVE OUR ROLES.
AND WE SHOULD NEVER STEP OUTSIDE OF THOSE ROLES?
OF COURSE WE SHOULD...
...JUST NOT THIS TIME.
C'MON! HELP ME! PLEASE!
STEPHEN. I *NEED* YOU TO HELP ME. I DON'T KNOW WHAT ELSE TO DO.
SIGH FINE.
BUT YOU CAN'T WEAR THAT RIDICULOUS UNIFORM. YOU'LL STICK OUT LIKE A SORE THUMB.
NO PROBLEM!

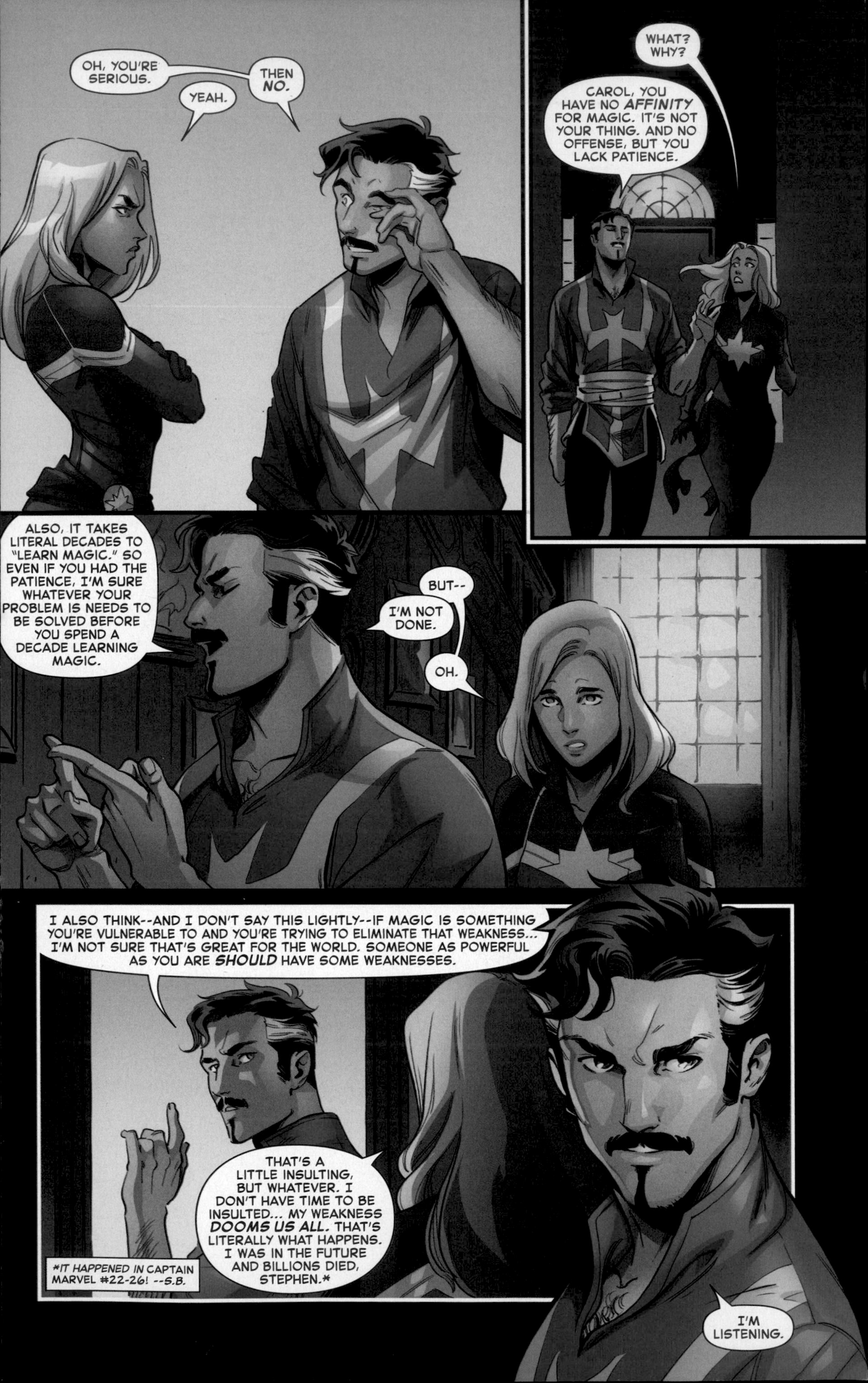
OH, YOU'RE SERIOUS.
YEAH.
THEN NO.
WHAT? WHY?
CAROL, YOU HAVE NO AFFINITY FOR MAGIC. IT'S NOT YOUR THING. AND NO OFFENSE, BUT YOU LACK PATIENCE.
ALSO, IT TAKES LITERAL DECADES TO "LEARN MAGIC." SO EVEN IF YOU HAD THE PATIENCE, I'M SURE WHATEVER YOUR PROBLEM IS NEEDS TO BE SOLVED BEFORE YOU SPEND A DECADE LEARNING MAGIC.
BUT--
I'M NOT DONE.
OH.
I ALSO THINK--AND I DON'T SAY THIS LIGHTLY--IF MAGIC IS SOMETHING YOU'RE VULNERABLE TO AND YOU'RE TRYING TO ELIMINATE THAT WEAKNESS... I'M NOT SURE THAT'S GREAT FOR THE WORLD. SOMEONE AS POWERFUL AS YOU ARE SHOULD HAVE SOME WEAKNESSES.
THAT'S A LITTLE INSULTING, BUT WHATEVER. I DON'T HAVE TIME TO BE INSULTED... MY WEAKNESS DOOMS US ALL. THAT'S LITERALLY WHAT HAPPENS. I WAS IN THE FUTURE AND BILLIONS DIED, STEPHEN.*
*IT HAPPENED IN CAPTAIN MARVEL #22-26! --S.B.
I'M LISTENING.

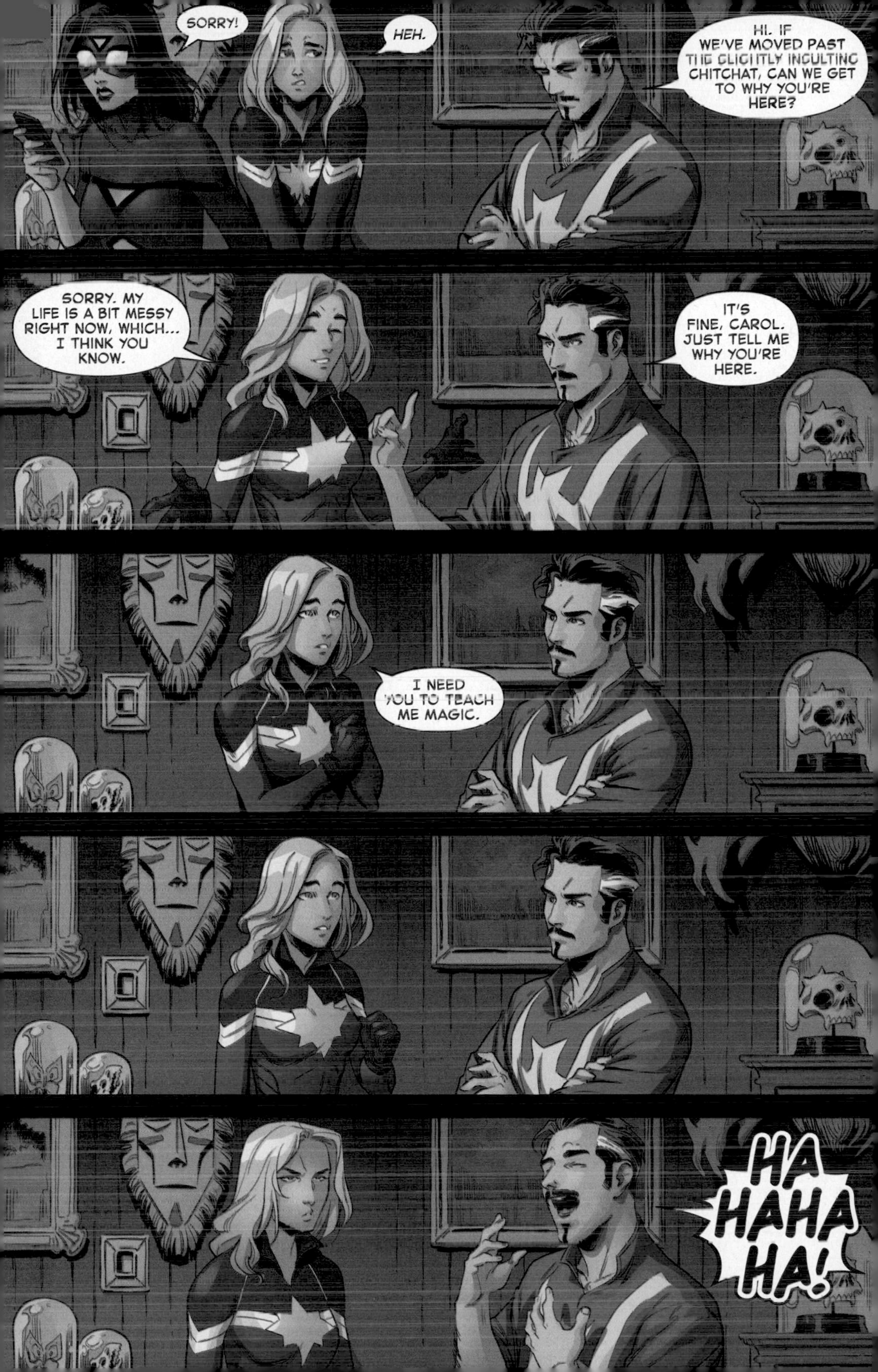
SORRY!
HEH.
HI. IF WE'VE MOVED PAST THE SLIGHTLY INSULTING CHITCHAT, CAN WE GET TO WHY YOU'RE HERE?
SORRY. MY LIFE IS A BIT MESSY RIGHT NOW, WHICH... I THINK YOU KNOW.
IT'S FINE, CAROL. JUST TELL ME WHY YOU'RE HERE.
I NEED YOU TO TEACH ME MAGIC.
HA HAHA HA!

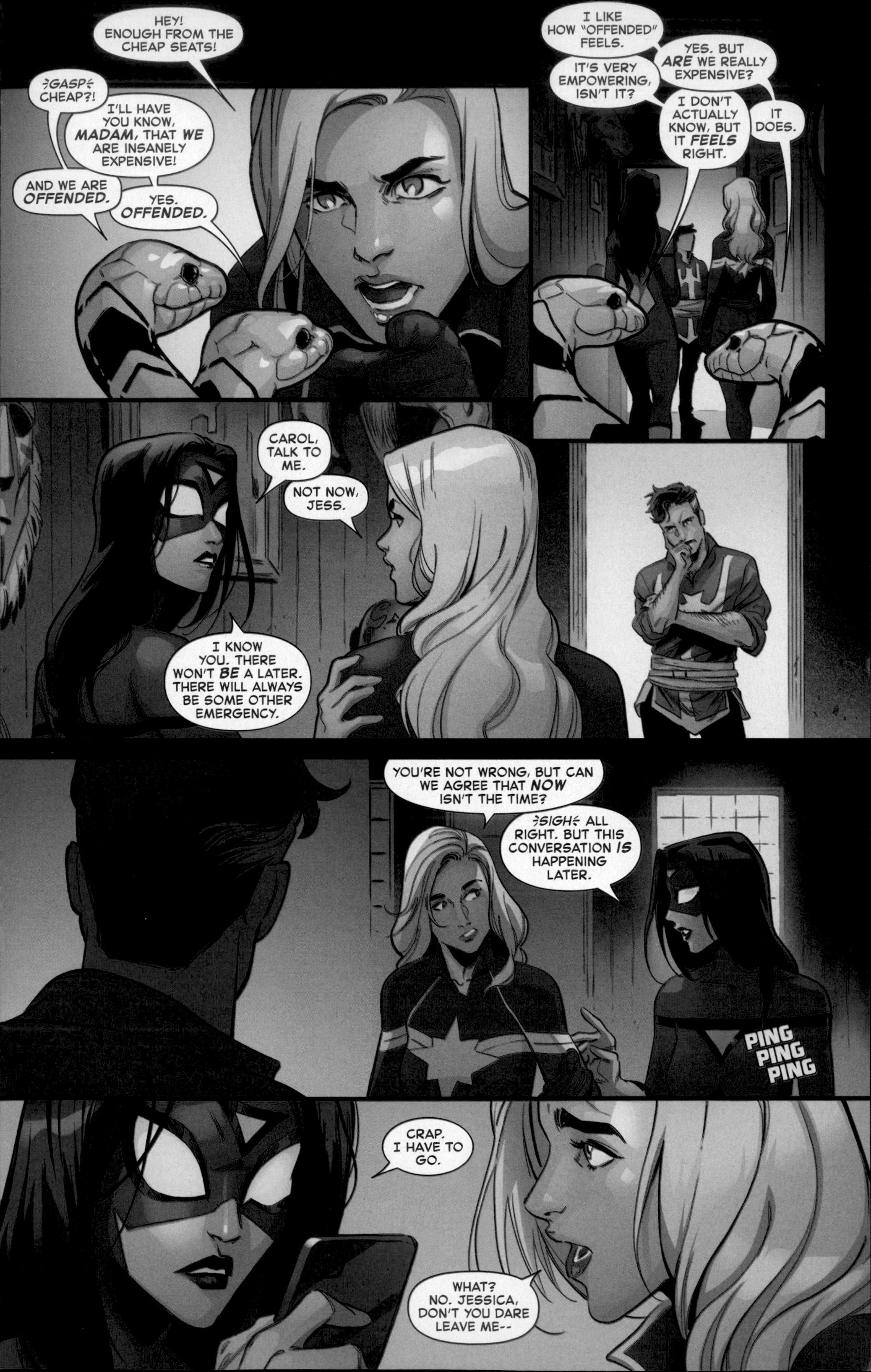
HEY! ENOUGH FROM THE CHEAP SEATS!
⚡GASP⚡ CHEAP?!
I'LL HAVE YOU KNOW, MADAM, THAT WE ARE INSANELY EXPENSIVE!
AND WE ARE OFFENDED.
YES. OFFENDED.
I LIKE HOW "OFFENDED" FEELS.
IT'S VERY EMPOWERING, ISN'T IT?
YES. BUT ARE WE REALLY EXPENSIVE?
I DON'T ACTUALLY KNOW, BUT IT FEELS RIGHT.
IT DOES.
CAROL, TALK TO ME.
NOT NOW, JESS.
I KNOW YOU. THERE WON'T BE A LATER. THERE WILL ALWAYS BE SOME OTHER EMERGENCY.
YOU'RE NOT WRONG, BUT CAN WE AGREE THAT NOW ISN'T THE TIME?
⚡SIGH⚡ ALL RIGHT. BUT THIS CONVERSATION IS HAPPENING LATER.
PING PING PING
CRAP. I HAVE TO GO.
WHAT? NO. JESSICA, DON'T YOU DARE LEAVE ME--

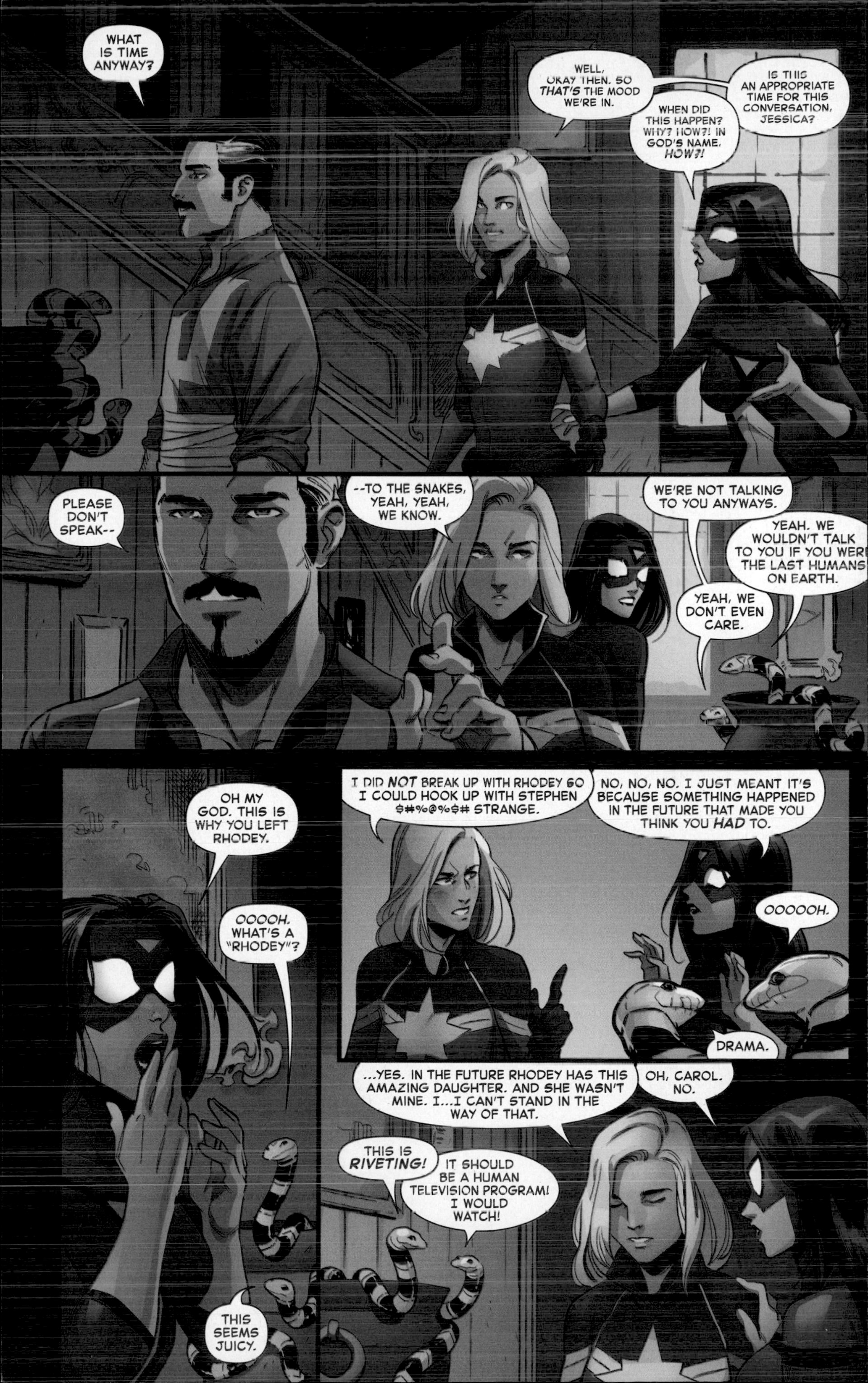
WHAT IS TIME ANYWAY?
WELL, OKAY THEN. SO THAT'S THE MOOD WE'RE IN.
IS THIS AN APPROPRIATE TIME FOR THIS CONVERSATION, JESSICA?
WHEN DID THIS HAPPEN? WHY? HOW?! IN GOD'S NAME, HOW?!
PLEASE DON'T SPEAK--
--TO THE SNAKES, YEAH, YEAH, WE KNOW.
WE'RE NOT TALKING TO YOU ANYWAYS.
YEAH. WE WOULDN'T TALK TO YOU IF YOU WERE THE LAST HUMANS ON EARTH.
YEAH, WE DON'T EVEN CARE.
OH MY GOD. THIS IS WHY YOU LEFT RHODEY.
OOOOH. WHAT'S A "RHODEY"?
I DID NOT BREAK UP WITH RHODEY SO I COULD HOOK UP WITH STEPHEN $#%@%$# STRANGE.
NO, NO, NO. I JUST MEANT IT'S BECAUSE SOMETHING HAPPENED IN THE FUTURE THAT MADE YOU THINK YOU HAD TO.
OOOOOH.
DRAMA.
...YES. IN THE FUTURE RHODEY HAS THIS AMAZING DAUGHTER. AND SHE WASN'T MINE. I...I CAN'T STAND IN THE WAY OF THAT.
OH, CAROL. NO.
THIS IS RIVETING!
IT SHOULD BE A HUMAN TELEVISION PROGRAM! I WOULD WATCH!
THIS SEEMS JUICY.

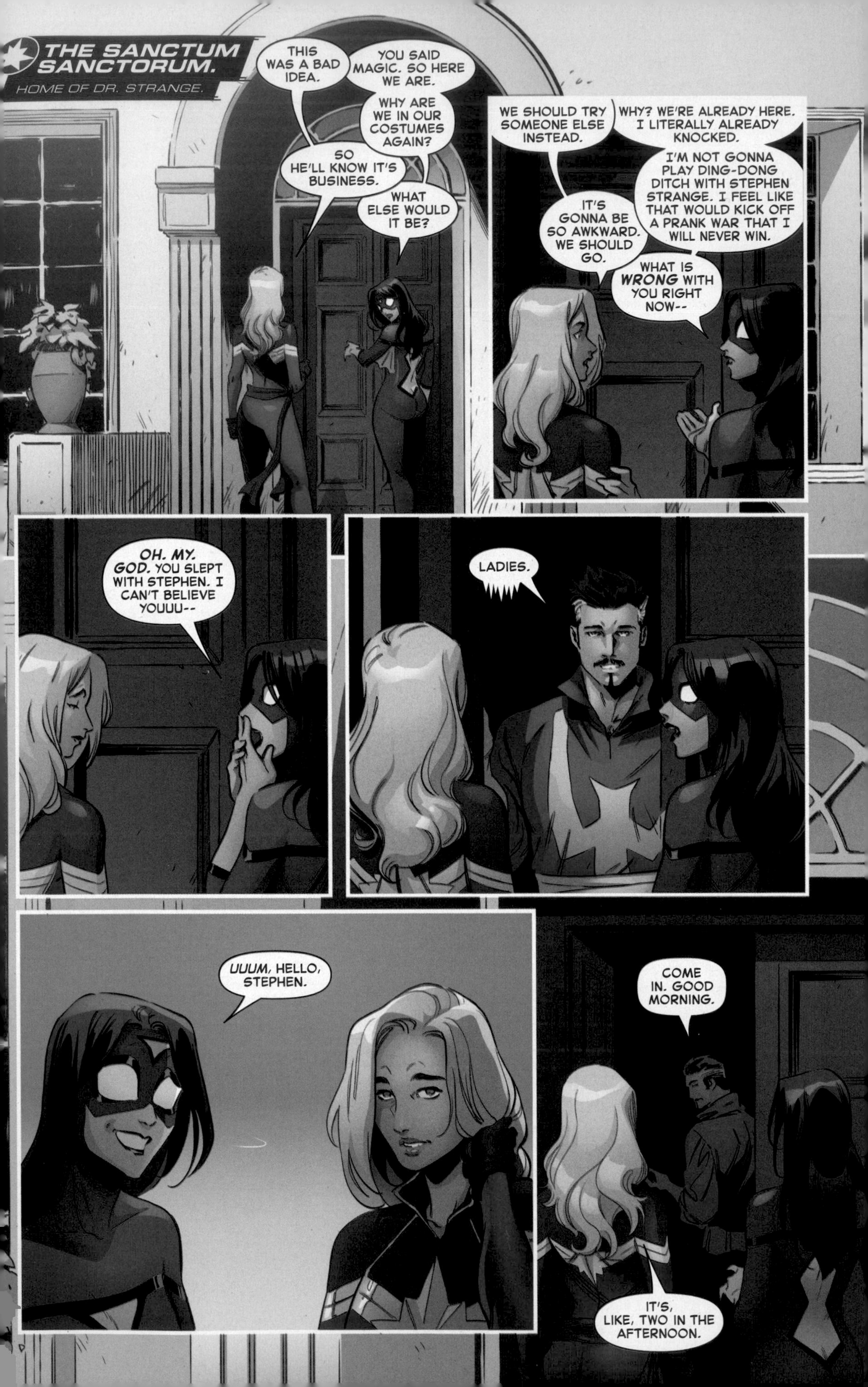
THE SANCTUM SANCTORUM.
HOME OF DR. STRANGE.
THIS WAS A BAD IDEA.
YOU SAID MAGIC. SO HERE WE ARE.
WHY ARE WE IN OUR COSTUMES AGAIN?
SO HE'LL KNOW IT'S BUSINESS.
WHAT ELSE WOULD IT BE?
WE SHOULD TRY SOMEONE ELSE INSTEAD.
WHY? WE'RE ALREADY HERE. I LITERALLY ALREADY KNOCKED.
I'M NOT GONNA PLAY DING-DONG DITCH WITH STEPHEN STRANGE. I FEEL LIKE THAT WOULD KICK OFF A PRANK WAR THAT I WILL NEVER WIN.
IT'S GONNA BE SO AWKWARD. WE SHOULD GO.
WHAT IS WRONG WITH YOU RIGHT NOW--
OH. MY. GOD. YOU SLEPT WITH STEPHEN. I CAN'T BELIEVE YOUUU--
LADIES.
UUUM, HELLO, STEPHEN.
COME IN. GOOD MORNING.
IT'S, LIKE, TWO IN THE AFTERNOON.

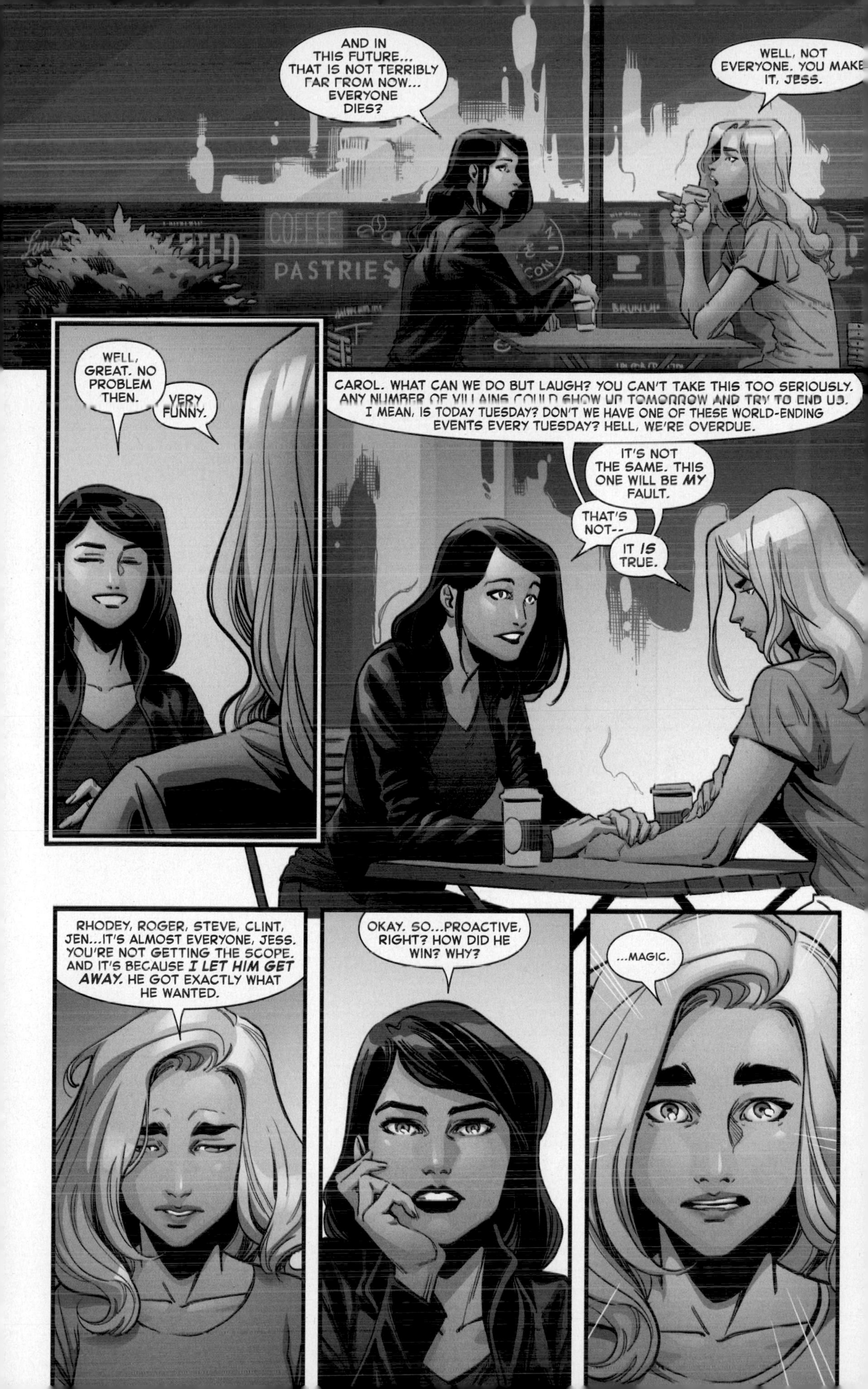
AND IN THIS FUTURE... THAT IS NOT TERRIBLY FAR FROM NOW... EVERYONE DIES?
WELL, NOT EVERYONE. YOU MAKE IT, JESS.
COFFEE
PASTRIES
WELL, GREAT. NO PROBLEM THEN.
VERY FUNNY.
CAROL. WHAT CAN WE DO BUT LAUGH? YOU CAN'T TAKE THIS TOO SERIOUSLY. ANY NUMBER OF VILLAINS COULD SHOW UP TOMORROW AND TRY TO END US. I MEAN, IS TODAY TUESDAY? DON'T WE HAVE ONE OF THESE WORLD-ENDING EVENTS EVERY TUESDAY? HELL, WE'RE OVERDUE.
IT'S NOT THE SAME. THIS ONE WILL BE *MY* FAULT.
THAT'S NOT--
IT *IS* TRUE.
RHODEY, ROGER, STEVE, CLINT, JEN...IT'S ALMOST EVERYONE, JESS. YOU'RE NOT GETTING THE SCOPE. AND IT'S BECAUSE ***I LET HIM GET AWAY.*** HE GOT EXACTLY WHAT HE WANTED.
OKAY. SO...PROACTIVE, RIGHT? HOW DID HE WIN? WHY?
...MAGIC.

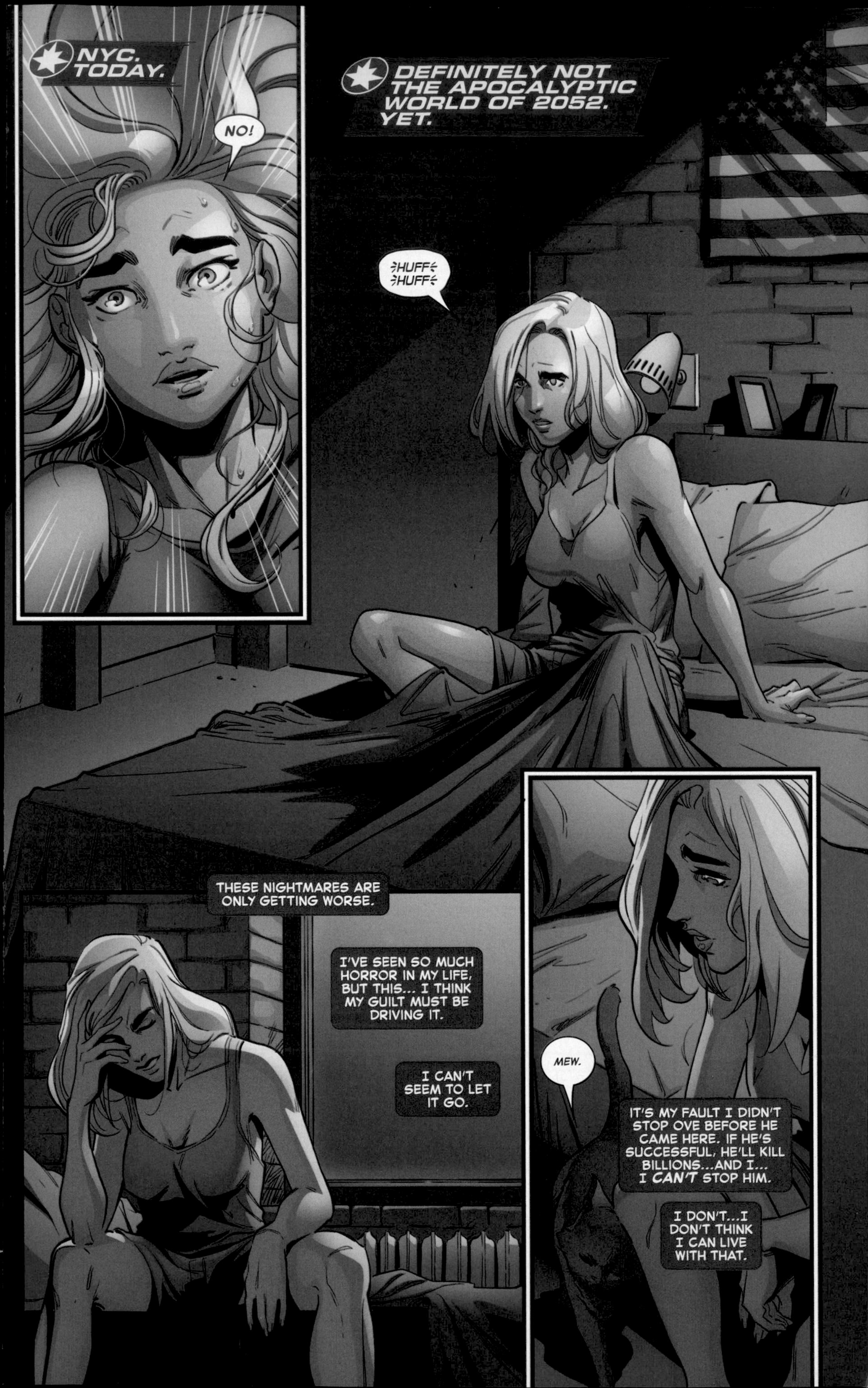

NYC. TODAY.
NO!
DEFINITELY NOT THE APOCALYPTIC WORLD OF 2052. YET.
HUFF HUFF
THESE NIGHTMARES ARE ONLY GETTING WORSE.
I'VE SEEN SO MUCH HORROR IN MY LIFE, BUT THIS... I THINK MY GUILT MUST BE DRIVING IT.
I CAN'T SEEM TO LET IT GO.
MEW.
IT'S MY FAULT I DIDN'T STOP OVE BEFORE HE CAME HERE. IF HE'S SUCCESSFUL, HE'LL KILL BILLIONS...AND I... I CAN'T STOP HIM.
I DON'T...I DON'T THINK I CAN LIVE WITH THAT.

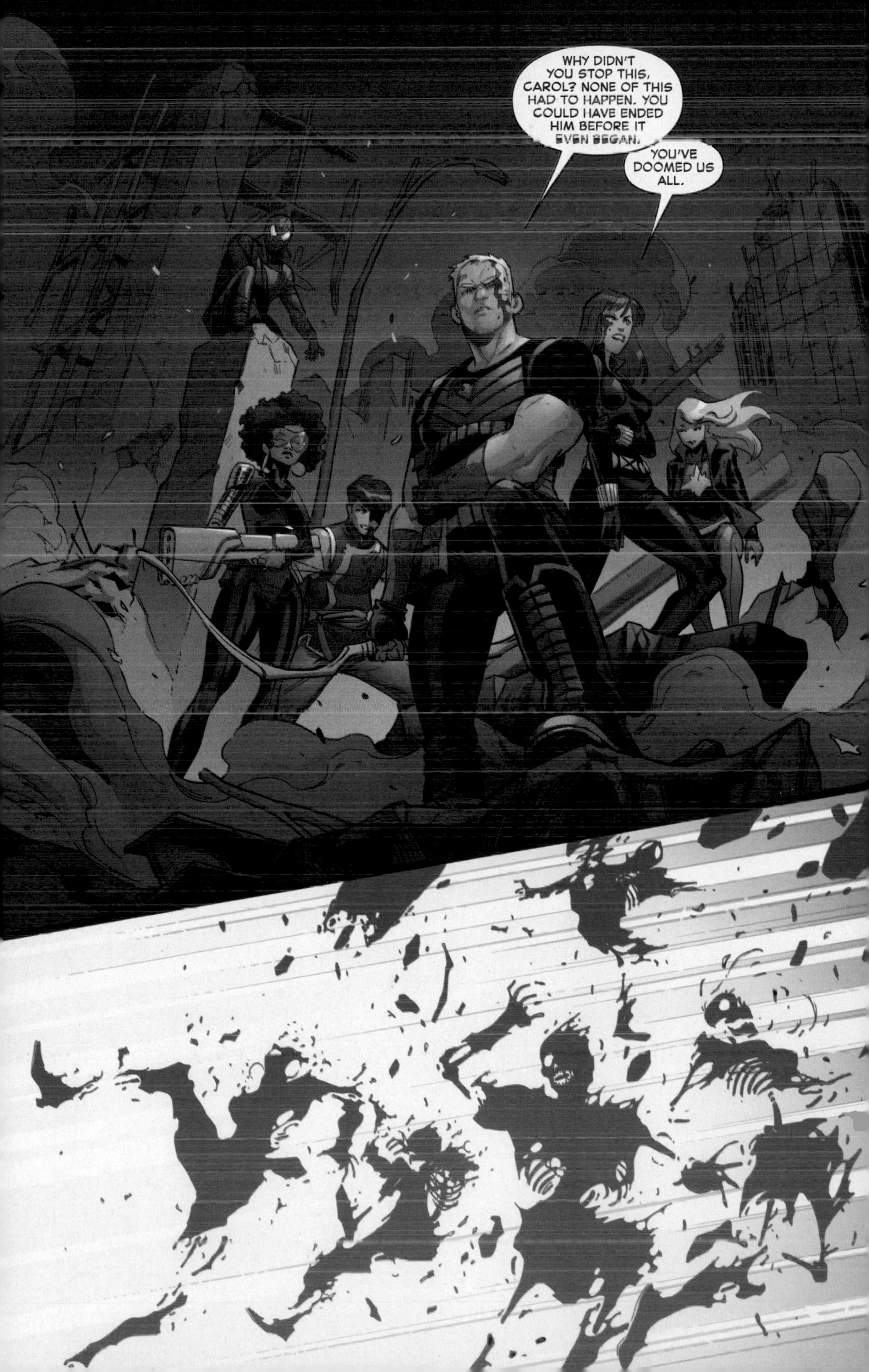
WHY DIDN'T YOU STOP THIS, CAROL? NONE OF THIS HAD TO HAPPEN. YOU COULD HAVE ENDED HIM BEFORE IT EVEN BEGAN.
YOU'VE DOOMED US ALL.

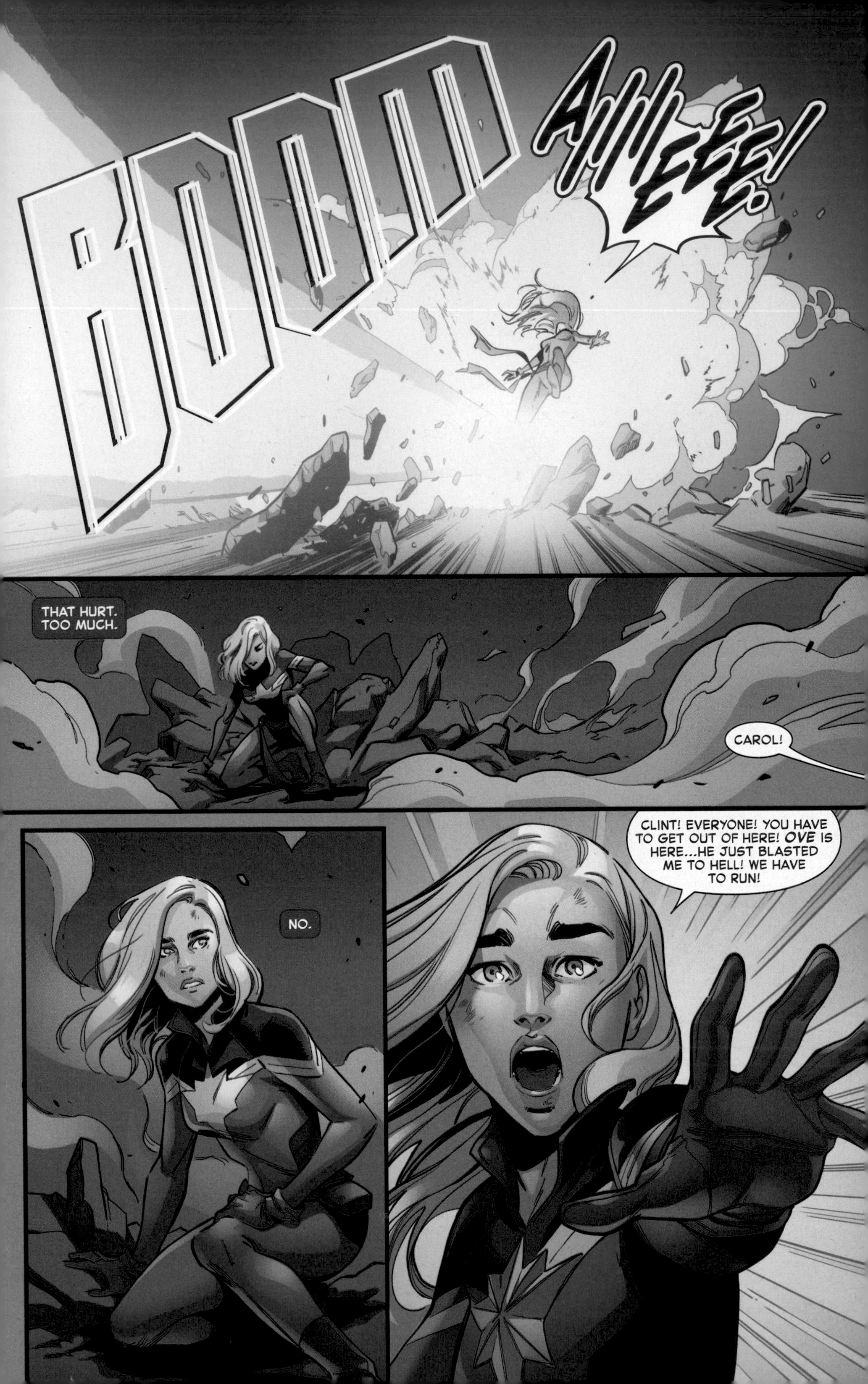
BOOM
AIIIEEEE!
THAT HURT. TOO MUCH.
CAROL!
NO.
CLINT! EVERYONE! YOU HAVE TO GET OUT OF HERE! OVE IS HERE...HE JUST BLASTED ME TO HELL! WE HAVE TO RUN!

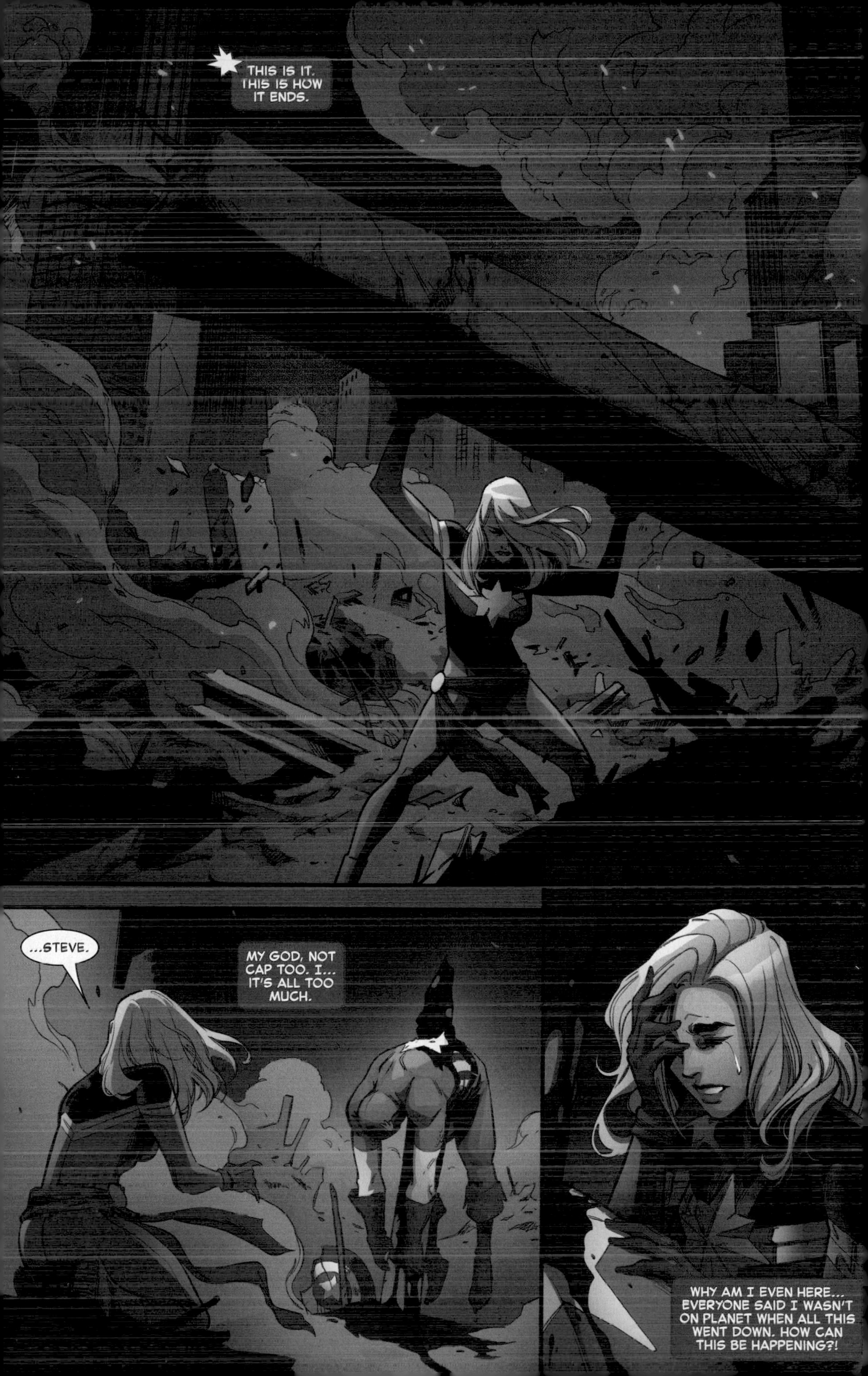
THIS IS IT. THIS IS HOW IT ENDS.
...STEVE.
MY GOD, NOT CAP TOO. I... IT'S ALL TOO MUCH.
WHY AM I EVEN HERE... EVERYONE SAID I WASN'T ON PLANET WHEN ALL THIS WENT DOWN. HOW CAN THIS BE HAPPENING?!

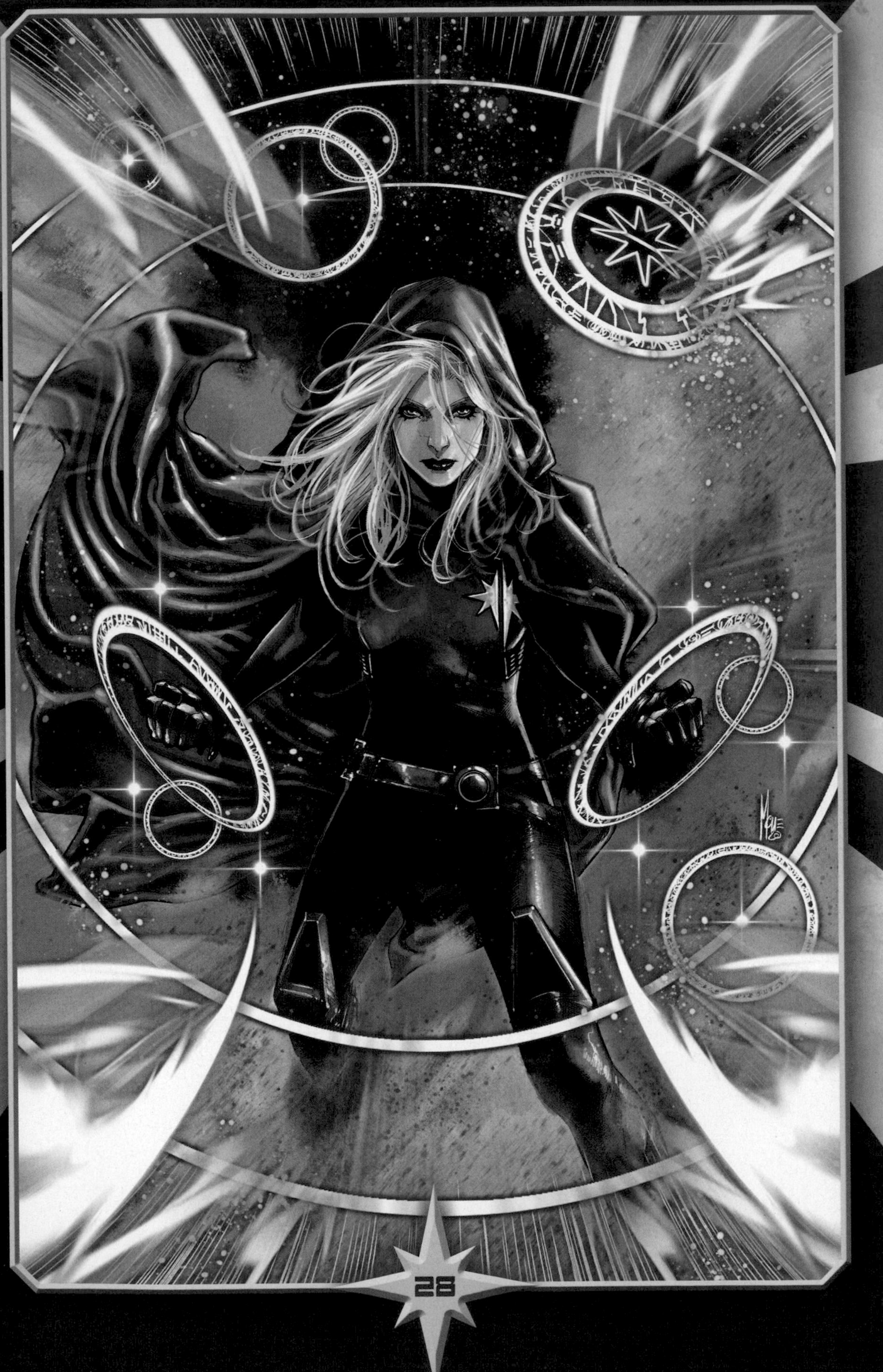
28

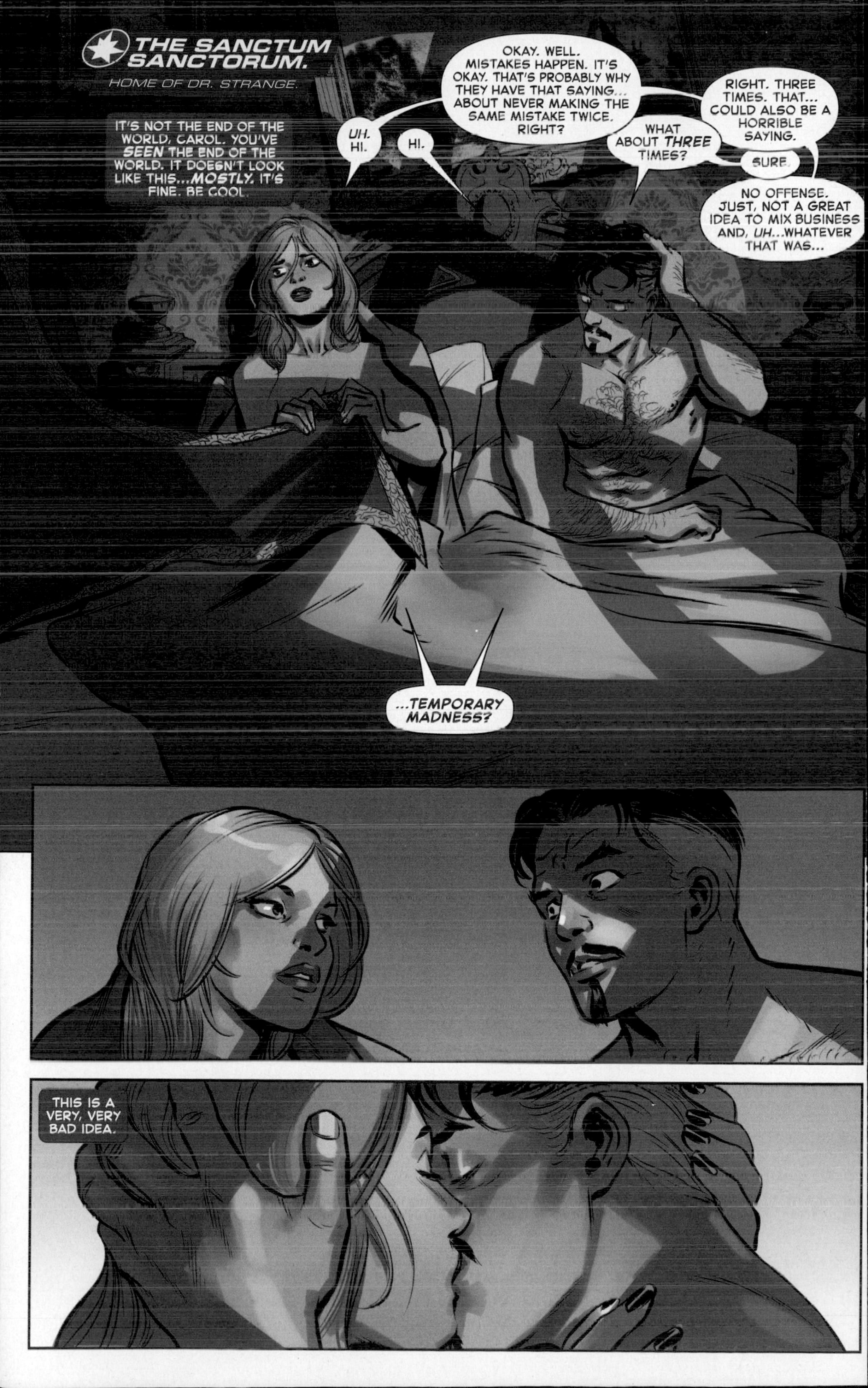
THE SANCTUM SANCTORUM.
HOME OF DR. STRANGE.
IT'S NOT THE END OF THE WORLD, CAROL. YOU'VE SEEN THE END OF THE WORLD. IT DOESN'T LOOK LIKE THIS...MOSTLY. IT'S FINE. BE COOL.
UH. HI.
HI.
OKAY. WELL. MISTAKES HAPPEN. IT'S OKAY. THAT'S PROBABLY WHY THEY HAVE THAT SAYING... ABOUT NEVER MAKING THE SAME MISTAKE TWICE. RIGHT?
WHAT ABOUT THREE TIMES?
RIGHT. THREE TIMES. THAT... COULD ALSO BE A HORRIBLE SAYING.
SURE.
NO OFFENSE. JUST, NOT A GREAT IDEA TO MIX BUSINESS AND, UH...WHATEVER THAT WAS...
...TEMPORARY MADNESS?
THIS IS A VERY, VERY BAD IDEA.

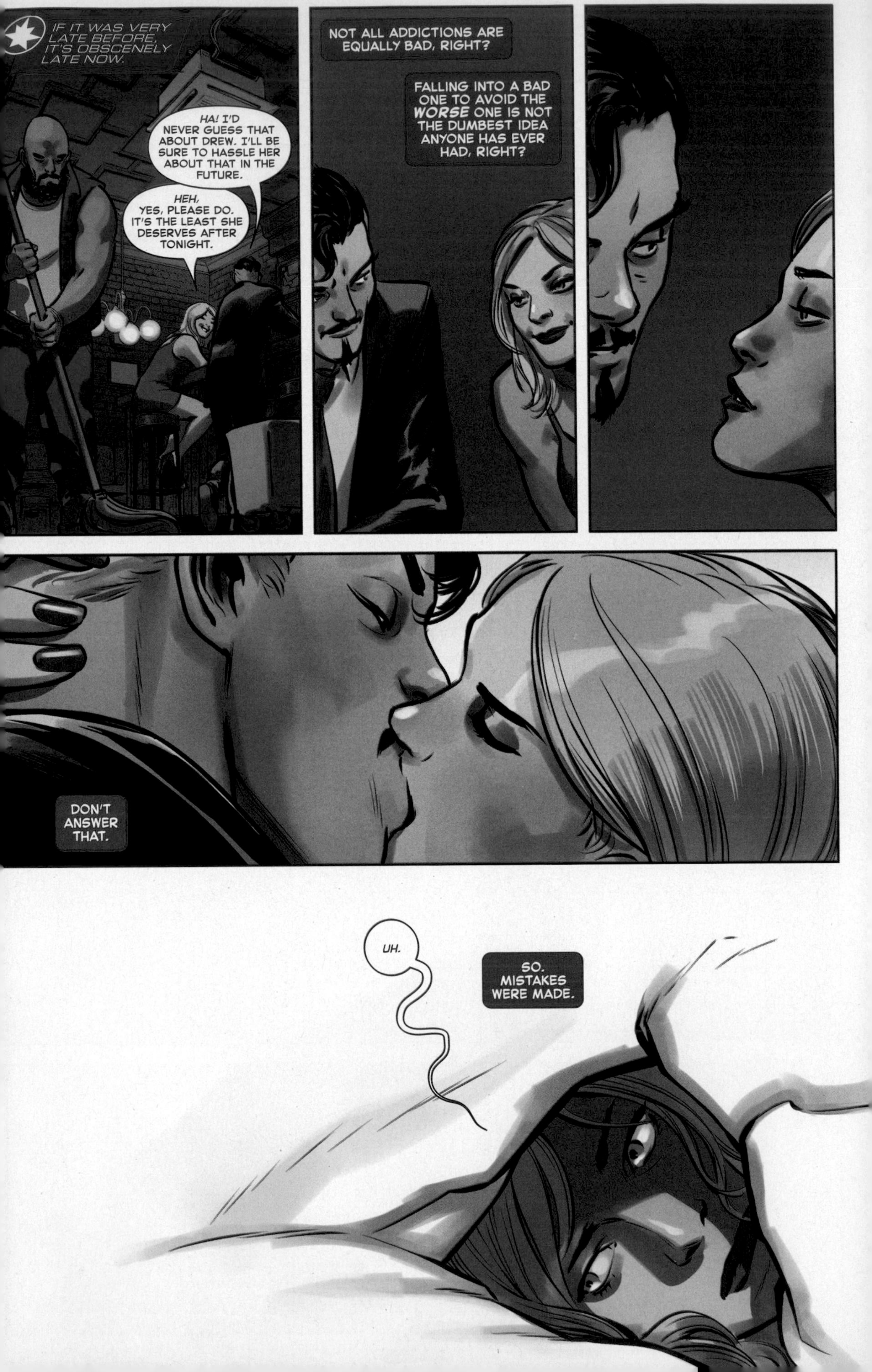
IF IT WAS VERY LATE BEFORE, IT'S OBSCENELY LATE NOW.
HA! I'D NEVER GUESS THAT ABOUT DREW. I'LL BE SURE TO HASSLE HER ABOUT THAT IN THE FUTURE.
HEH, YES, PLEASE DO. IT'S THE LEAST SHE DESERVES AFTER TONIGHT.
NOT ALL ADDICTIONS ARE EQUALLY BAD, RIGHT?
FALLING INTO A BAD ONE TO AVOID THE WORSE ONE IS NOT THE DUMBEST IDEA ANYONE HAS EVER HAD, RIGHT?
DON'T ANSWER THAT.
UH.
SO. MISTAKES WERE MADE.

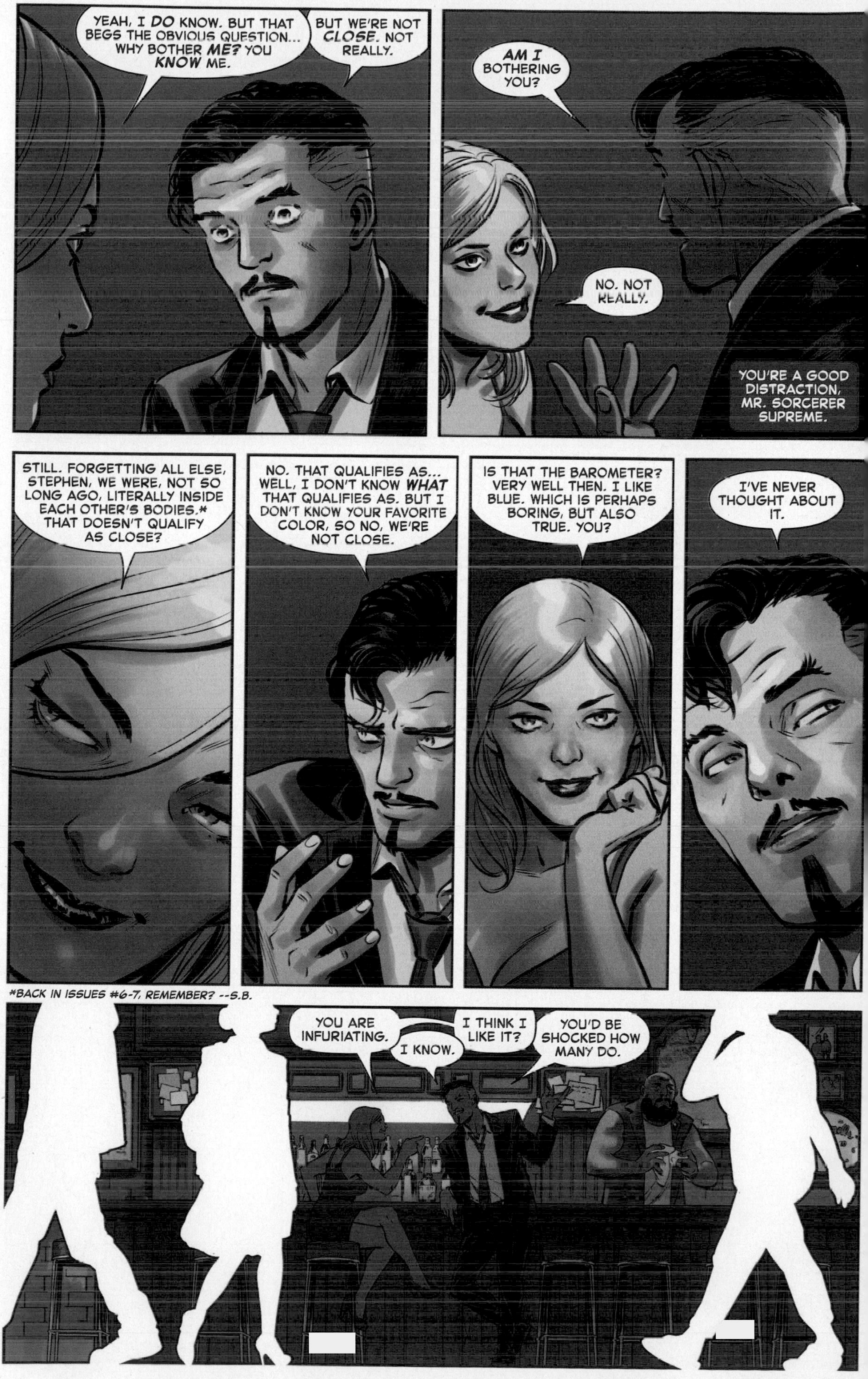
YEAH, I DO KNOW. BUT THAT BEGS THE OBVIOUS QUESTION... WHY BOTHER ME? YOU KNOW ME.
BUT WE'RE NOT CLOSE. NOT REALLY.
AM I BOTHERING YOU?
NO. NOT REALLY.
YOU'RE A GOOD DISTRACTION, MR. SORCERER SUPREME.
STILL. FORGETTING ALL ELSE, STEPHEN, WE WERE, NOT SO LONG AGO, LITERALLY INSIDE EACH OTHER'S BODIES.* THAT DOESN'T QUALIFY AS CLOSE?
NO. THAT QUALIFIES AS... WELL, I DON'T KNOW WHAT THAT QUALIFIES AS. BUT I DON'T KNOW YOUR FAVORITE COLOR, SO NO, WE'RE NOT CLOSE.
IS THAT THE BAROMETER? VERY WELL THEN. I LIKE BLUE. WHICH IS PERHAPS BORING, BUT ALSO TRUE. YOU?
I'VE NEVER THOUGHT ABOUT IT.
*BACK IN ISSUES #6-7, REMEMBER? --S.B.
YOU ARE INFURIATING.
I KNOW.
I THINK I LIKE IT?
YOU'D BE SHOCKED HOW MANY DO.

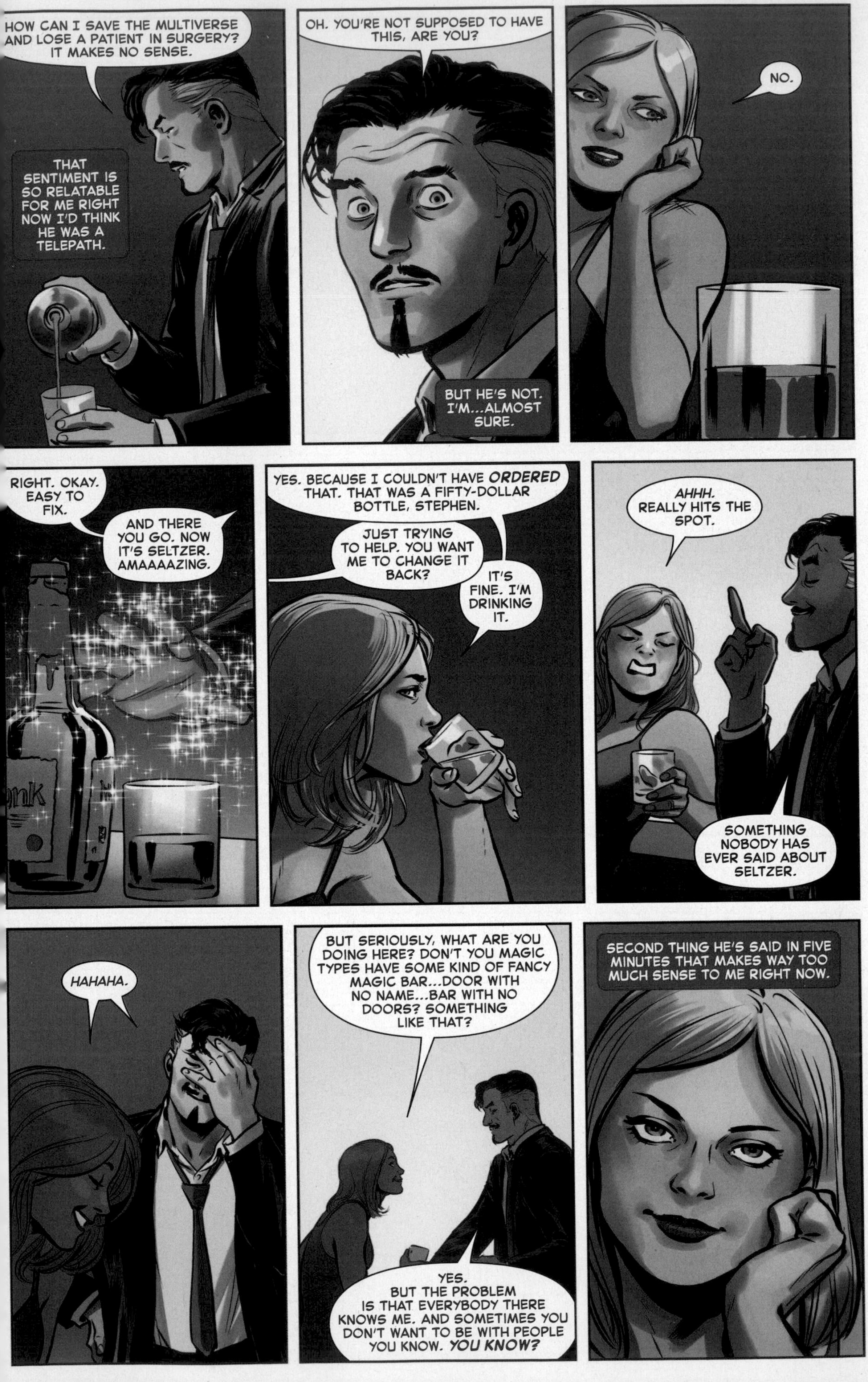

HOW CAN I SAVE THE MULTIVERSE AND LOSE A PATIENT IN SURGERY? IT MAKES NO SENSE.
THAT SENTIMENT IS SO RELATABLE FOR ME RIGHT NOW I'D THINK HE WAS A TELEPATH.
OH. YOU'RE NOT SUPPOSED TO HAVE THIS, ARE YOU?
BUT HE'S NOT. I'M...ALMOST SURE.
NO.
RIGHT. OKAY. EASY TO FIX.
AND THERE YOU GO. NOW IT'S SELTZER. AMAAAAZING.
YES. BECAUSE I COULDN'T HAVE *ORDERED* THAT. THAT WAS A FIFTY-DOLLAR BOTTLE, STEPHEN.
JUST TRYING TO HELP. YOU WANT ME TO CHANGE IT BACK?
IT'S FINE. I'M DRINKING IT.
AHHH. REALLY HITS THE SPOT.
SOMETHING NOBODY HAS EVER SAID ABOUT SELTZER.
HAHAHA.
BUT SERIOUSLY, WHAT ARE YOU DOING HERE? DON'T YOU MAGIC TYPES HAVE SOME KIND OF FANCY MAGIC BAR...DOOR WITH NO NAME...BAR WITH NO DOORS? SOMETHING LIKE THAT?
YES. BUT THE PROBLEM IS THAT EVERYBODY THERE KNOWS ME. AND SOMETIMES YOU DON'T WANT TO BE WITH PEOPLE YOU KNOW. *YOU KNOW?*
SECOND THING HE'S SAID IN FIVE MINUTES THAT MAKES WAY TOO MUCH SENSE TO ME RIGHT NOW.

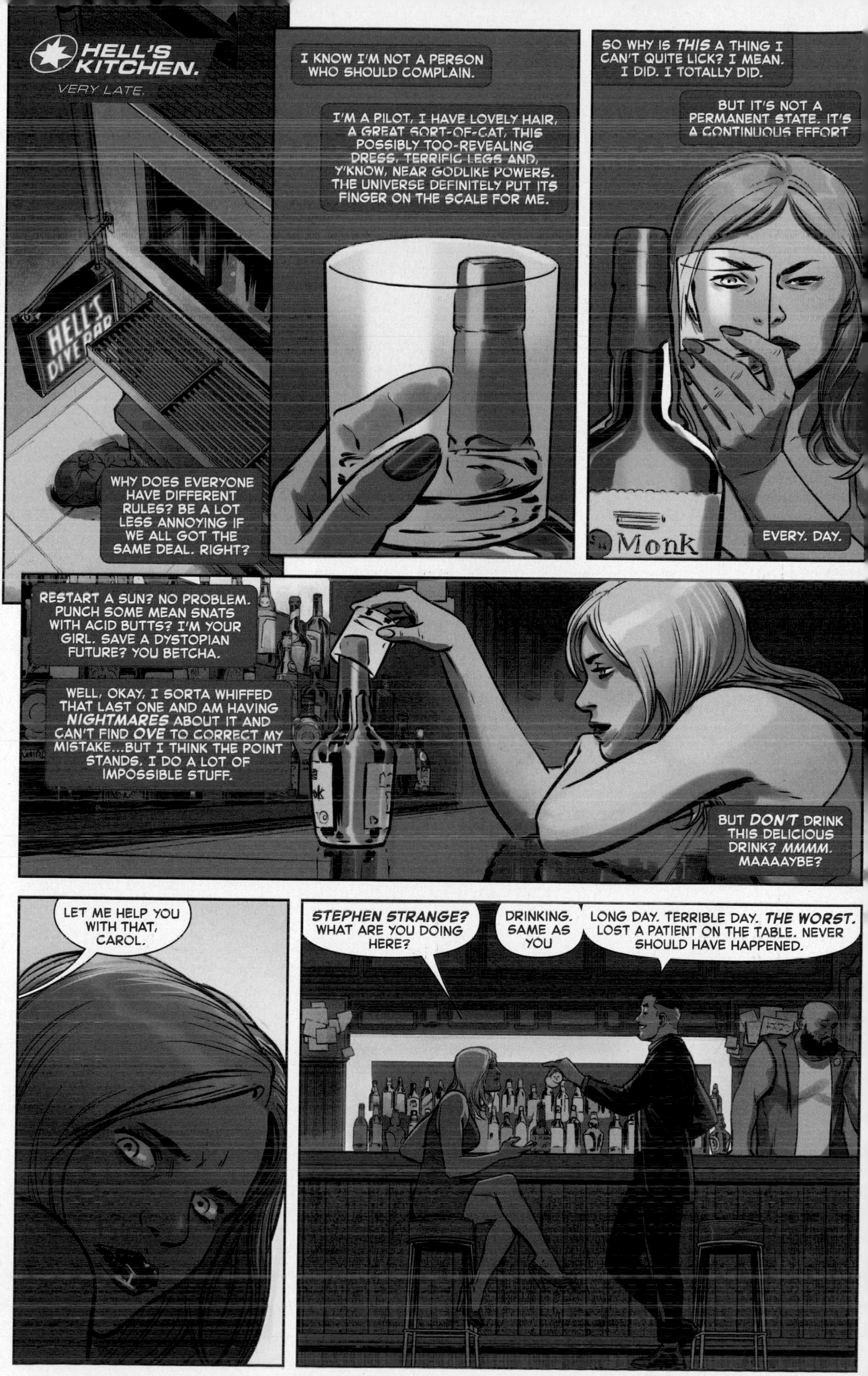
HELL'S KITCHEN.
VERY LATE.
HELL'S DIVE BAR
WHY DOES EVERYONE HAVE DIFFERENT RULES? BE A LOT LESS ANNOYING IF WE ALL GOT THE SAME DEAL. RIGHT?
I KNOW I'M NOT A PERSON WHO SHOULD COMPLAIN.
I'M A PILOT, I HAVE LOVELY HAIR, A GREAT SORT-OF-CAT, THIS POSSIBLY TOO-REVEALING DRESS, TERRIFIC LEGS AND, Y'KNOW, NEAR GODLIKE POWERS. THE UNIVERSE DEFINITELY PUT ITS FINGER ON THE SCALE FOR ME.
SO WHY IS THIS A THING I CAN'T QUITE LICK? I MEAN. I DID. I TOTALLY DID.
BUT IT'S NOT A PERMANENT STATE. IT'S A CONTINUOUS EFFORT
Monk
EVERY. DAY.
RESTART A SUN? NO PROBLEM. PUNCH SOME MEAN SNATS WITH ACID BUTTS? I'M YOUR GIRL. SAVE A DYSTOPIAN FUTURE? YOU BETCHA.
WELL, OKAY, I SORTA WHIFFED THAT LAST ONE AND AM HAVING NIGHTMARES ABOUT IT AND CAN'T FIND OVE TO CORRECT MY MISTAKE...BUT I THINK THE POINT STANDS. I DO A LOT OF IMPOSSIBLE STUFF.
BUT DON'T DRINK THIS DELICIOUS DRINK? MMMM. MAAAAYBE?
LET ME HELP YOU WITH THAT, CAROL.
STEPHEN STRANGE? WHAT ARE YOU DOING HERE?
DRINKING. SAME AS YOU
LONG DAY. TERRIBLE DAY. THE WORST. LOST A PATIENT ON THE TABLE. NEVER SHOULD HAVE HAPPENED.

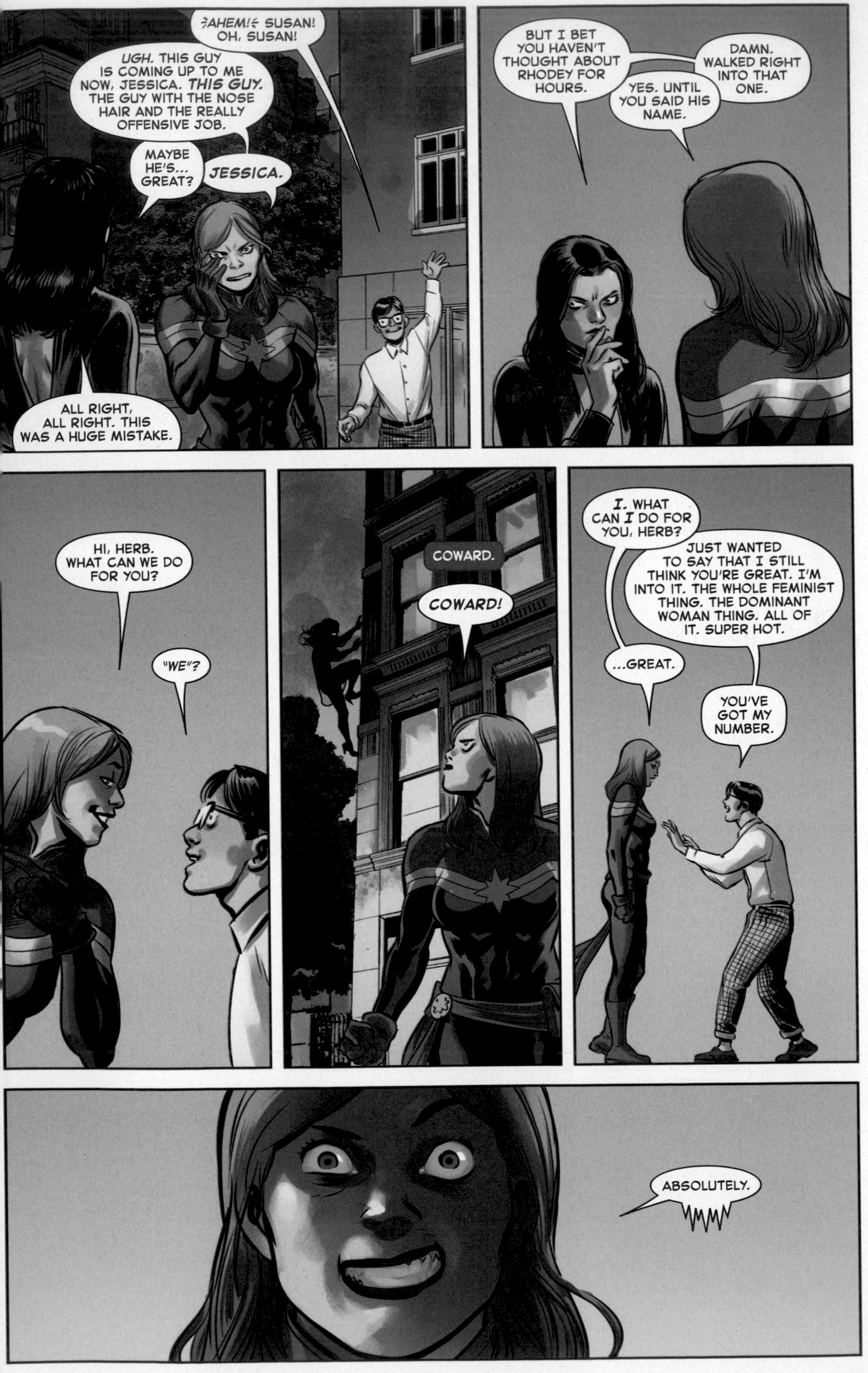

AHEM! SUSAN! OH, SUSAN!
UGH. THIS GUY IS COMING UP TO ME NOW, JESSICA. THIS GUY. THE GUY WITH THE NOSE HAIR AND THE REALLY OFFENSIVE JOB.
MAYBE HE'S... GREAT?
JESSICA.
ALL RIGHT, ALL RIGHT. THIS WAS A HUGE MISTAKE.
BUT I BET YOU HAVEN'T THOUGHT ABOUT RHODEY FOR HOURS.
YES. UNTIL YOU SAID HIS NAME.
DAMN. WALKED RIGHT INTO THAT ONE.
HI, HERB. WHAT CAN WE DO FOR YOU?
"WE"?
COWARD.
COWARD!
I. WHAT CAN I DO FOR YOU, HERB?
JUST WANTED TO SAY THAT I STILL THINK YOU'RE GREAT. I'M INTO IT. THE WHOLE FEMINIST THING. THE DOMINANT WOMAN THING. ALL OF IT. SUPER HOT.
...GREAT.
YOU'VE GOT MY NUMBER.
ABSOLUTELY.

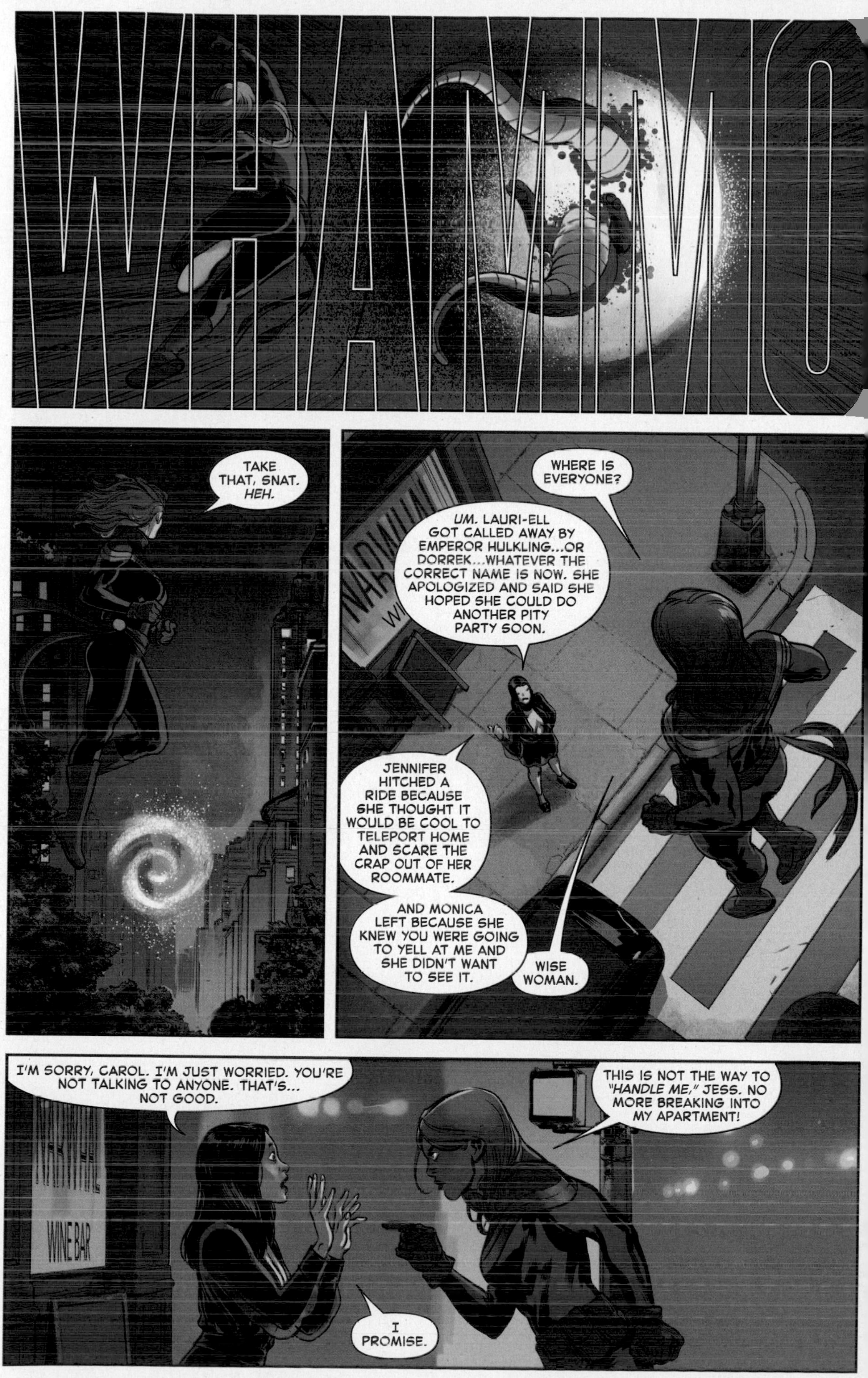
WHAAAMMO
TAKE THAT, SNAT. HEH.
WHERE IS EVERYONE?
UM. LAURI-ELL GOT CALLED AWAY BY EMPEROR HULKLING...OR DORREK...WHATEVER THE CORRECT NAME IS NOW. SHE APOLOGIZED AND SAID SHE HOPED SHE COULD DO ANOTHER PITY PARTY SOON.
JENNIFER HITCHED A RIDE BECAUSE SHE THOUGHT IT WOULD BE COOL TO TELEPORT HOME AND SCARE THE CRAP OUT OF HER ROOMMATE.
AND MONICA LEFT BECAUSE SHE KNEW YOU WERE GOING TO YELL AT ME AND SHE DIDN'T WANT TO SEE IT.
WISE WOMAN.
THIS IS NOT THE WAY TO "HANDLE ME," JESS. NO MORE BREAKING INTO MY APARTMENT!
I'M SORRY, CAROL. I'M JUST WORRIED. YOU'RE NOT TALKING TO ANYONE. THAT'S... NOT GOOD.
I PROMISE.
WINE BAR

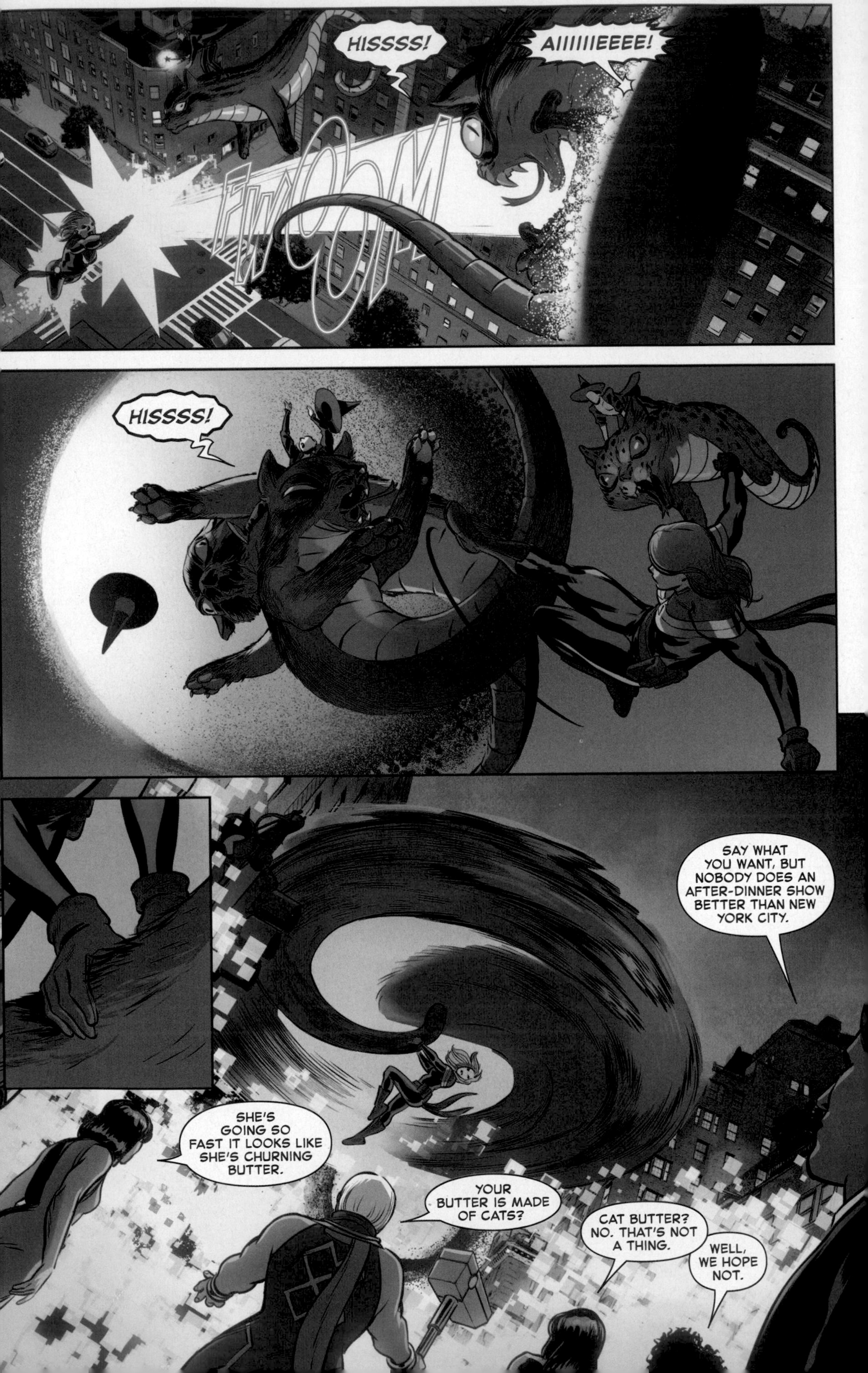
HISSSS!
AIIIIIEEEE!
FWOOM
HISSSS!
SAY WHAT YOU WANT, BUT NOBODY DOES AN AFTER-DINNER SHOW BETTER THAN NEW YORK CITY.
SHE'S GOING SO FAST IT LOOKS LIKE SHE'S CHURNING BUTTER.
YOUR BUTTER IS MADE OF CATS?
CAT BUTTER? NO. THAT'S NOT A THING.
WELL, WE HOPE NOT.

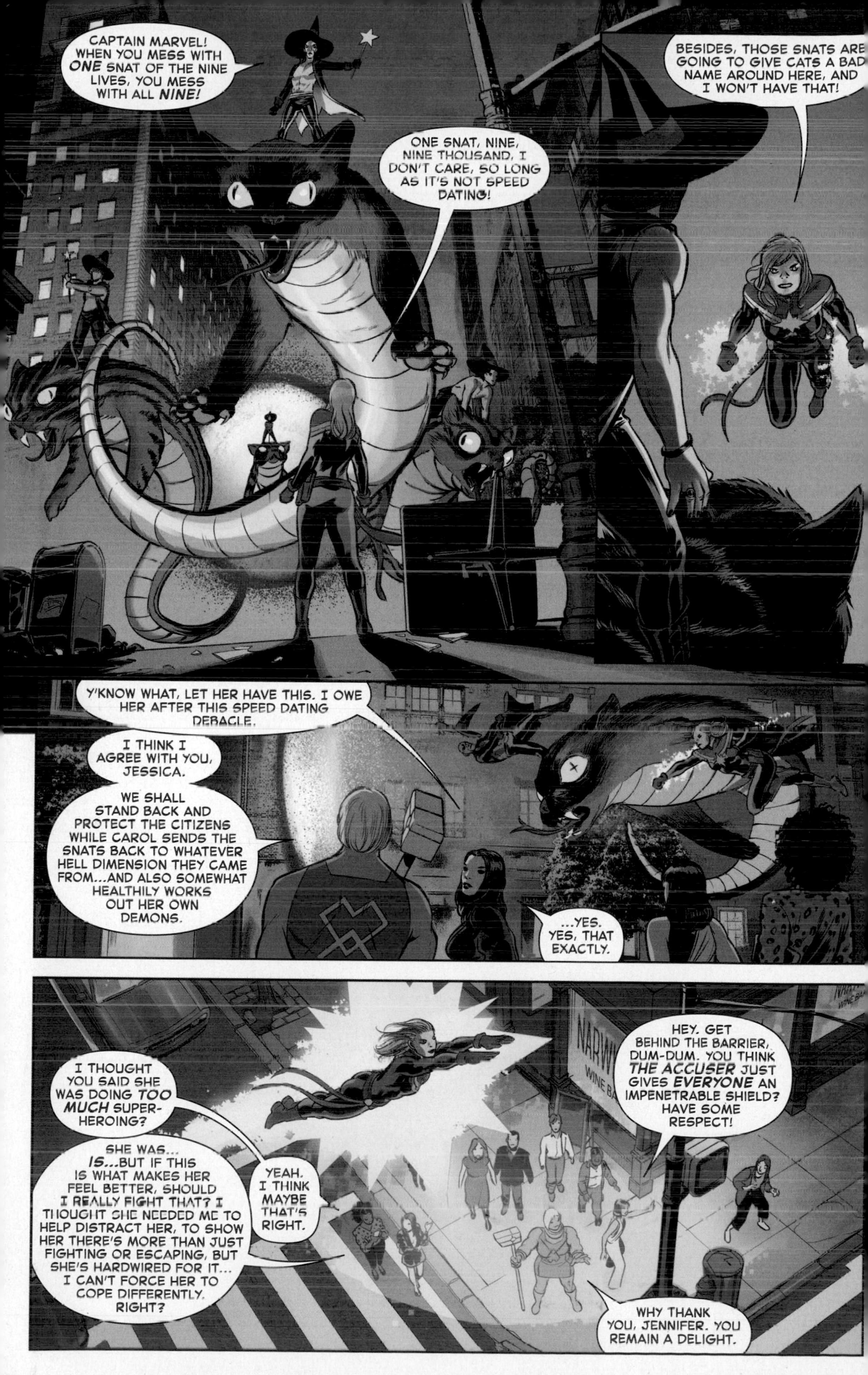
CAPTAIN MARVEL! WHEN YOU MESS WITH ONE SNAT OF THE NINE LIVES, YOU MESS WITH ALL NINE!
ONE SNAT, NINE, NINE THOUSAND, I DON'T CARE, SO LONG AS IT'S NOT SPEED DATING!
BESIDES, THOSE SNATS ARE GOING TO GIVE CATS A BAD NAME AROUND HERE, AND I WON'T HAVE THAT!
Y'KNOW WHAT, LET HER HAVE THIS. I OWE HER AFTER THIS SPEED DATING DEBACLE.
I THINK I AGREE WITH YOU, JESSICA.
WE SHALL STAND BACK AND PROTECT THE CITIZENS WHILE CAROL SENDS THE SNATS BACK TO WHATEVER HELL DIMENSION THEY CAME FROM...AND ALSO SOMEWHAT HEALTHILY WORKS OUT HER OWN DEMONS.
...YES. YES, THAT EXACTLY.
I THOUGHT YOU SAID SHE WAS DOING TOO MUCH SUPER-HEROING?
SHE WAS... IS...BUT IF THIS IS WHAT MAKES HER FEEL BETTER, SHOULD I REALLY FIGHT THAT? I THOUGHT SHE NEEDED ME TO HELP DISTRACT HER, TO SHOW HER THERE'S MORE THAN JUST FIGHTING OR ESCAPING, BUT SHE'S HARDWIRED FOR IT... I CAN'T FORCE HER TO COPE DIFFERENTLY. RIGHT?
YEAH. I THINK MAYBE THAT'S RIGHT.
HEY. GET BEHIND THE BARRIER, DUM-DUM. YOU THINK THE ACCUSER JUST GIVES EVERYONE AN IMPENETRABLE SHIELD? HAVE SOME RESPECT!
WHY THANK YOU, JENNIFER. YOU REMAIN A DELIGHT.

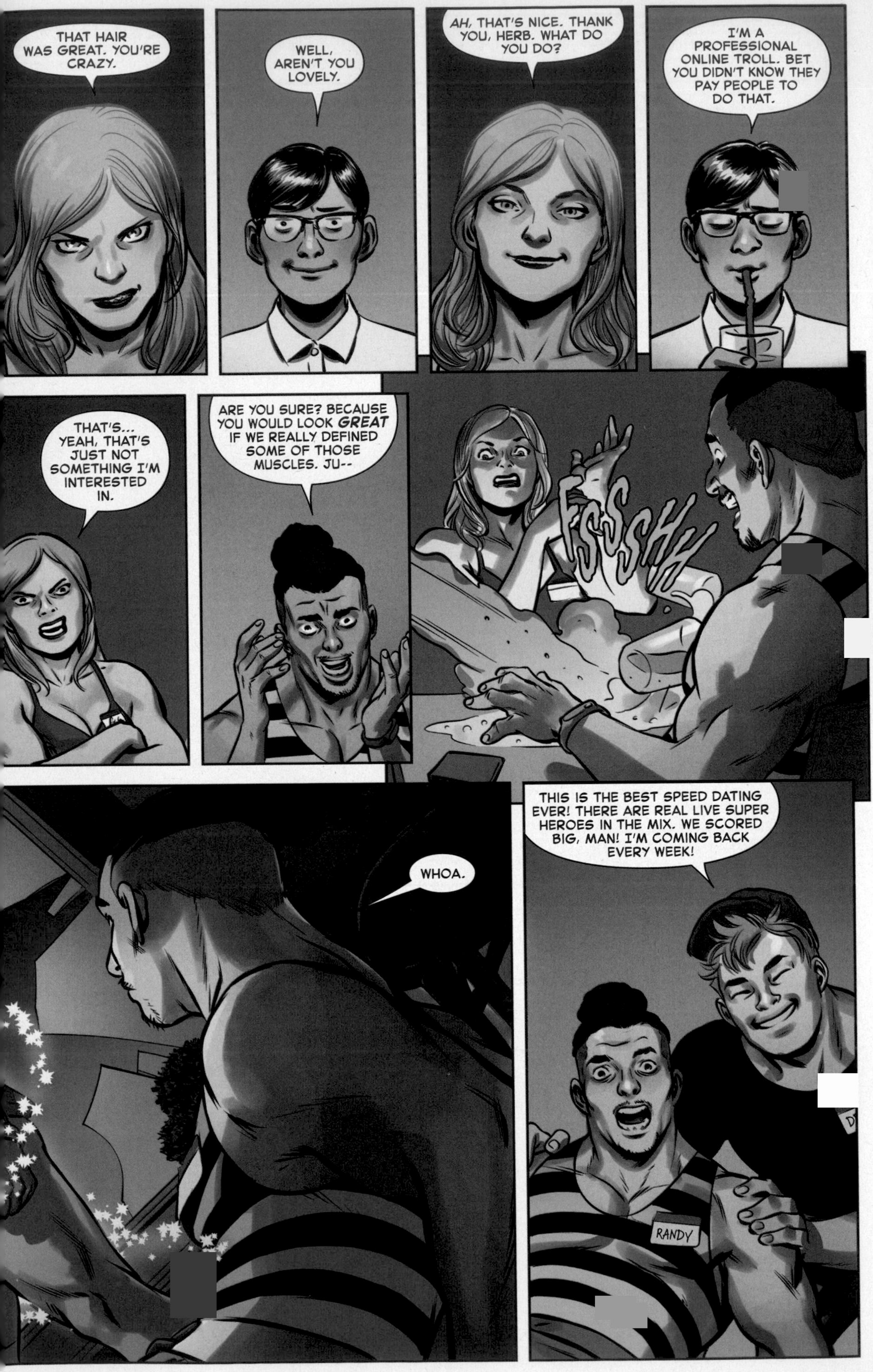
THAT HAIR WAS GREAT. YOU'RE CRAZY.
WELL, AREN'T YOU LOVELY.
AH, THAT'S NICE. THANK YOU, HERB. WHAT DO YOU DO?
I'M A PROFESSIONAL ONLINE TROLL. BET YOU DIDN'T KNOW THEY PAY PEOPLE TO DO THAT.
THAT'S... YEAH, THAT'S JUST NOT SOMETHING I'M INTERESTED IN.
ARE YOU SURE? BECAUSE YOU WOULD LOOK *GREAT* IF WE REALLY DEFINED SOME OF THOSE MUSCLES. JU--
FSSSHH
WHOA.
THIS IS THE BEST SPEED DATING EVER! THERE ARE REAL LIVE SUPER HEROES IN THE MIX. WE SCORED BIG, MAN! I'M COMING BACK EVERY WEEK!
RANDY

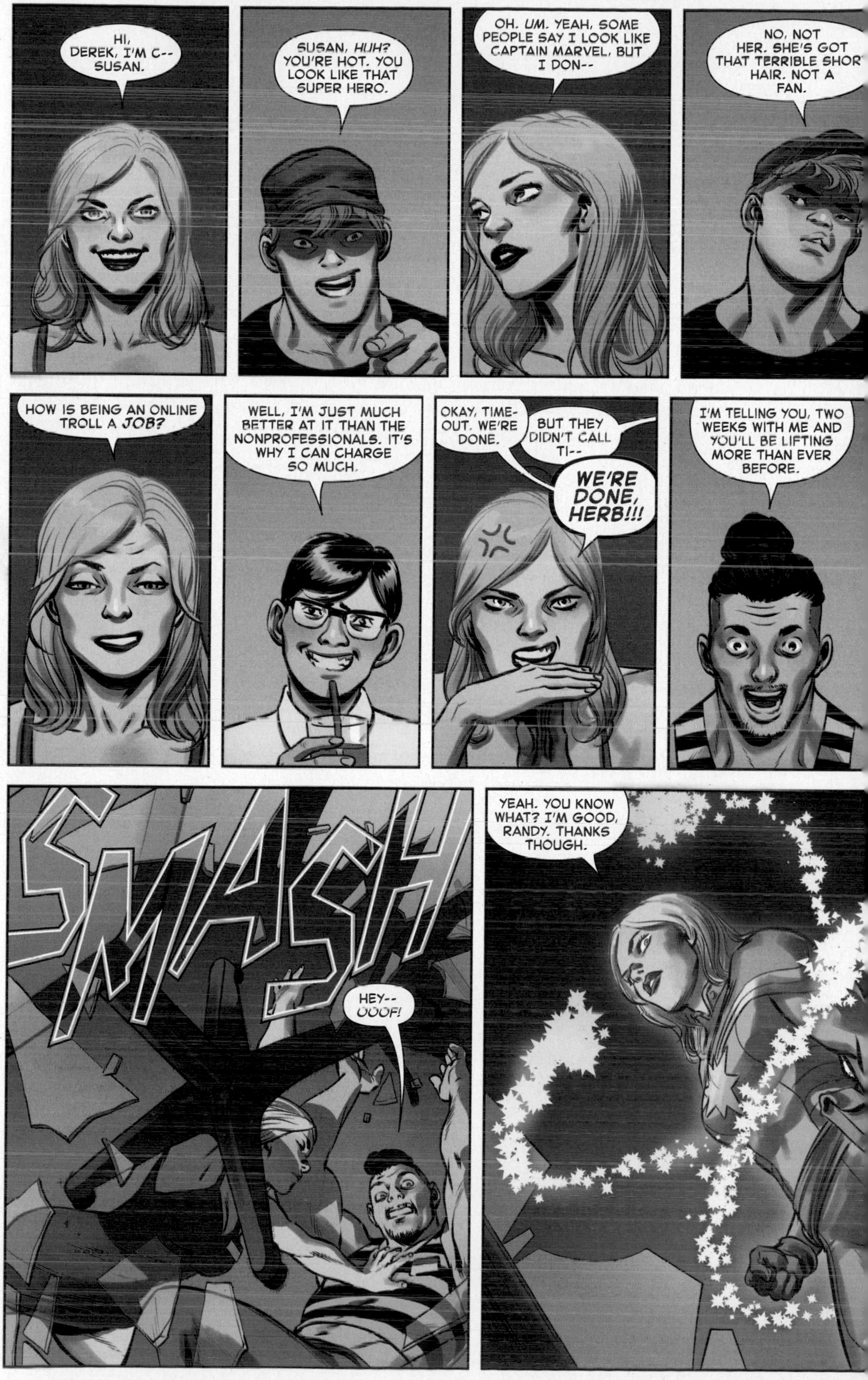

HI, DEREK, I'M C-- SUSAN.
SUSAN, HUH? YOU'RE HOT. YOU LOOK LIKE THAT SUPER HERO.
OH. UM. YEAH, SOME PEOPLE SAY I LOOK LIKE CAPTAIN MARVEL, BUT I DON--
NO, NOT HER. SHE'S GOT THAT TERRIBLE SHOR HAIR. NOT A FAN.
HOW IS BEING AN ONLINE TROLL A JOB?
WELL, I'M JUST MUCH BETTER AT IT THAN THE NONPROFESSIONALS. IT'S WHY I CAN CHARGE SO MUCH.
OKAY, TIME-OUT. WE'RE DONE.
BUT THEY DIDN'T CALL TI--
WE'RE DONE, HERB!!!
I'M TELLING YOU, TWO WEEKS WITH ME AND YOU'LL BE LIFTING MORE THAN EVER BEFORE.
SMASH
HEY-- OOOF!
YEAH. YOU KNOW WHAT? I'M GOOD, RANDY. THANKS THOUGH.

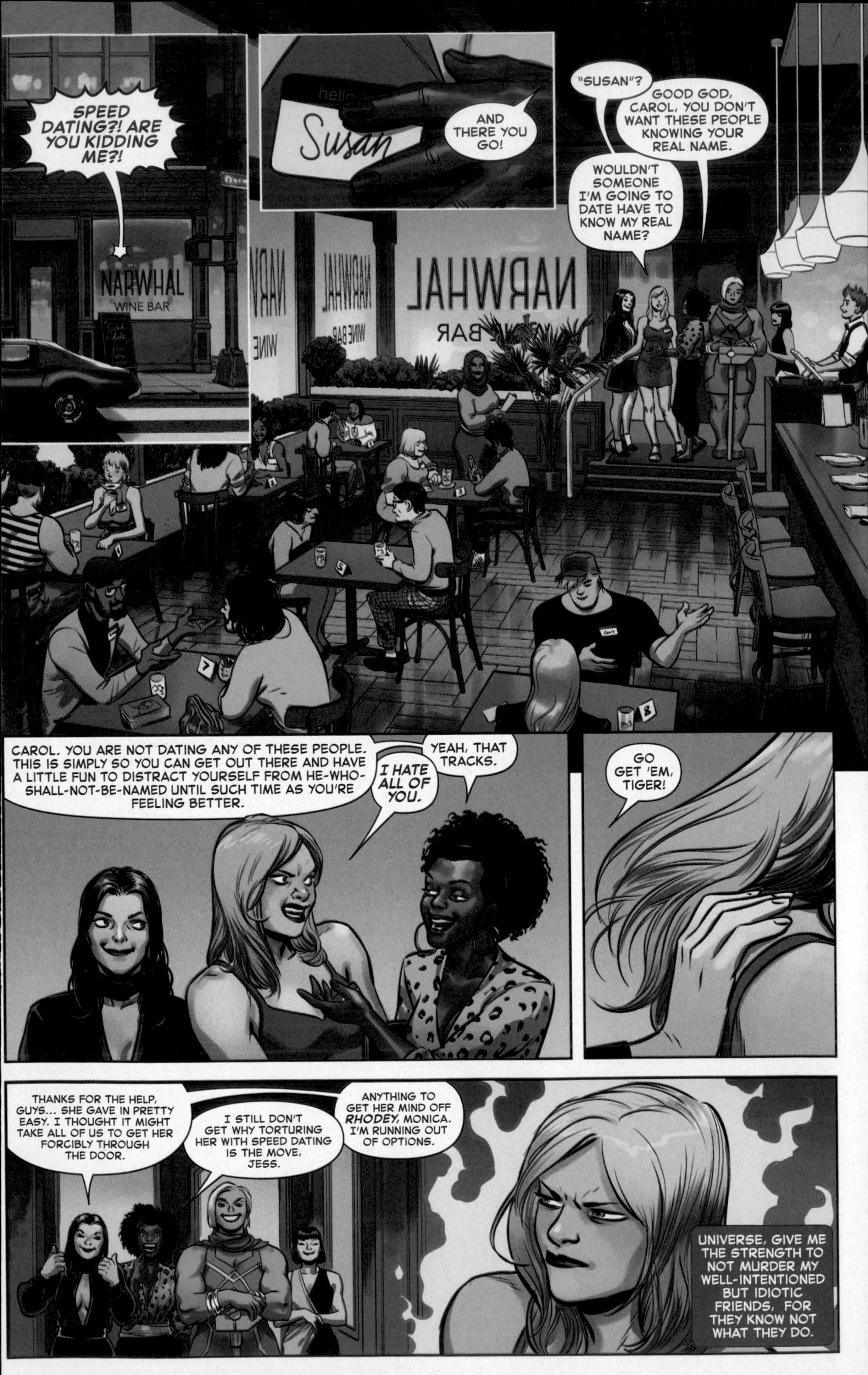
SPEED DATING?! ARE YOU KIDDING ME?!
NARWHAL
WINE BAR
hello
Susan
AND THERE YOU GO!
"SUSAN"?
GOOD GOD, CAROL, YOU DON'T WANT THESE PEOPLE KNOWING YOUR REAL NAME.
WOULDN'T SOMEONE I'M GOING TO DATE HAVE TO KNOW MY REAL NAME?
CAROL. YOU ARE NOT DATING ANY OF THESE PEOPLE. THIS IS SIMPLY SO YOU CAN GET OUT THERE AND HAVE A LITTLE FUN TO DISTRACT YOURSELF FROM HE-WHO-SHALL-NOT-BE-NAMED UNTIL SUCH TIME AS YOU'RE FEELING BETTER.
YEAH, THAT TRACKS.
I HATE ALL OF YOU.
GO GET 'EM, TIGER!
THANKS FOR THE HELP, GUYS... SHE GAVE IN PRETTY EASY. I THOUGHT IT MIGHT TAKE ALL OF US TO GET HER FORCIBLY THROUGH THE DOOR.
I STILL DON'T GET WHY TORTURING HER WITH SPEED DATING IS THE MOVE, JESS.
ANYTHING TO GET HER MIND OFF RHODEY, MONICA. I'M RUNNING OUT OF OPTIONS.
UNIVERSE, GIVE ME THE STRENGTH TO NOT MURDER MY WELL-INTENTIONED BUT IDIOTIC FRIENDS, FOR THEY KNOW NOT WHAT THEY DO.

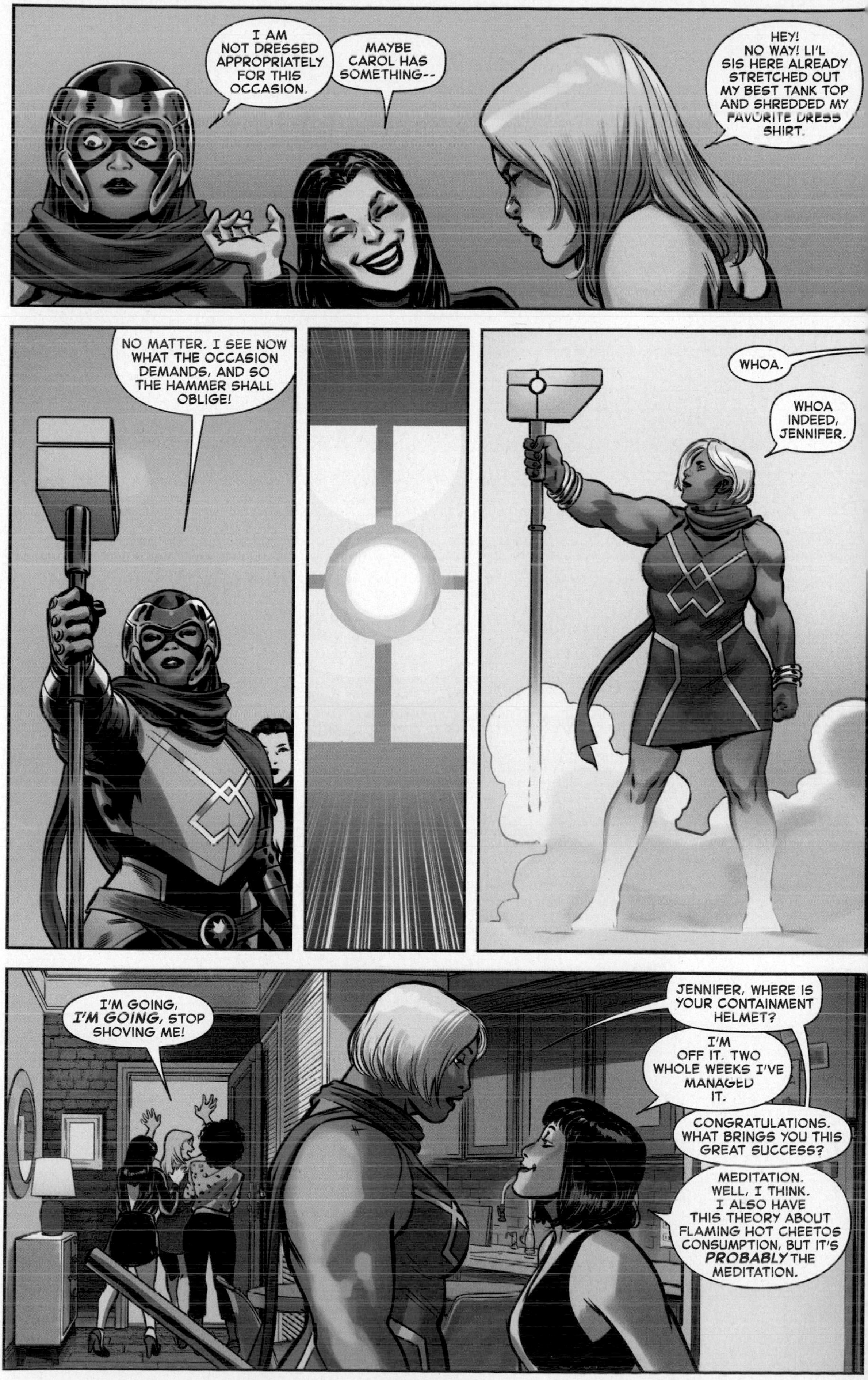
I AM NOT DRESSED APPROPRIATELY FOR THIS OCCASION.
MAYBE CAROL HAS SOMETHING--
HEY! NO WAY! LI'L SIS HERE ALREADY STRETCHED OUT MY BEST TANK TOP AND SHREDDED MY FAVORITE DRESS SHIRT.
NO MATTER. I SEE NOW WHAT THE OCCASION DEMANDS, AND SO THE HAMMER SHALL OBLIGE!
WHOA.
WHOA INDEED, JENNIFER.
I'M GOING, *I'M GOING,* STOP SHOVING ME!
JENNIFER, WHERE IS YOUR CONTAINMENT HELMET?
I'M OFF IT. TWO WHOLE WEEKS I'VE MANAGED IT.
CONGRATULATIONS. WHAT BRINGS YOU THIS GREAT SUCCESS?
MEDITATION. WELL, I THINK. I ALSO HAVE THIS THEORY ABOUT FLAMING HOT CHEETOS CONSUMPTION, BUT IT'S *PROBABLY* THE MEDITATION.

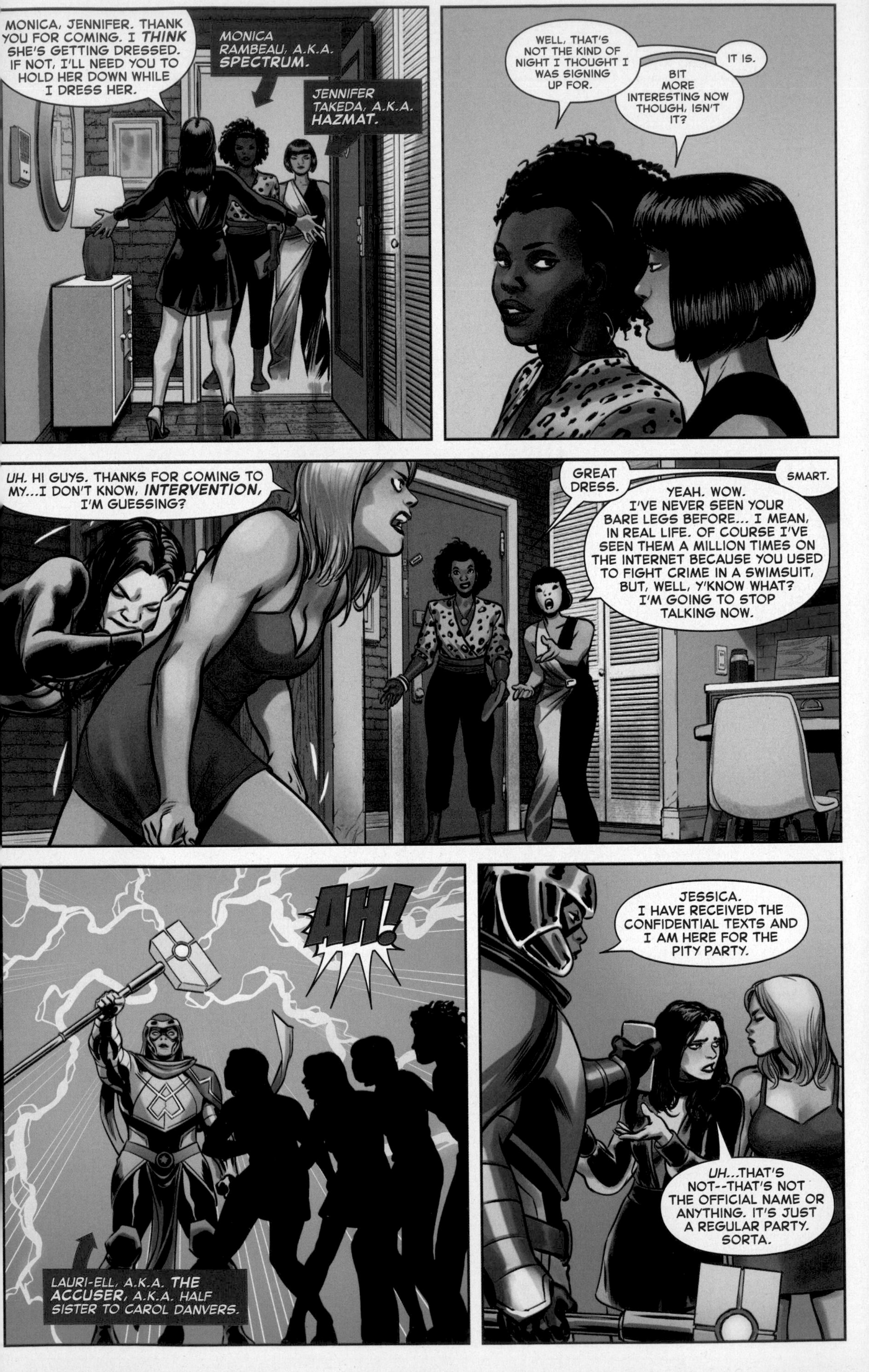
MONICA, JENNIFER. THANK YOU FOR COMING. I *THINK* SHE'S GETTING DRESSED. IF NOT, I'LL NEED YOU TO HOLD HER DOWN WHILE I DRESS HER.
MONICA RAMBEAU, A.K.A. **SPECTRUM.**
JENNIFER TAKEDA, A.K.A. **HAZMAT.**
WELL, THAT'S NOT THE KIND OF NIGHT I THOUGHT I WAS SIGNING UP FOR.
IT IS.
BIT MORE INTERESTING NOW THOUGH, ISN'T IT?
UH. HI GUYS. THANKS FOR COMING TO MY...I DON'T KNOW, ***INTERVENTION,*** I'M GUESSING?
GREAT DRESS.
SMART.
YEAH. WOW. I'VE NEVER SEEN YOUR BARE LEGS BEFORE... I MEAN, IN REAL LIFE. OF COURSE I'VE SEEN THEM A MILLION TIMES ON THE INTERNET BECAUSE YOU USED TO FIGHT CRIME IN A SWIMSUIT, BUT, WELL, Y'KNOW WHAT? I'M GOING TO STOP TALKING NOW.
AH!
LAURI-ELL, A.K.A. **THE ACCUSER,** A.K.A. HALF SISTER TO CAROL DANVERS.
JESSICA. I HAVE RECEIVED THE CONFIDENTIAL TEXTS AND I AM HERE FOR THE PITY PARTY.
*UH...*THAT'S NOT--THAT'S NOT THE OFFICIAL NAME OR ANYTHING. IT'S JUST A REGULAR PARTY. SORTA.

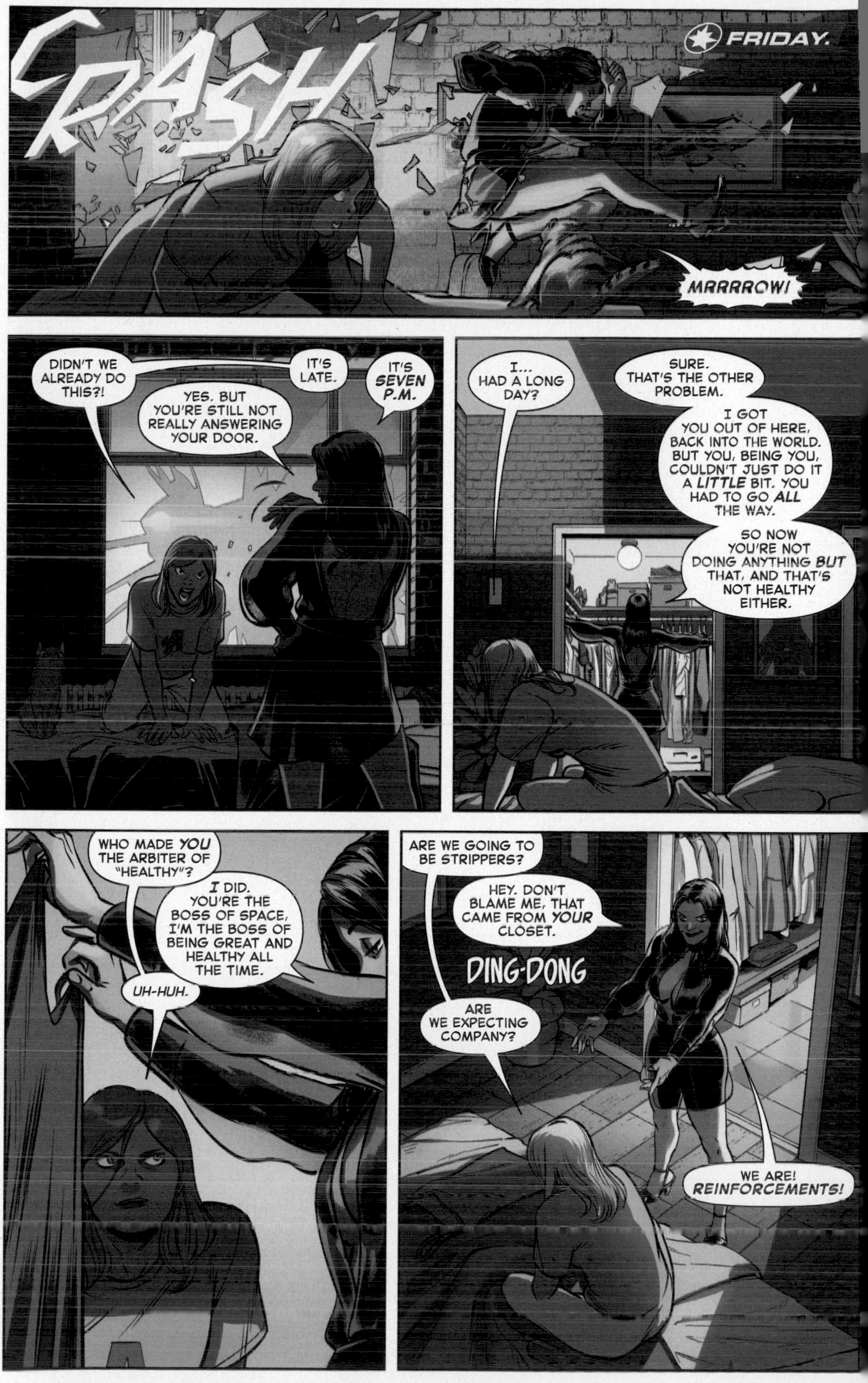
FRIDAY.
CRASH
MRRRROW!
DIDN'T WE ALREADY DO THIS?!
IT'S LATE.
IT'S SEVEN P.M.
YES. BUT YOU'RE STILL NOT REALLY ANSWERING YOUR DOOR.
I... HAD A LONG DAY?
SURE. THAT'S THE OTHER PROBLEM.
I GOT YOU OUT OF HERE, BACK INTO THE WORLD. BUT YOU, BEING YOU, COULDN'T JUST DO IT A LITTLE BIT. YOU HAD TO GO ALL THE WAY.
SO NOW YOU'RE NOT DOING ANYTHING BUT THAT, AND THAT'S NOT HEALTHY EITHER.
WHO MADE YOU THE ARBITER OF "HEALTHY"?
I DID. YOU'RE THE BOSS OF SPACE, I'M THE BOSS OF BEING GREAT AND HEALTHY ALL THE TIME.
UH-HUH.
ARE WE GOING TO BE STRIPPERS?
HEY. DON'T BLAME ME, THAT CAME FROM YOUR CLOSET.
DING-DONG
ARE WE EXPECTING COMPANY?
WE ARE! REINFORCEMENTS!

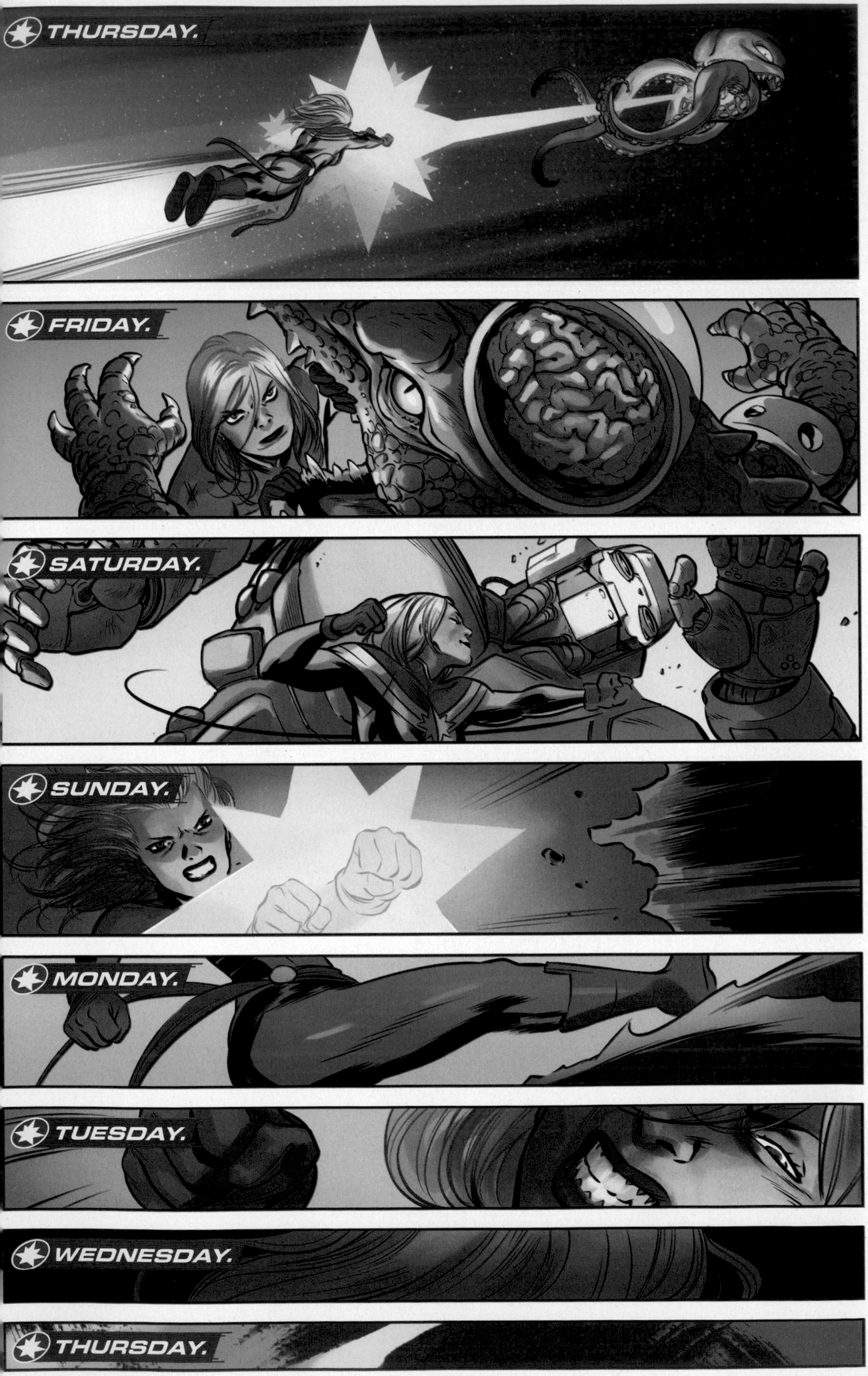
THURSDAY.
FRIDAY.
SATURDAY.
SUNDAY.
MONDAY.
TUESDAY.
WEDNESDAY.
THURSDAY.

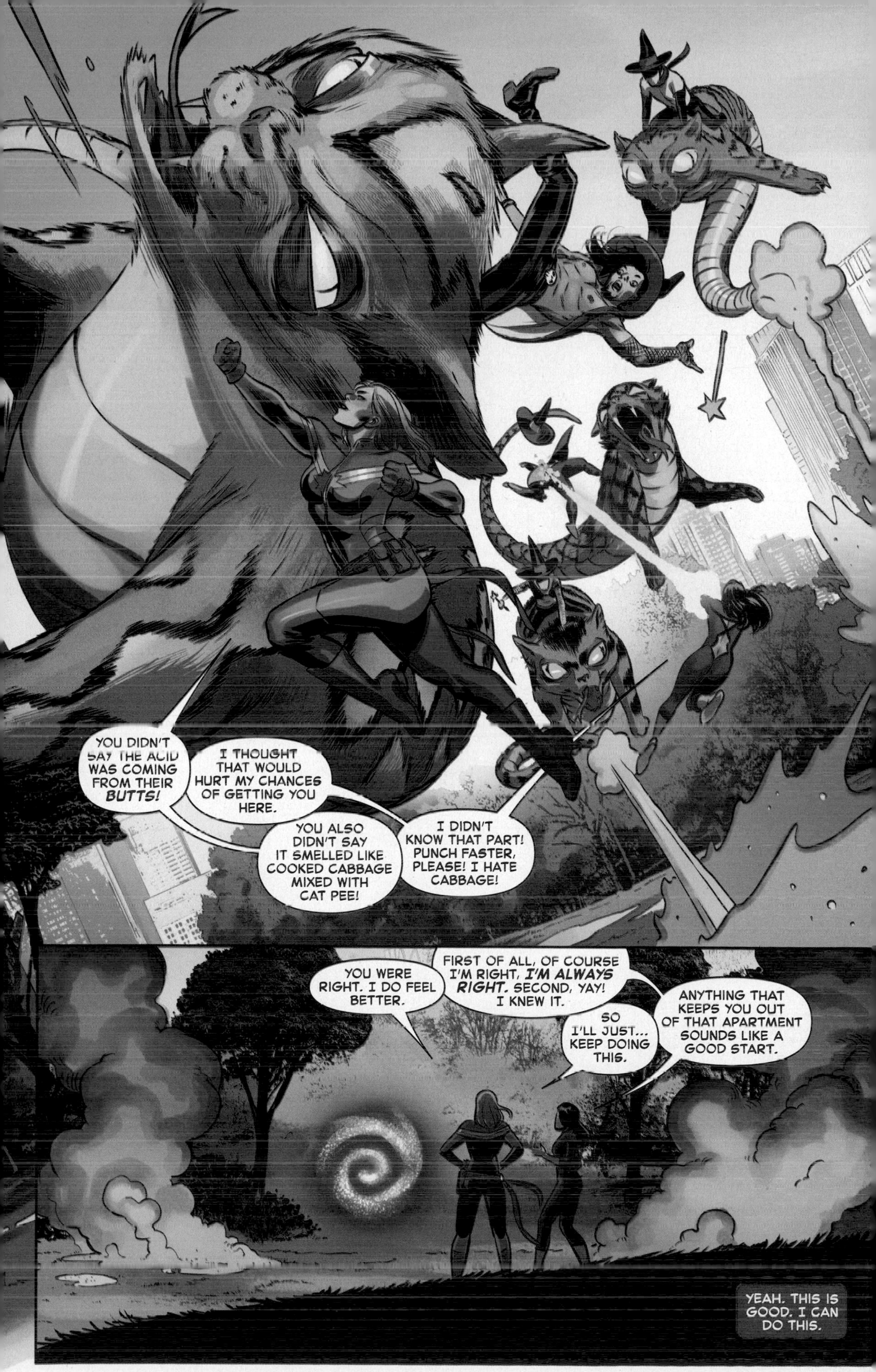
YOU DIDN'T SAY THE ACID WAS COMING FROM THEIR *BUTTS!*
I THOUGHT THAT WOULD HURT MY CHANCES OF GETTING YOU HERE.
YOU ALSO DIDN'T SAY IT SMELLED LIKE COOKED CABBAGE MIXED WITH CAT PEE!
I DIDN'T KNOW THAT PART! PUNCH FASTER, PLEASE! I HATE CABBAGE!
YOU WERE RIGHT. I DO FEEL BETTER.
FIRST OF ALL, OF COURSE I'M RIGHT, *I'M ALWAYS RIGHT.* SECOND, YAY! I KNEW IT.
SO I'LL JUST... KEEP DOING THIS.
ANYTHING THAT KEEPS YOU OUT OF THAT APARTMENT SOUNDS LIKE A GOOD START.
YEAH. THIS IS GOOD. I CAN DO THIS.

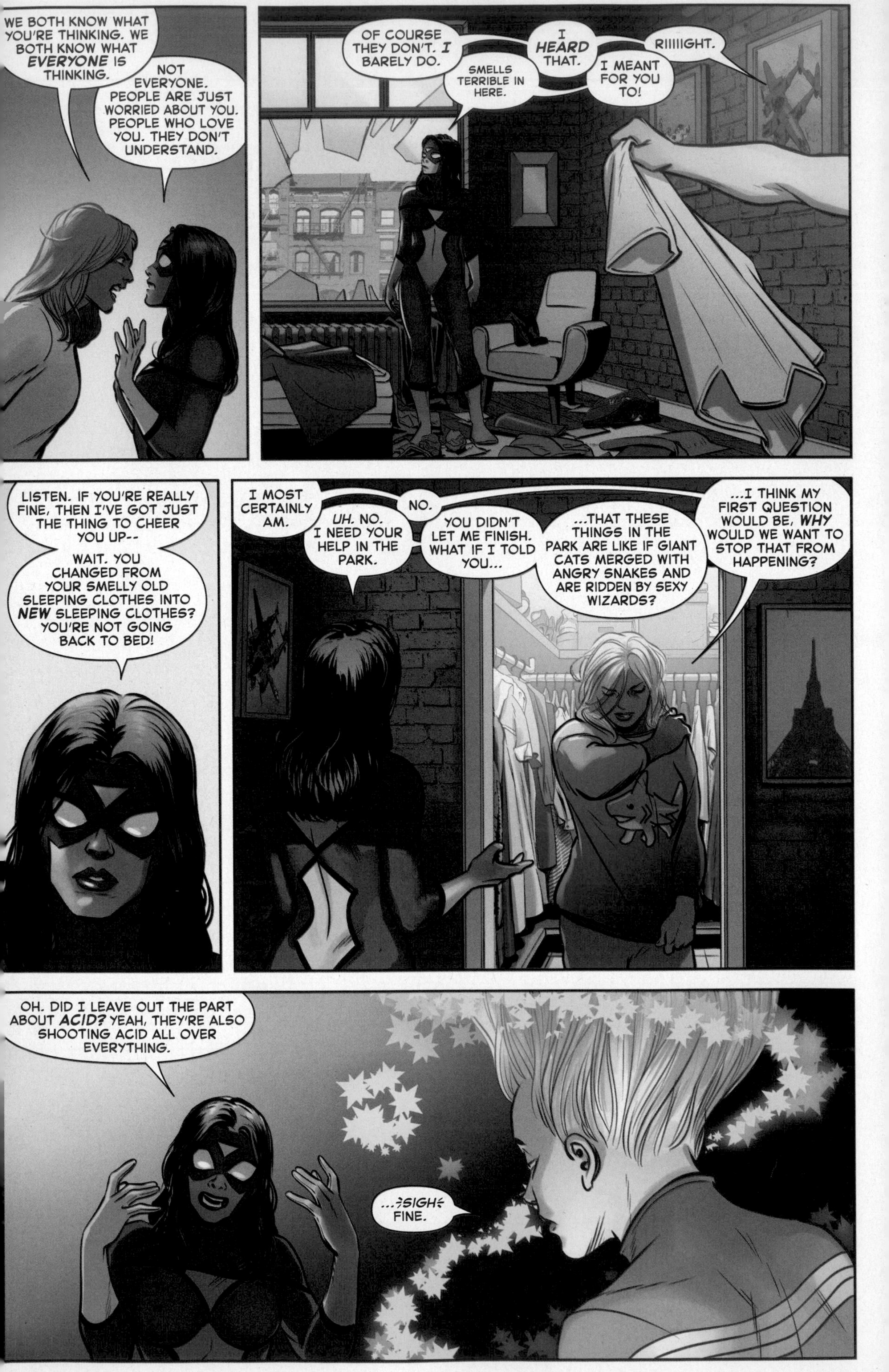
WE BOTH KNOW WHAT YOU'RE THINKING. WE BOTH KNOW WHAT EVERYONE IS THINKING.
NOT EVERYONE. PEOPLE ARE JUST WORRIED ABOUT YOU. PEOPLE WHO LOVE YOU. THEY DON'T UNDERSTAND.
OF COURSE THEY DON'T. I BARELY DO.
SMELLS TERRIBLE IN HERE.
I HEARD THAT.
I MEANT FOR YOU TO!
RIIIIIGHT.
LISTEN. IF YOU'RE REALLY FINE, THEN I'VE GOT JUST THE THING TO CHEER YOU UP--
WAIT. YOU CHANGED FROM YOUR SMELLY OLD SLEEPING CLOTHES INTO NEW SLEEPING CLOTHES? YOU'RE NOT GOING BACK TO BED!
I MOST CERTAINLY AM.
UH. NO. I NEED YOUR HELP IN THE PARK.
NO.
YOU DIDN'T LET ME FINISH. WHAT IF I TOLD YOU...
...THAT THESE THINGS IN THE PARK ARE LIKE IF GIANT CATS MERGED WITH ANGRY SNAKES AND ARE RIDDEN BY SEXY WIZARDS?
...I THINK MY FIRST QUESTION WOULD BE, WHY WOULD WE WANT TO STOP THAT FROM HAPPENING?
OH. DID I LEAVE OUT THE PART ABOUT ACID? YEAH, THEY'RE ALSO SHOOTING ACID ALL OVER EVERYTHING.
...SIGH FINE.

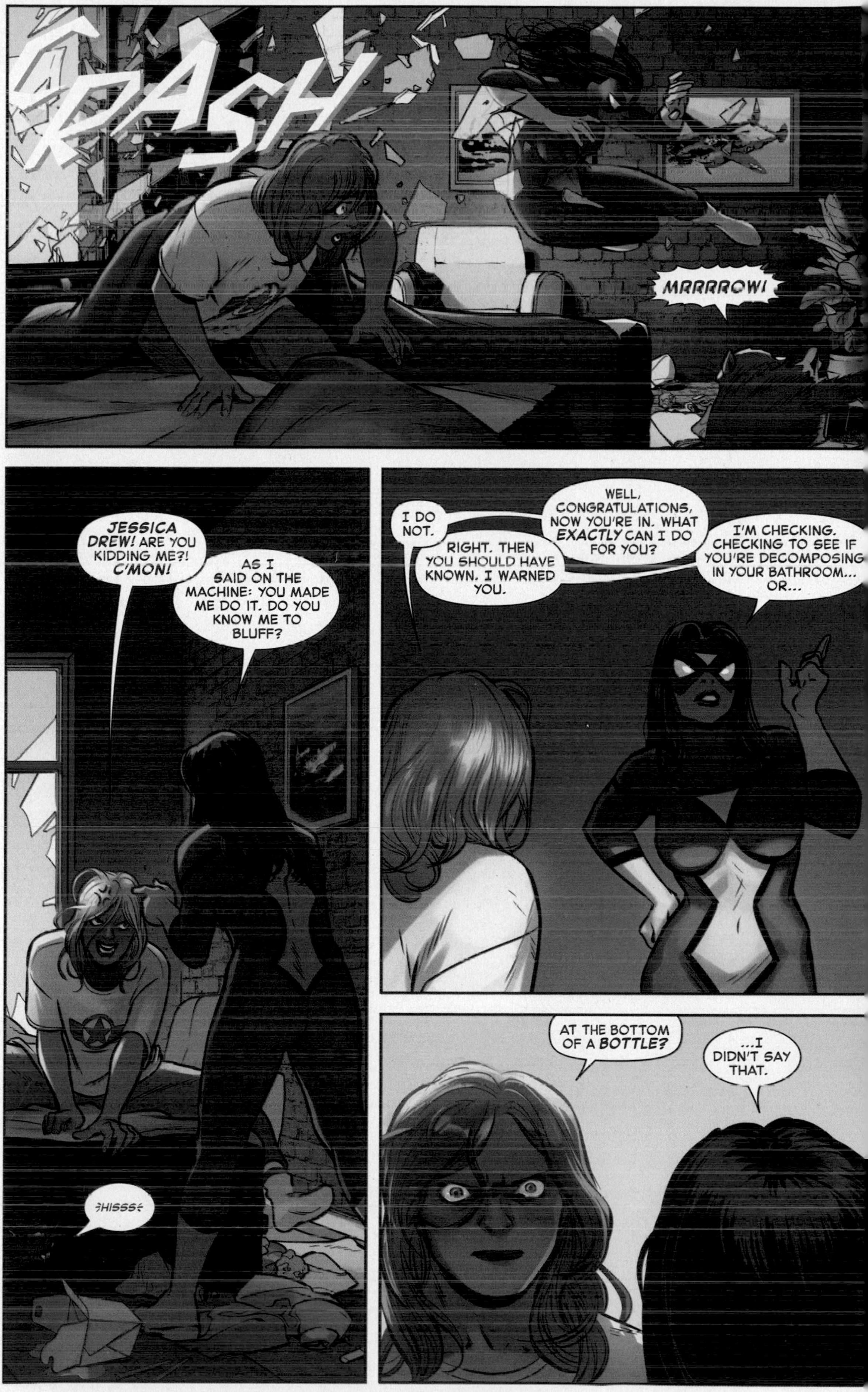
CRASH
MRRRROW!
JESSICA DREW! ARE YOU KIDDING ME?! C'MON!
AS I SAID ON THE MACHINE: YOU MADE ME DO IT. DO YOU KNOW ME TO BLUFF?
HISSS
I DO NOT.
RIGHT. THEN YOU SHOULD HAVE KNOWN. I WARNED YOU.
WELL, CONGRATULATIONS, NOW YOU'RE IN. WHAT EXACTLY CAN I DO FOR YOU?
I'M CHECKING. CHECKING TO SEE IF YOU'RE DECOMPOSING IN YOUR BATHROOM... OR...
AT THE BOTTOM OF A BOTTLE?
...I DIDN'T SAY THAT.

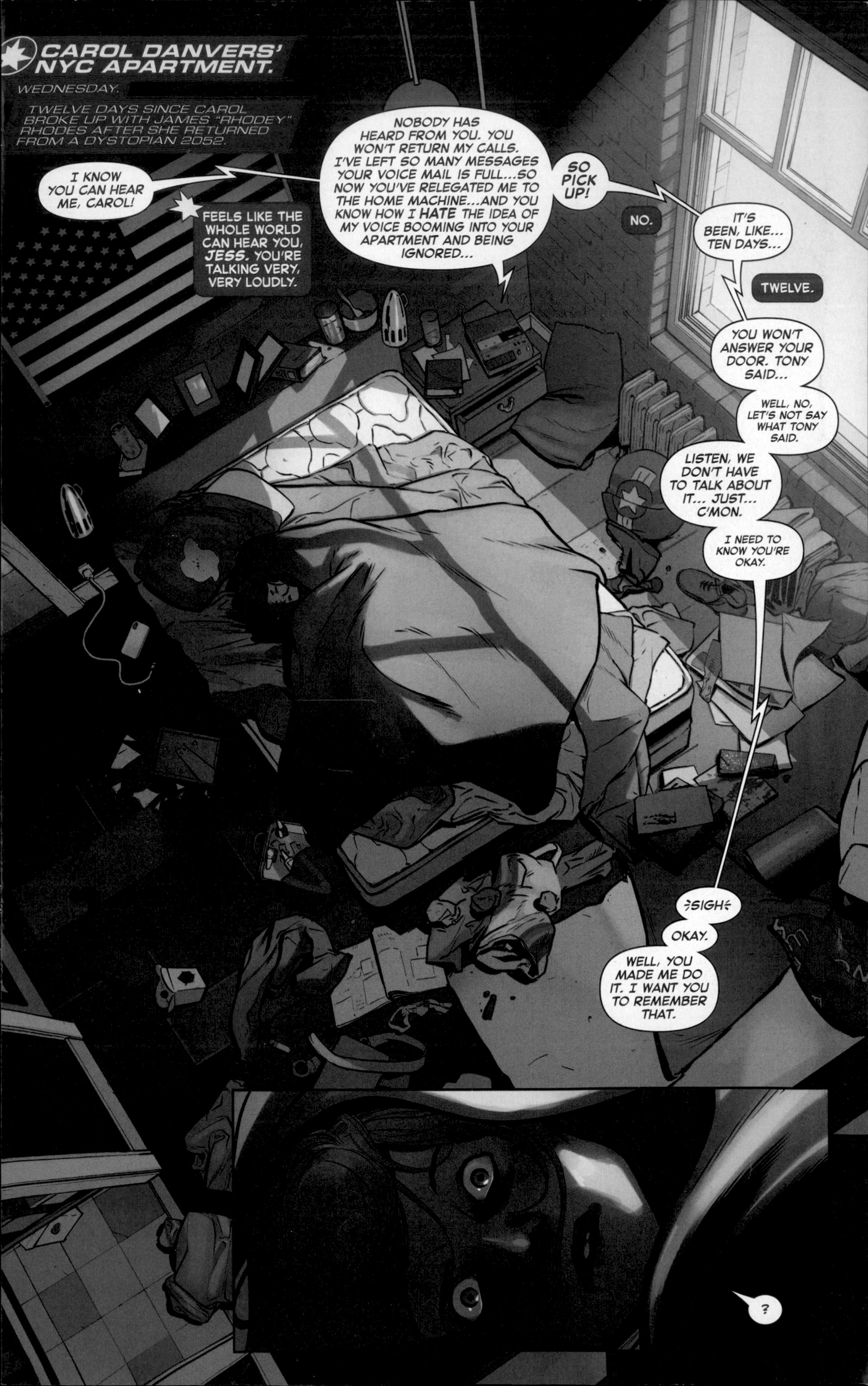
CAROL DANVERS' NYC APARTMENT.
WEDNESDAY.
TWELVE DAYS SINCE CAROL BROKE UP WITH JAMES "RHODEY" RHODES AFTER SHE RETURNED FROM A DYSTOPIAN 2052.
I KNOW YOU CAN HEAR ME, CAROL!
FEELS LIKE THE WHOLE WORLD CAN HEAR YOU, JESS. YOU'RE TALKING VERY, VERY LOUDLY.
NOBODY HAS HEARD FROM YOU. YOU WON'T RETURN MY CALLS. I'VE LEFT SO MANY MESSAGES YOUR VOICE MAIL IS FULL...SO NOW YOU'VE RELEGATED ME TO THE HOME MACHINE...AND YOU KNOW HOW I HATE THE IDEA OF MY VOICE BOOMING INTO YOUR APARTMENT AND BEING IGNORED...
SO PICK UP!
NO.
IT'S BEEN, LIKE... TEN DAYS...
TWELVE.
YOU WON'T ANSWER YOUR DOOR. TONY SAID...
WELL, NO, LET'S NOT SAY WHAT TONY SAID.
LISTEN, WE DON'T HAVE TO TALK ABOUT IT... JUST... C'MON.
I NEED TO KNOW YOU'RE OKAY.
SIGH
OKAY.
WELL, YOU MADE ME DO IT. I WANT YOU TO REMEMBER THAT.
?

PICTORIAL
ATLAS
OF THE
WORLD

The following flags are copyright by and used with permission from **The Flag Research Center**, Winchester, Mass. 01890:

p.10 – Albania, Andorra, Bosnia-Herzegovina; p.11 – Bulgaria, Croatia, Czech Republic, Estonia, Finland, Georgia; p.12 – Latvia; p.13 – Lithuania, Macedonia; p.14 – San Marino, Slovak Republic, Slovenia, Spain; p.15 – Azerbaijan, Kazakhstan, Kyrgyzstan, Russia, Tajikistan, Turkmenistan, Uzbekistan, Yugoslavia; p.18 – Afghanistan, Bahrain, Bangladesh, Cambodia; p.19 – Iraq; p.21 – Mongolia, Nepal; p.22 – Saudi Arabia; p.23 – United Arab Emirates; p.26 – Cape Verde; p.27 – Congo; p.28 – Djibouti, Equatorial Guinea; Ethiopia; p.33 – Zimbabwe; p.36 – Bermuda; p.37 – Brazil; p.38 – Dominica, El Salvador; p.39 – Haiti; p.40 – Nicaragua; p.44 – Kiribati; p.44/45 – Marshall Islands, Micronesia; p.45 – Tuvalu.

This revised fifth edition published 1996
Printed and bound in Italy

AT004G

ISBN 0 8241 1706 9

PICTORIAL
ATLAS
OF THE
WORLD

Ottenheimer Publishers, Inc.

FOREWORD

In 1636 a bound collection of maps was published by Gerard Mercator and John Hondt with a frontispiece illustrating the titan Atlas bearing the world on his shoulders. As a result, the word "atlas" entered the vocabulary as a synonym for a book of maps. In the seventeenth century only the very rich could afford the luxury of an atlas. Cartographic masterpieces by Dutch map engravers offered their patrons the first view of a world whose horizons were being swiftly broadened by maritime discovery.

Today, most households can afford an atlas even if they do not own one. Certainly, the need for and the attraction of the atlas have never been greater. Never have so many people been on the move around the world. Never have so many been concerned with the impact of world events. "Atlas-eaters," Dylan Thomas called those who were hungry for world news. The atlas, through its coordinates of latitude and longitude, can answer the question "Where?". Or, perhaps, more precisely, the index to the atlas provides the answer – hence the importance of the extended index to the *Pictorial Atlas of the World*.

In an atlas, the science of map-making is married to the art of map presentation. Techniques of production are increasingly refined; sources of information are increasingly precise. Satellite imagery, photogrammetry and computerization have transformed map production. Most of the *Pictorial Atlas of the World* consists of topographical maps. Additionally, the pictorial section provides useful and fascinating information on the world's nations and peoples.

An atlas is no substitute for a globe. The two are complementary, for not even the larger globes can include a fraction of the information that is packed into an atlas. The task of projecting the globe onto a flat surface has taxed the ingenuity of mathematicians since the Greeks first attempted to measure the circumference of the Earth. The variety of formidably-named projections employed in the *Pictorial Atlas of the World* illustrates the extended range of options available to present-day cartographers.

Atlases have a romantic appeal as well as a utilitarian value. The English novelist Alan Sillitoe, in a memorable essay on maps, recalls the flights of fancy set in motion by his "first cheap layer-tinted atlas." To turn the pages of the *Pictorial Atlas of the World* – to contemplate the controlling features of land and sea, to reflect upon the boundaries that define the outlines and shape the destinies of countries and to respond to the magic of the infinity of place-names – is to experience a stimulus to the imagination as well as to the intellect.

William R. Mead
PROFESSOR EMERITUS OF GEOGRAPHY, UNIVERSITY COLLEGE LONDON.

MAP LEGEND

SETTLEMENT

For scales larger than 1 inch : 30 miles | Population

🔺	**BIRMINGHAM**	>1,000,000
🔺	**GLASGOW**	500,000–1,000,000
🔺	**CARDIFF**	250,000–500,000
🔺	LIMERICK	50,000–250,000
•	Dover	10,000–50,000
•	Lossiemouth	5,000–10,000
○	Church Stretton	<5,000

🔺	CROYDON	London Borough

For scales between 1 inch : 30 miles and 1 inch : 190 miles

🔺	**NEW YORK**	>5,000,000
🔺	**MONTRÉAL**	2,500,000–5,000,000
■	**SAN DIEGO**	1,000,000–2,500,000
•	Hyderabad	500,000–1,000,000
•	Adelaide	100,000–500,000
○	Key West	<100,000

For scales smaller than 1 inch : 190 miles

■	LOS ANGELES	>1,000,000
•	Maracaibo	500,000–1,000,000
•	Santa Fe	<500,000

Washington National capital   Winnipeg State, provincial capital

COMMUNICATIONS

═════	Highway
═ ═ ═ ═	Highway under construction
───────	Principal road
- - - - - - -	Principal road under construction
───────	Other main road
─ ─ ─ ─ ─	Track, seasonal road
⟶ ⟵	Road tunnel
───────	Principal railroad
─ ─ ─ ─	Principal railroad under construction
⟶ ⟵	Railroad tunnel
✈	International, main airport

BOUNDARIES

▬▬▬	International
▬ ▬ ▬	Undefined, disputed
▬▬▬▬	Internal, state, provincial
─ ─ ─ ─	Armistice, ceasefire line

The representation of a boundary in this atlas does not denote its international recognition and therefore the de facto situation has been depicted.

HYDROGRAPHIC FEATURES

～～	River, stream
～～	Intermittent watercourse
～～	Waterfall, rapids
～～	Dam, barrage
∕∕	Irrigation, drainage channel
	Canal
～	Lake, reservoir
～	Intermittent, seasonal lake
～	Salt pan, mud flat
•	Oasis
▦	Marsh, swamp
～	Reef

Depth of sea in meters

Scales larger than 1 inch : 190 miles

| 0 |
| 200 |
| 3000 |

Scales smaller than 1 inch : 190 miles

| 0 |
| 1000 |
| 5000 |

OTHER FEATURES

▲ 3798	Elevation above sea level (meters)
▼ −133	Depression below sea level (meters)
⪥	Pass
●—●—●	Oil, gas pipeline with field

ENVIRONMENTAL TYPES

	Permanent ice and snow
	Mountain and moorland
	Tundra
	Coniferous forest
	Deciduous forest
	Tropical forest
	Prairie
	Temperate agriculture
	Mediterranean scrub
	Savannah
	Desert

This representation of the environment and its associated vegetation gives an overview of the landscape. It is not intended to be definitive.

CONVERSION SCALES

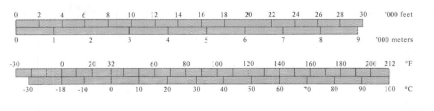

CONTENTS

PEOPLES AND PLACES OF THE WORLD

An A to Z of the World's Countries:

THE WORLD IN MAPS

EUROPE

First page: Victoria Falls span the Middle Zambezi River at one of its widest points. Title Page: the well-known resort of Bled, in the Slovenian Highlands.

◄ *Chicago, Illinois, one of the largest cities in the United States.*

EUROPE

As the cradle of Western civilization and the industrial revolution that now dominates the world economies, Europe may justly claim to be the historical heart of the modern world. It was in Europe that technological advances made mass-production industry possible for the first time. This led to an economic dominance over the rest of the world, which continued until the same processes were taken up by the booming population of North America and the industrial lead crossed the Atlantic.

Geographically, Europe is a highly diverse and fragmented continent without any of the vast plains, mountain ranges or deserts that characterize other land masses. In Europe everything is on a much smaller scale than elsewhere. The greatest mountain chain is the Alps, which stretch across northern Italy and on into eastern Europe, but these peaks are dwarfed by the Asian Himalayas or the South American Andes. The largest plain is that of the Ukraine, now devoted to the production of grain crops, but again this is far smaller than the North American plains or the Mongolian grasslands.

Europe is, however, immensely diverse, with a wide variety of landscape forms being found in relatively small areas. Fertile plains jostle with mountain ranges and dense forests with productive meadows. It is the sheer diversity of the geological makeup that gives the continent its characteristic appearance. Nowhere is it possible to travel far without coming across a change in scenery.

Hidden beneath this fragmented landscape is a wide variety of mineral wealth. Pockets of every conceivable metal ore are to be found scattered across Europe. Though none occurs in the kind of mass deposit encountered on other continents, these ores have provided the raw materials for European industry for centuries and only now are being surpassed by bulk ores from elsewhere.

Until the immigration of racial groups from other continents in large numbers during the late 20th century, the population of Europe was remarkably homogeneous. Almost the entire population was descended from Indo-Europeans, who spread across the continent in antiquity. Earlier peoples were swamped by these new cultures, only surviving in isolated pockets, such as that of the Basques of northern Spain.

However, the populations of Europe have strong historic cultures and concepts of nationhood that transcend the rather academic classification of Indo-European. These nationalist identities are a powerful cultural impetus within Europe and sources of much pride. They may also lead to factional violence, and attempts at supranational states have rarely survived. Among the most recent to fall before nationalist feelings is Yugoslavia, where civil war still rages after the secession of Croatia, Slovenia, Bosnia-Herzegovina and Macedonia. The colossal USSR, too, crumbled following severe economic difficulties and the political upheaval of 1991. The Baltic States took the opportunity of leaving the union first, followed by the other republics, which remained bound together, however, within the Commonwealth of Independent States.

The keynote of Europe is diversity. There is diversity in landscape, in geology and in human culture. Packed into the smallest of the continents are over thirty countries based around identifiable national groupings. Even within countries nationalist divisions are found. The nation state of Italy was united little more than a century ago, and strong regional differences of culture, language and lifestyle are still apparent. Europe is nothing if not a continent of contrasts.

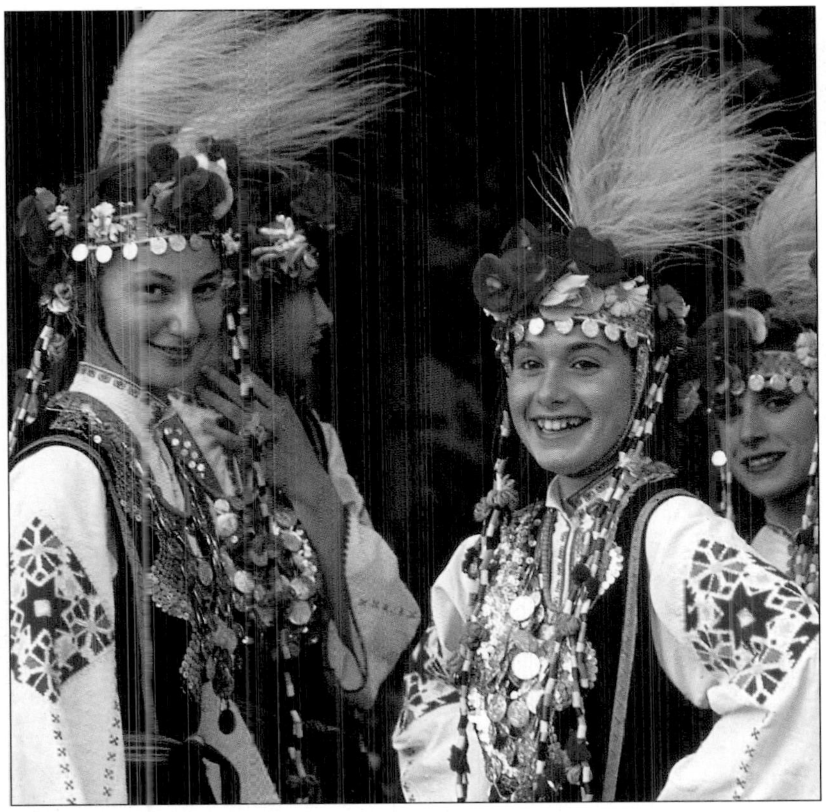

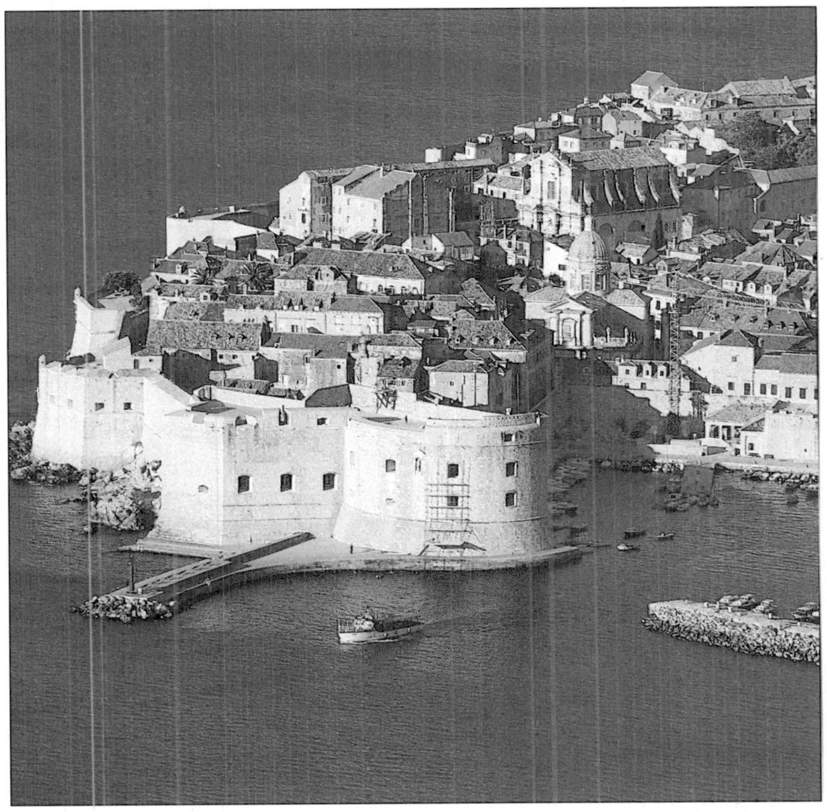

◄ Iceland – 'Land of fire and Ice'.

▲ Traditional costume, Bulgaria.

▲ Dubrovnik, Croatia.

▼ Pünderich, overlooking the Mosel, Germany.

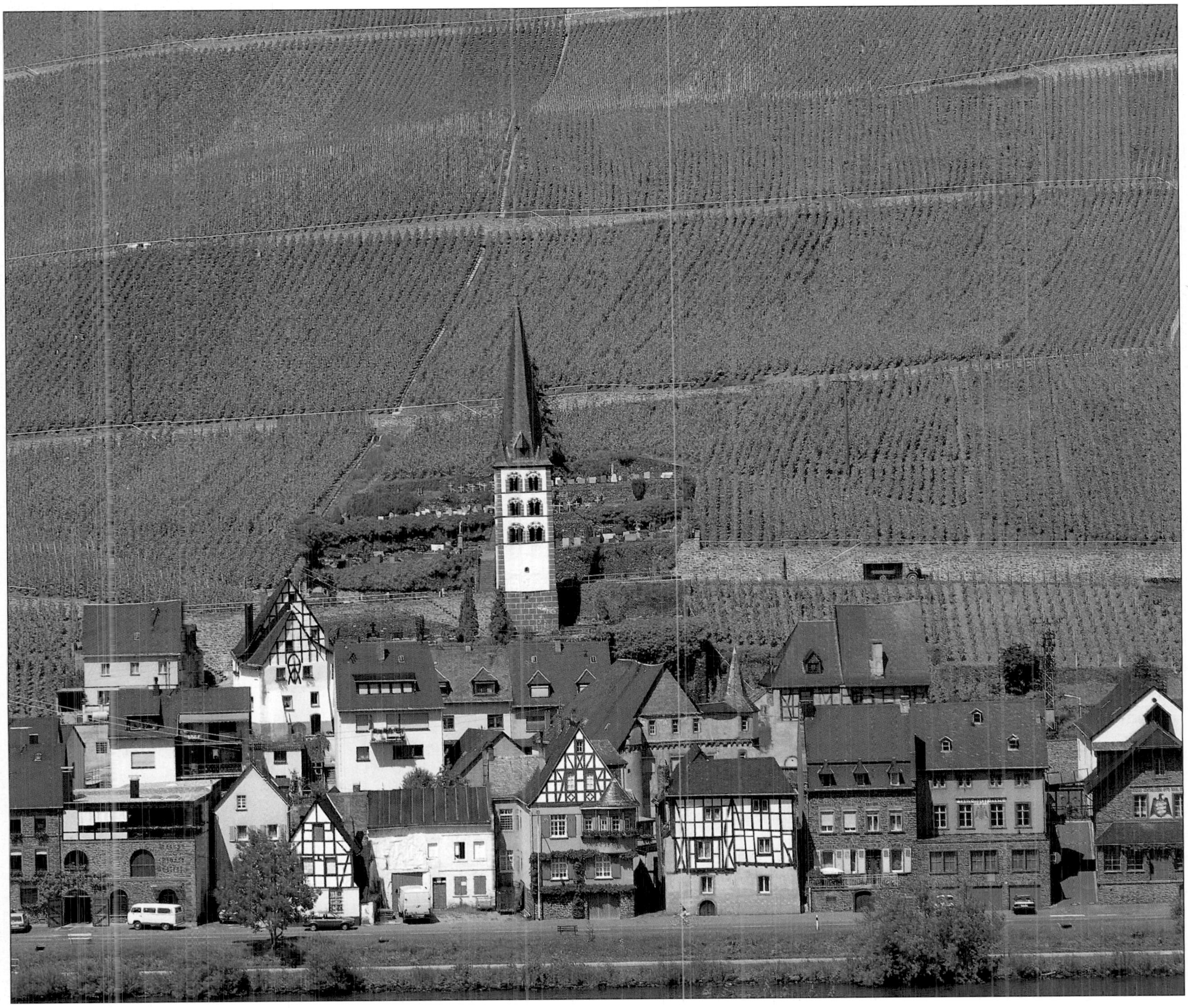

ALBANIA

Population: 3.4 million
Area: 11,000 square miles
Capital: Tirana
Language: Albanian and Greek
Currency: Lek

The rugged mountain nation of Albania has been virtually cut off from the rest of Europe for decades. A province of first the Byzantine and later the Ottoman Empires, Albania gained independence as a kingdom in 1912 and as a Communist republic in 1946. Until the early 1900s, the old-style Stalinist regime retained a tight grip on running the country. In 1992, however, a non-communist regime was elected. Under Communism the nation had tried to revolutionize its economy by abandoning the traditional farming techniques that formerly employed the population. Today, less than half the work force is in farming. Copper, steel and electronics are among the growth industries.

ANDORRA

Population: 57,000
Area: 180 square miles
Capital: Andorra La Vella
Language: Catalan and French
Currency: French Franc and Spanish Peseta

The independent mountain state of Andorra has retained its freedom unchanged since 1278, when the rival powers of the region agreed on a compromise. Under the 700-year-old arrangement the state is ruled jointly by Spain's Bishop of Urgel and the Count of Foix, represented by the President of France. In practice the native Andorrans, who number around 10,000, govern themselves through a democratic system, though the agreement of the joint rulers is needed for all actions. Tourism and duty-free shopping bolster the modern prosperity.

AUSTRIA

Population: 7.9 million
Area: 32,000 square miles
Capital: Vienna
Language: German
Currency: Schilling

Until 1918 the heart of the vast Hapsburg Empire, which encompassed the Danube Basin and much of the Balkans, Austria is now a democratic republic based upon the German-speaking parts of that Empire. The capital, Vienna, has a long tradition of sophisticated culture and excellence in the arts, music being strongly represented. The economy of Austria is broadly based, though agriculture is limited by the terrain. The mountains attract large numbers of tourists who enjoy winter skiing and summer hiking.

BELGIUM

Population: 10 million
Area: 12,000 square miles
Capital: Brussels
Language: Flemish, French and German
Currency: Belgian Franc

The present constitutional monarchy dates back to 1830, when the Belgian people rebelled against Dutch rule and invited a German prince to become their king. The government consists of a two-chamber Parliament acting under the monarch. The Flemish- and French-speaking areas each enjoy a degree of regional self-government. The nation is predominantly urban, with industry and services leading the economy. The coal and steel and other metal industries dominate the scene. Agriculture contributes only a small proportion to the economy, but Belgium is now almost self-sufficient in food.

▲ *An open-air restaurant, Brussels, Belgium.*

BOSNIA-HERZEGOVINA

Population: 4.3 million
Area: 20,000 square miles
Capital: Sarajevo
Language: Serbo-Croatian
Currency: Din

With the largest Serb minority of any of the breakaway Yugoslav republics, Bosnia-Herzegovina also shared a long border with Serbian-dominated Yugoslavia. The intent to become independent was approved in a 1992 referendum boycotted by ethnic Serbian voters. A savage civil war broke out in spring 1992 with Serbian separatists supported by Yugoslav forces annexing territory and shelling Bosnian cities such as Sarajevo despite the presence of a UN peace-keeping force in Bosnia and UN sanctions against Yugoslavia. The war decimated the Bosnian economy. Agriculture (corn, wheat) is often at a subsistence level. Manufacturing produces steel, aluminum and textiles.

▲ *Tranquil countryside, Finland.*

Above right: *The Schonbrunn Palace, Vienna, Austria.*

▼ *Old-world charm, Czech Republic.*

▼ *Nyhavn, in Copenhagen, Denmark.*

▲ *Corn harvest, Albania.*

▼ *An Orthodox priest, Cyprus.*

▲ *The Orthodox Cathedral, Tallinn, Estonia.*

▲ *Vineyards, Santenay, France.*

▲ *The mountain state of Andorra.*

BULGARIA

Population: 9 million
Area: 43,000 square miles
Capital: Sofia
Language: Bulgarian
Currency: Lev

Bulgaria became independent of the Moslem Ottoman Empire in 1908 as a kingdom, and became a Communist republic following the Russian occupation in 1946. In 1989 street protests and demands for reform led the National Assembly to approve a multiparty democracy and free elections. In 1990 the Communist government stepped down. The river valleys have fertile soils and a climate conducive to heavy grain crops and livestock rearing. The traditional dominance of agriculture has been overtaken by a growing industrial sector producing iron, steel, textiles and agricultural equipment.

CROATIA

Population: 4.7 million
Area: 22,000 square miles
Capital: Zagreb
Language: Croatian
Currency: Croatian Dinar

The former Yugoslav republic of Croatia seceded from the Yugoslav federation in October 1991. Internal conflict arose as long-standing tensions between Croats and ethnic Serbs erupted. Helped by Yugoslav troops, the Serbian minority tried to seize power by force. Fighting continued throughout 1991, and in 1992 UN peace-keeping troops intervened, establishing four peacekeeping zones. In 1993, Croatian forces launched an attack on one of these zones, an action that was widely condemned. The civil war continues.

CYPRUS

Population: 756,000
Area: 3,500 square miles
Capital: Nicosia (Lefkosia)
Language: Greek and Turkish
Currency: Cypriot Pound

For centuries part of the Ottoman Empire, Cyprus passed to Britain, which granted independence in 1960 under a constitution designed to calm ethnic rivalries between the Greek and Turkish populations. In 1974 a coup by the Greeks threatened to join Cyprus to Greece, and Turkey invaded to block the move. Today, the island is divided between the Turkish northern third, which has declared itself an independent state, and the southern Greek section. The traditional agricultural products of olives, grapes and fruits remain important. Tourists are attracted by the beautiful scenery and beaches, though this business has been disrupted by the partition.

CZECH REPUBLIC

Population: 10.3 million
Area: 30,000 square miles
Capital: Prague
Language: Czech and Slovak
Currency: Koruna

The Czech Republic occupies the western regions of what was Czechoslovakia until 1993 and has a predominantly urban culture with strong German influences. Formerly part of the Hapsburg Empire, Czechoslovakia became independent in 1918. Communists took power with Soviet aid in 1948, and an attempt at liberalization in 1968, known as the Prague Spring, was crushed by Russian tanks. In November 1989 mass public demonstrations led to the resignation of the Communist government. Unable to agree on ethnic and economic issues, the Czech and Slovak regions decided to separate. The Czech Republic is a heavily industrialized nation with iron and steel, chemicals and food processing being prominent.

DENMARK

Population: 5 million
Area: 16,500 square miles
Capital: Copenhagen
Language: Danish
Currency: Krone

The rich soil and temperate climate of Denmark have aided the traditionally-strong agricultural sector. Grains, potatoes and vegetables are grown, but livestock dominates. Recently, the industrial sector has grown significantly, using imported raw materials which are then processed for export as finished goods. Manufacturing now outstrips agriculture in terms of economic value by about four times. The constitution is based on the monarch, who cannot act without the consent of the democratically-elected Parliament.

ESTONIA

Population: 1.6 million
Area: 17,000 square miles
Capital: Tallinn
Language: Estonian and Russian
Currency: Rouble

In September 1991 Estonia was accepted as an independent nation for the first time since it annexation by the Soviet Union in 1939. The republic has been dominated by economic central planning from Moscow for over five decades and relies heavily on agriculture for employment and prosperity. Gasrich shale and phosphates represent the only mineral wealth and industrial base for this small nation. Cooperation with the other Baltic states is already established, and other foreign economic links are being vigorously pursued.

FINLAND

Population: 5 million
Area: 130,000 square miles
Capital: Helsinki
Language: Finnish
Currency: Markka

Ruled in turn by Denmark, Sweden and Russia, Finland gained independence in 1917, when the Finns took advantage of the chaos following the Russian Revolution to seize power. In 1940 war with Russia resulted in Finland losing much territory around Lake Ladoga to the Soviets. Modern foreign policy emphasizes the need for friendly relations with Russia and with Scandinavian nations. The economy of the nation is mixed and broadly based. Vast forests provide raw material for a lumber trade. The small area of land suitable for agriculture is heavily used for raising livestock, particularly cattle in the south and reindeer in the north. Industry is concentrated on the extraction and processing of iron deposits.

FRANCE

Population: 57 million
Area: 210,000 square miles
Capital: Paris
Language: French
Currency: French Franc

The modern state of France is generally traced back to the accession of the Capetian dynasty to the throne of the Western Franks in 987, though Frankish power was established in the region as early as 500 a.d. The monarchy was overthrown in the Revolution of 1789, after which France was ruled by republics, emperors and kings. The Fifth Republic was established in 1958. The present constitution allows for a democratically-elected Parliament, which operates under the guidance of an elected President. The economy of the nation is highly developed, with industry and services being dominant employers. Agriculture remains largely in the hands of small-scale farmers and produces quantities of grain and fruits, most notably grapes, from which the famous French wines are produced.

GEORGIA

Population: 5.5 million
Area: 27,000 square miles
Capital: Tbilisi
Language: Georgian, Armenian, Russian
Currency: Ruble

Vast manganese deposits form the basis for the prosperous mining industry of Georgia, though coal is also found in quantity and other minerals are expoited on a smaller scale. The warm climate enables production of silk, tea and wine in

11

large quantities. After becoming independent of the Soviet Union in 1991, Georgia refused to join the successor Commonwealth of Independent States.

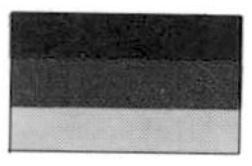

GERMANY

Population: 80 million
Area: 138,000 square miles
Capital: Berlin
Language: German
Currency: Mark

Unity and division have been the hallmarks of German history. The disparate German tribes were united under the Frankish Empire in the 9th century, but this fell apart, to be replaced by the Holy Roman Empire of the Middle Ages. Initially strong, the Empire broke up into dozens of petty feudal states and city republics. The Napoleonic Wars swept this pattern away, and in 1871 the German states were united under Prussian rule as the German Empire. This nation remained together until 1945, when Germany lost much territory and was divided as Communist East and democratic West Germany. In 1990 the overthrow of the Communist regime in East Germany led to reunification. The strong West German economy is concentrating on raising the prosperity of East Germany.

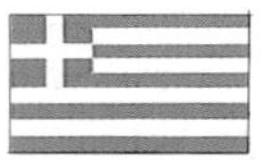

GREECE

Population: 10 million
Area: 51,000 square miles
Capital: Athens
Language: Greek
Currency: Drachma

Home of the ancient civilization that has had such a profound influence on all Western culture, Greece is today working to join the front runners in European economies. The magnificent history, fine climate and attractive beaches have made Greece a favorite tourist resort for generations. Tourism is now the largest single industry in terms of foreign earnings. The mountainous terrain limits agriculture, but there are extensive olive groves and citrus orchards. Industry is less dominant than in other European nations and is concentrated on food processing, textiles and leatherwork. After a period of military rule in the 1970s, Greece reverted to a democratic system.

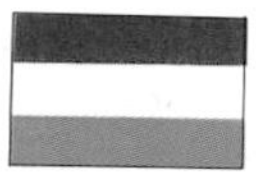

HUNGARY

Population: 10 million
Area: 36,000 square miles
Capital: Budapest
Language: Magyar
Currency: Forint

Formerly a dominant state within the Hapsburg Empire, Hungary became independent in 1918. In 1949 a Communist government was imposed, and the 1956 nationalist rising was put down by Russian tanks and troops. After popular protests and demands for reform, the Communist Party was disbanded in 1989 and opened the way for democratic elections in 1990. The great flat plain of Hungary has dominated the economy for generations. Its fertile soils and temperate climate make abundant crops possible. Wheat, corn and potatoes are the main crops, and large numbers of cattle and pigs are raised. In recent years industry has rapidly gained over agriculture and now dominates the economy, with metallurgy, chemicals and electronics predominating.

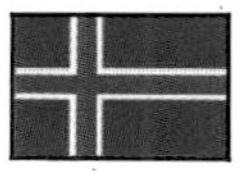

ICELAND

Population: 261,000
Area: 40,000 square miles
Capital: Reykjavik
Language: Icelandic
Currency: Icelandic Krona

Viking settlers began arriving in Iceland in the 9th century, ousting the few Irish monks there. An independent society existed based on Viking social rules until 1264, when Norway took control. In 1381 Iceland passed to the Danish crown, recovering full self-government in 1918 and severance from Denmark in 1946. The present republic operates with two chambers under an elected President. Only two percent of land is farmed, producing potatoes, turnips and hay. Livestock is kept in small numbers. Fishing provides the basis of the economy. Industry is very limited.

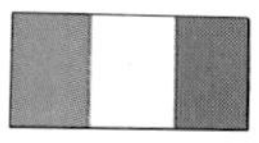

IRELAND

Population: 3.5 million
Area: 27,000 square miles
Capital: Dublin
Language: Gaelic and English
Currency: Irish Pound

After centuries of growing British influence, Ireland joined with Britain in 1801. In 1921 the Catholic southern counties of Ireland gained independence after an armed uprising and became the Republic of Eire in 1948, the Protestant counties of Ulster remaining part of Britain. Ongoing civil violence and terrorist activities have disrupted life in border counties and dominate Irish relations with Britain. The economy is traditionally agricultural. Large numbers of cattle produce dairy products, and sheep and pigs provide meat. Industrial activity has grown rapidly in recent years, and this is now more important to the economy than agriculture. Food processing, textiles and electrical engineering are the dominant industries.

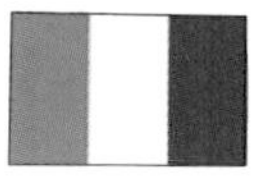

ITALY

Population: 57 million
Area: 116,000 square miles
Capital: Rome
Language: Italian
Currency: Italian Lira

The various city states, kingdoms and duchies of Italy were not united until 1861, and the republic was established in 1946. The present constitution allows for two chambers, the lower elected directly and the upper elected by the historic regions. The President is elected by the two houses of parliament. There are numerous political parties representing many shades of opinion, though fascism is banned. Southern parts of the country are generally less well developed than the north. Grapes are widely grown for wine production. Industry is concentrated in northern cities where textiles, food processing and the manufacture of machinery lead the sector.

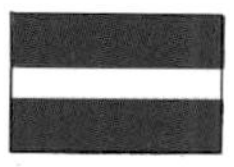

LATVIA

Population: 2.7 million
Area: 25,000 square miles
Capital: Riga
Language: Latvian and Russian
Currency: Rouble

The troubled history of Latvia as an independent nation began with a democratic government being installed in 1919 and came to an end in 1940 when Soviet power was imposed. Together with Lithuania and Estonia, Latvia became independent once again in 1991. Five decades of economic central planning has given Latvia a heritage of heavy industry, with steel, railroad equipment and textiles dominating.

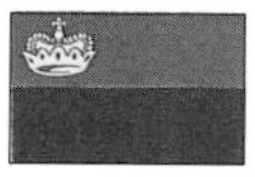

LIECHTENSTEIN

Population: 30,000
Area: 62 square miles
Capital: Vaduz
Language: German
Currency: Swiss Franc

The tiny principality of Liechtenstein dates back to 1434. In 1712 the principality passed to the Liechtenstein family, which held it from the Holy Roman Emperor. When that empire collapsed in 1806, the family retained their domains and in 1923 joined Switzerland in a customs and currency union. The present constitution places power in the hands of the Prince, though legislation needs approval of the democratically-elected Parliament. The economy is based on a mixture of agriculture, light industry and commerce. Many companies have their nominal headquarters in Liechtenstein, and their taxation contributes to the state income.

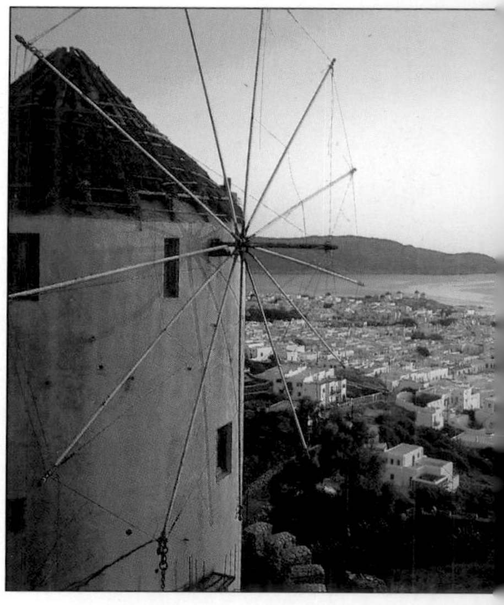

▲ *Dusk in Mykonos, Greece.*

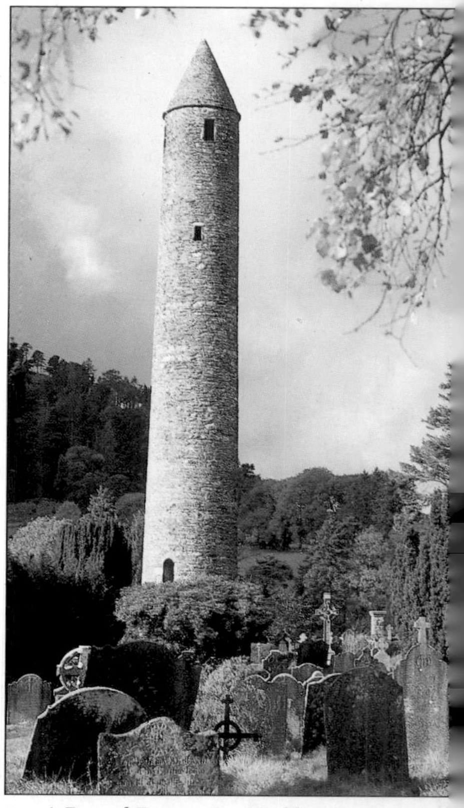

▲ *A Round Tower, Co. Wicklow, Ireland.*

▼ *Luxembourg, one of Europe's smallest nations.*

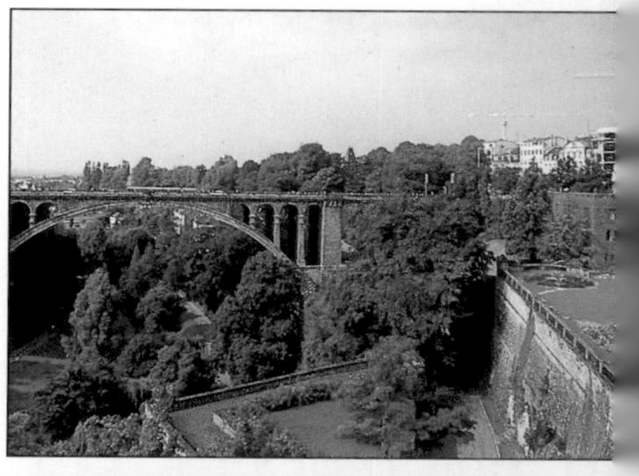

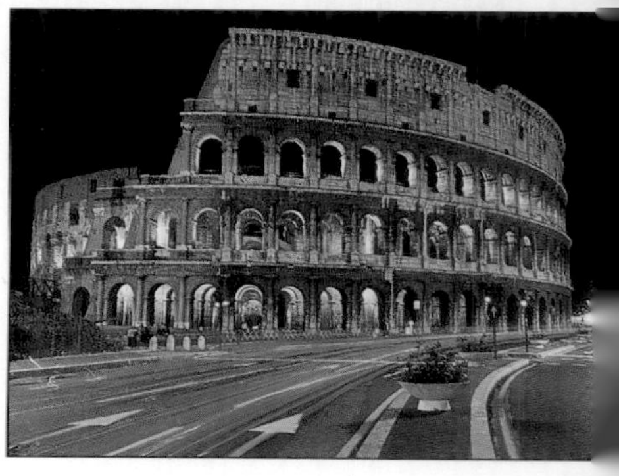

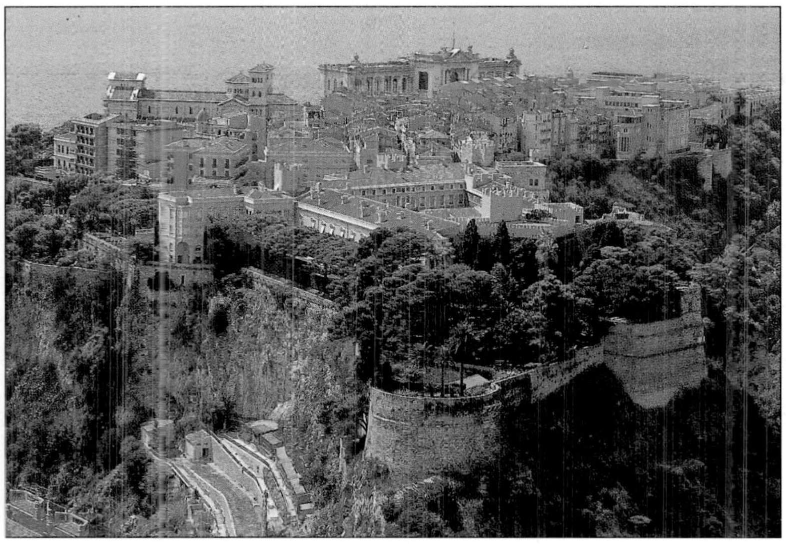

▼ *The Principality of Liechtenstein.*

▲ *The Principality of Monaco.*

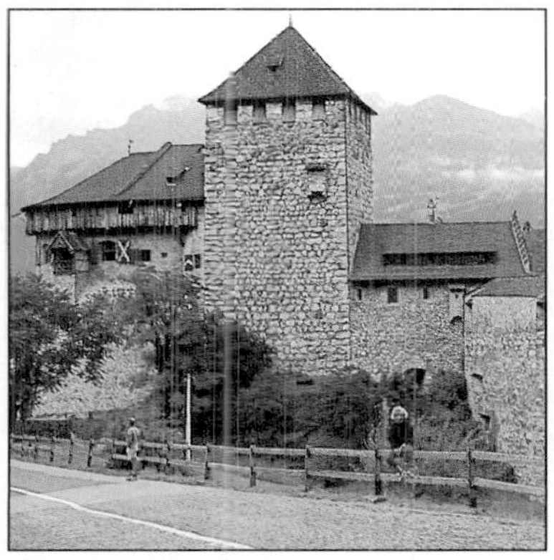

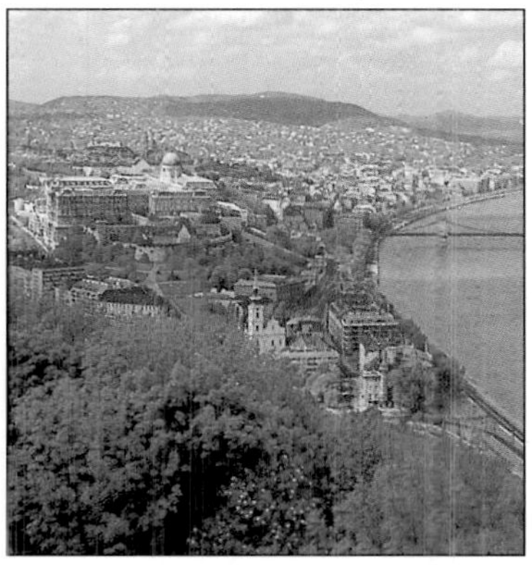

▲ *The Danube River, Budapest, Hungary.*

◄ *Heavy industry, Lithuania.*

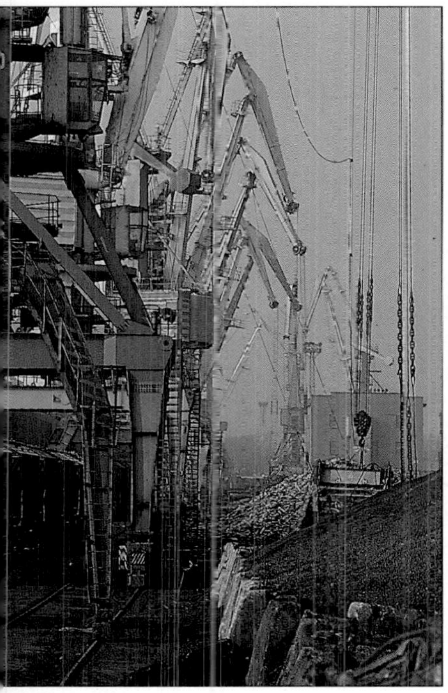

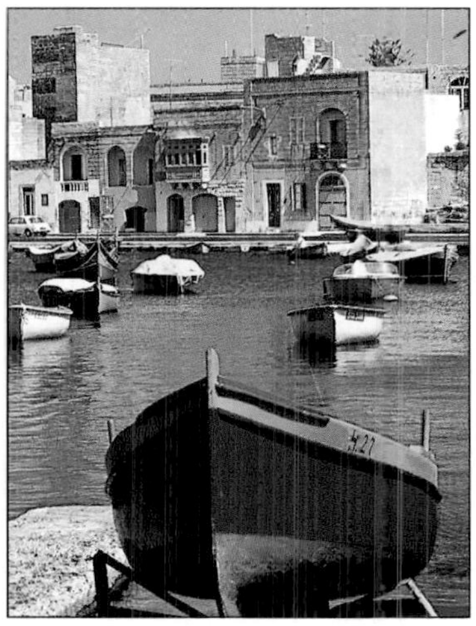

▲ *A characteristic view of Malta.*

▼ *The Old City, Riga, Latvia.*

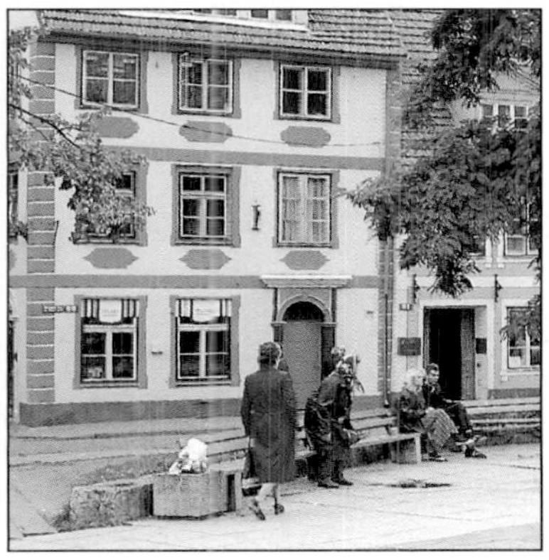

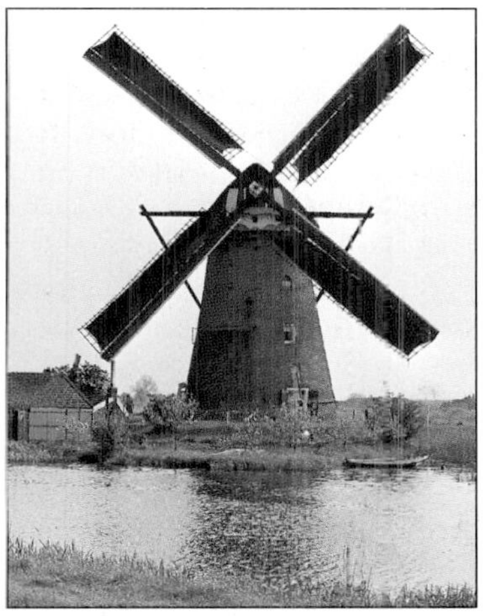

◄ *The Colosseum, Rome, Italy.*

▲ *Kinderdijk, east of Rotterdam, Netherlands.*

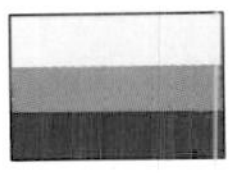

LITHUANIA

Population: 3.8 million
Area: 25,000 square miles
Capital: Vilnius
Language: Lithuanian and Russian
Currency: Rouble

With a population over 80 percent ethnic Lithuanians, the republic has long desired independence. In March 1991 an overwhelming majority voted for separation from the Soviet Union, achieved in August. Traditionally an agricultural nation, Lithuania is now dominated by industry. Heavy engineering and textiles dominate the economic scene, although forestry and agriculture are significant employers.

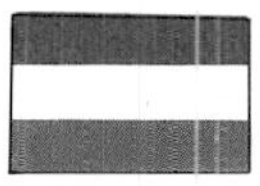

LUXEMBOURG

Population: 400,000
Area: 965 square miles
Capital: Luxembourg
Language: German and French
Currency: Luxembourg Franc

Tiny Luxembourg enjoyed varying degrees of self government until being conquered by France in 1795. In 1815 the current Grand Duchy came into being under the Dutch monarchy, and in 1890 full independence came. The Grand Duke is closely involved in administration with the democratically-elected Parliament. The nation is part of a customs union with Belgium. Industry is based on a thriving iron and steel business, though attempts are being made to diversify the economy. Agriculture plays a minor role in national life.

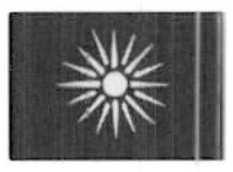

MACEDONIA

Population: 2 million
Area: 10,000 square miles
Capital: Skopje
Language: Macedonian
Currency: Denar

Although Macedonia declared its independence from Yugoslavia in 1991, it was not recognized by the international community (because of Greek objections to the use of the name "Macedonia") until 1993. Independence was the crowning achievement of the republic's efforts to create a nation. Landlocked and pressured by larger neighbors with claims on its territory–Greece, Bulgaria and Serbia–Macedonia confronts an uncertain future. Agriculture (wheat, grapes and corn) is important, and there are deposits of copper and other minerals, but manufacturing is limited.

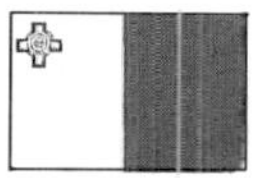

MALTA

Population: 360,000
Area: 122 square miles
Capital: Valletta
Language: Maltese and English
Currency: Maltese Lira

During World War II Malta was a vital British naval base and came under massive attack by German and Italian forces. In 1942 the people of Malta were awarded Britain's George Cross, which is featured on the Maltese flag, together with the colors of the religious Knights of Malta, who ruled between 1530 and 1798. Malta gained independence from Britain in 1964. Malta's strategic position in the Mediterranean makes commerce, trade and shipbuilding lucrative industries. Tourism has long been important and is the biggest single earner of foreign currency for Malta. Politically, the nation is a multiparty democracy.

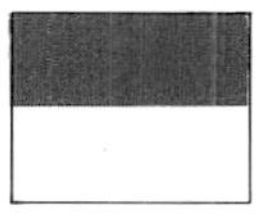

MONACO

Population: 30,000
Area: 0.6 square miles
Capital: Monaco
Language: Monegasque and French
Currency: French Franc

The small Principality of Monaco has been the domain of the Grimaldi family since 1297, placing itself under French protection in 1861. The constitution allows for democratic government though the Prince retains much influence. The main economic base of Monaco is tourism, with nearly ten times as many visitors as residents in the course of a year. The scenic coastline and fine beach delight many tourists, but it is the famous casino which is the major attraction. Agriculture is virtually nonexistent but the industrial sector is growing in importance.

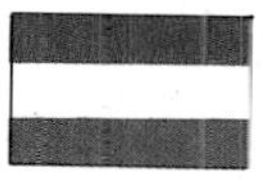

NETHERLANDS

Population: 15 million
Area: 16,000 square miles
Capital: Amsterdam and The Hague
Language: Dutch
Currency: Dutch Guilder

The nation came into being in the late 16th century, when the prosperous Protestant cities rebelled against oppressive Catholic rule from Spain. Much of the Netherlands has been reclaimed from the sea by massive reclamation projects. Much of this land is devoted to agriculture, with potatoes, sugar beet and grain being major crops. Cut flowers and flower bulbs are produced in large quantities for export, while dairy cattle graze on meadows to produce milk from which famous Dutch cheeses are made. The nation's position at the mouth of the Rhine has long ensured lucrative trade and commerce connections. The Netherlands still enjoys much transshipment trade and processes many raw materials for export as finished goods.

NORWAY

Population: 4.3 million
Area: 125,000 square miles
Capital: Oslo
Language: Norwegian
Currency: Norwegian Krone

In 1905 Norway gained independence from Sweden. The constitution places power in the hands of a democratically-elected Parliament called the *Storting*, though the monarch retains control of the armed forces and can veto legislation. The mountainous terrain makes agriculture difficult, and much food needs to be imported. Hydroelectric power is produced in quantity and supplies ninety-nine percent of domestic needs. Offshore oil and gas have added to the energy self-reliance of Norway. Industry is prosperous and is based on the processing of domestic metals, agricultural products and timber from the vast upland forests.

▲ *The Lofoten Islands, Norway.*

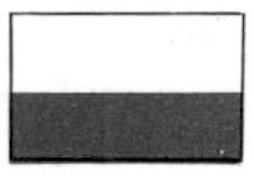

POLAND

Population: 38 million
Area: 120,000 square miles
Capital: Warsaw
Language: Polish
Currency: Zloty

The powerful kingdom of Poland collapsed in the late 18th century and was divided among the Prussian, Hapsburg and Russian empires. Reconstitution and independence did not occur until 1918. The German invasion of Poland in 1939 sparked World War II, and following liberation in 1945 Poland was ruled by a Communist regime imposed by the Soviet Union. Communist rule ended in 1989 after several years of opposition from the Solidarity trade union. Free elections were held in 1991, with opposition parties campaigning for the first time in decades. The Polish economy is industrially based, with iron and steel, textiles and machine manufacture being the most important. The formerly dominant

agricultural sector is still important, producing wheat, rye, potatoes and dairy products.

PORTUGAL

Population: 10 million
Area: 35,000 square miles
Capital: Lisbon
Language: Portuguese
Currency: Escudo

The coup of 1974 overthrew the dictatorship that had governed Portugal since 1933 and in 1976 introduced a democratic constitution. The present constitution, adopted in 1982, allows for an elected President who chooses the Prime Minister from the Assembly, which is elected by universal suffrage. The economy is presently dominated by the dismantling of government control and privatization of industry. Manufacturing is based on textiles, leather goods and ceramics. Agriculture is based on grains and potatoes, and wine, cork and olives are important export earners.

ROMANIA

Population: 23 million
Area: 92,000 square miles
Capital: Bucharest
Language: Romanian and Hungarian
Currency: Leu

The overthrow of the Communist regime of President Ceausescu was attended by street fighting and great confusion. A temporary government was elected in 1990 to draw up a new constitution based on democratic principles. Until the Communist takeover in 1947 Romania was a traditionally agricultural kingdom with little industry. The past decades have seen massive government encouragement of industry, which has overtaken agriculture and is concentrated on iron and steel, chemicals and textiles. The farms continue to produce large quantities of wheat and corn, while sheep raising is still important.

SAN MARINO

Population: 24,000
Area: 24 square miles
Capital: San Marino
Language: Italian
Currency: Italian Lira

Legend has it that the 4th-century Saint Marinus founded the republic as a self-governing Christian community to escape Roman persecution. The republic won full independence from the Pope in 1631 and in 1862 concluded a treaty with the newly-created Italian nation, which secured continued independence. Agriculture is an important source of employment, and wine is exported.

Small-scale industry includes chemicals, ceramics and paints. Much economic wealth comes from tourism and the sale of its unique coins and stamps.

SLOVAK REPUBLIC or SLOVAKIA

Population: 5.3 million
Area: 19,000 square miles
Capital: Bratislava
Language: Slovak, Czech
Currency: Slovak Koruna

Proud of their distinct heritage and determined to assert their sovereignty, the people of Slovakia separated from Czechoslovakia on Jan. 1, 1993, and became citizens of the Slovak Republic. Physically, it is dominated by the Carpathian Mountains, with fertile valleys leading toward the Hungarian Plain. The transition from an agricultural to an industrial economy has been complicated by the abandonment of a Communist system.

SLOVENIA

Population: 1.9 million
Area: 7,800 square miles
Capital: Ljubljana
Language: Slovenian
Currency: Tolar

Formerly a constituent republic of Yugoslavia, Slovenia declared its independence in June 1991. Less ethnically diverse than the other Yugoslav republics, with its own language and a strong Roman Catholic heritage, Slovenia led the drive for reforms in Yugoslavia. When these efforts failed, Slovenia was able to withdraw with a minimum of violence. Agriculture (potatoes, corn and wheat) remains important. Manufacturing produces steel, textiles and appliances.

SPAIN

Population: 40 million
Area: 190,000 square miles
Capital: Madrid
Language: Spanish and regional
Currency: Peseta

Spain regained its monarchy in 1975 after an interruption of forty-four years. King Juan Carlos is carefully leading his nation to democracy and stability. The constitution vests power in a two-chamber Parliament, the *Cortes*, with a main body elected by proportional representation and a senate elected by province. The traditional agricultural economic base has now been overtaken by industry, but remains important. Wheat and barley are the major crops. Industry is dominated by motor vehicles, textiles, paper, and iron and steel, which together account for the majority of exports.

SWEDEN

Population: 8.7 million
Area: 174,000 square miles
Capital: Stockholm
Language: Swedish
Currency: Swedish Krona

Sweden acquired approximately its present boundaries a thousand years ago and in the 17th century enjoyed Baltic hegemony. The present dynasty dates from 1809, when French general Jean Bernadotte was chosen to become king on the extinction of the native line. The constitution of 1975 reduced the role of monarch to ceremonial and gave power to the democratic Parliament. The highly-prosperous economy is based on iron ore deposits, the forests and immense hydroelectric power. Over half of all manufacturing is made up of metal smelting, metal machinery and other metal products. A further quarter of the sector is composed of timber, plywood and other wood products. Agriculture is well developed, but on a small scale.

SWITZERLAND

Population: 7 million
Area: 16,000 square miles
Capital: Bern
Language: German, French, Italian and Romansch
Currency: Swiss Franc

The confederation of twenty-three cantons that makes up Switzerland is famous for its neutrality. But the state had its origins in a defensive alliance in 1291 and saw many wars in its early centuries of existence. The constitution vests supreme power in the electorate, which can demand laws and changes to the constitution. Each canton is self-governing, with its own parliament; the federal government being responsible for war, peace and treaties. Most crops are grown on the fertile central plain. Manufacturing is a major activity and is based on textiles, chemicals and the processing of agricultural produce. Banking and finance is a well-established sector of the economy.

USSR – COMMONWEALTH OF INDEPENDENT STATES

Successor to the Soviet Union, the Commonwealth of Independent States (CIS) came into being following the collapse of the old regime in 1991. It is intended that this loose structure handle only major central issues such as nuclear weapon deployment, with other powers being assumed by the individual nations. There are separate listings for those republics that did not join the CIS: Estonia, Georgia, Latvia, and Lithuania.

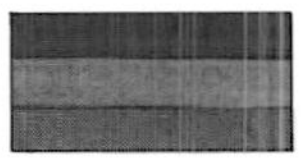

ARMENIA

Population: 3.3 million
Area: 11,500 square miles
Capital: Yerevan
Language: Armenian, Russian, Kurdish
Currency: Ruble

Armenia's rugged terrain allows only limited agriculture based on olive groves, cotton and subtropical fruits. Wide ranging mineral deposits are more promising for the economy, and efficient exploitation of these in the wake of freedom from central Soviet planning may lead to prosperity.

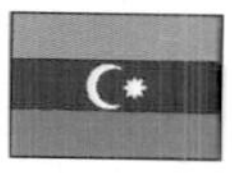

AZERBAIJAN

Population: 7 million
Area: 33,500 square miles
Capital: Baku
Language: Azerbaijani, Armenian, Russian
Currency: Ruble

Recently the scene of ethnic violence between the Azerbaijani majority and the Armenian minority, this republic is rich in natural resources. Industry is based on reserves of oil, iron ore, bauxite and various precious metals. Agriculturally, the republic produces rubber, grapes and tobacco along with other warm weather crops.

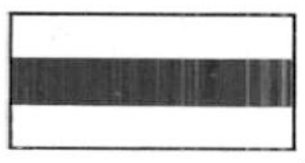

BELARUS

Population: 10 million
Area: 80,000 square miles
Capital: Minsk
Language: Russian, Polish and other languages
Currency: Ruble

Belarus, or Belorussia has taken a lead in the development of the CIS and its institutions. The economy of the republic is based on the rich pasture land and pockets of agricultural land. The processing of the farm output accounts for much of the industry, but there are also large chemical and steel concerns.

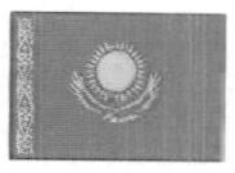

KAZAKHSTAN

Population: 16.5 million
Area: 1,000 000 square miles
Capital: Alma-Ata
Language: Russian, Kazakh
Currency: Ruble

Since the collapse of the USSR, Kazakhstan has emerged as one of the Central Asian Republics of the CIS, a region with interests that are distinct from the other states of the new Commonwealth. Formerly a pastoral economy, agriculture and the mineral wealth are now exploited on a large scale.

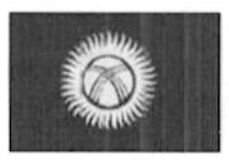

KYRGYZSTAN

Population: 4.2 million
Area: 77,000 square miles
Capital: Bishkek
Language: Kirghiz-Turkish, Russian, Jagatai
Currency: Ruble

Traditionally a pastoral region, the economy of Kyrgyzstan, or Kirghizia, remains firmly based on livestock, but grain crops and tobacco have become particularly important. Much of the industry is based on processing agricultural products, though mining contributes to the economy.

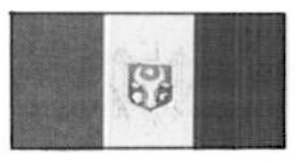

MOLDOVA

Population: 4.3 million
Area: 13,000 square miles
Capital: Chisinau
Language: Romanian, Russian, Gagauzi
Currency: Ruble

Populated mainly with ethnic Romanians, Moldova, or Moldavia, is economically dominated by agriculture and the processing of farm products. Only the production of concrete and other building materials breaks the pattern.

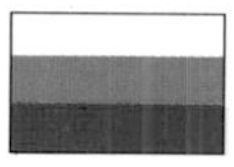

RUSSIA

Population: 147 million
Area: 6,600,00 square miles
Capital: Moscow
Language: Russian, numerous other languages
Currency: Ruble

Russia is the largest of the republics within the CIS. Industry is highly developed and is a major employer. Russia's economy has led the way in throwing off central state control and embracing the free market principles.

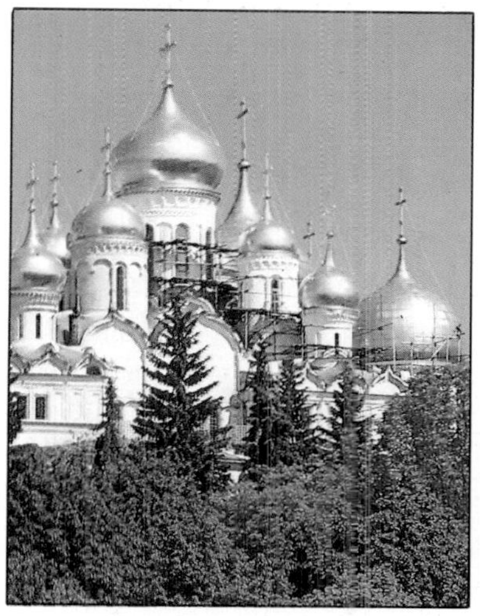

▲ *The golden domes of the Kremlin, Moscow, Russia.*

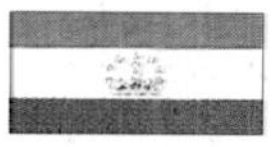

TAJIKISTAN

Population: 5 million
Area: 55,000 square miles
Capital: Dushandbe
Language: Tajik-Persian, Jagatai, Russian
Currency: Ruble

The republic is largely dependent on agriculture, with irrigation enabling the production of warm-climate fruits. Coal, lead and zinc mining account for most industrial activity in Tajikistan. In 1992 the volatile political situation erupted and civil war broke out.

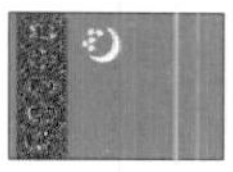

TURKMENISTAN

Population: 3.5 million
Area: 188,000 square miles
Capital: Ashkhabad
Language: Turkish, Russian, Jagatai
Currency: Ruble

Rich oil, coal and sulphur deposits form the basis for an industrial economy, although agriculture, notably cotton, corn, fruits and vegetables, provides the majority of the employment. Turkmenistan was the first of the Central Asian Republics to declare itself free of Moscow, in August 1990.

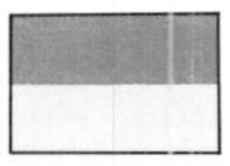

UKRAINE

Population: 52 million
Area: 233,000 square miles
Capital: Kiev
Language: Ukrainian and Russian
Currency: Ruble

The traditional grain basket of eastern Europe, the Ukraine is still a highly productive agricultural region, with nearly half of the crops of the CIS coming from it. Large deposits of coal and oil have boosted the industrial sector in recent years.

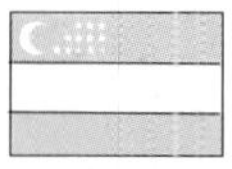

UZBEKISTAN

Population: 20 million
Area: 172,000 square miles
Capital: Tashkent
Language: Jagatai, Russian, Tatar
Currency: Ruble

The Uzbek economy is based on intensive agriculture producing silk, rice, subtropical fruits and grapes, with mineral exploitation on a modest scale. Industry is limited and is largely based on the rich deposits of oil, coal and copper.

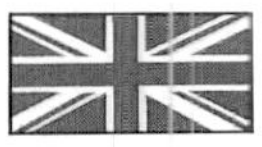

UNITED KINGDOM

Population: 57.5 million
Area: 94,000 square miles
Capital: London
Language: English, Welsh and Gaelic
Currency: Pound Sterling

The United Kingdom is a constitutional monarchy governing Britain, the northern counties of Ireland and neighboring islands. The kingdoms of England and Scotland were united in 1603 when King James VI of Scotland inherited the English throne. The constitution allows for a single elected chamber together with a part-appointed, part-inherited House of Lords. The monarch in practice follows the wishes of Parliament. Agriculture is well developed and produces about half the nation's requirements. Industry and commerse are the basis of the economic wealth.

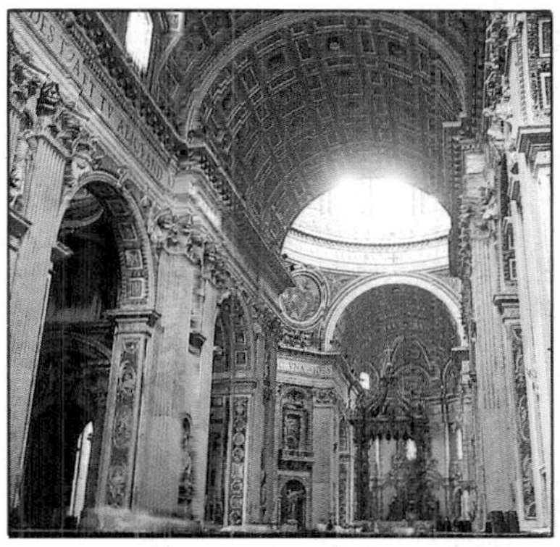

▲ *The interior of St Peter's, the Vatican.*

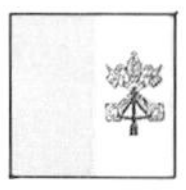

VATICAN

Population: 700
Area: 0.1 square miles
Capital: Vatican City
Language: Italian and Latin
Currency: Italian Lira

The Vatican is the smallest independent state in the world and exists solely as the residence of the Pope, the head of the Roman Catholic Church. Until 1860 the Pope ruled areas of central Italy, but these were incorporated into the Kingdom of Italy, which in 1870 invaded Rome and confined the Pope to the Vatican complex. In 1929 the Vatican was recognized as an independent state in return for the Pope relinquishing claims over Rome and surrounding territory. The Vatican is the administrative headquarters of the Catholic Church.

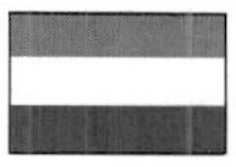

YUGOSLAVIA

(see separate listings for BOSNIA-HERZEGOVINA, CROATIA, MACEDONIA AND SLOVENIA)

Population: 10.2 million
Area: 40,000 square miles
Capital: Belgrade
Language: Serbo-Croatian
Currency: Yugoslav new Dinar

Yugoslavia came into being in 1918 as a confederation of southern Slavonic peoples newly independent of the Hapsburg Empire. A new constitution of 1946 made the nation a grouping of six republics, in which the Communist party was the only legal political party. Attempts in 1989-90 by the central government to curb the internal government of the republics led to widespread protest. When the republics of Slovenia, Croatia, Bosnia-Herzegovina and Macedonia seceded from Serbian-dominated Yugoslavia in 1991, a bloody civil war ensued. The new Yugoslavia was composed of Serbia, Montenegro and two formerly autonomous regions. The war continues, fueled by ancient political antagonisms and long-standing ethnic hostilities.

ASIA

*A*sia is the largest and most populated continent on Earth. Just two nations, China and India, between them account for nearly two billion inhabitants. An Asian country, Bangladesh is the most densely populated on Earth, with nearly 2,000 people to each square mile. This compares to about 65 per square mile in the United States.

The incredible population statistics are made possible by the remarkably fertile soils and productive climates of Asia. Bangladesh, for example, is almost ideal for rice cultivation. The monsoon climate provides the alternate wet and dry season needed by the cereal, while the flat landscape makes the flooding and draining of fields easy to accomplish. Massive crops are produced each year. Similar conditions prevail in eastern China, where rural populations have reached the saturation point in some areas.

But if Asia has been endowed with vast, life-giving resources, it also has its share of natural disasters. Earthquakes, floods and typhoons are common. Given the concentrated populations, these calamities claim horrendous death tolls among the local peoples. Many regions of Asia have a history scattered with the records of bumper crops leading to population booms, the children of which are then wiped out by disaster and famine.

Not only does Asia contain some of the densest populations in the world, it also boasts some of the emptiest regions anywhere. The vast expanses of Siberia consist of open tundra bordering the Arctic Ocean and, further south, extensive boreal forests. These great coniferous forests cover a staggering 2.7 billion acres and are thought to contain about one-quarter of all the world's trees.

In central eastern Asia there are extensive grasslands on which pastoral peoples lead traditional lives that have scarcely changed in centuries. Mongolia and neighboring sections of both China and the former Soviet Union are the home of ethnic Mongols, who herd cattle and horses on the open plains as their ancestors have done for millenia.

Ethnically, the population of Asia is incredibly diverse. In addition to recent immigrations of Europeans and Africans, there is a wide range of indigenous peoples. In the far east, Mongoloid races form the vast majority. In the subcontinent of India Indo-Europeans and Dravidians constitute the bulk of the population. Here, as elsewhere in Asia, there are remnant populations of far older peoples. The inland uplands of Sri Lanka are home to the Veddah, who are apparently unrelated to the majority population but have affinities with the Aboriginals of Australia. Similarly enigmatic are the Ainu of Japan.

Culturally, too, the Asians present a bewildering picture to the world. Asia has been the cradle of major world religions: Buddhism, Hinduism, Confucianism and Taoism all originated in Asia, and continue to find the bulk of their adherents on that continent. Islam, originating on the Arabian peninsula, has spread across much of southern Asia as far as the Pacific Ocean.

The vast continent of Asia is rich in both agricultural and human resources. However, much of the population continues to live at subsistence level. Great increases in the number of humans has kept pace with improved farming technology and crop increases, so that the per capita wealth remains low. National prosperity in most nations is devoted to finding food for their growing populations rather than improving living standards. So long as this cycle of improved food production and increased population continues, the traditional lifestyles and general impoverishment of Asia will probably continue.

▲ *The Himalayas, Nepal.*

▼ *Temple dancers, Bali, Indonesia.*

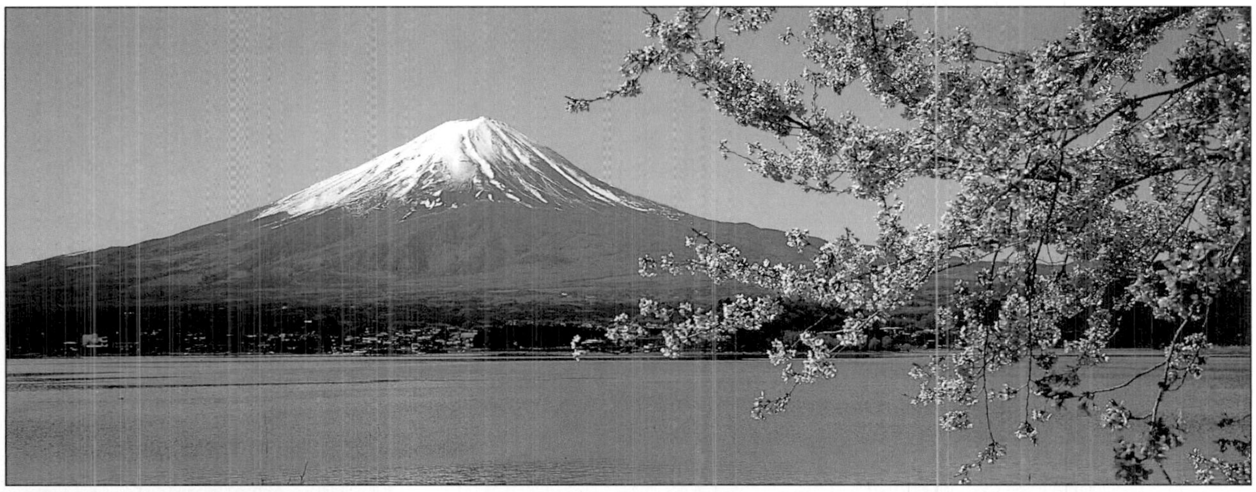

◀ *Lake Kawaguchi and Mount Fujiyama, Japan.*

▼ *A natural rock formation in Dukhan, Qatar.*

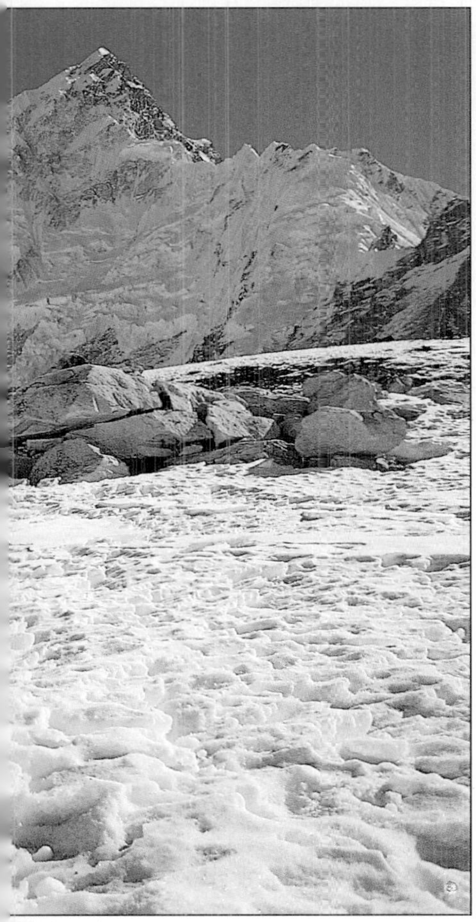

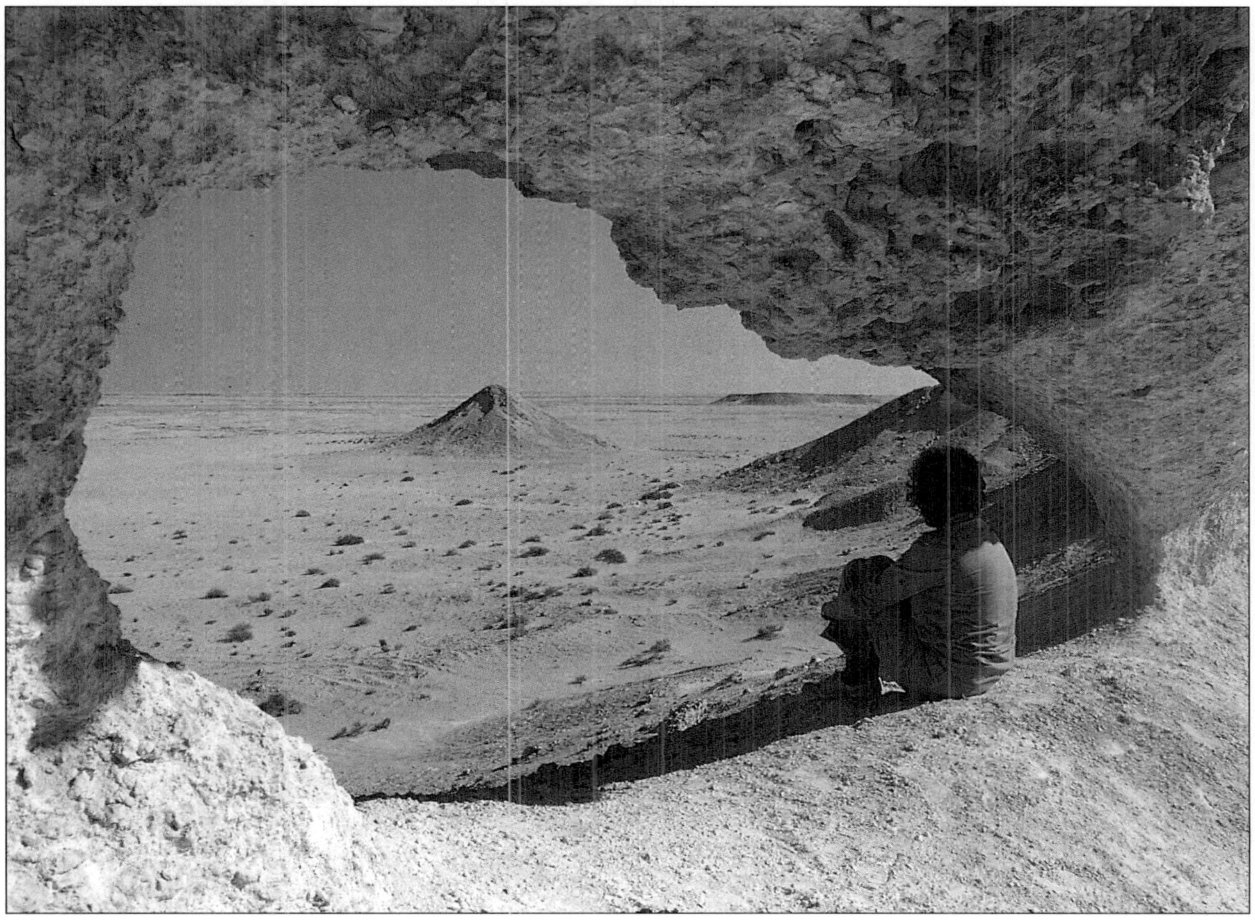

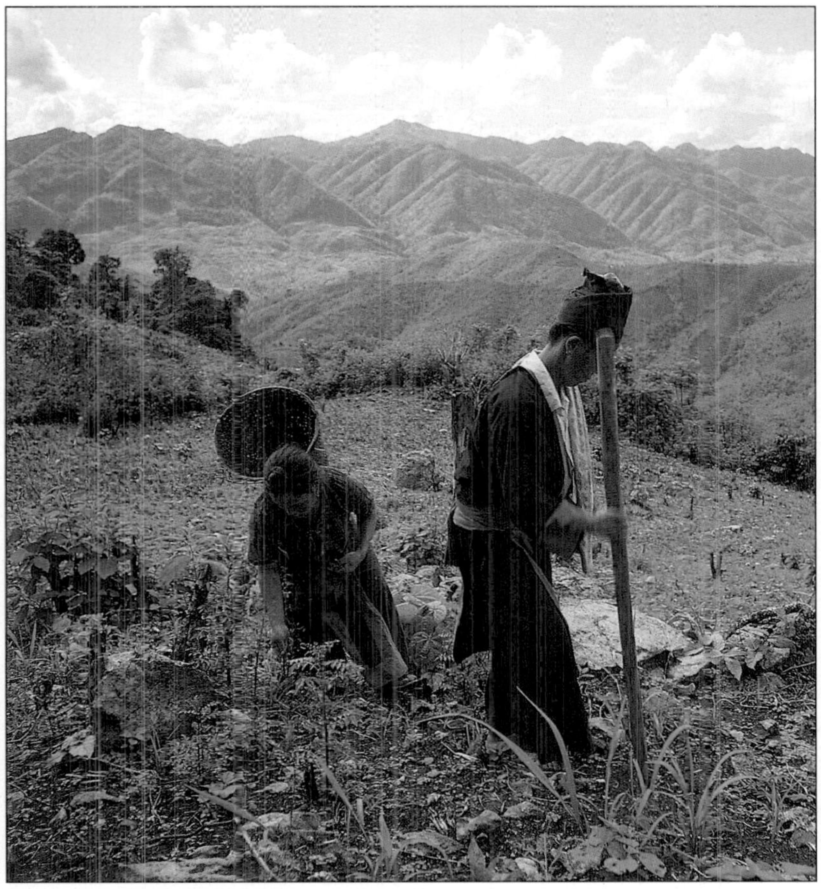

◀ *The back-breaking task of planting rice, Laos.*

▼ *The bustling city of Taipei, Taiwan.*

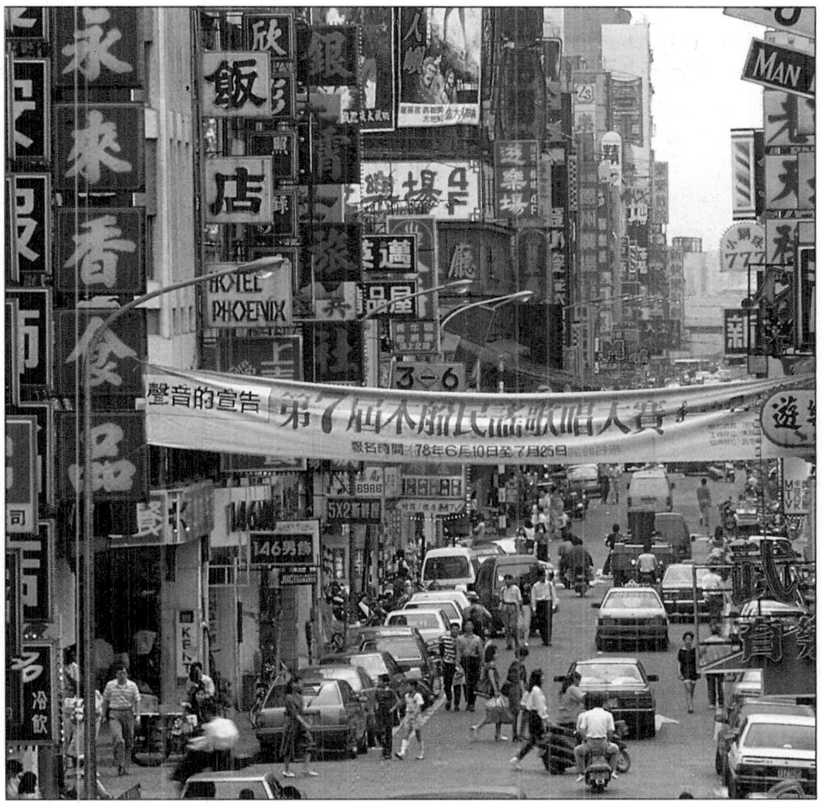
HOTEL PHOENIX

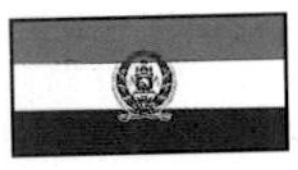

AFGHANISTAN

Population: 18 million
Area: 252,000 square miles
Capital: Kabul
Language: Pustu and Dari
Currency: Afghani

Afghanistan is a country in turmoil and has been for generations. The Soviet invasion of 1979 led to the various factions uniting against the aggressor. The withdrawal of Soviet troops has allowed the chieftains and religious leaders to resume their internal disputes. The mountainous republic has a long tradition of tribal independence and weak government control. The social structure remains fragmented, with most of the population belonging to distinctly different ethnic groups linked by the Islamic religion. The bulk of the population are subsistence farmers or nomadic herdsmen, the latter mainly in the south. Fruit, bread and sheep are the basis of the nation's self-produced food supply. The only mineral wealth is natural gas in the far north.

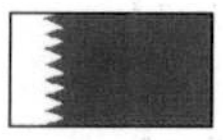

BAHRAIN

Population: 520,000
Area: 265 square miles
Capital: Manama
Language: Arabic
Currency: Bahraini Dinar

In 1882 the Emirate of Bahrain handed control of its foreign affairs to Britain, whose navy was in the process of suppressing the endemic piracy of the Arabian Gulf. In 1971 the arrangement was ended and the Emir proclaimed his nation's independence and soon after dismissed Parliament to rule the nation himself. Until 1931 Bahrain was an impoverished state subsisting on pearl fishing, small-scale agriculture and the profits of trade. The discovery of oil changed everything, and vast wealth poured into the nation. The thirty-three islands now support a flourishing manufacturing economy, including the production of aluminum alloys, ships and medical equipment. So many people now live in Bahrain that ninety percent of food needs to be imported and water supply is a chronic problem.

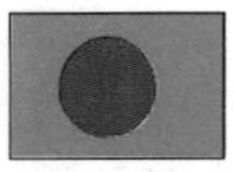

BANGLADESH

Population: 111 million
Area: 56,000 square miles
Capital: Dhaka
Language: Bangla and English
Currency: Taka

In a good year Bangladesh is almost ideally suited to intensive cultivation of rice. As many as three heavy crops can be grown on the rich soils within just twelve months. As a consequence, the nation is extremely densely populated by peasant farmers growing crops for their own consumption and for sale. Unfortunately, recurrent natural disasters, such as floods and cyclones, take a heavy toll in human life and destroy crops. The extremely high birth rate causes an ever-growing population that ensures that the agricultural wealth is fully used feeding the people rather than in improving their living conditions. Other than glass sand, mineral deposits scarcely exist, and industry is negligible. The government is notoriously unstable, having suffered numerous coups and military takeovers since independence from Pakistan in 1971.

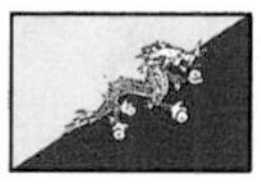

BHUTAN

Population: 1.5 million
Area: 18,000 square miles
Capital: Thimphu
Language: Dzongkha, Nepalese, English
Currency: Ngultrum

The mountain kingdom of Bhutan is an anomaly in India, having managed to retain its quasi-independence when Britain withdrew from the subcontinent, while other kingdoms became merged into the new state of India. Bhutan receives an annual subsidy from India in return for abiding by that country's foreign policy. Internal government is conducted by the king, with the advice of an elected assembly. The electoral system is unusual in that each family has one vote regardless of its number, and monks are separately represented. Bhutan is made up of a number of valleys isolated from each other by precipitous mountains and sheer cliffs. The different ethnic groups have scarcely mixed, and they retain their identities. The basis of the economy is agriculture, with many hill tribes surviving at subsistence level. Large mineral deposits have been found but the difficult terrain has hampered exploitation.

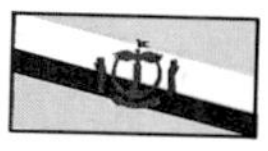

BRUNEI

Population: 268,000
Area: 2,000 square miles
Capital: Bandar Seri Begawan
Language: Malay and English
Currency: Brunei Dollar

The Sultan of Brunei is reputed to the be the richest man on earth, with a personal fortune of about $26 billion. This massive wealth is based on the oilfields of Brunei and on the fact that all national finance is conducted through the Sultan. The first oil well was drilled in 1929, and since that time fresh reserves have been continually identified. Oil production remains high and is the basis of the nation's wealth. The Sultan is currently encouraging the growth of other businesses in order to limit his people's dependence on international oil prices. The traditional industries of boat-building, silversmithing and weaving remain in operation, and the agriculture of the tropical country continues to produce rubber, fruits and rice.

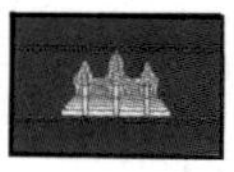

CAMBODIA (Formerly Kampuchea)

Population: 9 million
Area: 27,000 square miles
Capital: Phnom Penh
Language: Khmer and Chinese
Currency: Riel

In the last two decades the formerly wealthy kingdom of Cambodia, has been plunged into a vicious maelstrom of violence, hardship and poverty. In 1970 Prince Sihanouk was ousted from power by a republican movement. When the Vietnam war spilled into Cambodia in 1975, the Communist Khmer Rouge movement took power. This new regime abolished money, expelled foreigners, closed the borders and forced city dwellers to move to the countryside. Mass executions followed any attempt at protest, and it is thought that fifteen percent of the population died in these years. Vietnamese troops imposed a new government in 1979. Nationalist resistance under both Prince Sihanouk and the Khmer Rouge began a civil war interrupted by fragile peace agreements that continues to this day. The former cash crops and industries have been destroyed, and the population relies on subsistence agriculture.

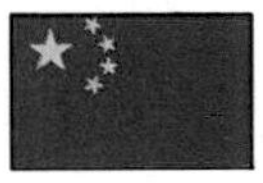

CHINA (PEOPLE'S REPUBLIC)

Population: 1.17 billion
Area: 3,700,000 square miles
Capital: Peking
Language: Mandarin and numerous dialects
Currency: Renminbi Yuan

With a civilization dating back at least 3,500 years, China has one of the oldest cultures on earth. Despite periods of civil war and instability, there has been a constant pressure for unity among the Chinese, principally to resist the incursions of foreign barbarians. The Empire collapsed in 1912, to be replaced by the rule of several warlords. The Communist Party restored unity in 1949 under Chairman Mao and has held power since. The violent repression by the government of a pro-democracy movement in 1989 triggered international condemnation of China's domestic policies. China's economy is based on intensive cultivation of rice, wheat and beans together with the raising of cattle, pigs and sheep. Small-scale, traditional industries are carried on within villages, but large, state-run factories in the cities produce silk, cotton and heavy industrial goods, both for internal consumption and export. Liberalized economic policies, such as the creation of special economic zones and of Western-style stock exchanges, helped to spur an expansion of the economy in the early 1990s.

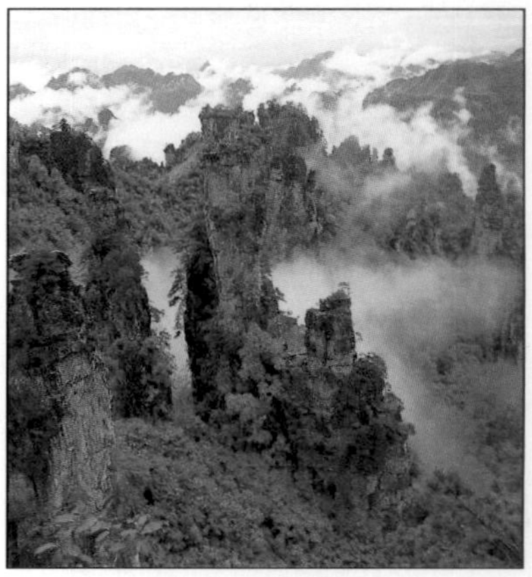

▲ *Tianzi Mountains, China.*

▼ *The ancient town of Dalĭ, China.*

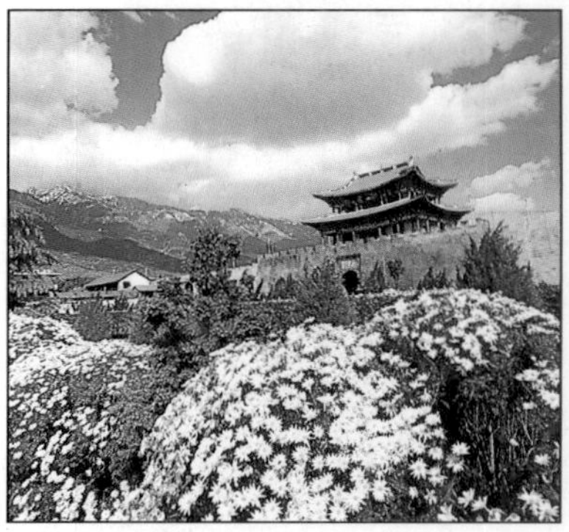

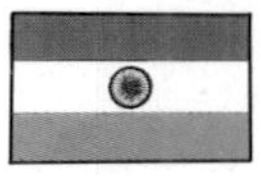

INDIA

Population: 890 million
Area: 1,222,000 square miles
Capital: New Delhi
Language: Hindi, English and various regional languages
Currency: Rupee

The most populous democracy in the world has experienced unrest in recent years with the assassination of two prime ministers and demands for independence by ethnic minorities. Despite this, however, the polyglot nation remains intact, and the processes of democracy have not been overthrown. The present Indian state originated in 1947, when the provinces of British India gained independence and joined with several semi-independent monarchies to form a federal union. The economic base of the nation is agriculture, which has benefited from modern technology in recent years, ensuring that famines are a thing of the past. Rice and wheat are the main crops, though beans and sugar are also produced. Tea is grown in large quantities for export, and coffee production is increasing. Industry has grown in recent years, but remains at a low technical level and chiefly supplies local demand.

▲ *Dusty hill-country, Afghanistan.*

▶ *Tropical rain forest, Brunei.*

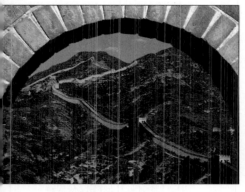

▲ *Zhang Jia Khou Pass, Great Wall, China.*

▲ *Ceremonial costumes, Bhutan.*

▼ *The 'Wailing Wall', Jerusalem, Israel.*

▲ *New development in oil-rich Bahrain.*

▼ *In the Golden Temple of Amritsar, India.*

▲ *Low-lying Bangladesh, veined by rivers.*

▼ *14th Ramadhan Mosque, Baghdad, Iraq.*

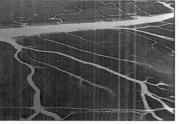

◀ *Tehran, capital of Iran.*

INDONESIA

Population: 185 million
Area: 741,000 square miles
Capital: Jakarta
Language: Malay, Indonesian, English and Dutch
Currency: Rupiah

The East Indies, of which area Indonesia occupies a large percentage, were previously famous as the Spice Islands, from which came mace, nutmeg, cinnamon and pepper to grace the cuisines of the world. So valuable was this trade that fierce battles were fought along the trade routes and for control of the islands themselves. In the early 17th century the Dutch gained dominance of the islands and remained the ruling power until the Japanese invasion of 1941. Independence came in 1949; since then the islands have experienced periods of both democracy and dictatorship. Spices are now negligible in the Indonesian economy. Oil fields are dominant, producing most of southern Asia's oil, backed by copper and manufactured goods. Agriculture employs many people in the production of rice, cassava and sweet potatoes for local consumption and coffee, rubber and coconuts for export.

IRAN

Population: 60 million
Area: 636,000 square miles
Capital: Tehran
Language: Persian, Kurdish and Arabic
Currency: Rial

In 1979 a popular revolution overthrew the monarchy and established an Islamic Republic under the religious control of the Ayatollah Khomeni. This event marked a fundamentalist revival of Islam, which has been felt elsewhere throughout the Islamic world. The basis of the modern Iranian economy is oil, which was discovered in 1908. The industry has suffered several setbacks with the destruction of refineries and ports during the Iran-Iraq War of 1980-88, but oil remains the chief export and currency earner. Other minerals exist in some quantity but are exploited on only a modest scale. Most of the country is unsuited to agriculture due to the lack of rain, but crops include wheat and barley. Millions of sheep, cattle and goats are grazed on the sparse grasslands.

IRAQ

Population: 19 million
Area: 168,000 square miles
Capital: Baghdad
Language: Arabic and Kurdish
Currency: Iraqi Dinar

The economy of Iraq was severely disrupted by the Persian Gulf War of 1990-91 and has not yet recovered. The war began in August 1990 when Iraq invaded Kuwait without warning and announced the annexation of that state. International forces gathered in Saudi Arabia while attempts were made to persuade Iraq to withdraw. On January 16, Operation Desert Storm began with allied air strikes on Iraqi positions, and in February a lightning land campaign crushed the Iraqi army and liberated Kuwait. International sanctions on Iraq crippled its economy, which before the war was based on oil exports. Internally, agriculture is a major employer, and large crops can be raised in the fertile Tigris-Euphrates Valley. Industry was poorly developed before hostilities. The nation is ruled by the Ba'th Party, led by Saddam Hussein, the country's President.

ISRAEL

Population: 5 million
Area: 8,000 square miles
Capital: Jerusalem
Language: Hebrew, Arabic and English
Currency: Shekel

The six pointed Star of David dominates the flag of Israel, symbolizing the overwhelming Jewish heritage of the nation. The state of Israel came into being in 1948 as a homeland for Jews from around the world. The demand for a Jewish state became especially strong after Jewish persecution by the Nazis. As soon as Israel came into being it was invaded by Arab states, and the nation's history has been dominated by intermittent warfare and constant terrorist activities to the present day. Israel currently occupies large areas of territory that officially belong to neighboring states. The nation has few mineral resources, and agriculture is only possible in irrigated areas. Israel produces much of its own food, and its manufacturing industries are healthy.

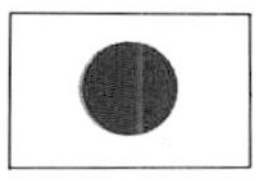

JAPAN

Population: 124 million
Area: 146,000 square miles
Capital: Tokyo
Language: Japanese
Currency: Yen

The Emperor of Japan belongs to a family that has occupied the throne for many centuries, reputedly since the sun goddess began the dynasty in around 600 BC. For many years the nation was actually ruled by powerful noblemen known as Shogun, but the Emperor regained power in 1867, and in 1947 the present democratic constitution was introduced. Since the devastation of World War II, Japan has fully revitalized its industry and is now a major economic world power. The most important industries are iron and steel, automobiles, electronics and chemicals, in which Japan leads the world in technical expertise as well as profitable productivity. The small area of land suitable for agriculture is intensively worked to produce rice, fruit and livestock, but the nation needs to import most of its food.

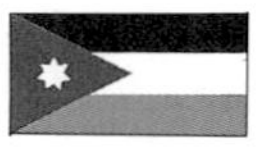

JORDAN

Population: 3.6 million
Area: 35,000 square miles
Capital: Amman
Language: Arabic
Currency: Jordanian Dinar

The Kingdom of Jordan is ruled by King Hussein, last surviving monarch of the four Arab kingdoms established following the collapse of the Ottoman Empire in 1918. Political parties have recently been legalized in the kingdom, though elections to Parliament have not been called. During the 1967 war with Israel, Jordan lost control of the West Bank of the Jordan River which remains under Israeli control. This entailed the loss of nearly half of the kingdom's fertile land, a serious blow to an economy dependent on agriculture. The farmland of Jordan produces large quantities of tomatoes, olives and citrus fruits. Livestock is grazed on the arid grasslands and near desert of the east. Industry is dependent on the mining and processing of phosphates and potash.

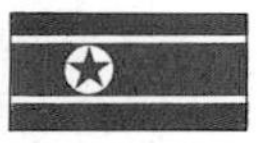

KOREA (NORTH)

Population: 22 million
Area: 47,000 square miles
Capital: Pyongyang
Language: Korean
Currency: Won

In 1945 the defeat of Japan in World War II led to a joint occupation of Korea by Russian and American forces. In 1948 the Russian zone declared itself the People's Democratic Republic of Korea and established a Communist state. Kim Il Sung took power at that time, ruling as Prime Minister until 1972 and as President thereafter. At elections only one Communist candidate is allowed and, it is claimed, these attract the votes of over ninety-five percent of the electorate. Industry, developed during the Japanese occupation, has been enhanced by government plans, and Korea now produces iron and steel in quantity and is a major shipbuilding power. Agriculture is also state-run, and rice, corn and potatoes are produced in large quantities.

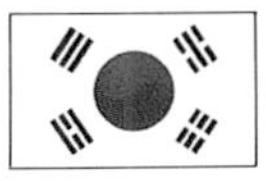

KOREA (SOUTH)

Population: 44 million
Area: 39,000 square miles
Capital: Seoul
Language: Korean
Currency: Won

Following liberation from Japan, Korea was divided into Russian and American areas. In 1948 the American zone became the Republic of Korea, with a democratic constitution. In 1950 North Korea invaded in an attempt to reunite the nation under Communism. International forces backed the South, while China supported the Communist forces. In 1953 a ceasefire was agreed upon, but no peace treaty has ever been signed. Political life in South Korea has been unstable, with military rule and political murders. The current democratic government began in 1980. Agriculture remains important in the South Korean economy, with large quantities of rice, radishes and fruits being produced. Industry has increased dramatically in recent years and now accounts for about half of the economy. Major industries include electronics, shipbuilding, textiles, apparel and motor vehicles.

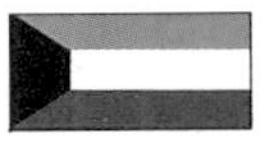

KUWAIT

Population: 1.2 million
Area: 7,000 square miles
Capital: Kuwait City
Language: Arabic
Currency: Kuwait Dinar

Kuwait is an hereditary Emirate on the Arabian Gulf that has been ruled by the same family since 1756. In 1899 the Emirate placed itself under British protection and regained full independence in 1961. In 1990 Kuwait was invaded and overrun by Iraqi forces that annexed the nation. American forces, together with allied troops under combined commands, liberated Kuwait in 1991 after Kuwait's oil wells were left flaming by the war, and many burned for months. The economy of Kuwait is almost entirely dependent on its vast oil reserves, which bring in large quantities of foreign money. The Emir was attempting to use this money to diversify the economy before the war. Postwar efforts were devoted to rebuilding Kuwait's infrastructure. There were also some tentative political reforms.

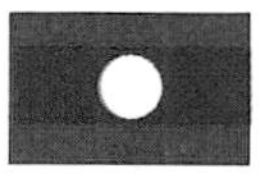

LAOS

Population: 4.4 million
Area: 92,000 square miles
Capital: Vientiane
Language: Lao and French
Currency: Kip

The modern state of Laos is unusual in having been founded

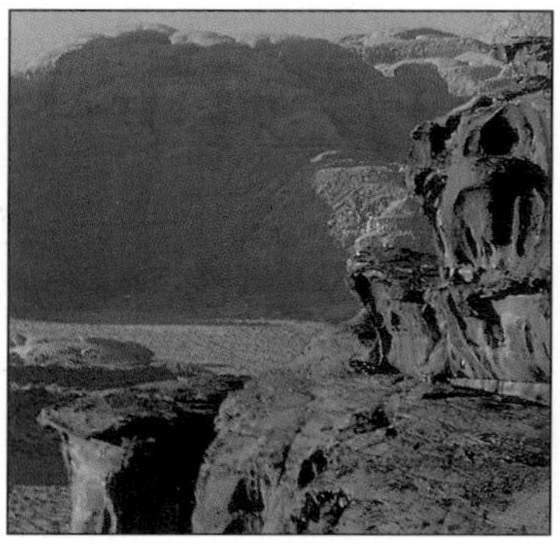

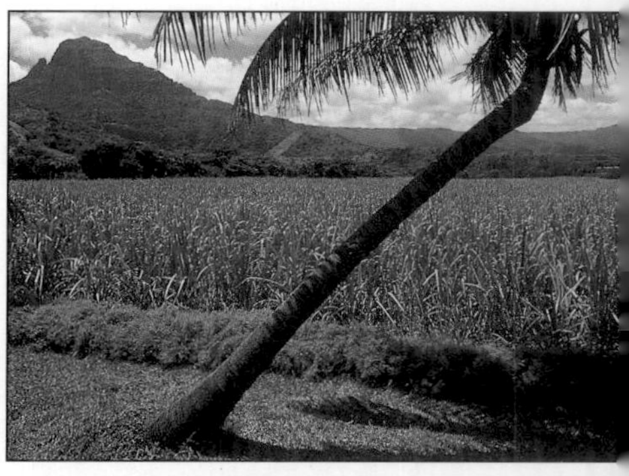

▲ *Wadi Kum, Jordan.*

Above right: *The volcanic islnd of Mauritius.*

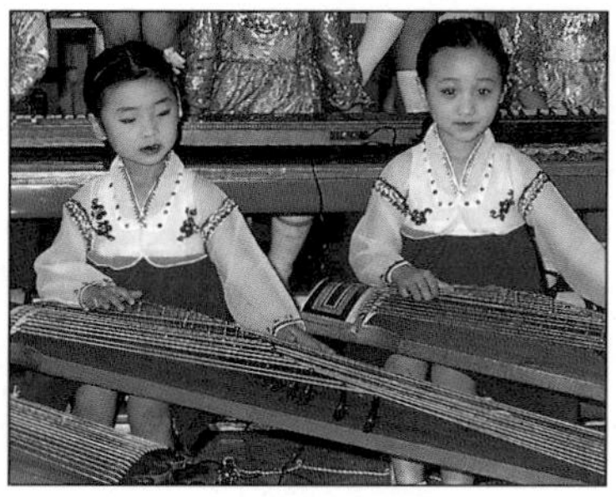

▲ *A children's orchestra, North Korea.*

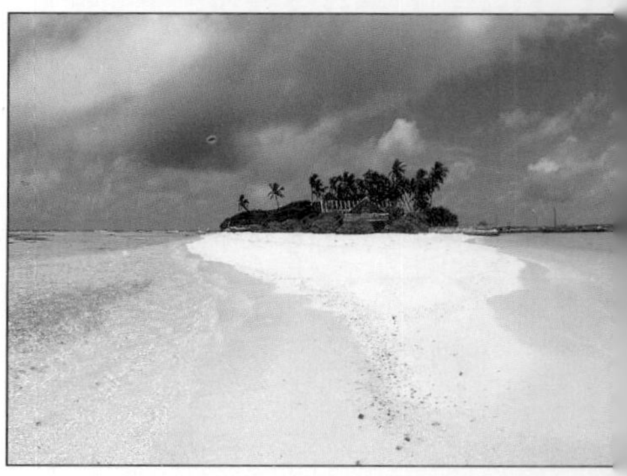

▲ *Stormy skies over the Maldives.*

▼ *Waiting for gasoline, Kuwait.*

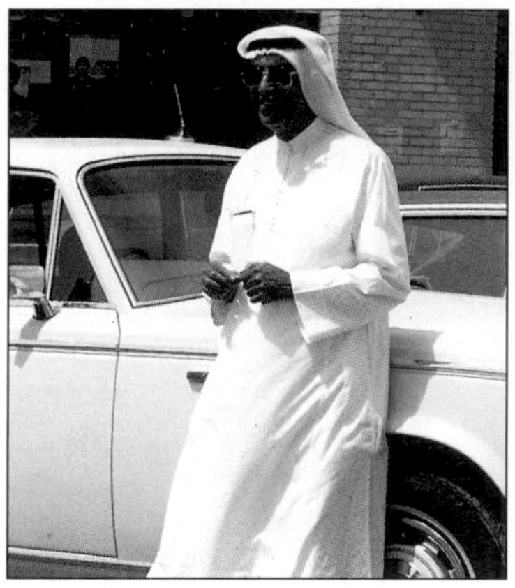

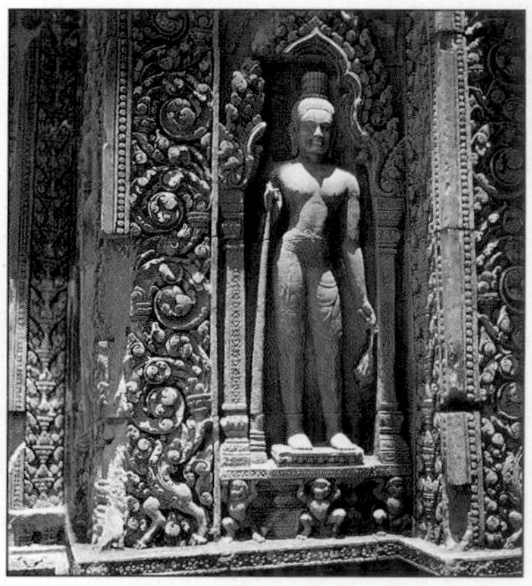

▲ *Angkor Wat, Cambodia.*

▼ *Rice field, Malaysia.*

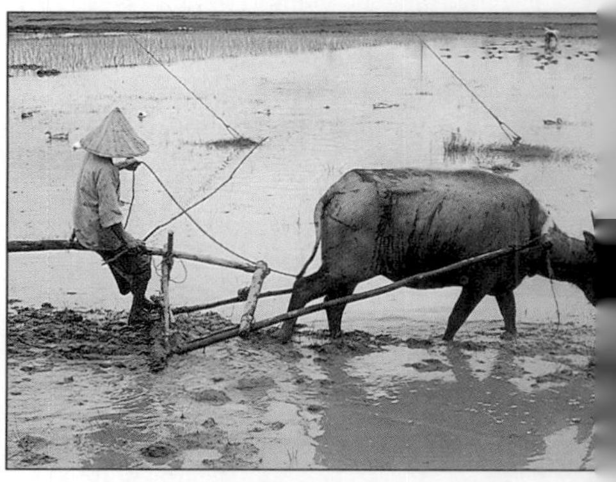

▼ *Misfat Oasis, Oman.*

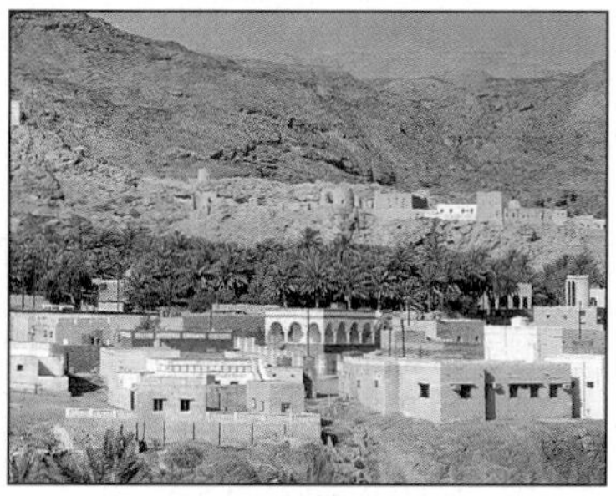

► *Beirut, capital of Lebanon.*

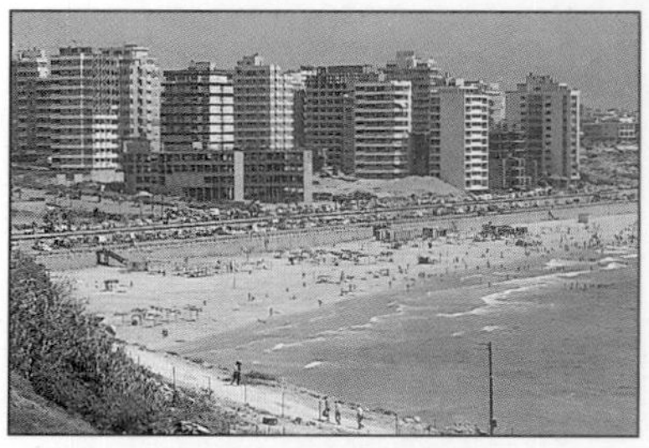

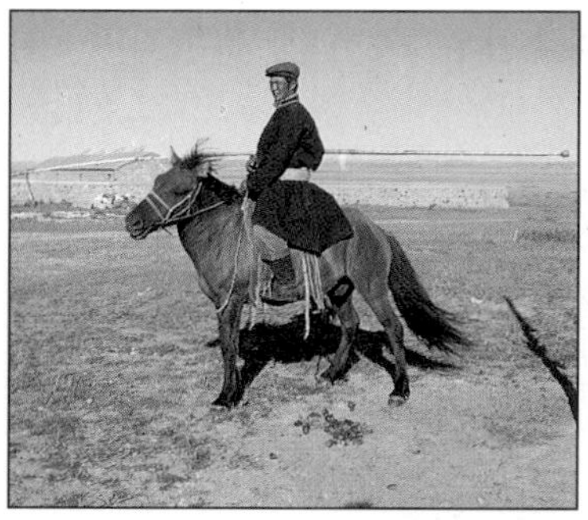

▲ *On the grass plains of Mongolia.*

► *Agriculture in South Korea.*

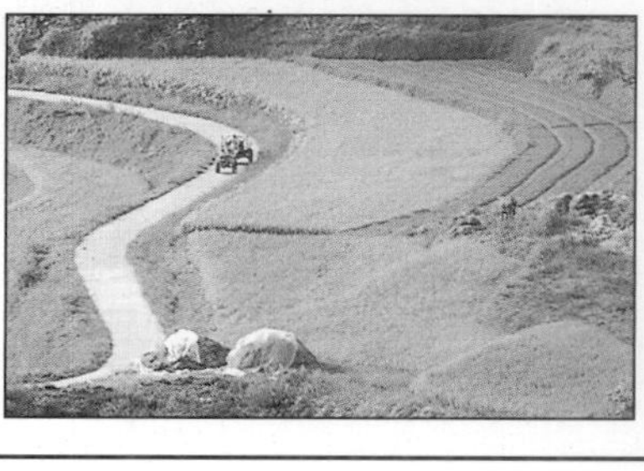

by a Communist movement led by a royal prince. When the French relinquished colonial control of the Lao people in 1947, a constitutional monarchy was established. The discontented Prince Souphanouvong, however, allied himself with Communists from North Vietnam and began a rebellion. This culminated in 1975 with the collapse of the Royal government and the installation of a Communist state under the Pathet Lao party. The nation is predominantly agricultural, with many of the Lao raising rice in the valleys of the various rivers of Laos. The mountainous interior and poor communications have made exploitation of mineral deposits difficult, and industry is at only a rudimentary level.

LEBANON

Population: 2.8 million
Area: 4,000 square miles
Capital: Beirut
Language: Arabic and French
Currency: Lebanese Pound

Lebanon is best known for the factional violence that has torn this previously-prosperous nation apart. During the 1960s the Moslem Palestinian Liberation Organization began using bases in southern Lebanon to attack Israel. This led to great tension between the Christians and Moslems within Lebanon, and civil war broke out in 1975. Israel invaded in 1982, occupying much of southern Lebanon. Syrian troops are present in many areas of the country in an attempt to enforce a ceasefire among the factions. Lebanon has a constitution with an elected Assembly and a President, but real power remains with the factional guerillas. Lebanon is now a basically agricultural nation, having lost its banking, manufacturing and tourist industries during the civil war.

MALAYSIA

Population: 19 million
Area: 127,000 square miles
Capital: Kuala Lumpur
Language: Malay, Chinese and English
Currency: Ringgit

The government of Malaysia is unique in that the nine rajahs and sultans meet every five years to elect one of their number to be the supreme ruler, or Yang de-Pertuan Agong. Operating under the head of state is a Parliament elected from the states, in which political power is vested. The nation is among the most prosperous of Southeast Asia, having a highly diversified economy. Exports are dominated in value by manufactured goods, though agri-

culture provides employment for most people. The lush farmland not only produces food for internal consumption but also exports cash crops such as rubber, cocoa, tobacco, sugar cane and tea. There are substantial deposits of tin in the country, together with oilfields, which add to the national wealth.

MALDIVES

Population: 230,000
Area: 116 square miles
Capital: Male
Language: Divehi
Currency: Rufiyaa

Scattered across the Indian Ocean, southwest of India, the Maldives number around 1,200 islands, but only 202 are inhabited. The islands were dominated by the Arabs from around 1100, and Islam is the dominant religion among the mixed population of Arabs and the Sinhalese from India. Britain established a protectorate over the local Sultanate in 1887 and returned full independence in 1965. The Sultan was overthrown and a republic established in 1968. The coral islands lack mineral wealth, and only small patches of land are suitable for farming. The economy is based on fishing, tourism and the processing of coconuts and reeds into craftwork for sale abroad.

MAURITIUS

Population: 1 million
Area: 772 square miles
Capital: Port Louis
Language: English
Currency: Mauritius Rupee

Mauritius is composed of a number of islands in the Indian Ocean. The two largest islands, Mauritius itself and Rodrigues, are separated by more than 300 miles of open ocean. The rocky volcanic islands have an economy based on the production of sugar. Sugar cane covers most of the arable land, and industry is dominated by sugar refineries. Tobacco and tea are also grown for export, while corn, beef and goat meat are produced for internal consumption. Fishing also provides employment. The government is a democracy based on universal suffrage, producing an assembly that elects a Prime Minister who appoints a cabinet.

MONGOLIA

Population: 2 million
Area: 605,000 square miles
Capital: Ulan Bator
Language: Mongol
Currency: Tugrik

During the early 13th century the Mongols conquered a massive

empire encompassing China, Central Asia and parts of eastern Europe. By the late 17th century, however, the Mongols had fallen under Chinese control. In 1924 the Mongols, with Soviet support, drove the Chinese out and declared an independent Mongolian nation. The new Communist government suppressed traditional Buddhist and Shamanist religions and pursued a policy of farm collectivization and industrialization, which has been partially successful. However, the majority of the population still leads a traditional nomadic lifestyle, caring for herds of livestock. Millions of cattle, horses, sheep and goats are driven across the vast grasslands by expert horsemen. In 1990 the Communist Party allowed free elections for the first time and retained power with a large majority.

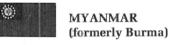

MYANMAR
(formerly Burma)

Population: 44 million
Area: 261,000 square miles
Capital: Yangon (Rangoon)
Language: Burmese, Thai, English
Currency: Kyat

Myanmar, long known as Burma, has a history of upheaval, fragmentation and unification. The process continues today, with vociferous separatist movements among the various minority populations which live in the country. Since Burma was granted its freedom by Britain in 1947, there have been numerous coups and attempted coups. The military junta which seized power in 1988 held democratic elections but power remains with the army, which numbers over 200,000. Myanmar is dominated by traditional agriculture, based on rice, cattle and pigs, which flourishes in the wet tropical climate of the region. Industrial activity is mainly concerned with processing cash crops of sugar and cotton or with manufacturing fertilizer and agricultural tools.

NEPAL

Population: 19.8 million
Area: 57,000 square miles
Capital: Kathmandu
Language: Nepali
Currency: Nepalese Rupee

The mountain kingdom of Nepal is unique in having the only flag that is not rectangular in shape. The traditional triangular banner carries a sun to represent the ruling Maharaja and a moon to symbolize the prime minister, until 1951 an hereditary post. Nepal pursued a policy of isolation until the mid-1950s; since then the economy has been slowly modernized. Many Nepalese live in inaccessible

mountain valleys where they continue to practice traditional farming techniques. Others produce cash crops of herbs and potatoes or keep cattle to produce ghee, a form of clarified butter. A valuable source of foreign currency comes from the Gurkha troops recruited in Nepal to serve in the British army. Under a constitution introduced in 1990 the Maharaja permits political parties and free elections.

OMAN

Population: 1.6 million
Area: 116,000 square miles
Capital: Muscat
Language: Arabic
Currency: Rial

Until 1937 the Sultanate of Oman was a somewhat impoverished Moslem state relying upon fishing and date production for its livelihood. In that year, however, oil was discovered, and although reserves are not vast it is the petrochemical industry that dominates. The Sultan is attempting to diversify the economy by improving agriculture and the fishing industry. Copper mining in the interior is being encouraged, but further mineral exploitation is hampered by the fact that Oman's borders with both Saudi Arabia and the Yemen are in dispute. Oman has no constitution and is ruled by decrees issued by the Sultan. There is, however, a State Council composed of prominent citizens that the Sultan may call for consultation on important issues.

▲ *Honeymoon Lake, Pakistan.*

PAKISTAN

Population: 130 million
Area: 307,000 square miles
Capital: Islamabad
Language: Urdu, Punjabi, Sindi and English
Currency: Pakistan Rupee

The nation of Pakistan was created in 1947 by the British as an Islamic homeland after fears were expressed by the Moslems about joining a Hindu-dominated India. The population is united by its religion, but otherwise is very diverse, with occasional calls for independence by various ethnic groups. Periods of democracy have alternated with military rule, and there have been frequent charges of corruption in both types of government. The economy is based upon agriculture, which employs over half the workforce. The irrigated plains around the Indus and its tributaries produce large quantities of rice, wheat and sugar for internal consumption and some cotton for export. Tax and economy laws favor the peasant smallholder with fewer than twenty-five acres to farm.

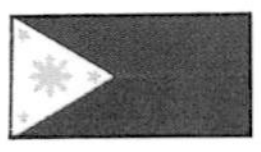

PHILIPPINES

Population: 64 million
Area: 116,000 square miles
Capital: Manila
Language: Filipino, Spanish, English and tribal languages
Currency: Philippine Peso

The Philippines contain over 7,000 islands, but very few of these are inhabited and most do not even have names. From about 1550 Spain gradually acquired control over the profitable Spice Islands of the Philippines and ruled until 1898, when the United States took over. Independence was achieved in 1946, and since that time a fragile democracy has been interrupted by military coups, fraudulent elections and massive corruption. The Philippines is an agricultural nation with rice, corn and coconuts as the main crops. Many coastal villages depend on fishing for income. The mining of nickel, zinc and copper lead the mining industry, while manufacturing is rapidly gaining in importance. The nation remains dependent on imported food and materials.

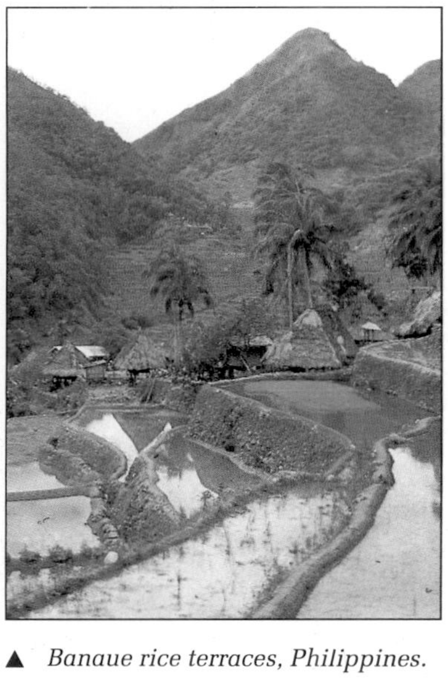

▲ *Banaue rice terraces, Philippines.*

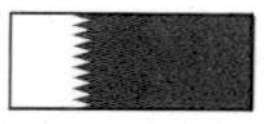

QATAR

Population: 520,000
Area: 4,000 square miles
Capital: Doha
Language: Arabic
Currency: Qatar Riyal

The long, streaming banner of the Emirate of Qatar is based upon the red and white banner imposed by Britain in the 19th century on all Gulf states that were party to an anti-pirate agreement. Britain controlled foreign policy until 1971, when the Emir was granted full independence. The Emir is an absolute monarch who rules by decree, but an Advisory Council of prominent citizens is consulted on major issues. Oil was first exploited during the 1950s and since then has come to dominate the economy. Oil revenue is being used to improve agriculture and fishing, with the long-term aim of the country becoming self-sufficient. Industry is also being encouraged. Most of Qatar is desert, thinly populated by nomadic Bedouin tribes. Lack of water is a perennial problem.

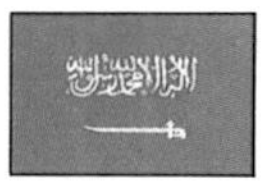

SAUDI ARABIA

Population: 15 million
Area: 850,000 square miles
Capital: Riyadh
Language: Arabic
Currency: Saudi Riyal

The religious kingdom of Saudi Arabia was carved out of the deserts by the aristocratic Saud family of the Wahhabi Islamic sect early in the 20th century and was internationally recognized as recently as 1927. The king is also custodian of the holy mosques, and the power structure is based upon Koranic law, though an assembly may be consulted by the king if he wishes. The desert kingdom began producing oil in 1937, and the economy rapidly shifted away from traditional reliance on dates and nomadic herds to concentrate on petrochemicals. There has also been some diversification into light industry and the production of plastics as a byproduct of oil refining. In 1990-91, U.S. and other foreign troops and Saudi forces forced Iraq out of Kuwait in the Persian Gulf War.

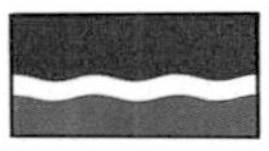

SEYCHELLES

Population: 71,000
Area: 175.6 square miles
Capital: Victoria
Language: English and French
Currency: Seychelles Rupee

When Portuguese sailors discovered the Seychelles in the 16th century, they were uninhabited, and not until the 1770s was permanent colonization begun by France. Britain acquired the islands in 1810, and independence was granted in 1976. A coup took place within a year of independence, and the Seychelles are now a one-party state. Tourism is the major industry on the islands, with about 100,000 people visiting each year. The idyllic coral islands, rugged granite peaks and tropical climate make the Seychelles a popular vacation resort for those able to reach them. The large fishing fleet catches tuna

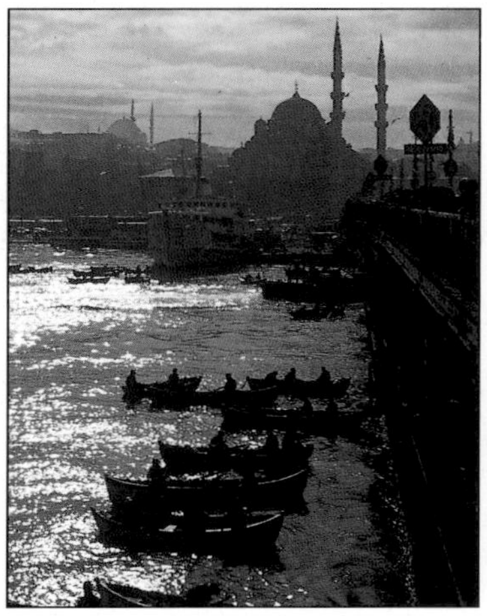

▲ *Istanbul, Turkey, at dusk.*

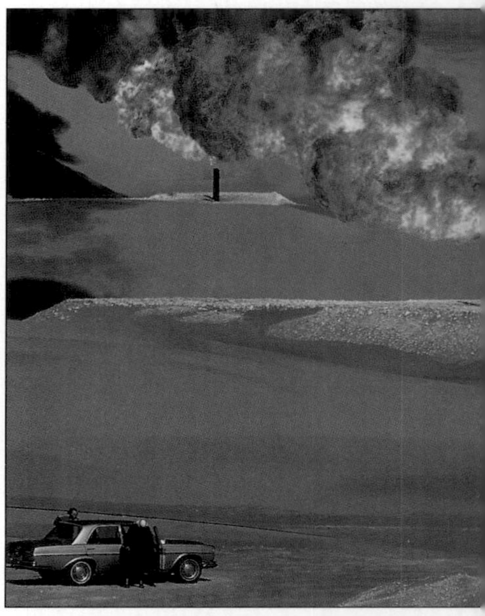

► *Abu Dhabi, United Arab Emirates.*

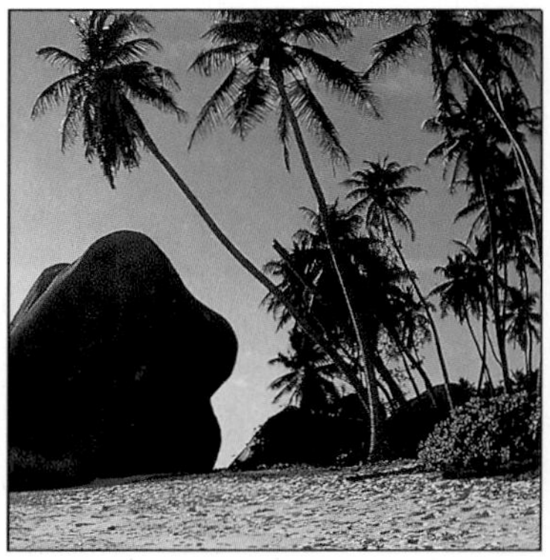

▲ *La Digue, Seychelles.*

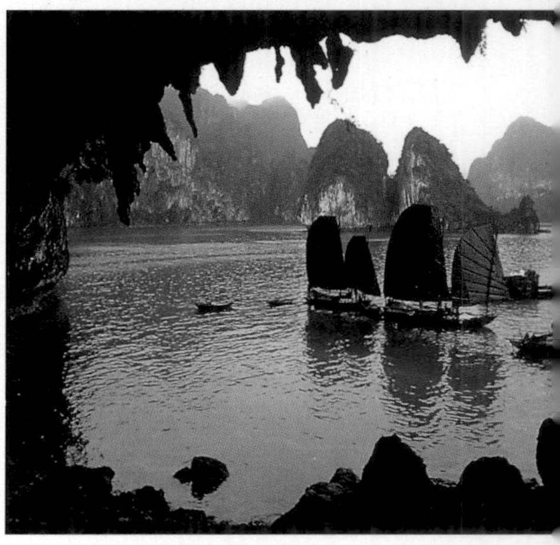

▲ *Sailing junks, Vietnam.*

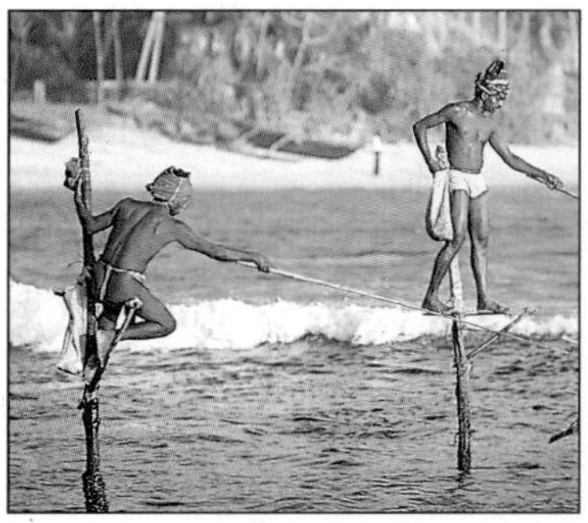

◄ *Stilt fishermen, Sri Lanka.*

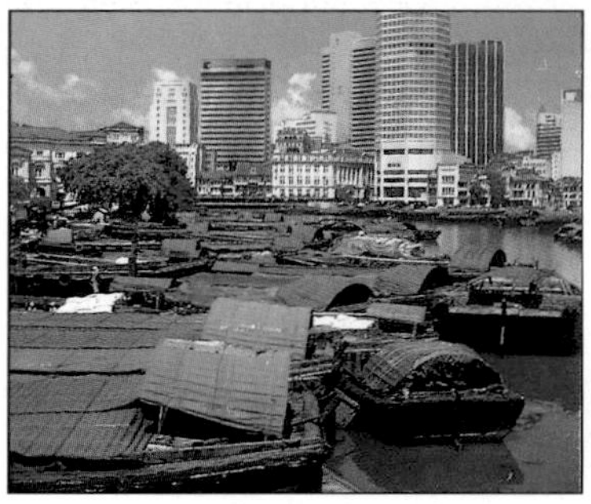

▲ *The Singapore River, Singapore.*

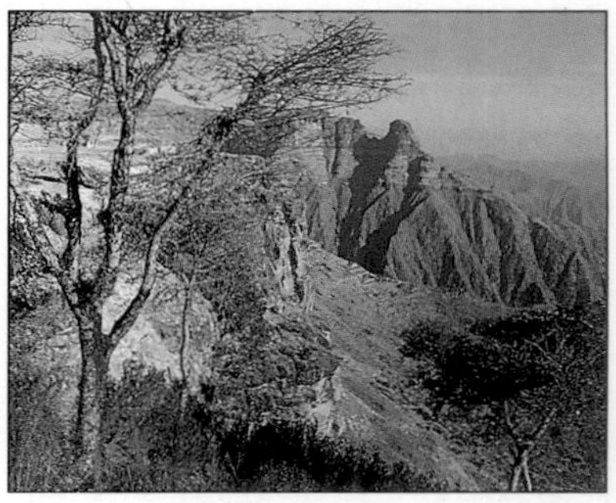

▲ *A Yemeni landscape.*

▼ *Damascus, Syria.*

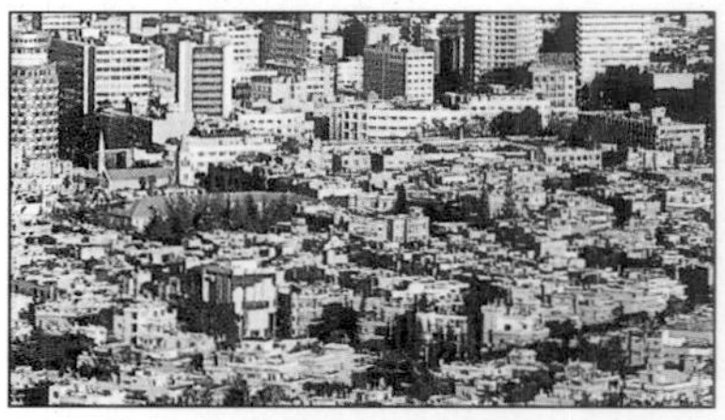

▼ *Mecca, Saudi Arabia.*

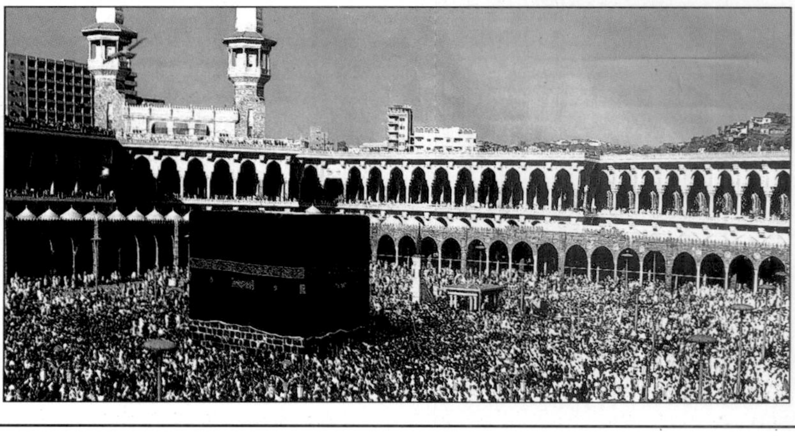

for canning and export, while coconuts and cinnamon are the main cash crops.

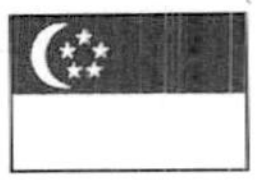

SINGAPORE

Population: 2.8 million
Area: 241.3 square miles
Capital: Singapore
Language: English, Chinese and Malay
Currency: Singapore Dollar

The city state of Singapore was founded by Sir Stamford Raffles in 1819 as a trading port of the British East India Company. Since that date the city has flourished as a trading and manufacturing center. Singapore passed from the Company to the British Government in the 19th century before acquiring independence in 1965. Though it has no mineral resources and virtually no farmland, Singapore is a leading economic power in Asia. Commercial and merchant banks number almost 200, and together provide the economic mainspring for much of Southeast Asia. The manufacturing base is diverse, including the processing of chemicals, food, rubber and textiles. The state is a democracy with free elections though power is almost monopolized by a single party.

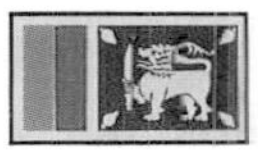

SRI LANKA

Population: 17 million
Area: 25,000 square miles
Capital: Colombo
Language: Sinhala, Tamil and English
Currency: Sri Lankan Rupee

Sri Lankan politics are dominated by ethnic violence between the majority Sinhalese and the Tamils, the largest minority. Many Tamils wish to form their own nation in the north of the island, and extremists undertake periodic terrorist action. Other minority groups include Europeans, Malays and the Veddah tribesmen who inhabit the forested mountains and are probably descendants of the original inhabitants. Agriculture dominates the economy, with rubber, coconuts and especially tea being grown as cash crops for export. Efforts are being made to improve rice production to reduce reliance on imported food. Industry centers on the processing of agricultural products, while precious stones are the only mineral resources of note.

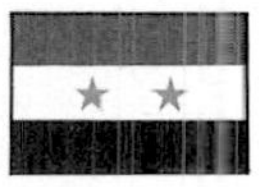

SYRIA

Population: 13 million
Area: 71,000 square miles
Capital: Damascus
Language: Arabic
Currency: Syrian Pound

Arabs form the overwhelming bulk of the Syrian population, and the Islamic religion is a strong unifying force. Government is by a democratically-elected Parliament, and the Arab Socialist Party has formed a majority since 1963, with President Assad holding executive power. Syria has been a major power in the Middle East, taking part in wars against Israel and maintaining a peace-keeping force in Lebanon. The economy is based on oil and textiles, which together make up about three-quarters of exports. Irrigated farmland in the Euphrates Valley and in the west produces quantities of wheat, barley and olives for domestic consumption. The southern deserts are sparsely populated by nomadic pastoralists raising livestock at subsistence level.

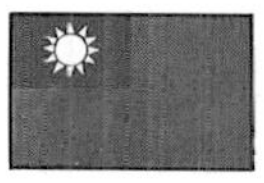

TAIWAN

Population: 21 million
Area: 14,000 square miles
Capital: Taipei
Language: Chinese dialects and Japanese
Currency: New Taiwan Dollar

When the Communist Party gained control of mainland China in 1949, the surviving nationalists fled to the island of Taiwan and set up a rival Republic of China, which is now usually referred to as Taiwan. Neither regime recognizes the other as legitimate, and a continual propaganda war has been carried on. Until the Nationalist takeover, Taiwan was an agricultural island with intensively-farmed pockets of fertile land. Rice, pineapples and bananas are still produced in quantity on the few areas suitable for agriculture amid the mountainous terrain. Industrial development has been the keynote of Taiwan's economy since 1949. Light industry was encouraged first, but iron and steel works and shipbuilding yards are now well established, together with electronics.

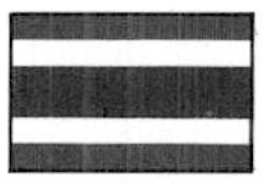

THAILAND

Population: 56.8 million
Area: 198,000 square miles
Capital: Bangkok
Language: Thai
Currency: Baht

The kingdom of Thailand dates back many centuries, but the present dynasty came to power in 1782, when the founder threw off Burmese control. The kingdom never succumbed to European colonialism but was overrun by Japan in World War II. The royal dynasty remains on the throne, but political power has changed hands rapidly between Parliament and army factions as coups have been common in recent years. The majority of the population lives in rural areas, where the fertile soil and ideal climate allow Thailand to produce far more food than it needs. Rice is a substantial export. The beautiful old temples and notorious nightlife of Bangkok make Thailand a popular tourist resort, attracting over five million visitors annually.

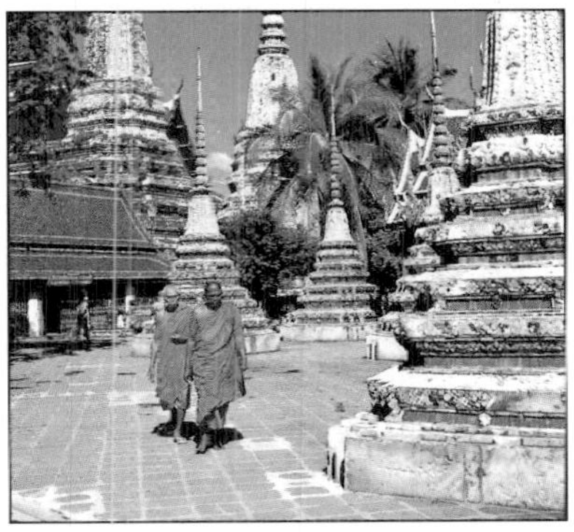

▲ *Buddhist priests, Bangkok, Thailand.*

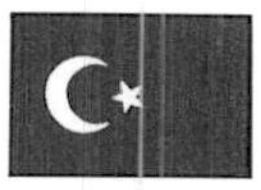

TURKEY

Population: 58.5 million
Area: 301,000 square miles
Capital: Ankara
Language: Turkish
Currency: Turkish Lira

The Turks formerly ruled the vast Ottoman Empire, embracing the Balkans, the Near East and much of North Africa, and modern Turkey has a flag derived from that of the Empire. The modern republic was founded in 1923, when the last emperor was deposed. Democratic government has been interrupted by periods of military control, most recently in 1980-83. The interior plateau has a fertile soil and produces large quantities of grain, while the warmer coast produces heavy crops of olives, figs and citrus fruits. Flax and cotton form the basis of a flourishing textile industry. Agriculture employs over half the work force, some at little above subsistence level. Industry is dominated by the production of iron and steel, motor vehicles and cement and is growing under state encouragement.

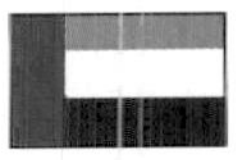

UNITED ARAB EMIRATES

Population: 2 million
Area: 32,000 square miles
Capital: Abu Dhabi
Language: Arabic
Currency: Dirham

As the name suggests, the United Arab Emirates is a confederation of seven independent nations: Abu Dhabi, Dubai, Ash Shariqah, Ajman, Umm al Qaywayn, Al Fujayrah and Ras al Khaymah. The federation is ruled jointly by the seven Emirs, who appoint ministers to legislate and agree upon a joint budget. The federation came into being when Britain gave the Emirs full independence after a period when Britain controlled foreign policy in return for giving military protection. The bulk of the territory is desert, with little opportunity for agriculture, though fishing has potential and there is a large export trade. The economy is basically dependent on oil, which is produced and exported in large quantities. Oil revenues are used to promote a more diversified economy and to improve living conditions.

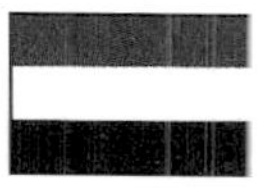

YEMEN

Population: 12 million
Area: 205,000 square miles
Capital: Sana'a
Language: Arabic
Currency: Riyal and Dinar

In May 1990 the former states of Yemen and the People's Democratic Republic of Yemen merged to form a single nation. The new constitution of the united Republic of Yemen allowed for free, multi-party elections after an interim period of two years, during which complicated arrangements for fusing the armies, administrations and economies would be put into effect. The two currencies, the Riyal of Yemen and the Dinar of the Peoples Republic remain in circulation side by side. The new nation has very little industry, and most of the population is engaged in agriculture, usually at subsistence level. The arid nature of much of Yemen restricts agriculture to river valleys. Coastal villages supplement farming with fishing, with much of the catch being dried and exported.

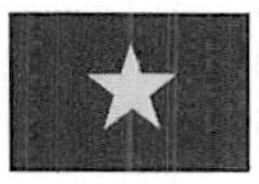

VIETNAM

Population: 69 million
Area: 127,000 square miles
Capital: Hanoi
Language: Vietnamese
Currency: Dong

Vietnam formally came into being in July 1976 with the union of the former nations of North and South Vietnam after the long and costly Vietnam War. Just two years later Vietnam invaded Cambodia, withdrawing only in 1988. The constitution states that Vietnam is a proletarian dictatorship under Marxist-Leninism. In effect, all power is in the hands of the Communist Party, which has followed a consistently pro-Russian stance, thus angering its neighbor China. This has led to border skirmishes in recent years. Well over half the population is directly dependent on agriculture. Although over fifteen million tons of rice and two million tons of sweet potatoes are produced each year, Vietnam still needs to import food. There is little heavy industry and light industry is small-scale.

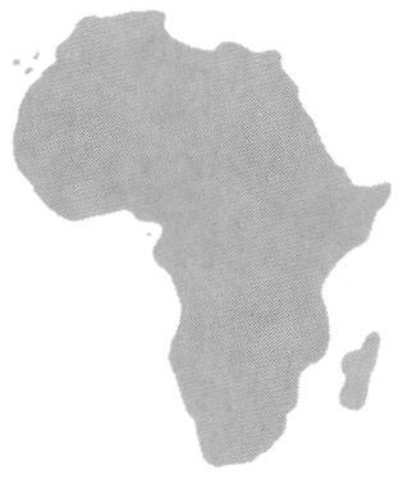

AFRICA

Africa is, in general, an underdeveloped continent, where political violence and dictatorships are common. It is also, however, a continent of great potential, with a magnificent environmental heritage and the possibility of significant improvements.

It is usual to divide Africa, for cultural and geographical reasons, into two distinct sections. The first, North Africa, includes the Islamic states that fringe the Mediterranean and northern Atlantic coasts. These nations are united by a common language and religion which is the result of their Islamic heritage. Most have fertile coastal regions backed by vast desert interiors inhabited only by nomadic tribesmen. Oilfields are present in most of these nations, ensuring a national wealth that pays for programs to improve the quality of life.

The second major region is sub-Saharan Africa, which stretches from the Sahara desert to the Cape of Good Hope. This is a more diverse region, ranging from dense rainforest through open savannah to desert conditions, but united by having a mainly black population and having only recently gained independence from European colonial rule. There are, however, distinct differences between the regions.

West Africa is characterized by settled farming communities of great tribal diversity, where mineral exploitation and industry is well developed compared to elsewhere in Africa. East Africa is dominated by plains originally populated by seminomadic pastoral tribes, where minerals are less common and farming plays a more dominant role in the economy. Southern Africa is as diverse as the entire continent, with areas of fertile farmland, dense forests and open plains to be found within a short distance of each other.

Nations bordering the Sahara are subject to periodic droughts, which bring great misery in their wake. Population booms over the past decades have led to a reliance on good crops, and when these fail famine follows. The worst of these famines were those that killed hundreds of thousands, possibly millions, of people in Ethiopia and neighboring countries such as Somalia. Elsewhere in Africa famine is not such a constant threat, but chronic poverty and poor medical services cause a low life expectancy.

Though the age of European colonization is now over, the signs of those times are still clear. The official language of most nations is still that of the colonizing power. The diverse tribal tongues of most nations (some have over 200 languages) make a lingua franca essential, and it has been found most convenient to maintain that of the former ruling European power.

Most former French colonies in sub-Saharan Africa share a common currency: the Franc CFA. This currency is issued by the Banque Centrale des Etats de l'Afrique de l'Ouest and is locked into the French Franc at a rate of 50 Francs CFA to one French Franc. This arrangement has advantages for those countries within it, but also has the effect of robbing them of total discretion over their own economies, which to some extent remain vulnerable to outside control.

In the aftermath of independence, many sub-Saharan states abandoned democracy. In some cases this was due to the total dominance of a single party, which then outlawed opposition, but was more normally produced by a military coup. Nearly all sub-Saharan African states have experienced dictatorship at some stage and many are still ruled without democracy. From the late 1980s, several nations returned to civilian multiparty rule. There have been numerous accusations of human rights violations by the governments in these states.

Most attention has been focused on South Africa, where a white minority holds total control over the nation, without the right to vote being given to the black majority. International pressure has been brought to bear on the nation, and the government has abandoned the policies of apartheid that enforced this control.

The mineral wealth of Africa is vast and underexploited. Effective capital investment and improved transportation would bring this wealth into the economy, but international companies are unwilling to invest heavily in nations subject to civil war or frequent coups.

Africa is undoubtedly a beautiful and potentially wealthy continent, but its endemic problems and recurring violence have locked it into a cycle of poverty that will prove difficult to break.

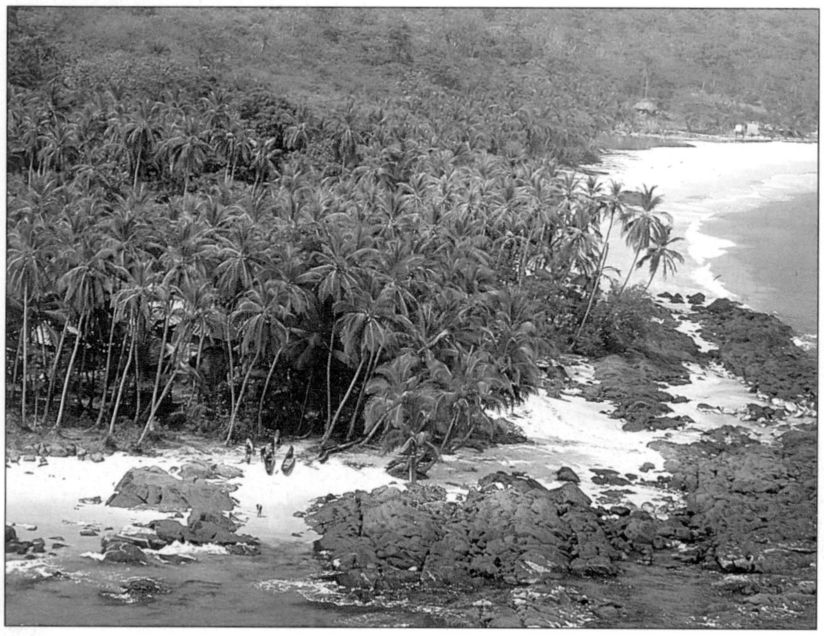

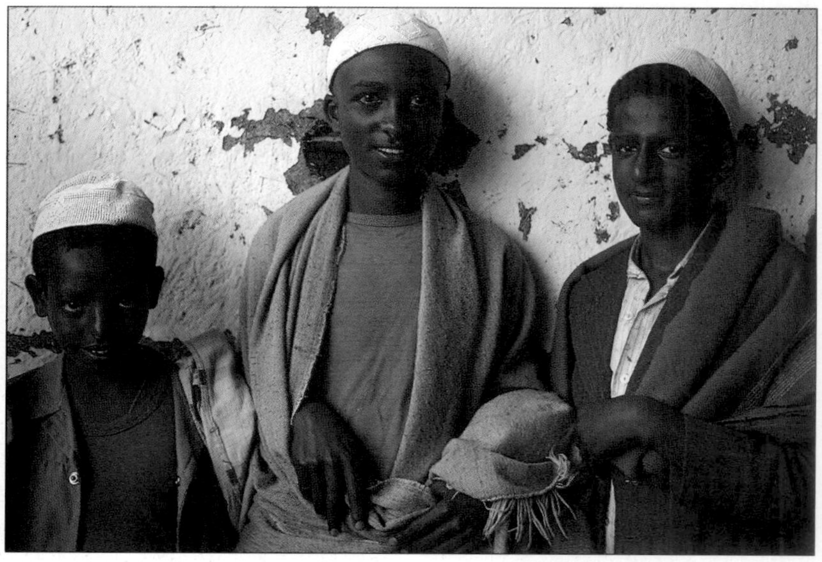

◄ Sierra Leone beaches.

▲ People of Ethiopa.

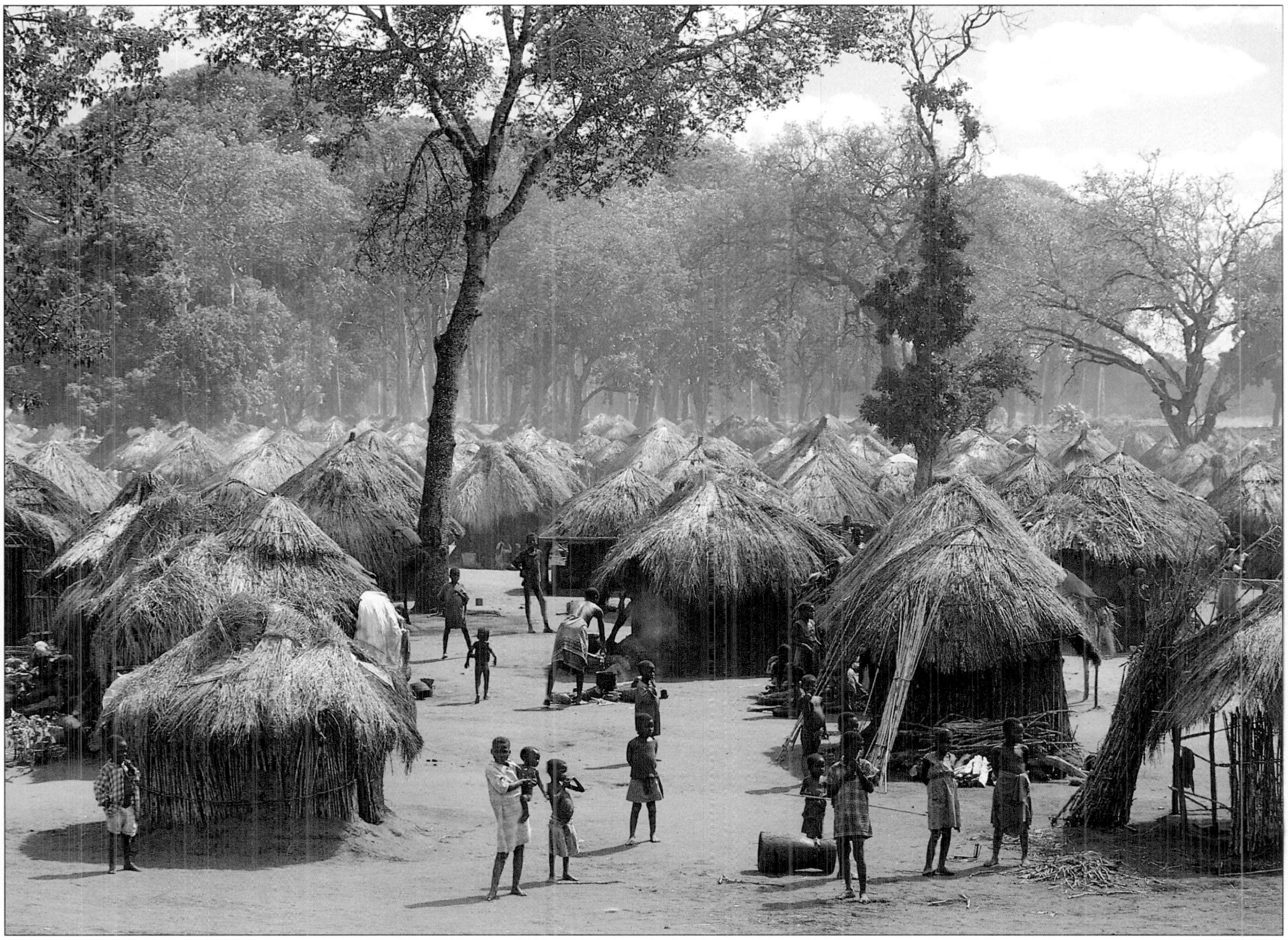

▲ *A village in Mozambique.*

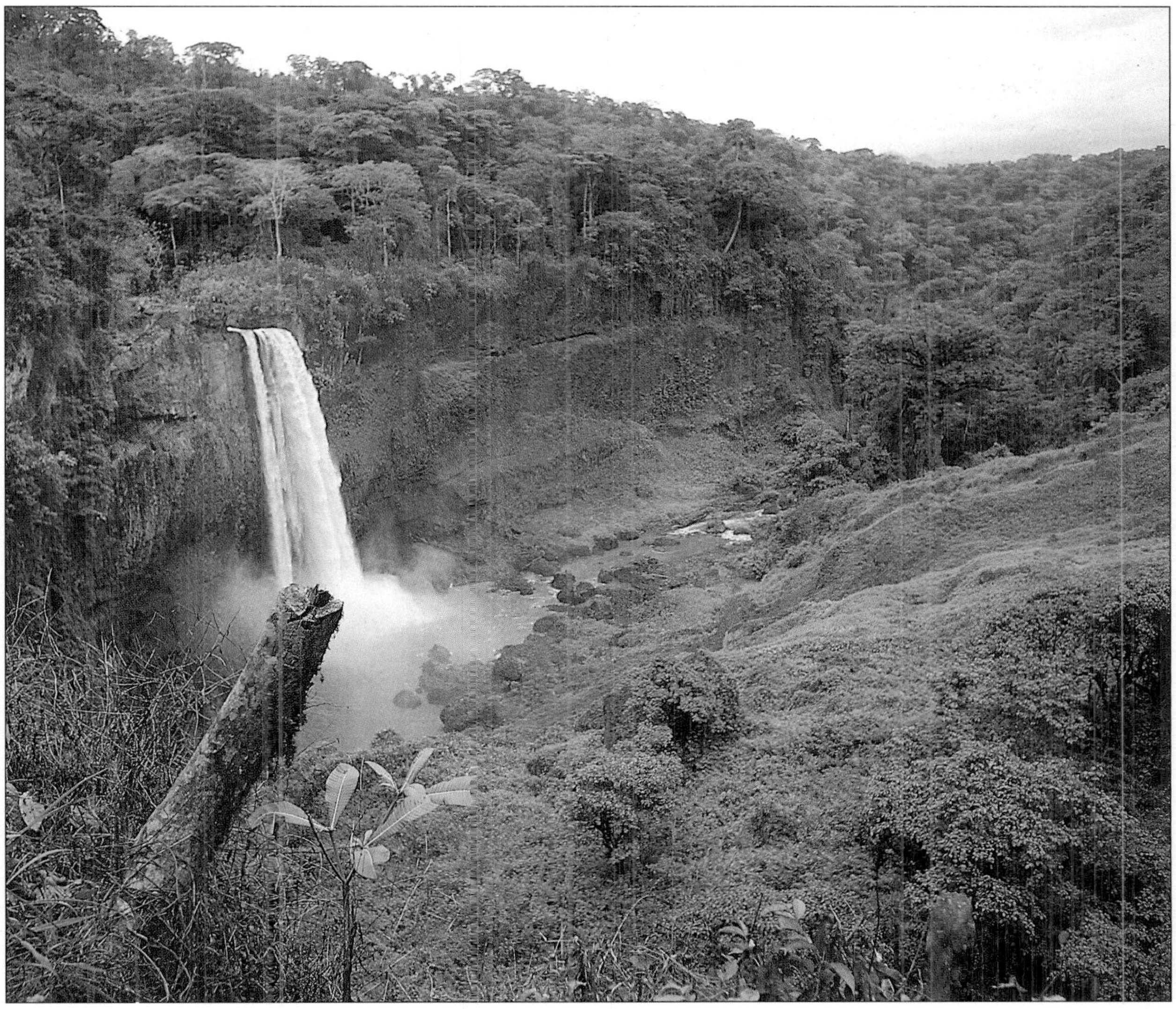

► *A waterfall in Cameroon.*

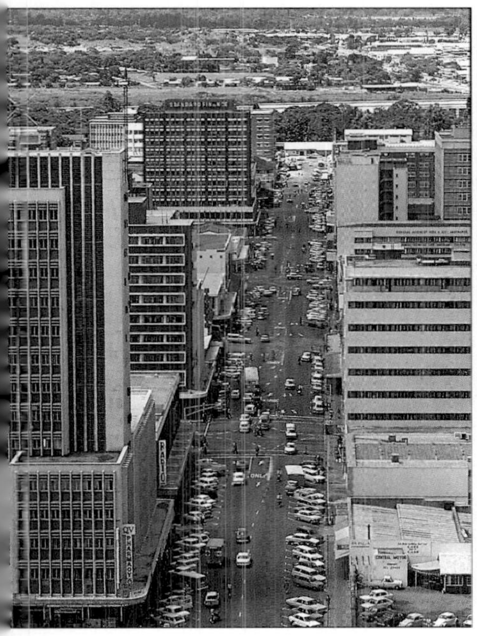

▼ *Salisbury, Zimbabwe.*

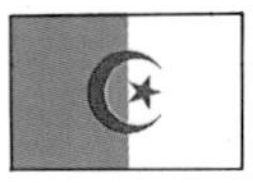

ALGERIA

Population: 26 million
Area: 927,000 square miles
Capital: Algiers
Language: Arabic
Currency: Dinar

Algeria gained its independence from France in 1962 after nearly a decade of guerilla warfare. The bulk of the population lives along the Mediterranean coast and in the Atlas Mountains, where the climate is milder and the land more fertile than in the arid Sahara which makes up most of the country. The discovery of large natural gas fields has made Algeria relatively wealthy, and some of these resources are spent on free health treatment and high quality education. Many people continue to lead a traditional Islamic lifestyle, though European influences are strong in coastal towns. The country's first multiparty elections in 1991 showed the strength of the fundamentalist Islamic opposition, and the military took a more direct role in running the government.

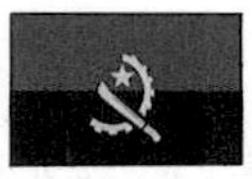

ANGOLA

Population: 10.6 million
Area: 463,000 square miles
Capital: Luanda
Language: Portuguese and various tribal languages
Currency: Kwanza

For most of its independent existence Angola has been torn by civil war between the communist MPLA party, which forms the central government, and the rebel UNITA organization, which controls much of southern Angola. The first free multiparty elections were held in 1992. The long years of warfare caused much hardship and seriously disrupted the economy, making this one of the poorer African nations. However, oil production in the north and diamond mining may lead to economic revival. The coastal region is the center for industrialization and urban lifestyles. The high plateau of the interior is heavily forested and inhabited by tribes which live in a traditional way.

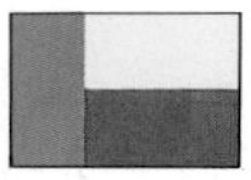

BENIN

Population: 5 million
Area: 43,000 square miles
Capital: Porto Novo
Language: French and tribal languages
Currency: Franc CFA

The ideal of a revolutionary socialist state was recently abandoned in Benin, with the holding of free elections and the founding of several political parties. For the vast majority of the population the change probably meant little. Traditional agricultural lifestyles dominate in the interior, where tribal culture and animist cults are common. It is thought that about ninety percent of the population practice subsistence farming. In the mountainous far north Islamic culture has filtered down from the desert regions. Only on the coast is industry to be found, and even this is heavily based on the agricultural produce of the interior, particularly sugar and palm oil. A recently-exploited oilfield off the coast is expected to help boost the economy.

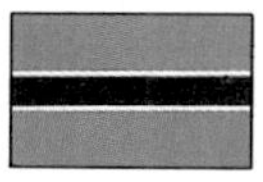

BOTSWANA

Population: 1.3 million
Area: 225,000 square miles
Capital: Gaborone
Language: English, Setswana
Currency: Pula

Botswana is rare among African nations in having maintained its democratic constitution throughout its period of independence. The constitution granted in 1966 allowed for an Elected Assembly of thirty-eight members and a House of Chiefs comprised of the twelve tribal chiefs, and this arrangement is still in place. The vast majority of the population lives in traditional villages, where cattle farming is the main activity, though some crops are also sown. Industry is limited to diamond and copper mining, and many young men work in South Africa for some years in order to earn money for their families at home. The vast Kalahari Desert in the southwest of the nation is inhabited by nomadic bushmen tribes, and they have little to do with national life.

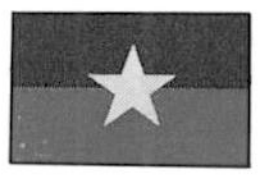

BURKINA FASO

Population: 9.5 million
Area: 106,000 square miles
Capital: Ouagadougou
Language: French and tribal languages
Currency: Franc CFA

As one of the poorest and most unstable countries in Africa, Burkina Faso has experienced much hardship. Numerous coups and government changes have occurred, most recently in 1989. The nation is a largely artificial creation, being a former French administrative district covering the territory of several indigenous tribes. The vast majority of the population is engaged in subsistence farming in traditional tribal society. The country is periodically struck by drought and famine, being on the southern fringe of the Sahara. The recent discoveries of gold and manganese deposits are unlikely to be exploited due to a poor transportation system and lack of capital. The nation depends largely on foreign aid and remains chronically depressed.

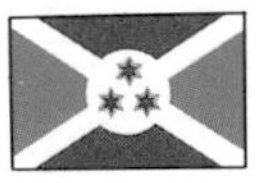

BURUNDI

Population: 5.6 million
Area: 10,000 square miles
Capital: Bujumbura
Language: French, Kirundi and Swahili
Currency: Burundi Franc

Sometime in the 16th century Tutsi tribes invaded the area and conquered the Hutu peoples. Even today the nation is divided into the two ethnic groups, with the Tutsi wielding power. After a period of German and Belgian rule Burundi became independent in 1962 under a Tutsi monarch. In 1966 the king was overthrown by the Tutsi-dominated army, which has since suppressed Hutu unrest and dismissed Presidents at will. Tea and coffee plantations are the mainstays of both industry and the export economy. The majority of the population, however, remains dependent on subsistence agriculture based on bananas, corn and cattle. Less than one percent of the population is composed of pygmies, who inhabit dense forest and take little active part in national life.

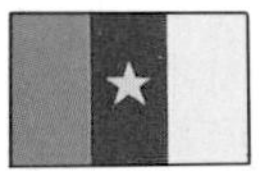

CAMEROON

Population: 12.6 million
Area: 183,000 square miles
Capital: Yaounde
Language: English, French and tribal languages
Currency: Franc CFA

Much of the interior of Cameroon is virtually inaccessible during the rainy season, when torrential downpours wash away roads and flood large areas. This isolation is emphasized by ethnic diversity, with twenty-four languages and as many as 200 tribes. The fragmentation has slowed economic development, though the nation is relatively wealthy by African standards. The economy is based largely on agriculture, with coffee, cocoa and palm oil forming the bulk of export crops. The majority of farmland is, however, devoted to producing foods such as cassava, corn and groundnuts for local consumption. Industry is concentrated on aluminum smelting and the processing of agricultural products. Oil revenue has helped the government to invest in new projects.

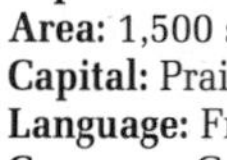

CAPE VERDE

Population: 346,000
Area: 1,500 square miles
Capital: Praia
Language: French and Sangho
Currency: Cape Verde Escudo

The Cape Verde Islands have been independent only since 1975, when Portugal relinquished control. The islands have strong historical links with Guinea-Bissau, also formerly Portuguese controlled, and have similar flags. The government is a

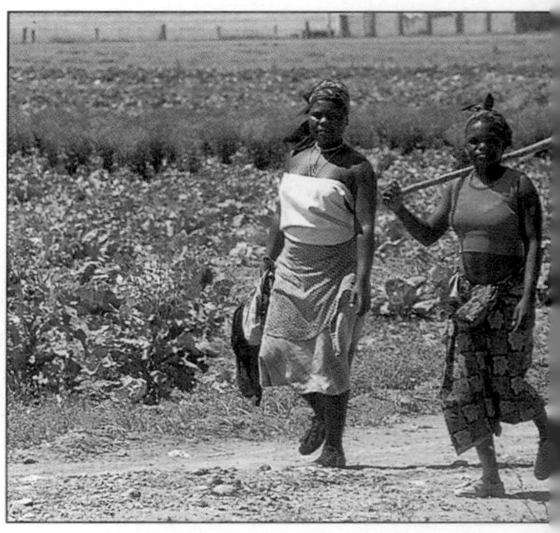

▲ *Farm workers in Angola.*

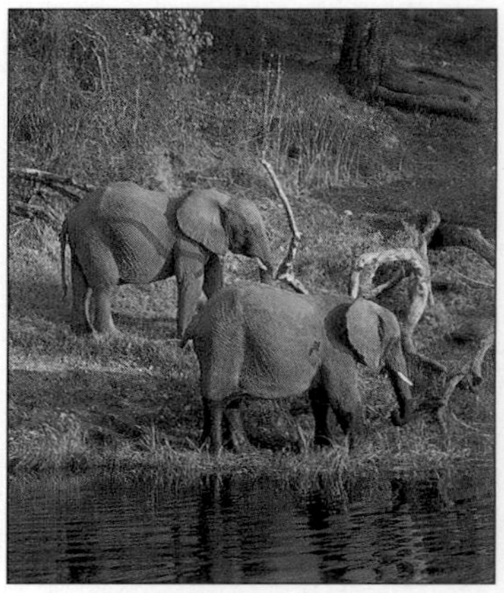

▲ *A scene on the Chobe River, Botswana.*

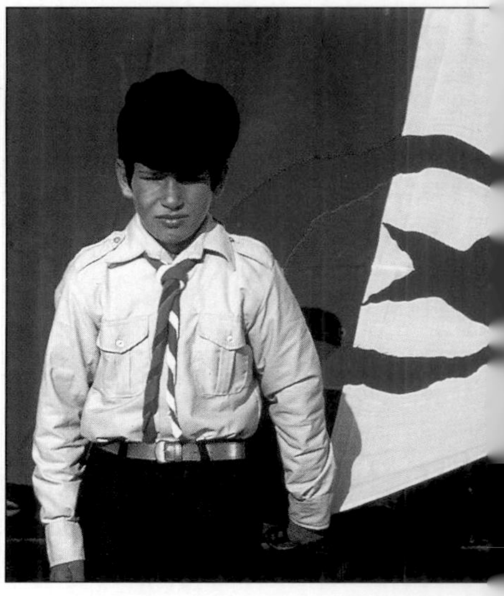

▲ *Celebrations on the anniversary of the Algerian Revolution.*

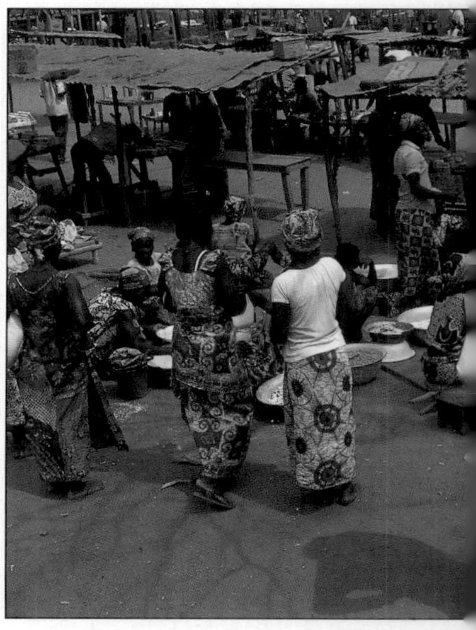

▲ A village in Chad.

▲ Barren, drought-scarred landscape, Cape Verde.

▼ A domestic scene in Burkina Faso.

▲ Riverboat merchant, Benin.

▼ The Central African Republic.

▲ Bathers in the Comoros.

single-party state, though the ruling elite joined several other African nations in 1990 by announcing an intention to allow democracy. The islands are small, rugged and arid, with little opportunity for farming. Coconuts, coffee and sugar are produced in small quantities on irrigated land. Fishing is far more productive for the local population, with large numbers of tuna being landed each year. The climate and scenic coastline hold out the promise of an increase in tourism for the islands, though as yet this is under-developed.

CENTRAL AFRICAN REPUBLIC

Population: 2.9 million
Area: 240,000 square miles
Capital: Bangui
Language: French and tribal languages
Currency: Franc CFA

For thirteen years until 1979 this nation was ruled by Jean-Bedel Bokassa, who proclaimed himself Emperor and staged a lavish coronation ceremony. Bokassa was overthrown by the army, and today the nation is a one-party state ostensibly committed to intro-ducing democratic government. After a brief period of multi-party democracy in 1992 the President set up the Provisional National Political Council of the Republic. Though potentially rich in minerals and agriculture, the economy has been held back by political in-stability, by poor communications, and particularly by the lack of a coastline. Diamond, gold and uranium mining lead the small industrial sector, while the majority of the population remain employed in subsistence agriculture.

CHAD

Population: 5.9 million
Area: 496,000 square miles
Capital: N'djamena
Language: French, Arabic and tribal languages
Currency: Franc CFA

Endemic civil war has marked the history of Chad since independence from France in 1960. The fighting between various ethnic factions is based upon a struggle between the nomadic, Moslem north and the agricultural and animist south. The situation has been confused by shifting alliances and foreign inter-vention. Chad remains unstable, and French troops have intervened several times to restore order. The warfare has prevented exploitation of recently-discovered oilfields and deposits of gold and uranium. The population remains desperately poor and is dependent on sub-sistence agriculture varied by fishing on the shores of Lake Chad. A new government was installed in March 1991, and it is to be hoped that this leads to some stability.

COMOROS

Population: 500,000
Area: 695 square miles
Capital: Moroni
Language: Arabic, French and Swahili
Currency: Franc CFA

When the three Comoros islands of Mwali, Njazidja and Nzwani declared themselves to be indep-endent of France in 1975, the fourth island, Mayotte, refused to join them. The newly-independent nation has suffered three successful coups and has chronic problems of disease and poverty. The islands have, over the centuries, received influxes of Africans, Indonesian, Arabic and European peoples and today have a mixed population. The majority of the population engages in subsistence farming, producing such crops as cassava, bananas, coconuts and corn. In recent years commercial production of vanilla, cloves and coffee has been undertaken and these now account for much of the nation's exports. Though independent, the Comoros remain economically dependent on France.

▲ The Congo's Sangha River.

CONGO

Population: 2.7 million
Area: 132,000 square miles
Capital: Brazzaville
Language: French and tribal languages
Currency: Franc CFA

Formerly a French colony, the Congo was a single-party, Marxist-Leninist state until 1992 when multi-party democracy was re-stored. The army has engineered a total of four coups since inde-pendence. The nation is relatively wealthy by African standards, with oil reserves offshore and productive gold mines. Industry is well established around the capital and produces cement and textiles among other products. However, more than three-quarters of the population remains engaged in farming, much of it at subsistence level. The vast bulk of the population is found in the southern parts of the country, for the northern regions are covered by dense forests and unfertile land.

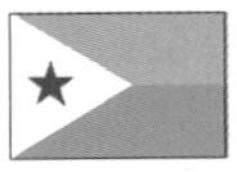

DJIBOUTI

Population: 557,000
Area: 9,000 square miles
Capital: Djibouti City
Language: Somali, Afar, French
Currency: Djibouti Franc

The state of Djibouti is dominated by disputes between its ethnic Somalis and Afars. The hinterland is composed of arid grazing lands, although the bulk of the population, lives in or around Djibouti City. The city has a long history as a trading center, and the economy is largely dependent on the port. Djibouti was a one-party state until 1992, when a constitution paved the way for democracy.

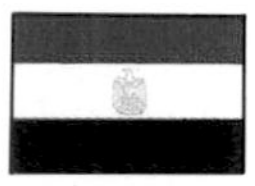

EGYPT

Population: 56 million
Area: 386,000 square miles
Capital: Cairo
Language: Arabic
Currency: Egyptian Pound

Egypt was conquered by the Arabs in the 7th century, and today the nation is firmly Moslem in culture and outlook. People and prosperity are concentrated in the Nile Valley, as they have been since recorded history began here in 3,000 BC. The waters of the Nile allow irrigation of the farmland that produces the bulk of the nation's food as well as export crops. Industry is well advanced in the major towns and cities. Tourism plays a major role in the economy. Egypt has a relatively stable political system but faces internal opposition from Islamic fundamentalists.

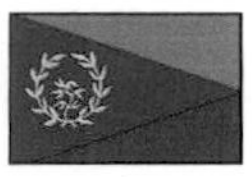

ERITREA

Population: 3.5 million
Area: 48,000 square miles
Capital: Asmara
Language: Arabic and tribal languages
Currency: Birr

Eritrea, a country with a diverse climate and geography, has been under Italian, British and Ethiopian rule. In 1991, after thirty years of armed struggle by the Eritrean People's Liberation Front, the country won its right to self-determination. Two years of provisional government followed, and after an internationally monitored referendum in April 1993, full independence was achieved.

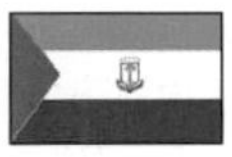

EQUATORIAL GUINEA

Population: 367,000
Area: 11,000 square miles
Capital: Malabo
Language: Spanish and tribal languages
Currency: Franc CFA

Equatorial Guinea is divided between the mainland territory on the Mbini River and the island of Bioko. Cocoa and coffee remain important export crops, although the majority of farmland is used for subsistence agriculture, with cassava and sweet potatoes being the chief products. The wet, hot tropical climate produces vast forests in the interior, and these are beginning to be exploited for their timber, which accounts for one quarter of all exports. Although over half the population lives in towns, there is virtually no industry in the nation.

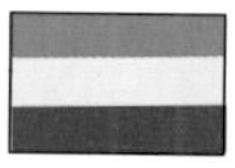

ETHIOPIA

Population: 53.8 million
Area: 471,000 square miles
Capital: Addis Ababa
Language: Arabic and tribal languages
Currency: Birr

Drought, famine and civil war dogged Ethiopia for many years. Much of the country is in the hands of rebel factions, one of which recently overthrew the central government. The violence is largely due to the many ethnic groups included within the nation, many of which desire independence from strong central rule.Famine has claimed hundreds of thousands of lives, and internal political unrest has undoubtedly worsened the situation. Despite this, farming is generally in good condition and in productive years can account for valuable exports of coffee and sugar. Much potentially fertile ground remains untilled due to political instability. Peace would undoubtedly help ease the desperate plight of the Ethiopian peoples.

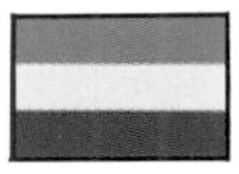

GABON

Population: 1 million
Area: 103,000 square miles
Capital: Libreville
Language: French and tribal languages
Currency: Franc CFA

Made up largely of the drainage basin of the Ogooue River, Gabon has numerous natural resources but lacks the finance and population to take best advantage of them. Offshore oil is being exploited, as are deposits of uranium and manganese, but the economy remains based chiefly on agriculture. The Equator runs through the center of Gabon, and this dictates the climate and range of crops that can be produced. Most of the population supports itself on subsistence agriculture, though sugar cane is grown in large quantities near the coast for export. Government under a single-party state has been stable since 1967, but this was recently dismantled and free elections were held in 1990, though allegations of ballot-rigging were made.

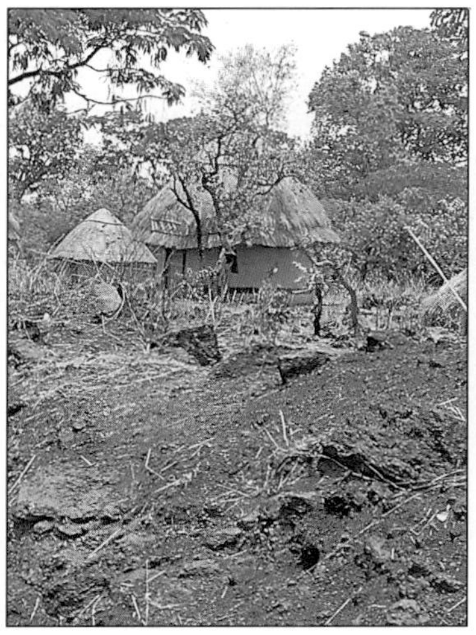

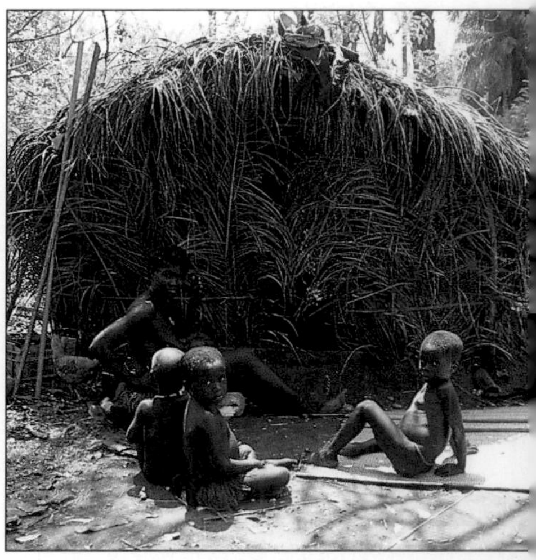

▲ *Thatched huts in Equatorial Guinea.*

Above right: *Children in Guinea-Bissau.*

▼ *Filling water pots, Ghana.*

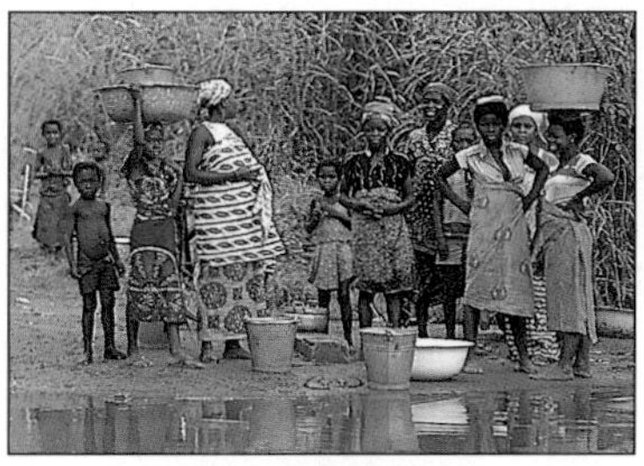

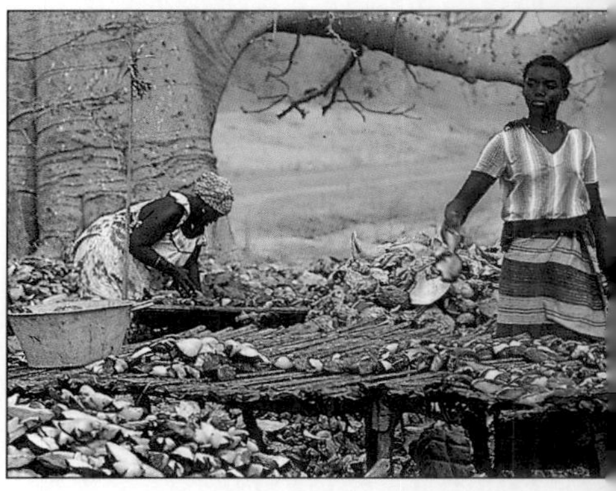

▲ *Women cleaning groundnuts, Gambia.*

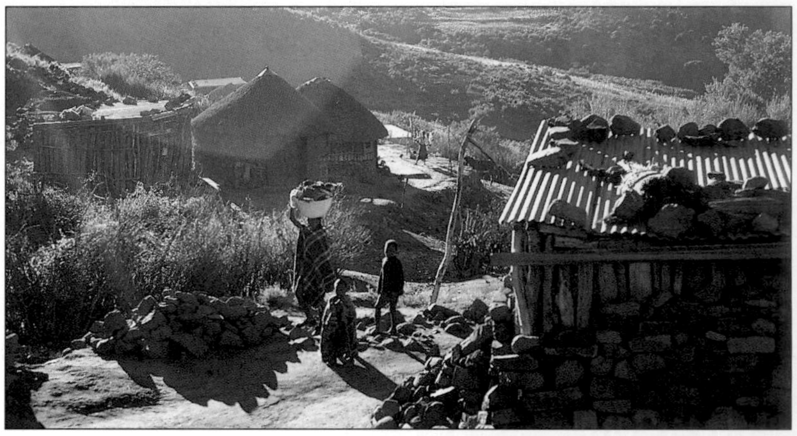

▲ *The mountain village of Ha Thuhlo, Lesotho.*

► *Landscape of Gabon.*

▼ *Kenyatta Centre, Nairobi, Kenya.*

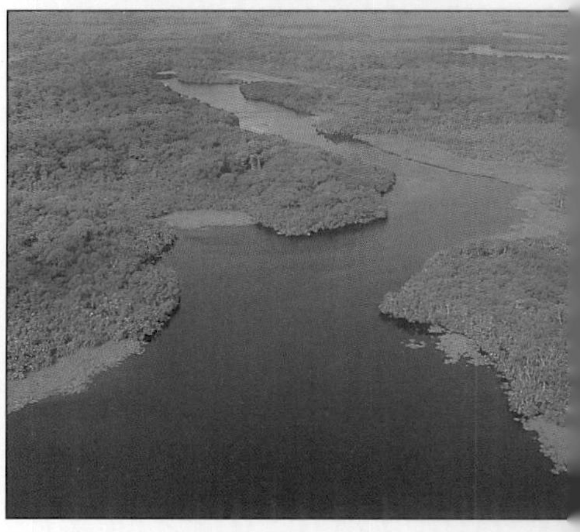

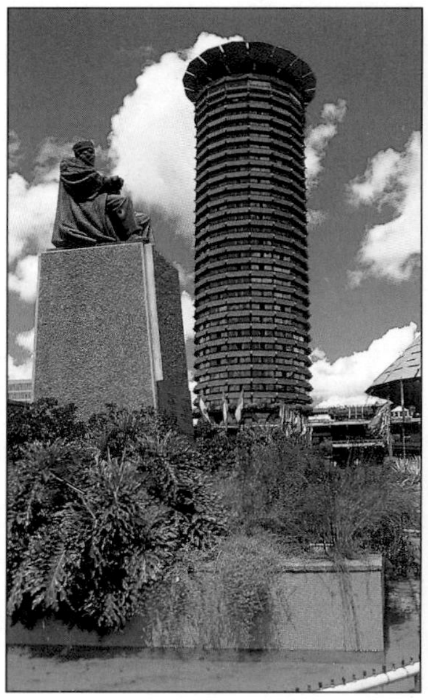

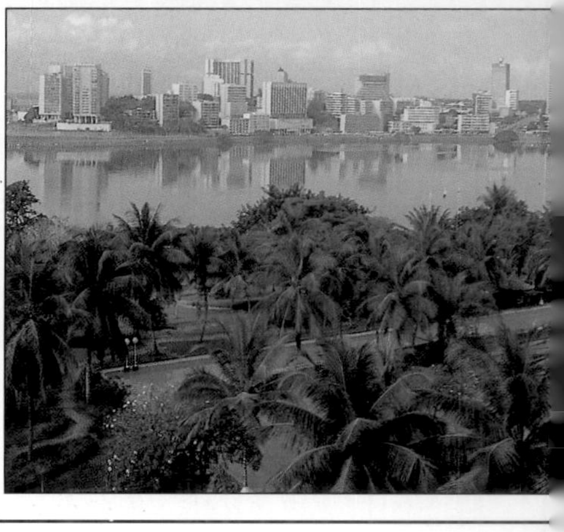

► *Abidjan, Ivory Coast.*

GAMBIA

Population: 921,000
Area: 4,000 square miles
Capital: Banjul
Language: English and tribal languages
Currency: Dalasi

The Gambia exists because of the river from which it takes its name. The nation is made up of a narrow strip of land rarely more than twelve miles wide that follows the twists and turns of the river from Koina to the ocean. Several tribes have their territories along the river, and their chiefs have an established position within the constitution. The nation is basically agricultural and has only one export of any importance. This is the groundnut, thousands of tons of which are shipped out each year. More recently the government has tried to break this hazardous dependence on a single crop. In 1982 Gambia joined with Senegal, which virtually surrounds it, to form the Confederation of Senegambia, but this was dissolved in 1989.

GHANA

Population: 15 million
Area: 92,000 square miles
Capital: Accra
Language: English and tribal languages
Currency: Cedi

As the first black African state to become independent of a European colonial power, in 1957, Ghana has set several trends in African history. The colors of the Ghanaian flag – red, green and yellow – have been adopted by several other nations, while the black star of African freedom has also become a popular motif. Ghana has experienced several coups and was long ruled by a Provisional Council led by Flight Lieutenant Jerry Rawlings, who was elected president in 1992 under a democratic constitution. The economy is relatively healthy and is based on cash crop agriculture, with cocoa the most important, though tobacco, coffee and tropical fruits are catching up. Industrial activities are based around the mining of gold, diamonds and, more recently, oil.

GUINEA

Population: 7 million
Area: 95,000 square miles
Capital: Conakry
Language: French and tribal languages
Currency: Syli

Guinea followed Ghana to independence one year later and adopted the same colors for its flag, though they are arranged in vertical rather than horizontal stripes. Several tribal groupings are included within Guinea, with the Fulani being the largest at around

forty percent of the population. The nation was under military and single-party control from 1984 until the early 1990s, when it was replaced by a Transitional Committee for National Rectification. The nation has a tropical climate, with a summer monsoon which brings heavy rain and high temperatures. Combined with fertile soils this creates ideal conditions for a variety of crops, including rice, sugar cane and tropical fruits. Vast reserves of bauxite are now being mined as are iron ore deposits and diamonds.

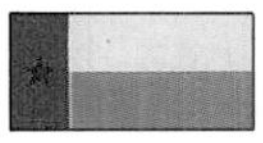

GUINEA-BISSAU

Population: 1 million
Area: 14,000 square miles
Capital: Bissau
Language: Portuguese and tribal languages
Currency: Peso

For many years a one-party state, Guinea-Bissau became a multi-party democracy in 1991. The fertile soil and tropical climate allow the production of large quantities of rice, rubber and groundnuts, much of which is exported. A third of the country is forested, and timber production remains an important source of income. Most of the population remains dependent on subsistence agriculture, and industry is virtually nonexistent. Guinea-Bissau has a crushing foreign debt more than one hundred times the size of the government's annual budget. Ethnically the population is divided between the coastal Balanta and the Muslim Fulani of the inland regions, though there are several smaller tribes.

IVORY COAST

Population: 12.1 million
Area: 124,000 square miles
Capital: Abidjan
Language: French and tribal languages
Currency: Franc CFA

This nation takes its name from the early trade in ivory that dominated the region when it was first discovered by Europeans in the 15th century. Since then slavery, and more recently coffee, have been the mainstays of the economy. Today the rich soil of the coastal regions has been turned to support a wide variety of crops including yams, cassava and a number of tropical fruits for export. Despite this fertility the economy of the Ivory Coast is held back by massive foreign debts and limited mineral resources. The single party state that has existed for many years recently announced that it would begin a process of democratization, and free elections have been held. The former sole party still retains power, having won over ninety percent of the seats in Parliament.

KENYA

Population: 27 million
Area: 225,000 square miles
Capital: Nairobi
Language: English, Swahili and tribal languages
Currency: Kenya Shilling

Committed until 1990 to the concept of "democracy with one party," the state of Kenya has enjoyed more stability than many other African nations since it achieved independence in 1963. This has combined with rich natural resources and a long history of international trade to make it economically viable, though not particularly wealthy. Most of the population inhabits the interior highlands, where coffee, tea and sugar are grown in large quantities for export, or the lower hills, where corn, cassava and sweet potatoes are produced for local consumption. The vast semi-arid plains are the home of gazelles, zebras and lions, which attract over half-a-million tourists each year, boosting the economy. The coastal towns have been trading with foreigners since the Arabs first arrived about the time of Christ and are thriving commercial centers.

LESOTHO

Population: 1.8 million
Area: 12,000 square miles
Capital: Maseru
Language: English, Sesotho
Currency: Loti

Lesotho is one of the few African tribal kingdoms to survive into modern times. Since a coup in 1986 the king acts on the advice of the army. In the early 19th century refugees from vicious warfare in the north fled to the mountains of Lesotho and became welded into a kingdom under Moshoeshoe I, who placed himself under British protection. This wise move ensured that the Sotho clans retained some form of self-government throughout the colonial era and in 1966 became independent outside the Union of South Africa. The country has few natural resources and little agricultural land. The young men work in South Africa for long periods of time, earning enough money to support their families and keep the fragile economy of the kingdom in balance.

LIBERIA

Population: 2.8 million
Area: 43,000 square miles
Capital: Monrovia
Language: English and tribal languages
Currency: Liberian Dollar

The flag of Liberia is similar to that of the United States, indicating the

origins of the nation. In 1822 an American society landed a party of freed slaves on the coast in Monrovia in an attempt to establish a haven for such people. In 1847 the nation declared itself independent and adopted a constitution similar to that of the United States. Recent years have witnessed violent upheavals, with coups and civil war raging fiercely. The situation is not yet stable. Liberia has rich mineral resources, in particular massive iron ore deposits, which make up seventy percent of exports, together with gold and diamonds. The vast bulk of the population is engaged in farming, with numerous commercial farms growing coffee, rice and sugar cane.

▲ *A lake in the Fezzan desert, Libya.*

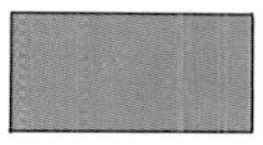

LIBYA

Population: 4.4 million
Area: 680,000 square miles
Capital: Tripoli
Language: Arabic
Currency: Libyan Dinar

Until recently one of the poorest Mediterranean nations, Libya is now one of the richest, following the discovery of massive oil fields in 1959. In 1969 King Idris was overthrown by an army faction led by Colonel Muammar Gadaffi, who established Libya as an Arab republic. The country has since vociferously supported Arab unity and nationalism, lending aid to various organizations such as the PLO and so earning Western enmity. The economy is based on natural oil and gas, which account for nearly all exports. Internally, however, agriculture dominates, with the most fertile lands of North Africa producing rich harvests of dates, citrus fruits and cereals. Ambitious irrigation projects are under way which aim at adding hundreds of square miles to the farmland.

MADAGASCAR

Population: 12.8 million
Area: 228,000 square miles
Capital: Antananarivo
Language: Malagasy and French
Currency: Malagasy Franc

The original kingdom, comprising a mixed population of Malaysians and Africans, was overrun by the French in 1897. In 1960 the island became an independent republic, and since then has undergone several coups. The country was ruled by the Supreme Revolutionary Council and the President from 1975-1991, when anti-government unrest led to political changes. The economy is based on tropical agriculture and the exploitation of forests, both natural and planted. The fertile soils produce heavy crops of coffee, tobacco and tropical fruits, the processing of which forms the basis of the island's small-scale industries. Cattle breeding is a major activity in the highlands, and there are nearly as many cattle as people.

MALAWI

Population: 9.4 million
Area: 46,000 square miles
Capital: Lilongwe
Language: Chichewa and English
Currency: Kwacha

Ruled as a one-party state by Dr Kamuzu Banda, Malawi is a land-locked nation with few resources. Agriculture is the basic activity, with most of the population relying on subsistence farming for a livelihood. Tobacco and tea are grown for export, but occupy only a small part of the total agricultural land. Marble is the only major quarrying material, and industry is restricted to local consumer goods. As a mountainous nation, however, Malawi has massive potential for hydroelectricity, and this is now being exploited on a large scale. The economy remains reliant on its migrant workers, who leave Malawi for South Africa or Zambia to work in mines and factories to earn much needed income.

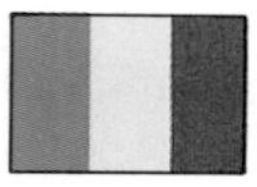

MALI

Population: 8.4 million
Area: 479,000 square miles
Capital: Bamako
Language: French, Bambara and tribal languages
Currency: Franc CFA

Mali is one of the world's poorest nations, being dependent on an agriculture at the mercy of drought and semidesert conditions. The majority of the diverse population is concentrated in the southwest, where the Senegal and Niger rivers give a semblance of reliability to the water supply for irrigation. Millet,

cassava and sweet potatoes are the chief crops for local consumption, while cotton is produced on a modest scale for export. The northern and eastern regions are covered by desert and are virtually uninhabited. Mineral wealth remains untapped due to poor transport and a lack of capital. The military coup of 1968 produced a stable government headed by General Traore. The nation's first democratic elections, in 1992, resulted in a civilian president.

MAURITANIA

Population: 2 million
Area: 400,000 square miles
Capital: Nouakchott
Language: Arabic and French
Currency: Ouguiya

The crescent and star on Mauritania's green flag indicate the Islamic heritage of this desert nation. The vast desert region of the north and east is the home of nomadic herdsmen, but the majority of the population inhabits the Senegal Valley in the southwest. In this region millet, rice and dates are produced in large quantities for local consumption. Coastal villages land large catches of Atlantic fish, which are dried or salted locally to form the bulk of exports by value. Industry is virtually nonexistent, what there is being restricted to iron-ore mining or food processing. A long-running war with Morocco over the Western Sahara territory, which ended in 1979, drained the Mauritanian economy, which is still attempting to recover. The country held its first democratic multiparty elections in 1992.

MOROCCO

Population: 26 million
Area: 172,000 square miles
Capital: Rabat
Language: Arabic, Berber, French
Currency: Dirham

The Islamic kingdom of Morocco became independent of France in 1956, though the Sultan had always enjoyed some degree of control. The Sultanate became a Kingdom in 1957. The king holds supreme authority over both secular and religious life, though the government is actually carried out by a democratically-elected Parliament. The bulk of the nation's wealth is based on its rich mineral deposits, particularly phosphates and lead ore, which are extensively mined and provide much employment. Most of the population remains dependent on agriculture, however, and traditional crops of cereals, fruits and tomatoes dominate. Morocco has been involved in a lengthy war in the

Western Sahara, where it claims large areas of territory.

MOZAMBIQUE

Population: 14.8 million
Area: 302,000 square miles
Capital: Maputo
Language: Portuguese and tribal languages
Currency: Metical

The national flag of Mozambique features a book, a hoe and a gun; symbols that are apt for this poverty-ridden nation in southern Africa. Since 1977 the Marxist Frelimo Party has been the only legal political party in Mozambique, though it recently announced its intention of allowing opposition. Opposition of a more violent kind has been maintained by the Renamo movement, which has been carrying on an armed struggle for many years. In 1992 the two factions signed a peace treaty that held promise of ending the long civil war. The hoe symbolizes the agricultural base of the national economy, which relies on cereals, bananas and various types of nuts. The long coastline on the Indian Ocean offers fine fishing opportunities, and the catch is substantial.

NAMIBIA

Population: 1.5 million
Area: 319,000 square miles
Capital: Windhoek
Language: English, Afrikaans and tribal languages
Currency: South African Rand

The vast desert nation of Namibia gained independence from South Africa in 1990, after many years of confused political instability. Cuban mercenaries from Communist Angola backed the SWAPO guerilla movement, while South Africa attempted to maintain its influence by enforcing a constitution. The independence elections resulted in victory for SWAPO, but not by the margin needed for them to fulfill its goal of one-party rule. The political struggle was made more bitter by the vast mineral wealth of Namibia, which provides one the highest average incomes on the continent. Diamonds and uranium form the basis of the mineral industry. Most of the people are engaged in stock ranching of either cattle or sheep, which together outnumber humans in Namibia by six to one.

NIGER

Population: 8 million
Area: 490,000 square miles
Capital: Niamey
Language: French, Hausa and tribal languages
Currency: Franc CFA

Only around the southwestern borders is Niger a productive

▲ *A typical Senegalese, Senegal.*

▲ *Fertile river banks, Morocco.*

▼ *Terraced hillsides, Rwanda.*

▲ *Tanandava, Madagascar.*

▲ *Djenné, Mali.*

▲ *A young girl, Mauritania.*

◄ *Lumber workers, Lagos, Nigeria.*

▼ *Village in Malawi.*

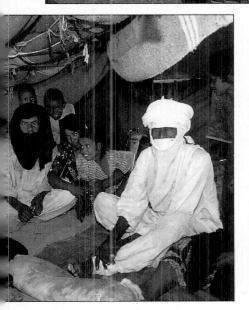

▲ *Refugees in Niger.*

▲ *Oranjemund, Namibia.*

agricultural country. Here the Niger River provides water for irrigation and drinking. The bulk of the population is concentrated in this region, where they farm at a subsistence level. The capital, Niamey, stands on the banks of the Niger River and has some small-scale industry. Elsewhere through southern Niger a number of oases permit farming, but away from the Niger the land is generally devoted to grazing livestock. In the north the Sahara makes even grazing virtually impossible. In 1974 the government was overthrown by a military coup, and the nation was ruled by a supreme military council. In 1992 a new constitution was adopted.

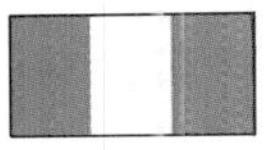

NIGERIA

Population: 89.6 million
Area: 365,000 square miles
Capital: Abuja
Language: English, Hausa and tribal languages
Currency: Naira

Great confusion exists about Nigeria, its population and resources, due to decades of political instability and civil war. The population was estimated in 1963 to be 55,670,000. Recent massive growths in population are known to have taken place, but estimates of the present number range from 90 to 120 million. Equally uncertain are the country's economic figures. The rich agricultural soil supports thriving farming communities, which produce heavy crops of millet, cassava and yams for local consumption. Export crops include cocoa and groundnuts. Industrial activity has been boosted by rich oil reserves, but no accurate picture of this sector is possible. The political instability accelerated in 1983 with a military coup, followed by another in 1985. A subsequent promised return to democratic civilian government was postponed several times.

RWANDA

Population: 7.3 million
Area: 10,000 square miles
Capital: Kigali
Language: Kinyarwanda and French
Currency: Rwanda Franc

The independence celebrations of Rwanda in 1962 were nearly marred when it was realized that the intended national flag was almost identical to that already chosen by Mali. A large 'R' was hurriedly added and the events went ahead as planned. Independence from Belgium came in the wake of a savage internal struggle between the agricultural Hutu and the pastoral Watutsi. The latter had held power for centuries but were overthrown in the fighting, many fleeing to neighboring countries. Rwanda is a densely-populated agricultural country producing sweet potatoes and cassava for local use and coffee for sale abroad. The coup of 1973 brought the military to power, and today there is only one political party allowed in the country.

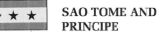

SAO TOME AND PRINCIPE

Population: 126,000
Area: 326 square miles
Capital: Sao Tome
Language: Portuguese and Fang
Currency: Dobra

As with many African nations, Sao Tome has announced that it will abandon the one-party form of government for democracy. The move was agreed to in 1990, but in the Presidential elections of 1991 there was, as usual, only one candidate. The economy of the islands is heavily dependent on two agricultural crops, cocoa and copra, and fluctuations in the international markets have great effects in Sao Tome and Principe. The government has recently tried to diversify crop production, but has had more success in building up a fishing industry to exploit the vast tuna shoals of the Gulf of Guinea. The flag of the republic features two black stars to symbolize the two islands and carries the green, red, and yellow colors common to many African nations.

▲ *Sao Tome, capital of Sao Tome and Principe.*

SENEGAL

Population: 7.7 million
Area: 76,000 square miles
Capital: Dakar
Language: French, Wolof and tribal languages
Currency: Franc CFA

In 1960 Senegal became independent of France as part of the Mali Confederacy. After only a few months Senegal withdrew, adding a green star to the Mali flag to proclaim its independence. The nation was a one-party state for some years, but is now a democracy despite several coup attempts. The groundnut, or peanut, was introduced in the 1600s as a cheap food for slaves being transported to the Caribbean, and it remains the country's most important crop.

Cotton is also grown for export, and attempts at diversifying into other areas have been made. The nation has a good transportation system, and this has encouraged modest industrialization, though this is still largely confined to Dakar, which is an extremely busy port, handling both trade and fishing vessels.

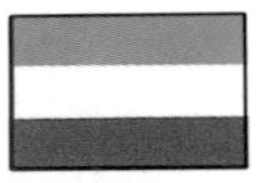

SIERRA LEONE

Population: 4.4 million
Area: 28,000 square miles
Capital: Freetown
Language: English, Krio and tribal languages
Currency: Leone

Freetown was founded as a settlement for freed slaves by the British in 1787, but the area was not formally taken over as a colony until 1808. When independence came in 1961, Sierra Leone adopted a flag showing blue for the ocean, white for unity and green for agriculture. The nation is now a one-party state under the leadership of the army. The vast majority of the population engages in subsistence farming, with rice, cassava and livestock being the primary products. A small amount of both coffee and cocoa is exported, but the nation's economy is based on the mining of bauxite, diamonds and molybdenite. Local government in Sierra Leone is based on tribal units. Each chief is supported by a Council of Elders that is responsible for law and order in the area and that has limited powers to raise and spend taxes.

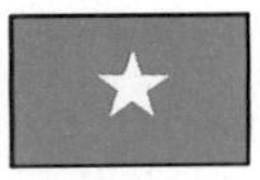

SOMALIA

Population: 7.9 million
Area: 246,000 square miles
Capital: Mogadishu
Language: Somali, Arabic, English and Italian
Currency: Somali Shilling

The Somali people are a widely-scattered nation of herdsmen whose members range widely across the arid grazing lands of the Horn of Africa. Somalia came into being when British Somaliland merged with Italian Somalia and became independent. In 1969 General Barre seized power in a coup. A long-running civil war caused Barre to flee the nation in 1991. The escalating civil war, complicated by a severe famine, led to a breakdown of the government in 1992 that caused the UN to approve intervention by troops of the United States and other nations. The internal troubles have prevented exploitation of the iron ore and gypsum and the development of industry. Over three-quarters of the Somalis lead a traditional lifestyle based on cattle, goats, sheep and camels. A few engage in agriculture along the river banks.

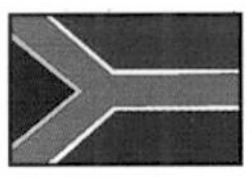

SOUTH AFRICA

Population: 32 million
Area: 434,000 square miles
Capital: Pretoria
Language: Afrikaans, English and tribal languages
Currency: Rand

Conflict between the white minority and various factions among the black majority, most noticeably the ANC and Inkatha, have overshadowed South African history in recent years. In 1991 the government announced the end of *Apartheid*, a policy of separate racial development. In 1994 the country held its first non-racial elections, with the ANC winning the largest proportion of the vote. South Africa is the wealthiest nation in Africa. Its prosperity is founded on the efficient exploitation of vast mineral wealth and large agricultural potential. Gold is mined in staggering quantity (600 metric tons in 1990) and is only the most valuable of several mining exports. Industry is well developed, with food processing, metal smelting and machinery manufacture being the most productive. The massive economic base of South Africa makes several neighboring nations dependent upon it and attracts large numbers of migrant workers. An unreliable climate ensures that agriculture remains unpredictable, though highly productive.

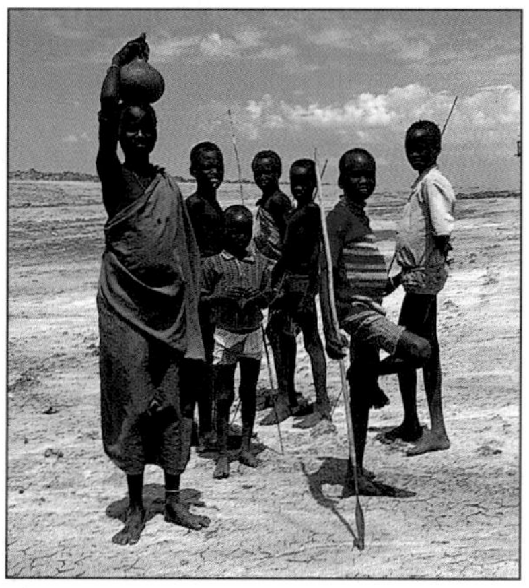

▲ *A Sudanese group, near Jonglei Canal, Sudan.*

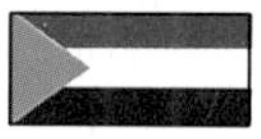

SUDAN

Population: 30 million
Area: 967,000 square miles
Capital: Khartoum
Language: Arabic, English, tribal languages
Currency: Sudanese Pound

In 1989 the army overthrew the government and pledged itself to ending the bitter civil war between the Arabic and Islamic north, and the south, where black Africans practicing tribal religions form the majority. Despite this pledge the war continues to bring misery to millions of Sudanese. The war, combined with government control of the economy, led to drastic food shortages in 1991-92. The nation is mainly desert or arid grassland, where cattle, goats and sheep are grazed. Agriculture is concentrated along the Nile and in the south, where irrigation is possible. Cotton and sugar are grown for export, as is gum arabic in the forested southwest. Land devoted to producing food is vulnerable to the periodic droughts of the region. The large mineral reserves are undeveloped due to political instability.

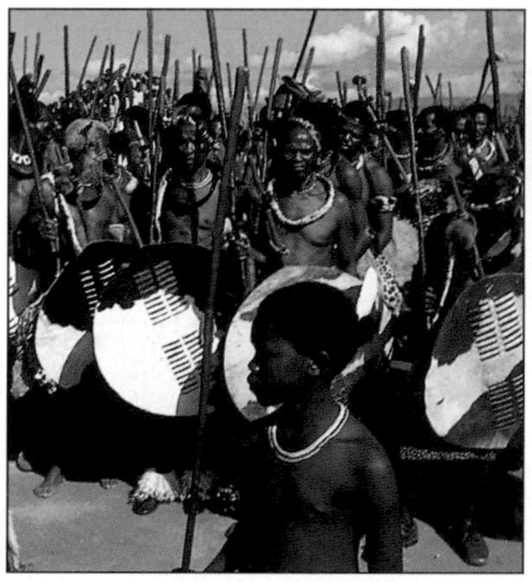

▲ *The coronation of Mswati III, Swaziland.*

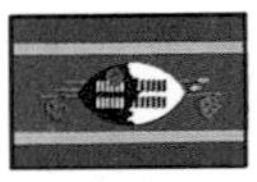

SWAZILAND

Population: 826,000
Area: 7,000 square miles
Capital: Mbabane
Language: siSwati and English
Currency: Lilangeni

Sandwiched between Mozambique and South Africa, the Kingdom of Swaziland gained independence from Britain in 1968. Since 1973 the king has ruled without Parliament, though the new king, Mswati III, has allowed an advisory college to be elected. The flag depicts the traditional shield and spears with which the Swazi successfully defended themselves against Zulu aggression in the early 19th century. Today, Swaziland is a predominantly agricultural country with the bulk of the population being engaged in subsistence agriculture. European settlers operate large-scale farms producing sugar cane, citrus fruits and cotton for export. Industry is limited to the mining of asbestos, coal and iron ore, chiefly for export.

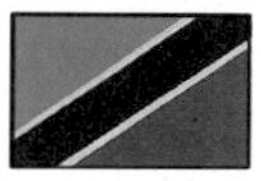

TANZANIA

Population: 25.8 million
Area: 365,000 square miles
Capital: Dodoma
Language: English, Swahili and tribal languages
Currency: Tanzanian Shilling

The republic of Tanzania is made up of over 100 tribes, each with its own language and customs. Since 1977 this diverse population has been kept together by a government based on a single political party, the leader of which, Ali Mwinyi, won the 1990 presidential election. He was the only candidate. The nation came into being in 1964, when the African majority on Zanzibar overthrew the Islamic Sultan and joined mainland Tanganyika to form a new republic. Most of the population is engaged in agriculture, though the tsetse fly and drought make this difficult across much of the mainland. Crops such as coconuts, cardamoms and cocoa have been introduced in an attempt to gain much-needed export sales. Deposits of several metal ores have been found but they remain unexploited.

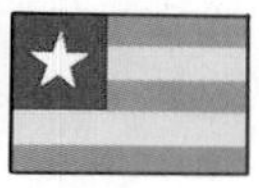

TOGO

Population: 3.7 million
Area: 22,000 square miles
Capital: Lome
Language: French and tribal languages
Currency: Franc CFA

A white star for hope dominates the flag of Togo. This former German colony passed through French control after World War I before achieving independence in 1960. The first decade of freedom was marred by internal violence, but since 1969 power has been centralized in the hands of a single party under military control. Vast reserves of phosphates, bauxite and iron ore have provided a mineral backbone to the Togo economy since exploitation began in 1953. Most of the population is engaged in agriculture on the pockets of fertile land among the inland hills. Corn and cassava are the bulk crops for local consumption, though coffee, cocoa and cotton are produced for export. The short coastline is dotted with fishing villages that reap rich harvests in the tropical waters.

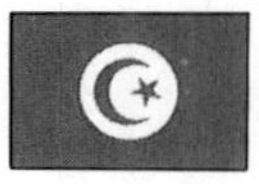

TUNISIA

Population: 8.4 million
Area: 63,000 square miles
Capital: Tunis
Language: Arabic and French
Currency: Tunisian Dinar

The Tunisian flag has been in use since 1835 when Tunisia was a province of the Turks' Ottoman Empire, and it retains the crescent, star and red field of the Turkish flag. After a period as a French protectorate, Tunisia became an independent kingdom in 1956 and a republic the following year. Oil fields exist in Tunisia, but are not rich enough to dominate the economy in the same way as in other Arab countries. Mining of lead, iron and zinc ores is also an important source of mineral wealth. Tunisia remains, however, an agricultural nation, with nearly half the working population occupied on farms, mostly in the northern half of the country. Tomatoes, olives and citrus fruits are among the most important crops. Fishing is an important employment along the coast.

▲ *A crowded market, Togo*

▲ *Mogadishu, Somalia.*

▼ *Ngorongoro Conservation Area, Tanzania.*

▲ *Typical Tunisian architecture.*

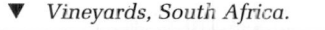

▲ *Kampala, Uganda's capital.*

▼ *Vineyards, South Africa.*

UGANDA

Population: 17 million
Area: 91,000 square miles
Capital: Kampala
Language: English, Swahili and tribal languages
Currency: Uganda Shilling

Uganda has experienced several coups and foreign invasions since independence, giving rise to numerous regimes, the most notorious being that of Idi Amin in the 1970s. The nation is made up of numerous tribes, none constituting more than one fifth of the total population, and each with its own language and culture. The political troubles have prevented the development of an industrial economy, though there is some copper mining. By contrast, agriculture is well developed and Uganda can feed itself while still producing cotton, sugar cane and coffee for export. Fishing on Lake Victoria is also a major occupation. Uganda was a British colony from 1894 to 1961. English is still widely spoken and the bulk of the population is Christian.

ZAIRE

Population: 41 million
Area: 905,000 square miles
Capital: Kinshasa
Language: French, Lingala, Swahili and tribal languages
Currency: Zaire

The flag of Zaire is based on the emblem of the Popular Movement of the Revolution, the only legal political party in the country. The party held power from 1978 until 1990, when the transition to multiparty democracy began. The vast interior of Zaire is largely covered by the Congo Basin, in which flourishes dense rain forest. Much of this area has never been properly explored and remains home to tribes leading traditional lifestyles. Best known are the pygmies, but several hundred other peoples maintain their languages and cultures. Government control is limited to regions along the Congo River and the more open regions. Here mineral mining is the mainstay of the economy, with exploitation of rich deposits of copper, oil and cobalt.

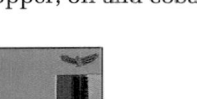

ZAMBIA

Population: 8.3 million
Area: 290,000 square miles
Capital: Lusaka
Language: English and tribal languages
Currency: Kwacha

The Zambian economy is almost entirely dependent on copper, over 500,000 metric tons of which are produced each year. The nation is therefore vulnerable to changes on the international commodities market. The bulk of the population

is employed in agriculture, much of it subsistence. Corn and livestock are the main agricultural products, though some sugar cane is produced for export. The development of more sophisticated agriculture is hampered by the tsetse fly and occasional droughts. Forests cover nearly half the total land area, but there is no forestry industry. Independence from Britain came to Zambia in 1964, and until the 1991 multiparty elections it was ruled by the United National Independence Party of Kenneth Kaunda.

▲ *Kapenta drying racks, Zambia.*

▲ *Plantation worker harvesting tea, Zaire.*

ZIMBABWE

Population: 9.9 million
Area: 151,000 square miles
Capital: Harare
Language: English, Shona and Ndebele
Currency: Zimbabwe Dollar

Zimbabwe came into being in 1980, when the former white-ruled Rhodesia became a democracy under black rule. President Mugabe moved the nation towards Marxism. The new nation was named after stone ruins discovered in the region, which indicated an advanced civilization that had vanished some centuries earlier. The country has a balanced economy, with mining, industry and agriculture all playing their part. Mining is based on the exploitation of gold, nickel and coal deposits. Agriculture is largely conducted by subsistence farmers producing corn and sorghum. Larger scale farms produce tobacco for export and fruits. The extensive industrial scene is dominated by the processing of mining and agricultural products.

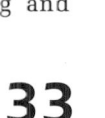

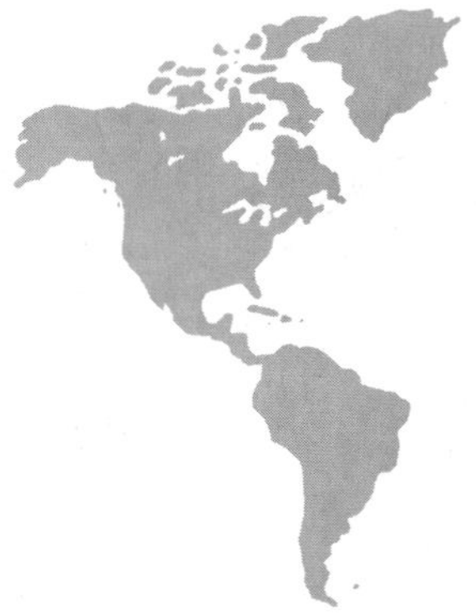

The AMERICAS

The Americas are continents of contrast, where wealth and poverty, wilderness and human-engineered landscapes can be found in the greatest diversity and extremes.

Stretching from the Arctic Ocean to the chill, stormy waters off Cape Horn, the Americas embrace the full range of climatic zones, from frozen tundra to tropical heat and then to bare, frozen plains again. Nor is the physical geology any less diverse. The central regions of North America, long characterized by vast prairies, are flat and featureless, and the Amazon Basin is a vast, alluvial depression where no land is more than several feet above sea level. But in the Andes and Rockies the Americas can also boast one of the longest and most rugged mountain chains in the world. Heights exceed 22,000 feet in the southern Andes and top 20,000 feet in Alaska.

Associated with climatic and geographical variation are those of ecology and habitat. The tropical regions of South and Central America are the site of the largest and most diverse rainforests in the world. These forests cover vast areas of land and contain more species of plants and animals than the rest of the world put together. The sheer beauty and diversity of the rainforests are staggering. Yet, it is in the Americas that destruction of the rainforests is at its most widespread. The vast boreal forests of the far north are less threatened, though they are heavily exploited for timber and pulp. Elsewhere, a combination of semiaridity and suitable temperature produce vast grasslands on which graze huge herds of animals.

The human impact on the Americas has been immense. North America is generally more prosperous and has felt the influence of humans more widely than either Central or South America. The once open prairies have been emptied of the millions of bison and are now plowed to produce massive crops of grain to feed the world. Those areas unsuited to grain agriculture are grazed by cattle and sheep, banishing the native fauna to special reserves.

The mineral wealth of the north has been exploited and is still being extracted on a massive scale. Gold, silver, copper, iron and other metals are gouged from the ground in huge quantities by large companies.

These changes have resulted in a highly developed and prosperous economy for the peoples of North America. Large cities have sprung up across the continent, with populations numbering into the millions. Roads, railroads and flightpaths provide good communications across the northern continent, allowing free trade and transportation links to aid prosperity further.

By contrast, much of Central and South America is less altered by human progress, and living conditions are generally poorer. Though large areas of rainforest are being developed or destroyed, much of it still stands untouched by anything except the activities of hunter-gatherer societies that have coexisted with the forests for millenia. Industry and mining are poorly developed, and the bulk of the population rely on farming for a livelihood. Often the farmers operate at subsistence level, barely producing enough for their own needs. Many of the peoples of the interior have little contact with European-style civilization. Both in the high Andes and in the dense forests there exist settlements that continue to live as their ancestors have done for generations. Technology and beliefs are much as they have always been, preserving cultures in tune with their surroundings, but giving poor life expectancy and low standards of living.

Many of the nations are poverty stricken and have fragile economies. Though the dominant and more prosperous nations give aid and help, the tiny island republics of the Caribbean remain devoid of natural resources and have economies based on the growing of bananas or coconuts and on tourism.

Taken together, the Americas provide a startling contrast of landscapes, natural ecologies and human activities. If they are continents of wealth, plenty and beauty, they are also lands where poverty, deprivation and squalor are equally common.

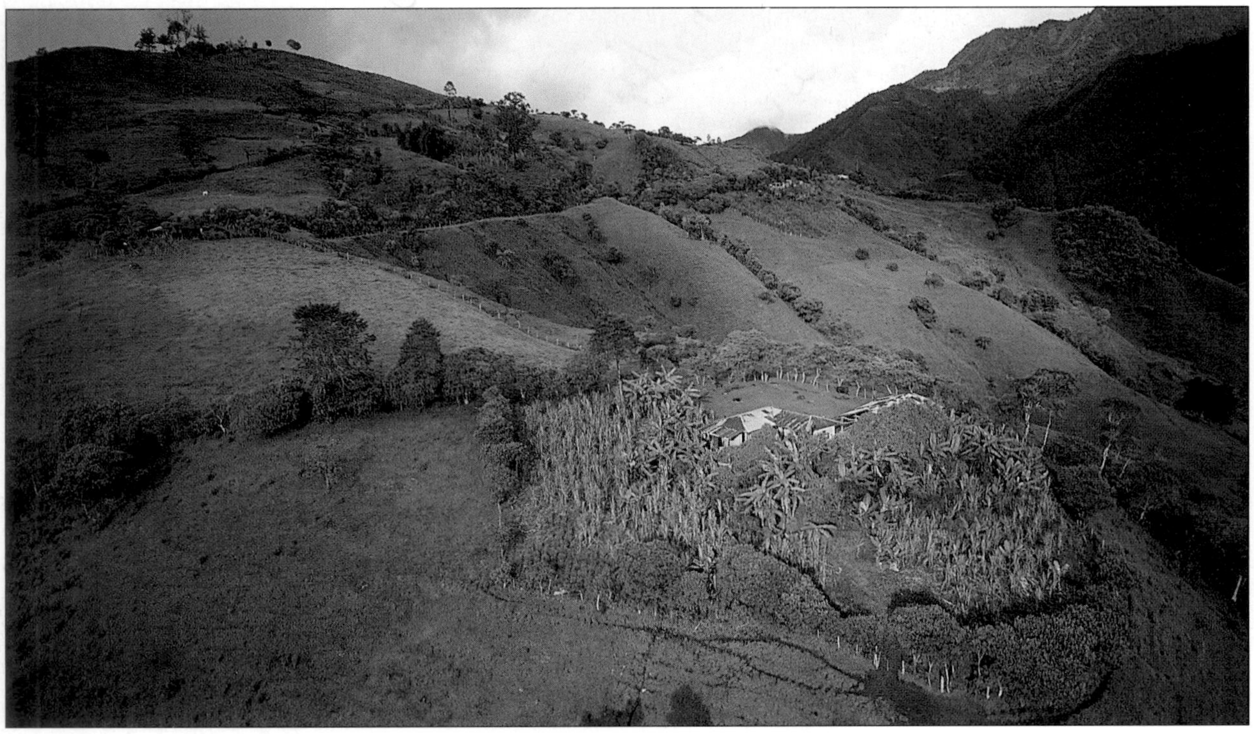

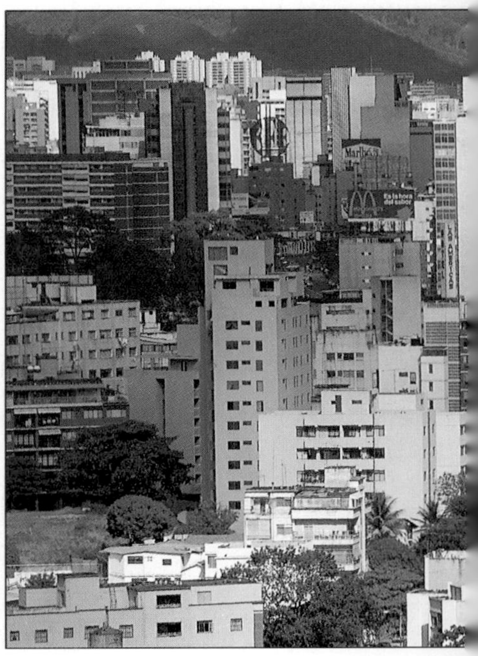

◄ *A hillside dwelling, Colombia.*

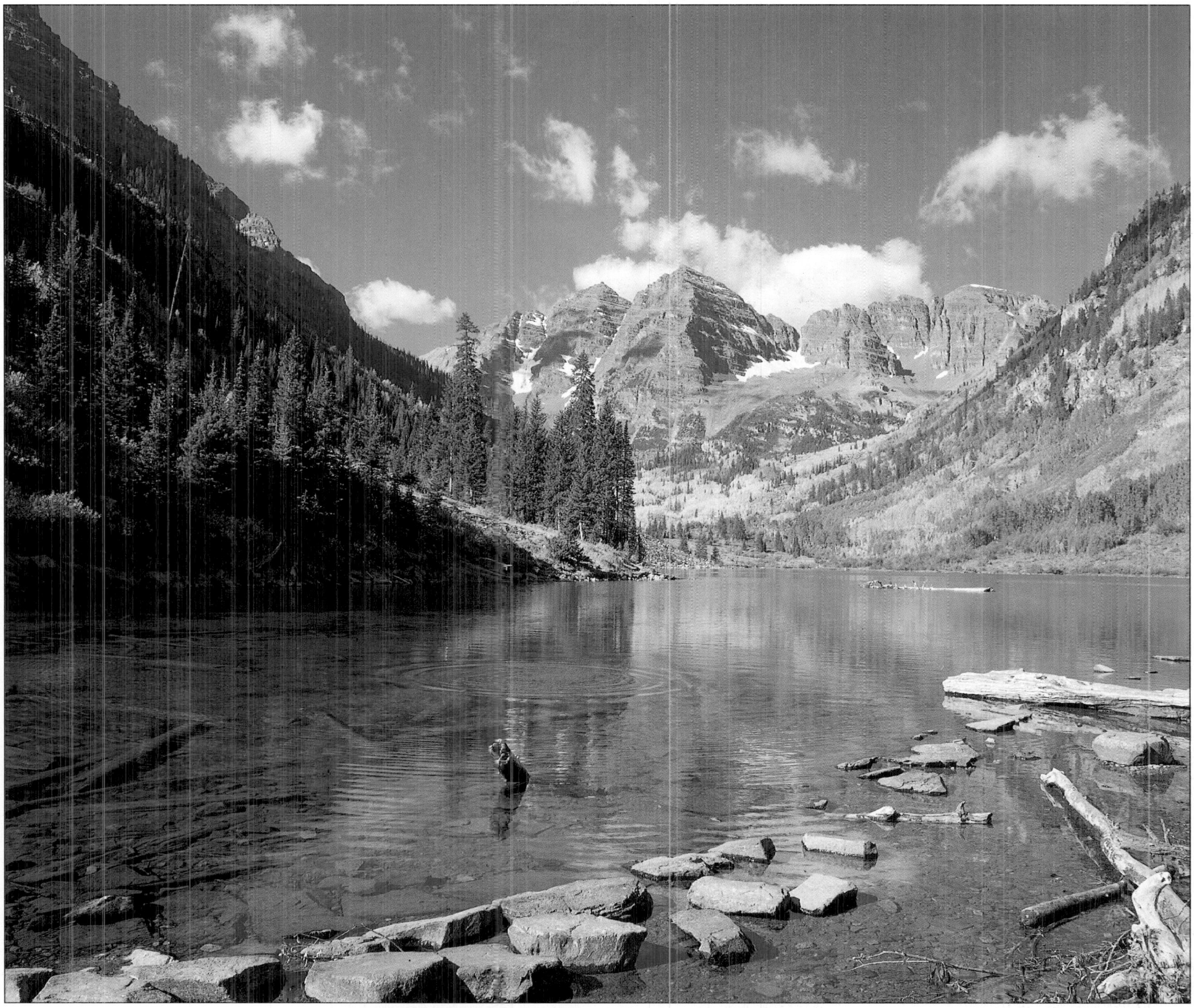

▲ *Lake and mountain scenery, Colorado, USA.*

▶ *Prickly Bay beach, Grenada.*

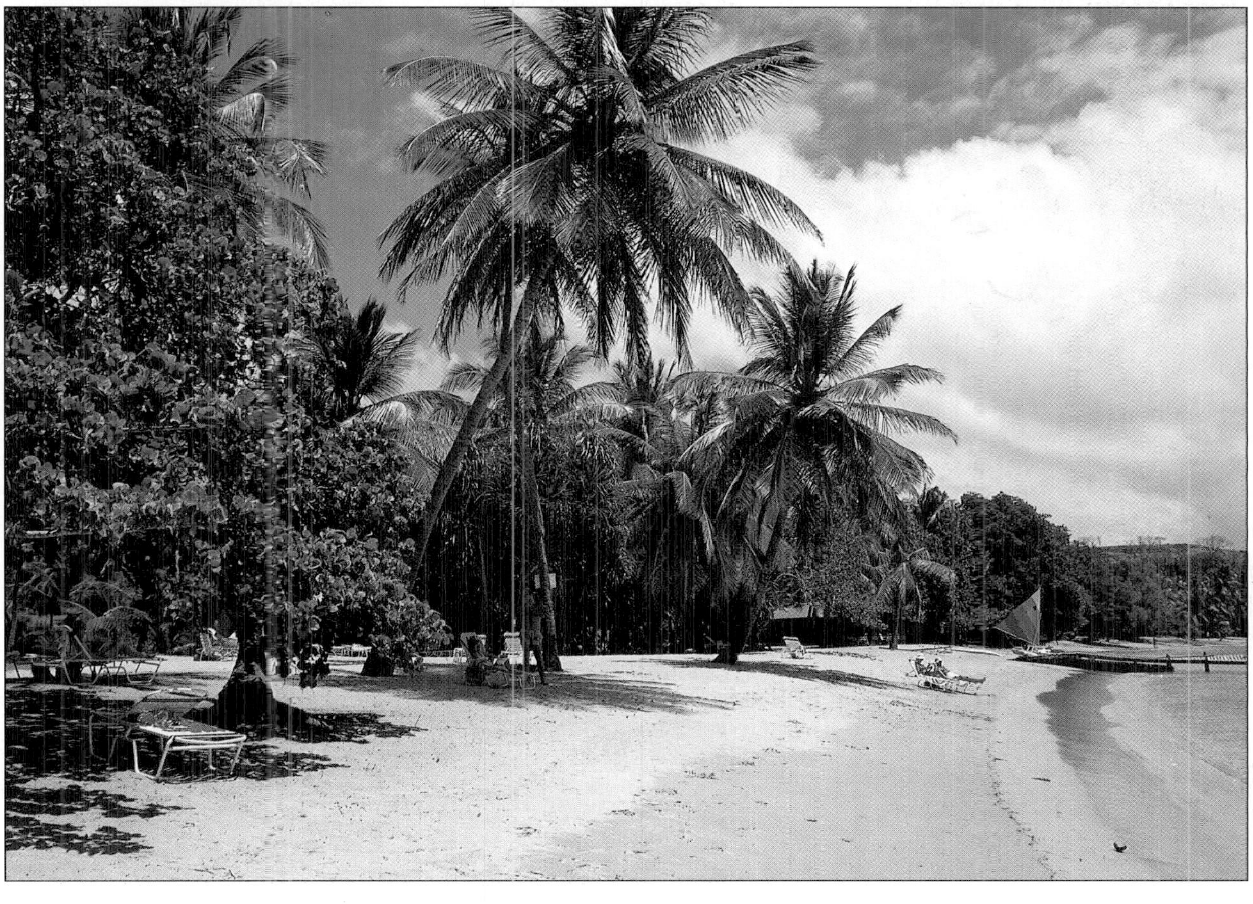

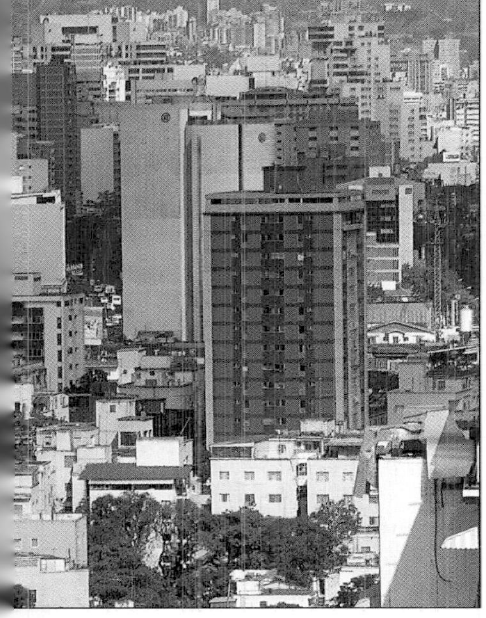

▲ *Caracas, capital of Venezuela.*

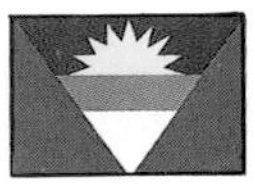

ANTIGUA AND BARBUDA

Population: 64,000
Area: 169.8 square miles
Capital: St John's
Language: English
Currency: East Caribbean Dollar

This nation of three islands take its name from the two populated islands, the third being Redonda. The islands were discovered by Christopher Columbus in 1493 but Spanish attempts at colonization failed, as did those of France. Only when British settlers arrived to grow sugar cane in the late 17th century did a permanent settlement result. The sugar crop was abandoned in the 1970s in favor of more diversified agriculture, with cotton and fruit ranking high. The wealth of the nation, however, lies in tourism. The glittering white beaches and warm seas make this a paradise for those seeking a relaxing vacation. The government is a democracy based on universal suffrage, with a Prime Minister and a two-chamber legislature.

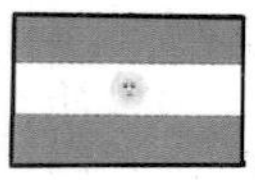

ARGENTINA

Population: 33 million
Area: 1,068,000 square miles
Capital: Buenos Aires
Language: Spanish
Currency: Austral

As one of the largest and richest countries in South America, Argentina has the potential to become a dominant influence in that region. Internal political troubles, however, have held back the massive growth that is still possible. The most recent military rule began in a coup of 1976, and collapsed after defeat in the Falklands War against Britain in 1982. The government has attempted to bring together in harmony the mixed population. The largest ethnic groups are the native Indian peoples, the descendants of Spanish settlers, and more recent European arrivals. Agricultural fertility is noticeable. Sunflower oil and wheat are both produced in quantity, but the largest exports are beef and lamb from the pampas grasslands. Mining is a major contributor to national wealth, with coal, gold, silver and copper all being worked in quantity.

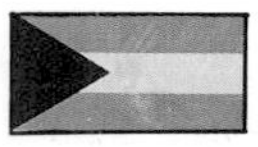

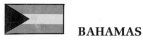

BAHAMAS

Population: 264,000
Area: 5,000 square miles
Capital: Nassau
Language: English
Currency: Bahamian Dollar

There may be as many as 1,700 islands and cays in the Bahamas, but only 700 are of any size, and only 30 are permanently inhabited. The low-lying coral islands support only a thin soil, a fact which has long hampered a more dynamic economy. The agricultural base of the islands remains sugar cane, though livestock and egg production for local consumption are important. Fishing the shallow tropical waters is a thriving industry, and modern techniques of fish farming are boosting the catch. The business community is much larger than might be expected, due to the liberal tax laws that have turned the islands into a tax haven for foreign businesses. The balmy climate and open beaches have made the islands a center for tourism, which brings large quantities of foreign currency into the islands.

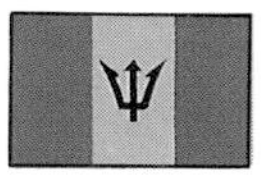

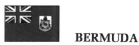

BARBADOS

Population: 259,000
Area: 166 square miles
Capital: Bridgetown
Language: English
Currency: Barbados Dollar

The trident dominates the flag of Barbados, symbolizing the wealth of the sea. This is apt, for the island has long depended on the sea for its livelihood. The delectable flying fish of the island's waters are a noted delicacy, and during the season hundreds of boats put out in search of these creatures and the high prices they fetch. Recent tourist promotions have boosted the economy, with outsiders flocking to Barbados in search of the warm sea and wide beaches. The island is densely populated, ranking high in the world's population density, though most of the people live in the countryside. The traditional sugar cane crop, part of which is turned to rum, remains important to the local economy. The country has a democratic constitution with a Prime Minister and a two-chamber legislature.

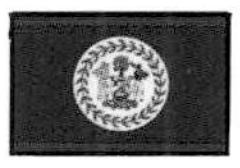

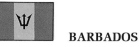

BELIZE

Population: 196,000
Area: 9,000 square miles
Capital: Belmopan
Language: English and Spanish
Currency: Belize Dollar

The small nation of Belize gained its independence from Great Britain in 1981. A British military garrison remains, however, to provide protection against Guatemala, which claims Belize for its own, as the latter's army consists of a single battalion and two small naval craft. Belize has a democratic government operating under a Prime Minister and a two-chamber legislature. Only the coastal region is heavily populated, with the interior being blanketed in dense forests that are, as yet, unexploited. The mainstay of the economy is agriculture, which accounts for over half of export values. Sugar cane is the chief crop, followed by citrus fruits, which are processed into juice concentrates for export. Corn, rice and livestock are raised for local consumption, making Belize self-sufficient in food.

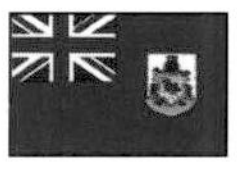

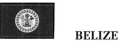

BERMUDA

Population: 60,000
Area: 20.4 square miles
Capital: Hamilton
Language: English
Currency: Bermuda Dollar

The islands of Bermuda lie in the Western Atlantic some 500 miles from the North American coast. Only about 20 of the 150 islands are inhabited, the rest being isolated islets and rocky outcrops. The economy is almost entirely reliant on tourism and insurance for survival. Over half a million tourists come to Bermuda each year to enjoy the balmy climate and excellent swimming waters Several major insurance companies are based here to take advantage of favorable local laws. The islands are officially a colony of the United Kingdom, with a Governor General being appointed by the Crown. However, the democratically-elected Parliament is free to take what action it wishes in all matters other than foreign affairs, defense and the police. The Governor General is responsible for these matters.

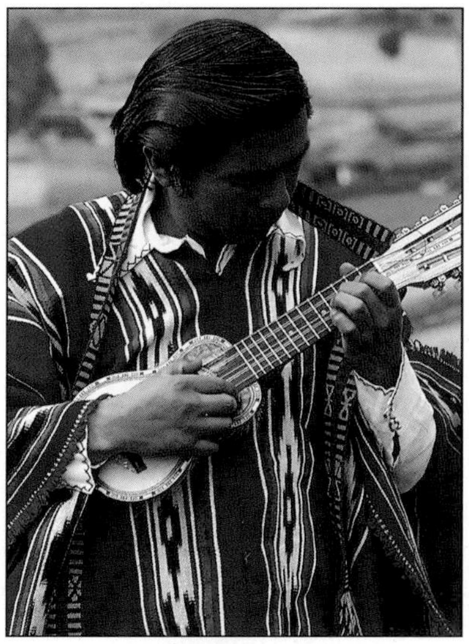

▲ *A musician performing at a festival, Bolivia.*

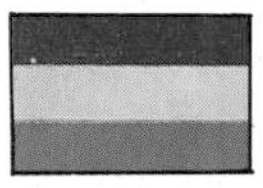

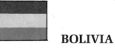

BOLIVIA

Population: 7.7 million
Area: 424,000 square miles
Capital: Sucre
Language: Spanish and tribal languages
Currency: Boliviano

Bolivia has been landlocked since it lost its coastline to Chile in 1884, and all exports must leave via other nations, predominantly along the

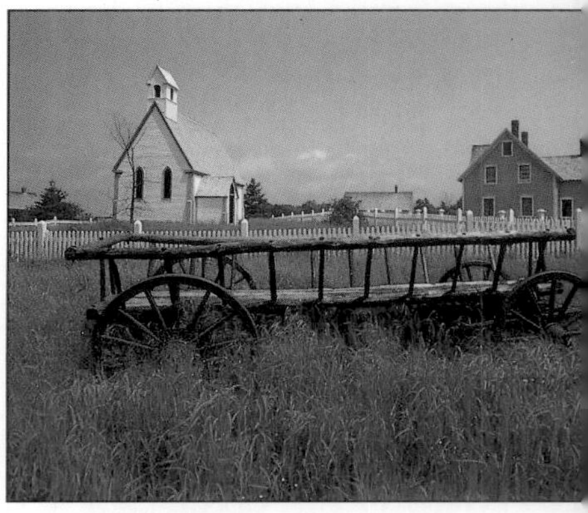

▲ *Kings Landing Historical Settlement, Canada.*

▼ *English Harbour, Antigua.*

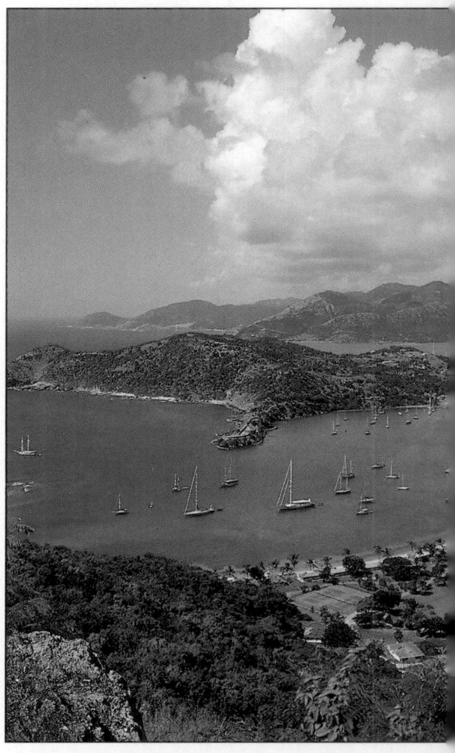

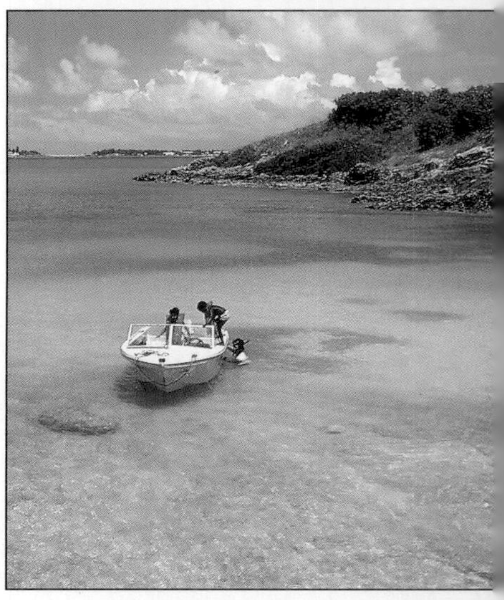

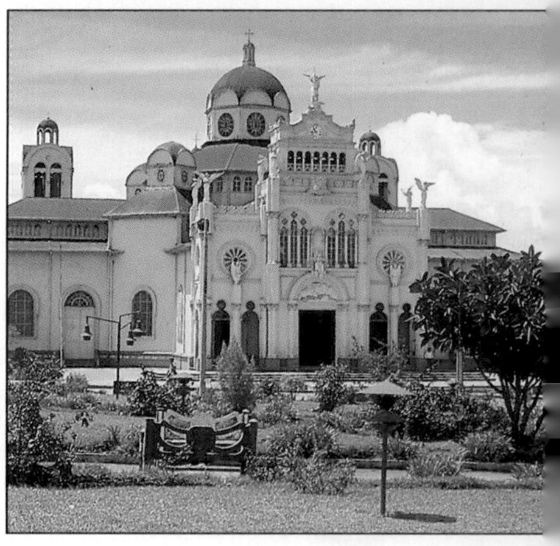

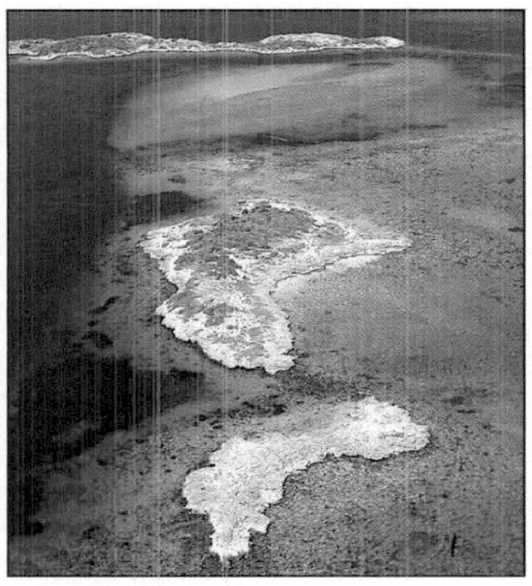

▲ *Normans Cays and Exuma Cays, Bahamas.*

▼ *Village children in Belize.*

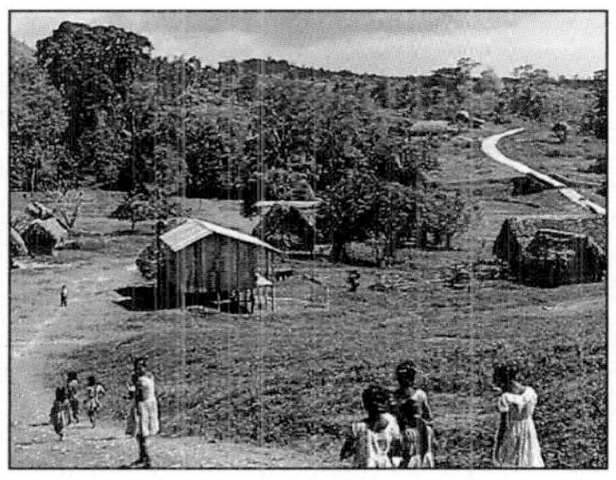

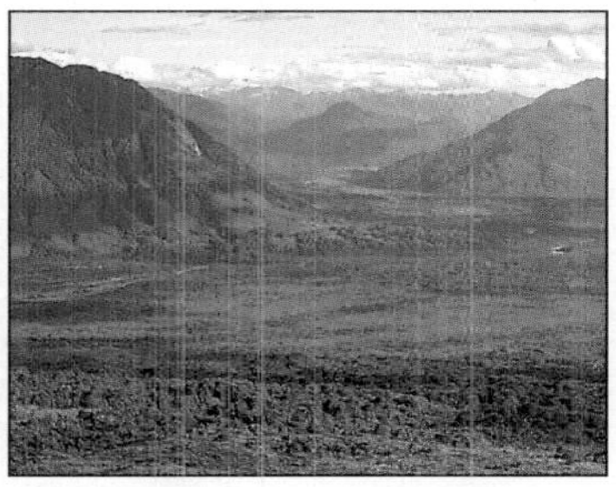

▲ *A landscape in southern Chile.*

Below left: *Hawkins Island, Bermuda.*

▼ *The Careenage, Bridgetown, Barbados.*

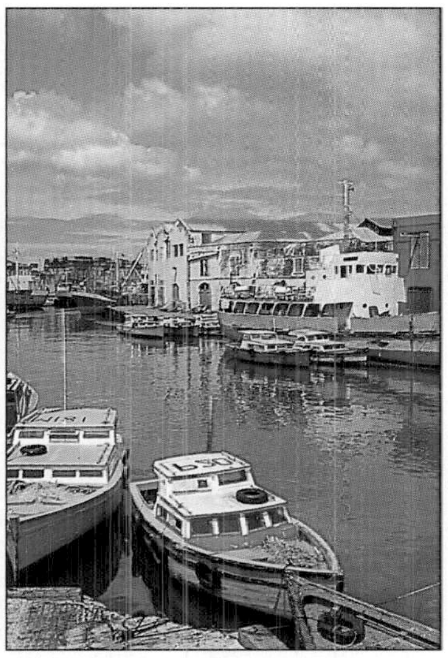

◄ *Cartago, former capital of Costa Rica.*

▼ *Buenos Aires, Argentina.*

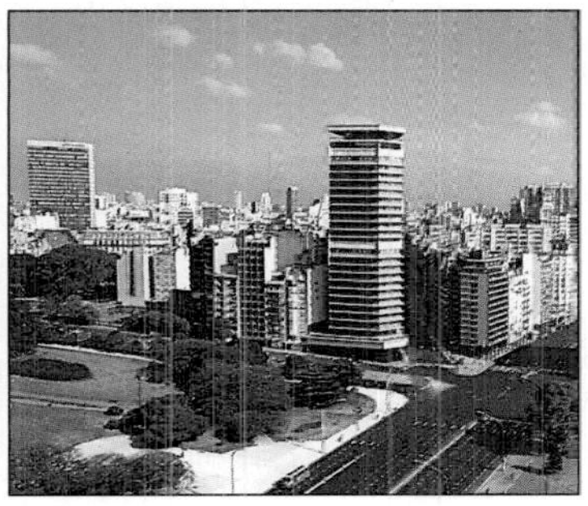

rail link to the Chilean town of Arica. The vast bulk of these exports are minerals, with tin leading the field by a large margin. It is planned to expand the smelting capacity of Bolivia so that more tin ore can be processed before export. Silver and gold are exploited in smaller quantities, as is zinc. The agricultural output includes coffee and potatoes grown in the mountains, together with increasing quantities of sugar cane and cotton in the eastern lowlands. Coca is a traditional crop which has recently boomed as a source of cocaine. The United States is sponsoring a government program to destroy the coca crop. Bolivia is notoriously unstable politically, having experienced fourteen presidents and a military junta since 1966.

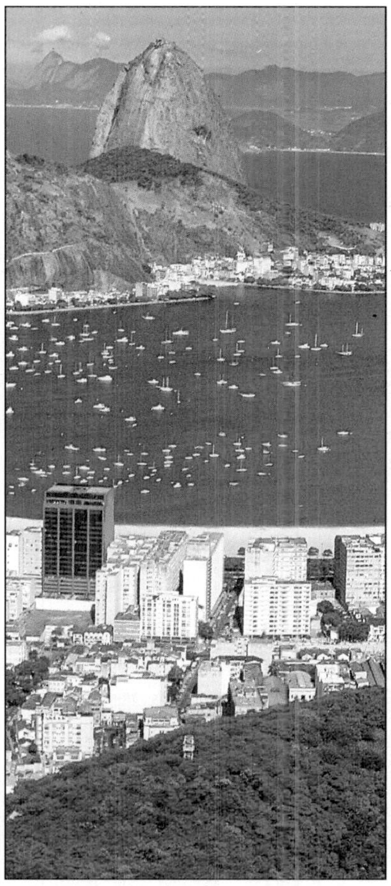

▲ *Rio de Janeiro, Brazil.*

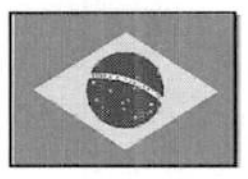

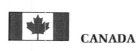

BRAZIL

Population: 151 million
Area: 3,286,000 square miles
Capital: Brasilia
Language: Portuguese and tribal languages
Currency: Cruzeiro

The present democratic constitution of Brazil came into being in 1988 after two decades of military rule. The nation is the only South American state with Portuguese as the official language, a fact that dates back to a treaty between Spain and Portugal in 1494. The southern and eastern regions are the best developed, and it is here that agriculture and industry are most heavily concentrated. Coffee is by far the most important crop, producing over 3 million metric tons annually. Various other tropical crops such as sugar cane, cotton, cassava and citrus fruits are also important. Industry is based on the exploitation of crops and minerals such as quartz, thorium, zirconium and chromium. The vast Amazon Basin contains the largest rainforest in the world, with an incredible diversity of wildlife. Conservationists throughout the world are concerned as large areas of this forest are felled each year to make way for agriculture and to extract the valuable timber.

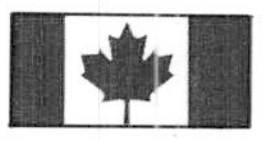

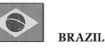

CANADA

Population: 27.7 million
Area: 4,000,000 square miles
Capital: Ottawa
Language: English and French
Currency: Canadian Dollar

As the second largest country in area in the world, Canada has a surprisingly small population. The reason for this is that the vast majority of Canada's land lies in the harsh northern latitudes, where tundra or boreal forest cover the ground. The population is concentrated in the southern region, where the climate is kinder and agriculture is possible. Wheat production is the basis of the agricultural economy, with nearly 900 million bushels being produced each year. Beef output is almost as important, while market gardening and fur farming are important in certain localities. Vast mineral reserves include nickel, zinc, copper and gold. The forestry sector is a major employer. The industrial scene is highly diversified, with a wide range of products being produced both for internal consumption and for export. Canada is a federal democracy with each of the provinces retaining considerable powers. There have been demands for provincial independence, especially from Quebec.

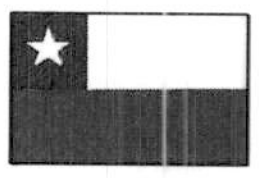

CHILE

Population: 13.6 million
Area: 284,000 square miles
Capital: Santiago
Language: Spanish
Currency: Chilean Peso

The long, narrow strip of territory which makes up Chile is defined by the Pacific Ocean on the west and the watershed of the Andes on the east. The mountainous terrain has inhibited both communications and economic development, and Chile remains one of the poorer South American states. Nonetheless, the nation has some potential. The north has rich mineral deposits, and these are being exploited on a large scale, especially copper, which accounts for forty percent of exports by value. Agriculture is restricted to valleys and terraced highlands. The most important crops are fruits such as apples, plums and citrus. Chile has had a checkered political history, with military coups and a Marxist government featuring strongly. In 1989 the military regime handed rule over to a democratically elected civilian government, but retained some powers for itself.

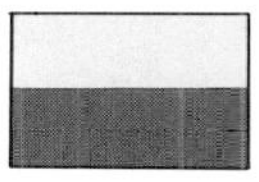

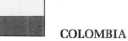

COLOMBIA

Population: 33.4 million
Area: 441,000 square miles
Capital: Bogota
Language: Spanish
Currency: Colombian Peso

When Colombia won its independence from Spain in 1819, it included modern Panama, Venezuela and Ecuador within its frontiers. These states broke away in 1830 and 1903, while an internal revolution stripped the remaining areas of power and centralized it in Bogota. Earlier political violence appears to have ended, and the government now concentrates on improving the economy. The nation is perhaps best known for its coffee, which remains an important crop. Rubber is also cultivated, but the dominant food crops are potatoes and rice. The coca crop forms the basis of a flourishing cocaine trade, and the government is engaged in a bitter struggle with drug barons to stamp out the industry. Minerals are found in abundance in Colombia, with gold and silver being the most important. The mountains produce half the world's emeralds, which are exported in quantity.

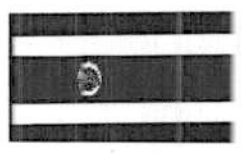

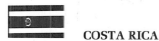

COSTA RICA

Population: 3.1 million
Area: 20,000 square miles
Capital: San Jose
Language: Spanish
Currency: Costa Rican Colon

Named 'The Rich Coast' when first discovered by Spain in the 16th century, Costa Rica has continued to support a thriving economy despite periodic disturbances. The nation is unusual in that its constitution forbids the raising of an army for any reason. However, the para-military Civil Guard undertakes many duties usually carried out by the army in other nations. Agriculture forms the basis of the economy, with the traditional crops of coffee and bananas still dominating. The two million cattle that roam the interior grasslands make an increasing contribution to the economy, as does a burgeoning industrial sector which concentrates on processing local products. Since a civil war in 1948 government has been relatively stable, and the constitution of 1949 is still in force.

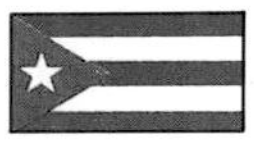

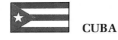

CUBA

Population: 10.8 million
Area: 44,000 square miles
Capital: Havana
Language: Spanish
Currency: Cuban Peso

It is ironic that the Cuban flag is based on that of the United States, with a triangle added to symbolize Freemasonry, for the present regime is openly hostile to the United States and has a Communist system. The present flag dates to 1849 and remained unchanged when Fidel Castro seized power in 1959. Since then Castro has pursued a Marxist-Leninist program and has given support to similar movements in Third World nations. Agriculture remains the basis of the Cuban economy, with the traditional sugar cane being the chief crop. Tobacco growing is also important, as is cotton. Fishing is a major export earner, with numerous small craft putting out to fish the surrounding waters. Mining and associated processes make up the bulk of the industrial sector, with iron and nickel leading the production tables.

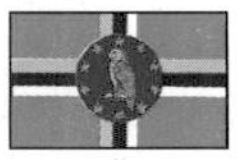

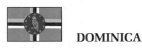

DOMINICA

Population: 71,500
Area: 290 square miles
Capital: Roseau
Language: English and French
Currency: East Caribbean Dollar

The tiny nation state of Dominica is a democratic republic within the Commonwealth and is one of the poorer Caribbean states. The economy is heavily reliant on agriculture. Bananas and coconuts are the principal crops, both of which are vulnerable to international price fluctuations. Citrus fruits are also important. The crops are periodically devastated by hurricanes, bringing disaster to the country. Fishing promises to increase significantly and remove the dangerous reliance on agriculture. Tourism is also growing as visitors come to enjoy the sun on the broad sandy beaches of the island. The inland mountains have a diverse wildlife population, including a unique species of parrot, the sisserou, which features on the national flag.

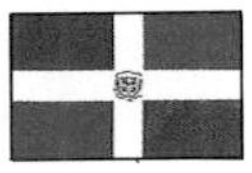

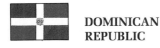

DOMINICAN REPUBLIC

Population: 7.5 million
Area: 19,000 square miles
Capital: Santo Domingo
Language: Spanish
Currency: Dominica Peso

The capital city of the Dominican Republic is the oldest European city in the Americas, having been founded by Bartholomew Columbus in 1496. During the bitter colonial struggles of the 18th century the western area of Hispaniola was captured by France, but the eastern section remained under Spanish control, and this now forms the Dominican Republic. The nation became independent in 1844, and since that time the nation has experienced political instability and periods of occupation by United States troops. The economy remains dependent on sugar cane, with sugar refining the main industry. Sugar accounts for about a quarter of all exports, though coffee and cocoa also earn foreign cash. Minerals being exploited include bauxite, gold and silver.

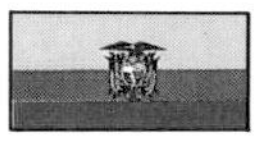

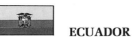

ECUADOR

Population: 10.6 million
Area: 116,000 square miles
Capital: Quito
Language: Spanish and Quechua
Currency: Sucre

Perched high in the Andes, the capital of Ecuador, Quito, has witnessed much political instability since independence from Colombia in 1830. The past forty years have seen fifteen changes of government, and confused party loyalties continue to complicate the power structure. There have been continual disputes with Peru over the border territories in the rainforest, and this quarrel most recently erupted into war in 1981, when the present border was grudgingly accepted. The discovery of oil in the rainforest region has helped boost the underdeveloped economy but has added fuel to the dispute with Peru. The mountains and coastal regions are the center of agriculture, much of which is carried out at subsistence level by the Quechua Indians. Foreign cash is earned by the export of coffee, bananas and cocoa.

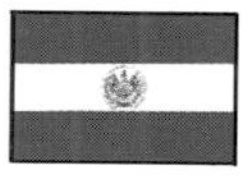

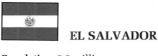

EL SALVADOR

Population: 5.5 million
Area: 8,000 square miles
Capital: San Salvador
Language: Spanish
Currency: Salvadoran Colon

Civil war and terrorism have dominated the political scene of El Salvador for over a decade. Despite this the nation is densely populated, and nearly every piece of fertile land is now under cultivation. Coffee and sugar are the main cash crops for export but large quantities of corn, beans and sorghum are produced for local consumption. There are few mineral resources and industry is based on food processing and the supply of internal requirements for clothing and other similar items. The interior forests are being exploited for

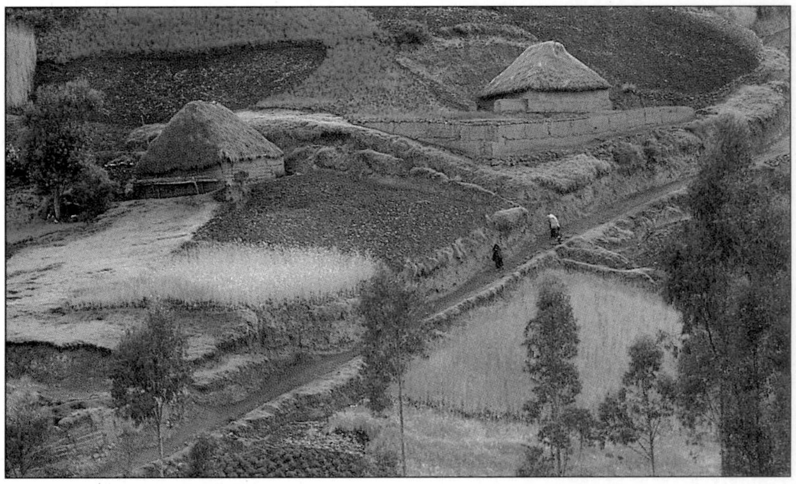

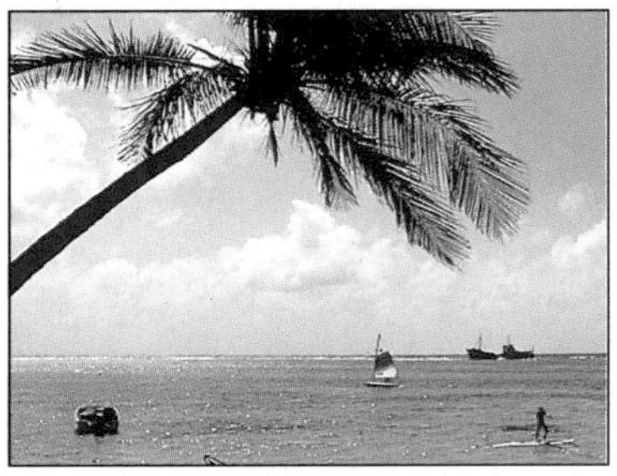

▲ *A rural scene in Ecuador.*

◀ *Punta Cana, Dominican Republic.*

▶ *A diver at Acapulco, Mexico.*

▼ *Scotts Head Peninsula, Dominica.*

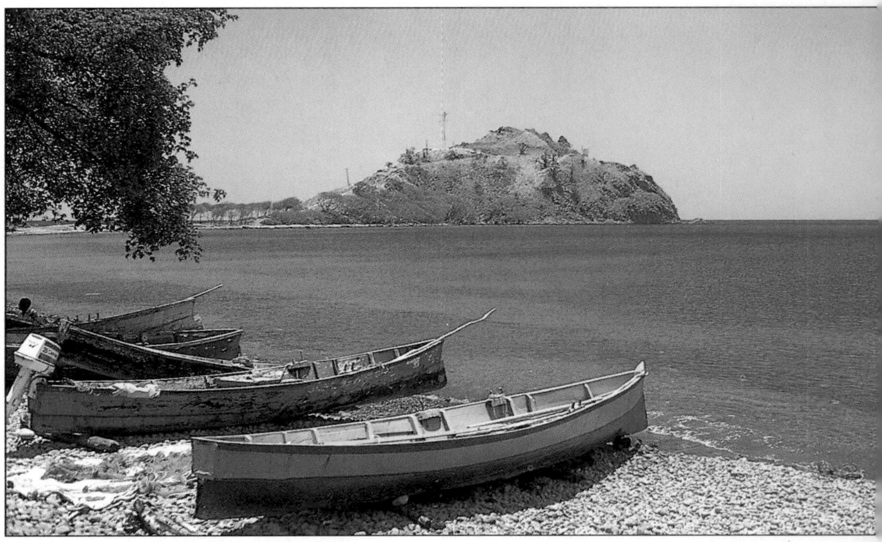

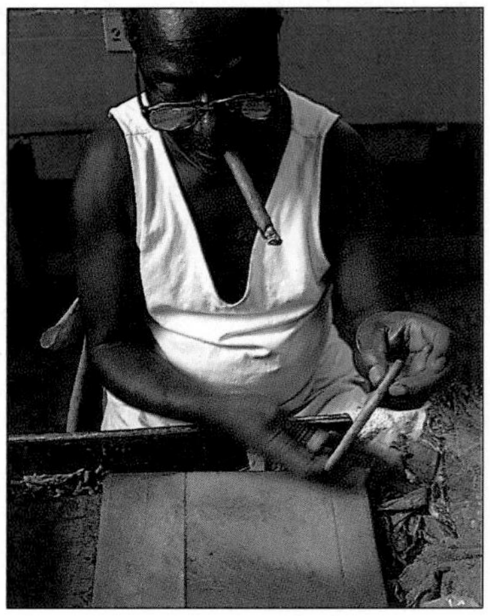

▲ *Cigar making in Havana, Cuba.*

▼ *Women washing clothes, Guatemala.*

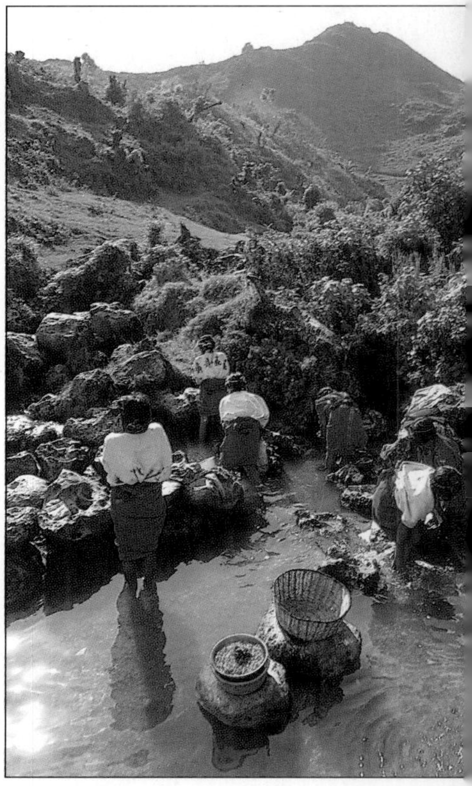

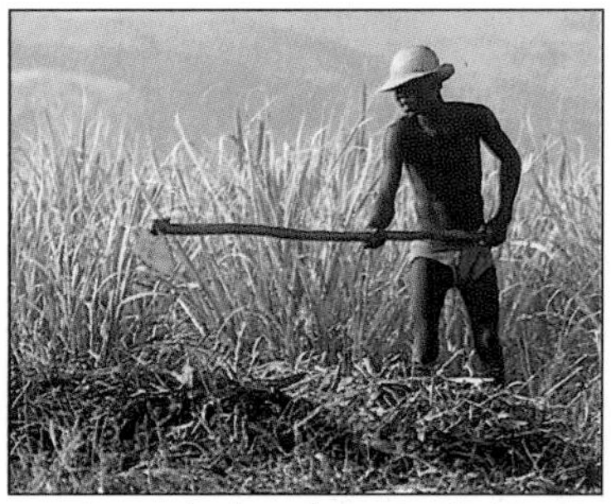

▲ *An agricultural scene, Haiti.*

▶ *Cutting cane, El Salvador.*

▲ *A coconut palm plantation, Guyana.*

▲ *Tegucigalpa, capital of Honduras.*

commercial gain, principally for timber and tropical gums. The majority of the population is descended from Spanish settlers and indigenous tribesmen, the mixed-blood mestizos forming the large majority of the people.

GRENADA

Population: 91,000
Area: 133 square miles
Capital: St George's
Language: English and French
Currency: Eastern Caribbean Dollar

Since independence from Britain in 1974, Grenada has remained within the Commonwealth but has experienced violent changes of government. In 1979 the democratic government was overthrown by a Marxist coup, which was followed by an army takeover in 1983 and an almost immediate invasion by United States troops at the request of neighboring nations worried by the turn of events. Democracy was soon restored. The economy is based on agriculture and tourism, which together account for almost all foreign earnings. The local agriculture has traditionally specialized in tropical spices, with nutmeg and mace remaining valuable crops. More usual Caribbean crops of cocoa, coconuts and bananas are also grown in quantity.

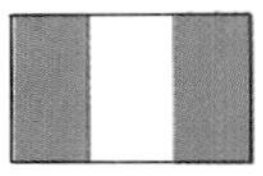

GUATEMALA

Population: 9.4 million
Area: 42,000 square miles
Capital: Guatemala City
Language: Spanish and Mayan
Currency: Quetzal

As with most Central American states, Guatemala has experienced periods of revolution, civil war and dictatorship. A constitution introduced in 1986 restored democracy, and free elections were held in 1990. The ancient Mayan civilization dominated the region before the arrival of Spanish colonists, and Mayan is still spoken by the minority Indian population. Most of the people are of Spanish descent or have adopted Spanish culture. The nation relies on agricultural produce for export earnings. Coffee alone accounts for nearly half of exports by value, with cotton, bananas and sugar making up much of the remainder. The bulk of the population is concentrated in the farming regions of the south, while the northern forests are sparsely inhabited.

GUYANA

Population: 748,000
Area: 83,000 square miles
Capital: Georgetown
Language: English
Currency: Guyana Dollar

The original inhabitants of Guyana,

the local Indian tribes, now make up barely ten percent of the population and live mainly in the southern highlands. The fertile coastal region is densely populated by the descendants of settlers and slaves of African, Indonesian, European and Chinese racial origins. These racial divides are reflected in the nation's politics, with parties often basing their support on the interests of sections of the population. The wealth of the nation lies in the agriculture of the coastal plain, where sugar cane and rice are grown in large quantities. Tropical fruits are also important crops, and much is exported. The exploitation of minerals, particularly bauxite and diamonds, adds to the export drive.

HAITI

Population: 6.8 million
Area: 11,000 square miles
Capital: Port-au-Prince
Language: French and Creole
Currency: Gourde

With an economy based on subsistence farming mixed with some cash crops, Haiti is one of the poorest American nations. Haitian coffee is considered to be of good quality and commands a high price; however, inefficient farming methods ensure that the business is of only limited profitability. Sugar and rum are also exported, but again without producing dramatic profits. The nation may have extensive mineral deposits, but these have never been confirmed. Haiti became the world's first black-governed republic when the slaves revolted in 1791 and won independence from France in 1804. After periods as a republic, kingdom and empire, Haiti fell under United States occupation before regaining independence in 1934. Between 1957 and 1986 the nation was ruled by the notorious Duvalier regime; since then the government structure has been unstable.

HONDURAS

Population: 5 million
Area: 43,000 square miles
Capital: Tegucigalpa
Language: Spanish
Currency: Lempira

In 1821 Honduras joined with El Salvador, Guatemala, Costa Rica and Nicaragua to declare independence from Spain. Once colonial rule had been ended, however, the union fell apart, and Honduras became fully independent in 1838. Since then the nation has been subject to coups and military rule alternating with periods of democracy, one of which began in 1982. The mountainous interior and continual troubles have combined to ensure that Honduras remains

economically backward. The wealth of the nation is derived from two crops, bananas and coffee, which together account for nearly all exports by value. Increasingly heavy catches of lobster and shrimp are beginning to feature in the economy. There is some small-scale mining and industrial activity.

JAMAICA

Population: 2.4 million
Area: 4,000 square miles
Capital: Kingston
Language: English
Currency: Jamaican Dollar

Though comparatively wealthy by Caribbean standards, Jamaica has continued to be troubled by a degree of poverty and periodic unemployment. The democracy established on independence in 1962 remains in force. The island nation has a mixed economy better able to withstand international price fluctuations than others in the region. Agriculture is dominated by the traditional Caribbean crops of sugar cane, bananas and citrus fruits, though less usual products such as spices are also to be found. The bulk of exports, however, are created through the mining of bauxite and gypsum. A substantial influence in the local business community, and the island's culture, is tourism. Over a million visitors come to the island each year and pump large quantities of cash into the economy.

▲ *St Elizabeth, Jamaica.*

MEXICO

Population: 84.4 million
Area: 761,000 square miles
Capital: Mexico City
Language: Spanish
Currency: Mexican Peso

Carved out of central America by invading Spaniards, Mexico was formerly the territory of the Aztecs and other tribes, who practiced human sacrifice and sun worship. The bulk of the population, known as Mestizos, is today of mixed blood though substantial minorities of both Indians and Spaniards remain. Once notorious for revolutions, Mexico has preserved its democratic constitution since 1917 and is now a relatively wealthy Central American nation. This wealth is largely based on oil reserves and a booming tourist business, though industry is growing. Silver, iron and uranium are also important minerals. Many people live on the land, producing corn, potatoes, fruits and wheat for internal markets.

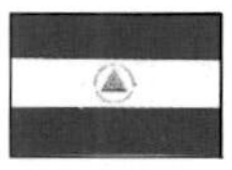

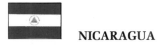

NICARAGUA

Population: 4.1 million
Area: 49,000 square miles
Capital: Managua
Language: Spanish and English
Currency: Cordoba

Nicaragua has a democratic constitution, but a state of emergency long curtailed civil liberties and democracy. The cause of the move was the long-running civil war between the Sandinista government and supporters of the previous Somoza regime. Dissension continued between rival groups after the Sandinistas were voted out of office in 1990. The continuing troubles have ensured that Nicaragua has remained underdeveloped, with agriculture continuing to employ most of the population. Coffee, cotton and sugar make up the bulk of exports, though gold, silver and copper are being mined on a small scale. Crops of corn, rice and beans are raised for internal consumption.

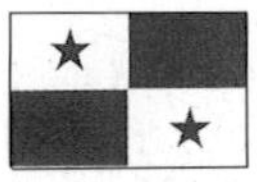

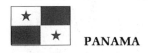

PANAMA

Population: 2.5 million
Area: 30,000 square miles
Capital: Panama City
Language: Spanish
Currency: Balboa

The Panama Canal has dominated Panamanian history and its economy ever since the nation came into being. Indeed, the province of Panama declared itself independent of Colombia in 1903 because the Colombian government had refused to sanction the construction of the Canal. The Canal eventually opened in 1914, providing both jobs and an incentive to local business. The land flanking it was held by the United States, but was returned to Panama in 1979. The late 1980s saw a succession of Presidents as power was manipulated by General Noriega. In 1989 the United States invaded the country and removed Noriega from control. Despite the economic dominance of the Canal, local food processing and manufacturing industries are important. Agriculture is restricted due to the lack of fertile ground and provides less than half of the nation's food.

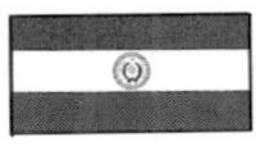

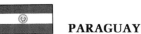

PARAGUAY

Population: 4.5 million
Area: 157,000 square miles
Capital: Asuncion
Language: Spanish and Guarani
Currency: Guarani

West of the Paraguay River is a vast region of open grasslands known as the Chaco, where the indigenous Guarani Indians ranch millions of cattle. The bulk of the population is of mixed Guarani and Spanish ancestry and inhabits the more fertile southeastern parts of the country. Here cassava, corn and beans are produced in large quantities for local consumption, though coffee and tobacco are raised as cash crops. Industry is chiefly concerned with processing agricultural products as the mineral wealth of Paraguay is negligible. There is great potential for hydroelectricity, and the largest such hydroelectric complex in the world stands at Itaipu. A 1989 coup overthrew General Stroessner, who had held power since 1956, and in 1992 a new constitution was adopted.

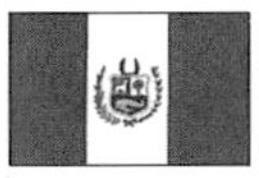

PERU

Population: 22.5 million
Area: 496,000 square miles
Capital: Lima
Language: Spanish, Aymara, Quechua
Currency: Sol

The mountain republic of Peru is unusual in that the bulk of its population is composed of indigenous Indians, with the Europeans and mixed-ancestry Mestizo in the minority. The Indians belong to the Aymara and Quechua tribal groups and generally lead traditional lifestyles in the Andes. The isolated villages and subsistence economy of the Indians have kept them outside the mainstream of Peruvian politics and national life. Along the coastal fringe coffee, cotton and sugar are produced as cash crops. Industrial activity is concentrated around the capital and is composed largely of iron and zinc works. The government of Peru has been notoriously volatile. A democratic constitution was in place from 1980 until 1992, when it was suspended by the President.

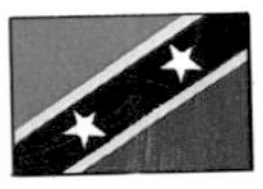

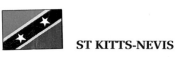

ST KITTS-NEVIS

Population: 43,000
Area: 103 square miles
Capital: Basseterre
Language: English
Currency: East Caribbean Dollar

The tiny state of St Kitts-Nevis, a Commonwealth member, is populated almost entirely by the descendants of African slaves brought to the Caribbean during the 18th century, when sugar cane was the economic mainstay of the area. Sugar remains the major crop on the islands and industry concentrates on sugar refining. Cotton is the secondary crop, and livestock is raised for local uses. Tourists, especially those from cruise ships stopping at the islands, are a welcome source of income for many of the citizens. The islands have a democratic constitution that guarantees Nevis the right to secede under certain conditions. After gaining internal self-government in 1967, the islands became fully independent in 1983.

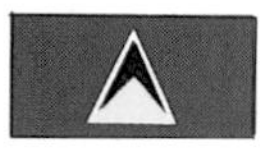

SAINT LUCIA

Population: 135,000
Area: 238 square miles
Capital: Castries
Language: English and French
Currency: East Caribbean Dollar

When Saint Lucia was granted self-government in 1967, a competition was launched to design a flag, and the winning entry remains the national flag now that full independence has been achieved. The blue ground symbolises the ocean while the black triangle represents the volcanic peak of Mount Gimie, and the yellow signifies the sun. Since independence in 1979, Saint Lucia has struggled to diversify its economy and prevent urban deprivation. Despite a move into the production of spices and citrus fruits, bananas, cocoa and coconuts remain the three dominant factors in the economy. Industry is limited to the processing of these foods. Tourism is significant, with more people visiting the island annually than actually live there.

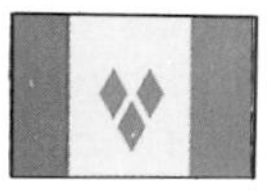

ST VINCENT AND THE GRENADINES

Population: 109,000
Area: 150 square miles
Capital: Kingstown
Language: English and French
Currency: East Caribbean Dollar

During the 18th century the sugar plantations of the Caribbean were a rich source of wealth, and they prompted rivalries between European powers. St Vincent was agreed to be neutral territory, but fighting between the British and French soon reached the island, which became a British colony in 1783. The islands achieved independence in 1979; since then the agricultural and tourist industries have continued to flourish. Agriculture is based upon bananas, cocoa, avocado pears and other tropical crops. Tourism attracts over 120,000 visitors each year, who come in search of the balmy climate and broad beaches lapped by warm waters. The constitution allows for a single elected chamber under the Prime Minister, who is appointed by the Governor General.

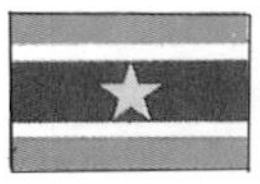

SURINAME

Population: 404,000
Area: 63,000 square miles
Capital: Parmaribo
Language: Dutch, English and others
Currency: Surinam Guilder

In 1667 Britain exchanged Suriname for Manhattan in a deal with the Netherlands. Dutch rule continued until 1975, when the nation gained independence. Since that time Suriname has been troubled by volatile politics and ethnic diversity. The major population groups are Indonesians and Creoles, with mixed European and black ancestry, but significant numbers of Chinese, Javanese and blacks form minority communities. The dense inland forests are inhabited by indigenous Indian tribes. After independence there were several coups before democracy was established in 1988, to be ousted by a military coup in 1990. The country has a flourishing economy based on mining for bauxite, together with the growing of rice and bananas, as well as fishing.

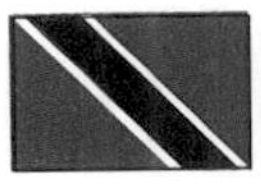

TRINIDAD AND TOBAGO

Population: 1.3 million
Area: 2,000 square miles
Capital: Port-of-Spain
Language: English
Currency: Trinidad and Tobago Dollar

The two islands that make up this nation were joined administratively by Britain in 1889, but differences remain marked. Tobago has gained the right of limited self-government after agitation against control from Trinidad. The population of Tobago is almost entirely composed of the descendants of African slaves, while Trinidad has a more mixed people. As with other Caribbean islands, Trinidad and Tobago produce quantities of cocoa, sugar and other tropical products and enjoy a thriving tourist business. However, the basis of the economy is oil, with major fields existing both on Trinidad and offshore. Unemployment remains high, and substantial parts of the population suffer poverty despite government attempts to alleviate the situation.

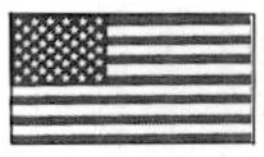

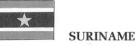

UNITED STATES OF AMERICA

Population: 255.4 million
Area: 3,680,000 square miles
Capital: Washington, D.C.
Language: English
Currency: US Dollar

The United States is the dominant economic power in the world. All sectors of the economy are highly developed and extremely

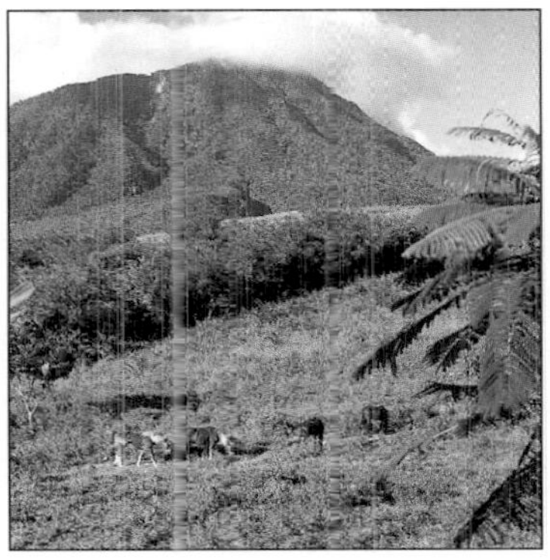

▲ *Nevis Peak, St Kitts-Nevis.*

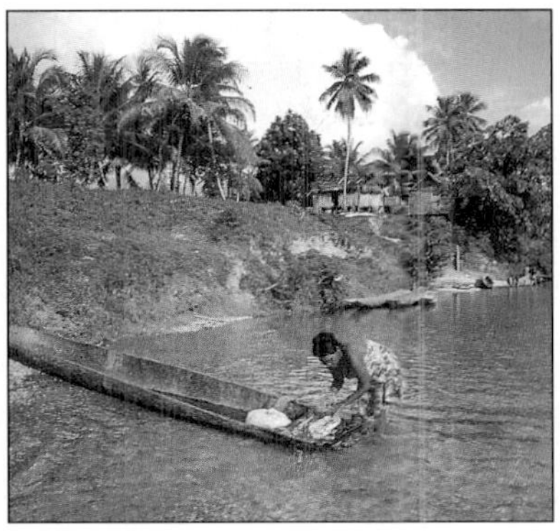

▲ *Washing clothes, Nicaragua.*

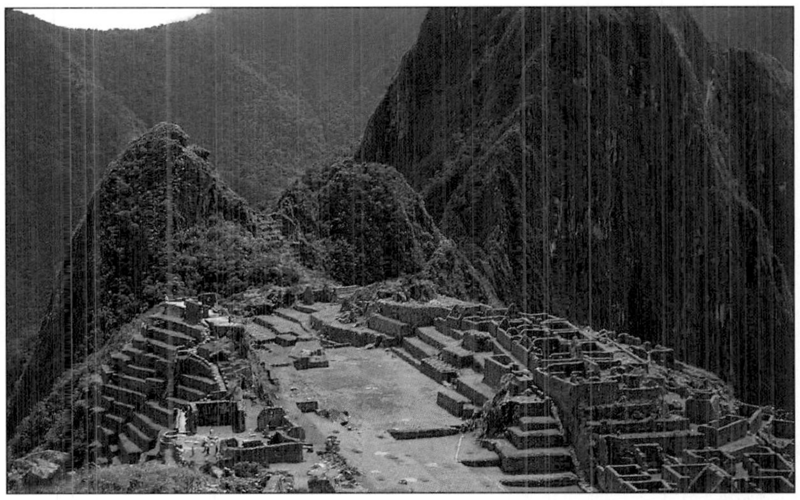

▲ *Machu Picchu, Peru.*

▼ *Loading a schooner, St Vincent.*

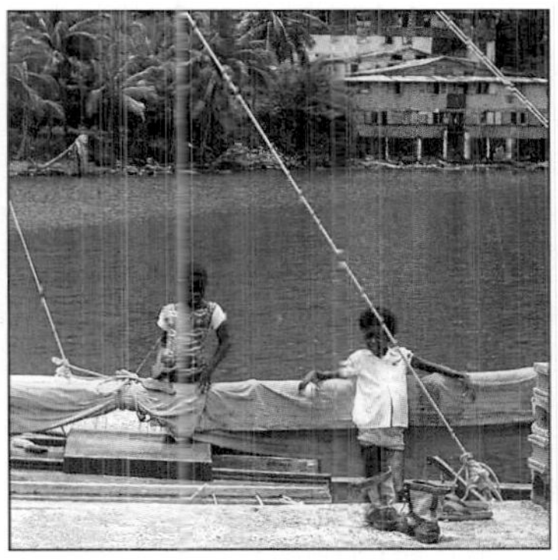

▼ *Punta del Este, Uruguay*

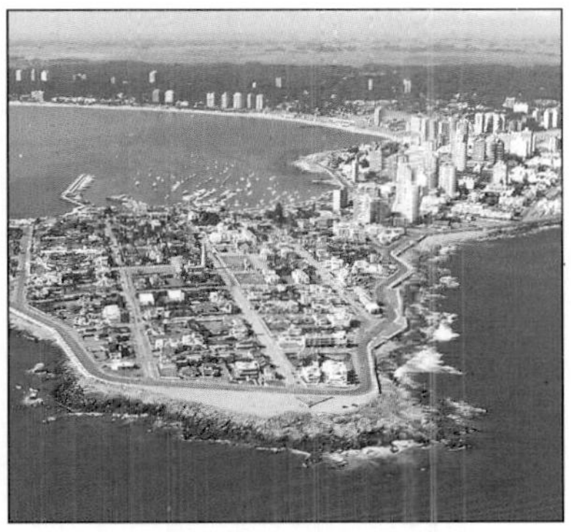

▼ *Paramaribo, Suriname.*

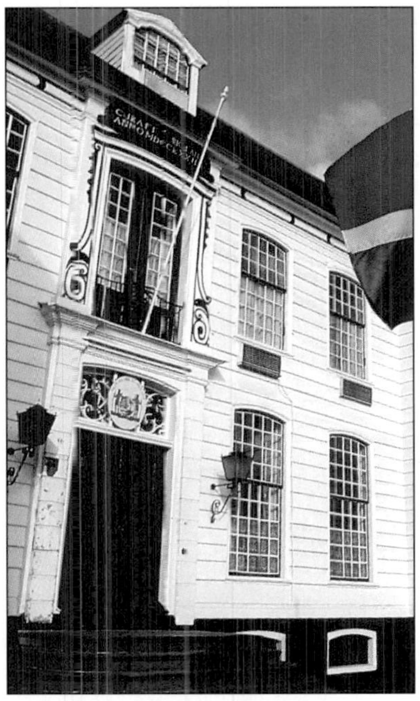

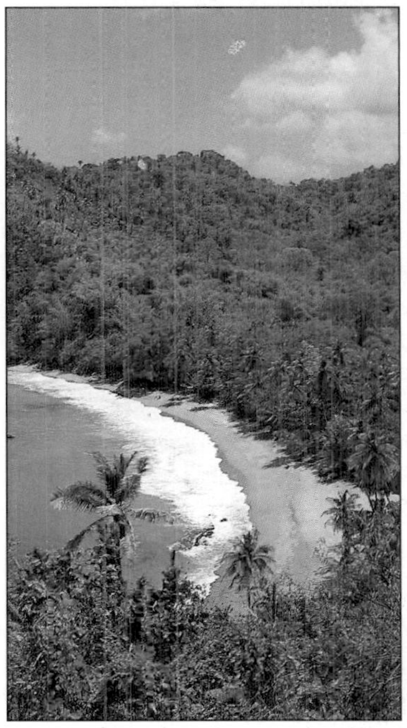

▲ *Englishman's Bay, Trinidad and Tobago.*

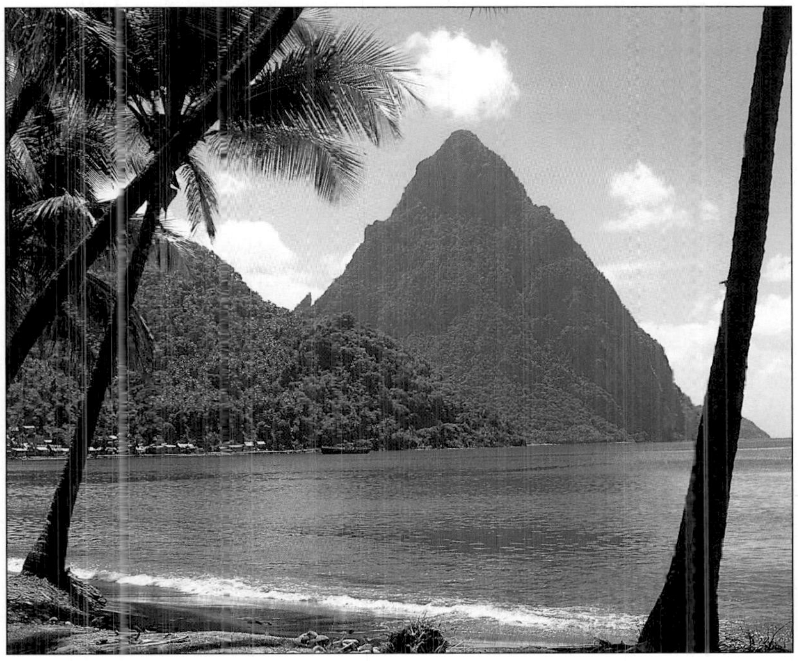

▲ *Petit Piton and Soufrière, St Lucia.*

▶ *Asuncion, Paraguay.*

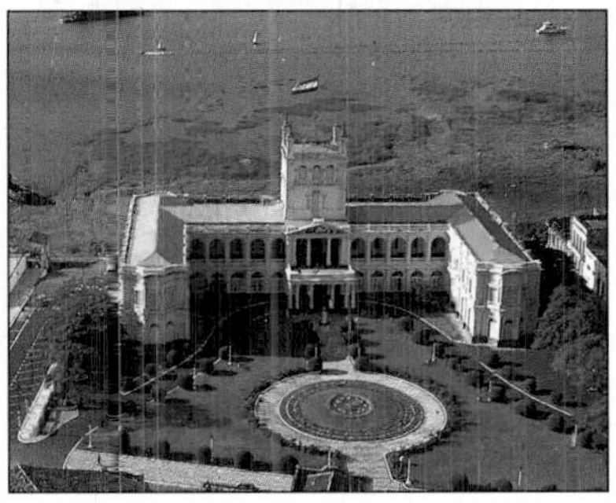

▼ *The Panama Canal, Panama.*

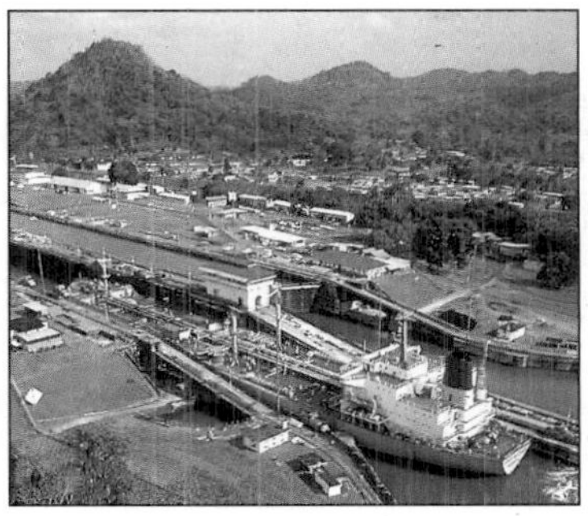

productive. Throughout the large area occupied by the nation are to be found deposits of a wide range of minerals, including oil, coal and various metals. The fertile soils are extensively farmed to produce huge crops; over two billion bushels of wheat alone. Industry is highly developed with high-tech industries leading the world in developing new processes. In other fields, too, the United States leads the industries of the world with a highly diversified range of businesses producing almost every type of goods imaginable. The nation is a democratic federal union of fifty states in which individual states have some rights of self-government, but the most important powers are held by the central government.

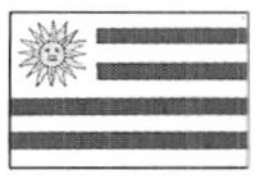

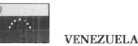

URUGUAY

Population: 3.1 million
Area: 68,000 square miles
Capital: Montevideo
Language: Spanish
Currency: Uruguayan Nuevo Peso

Uruguay was a province of Brazil until it won its independence in 1828 after a brief war, in which Uruguay enjoyed Argentinian support. Uruguay then adopted a flag sharing the same colors and the Sun of May symbol as Argentina's. In 1989 democratic elections were held after more than a decade of military intervention in government. The chief wealth of Uruguay is its land, which supports a flourishing pastoral economy. There are about 11 million cattle and 25 million sheep grazing on the rich grasslands of Uruguay, together with large numbers of farm animals. The processing of meat and leather are major industries in Uruguay, as is the spinning and weaving of wool. The nation has virtually no mineral resources and only a limited industrial base.

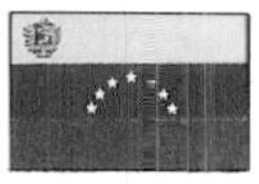

VENEZUELA

Population: 20.2 million
Area: 352,000 square miles
Capital: Caracas
Language: Spanish
Currency: Bolivar

The Republic of Venezuela came into being in 1830, when the area broke away from Colombia just nine years after the two countries had jointly won their independence from Spain. Venezuela is more heavily dependent on industry than most other South American nations and has large cities. Nearly ninety percent of the population lives in towns, far more than in neighboring states. Vast oil reserves have been discovered and are being exploited. More established is the mining of bauxtie, which supports an aluminum smelting business. Iron ore similarly forms the basis of a metal working industry. Agriculture has steadily declined in importance, with more than half of those now employed in agriculture living at subsistence level.

AUSTRALASIA

*T*he nations of Australasia do not occupy a single continental entity, as do those of Asia, Africa or Europe. Instead they are united by cultural and ethnic traits more closely linked to the human populations than to the geographical limits of that region commonly called Australasia.

Strictly speaking, Australasia consists of the island continent of Australia, New Guinea, the Solomon Islands and possibly New Caledonia and New Zealand, though these latter are separate geological entities. The remaining islands strung across the vast spaces of the Pacific are isolated outcrops of volcanic rock or coral reefs with no geological or geographical connection to each other.

These far-flung islands and islets are, however, united by their human inhabitants. Several centuries ago, the ancestors of Polynesian and Melanesian islanders sailed across the vast, open stretches of the Pacific Ocean from Southeast Asia to colonize the remote islands of the tropical and subtropical regions. With them they brought taro, yams and other tropical crops with which to support themselves. Common ties of culture and religion bound these peoples together. Long voyages in open canoes were often undertaken between the various islands, preserving ties of technology and belief.

When European seamen arrived, from the 16th century onwards, they found the islands densely inhabited by peoples so similar that the entire region of Oceania came to be viewed as a cultural entity. European settlers and missionaries radically altered the society and cultures of the islands, though many features of Polynesian society remain even today.

The modern nations of Australasia are clearly divided into cultural and physical regions. The divides between the regions have as much to do with the economies and lifestyles of the peoples as with the physical location of the islands.

Dominating all is the great landmass of Australia. The Australian nation has a mixed culture based on the various immigrant groups, chiefly from Europe. To a much lesser extent Australian culture rests on the indigenous Aboriginal peoples who are now largely restricted to the Outback. The bulk of Australia is covered by arid deserts, where settlements are few and far between. The only populous centers are mining towns thriving on the exploitation of the rich mineral content of the nation's rocks.

Kinder climatic regions around the coasts are more densely populated, with farming communities producing crops according to the prevailing climate. All the major cities are on the coast, centered on the sites of historic ports. Here the population is engaged in industrial and service occupations more akin to developed Western economies than to the prevailing culture of Australasia.

Sharing much of the flavor of Australia is New Zealand, with its largely European population and small indigenous element. The economy and lifestyle here is more rural than in Australia, while the temperate climate dictates the crops and livestock that can be produced.

Away from these economic giants of the region, the nations are far smaller and less developed, though the original cultures are more apparent. Nations may be as small as a single island with a population of just 7,000. The largest consist of archipelagoes spread across thousands of square miles of ocean, but even these never top one million in population. The cultures of the smaller nations are closely allied to the indigenous peoples. Christianity has generally replaced the ceremonies and beliefs of the former religions, and settlers from Europe and elsewhere often form sizeable minorities among the population.

The disparate nations of Australasia form a complex pattern of human adaptation to harsh environments. From the Australian deserts to the open ocean, Australasia is a place of extremes and superlatives. The differing cultures of European settlers and native populations are sometimes blended together and elsewhere stand in stark contrast to each other. But everywhere there is the great Pacific Ocean, dividing the nations and yet uniting them.

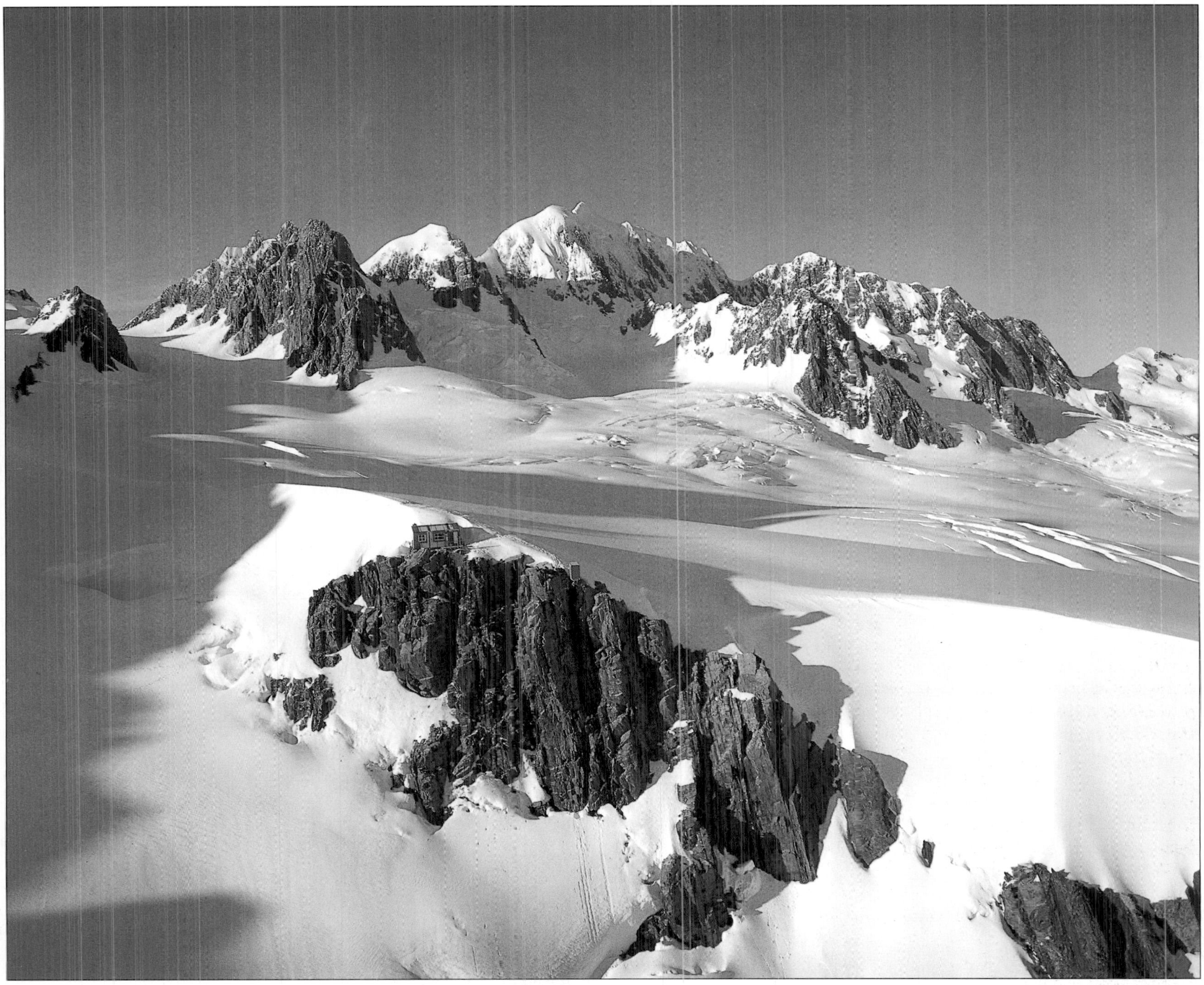

▲ *Mount Tasman, New Zealand.*

► *A native girl on the beach, Kiribati.*

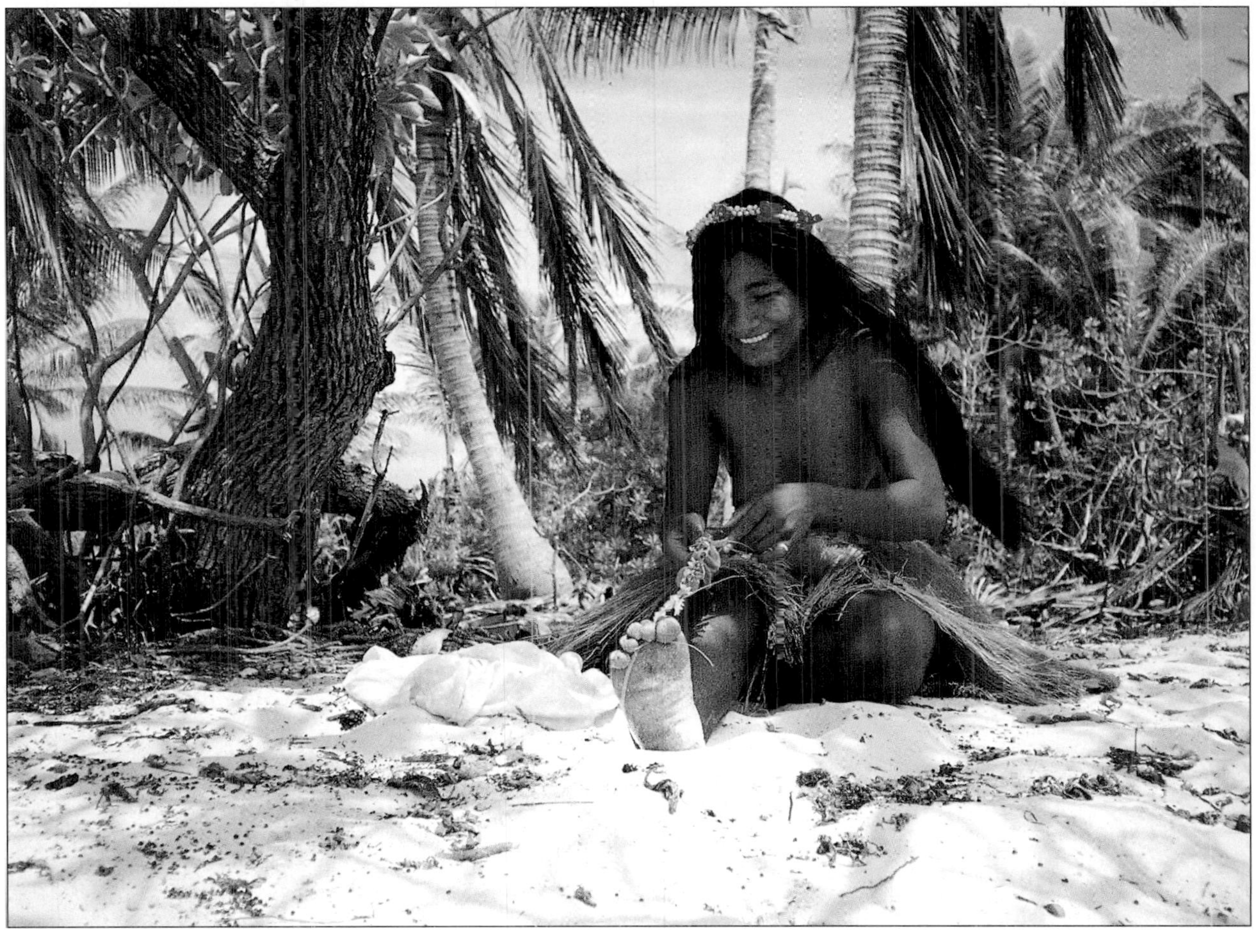

◄ *The world-famed Opera House, Sydney, Australia.*

AUSTRALIA

Population: 17.6 million
Area: 3,000,000 square miles
Capital: Canberra
Language: English
Currency: Australian Dollar

The vast nation continent of Australia was the last major land mass to be discovered by Europeans, remaining largely unknown until the 18th century. Immigration, initially from Great Britain but later from the rest of Europe, and most recently from Asia, produced the dominant social profile of modern Australia. The extensive grazing lands support large numbers of sheep and cattle, while the smaller areas of arable land produce wheat, rice and market crops. The large desert regions are rich in mineral deposits. Industry is well developed, with a wide range of consumer goods and engineering equipment being produced. The nation is a federation of six states, with the central government being responsible for the Northern Territory. It came into being on the first day of the 20th century, when former British colonies joined to form the Commonwealth of Australia.

FIJI

Population: 748,000
Area: 7,000 square miles
Capital: Suva
Language: English, Fijian and Hindustani
Currency: Fijian Dollar

Britain annexed the 330 islands of Fiji in 1874 and stamped out the endemic tribal warfare. Independence was granted in 1970, and a troubled history has resulted. The population is almost equally divided between native Fijians of Melanesian and Polynesian ancestry and immigrants from India, who arrived during British rule. In 1987 an Indian coalition won power in Parliament. Within months a coup organized by the native Fijians placed the army in power. A new constitution has been imposed, which places political power in the hands of the native Fijians. The economy is based on agriculture, with sugar cane, coconuts and ginger being the primary crops. Industry is concentrated on processing the crops.

KIRIBATI

Population: 75,000
Area: 277 square miles
Capital: Tarawa
Language: English, Gilbertese
Currency: Australian Dollar

Although Kiribati is independent, it has no currency of its own, and its citizens use the Australian dollar.

The islands are generally small but are spread over an immense area of the Pacific Ocean, being grouped into three coral archipelagos and one volcanic island. The islands voluntarily became British protectorates in 1892 and regained independence in 1979. The democratically-elected government consists of one-chamber legislature and a President. The agricultural economy relies almost exclusively on coconuts and copra, which make up over ninety percent of exports by value. The coconut tree grows well in the thin soil and tropical climate of Kiribati.

MARSHALL ISLANDS

Population: 50,000
Area: 68 square miles
Capital: Majuro
Language: English
Currency: U.S. Dollar

The republic of the Marshall Islands, independent and a member of the United Nations since 1991, consist of two chains (Radak and Ralik) of small coral atolls in the western Pacific. The form of government is a republic, headed by a President. Tourism and agriculture sustain the economy. U.S. atom bomb testing was conducted on Bikini and Eniwetok atolls.

MICRONESIA

Population: 110,000
Area: 270 square miles
Capital: Palikir
Language: English
Currency: U.S. Dollar

Better known as the Caroline Islands until independence was achieved in 1991, the Federated States of Micronesia had been under U.S. rule since World War II. The islands had previously been controlled by Spain, Germany and Japan. Made up of more than 500 islands in the western Pacific, north of Papa New Guinea, the primarily agricultural nation (coconuts, fruit) is a member of the United Nations.

NAURU

Population: 8,100
Area: 8 square miles
Capital: Yaren
Language: Nauruan and English
Currency: Australian Dollar

With a population among the lowest in the world, Nauru does not support its own currency, using instead the Australian dollar. The population is a mix of Polynesians and Melanesians who arrived generations ago and have merged to produce a single racial group. The island fell under German control in 1881, passed to Australia in 1914,

▲ *An isolated beach, Nauru.*

▶ *A highly-decorated native, Papua New Guinea.*

▼ *Niutao Island church, Tuvalu.*

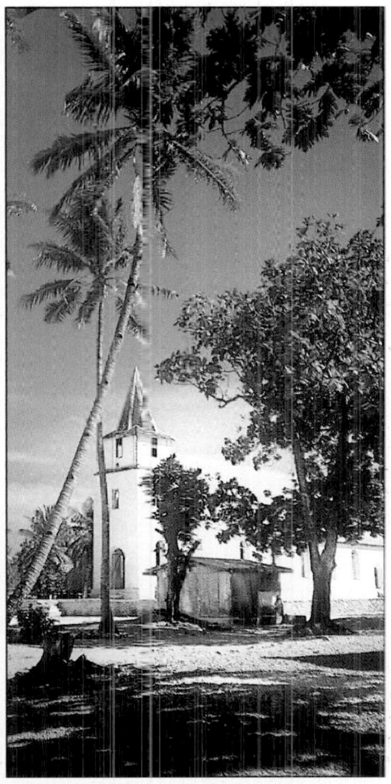

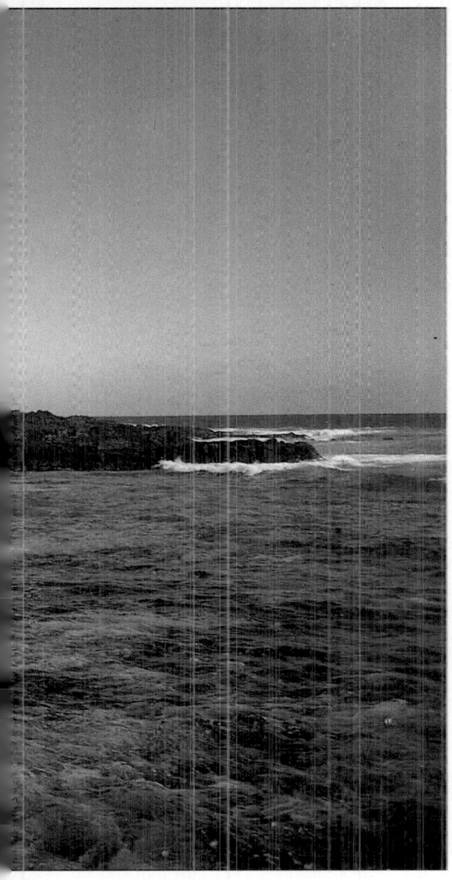

▲ *Lefaga Beach, Upolu, Western Samoa.*

◄ *Yasur volcano, Vanuatu.*

▼ *Mananuca Islands, Fiji.*

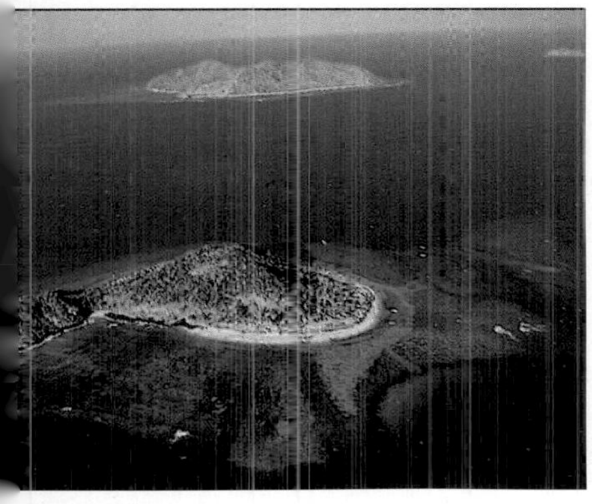

and became independent in 1968. The constitution allows an assembly elected every three years under a President. Nauru remains within the Commonwealth. The traditional crop of coconuts is widely grown and exported, while vegetables and livestock are kept for local consumption. Tourism is a growing business. The island nation's wealth, however, depends on phosphates mined on the island. This gives Nauru the highest per capita income in the Pacific islands.

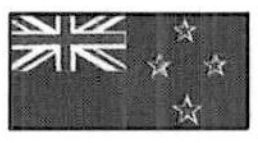

NEW ZEALAND

Population: 3.5 million
Area: 103,000 square miles
Capital: Wellington
Language: English and Maori
Currency: New Zealand Dollar

Descendants of European immigrants form the bulk of New Zealand's population, though the native Maori form the largest minority. The exports of New Zealand have traditionally been agricultural, and the pattern continues, with refrigerated meat, live animals, dairy products and wool far outstripping manufactured goods in value. However, industry is of growing importance internally, with iron and steel works and aluminum smelting being the largest heavy industrial works. The attractive scenery and relaxed lifestyle of the islands make New Zealand an increasingly popular vacation destination, with nearly a million tourists visiting each year. The government is based on universal suffrage, though some seats in the Assembly are reserved for Maoris and have an exclusively Maori electorate.

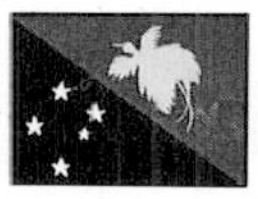

PAPUA NEW GUINEA

Population: 3.8 million
Area: 179,000 square miles
Capital: Port Moresby
Language: English, Motu and tribal languages
Currency: Kina

The rugged highlands of New Guinea are divided into isolated valleys covered by dense forests in which travel is difficult and communications are poor. The numerous tribes speak as many as 700 different languages, though the Motu form of pidgin English is a common *lingua franca*. Many of these tribes were untouched by the outside world, having no knowledge of whites until the 1940s, and they still lead traditional lifestyles. Agriculture for export is concentrated around the coasts and produces coffee, copra and cocoa. Gold is mined on a commercial scale, and there are large copper reserves on the island of Bougainville, though an active secessionist movement has disrupted mining. There is a Prime Minister and a single-chamber legislature.

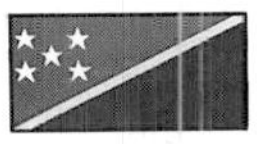

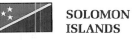

SOLOMON ISLANDS

Population: 339,000
Area: 11,000 square miles
Capital: Honiara
Language: English and tribal languages
Currency: Solomon Island Dollar

The Melanesian tribes of the Solomons retained their freedom until Britain declared a protectorate in 1893. The Japanese invaded during World War II, and Britain granted full independence in 1978. The country, a member of the Commonwealth, is governed by a Parliament elected by universal suffrage, under a Prime Minister and his cabinet. The islands are predominantly agricultural, with property ownership held collectively by tribes and clans. Cocoa and coconuts are grown for export while yams, taro and sweet potatoes are consumed locally. The large fishing fleet exploits the tuna shoals of the region and the catch is canned before export.

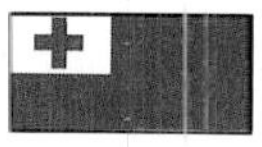

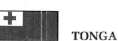

TONGA

Population: 97,000
Area: 270 square miles
Capital: Nuku'alofa
Language: Tongan and English
Currency: Pa'anga

The kingdom of Tonga dates back to the early 19th century, when the warlike King Tupou of the Ha'apai conquered all the island tribes. Tupou overthrew the rule of petty chiefs and established a rudimentary democracy before Britain declared a protectorate in 1899. Internal government continued under the royal family, and full independence came in 1970. The present constitution is based on that of King Tupou. The Assembly consists of nine chiefs elected by the chiefs, nine representatives elected by the people and eleven privy councillors appointed by the king. The main exports are coconuts, fish and vanilla, while tourism brings in substantial quantities of foreign capital.

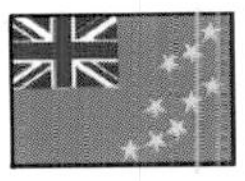

TUVALU

Population: 9,500
Area: 9.2 square miles
Capital: Funafuti
Language: Tuvaluan and English
Currency: Australian Dollar

As with other tiny Pacific states, Tuvalu uses the Australian dollar. However, it mints its own coins with unique and attractive designs. A British protectorate from 1892 to 1968, Tuvalu has a Parliament elected by universal suffrage and consisting of just twelve members, four of whom are government ministers. There are no political parties, and candidates for office run as individuals. Its nine islands are coral atolls with thin soils capable of supporting little other than coconut trees. Coconuts and copra comprise the main exports, with vegetables being grown for local consumption. The flag is highly symbolic, with the blue field representing the Pacific Ocean, the nine stars the nine islands, and the Union Jack the Commonwealth.

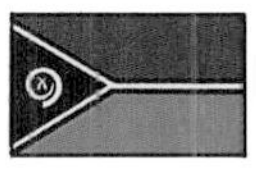

VANUATU

Population: 154,000
Area: 5,000 square miles
Capital: Vila
Language: Bislama and English
Currency: Vatu

On independence in 1980 the islands changed their name from New Hebrides to Vanuatu. The former name was given by Captain Cook because the rugged mountainous interiors reminded him of the Scottish islands, though the tropical climate is very different from that of the Scottish Hebrides. Power resides in an elected Parliament together with the tribal chiefs who sit in a separate Council. The Council advises primarily on matters of custom and tradition. The basis of the economy is the coconut tree, cocoa and coffee, which flourish in the hot, moist climate. A livestock industry based on cattle is becoming established. Tropical crops such as yams and taro are grown for local markets. Industry is limited to processing export crops and freezing the plentiful fish catch.

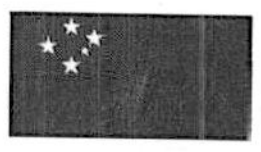

WESTERN SAMOA

Population: 160,000
Area: 1,080 square miles
Capital: Apia
Language: English and Samoan
Currency: Tala

Formerly a German colony governed from 1920 by New Zealand, Western Samoa became independent in 1962. His Highness Malietoa Manumalfili became head of state for life, but after his death future heads of state are due to be elected. Though now independent, Western Samoa maintains direct diplomatic links only within the Pacific. Elsewhere New Zealand acts on its behalf. The economy of the islands is basically agricultural, with coconuts, bananas and cocoa being among the most important crops. Despite the tropical climate and a marked dry season, tourism is only poorly developed. Industy is limited to the processing of agricultural products.

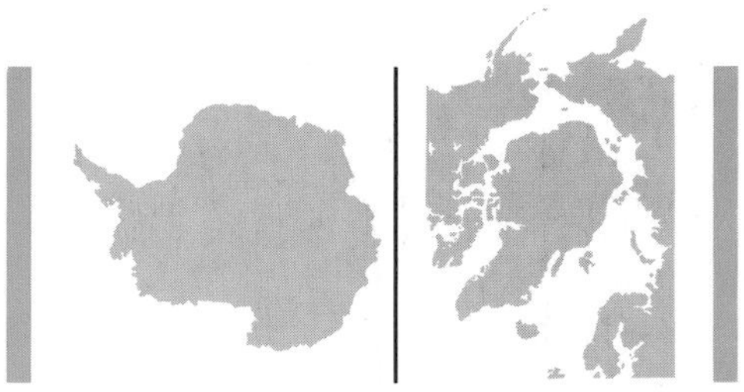

POLAR REGIONS

The polar regions have an image of being blizzard-swept wastes inhabited only by penguins and polar bears. In fact the polar regions are far more than that. It is true that both the North and South Poles are ice-bound throughout the year, but the wildlife of the regions is incredibly varied. In the north polar bears, seals and whales make up the mammal population, and the oceans are teeming with fish. The south, which has the advantage of a solid rock continent, is home to a variety of fauna, including penguins.

Both poles have been divided among various nations that maintain scientific bases and conduct research. As the Arctic is open ocean beneath the ice, it is technically not subject to any state. However, those nations that have Arctic coasts maintain various bases, often military, in the area and patrol it regularly.

The political situation of Antarctica is more complicated. Officially, the vast continent is divided among Australia, New Zealand, France, Norway and Britain. Other nations, however, including Chile and Argentina, claim sections of the continent. All these nations, and others, maintain scientific research stations on Antarctica. The population of these outposts varies greatly with the season and from year to year, but there are rarely more than a thousand people on the continent. English is now the recognized scientific language, but each nationality speaks its own language on the continent.

In 1959 the Antarctic Treaty was signed by nations involved on the continent, and in 1991 a new environmental protocol was added. The Treaty bans military activity and tightly regulates commercial and scientific activity in Antarctica. It is unlikely that either polar region will ever maintain a sizeable human population, but both remain rich in wildlife and environmental interest. It is to be hoped that international cooperation will ensure the continued existence of these great wilderness areas.

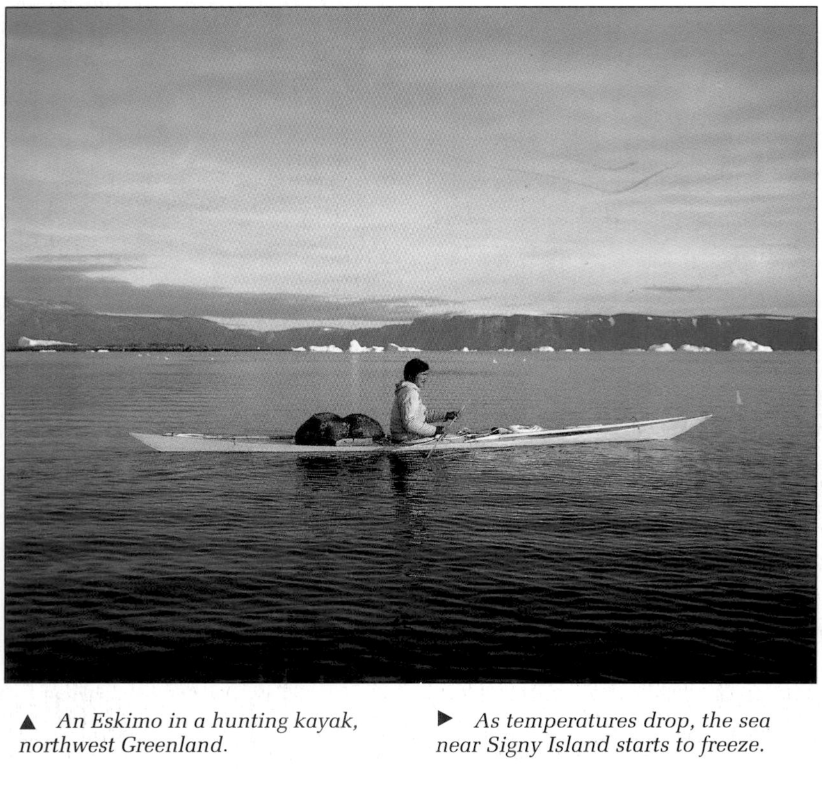

▲ *An Eskimo in a hunting kayak, northwest Greenland.*

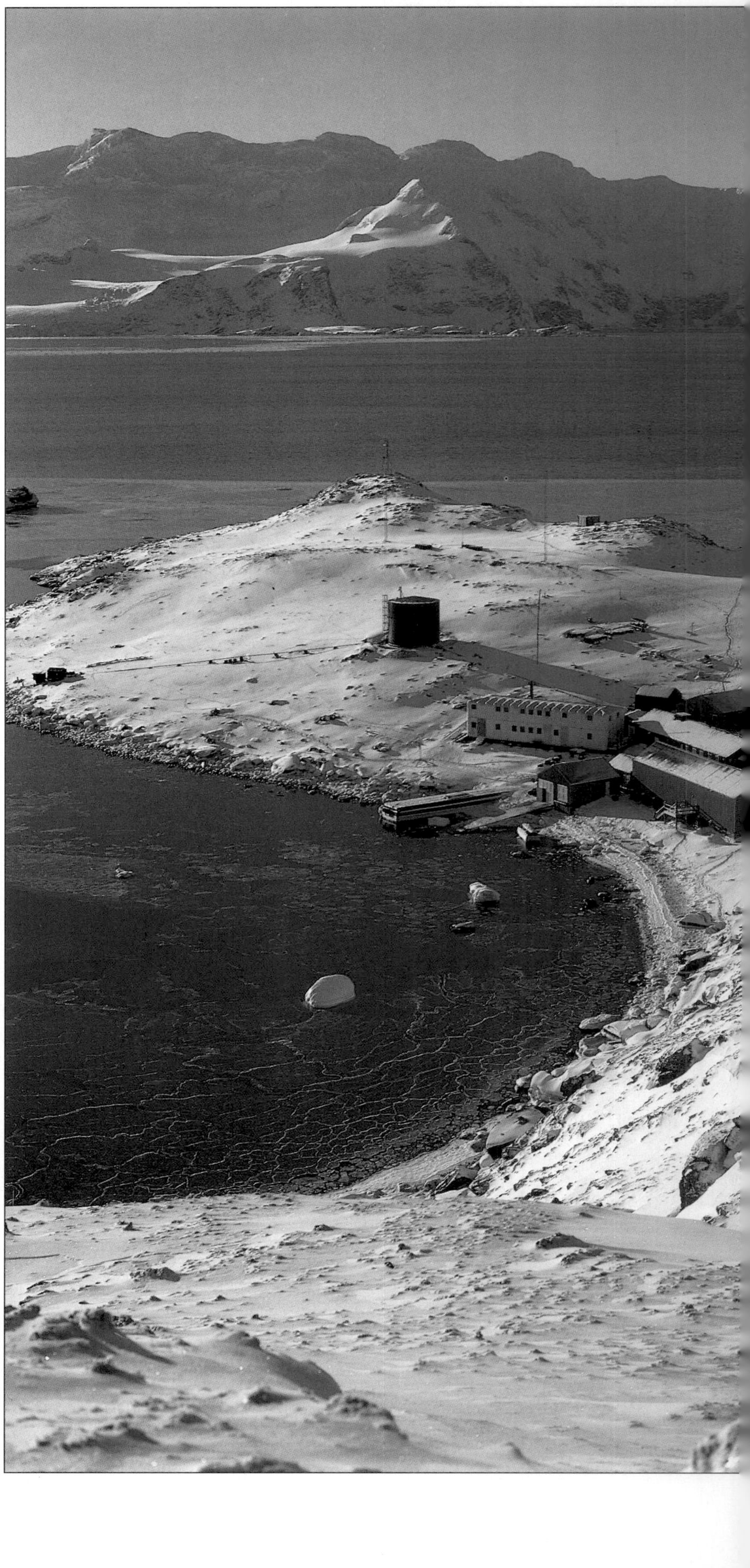

▶ *As temperatures drop, the sea near Signy Island starts to freeze.*

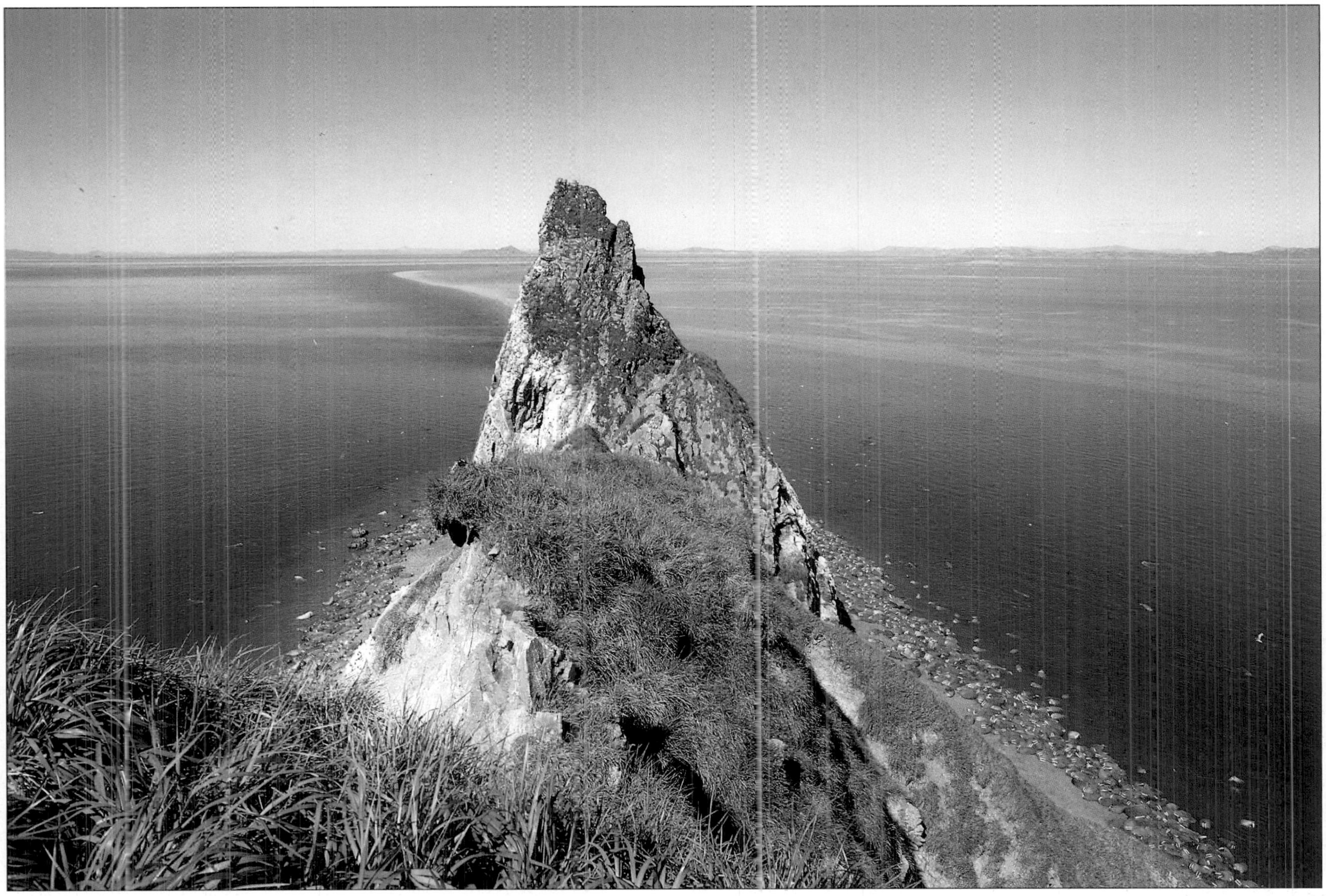

▼ Macaroni penguins on Bird Island, South Georgia.

▲ Heavy-bodied walruses resting on the beaches at Round Island, Alaska.

▼ Probing newly-formed ice in Antarctica.

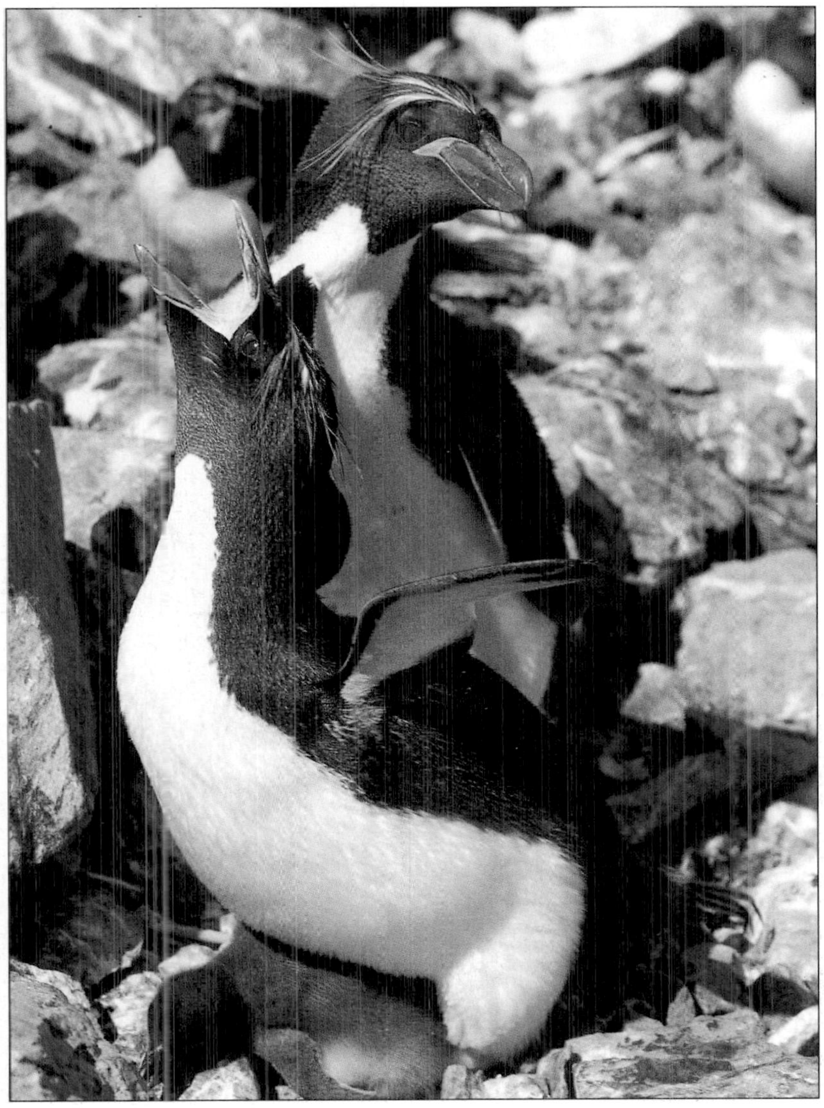

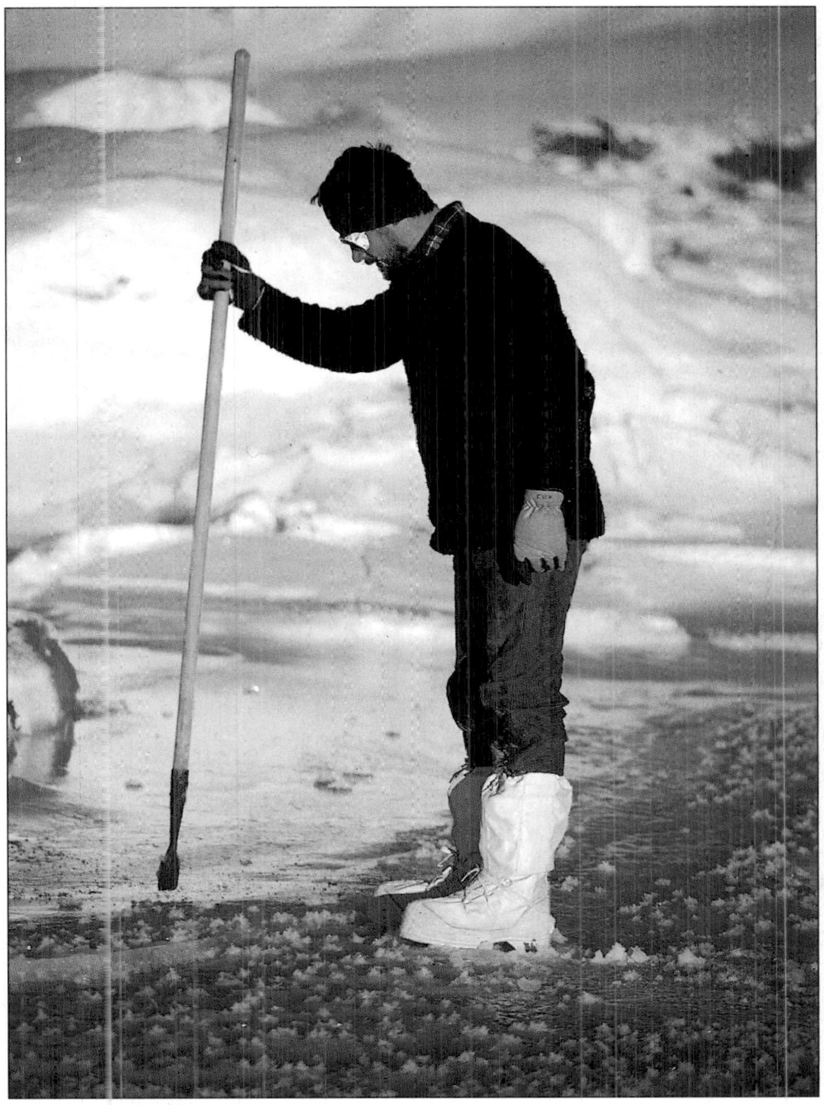

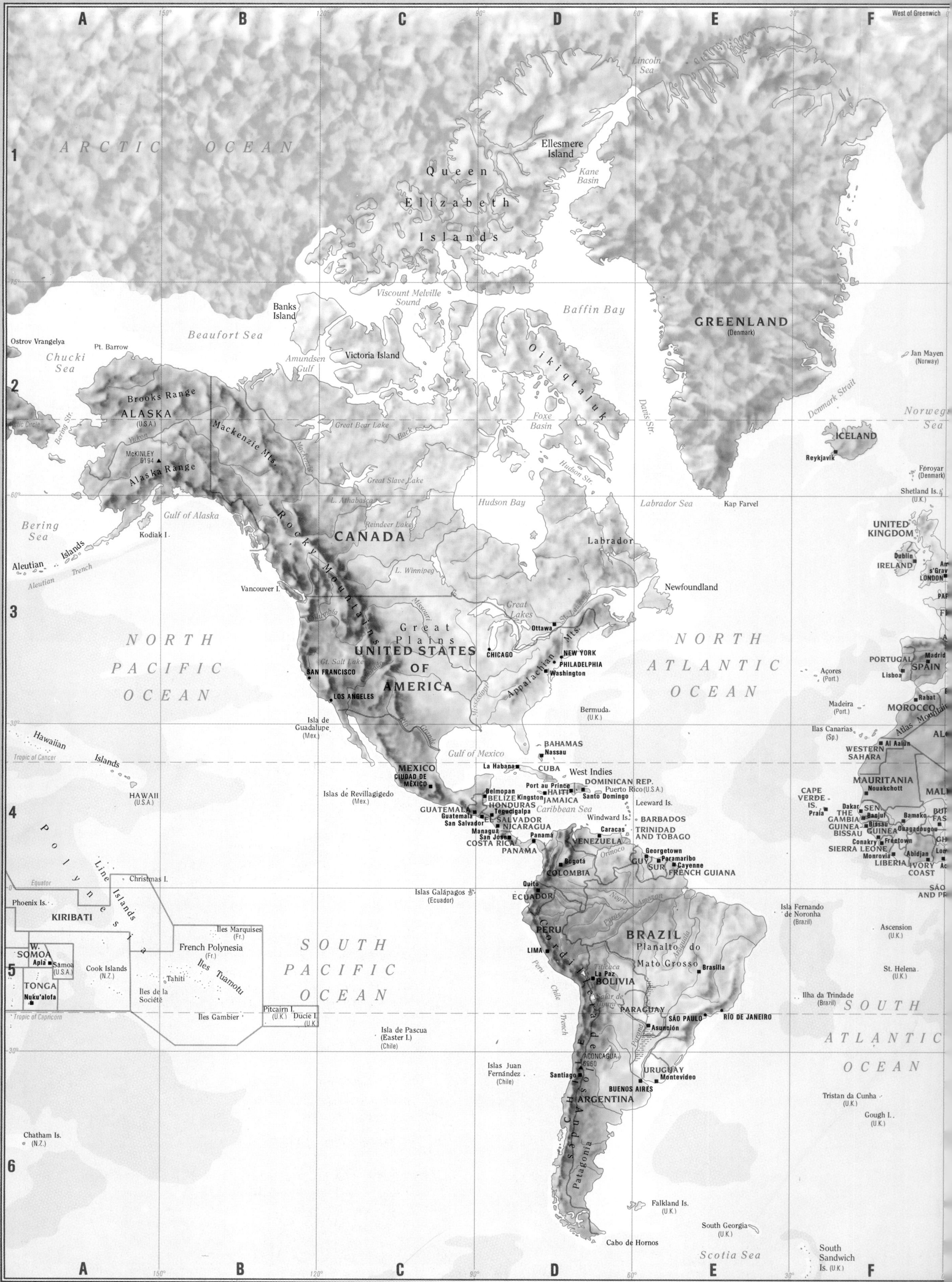
West of Greenwich
ARCTIC OCEAN
Queen Elizabeth Islands
Ellesmere Island
Lincoln Sea
Kane Basin
Baffin Bay
GREENLAND
(Denmark)
Banks Island
Viscount Melville Sound
Beaufort Sea
Ostrov Vrangelya
Pt. Barrow
Chukchi Sea
Amundsen Gulf
Victoria Island
Oikiqtaluk
Jan Mayen
(Norway)
Brooks Range
ALASKA
(U.S.A.)
Bering Str.
Yukon
Mackenzie Mts.
Great Bear Lake
Foxe Basin
Davis Str.
Denmark Strait
Norwegian Sea
ICELAND
Reykjavik
McKINLEY
6194
Alaska Range
Great Slave Lake
Hudson Str.
Føroyar
(Denmark)
Shetland Is.
(U.K.)
Hudson Bay
Labrador Sea
Kap Farvel
L. Athabasca
Gulf of Alaska
Bering Sea
Kodiak I.
Reindeer Lake
CANADA
Rocky Mountains
Labrador
UNITED KINGDOM
Dublin
IRELAND
LONDON
Aleutian Islands
Aleutian Trench
L. Winnipeg
Newfoundland
Vancouver I.
Missouri
Great Lakes
Ottawa
NORTH PACIFIC OCEAN
Great Plains
UNITED STATES OF AMERICA
CHICAGO
NEW YORK
PHILADELPHIA
Washington
Appalachian Mts.
NORTH ATLANTIC OCEAN
PORTUGAL
Madrid
SPAIN
Lisboa
Açores
(Port.)
Gt. Salt Lake
SAN FRANCISCO
LOS ANGELES
Mississippi
Bermuda
(U.K.)
Madeira
(Port.)
Rabat
MOROCCO
Atlas Mountains
Isla de Guadalupe
(Mex.)
Rio Grande
Ilas Canarias
(Sp.)
Hawaiian Islands
Tropic of Cancer
Gulf of Mexico
BAHAMAS
Nassau
WESTERN SAHARA
Al Aaiún
La Habana
CUBA
West Indies
MEXICO
CIUDAD DE MÉXICO
DOMINICAN REP.
Puerto Rico (U.S.A.)
Port au Prince
HAITI
Santo Domingo
Kingston
JAMAICA
Belmopan
BELIZE
HONDURAS
Tegucigalpa
Caribbean Sea
Leeward Is.
MAURITANIA
Nouakchott
Islas de Revillagigedo
(Mex.)
HAWAII
(U.S.A.)
CAPE VERDE IS.
Praia
GUATEMALA
Guatemala
San Salvador
EL SALVADOR
NICARAGUA
Managua
San José
COSTA RICA
Panamá
PANAMA
Windward Is.
BARBADOS
Caracas
TRINIDAD AND TOBAGO
VENEZUELA
Georgetown
Paramaribo
Cayenne
GUY.
SUR.
FRENCH GUIANA
Orinoco
Dakar
SEN.
THE GAMBIA
Banjul
GUINEA-BISSAU
Bissau
GUINEA
Conakry
Freetown
SIERRA LEONE
Monrovia
LIBERIA
Bamako
Ouagadougou
Abidjan
IVORY COAST
Polynesia
Line Islands
Christmas I.
Equator
Bogotá
COLOMBIA
Quito
ECUADOR
Islas Galápagos
(Ecuador)
Negro
Amazon
Phoenix Is.
KIRIBATI
Isla Fernando de Noronha
(Brazil)
PERU
BRAZIL
Planalto do Mato Grosso
Brasília
LIMA
Cordillera de los Andes
Ascension
(U.K.)
Iles Marquises
(Fr.)
French Polynesia
(Fr.)
W. SOMOA
Apia
Samoa
(U.S.A.)
SOUTH PACIFIC OCEAN
Cook Islands
(N.Z.)
Tahiti
Iles Tuamotu
Iles de la Société
TONGA
Nuku'alofa
Titicaca
La Paz
BOLIVIA
St. Helena
(U.K.)
Peru Chile Trench
Salar de Uyuni
PARAGUAY
SÃO PAULO
RIO DE JANEIRO
Ilha da Trindade
(Brazil)
SOUTH ATLANTIC OCEAN
Tropic of Capricorn
Iles Gambier
Pitcairn I.
(U.K.)
Ducie I.
(U.K.)
Asunción
Paraná
Isla de Pascua
(Easter I.)
(Chile)
ACONCAGUA
6960
Islas Juan Fernández
(Chile)
Santiago
URUGUAY
Montevideo
BUENOS AIRES
ARGENTINA
CHILE
Tristan da Cunha
(U.K.)
Gough I.
(U.K.)
Chatham Is.
(N.Z.)
Patagonia
Falkland Is.
(U.K.)
South Georgia
(U.K.)
Cabo de Hornos
Scotia Sea
South Sandwich Is. (U.K.)
A
B
C
D
E
F
1
2
3
4
5
6

Mercator Projection

1:85,000,000 (Scale at the Equator)

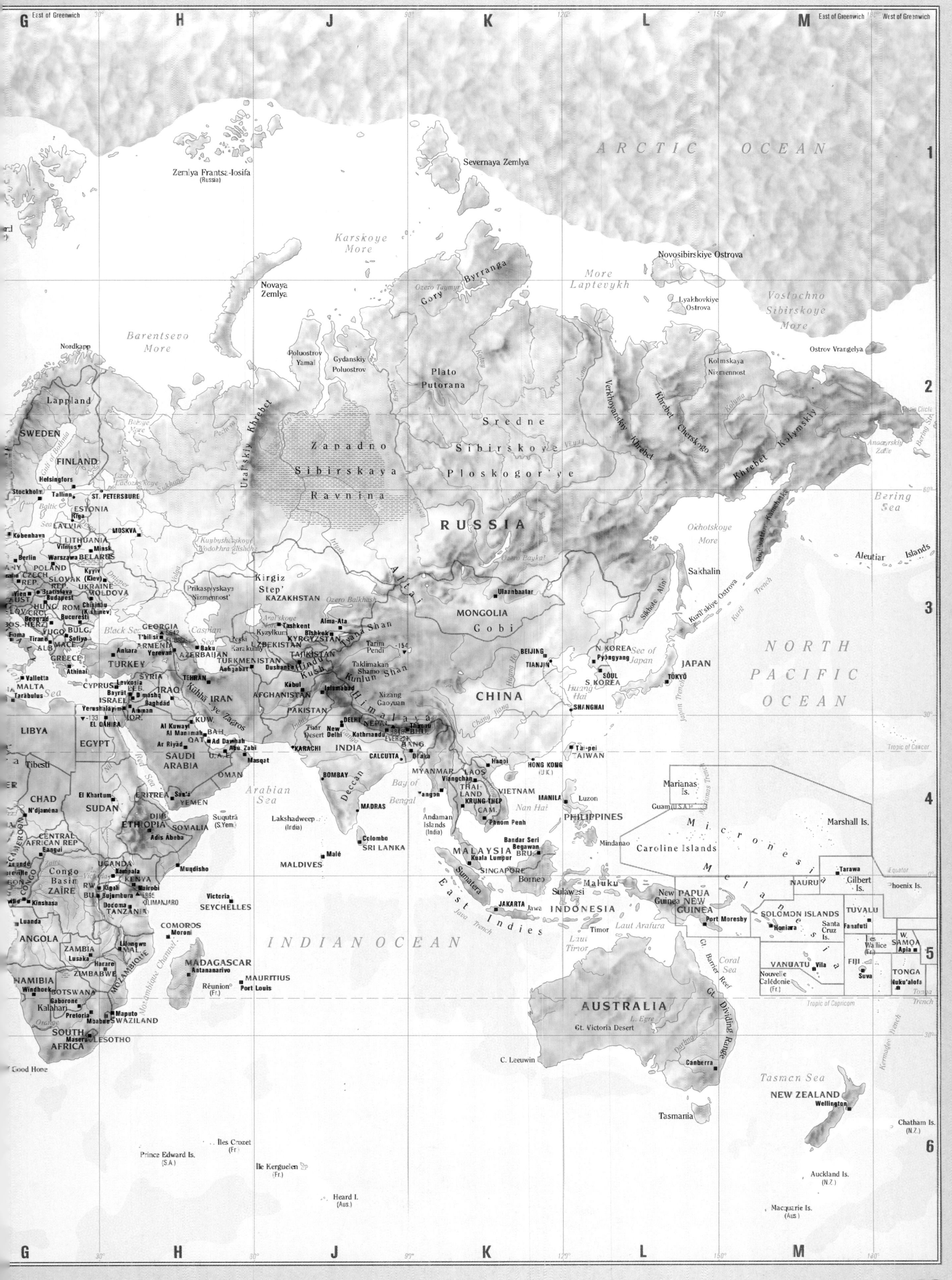

G H J K L M
East of Greenwich
West of Greenwich
1 2 3 4 5 6
ARCTIC OCEAN
Severnaya Zemlya
Zemlya Frantsa-Iosifa
(Russia)
Karskoye More
Novaya Zemlya
Novosibirskiye Ostrova
More Laptevykh
Lyakhovkiye Ostrova
Vostochno Sibirskoye More
Ostrov Vrangelya
Barentsevo More
Nordkapp
Poluostrov Yamal
Gydanskiy Poluostrov
Gory Byrranga
Plato Putorana
Kolmskaya Nizmennost
Lappland
SWEDEN
FINLAND
Helsingfors
Stockholm
Tallinn
ST. PETERSBURG
ESTONIA
Riga
LATVIA
MOSKVA
København
LITHUANIA
Vilnius
Minsk
Berlin
Warszawa
BELARUS
POLAND
CZECH REP.
SLOVAK REP.
Kyyiv (Kiev)
UKRAINE
MOLDOVA
Wien
Bratislava
Budapest
HUNG.
ROM.
Bucuresti
Chisinau (Kishinev)
Beograd
YUGO.
BULG.
Sofiya
Tirane
ALB.
MACE.
GREECE
Athinai
Roma
Valletta
MALTA
Tarabulus
Uralskiy Khrebet
Zapadno Sibirskaya Ravnina
Sredne Sibirskoye Ploskogor'ye
Verkhoyanskiy Khrebet
Khrebet Cherskogo
Khrebet Kolymskiy
Bering Sea
Okhotskoye More
RUSSIA
Ozero Baykal
Sakhalin
Aleutian Islands
Kuril'skiye Ostrova
Kuril Trench
Kirgiz Step'
KAZAKHSTAN
Prikaspiyskaya Nizmennost'
Ozero Balkhash
Altai
Ulaanbaatar
MONGOLIA
Gobi
Alma-Ata
Tashkent
Bishkek
KYRGYZSTAN
Tyan Shan
Aral'skoye More
Kyzylkum
UZBEKISTAN
TAJIKISTAN
TURKMENISTAN
Ashgabat
Dushanbe
Peski Karakumy
Caspian Sea
GEORGIA
T'bilisi
ARMENIA
Yerevan
AZERBAIJAN
Baku
Black Sea
Ankara
TURKEY
CYPRUS
Levkosia
SYRIA
Bayrut
LEB.
Dimashq
ISRAEL
Yerushalayim
Amman
JOR.
IRAQ
Baghdad
TEHRAN
IRAN
Kuhha-ye Zagros
KUW.
Al Kuwayt
BAH.
Al Manamah
QAT.
Ad Dawhah
Abu Zabi
U.A.E.
Masqat
OMAN
Ar Riyad
SAUDI ARABIA
Kabul
AFGHANISTAN
Islamabad
PAKISTAN
Hindu Kush
KARACHI
Tarim Pendi
Taklimakan Shamo
Kunlun Shan
Xizang Gaoyuan
Himalaya
DELHI
New Delhi
Thar Desert
NEPAL
Kathmandu
EVEREST
Thimphu
BHU.
BANG.
Dhaka
CALCUTTA
INDIA
BOMBAY
Deccan
MADRAS
Arabian Sea
Bay of Bengal
Lakshadweep (India)
MALDIVES
Male
Colombo
SRI LANKA
Andaman Islands (India)
BEIJING
TIANJIN
CHINA
Huang He
Chang Jiang
SHANGHAI
Huang Hai
N. KOREA
Pyongyang
SOUL
S. KOREA
Sea of Japan
JAPAN
TOKYO
Japan Trench
Sikhote Alin'
NORTH PACIFIC OCEAN
Tai-pei
TAIWAN
HONG KONG (U.K.)
Hanoi
MYANMAR
Viangchan
LAOS
THAILAND
Yangon
KRUNG THEP
CAM.
Phnom Penh
VIETNAM
Nan Hai
MANILA
Luzon
PHILIPPINES
Mindanao
Bandar Seri Begawan
BRU.
MALAYSIA
Kuala Lumpur
SINGAPORE
Borneo
Sumatera
East Indies
JAKARTA
Jawa
Java Trench
INDONESIA
Sulawesi
Maluku
Timor
Laut Arafura
Laut Timor
New Guinea
PAPUA NEW GUINEA
Port Moresby
Marianas Is.
Marianas Trench
Guam (U.S.A.)
Micronesia
Marshall Is.
Caroline Islands
Melanesia
Tarawa
NAURU
Gilbert Is.
Phoenix Is.
Equator
SOLOMON ISLANDS
Honiara
Santa Cruz Is.
TUVALU
Fanafuti
Îles Wallice (Fr.)
W. SAMOA
Apia
FIJI
Suva
VANUATU
Vila
Nouvelle Calédonie (Fr.)
TONGA
Nuku'alofa
Tonga Trench
Kermadec Trench
Coral Sea
Gt. Barrier Reef
Gt. Dividing Range
AUSTRALIA
L. Eyre
Gt. Victoria Desert
Darling
C. Leeuwin
Canberra
Tasmania
Tasman Sea
NEW ZEALAND
Wellington
Chatham Is. (N.Z.)
Auckland Is. (N.Z.)
Macquarie Is. (Aus.)
Tropic of Cancer
Tropic of Capricorn
Arctic Circle
Bering Str.
Anadyrskiy Zaliv
Tibesti
LIBYA
EGYPT
EL QAHIRA
Red Sea
Nile
CHAD
N'djaména
El Khartum
SUDAN
ERITREA
San'a
YEMEN
DJIB.
ETHIOPIA
Adis Abeba
SOMALIA
Suqutra (S.Yem.)
Muqdisho
CENTRAL AFRICAN REP.
Bangui
CAMEROON
UGANDA
Kampala
KENYA
Nairobi
Kigali
RW.
BU.
Bujumbura
KILIMANJARO
Dodoma
TANZANIA
Congo Basin
ZAIRE
CONGO
Kinshasa
Victoria
SEYCHELLES
Luanda
ANGOLA
COMOROS
Moroni
Lilongwe
MAL.
ZAMBIA
Lusaka
Harare
ZIMBABWE
MOZAMBIQUE
Mozambique Channel
MADAGASCAR
Antananarivo
MAURITIUS
Port Louis
Réunion (Fr.)
NAMIBIA
Windhoek
BOTSWANA
Gaborone
Kalahari
Pretoria
Maputo
Mbabane
SWAZILAND
Orange
SOUTH AFRICA
Maseru
LESOTHO
Good Hope
INDIAN OCEAN
Prince Edward Is. (S.A.)
Îles Crozet (Fr.)
Île Kerguelen (Fr.)
Heard I. (Aus.)

Designed and produced by E.S.R.

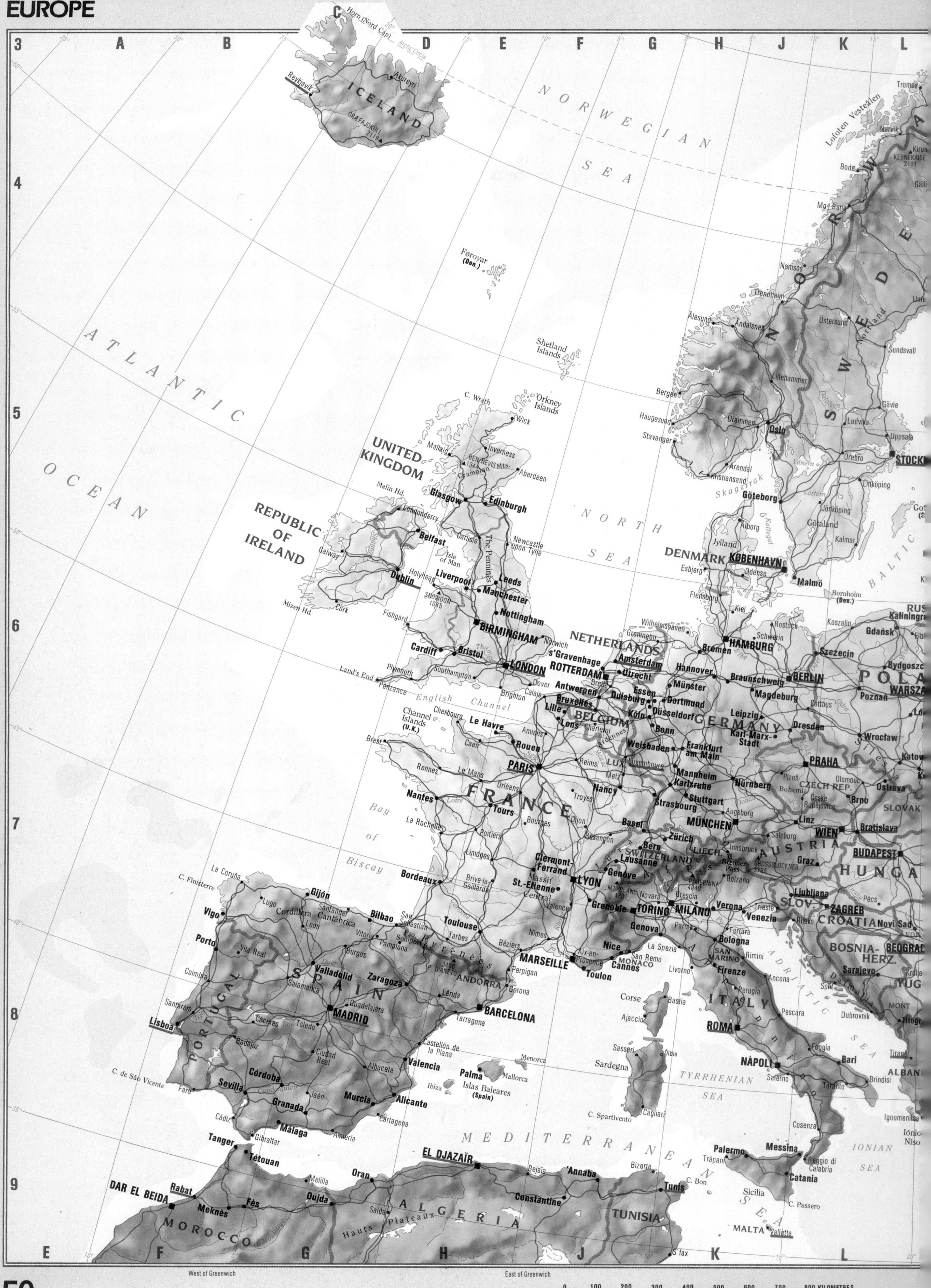

ICELAND
Reykjavík
Akureyri
ÖRÆFAJÖKULL 2119
Horn (Nord Cap)
Arctic Circle
NORWEGIAN SEA
Føroyar (Den.)
Shetland Islands
Orkney Islands
ATLANTIC OCEAN
UNITED KINGDOM
REPUBLIC OF IRELAND
C. Wrath
Wick
Mallaig
Inverness
BEN NEVIS 1344
Grampian Mts.
Aberdeen
Malin Hd.
Londonderry
Glasgow
Edinburgh
Belfast
Galway
Carlisle
The Pennines
Newcastle upon Tyne
Isle of Man
Holyhead
Dublin
Liverpool
Leeds
Manchester
SNOWDON 1085
Cork
Mizen Hd.
Fishguard
Nottingham
BIRMINGHAM
Norwich
Cardiff
Bristol
LONDON
Land's End
Plymouth
Penzance
Southampton
Brighton
Dover
Calais
English Channel
NORTH SEA
DENMARK
KØBENHAVN
Esbjerg
Odense
Jylland
Ålborg
Kattegat
Skagerrak
Malmö
Bornholm (Den.)
Flensburg
Kiel
NORWAY
SWEDEN
Tromsø
Lofoten Vesterålen
Narvik
Kiruna
KEBNEKAISE 2111
Bodø
Mo i Rana
Namsos
Trondheim
Ålesund
Åndalsnes
Östersund
Sundsvall
Lillehammer
Bergen
Haugesund
Stavanger
Drammen
Oslo
Gävle
Uppsala
Ludvika
Örebro
STOCKHOLM
Arendal
Kristiansand
Göteborg
Vänern
Vättern
Linköping
Jönköping
Götaland
Kalmar
BALTIC
NETHERLANDS
Amsterdam
s'Gravenhage
ROTTERDAM
Utrecht
Groningen
Wilhelmshaven
Bremen
HAMBURG
Rostock
Schwerin
Hannover
Braunschweig
BERLIN
Magdeburg
Münster
Essen
Duisburg
Dortmund
Düsseldorf
Köln
Bonn
Antwerpen
Bruxelles
BELGIUM
Lille
Lens
Charleroi
Ardennes
GERMANY
Leipzig
Dresden
Karl-Marx-Stadt
Cottbus
Frankfurt am Main
Wiesbaden
LUX.
Luxembourg
Mannheim
Karlsruhe
Nürnberg
Stuttgart
Strasbourg
Augsburg
MÜNCHEN
Gdańsk
Kaliningrad
Koszalin
Szczecin
Bydgoszcz
Poznań
POLAND
WARSZAWA
Wrocław
Katowice
PRAHA
Plzeň
Bohemia
CZECH REP.
Olomouc
Ostrava
České Budějovice
Brno
SLOVAKIA
Linz
WIEN
Bratislava
Salzburg
AUSTRIA
Innsbruck
Graz
GROSSGLOCKNER 3798
BUDAPEST
HUNGARY
Cherbourg
Channel Islands (U.K.)
Le Havre
Amiens
Caen
Rouen
Brest
Rennes
Le Mans
PARIS
Reims
Metz
Nancy
Orléans
Troyes
FRANCE
Nantes
Loire
Tours
Bourges
Dijon
Besançon
Bay of Biscay
La Rochelle
Poitiers
Limoges
Clermont-Ferrand
Bordeaux
Brive-la-Gaillarde
Massif Central
St.-Étienne
LYON
Genève
Lausanne
Bern
Basel
Zürich
SWITZERLAND
LIECH.
MT. BLANC 4807
Grenoble
Valence
Toulouse
Tarbes
Nîmes
Béziers
MARSEILLE
Aix-en-Provence
Toulon
Nice
Cannes
MONACO
San Remo
Perpignan
ANDORRA
Pyrénées
PIC D'ANETO 3404
TORINO
MILANO
Novara
Brescia
Verona
Venezia
Trieste
Bolzano
Genova
La Spezia
Parma
Ferrara
Bologna
SAN MARINO
Rimini
Firenze
Livorno
Perugia
Ancona
ITALY
Apennines
ROMA
Pescara
NÁPOLI
Salerno
Foggia
Bari
Brindisi
Taranto
Cosenza
Reggio di Calabria
Messina
Palermo
Trapani
Catania
Sicilia
C. Passero
MALTA
Valletta
Corse
Bastia
Ajaccio
Sardegna
Sassari
Olbia
Cagliari
C. Spartivento
TYRRHENIAN SEA
ADRIATIC SEA
IONIAN SEA
SLOV.
Ljubljana
ZAGREB
Rijeka
CROATIA
Novi Sad
BEOGRAD
BOSNIA-HERZ.
Sarajevo
Split
Dubrovnik
MONT.
Titograd
Tiranë
ALBANIA
Igoumenitsa
Iónio Nísoi
La Coruña
C. Finisterre
Lugo
Gijón
Cordillera Cantábrica
Santander
Bilbao
San Sebastián
Vigo
León
Vitoria
Pamplona
Porto
Vila Real
Burgos
Duero
Valladolid
Salamanca
Zaragoza
Ebro
Lérida
Gerona
BARCELONA
Tarragona
Coimbra
PORTUGAL
SPAIN
Guadalajara
MADRID
Santarém
Lisboa
Cáceres
Tajo
Toledo
Badajoz
Ciudad Real
Castellón de la Plana
Valencia
Albacete
Menorca
Mallorca
Palma
Islas Baleares (Spain)
Ibiza
C. de São Vicente
Faro
Córdoba
Sevilla
Guadalquivir
Jaén
Granada
Murcia
Alicante
Cartagena
Cádiz
Málaga
Almería
Gibraltar
Tanger
Tétouan
MEDITERRANEAN SEA
Melilla
Oran
EL DJAZAÏR
Bejaïa
'Annaba
Bizerte
Tunis
C. Bon
Rabat
DAR EL BEIDA
Meknès
Fès
Oujda
Saïda
Hauts Plateaux
Constantine
ALGERIA
TUNISIA
MOROCCO
Sfax
West of Greenwich
East of Greenwich

1:12,500,000

0 100 200 300 400 500 600 700 800 KILOMETRES

0 100 200 300 400 500 STATUTE MILES

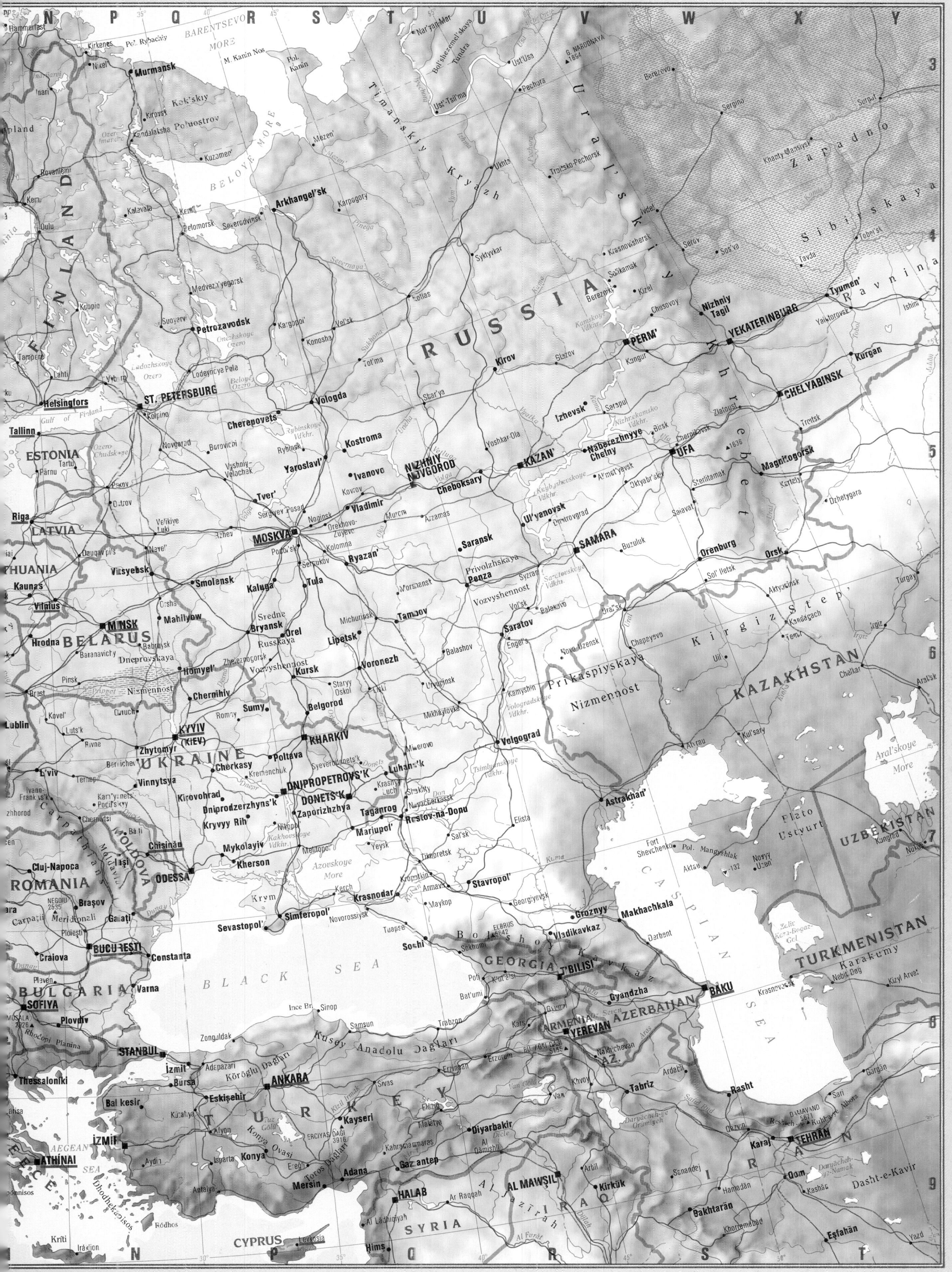

N P Q R S T U V W X Y
BARENTSEVO MORE
RUSSIA
FINLAND
ESTONIA
LATVIA
LITHUANIA
BELARUS
UKRAINE
MOLDOVA
ROMANIA
BULGARIA
GEORGIA
ARMENIA
AZERBAIJAN
KAZAKHSTAN
UZBEKISTAN
TURKMENISTAN
TURKEY
SYRIA
IRAQ
IRAN
CYPRUS
BLACK SEA
CASPIAN SEA
Aral'skoye More
Azovskoye More
BELOYE MORE
Murmansk
Arkhangel'sk
Petrozavodsk
ST. PETERSBURG
Helsingfors
Tallinn
Riga
Vilnius
MINSK
MOSKVA
Vologda
Yaroslavl'
Kostroma
Ivanovo
NIZHNIY NOVGOROD
Kirov
PERM'
YEKATERINBURG
CHELYABINSK
Tyumen'
Kurgan
KAZAN'
UFA
Magnitogorsk
SAMARA
Orenburg
Orsk
Saratov
Volgograd
Astrakhan'
Penza
Ul'yanovsk
Tula
Ryazan'
Smolensk
Bryansk
Orel
Kursk
Voronezh
Lipetsk
Tambov
Belgorod
KHARKIV
KYYIV (KIEV)
DNIPROPETROVS'K
DONETS'K
Luhans'k
Zaporizhzhya
Rostov-na-Donu
Krasnodar
Stavropol'
Simferopol'
Sevastopol'
ODESSA
Chişinău
BUCUREŞTI
Constanta
Varna
SOFIYA
ISTANBUL
ANKARA
İZMİR
ATHINAI
Thessaloniki
Kayseri
Konya
Adana
HALAB
AL MAWŞIL
T'BILISI
YEREVAN
BAKU
Makhachkala
Groznyy
Tabriz
TEHRAN
Rasht
Qom
Eşfahān
Sochi
Trabzon
Samsun

Miller Oblated Stereographic Projection

Designed and produced by E.S.R.

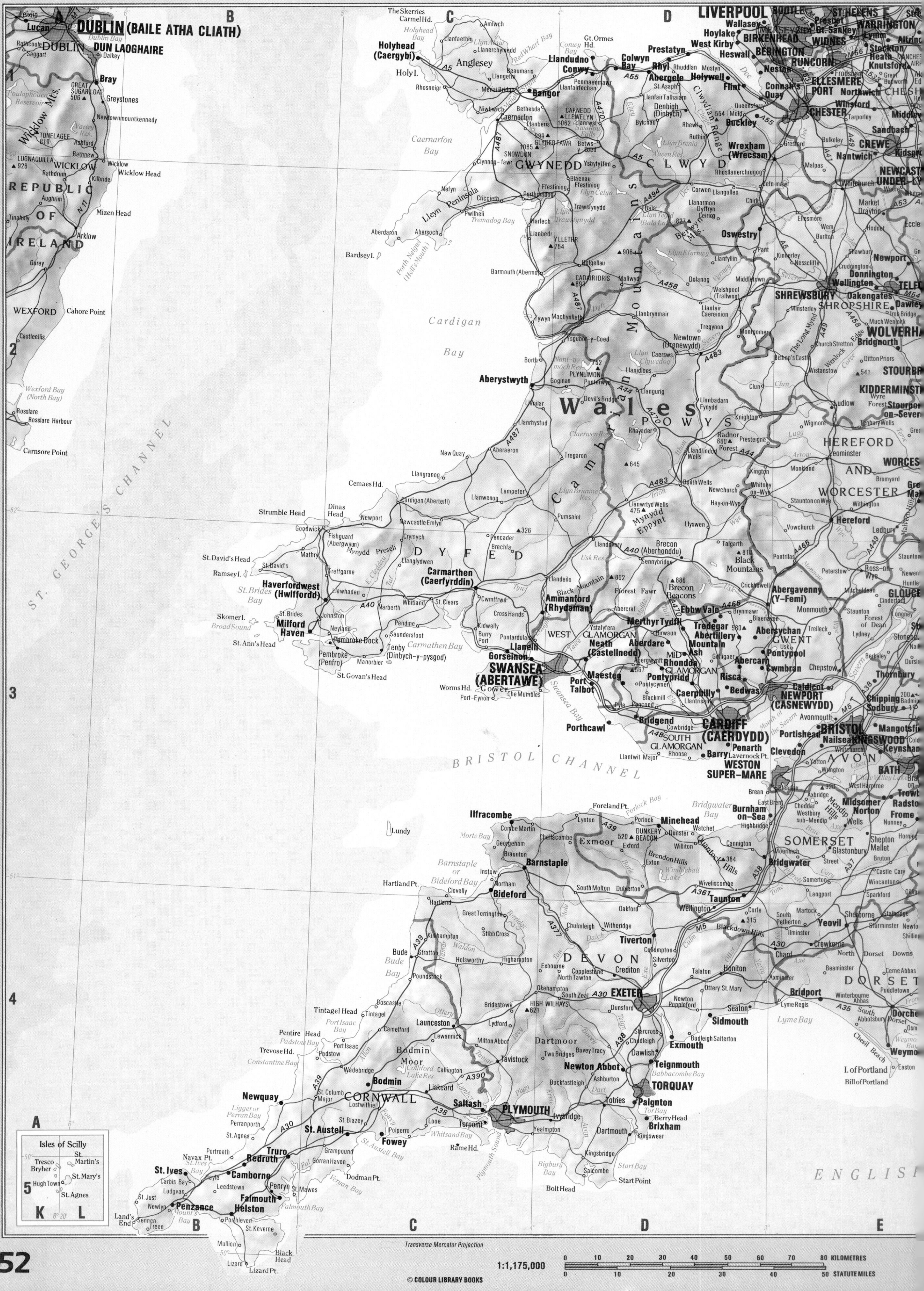
DUBLIN (BAILE ATHA CLIATH)
DUN LAOGHAIRE
Dublin Bay
Bray
Greystones
Wicklow Mts.
WICKLOW
Wicklow Head
REPUBLIC OF IRELAND
Arklow
Mizen Head
Gorey
WEXFORD
Cahore Point
Castleellis
Wexford Bay (North Bay)
Rosslare
Rosslare Harbour
Carnsore Point
ST. GEORGE'S CHANNEL
LIVERPOOL
BOOTLE
ST. HELENS
WARRINGTON
Wallasey
Hoylake
BIRKENHEAD
WIDNES
West Kirby
Heswall
BEBINGTON
RUNCORN
Neston
ELLESMERE PORT
Northwich
Connah's Quay
CHESTER
Winsford
Middlewich
Sandbach
CREWE
Nantwich
NEWCASTLE UNDER LYME
Holyhead (Caergybi)
Holy I.
Anglesey
Amlwch
The Skerries
Carmel Hd.
Holyhead Bay
Red Wharf Bay
Beaumaris
Bangor
Llandudno
Conwy
Colwyn Bay
Prestatyn
Rhyl
Abergele
Holywell
Flint
Denbigh (Dinbych)
Mold
Buckley
Wrexham (Wrecsam)
Caernarfon
Caernarfon Bay
CARNEDD LLEWELYN 1062
SNOWDON 1085
GWYNEDD
CLWYD
Clwydian Range
Blaenau Ffestiniog
Llyn Celyn
Criccieth
Pwllheli
Porthmadog
Lleyn Peninsula
Tremadog Bay
Nefyn
Aberdaron
Abersoch
Bardsey I.
Harlech
Bala
Berwyn Mts.
Oswestry
Llangollen
Chirk
Ellesmere
Wem
Market Drayton
Newport
Donnington
Wellington
Oakengates
TELFORD
Dawley
SHREWSBURY
SHROPSHIRE
Dolgellau
CADAIR IDRIS 892
Barmouth (Abermaw)
Welshpool (Trallwng)
Machynlleth
Tywyn
Cardigan Bay
Cambrian Mountains
Newtown (Drenewydd)
Montgomery
The Long Mynd
Church Stretton
Wenlock Edge
Bishop's Castle
Much Wenlock
WOLVERHAMPTON
Bridgnorth
STOURBRIDGE
KIDDERMINSTER
Stourport-on-Severn
Aberystwyth
PLYNLIMON 752
Llanidloes
Llangurig
Devil's Bridge
Wales
POWYS
Rhayader
Llanbadarn Fynydd
Knighton
Radnor Forest 660
Presteigne
Ludlow
Llanon
Llanrhystud
Aberaeron
New Quay
Llangranog
Tregaron
Lampeter
Llandrindod Wells
Builth Wells
Kington
Leominster
HEREFORD AND WORCESTER
WORCESTER
Bromyard
Hay-on-Wye
Hereford
Ledbury
Cemaes Hd.
Cardigan (Aberteifi)
Newport
Newcastle Emlyn
Llanwrtyd Wells
Mynydd Eppynt
Pumsaint
Llandovery
Brecon (Aberhonddu)
Sennybridge
Talgarth
Black Mountains
Brecon Beacons 886
Crickhowell
Abergavenny (Y-Fenni)
Monmouth
Ross-on-Wye
Forest of Dean
Lydney
Strumble Head
Dinas Head
Fishguard (Abergwaun)
Goodwick
Mynydd Preseli
DYFED
St. David's Head
St. David's
Ramsey I.
Haverfordwest (Hwlffordd)
St. Brides Bay
Skomer I.
Milford Haven
Neyland
Pembroke Dock
Pembroke (Penfro)
Tenby (Dinbych-y-pysgod)
St. Govan's Head
St. Ann's Head
Carmarthen (Caerfyrddin)
Carmarthen Bay
Whitland
St. Clears
Narberth
Llandeilo
Ammanford (Rhydaman)
Black Mountain 802
Llanelli
Gorseinon
SWANSEA (ABERTAWE)
Gower
Worms Hd.
Port-Eynon
The Mumbles
Swansea Bay
Neath (Castellnedd)
Port Talbot
Maesteg
WEST GLAMORGAN
MID GLAMORGAN
SOUTH GLAMORGAN
Merthyr Tydfil
Aberdare
Ebbw Vale
Tredegar
Abertillery
Mountain Ash
Rhondda
Pontypridd
Pontypool
Cwmbran
Abercarn
Risca
Caerphilly
Bedwas
Abersychan
GWENT
Chepstow
Caldicot
NEWPORT (CASNEWYDD)
Bridgend
Porthcawl
Cowbridge
CARDIFF (CAERDYDD)
Penarth
Barry
Lavernock Pt.
Llantwit Major
Thornbury
Chipping Sodbury
Avonmouth
Portishead
BRISTOL
KINGSWOOD
Mangotsfield
Keynsham
Nailsea
Clevedon
AVON
BATH
WESTON SUPER-MARE
BRISTOL CHANNEL
Lundy
Ilfracombe
Foreland Pt.
Porlock Bay
Lynton
Minehead
Watchet
DUNKERY BEACON 520
Exmoor
Quantock Hills
Bridgwater Bay
Burnham on-Sea
Bridgwater
SOMERSET
Glastonbury
Street
Wells
Shepton Mallet
Frome
Mendip Hills
Cheddar
Morte Bay
Barnstaple
Barnstaple or Bideford Bay
Bideford
Hartland Pt.
Clovelly
Great Torrington
South Molton
Dulverton
Brendon Hills
Taunton
Wellington
Blackdown Hills
Yeovil
Crewkerne
Chard
Sherborne
Tiverton
DEVON
Crediton
EXETER
Honiton
Axminster
Bridport
Lyme Regis
Lyme Bay
DORSET
Dorchester
Weymouth
Chesil Beach
I. of Portland
Bill of Portland
Sidmouth
Exmouth
Budleigh Salterton
Dawlish
Teignmouth
Babbacombe Bay
TORQUAY
Paignton
Brixham
Berry Head
Dartmouth
Totnes
Newton Abbot
Dartmoor
HIGH WILHAYS 621
Okehampton
Tavistock
Bude
Bude Bay
Stratton
Holsworthy
Launceston
Tintagel Head
Tintagel
Camelford
Port Isaac Bay
Pentire Head
Padstow Bay
Trevose Hd.
Constantine Bay
Bodmin
Bodmin Moor
Liskeard
Saltash
PLYMOUTH
Plymouth Sound
Torpoint
Rame Hd.
Ivybridge
Kingsbridge
Salcombe
Bolt Head
Start Point
Start Bay
Bigbury Bay
Newquay
CORNWALL
St. Austell
St. Austell Bay
Fowey
Lostwithiel
Polperro
Looe
Whitsand Bay
Truro
Redruth
Camborne
Falmouth
Falmouth Bay
Penryn
St. Mawes
Helston
St. Ives
St. Ives Bay
Hayle
Penzance
Mount's Bay
Newlyn
St. Just
Land's End
Porthleven
Mullion
Lizard
Lizard Pt.
Black Head
Dodman Pt.
Navax Pt.
Isles of Scilly
Tresco
Bryher
St. Martin's
St. Mary's
Hugh Town
St. Agnes
ENGLISH
A
B
C
D
E
1
2
3
4
5
K
L
Transverse Mercator Projection
1:1,175,000
KILOMETRES
STATUTE MILES

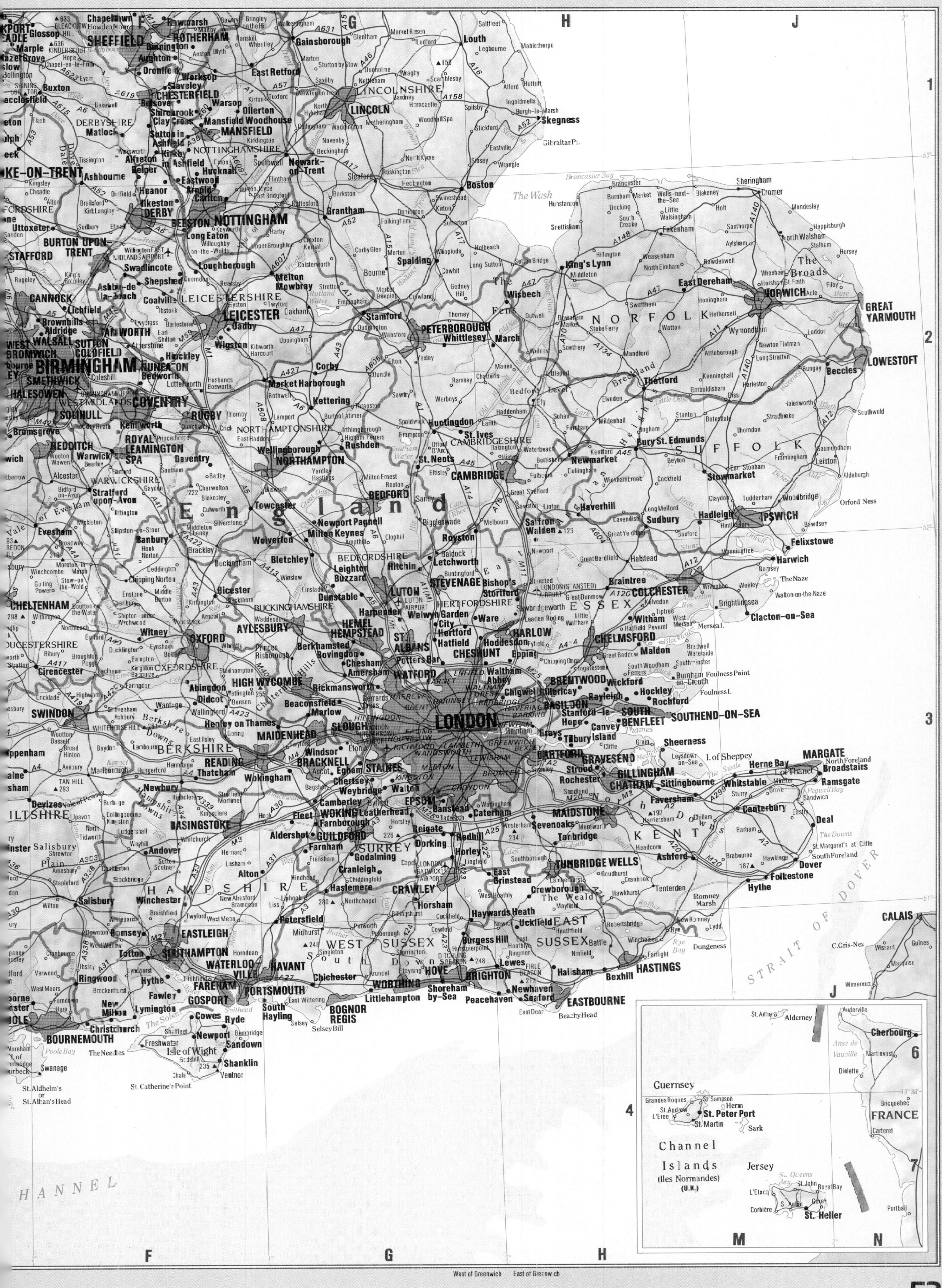

SHEFFIELD
ROTHERHAM
Gainsborough
Louth
Chesterfield
LINCOLNSHIRE
LINCOLN
Skegness
Mansfield
NOTTINGHAMSHIRE
Newark-on-Trent
Boston
The Wash
NOTTINGHAM
DERBY
Grantham
King's Lynn
Sheringham
Cromer
LEICESTERSHIRE
LEICESTER
PETERBOROUGH
NORFOLK
NORWICH
GREAT YARMOUTH
LOWESTOFT
BIRMINGHAM
COVENTRY
Kettering
Thetford
SUFFOLK
NORTHAMPTONSHIRE
NORTHAMPTON
CAMBRIDGESHIRE
CAMBRIDGE
Bury St. Edmunds
IPSWICH
England
BEDFORD
Milton Keynes
Felixstowe
Harwich
LUTON
COLCHESTER
Clacton-on-Sea
HERTFORDSHIRE
ESSEX
OXFORD
AYLESBURY
BUCKINGHAMSHIRE
CHELMSFORD
SWINDON
LONDON
SOUTHEND-ON-SEA
READING
BERKSHIRE
MARGATE
Broadstairs
Ramsgate
Canterbury
GILLINGHAM
CHATHAM
MAIDSTONE
KENT
Dover
Folkestone
SURREY
GUILDFORD
CRAWLEY
TUNBRIDGE WELLS
HAMPSHIRE
Salisbury
Winchester
SOUTHAMPTON
PORTSMOUTH
WEST SUSSEX
EAST SUSSEX
BRIGHTON
HASTINGS
EASTBOURNE
STRAIT OF DOVER
CALAIS
BOURNEMOUTH
Isle of Wight
CHANNEL
Alderney
Cherbourg
Guernsey
St. Peter Port
Sark
Channel Islands
(Iles Normandes)
(U.K.)
Jersey
St. Helier
FRANCE

Designed and produced by E.S.R.

NORTHERN ENGLAND AND NORTHERN IRELAND

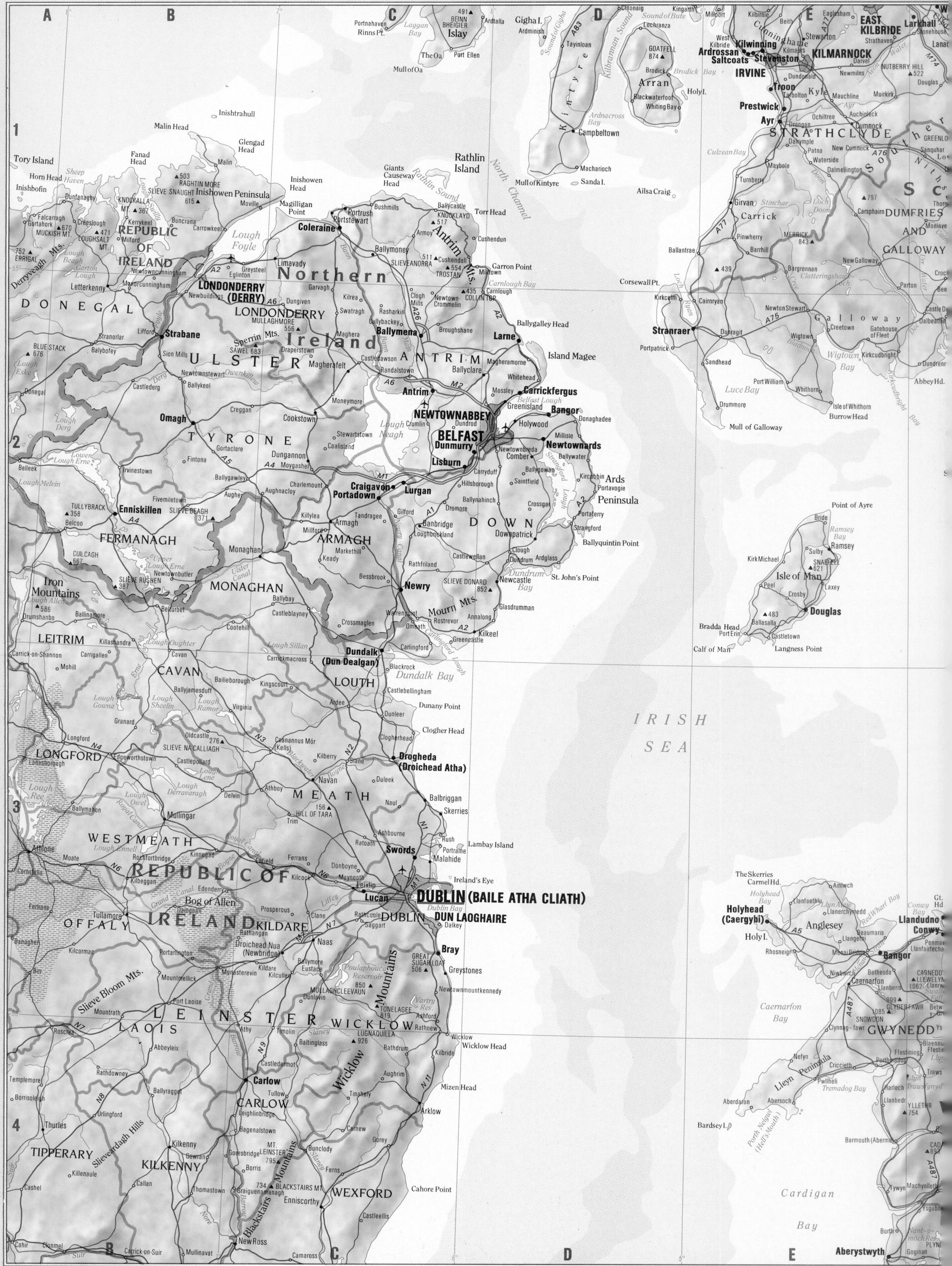
A
B
C
D
E
1
2
3
4
Malin Head
Inishtrahull
Glengad Head
Tory Island
Fanad Head
Horn Head
Sheep Haven
Inishbofin
Malin
RAGHTIN MORE
SLIEVE SNAUGHT
Inishowen Peninsula
Inishowen Head
Moville
Magilligan Point
Buncrana
Carrowkeel
Lough Foyle
REPUBLIC OF IRELAND
ERRIGAL
Derryveagh Mts.
Letterkenny
Manorcunningham
Newtowncunningham
LONDONDERRY (DERRY)
Limavady
Eglinton
Greysteel
Coleraine
Portrush
Portstewart
Bushmills
Giants Causeway Head
Rathlin Island
Rathlin Sound
Ballycastle
KNOCKLAYD
Torr Head
Cushendun
Cushendall
TROSTAN
Antrim Mts.
Garron Point
Carnlough
Carnlough Bay
Ballymoney
SLIEVEANORRA
Northern Ireland
DONEGAL
Strabane
Lifford
Stranorlar
Ballybofey
BLUE STACK
Lough Eske
Donegal
Sperrin Mts.
SAWEL
LONDONDERRY
Dungiven
Garvagh
Kilrea
MULLAGHMORE
Draperstown
Maghera
Swatragh
Rasharkin
Cullybackey
Ballymena
Clough Mills
Newtown-Crommelin
COLLIN TOP
Broughshane
Larne
Ballygalley Head
Island Magee
ULSTER
Magherafelt
Castledawson
Randalstown
ANTRIM
Ballyclare
Magheramorne
Whitehead
Antrim
Carrickfergus
Mossley
Greenisland
Belfast Lough
Bangor
Donaghadee
Holywood
NEWTOWNABBEY
Dundrod
Crumlin
Lough Neagh
BELFAST
Dunmurry
Lisburn
Milliste
Newtownards
Comber
Ballywater
Ballygowan
Kircubbin
Portavogie
Ards Peninsula
Saintfield
Strangford Lough
Hillsborough
Carryduff
Ballynahinch
Crossgar
Portaferry
Strangford
Ballyquintin Point
Omagh
Newtownstewart
Castlederg
Ballykeel
Creggan
Cookstown
Moneymore
TYRONE
Fintona
Gortaclare
Dungannon
Moygashel
Coalisland
Stewartstown
Lough Erne
Belleek
Lough Melvin
Irvinestown
Ballygawley
Augher
Aughnacloy
Charlemont
Craigavon
Portadown
Lurgan
Enniskillen
Fivemiletown
SLIEVE BEAGH
TULLYBRACK
Belcoo
FERMANAGH
Tandragee
Killylea
Armagh
Millford
Gilford
Dromore
Banbridge
Loughbrickland
DOWN
Downpatrick
ARMAGH
Markethill
Keady
Monaghan
CUILCAGH
Upper Lough Erne
Newtownbutler
SLIEVE RUSHEN
Iron Mountains
MONAGHAN
Rathfriland
Castlewellan
Clough
Dundrum
Ardglass
Dundrum Bay
SLIEVE DONARD
Newcastle
St. John's Point
Bessbrook
Newry
Mourn Mts.
Ballybay
Castleblayney
Ballinamore
Drumshanbo
Belturbet
Cootehill
Crossmaglen
Warrenpoint
Rostrevor
Annalong
Glasdrumman
Kilkeel
Greencastle
Omeath
LEITRIM
Killashandra
Lough Oughter
Carrick-on-Shannon
Carrigallen
Mohill
Cavan
Lough Sillan
Carrickmacross
Dundalk (Dun Dealgan)
Carlingford
Carlingford Lough
Blackrock
CAVAN
Bailieborough
Kingscourt
LOUTH
Dundalk Bay
Castlebellingham
Ballyjamesduff
Lough Gowna
Lough Sheelin
Lough Ramor
Virginia
Ardee
Dunany Point
Granard
Dunleer
Clogherhead
Clogher Head
Longford
Oldcastle
SLIEVE NA CALLIAGH
Ceanannus Mór (Kells)
LONGFORD
Edgeworthstown
Castlepollard
Kilberry
Slane
Drogheda (Droichead Atha)
Lough Ree
Lough Lene
Navan
Duleek
Lough Owel
Lough Derravaragh
Delvin
Athboy
MEATH
Ballymahon
Naul
Balbriggan
Skerries
HILL OF TARA
Trim
Mullingar
WESTMEATH
Lough Ennell
Athlone
Moate
Kinnegad
Rochfortbridge
Ratoath
Ashbourne
Rush
Lambay Island
Portrane
Swords
Malahide
REPUBLIC OF IRELAND
Kilbeggan
Enfield
Ferrans
Dunboyne
Maynooth
Kilcock
Leixlip
Ireland's Eye
Lucan
DUBLIN (BAILE ATHA CLIATH)
DUN LAOGHAIRE
Dublin Bay
Dalkey
Edenderry
Bog of Allen
Grand Canal
Daingean
Prosperous
Clane
Rathcoole
Saggart
Tullamore
OFFALY
KILDARE
Rathangan
Droichead Nua (Newbridge)
Naas
Bray
Banagher
Kilcormac
Portarlington
GREAT SUGAR LOAF
Greystones
Ballymore Eustace
Poulaphouca Reservoir
Kildare
Monasterevin
Kilcullen
Mountmellick
Slieve Bloom Mts.
Newtownmountkennedy
Birr
Dunlavin
MULLAGHCLEEVAUN
Mountains
Port Laoise
Vartry Res.
TONELAGEE
Ashford
Mountrath
LEINSTER
WICKLOW
Rathnew
Wicklow
Wicklow Head
LAOIS
Roscrea
Athy
Timolin
LUGNAQUILLA
Baltinglass
Abbeyleix
Castledermot
Rathdrum
Kilbride
Rathdowney
Carlow
Tullow
Aughrim
Tinahely
Mizen Head
Templemore
Borrisoleigh
Ballyragget
CARLOW
Arklow
Leighlinbridge
Urlingford
Bagenalstown
Thurles
Slieveardagh Hills
Carnew
Gorey
TIPPERARY
Kilkenny
Gowran
Goresbridge
MT. LEINSTER
Bunclody
KILKENNY
Borris
Ferns
Killenaule
Callan
Cashel
Thomastown
Graiguenamanagh
BLACKSTAIRS MT
Blackstairs Mountains
Enniscorthy
WEXFORD
Cahore Point
Castleellis
Cahir
Clonmel
Carrick-on-Suir
Mullinavat
New Ross
Camaross
Portnahaven
Rinns Pt.
Laggan Bay
BEINN BHEIGIER
Islay
Ardtalla
The Oa
Port Ellen
Mull of Oa
Gigha I.
Ardminish
Sound of Gigha
Tayinloan
Kintyre
Kilbrannan Sound
Campbeltown
Ardnacross Bay
Machariod
Mull of Kintyre
Sanda I.
Claonaig
Sound of Bute
Lochranza
GOATFELL
Arran
Brodick
Brodick Bay
Blackwaterfoot
Whiting Bay
Holy I.
Ailsa Craig
Kingarth
Millport
Kilbirnie
Beith
West Kilbride
Kilwinning
Ardrossan
Saltcoats
Stevenston
Stewarton
KILMARNOCK
EAST KILBRIDE
Larkhall
IRVINE
Troon
Dundonald
Tarbolton
Kyle
Prestwick
Ayr
STRATHCLYDE
Darvel
Newmilns
Mauchline
Auchinleck
Cumnock
Ochiltree
Culzean Bay
Dalrymple
Maybole
Patna
Dalmellington
New Cumnock
Turnberry
Girvan
Stinchar
Carrick
DUMFRIES AND GALLOWAY
Carsphairn
MERRICK
Pinwherry
Barrhill
Ballantrae
Bargrennan
New Galloway
Clatteringshaws Loch
Corsewall Pt.
Loch Ryan
Kirkcolm
Cairnryan
Stranraer
Portpatrick
Dunragit
Newton Stewart
Wigtown
Creetown
Gatehouse of Fleet
Galloway
Wigtown Bay
Kirkcudbright
Sandhead
Port William
Luce Bay
Whithorn
Isle of Whithorn
Burrow Head
Drummore
Mull of Galloway
Abbey Hd.
North Channel
Point of Ayre
Bride
Ramsey Bay
Ramsey
Sulby
SNAEFELL
Kirk Michael
Isle of Man
Peel
Laxey
Crosby
Douglas
Ballasalla
Bradda Head
Port Erin
Castletown
Calf of Man
Langness Point
IRISH SEA
The Skerries
Carmel Hd.
Amlwch
Holyhead Bay
Llanfaethlu
Llanerchymedd
Red Wharf Bay
Holyhead (Caergybi)
Holy I.
Anglesey
Beaumaris
Llangefni
Rhosneigr
Menai Bridge
Bangor
Llandudno
Conwy
Conwy Bay
Bethesda
Caernarfon
Llanberis
Caernarfon Bay
SNOWDON
GWYNEDD
Nefyn
Lleyn Peninsula
Criccieth
Pwllheli
Tremadog Bay
Porthmadog
Harlech
Llanbedr
Aberdaron
Abersoch
Bardsey I.
Porth Neigwl (Hell's Mouth)
Barmouth
Cardigan Bay
Tywyn
Machynlleth
Borth
Aberystwyth

Transverse Mercator Projection

1:1,175,000

0 10 20 30 40 50 60 70 80 KILOMETRES

0 10 20 30 40 50 STATUTE MILES

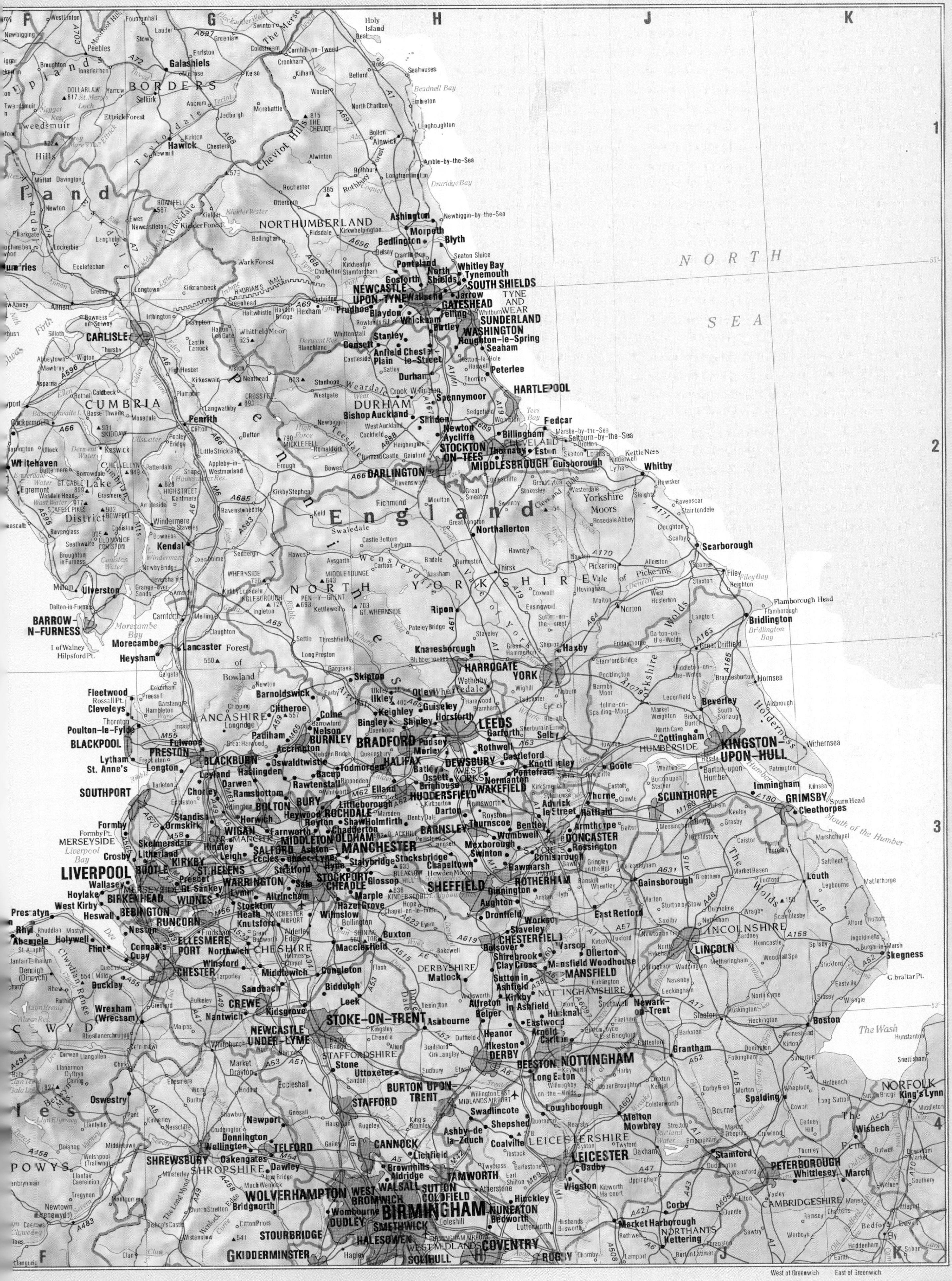
F
G
H
J
K
1
2
3
4
NORTH SEA
BORDERS
NORTHUMBERLAND
TYNE AND WEAR
DURHAM
CUMBRIA
CLEVELAND
NORTH YORKSHIRE
England
LANCASHIRE
WEST YORKS
HUMBERSIDE
MERSEYSIDE
CHESHIRE
DERBYSHIRE
NOTTINGHAMSHIRE
LINCOLNSHIRE
STAFFORDSHIRE
SHROPSHIRE
LEICESTERSHIRE
WEST MIDLANDS
NORTHANTS
CAMBRIDGESHIRE
NORFOLK
POWYS
CLWYD
Cheviot Hills
The Wash
Mouth of the Humber
NEWCASTLE UPON TYNE
GATESHEAD
SOUTH SHIELDS
SUNDERLAND
WASHINGTON
CARLISLE
HARTLEPOOL
DARLINGTON
STOCKTON ON-TEES
MIDDLESBROUGH
HARROGATE
YORK
LEEDS
BRADFORD
KINGSTON-UPON-HULL
BLACKPOOL
PRESTON
BLACKBURN
BARROW-N-FURNESS
SOUTHPORT
LIVERPOOL
BOLTON
WIGAN
MANCHESTER
STOCKPORT
SHEFFIELD
ROTHERHAM
DONCASTER
SCUNTHORPE
GRIMSBY
LINCOLN
CHESTERFIELD
MANSFIELD
CHESTER
CREWE
STOKE-ON-TRENT
DERBY
NOTTINGHAM
LEICESTER
PETERBOROUGH
WOLVERHAMPTON
BIRMINGHAM
COVENTRY
TELFORD
SHREWSBURY
West of Greenwich
East of Greenwich

Designed and produced by E.S.R.

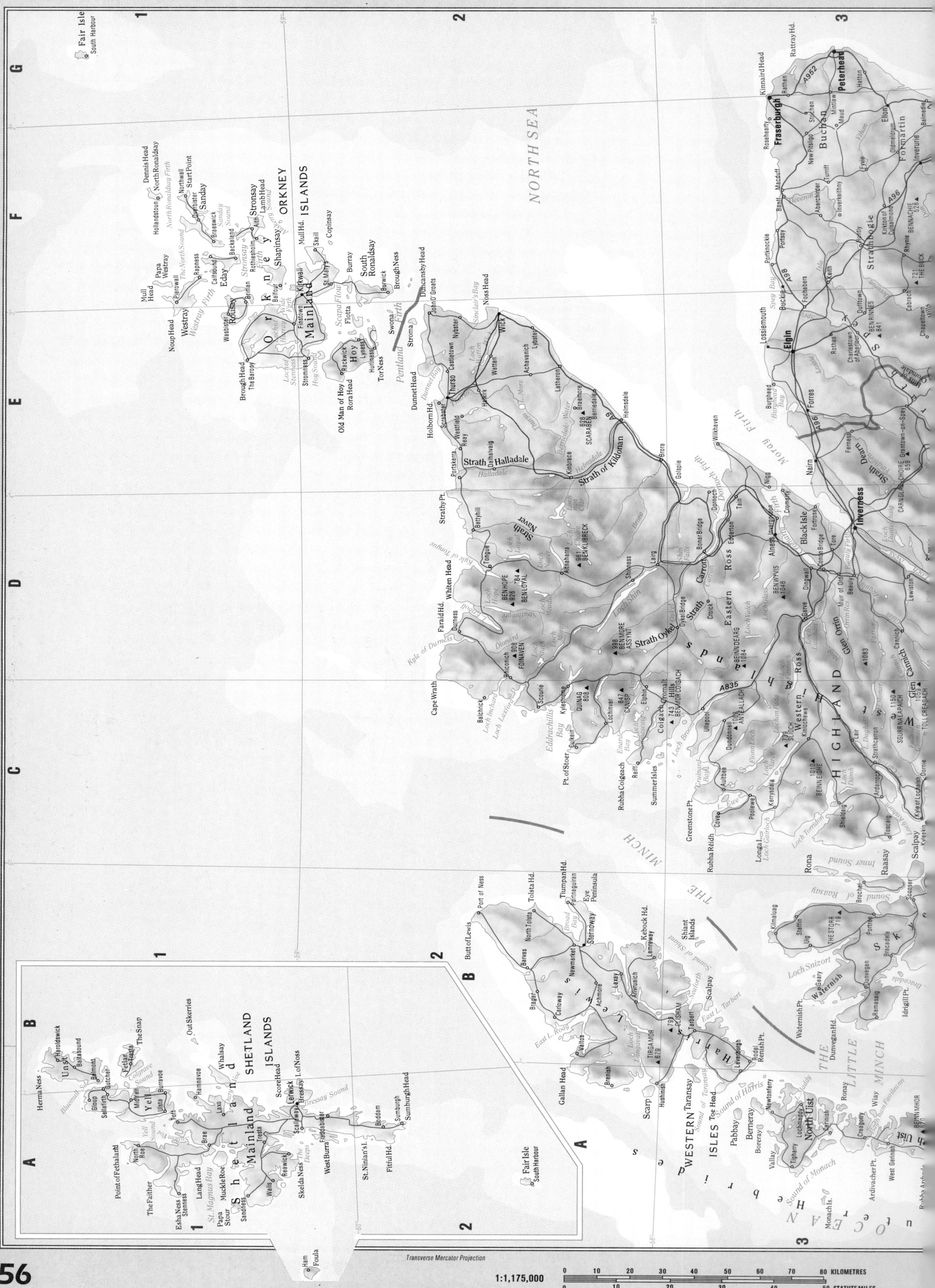
NORTH SEA
ORKNEY ISLANDS
Mainland
Hoy
Westray
Sanday
Stronsay
Shapinsay
Rousay
Eday
South Ronaldsay
Kirkwall
Stromness
Pentland Firth
Scapa Flow
Fair Isle
Thurso
Wick
Dunnet Head
Duncansby Head
John O'Groats
Cape Wrath
Strath Halladale
Strath of Kildonan
Strath Naver
Strath Oykel
Loch Shin
Tongue
Lairg
Durness
Ullapool
Dornoch Firth
Moray Firth
Inverness
Nairn
Forres
Elgin
Lossiemouth
Fraserburgh
Peterhead
Buchan
Strathbogie
Black Isle
Eastern Ross
Wester Ross
HIGHLAND
Glen Affric
Kyle of Lochalsh
Loch Broom
Loch Ewe
Loch Torridon
THE MINCH
THE LITTLE MINCH
Butt of Lewis
Stornoway
Lewis
Harris
North Uist
WESTERN ISLES
Sound of Harris
Skye
Raasay
Rona
Scalpay
Shiant Islands
Hebridean Sea
OCEAN
SHETLAND ISLANDS
Unst
Yell
Fetlar
Whalsay
Mainland
Lerwick
Sumburgh Head
Foula
Out Skerries
Transverse Mercator Projection
1:1,175,000
0 10 20 30 40 50 60 70 80 KILOMETRES
0 10 20 30 40 50 STATUTE MILES

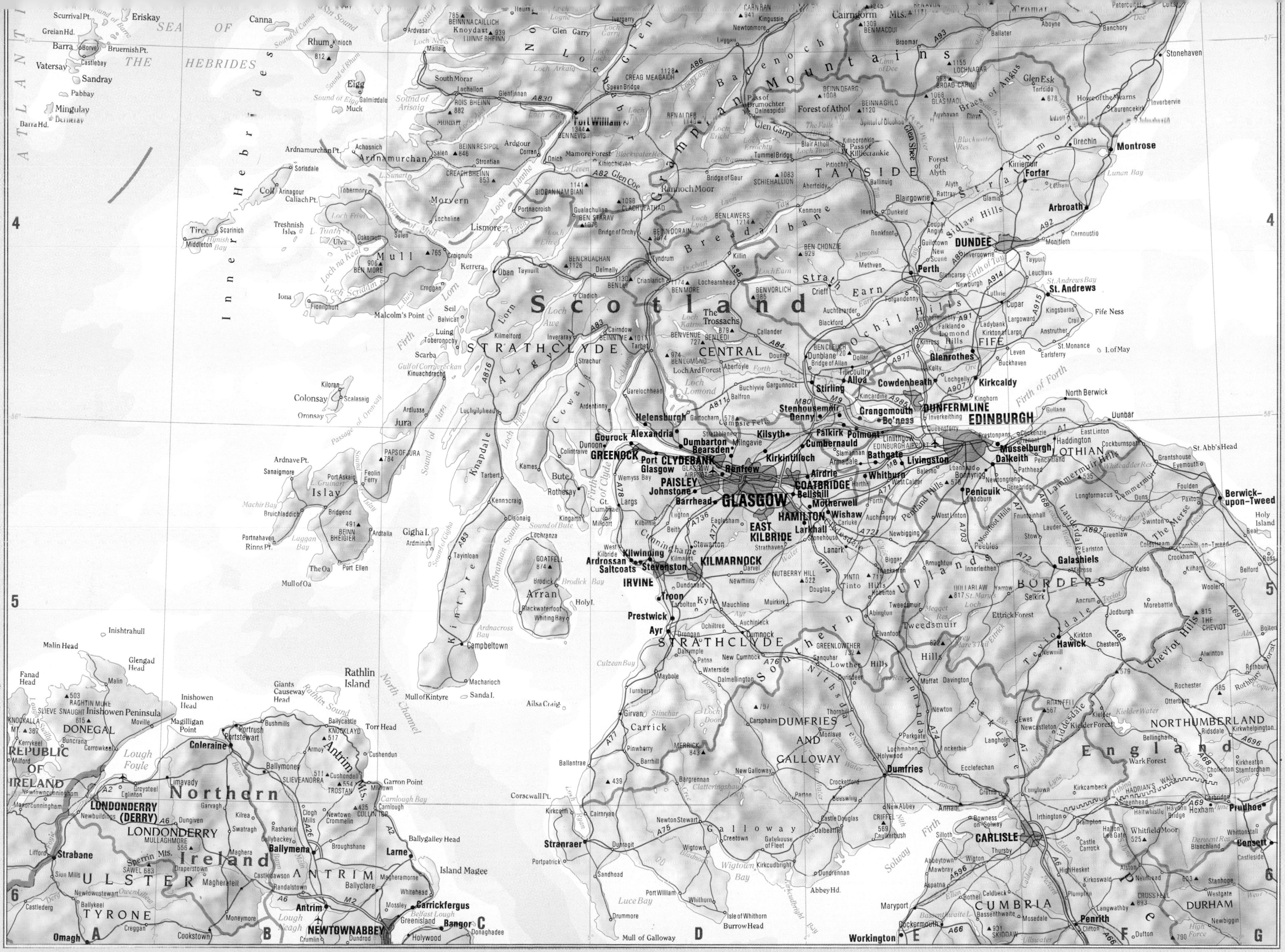
Scotland
STRATHCLYDE
CENTRAL
TAYSIDE
FIFE
LOTHIAN
BORDERS
DUMFRIES AND GALLOWAY
NORTHUMBERLAND
CUMBRIA
DURHAM
England
Northern Ireland
ULSTER
REPUBLIC OF IRELAND
DONEGAL
LONDONDERRY
ANTRIM
TYRONE
GLASGOW
EDINBURGH
DUNDEE
Perth
Stirling
DUNFERMLINE
Kirkcaldy
Glenrothes
Motherwell
HAMILTON
EAST KILBRIDE
PAISLEY
GREENOCK
KILMARNOCK
IRVINE
Ayr
Dumfries
CARLISLE
Penrith
Workington
Hawick
Galashiels
Berwick-upon-Tweed
Montrose
Arbroath
Forfar
St. Andrews
Fort William
Oban
Campbeltown
Stranraer
LONDONDERRY (DERRY)
Coleraine
Ballymena
Antrim
Larne
NEWTOWNABBEY
Carrickfergus
Bangor
Omagh
Strabane
Mull
Jura
Islay
Arran
Bute
Kintyre
Tiree
Coll
Colonsay
Rathlin Island
Inner Hebrides
SEA OF THE HEBRIDES
North Channel
Firth of Clyde
Firth of Forth
Solway Firth
Cheviot Hills
Southern Uplands
Grampian Mountains
Lammermuir Hills
West of Greenwich

Designed and produced by E.S.F.

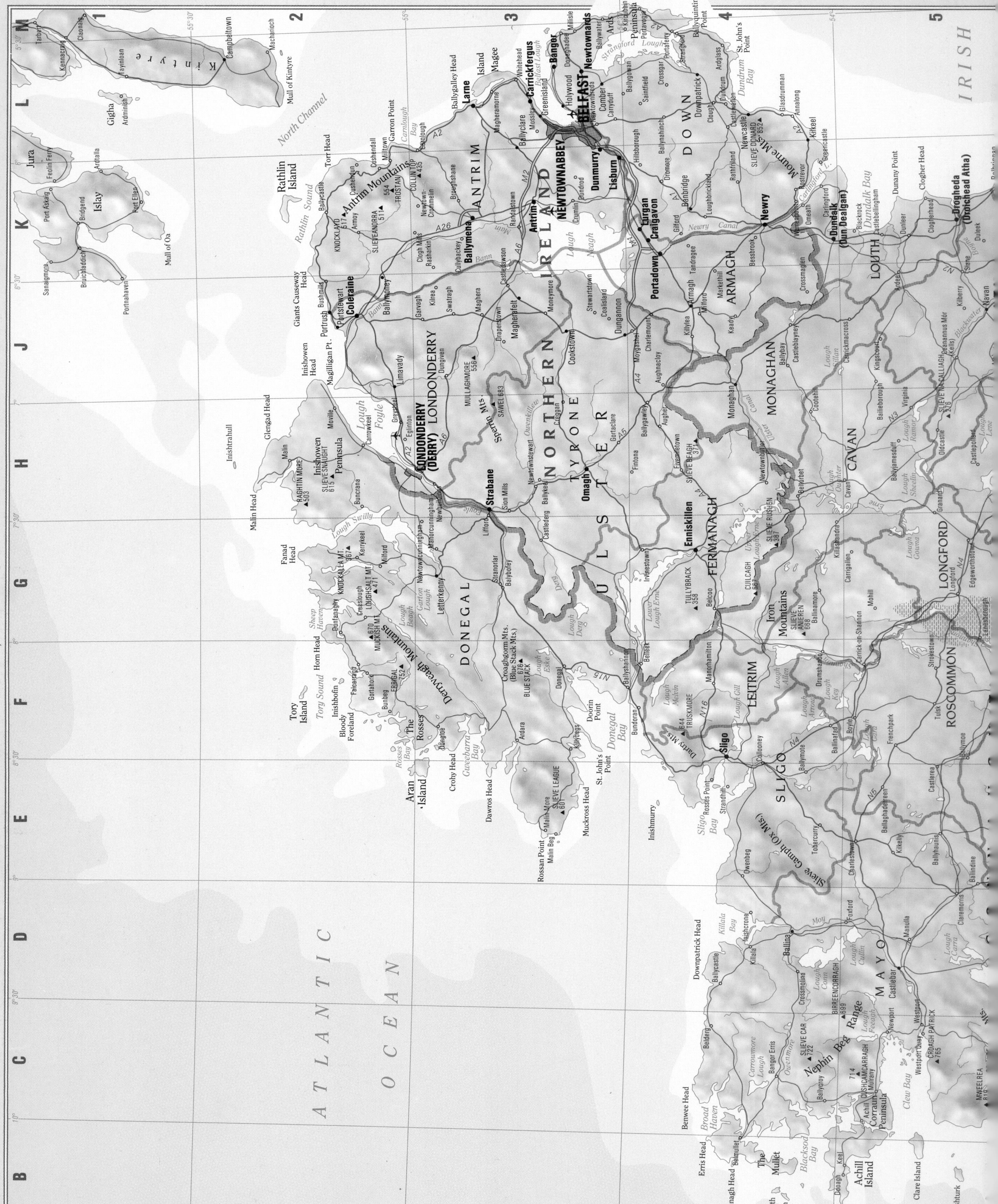
ATLANTIC OCEAN
NORTHERN IRELAND
ULSTER
ANTRIM
LONDONDERRY
TYRONE
FERMANAGH
ARMAGH
DOWN
DONEGAL
MONAGHAN
CAVAN
LOUTH
LONGFORD
LEITRIM
SLIGO
ROSCOMMON
MAYO
BELFAST
LONDONDERRY (DERRY)
NEWTOWNABBEY
Lisburn
Bangor
Newtownards
Carrickfergus
Larne
Ballymena
Coleraine
Antrim
Lurgan
Craigavon
Portadown
Newry
Dundalk (Dún Dealgan)
Drogheda (Droichead Átha)
Strabane
Omagh
Enniskillen
Sligo
North Channel
Lough Neagh
Lough Foyle
Lough Swilly
Donegal Bay
Tory Island
Aran Island
Achill Island
Inishowen Peninsula
Antrim Mountains
Sperrin Mts
Derryveagh Mountains
Mourne Mts
Iron Mountains
Kintyre
Islay
Jura
Gigha
Rathlin Island
IRISH

Lambert Conformal Conic Projection

1:1,000,000

0 10 20 30 40 50 60 70 80 KILOMETRES

0 10 20 30 40 50 STATUTE MILES

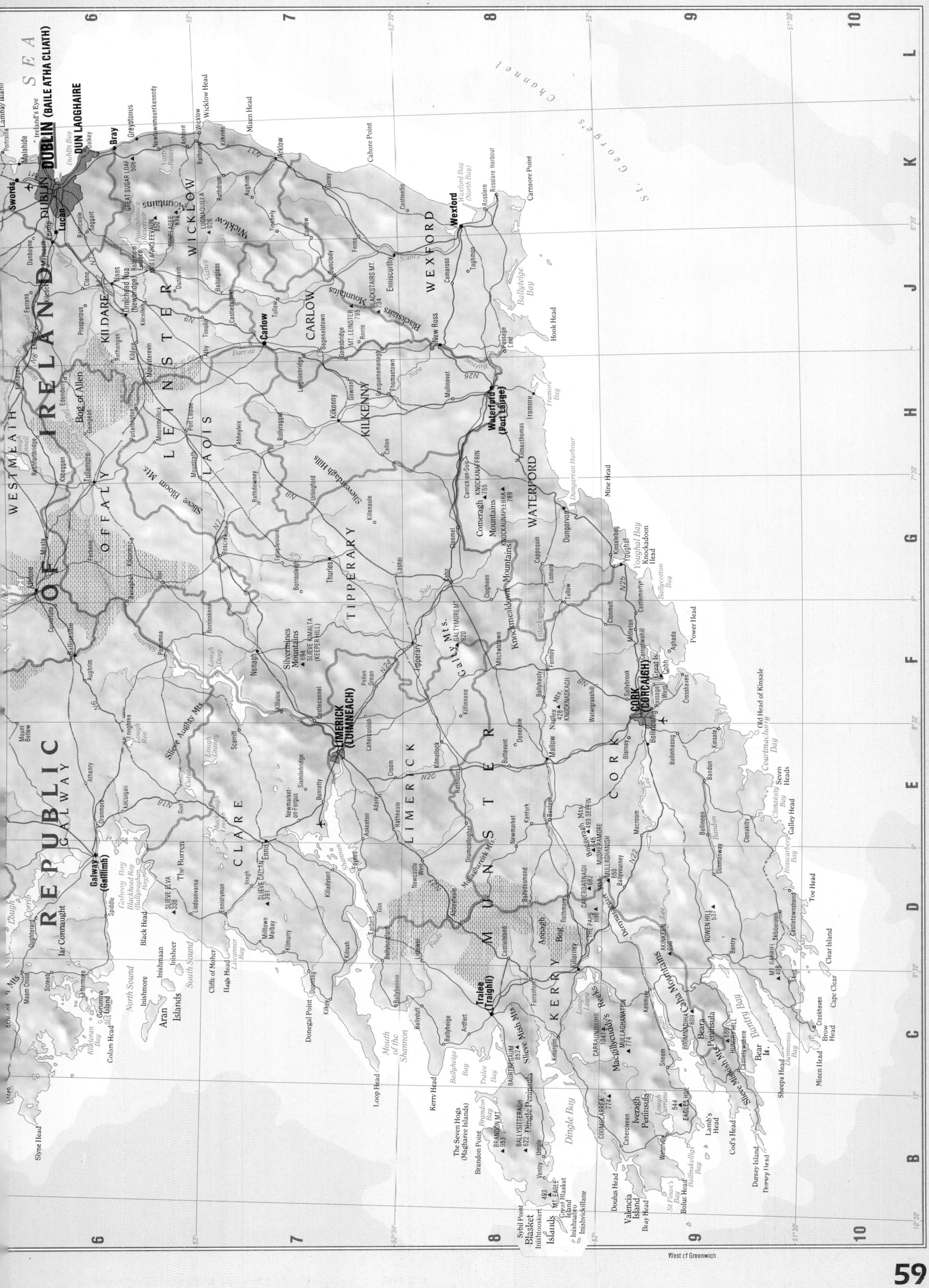

REPUBLIC OF IRELAND
LEINSTER
MUNSTER
GALWAY
WESTMEATH
OFFALY
KILDARE
LAOIS
WICKLOW
CARLOW
KILKENNY
WEXFORD
TIPPERARY
WATERFORD
LIMERICK
CLARE
CORK
KERRY
SEA
St. George's Channel
DUBLIN (BAILE ATHA CLIATH)
DUN LAOGHAIRE
Dublin Bay
Lambay Island
Ireland's Eye
Malahide
Portrane
Swords
Lucan
Dalkey
Bray
Greystones
Wicklow
Wicklow Head
Mizen Head
Arklow
Cahore Point
Gorey
Wexford
Wexford Bay (North Bay)
Rosslare
Rosslare Harbour
Carnsore Point
Wicklow Mountains
LUGNAQUILLA 926
GREAT SUGAR LOAF 506
Naas
Kildare
Maynooth
Celbridge
Athy
Carlow
Tullow
Enniscorthy
Blackstairs Mountains
MT. LEINSTER 795
BLACKSTAIRS MT. 734
New Ross
Ballyteige Bay
Hook Head
Bog of Allen
Edenderry
Tullamore
Portlaoise
Mountmellick
Portarlington
Slieve Bloom Mts.
Kilkenny
Callan
Thomastown
Waterford (Port Láirge)
Tramore
Tramore Bay
Dungarvan
Dungarvan Harbour
Mine Head
Comeragh Mountains
KNOCKANAFFRIN 755
Knockmealdown Mountains
Carrick-on-Suir
Clonmel
Cahir
Cashel
Thurles
Slieveardagh Hills
Athlone
Moate
Ballinasloe
Birr
Shannon
Lough Derg
Nenagh
Silvermines Mountains
KEEPER HILL
Galty Mts.
GALTYMORE MT. 920
Tipperary
Mitchelstown
Fermoy
Lismore
Youghal
Youghal Bay
Knockadoon Head
Ballycotton Bay
Power Head
Midleton
Cobh
Great Is.
CORK (CORCAIGH)
Blarney
Mallow
Kinsale
Old Head of Kinsale
Courtmacsherry Bay
Seven Heads
Galley Head
Clonakilty
Bandon
Dunmanway
Skibbereen
Toe Head
Clear Island
Cape Clear
Bantry
Bantry Bay
Mizen Head
Brow Head
Crookhaven
Sheeps Head
Bear Is.
Beara Peninsula
Dursey Island
Dursey Head
Slieve Miskish Mts.
Caha Mountains
Kenmare
Killarney
Macgillycuddy's Reeks
CARRAUNTUOHILL 1041
Iveragh Peninsula
Lough Currane
Valencia Island
Bray Head
Bolus Head
Ballinskelligs Bay
Cahersiveen
Waterville
Lamb's Head
Cod's Head
Dingle Bay
Dingle Peninsula
BRANDON MT. 953
Brandon Bay
Brandon Point
Tralee (Trá Lí)
Tralee Bay
Slieve Mish Mts.
Castleisland
Listowel
Ballybunion
Kerry Head
Loop Head
Mouth of the Shannon
The Seven Hogs (Magharee Islands)
Blasket Islands
Great Blasket Island
Inishtooskert
Inishvickillane
Sybil Point
LIMERICK (LUIMNEACH)
Newcastle West
Abbeyfeale
Kilrush
Kilkee
Ennis
Ennistymon
Lisdoonvarna
The Burren
Cliffs of Moher
Hag's Head
Liscannor Bay
Doonbeg
Donegal Point
Aran Islands
Inishmore
Inishmaan
Inisheer
North Sound
South Sound
Galway (Gaillimh)
Galway Bay
Black Head
Spiddle
Iar Connaught
Oughterard
Lough Corrib
Athenry
Loughrea
Gort
Slieve Aughty Mts.
Golam Head
Kilkieran Bay
Slyne Head
Clifden
Mount Bellew
Banagher
West of Greenwich
6
7
8
9
10
B
C
D
E
F
G
H
J
K
L

Designed and produced by E.S.R.

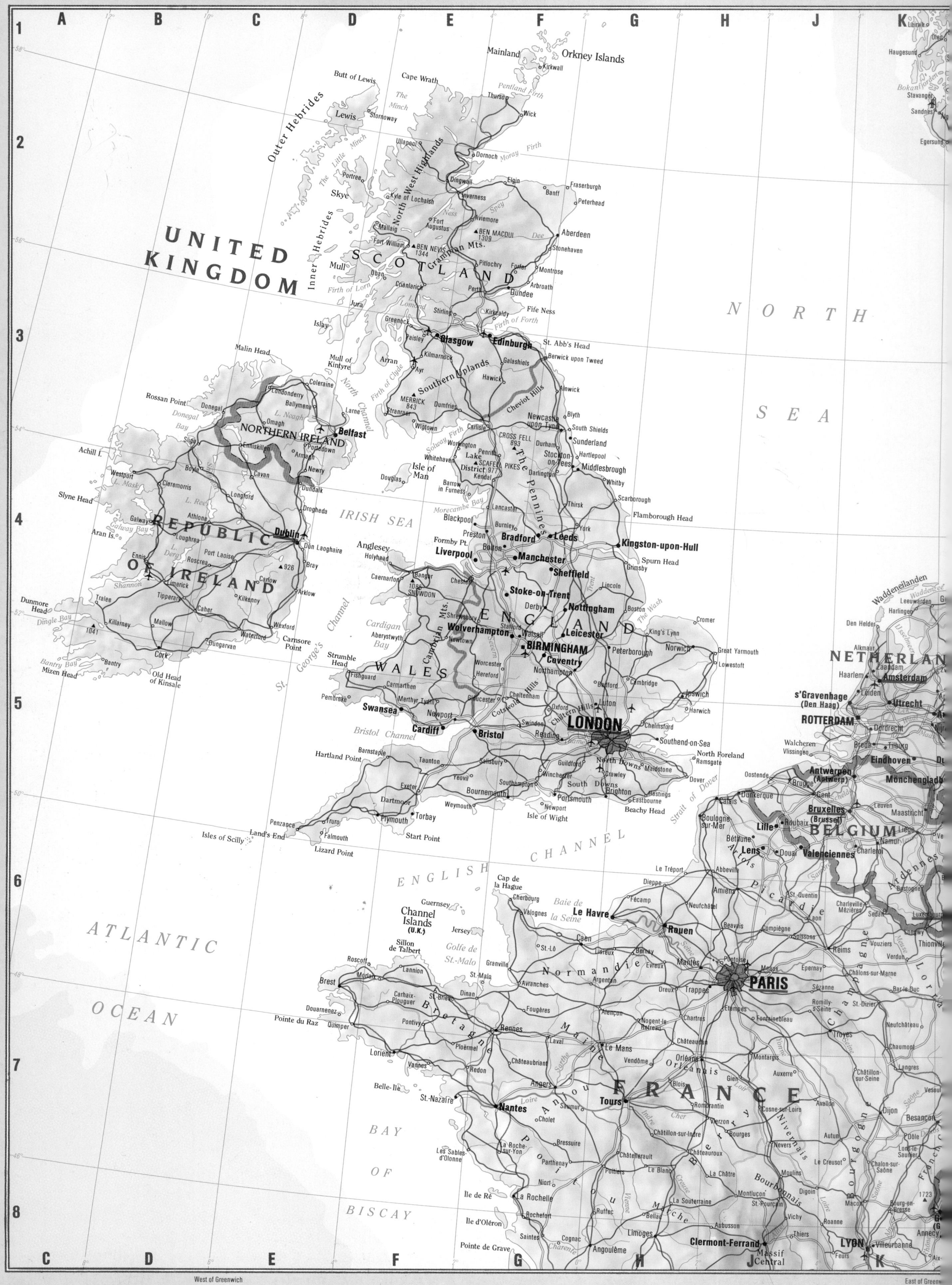
UNITED KINGDOM
SCOTLAND
NORTHERN IRELAND
REPUBLIC OF IRELAND
ENGLAND
WALES
FRANCE
BELGIUM
NETHERLAN
NORTH SEA
ATLANTIC OCEAN
IRISH SEA
ENGLISH CHANNEL
BAY OF BISCAY
Bristol Channel
St. George's Channel
Strait of Dover
North Channel
Orkney Islands
Mainland
Kirkwall
Pentland Firth
Thurso
Wick
Butt of Lewis
Cape Wrath
The Minch
Lewis
Stornoway
Outer Hebrides
The Little Minch
Ullapool
North West Highlands
Dornoch
Moray Firth
Portree
Skye
Dingwall
Elgin
Banff
Fraserburgh
Peterhead
Inverness
Kyle of Lochalsh
Inner Hebrides
Mallaig
Fort Augustus
Aviemore
BEN MACDUI 1309
Aberdeen
Fort William
BEN NEVIS 1344
Grampian Mts.
Stonehaven
Pitlochry
Forfar
Montrose
Mull
Oban
Firth of Lorn
Arbroath
Perth
Dundee
Jura
Fife Ness
Stirling
Kirkcaldy
Firth of Forth
Islay
Greenock
Paisley
Glasgow
Edinburgh
St. Abb's Head
Berwick upon Tweed
Malin Head
Mull of Kintyre
Arran
Kilmarnock
Galashiels
Ayr
Southern Uplands
Hawick
Firth of Clyde
Coleraine
Londonderry
Ballymena
L. Neagh
Larne
MERRICK 843
Dumfries
Cheviot Hills
Alnwick
Rossan Point
Donegal
Donegal Bay
Omagh
Stranraer
Belfast
Wigtown
Carlisle
Newcastle upon Tyne
Blyth
South Shields
Sunderland
Solway Firth
Workington
Penrith
CROSS FELL 893
Durham
Hartlepool
Sligo
Enniskillen
Portadown
Armagh
Whitehaven
Lake District
SCAFELL PIKES 977
Stockton-on-Tees
Middlesbrough
Achill I.
Boyle
Newry
Isle of Man
Douglas
Kendal
Darlington
Whitby
Westport
L. Mask
Claremorris
Cavan
Dundalk
Barrow in Furness
The Pennines
Scarborough
L. Ree
Longford
Morecambe Bay
Thirsk
Flamborough Head
Slyne Head
Galway
Galway Bay
Athlone
Drogheda
Lancaster
Blackpool
Burnley
York
Aran Is.
Loughrea
Dublin
Preston
Bradford
Leeds
Formby Pt.
Bolton
Kingston-upon-Hull
Anglesey
Holyhead
Liverpool
Manchester
Spurn Head
Dun Laoghaire
Ennis
L. Derg
Port Laoise
Roscrea
Bray
Sheffield
Grimsby
Caernarfon
Bangor
Chester
Shannon
Limerick
Carlow
Tipperary
Kilkenny
1085 SNOWDON
Stoke-on-Trent
Lincoln
Trent
Arklow
Derby
Nottingham
Tralee
Dunmore Head
Dingle Bay
Killarney
Mallow
Caher
Cambrian Mts.
Boston
The Wash
Cromer
Cardigan Bay
Aberystwyth
Shrewsbury
Stafford
Wolverhampton
Walsall
Leicester
King's Lynn
1041
Waterford
Wexford
Newtown
BIRMINGHAM
Norwich
Great Yarmouth
Dungarvan
Carnsore Point
Coventry
Peterborough
Lowestoft
Cork
Bantry Bay
Bantry
Mizen Head
Old Head of Kinsale
Strumble Head
Worcester
Northampton
Hereford
Bedford
Cambridge
Fishguard
Carmarthen
Cotswold Hills
Cheltenham
Ipswich
Gloucester
Luton
Pembroke
Merthyr Tydfil
Oxford
Chiltern Hills
Harwich
Swansea
Newport
Swindon
LONDON
Cardiff
Bristol
Reading
Chelmsford
Southend-on-Sea
Barnstaple
North Foreland
Hartland Point
Ramsgate
Taunton
Salisbury
Guildford
North Downs
Maidstone
Crawley
Dover
Exeter
Yeovil
Winchester
Southampton
South Downs
Bournemouth
Portsmouth
Brighton
Hastings
Eastbourne
Dartmoor
Weymouth
Newport
Isle of Wight
Beachy Head
Torbay
Penzance
Truro
Plymouth
Isles of Scilly
Land's End
Falmouth
Start Point
Lizard Point
Le Tréport
Abbeville
Cap de la Hague
Dieppe
Amiens
Picardie
Cherbourg
Baie de la Seine
Fécamp
Neufchâtel
Guernsey
Channel Islands (U.K.)
Valognes
Le Havre
Jersey
Rouen
Beauvais
Compiègne
Soissons
Sillon de Talbert
Caen
Golfe de St.-Malo
St.-Lô
Lisieux
Bernay
Evreux
Pontoise
Reims
Roscoff
Morlaix
Lannion
Granville
Normandie
Mantes
Meaux
Epernay
Châlons-sur-Marne
St.-Malo
Argentan
Avranches
Brest
Carhaix-Plouguer
St.-Brieuc
Dinan
Dreux
Trappes
PARIS
Sézanne
Bar-le-Duc
Fougères
Étampes
Romilly-s-Seine
St.-Dizier
Douarnenez
Pointe du Raz
Quimper
Bretagne
Pontivy
Rennes
Alençon
Nogent-le-Rotrou
Chartres
Fontainebleau
Troyes
Neufchâteau
Laval
Maine
Châteaudun
Champagne
Chaumont
Lorient
Ploërmel
Le Mans
Vendôme
Orléans
Orléanais
Montargis
Châteaubriant
Vannes
Redon
Langres
Auxerre
Belle-Île
Angers
Blois
Gien
Châtillon-sur-Seine
St.-Nazaire
Nantes
Anjou
Saumur
Tours
Romorantin
Cosne-sur-Loire
Avallon
Dijon
Cholet
Cher
Vierzon
Nivernais
Besançon
Bressuire
Châtillon-sur-Indre
Bourges
Dôle
Autun
La Roche-sur-Yon
Les Sables-d'Olonne
Parthenay
Châteauroux
Nevers
Le Creusot
Lons-le-Saunier
Poitou
Châtellerault
Berry
Chalon-sur-Saône
Niort
Poitiers
Le Blanc
La Châtre
Bourbonnais
Moulins
Île de Ré
La Rochelle
Montluçon
Digoin
Mâcon
Bourg-en-Bresse
La Souterraine
St.-Pourçain
Rochefort
Ruffec
Marche
Bellac
Vichy
Roanne
Île d'Oléron
Limoges
Aubusson
Saintes
Cognac
Clermont-Ferrand
Thiers
LYON
Villeurbanne
Pointe de Grave
Angoulême
Massif Central
Feurs
Calais
Dunkerque
Boulogne-sur-Mer
Brugge
Gent
Oostende
Antwerpen (Antwerp)
Bruxelles (Brussel)
Lille
Roubaix
Béthune
Lens
Douai
Valenciennes
Artois
Charleroi
Namur
Liège
Maastricht
Leuven
Eindhoven
Mönchengladb
Tilburg
Breda
Dordrecht
Walcheren
Vlissingen
ROTTERDAM
s'Gravenhage (Den Haag)
Utrecht
Leiden
Haarlem
Amsterdam
Zaandam
Alkmaar
Den Helder
Harlingen
Leeuwarden
Waddeneilanden
Ardennes
St.-Quentin
Laon
Charleville-Mézières
Sedan
Vouziers
Verdun
Thionville
Lorraine
Haugesund
Stavanger
Sandnes
Egersund
Bokanfjorden
West of Greenwich
East of Greenwich

1:5,000,000

0 50 100 150 200 250 300 350 400 KILOMETRES

0 50 100 150 200 250 STATUTE MILES

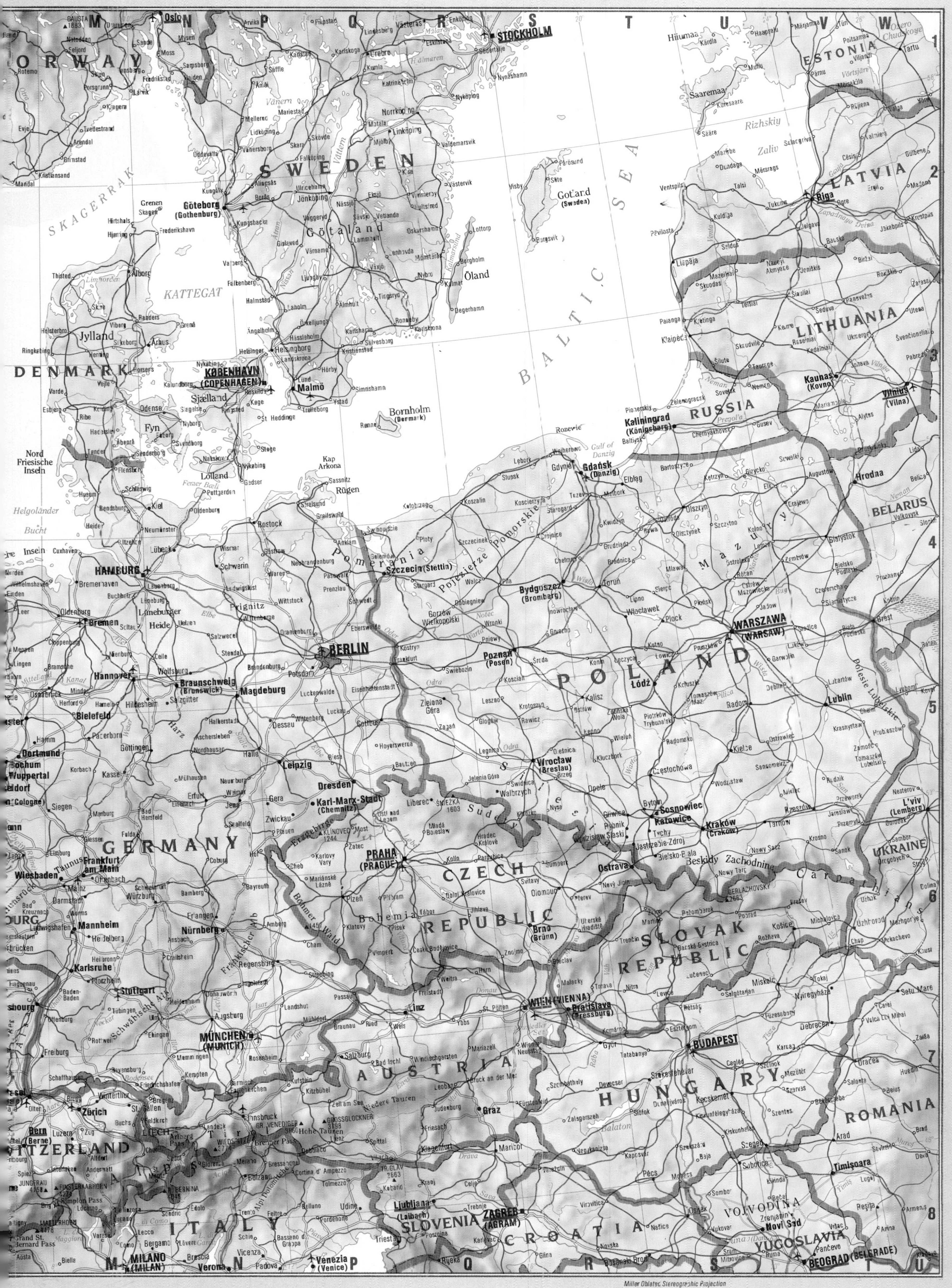
SWEDEN
Götaland
STOCKHOLM
Göteborg (Gothenburg)
Oslo
NORWAY
SKAGERRAK
KATTEGAT
DENMARK
Jylland
Sjælland
Fyn
Lolland
KØBENHAVN (COPENHAGEN)
Malmö
Bornholm (Denmark)
Öland
Gotland (Sweden)
BALTIC SEA
Saaremaa
Hiiumaa
Rizhskiy Zaliv
ESTONIA
LATVIA
Riga
LITHUANIA
Kaunas (Kovno)
Vilnius (Vilna)
Kaliningrad (Königsberg)
RUSSIA
BELARUS
Hrodna
Brest
Gulf of Danzig
Gdańsk (Danzig)
Rügen
Pomerania
Pojezierze Pomorskie
Mazury
Szczecin (Stettin)
Bydgoszcz (Bromberg)
Poznań (Posen)
WARSZAWA (WARSAW)
POLAND
Łódź
Lublin
Wrocław (Breslau)
Kraków (Cracow)
Katowice
Ostrava
Sudety
L'viv (Lemberg)
UKRAINE
Carpathians
Beskidy Zachodnie
BERLIN
HAMBURG
Bremen
Hannover
Braunschweig (Brunswick)
Magdeburg
Leipzig
Dresden
Karl-Marx-Stadt (Chemnitz)
GERMANY
Frankfurt am Main
Wiesbaden
Mannheim
Nürnberg
Stuttgart
Karlsruhe
MÜNCHEN (MUNICH)
Schwäbische Alb
Fränkischer Alb
PRAHA (PRAGUE)
CZECH REPUBLIC
Bohemia
Böhmer Wald
Brno (Brünn)
SLOVAK REPUBLIC
Bratislava (Pressburg)
WIEN (VIENNA)
AUSTRIA
Linz
Salzburg
Graz
Innsbruck
Tirol
Niedere Tauern
HUNGARY
BUDAPEST
Balaton
ROMANIA
Timişoara
YUGOSLAVIA
BEOGRAD (BELGRADE)
Novi Sad
VOJVODINA
CROATIA
ZAGREB (AGRAM)
SLOVENIA
Ljubljana (Laibach)
ITALY
MILANO (MILAN)
Venezia (Venice)
Verona
Trieste
Alps
SWITZERLAND
Bern (Berne)
Zürich
Helgoländer Bucht
Nord Friesische Inseln
M N P Q R S T U V W
1 2 3 4 5 6 7 8
Miller Oblated Stereographic Projection

Designed and produced by E.S.R.

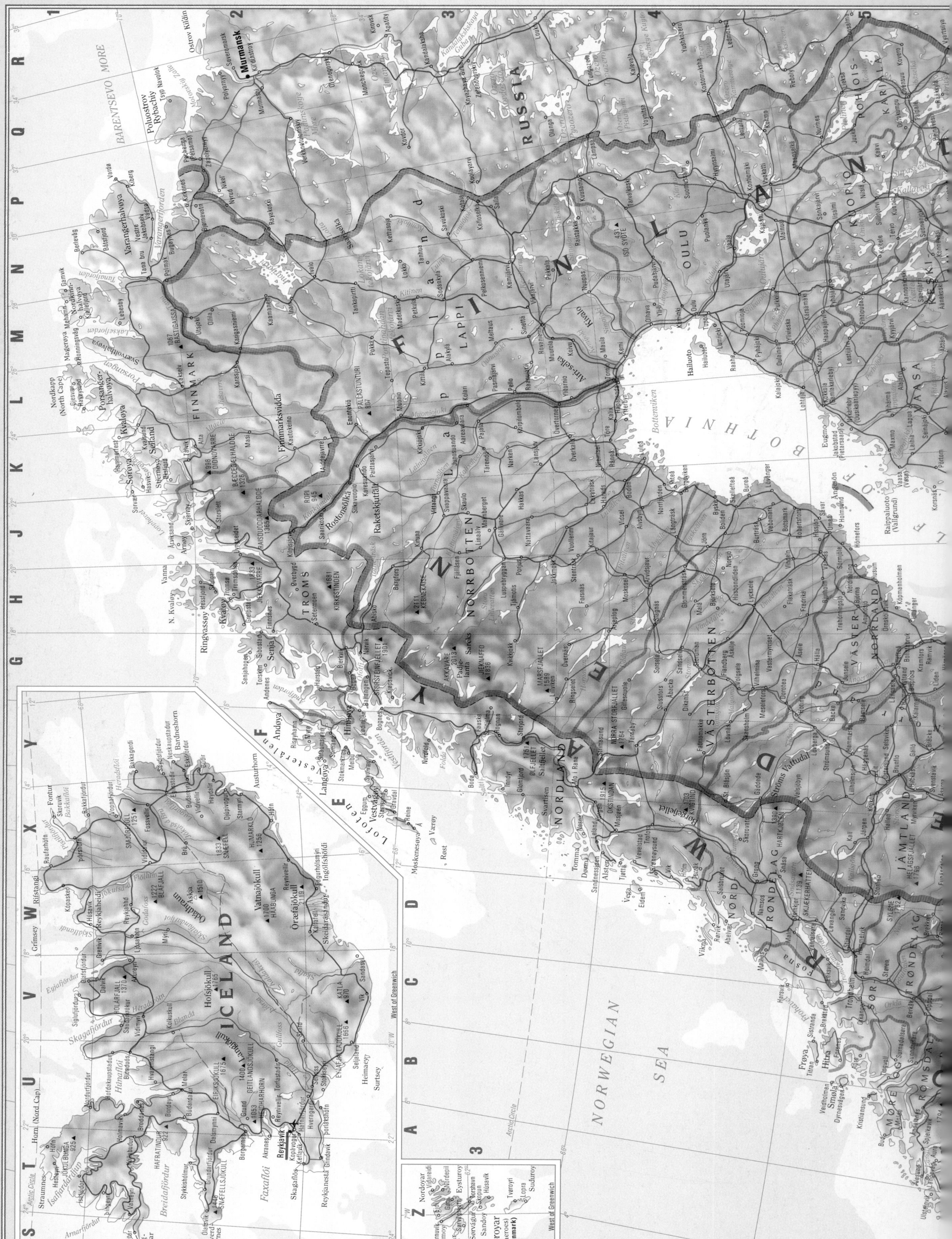
BARENTSEVO MORE
RUSSIA
FINLAND
LAPPI
OULU
VAASA
KUOPIO
NORRBOTTEN
VÄSTERBOTTEN
VÄSTERNORRLAND
JÄMTLAND
NORDLAND
TROMS
FINNMARK
NORD TRØNDELAG
SØR TRØNDELAG
MØRE OG ROMSDAL
NORWEGIAN SEA
BOTHNIA
Bottenviken
ICELAND
Vatnajökull
Hofsjökull
Langjökull
Reykjavík
Faxaflói
Føroyar (Faeroes) (Denmark)
Lofoten
Vesterålen
Murmansk
West of Greenwich
Arctic Circle

Miller Oblated Stereographic Projection

1:4,500,000

0 50 100 150 200 250 300 KILOMETRES

0 50 100 150 200 STATUTE MILES

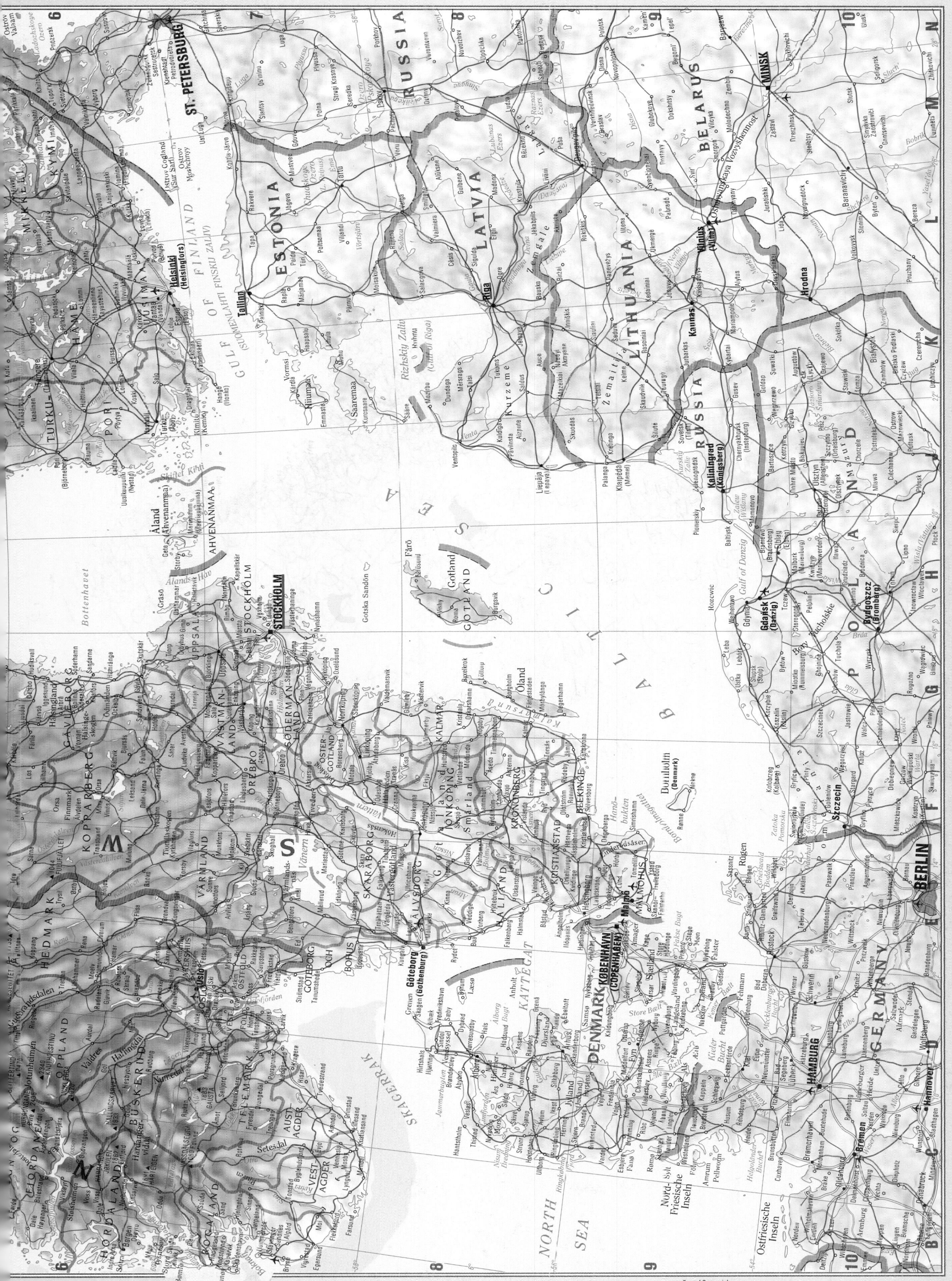

RUSSIA
ESTONIA
LATVIA
LITHUANIA
BELARUS
POLAND
GERMANY
DENMARK
ST. PETERSBURG
Tallinn
Riga
Vilnius (Vilna)
Kaunas
MINSK
Hrodna
Kaliningrad (Königsberg)
Gdańsk (Danzig)
Szczecin
BERLIN
HAMBURG
Bremen
Hannover
KØBENHAVN (COPENHAGEN)
Malmö
Göteborg (Gothenburg)
Oslo
STOCKHOLM
Helsinki (Helsingfors)
GULF OF FINLAND
BALTIC SEA
Gulf of Danzig
Gotland
Öland
Bornholm (Denmark)
KATTEGAT
SKAGERRAK
NORTH SEA
Åland (Ahvenanmaa)
Saaremaa
Hiiumaa
Rīzhskiy Zaliv (Gulf of Riga)

East of Greenwich

Designed and produced by E.S.R.

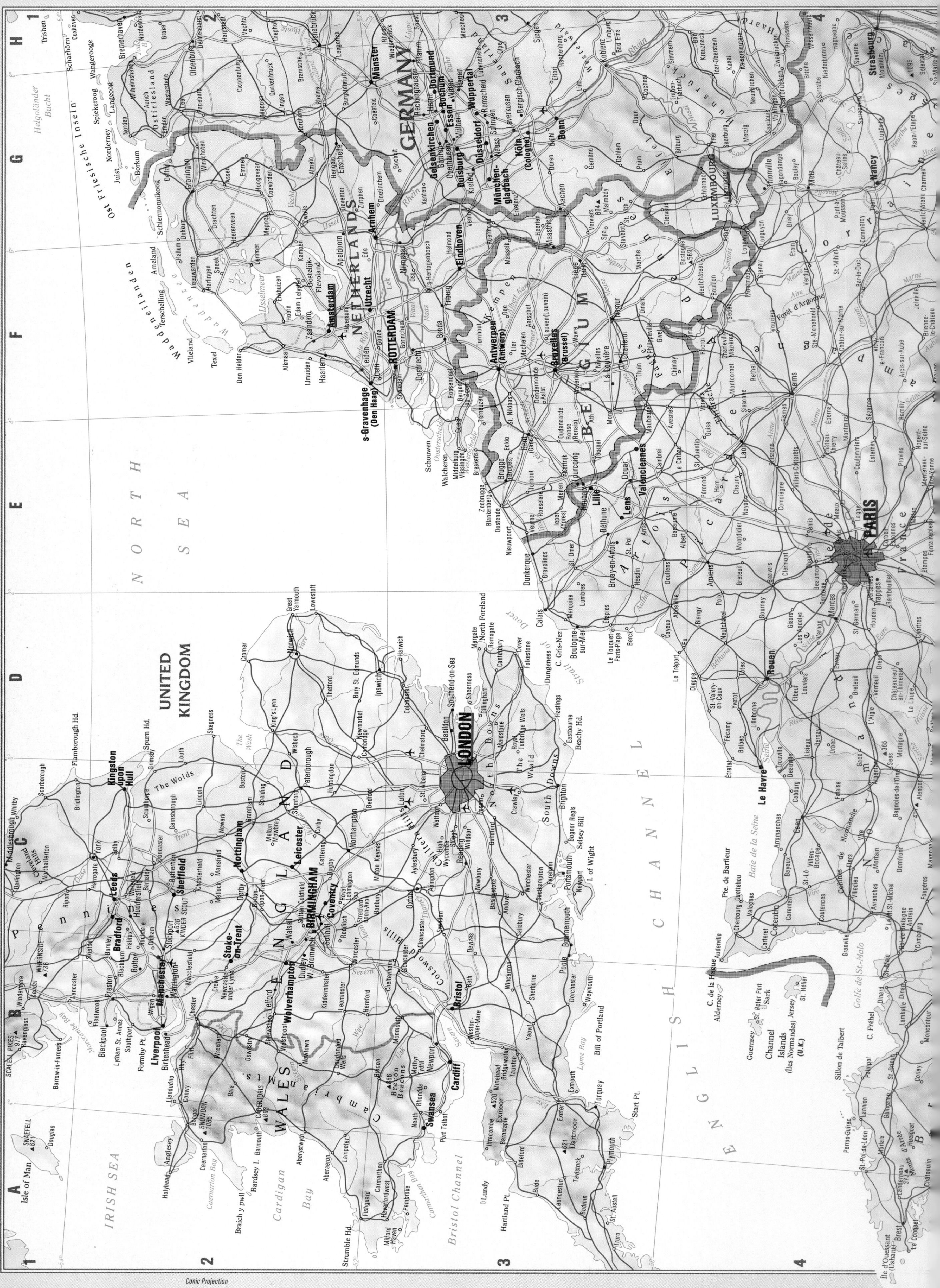
UNITED KINGDOM
NORTH SEA
ENGLISH CHANNEL
IRISH SEA
NETHERLANDS
BELGIUM
LUXEMBOURG
GERMANY
WALES
ENGLAND
LONDON
PARIS
AMSTERDAM
ROTTERDAM
Utrecht
's-Gravenhage (Den Haag)
Antwerpen (Antwerp)
Bruxelles (Brussel)
Lille
Rouen
Le Havre
Birmingham
Manchester
Liverpool
Leeds
Sheffield
Bristol
Cardiff
Köln (Cologne)
Düsseldorf
Essen
Dortmund
Strasbourg
Nancy
Metz
Reims
Channel Islands (Iles Normandes) (U.K.)
Bristol Channel
Cardigan Bay
The Wash
Strait of Dover
Baie de la Seine
Golfe de St-Malo
Ost Friesische Inseln
Waddeneilanden
Helgoländer Bucht

Conic Projection

1:3,000,000

0 25 50 75 100 125 150 175 200 KILOMETRES

0 25 50 75 100 125 STATUTE MILES

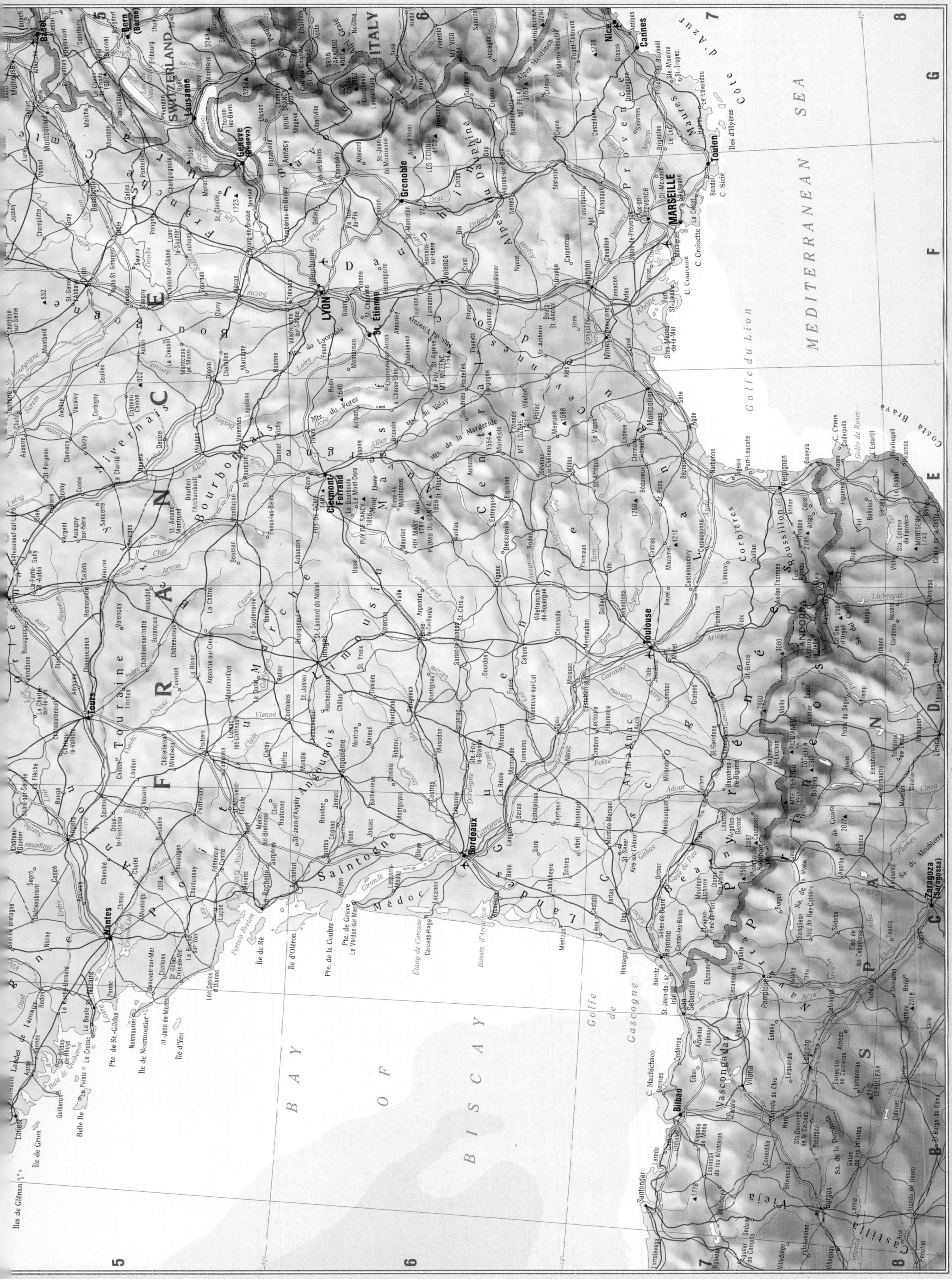
FRANCE
SWITZERLAND
ITALY
SPAIN
ANDORRA
BAY OF BISCAY
MEDITERRANEAN SEA
Golfe de Gascogne
Golfe du Lion
Massif Central
Pyrénées
Bern (Berne)
Basel
Lausanne
Genève (Geneva)
Nice
Cannes
Grenoble
Marseille
Toulon
Lyon
St-Étienne
Valence
Avignon
Montpellier
Nîmes
Toulouse
Perpignan
Clermont-Ferrand
Limoges
Bordeaux
Tours
Nantes
Angers
Angoulême
Pau
Bayonne
Biarritz
San Sebastián
Pamplona
Bilbao
Vitoria
Burgos
Santander
Zaragoza (Saragossa)
Lérida
Huesca
Lorient
Belle Île
Île de Ré
Île d'Oléron
Île d'Yeu
Île de Noirmoutier
Îles d'Hyères
Mt. Viso
Mt. Pelat
Mt. Lozère
Puy de Dôme
Mte. Perdido
Pic d'Aneto
West of Greenwich
East of Greenwich

Designed and produced by E.S.R.

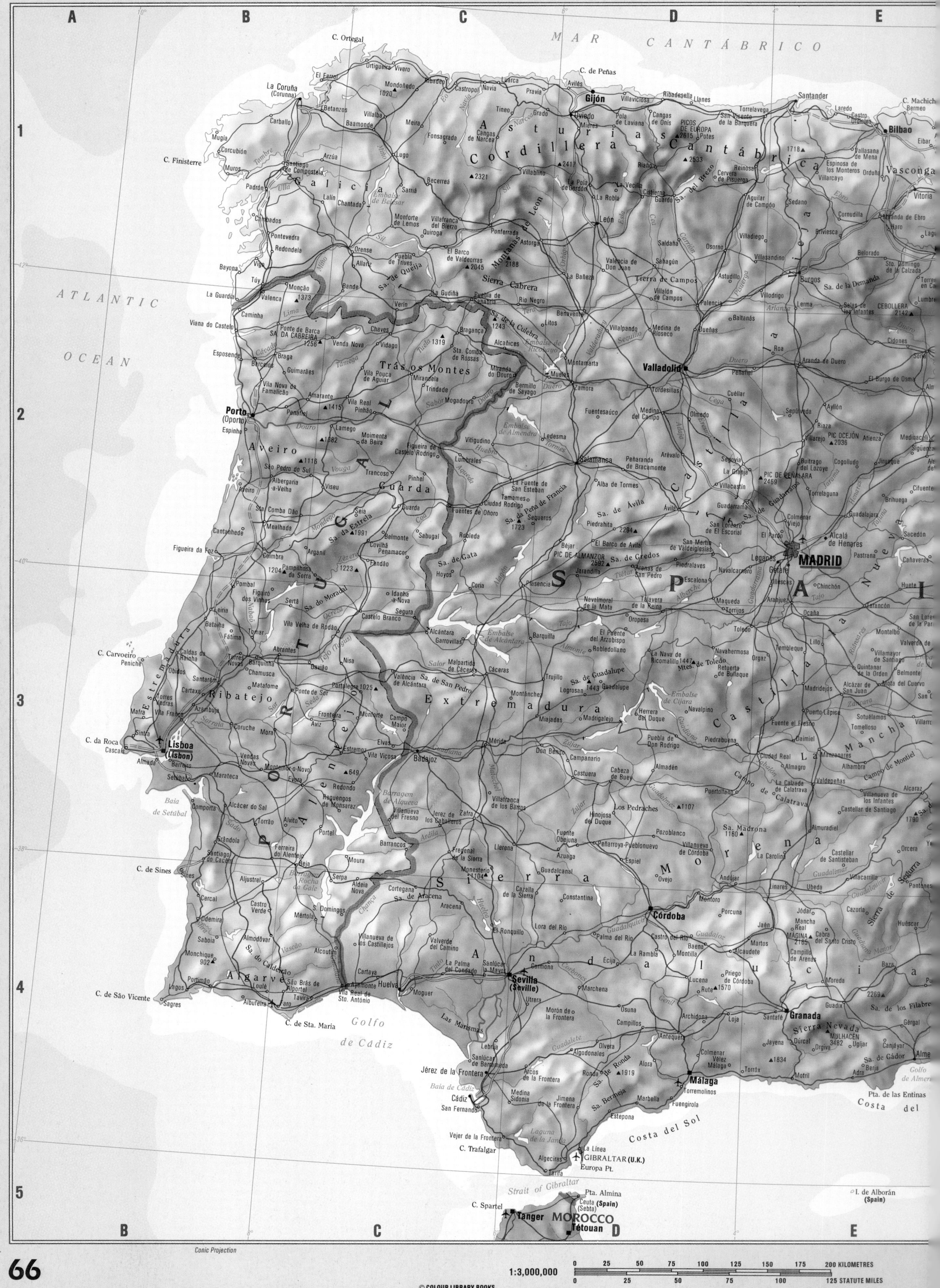
MAR CANTÁBRICO
ATLANTIC OCEAN
C. Ortegal
C. Finisterre
La Coruña (Corunna)
El Ferrol
Santiago de Compostela
Lugo
Orense
Vigo
Pontevedra
Galicia
Asturias
Cordillera Cantábrica
Oviedo
Gijón
Avilés
C. de Peñas
Santander
Bilbao
Vitoria
León
Astorga
Ponferrada
Burgos
Palencia
Valladolid
Zamora
Salamanca
Segovia
Ávila
MADRID
Toledo
Guadalajara
Alcalá de Henares
Aranjuez
Castilla la Vieja
Castilla la Nueva
Tierra de Campos
Sierra de Guadarrama
Sierra de Gredos
PIC DE ALMANZOR 2592
Sa. de Gata
PORTUGAL
Trás os Montes
Porto (Oporto)
Braga
Viana do Castelo
Aveiro
Coimbra
Viseu
Guarda
Sa. da Estrela 1991
Leiria
Castelo Branco
Santarém
Ribatejo
Estremadura
C. Carvoeiro
Peniche
C. da Roca
Lisboa (Lisbon)
Setúbal
Baia de Setúbal
Évora
Alentejo
Beja
C. de Sines
Algarve
Faro
Lagos
C. de São Vicente
Sagres
C. de Sta. Maria
Badajoz
Mérida
Cáceres
Extremadura
Plasencia
Sierra Morena
Ciudad Real
La Mancha
Campo de Calatrava
Sierra Madrona
Córdoba
Sevilla (Seville)
Huelva
Golfo de Cádiz
Las Marismas
Jérez de la Frontera
Cádiz
San Fernando
Baia de Cádiz
C. Trafalgar
Andalucia
Granada
Sierra Nevada
MULHACÉN 3482
Málaga
Torremolinos
Marbella
Costa del Sol
La Línea
GIBRALTAR (U.K.)
Europa Pt.
Algeciras
Tarifa
Strait of Gibraltar
Pta. Almina
Ceuta (Sebta) (Spain)
C. Spartel
Tanger
MOROCCO
Tétouan
I. de Alborán (Spain)
Almería
Pta. de las Entinas
Jaén
Úbeda
Linares
Sa. de Segura
SPAIN
Rio Tajo
Guadiana
Guadalquivir
Duero
Douro
Tajo (Tejo)
Miño
Conic Projection
1:3,000,000
0 25 50 75 100 125 150 175 200 KILOMETRES
0 25 50 75 100 125 STATUTE MILES

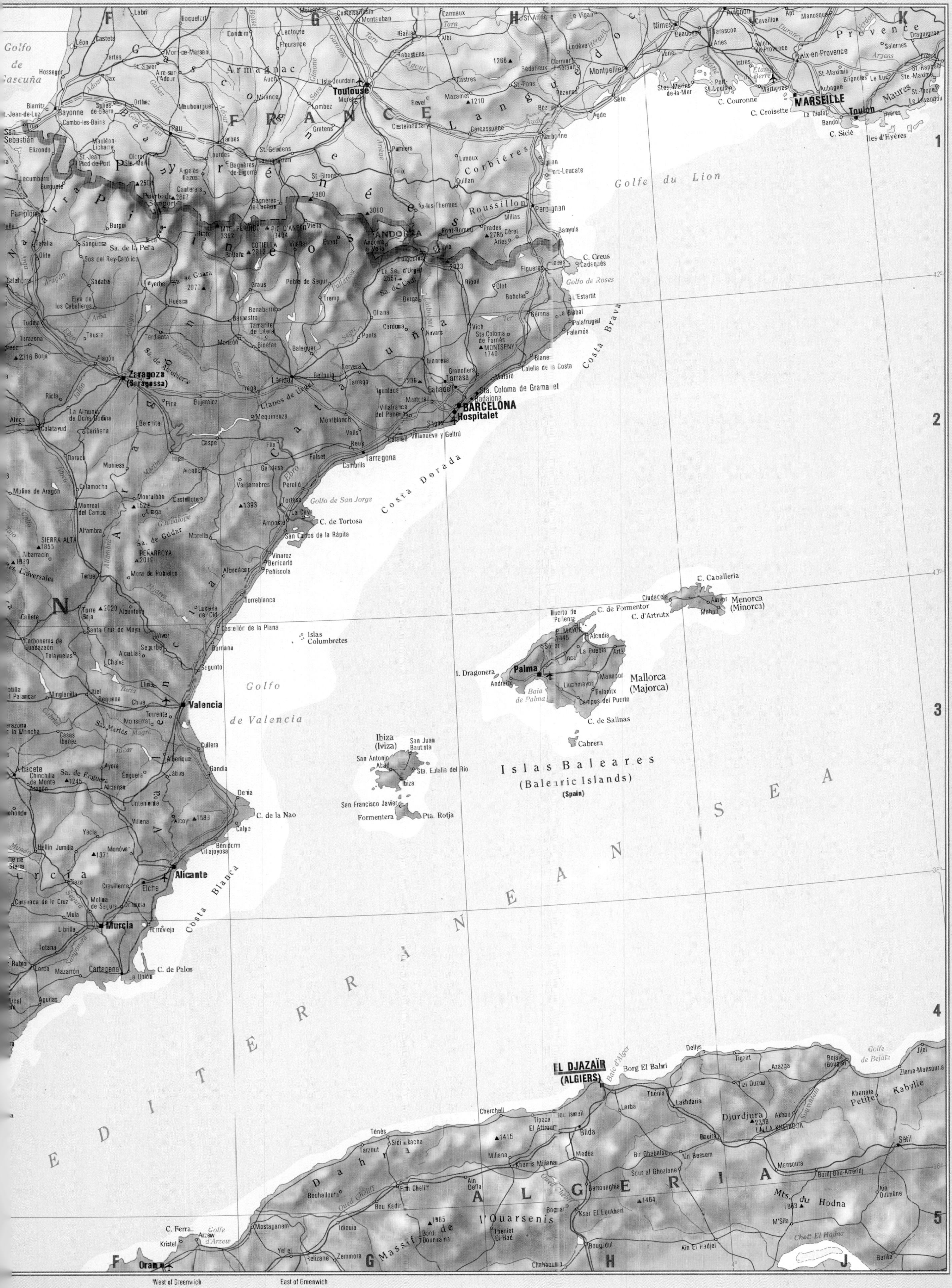
FRANCE
Languedoc
Armagnac
Gascogne
Provence
Pyrénées
Golfe de Gascuña
Golfe du Lion
Toulouse
MARSEILLE
Toulon
Montpellier
Nîmes
Avignon
Aix-en-Provence
Carcassonne
Narbonne
Perpignan
Pau
Tarbes
Bayonne
Biarritz
Roussillon
Corbières
ANDORRA
Andorra la Vella
Pamplona
Zaragoza (Saragossa)
Huesca
Lérida
Cataluña
Costa Brava
Golfo de Roses
Figueres
Gerona
Vich
Manresa
Tarrasa
Sabadell
BARCELONA
Hospitalet
Sta. Coloma de Gramanet
Vilanueva y Geltrú
Tarragona
Reus
Costa Dorada
Golfo de San Jorge
Tortosa
C. de Tortosa
San Carlos de la Rápita
Vinaroz
Benicarló
Peñíscola
Castellón de la Plana
Islas Columbretes
Teruel
Sagunto
Valencia
Golfo de Valencia
Gandia
Denia
C. de la Nao
Calpe
Benidorm
Alicante
Elche
Costa Blanca
Murcia
Cartagena
C. de Palos
Torrevieja
Albacete
Calatayud
Mallorca (Majorca)
Palma
I. Dragonera
Bahía de Palma
C. de Salinas
Cabrera
C. de Formentor
Menorca (Minorca)
Ciudadela
Mahón
C. Caballeria
C. d'Artrutx
Ibiza (Iviza)
San Antonio Abad
San Juan Bautista
Formentera
Pta. Rotja
Islas Baleares (Balearic Islands) (Spain)
MEDITERRANEAN SEA
EL DJAZAÏR (ALGIERS)
Borg El Bahri
Baie d'Alger
Blida
Médéa
Tipaza
Cherchell
Ténès
Miliana
Tizi Ouzou
Dellys
Bejaïa (Bougie)
Golfe de Bejaïa
Jijel
Kabylie
Petite Kabylie
Djurdjura
Sétif
Mts. du Hodna
Chott El Hodna
M'Sila
Dahra
l'Ouarsenis
Massif de l'Ouarsenis
ALGERIA
Mostaganem
Oran
Golfe d'Arzew
Relizane
Chlef
West of Greenwich
East of Greenwich

Designed and produced by E.S.R.

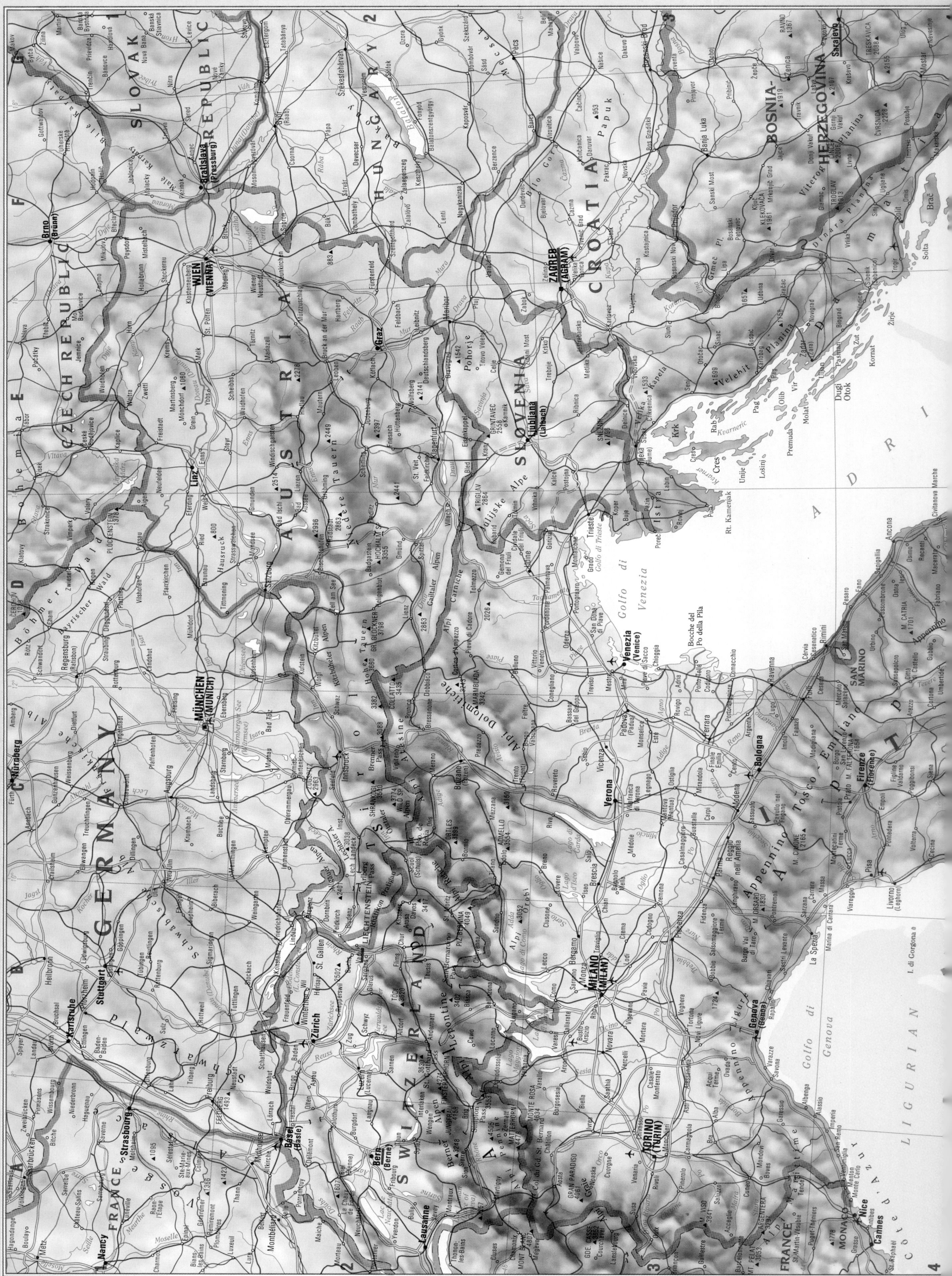
GERMANY
AUSTRIA
SWITZERLAND
CZECH REPUBLIC
SLOVAK REPUBLIC
HUNGARY
SLOVENIA
CROATIA
BOSNIA-HERZEGOVINA
FRANCE
LIECHTENSTEIN
SAN MARINO
MONACO
München (Munich)
Wien (Vienna)
Zagreb (Agram)
Ljubljana (Laibach)
Bratislava (Pressburg)
Brno (Brünn)
Graz
Linz
Salzburg
Innsbruck
Zürich
Basel (Bâle)
Bern (Berne)
Lausanne
Milano (Milan)
Torino (Turin)
Genova (Genoa)
Venezia (Venice)
Verona
Bologna
Firenze (Florence)
Trieste
Stuttgart
Karlsruhe
Strasbourg
Nancy
Nice
Cannes
Sarajevo
Golfo di Venezia
Golfo di Genova
Conic Projection

1:3,000,000

0 25 50 75 100 125 150 175 200 KILOMETRES

0 25 50 75 100 125 STATUTE MILES

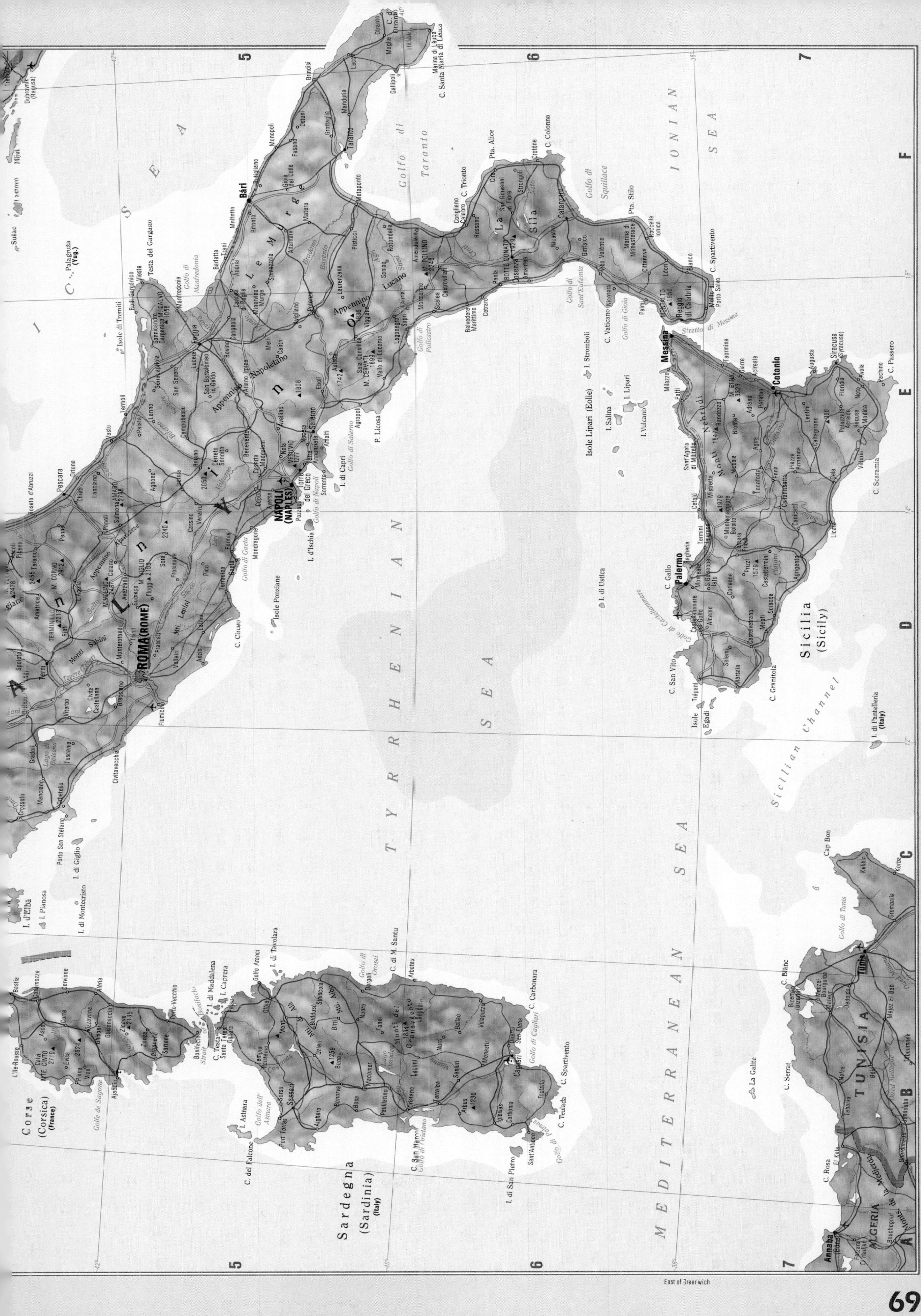
Corse
(Corsica)
(France)
Sardegna
(Sardinia)
(Italy)
Sicilia
(Sicily)
T Y R R H E N I A N
S E A
M E D I T E R R A N E A N
S E A
I O N I A N
S E A
Sicilian Channel
TUNISIA
ALGERIA
ROMA (ROME)
NAPOLI (NAPLES)
Bari
Palermo
Messina
Catania
Taranto
Brindisi
Pescara
Cagliari
Sassari
Tunis
Annaba
Siracusa (Syracuse)
Reggio di Calabria
Golfo di Taranto
Golfo di Squillace
Stretto di Messina
Isole Lipari (Eolie)
I. di Ustica
I. di Pantelleria (Italy)
Cap Bon
La Sila
Appennino
Monti Nebrodi
East of Greerwich

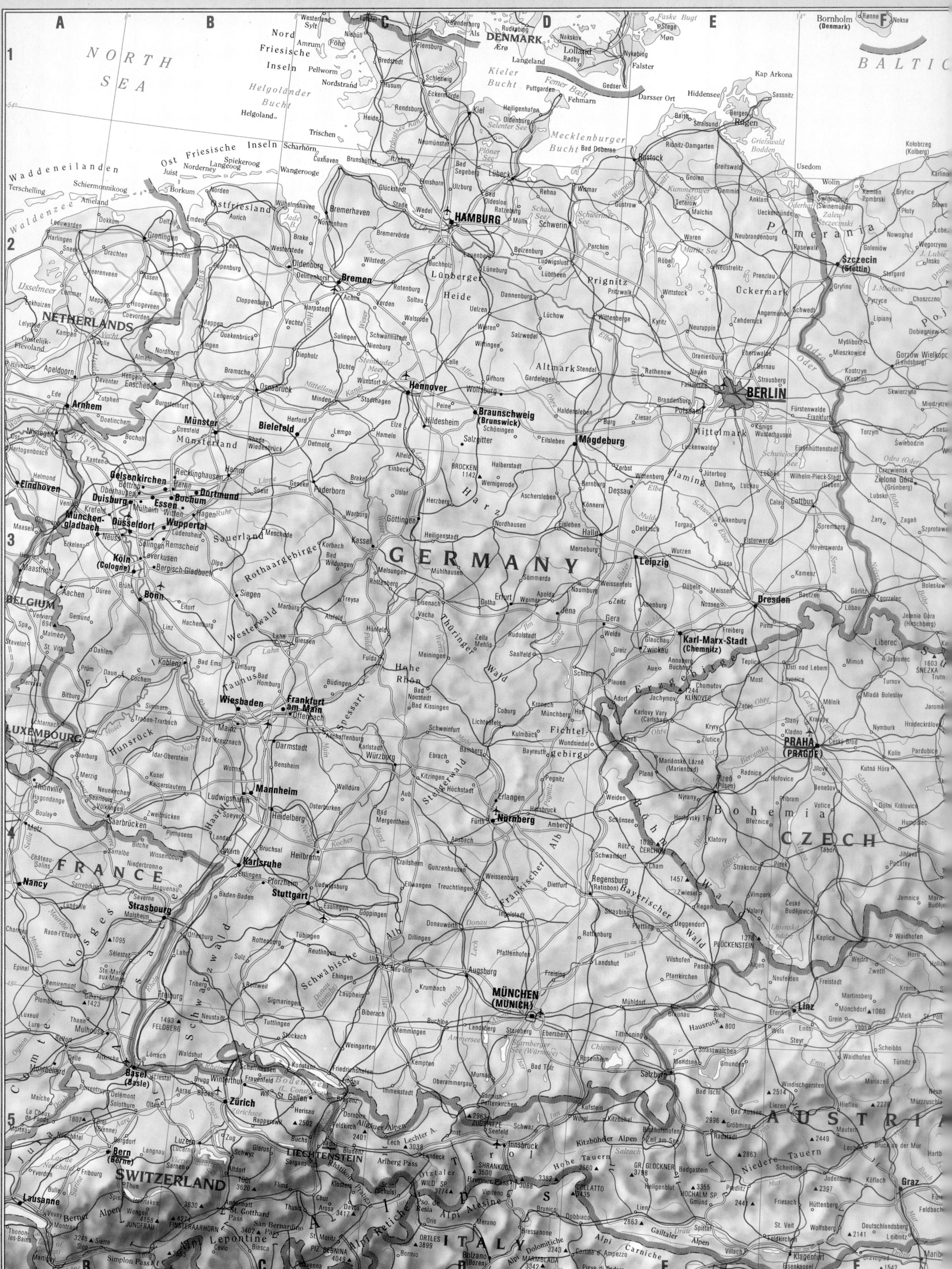
NORTH SEA
BALTIC
DENMARK
NETHERLANDS
BELGIUM
LUXEMBOURG
FRANCE
SWITZERLAND
LIECHTENSTEIN
AUSTRIA
ITALY
CZECH
GERMANY
HAMBURG
BERLIN
Bremen
Hannover
Braunschweig (Brunswick)
Magdeburg
Leipzig
Dresden
Karl-Marx-Stadt (Chemnitz)
Köln (Cologne)
Düsseldorf
Essen
Dortmund
Bochum
Duisburg
Gelsenkirchen
Wuppertal
Bonn
Münster
Bielefeld
Frankfurt am Main
Wiesbaden
Mannheim
Karlsruhe
Stuttgart
Nürnberg
MÜNCHEN (MUNICH)
Strasbourg
Basel (Basle)
Zürich
Bern (Berne)
Lausanne
Nancy
Arnhem
Eindhoven
Szczecin (Stettin)
PRAHA (PRAGUE)
Linz
Graz
Innsbruck
Salzburg
Harz
Erzgebirge
Bohemia
Pomerania
Schwarzwald
Alpen
Conic Projection

1:3,000,000

0 25 50 75 100 125 150 175 200 KILOMETRES

0 25 50 75 125 STATUTE MILES

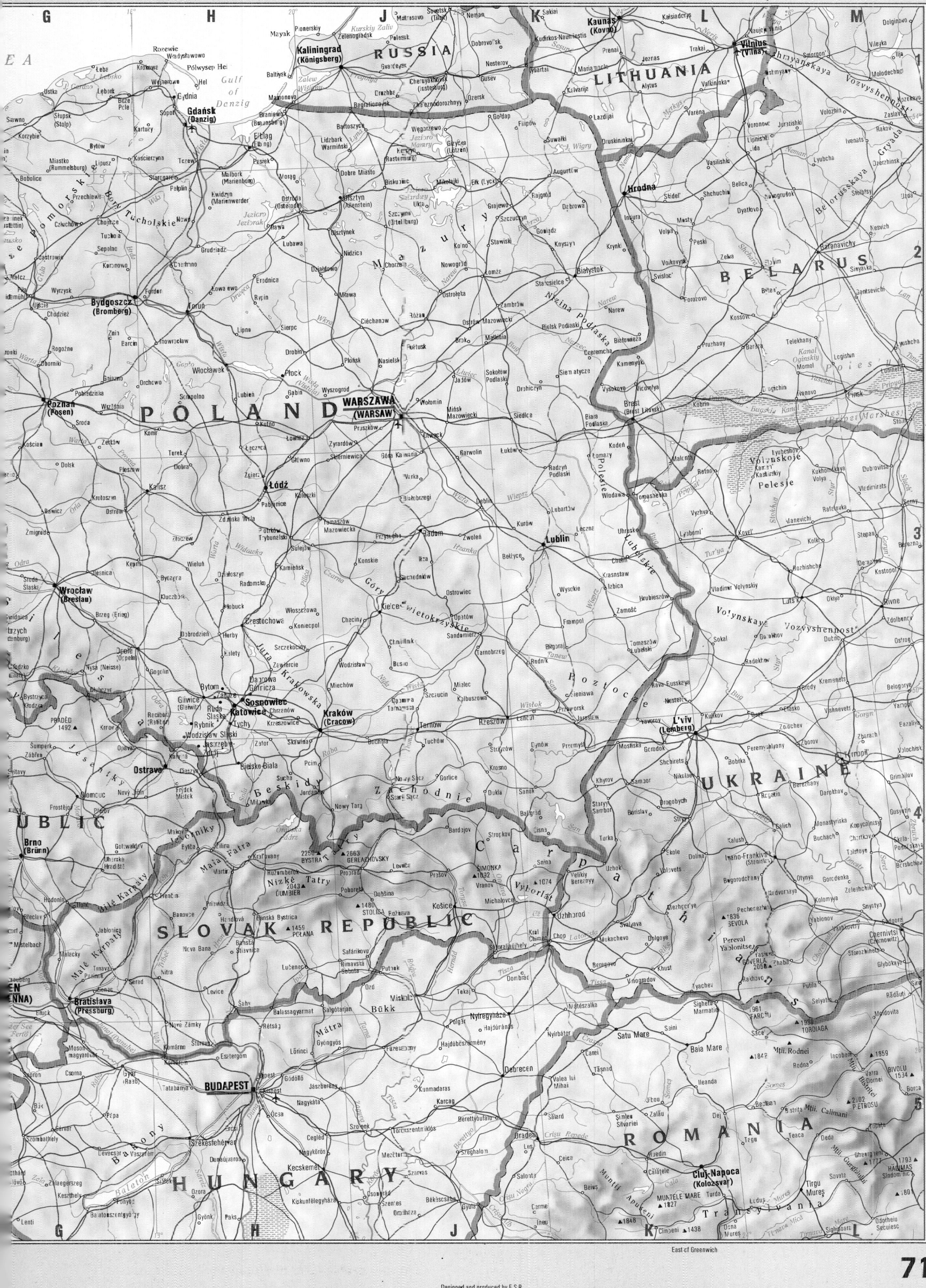

RUSSIA
LITHUANIA
BELARUS
POLAND
UKRAINE
SLOVAK REPUBLIC
HUNGARY
ROMANIA
Kaliningrad (Königsberg)
Gulf of Danzig
Gdańsk (Danzig)
Kaunas (Kovno)
Vilnius (Vilna)
Hrodna
Bydgoszcz (Bromberg)
Toruń
Poznań (Posen)
WARSZAWA (WARSAW)
Białystok
Brest (Brest Litovsk)
Łódź
Lublin
Wrocław (Breslau)
Katowice
Sosnowiec
Kraków (Cracow)
L'viv (Lemberg)
Ostrava
Brno (Brünn)
Bratislava (Pressburg)
BUDAPEST
Košice
Uzhhorod
Debrecen
Cluj-Napoca (Kolozsvar)
Mazury
Nizina Podlaska
Góry Świętokrzyskie
Beskidy Zachodnie
Nizke Tatry
Carpathians
Transylvania
East of Greenwich

Designed and produced by E.S.R.

THE BALKAN REPUBLICS, HUNGARY, ROMANIA AND BULGARIA

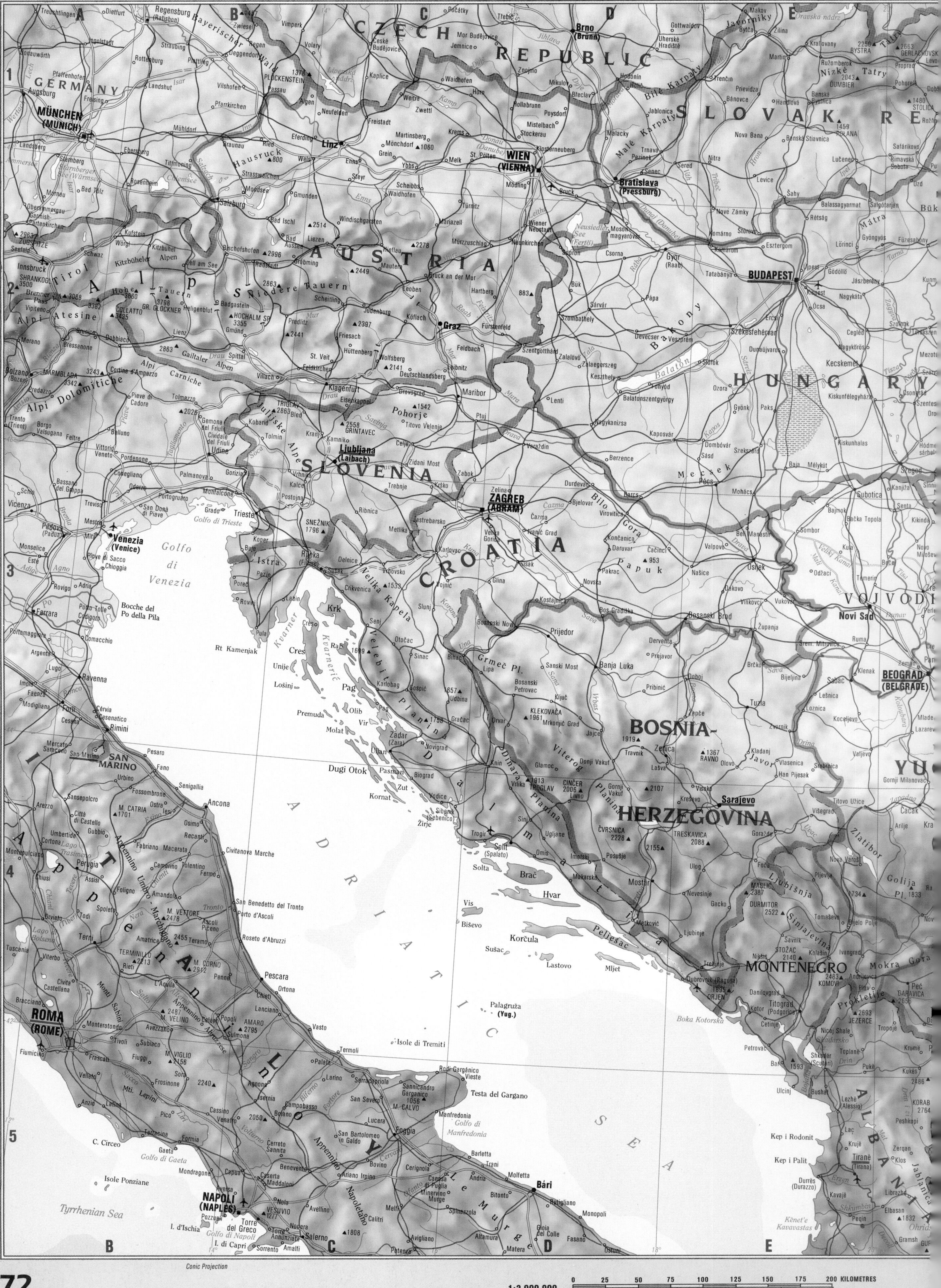

CZECH REPUBLIC
GERMANY
SLOVAK
AUSTRIA
SLOVENIA
CROATIA
HUNGARY
BOSNIA-
HERZEGOVINA
MONTENEGRO
ALBANIA
SAN MARINO
VOJVODI
München
(Munich)
Wien
(Vienna)
Bratislava
(Pressburg)
Budapest
Ljubljana
(Laibach)
Zagreb
(Agram)
Sarajevo
Beograd
(Belgrade)
Roma
(Rome)
Napoli
(Naples)
Bári
Venezia
(Venice)
Trieste
Graz
Linz
Salzburg
Innsbruck
Brno
(Brünn)
Novi Sad
Tiranë
(Tirana)
Split
(Spalato)
Dubrovnik (Ragusa)
Titograd
(Podgorica)
Golfo di Venezia
ADRIATIC SEA
Tyrrhenian Sea
Golfo di Gaeta
Golfo di Manfredonia
Golfo di Trieste
Balaton
Dunaj (Danube)
Donau (Danube)
Alpi Dolomitiche
Alpi Atesine
Niedere Tauern
Karlovac
Rijeka
Pula
Zadar
(Zara)
Šibenik
(Sebenico)
Mostar
Banja Luka
Osijek
Pécs
Szeged
Ancona
Pescara
Foggia
Perugia
Ravenna
Ferrara
Padova
(Padua)
A
B
C
D
E
1
2
3
4
5

Conic Projection

1:3,000,000

0 25 50 75 100 125 150 175 200 KILOMETRES

0 25 50 75 100 125 STATUTE MILES

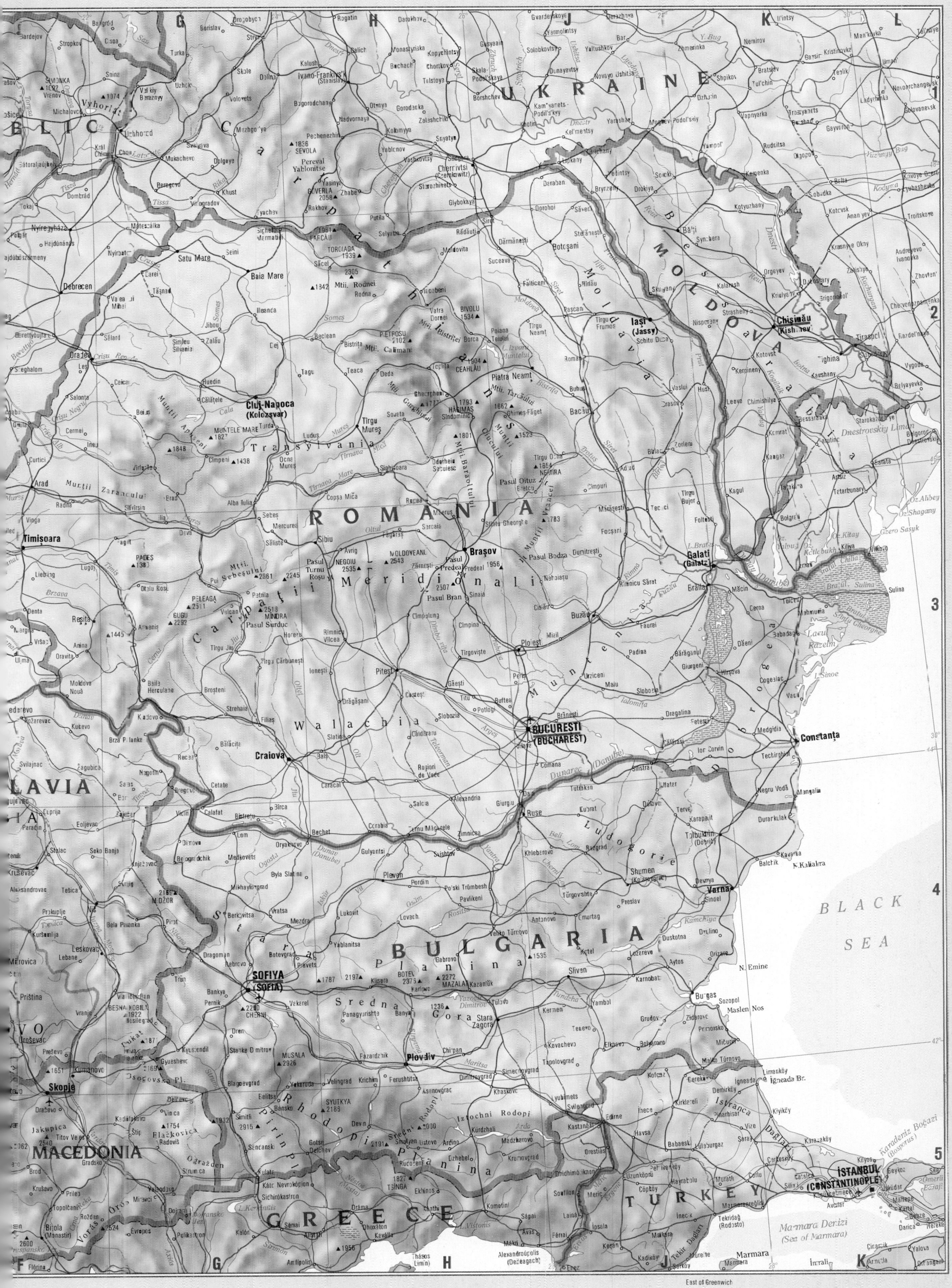
UKRAINE
MOLDOVA
ROMANIA
BULGARIA
TURKEY
GREECE
MACEDONIA
BLACK SEA
Transylvania
Walachia
Carpaţii Meridionali
Stara Planina
Rhodopi Planina
Sredna Gora
Ludogorie
Dobrogea
Muntenia
Moldavia
Bessarabia
BUCUREŞTI (BUCHAREST)
SOFIYA (SOFIA)
ISTANBUL (CONSTANTINOPLE)
Chişinău (Kishinev)
Cluj-Napoca (Kolozsvar)
Iaşi (Jassy)
Galaţi (Galatz)
Braşov
Craiova
Timişoara
Constanţa
Varna
Burgas
Plovdiv
Skopje
Ruse
Ploieşti
Sibiu
Marmara Denizi (Sea of Marmara)
G
H
J
K
L
F
1
2
3
4
5
East of Greenwich

Designed and produced by E.S.R.

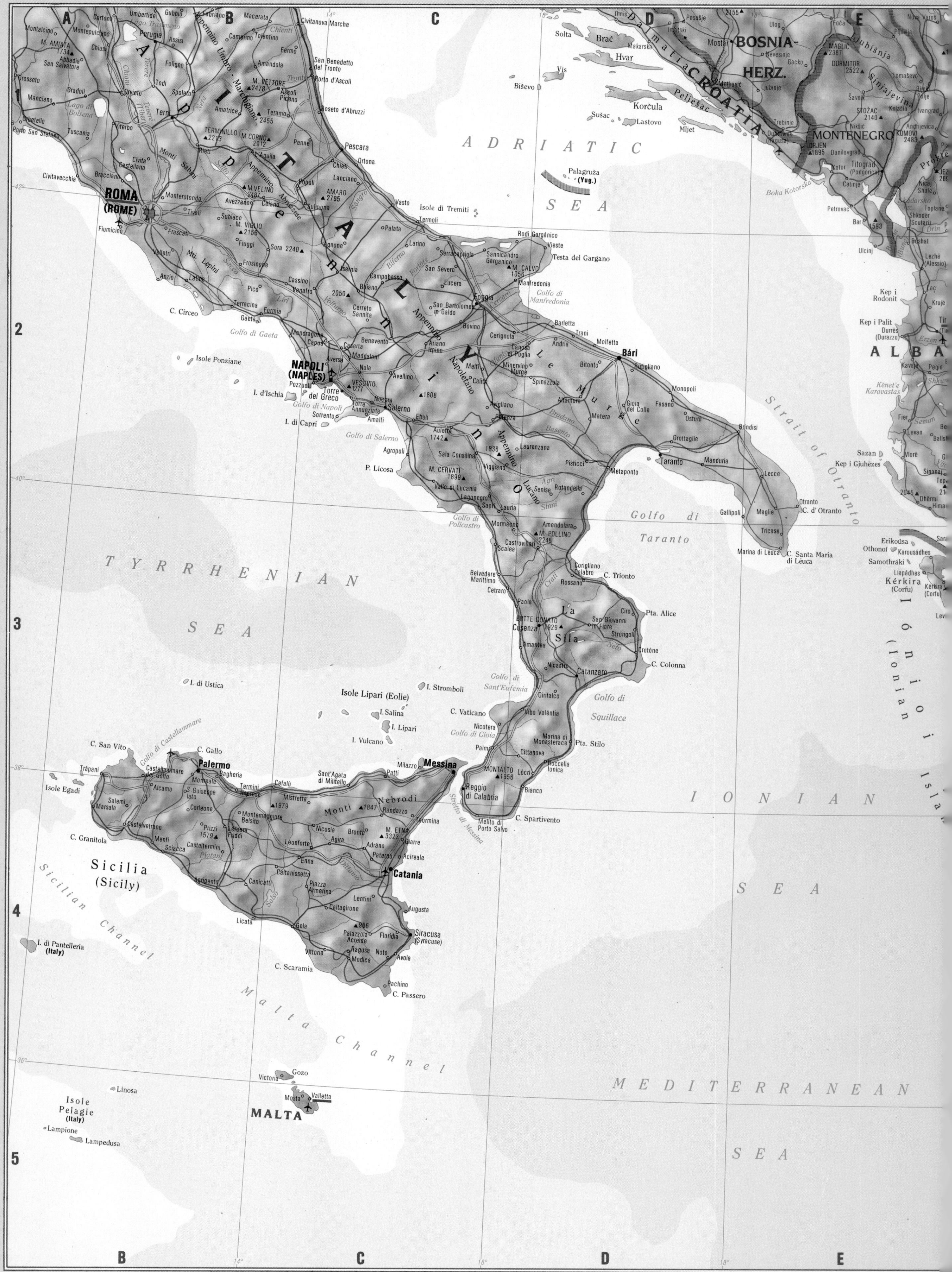
ITALY
ADRIATIC SEA
TYRRHENIAN SEA
IONIAN SEA
MEDITERRANEAN SEA
Strait of Otranto
Sicilian Channel
Malta Channel
Golfo di Taranto
Golfo di Squillace
Golfo di Sant'Eufemia
Golfo di Gioia
Golfo di Policastro
Golfo di Salerno
Golfo di Napoli
Golfo di Gaeta
Golfo di Manfredonia
Golfo di Castellammare
Stretto di Messina
Appennino
Appennino Napoletano
Appennino Lucano
Le Murge
La Sila
Monti Nebrodi
ROMA
(ROME)
NAPOLI
(NAPLES)
Bári
Taranto
Brindisi
Lecce
Foggia
Pescara
Perugia
Messina
Palermo
Catania
Siracusa
(Syracuse)
Reggio di Calabria
Catanzaro
Cosenza
Salerno
Sicilia
(Sicily)
MALTA
Valletta
Gozo
Isole Lipari (Eolie)
I. Stromboli
I. Salina
I. Lipari
I. Vulcano
I. di Ustica
Isole Egadi
I. di Pantelleria
(Italy)
Isole Pelagie
(Italy)
Linosa
Lampione
Lampedusa
Isole Ponziane
I. d'Ischia
I. di Capri
Isole di Tremiti
Palagruža
(Yug.)
C. Circeo
C. San Vito
C. Gallo
C. Granitola
C. Scaramia
C. Passero
C. Vaticano
C. Spartivento
C. Colonna
C. Trionto
Pta. Alice
Pta. Stilo
C. Santa Maria di Léuca
C. d'Otranto
P. Licosa
Testa del Gargano
M. ETNA 3323
VESUVIO 1277
M. POLLINO 2248
M. CALVO 1056
M. CERVATI 1899
M. VETTORE 2478
M. VELINO 2487
M. CORNO 2912
MONTALTO 1956
BOSNIA-HERZ.
CROATIA
MONTENEGRO
ALBA
Dalmatia
Brač
Hvar
Korčula
Lastovo
Mljet
Solta
Vis
Biševo
Sušac
Pelješac
Titograd
(Podgorica)
Kérkira
(Corfu)
Ióniо (Ionian Isla
A
B
C
D
E
1
2
3
4
5
14°
16°
18°
42°
40°
38°
36°

Conic Projection

1:3,000,000

0	25	50	75	100	125	150	175	200 KILOMETRES
0		25		50	75		100	125 STATUTE MILES

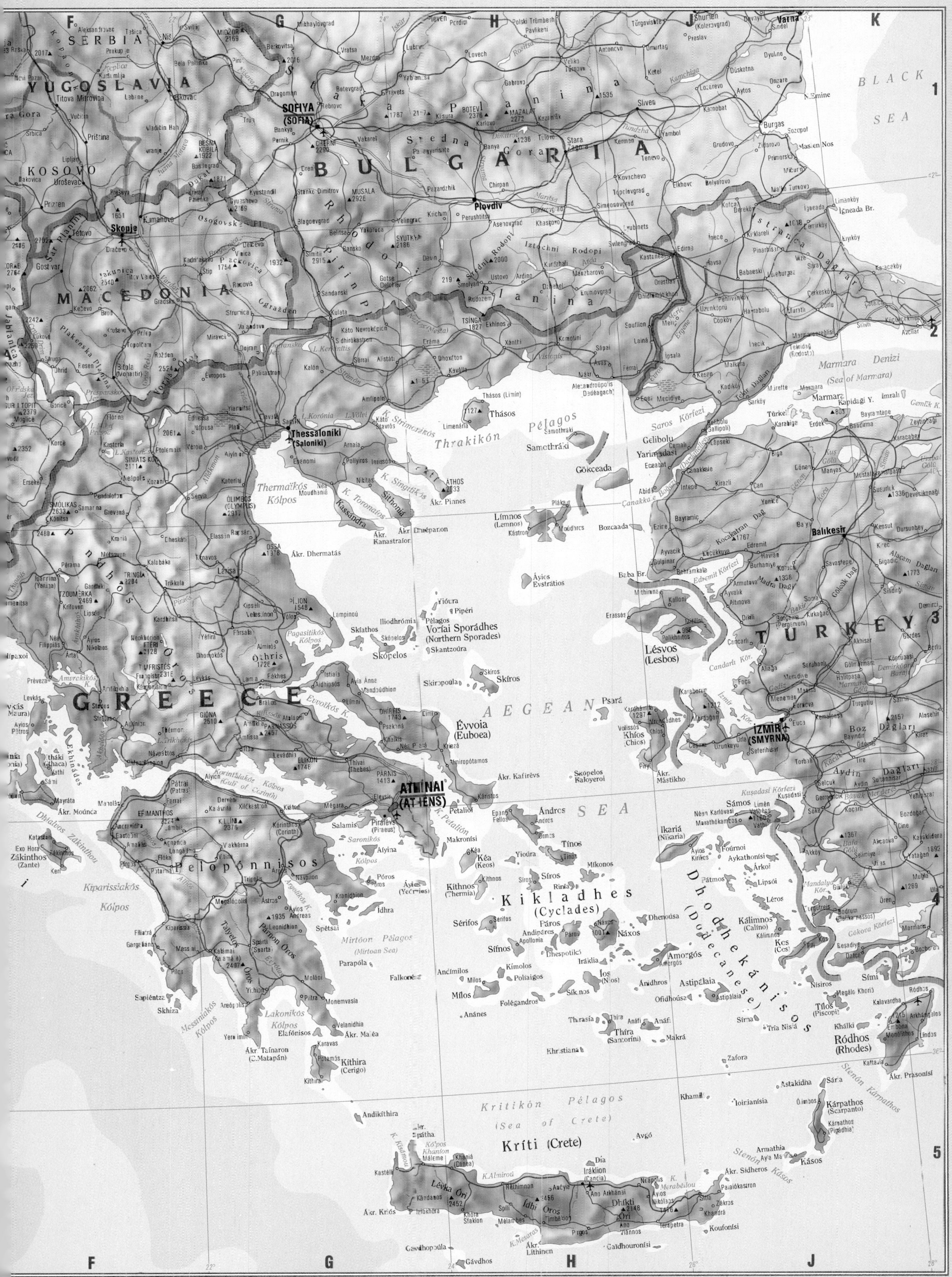
SERBIA
YUGOSLAVIA
KOSOVO
MACEDONIA
BULGARIA
GREECE
TURKEY
SOFIYA (SOFIA)
Plovdiv
Varna
Burgas
Skopje
Thessaloníki (Salonika)
ATHINAI (ATHENS)
Piraiévs (Piraeus)
İZMIR (SMYRNA)
Edirne
Balıkesir
BLACK SEA
AEGEAN SEA
Marmara Denizi (Sea of Marmara)
Thrakikón Pélagos
Thermaïkós Kólpos
Kritikón Pélagos (Sea of Crete)
Mirtóon Pélagos (Mirtoan Sea)
Kíkladhes (Cyclades)
Dhodhekánisos (Dodecanese)
Voríai Sporádhes (Northern Sporades)
Kríti (Crete)
Rhodopi Planina
Stara Planina
Pelopónnisos
Évvoia (Euboea)
Lésvos (Lesbos)
Límnos (Lemnos)
Thásos
Samothráki
Gökçeada
Bozcaada
Khíos (Chios)
Sámos
Ikaría (Nikaria)
Náxos
Páros
Thíra (Santorini)
Mílos
Kárpathos (Scarpanto)
Ródhos (Rhodes)
Kíthira (Cerigo)
Zákinthos (Zante)
Gelibolu Yarımadası
East of Greenwich

Designed and produced by E.S.R.

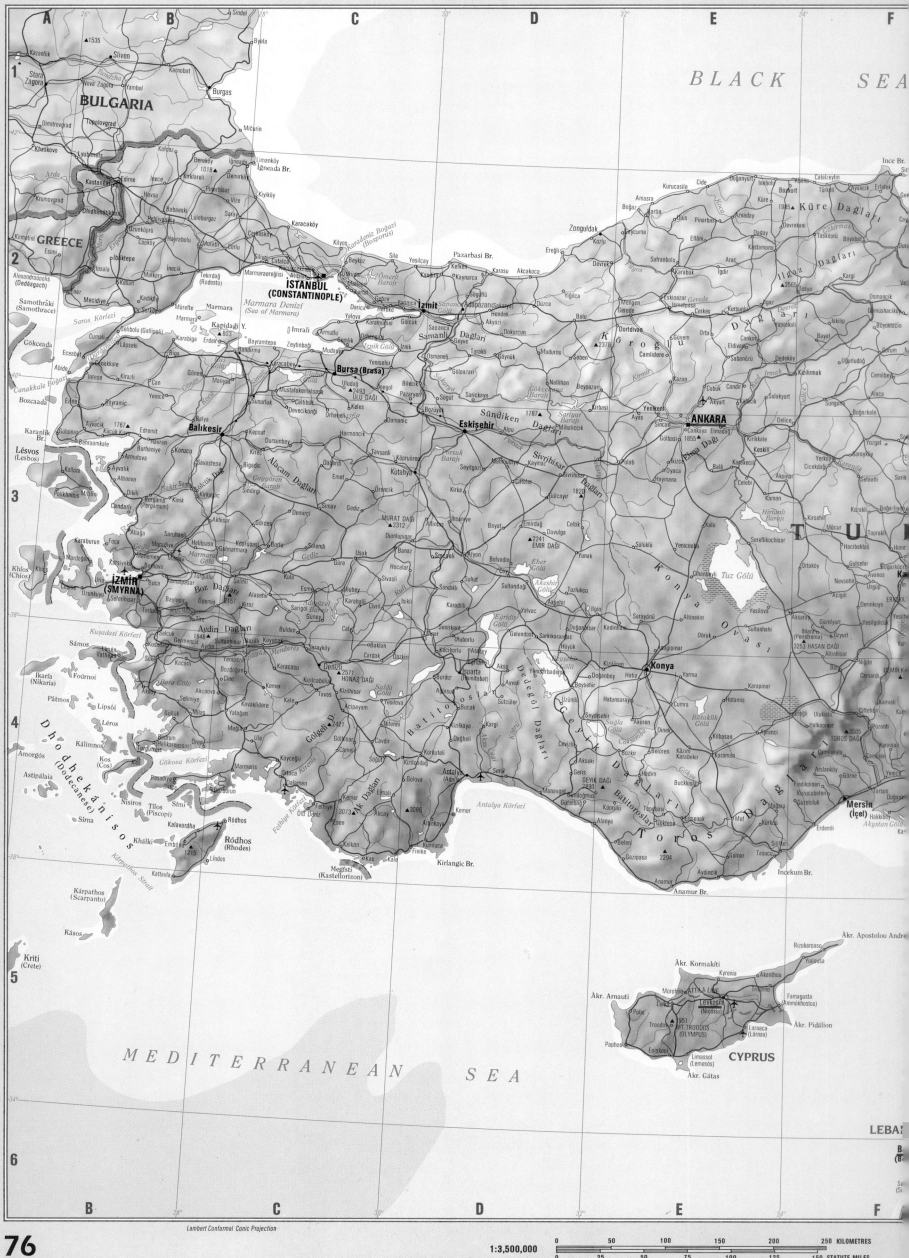

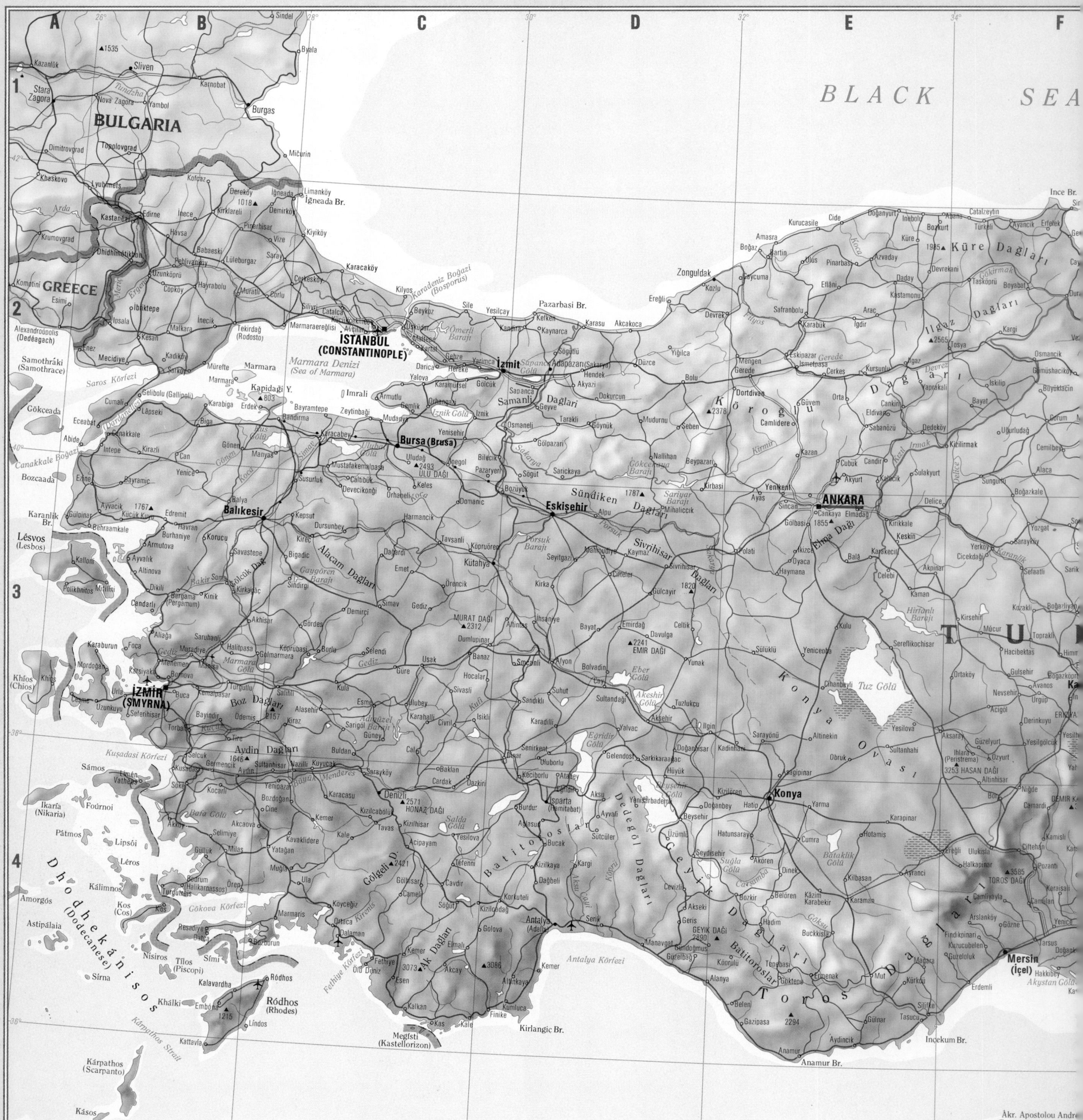
BLACK SEA
MEDITERRANEAN SEA
BULGARIA
GREECE
CYPRUS
LEBAN
İSTANBUL (CONSTANTINOPLE)
İZMİR (SMYRNA)
ANKARA
Bursa (Brusa)
Balıkesir
Eskişehir
İzmit
Kütahya
Denizli
Konya
Antalya
Mersin (İçel)
Sliven
Burgas
Edirne
Marmara Denizi (Sea of Marmara)
Karadeniz Boğazi (Bosporus)
Çanakkale Boğazi
Saros Körfezi
Kuşadasi Körfezi
Gökova Körfezi
Antalya Körfezi
Fethiye Körfezi
Tuz Gölü
Köroğlu Dağları
Küre Dağları
Ilgaz Dağları
Sündiken Dağları
Sivrihisar Dağları
Alaçam Dağları
Boz Dağları
Aydın Dağları
Batı Toroslar
Toros Dağları
Geyik Dağları
Dedegöl Dağları
Konya Ovası
Lésvos (Lesbos)
Khíos (Chios)
Sámos
Ikaría (Nikaria)
Dhodhekánisos (Dodecanese)
Kos (Cos)
Ródhos (Rhodes)
Kárpathos (Scarpanto)
Kríti (Crete)
Gökçeada
Bozcaada
Samothráki (Samothrace)
Megísti (Kastellorizon)
Zonguldak
Sinop
Kastamonu
Bolu
Akr. Apostolou Andreas
Akr. Kormakíti
Akr. Arnauti
Akr. Pidálion
Akr. Gátas
Levkosía (Nicosia)
Famagusta (Ammókhostos)
Larnaca (Lárnax)
Limassol (Lemesós)
Paphos
Kyrenia
MT. TROODOS (OLYMPUS)
ATTILA LINE

Lambert Conformal Conic Projection

1:3,500,000

0 50 100 150 200 250 KILOMETRES

0 25 50 75 100 125 150 STATUTE MILES

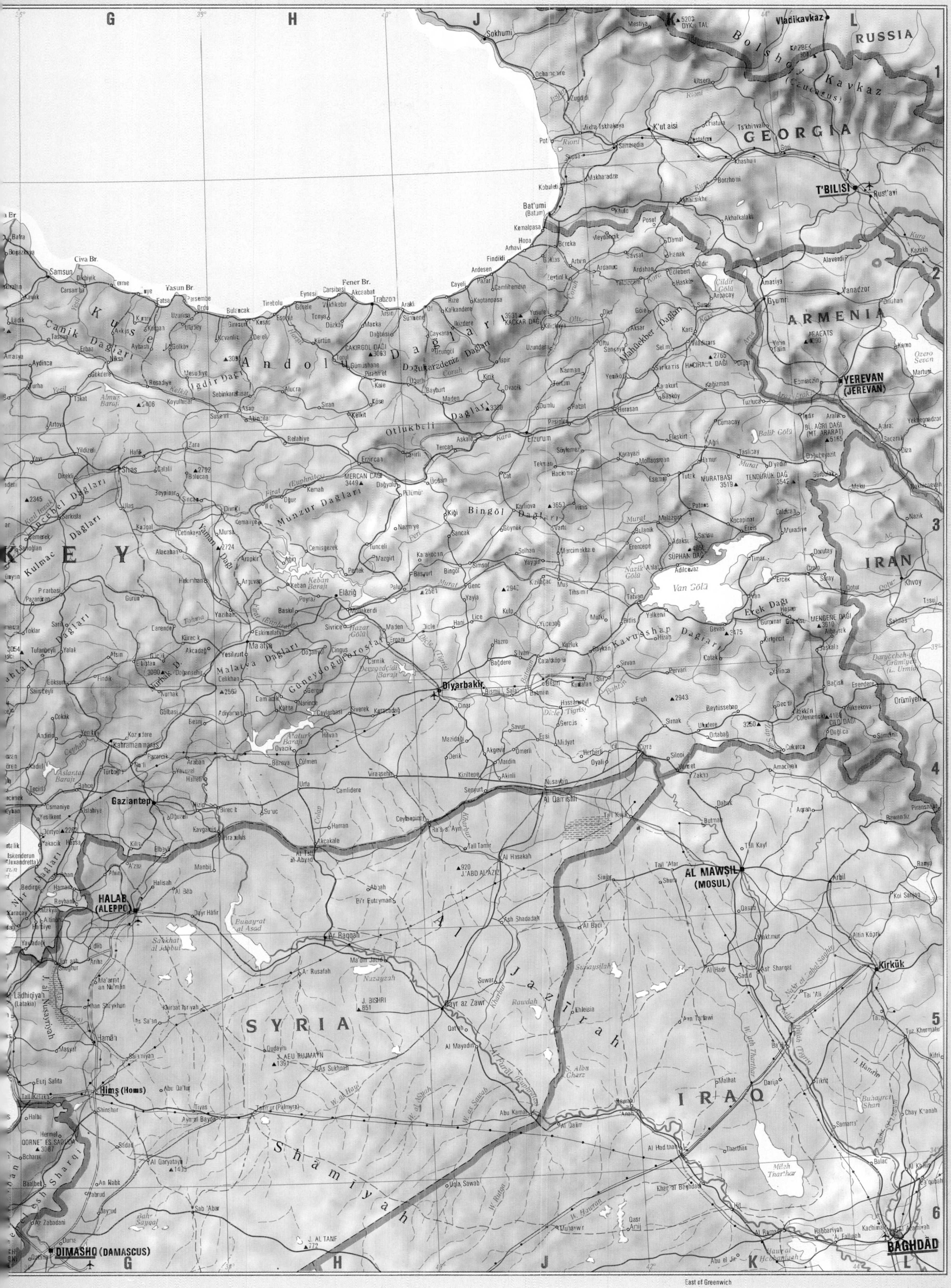

G
H
J
K
L
1
2
3
4
5
6
RUSSIA
GEORGIA
ARMENIA
IRAN
IRAQ
SYRIA
K E Y
Vladikavkaz
Sokhumi
Bol'shoy Kavkaz
T'BILISI
YEREVAN (JEREVAN)
Bat'umi (Batum)
Trabzon
Samsun
Erzurum
Sivas
Malatya
Elâzığ
Diyarbakır
Van Gölü
Gaziantep
Kahramanmaraş
HALAB (ALEPPO)
AL MAWSIL (MOSUL)
Kirkūk
Ar Raqqah
Dayr az Zawr
Ḥimş (Homs)
Ḥamāh
DIMASHQ (DAMASCUS)
BAGHDĀD
Al Jazīrah
Shāmiyah
Otlukbeli
Bingöl Dağları
Munzur Dağları
Andolu Dağları
BL. AGRI DAĞI (MT. ARARAT) 5165
Ozero Sevan
Buḥayrat al Asad
Milḥ Tharthār

East of Greenwich

Designed and produced by E.S.R.

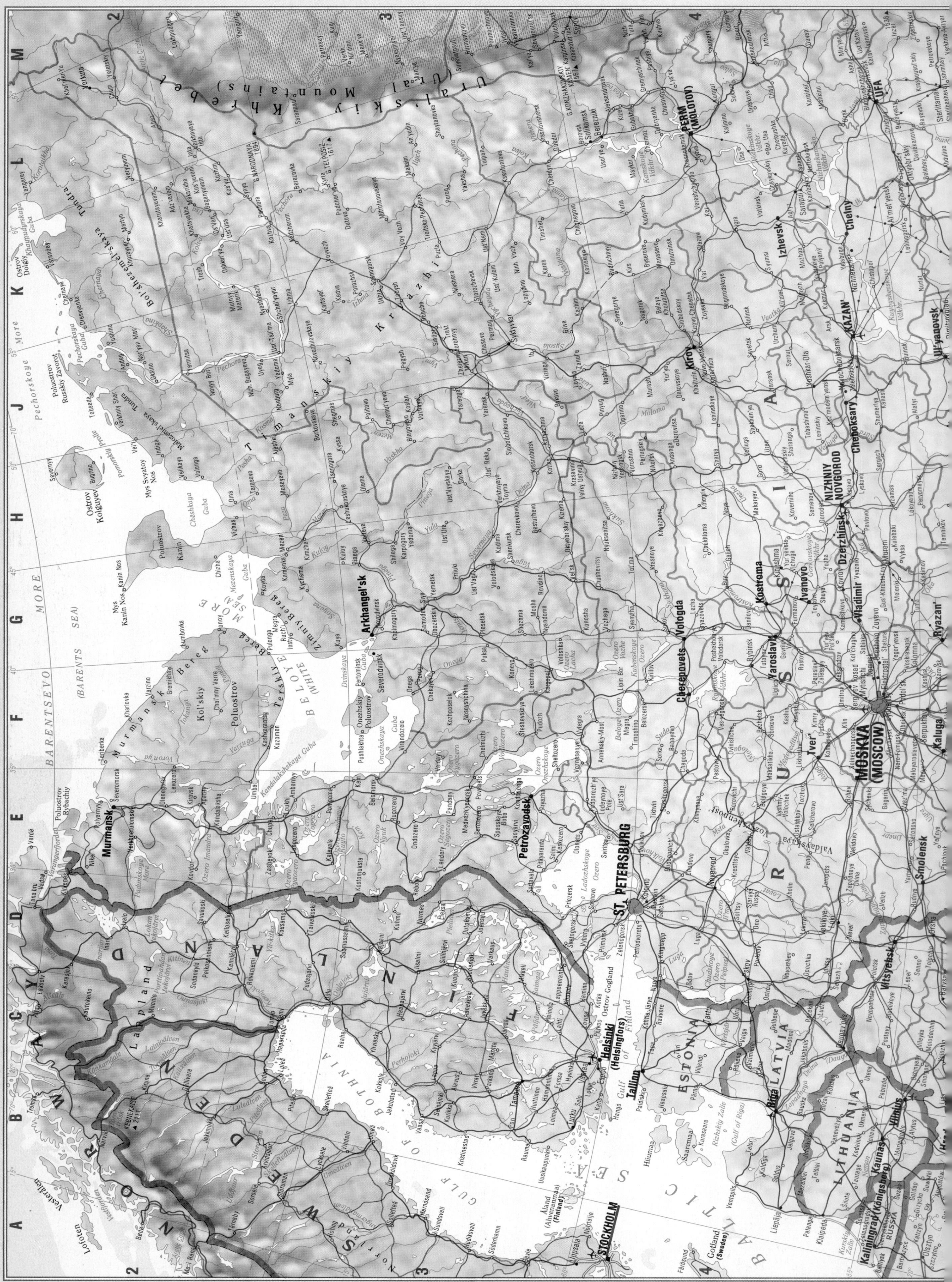
Ural'skiy Khrebet (Ural Mountains)
Timanskiy Kryazh
BARENTSEVO MORE (BARENTS SEA)
BELOYE MORE (WHITE SEA)
GULF OF BOTHNIA
BALTIC SEA
Gulf of Finland
Rizhskiy Zaliv (Gulf of Riga)
Poluostrov Kanin
Ostrov Kolguyev
Kol'skiy Poluostrov
Lappland
FINLAND
SWEDEN
NORWAY
ESTONIA
LATVIA
LITHUANIA
RUSSIA
Murmansk
Arkhangel'sk
Petrozavodsk
ST. PETERSBURG
Helsinki (Helsingfors)
Tallinn
Riga
Vilnius
Kaunas
Kaliningrad (Königsberg)
STOCKHOLM
MOSKVA (MOSCOW)
Vologda
Cherepovets
Yaroslavl'
Kostroma
Ivanovo
Vladimir
Dzerzhinsk
NIZHNIY NOVGOROD
Cheboksary
KAZAN'
Ul'yanovsk
Izhevsk
Chelny
UFA
PERM (MOLOTOV)
Kirov
Syktyvkar
Tver'
Smolensk
Vitsyebsk
Kaluga
Ryazan'
Gotland (Sweden)
Åland (Ahvenanmaa) (Finland)
Lofoten

Miller Oblated Stereographic Projection

1:8,000,000

0 100 200 300 400 500 600 KILOMETRES
0 50 100 150 200 250 300 350 400 STATUTE MILES

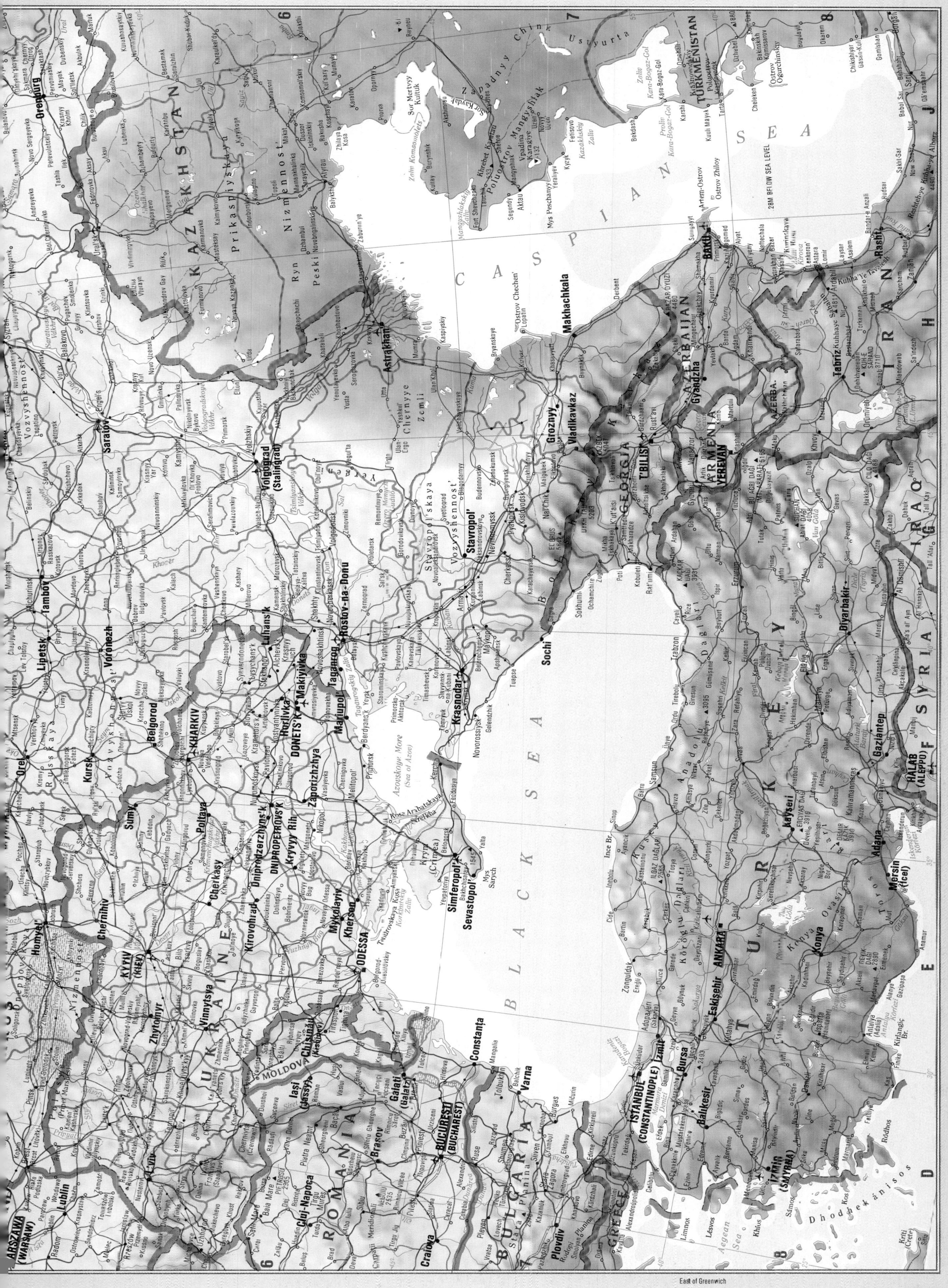

KAZAKHSTAN
CASPIAN SEA
BLACK SEA
UKRAINE
ROMANIA
MOLDOVA
BULGARIA
GREECE
TURKEY
GEORGIA
ARMENIA
AZERBAIJAN
AZERBA.
IRAN
IRAQ
SYRIA
TURKMENISTAN
Azovskoye More (Sea of Azov)
Aegean Sea
Dhodhekánisos
Orenburg
Saratov
Volgograd (Stalingrad)
Astrakhan'
Makhachkala
Baku
T'BILISI
YEREVAN
Rostov-na-Donu
Voronezh
KHARKIV
DNIPROPETROVS'K
DONETS'K
Luhans'k
KYIV (KIEV)
ODESSA
Sevastopol'
Simferopol'
Krasnodar
Stavropol'
Sochi
Groznyy
Vladikavkaz
Tabriz
Rasht
Kayseri
Adana
Mersin (Içel)
Konya
ANKARA
ISTANBUL (CONSTANTINOPLE)
Bursa
İzmir (SMYRNA)
BUCUREŞTI (BUCHAREST)
Constanţa
Varna
Plovdiv
Chişinău (Kishinev)
Iaşi (Jassy)
Galaţi
Braşov
Cluj-Napoca
Craiova
L'viv
Lublin
WARSZAWA (WARSAW)
Homyel'
Chernihiv
Vinnytsya
Zhytomyr
Kirovohrad
Mykolayiv
Kherson
Zaporizhzhya
Mariupol'
Taganrog
Lipetsk
Tambov
Kursk
Orel
Belgorod
Sumy
Poltava
Cherkasy
Kryvyy Rih
Trabzon
Samsun
Erzurum
Diyarbakir
Gaziantep
HALAB (ALEPPO)
Gyandzha
6
7
8
9
D
E
F
G
H
J

East of Greenwich

Designed and produced by E.S.R.

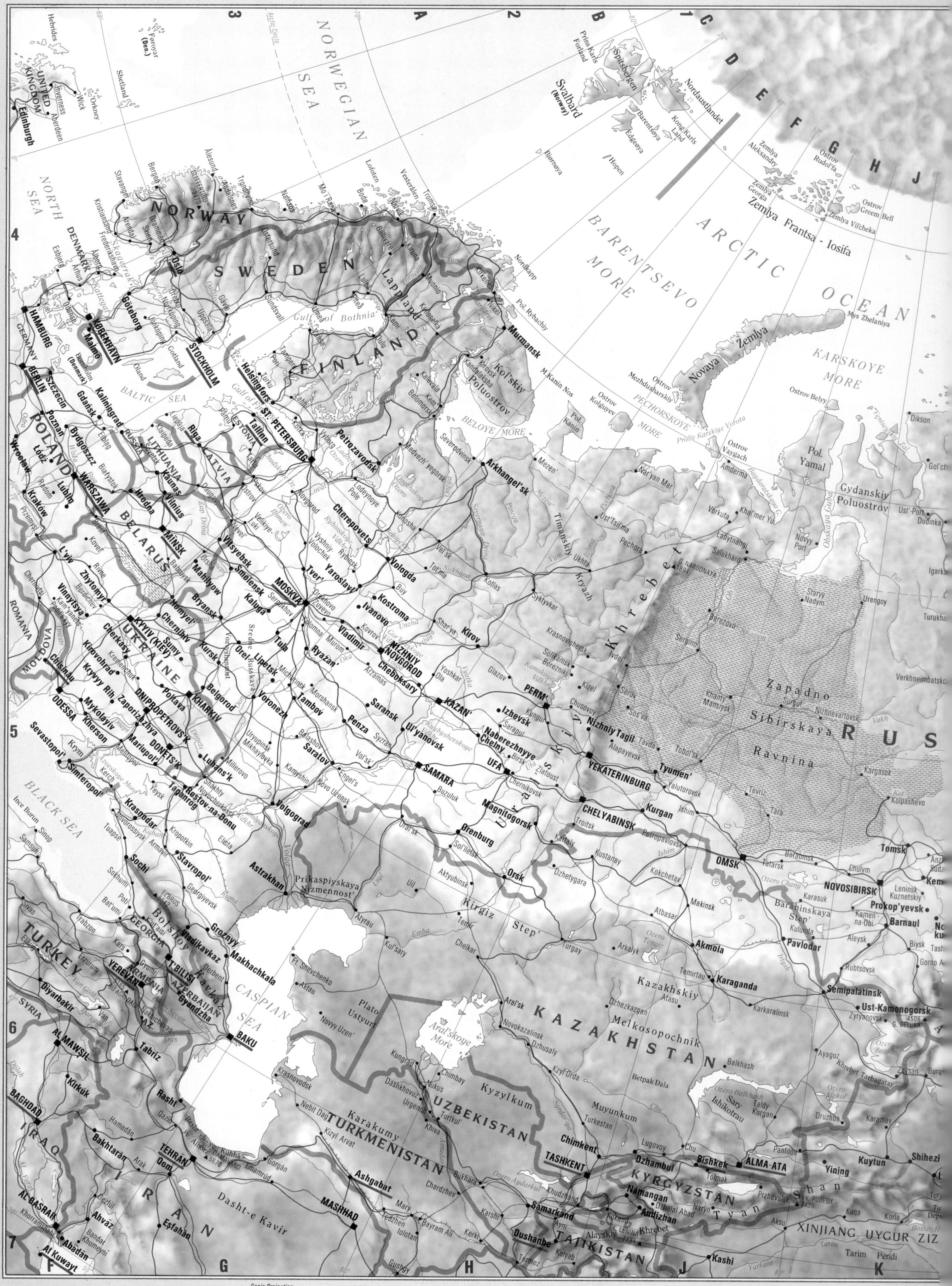
NORWEGIAN SEA
NORTH SEA
NORWAY
SWEDEN
FINLAND
DENMARK
UNITED KINGDOM
Svalbard (Norway)
Spitsbergen
Nordaustlandet
Zemlya Frantsa - Iosifa
ARCTIC OCEAN
BARENTSEVO MORE
KARSKOYE MORE
PECHORSKOYE MORE
BELOYE MORE
Novaya Zemlya
Gulf of Bothnia
BALTIC SEA
ESTONIA
LATVIA
LITHUANIA
POLAND
BELARUS
UKRAINE
MOLDOVA
ROMANIA
GERMANY
BLACK SEA
CASPIAN SEA
Aral'skoye More
GEORGIA
ARMENIA
AZERBAIJAN
TURKEY
SYRIA
IRAQ
IRAN
KAZAKHSTAN
UZBEKISTAN
TURKMENISTAN
KYRGYZSTAN
TAJIKISTAN
XINJIANG UYGUR ZIZ
Zapadno Sibirskaya Ravnina
Kirgiz Step'
Kazakhskiy Melkosopochnik
Kyzylkum
Karakumy
Dasht-e Kavir
Prikaspiyskaya Nizmennost'
Ural'skiy Khrebet
Tyan Shan
Oslo
STOCKHOLM
KØBENHAVN
Helsingfors
Tallinn
Riga
Vilnius
MINSK
WARSZAWA
BERLIN
HAMBURG
ST. PETERSBURG
MOSKVA
KYYIV (KIEV)
Odessa
Murmansk
Arkhangel'sk
NIZHNIY NOVGOROD
KAZAN'
SAMARA
PERM'
UFA
YEKATERINBURG
CHELYABINSK
OMSK
NOVOSIBIRSK
Volgograd
Astrakhan
Rostov-na-Donu
TBILISI
YEREVAN
BAKU
TEHRAN
BAGHDAD
AL KUWAYT
Ashgabat
TASHKENT
Dushanbe
Bishkek
ALMA-ATA
Akmola
Karaganda
Semipalatinsk
1

Conic Projection

1:17,000,000

0 100 200 300 400 500 600 700 800 KILOMETRES
0 100 200 300 400 500 STATUTE MILES

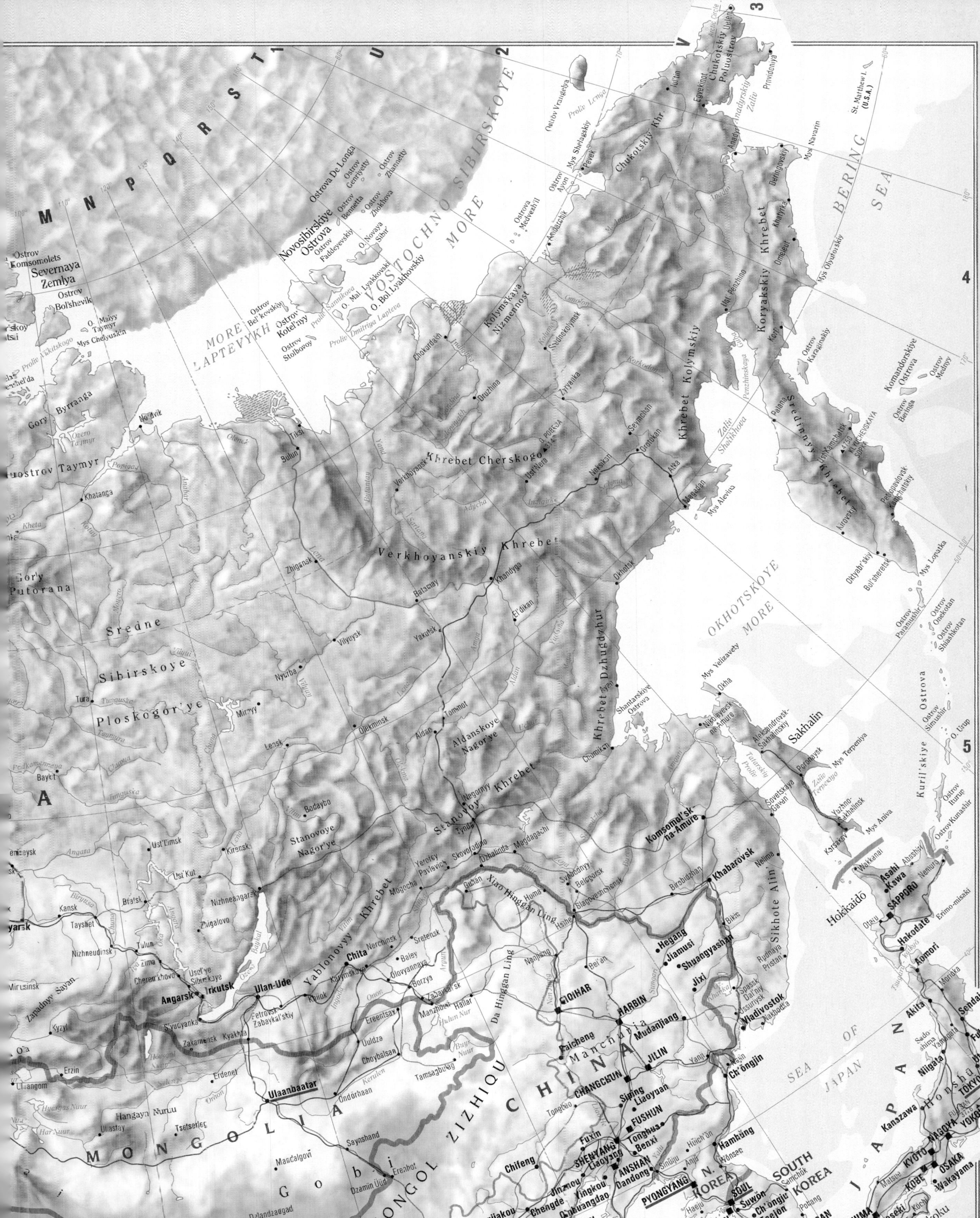
Severnaya Zemlya
Novosibirskiye Ostrova
Ostrova De Longa
MORE LAPTEVYKH
VOSTOCHNO SIBIRSKOYE MORE
BERING SEA
Chukotskiy Poluostrov
Chukotskiy Khr.
Koryakskiy Khrebet
Khrebet Kolymskiy
Kolymskaya Nizmennost
Khrebet Cherskogo
Verkhoyanskiy Khrebet
Gory Byrranga
Poluostrov Taymyr
Gory Putorana
Sredne Sibirskoye Ploskogor'ye
Aldanskoye Nagor'ye
Stanovoy Khrebet
Stanovoye Nagor'ye
Khrebet Dzhugdzhur
OKHOTSKOYE MORE
Sredinnyy Khrebet
Komandorskiye Ostrova
Kuril'skiye Ostrova
Sakhalin
Sikhote Alin'
Xiao Hinggan Ling
Da Hinggan Ling
Yablonovyy Khrebet
Manchuria
Hokkaido
Honshu
Shikoku
Kyushu
SEA OF JAPAN
HUANG HAI
BO HAI
Gobi
NEI MONGOL ZIZHIQU
MONGOLIA
CHINA
JAPAN
N. KOREA
SOUTH KOREA
Tiksi
Khatanga
Yakutsk
Magadan
Okhotsk
Verkhoyansk
Mirnyy
Tynda
Irkutsk
Angarsk
Ulan-Ude
Chita
Khabarovsk
Komsomol'sk na-Amure
Vladivostok
Nakhodka
Ulaanbaatar
Harbin
Qiqihar
Changchun
Jilin
Shenyang
Fushun
Anshan
Dalian
Beijing
Tianjin
Tangshan
Hohhot
Baotou
Datong
Shijiazhuang
Taiyuan
Jinan
Qingdao
Pyongyang
Seoul
Inch'on
Taegu
Pusan
Kwangju
Sapporo
Hakodate
Aomori
Sendai
Tokyo
Yokohama
Nagoya
Kyoto
Osaka
Kobe
Hiroshima
Kita-Kyushu
Fukuoka
Nagasaki
Kagoshima
Petropavlovsk-Kamchatskiy
Yuzhno-Sakhalinsk
Arctic Circle
St. Matthew I. (U.S.A.)
L M N P Q
East of Greenwich

Designed and produced by E.S.R.

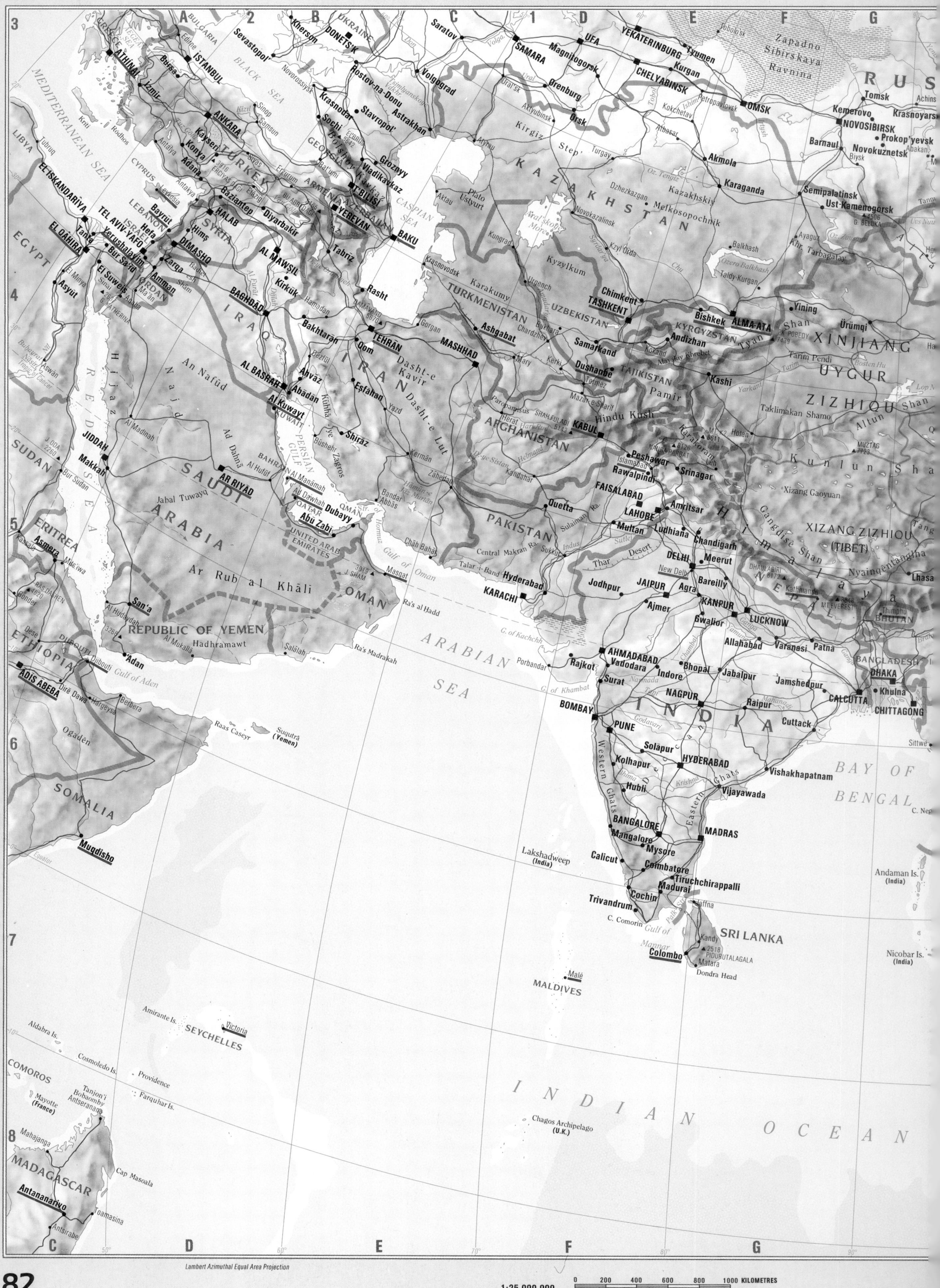
MEDITERRANEAN SEA
BLACK SEA
CASPIAN SEA
ARABIAN SEA
BAY OF BENGAL
INDIAN OCEAN
RED SEA
PERSIAN GULF
Gulf of Aden
Gulf of Oman
TURKEY
SYRIA
IRAQ
IRAN
SAUDI ARABIA
KAZAKHSTAN
TURKMENISTAN
UZBEKISTAN
AFGHANISTAN
PAKISTAN
INDIA
SRI LANKA
REPUBLIC OF YEMEN
OMAN
EGYPT
SUDAN
ERITREA
ETHIOPIA
SOMALIA
MADAGASCAR
SEYCHELLES
MALDIVES
COMOROS
BANGLADESH
BHUTAN
XINJIANG UYGUR ZIZHIQU
XIZANG ZIZHIQU (TIBET)
UNITED ARAB EMIRATES
ISTANBUL
ANKARA
TEHRĀN
BAGHDĀD
AR RIYĀD
KABUL
KARACHI
DELHI
BOMBAY
CALCUTTA
MADRAS
BANGALORE
HYDERABAD
TASHKENT
ALMA-ATA
BAKU
Colombo
Muqdisho
ADIS ABEBA
Antananarivo
Himalaya
Hindu Kush
Ar Rub al Khāli
Dasht-e Kavir
Dasht-e Lut
Thar Desert

Lambert Azimuthal Equal Area Projection

1:25,000,000

0 200 400 600 800 1000 KILOMETRES

0 100 200 300 400 500 600 STATUTE MILES

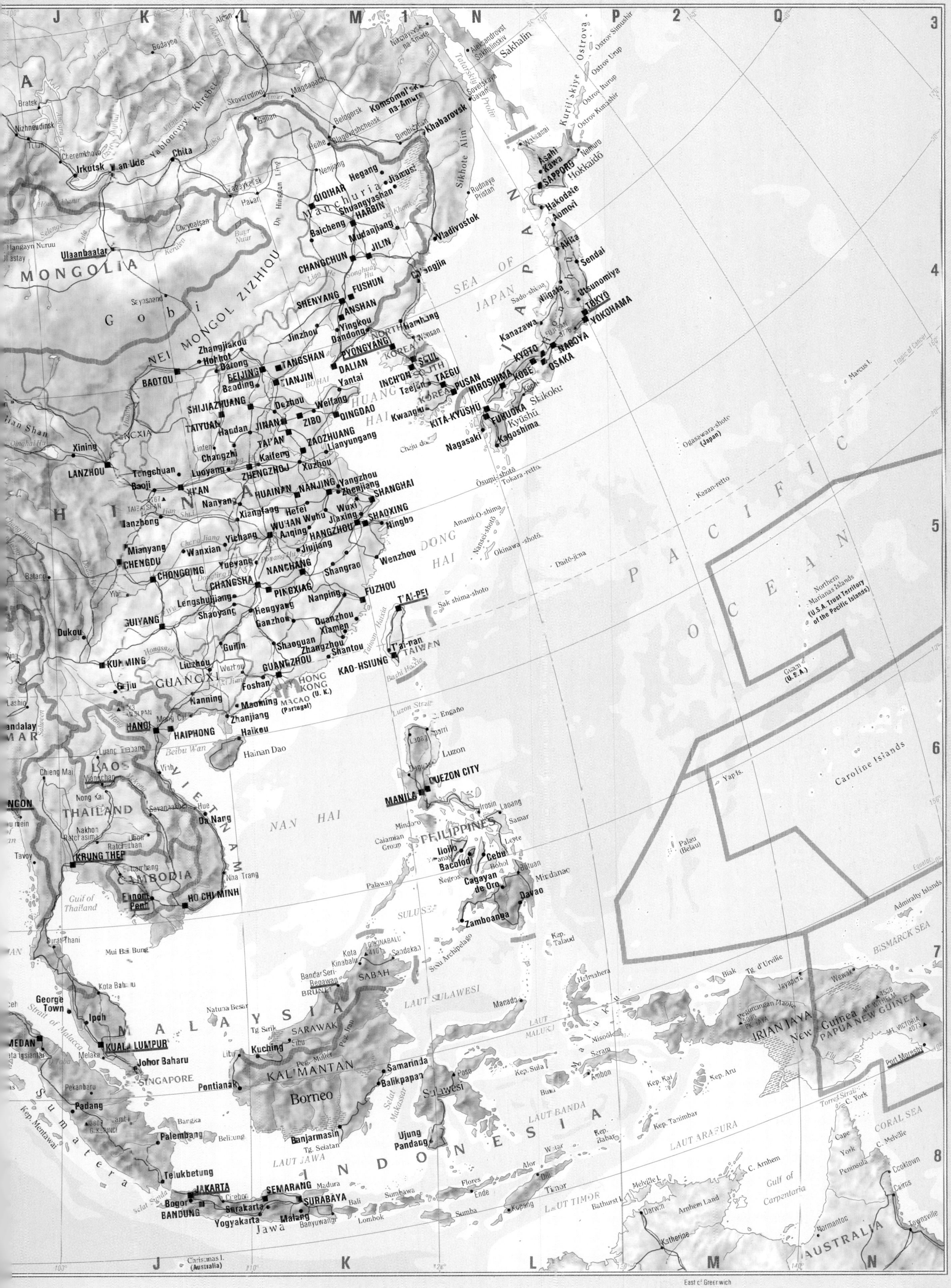
MONGOLIA
Gobi
NEI MONGOL ZIZHIQU
CHINA
Manchuria
SEA OF JAPAN
JAPAN
HUANG HAI
DONG HAI
KOREA
PACIFIC OCEAN
NAN HAI
PHILIPPINES
LAOS
THAILAND
VIETNAM
CAMBODIA
MALAYSIA
INDONESIA
Borneo
KALIMANTAN
Sulawesi
Jawa
IRIAN JAYA
PAPUA NEW GUINEA
New Guinea
AUSTRALIA
CORAL SEA
BISMARCK SEA
Caroline Islands
Northern Marianas Islands (U.S.A. Trust Territory of the Pacific Islands)
Guam (U.S.A.)
Sakhalin
Hokkaido
Honshu
Kyushu
Shikoku
Luzon
Mindanao
Hainan Dao
Ulaanbaatar
Irkutsk
Chita
Khabarovsk
Vladivostok
HARBIN
CHANGCHUN
SHENYANG
BEIJING
TIANJIN
PYONGYANG
SEOUL
PUSAN
TOKYO
YOKOHAMA
NAGOYA
OSAKA
KYOTO
SAPPORO
SHANGHAI
NANJING
WUHAN
CHONGQING
CHENGDU
XI'AN
LANZHOU
KUNMING
GUANGZHOU
HONG KONG (U.K.)
MACAO (Portugal)
T'AI-PEI
KAO-HSIUNG
HANOI
HAIPHONG
KRUNG THEP
HO CHI MINH
MANILA
QUEZON CITY
KUALA LUMPUR
SINGAPORE
MEDAN
JAKARTA
BANDUNG
SEMARANG
SURABAYA
Port Moresby
East of Greenwich

Designed and produced by E.S.R.

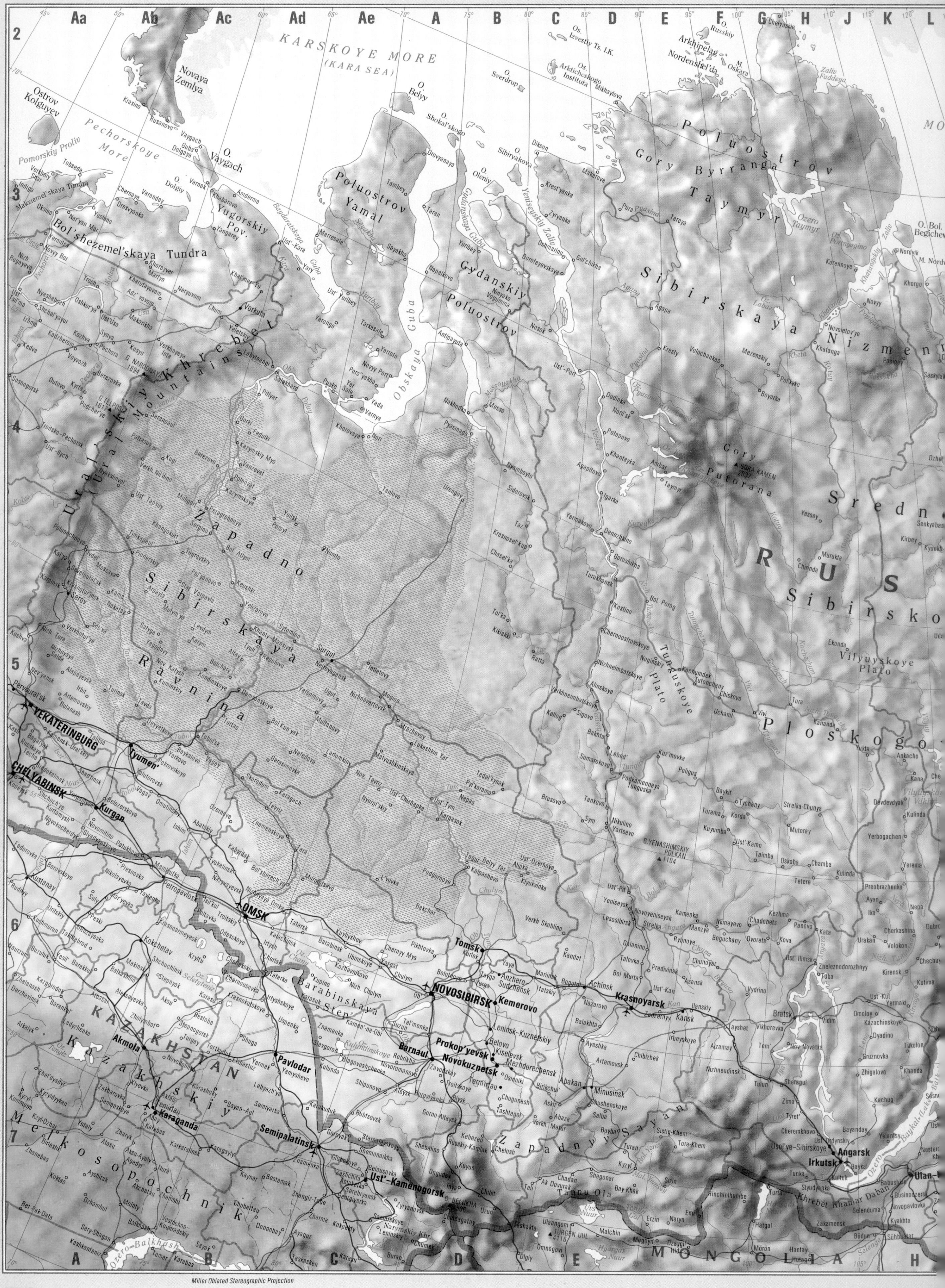
KARSKOYE MORE
(KARA SEA)
Novaya Zemlya
Ostrov Kolguyev
Pechorskoye More
O. Vaygach
Poluostrov Yamal
Gydanskiy Poluostrov
Obskaya Guba
Poluostrov Taymyr
Gory Byrranga
Sibirskaya Nizmennost
Gory Putorana
Bol'shezemel'skaya Tundra
Ural'skiy Khrebet
(Ural Mountains)
Zapadno Sibirskaya Ravnina
Tunguskoye Plato
Vilyuyskoye Plato
Barabinskaya Step'
KAZAKHSTAN
Kazakhskiy Melkosopochnik
Zapadnyy Sayan
MONGOLIA
YEKATERINBURG
CHELYABINSK
Tyumen'
Kurgan
OMSK
NOVOSIBIRSK
Tomsk
Kemerovo
Barnaul
Novokuznetsk
Krasnoyarsk
Irkutsk
Angarsk
Akmola
Pavlodar
Karaganda
Semipalatinsk
Ust'-Kamenogorsk
Surgut
Vorkuta
Noril'sk
Ozero Balkhash
Ozero Baykal
Miller Oblated Stereographic Projection

1:11,500,000

0 100 200 300 400 500 600 700 800 KILOMETRES
0 50 100 150 200 250 300 350 400 450 500 STATUTE MILES

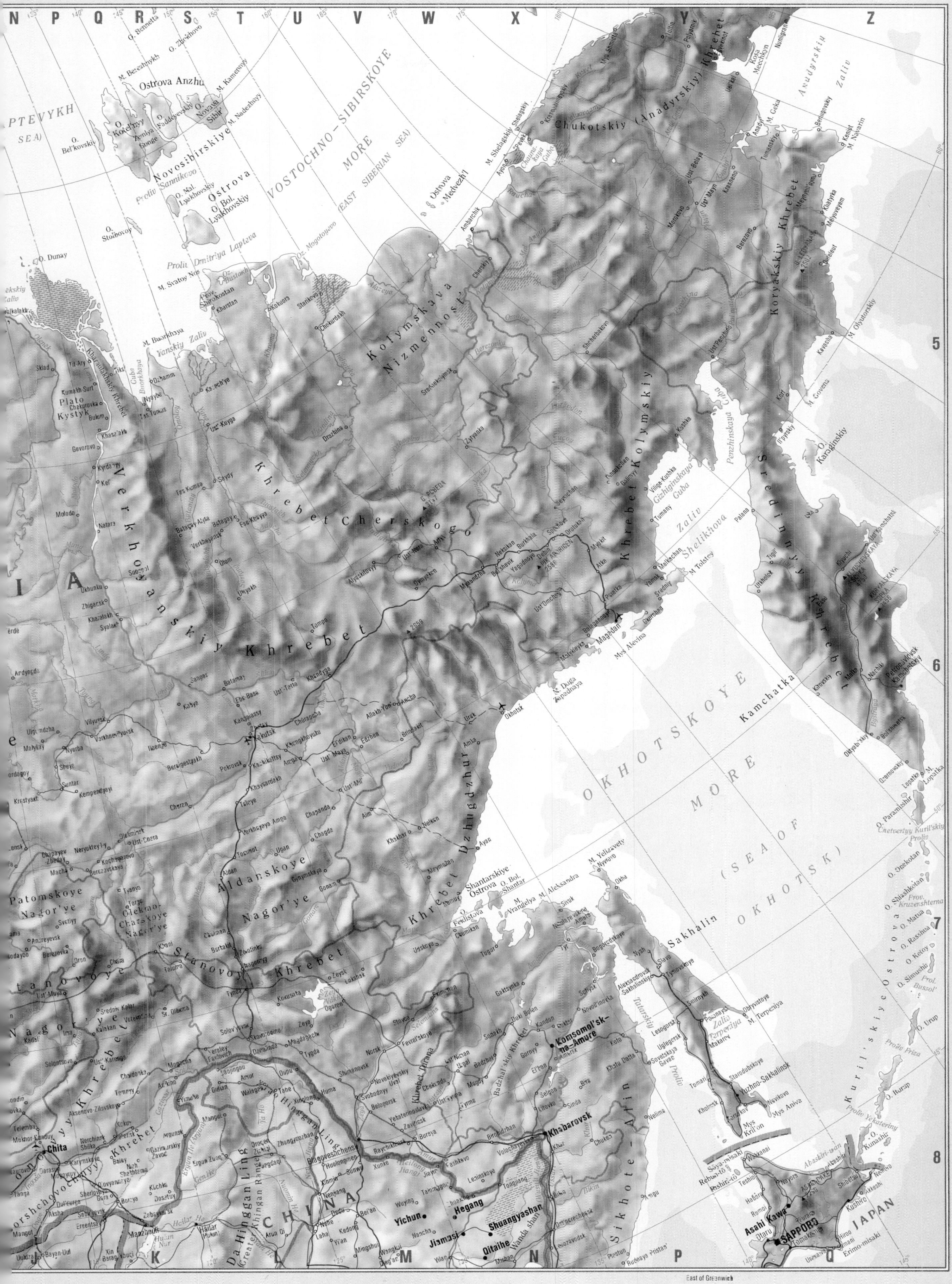

N P Q R S T U V W X Y Z
Ostrova Anzhu
Novosibirskiye Ostrova
VOSTOCHNO-SIBIRSKOYE MORE
(EAST SIBERIAN SEA)
Proliv Dmitriya Lapteva
Yanskiy Zaliv
Chukotskiy (Anadyrskiy) Khrebet
Anadyrskiy Zaliv
Kolymskaya Nizmennost'
Khrebet Cherskogo
Verkhoyanskiy Khrebet
Khrebet Kolymskiy
Koryakskiy Khrebet
Sredinnyy Khrebet
Kamchatka
Shelikhova Zaliv
Gizhiginskaya Guba
Penzhinskaya Guba
Magadan
Okhotsk
Yakutsk
OKHOTSKOYE MORE
(SEA OF OKHOTSK)
Khrebet Dzhugdzhur
Aldanskoye Nagor'ye
Patomskoye Nagor'ye
Olekmo-Charskoye Nagor'ye
Stanovoy Khrebet
Sakhalin
Tatarskiy Proliv
Zaliv Terpeniya
Yuzhno-Sakhalinsk
Kuril'skiye Ostrova
Komsomol'sk-na-Amure
Khabarovsk
Blagoveshchensk
Chita
Sikhote-Alin
CHINA
Da Hinggan Ling
Yichun
Hegang
Shuangyashan
Jiamusi
Qitaihe
Asahi Kawa
SAPPORO
JAPAN
Petropavlovsk Kamchatskiy
K L M N P Q
5
6
7
8

East of Greenwich

Designed and produced by E.S.R.

CHINA, MONGOLIA, NORTH AND SOUTH KOREA

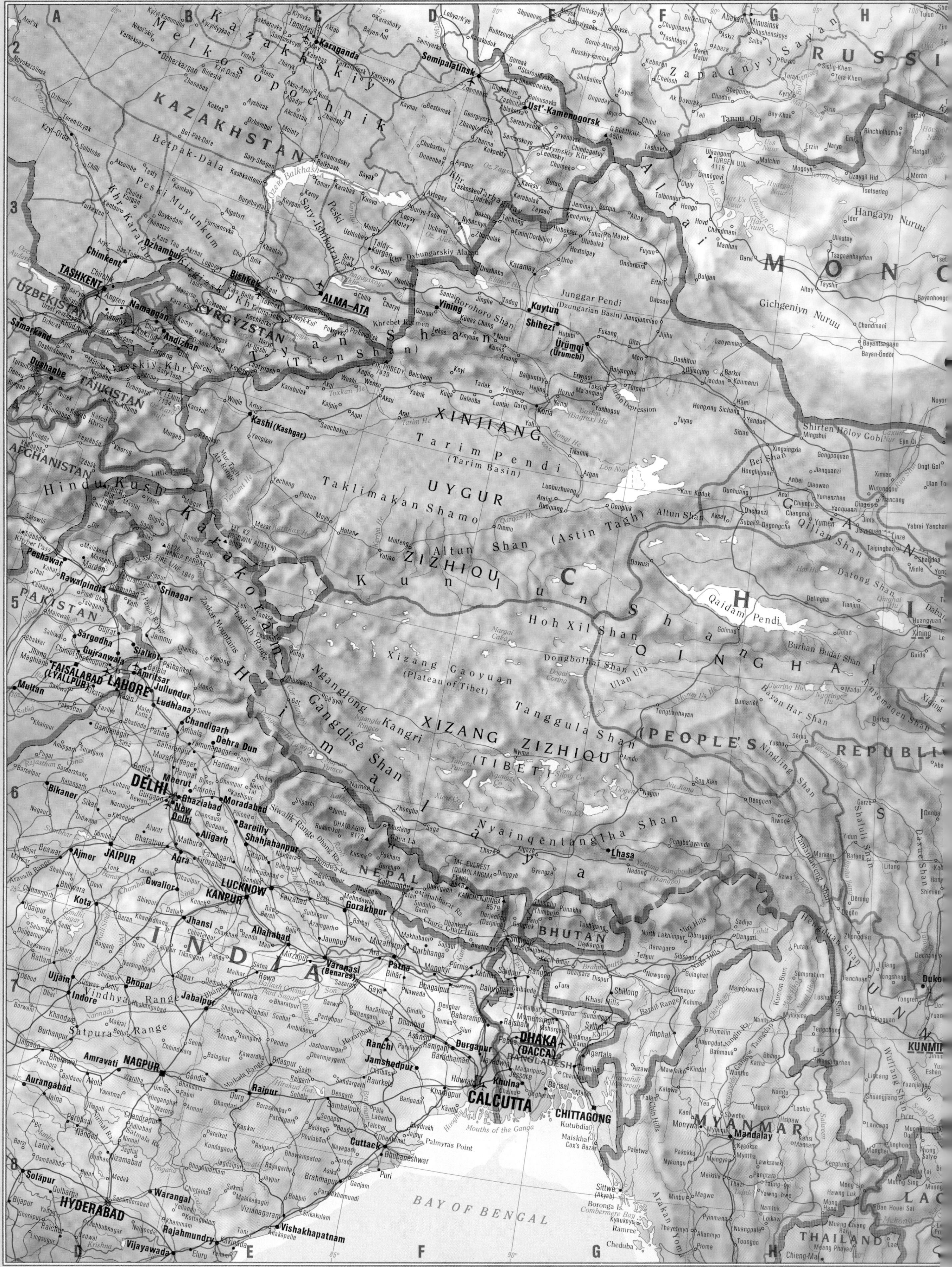

KAZAKHSTAN
UZBEKISTAN
KYRGYZSTAN
TAJIKISTAN
AFGHANISTAN
PAKISTAN
INDIA
NEPAL
BHUTAN
BANGLADESH
MYANMAR
THAILAND
MONGOLIA
RUSSIA
CHINA (PEOPLE'S REPUBLIC)
XINJIANG UYGUR ZIZHIQU
XIZANG ZIZHIQU (TIBET)
QINGHAI
Melkosopochnik
Kazakhskiy
Tien Shan
Altai
Hindu Kush
Karakoram
Himalaya
Kunlun Shan
Altun Shan (Astin Tagh)
Tanggula Shan
Nyainqêntanglha Shan
Gangdisê Shan
Tarim Pendi (Tarim Basin)
Taklimakan Shamo
Xizang Gaoyuan (Plateau of Tibet)
Qaidam Pendi
Junggar Pendi (Dzungarian Basin)
BAY OF BENGAL
Karaganda
Semipalatinsk
Ust'-Kamenogorsk
Alma-Ata
Bishkek
Tashkent
Dushanbe
Samarkand
Kashi (Kashgar)
Ürümqi (Urumchi)
Lhasa
Islamabad
Rawalpindi
Peshawar
Lahore
Faisalabad (Lyallpur)
Srinagar
Delhi
New Delhi
Jaipur
Lucknow
Kanpur
Varanasi (Benares)
Patna
Calcutta
Dhaka (Dacca)
Chittagong
Mandalay
Kunming
Nagpur
Hyderabad
Vishakhapatnam
MT. EVEREST (QOMOLANGMA FENG) 8848
K2 (GODWIN AUSTEN) 8611

Miller Oblated Stereographic Projection

1:11,500,000

0 100 200 300 400 500 600 700 800 KILOMETRES

0 50 100 150 200 250 300 350 400 450 500 STATUTE MILES

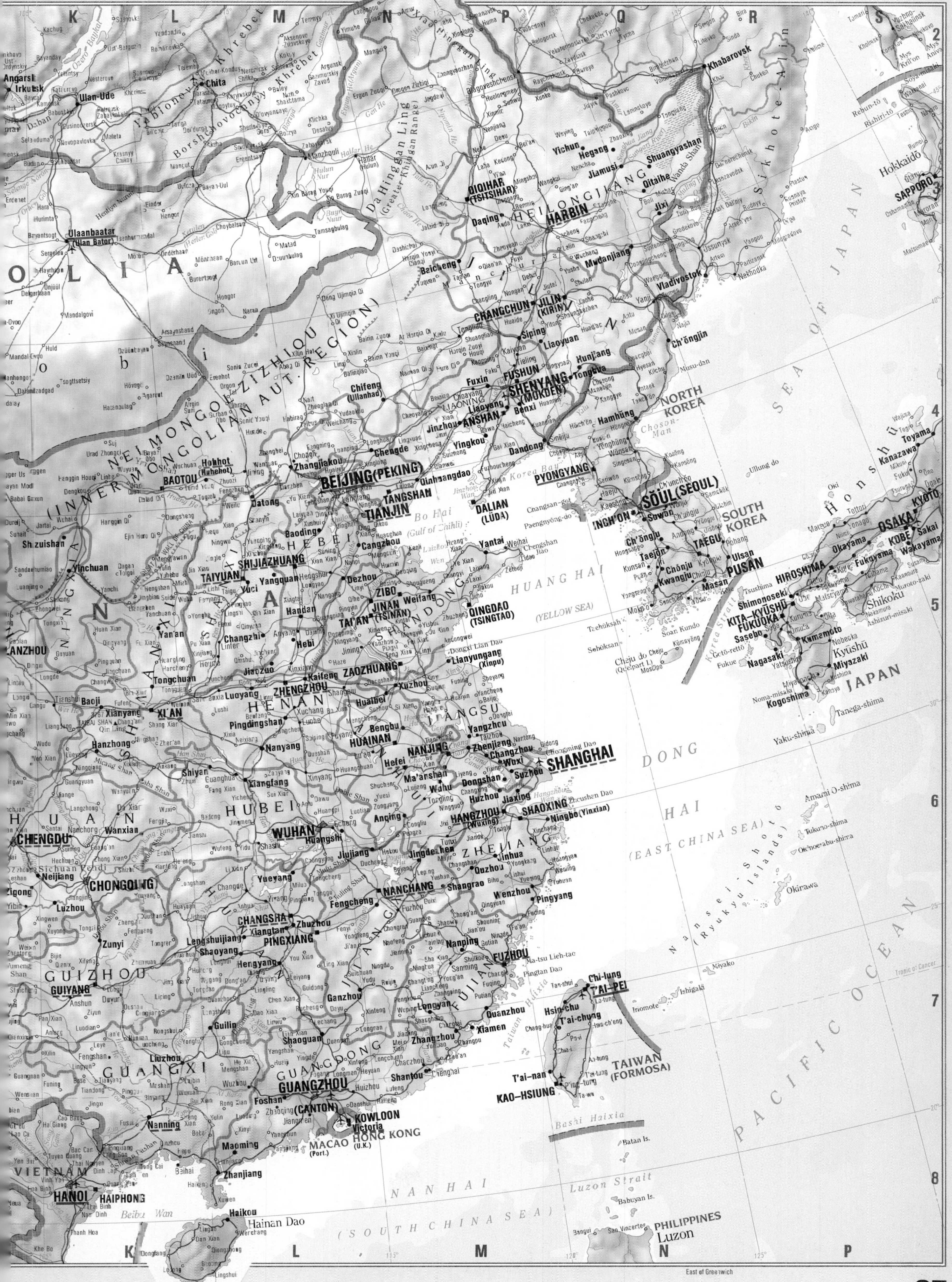
K L M N P Q R S
MONGOLIA
Gobi
NEI MONGOL ZIZHIQU (INNER MONGOLIAN AUT. REGION)
HEILONGJIANG
JILIN
LIAONING
HEBEI
SHANXI
SHAANXI
SHANDONG
HENAN
JIANGSU
ANHUI
HUBEI
ZHEJIANG
JIANGXI
HUNAN
FUJIAN
GUANGDONG
GUANGXI
GUIZHOU
SICHUAN
NINGXIA
Manchuria
Da Hinggan Ling (Greater Khingan Range)
Sikhote-Alin
Ulaanbaatar (Ulan Bator)
Irkutsk
Ulan-Ude
Chita
Khabarovsk
Vladivostok
QIQIHAR (TSITSIHAR)
HARBIN
Daqing
Jiamusi
Shuangyashan
Qitaihe
Jixi
Mudanjiang
CHANGCHUN
JILIN (KIRIN)
Siping
Liaoyuan
FUSHUN
SHENYANG (MUKDEN)
Benxi
ANSHAN
Liaoyang
Fuxin
Jinzhou
Yingkou
Dandong
DALIAN (LÜDA)
Chifeng (Ulanhad)
Zhangjiakou
Chengde
BEIJING (PEKING)
TANGSHAN
TIANJIN
Qinhuangdao
Baoding
Cangzhou
BAOTOU
Hohhot (Huhehot)
Datong
Yinchuan
SHIJIAZHUANG
TAIYUAN
Yangquan
Yuci
Handan
Changzhi
Yan'an
LANZHOU
Tongchuan
XI'AN
Baoji
Xianyang
Hanzhong
Luoyang
ZHENGZHOU
Kaifeng
Jiaozuo
Hebi
Pingdingshan
Nanyang
Dezhou
ZIBO
JINAN (TSINAN)
Weifang
TAI'AN
Yantai
QINGDAO (TSINGTAO)
ZAOZHUANG
Xuzhou
Lianyungang (Xinpu)
Huaibei
Bengbu
HUAINAN
Hefei
NANJING
Yangzhou
Zhenjiang
Changzhou
Wuxi
Suzhou
SHANGHAI
Ma'anshan
Wuhu
Huzhou
Jiaxing
HANGZHOU
SHAOXING
Ningbo (Yinxian)
Jinhua
Quzhou
Wenzhou
Shiyan
Xiangfang
WUHAN
Huangshi
Anqing
Jiujiang
Jingdezhen
Yueyang
NANCHANG
Shangrao
Fengcheng
CHENGDU
CHONGQING
Neijiang
Luzhou
Wanxian
CHANGSHA
Xiangtan
Zhuzhou
PINGXIANG
Lengshuijiang
Shaoyang
Hengyang
GUIYANG
Zunyi
Nanping
FUZHOU
Pingyang
Longyan
Quanzhou
Xiamen
Zhangzhou
Ganzhou
Shaoguan
Guilin
Liuzhou
Nanning
GUANGZHOU (CANTON)
Foshan
Shantou
KOWLOON
Victoria
MACAO (Port.)
HONG KONG (U.K.)
Maoming
Zhanjiang
Haikou
Hainan Dao
VIETNAM
HANOI
HAIPHONG
NORTH KOREA
PYONGYANG
Hamhŭng
Ch'ŏngjin
SOUTH KOREA
SŎUL (SEOUL)
INCH'ŎN
Suwŏn
TAEGU
PUSAN
Ulsan
Masan
Kwangju
Chŏnju
Taejŏn
Ch'ŏngju
JAPAN
SAPPORO
Hokkaidō
Honshū
Shikoku
Kyūshū
Toyama
Kanazawa
KYOTO
OSAKA
KOBE
Sakai
Wakayama
Okayama
Fukuyama
HIROSHIMA
Shimonoseki
KITA-KYUSHU
FUKUOKA
Sasebo
Nagasaki
Kumamoto
Miyazaki
Kagoshima
TAIWAN (FORMOSA)
T'AI-PEI
Chi-lung
Hsin-chu
T'ai-chung
T'ai-nan
KAO-HSIUNG
PHILIPPINES
Luzon
SEA OF JAPAN
Bo Hai (Gulf of Chihli)
Korea Bay
HUANG HAI (YELLOW SEA)
DONG HAI (EAST CHINA SEA)
Nansei-shotō (Ryukyu Islands)
Okinawa
PACIFIC OCEAN
Taiwan Haixia
Bashi Haixia
Luzon Strait
NAN HAI (SOUTH CHINA SEA)
Beibu Wan
Korea Strait
Tropic of Cancer
East of Greenwich
2 3 4 5 6 7 8

Designed and produced by E.S.R.

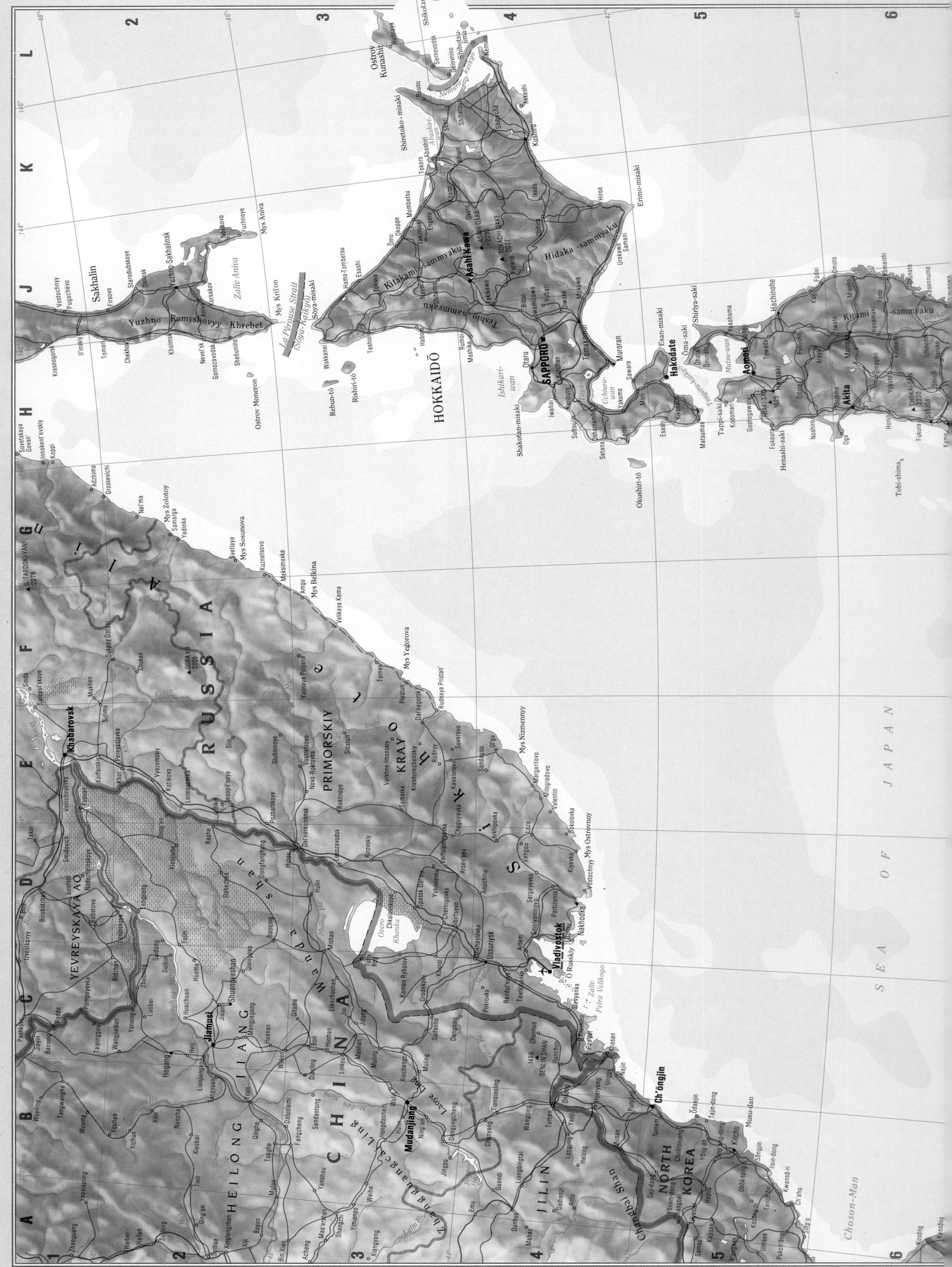
SEA OF JAPAN
RUSSIA
CHINA
HOKKAIDŌ
NORTH KOREA
PRIMORSKIY KRAY
HEILONG JIANG
JILIN
YEVREYSKAYA AO
Sakhalin
Yuzhno Kamyshovyy Khrebet
La Pérouse Strait (Soya-Kaikyō)
Zaliv Aniva
Ostrov Kunashir
Hidaka -sammyaku
Kitakami -sammyaku
Teshio -sammyaku
Ozero Khanka
Changbai Shan
Zhangguangcai Ling
Wanda Shan
Choson-Man
Khabarovsk
Vladivostok
Nakhodka
Ussuriysk
SAPPORO
Asahikawa
Hakodate
Muroran
Otaru
Kushiro
Aomori
Akita
Hachinohe
Ch'ŏngjin
Jiamusi
Mudanjiang
Yuzhno-Sakhalinsk
Rishiri-tō
Rebun-tō
Okushiri-tō
Tobi-shima
Soya-misaki
Erimo-misaki
Shiretoko-misaki

Miller Oblated Stereographic Projection

1:4,500,000

0 50 100 150 200 250 300 KILOMETRES

0 50 100 150 200 STATUTE MILES

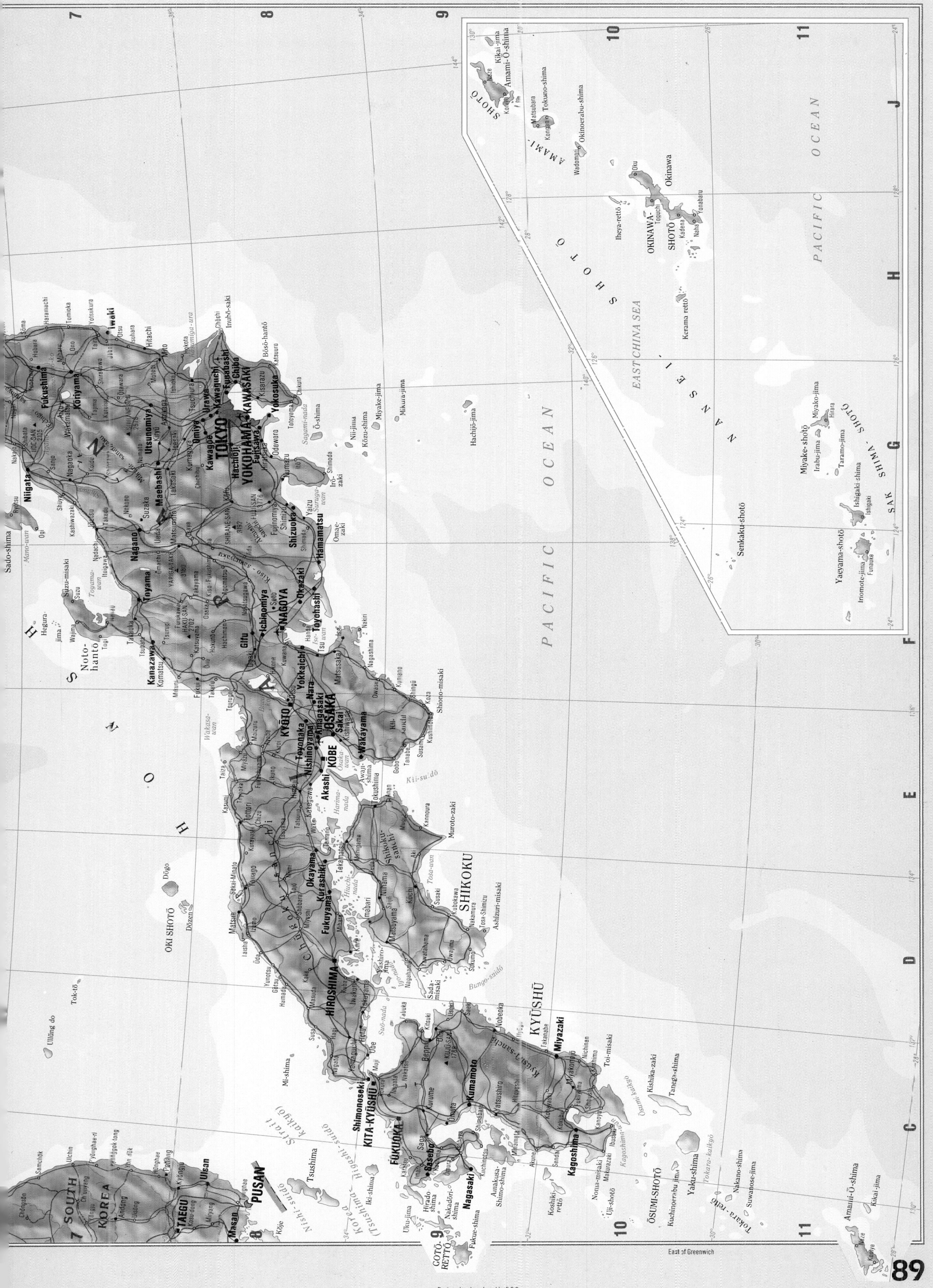

PACIFIC OCEAN
EAST CHINA SEA
NANSEI SHOTŌ
SHIKOKU
KYŪSHŪ
SOUTH KOREA
TOKYO
YOKOHAMA
KAWASAKI
NAGOYA
KYŌTO
ŌSAKA
KŌBE
HIROSHIMA
FUKUOKA
KITA-KYŪSHŪ
PUSAN
TAEGU
OKI SHOTŌ
GOTŌ-RETTŌ
ŌSUMI-SHOTŌ
OKINAWA-SHOTŌ
AMAMI-SHOTŌ
SAKISHIMA-SHOTŌ
Tsushima
Okinawa
Amami-Ō-shima
Kikai-jima
Tokuno-shima
Miyako-jima
Ishigaki-shima
Iriomote-jima
Yaku-shima
Tanega-shima
Hachijō-jima
Miyake-jima
Sado-shima
Niigata
Nagano
Toyama
Kanazawa
Gifu
Shizuoka
Hamamatsu
Okayama
Kumamoto
Kagoshima
Miyazaki
Nagasaki
Sasebo
Shimonoseki
Wakayama
Sakai
Iwaki
Koriyama
Fukushima
Utsunomiya
Maebashi
Chiba
Yokosuka
East of Greenwich

Designed and produced by E.S.R.

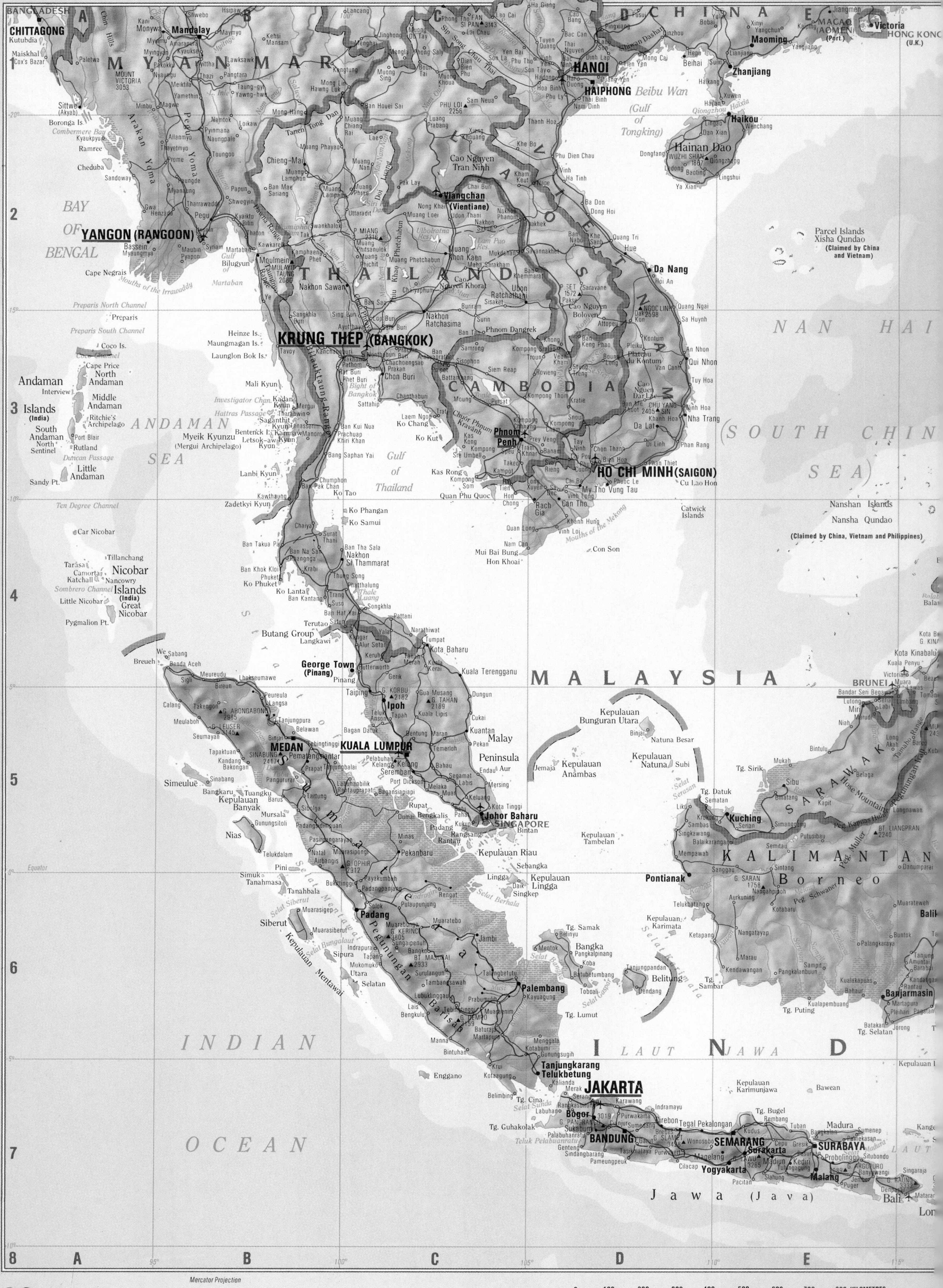
MYANMAR
THAILAND
CAMBODIA
LAOS
VIETNAM
MALAYSIA
CHINA
BANGLADESH
CHITTAGONG
Mandalay
YANGON (RANGOON)
HANOI
HAIPHONG
Viangchan (Vientiane)
KRUNG THEP (BANGKOK)
Phnom Penh
HO CHI MINH (SAIGON)
Da Nang
Hue
KUALA LUMPUR
George Town (Pinang)
Ipoh
Johor Baharu
SINGAPORE
MEDAN
Padang
Palembang
JAKARTA
Bandung
SEMARANG
SURABAYA
Yogyakarta
Kuching
Pontianak
Banjarmasin
Haikou
Hainan Dao
Zhanjiang
Maoming
MACAO (AOMEN) (Port.)
Victoria
HONG KONG (U.K.)
BAY OF BENGAL
ANDAMAN SEA
Andaman Islands (India)
Nicobar Islands (India)
Gulf of Martaban
Gulf of Thailand
Gulf of Tongking
Beibu Wan
Paracel Islands
Xisha Qundao
(Claimed by China and Vietnam)
Nanshan Islands
Nansha Qundao
(Claimed by China, Vietnam and Philippines)
NAN HAI
(SOUTH CHINA SEA)
Malay Peninsula
SARAWAK
BRUNEI
KALIMANTAN
Borneo
Sumatera
Jawa (Java)
LAUT JAWA
INDIAN OCEAN
Equator
A
B
C
D
E
1
2
3
4
5
6
7
8

Mercator Projection

1:12,000,000

0 100 200 300 400 500 600 700 800 KILOMETRES

0 100 200 300 400 500 STATUTE MILES

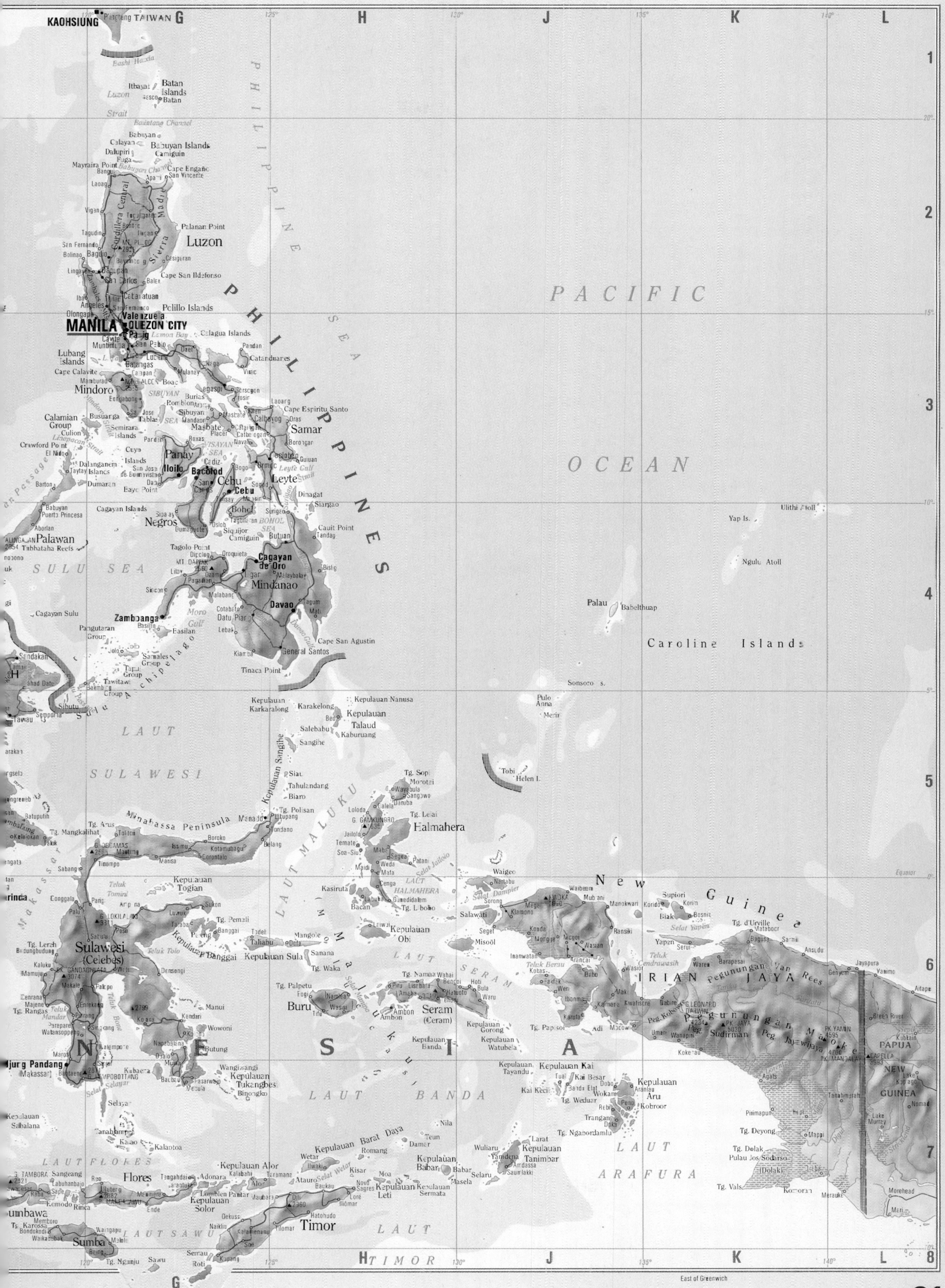

KAOHSIUNG
TAIWAN
Batan Islands
Luzon Strait
Bashi Channel
Babuyan Islands
Camiguin
Cape Engaño
Luzon
Baguio
Dagupan
San Carlos
Cabanatuan
Polillo Islands
MANILA
QUEZON CITY
Calagua Islands
PHILIPPINES
PHILIPPINE SEA
Lubang Islands
Cape Calavite
Batangas
Catanduanes
Mindoro
SIBUYAN SEA
Romblon
Sibuyan
Masbate
Calamian Group
Culion
Busuanga
Semirara Islands
Samar
Catbalogan
Leyte
Panay
Iloilo
Bacolod
Cebu
VISAYAN SEA
Negros
Bohol
BOHOL SEA
Siquijor
Camiguin
Dinagat
Siargao
Palawan
Puerto Princesa
Cagayan Islands
SULU SEA
Cagayan de Oro
Mindanao
Davao
Butuan
Cotabato
Zamboanga
Moro Gulf
Basilan
Cape San Agustin
General Santos
Cagayan Sulu
Pangutaran Group
Jolo
Tawitawi Group
Sulu Archipelago
Sandakan
Tawau
PACIFIC
OCEAN
Yap Is.
Ulithi Atoll
Ngulu Atoll
Palau
Babelthuap
Caroline Islands
Sonsorol Is.
Pulo Anna
Merir
Tobi
Helen I.
Kepulauan Karkaralong
Kepulauan Nanusa
Kepulauan Talaud
Karakelong
Salebabu
Kaburuang
Sangihe
Kepulauan Sangihe
Siau
Tahulandang
Biaro
LAUT SULAWESI
Minahassa Peninsula
Manado
Gorontalo
Tg. Mangkalihat
Teluk Tomini
Kepulauan Togian
Sulawesi (Celebes)
Palu
Kepulauan Banggai
Teluk Tolo
Kendari
Wowoni
Muna
Butung
Ujung Pandang (Makassar)
Selat Makassar
Selayar
Kalaotoa
LAUT FLORES
LAUT MALUKU
Morotai
Halmahera
Ternate
Tidore
Bacan
LAUT HALMAHERA
Kepulauan Obi
Kepulauan Sula
Mangole
Taliabu
Sanana
Maluku (Moluccas)
LAUT SERAM
Buru
Seram (Ceram)
Ambon
Kepulauan Gorong
Kepulauan Watubela
Kepulauan Banda
Kepulauan Tukangbesi
LAUT BANDA
Kepulauan Kai
Kepulauan Aru
Kepulauan Tanimbar
Kepulauan Barat Daya
Wetar
Kepulauan Alor
Flores
Sumbawa
Sumba
Kepulauan Solor
Timor
Kupang
Roti
Sawu
LAUT SAWU
TIMOR LAUT
Kepulauan Babar
Kepulauan Leti
Kepulauan Sermata
Waigeo
Salawati
Misool
Sorong
New Guinea
Supiori
Biak
Yapen
Manokwari
Teluk Cendrawasih
Teluk Berau
IRIAN JAYA
Pegunungan Van Rees
Pegunungan Maoke
Peg. Sudirman
Peg. Jayawijaya
Jayapura
Tg. d'Urville
LAUT ARAFURA
Pulau Jos Sodarso (Dolak)
Merauke
PAPUA NEW GUINEA
Tg. Vals
S I A
Equator
G H J K L
1 2 3 4 5 6 7 8
120° 125° 130° 135° 140°
East of Greenwich

Designed and produced by E.S.R.

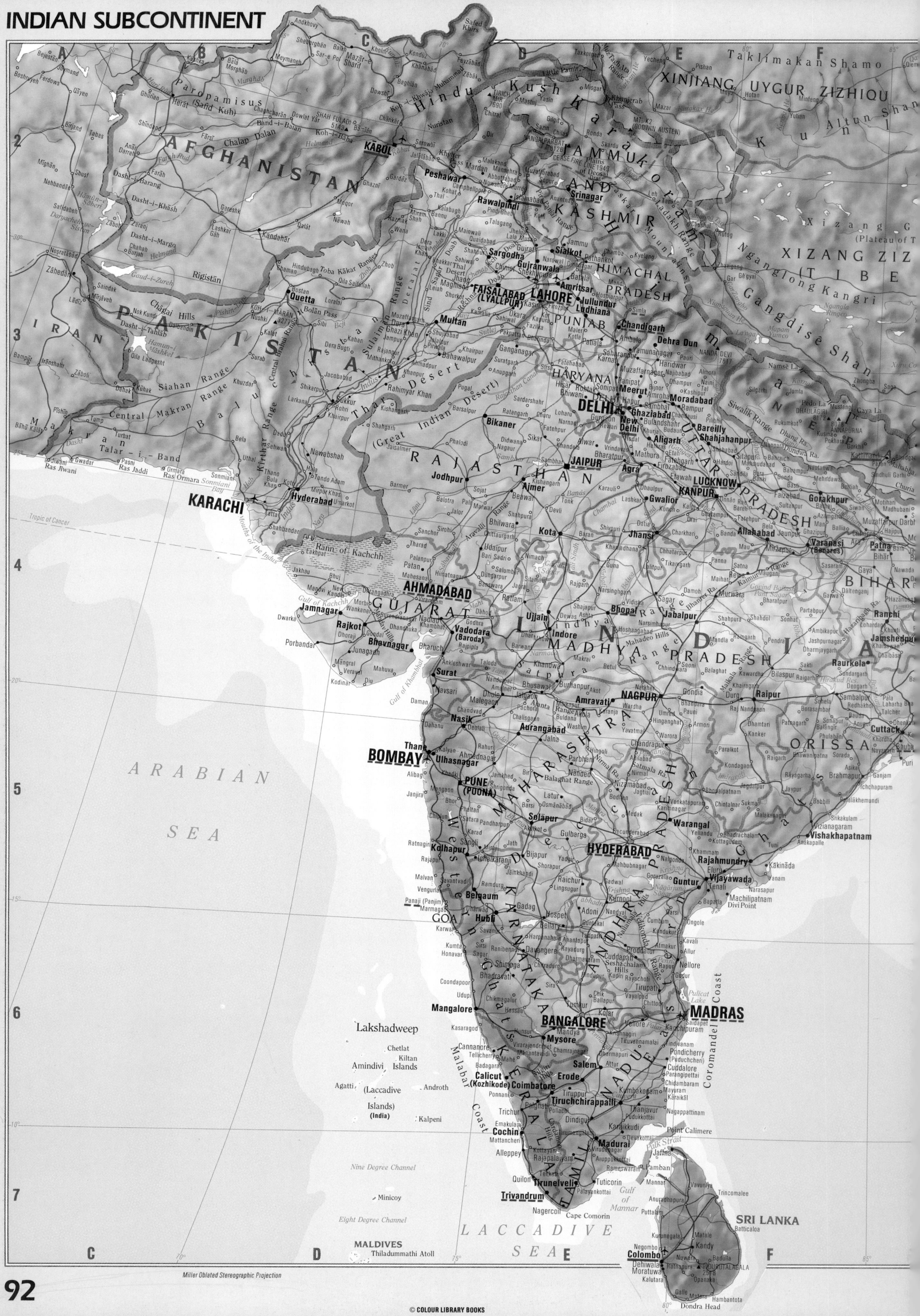
AFGHANISTAN
PAKISTAN
IRAN
JAMMU AND KASHMIR
HIMACHAL PRADESH
PUNJAB
HARYANA
DELHI
RAJASTHAN
GUJARAT
UTTAR PRADESH
MADHYA PRADESH
BIHAR
ORISSA
MAHARASHTRA
ANDHRA PRADESH
KARNATAKA
TAMIL NADU
KERALA
GOA
INDIA
NEPAL
SRI LANKA
XINJIANG UYGUR ZIZHIQU
XIZANG ZIZ
(TIBE
Taklimakan Shamo
Kunlun Shan
Altun Shan
Hindu Kush
Karakoram
Paropamisus (Safid Kuh)
Dasht-i-Margo
Rigistān
Thar Desert
(Great Indian Desert)
Rann of Kachchh
Gulf of Kachchh
Gulf of Khambhat
Western Ghats
Eastern Ghats
Malabar Coast
Coromandel Coast
Gangdisê Shan
Nganglong Kangri
Siwalik Range
Satpura Range
Vindhya Range
Deccan
ARABIAN SEA
LACCADIVE SEA
Lakshadweep
(Laccadive Islands)
(India)
Amindivi Islands
Nine Degree Channel
Eight Degree Channel
MALDIVES
Palk Strait
Gulf of Mannar
Tropic of Cancer
KĀBUL
Peshawar
Rawalpindi
Islamabad
Srinagar
Quetta
Multan
LAHORE
FAISALABAD (LYALLPUR)
KARACHI
Hyderabad
Amritsar
Chandigarh
Dehra Dun
NEW DELHI
Meerut
Agra
JAIPUR
Jodhpur
Bikaner
LUCKNOW
KANPUR
Allahabad
Varanasi (Benares)
Patna
AHMADABAD
Rajkot
Vadodara (Baroda)
Surat
Bhopal
Indore
Jabalpur
NAGPUR
BOMBAY
PUNE (POONA)
Solapur
HYDERABAD
Vishakhapatnam
Vijayawada
Panaji (Panjim)
Hubli
BANGALORE
MADRAS
Mysore
Mangalore
Calicut (Kozhikode)
Coimbatore
Cochin
Madurai
Tiruchchirappalli
Trivandrum
Cape Comorin
Colombo
Kandy
Jaffna
Trincomalee
Batticaloa
Dondra Head

Miller Oblated Stereographic Projection

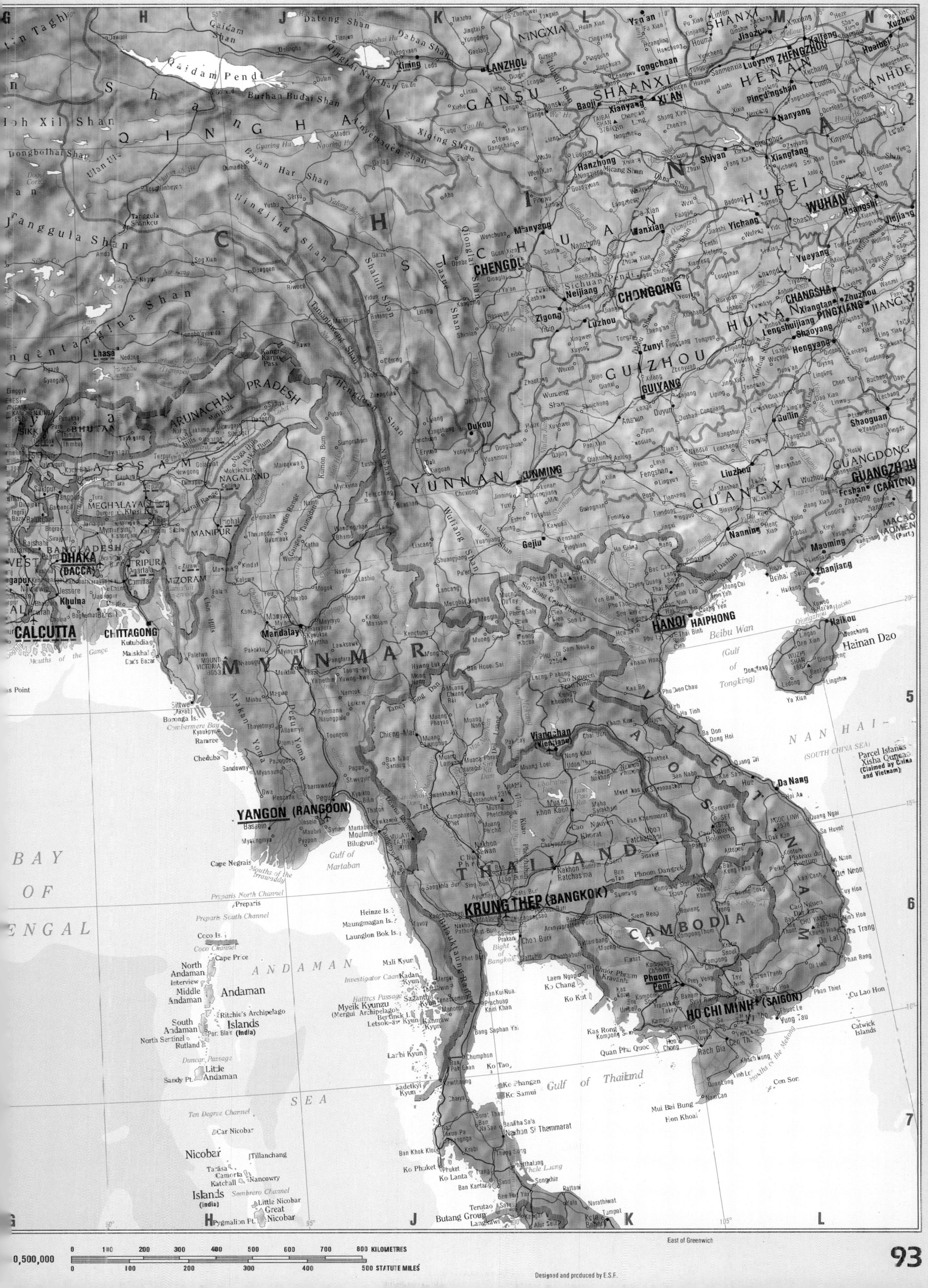
QINGHAI
GANSU
NINGXIA
SHAANXI
SHANXI
HENAN
ANHUI
HUBEI
SICHUAN
CHINA
GUIZHOU
HUNAN
JIANGXI
YUNNAN
GUANGXI
GUANGDONG
MYANMAR
THAILAND
LAOS
VIETNAM
CAMBODIA
BANGLADESH
BHUTAN
ARUNACHAL PRADESH
ASSAM
NAGALAND
MEGHALAYA
MANIPUR
TRIPURA
MIZORAM
LANZHOU
XI'AN
CHENGDU
CHONGQING
GUIYANG
KUNMING
WUHAN
CHANGSHA
GUANGZHOU (CANTON)
MACAO (AOMEN) (Part)
HANOI
HAIPHONG
DHAKA (DACCA)
CALCUTTA
CHITTAGONG
Mandalay
YANGON (RANGOON)
KRUNG THEP (BANGKOK)
Vientiane
Phnom Penh
HO CHI MINH (SAIGON)
Da Nang
Lhasa
Qaidam Pendi
Hainan Dao
Beibu Wan (Gulf of Tongking)
NAN HAI (SOUTH CHINA SEA)
Parcel Islands Xisha Qundao (Claimed by China and Vietnam)
Gulf of Martaban
Gulf of Thailand
BAY OF BENGAL
ANDAMAN SEA
Andaman Islands (India)
Nicobar Islands (India)
Myeik Kyunzu (Mergui Archipelago)
Mouths of the Mekong
Mouths of the Ganges
Mouths of the Irrawaddy
Ten Degree Channel
Sombrero Channel
Duncan Passage
Preparis North Channel
Preparis South Channel
Coco Channel
Tanggula Shankou
Hengduan Shan
Arakan Yoma
Pegu Yoma
Sichuan Pendi

0,500,000

0 100 200 300 400 500 600 700 800 KILOMETRES

0 100 200 300 400 500 STATUTE MILES

East of Greenwich

Designed and produced by E.S.F.

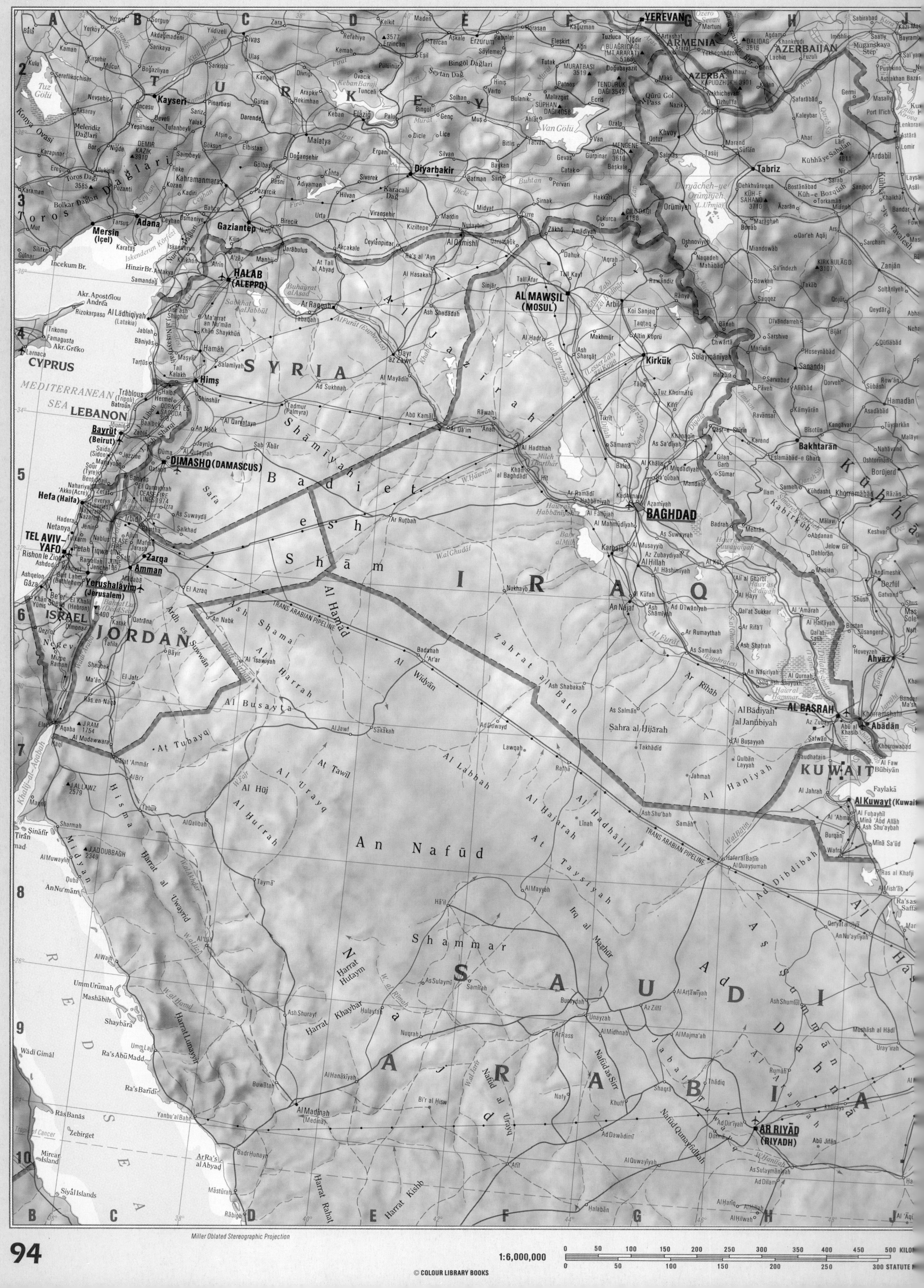
TURKEY
SYRIA
IRAQ
JORDAN
ISRAEL
LEBANON
CYPRUS
KUWAIT
SAUDI ARABIA
ARMENIA
AZERBAIJAN
MEDITERRANEAN SEA
RED SEA
YEREVAN
Kayseri
Adana
Mersin (Içel)
Gaziantep
Diyarbakir
Malatya
Erzurum
Sivas
Tabriz
HALAB (ALEPPO)
Ḩimş
Ḩamāh
Al Lādhiqīyah (Latakia)
Ţarābulus (Tripoli)
Bayrūt (Beirut)
DIMASHQ (DAMASCUS)
Hefa (Haifa)
TEL AVIV-YAFO
Yerushalayim (Jerusalem)
Amman
Zarqa
AL MAWŞIL (MOSUL)
Kirkūk
Arbīl
BAGHDAD
Karbalā
An Najaf
Al Ḩillah
AL BASRAH
Ābādān
Khorramshahr
Al Kuwayt (Kuwait)
Sulaymānīyah
Bakhtaran
Sanandaj
Ar Raqqah
Dayr az Zawr
Tadmur (Palmyra)
Al Jazīrah
Bādiet esh Shām
Shāmīyah
Al Ḩamād
An Nafūd
Shammar
Ḩā'il
Al Madīnah (Medina)
AR RIYĀD (RIYADH)
Buraydah
Unayzah
Tabūk
Al Jawf
Ad Dahnā
Ad Dibdibah
TRANS ARABIAN PIPELINE
Tropic of Cancer
A B C D E F G H J
2 3 4 5 6 7 8 9 10

Miller Oblated Stereographic Projection

1:6,000,000

0 50 100 150 200 250 300 350 400 450 500 KILOMETRES

0 50 100 150 200 250 300 STATUTE MILES

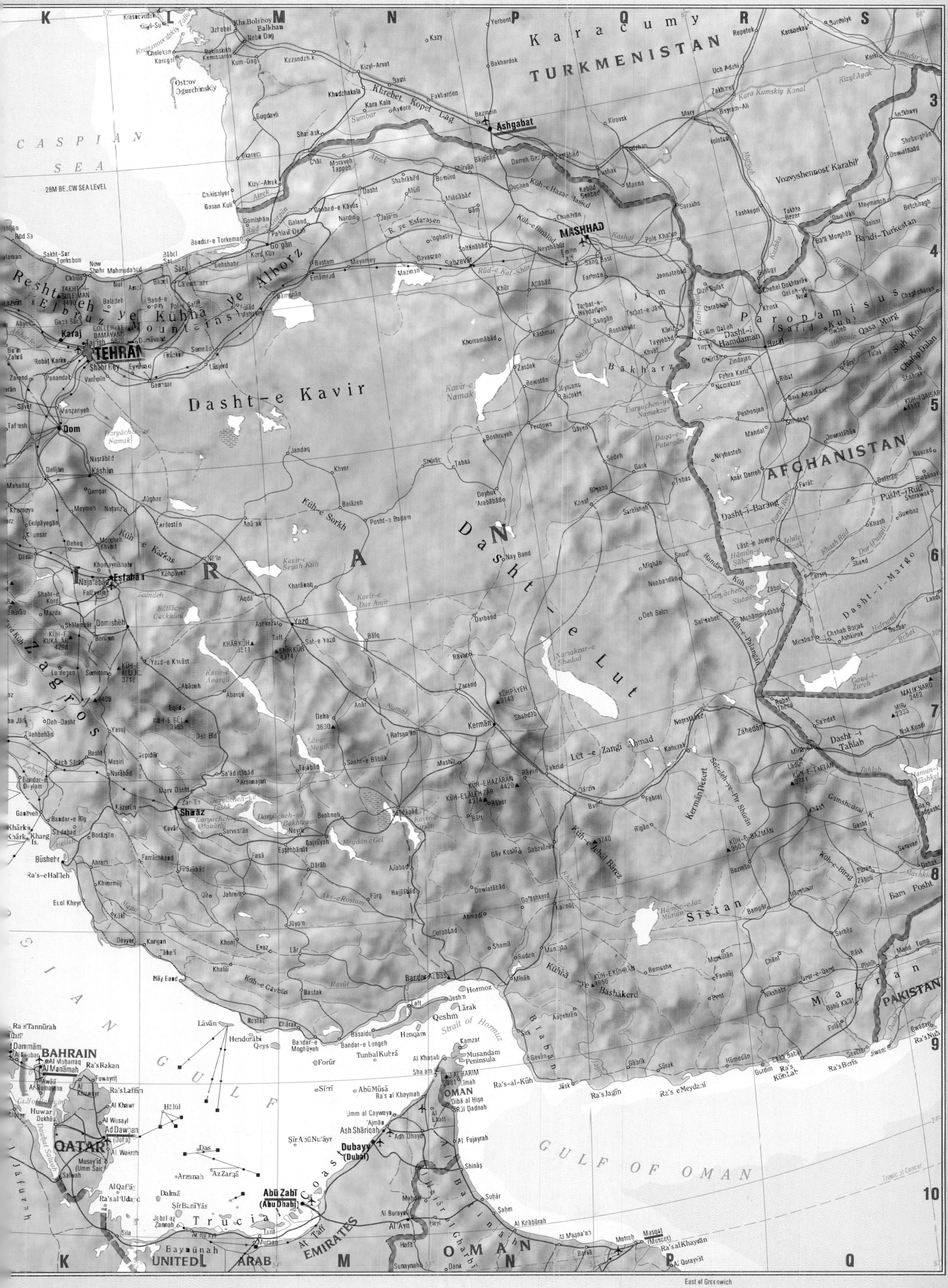

K
L
M
N
P
Q
R
S
Karacumy
TURKMENISTAN
Krasnovodsk
Dzhebel
Nebit Dag
Cheleken
Kazandzhik
Kizyl-Arvat
Bami
Bakhardok
Yerbent
Repetek
Kazy
Khrebet Kopet Dag
Bezmein
Ashgabat
Kirovsk
Mary
Bayram-Ali
Karo Kumskiy Kanal
Uch Adzhi
Zakhmet
Kizyl Ayak
Amudar'ya
Kerki
Andkhvoy
Sheberghan
Dowlatabad
Vozvyshennost' Karabil'
Kushka
Meymaneh
Belchiragh
Bandi-Turkestan
Gumbadli
Ostrov Ogurchinskiy
CASPIAN SEA
28M BELOW SEA LEVEL
Gasan Kuli
Kizyl-Atrek
Atrek
Gomishan
Gonbad-e Kavus
Bandar-e Torkeman
Babol Sar
Sari
Behshahr
Bastam
Shahrud
Damghan
Semnan
Quchan
Kuh-e Hazar Masjed
Shirvan
Bojnurd
Esfarayen
MASHHAD
Neyshabur
Sabzevar
Sarakhs
Kashaf
Torbat-e Heydariyeh
Torbat-e Jam
Kashmar
Jannatabad
Jam
Paropamisus
(Safid Kuh)
Herat
Dasht-i Hamdaman
Qasa Murg
Chaghcharan
Siah Koh
Chalap Dalan
Resht
Elburz Mountains
Reshteh-ye Kuhha-ye Alborz
Chalus
TAKHT-I-SULEIMAN 4490
Karaj
Qazvin
TEHRAN
QOLLEH-YE DAMAVAND 5670
Varamin
Zarand
Saveh
Tafresh
Qom
Daryacheh-ye Namak
Dasht-e Kavir
Kavir-e Namak
Jandaq
Khvor
Tabas
Bakharz
Boshruyeh
Ferdows
Qayen
Daryacheh-ye Namakzar
Daqq-e Patargan
AFGHANISTAN
Mandal
Shindand
Farah
Farah Rud
Dasht-i Bakwa
Pusht-i Rud
Kuh-e Karkas
Kashan
Natanz
Ardestan
Anarak
Kuh-e Sorkh
Khomeyni Shahr
Najafabad
Esfahan
Nain
Kavir-e Seyah Kuh
Kharanaq
IRAN
Dasht-e Lut
Nay Band
Zabol
Daryacheh-ye Sistan
Hamun-e Saberi
Dasht-i-Margo
Helmand
Shahr-e Kord
Zagros
Qomsheh
Yazd
Kavir-e Dar Anjir
Bafq
Ravar
Kuh-e Palangan
Namakzar-e Shadad
Gaud-i-Zirreh
MALIK NARO 2462
Zahedan
Nosratabad
Kerman
Zarand
Shahdad
Anar
Mehriz
Abarqu
Yasuj
Dehaj 3600
Rafsanjan
Sirjan
Lut-e Zangi Ahmad
Dasht-i-Tahlab
Tahlab
Nok Kundi
KUH-E TAFTAN
Hamun-i-Mashkel
Marv Dasht
Shiraz
Daryacheh-ye Tashk
Daryacheh-ye Bakhtegan
Daryacheh-ye Maharlu
Bam
Fahraj
Kerman Desert
Kuh-e Jebal Barez
KUH-E BAZMAN 3503
Saravan
Bushehr
Khark
Fasa
Darab
Jiroft
Iranshahr
Bampur
Sistan
Bam Posht
Kuh-e Birag
Lar
Bandar Abbas
Minab
Kuhha-ye Bashakerd
Makran
PAKISTAN
Hormoz
Qeshm
Strait of Hormuz
Musandam Peninsula
Jask
Ras Jagin
Ras e Meydani
Gwadar
Jiwani
Chah Bahar
Kish
Lavan
Hendorabi
Bandar-e Lengeh
Forur
Tunbal Kubra
Abu Musa
Sirri
PERSIAN GULF
BAHRAIN
Al Manamah
Al Muharraq
QATAR
Ad Dawhah (Doha)
Dukhan
Ras Laffan
OMAN
Ras al Khaymah
Umm al Qaywayn
Ash Shariqah
Ajman
Dubayy (Dubai)
Abu Zabi (Abu Dhabi)
Trucial Coast
UNITED ARAB EMIRATES
Al Fujayrah
Al Buraymi
Al Ayn
Suhar
Al Batinah
Al Gharbi
Masqat (Muscat)
Matrah
GULF OF OMAN
Tropic of Cancer
Das
Dalma
Sir Bani Yas
Jabal az Zannah
3
4
5
6
7
8
9
10
East of Greenwich

Designed and produced by E.S.R.

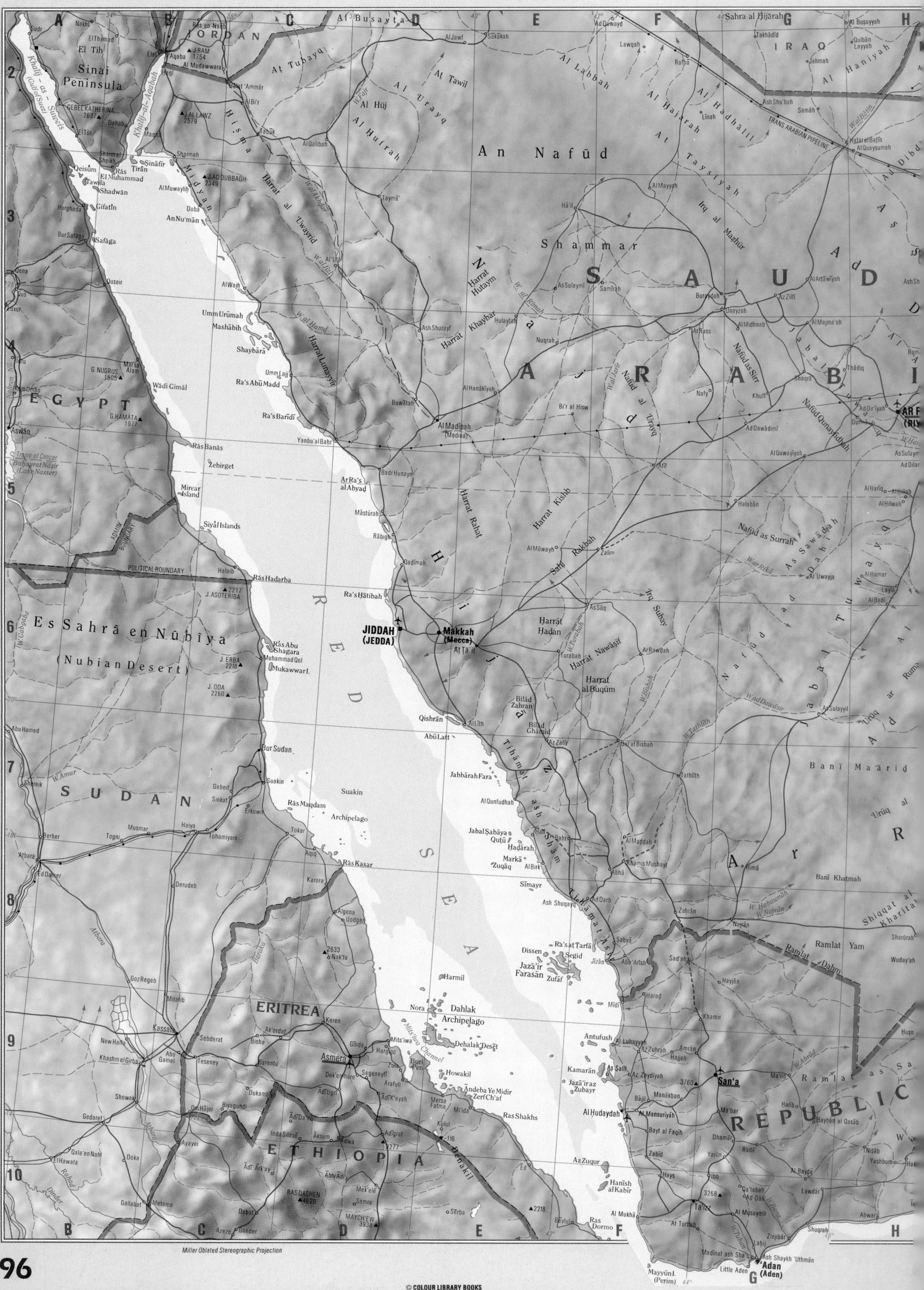
Sinai Peninsula
El Tih
JORDAN
IRAQ
An Nafūd
Shammar
SAUDI ARABIA
Najd
Hijaz
EGYPT
SUDAN
ERITREA
ETHIOPIA
REPUBLIC
Es Sahrâ en Nûbîya
(Nubian Desert)
RED SEA
JIDDAH
(JEDDA)
Makkah
(Mecca)
Al Madīnah
(Medina)
San'a
Adan
(Aden)
At Tā'if
Tabūk
Taymā'
Hā'il
Buraydah
Unayzah
Yanbu' al Bahr
Al Wajh
Aqaba
Elat
Bur Sudan
Suakin
Kassala
Asmera
Aswân
Luxor
Qena
Hurghada
Safâga
Quseir
Dahlak Archipelago
Jazā'ir Farasān
Kamarān
Al Hudaydah
Al Mukhā
Ta'izz
Mayyūn I.
(Perim)
Trans Arabian Pipeline
Tropic of Cancer
Buhayrat Nâsir
(Lake Nasser)
Political Boundary
Admin. Boundary
Gulf of Suez
Gulf of Aqaba
Harrat Khaybar
Harrat Rahat
Harrat Kishb
Nafūd as Surrah
Jabal Tuwayq
Tihāmat ash Shām
Tihāmat 'Asīr
Ramlat Dahm
Bani Ma'ārid
Bani Khatmah
J. Ram 1754
J. Al Lawz 2579
J. Ad Dubbagh 2349
Gebel Katherina 2637
G. Nugrus 1505
G. Hamâta 1977
J. Asoteriba 2217
J. Erba 2218
J. Oda 2260
Ras Dashen 4620
A B C D E F G H

Miller Oblated Stereographic Projection

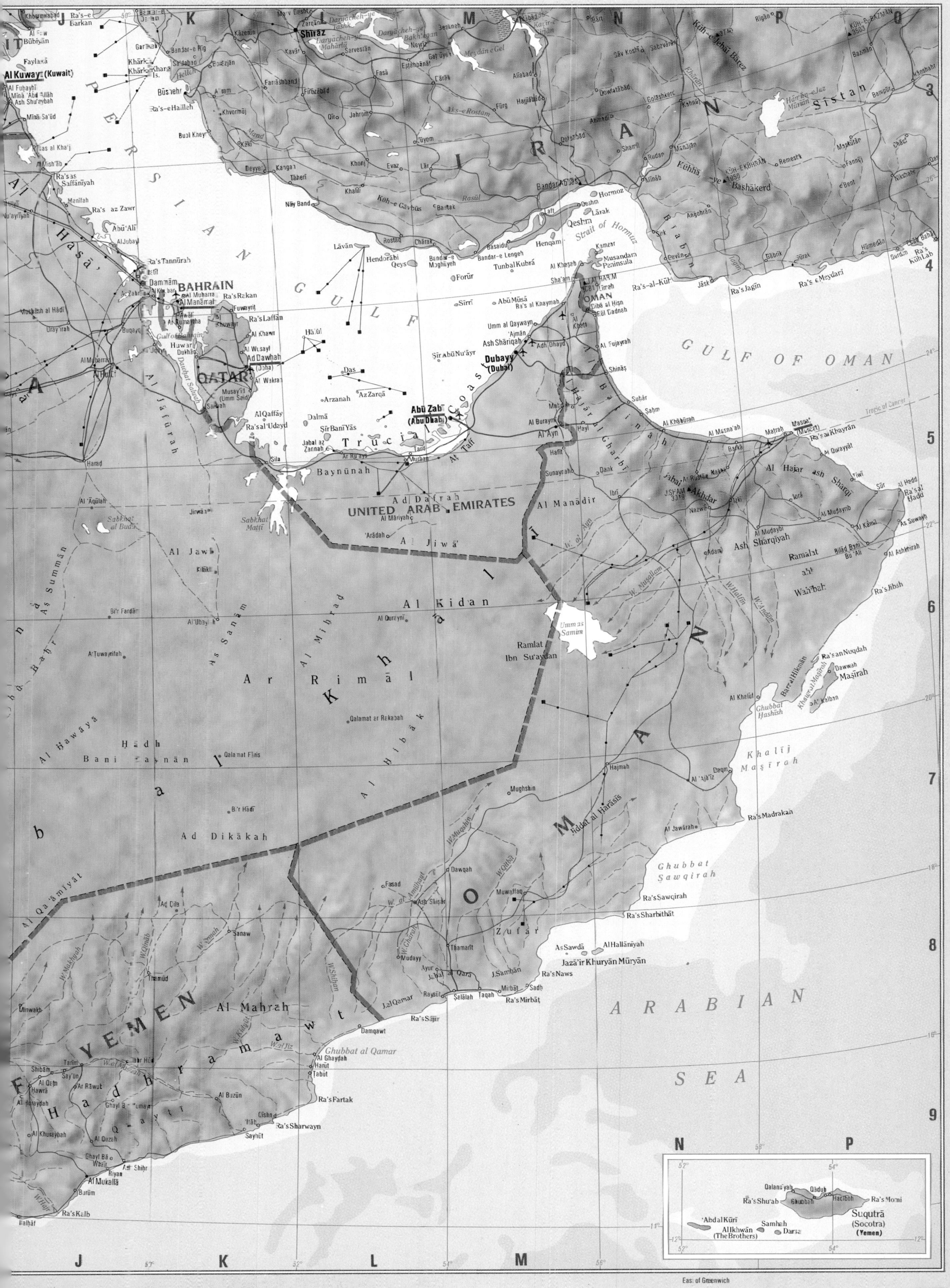
IRAN
PERSIAN GULF
GULF OF OMAN
ARABIAN SEA
Strait of Hormuz
BAHRAIN
QATAR
UNITED ARAB EMIRATES
OMAN
YEMEN
Al Kuwayt (Kuwait)
Shīrāz
Bandar Abbas
Hormoz
Qeshm
Musandam Peninsula
Ad Dawhah (Doha)
Al Manāmah
Abū Zabī (Abu Dhabi)
Dubayy (Dubai)
Ash Shāriqah
'Ajmān
Umm al Qaywayn
Ra's al Khaymah
Al Fujayrah
Masqat (Muscat)
Maţraḩ
Şūr
Ra's al Ḩadd
Trucial Coast
Al Jiwā'
Al Kidan
Ar Rimāl
Rub' al Khali
Ad Dikākah
Umm as Samīm
Ramlat Ibn Su'aydan
Ramlat al Wahībah
Ash Sharqīyah
Al Ḩajar ash Sharqī
Jabal Akhdar
Al Bāţinah
Maşīrah
Khalīj Maşīrah
Ghubbat Ḩashīsh
Jiddat al Ḩarāsīs
Ghubbat Sawqirah
Ra's Madrakah
Ra's Sawqirah
Ra's Sharbithāt
Ẓufār
Jazā'ir Khuryān Mūryān
Şalālah
Ra's Mirbāţ
Ra's Sājir
Al Mahrah
Ḩaḑramawt
Ghubbat al Qamar
Ra's Fartak
Ra's Sharwayn
Al Mukallā
Ra's Kalb
Sistan
Bashākerd
Ra's Jagīn
Ra's e Meydānī
Jāsk
Suquţrā (Socotra) (Yemen)
'Abd al Kūrī
Al Ikhwān (The Brothers)
Samḩah
Darsa
Ra's Shu'ab
Ra's Momi
Qalanīyah
Ḩadībōh

East of Greenwich

0 50 100 150 200 250 300 350 400 450 500 KILOMETRES
0 50 100 150 200 250 300 STATUTE MILES

Designed and produced by E.S.R.

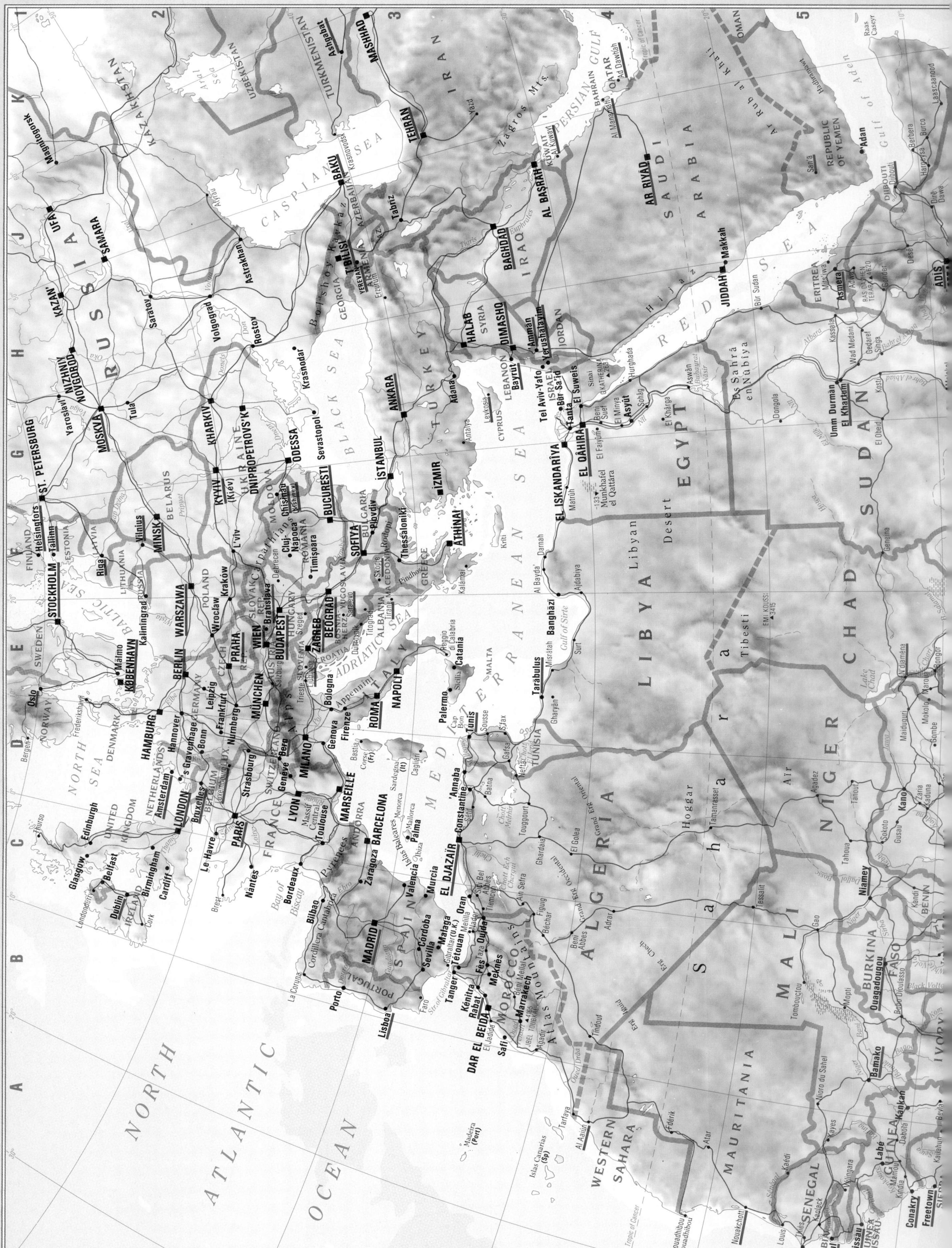
NORTH ATLANTIC OCEAN
NORTH SEA
BALTIC SEA
BLACK SEA
CASPIAN SEA
MEDITERRANEAN SEA
RED SEA
PERSIAN GULF
Gulf of Aden
ADRIATIC SEA
Bay of Biscay
UNITED KINGDOM
IRELAND
FRANCE
SPAIN
PORTUGAL
ITALY
GERMANY
POLAND
RUSSIA
UKRAINE
BELARUS
TURKEY
GREECE
SYRIA
IRAQ
IRAN
SAUDI ARABIA
EGYPT
LIBYA
ALGERIA
MOROCCO
TUNISIA
WESTERN SAHARA
MAURITANIA
MALI
NIGER
CHAD
SUDAN
SENEGAL
GUINEA
BURKINA FASO
REPUBLIC OF YEMEN
ERITREA
Sahara
Libyan Desert
Atlas Mountains
Alps
Pyrenees
LONDON
PARIS
MADRID
LISBOA
ROMA
BERLIN
WIEN
PRAHA
WARSZAWA
BUDAPEST
BEOGRAD
BUCUREŞTI
SOFIYA
ATHÍNAI
İSTANBUL
ANKARA
MOSKVA
ST. PETERSBURG
KYIV
DIMASHQ
BAGHDAD
TEHRAN
AR RIYĀD
EL QÂHIRA
EL ISKANDARÎYA
TARĀBULUS
TUNIS
EL DJAZAÏR
DAR EL BEIDA
DAKAR
BAMAKO
NIAMEY
EL KHARTUM
JIDDAH
Makkah

Miller Oblated Stereographic Projection

1:23,000,000

0	250	500	750	1000	1250	1500	KILOMETRES

0	100	200	300	400	500	600	700	800	900	1000	STATUTE MILES

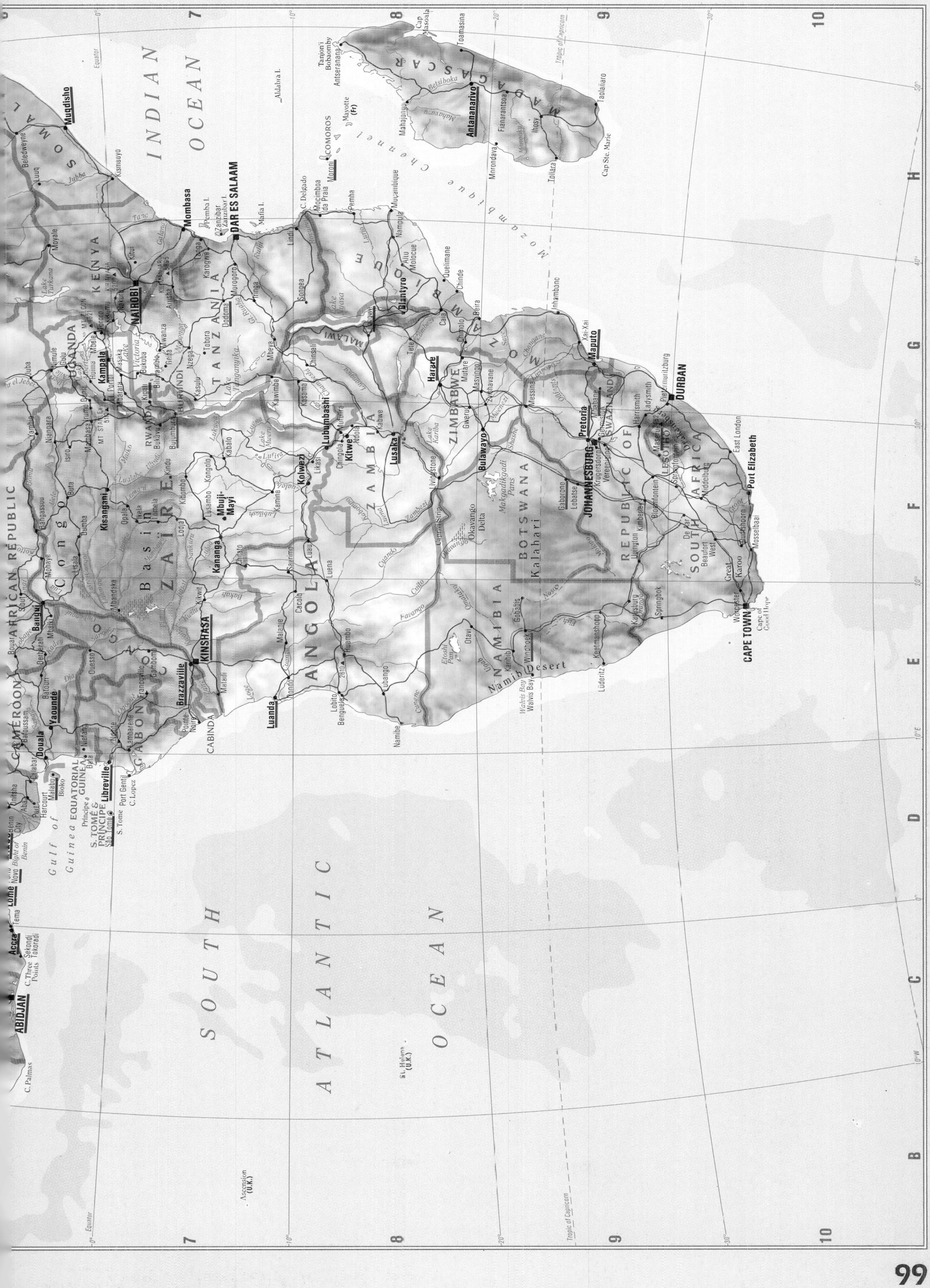

INDIAN OCEAN
SOUTH ATLANTIC OCEAN
Gulf of Guinea
Mozambique Channel
CENTRAL AFRICAN REPUBLIC
CAMEROON
EQUATORIAL GUINEA
GABON
CONGO
ZAIRE
Congo Basin
UGANDA
KENYA
SOMALIA
RWANDA
BURUNDI
TANZANIA
MALAWI
ZAMBIA
ANGOLA
MOZAMBIQUE
ZIMBABWE
BOTSWANA
NAMIBIA
REPUBLIC OF SOUTH AFRICA
LESOTHO
SWAZILAND
MADAGASCAR
COMOROS
S. TOMÉ & PRINCIPE
CABINDA
Kalahari
Namib Desert
Great Karoo
Okavango Delta
Makgadikgadi Pans
Tropic of Capricorn
Equator
ABIDJAN
Accra
Lomé
Douala
Yaoundé
Libreville
Brazzaville
KINSHASA
Luanda
Bangui
Kisangani
Kampala
NAIROBI
Mombasa
Mogadisho
DAR ES SALAAM
Dodoma
Lubumbashi
Lusaka
Harare
Bulawayo
Maputo
Pretoria
JOHANNESBURG
DURBAN
Port Elizabeth
CAPE TOWN
Windhoek
Gaborone
Antananarivo
Mbuji-Mayi
Kananga
Kolwezi
Kitwe
Blantyre
Beira
Ascension (U.K.)
St. Helena (U.K.)
Aldabra I.
Mayotte (Fr)
C. Palmas
Cape of Good Hope

Designed and produced by E.S.R.

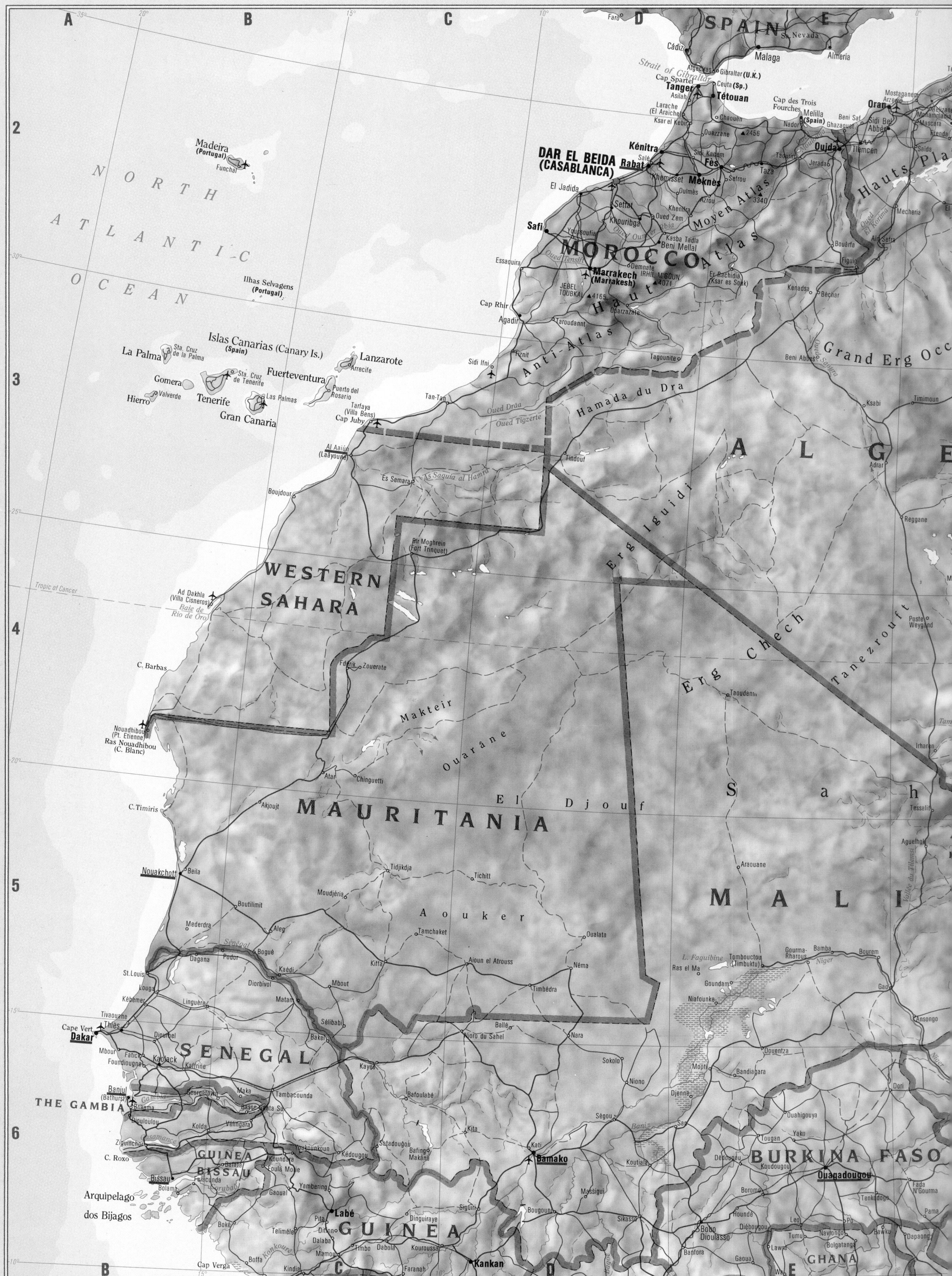
SPAIN
Sa. Nevada
Faro
Cádiz
Malaga
Almería
Strait of Gibraltar
Algeciras
Gibraltar (U.K.)
Cap Spartel
Tanger
Ceuta (Sp.)
Asilah
Tétouan
Larache (El Araiche)
Ksar el Kebir
Chaouèn
Cap des Trois Fourches
Melilla (Spain)
Nador
Oran
Mostaganem
Arzew
Beni Saf
Ghazaouet
Sidi Bel Abbès
Mascara
Tlemcen
Oujda
Ouezzane
Kénitra
Salé
DAR EL BEIDA (CASABLANCA)
Rabat
Sidi Kacem
Fès
Meknès
Khemisset
Sefrou
Taza
Taourirt
Jerada
Saïda
El Jadida
Settat
Oulmès
Azrou
Khouribga
Oued Zem
Khenifra
Moyen Atlas
Hauts Plat
Safi
Youssoufia
Kasba Tadla
Beni Mellal
MOROCCO
Atlas
Oued Tensift
Essaouira
Demnate
Marrakech (Marrakesh)
IRHIL M'GOUN 4071
JEBEL TOUBKAL 4165
Er Rachidia (Ksar es Souk)
Haut
Ouarzazate
Cap Rhir
Agadir
Taroudannt
Mecheria
Aïn Sefra
Bouârfa
Figuig
Kenadsa
Béchar
Sidi Ifni
Tiznit
Anti-Atlas
Tagounite
Beni Abbès
Grand Erg Occ
Madeira (Portugal)
Funchal
NORTH ATLANTIC OCEAN
Ilhas Selvagens (Portugal)
Islas Canarias (Canary Is.) (Spain)
La Palma
Sta. Cruz de la Palma
Lanzarote
Arrecife
Fuerteventura
Gomera
Sta. Cruz de Tenerife
Puerto del Rosario
Hierro
Valverde
Tenerife
Las Palmas
Gran Canaria
Tarfaya (Villa Bens)
Cap Juby
Tan-Tan
Oued Drâa
Oued Tigzerte
Hamada du Dra
Ksabi
Timimoun
Al Aaiún (Laâyoune)
Es Semara
As Saguia al Hamra
Tindouf
ALGE
Adrar
Boujdour
Erg Iguidi
Reggane
Bîr Moghrein (Fort Trinquet)
WESTERN SAHARA
Tropic of Cancer
Ad Dakhla (Villa Cisneros)
Baie de Rio de Oro
Erg Chech
Poste Weygand
Tanezrouft
C. Barbas
Fdérik
Zouerate
Taoudenni
Makteir
Nouadhibou (Pt. Etienne)
Ras Nouadhibou (C. Blanc)
Ouarâne
Irharen
Atar
Chinguetti
El Djouf
Sah
C. Timiris
Akjoujt
MAURITANIA
Tessalit
Aguelhok
Nouakchott
Beïla
Tidjikdja
Tichitt
Araouane
Moudjéria
Boutilimit
Aouker
MALI
Mederdra
Aleg
Tamchaket
Oualata
Sénégal
Dagana
Podor
Bogué
Kaédi
Kiffa
Aioun el Atrouss
Néma
L. Faguibine
Tombouctou (Timbuktu)
Gourma-Rharous
Bamba
Bourem
Ras el Ma
Niger
St. Louis
Diorbivol
Mbout
Goundam
Louga
Kébémer
Linguère
Matam
Timbédra
Niafounké
Gao
Tivaouane
Cape Vert
Thiès
Dakar
Diourbel
Sélibabi
Ansongo
Bakel
Nioro du Sahel
Nara
Mbour
Fatick
Kaolack
Foundiougne
Kaffrine
SENEGAL
Kayes
Sokolo
Douentza
Banjul (Bathurst)
THE GAMBIA
Georgetown
Maka
Tambacounda
Bafoulabé
Niono
Mopti
Bandiagara
Dori
Brikama
Ziguinchor
Kolda
Vélingara
Basse Santa Su
Casamance
Ouahigouya
Djenne
Ségou
Kita
Tougan
Yako
C. Roxo
GUINEA BISSAU
Bissau
Bolama
Bafatá
Fulacunda
Kédougou
Youkounkoun
Koula Mouse
Bafing Makana
Kati
Bamako
Koutiala
Dédougou
Koudougou
BURKINA FASO
Ouagadougou
Arquipelago dos Bijagos
Yambering
Gaoual
Labé
Siguiri
Bougouni
Massigui
Boromo
Fada N'Gourma
Tenkodogo
Boké
Télimélé
Pita
Dinguiraye
Sikasso
Houndé
Diébougou
Bobo Dioulasso
Leo
Po
Pama
Dalaba
Mamou
Timbo
Dabola
Kouroussa
Banfora
Tumu
Navrongo
Bolgatanga
Bawku
Dapaong
GUINEA
Boffa
Kindia
Faranah
Kankan
Gaoua
Lawra
Wa
GHANA
Cap Verga
A
B
C
D
E
2
3
4
5
6

Miller Oblated Stereographic Projection

West of Greenwich

1:9,000,000

0 100 200 300 400 500 600 KILOMETRES

0 50 100 150 200 250 300 350 400 STATUTE MILES

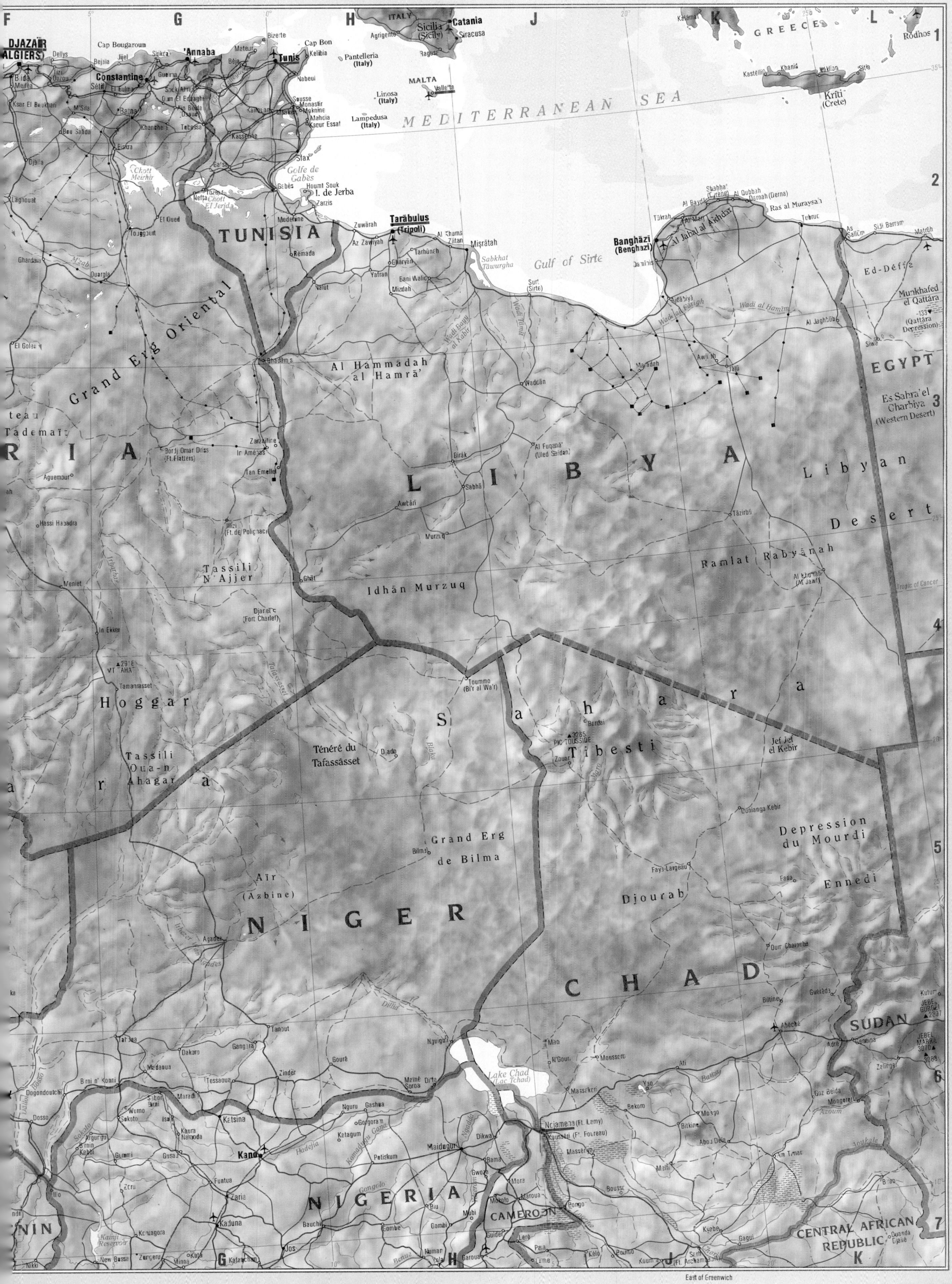
DJAZAÏR
ALGIERS
Dellys
Bejaia
Jijel
Skikda
'Annaba
Constantine
Sétif
El Eulma
Guelma
Souk Ahras
Batna
Khenchela
Tebessa
M'Sila
Bou Saada
Biskra
Djelfa
Chott Melrhir
Chott El Jerid
Laghouat
El Oued
Touggourt
Ghardaïa
Ouargla
El Golea
Grand Erg Oriental
Tademaït
Aguemour
Hassi Habadra
Meniet
In Ekker
Hoggar
Tamanrasset
VT 'AHA
Tassili Oua-n Ahagar
Tassili N'Ajjer
Illizi (Ft. de Polignac)
Djanet (Fort Charlet)
Bordj Omar Driss (Ft. Flatters)
In Amenas
Zarzaitine
Tan Emellel
Cap Bougaroun
Bizerte
Cap Bon
Tunis
Kelibia
Nabeul
Sousse
Monastir
Mahdia
Ksour Essaf
Sfax
Kairouan
Kasserine
Gafsa
Gabès
Golfe de Gabès
Houmt Souk
I. de Jerba
Zarzis
Medenine
Remada
Tozeur
Nefta
TUNISIA
Pantelleria (Italy)
Linosa (Italy)
Lampedusa (Italy)
MALTA
Valletta
ITALY
Sicilia (Sicily)
Catania
Siracusa
Agrigento
Ragusa
MEDITERRANEAN SEA
GREECE
Kalamata
Kriti (Crete)
Kastelli
Khania
Iraklion
Sitia
Rodhos
Tarābulus (Tripoli)
Zuwārah
Az Zawiyah
Al Khums
Zlitan
Misrātah
Tarhūnah
Gharyān
Yafran
Bani Walid
Mizdah
Nalut
Ghadamis
Al Hammadah al Hamrā'
Sabkhat Tawurgha
Gulf of Sirte
Surt (Sirte)
Wadi Bayy al Kabir
Banghāzī (Benghazi)
Al Marj
Al Bayda
Shahhat (Cyrene)
Al Jabal al Akhdar
Darnah (Derna)
Ras al Muraysah
Al Qubbah
Tubruq
Tūkrah
Ajdābiyā
Wadi al Farigh
Wadi al Hamim
Al Jaghbūb
Awjilah
Jalū
Marādah
Waddān
Al Fuqahā' (Uled Seidan)
Birāk
Sabhā
Awbārī
Murzuq
Ghāt
Idhān Murzuq
LIBYA
Tāzirbū
Ramlat Rabyānah
Al Khufrah (Al Jawf)
Libyan Desert
As Sallūm
Sidi Barrani
Matrūh
Ed-Déffa
Munkhafed el Qattâra
Siwa
EGYPT
Es Sahra'el Gharbiya (Western Desert)
Tropic of Cancer
Toummo (Bi'r al Wa'r)
Sahara
Bardai
PIC TOUSSIDE
Tibesti
Zouar
Jef Jef el Kebir
Ounianga Kebir
Depression du Mourdi
Ennedi
Faya-Largeau
Fada
Djourab
Oum Chalouba
CHAD
Biltine
Guereda
Abéché
Adré
Ténéré du Tafassâsset
Djado
Grand Erg de Bilma
Bilma
Aïr (Azbine)
Agadez
NIGER
Tahoua
Dakoro
Madaoua
Tanout
Gangara
Zinder
Gouré
N'guigmi
Mainé Soroa
Tessaoua
Birni n' Konni
Dogondoutchi
Dosso
Lake Chad (Lac Tchad)
Mao
Moussoro
N'Gouri
Massakori
Ndjamena (Ft. Lamy)
Kousseri (Ft. Foureau)
Bokoro
Mongo
Bitkine
Abou Deïa
Ati
Mongororo
Goz Beïda
Am Timan
Massenya
Melfi
Bousso
Kyabé
Sarh (Ft. Archambault)
Koumra
Moundou
Pala
Léré
Bongor
Kumbo
Gagal
Batha
NIGERIA
Sokoto
Katsina
Kano
Kaura Namoda
Gusau
Zaria
Kaduna
Funtua
Maiduguri
Nguru
Gashua
Potiskum
Dikwa
Bama
Gwoza
Mubi
Yola
Bauchi
Gombe
Biu
Jos
Kontagora
Minna
New Bussa
Kainji Reservoir
Nikki
Zungeru
Katagum
Gorgoram
Mokolo
Maroua
Garoua
Guider
CAMEROON
Numan
Jalingo
SUDAN
Geneina
Zalingei
JEBEL MARRA
CENTRAL AFRICAN REPUBLIC
Birao
Ouanda Djallé
East of Greenwich
F
G
H
J
K
L
1
2
3
4
5
6
7

Designed and produced by E.S.R.

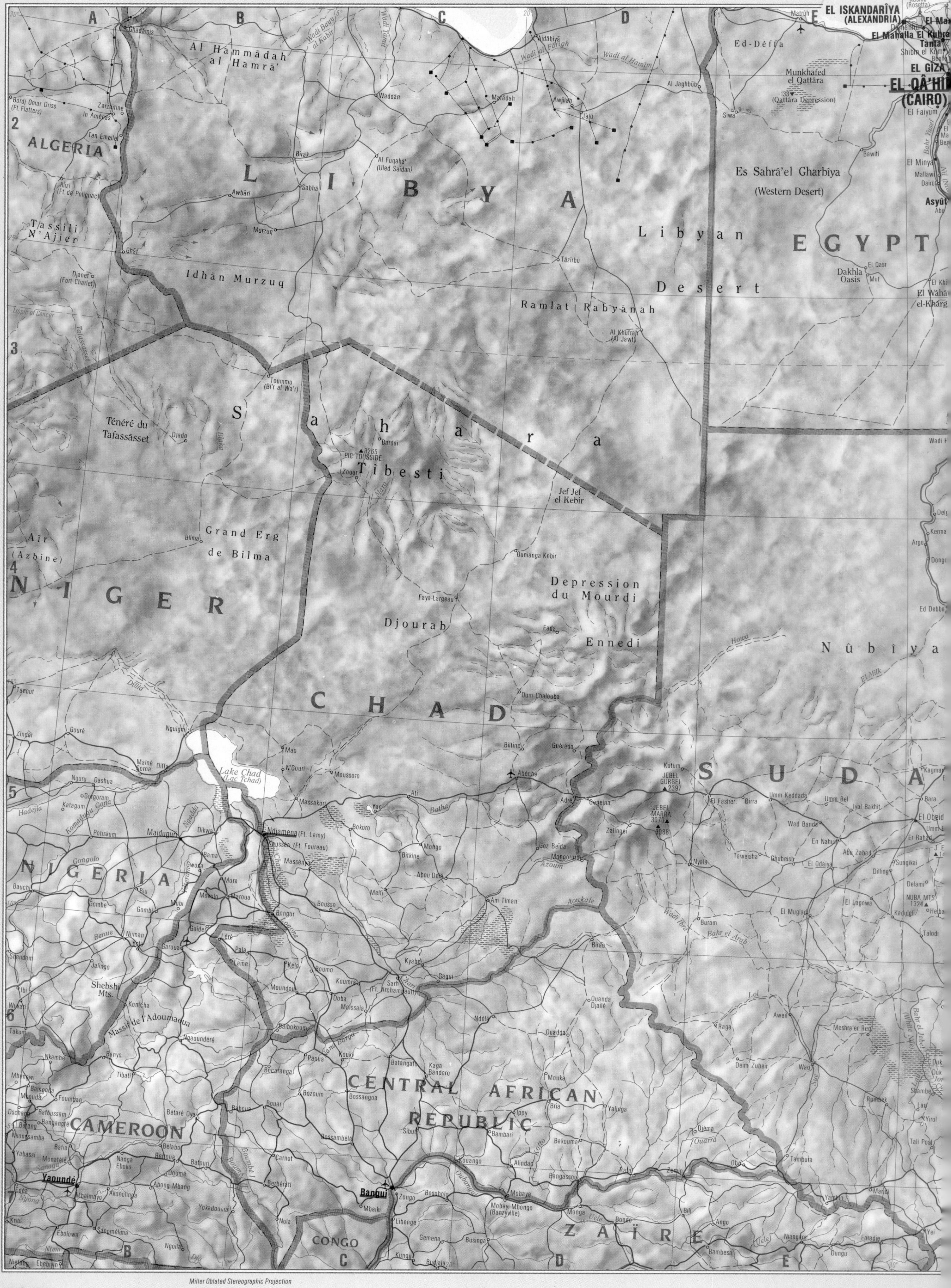
A
B
C
D
E
2
3
4
5
6
7
ALGERIA
L I B Y A
E G Y P T
N I G E R
C H A D
S U D A
NIGERIA
CAMEROON
CENTRAL AFRICAN REPUBLIC
CONGO
ZAÏRE
EL ISKANDARÎYA (ALEXANDRIA)
EL QÂ'HIR (CAIRO)
EL GÎZA
Tanta
Matrûh
Rashîd (Rosetta)
Ed-Déffa
Munkhafed el Qattâra
-133 (Qattâra Depression)
Siwa
Al Jaghbûb
El Faiyum
Bawîti
El Minya
Mallawi
Dairût
Asyût
Es Sahrâ'el Gharbîya
(Western Desert)
Libyan Desert
Dakhla Oasis
El Qasr
Mut
Al Hammâdah al Hamrâ'
Ghadâmis
Bordj Omar Driss (Ft. Flatters)
Zarzaïtine
In Amenas
Tan Emellel
Illizi (Ft. de Polignac)
Tassili N'Ajjer
Ghât
Djanet (Fort Charlet)
Tropic of Cancer
Idhân Murzuq
Murzuq
Awbârî
Sabhâ
Birâk
Al Fuqahâ' (Uled Saidan)
Waddân
Marâdah
Ajdâbiyâ
Awjilah
Jâlû
Wadi al Fârigh
Wadi al Hamim
Tâzirbû
Ramlat Rabyânah
Al Khufrah (Al Jawf)
Toummo (Bi'r al Wa'r)
Ténéré du Tafassâsset
Djado
S a h a r a
PIC TOUSSIDE 3265
Bardai
Zouar
Tibesti
Jef Jef el Kebir
Aïr (Azbine)
Bilma
Grand Erg de Bilma
Ounianga Kebir
Depression du Mourdi
Faya-Largeau
Djourab
Fada
Ennedi
Oum Chalouba
Biltine
Guéréda
Abéché
Tanout
Zinder
Gouré
Nguigmi
Mainé Soroa
Mao
N'Gouri
Moussoro
Lake Chad (Lac Tchad)
Nguru
Gashua
Katagum
Potiskum
Maiduguri
Dikwa
Ndjamena (Ft. Lamy)
Kousséri (Ft. Foureau)
Massakori
Ati
Yao
Batha
Bokoro
Bitkine
Mongo
Massénya
Abou Deïa
Melfi
Am Timan
Goz Beïda
Mongororo
Azoum
Adré
Geneina
Kutum
JEBEL GURGEI 2387
JEBEL MARRA 3070
3088
Zalingei
El Fasher
Dirra
Umm Keddada
Umm Bel
Iyal Bakhit
Wad Banda
En Nahud
El Obeid
Er Rahad
Taweisha
Ghubeish
Abu Zabad
Nyala
El Odaiya
Sungikai
Dilling
Delami
NUBA MTS 1324
Kadugli
Heiban
El Lagowa
El Muglad
Buram
Wadi Ibra
Bahr el Arab
Talodi
Aoukalé
Birao
Nûbîya
Wadi el Milk
Howa
Ed Debba
Dongola
Kerma
Argo
Wadi Halfa
Gombe
Bauchi
Mubi
Gongola
Biu
Bama
Gwoza
Mora
Maroua
Bongor
Bousso
Numan
Yola
Garoua
Guider
Léré
Pala
Lamé
Kélo
Laï
Moundou
Koumra
Doba
Sarh (Ft. Archambault)
Kyabé
Gagui
Jalingo
Shebshi Mts.
Massif de l'Adoumaoua
Ngaoundéré
Baïbokoum
Ouanda Djallé
Ndélé
Ouadda
Raga
Aweil
Meshra'er Req
Deim Zubeir
Wau
Rumbek
Batangafo
Kaga Bandoro
Bossangoa
Bozoum
Bouar
Baboua
Bocaranga
Paoua
Mouka
Bria
Yalinga
Ippy
Bambari
Sibut
Bossambélé
Bakouma
Djéma
Bangassou
Rafaï
Zémio
Obo
Tambura
Yambio
Maridi
Kouango
Alindao
Bangui
Zongo
Bosobolo
Mobaye
Mobayi-Mbongo (Banzyville)
Mbaïki
Libenge
Gemena
Businga
Kungu
Budjala
Monga
Bondo
Bili
Ango
Bambesa
Dungu
Faradje
Yei
Niangara
Nola
Berbérati
Carnot
Batouri
Bertoua
Bélabo
Bétaré Oya
Tibati
Banyo
Nkambe
Kontcha
Foumban
Bafoussam
Bangangté
Bafia
Yabassi
Monatélé
Yaounde
Eboko
Doumé
Abong Mbang
Akonolinga
Mbalmayo
Sangmélima
Ebolowa
Yokadouma
Ngoila
Kribi
Edéa
Nyong
Ntem
Sanaga
Benue
Takum
Wukari
Shendam
Ibi
Mbengwi
Nkongsamba
Dschang
Hadejia
Komadugu Gana
Ngadda
Dillia
Logone
Chari
Ouham
Bamingui
Kotto
Ouarra
Oubangui
Uele
Boumbé I
Boumbé II
Mambéré
Lol
Sue
Bahr el Jebel (White Nile)
Yirol
Tali Post
Juba

Miller Oblated Stereographic Projection

1:9,000,000

0 100 200 300 400 500 600 KILOMETRES

0 50 100 150 200 250 300 350 400 STATUTE MILES

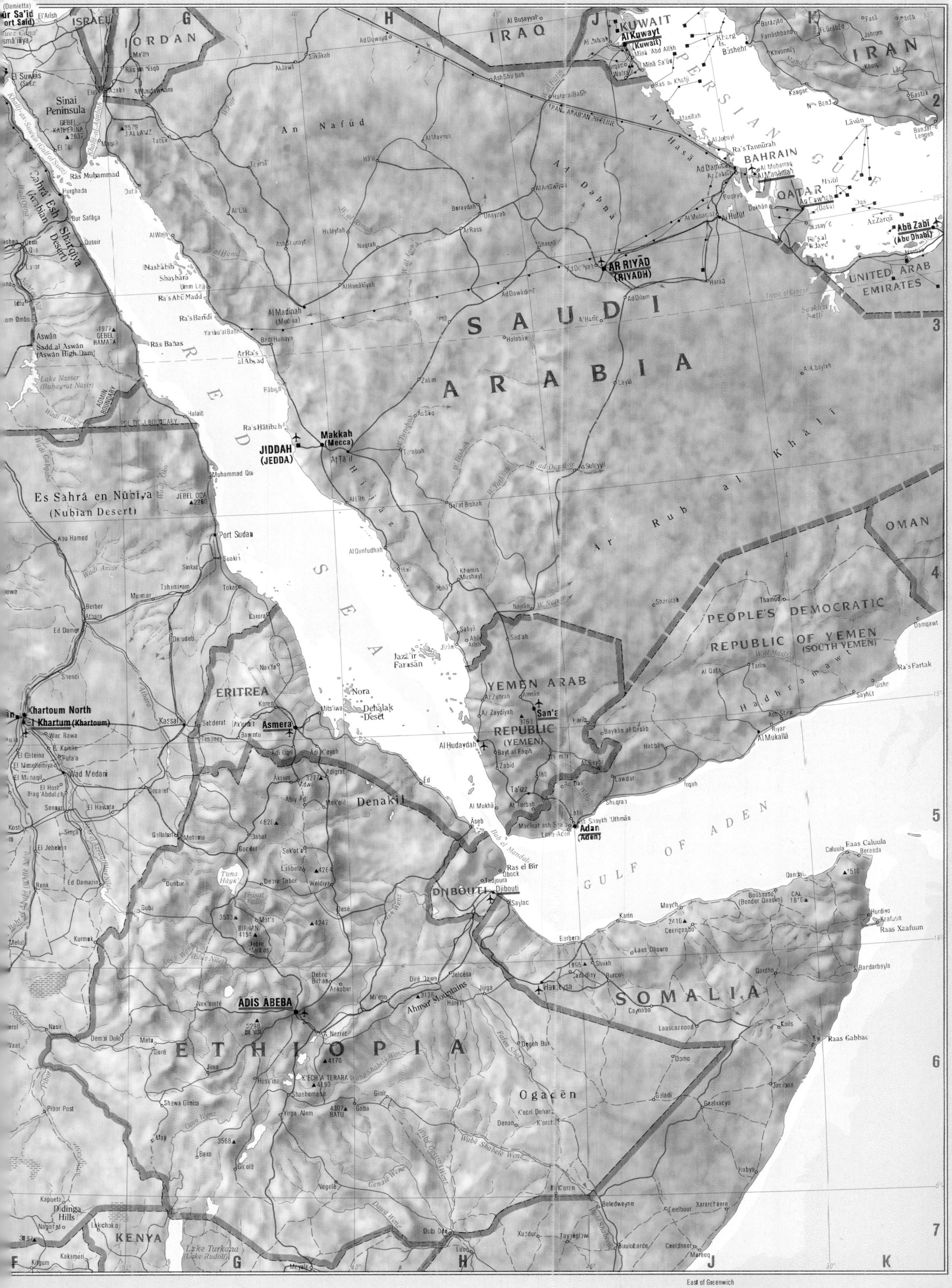
ISRAEL
JORDAN
IRAQ
KUWAIT
Al Kuwayt
(Kuwait)
IRAN
PERSIAN GULF
BAHRAIN
Al Manamah
QATAR
Ad Dawhah
(Doha)
Abū Zabī
(Abu Dhabi)
UNITED ARAB EMIRATES
Sinai Peninsula
An Nafūd
Ad Dahna
SAUDI ARABIA
AR RIYĀD
(RIYADH)
Al Madīnah
(Medina)
Makkah
(Mecca)
JIDDAH
(JEDDA)
At Tā'if
ar Rub al Khālī
OMAN
Tropic of Cancer
RED SEA
Port Sudan
Es Sahrâ en Nûbîya
(Nubian Desert)
Lake Nasser
Aswān
Sadd al Aswān
(Aswān High Dam)
Khartoum North
El Khartum (Khartoum)
Wad Medani
ERITREA
Asmera
Denakil
Jazā'ir Farasān
Dehalak Deset
YEMEN ARAB REPUBLIC
(YEMEN)
San'a
Al Hudaydah
PEOPLE'S DEMOCRATIC REPUBLIC OF YEMEN
(SOUTH YEMEN)
Hadhramawt
Al Mukallā
Adan
(Aden)
Bab el Mandab
GULF OF ADEN
DJIBOUTI
Djibouti
SOMALIA
Hargeysa
Berbera
Raas Caluula
ADIS ABEBA
ETHIOPIA
Ogaden
Ahmar Mountains
Dirē Dawa
Tana Hāyk'
KENYA
Lake Turkana
(Lake Rudolf)
Didinga Hills
Beledweyne
F
G
H
J
K
2
3
4
5
6
7
East of Greenwich

Designed and produced by E.S.R.

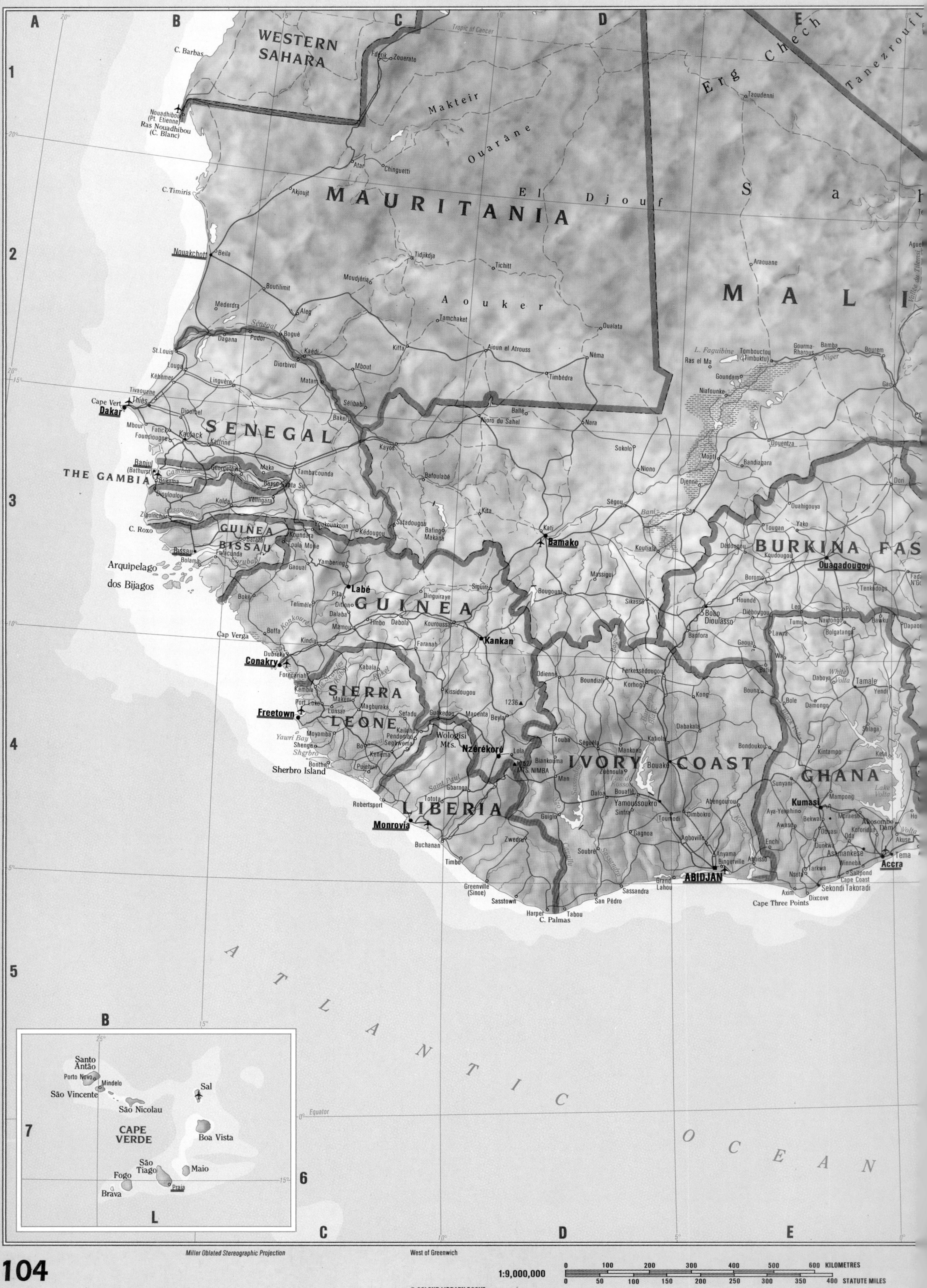
WESTERN SAHARA
MAURITANIA
MALI
SENEGAL
THE GAMBIA
GUINEA BISSAU
GUINEA
SIERRA LEONE
LIBERIA
IVORY COAST
BURKINA FASO
GHANA
CAPE VERDE
ATLANTIC OCEAN
Tropic of Cancer
Equator
Erg Chech
Tanezrouft
Makteir
Ouarâne
El Djouf
Aouker
Sahara
C. Barbas
Fderik
Zouerate
Taoudenni
Nouadhibou (Pt. Etienne)
Ras Nouadhibou (C. Blanc)
Atar
Chinguetti
C. Timiris
Akjoujt
Nouakchott
Beila
Tidjikdja
Tichitt
Araouane
Boutilimit
Moudjéria
Mederdra
Aleg
Tamchaket
Oualata
Dagana
Podor
Bogué
Kaédi
Kiffa
Aioun el Atrouss
Néma
St. Louis
Louga
Kébémer
Diorbivol
Mbout
Timbédra
Linguère
Matam
Tivaouane
Thiès
Cape Vert
Dakar
Diourbel
Sélibabi
Bakel
Ballé
Nioro du Sahel
Nara
Mbour
Fatick
Kaolack
Foundiougne
Kaffrine
Kayes
Banjul (Bathurst)
Brikama
Georgetown
Maka
Tambacounda
Basse Santa Su
Bafoulabé
Sokolo
Niono
Mopti
Bandiagara
Douentza
Djenné
Bignona
Kolda
Vélingara
Ziguinchor
C. Roxo
Kita
Ségou
Youkounkoun
Kédougou
Satadougou
Bafing Makana
Kati
Bamako
San
Koutiala
Bissau
Bolama
Bafatá
Koundara
Arquipelago dos Bijagos
Labé
Pita
Télimélé
Dalaba
Mamou
Boké
Kindia
Dabola
Kouroussa
Kankan
Faranah
Siguiri
Bougouni
Sikasso
Bobo Dioulasso
Banfora
Gaoua
Cap Verga
Boffa
Dubréka
Conakry
Forécariah
Kambia
Port Loko
Freetown
Makeni
Magburaka
Kabala
Kissidougou
Guéckédou
Macenta
Beyla
Odienné
Boundiali
Korhogo
Ferkessédougou
Kong
Bouna
Dabakala
Bondoukou
Katiola
Touba
Séguéla
Bouaké
Man
Daloa
Bouaflé
Yamoussoukro
Sinfra
Toumodi
Dimbokro
Abengourou
Gagnoa
Agboville
Guiglo
Soubré
Anyama
Bingerville
Aboisso
ABIDJAN
Grand Lahou
Sassandra
San Pédro
Tabou
Harper
C. Palmas
Sasstown
Greenville (Sinoe)
Timbo
Buchanan
Monrovia
Robertsport
Gbarnga
Zwedru
Nzérékoré
Lola
Wologisi Mts.
MTS. NIMBA
Sefadu
Kailahun
Kenema
Bo
Moyamba
Shenge
Bonthe
Sherbro Island
Yawri Bay
Pujehun
Tombouctou (Timbuktu)
Ras el Ma
L. Faguibine
Goundam
Niafounké
Gourma-Rharous
Bamba
Bourem
Niger
Ouahigouya
Tougan
Yako
Dédougou
Koudougou
Ouagadougou
Boromo
Tenkodogo
Houndé
Diébougou
Léo
Tumu
Navrongo
Bolgatanga
Lawra
Wa
Daboya
Tamale
Yendi
White Volta
Black Volta
Bole
Damongo
Salaga
Kintampo
Sunyani
Kumasi
Mampong
Bekwai
Obuasi
Akosombo Dam
Lake Volta
Tema
Accra
Winneba
Saltpond
Cape Coast
Sekondi Takoradi
Dixcove
Axim
Cape Three Points
Nsuta
Tarkwa
Dunkwa
Awaso
Aya-Yenahino
Enchi
1236
Santo Antão
Porto Novo
Mindelo
São Vincente
São Nicolau
Sal
Boa Vista
São Tiago
Maio
Fogo
Brava
Praia
Miller Oblated Stereographic Projection
West of Greenwich

1:9,000,000

0 100 200 300 400 500 600 KILOMETRES

0 50 100 150 200 250 300 350 400 STATUTE MILES

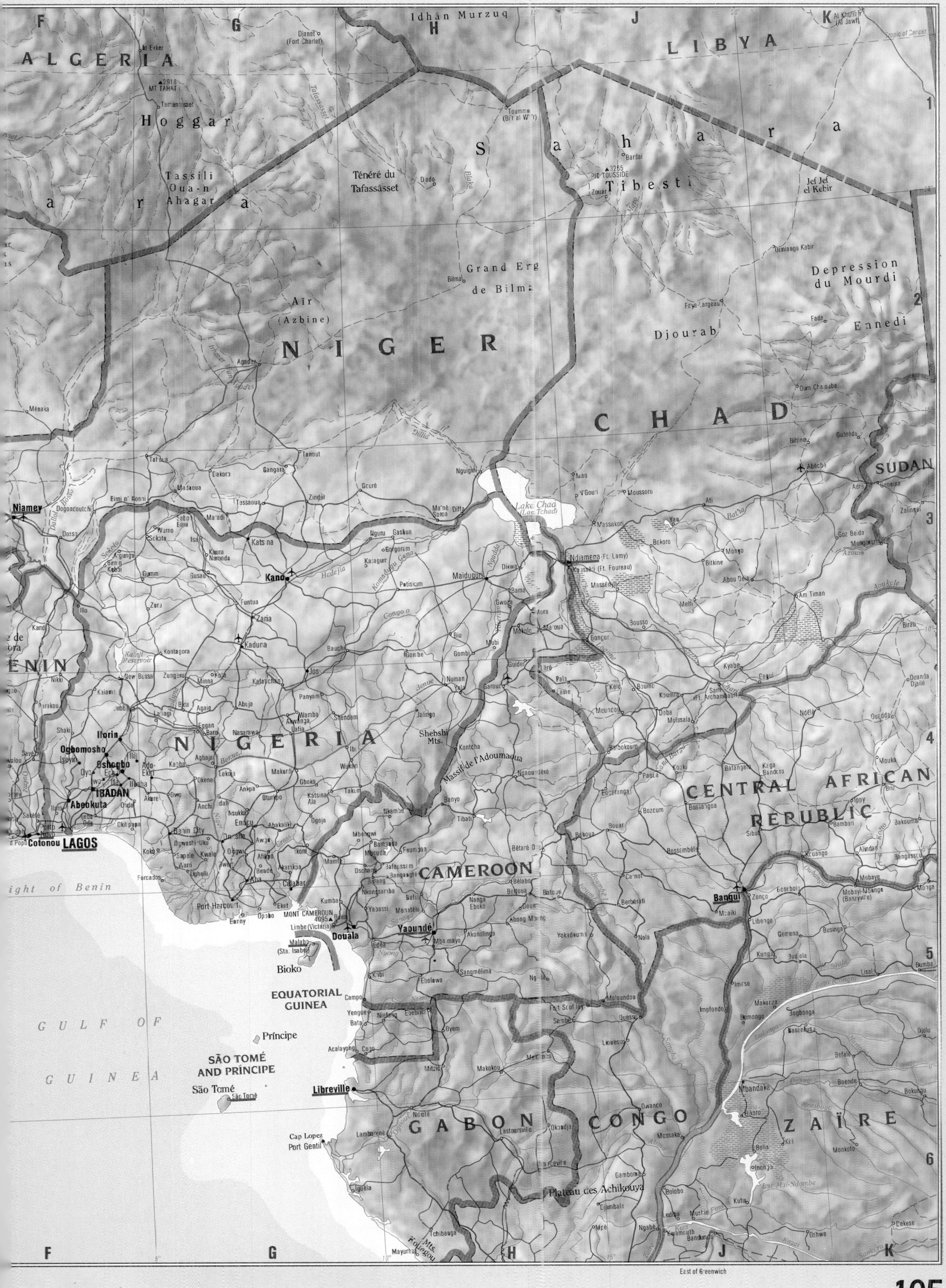

F
G
H
J
K
Idhan Murzuq
ALGERIA
LIBYA
Djanet (Fort Charlet)
In Ekker
2918 MT TAHAT
Tamanrasset
Hoggar
Tassili Oua-n Ahagar
Ténéré du Tafassasset
Dado
Toummo (Bi'r al W...)
Sahara
Bardai
3265 PIC TOUSSIDE
Zouar
Tibesti
Jef Jef el Kebir
Ounianga Kabir
Depression du Mourdi
Grand Erg de Bilma
Bilma
Aïr (Azbine)
Agadez
NIGER
Faya Largeau
Djourab
Fada
Ennedi
Oum Chalouba
CHAD
Ménaka
Tahoua
Tanout
Dakoro
Gangara
Nguigmi
Mao
Niamey
Madaoua
Birni n' Konni
Dogondoutchi
Zinder
Gouré
Mainé Soroa
Diffa
N'Gouri
Moussoro
Abéché
SUDAN
Adré
Geneina
Lake Chad (Lac Tchad)
Tessaoua
Maradi
Katsina
Sokoto
Kano
Nguru
Gashua
Massakori
Bokoro
Ati
Batha
Zalingei
Goz Beïda
Mongororo
Azoum
Ndjamena (Ft. Lamy)
Kousséri (Ft. Foureau)
Massénya
Bitkine
Mongo
Abou Deïa
Melfi
Am Timan
Aoukale
Birao
Dikwa
Maiduguri
Potiskum
Bama
Gwoza
Mora
Maroua
Mokolo
Bousso
Gongor
Zaria
Funtua
Kaduna
Kontagora
Bauchi
Biu
Gombe
Mubi
Guider
Jos
Numan
Yola
Garoua
Léré
Pala
Laï
Kelo
Moundou
Koumra
Sarh (Ft. Archambault)
Kyabé
Ndélé
Ouadda
Ouanda Djallé
BENIN
New Bussa
Minna
Abuja
Kafanchan
Wamba
Awanga
Lafia
Shendam
Jalingo
Shebshi Mts.
Kontcha
Massif de l'Adoumaoua
Ngaoundéré
Doba
Moissala
Baibokoum
Paoua
Batangafo
Kaga Bandoro
NIGERIA
Ilorin
Ogbomosho
Oshogbo
Ado-Ekiti
Ilesha
Ibadan
Abeokuta
Lokoja
Makurdi
Oturkpo
Ogoja
Gboko
Takum
Wukari
Banyo
Tibati
Bétaré Oya
Bouar
Bozoum
Bossangoa
Bossembélé
Sibut
CENTRAL AFRICAN REPUBLIC
Ippy
Bria
Bambari
Bakouma
Alindao
Bangassou
Kouango
Cotonou
LAGOS
Benin City
Onitsha
Enugu
Abakaliki
Warri
Aba
Calabar
Port Harcourt
Mamfe
Bamenda
Foumban
Bafoussam
Dschang
Nkongsamba
Bafia
CAMEROON
Bélabo
Bertoua
Batouri
Carnot
Berbérati
Bangui
Mobaye
Mobayi-Mbongo (Banzyville)
Zongo
Libenga
Gemena
Businga
Lisala
Bumba
Bight of Benin
Forcados
Opobo
Ekeet
MONT CAMEROUN 4095
Kumba
Limbe (Victoria)
Douala
Edéa
Yaoundé
Mbalmayo
Nanga Eboko
Abong Mbang
Yokadouma
Akonolinga
Sangmélima
Ebolowa
Kribi
Malabo (Sta. Isabel)
Bioko
EQUATORIAL GUINEA
Campo
Bata
Ebebiyin
Nola
Ouesso
Moloundou
Fort Soufflay
Souanké
Impfondo
Makanza
Bomongo
Basankusu
GULF OF GUINEA
Príncipe
SÃO TOMÉ AND PRÍNCIPE
São Tomé
Libreville
Oyem
Mitzic
Makokou
Mékambo
Ouesso
Liouesso
Mbandaka
Boende
Bokungu
Djolu
Betale
Cap Lopez
Port Gentil
Lambaréné
GABON
CONGO
Owando
Okondja
Lastoursville
Mossaka
Bikoro
Inongo
ZAÏRE
Kiri
Monkoto
Franceville
Gamboma
Plateau des Achikouya
Djambala
Lac Mai-Ndombe
Bolobo
Mushie
Kutu
Iguéla
Tchibanga
Mayumba
Mts. Kolingou
Mpé
Ngabé
Kwamouth
Bandundu
Oshwe
Dekese
Tropic of Cancer
1
2
3
4
5
6

East of Greenwich

Designed and produced by E.S.R.

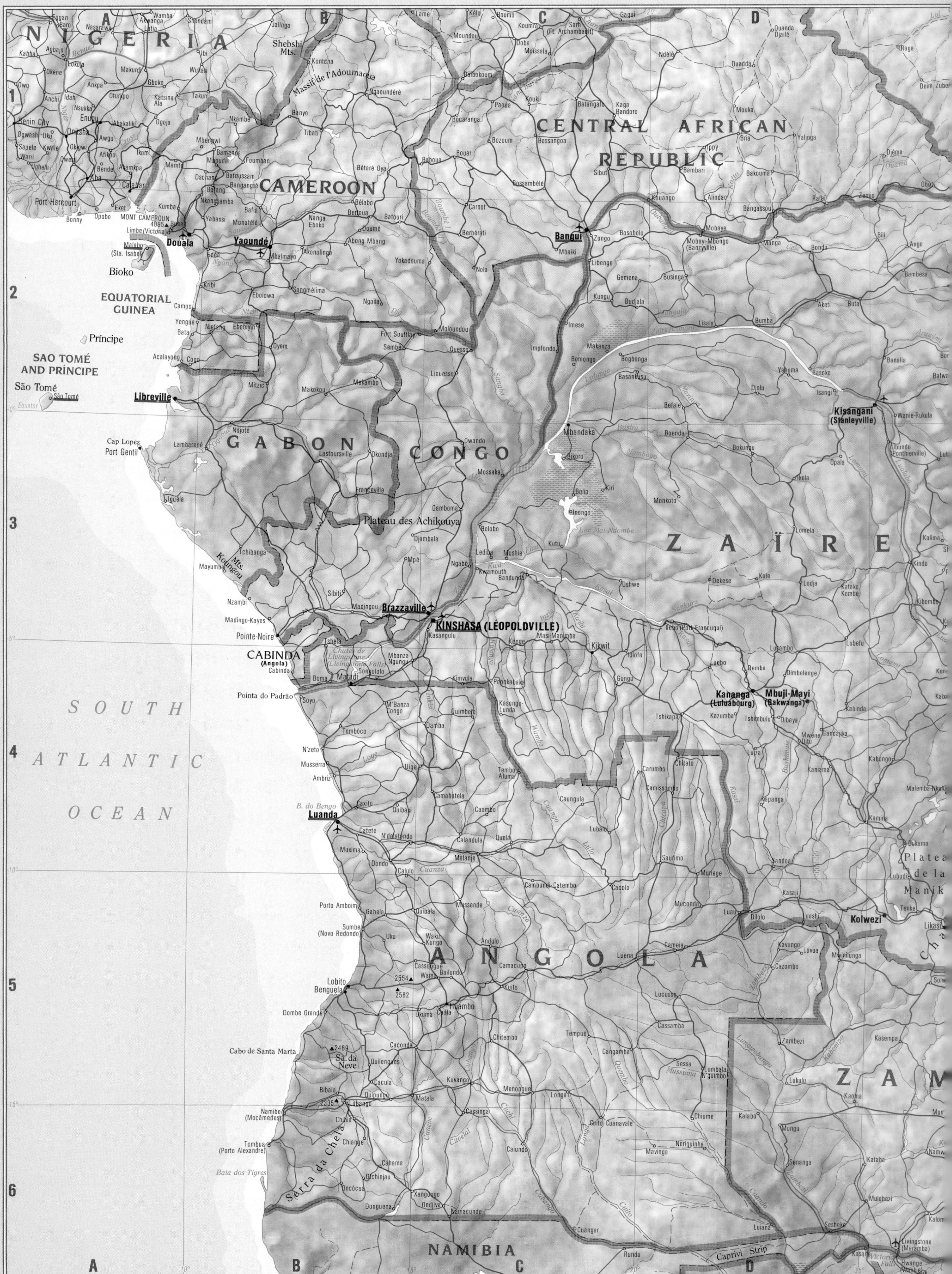

A
B
C
D
1
2
3
4
5
6
NIGERIA
CAMEROON
CENTRAL AFRICAN REPUBLIC
EQUATORIAL GUINEA
SAO TOMÉ AND PRÍNCIPE
GABON
CONGO
ZAÏRE
CABINDA (Angola)
ANGOLA
NAMIBIA
ZAM
SOUTH ATLANTIC OCEAN
Bioko
Príncipe
São Tomé
Equator
Shebshi Mts.
Massif de l'Adoumaoua
Plateau des Achikouya
Mts Koungou
Serra da Chela
Sa. da Neve
Caprivi Strip
Plateau de la Manika
Port Harcourt
Enugu
Benin City
Onitsha
Aba
Calabar
Bonny
Opobo
MONT CAMEROUN
Limbe (Victoria)
Douala
Yaoundé
Malabo (Sta. Isabel)
Kribi
Ebolowa
Campo
Bata
Mbalmayo
Foumban
Bafoussam
Nkongsamba
Kumba
Bafia
Bertoua
Batouri
Bélabo
Nanga Eboko
Doumé
Abong Mbang
Yokadouma
Ngaoundéré
Tibati
Banyo
Meiganga
Garoua
Bétaré Oya
Moundou
Sarh (Ft. Archambault)
Bocaranga
Bouar
Baboua
Bozoum
Bossangoa
Bossambélé
Carnot
Berbérati
Nola
Bangui
Zongo
Mbaiki
Libenge
Gemena
Businga
Kaga Bandoro
Batangafo
Sibut
Bambari
Ippy
Bria
Yalinga
Djéma
Obo
Rafaï
Bangassou
Alindao
Kouango
Mobaye
Mobayi-Mbongo (Banzyville)
Bakouma
Ouadda
Ndélé
Ouanda Djailé
Birao
Bondo
Monga
Bili
Ango
Bambesa
Aketi
Buta
Bumba
Lisala
Kungu
Budjala
Imese
Impfondo
Ouesso
Moloundou
Fort Soufflay
Sembé
Souanké
Liouesso
Makoua
Owando
Mossaka
Gamboma
Djambala
Bolobo
Mushie
Ngabé
Kwamouth
Bandundu
Brazzaville
KINSHASA (LÉOPOLDVILLE)
Kasangulu
Madingou
Sibiti
Mpé
Nzambi
Madingo-Kayes
Pointe-Noire
Cabinda
Tshela
Boma
Matadi
Mbanza-Ngungu
Songololo
Chutes de Livingstone (Livingstone Falls)
Libreville
Cocobeach
Acalayong
Cogo
Oyem
Ebebiyin
Mitzic
Makokou
Mekambo
Ndjolé
Lambaréné
Cap Lopez
Port Gentil
Lastoursville
Okondja
Franceville
Iguéla
Tchibanga
Mayumba
Mbandaka
Bikoro
Bolia
Inongo
Lac Mai-Ndombe
Kutu
Kiri
Boende
Befale
Basankusu
Bogbonga
Makanza
Bomongo
Djolu
Yahuma
Basoko
Isangi
Kisangani (Stanleyville)
Wanie-Rukula
Ubundu (Ponthierville)
Opala
Ikela
Bokungu
Monkoto
Lomela
Dekese
Kole
Lodja
Katako Kombe
Kindu
Kibombo
Oshwe
Ilebo (Port Francqui)
Kikwit
Idiofa
Masi-Manimba
Kenge
Gungu
Popokabaka
Kasongo-Lunda
Tshikapa
Luebo
Demba
Dimbelenge
Lusambo
Lubefu
Kananga (Luluabourg)
Mbuji-Mayi (Bakwanga)
Kabinda
Tshimbulu
Kazumba
Dibaya
Mwene Ditu
Gandajika
Kabongo
Kaniama
Luiza
Kapanga
Kamina
Bukama
Malemba-Nkulu
Lubudi
Sandoa
Kasaji
Dilolo
Luashi
Kolwezi
Tenke
Likasi
Soyo
Pointa do Padrão
M'Banza Congo
Quimbele
Damba
Tomboco
N'zeto
Musserra
Ambriz
Uige
Tembo Aluma
Carumbo
Chitato
Camissombo
Caungula
Lubalo
Camabatela
Caxito
Quibaxi
B. do Bengo
Luanda
Catete
N'dalatando
Caombo
Quela
Calandula
Malanje
Muxima
Dondo
Calulo
Saurimo
Muriege
Cacolo
Cambundi-Catembo
Mucondo
Luau
Porto Amboim
Gabela
Quibala
Mussende
Sumbe (Novo Redondo)
Uku
Waku Kungo
Andulo
Cameia
Luena
Cazombo
Kavungo
Lôvua
Mwinilunga
Cassongue
Wama
Bailundo
Camacupa
Kuito
Lobito
Benguela
2554
2582
Dombe Grande
Ukuma
Caála
Huambo
Lucusso
Cassamba
Tempué
Chitembo
Cangamba
Sessa
Mussuma
Lumbala N'guimbo
Zambezi
Kasempa
Lukulu
Kaoma
Cabo de Santa Marta
2489
Caconda
Quilengues
Cacula
Bibala
2335
Lubango
Quipungo
Matala
Kuvango
Menongue
Longa
Namibe (Moçâmedes)
Chibia
Cassinga
Cuito Cuanavale
Chiume
Kalabo
Mongu
Tombua (Porto Alexandre)
Chiange
Caiundo
Mavinga
Neriquinha
Senanga
Kataba
Baia dos Tigres
Cahama
Chinjau
Oncócua
Xangongo
Ondjiva
Donguena
Namacunde
Cuangar
Rundu
Luiana
Sesheke
Mulobezi
Kasane
Livingstone (Maramba)
Hwange
Zaïre (Congo)
Ubangi
Sangha
Likouala
Lulonga
Kasai
Sankuru
Kwango
Kwilu
Cuanza
Cuango
Chicapa
Cuito
Cubango
Cuando
Zambezi
Lualaba
Lomami
Kunene
Benue
Niger
Cross
Sanaga
Nyong
Ntem
Ogooué
Alima
Lungwebungu
Kabompo
Cuvelai
Cuchi

Miller Oblated Stereographic Projection

1:9,000,000

0 100 200 300 400 500 600 KILOMETRES

0 50 100 150 200 250 300 350 400 STATUTE MILES

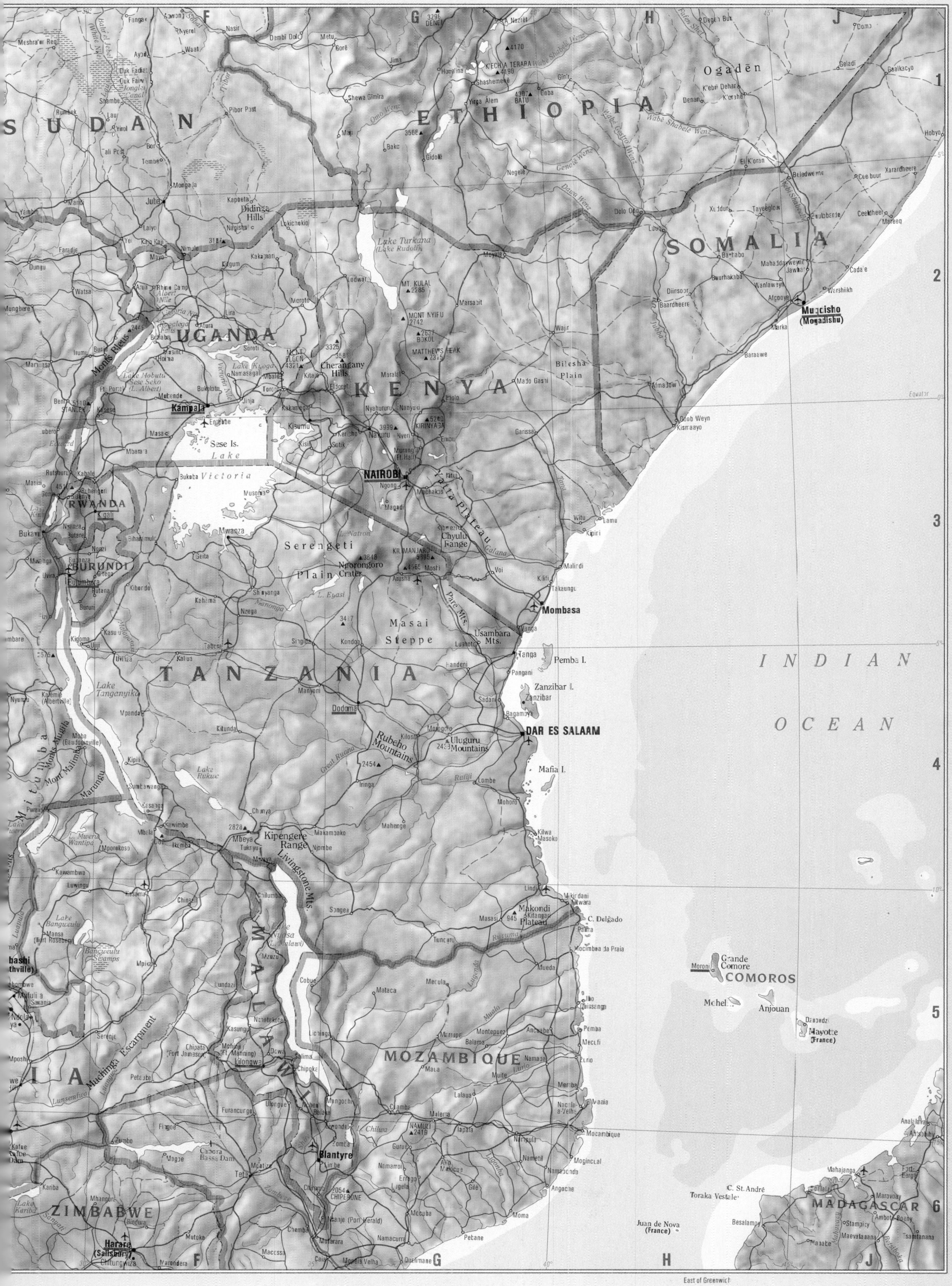

SUDAN
ETHIOPIA
SOMALIA
UGANDA
KENYA
RWANDA
BURUNDI
TANZANIA
MALAWI
MOZAMBIQUE
ZIMBABWE
COMOROS
MADAGASCAR
INDIAN
OCEAN
Ogadēn
Lake Turkana
(Lake Rudolf)
Lake Victoria
Sese Is.
Lake Tanganyika
Lake Rukwa
Lake Kyoga
Lake Mobutu Sese Seko
(L. Albert)
Lake Bangweulu
Lake Kariba
L. Natron
L. Eyasi
L. Chilwa
Serengeti Plain
Ngorongoro Crater
KILIMANJARO 5895
Masai Steppe
Usambara Mts.
Pare Mts.
Uluguru Mountains
Rubeho Mountains
Kipengere Range
Livingstone Mts.
Makondi Plateau
Muchinga Escarpment
Mitumba
Monts Mugila
Mont Malimba
Bilesha Plain
Yatta Plateau
Chyulu Range
Cherangany Hills
Didinga Hills
MT. KULAL 2285
MONT NYIFU 2742
MATTHEW'S PEAK
MT. ELGON 4321
KIRINYAGA 5200
Kagera
Rufiji
Ruvuma
Zambeze
Equator
Mugdisho
(Mogadishu)
NAIROBI
Kampala
Mombasa
DAR ES SALAAM
Dodoma
Kigali
Bujumbura
Blantyre
Lilongwe
Harare
(Salisbury)
Moroni
Zanzibar I.
Pemba I.
Mafia I.
Grande Comore
Mohéli
Anjouan
Mayotte
(France)
Juan de Nova
(France)
C. Delgado
C. St. André
Mahajanga
Juba
Kismaayo
Tanga
Lindi
Moçambique
Quelimane
Tete
Nampula
Kisumu
Nakuru
Arusha
Moshi
Mwanza
Tabora
Kigoma
Mbeya
Iringa
Malindi
Lamu
Marka
Baraawe
East of Greenwich

Designed and produced by E.S.R.

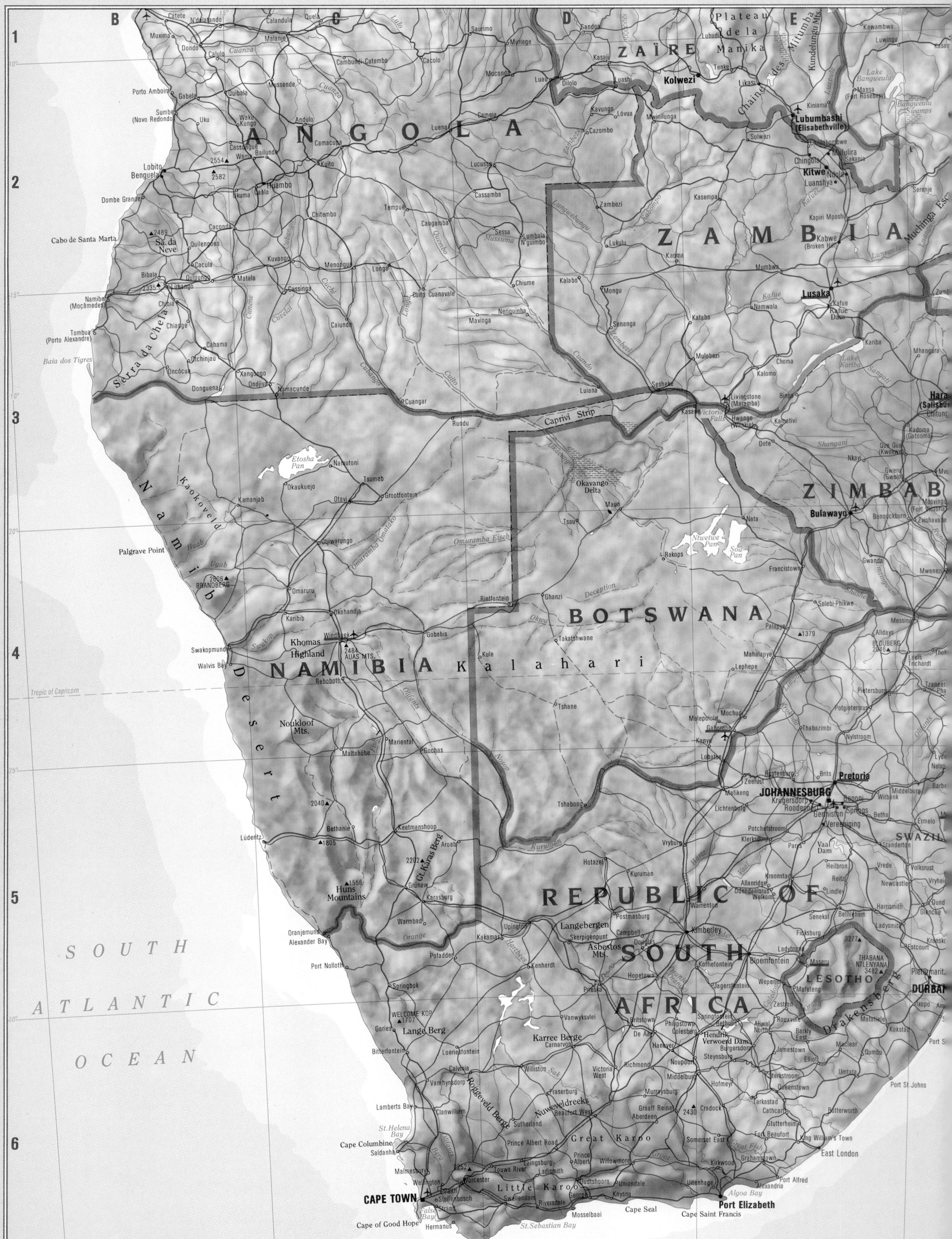
ANGOLA
ZAÏRE
ZAMBIA
ZIMBAB
BOTSWANA
NAMIBIA
REPUBLIC OF SOUTH AFRICA
LESOTHO
SWAZIL
SOUTH ATLANTIC OCEAN
Plateau de la Manika
Kalahari
Namib Desert
Great Karoo
Little Karoo
Caprivi Strip
Okavango Delta
Etosha Pan
Ntwetwe Pan
Sua Pan
Lake Kariba
Lake Bangweulu
Bangweulu Swamps
Khomas Highland
Noukloof Mts.
Huns Mountains
Kaokoveld
Tropic of Capricorn
Drakensberg
Nuweveldreeks
Roggeveld Berge
Lange Berg
Karree Berge
Asbestos Mts.
Langebergen
Gt. Karas Berg
Zambezi
Orange
Cuanza
Cubango
Cuito
Kafue
Limpopo
Vaal
Baia dos Tigres
Cabo de Santa Marta
Palgrave Point
Cape Columbine
Cape of Good Hope
Cape Seal
Cape Saint Francis
Quoin Point
Kaap Agulhas
St. Helena Bay
False Bay
Algoa Bay
St. Sebastian Bay
Luanda
Lobito
Benguela
Huambo
Kuito
Namibe (Moçâmedes)
Tombua (Porto Alexandre)
Sumbe (Novo Redondo)
Porto Amboim
Lubango
Menongue
Cuito Cuanavale
Luena
Saurimo
Kolwezi
Lubumbashi (Elisabethville)
Likasi
Kitwe
Ndola
Chingola
Luanshya
Kabwe (Broken Hill)
Lusaka
Livingstone (Maramba)
Victoria Falls
Hwange (Wankie)
Mongu
Senanga
Kasane
Maun
Nata
Francistown
Ghanzi
Rakops
Serowe
Mahalapye
Palapye
Mochudi
Molepolole
Gaborone
Kanye
Lobatse
Tshabong
Tshane
Tsumeb
Grootfontein
Otavi
Outjo
Okaukuejo
Kamanjab
Otjiwarongo
Omaruru
Okahandja
Karibib
Windhoek
Swakopmund
Walvis Bay
Rehoboth
Gobabis
Mariental
Maltahöhe
Gochas
Keetmanshoop
Bethanie
Lüdentz
Aroab
Karasburg
Grünau
Warmbad
Oranjemund
Alexander Bay
Port Nolloth
Springbok
Rundu
Bulawayo
Gweru (Gwelo)
Kadoma (Gatooma)
Que Que (Kwekwe)
Harare (Salisbury)
Messina
Louis Trichardt
Pietersburg
Potgietersrus
Nylstroom
Thabazimbi
Rustenburg
Zeerust
Mafikeng
Lichtenburg
Pretoria
JOHANNESBURG
Krugersdorp
Roodepoort
Germiston
Benoni
Springs
Vereeniging
Vaal Dam
Witbank
Middelburg
Ermelo
Standerton
Potchefstroom
Klerksdorp
Vryburg
Kuruman
Hotazel
Postmasburg
Kimberley
Warrenton
Welkom
Kroonstad
Bethlehem
Harrismith
Ladysmith
Newcastle
Vryheid
Bloemfontein
Maseru
THABANA NTLENYANA 3482
Pietermaritzburg
DURBAN
Upington
Kakamas
Kenhardt
Prieska
Hopetown
Britstown
De Aar
Colesberg
Hendrik Verwoerd Dam
Burgersdorp
Aliwal North
Queenstown
East London
King William's Town
Grahamstown
Port Alfred
Port Elizabeth
Uitenhage
Graaff Reinet
Aberdeen
Beaufort West
Prince Albert
Oudtshoorn
George
Knysna
Mosselbaai
Riversdale
Swellendam
Worcester
Paarl
Stellenbosch
Strand
Hermanus
CAPE TOWN
Malmesbury
Saldanha
Clanwilliam
Lamberts Bay
Vanrhynsdorp
Calvinia
Sutherland
Fraserburg
Williston
Carnarvon
Victoria West
Richmond
Middelburg
Cradock
Somerset East
Port St. Johns
Umtata
Kokstad
A B C D E
1 2 3 4 5 6

Miller Oblated Stereographic Projection

1:9,000,000

0 100 200 300 400 500 600 KILOMETRES

0 50 100 150 200 250 300 350 400 STATUTE MILES

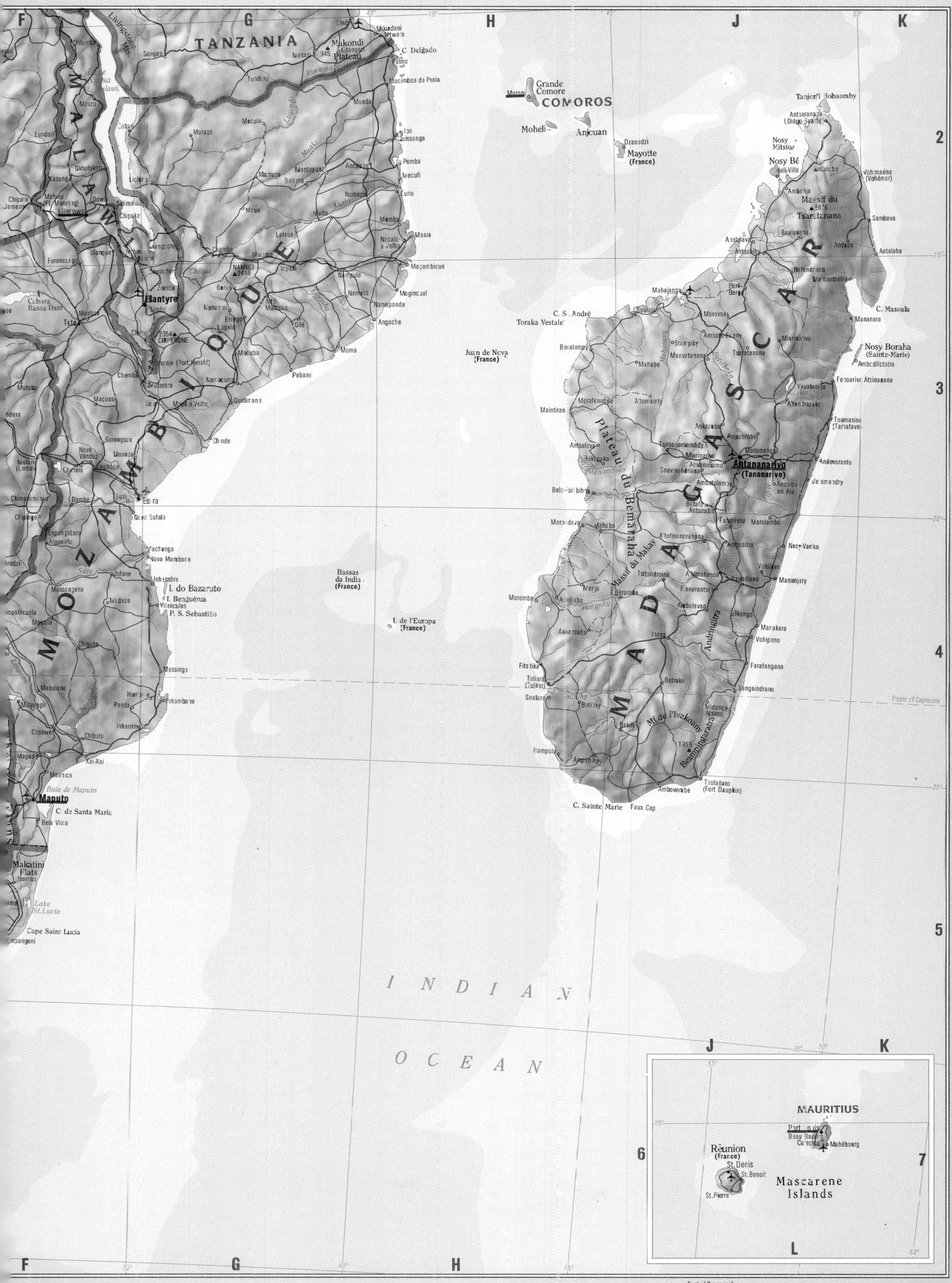

TANZANIA
MALAWI
MOZAMBIQUE
MADAGASCAR
COMOROS
Grande Comore
Moroni
Moheli
Anjouan
Dzaoudzi
Mayotte (France)
Makondi Plateau
C. Delgado
Mocimboa da Praia
Pemba
Nacala
Moçambique
Nampula
Angoche
Quelimane
Chinde
Beira
Nova Sofala
Blantyre
Zomba
Lilongwe
Tete
Cabora Bassa Dam
Inhambane
Xai-Xai
Maputo
Baia de Maputo
C. de Santa Maria
Bela Vista
Makatini Flats
Lake St. Lucia
Cape Saint Lucia
I. do Bazaruto
I. Benguérua
Vilanculos
P. S. Sebastião
Juan de Nova (France)
Bassas da India (France)
I. de l'Europa (France)
Antsiranana (Diégo-Suarez)
Nosy Bé
Hell-Ville
Massif du Tsaratanana
Sambava
Antalaha
Vohémar
Mahajanga
C. S. André
Toraka Vestale
C. Masoala
Nosy Boraha (Sainte-Marie)
Toamasina (Tamatave)
Antananarivo (Tananarive)
Plateau du Bemaraha
Massif du Makay
Antsirabe
Fianarantsoa
Morondava
Morombe
Mananjary
Manakara
Farafangana
Andringitra
Toliara (Tulear)
Mt. de l'Ivakoany
Taolañaro (Fort Dauphin)
C. Sainte Marie
Faux Cap
Ambovombe
Tropic of Capricorn
INDIAN OCEAN
MAURITIUS
Port Louis
Mahébourg
Réunion (France)
St. Denis
St. Benoit
St. Pierre
Mascarene Islands
East of Greenwich

Designed and produced by E.S.R

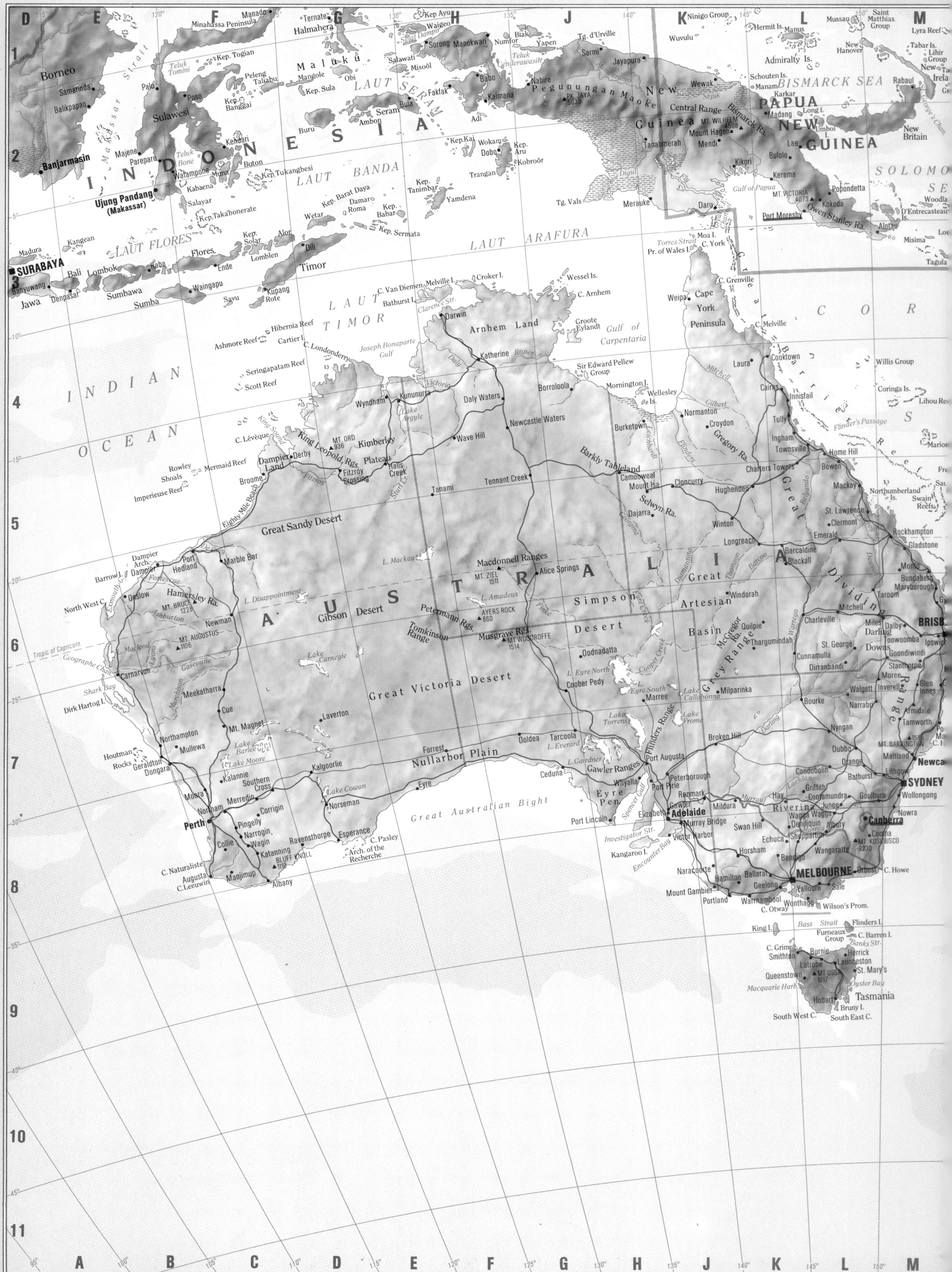
D
E
F
G
H
J
K
L
M
Borneo
Samarinda
Balikpapan
Banjarmasin
Makassar Strait
Manado
Minahassa Peninsula
Ternate
Halmahera
Kep Ayu
Waigeo
Selat Dampir
Sorong
Manokwari
Numfor
Biak
Yapen
Tg. d'Urville
Ninigo Group
Wuvulu
Hermit Is.
Manus
Mussau
Saint Matthias Group
Lyra Reef
Tabar Is.
Lihir Group
New Hanover
New Irela
Admiralty Is.
Teluk Tomini
Kep. Togian
Palu
Poso
Peleng
Taliabu
Kep. Banggai
Sulawesi
Maluku
Mangole
Obi
Kep. Sula
Salawati
Misoöl
LAUT SERAM
Fakfak
Babo
Kaimana
Nabire
Teluk Cenderawasih
Sarmi
Jayapura
Pegunungan Maoke
PK. JAYA 5030
New Guinea
Wewak
Sepik
Schouten Is.
Manam
Karkar
BISMARCK SEA
Rabaul
Central Range
MT. WILHELM 4508
Mount Hagen
Mendi
Tanahmerah
Bismarck Ra.
PAPUA NEW GUINEA
Madang
Long I.
Umboi I.
New Britain
George's Chan.
Lae
Bulolo
Seram
Bula
Buru
Ambon
Adi
I N D O N E S I A
Majene
Parepare
Teluk Bone
Kendari
Buton
Watampone
Muna
Kabaena
Kep. Tukangbesi
LAUT BANDA
Kep. Kai
Wokam
Dobo
Kep. Aru
Kobroör
Trangan
Kep. Tanimbar
Yamdena
Ujung Pandang (Makassar)
Salayar
Kep. Takabonerate
Kep. Barat Daya
Damar
Roma
Wetar
Kep. Babar
Kep. Sermata
Digul
Fly
Kikori
Kerema
Gulf of Papua
MT. VICTORIA 4073
Kokoda
Popondetta
Owen Stanley Ra.
Port Moresby
Alotau
SOLOMON SEA
Woodlark
D'Entrecasteaux Is.
Misima
Tagula
Tg. Vals
Merauke
Daru
Madura
Kangean
LAUT FLORES
Kep. Solar
Alor
Lomblen
Flores
Ende
Dili
Timor
SURABAYA
Bali
Lombok
Raba
Sumbawa
Waingapu
Sumba
Banyuwang
Denpasar
Jawa
Savu
Kupang
Rote
LAUT ARAFURA
Torres Strait
Moa I.
Pr. of Wales I.
C. York
C. Grenville
Weipa
Cape York Peninsula
C. Melville
Great Barrier Reef
C O R
C. Van Diemen
Melville I.
Bathurst I.
Croker I.
Wessel Is.
C. Arnhem
Clarence Str.
Darwin
Arnhem Land
Groote Eylandt
Gulf of Carpentaria
LAUT TIMOR
Hibernia Reef
Ashmore Reef
Cartier I.
C. Londonderry
Joseph Bonaparte Gulf
Katherine
Roper
Daly
Sir Edward Pellew Group
Mornington I.
Wellesley Is.
Borroloola
Laura
Cooktown
Willis Group
Seringapatam Reef
Scott Reef
INDIAN OCEAN
Victoria
Wyndham
Kununurra
Lake Argyle
Daly Waters
Mitchell
Gilbert
Normanton
Croydon
Cairns
Innisfail
Coringa Is.
Lihou Reef
Tully
Ingham
Townsville
Flinders Passage
King Sound
C. Lévêque
MT. ORD 936
Kimberley
King Leopold Rgs.
Plateau
Wave Hill
Newcastle Waters
Burketown
Leichhardt
Flinders
Gregory Ra.
Home Hill
Bowen
Rowley Shoals
Mermaid Reef
Dampier Land
Derby
Fitzroy Crossing
Halls Creek
Sturt Cr.
Barkly Tableland
Camooweal
Mount Isa
Cloncurry
Charters Towers
Mackay
Broome
Imperieuse Reef
Tanami
Tennant Creek
Selwyn Ra.
Hughenden
Northumberland Is.
Swain Reefs
Eighty Mile Beach
Great Sandy Desert
Dajarra
Georgina
Winton
St. Lawrence
Clermont
Burdekin
Belyando
Rockhampton
Gladstone
Longreach
Emerald
Barcaldine
Blackall
Great Dividing Range
L. Mackay
Macdonnell Ranges
MT. ZIEL 1511
Alice Springs
Dampier Arch.
Dampier
Port Hedland
De Grey
Marble Bar
Barrow I.
Fortescue
Hamersley Ra.
MT. BRUCE 1228
Onslow
Exmouth G.
North West C.
Ashburton
L. Disappointment
Gibson Desert
A U S T R A L I A
Petermann Rgs.
L. Amadeus
AYERS ROCK 860
Simpson Desert
Great Artesian Basin
Windorah
Diamantina
Thomson
Barcoo
Dawson
Monto
Bundaberg
Maryborough
Taroom
Mitchell
Charleville
Miles
Dalby
BRISB
Darling Downs
Toowoomba
Ipswich
Newman
MT. AUGUSTUS 1106
Tropic of Capricorn
Tomkinson Range
Musgrave Rgs.
MT. WOODROFFE 1514
Finke
Oodnadatta
McGregor Ra.
Quilpie
Thargomindah
Warrego
St. George
Goondiwindi
Cunnamulla
Dirranbandi
Stanthorpe
Moree
L. Macleod
Lyons
Gascoyne
Geographe Chan.
Carnarvon
Lake Carnegie
Great Victoria Desert
L. Eyre North
Cooper Creek
Grey Range
Milparinka
Gwydir
Inverell
Glen Innes
Shark Bay
Murchison
Meekatharra
Coober Pedy
Eyre South
Marree
Lake Callabonna
Walgett
Dirk Hartog I.
Cue
Laverton
Lake Torrens
Lake Frome
Bourke
Narrabri
Armidale
Tamworth
Mt. Magnet
Darling
Northampton
Mullewa
Lake Barlee
Lake Moore
Forrest
Ooldea
Tarcoola
L. Everard
Flinders Range
Broken Hill
Nyngan
MT. BARRINGTON 1585
Houtman Rocks
Geraldton
Dongara
Kalannie
Southern Cross
Kalgoorlie
Nullarbor Plain
L. Gairdner
Gawler Ranges
Port Augusta
Dubbo
Orange
Maitland
Newcastle
Ceduna
Peterborough
Port Pirie
Whyalla
Condobolin
Lithgow
Bathurst
SYDNEY
Moora
Merredin
Lake Cowan
Eyre
Eyre Pen.
Spencer Gulf
Renmark
Hay
Lachlan
Griffith
Cootamundra
Goulburn
Wollongong
Northam
Corrigin
Norseman
Great Australian Bight
Gawler
Adelaide
Mildura
Murray
Riverina
Junee
Wagga Wagga
Nowra
Perth
Pingelly
Narrogin
Wagin
Ravensthorpe
Esperance
C. Pasley
Port Lincoln
Elizabeth
Murray Bridge
Swan Hill
Deniliquin
Albury
Canberra
Collie
Katanning
BLUFF KNOLL 1110
Arch. of the Recherche
Investigator Str.
Victor Harbor
Encounter Bay
Echuca
Shepparton
Cooma
MT. KOSCIUSKO 2230
Kangaroo I.
Horsham
Bendigo
Wangaratta
C. Naturaliste
Augusta
C. Leeuwin
Manjimup
Albany
Naracoorte
Hamilton
Ballarat
MELBOURNE
Orbost
C. Howe
Geelong
Yallourn
Sale
Mount Gambier
Portland
Warrnambool
Wonthaggi
C. Otway
Wilson's Prom.
Bass Strait
Flinders I.
King I.
Furneaux Group
C. Barren I.
Banks Str.
C. Grim
Smithton
Burnie
Herrick
Launceston
Latrobe
St. Mary's
Queenstown
MT. OSSA 1617
Oyster Bay
Macquarie Harb.
Tasmania
Hobart
Bruny I.
South West C.
South East C.
1
2
3
4
5
6
7
8
9
10
11
A
B
C
D
E
F
G
H
J
K
L
M
120°
125°
130°
135°
140°
145°
150°
95°
100°
105°
110°
115°
5°
10°
15°
20°
25°
30°
35°
40°
45°

Bonne Projection

East of Greenwich

1:19,000,000

0 200 400 600 800 KILOMETRES

0 100 200 300 400 500 STATUTE MILES

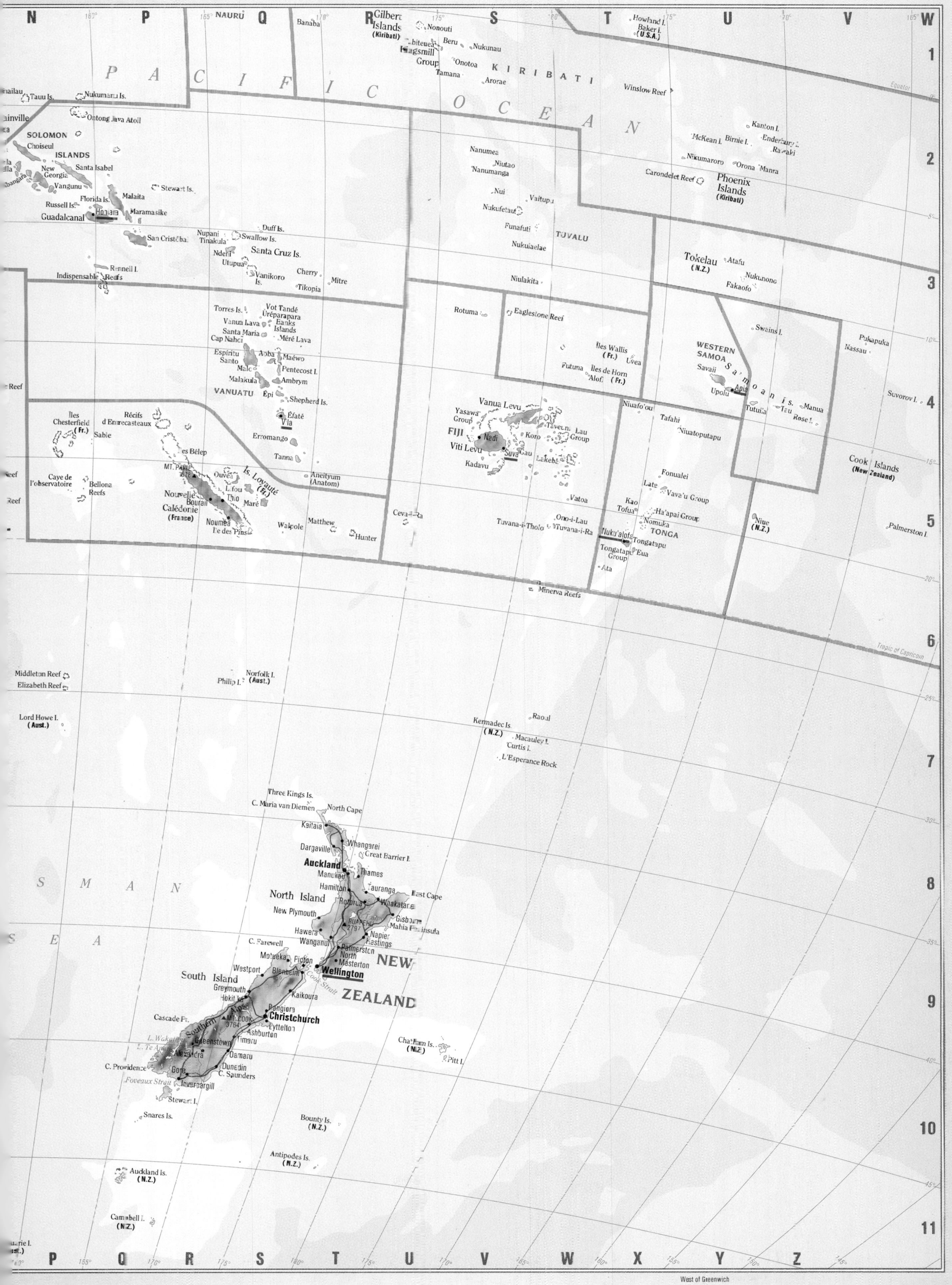

NAURU
Banaba
Gilbert Islands (Kiribati)
Nonouti
Beru
Nukunau
Kingsmill Group
Onotoa
Tamana
Arorae
KIRIBATI
Howland I.
Baker I.
(U.S.A.)
Winslow Reef
Equator
PACIFIC OCEAN
Tauu Is.
Nukumanu Is.
Ontong Java Atoll
SOLOMON ISLANDS
Choiseul
Santa Isabel
New Georgia
Vangunu
Stewart Is.
Malaita
Florida Is.
Russell Is.
Honiara
Maramasike
Guadalcanal
San Cristobal
Duff Is.
Nupani
Tinakula
Swallow Is.
Santa Cruz Is.
Ndeni
Utupua
Vanikoro Is.
Cherry
Mitre
Tikopia
Rennell I.
Indispensable Reefs
Kanton I.
McKean I.
Birnie I.
Enderbury I.
Rawaki
Nikumaroro
Orona
Manra
Carondelet Reef
Phoenix Islands (Kiribati)
Nanumea
Niutao
Nanumanga
Nui
Vaitupu
Nukufetau
Funafuti
TUVALU
Nukulaelae
Niulakita
Tokelau (N.Z.)
Atafu
Nukunono
Fakaofo
Torres Is.
Vot Tandé
Uréparapara
Vanua Lava
Banks Islands
Santa Maria
Cap Nahoi
Méré Lava
Espiritu Santo
Aoba
Maéwo
Malo
Pentecost I.
Malakula
Ambrym
VANUATU
Epi
Shepherd Is.
Efaté
Vila
Erromango
Tanna
Aneityum (Anatom)
Îles Chesterfield (Fr.)
Récifs d'Entrecasteaux
Sable
Bélep
MT. PANIE 1628
Ouvéa
Is. Loyauté (Fr.)
Lifou
Tiga
Maré
Caye de l'observatoire
Bellona Reefs
Nouvelle Calédonie (France)
Bourail
Nouméa
Île des Pins
Walpole
Matthew
Hunter
Rotuma
Eaglestone Reef
Îles Wallis (Fr.)
Uvea
Futuna
Îles de Horn
Alofi (Fr.)
WESTERN SAMOA
Samoa Is.
Savaii
Upolu
Apia
Tutuila
Tau
Manua
Rose I.
Swains I.
Pukapuka
Nassau
Suvorov I.
Vanua Levu
Yasawa Group
FIJI
Nadi
Viti Levu
Suva
Kadavu
Koro
Taveuni
Lau Group
Gau
Lakeba
Niuafo'ou
Tafahi
Niuatoputapu
Fonualei
Late
Vava'u Group
Kao
Tofua
Ha'apai Group
Nomuka
TONGA
Nuku'alofa
Tongatapu
Tongatapu Group
'Eua
Ata
Vatoa
Ono-i-Lau
Tuvana-i-Tholo
Tuvana-i-Ra
Ceva-i-Ra
Niue (N.Z.)
Cook Islands (New Zealand)
Palmerston I.
Minerva Reefs
Tropic of Capricorn
Middleton Reef
Elizabeth Reef
Norfolk I. (Aust.)
Philip I.
Lord Howe I. (Aust.)
Raoul
Kermadec Is. (N.Z.)
Macauley I.
Curtis I.
L'Esperance Rock
Three Kings Is.
C. Maria van Diemen
North Cape
Kaitaia
Whangarei
Dargaville
Great Barrier I.
Auckland
Manukau
Thames
Hamilton
Tauranga
North Island
Rotorua
Whakatane
East Cape
New Plymouth
RUAPEHU 2797
Gisborne
Mahia Peninsula
Hawera
Wanganui
Napier
Hastings
Palmerston North
Masterton
C. Farewell
Motueka
Picton
Wellington
NEW ZEALAND
Westport
Blenheim
Cook Strait
South Island
Greymouth
Kaikoura
Hokitika
Southern Alps
MT. COOK 3764
Rangiora
Christchurch
Lyttelton
Cascade Pt.
Ashburton
Timaru
Queenstown
Alexandra
Oamaru
Chatham Is. (N.Z.)
Pitt I.
C. Providence
Gore
Dunedin
C. Saunders
Foveaux Strait
Invercargill
Stewart I.
Snares Is.
Bounty Is. (N.Z.)
Antipodes Is. (N.Z.)
Auckland Is. (N.Z.)
Campbell I. (N.Z.)
TASMAN SEA
West of Greenwich

Designed and produced by E.S.R.

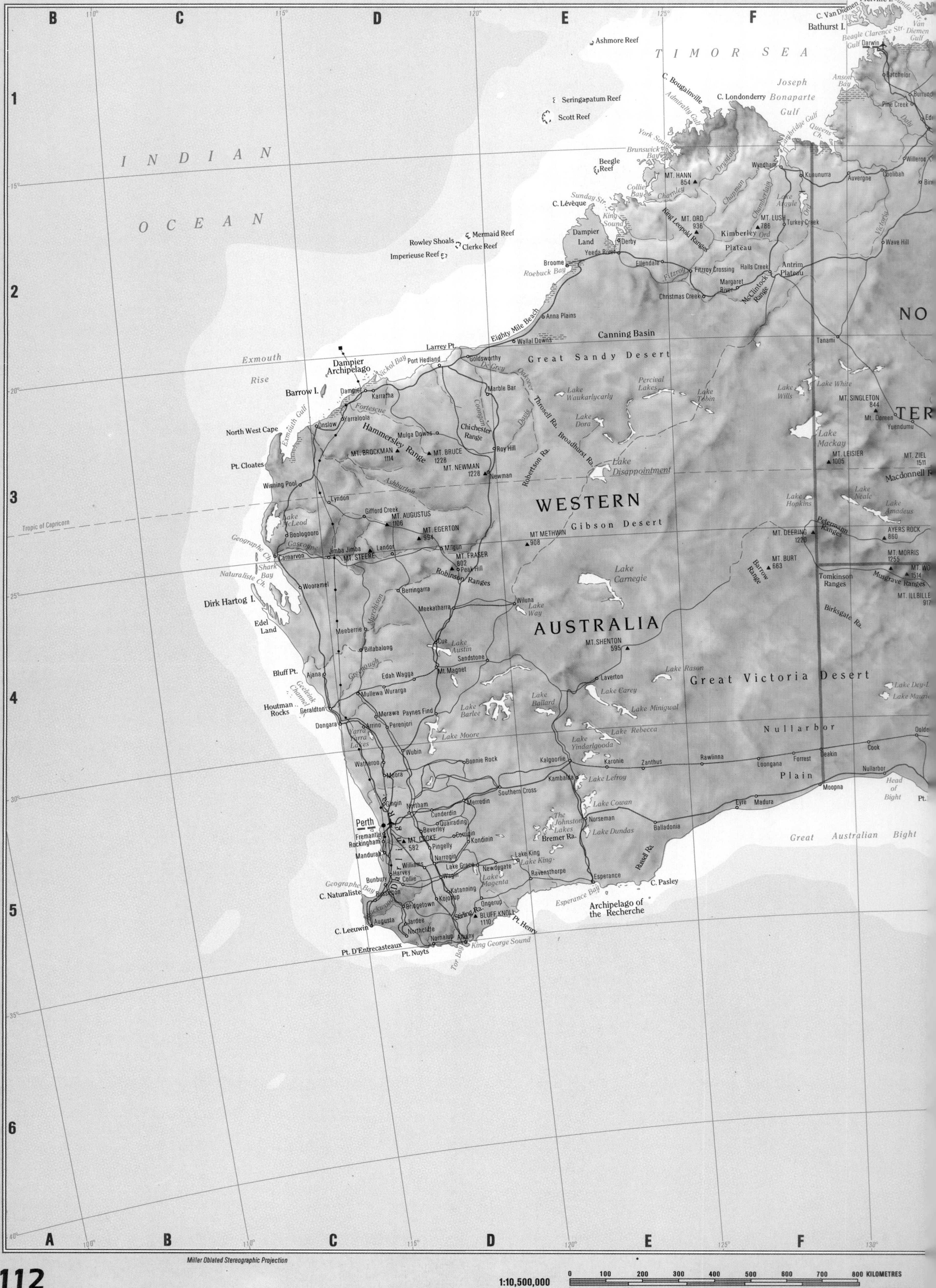
INDIAN
OCEAN
TIMOR SEA
Ashmore Reef
Seringapatam Reef
Scott Reef
Rowley Shoals
Mermaid Reef
Clerke Reef
Imperieuse Reef
Melville I.
C. Van Diemen
Bathurst I.
Beagle Clarence Str.
Van Diemen Gulf
Darwin
C. Bougainville
Admiralty Gulf
C. Londonderry
Joseph Bonaparte Gulf
Cambridge Gulf
Queens Ch.
Anson Bay
Batchelor
Pine Creek
York Sound
Brunswick Bay
Beegle Reef
MT. HANN 854
Drysdale
Wyndham
Kununurra
Auvergne
Willeroo
Collier Bay
Charnley
Chapman
Chamberlain
Lake Argyle
Ord
Sunday Str.
C. Lévêque
King Sound
King Leopold Ranges
MT. ORD 936
MT. LUSH 786
Turkey Creek
Victoria
Dampier Land
Derby
Kimberley Plateau
Yeeda River
Wave Hill
Broome
Roebuck Bay
Ellendale
Fitzroy
Fitzroy Crossing
Halls Creek
Antrim Plateau
Margaret River
McClintock Range
Christmas Creek
Eighty Mile Beach
Anna Plains
Wallal Downs
Canning Basin
Tanami
Larrey Pt.
Port Hedland
Goldsworthy
Great Sandy Desert
Exmouth Rise
Dampier Archipelago
Nickol Bay
De Grey
Oakover
Percival Lakes
Lake Tobin
Lake White
Lake Wills
MT. SINGLETON 844
Mt. Doreen
Yuendumu
Barrow I.
Dampier
Karratha
Marble Bar
Coongan
Lake Waukarlycarly
Exmouth Gulf
Fortescue
Yarraloola
Onslow
North West Cape
Mulga Downs
Hammersley Range
Chichester Range
Throssell Ra.
Lake Dora
Broadhurst Ra.
Lake Mackay
MT. BROCKMAN 1114
MT. BRUCE 1228
Roy Hill
MT. LEISIER 1005
MT. ZIEL 1511
Pt. Cloates
MT. NEWMAN 1228
Newman
Robertson Ra.
Lake Disappointment
Macdonnell Ra.
Winning Pool
Ashburton
Lyndon
WESTERN
AUSTRALIA
Lake Hopkins
Lake Neale
Lake Amadeus
Tropic of Capricorn
Gifford Creek
MT. AUGUSTUS 1106
Lake McLeod
MT. EGERTON 994
Gibson Desert
MT. METHWIN 908
MT. DEERING 1220
Petermann Ranges
AYERS ROCK 860
Boologooro
Geographe Ch.
Gascoyne
Jimba Jimba
Landor
Milgun
Carnarvon
MT. STEERE
MT. FRASER 802
Peak Hill
MT. BURT 663
Barrow Range
MT. MORRIS 1255
Shark Bay
Naturaliste Ch.
Robinson Ranges
Lake Carnegie
Tomkinson Ranges
Musgrave Ranges
MT. ILLBILLE
Wooramel
Berringarra
Dirk Hartog I.
Murchison
Meekatharra
Wiluna
Lake Way
Birksgate Ra.
Edel Land
Meeberrie
Cue
Lake Austin
MT. SHENTON 595
Billabalong
Sandstone
Bluff Pt.
Ajana
Greenough
Edah Wagga
Mt. Magnet
Laverton
Lake Rason
Great Victoria Desert
Geelvink Channel
Mullewa
Wurarga
Lake Carey
Lake Ballard
Lake Minigwal
Houtman Rocks
Geraldton
Morawa
Paynes Find
Lake Barlee
Dongara
Arrino
Perenjori
Lake Moore
Lake Rebecca
Nullarbor
Yarra Yarra Lakes
Lake Yindarlgooda
Wubin
Bonnie Rock
Kalgoorlie
Karonie
Zanthus
Rawlinna
Loongana
Forrest
Deakin
Cook
Watheroo
Moora
Kambalda
Lake Lefroy
Nullarbor Plain
Head of Bight
Southern Cross
Moopna
Gingin
Northam
Merredin
Lake Cowan
Eyre
Madura
Perth
Cunderdin
Quairading
The Johnston Lakes
Norseman
Lake Dundas
Balladonia
Fremantle
Rockingham
Beverley
Corrigin
Kondinin
Bremer Ra.
Great Australian Bight
MT. COOKE 582
Mandurah
Pingelly
Narrogin
Williams
Lake Grace
Newdegate
Lake King
Russell Ra.
Bunbury
Harvey
Collie
Wagin
Lake Magenta
Ravensthorpe
Esperance
C. Pasley
Geographe Bay
C. Naturaliste
Busselton
Katanning
Kojonup
Esperance Bay
Archipelago of the Recherche
Bridgetown
Ongerup
Stirling Ra.
BLUFF KNOLL 1110
Pt. Henry
C. Leeuwin
Augusta
Jardee
Northcliffe
Nornalup
Albany
King George Sound
Pt. D'Entrecasteaux
Pt. Nuyts
Torbay
NO
TER

Miller Oblated Stereographic Projection

1:10,500,000

0 100 200 300 400 500 600 700 800 KILOMETRES

0 100 200 300 400 500 STATUTE MILES

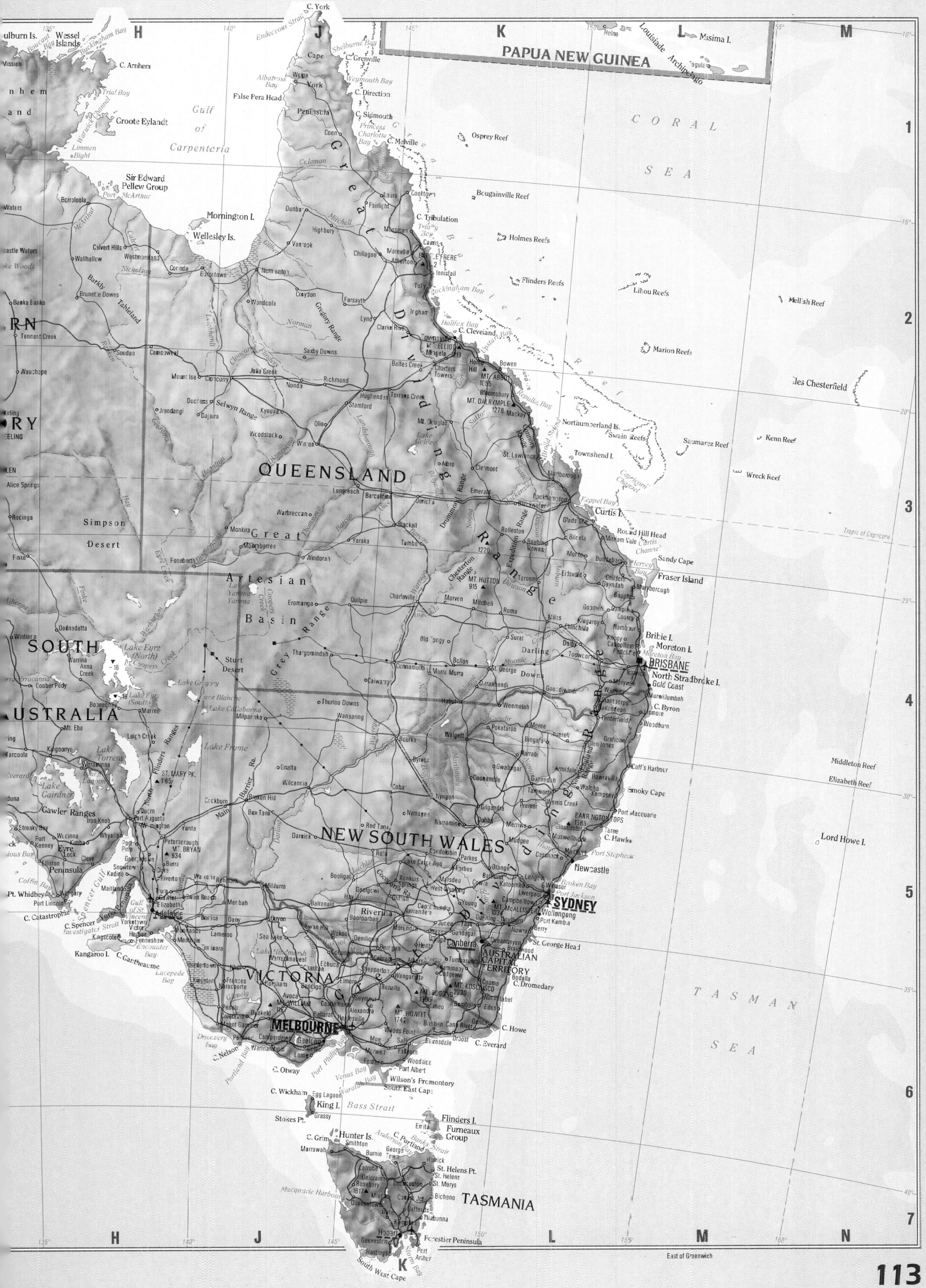
PAPUA NEW GUINEA
CORAL SEA
TASMAN SEA
QUEENSLAND
NEW SOUTH WALES
VICTORIA
TASMANIA
SOUTH AUSTRALIA
AUSTRALIAN CAPITAL TERRITORY
Great Dividing Range
Great Artesian Basin
Simpson Desert
Sturt Desert
Gulf of Carpentaria
Great Barrier Reef
Cape York Peninsula
BRISBANE
SYDNEY
MELBOURNE
Canberra
Adelaide
Newcastle
Wollongong
Hobart
Townsville
Cairns
Mackay
Rockhampton
Bundaberg
Maryborough
Gold Coast
Toowoomba
Mount Isa
Cloncurry
Longreach
Charleville
Roma
Broken Hill
Wilcannia
Bourke
Dubbo
Orange
Bathurst
Wagga Wagga
Albury
Bendigo
Ballarat
Geelong
Launceston
Riverina
Lake Eyre (North)
Lake Eyre (South)
Lake Torrens
Lake Gairdner
Lake Frome
Bass Strait
King I.
Flinders I.
Furneaux Group
Kangaroo I.
Fraser Island
Moreton I.
North Stradbroke I.
Groote Eylandt
Mornington I.
Wellesley Is.
Sir Edward Pellew Group
Lord Howe I.
Middleton Reef
Elizabeth Reef
Osprey Reef
Bougainville Reef
Holmes Reefs
Flinders Reefs
Lihou Reefs
Mellish Reef
Marion Reefs
Kenn Reef
Saumarez Reef
Wreck Reef
Louisiade Archipelago
Misima I.
C. York
C. Melville
C. Byron
C. Howe
C. Otway
Wilson's Promontory
South East Cape
South West Cape
Tropic of Capricorn
MT. KOSCIUSKO 2230
East of Greenwich

Designed and produced by E.S.R.

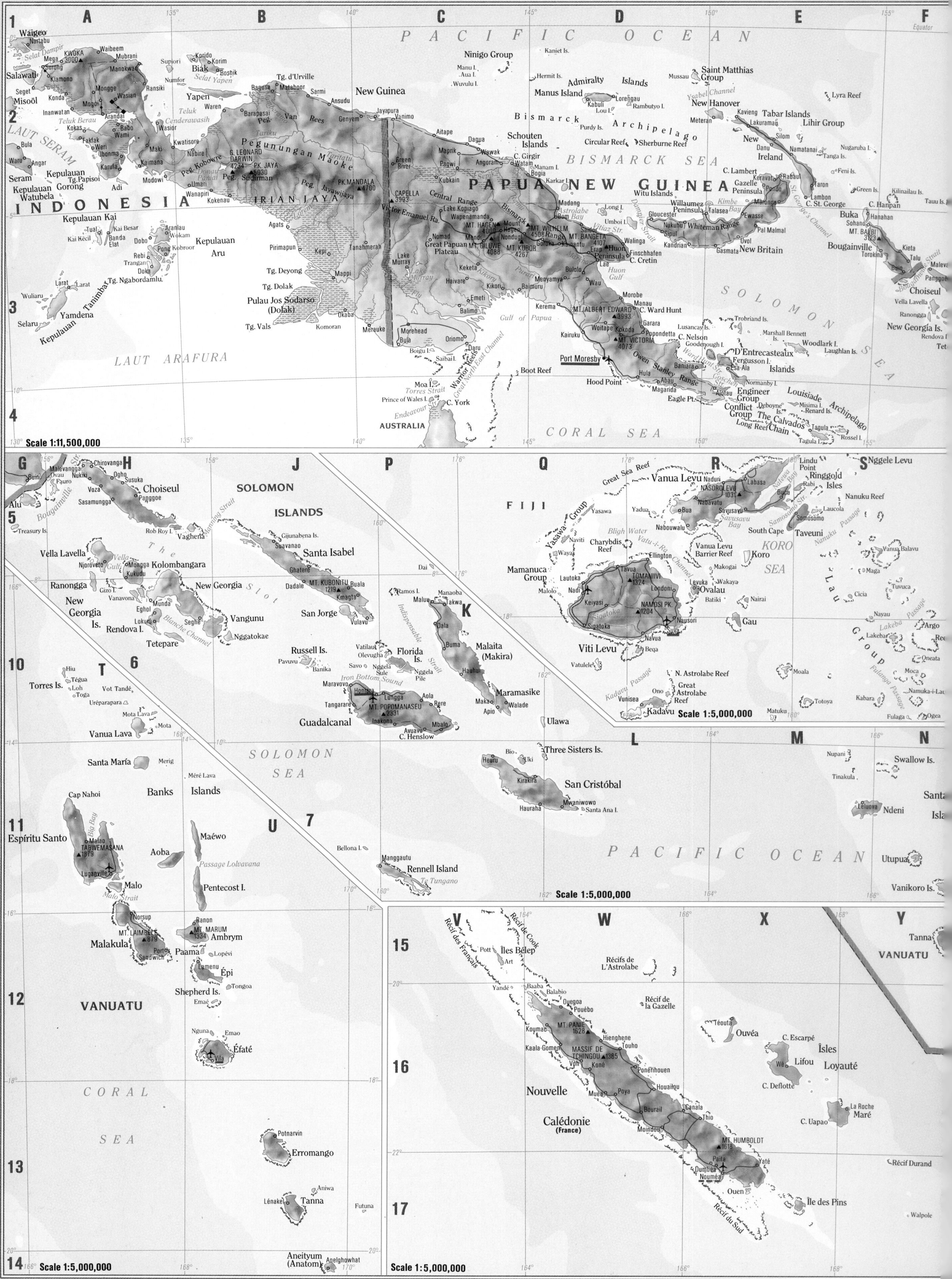
PACIFIC OCEAN
Equator
Ninigo Group
Admiralty Islands
Manus Island
Saint Matthias Group
New Hanover
Lyra Reef
Tabar Islands
Lihir Group
Bismarck Archipelago
BISMARCK SEA
New Ireland
Schouten Islands
New Guinea
Waigeo
Salawati
Misoöl
Biak
Yapen
Teluk Cenderawasih
LAUT SERAM
Seram
Kepulauan Gorong
Kepulauan Watubela
INDONESIA
IRIAN JAYA
Pegunungan Maoke
PK. JAYA 5030
Kepulauan Kai
Kepulauan Aru
Kepulauan Tanimbar
Yamdena
LAUT ARAFURA
Pulau Jos Sodarso (Dolak)
Tg. Vals
PAPUA NEW GUINEA
Central Range
MT. WILHELM 4508
Victor Emanuel Ra.
Great Papuan Plateau
Gulf of Papua
Port Moresby
Owen Stanley Range
MT. VICTORIA 4073
MT. ALBERT EDWARD 3993
Huon Gulf
Boot Reef
Torres Strait
C. York
AUSTRALIA
CORAL SEA
New Britain
Whiteman Range
Witu Islands
Trobriand Is.
Woodlark I.
D'Entrecasteaux Islands
Louisiade Archipelago
Buka
Bougainville
MT. BALBI 3123
Choiseul
New Georgia Is.
SOLOMON SEA
Scale 1:11,500,000
SOLOMON ISLANDS
Santa Isabel
Vella Lavella
Kolombangara
New Georgia
Vangunu
Rendova I.
Tetepare
The Slot
Russell Is.
Florida Is.
Guadalcanal
MT. POPOMANASEU 2331
Honiara
Malaita (Makira)
Maramasike
Ulawa
Three Sisters Is.
San Cristóbal
SOLOMON SEA
Rennell Island
Bellona I.
Santa Cruz Islands
Ndeni
Utupua
Vanikoro Is.
PACIFIC OCEAN
Scale 1:5,000,000
FIJI
Vanua Levu
Taveuni
Yasawa Group
Viti Levu
TOMANIIVI 1324
Suva
Nadi
Lautoka
Ovalau
KORO SEA
Koro
Lau Group
Kadavu
Great Astrolabe Reef
Scale 1:5,000,000
Torres Is.
Vanua Lava
Banks Islands
Espíritu Santo
TABWEMASANA 1879
Maéwo
Aoba
Pentecost I.
Malo
Malakula
Ambrym
Paama
Épi
Shepherd Is.
VANUATU
Éfaté
Vila
CORAL SEA
Erromango
Tanna
Aneityum (Anatom)
Scale 1:5,000,000
Récif de Cook
Récif des Français
Îles Belep
Récifs de L'Astrolabe
Récif de la Gazelle
Ouvéa
Îles Loyauté
Lifou
Maré
Nouvelle Calédonie (France)
MT. PANIÉ 1628
MT. HUMBOLDT 1618
Nouméa
Île des Pins
Récif du Sud
Récif Durand
Walpole
VANUATU
Tanna
Scale 1:5,000,000

Miller Oblated Stereographic Projection

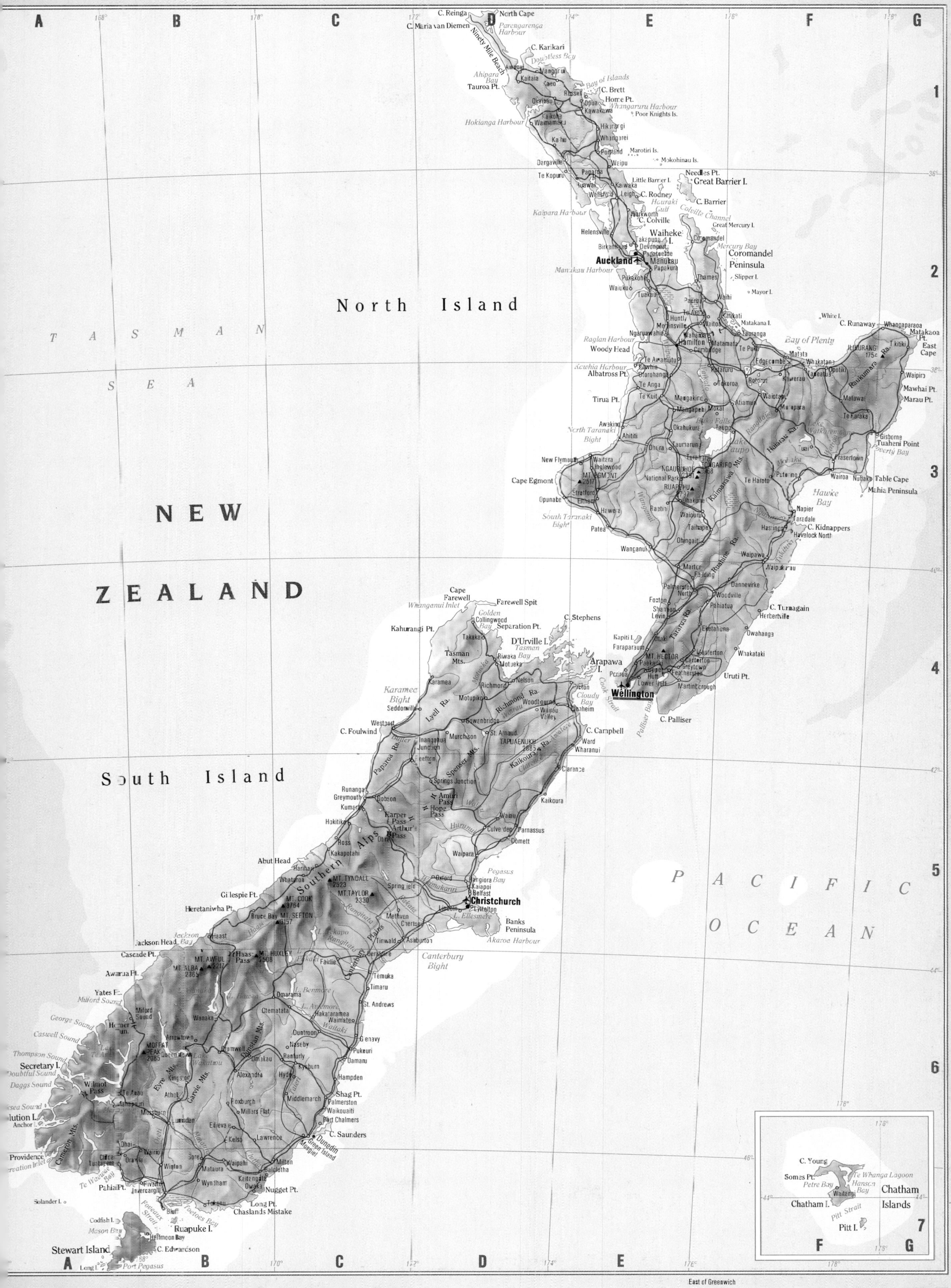
A
B
C
D
E
F
G
1
2
3
4
5
6
7
North Island
South Island
NEW ZEALAND
TASMAN SEA
PACIFIC OCEAN
C. Reinga
North Cape
C. Maria van Diemen
Parengarenga Harbour
Ninety Mile Beach
C. Karikari
Doubtless Bay
Ahipara Bay
Tauroa Pt.
Kaitaia
Bay of Islands
C. Brett
Russell
Opua
Kawakawa
Whangaruru Harbour
Poor Knights Is.
Hokianga Harbour
Kaikohe
Hikurangi
Whangarei
Marotiri Is.
Mokohinau Is.
Dargaville
Te Kopuru
Paparoa
Needles Pt.
Great Barrier I.
Little Barrier I.
C. Rodney
Hauraki Gulf
C. Barrier
Colville Channel
Kaipara Harbour
Warkworth
C. Colville
Great Mercury I.
Helensville
Waiheke I.
Coromandel
Mercury Bay
Auckland
Manukau
Papakura
Coromandel Peninsula
Manukau Harbour
Pukekohe
Thames
Slipper I.
Waiuku
Tuakau
Waihi
Mayor I.
Katikati
White I.
C. Runaway
Whangaparaoa
Matakaoa Pt.
East Cape
Huntly
Matakana I.
Tauranga
Bay of Plenty
Raglan Harbour
Hamilton
Woody Head
Cambridge
Te Puke
Matata
Edgecumbe
Whakatane
Opotiki
HIKURANGI 1754
Raukumara Ra.
Te Awamutu
Kawhia Harbour
Kawhia
Albatross Pt.
Otorohanga
Putaruru
Rotorua
Tokoroa
Te Kuiti
Waipiro
Mawhai Pt.
Marau Pt.
Tirua Pt.
Mangakino
Atiamuri
Mangapehi
Murupara
Te Karaka
Awakino
North Taranaki Bight
Okahukura
Huka Falls
Taupo
Lake Taupo
Gisborne
Tuaheni Point
Poverty Bay
Ohura
Taumarunui
New Plymouth
Waitara
Inglewood
TONGARIRO
NGAURUHOE
National Park
RUAPEHU
MT. EGMONT 2517
Cape Egmont
Opunake
Stratford
Eltham
Hawera
Raetihi
Waiouru
Kaimanawa Mts.
Te Haroto
Frasertown
Wairoa
Nuhaka
Table Cape
Mahia Peninsula
Hawke Bay
Napier
Taradale
Hastings
C. Kidnappers
Havelock North
South Taranaki Bight
Patea
Taihape
Wanganui
Ohingaiti
Waipawa
Waipukurau
Marton
Feilding
Ruahine Ra.
Palmerston North
Dannevirke
Woodville
Foxton
Shannon
Levin
Pahiatua
C. Turnagain
Herbertville
Tararua Ra.
Eketahuna
Owahanga
Kapiti I.
Paraparaumu
Otaki
MT. HECTOR
Masterton
Carterton
Greytown
Featherston
Whakataki
Uruti Pt.
Porirua
Upper Hutt
Lower Hutt
Martinborough
Wellington
Palliser Bay
C. Palliser
Cape Farewell
Farewell Spit
Whanganui Inlet
Golden Bay
Collingwood
Separation Pt.
C. Stephens
Kahurangi Pt.
Takaka
D'Urville I.
Tasman Bay
Tasman Mts.
Riwaka
Motueka
Arapawa I.
Cook Strait
Karamea
Nelson
Richmond
Picton
Karamea Bight
Motupiko
Richmond Ra.
Cloudy Bay
Seddonville
Lyell Ra.
Blenheim
Westport
C. Foulwind
Murchison
St. Arnaud
C. Campbell
TAPUAENUKU 2885
Ward
Paparoa Ra.
Inangahua Junction
Spenser Mts.
Kaikoura Ra.
Reefton
Clarence
Springs Junction
Runanga
Greymouth
Kumara
Amuri Pass
Hope Pass
Kaikoura
Hokitika
Harper Pass
Arthur's Pass
Culverden
Parnassus
Domett
Ross
Kakapotahi
Southern Alps
Waipara
Abut Head
Harihari
Whataroa
MT. TYNDALL 2523
MT. TAYLOR 2330
Oxford
Rangiora
Kaiapoi
Belfast
Pegasus Bay
Gillespie Pt.
MT. COOK 3764
Springfield
Christchurch
Lyttelton
Heretaniwha Pt.
Bruce Bay
MT. SEFTON 3157
Methven
Lincoln
L. Ellesmere
Banks Peninsula
Akaroa Harbour
Jackson Head
Jackson Bay
Haast
Tinwald
Ashburton
Canterbury Plains
Cascade Pt.
MT. ASPIRING
Haast Pass
MT. HUXLEY 2505
Geraldine
Canterbury Bight
MT. ALBA 2365
Fairlie
Awarua Pt.
Temuka
Timaru
Yates Pt.
Milford Sound
Omarama
L. Benmore
Otematata
L. Aviemore
St. Andrews
Hakataramea
Waimate
Wanaka
George Sound
Homer Tun.
Waitaki
Caswell Sound
Arrowtown
Glenavy
MOFFAT PEAK 2085
Queenstown
Naseby
Thompson Sound
Cromwell
Dunstan Mts.
Pukeuri
Oamaru
Secretary I.
Doubtful Sound
Omakau
Ranfurly
Kyeburn
Hampden
Daggs Sound
Wilmot Pass
Kingston
Alexandra
Hyde
Eyre Mts.
Garvie Mts.
Shag Pt.
Palmerston
Waikouaiti
Port Chalmers
Te Anau
Athol
Middlemarch
Manapouri
Dusky Sound
Resolution I.
Mossburn
Lumsden
Millers Flat
Anchor I.
Edievale
Kelso
Lawrence
C. Saunders
Dunedin
Mosgiel
Cameron Mts.
Green Island
Providence
Preservation Inlet
Tuatapere
Ohai
Otautau
Winton
Gore
Mataura
Milton
Balclutha
Te Waewae Bay
Pahia Pt.
Riverton
Invercargill
Wyndham
Kaitangata
Owaka
Nugget Pt.
Solander I.
Bluff
Foveaux Strait
Toetoes Bay
Tokanui
Long Pt.
Chaslands Mistake
Codfish I.
Mason Bay
Ruapuke I.
Halfmoon Bay
C. Edwardson
Stewart Island
Long I.
Port Pegasus
C. Young
Somes Pt.
Petre Bay
Te Whanga Lagoon
Hanson Bay
Waitangi
Chatham I.
Chatham Islands
Pitt Strait
Pitt I.
East of Greenwich

1:4,500,000

0 50 100 150 200 250 300 KILOMETRES

0 50 100 150 200 STATUTE MILES

Designed and produced by E.S.R.

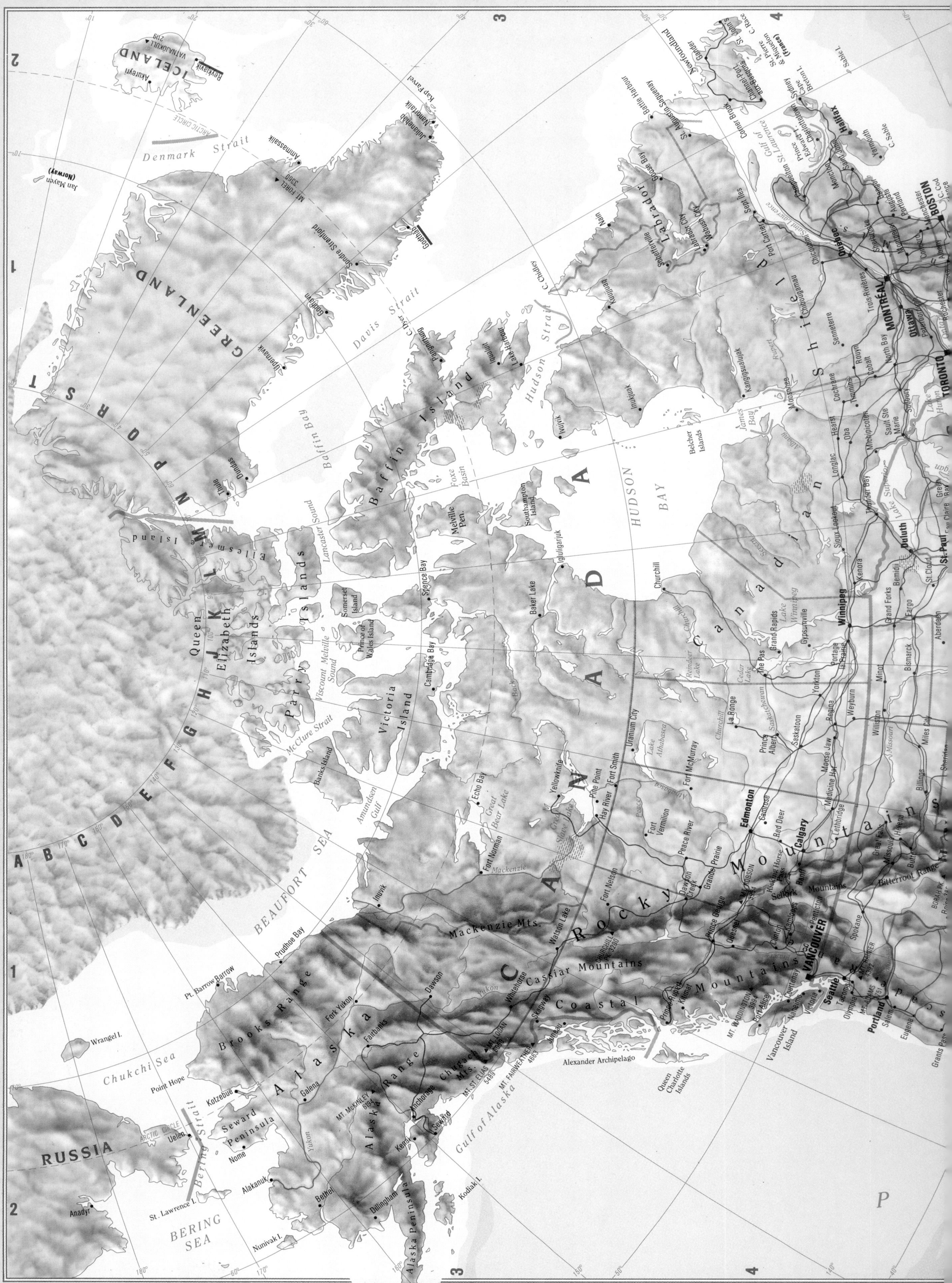
GREENLAND
ICELAND
CANADA
Alaska
RUSSIA
HUDSON BAY
BEAUFORT SEA
BERING SEA
Chukchi Sea
Gulf of Alaska
Baffin Bay
Davis Strait
Denmark Strait
Hudson Strait
Bering Strait
Baffin Island
Victoria Island
Banks Island
Ellesmere Island
Queen Elizabeth Islands
Parry Islands
Southampton Island
Vancouver Island
Queen Charlotte Islands
Alexander Archipelago
Labrador
Seward Peninsula
Alaska Peninsula
Brooks Range
Alaska Range
Mackenzie Mts.
Cassiar Mountains
Coastal Mountains
Rocky Mountains
Selkirk Mountains
Great Bear Lake
Great Slave Lake
Lake Athabasca
Lake Winnipeg
Lake Superior
Wrangel I.
Kodiak I.
Nunivak I.
St. Lawrence I.
Jan Mayen (Norway)
St. Pierre & Miquelon (France)
Newfoundland
Anadyr
Nome
Kotzebue
Point Hope
Pt. Barrow
Prudhoe Bay
Inuvik
Fairbanks
Anchorage
Dawson
Whitehorse
Juneau
Yellowknife
Churchill
Baker Lake
Winnipeg
Edmonton
Calgary
Saskatoon
Regina
VANCOUVER
Seattle
Portland
Spokane
Duluth
Thunder Bay
Sudbury
TORONTO
Ottawa
MONTRÉAL
Québec
Halifax
BOSTON
Lambert Azimuthal Equal Area Projection

1:20,000,000

0 100 200 300 400 500 600 700 800 900 1000 KILOMETRES

0 100 200 300 400 500 600 STATUTE MILES

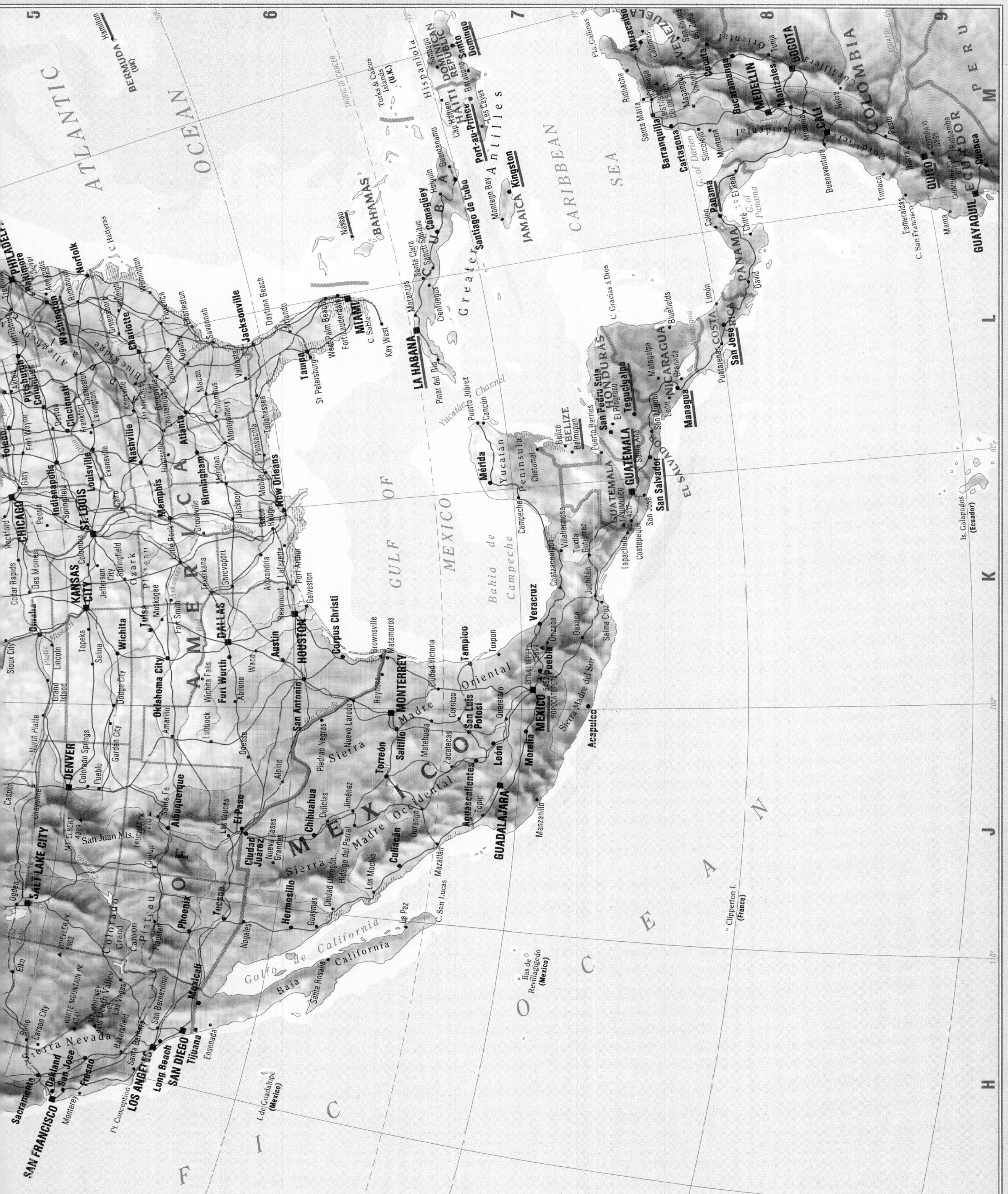
ATLANTIC
OCEAN
BERMUDA (UK)
Hamilton
BAHAMAS
Nassau
Greater Antilles
Hispaniola
HAITI
DOMINICAN REPUBLIC
Santo Domingo
Port-au-Prince
JAMAICA
Kingston
CARIBBEAN
SEA
LA HABANA
Santiago de Cuba
Camagüey
GULF OF MEXICO
Bahía de Campeche
Yucatán Peninsula
Mérida
BELIZE
Belmopan
GUATEMALA
HONDURAS
Tegucigalpa
EL SALVADOR
San Salvador
NICARAGUA
Managua
COSTA RICA
San José
PANAMA
Panamá
G. of Panama
COLOMBIA
BOGOTA
MEDELLIN
CALI
Barranquilla
Cartagena
ECUADOR
QUITO
GUAYAQUIL
PERU
MEXICO
MEXICO
Guadalajara
Monterrey
Chihuahua
Acapulco
Veracruz
Puebla
Sierra Madre Occidental
Sierra Madre Oriental
Sierra Madre del Sur
Baja California
Golfo de California
Is. Galapagos (Ecuador)
Clipperton I. (France)
Islas de Revillagigedo (Mexico)
I. de Guadalupe (Mexico)
PACIFIC OCEAN
AMERICA
CHICAGO
ST LOUIS
KANSAS CITY
DENVER
SALT LAKE CITY
SAN FRANCISCO
LOS ANGELES
SAN DIEGO
HOUSTON
DALLAS
MIAMI
Washington
PHILADELPHIA
New Orleans
Atlanta
Jacksonville
Tropic of Cancer
Equator
West of Greenwich

Designed and produced by E.S.R.

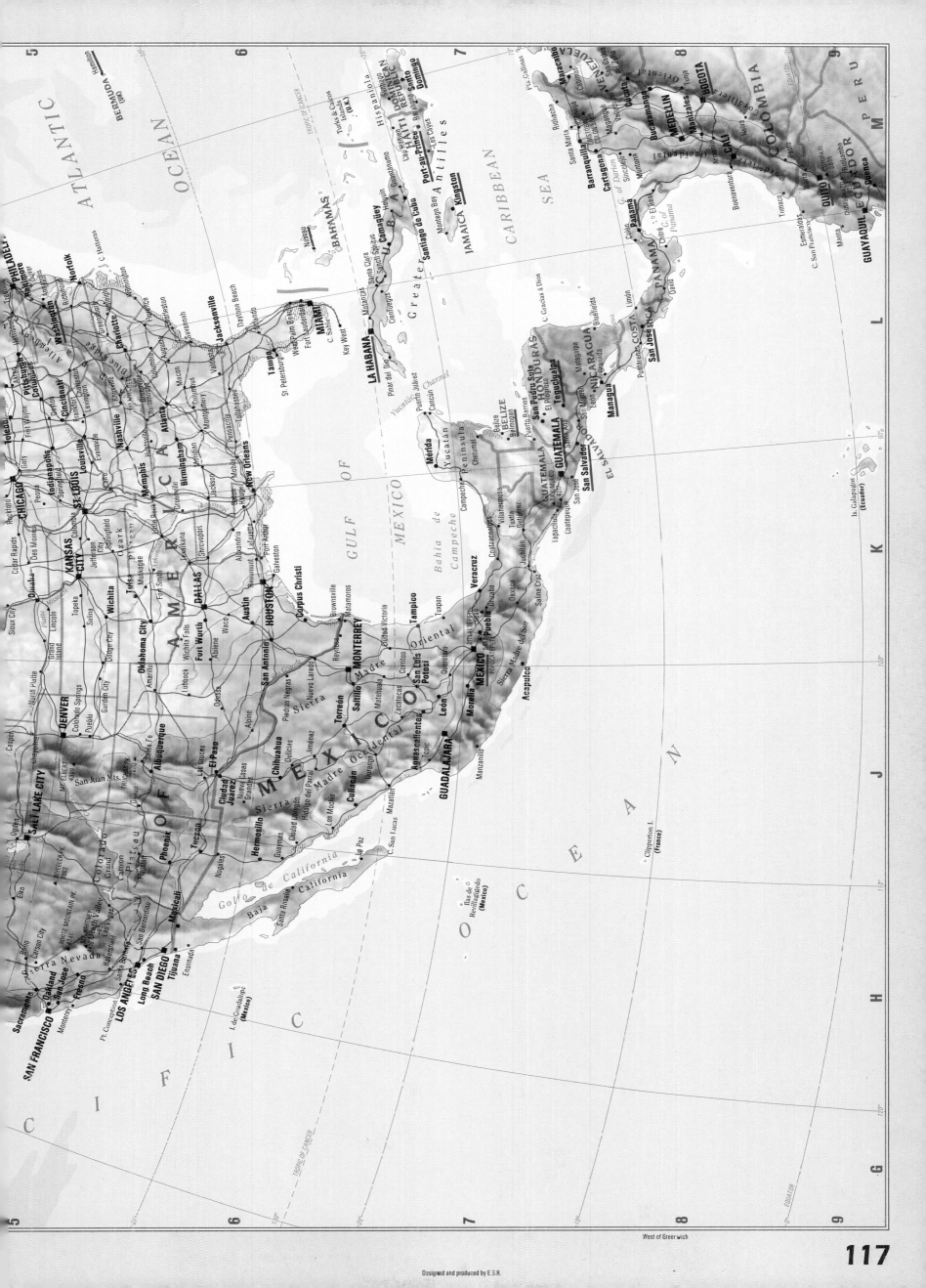

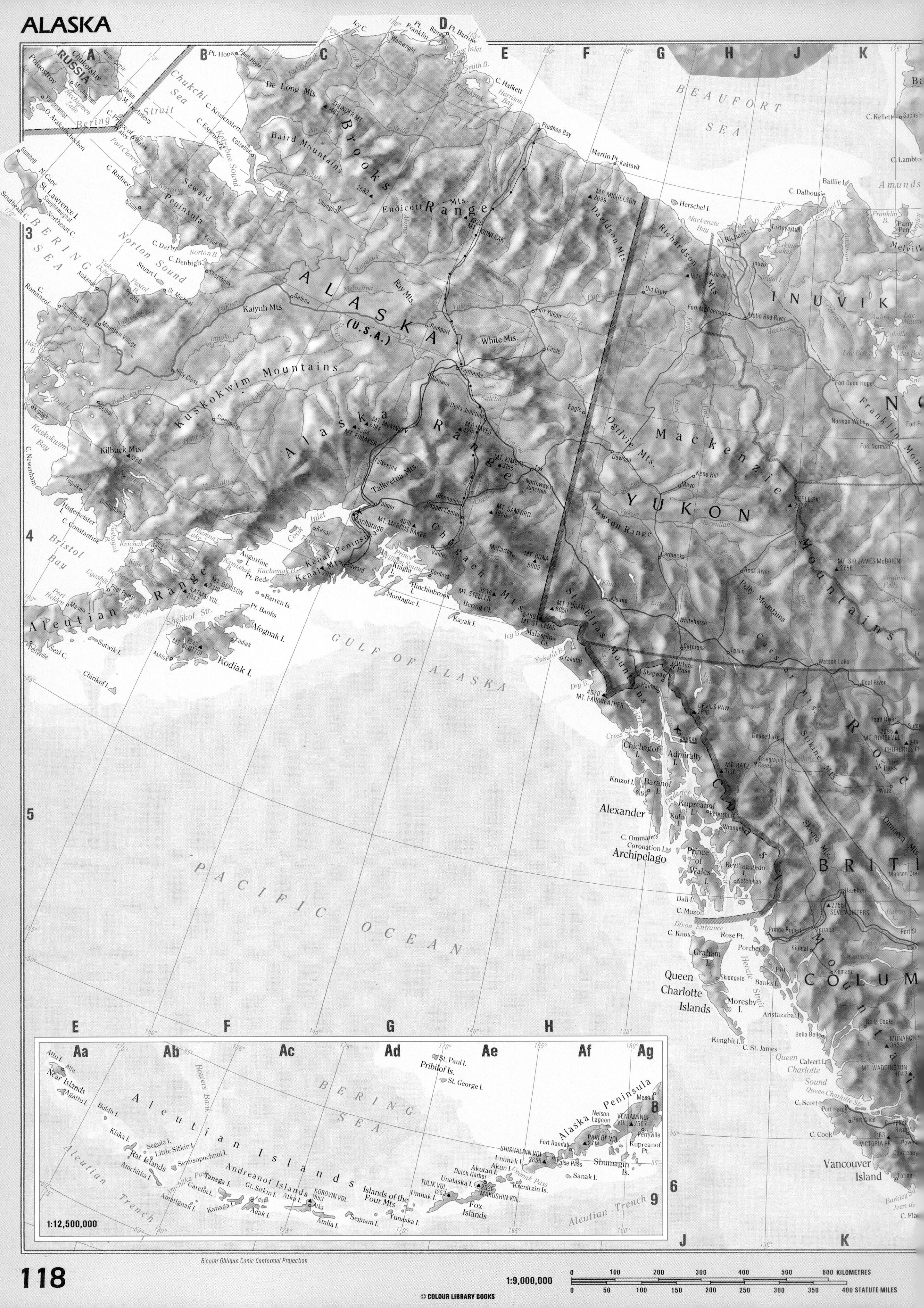
ALASKA (U.S.A.)
RUSSIA
BEAUFORT SEA
BERING SEA
GULF OF ALASKA
PACIFIC OCEAN
Chukchi Sea
Bering Strait
Norton Sound
Bristol Bay
Brooks Range
Baird Mountains
De Long Mts.
Endicott Mts.
Seward Peninsula
Kuskokwim Mountains
Alaska Range
Chugach Mts.
St. Elias Mountains
Aleutian Range
Kenai Peninsula
Kodiak I.
Afognak I.
Alexander Archipelago
Queen Charlotte Islands
Vancouver Island
YUKON
Mackenzie Mountains
Ogilvie Mts.
Richardson Mts.
Davidson Mts.
Dawson Range
Pelly Mountains
Cassiar Mts.
INUVIK
Prudhoe Bay
Fairbanks
Anchorage
Nome
Juneau
Whitehorse
Dawson
MT. McKINLEY 6194
MT. LOGAN 6050
MT. ST. ELIAS 5489
MT. FAIRWEATHER 4670
Aleutian Islands
Andreanof Islands
Rat Islands
Near Islands
Fox Islands
Islands of the Four Mts
Pribilof Is.
Alaska Peninsula
Shumagin Is.
Aleutian Trench
1:12,500,000
Bipolar Oblique Conic Conformal Projection
1:9,000,000
0 100 200 300 400 500 600 KILOMETRES
0 50 100 150 200 250 300 350 400 STATUTE MILES

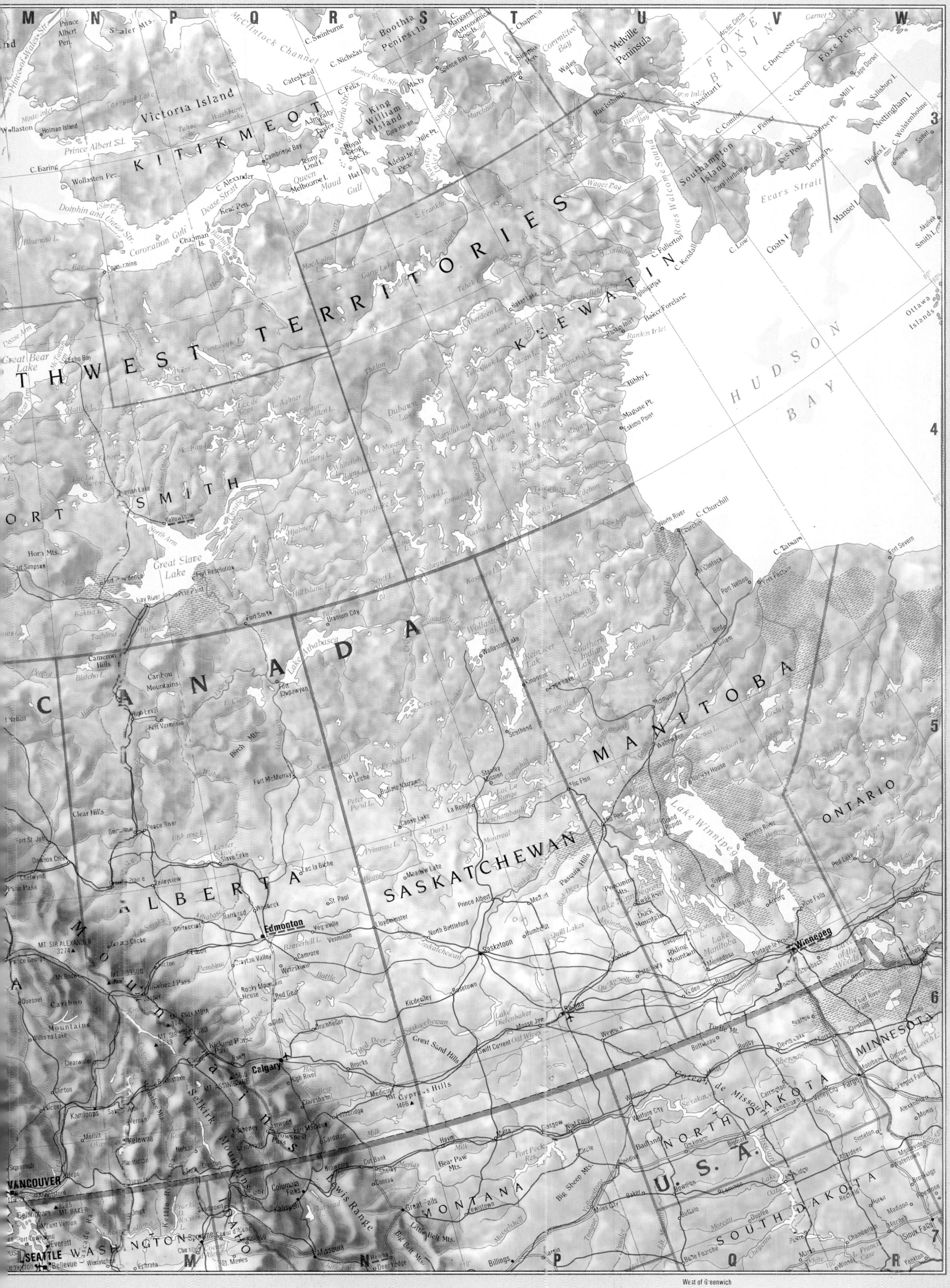
Victoria Island
KITIKMEOT
Boothia Peninsula
King William Island
Melville Peninsula
FOXE BASIN
Southampton Island
NORTHWEST TERRITORIES
KEEWATIN
HUDSON BAY
Great Bear Lake
FORT SMITH
Great Slave Lake
Yellowknife
Hay River
Fort Smith
Uranium City
Lake Athabasca
Wollaston Lake
Reindeer Lake
Southern Indian Lake
Churchill
C. Churchill
Port Nelson
York Factory
Fort Severn
CANADA
MANITOBA
ONTARIO
ALBERTA
SASKATCHEWAN
Fort McMurray
Peace River
Grande Prairie
Dawson Creek
Fort St. John
Edmonton
Calgary
Lethbridge
Medicine Hat
Saskatoon
Prince Albert
North Battleford
Regina
Moose Jaw
Swift Current
Lake Winnipeg
Lake Manitoba
Winnipeg
Brandon
Flin Flon
The Pas
Lake of the Woods
Kamloops
VANCOUVER
SEATTLE
Bellingham
Rocky Mountains
Selkirk Mountains
Cariboo Mountains
MT. SIR ALEXANDER 3274
Prince George
Quesnel
WASHINGTON
IDAHO
MONTANA
NORTH DAKOTA
SOUTH DAKOTA
MINNESOTA
U.S.A.
Great Falls
Helena
Missoula
Kalispell
Billings
Havre
Williston
Minot
Bismarck
Fargo
Grand Forks
Cypress Hills
Great Sand Hills
Coteau de Missouri
Lewis Range
West of Greenwich

Designed and produced by E.S.R.

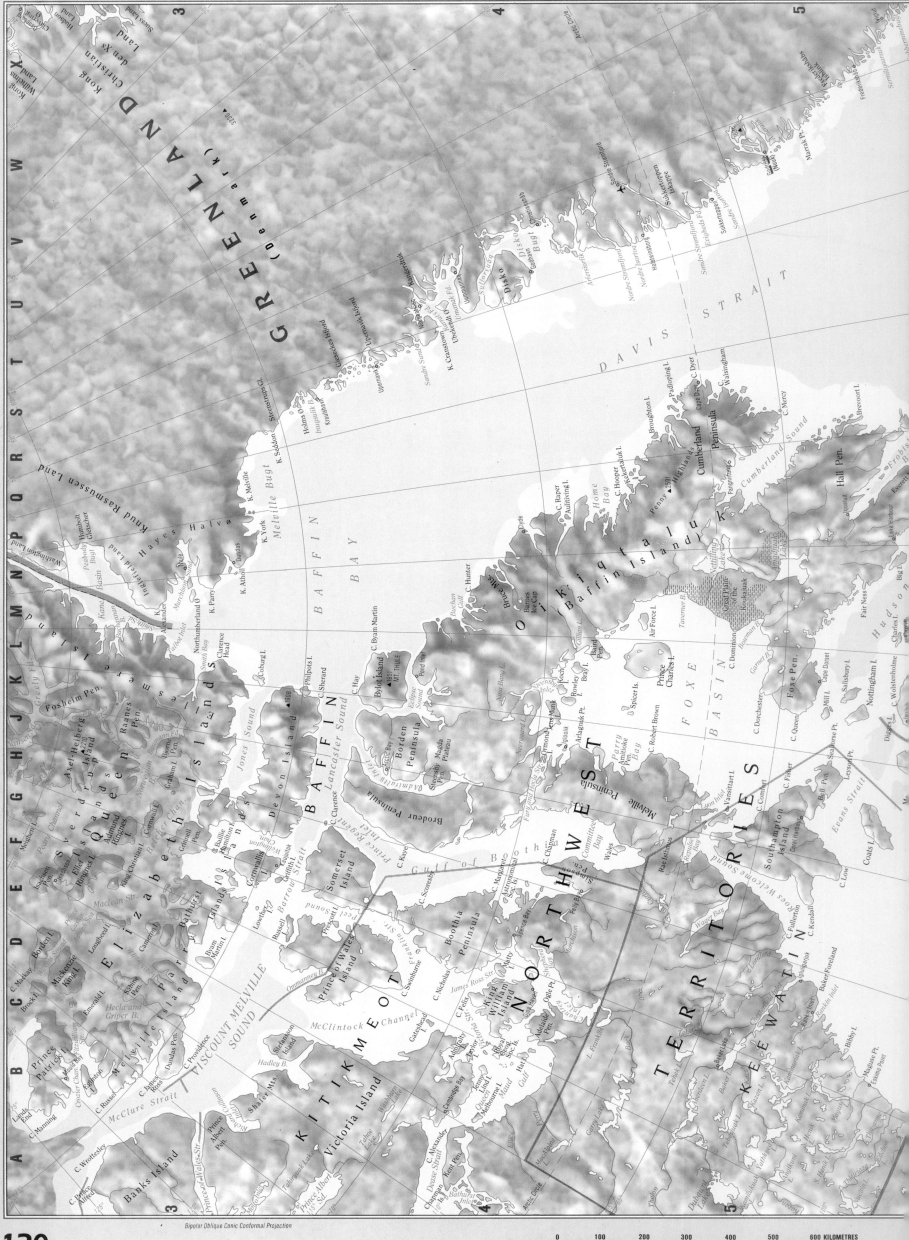

GREENLAND (Denmark)

DAVIS STRAIT

BAFFIN BAY

Qikiqtaaluk Baffin Island

Cumberland Peninsula

Cumberland Sound

Hall Pen.

Home Bay

Foxe Basin

Foxe Peninsula

Melville Peninsula

Brodeur Peninsula

Borden Peninsula

BAFFIN

Lancaster Sound

Devon Island

Jones Sound

Ellesmere Island

Queen Elizabeth Islands

Fosheim Pen.

Axel Heiberg Island

Sverdrup Islands

Parry Islands

Bathurst Island

Melville Island

Prince Patrick Island

Banks Island

Victoria Island

Prince of Wales Island

Somerset Island

Boothia Peninsula

King William Island

NORTHWEST TERRITORIES

KITIKMEOT

KEEWATIN

Southampton Island

Hudson Bay

VISCOUNT MELVILLE SOUND

McClure Strait

McClintock Channel

Gulf of Boothia

Prince Regent Inlet

Knud Rasmussen Land

Kong Christian den Xs Land

Hayes Halvø

Bipolar Oblique Conic Conformal Projection

1:9,000,000

| 0 | 100 | 200 | 300 | 400 | 500 | 600 KILOMETRES |

| 0 | 50 | 100 | 150 | 200 | 250 | 300 | 350 | 400 STATUTE MILES |

© COLOUR LIBRARY BOOKS

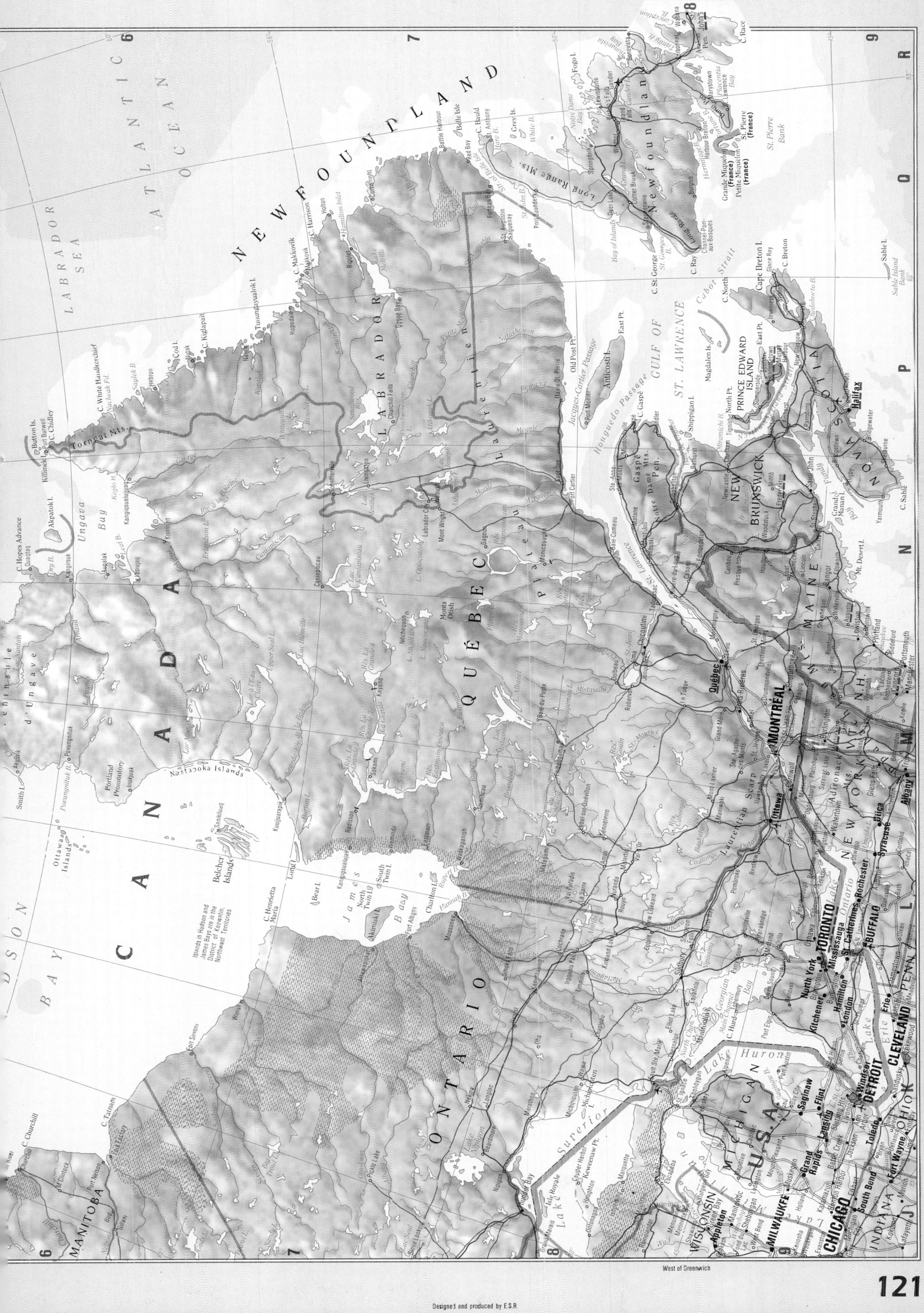
CANADA
NEWFOUNDLAND
LABRADOR
QUÉBEC
ONTARIO
MANITOBA
U.S.A.
LABRADOR SEA
ATLANTIC OCEAN
HUDSON BAY
James Bay
Ungava Bay
GULF OF ST. LAWRENCE
NEW BRUNSWICK
NOVA SCOTIA
PRINCE EDWARD ISLAND
MAINE
NEW YORK
MICHIGAN
WISCONSIN
Lake Superior
Lake Huron
Lake Ontario
Lake Erie
MONTREAL
TORONTO
Québec
Ottawa
Halifax
DETROIT
CLEVELAND
CHICAGO
MILWAUKEE
BUFFALO
Anticosti I.
Belcher Islands
Islands in Hudson and James Bays are in the District of Keewatin, Northwest Territories
West of Greenwich

Designed and produced by E.S.R

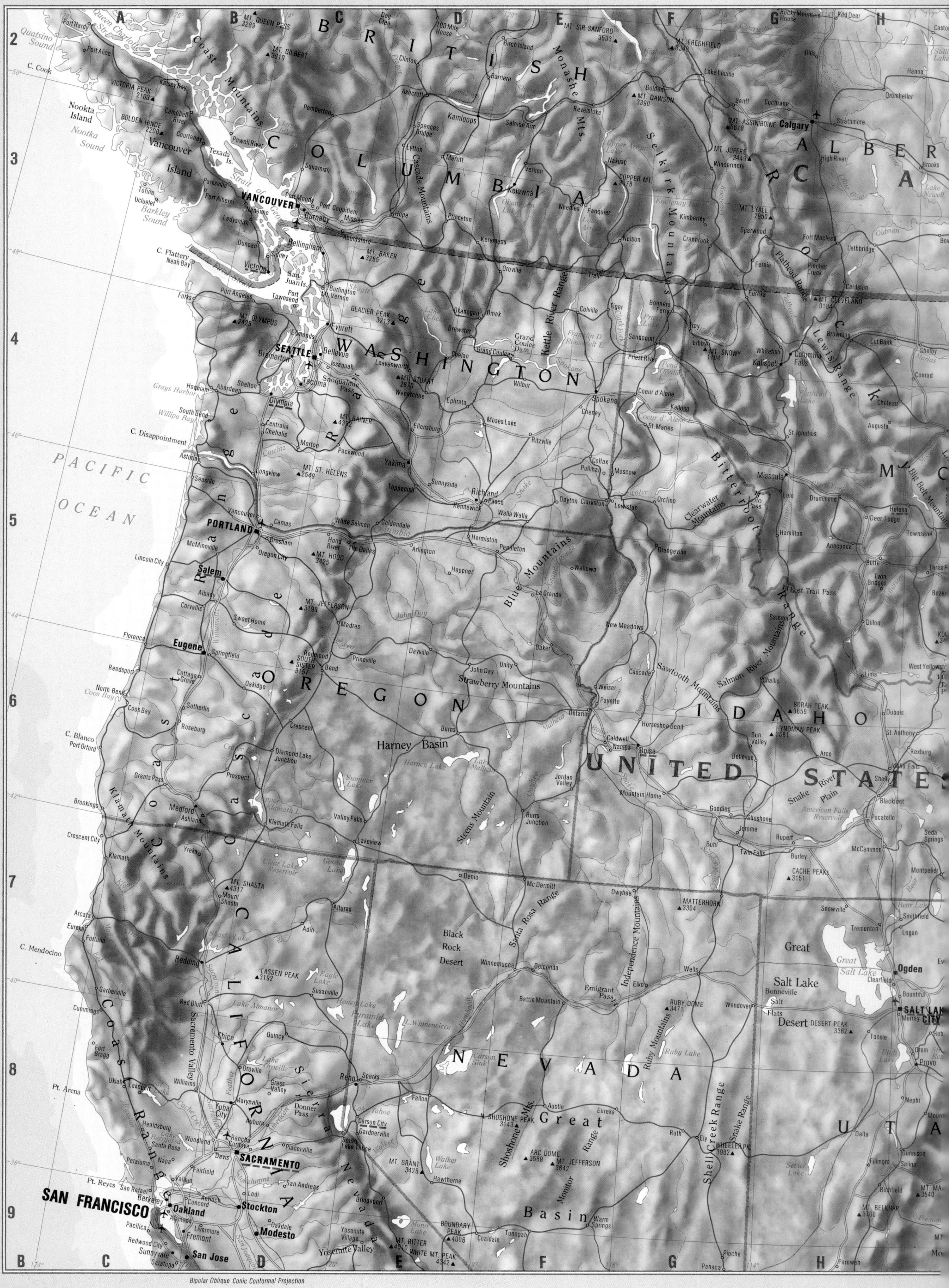
BRITISH COLUMBIA
ALBERTA
WASHINGTON
OREGON
IDAHO
NEVADA
CALIFORNIA
UTAH
MONTANA
UNITED STATES
PACIFIC OCEAN
Coast Mountains
Cascade Range
Coast Ranges
Klamath Mountains
Sierra Nevada
Monashee Mts.
Selkirk Mountains
Kettle River Range
Bitterroot Range
Clearwater Mountains
Salmon River Mountains
Sawtooth Mountains
Blue Mountains
Strawberry Mountains
Steens Mountain
Santa Rosa Range
Independence Mountains
Ruby Mountains
Shoshone Mts.
Monitor Range
Shell Creek Range
Snake Range
Lewis Range
Flathead Range
Harney Basin
Black Rock Desert
Great Basin
Great Salt Lake Desert
Bonneville Salt Flats
Snake River Plain
Vancouver Island
VANCOUVER
Victoria
SEATTLE
Tacoma
Olympia
Spokane
PORTLAND
Salem
Eugene
Boise
Calgary
Ogden
SALT LAKE CITY
Provo
Reno
Carson City
SACRAMENTO
SAN FRANCISCO
Oakland
San Jose
Stockton
Modesto
Fresno
MT. OLYMPUS 2428
MT. RAINIER 4392
MT. ST. HELENS 2549
MT. HOOD 3425
MT. SHASTA 4317
LASSEN PEAK 3192
MT. BAKER 3285
GLACIER PEAK 3213
BORAH PEAK 3859
MATTERHORN 3304
RUBY DOME 3471
WHEELER PK. 3982
BOUNDARY PEAK 4006
WHITE MT. PEAK 4342
MT. ASSINIBOINE 3618
Bipolar Oblique Conic Conformal Projection

1:5,000,000
0 50 100 150 200 250 300 350 400 KILOMETRES
0 50 100 150 200 250 STATUTE MILES

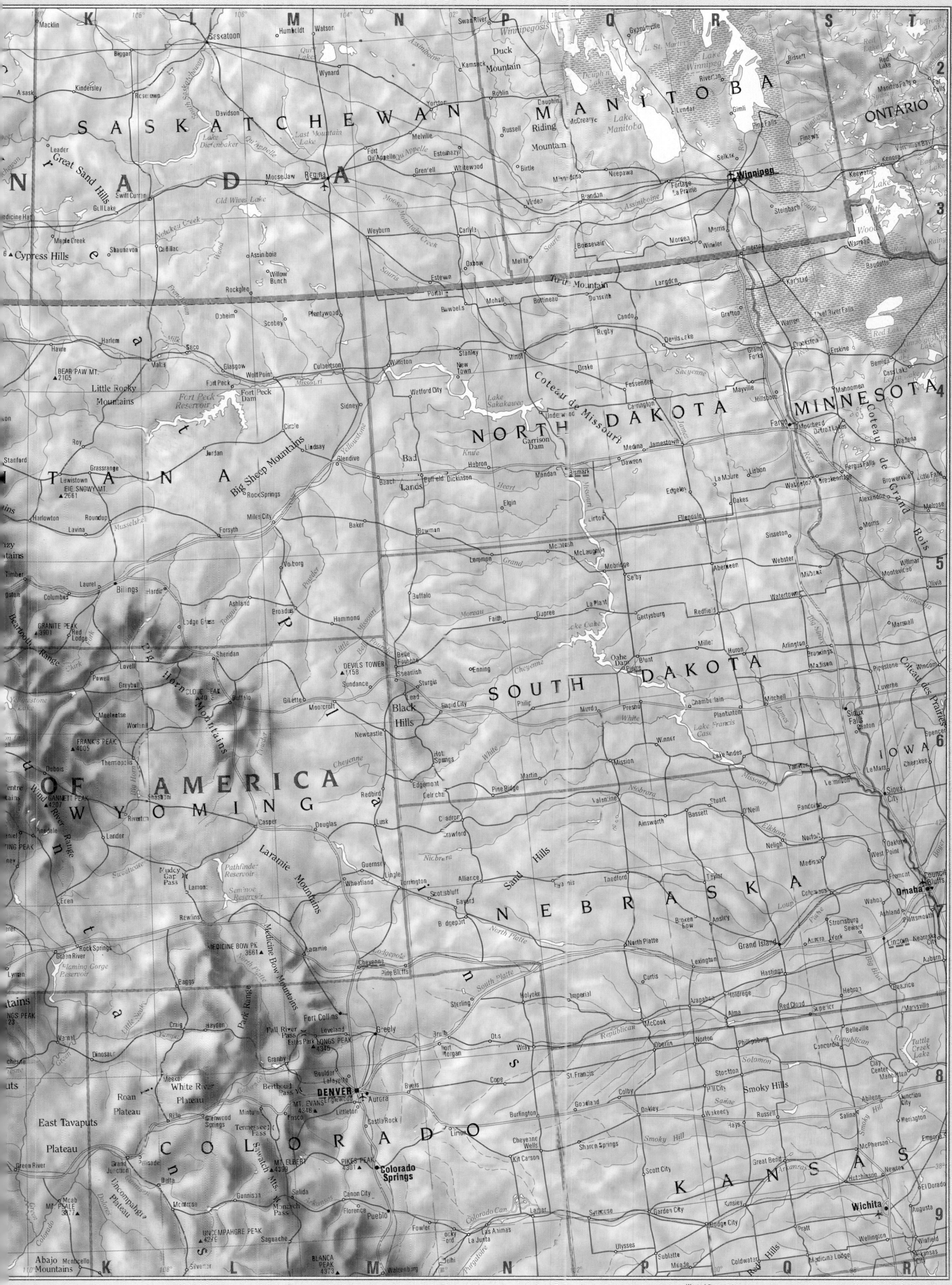
SASKATCHEWAN
MANITOBA
ONTARIO
CANADA
UNITED STATES OF AMERICA
NORTH DAKOTA
SOUTH DAKOTA
MINNESOTA
IOWA
NEBRASKA
KANSAS
WYOMING
COLORADO
Montana
Saskatoon
Regina
Moose Jaw
Swift Current
Medicine Hat
Cypress Hills
Great Sand Hills
Winnipeg
Lake Winnipeg
Lake Manitoba
Lake Winnipegosis
Riding Mountain
Duck Mountain
Lake of the Woods
Brandon
Weyburn
Estevan
Minot
Bismarck
Fargo
Grand Forks
Devils Lake
Jamestown
Dickinson
Williston
Lake Sakakawea
Coteau du Missouri
Billings
Glasgow
Fort Peck Reservoir
Little Rocky Mountains
Big Sheep Mountains
Miles City
Glendive
Sheridan
Big Horn Mountains
Black Hills
Rapid City
Pierre
Aberdeen
Watertown
Huron
Sioux Falls
Mitchell
Yankton
Sioux City
Omaha
Council Bluffs
Lincoln
Grand Island
North Platte
Scottsbluff
Sand Hills
Casper
Cheyenne
Laramie
Laramie Mountains
Medicine Bow Mountains
Rock Springs
Fort Collins
Greeley
Boulder
DENVER
Colorado Springs
Pueblo
Grand Junction
PIKES PEAK 4301
MT. ELBERT 4399
LONGS PEAK 4345
MT. EVANS 4348
Smoky Hills
Wichita
Dodge City
Garden City
Hutchinson
Salina

West of Greenwich

Designed and produced by E.S.R.

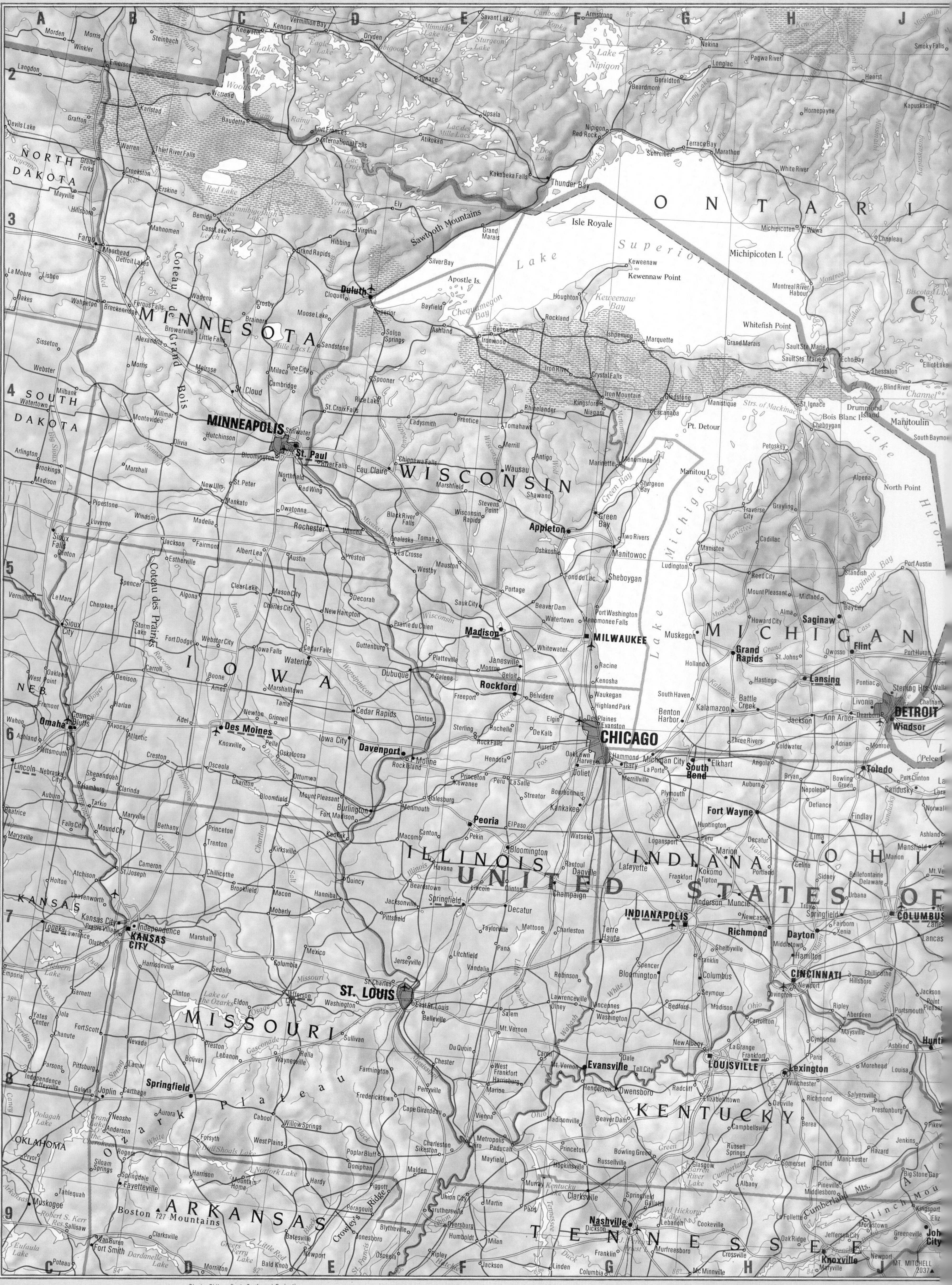
MINNESOTA
WISCONSIN
MICHIGAN
IOWA
ILLINOIS
INDIANA
MISSOURI
KENTUCKY
ARKANSAS
TENNESSEE
NORTH DAKOTA
SOUTH DAKOTA
NEB.
KANSAS
OKLAHOMA
ONTARIO
UNITED STATES OF
Lake Superior
Lake Michigan
Lake Huron
MINNEAPOLIS
St. Paul
CHICAGO
MILWAUKEE
DETROIT
ST. LOUIS
KANSAS CITY
INDIANAPOLIS
CINCINNATI
LOUISVILLE
COLUMBUS
Des Moines
Omaha
Duluth
Madison
Nashville
Springfield
Lexington
Ozark Plateau
Bipolar Oblique Conic Conformal Projection
1:5,000,000
0 50 100 150 200 250 300 350 400 KILOMETRES
0 50 100 150 200 250 STATUTE MI

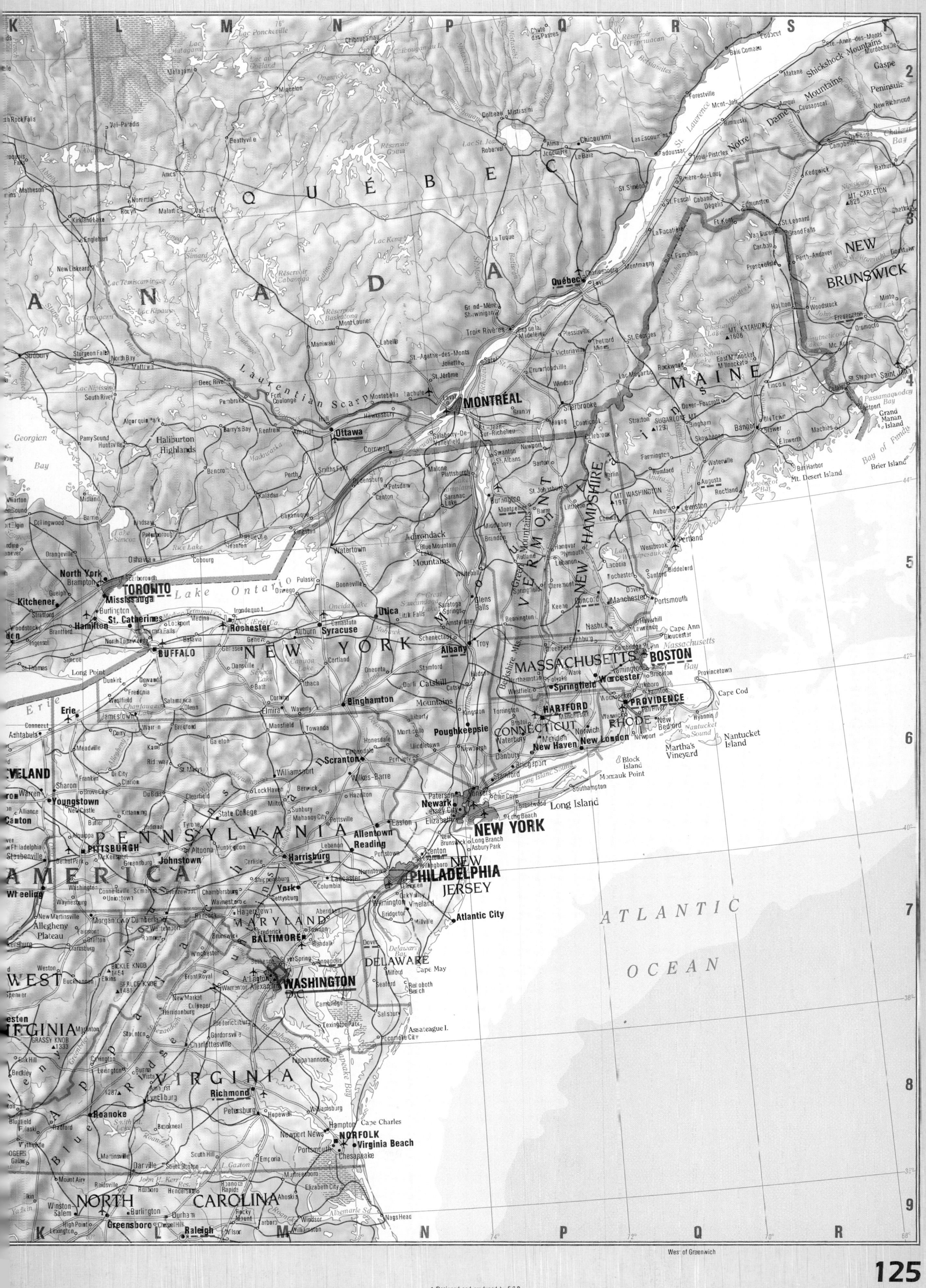
K L M N P Q R S T
CANADA
QUÉBEC
Lac Mistassini
Lac St Jean
Québec
Trois Rivières
MONTRÉAL
Ottawa
Laurentian Scarp
Georgian Bay
Haliburton Highlands
Lake Ontario
TORONTO
Mississauga
North York
Brampton
Kitchener
Hamilton
St. Catherines
BUFFALO
Rochester
Syracuse
Utica
Albany
NEW YORK
Binghamton
Erie
Lake Erie
Adirondack Mountains
Catskill Mountains
VERMONT
Green Mountains
Montpelier
Burlington
NEW HAMPSHIRE
Concord
Manchester
MT. WASHINGTON 1917
MAINE
Augusta
Portland
Bangor
MT. KATAHDIN 1606
NEW BRUNSWICK
Notre Dame Mountains
Shickshock Mountains
Gaspe Peninsula
St. Lawrence
Bay of Fundy
MASSACHUSETTS
BOSTON
Worcester
Springfield
Cape Cod
Nantucket Island
Martha's Vineyard
RHODE ISLAND
PROVIDENCE
CONNECTICUT
HARTFORD
New Haven
New London
Long Island
Long Island Sound
NEW YORK
Newark
Poughkeepsie
Scranton
Allentown
Reading
Harrisburg
PENNSYLVANIA
PITTSBURGH
Johnstown
Youngstown
PHILADELPHIA
NEW JERSEY
Atlantic City
DELAWARE
Dover
Cape May
MARYLAND
BALTIMORE
WASHINGTON D.C.
WEST VIRGINIA
Allegheny Plateau
VIRGINIA
Richmond
Roanoke
NORFOLK
Virginia Beach
Chesapeake Bay
Blue Ridge
Appalachian Mountains
NORTH CAROLINA
Greensboro
Raleigh
Winston-Salem
ATLANTIC OCEAN
AMERICA
West of Greenwich

* Designed and produced by ESR

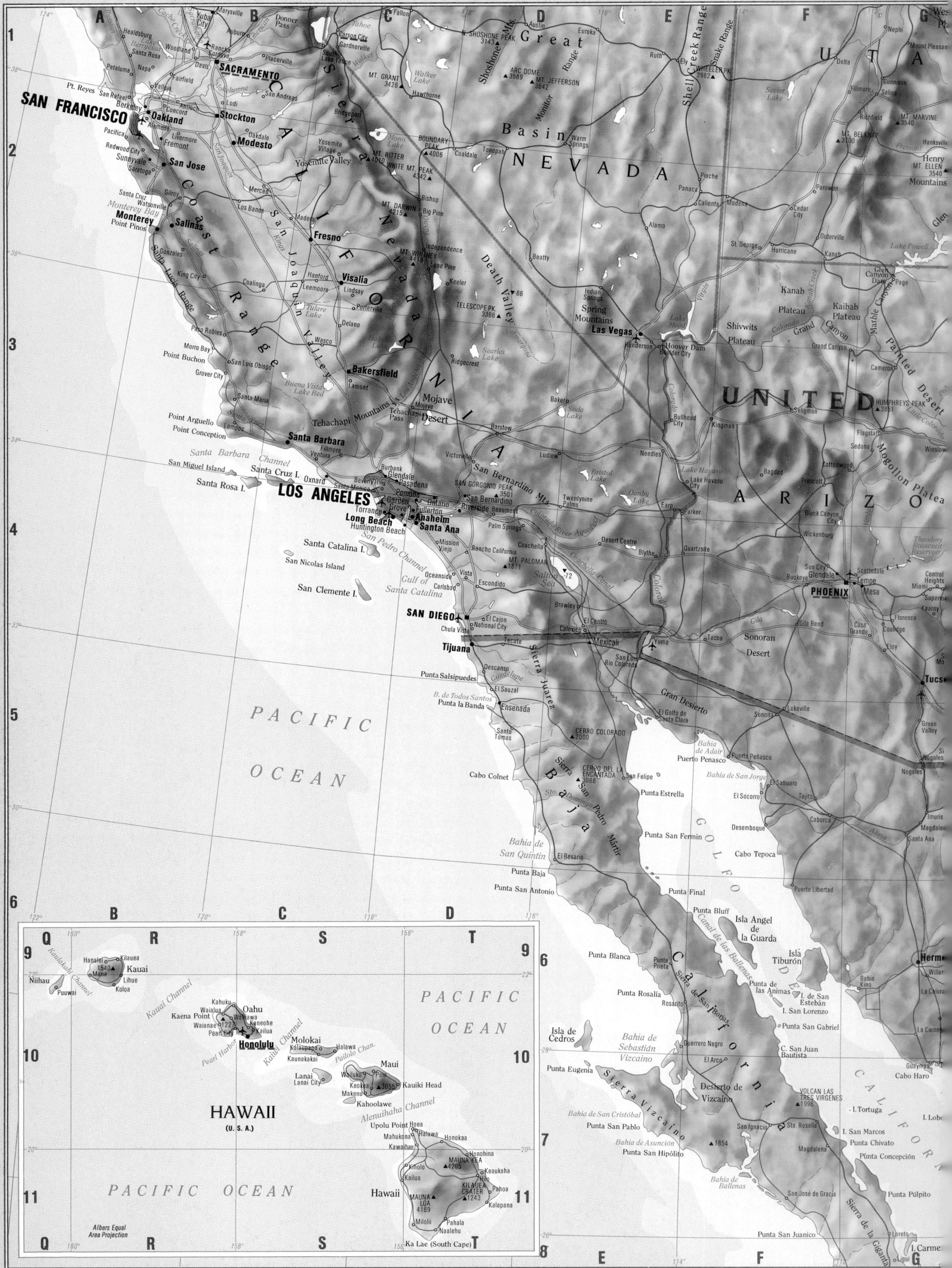

SAN FRANCISCO
SACRAMENTO
Oakland
Stockton
Modesto
San Jose
Fresno
Visalia
Bakersfield
Santa Barbara
LOS ANGELES
Long Beach
Anaheim
Santa Ana
SAN DIEGO
Tijuana
Las Vegas
PHOENIX
Tucson
C A L I F O R N I A
N E V A D A
U T A H
A R I Z O N A
UNITED
Great Basin
Sierra Nevada
Coast Range
San Joaquin Valley
Death Valley
Mojave Desert
Sonoran Desert
Gran Desierto
Baja California
Sierra Juarez
Sierra San Pedro Martir
Sierra Vizcaino
Desierto de Vizcaino
Golfo de California
Canal de las Ballenas
Sierra de la Giganta
Monterey Bay
Santa Barbara Channel
San Pedro Channel
Gulf of Santa Catalina
Santa Cruz I.
Santa Rosa I.
San Miguel Island
Santa Catalina I.
San Nicolas Island
San Clemente I.
Isla Angel de la Guarda
Isla Tiburón
Isla de Cedros
Bahia de Sebastián Vizcaíno
Salton Sea
Lake Mead
Lake Havasu
Lake Powell
Kaibab Plateau
Kanab Plateau
Shivwits Plateau
Grand Canyon
Painted Desert
Mogollon Plateau
Spring Mountains
Shell Creek Range
Snake Range
Tehachapi Mountains
San Bernardino Mts.
MT. WHITNEY 4418
MT. RITTER 4010
WHITE MT. PEAK 4342
BOUNDARY PEAK 4006
MT. DARWIN 4215
MT. GRANT 3426
SHOSHONE PEAK 3143
ARC DOME 3589
MT. JEFFERSON 3642
WHEELER PK. 3982
TELESCOPE PK. 3366
SAN GORGONIO PEAK 3501
MT. PALOMAR 1871
HUMPHREYS PEAK 3851
CERRO COLORADO 2000
CERRO DEL LA ENCANTADA 3088
VOLCAN LAS TRES VIRGENES 1996
PACIFIC OCEAN
HAWAII (U. S. A.)
Kauai
Niihau
Oahu
Honolulu
Molokai
Lanai
Maui
Kahoolawe
Hawaii
Kauai Channel
Kaulakahi Channel
Kaiwi Channel
Pailolo Chan.
Alenuihaha Channel
MAUNA KEA 4205
MAUNA LOA 4169
KILAUEA CRATER 1243
Ka Lae (South Cape)
PACIFIC OCEAN
Albers Equal Area Projection

1:5,000,000

0 50 100 150 200 250 300 350 400 KILOMETRES

0 50 100 150 200 250 STATUTE MILES

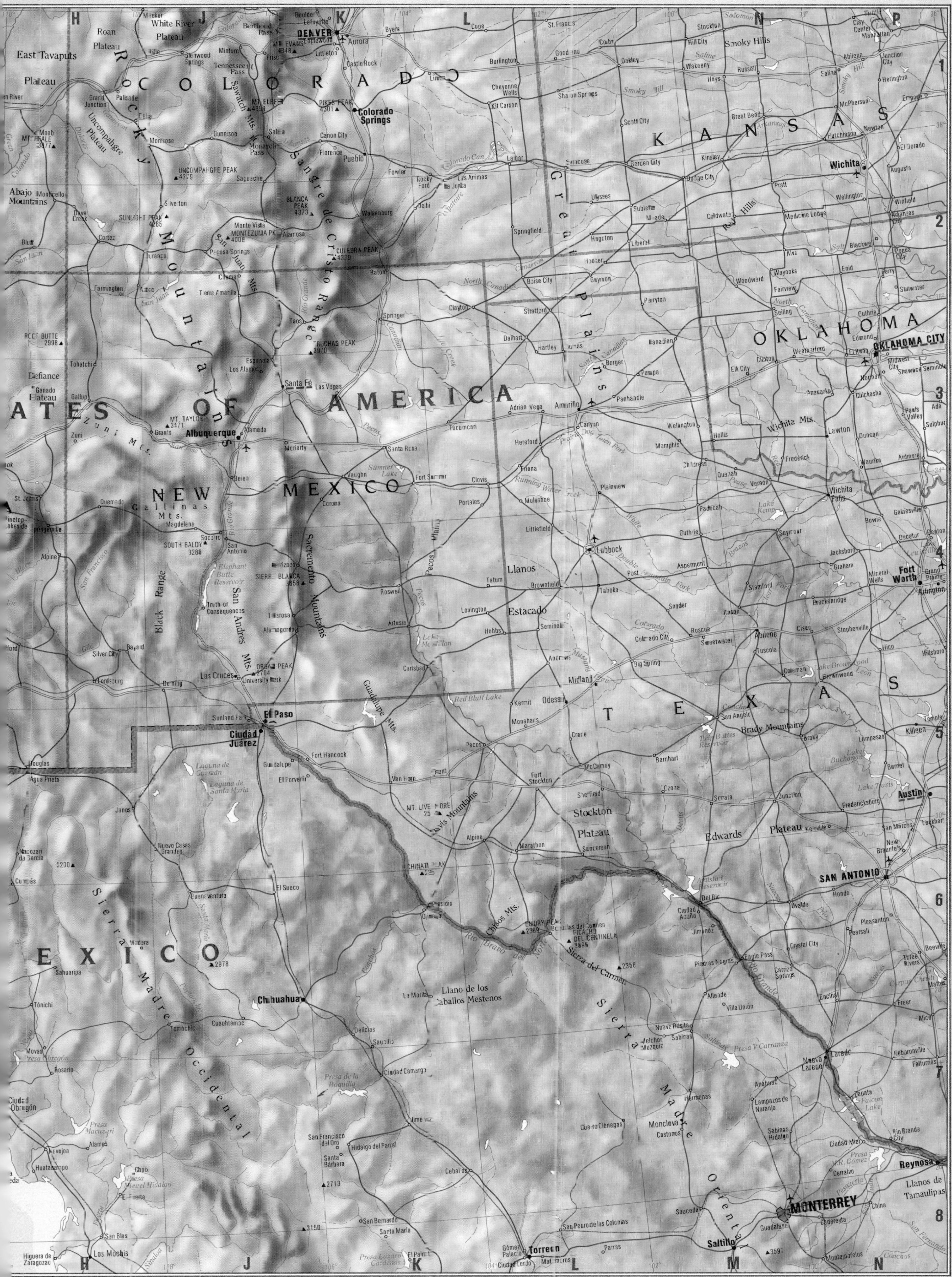
COLORADO
KANSAS
OKLAHOMA
NEW MEXICO
TEXAS
STATES OF AMERICA
MEXICO
Rocky Mountains
Sangre de Cristo Range
Great Plains
Sierra Madre Occidental
Sierra Madre Oriental
Llano Estacado
Edwards Plateau
Stockton Plateau
Smoky Hills
Denver
Colorado Springs
Pueblo
Wichita
Oklahoma City
Santa Fe
Albuquerque
Amarillo
Lubbock
Fort Worth
Austin
San Antonio
El Paso
Ciudad Juárez
Chihuahua
Torreón
Saltillo
Monterrey
Reynosa
Laredo
Nuevo Laredo
Wichita Falls
Abilene
San Angelo
Midland
Odessa
Roswell
Las Cruces
Pikes Peak
Rio Grande
Pecos
Llanos de Tamaulipas
Llano de los Caballos Mestenos
Chisos Mts.
Davis Mountains
Guadalupe Mts.
Sacramento Mountains
San Andres Mts.
Wichita Mts.
Brady Mountains
H
J
K
L
M
N
P
1
2
3
4
5
6
7
8

Bipolar Oblique Conic Conformal Projection

West of Greenwich

Designed and produced by E.S.R.

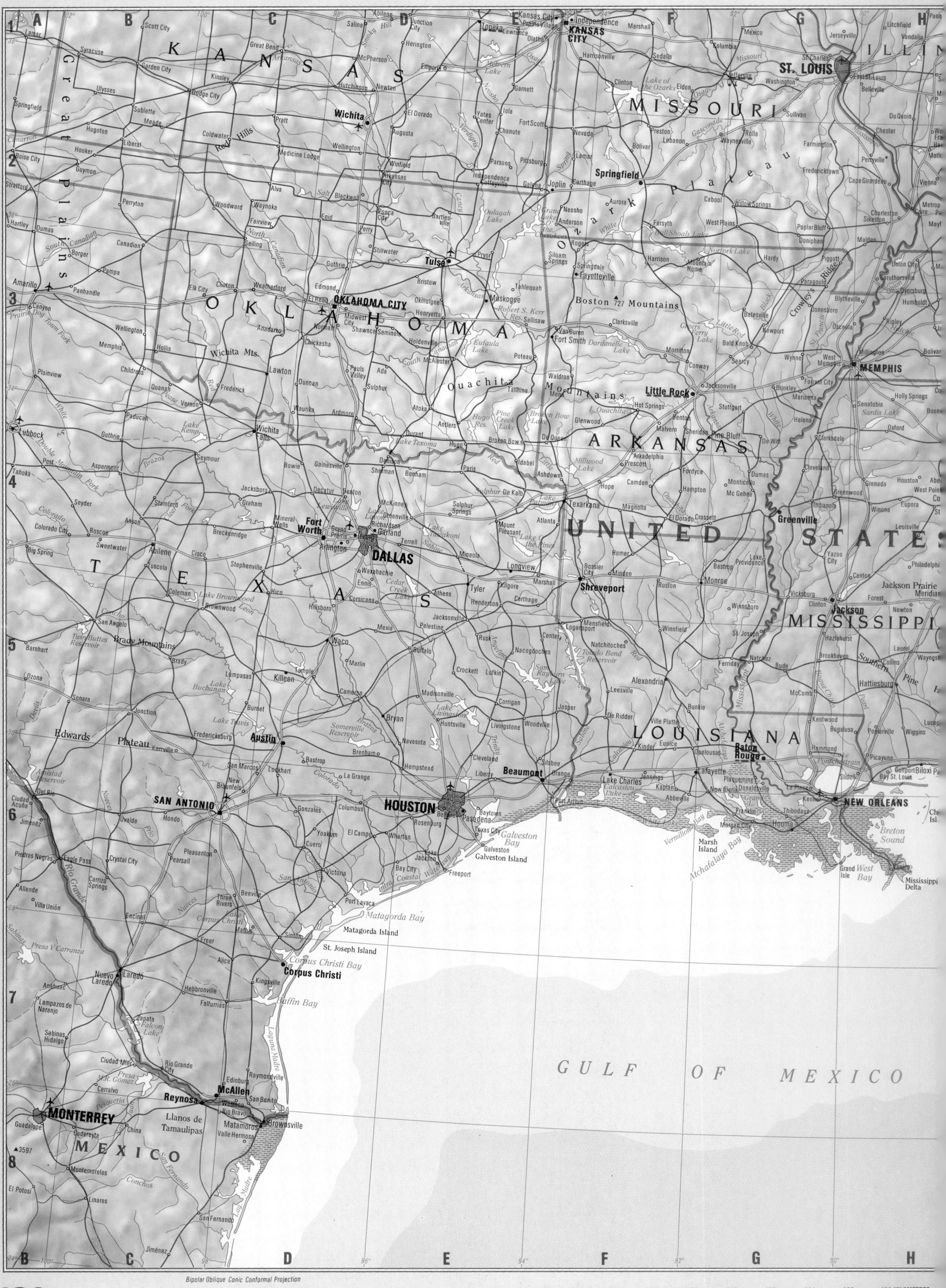
KANSAS
MISSOURI
OKLAHOMA
ARKANSAS
TEXAS
LOUISIANA
MISSISSIPPI
UNITED STATES
MEXICO
GULF OF MEXICO
Great Plains
Ozark Plateau
Ouachita Mountains
Edwards Plateau
Boston Mountains
Wichita Mts.
Brady Mountains
KANSAS CITY
Independence
Topeka
Wichita
Salina
Emporia
Hutchinson
Dodge City
Garden City
Liberal
ST. LOUIS
Springfield
Joplin
Jefferson City
Columbia
Sedalia
Cape Girardeau
Tulsa
OKLAHOMA CITY
Muskogee
Lawton
Enid
Norman
Ardmore
Fort Smith
Little Rock
Fayetteville
Hot Springs
Pine Bluff
Texarkana
El Dorado
Jonesboro
MEMPHIS
Greenville
Jackson
Vicksburg
Hattiesburg
Natchez
Biloxi
Gulfport
Shreveport
Monroe
Alexandria
Lafayette
Baton Rouge
NEW ORLEANS
Lake Charles
Houma
Amarillo
Lubbock
Wichita Falls
Abilene
San Angelo
Fort Worth
DALLAS
Arlington
Tyler
Longview
Waco
Austin
Bryan
SAN ANTONIO
HOUSTON
Pasadena
Beaumont
Port Arthur
Galveston
Victoria
Laredo
Nuevo Laredo
Corpus Christi
McAllen
Reynosa
Brownsville
Matamoros
MONTERREY
Del Rio
Galveston Bay
Matagorda Bay
Matagorda Island
St. Joseph Island
Corpus Christi Bay
Baffin Bay
Laguna Madre
Atchafalaya Bay
Breton Sound
Mississippi Delta
Lake Pontchartrain
Lake Texoma
Toledo Bend Reservoir
Sam Rayburn Lake
Amistad Reservoir
Rio Grande
Red
Arkansas
Mississippi
Brazos
Colorado
Sabine
Llanos de Tamaulipas

Bipolar Oblique Conic Conformal Projection

1:5,000,000

0 50 100 150 200 250 300 350 400 KILOMETRES

0 50 100 150 200 250 STATUTE MILES

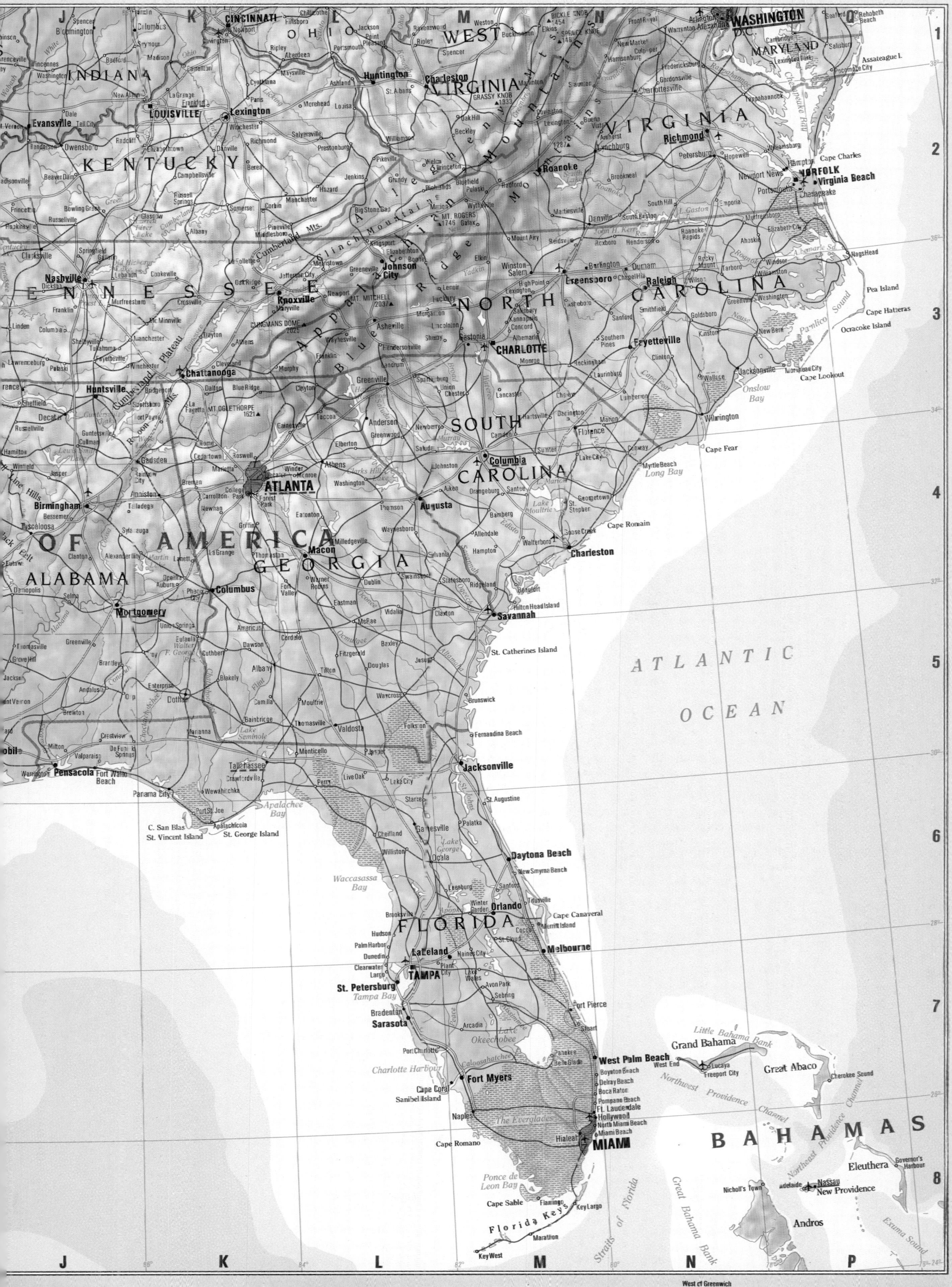
WASHINGTON D.C.
MARYLAND
OHIO
INDIANA
KENTUCKY
WEST VIRGINIA
VIRGINIA
TENNESSEE
NORTH CAROLINA
SOUTH CAROLINA
GEORGIA
ALABAMA
FLORIDA
OF AMERICA
BAHAMAS
ATLANTIC OCEAN
Appalachian Mountains
Allegheny Mountains
Blue Ridge Mountains
Cumberland Plateau
CINCINNATI
LOUISVILLE
Lexington
Evansville
Huntington
Charleston
Richmond
NORFOLK
Virginia Beach
Roanoke
Nashville
Knoxville
Johnson City
Chattanooga
Huntsville
Birmingham
ATLANTA
Greensboro
Raleigh
Fayetteville
CHARLOTTE
Wilmington
Columbia
Augusta
Charleston
Savannah
Macon
Columbus
Montgomery
Pensacola
Jacksonville
Daytona Beach
Orlando
Melbourne
Lakeland
TAMPA
St. Petersburg
Sarasota
Fort Myers
West Palm Beach
Ft. Lauderdale
Hollywood
MIAMI
Cape Hatteras
Cape Lookout
Cape Fear
Cape Canaveral
Cape Sable
Florida Keys
Key West
Grand Bahama
Great Abaco
Andros
Eleuthera
Nassau
New Providence
Straits of Florida
Great Bahama Bank
Northwest Providence Channel
J
K
L
M
N
P
1
2
3
4
5
6
7
8
West of Greenwich

Designed and produced by E.S.R

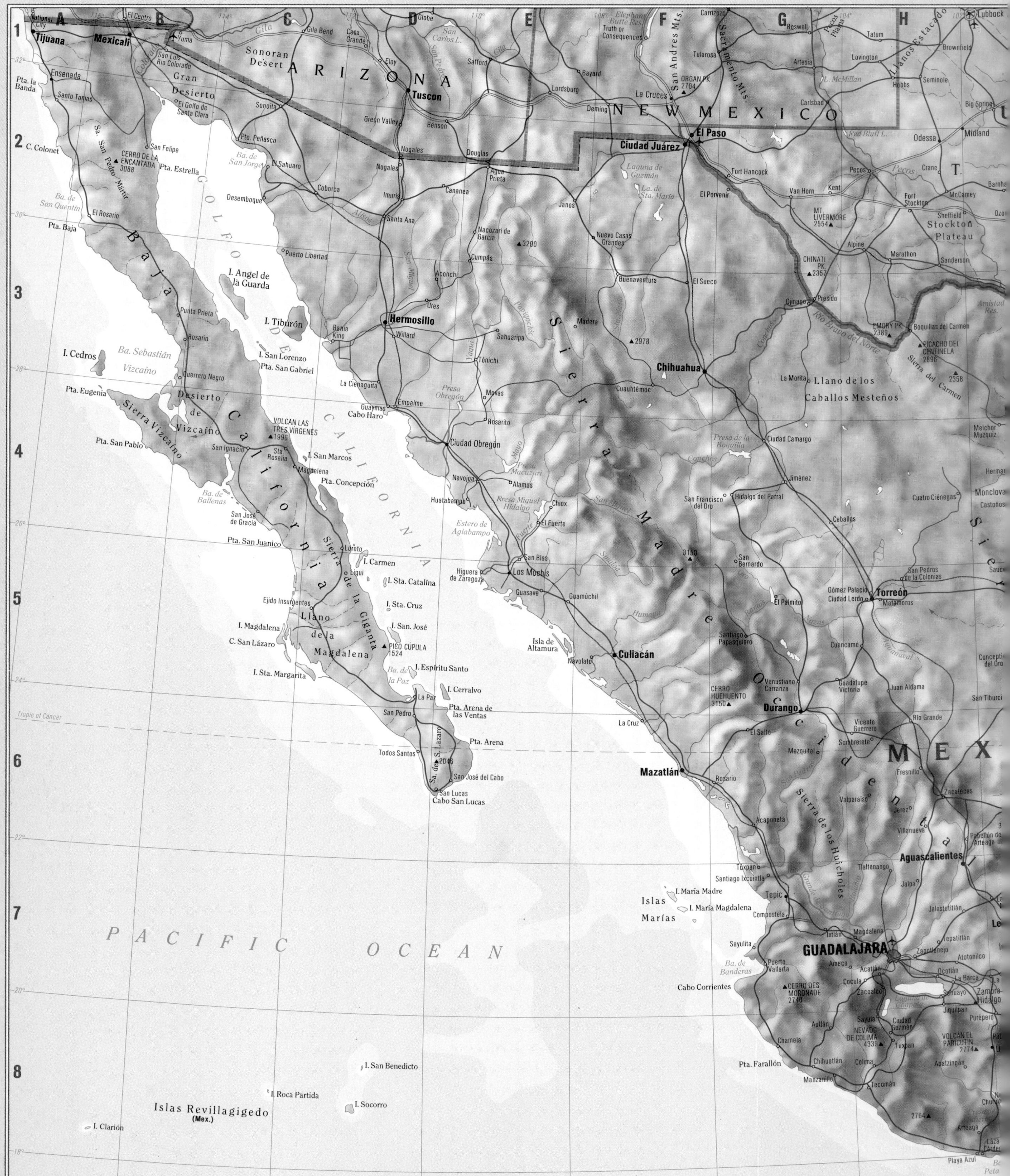

A
B
C
D
E
F
G
H
1
2
3
4
5
6
7
8
9
10
National City
Tijuana
Mexicali
El Centro
Yuma
San Luis Rio Colorado
Gila
Gila Bend
Casa Grande
Globe
San Carlos L.
Sonoran Desert
A R I Z O N A
Eloy
Tuscon
Safford
Green Valley
Benson
Nogales
Douglas
Sonoita
Lordsburg
Bayard
Deming
Elephant Butte Res.
Truth or Consequences
La Cruces
San Andres Mts.
ORGAN PK 2704
Carrizozo
Sacramento Mts.
Tularosa
N E W M E X I C O
Roswell
Pecos Plains
Artesia
Carlsbad
Tatum
Lovington
L. McMillan
Hobbs
Llanos Estacado
Lubbock
Brownfield
Seminole
Big Spring
Midland
Odessa
Red Bluff L.
El Paso
Ciudad Juárez
Fort Hancock
Pecos
Crane
Van Horn
Kent
El Porvenir
Fort Stockton
McCamey
MT LIVERMORE 2554
Sheffield
Stockton Plateau
Alpine
Marathon
Sanderson
CHINATI PK. 2357
Ojinaga
Presidio
Rio Bravo del Norte
EMORY PK. 2389
Boquillas del Carmen
PICACHO DEL CENTINELA 2896
Sierra del Carmen
2358
Amistad Res.
Ensenada
Pta. la Banda
Santo Tomas
Gran Desierto
El Golfo de Santa Clara
Colorado
C. Colonet
San Felipe
Sa. San Pedro Mártir
CERRO DE LA ENCANTADA 3088
Pta. Estrella
Pto. Peñasco
Ba. de San Jorge
El Sahuaro
Caborca
Cananea
Agua Prieta
Imuris
Santa Ana
Alisos
Desemboque
Ba. de San Quentín
El Rosario
Pta. Baja
GOLFO DE CALIFORNIA
Puerto Libertad
Nacozari de Garcia
3200
Cumpás
Aconchi
San Miguel
Ures
Janos
Laguna de Guzmán
La. de Sta. María
Nuevo Casas Grandes
Buenaventura
El Sueco
I. Angel de la Guarda
Punta Prieta
I. Tiburón
Hermosillo
Bahía Kino
Willard
Sahuaripa
Papigochic
Madera
Sierra Madre Occidental
2978
Chihuahua
Rosario
I. Cedros
Ba. Sebastián Vizcaíno
I. San Lorenzo
Pta. San Gabriel
Guerrero Negro
Tónichi
Yaqui
La Cienaguita
Presa Obregón
Movas
Cuauhtémoc
La Morita
Llano de los Caballos Mesteños
Conchos
Pta. Eugenia
Desierto de Vizcaíno
Sierra Vizcaíno
Baja California
Guaymas
Cabo Haro
Empalme
Rosarito
VOLCAN LAS TRES VIRGENES 1996
Pta. San Pablo
San Ignacio
Sta. Rosalia
I. San Marcos
Ciudad Obregón
Mayo
Presa de la Boquilla
Ciudad Camargo
Melchor Muzquiz
Mulegé
Magdalena
Pta. Concepción
Navojoa
Presa Macuzari
Alamos
Jiménez
Hermar
Ba. de Ballenas
San José de Gracia
Huatabampo
Presa Miguel Hidalgo
Chiox
San Francisco del Oro
Hidalgo del Parral
Cuatro Ciénegas
Monclova
Castaños
Estero de Agiabampo
El Fuerte
Fuerte
Ceballos
Pta. San Juanico
Loreto
Sierra de la Giganta
I. Carmen
Ligui
San Blas
Sinaloa
3150
San Bernardo
I. Sta. Catalina
Higuera de Zaragoza
Los Mochis
San Pedros de la Colonias
Gómez Palacio
Ciudad Lerdo
Torreón
Matamoros
Ejido Insurgentes
I. Sta. Cruz
Guasave
Guamúchil
Humaya
El Palmito
Ramos
Nazas
I. Magdalena
Llano de la Magdalena
I. San José
C. San Lázaro
PICO CUPULA 1524
Isla de Altamura
Culiacán
Santiago Papasquiaro
Cuencamé
Aguanaval
Navolato
I. Sta. Margarita
Ba. de la Paz
I. Espíritu Santo
I. Cerralvo
La Paz
Pta. Arena de las Ventas
CERRO HUEHUENTO 3150
Venustiano Carranza
Guadalupe Victoria
Juan Aldama
Concepción del Oro
San Tiburci
Tropic of Cancer
San Pedro
Durango
La Cruz
Rio Grande
El Salto
Vicente Guerrero
Sombrerete
Pta. Arena
Todos Santos
Sa. de S. Lazaro
2046
Mezquital
M E X
San José del Cabo
Mazatlán
Rosario
Fresnillo
Zacatecas
San Lucas
Cabo San Lucas
Sierra de los Huicholes
Valparaíso
Jerez
Acaponeta
Villanueva
Pabellón de Arteaga
Aguascalientes
Túxpan
Santiago Ixcuintla
Tlaltenango
Jalpa
I. María Madre
Islas Marías
I. María Magdalena
Tepic
Compostela
Jalostotitlán
Ixtlán
Magdalena
Tepatitlán
PACIFIC OCEAN
Sayulita
GUADALAJARA
Zapotlanejo
Atotonico
Ba. de Banderas
Puerto Vallarta
Ameca
Acatlán
Ocotlán
La Barca
Cabo Corrientes
CERRO DES MORONADE 2740
Cocula
Zacoalco
Sahuayo
Zamora Hidalgo
Laguna de Chapala
Jiquilpan
Purépero
Autlán
Sayula
Ciudad Guzmán
NEVADO DE COLIMA 4339
Tuxpan
VOLCAN EL PARICUTIN 2774
Chamela
I. San Benedicto
Pta. Farallón
Chihuatlán
Colima
Apatzingán
Manzanillo
Tecomán
I. Roca Partida
I. Socorro
Islas Revillagigedo (Mex.)
I. Clarión
2764
Playa Azul

Bipolar Oblique Conic Conformal Projection

1:6,500,000

0 50 100 150 200 250 300 350 400 KILOMETRES

0 50 100 150 200 250 STATUTE MILES

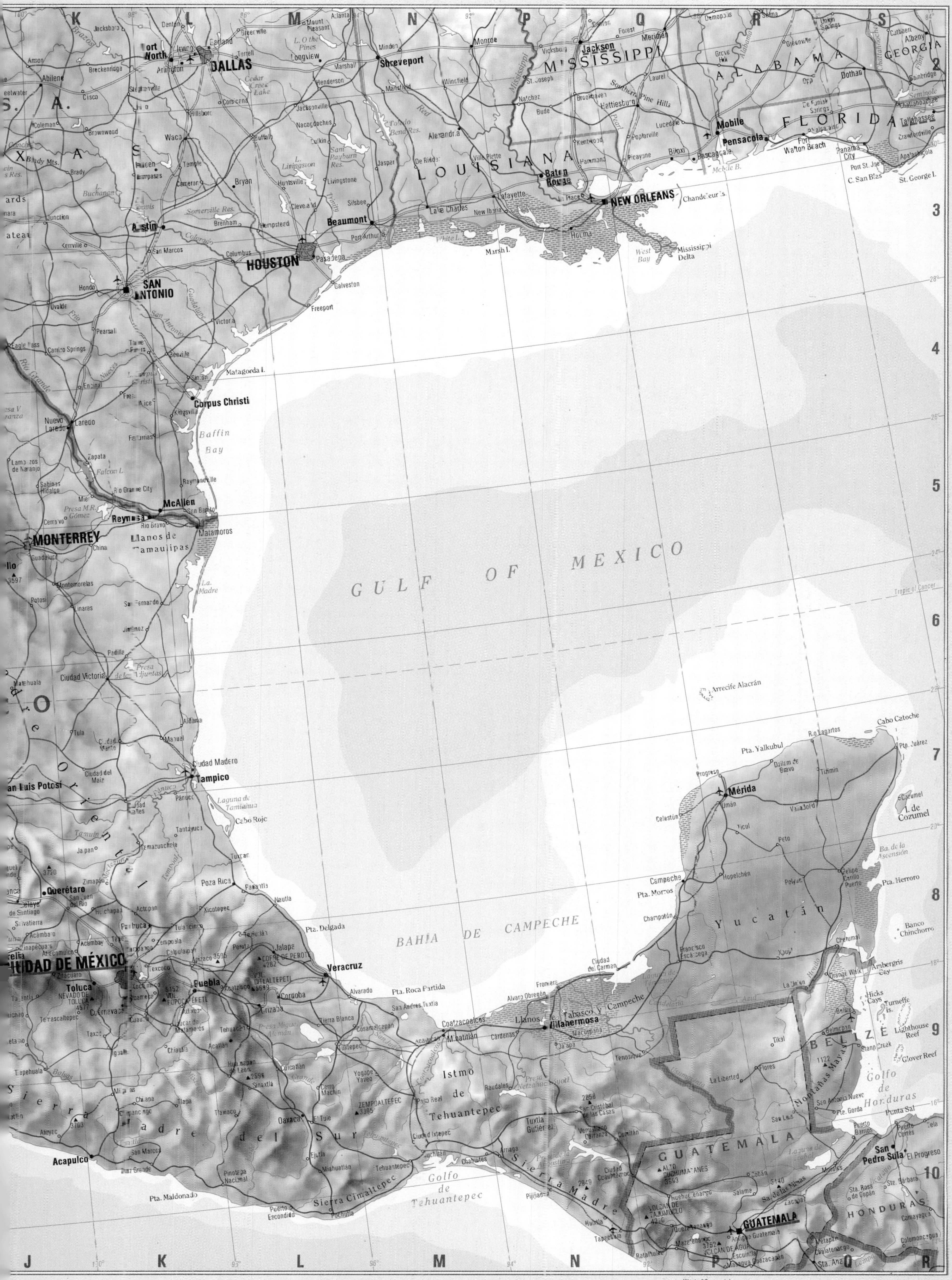
GULF OF MEXICO
BAHIA DE CAMPECHE
Golfo de Tehuantepec
Golfo de Honduras
Tropic of Cancer
MISSISSIPPI
ALABAMA
GEORGIA
FLORIDA
LOUISIANA
GUATEMALA
HONDURAS
BELIZE
Yucatán
Istmo de Tehuantepec
Sierra Madre del Sur
Sierra Madre
Sierra Madre Oriental
DALLAS
Fort Worth
HOUSTON
SAN ANTONIO
Austin
Corpus Christi
McAllen
Laredo
Nuevo Laredo
MONTERREY
Matamoros
Reynosa
Llanos de Tamaulipas
Ciudad Victoria
Tampico
Ciudad Madero
San Luis Potosí
Querétaro
CIUDAD DE MÉXICO
Toluca
Puebla
Cuernavaca
Acapulco
Oaxaca
Veracruz
Jalapa
Córdoba
Orizaba
Poza Rica
Coatzacoalcos
Minatitlán
Villahermosa
Ciudad del Carmen
Campeche
Mérida
Progreso
Chetumal
I. de Cozumel
Cabo Catoche
Arrecife Alacrán
Tuxtla Gutiérrez
San Cristóbal de las Casas
GUATEMALA
Quezaltenango
Cobán
Flores
Tikal
San Pedro Sula
El Progreso
Puerto Cortés
Belize
Lighthouse Reef
Glover Reef
Ambergris Cay
Banco Chinchorro
Shreveport
Jackson
Mobile
Pensacola
Baton Rouge
NEW ORLEANS
Mississippi Delta
Chandeleur Is.
Beaumont
Lafayette
Lake Charles
Galveston
Freeport
Matagorda I.
Baffin Bay
Laguna Madre
Laguna de Tamiahua
Cabo Rojo
Pta. Delgada
Pta. Roca Partida
Pta. Maldonado
Puerto Escondido
Salina Cruz
Tehuantepec
Tapachula
Mississippi
Red
Rio Grande
West of Greenwich
J K L M N P Q R
K L M N P Q R S
2 3 4 5 6 7 8 9 10

Designed and produced by E.S.R.

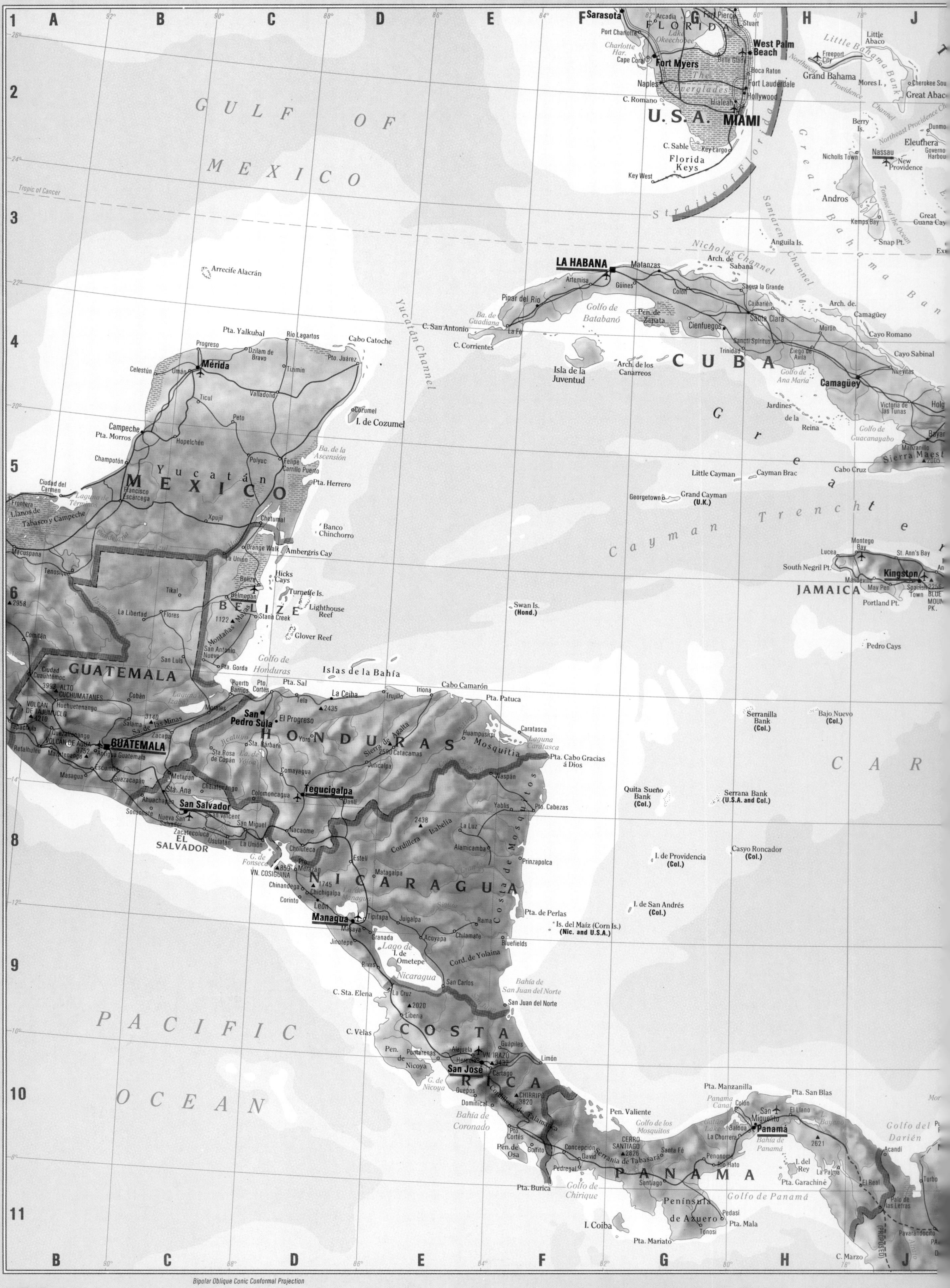
GULF OF MEXICO
Tropic of Cancer
Straits of Florida
FLORIDA
U.S.A.
MIAMI
Sarasota
Arcadia
Fort Pierce
Stuart
Port Charlotte
Lake Okeechobee
Charlotte Har.
Cape Coral
Fort Myers
West Palm Beach
Belle Glade
Boca Raton
Naples
The Everglades
Fort Lauderdale
Hollywood
C. Romano
Hialeah
C. Sable
Key Largo
Florida Keys
Key West
Little Bahama Bank
Little Abaco
Freeport City
Grand Bahama
Northwest Providence Channel
Mores I.
Cherokee Sound
Great Abaco
Berry Is.
Northeast Providence Channel
Eleuthera
Nicholls Town
Nassau
New Providence
Andros
Great Bahama Bank
Tongue of the Ocean
Great Guana Cay
Kemps Bay
Snap Pt.
Santaren Channel
Anguila Is.
Nicholas Channel
Arch. de Sabana
LA HABANA
Matanzas
Artemisa
Güines
Colón
Sagua la Grande
Pinar del Río
Caibarién
Golfo de Batabanó
Ba. de Guadiana
Pen. de Zapata
Cienfuegos
Santa Clara
Arch. de Camagüey
Morón
Cayo Romano
C. San Antonio
La Fe
C. Corrientes
Sancti Spíritus
Trinidad
Ciego de Ávila
Cayo Sabinal
Isla de la Juventud
Arch. de los Canarreos
CUBA
Golfo de Ana María
Camagüey
Nuevitas
Jardines de la Reina
Victoria de las Tunas
Holguín
Golfo de Guacanayabo
Bayamo
Manzanillo
Sierra Maestra
2005
Cabo Cruz
Little Cayman
Cayman Brac
Georgetown
Grand Cayman (U.K.)
Cayman Trench
Caribbean
Montego Bay
Lucea
St. Ann's Bay
South Negril Pt.
Kingston
Mandeville
May Pen
Spanish Town
2256 BLUE MOUNTAIN PK.
JAMAICA
Portland Pt.
Pedro Cays
Yucatán Channel
Arrecife Alacrán
Pta. Yalkubal
Río Lagartos
Cabo Catoche
Progreso
Dzilam de Bravo
Pto. Juárez
Celestún
Umán
Mérida
Tizimín
Valladolid
Ticul
Cozumel
I. de Cozumel
Peto
Campeche
Pta. Morros
Hopelchén
Ba. de la Ascensión
Champotón
Polyuc
Felipe Carrillo Puerto
Yucatán
Pta. Herrero
MEXICO
Ciudad del Carmen
Laguna de Términos
Francisco Escárcega
Frontera
Llanos de Tabasco y Campeche
Xpujil
Chetumal
Banco Chinchorro
Macuspana
Orange Walk
Ambergris Cay
Tenosique
La Unión
Hicks Cays
Belize
Turneffe Is.
Tikal
Belmopan
Lighthouse Reef
2958
La Libertad
Flores
BELIZE
1122
Stann Creek
Swan Is. (Hond.)
Montañas Mayas
Glover Reef
Comitán
San Luis
San Antonio Nuevo
Pta. Gorda
Golfo de Honduras
Islas de la Bahía
GUATEMALA
Ciudad Cuauhtémoc
3998 ALTO CUCHUMATANES
Puerto Barrios
Pto. Cortés
Pta. Sal
La Ceiba
Trujillo
Irioná
Cabo Camarón
Pta. Patuca
Cobán
Laguna de Izabal
Tela
2435
VOLCÁN DE TAJUMULCO 4210
Huehuetenango
San Pedro Sula
El Progreso
Salamá
3140
Sa. de las Minas
Tapachula
Quezaltenango
HONDURAS
Sierra de Agalta
Caratasca
Laguna Caratasca
Huampusirpi
Zacapa
Yoro
Retalhuleu
VOLCÁN DE AGUA
3752
GUATEMALA
Antigua Guatemala
Sta. Bárbara
2590 Catacamas
Mosquitia
Pta. Cabo Gracias á Dios
Mazatenango
Escuintla
Sta. Rosa de Copán
Juticalpa
Masagua
Guazacapán
Metapán
Comayagua
Waspán
Sta. Ana
Chalatenango
Colomoncagua
Tegucigalpa
Quita Sueño Bank (Col.)
Serrana Bank (U.S.A. and Col.)
Serranilla Bank (Col.)
Bajo Nuevo (Col.)
Ahuachapán
San Salvador
Danlí
Yablis
Pto. Cabezas
Sonsonate
Nueva San Salvador
San Vicent
San Miguel
2438
Zacatecoluca
Usulatán
La Unión
Nacaome
Cordillera Isabelia
La Luz
EL SALVADOR
Alamicamba
G. de Fonseca
Choluteca
Estelí
Prinzapolca
VN. COSIGÜINA
Pto. Morazán
I. de Providencia (Col.)
Casyo Roncador (Col.)
Chinandega
1745
Matagalpa
NICARAGUA
Costa de Mosquitos
Chichigalpa
Lago de Managua
Corinto
León
I. de San Andrés (Col.)
Managua
Tipitapa
Juigalpa
Rama
Pta. de Perlas
Is. del Maíz (Corn Is.) (Nic. and U.S.A.)
Masaya
Granada
Acoyapa
Chilamate
Jinotepe
Bluefields
Lago de Nicaragua
I. de Ometepe
Cord. de Yolaina
Rivas
San Carlos
Bahía de San Juan del Norte
C. Sta. Elena
La Cruz
San Juan del Norte
2020
Liberia
PACIFIC OCEAN
C. Velas
COSTA RICA
Guápiles
Pen. de Nicoya
Puntarenas
Alajuela
VN. IRAZÚ
3432
Heredia
Limón
San José
Cartago
G. de Nicoya
Quepos
CHIRRIPÓ 3820
Dominical
Cordillera de Talamanca
Bahía de Coronado
Pto. Cortés
Pen. de Osa
Golfito
Concepción
CERRO SANTIAGO 2826
David
Serranía de Tabasará
Pen. Valiente
Golfo de los Mosquitos
Panamá Canal
Colón
Gatún Lake
Balboa
La Chorrera
San Miguelito
Panamá
Bahía de Panamá
El Llano
Río Bayano
2621
Golfo del Darién
Acandí
Santa Fé
Penonomé
Río Hato
I. del Rey
La Palma
Pedregal
PANAMA
Pta. Garachiné
El Real
Turbo
Pta. Burica
Golfo de Chiriquí
Santiago
Golfo de Panamá
Península de Azuero
Pedasí
Pta. Mala
Tonosí
I. Coiba
Pta. Mariato
Palo de las Letras
Pavarandocito
(PROPOSED)
C. Marzo
Pta. Manzanilla
Pta. San Blas

Bipolar Oblique Conic Conformal Projection

1:7,000,000

0 50 100 150 200 250 300 350 400 KILOMETRES

0 50 100 150 200 250 STATUTE MILES

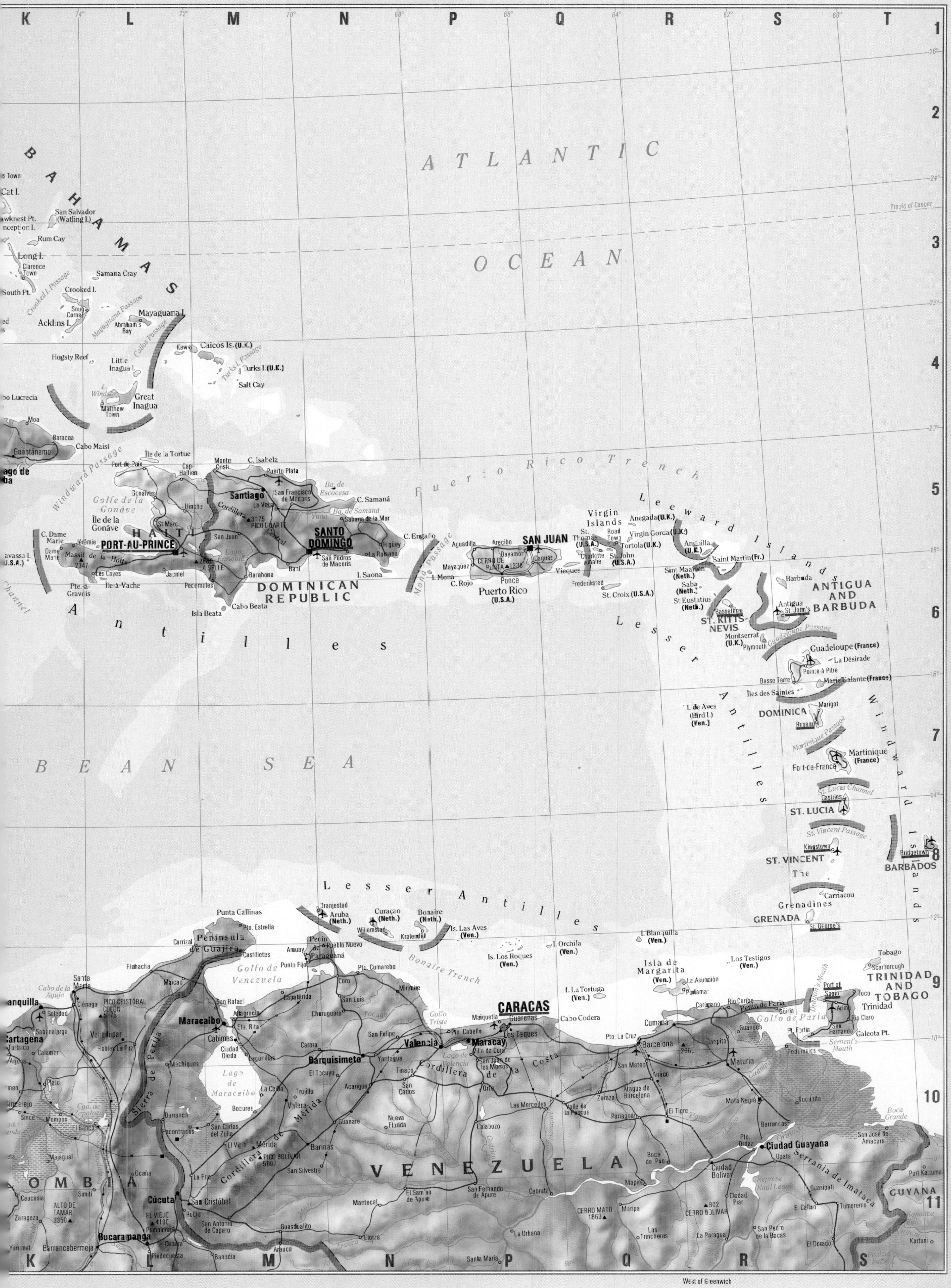
ATLANTIC OCEAN
Tropic of Cancer
BAHAMAS
Cat I.
San Salvador (Watling I.)
Rum Cay
Long I.
Clarence Town
Samana Cay
Crooked I.
Crooked I. Passage
Acklins I.
Mayaguana I.
Mayaguana Passage
Caicos Passage
Abraham's Bay
Caicos Is. (U.K.)
Turks I. (U.K.)
Turks I. Passage
Salt Cay
Hogsty Reef
Little Inagua I.
Great Inagua
Matthew Town
Moa
Baracoa
Cabo Maisí
Guantánamo
Windward Passage
Île de la Tortue
Fort de Paix
Cap-Haïtien
Monte Cristi
C. Isabela
Puerto Plata
Golfe de la Gonâve
Île de la Gonâve
Gonaïves
Hinche
St. Marc
HAITI
PORT-AU-PRINCE
C. Dame Marie
Jérémie
Massif de la Hotte
2347
Les Cayes
Île-à-Vache
Jacmel
Pte.-à-Gravois
Santiago
La Vega
PICO DUARTE
3175
Cordillera Central
San Francisco de Macorís
Ba. de Escocesa
C. Samaná
Ba. de Samaná
Sabana de la Mar
Yuna
SANTO DOMINGO
San Pedro de Macorís
La Romana
Higüey
San Juan
Lago Enriquillo
Barahona
Baní
Pedernales
Cabo Beata
Isla Beata
DOMINICAN REPUBLIC
I. Saona
C. Engaño
Mona Passage
I. Mona
C. Rojo
Puerto Rico Trench
Aguadilla
Arecibo
SAN JUAN
Bayamón
Caguas
CERRO DE PUNTA 1338
Mayagüez
Ponce
Puerto Rico (U.S.A.)
Vieques
Virgin Islands
St. Thomas (U.S.A.)
Charlotte Amalie
St. John (U.S.A.)
Road Town
Tortola (U.K.)
Anegada (U.K.)
Virgin Gorda (U.K.)
Frederiksted
St. Croix (U.S.A.)
Leeward Islands
Anguilla (U.K.)
Saint Martin (Fr.)
Sint Maarten (Neth.)
Saba (Neth.)
St. Eustatius (Neth.)
Basseterre
ST. KITTS-NEVIS
Barbuda
Antigua
St. John's
ANTIGUA AND BARBUDA
Montserrat (U.K.)
Plymouth
Guadeloupe Passage
Guadeloupe (France)
La Désirade
Pointe-à-Pitre
Basse Terre
Marie Galante (France)
Îles des Saintes
Lesser Antilles
I. de Aves (Bird I.) (Ven.)
DOMINICA
Marigot
Roseau
Martinique Passage
Martinique (France)
Fort-de-France
St. Lucia Channel
Castries
ST. LUCIA
St. Vincent Passage
Kingstown
ST. VINCENT
The Grenadines
Carriacou
GRENADA
St. George's
Bridgetown
BARBADOS
Windward Islands
Antilles
CARIBBEAN SEA
Oranjestad
Aruba (Neth.)
Curaçao (Neth.)
Willemstad
Bonaire (Neth.)
Kralendijk
Is. Las Aves (Ven.)
Bonaire Trench
Is. Los Roques (Ven.)
I. Orchila (Ven.)
I. Blanquilla (Ven.)
Los Testigos (Ven.)
Isla de Margarita (Ven.)
La Asunción
Porlamar
I. La Tortuga (Ven.)
Tobago
Scarborough
TRINIDAD AND TOBAGO
Port of Spain
Trinidad
Arima
Toco
Dragon's Mouth
Golfo de Paria
Rio Claro
San Fernando
Galeota Pt.
Serpent's Mouth
Punta Gallinas
Pto. Estrella
Península de Guajira
Carrizal
Castilletes
Riohacha
Maicao
Golfo de Venezuela
Punto Fijo
Amuay
Península de Paraguaná
Pueblo Nuevo
Pto. Cumarebo
Coro
Mirimire
Golfo Triste
Santa Marta
Ciénaga
Barranquilla
Soledad
Cartagena
Sabanalarga
Valledupar
Calamar
PICO CRISTOBAL COLON 5775
San Rafael
Altagracia
Maracaibo
Sta. Rita
Cabimas
Ciudad Ojeda
Lagunillas
Machiques
Lago de Maracaibo
Sierra de Perijá
Capatárida
Churuguara
San Luis
Tocuyo
San Felipe
Carora
Barquisimeto
Yaritagua
Valencia
Pto. Cabello
Maracay
Maiquetía
CARACAS
Guarenas
Los Teques
Cabo Codera
Lago de Valencia
Cordillera de la Costa
El Tocuyo
Tinaco
San Carlos
Acarigua
Trujillo
Valera
La Ceiba
Bobures
Barranca
San Carlos del Zulia
Encontrados
El Vigía
Mérida
Cordillera de Mérida
PICO BOLIVAR 5007
Guanare
Nueva Florida
Barinas
San Silvestre
La Fría
San Cristóbal
Cúcuta
Ocaña
EL VIEJO 4100
Pamplona
San Antonio de Caparo
Bucaramanga
Barrancabermeja
Piedecuesta
Guasdualito
Elorza
Arauca
Banadia
Santa María
Las Mercedes
Calabozo
Ortiz
El Sombrero
Valle de la Pascua
Zaraza
Pariaguán
Atagua de Barcelona
Anaco
El Tigre
Barcelona
Cumaná
Pto. La Cruz
Carúpano
Río Caribe
Penín de Paria
Güiria
Caripito
Maturín
Guanoco
Pedernales
Mata Negra
Tucupita
Barrancas
Boca Grande
San José de Amacuro
Pto. Ordaz
Ciudad Guayana
Upata
Serranía de Imataca
Boca de Pao
Ciudad Bolívar
Represa Raúl Leoni
Ciudad Piar
Guasipati
El Callao
Tumeremo
Mapire
Cabruta
San Fernando de Apure
El Samán de Apure
Mantecal
CERRO MATO 1863
Maripa
CERRO BOLIVAR 802
Las Trincheras
La Paragua
San Pedro de la Bocas
El Dorado
La Urbana
VENEZUELA
Port Kaituma
GUYANA
Kartuni
COLOMBIA
Sincelejo
Mompós
El Banco
Majagual
Simití
Caucasia
ALTO DE TAMAR 2350
Zaragoza
Yarumal
74°
72°
70°
68°
66°
64°
62°
60°
26°
24°
22°
20°
18°
16°
14°
12°
10°
8°
K L M N P Q R S T
1 2 3 4 5 6 7 8 9 10 11

West of Greenwich

Designed and produced by E.S.R.

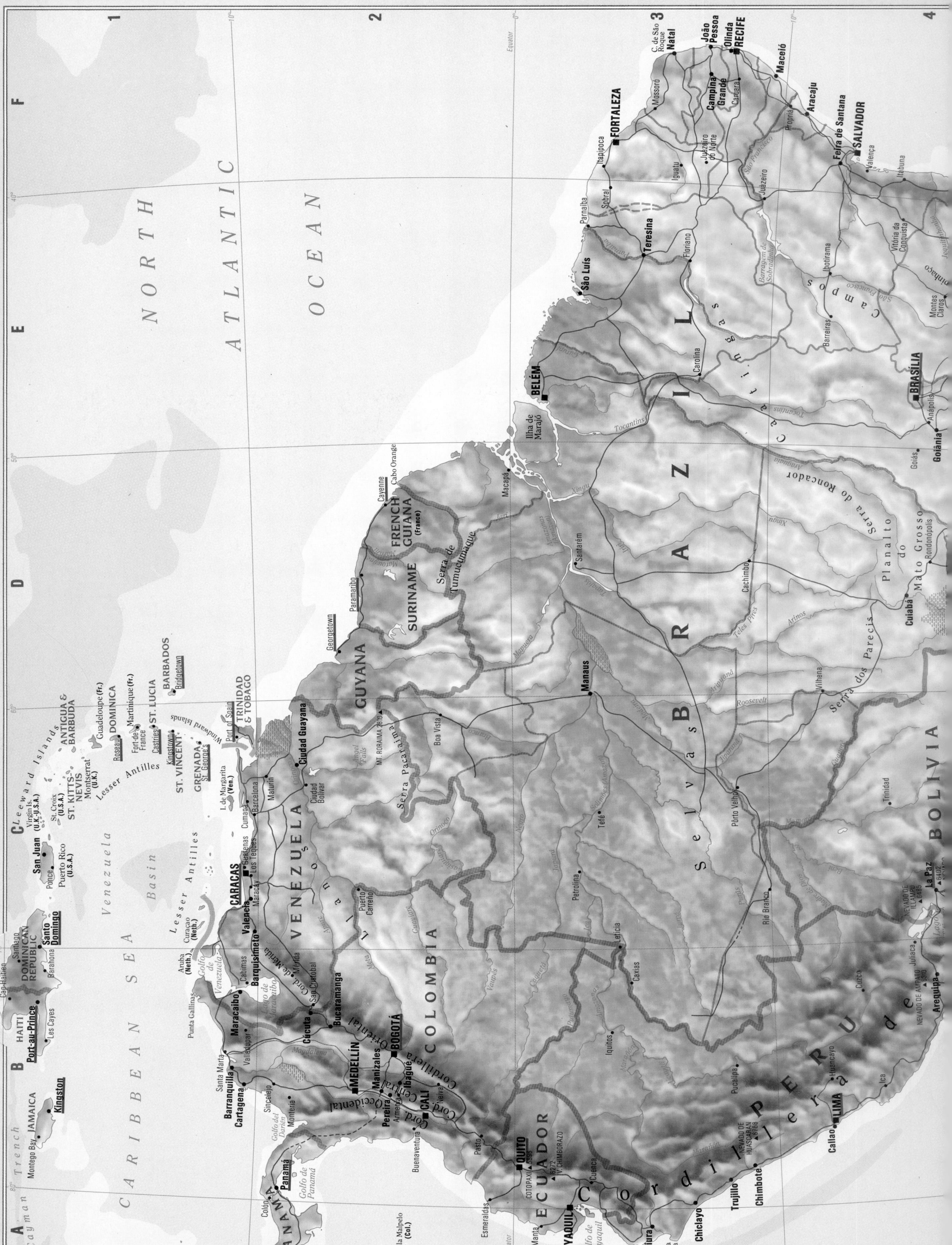
NORTH ATLANTIC OCEAN
CARIBBEAN SEA
Venezuela Basin
Cayman Trench
Leeward Islands
Lesser Antilles
Windward Islands
JAMAICA
Kingston
Montego Bay
HAITI
Port-au-Prince
Les Cayes
Cap-Haïtien
DOMINICAN REPUBLIC
Santo Domingo
Santiago
Barahona
San Juan
Ponce
Puerto Rico (U.S.A.)
Virgin Is. (U.K.-U.S.A.)
St. Croix (U.S.A.)
ST. KITTS-NEVIS
ANTIGUA & BARBUDA
Montserrat (U.K.)
Guadeloupe (Fr.)
DOMINICA
Roseau
Martinique (Fr.)
Fort-de-France
ST. LUCIA
Castries
BARBADOS
Bridgetown
ST. VINCENT
Kingstown
GRENADA
St. George's
TRINIDAD & TOBAGO
Port of Spain
I. de Margarita (Ven.)
Aruba (Neth.)
Curaçao (Neth.)
Punta Gallinas
Golfo de Venezuela
PANAMA
Panamá
Colón
Golfo de Panamá
Golfo del Darién
Isla Malpelo (Col.)
COLOMBIA
BOGOTÁ
MEDELLÍN
CALI
Barranquilla
Cartagena
Santa Marta
Cúcuta
Bucaramanga
Manizales
Pereira
Ibagué
Armenia
Neiva
Pasto
Buenaventura
Montería
Sincelejo
Valledupar
Leticia
Puerto Carreño
Cordillera Occidental
Cordillera Central
Cordillera Oriental
VENEZUELA
CARACAS
Maracaibo
Barquisimeto
Valencia
Maracay
Los Teques
Cumaná
Barcelona
Maturín
Ciudad Bolívar
Ciudad Guayana
Mérida
San Cristóbal
Cabimas
Llanos
GUYANA
Georgetown
SURINAME
Paramaribo
FRENCH GUIANA (France)
Cayenne
Cabo Orange
Serra de Tumucumaque
Serra Pacaraima
Mt. RORAIMA 2810
ECUADOR
QUITO
GUAYAQUIL
Cuenca
Esmeraldas
Manta
Golfo de Guayaquil
COTOPAXI 5896
CHIMBORAZO 6272
PERU
LIMA
Callao
Arequipa
Cuzco
Iquitos
Pucallpa
Chiclayo
Trujillo
Chimbote
Piura
Punta Aguja
Huancayo
Juliaca
Ica
NEVADO DE HUASCARÁN 6768
BOLIVIA
La Paz
Trinidad
Cordillera de los Andes
BRAZIL
BRASÍLIA
BELÉM
FORTALEZA
RECIFE
SALVADOR
Manaus
Natal
João Pessoa
Olinda
Maceió
Aracaju
Campina Grande
Teresina
São Luís
Macapá
Santarém
Boa Vista
Pôrto Velho
Rio Branco
Cuiabá
Goiânia
Anápolis
Feira de Santana
Vitória da Conquista
Montes Claros
Juàzeiro
Carolina
Floriano
Sobral
Parnaíba
Mossoró
Tefé
Cachimbo
Vilhena
Ilha de Marajó
C. de São Roque
Selvas
Campos
Caatingas
Planalto do Mato Grosso
Serra dos Parecis
Serra do Roncador
Tocantins
Xingu
Amazonas
Madeira
Equator

Bipolar Oblique Conic Conformal Projection

1:16,000,000

0 100 200 300 400 500 600 700 800 KILOMETRES

0 100 200 300 400 500 STATUTE MILES

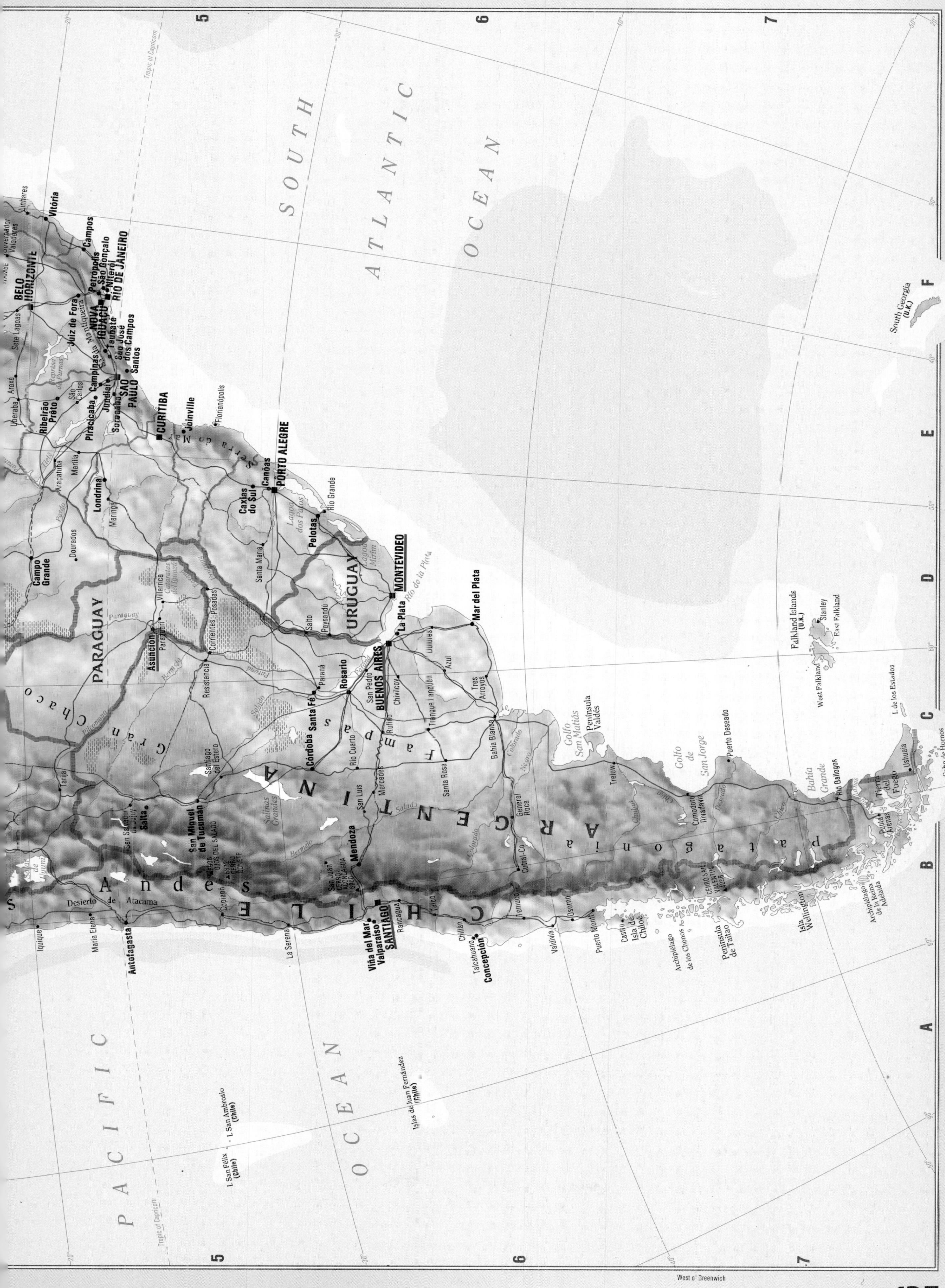
SOUTH ATLANTIC OCEAN
PACIFIC OCEAN
PARAGUAY
URUGUAY
ARGENTINA
CHILE
Gran Chaco
Pampas
Patagonia
Andes
Desierto de Atacama
Tropic of Capricorn
BELO HORIZONTE
Vitória
Campos
Petrópolis
RIO DE JANEIRO
Juiz de Fora
SÃO PAULO
Santos
Campinas
Ribeirão Prêto
Piracicaba
CURITIBA
Joinville
Florianópolis
Londrina
Campo Grande
Dourados
PÔRTO ALEGRE
Caxias do Sul
Canoas
Pelotas
Rio Grande
Santa Maria
MONTEVIDEO
Río de la Plata
Asunción
Corrientes
Posadas
Resistencia
Paysandú
Salto
La Plata
BUENOS AIRES
Mar del Plata
Rosario
Paraná
Santa Fé
Córdoba
Río Cuarto
Tandil
Azul
Tres Arroyos
Bahía Blanca
Santa Rosa
Mercedes
San Luis
Mendoza
San Juan
San Miguel de Tucumán
Santiago del Estero
Salta
Tarija
Iquique
Antofagasta
María Elena
Copiapó
La Serena
Viña del Mar
Valparaíso
SANTIAGO
Rancagua
Talca
Chillán
Talcahuano
Concepción
Temuco
Valdivia
Osorno
Puerto Montt
Isla de Chiloé
Archipiélago de los Chonos
Península de Taitao
Isla Wellington
Archipiélago de la Reina Adelaida
Punta Arenas
Tierra del Fuego
Ushuaia
Cabo de Hornos
Río Gallegos
Bahía Grande
Comodoro Rivadavia
Golfo de San Jorge
Puerto Deseado
Trelew
Península Valdés
Golfo San Matías
General Roca
Neuquén
Falkland Islands (U.K.)
Stanley
West Falkland
East Falkland
I. de los Estados
South Georgia (U.K.)
I. San Félix (Chile)
I. San Ambrosio (Chile)
Islas de Juan Fernández (Chile)
A
B
C
D
E
F
5
6
7

West of Greenwich

Designed and produced by E.S.R.

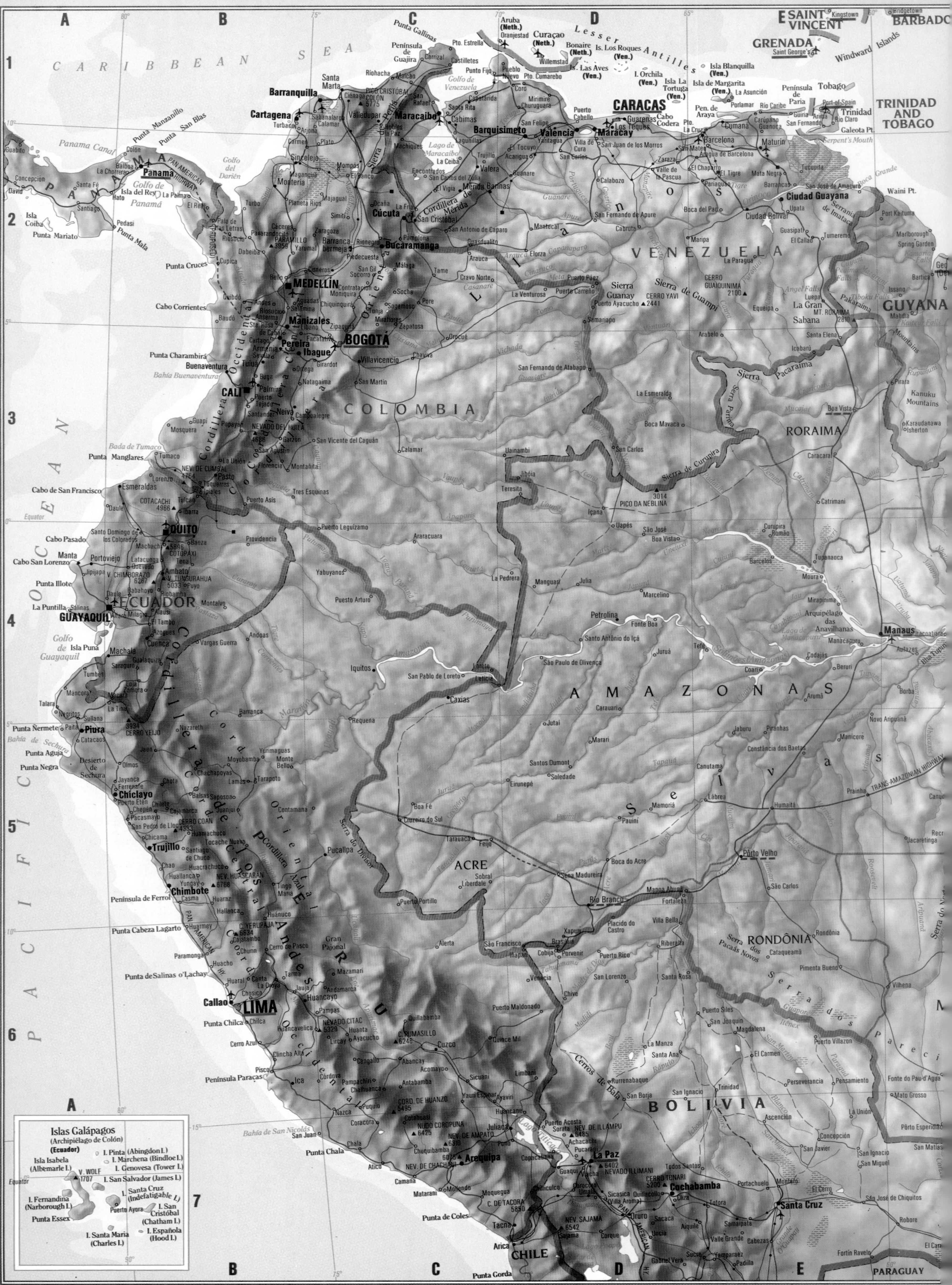
CARIBBEAN SEA
PACIFIC OCEAN
Lesser Antilles
SAINT VINCENT
BARBADOS
GRENADA
TRINIDAD AND TOBAGO
Windward Islands
Aruba (Neth.)
Curaçao (Neth.)
Bonaire (Neth.)
Is. Los Roques (Ven.)
Isla de Margarita (Ven.)
CARACAS
Maracaibo
Barquisimeto
Valencia
Maracay
Barcelona
Cumaná
Ciudad Guayana
Ciudad Bolívar
Lago de Maracaibo
Golfo de Venezuela
Península de Guajira
Barranquilla
Cartagena
Santa Marta
PICO CRISTOBAL COLON 5775
Cúcuta
Bucaramanga
MEDELLÍN
Manizales
Pereira
Ibagué
BOGOTÁ
Villavicencio
CALI
Buenaventura
Panama Canal
Panamá
Golfo de Panamá
PANAMA
Golfo del Darién
Llanos
VENEZUELA
COLOMBIA
GUYANA
RORAIMA
Boa Vista
Sierra Pacaraima
MT. RORAIMA 2810
Angel Falls
PICO DA NEBLINA 3014
Serra de Curupira
Cordillera Occidental
Cordillera Central
Cordillera Oriental
NEVADO DEL HUILA 4686
ECUADOR
QUITO
GUAYAQUIL
Golfo de Guayaquil
Equator
COTOPAXI 5896
V. CHIMBORAZO 6267
Cuenca
Machala
Iquitos
Leticia
Manaus
AMAZONAS
Selvas
Amazonas
TRANS AMAZONIAN HIGHWAY
ACRE
Rio Branco
Porto Velho
RONDÔNIA
Piura
Chiclayo
Trujillo
Chimbote
NEV. HUASCARAN 6768
PERU
Cordillera de los Andes
LIMA
Callao
Huancayo
Cuzco
Arequipa
Lago Titicaca
La Paz
NEVADO ILLIMANI
Cochabamba
Santa Cruz
Oruro
Sucre
BOLIVIA
CHILE
PARAGUAY
Arica
Tacna
Islas Galápagos (Archipiélago de Colón) (Ecuador)
I. Isabela (Albemarle I.)
I. Fernandina (Narborough I.)
I. Santa Cruz (Indefatigable I.)
I. San Cristóbal (Chatham I.)
I. Española (Hood I.)
I. Santa María (Charles I.)
I. San Salvador (James I.)
I. Pinta (Abingdon I.)
I. Marchena (Bindloe I.)
I. Genovesa (Tower I.)
Puerto Ayora
Punta Essex
V. WOLF 1707

Bipolar Oblique Conic Conformal Projection

1:11,000,000

0 100 200 300 400 500 600 700 800 KILOMETRES
0 100 200 300 400 500 STATUTE MILES

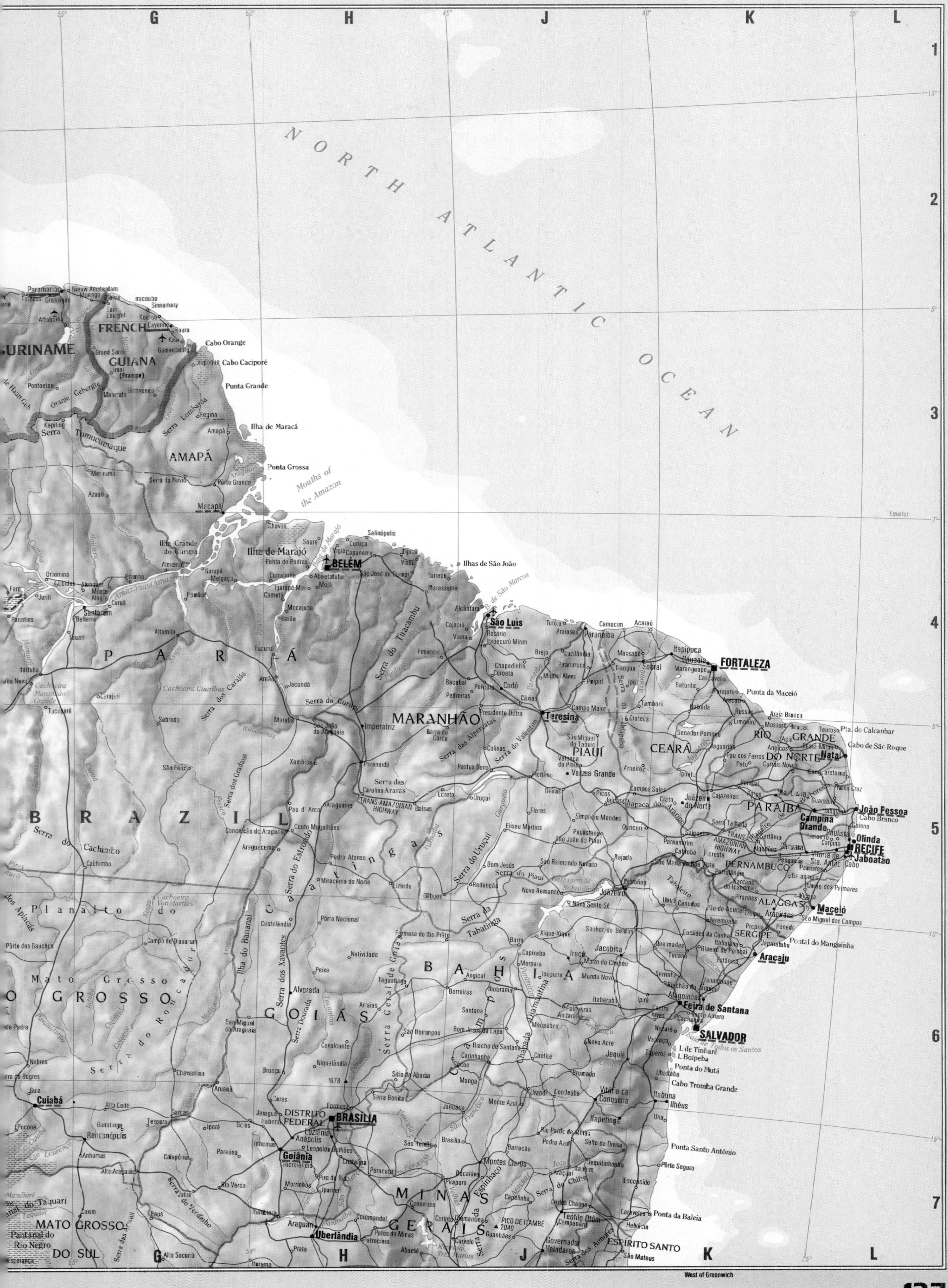
G
H
J
K
L
1
2
3
4
5
6
7
NORTH ATLANTIC OCEAN
SURINAME
FRENCH GUIANA (France)
AMAPÁ
Mouths of the Amazon
Ilha de Marajó
PARÁ
MARANHÃO
PIAUÍ
CEARÁ
RIO GRANDE DO NORTE
PARAÍBA
PERNAMBUCO
ALAGOAS
SERGIPE
BAHIA
GOIÁS
DISTRITO FEDERAL
MINAS GERAIS
ESPÍRITO SANTO
MATO GROSSO
MATO GROSSO DO SUL
BRAZIL
Planalto do Mato Grosso
Serra do Roncador
Serra do Cachimbo
Serra Tumucumaque
Caatinga
Chapada Diamantina
Serra do Espinhaço
TRANS-AMAZONIAN HIGHWAY
Paramaribo
Cabo Orange
Cabo Caciporé
Punta Grande
Ilha de Maracá
Ponta Grossa
Macapá
Salinópolis
Ilhas de São João
BELÉM
São Luís
FORTALEZA
Punta da Maceió
Teresina
Pta. do Calcanhar
Cabo de São Roque
Natal
João Pessoa
Cabo Branco
Campina Grande
Olinda
RECIFE
Jaboatão
Maceió
Aracaju
Pontal do Manguinha
Feira de Santana
SALVADOR
Baía de Todos os Santos
I. de Tinharé
I. Boipeba
Ponta do Mutá
Cabo Tromba Grande
Ilhéus
Ponta Santo Antônio
Pôrto Seguro
Ponta da Baleia
BRASÍLIA
Goiânia
Uberlândia
Cuiabá
Santarém
Imperatriz
Juazeiro
Petrolina
Montes Claros
Governador Valadares
PICO DE ITAMBÉ 2040
Equator
West of Greenwich

Designed and produced by E.S.R.

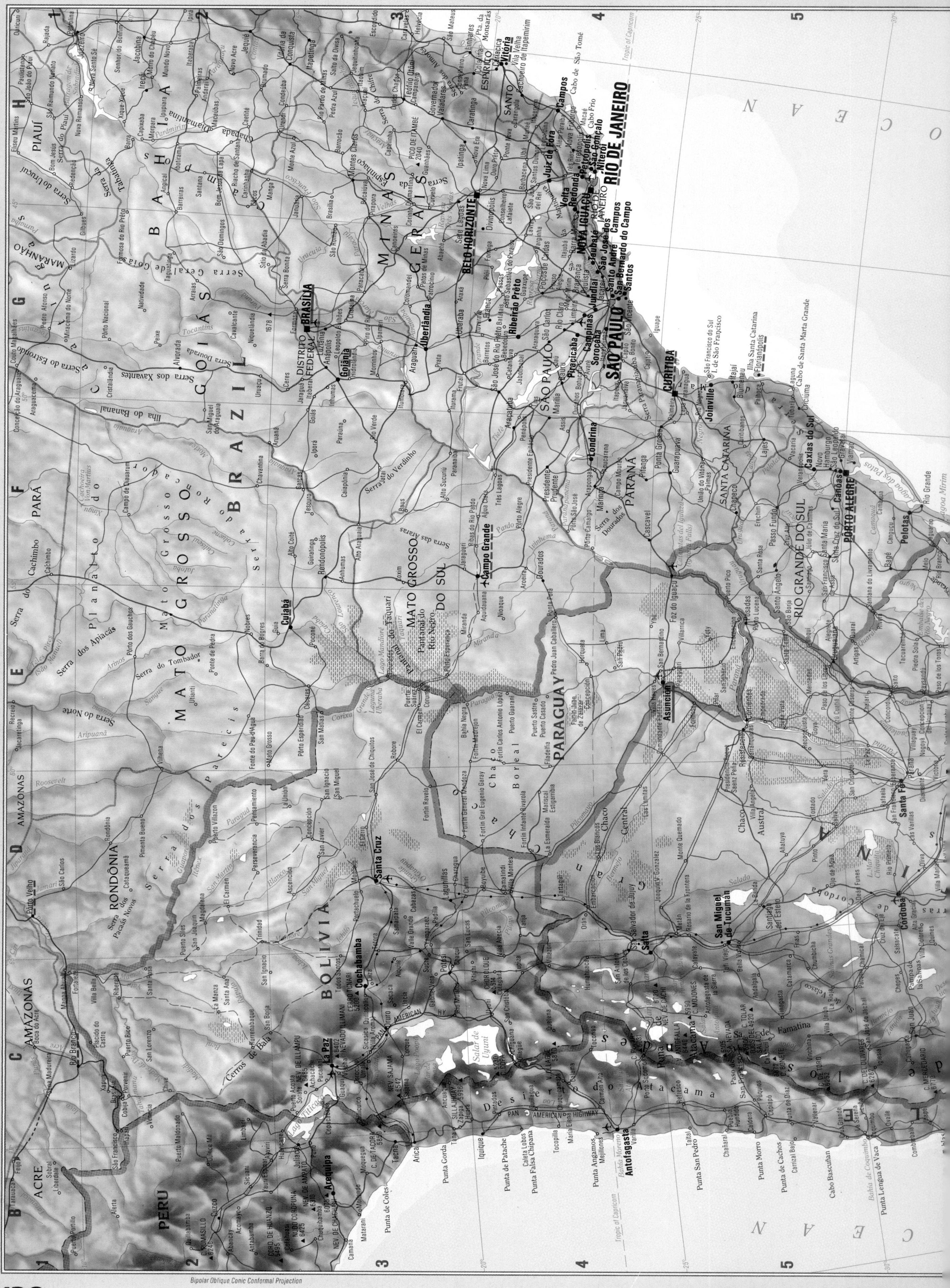
BRAZIL
BOLIVIA
PARAGUAY
PERU
BAHIA
MINAS GERAIS
GOIÁS
MATO GROSSO
MATO GROSSO DO SUL
SÃO PAULO
PARANÁ
SANTA CATARINA
RIO GRANDE DO SUL
RIO DE JANEIRO
ESPÍRITO SANTO
RONDÔNIA
AMAZONAS
ACRE
PARÁ
PIAUÍ
MARANHÃO
DISTRITO FEDERAL
BRASÍLIA
RIO DE JANEIRO
SÃO PAULO
BELO HORIZONTE
CURITIBA
PORTO ALEGRE
Campo Grande
Cuiabá
Goiânia
Uberlândia
Ribeirão Prêto
Campinas
Santos
Londrina
Joinville
Florianópolis
Pelotas
Caxias do Sul
Vitória
Campos
Juiz de Fora
Asunción
Santa Cruz
Cochabamba
La Paz
Arequipa
Antofagasta
Salta
San Miguel de Tucumán
Córdoba
Santa Fe
Corrientes
Posadas
Arica
Iquique
Tacna
Lago Titicaca
Salar de Uyuni
Desierto de Atacama
PAN AMERICAN HIGHWAY
Chaco Boreal
Chaco Central
Chaco Austral
Pantanal do Rio Negro
Pantanal do Taquari
Serra dos Parecis
Serra do Roncador
Serra Geral de Goiás
Serra do Espinhaço
Ilha do Bananal
Ilha Santa Catarina
Lagoa dos Patos
Lagoa Mirim
Tropic of Capricorn
OCEAN
Cabo de São Tomé
Cabo Frio

Bipolar Oblique Conic Conformal Projection

1:11,000,000

0 100 200 300 400 500 600 700 800 KILOMETRES

0 100 200 300 400 500 STATUTE MILES

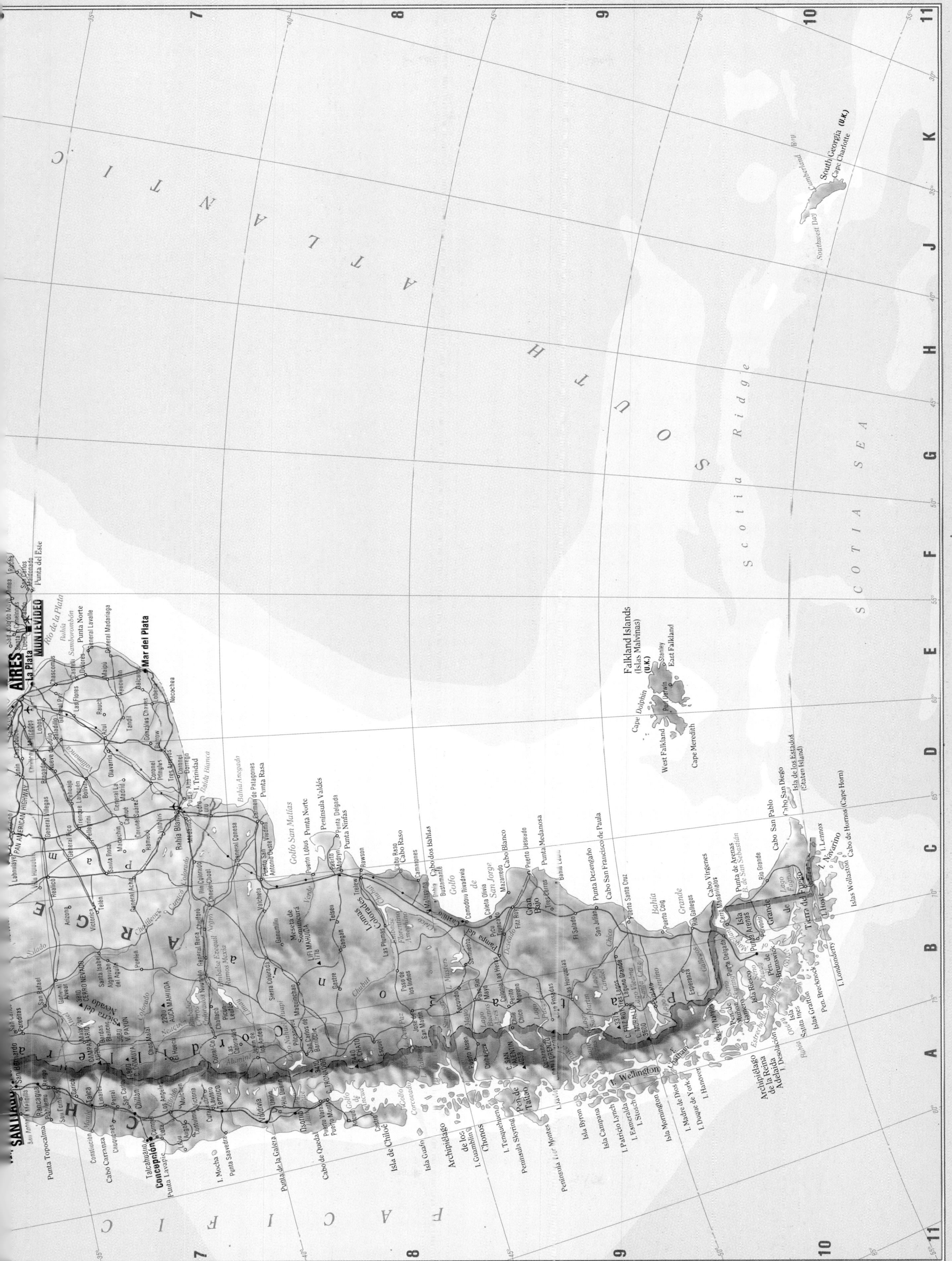
SOUTH ATLANTIC
PACIFIC
SCOTIA SEA
Scotia Ridge
Falkland Islands
(Islas Malvinas)
(U.K.)
West Falkland
East Falkland
Stanley
Cape Dolphin
Cape Meredith
South Georgia (U.K.)
Cape Charlotte
Cumberland Bay
Southwest Bay
ARGENTINA
CHILE
PATAGONIA
MONTEVIDEO
La Plata
Mar del Plata
Punta del Este
Río de la Plata
Bahía Blanca
Golfo San Matías
Península Valdés
Golfo San Jorge
Comodoro Rivadavia
Rawson
Trelew
Puerto Madryn
Viedma
Neuquén
Concepción
Talcahuano
Temuco
Valdivia
Osorno
Puerto Montt
Isla de Chiloé
Archipiélago de los Chonos
Península de Taitao
Golfo de Penas
I. Wellington
Punta Arenas
Isla Grande de Tierra del Fuego
Estrecho de Magallanes
Río Gallegos
Puerto Santa Cruz
Bahía Grande
Cabo Vírgenes
Isla de los Estados (Staten Island)
Cabo de Hornos (Cape Horn)
Islas Wollaston
I. Navarino
Ushuaia
Archipiélago de la Reina Adelaida
Isla Desolación
Isla Santa Inés
Pen. Brunswick
Pen. Brecknock
Gran Bajo
Pampa del Castillo
Meseta de Somuncurá
PAN AMERICAN HIGHWAY
West of Greenwich

Designed and produced by E.S.R.

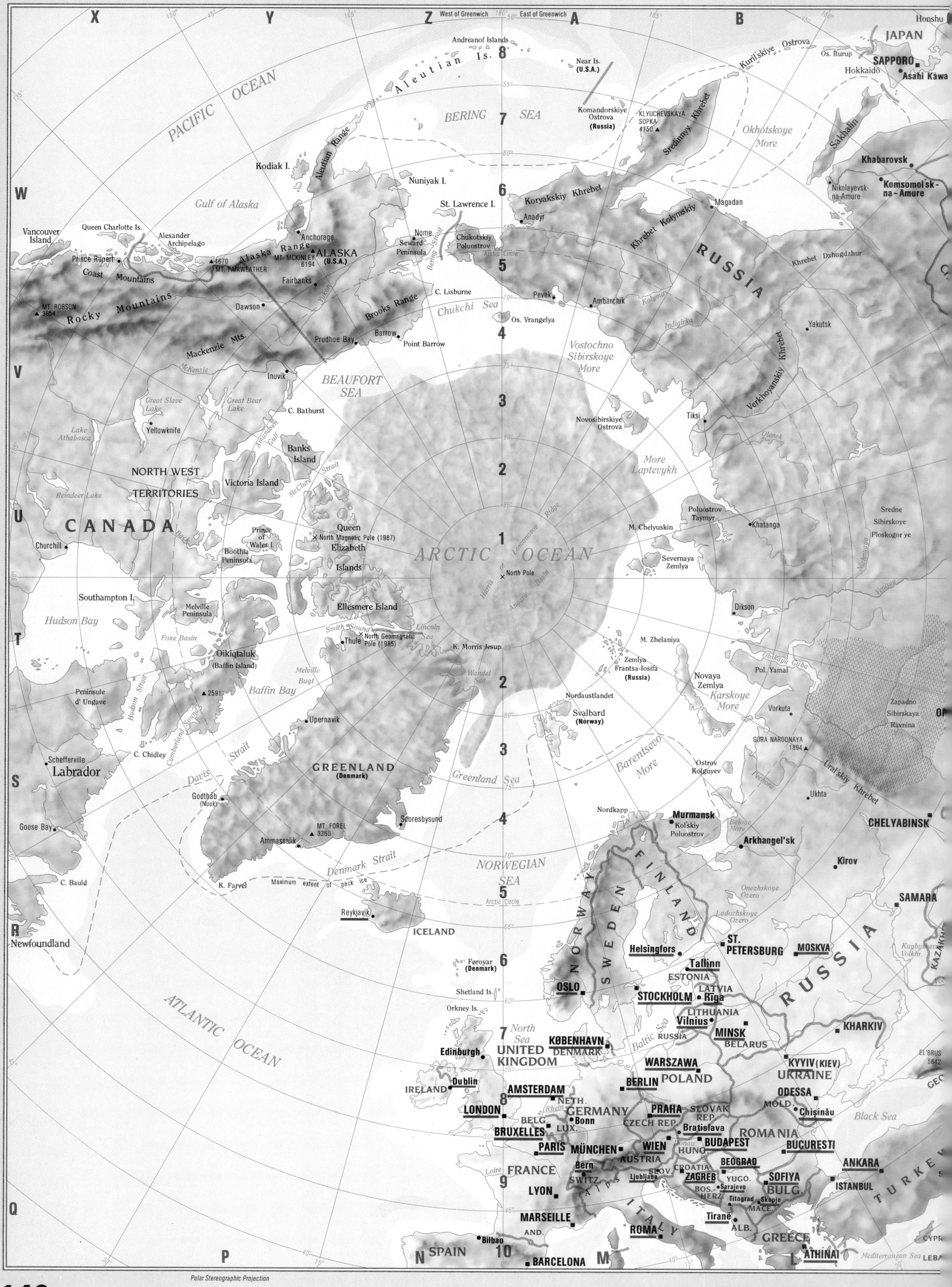
PACIFIC OCEAN
Aleutian Is.
Andreanof Islands
Near Is. (U.S.A.)
BERING SEA
Komandorskiye Ostrova (Russia)
KLYUCHEVSKAYA SOPKA 4750
Sredinnyy Khrebet
Kuril'skiye Ostrova
Os. Iturup
JAPAN
Honshu
SAPPORO
Hokkaido
Asahi Kawa
Sakhalin
Okhotskoye More
Khabarovsk
Komsomol'sk-na-Amure
Nikolayevsk-na-Amure
Kodiak I.
Aleutian Range
Nuniyak I.
Gulf of Alaska
St. Lawrence I.
Koryakskiy Khrebet
Anadyr
Magadan
Khrebet Kolymskiy
Vancouver Island
Queen Charlotte Is.
Alexander Archipelago
Anchorage
Alaska Range
ALASKA (U.S.A.)
MT. MCKINLEY 6194
Nome
Seward Peninsula
Bering Strait
Chukotskiy Poluostrov
Arctic Circle
RUSSIA
Khrebet Dzhugdzhur
Prince Rupert
Coast Mountains
4670 MT. FAIRWEATHER
Fairbanks
Yukon
C. Lisburne
Pevek
Ambarchik
Kolyma
MT. ROBSON 3954
Rocky Mountains
Dawson
Brooks Range
Chukchi Sea
Os. Vrangelya
Indigirka
Yakutsk
Mackenzie Mts.
Prudhoe Bay
Barrow
Point Barrow
Vostochno Sibirskoye More
Verkhoyanskiy Khrebet
McKenzie
Inuvik
BEAUFORT SEA
Great Slave Lake
Great Bear Lake
C. Bathurst
Novosibirskiye Ostrova
Tiksi
Lena
Yellowknife
Lake Athabasca
Amundsen Gulf
Banks Island
McClure Strait
Olenek
NORTH WEST TERRITORIES
Victoria Island
More Laptevykh
Reindeer Lake
CANADA
Back
Prince of Wales I.
Queen Elizabeth Islands
North Magnetic Pole (1987)
Lomonosov Ridge
Poluostrov Taymyr
M. Chelyuskin
Khatanga
Sredne Sibirskoye Ploskogor'ye
Churchill
Boothia Peninsula
ARCTIC OCEAN
North Pole
Severnaya Zemlya
Nizhnyaya
Yenisey
Southampton I.
Melville Peninsula
Ellesmere Island
Harris
Angara Basin
Dikson
Hudson Bay
Foxe Basin
Smith Sound
Thule
North Geomagnetic Pole (1985)
Lincoln Sea
K. Morris Jesup
M. Zhelaniya
Zemlya Frantsa-Iosifa (Russia)
Obskaya Guba
Pol. Yamal
Oikiqtaluk (Baffin Island)
Melville Bugt
Wandel Sea
Novaya Zemlya
Peninsule d' Ungave
Hudson Strait
2591
Baffin Bay
Nordaustlandet
Svalbard (Norway)
Karskoye More
Vorkuta
Zapadno Sibirskaya Ravnina
Upernavik
Cumberland Sound
C. Chidley
Davis Strait
GORA NARODNAYA 1894
Schefferville
Labrador
GREENLAND (Denmark)
Greenland Sea
Barentsevo More
Ostrov Kolguyev
Pechora
Ural'skiy Khrebet
Ob
Godthåb (Nuuk)
Ukhta
Goose Bay
MT. FOREL 3360
Scoresbysund
Nordkapp
Murmansk
Kol'skiy Poluostrov
Beloye More
CHELYABINSK
Ammassalik
Arkhangel'sk
Denmark Strait
NORWEGIAN SEA
Kirov
C. Bauld
K. Farvel
Maximum extent of pack ice
NORWAY
FINLAND
SWEDEN
Onezhskoye Ozero
SAMARA
Reykjavik
ICELAND
Ladozhskoye Ozero
Newfoundland
Helsingfors
ST. PETERSBURG
MOSKVA
Kuybyshevskoye Vdkhr.
KAZAKHSTAN
Føroyar (Denmark)
Tallinn
ESTONIA
OSLO
Shetland Is.
STOCKHOLM
LATVIA
Riga
ATLANTIC OCEAN
Orkney Is.
LITHUANIA
Vilnius
MINSK
KHARKIV
North Sea
KØBENHAVN
DENMARK
RUSSIA
BELARUS
Baltic Sea
Edinburgh
UNITED KINGDOM
WARSZAWA
KYYIV (KIEV)
EL'BRUS 5642
UKRAINE
IRELAND
Dublin
AMSTERDAM
BERLIN
POLAND
ODESSA
NETH.
Rhein
GERMANY
PRAHA
SLOVAK REP.
MOLD.
Chişinău
LONDON
BELG.
Bonn
Black Sea
LUX.
CZECH REP.
Bratislava
ROMANIA
BRUXELLES
PARIS
MÜNCHEN
WIEN
BUDAPEST
BUCURESTI
AUSTRIA
Donau
HUNG.
Loire
FRANCE
Bern
CROATIA
BEOGRAD
ANKARA
SWITZ.
Ljubljana
SLOV.
ZAGREB
YUGO.
SOFIYA
Alps
BOS.-HERZ.
Sarajevo
BULG.
ISTANBUL
TURKEY
LYON
Titograd
Skopje
MACE.
MARSEILLE
ITALY
Tirane
ALB.
AND.
ROMA
Bilbao
GREECE
SPAIN
BARCELONA
ATHINAI
Mediterranean Sea
CYPRUS
LEBANON
West of Greenwich
East of Greenwich
X
Y
Z
A
B
W
V
U
T
S
R
Q
P
N
M
L
1
2
3
4
5
6
7
8
9
10

Polar Stereographic Projection

Scale 1:30,000,000 (Approx.)

0 250 500 750 1000 1250 1500 KILOMETRES

0 250 500 750 1000 STATUTE MILES

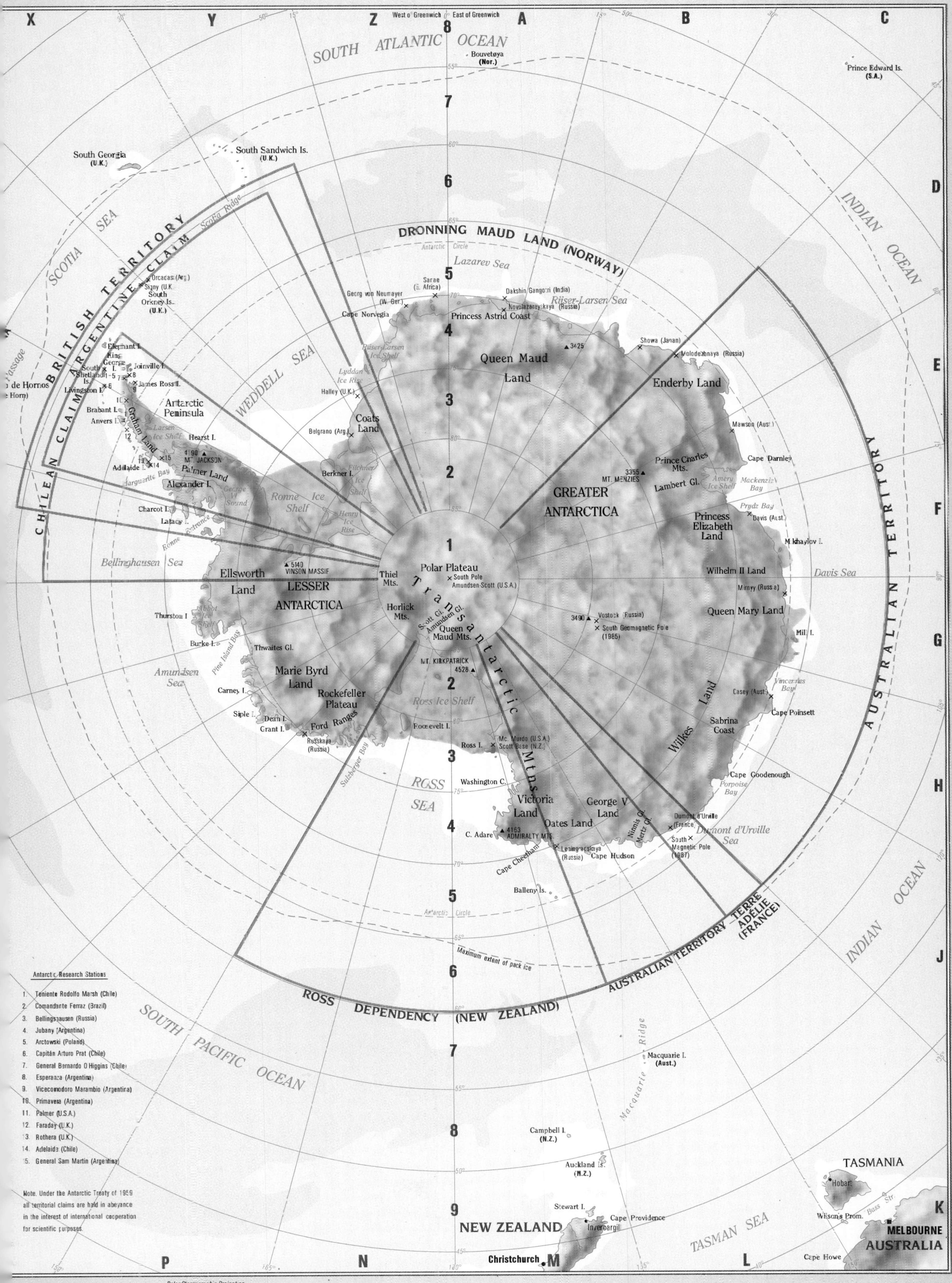
SOUTH ATLANTIC OCEAN
West of Greenwich
East of Greenwich
Bouvetøya (Nor.)
Prince Edward Is. (S.A.)
South Georgia (U.K.)
South Sandwich Is. (U.K.)
SCOTIA SEA
Scotia Ridge
BRITISH TERRITORY
ARGENTINE CLAIM
CHILEAN CLAIM
Orcadas (Arg.)
Signy (U.K.)
South Orkney Is. (U.K.)
WEDDELL SEA
DRONNING MAUD LAND (NORWAY)
Antarctic Circle
Lazarev Sea
Riiser-Larsen Sea
INDIAN OCEAN
Sanae (S. Africa)
Georg von Neumayer (W. Ger.)
Dakshin Gangotri (India)
Novolazarevskaya (Russia)
Cape Norvegia
Princess Astrid Coast
Riiser-Larsen Ice Shelf
Lyddan Ice Rise
Halley (U.K.)
Queen Maud Land
Showa (Japan)
Molodezhnaya (Russia)
Enderby Land
Elephant I.
King George I.
South Shetland Is.
Joinville I.
James Ross I.
Livingston I.
Cabo de Hornos (Cape Horn)
Drake Passage
Brabant I.
Anvers I.
Antarctic Peninsula
Graham Land
Larsen Ice Shelf
Hearst I.
Adelaide I.
Marguerite Bay
1190 MT. JACKSON
Palmer Land
Alexander I.
George VI Sound
Charcot I.
Latady I.
Ronne Entrance
Ronne Ice Shelf
Coats Land
Belgrano (Arg.)
Berkner I.
Filchner Ice Shelf
Henry Ice Rise
Mawson (Aust.)
Cape Darnley
Prince Charles Mts.
3355 MT. MENZIES
Lambert Gl.
Amery Ice Shelf
Mackenzie Bay
GREATER ANTARCTICA
Prydz Bay
Davis (Aust.)
Princess Elizabeth Land
Mikhaylov I.
Bellingshausen Sea
5140 VINSON MASSIF
Ellsworth Land
LESSER ANTARCTICA
Thiel Mts.
Polar Plateau
South Pole
Amundsen-Scott (U.S.A.)
Transantarctic Mtns.
Horlick Mts.
Scott Gl.
Amundsen Gl.
Queen Maud Mts.
Wilhelm II Land
Davis Sea
Mirnyy (Russia)
Queen Mary Land
3490
Vostock (Russia)
South Geomagnetic Pole (1985)
Mill I.
Thurston I.
Abbot Ice Shelf
Burke I.
Pine Island Bay
Thwaites Gl.
Amundsen Sea
Marie Byrd Land
MT. KIRKPATRICK 4528
Carney I.
Rockefeller Plateau
Ross Ice Shelf
Siple I.
Dean I.
Grant I.
Ford Ranges
Russkaya (Russia)
Roosevelt I.
Sulzberger Bay
Ross I.
Mc. Murdo (U.S.A.)
Scott Base (N.Z.)
Wilkes Land
Vincennes Bay
Casey (Aust.)
Cape Poinsett
Sabrina Coast
AUSTRALIAN TERRITORY
ROSS SEA
Washington C.
Cape Goodenough
Porpoise Bay
Victoria Land
George V Land
Oates Land
Ninnis Gl.
Mertz Gl.
Dumont d'Urville (France)
Dumont d'Urville Sea
4163 ADMIRALTY MTS.
C. Adare
Leningradskaya (Russia)
Cape Cheetham
Cape Hudson
South Magnetic Pole (1987)
Balleny Is.
Maximum extent of pack ice
TERRE ADÉLIE (FRANCE)
AUSTRALIAN TERRITORY
ROSS DEPENDENCY (NEW ZEALAND)
SOUTH PACIFIC OCEAN
Macquarie Ridge
Macquarie I. (Aust.)
Campbell I. (N.Z.)
Auckland Is. (N.Z.)
Stewart I.
Invercargill
Cape Providence
NEW ZEALAND
Christchurch
TASMAN SEA
TASMANIA
Hobart
Bass Str.
Wilson's Prom.
MELBOURNE
AUSTRALIA
Cape Howe
Antarctic Research Stations
1. Teniente Rodolfo Marsh (Chile)
2. Comandante Ferraz (Brazil)
3. Bellingshausen (Russia)
4. Jubany (Argentina)
5. Arctowski (Poland)
6. Capitán Arturo Prat (Chile)
7. General Bernardo O'Higgins (Chile)
8. Esperanza (Argentina)
9. Vicecomodoro Marambio (Argentina)
10. Primavera (Argentina)
11. Palmer (U.S.A.)
12. Faraday (U.K.)
13. Rothera (U.K.)
14. Adelaide (Chile)
15. General Sam Martin (Argentina)
Note. Under the Antarctic Treaty of 1959 all territorial claims are held in abeyance in the interest of international cooperation for scientific purposes.
Polar Stereographic Projection

Designed and produced by E.S.R.

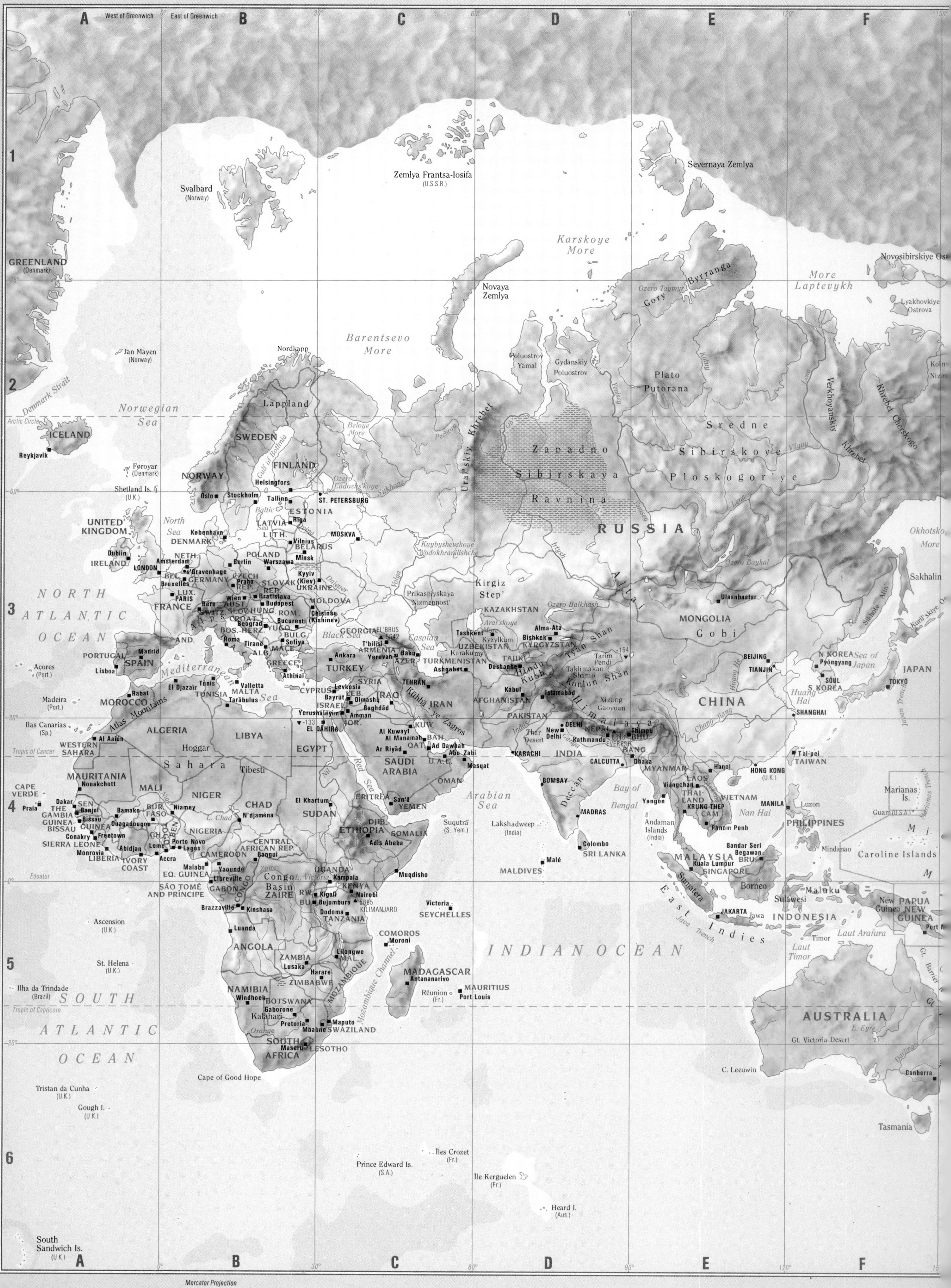
West of Greenwich
East of Greenwich
A
B
C
D
E
F
1
2
3
4
5
6
Svalbard
(Norway)
Zemlya Frantsa-Iosifa
(U.S.S.R.)
Severnaya Zemlya
Karskoye More
GREENLAND
(Denmark)
Novaya Zemlya
Ozero Taymyr
Gory Byrranga
More Laptevykh
Novosibirskiye Ostrova
Lyakhovskiye Ostrova
Jan Mayen
(Norway)
Nordkapp
Barentsevo More
Poluostrov Yamal
Gydanskiy Poluostrov
Plato Putorana
Denmark Strait
Norwegian Sea
Lappland
Arctic Circle
ICELAND
Reykjavik
SWEDEN
FINLAND
Beloye More
Gulf of Bothnia
Ural'skiy Khrebet
Zapadno Sibirskaya Ravnina
Sredne Sibirskoye Ploskogor'ye
Verkhoyanskiy Khrebet
Khrebet Cherskogo
Føroyar
(Denmark)
NORWAY
Helsingfors
Ozero Ladozhs'koye
Shetland Is.
(U.K.)
Oslo
Stockholm
Tallinn
ST. PETERSBURG
ESTONIA
Baltic Sea
LATVIA
Riga
North Sea
UNITED KINGDOM
København
DENMARK
LITH.
Vilnius
MOSKVA
BELARUS
RUSSIA
Okhotskoye More
Dublin
IRELAND
NETH.
Amsterdam
POLAND
Minsk
Kuybyshevskoye Vodokhranilishche
Irtysh
Ozero Baykal
LONDON
s'Gravenhage
Berlin
Warszawa
Volga
BEL.
Bruxelles
GERMANY
CZECH REP.
Praha
SLOVAK REP.
Kyyiv (Kiev)
UKRAINE
Dniepr
Kirgiz Step'
Altai
Sakhalin
NORTH ATLANTIC OCEAN
LUX.
PARIS
Wien
Bratislava
Budapest
MOLDOVA
Prikaspiyskaya Nizmennost'
KAZAKHSTAN
Ozero Balkhash
Ulaanbaatar
FRANCE
Bern
SWITZ.
AUST.
SLOV.
HUNG.
CROAT.
ROM.
Chisinau (Kishinev)
Bucuresti
MONGOLIA
Gobi
Beograd
BOS.-HERZ.
YUGO.
BULG.
Sofiya
Black Sea
GEORGIA
EL'BRUS
Aral'skoye More
Alma-Ata
Bishkek
KYRGYZSTAN
Tashkent
UZBEKISTAN
Kuril'skiye Ostrova
Açores
(Port.)
PORTUGAL
Lisboa
Madrid
SPAIN
AND.
Roma
Tirane
ALB.
MACE.
GREECE
Athinai
T'bilisi
ARMENIA
Yerevan
Baku
AZER.
Caspian Sea
TURKMENISTAN
Ashgabat
Dushanbe
TAJIK.
Tarim Pendi
Taklimakan Shamo
Kunlun Shan
Tyan Shan
BEIJING
TIANJIN
N. KOREA
Pyŏngyang
Sea of Japan
JAPAN
Ankara
TURKEY
Mediterranean Sea
Tunis
Valletta
MALTA
El Djazair
TUNISIA
CYPRUS
Levkosia
SYRIA
LEB.
Bayrūt
Dimashq
TEHRAN
IRAN
Kābul
Hindu Kush
Islamabad
SŎUL
S. KOREA
TŌKYŌ
Madeira
(Port.)
Rabat
MOROCCO
Atlas Mountains
Tarābulus
ISRAEL
Yerushalayim
Amman
JOR.
IRAQ
Baghdād
Kūhhā-ye Zagros
AFGHANISTAN
PAKISTAN
Xizang Gaoyuan
Himalaya
CHINA
Huang Hai
SHANGHAI
Ilas Canarias
(Sp.)
Al Aaiūn
ALGERIA
LIBYA
EL QAHIRA
Al Kuwayt
KUW.
Al Manamah
BAH.
DELHI
New Delhi
Kathmandu
NEPAL
EVEREST
Thimphu
BHU.
Thar Desert
Tropic of Cancer
WESTERN SAHARA
Hoggar
EGYPT
Ar Riyāḍ
QAT.
Ad Dawhah
Abū Zabi
U.A.E.
Masqat
KARACHI
INDIA
BANG.
Dhaka
Tai-pei
TAIWAN
HONG KONG
(U.K.)
MAURITANIA
Nouakchott
Sahara
Tibesti
SAUDI ARABIA
OMAN
CALCUTTA
MYANMAR
Hanoi
CAPE VERDE
Praia
MALI
NIGER
BOMBAY
Deccan
Bay of Bengal
LAOS
Viangchan
Marianas Is.
Dakar
SEN.
THE GAMBIA
Banjul
GUINEA-BISSAU
Bissau
GUINEA
Bamako
BUR. FASO
Niamey
Ouagadougou
CHAD
Nile
Red Sea
ERITREA
Sanʿa
YEMEN
Arabian Sea
THAILAND
KRUNG THEP
Yangon
VIETNAM
MANILA
Luzon
Guam (U.S.A.)
El Khartum
SUDAN
N'djaména
Conakry
Freetown
SIERRA LEONE
Monrovia
LIBERIA
Abidjan
IVORY COAST
GHANA
Accra
Lomé
Porto Novo
Lagos
NIGERIA
CENTRAL AFRICAN REP.
Bangui
CAMEROON
ETHIOPIA
Adis Abeba
DJIB.
SOMALIA
Suqutrā
(S. Yem.)
Lakshadweep
(India)
MADRAS
Andaman Islands
(India)
CAM.
Phnom Penh
Nan Hai
PHILIPPINES
Malabo
EQ. GUINEA
Yaoundé
Libreville
GABON
CONGO
Congo Basin
ZAIRE
UGANDA
Kampala
L. Victoria
KENYA
Nairobi
Muqdisho
Colombo
SRI LANKA
Malé
MALDIVES
MALAYSIA
Kuala Lumpur
SINGAPORE
Bandar Seri Begawan
BRU.
Mindanao
Caroline Islands
Equator
SÃO TOMÉ AND PRÍNCIPE
Brazzaville
Kinshasa
RWANDA
Kigali
BURUNDI
Bujumbura
5895
KILIMANJARO
Dodoma
TANZANIA
Victoria
SEYCHELLES
Sumatera
Borneo
Sulawesi
Maluku
New Guinea
PAPUA NEW GUINEA
Ascension
(U.K.)
Luanda
ANGOLA
COMOROS
Moroni
JAKARTA
Jawa
INDONESIA
Java Trench
East Indies
Timor
Laut Timor
Laut Arafura
INDIAN OCEAN
St. Helena
(U.K.)
ZAMBIA
Lusaka
Lilongwe
Harare
ZIMBABWE
MOZAMBIQUE
Mozambique Channel
MADAGASCAR
Antananarivo
Ilha da Trindade
(Brazil)
SOUTH ATLANTIC OCEAN
NAMIBIA
Windhoek
BOTSWANA
Gaborone
Kalahari
Pretoria
Maputo
Mbabane
SWAZILAND
Réunion
(Fr.)
MAURITIUS
Port Louis
Tropic of Capricorn
AUSTRALIA
L. Eyre
Gt. Victoria Desert
Orange
SOUTH AFRICA
Maseru
LESOTHO
Cape of Good Hope
C. Leeuwin
Canberra
Tristan da Cunha
(U.K.)
Gough I.
(U.K.)
Tasmania
Îles Crozet
(Fr.)
Prince Edward Is.
(S.A.)
Île Kerguelen
(Fr.)
Heard I.
(Aus.)
South Sandwich Is.
(U.K.)
Mercator Projection

1:85,000,000 (Scale at the Equator)

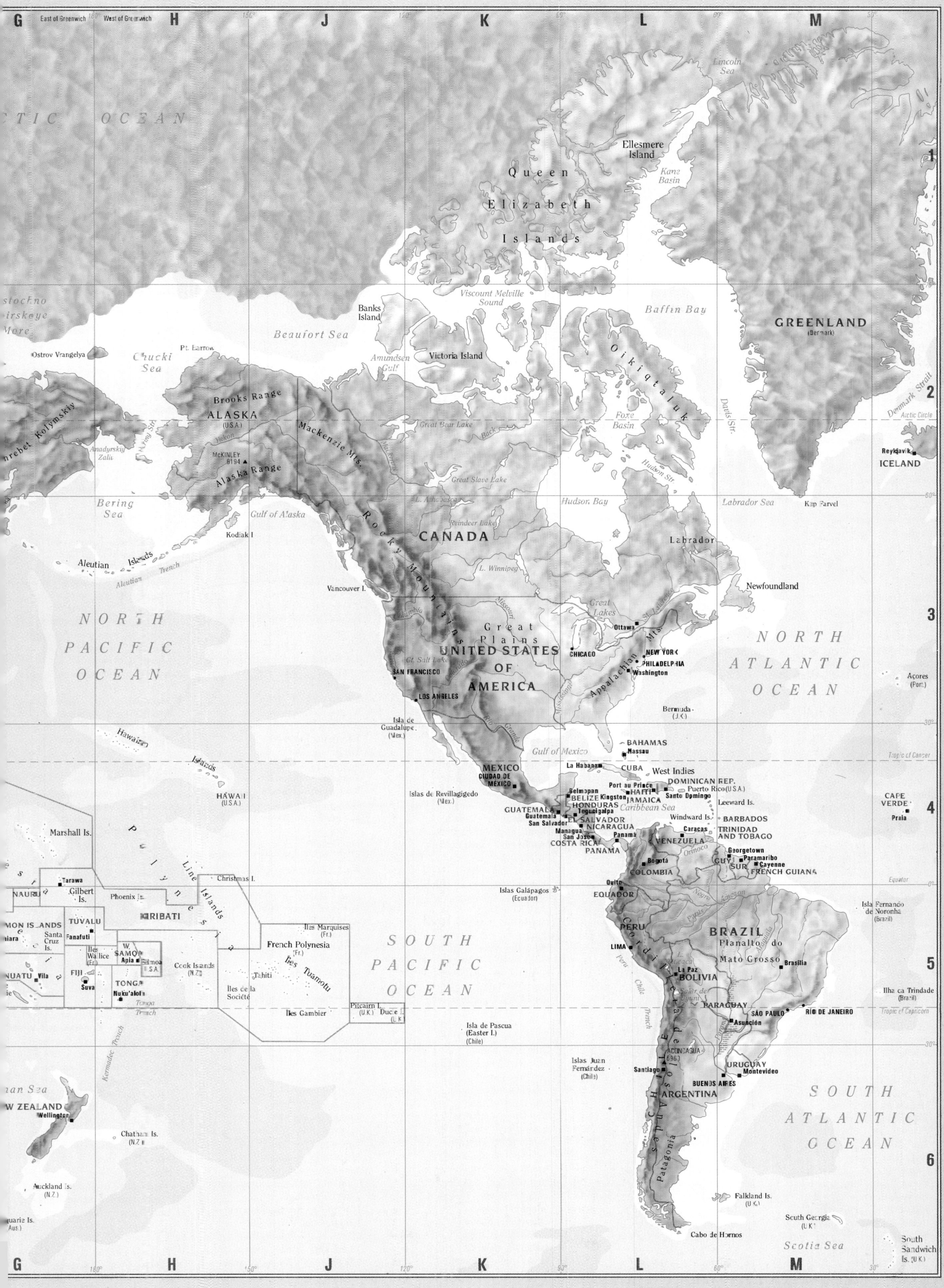
G
East of Greenwich
West of Greenwich
H
J
K
L
M
OCEAN
Lincoln Sea
Ellesmere Island
Kane Basin
Queen Elizabeth Islands
Banks Island
Viscount Melville Sound
Baffin Bay
GREENLAND
(Denmark)
Ostrov Vrangelya
Pt. Barrow
Chucki Sea
Beaufort Sea
Amundsen Gulf
Victoria Island
Oikiqtaluk
Brooks Range
ALASKA
(U.S.A.)
Mackenzie Mts.
Great Bear Lake
Foxe Basin
Davis Str.
Denmark Strait
Arctic Circle
Reykjavik
ICELAND
McKINLEY
6194
Alaska Range
Anadyrskiy Zaliv
Great Slave Lake
Hudson Str.
Bering Sea
Gulf of Alaska
Hudson Bay
Labrador Sea
Kap Farvel
Kodiak I.
Rocky Mountains
Reindeer Lake
CANADA
Labrador
Aleutian Islands
Aleutian Trench
L. Winnipeg
Newfoundland
Vancouver I.
Great Lakes
NORTH PACIFIC OCEAN
Great Plains
Ottawa
NORTH ATLANTIC OCEAN
UNITED STATES OF AMERICA
CHICAGO
NEW YORK
PHILADELPHIA
Washington
Gt. Salt Lake
SAN FRANCISCO
LOS ANGELES
Appalachian Mts.
Açores
(Port.)
Bermuda
(U.K.)
Isla de Guadalupe
(Mex.)
Hawaiian Islands
BAHAMAS
Nassau
Gulf of Mexico
Tropic of Cancer
La Habana
CUBA
West Indies
MEXICO
CIUDAD DE MÉXICO
Port au Prince
HAITI
DOMINICAN REP.
Puerto Rico (U.S.A.)
Santo Domingo
Belmopan
BELIZE
Kingston
JAMAICA
Caribbean Sea
Leeward Is.
CAPE VERDE
Praia
HAWAII
(U.S.A.)
Islas de Revillagigedo
(Mex.)
GUATEMALA
Guatemala
San Salvador
HONDURAS
Tegucigalpa
EL SALVADOR
NICARAGUA
Managua
San José
COSTA RICA
Panamá
PANAMA
Windward Is.
BARBADOS
Caracas
TRINIDAD AND TOBAGO
VENEZUELA
Marshall Is.
Polynesia
Georgetown
Paramaribo
Cayenne
GUYANA
SUR
FRENCH GUIANA
Bogotá
COLOMBIA
Tarawa
Christmas I.
Line Islands
Quito
EQUADOR
Equator
Gilbert Is.
Phoenix Is.
KIRIBATI
Islas Galápagos
(Ecuador)
Isla Fernando de Noronha
(Brazil)
TUVALU
Funafuti
Santa Cruz Is.
Îles Marquises
(Fr.)
PERU
BRAZIL
Planalto do Mato Grosso
French Polynesia
(Fr.)
Îles Tuamotu
SOUTH PACIFIC OCEAN
LIMA
Brasília
W. SAMOA
Apia
Samoa
(U.S.A.)
Îles Wallice
(Fr.)
Cook Islands
(N.Z.)
La Paz
BOLIVIA
FIJI
Vila
Suva
TONGA
Nuku'alofa
Tahiti
Îles de la Société
Ilha da Trindade
(Brazil)
PARAGUAY
SÃO PAULO
RIO DE JANEIRO
Tropic of Capricorn
Tonga Trench
Îles Gambier
Pitcairn I.
(U.K.)
Ducie I.
(U.K.)
Asunción
Isla de Pascua
(Easter I.)
(Chile)
Kermadec Trench
ACONCAGUA
6960
Islas Juan Fernández
(Chile)
Santiago
URUGUAY
Montevideo
BUENOS AIRES
ARGENTINA
NEW ZEALAND
Wellington
SOUTH ATLANTIC OCEAN
Chatham Is.
(N.Z.)
Patagonia
Auckland Is.
(N.Z.)
Falkland Is.
(U.K.)
South Georgia
(U.K.)
Cabo de Hornos
Scotia Sea
South Sandwich Is. (U.K.)
1
2
3
4
5
6

Designed and produced by E.S.R.

GLOSSARY AND ABBREVIATIONS

Language abbreviations in glossary

Afr	Afrikaans	*Dut*	Dutch	*I-C*	Indo-Chinese	*Mal*	Malay	*S-C*	Serbo-Croat
Alb	Albanian	*Fin*	Finnish	*Ice*	Icelandic	*Mlg*	Malagasy	*Som*	Somali
Ar	Arabic	*Fr*	French	*Ind*	Indonesian	*Mon*	Mongolian	*Sp*	Spanish
Ber	Berber	*Gae*	Gaelic	*It*	Italian	*Nor*	Norwegian	*Swe*	Swedish
Bul	Bulgarian	*Ger*	German	*Jap*	Japanese	*Per*	Persian	*Th*	Thai
Bur	Burmese	*Gr*	Greek	*Khm*	Khmer	*Pol*	Polish	*Tib*	Tibetan
Ch	Chinese	*Heb*	Hebrew	*Kor*	Korean	*Por*	Portuguese	*Tu*	Turkish
Cz	Czech	*Hin*	Hindi	*Lao*	Laotian	*Rom*	Romanian	*Vt*	Vietnamese
Dan	Danish	*Hun*	Hungarian	*Lat*	Latvian	*Rus*	Russian	*Wel*	Welsh

Glossary

A

Abar (*Ar*) – wells
Abyar (*Ar*) – wells
Adasi (*Tu*) – island
Adrar (*Ber*) – mountains
Ain (*Ar*) – spring, well
Akra (*Gr*) – cape, point
Alb (*Ger*) – mountains
Alpen (*Ger*) – mountains
Alpes (*Fr*) – mountains
Alpi (*It*) – mountains
Alto (*Por*) – high
-alv (*Swe*) – river
-alven (*Swe*) – river
Appenino (*It*) – mountain range
Aqabat (*Ar*) – pass
Archipielago (*Sp*) – archipelago
Arquipielago (*Por*) – archipelago
Arrecife (*Sp*) – reef
Ayia (*Gr*) – saint
Ayios (*Gr*) – saint
Ayn (*Ar*) – spring, well

B

Bab (*Ar*) – strait
Bad (*Ger*) – spa
Badiyah (*Ar*) – desert
Bælt (*Dan*) – strait
Baharu (*Mal*) – new
Bahia (*Sp*) – bay
Bahr (*Ar*) – bay, canal, lake, stream
Bahrat (*Ar*) – lake
Baia (*Por*) – bay
Baie (*Fr*) – bay
Baja (*Sp*) – lower
Ban (*Khm, Lao, Th*) – village
-bana (*Jap*) – cape, point
Banco (*Sp*) – bank
-bandao (*Ch*) – peninsula
Bandar (*Per*) – bay
Baraji (*Tu*) – reservoir
Barqa (*Ar*) – hill
Barragem (*Por*) – reservoir
Bassin (*Fr*) – basin, bay
Batin (*Ar*) – depression
Beinn (*Gae*) – mountain
Beloyy (*Rus*) – white
Ben (*Gae*) – mountain
Bereg (*Rus*) – bank, shore
Berg (*Ger*) – mountain
Berge (*Afr*) – mountains
Bheinn (*Gae*) – mountain
Biar (*Ar*) – wells
Bir (*Ar*) – well
Bi'r (*Ar*) – well
Birkat (*Ar*) – well
Birket (*Ar*) – well
Boca (*Sp*) – river mouth
Bocche (*It*) – mouths, estuary
Bodden (*Ger*) – bay
Bogazi (*Tu*) – strait
Boka (*S-C*) – gulf, inlet
Bol'shoy (*Rus*) – big
Bol'shoye (*Rus*) – big
Bory (*Pol*) – forest
Bratul (*Rom*) – river channel
Bucht (*Ger*) – bay
Bugt (*Dan*) – bay
Buhayrat (*Ar*) – lagoon, lake
Bukit (*Mal*) – hill, mountain
Bukt (*Nor*) – bay
Bulak (*Rus*) – spring
Burnu (*Tu*) – cape, point
Burun (*Tu*) – cape, point
Busen (*Ger*) – bay
Buyuk (*Tu*) – big

C

Cabo (*Por, Sp*) – cape, point
Cachoeira (*Sp*) – waterfall
Cap (*Fr*) – cape, point
Campos (*Sp*) – upland
Cao Nguyen (*Th*) – plateau, tableland
Cataratas (*Sp*) – waterfall
Cayi (*Tu*) – stream
Cayo (*Sp*) – islet, rock
Cerro (*Sp*) – hill
Chaco (*Sp*) – jungle
Chaine (*Fr*) – mountain chain
Chapada (*Por*) – hills
Ch'eng (*Ch*) – town
Chiang (*Ch*) – river
Chiang (*Th*) – town
Chott (*Ar*) – marsh, salt lake
Chute (*Fr*) – waterfall
Cienaga (*Sp*) – marshy lake
Ciudad (*Sp*) – city, town
Co (*Tib*) – lake
Col (*Fr*) – pass
Colinas (*Sp*) – hills
Cordillera (*Sp*) – mountain range
Costa (*Sp*) – coast, shore
Cote (*Fr*) – coast, slope
Coteau (*Fr*) – hill, slope
Coxilha (*Por*) – mountain pasture
Cuchillas (*Sp*) – hills

D

Dag (*Tu*) – mountain
Dagi (*Tu*) – mountain
Daglari (*Tu*) – mountains
-dake (*Jap*) – peak
-dal (*Nor*) – valley
Dao (*Ch*) – island
Darreh (*Per*) – valley
Daryacheh (*Per*) – lake
Dasht (*Per*) – desert
Denizi (*Tu*) – sea
Desierto (*Sp*) – desert
Djebel (*Ar*) – mountain
-djik (*Dut*) – dyke
Do (*Kor, Jap, Vt*) – island
Dolina (*Rus*) – valley
Dolok (*Ind*) – mountain
Dolna (*Bul*) – lower
Dolni (*Cz*) – lower
-dong (*Kor*) – village
-dorp (*Afr*) – village
Dur (*Ar*) – mountains

E

Eiland (*Dut*) – island
Eilanden (*Dut*) – islands
-elva (*Nor*) – river
Embalse (*Sp*) – reservoir
Erg (*Ar*) – sandy desert
Estero (*Sp*) – bay, estuary, inlet
Estrecho (*Sp*) – strait
Etang (*Fr*) – lagoon, pond
Ezers (*Lat*) – lake

F

Feng (*Ch*) – mountain, peak
Fels (*Ger*) – rock
Firth (*Gae*) – estuary
-fjall (*Swe*) – mountains
Fjeld (*Dan*) – mountain
-fjell (*Nor*) – mountain
-floi (*Ice*) – bay
-fjoraur (*Ice*) – fjord
Forde (*Ger*) – inlet
Foret (*Fr*) – forest
-foss (*Ice*) – waterfall

G

-gan (*Jap*) – rock
Gang (*Ch*) – harbour
Ganga (*Hin*) – river
Gata (*Jap*) – inlet, lagoon
Gave (*Fr*) – torrent
Gebel (*Ar*) – mountain
Gebirge (*Ger*) – mountains
Ghat (*Hin*) – range of hills
Ghubbat (*Ar*) – bay
Glen (*Gae*) – valley
Gletscher (*Ger*) – glacier
Gobi (*Mon*) – desert
Golfe (*Fr*) – bay, gulf
Golfo (*It, Sp*) – bay, gulf
Golu (*Tu*) – lake
Gora (*Bul*) – forest
Gora (*Pol, Rus*) – mountain
-gorod (*Rus*) – small town
Gory (*Pol, Rus*) – mountains
Grada (*Rus*) – mountain range
Grad (*Bul, Rus, S-C*) – city, town
Gross (*Ger*) – big
Gryada (*Rus*) – ridge
Guba (*Rus*) – bay
-gunto (*Jap*) – island group
Gunung (*Ind, Mal*) – mountain

H

Hadh (*Ar*) – sand dunes
Hafen (*Ger*) – harbour, port
Haff (*Ger*) – bay, lagoon
Hai (*Ch*) – sea
Haixia (*Ch*) – strait
-holm (*Dan*) – island
Halvo (*Dan*) – peninsula
-hama (*Jap*) – beach
Hamada (*Ar*) – plateau
-hamar (*Ice*) – mountain
Hammadah (*Ar*) – plain, stony desert
Hamun (*Per*) – marsh
-hanto (*Jap*) – peninsula
Harrat (*Ar*) – lava field
Hav (*Swe*) – gulf
Havet (*Nor*) – sea
-havn (*Dan, Nor*) – harbour
Hawr (*Ar*) – lake
He (*Ch*) – river
Heide (*Ger*) – heath, moor
-hisar (*Tu*) – castle
Ho (*Ch*) – river
Hohe (*Ger*) – hills
Horn (*Ger*) – peak, summit
Hu (*Ch*) – lake
-huk (*Swe*) – cape, point

I

Idd (*Ar*) – well
Idhan (*Ar*) – sand dunes
Ile (*Fr*) – island
Iles (*Fr*) – islands
Ilha (*Por*) – island
Ilhas (*Por*) – islands
Insel (*Ger*) – island
Inseln (*Ger*) – islands
Irq (*Ar*) – sand dunes
Irmak (*Tu*) – large river
Isfjord (*Dan*) – glacier
Iskappe (*Dan*) – icecap
Isla (*Sp*) – island
Islas (*Sp*) – islands
Isola (*It*) – island
Isole (*It*) – islands
Istmo (*Sp*) – isthmus

J

Jabal (*Ar*) – mountain
-jarvi (*Fin*) – lake
Jaza 'ir (*Ar*) – islands
Jazirat (*Ar*) – island
Jazovir (*Bul*) – reservoir
Jbel (*Ar*) – mountain
Jebel (*Ar*) – mountain
Jezero (*Alb, S-C*) – lake
Jezioro (*Pol*) – lagoon, lake
Jezirat (*Ar*) – island
-jiang (*Ch*) – river
Jibal (*Ar*) – mountain
Jiddat (*Ar*) – gravel plain
-jima (*Jap*) – island
-joki (*Fin*) – river
-jokull (*Ice*) – glacier

K

Kaap (*Afr*) – cape, point
-kai (*Jap*) – bay, sea
-kaikyo (*Jap*) – strait
Kanaal (*Dut*) – canal
Kap (*Ger*) – cape, point
-kapp (*Nor*) – cape, point
Kas (*Khm*) – island
Kavir (*Per*) – desert
-kawa (*Jap*) – river
Kenet (*Alb*) – inlet
Kep (*Alb*) – cape, point
Kepulauan (*Ind*) – archipelago, islands
Kereb (*Ar*) – hill, ridge
Khalij (*Ar*) – bay, gulf
Khawr (*Ar*) – wadi
Khrebet (*Ru*) – mountain range
Kiang (*Ch*) – river
Klein (*Afr, Ger*) – small
Ko (*Th*) – island
-ko (*Jap*) – inlet, lake
Koh (*Khm*) – island
Kolpos (*Gr*) – gulf
Kolymskoye (*Rus*) – mountain range
Korfezi (*Tu*) – bay, gulf
Kosa (*Rus*) – spit
Kotlina (*Cz, Pol*) – basin, depression
Kraj (*Cz, Pol, S-C*) – region
Krasnyy (*Rus*) – red
Kray (*Rus*) – region
Kreis (*Ger*) – district
Kryazh (*Rus*) – mountains
Kucuk (*Tu*) – small
Kuh (*Per*) – mountain
Kuhha (*Per*) – mountains
Kum (*Rus*) – sandy desert
Kyst (*Dan*) – coast
Kyun (*Bur*) – island
Kyunzu (*Bur*) – islands

L

La (*Tib*) – pass
Lac (*Fr*) – lake
Lacul (*Rom*) – lake
Laem (*Th*) – point
Lago (*It, Por, Sp*) – lake
Lagoa (*Por*) – lagoon
Laguna (*Sp*) – lagoon, lake
Lam (*Ar*) – stream
Lande (*Fr*) – heath, sandy moor
Laut (*Ind*) – sea
Ling (*Ch*) – mountain range
Liman (*Rus*) – bay, gulf
Limni (*Gr*) – lagoon, lake
Llano (*Sp*) – plain, prairie
Llanos (*Sp*) – plains, prairies

M

Mae Nam (*Th*) – river
Mala (*S-C*) – small
Malaya (*Rus*) – small
Male (*Cz*) – small
Maloye (*Rus*) – small
Malyy (*Rus*) – small
Mar (*Por, Sp*) – sea
Mare (*It*) – sea
Masirah (*Ar*) – channel
Massif (*Fr*) – mountains
Mato (*Por*) – forest
Meer (*Afr, Dut, Ger*) – lake, sea
Menor (*Por, Sp*) – lesser, smaller
Mer (*Fr*) – sea
Mesa (*Sp*) – tableland
Minami (*Jap*) – south
-misaki (*Jap*) – cape, point
Mont (*Fr*) – mountain
Montagna (*It*) – mountain
Montagne (*Fr*) – mountain
Montagnes (*Fr*) – mountains
Montana (*Sp*) – mountain
Montanas (*Sp*) – mountains
Monte (*It, Por, Sp*) – mountain
Monti (*It*) – mountains
More (*Rus*) – sea
Mull (*Gae*) – cape, point, promontory
Munkhafad (*Ar*) – depression
Muntii (*Rom*) – mountains
Mynydd (*Wel*) – mountain
Mys (*Rus*) – cape, point

N

-nada (*Jap*) – gulf, sea
Nadrz (*Cz*) – reservoir
Nafud (*Ar*) – desert, dune
Nagor'ye (*Rus*) – highland, uplands
Nagy- (*Hun*) – great
Nahr (*Ar*) – river
Namakzar (*Per*) – desert, salt flat
Nei (*Ch*) – inner
Ness (*Gae*) – cape, promontory
Neu (*Ger*) – new
Nevada (*Sp*) – snow capped mountains
Nevado (*Sp*) – mountain
Ngoc (*Vt*) – mountain peak
-nisi (*Gr*) – island
Nisoi (*Gr*) – islands
Nisos (*Gr*) – island
Nizhnyaya (*Rus*) – lower
Nizina (*Pol*) – depression, lowland
Nizmennost' (*Rus*) – lowland
Noord (*Dut*) – north
Nord (*Dan, Fr, Ger*) – north
Norte (*Por, Sp*) – north
Nos (*Bul, Rus*) – point, spit
Nosy (*Mlg*) – island
Nova (*Bul*) – new
Nova (*Cz*) – new
Novaya (*Rus*) – new
Nove (*Cz*) – new
Novi (*Bul*) – new
Nudo (*Sp*) – mountain
Nuruu (*Mon*) – mountain range
Nuur (*Mon*) – lake

O

Ø (*Dan*) – island
Oblast' (*Rus*) – province

Llyn (*Wel*) – lake
Loch (*Gae*) – lake
Lough (*Gae*) – lake

Occidental (Fr, Rom, Sp) – western
Oki (Jap) – bay
-oog (Ger) – island
Ojo (Sp) – spring
Orasul (Rom) – city
Ori (Gr) – mountains
Oriental (Fr, Rom, Sp) – eastern
Ormos (Gr) – bay
Oros (Gr) – island
Ort (Ger) – cape, point
Ostrov (Rus) – island
Ostrova (Rus) – islands
Otok (S-C) – island
Otoki (S-C) – islands
Ouadi (Ar) – wadi, dry watercourse
Oued (Ar) – dry river bed, wadi
Ovasi (Tu) – plain
Ozero (Rus) – lake

P

Pampa (Sp) – plain
Paniai (Ind) – lake
Paso (Sp) – pass
Passage (Fr) – pass
Passo (It) – pass
Pasul (Rom) – pass
Pelagos (Gr) – sea
Pendi (Ch) – basin
Pengunungnan (Ind) – mountain range
Peninsola (It) – peninsula
Peninsule (Fr) – peninsula
Pereval (Rus) – pass
Peski (Rus) – desert, sands
Phnom (Khm) – hill, mountain
Phu (Vt) – mountain
Pic (Fr) – peak
Picacho (Sp) – peak
Pico (Sp) – peak
Pik (Rus) – peak
Pingyuan (Ch) – plain
Pizzo (It) – peak
Planalto (Por) – plateau
Plana (S-C, Sp) – plain
Planina (Bul, S-C) – mountains
Plato (Afr, Bul, Rus) – plateau
Ploskogor'ye (Rus) – plateau
Ploskogorje (Rus) – plateau
Poco (Ind) – peak

Pohorie (Cz) – mountain range
Pointe (Fr) – cape, point
Pojezierze (Pol) – plateau
Poluostrov (Rus) – peninsula
Polwysep (Pol) – peninsula
Ponta (Por) – cape, point
Presa (Sp) – reservoir
Proliv (Sp) – strait
Pueblo (Sp) – village
Puerto (Sp) – harbour, pass
Pulau (Ind, Mal) – island
Puna (Sp) – desert plateau
Puncak (Ind) – peak
Punta (It, Sp) – cape, point
Puy (Fr) – peak

Q

Qalamat (Ar) – well
Qalib (Ar) – well
Qararat (Ar) – depression
Qolleh (Per) – mountain
Qornet (Ar) – peak
Qundao (Ch) – archipelago

R

Ramlat (Ar) – dunes
Ra's (Ar, Per) – cape, point
Ras (Ar) – cape, point
Rass (Som) – cape, point
Ravnina (Rus) – plain
Recife (Por) – reef
Represa (Por) – dam
Reshteh (Per) – mountain range
-retto (Jap) – island chain
Rijeka (S-C) – river
Rio (Por, Sp) – river
Riviere (Fr) – river
Rt (S-C) – cape, point
Rubha (Gae) – cape, point
Ruck (Ger) – mountain
Rucken (Ger) – ridge
Rud (Per) – river
Rudohorie (Cz) – mountains
Rzeka (Pol) – river

S

Sabkhat (Ar) – salt flat
Sagar (Hin) – lake
Sahara (Ar) – desert

Sahl (Ar) – plain
Sahra (Ar) – desert
Sa'id (Ar) – highland
-saki (Jap) – cape, point
Salar (Sp) – salt pan
Salina (Sp) – salt pan
San (Sp) – saint
-san (Jap) – mountain
-sanchi (Jap) – mountainous area
Sankt (Ger, Swe) – saint
-sanmyaku (Jap) – mountain range
Santa (Sp) – saint
Sao (Por) – saint
Sar (Kur) – mountain
Satu (Rom) – village
Sawqirah (Ar) – bay
Se (I-C) – river
See (Ger) – lake
-sehir (Tu) – town
Selat (Ind) – channel, strait
-selka (Fin) – bay
Selva (Sp) – forest
Serra (Por) – mountain range
Serrania (Sp) – mountains
-seto (Jap) – channel, strait
Severnaya (Rus) – southern
Sfintu (Rom) – saint
Shamo (Ch) – desert
Shan (Ch) – mountains
Shandi (Ch) – mountainous area
Shatt (Ar) – river mouth, river
-shima (Jap) – islands
Shiqqat (Ar) – interdune trough
-shoto (Jap) – group of islands
Sierra (Sp) – mountain range
Sint (Afr, Dut) – saint
Slieve (Gae) – range of hills
So (Dan, Nor) – lake
Soder- (Swe) – southern
Sondre (Dan, Nor) – southern
Song (Vt) – river
Spitze (Ger) – peak
Srednе (Rus) – middle
Stadt (Ger) – town
Stara (Cz) – old
Staraya (Rus) – old
Stenon (Gr) – strait, pass
Step' (Rus) – plain, steppe
Strelka (Rus) – spit
Stretto (It) – strait

-suido (Jap) – channel, strait
Sund (Swe) – sound, strait
Szent- (Hun) – saint

T

-take (Jap) – peak
Tall (Ar) – hill
Tallat (Ar) – hills
Tanggula (Tib) – pass
Tanjong (Ind, Mal) – cape, point
Tanjon'i (Mlg) – cape, point
Tanjung (Ind, Mal) – cape, point
Tao (Ch) – island
Taraq (Ar) – hills
Tassili (Ber) – rocky plateau
Tau (Rus) – mountains
Taung (Bur) – mountain, south
Tekojarvi (Fin) – reservoir
Tell (Ar) – hill
Teluk (Ind) – bay
Tenere (Fr) – desert
Terre (Fr) – land
Thale (Th) – lake
Thamad (Ar) – well
Tirat (Ar) – canal
Tjarn (Swe) – lake
Tso (Tib) – lake
Tonle (Khm) – lake
Tutul (Ar) – hills

U

Ujung (Ind) – cape, point
-ura (Jap) – inlet
Urayq (Ar) – sand ridge
Uruq (Ar) – dunes
Ust (Rus) – river mouth
Uul (Mon) – mountain

V

Valea (Rom) – valley
-varos (Hun) – town
-varre (Nor) – mountain
-vatten (Swe) – lake
Vaux (Fr) – valleys
Velika (S-C) – big
Velikaya (Rus) – big
Verkhne (Rus) – upper
-vesi (Fin) – lake, water
Ville (Fr) – town
Vinh (Vt) – bay

Virful (Rom) – peak
Vodokhranilishche (Rus) – reservoir
Volcan (Sp) – volcano
Vorota (Rus) – strait
Vostochnyy (Rus) – eastern
Vozvyshennost' (Rus) hills, upland
Vpadina (Rus) – depression

W

Wadi (Ar) – river, stream
Wahat (Ar) – oasis
Wai (Ch) – outer
Wald (Ger) – forest
Wan (Ch) – bay
Wasser (Ger) – lake, water
Wenz (Ar) – river
Wielka (Pol) – big

X

Xan (Ch) – strait
Xi (Ch) – stream, west
Xia (Ch) – gorge, lower
Xian (Ch) – county
Xiao (Ch) – small
Xu (Ch) – island

Y

Yam (Heb) – lake
-yama (Jap) – mountain
Yarimadasi (Tu) – peninsula
Yazovir (Bul) – reservoir
Ye (Bur) – island
Yoma (Bur) – mountain range
Yugo- (Rus) – southern
Yuzhnyy (Rus) – southern

Z

Zaki (Jap) – cape, point
Zalew (Pol) – bay, inlet
Zaliv (Rus) – bay
-zan (Jap) – mountain
Zapadno (Rus) – western
Zatoka (Pol) – bay
Zee (Dut) – sea
Zemlya (Rus) – island, land
-zhen (Ch) – town

Abbreviations

A

A. – Alp, Alpen, Alpi
Akr. – Akra
And. – Andorra
Arch. – Archipelago
Arr. – Arrecife
Aust. – Australia
Ay. – Ayios

B

B. – Bahia, Baia, Baie, Bay, Bucht, Bukt
Ba. – Bahia
Bang. – Bangladesh
Bah. – Bahrain
Bel. – Belgium
Ben. – Benin
Bg. – Berg
Bhu. – Bhutan
Bk. – Bukit
Bol. – Bol'shoy, Bol'shoye
Bos. – Bosnia-Herzegovina
Br. – Burnu, Burun
Bru. – Brunei
Bt. – Bukit
Bu. – Burundi
Bü. – Büyük
Bulg. – Bulgaria
Bur. Faso – Burkina Faso

C

C. – Cabo, Cap, Cape, Cerro
Cam. – Cambodia
Can. – Canal, Canale
Cga. – Cienaga
Chan. – Channel
Co. – Cerro
Col. – Columbia
Cord. – Cordillera
Cr. – Creek
Czech. – Czech Rep.

D

D. – Dag, Dagi, Daglari, Daryacheh
D.C. – District of Columbia
Den. – Denmark
Djib. – Djibouti

E

E. – East
Eq. – Equatorial
Est. – Estrecho

F

Fd. – Fjord
Fk. – Fork
Fr. – France
Ft. – Fort

G

G. – Golfe, Golfo, Guba, Gulf, Gora, Gunung
Gd. – Grand
Gde – Grande
Geb. – Gebirge
Gen. – General
Geog. – Geographical
Ger. – Germany
Gh. – Ghana
Gl. – Glacier
Gr. – Grande, Gross
Gt. – Great
Guy. – Guyana

H

Har. – Harbor
Hd. – Head
Hung. – Hungary

I

I. – Ile, Ilha, Insel, Isla, Island, Isle, Isola, Isole

Is. – Ilhas, Iles, Islands, Islas, Isles
Isth. – Isthmus

J

J. – Jabal, Jbel, Jebel, Jezioro, Jezero, Jazair
Jor. – Jordan

K

K. – Kap, Kuh, Kuhha, Koh, Kolpos
Kan. – Kanal, Kanaal
Kep. – Kepulauan
Khr. – Khrebet
Kör. – Körfezi
Kuw. – Kuwait

L

L. – Lac, Lacul, Lago, Lake, Limni, Llyn, Loch, Lough
Lag. – Lagoon, Laguna
Leb. – Lebanon
Liech. – Liechtenstein
Lit. – Little
Lux. – Luxembourg

M

M. – Mys
Mal. – Malawi
Mex. – Mexico
Mgne. – Montagne
Mt. – Mont, Mount, Mountain
Mti. – Monti
Mtii. – Muntii
Mts. – Monts, Mounts, Mountains

N

N. – Nord, North, Nos
Neb. – Nebraska
Neth. – Netherlands

Nev. – Nevado
N.H. – New Hampshire
Nizh. – Nizhnyaya
Nizm. – Nizmennost
Nor. – Norway
N.Z. – New Zealand

O

O. – Ost, Ostrov
Os. – Ostova
Oz. – Ozero

P

P. – Point
Pass. – Passage
Peg. – Peganungan
Penn. – Pennsylvania
Pen. – Peninsola, Peninsula, Peninsule
Pk. – Peak, Puncak
Pl. – Planina
Pol. – Poluostrov
Port. – Portugal
Prom. – Promontory
Pt. – Point
Pta. – Ponta, Punta
Pte. – Pointe
Pto. – Puerto, Punto

Q

Qat. – Qatar

R

R. – Reshteh
Ra. – Range
Rep. – Republic
Res. – Reservoir
Rés. – Réservoir
Rom. – Romania
Rw. – Rwanda

S

S. – Shatt, South
Sa. – Serra, Sierra
S.A. – South Africa
Sd. – Sound, Sund
Sp. – Spain
Sps. – Springs
St. – Saint, Sint
Sta – Santa
Ste – Sainte
Str. – Strait
Sur. – Suriname
Switz. – Switzerland

T

Tg. – Tanjong, Tanjung
Tk. – Teluk

U

U.A.E. – United Arab Emirates
U.K. – United Kingdom
U.S.A. – United States of America

V

V. – Volcano
Vdkhr. – Vodokhranilishche
Ven. – Venezuela
Verkh. – Verkhne
Vn. – Volcan
Vol. – Volcan, Volcano

W

W. – Wadi, Wald, West

Y

Y. – Yarimadasi

Z

Zal. – Zaliv

INDEX

The index includes an alphabetical list of all names appearing in the map section of the atlas. Names on the maps and in the index are generally in the local language. For names in languages not written in the Roman alphabet, the officially accepted transliteration system has been used.

Most features are indexed to the largest scale map on which they appear. Extensive features are usually indexed to maps that show the features completely or show them in their relationship to surrounding areas. For extensive regional features, locations are given for the approximate center of the feature, those for linear features are given at the position of the name.

Each entry in the index is located by a page number and an alphanumeric grid reference on that particular page. The grid is defined by letters, positioned at the top and at the bottom of the map spread, and numbers, shown at the sides of the spread. For example, Bandung in Indonesia has the reference 90 D7. It can thus be found on page 90 in the grid square D7.

Where two identical names are referenced to the same page and grid square, it should be noted that they relate to different adjacent features. For example, the name Avon appears twice in the index and in both cases it is referenced to 52 E3. These two entries locate firstly the county of Avon and secondly the River Avon.

Name	Page	Grid
Adda	68	B2
Adda	68	B3
Ad Dakhla	100	B4
Ad Dali	96	G10
Ad Dammam	97	K3
Ad Darb	96	F8
Ad Dawadimi	96	G4
Ad Dawhah	97	K4
Ad Dila	97	K7
Ad Dilam	96	H5
Ad Diriyah	96	H4
Ad Duwaniyah	94	G6
Ad Duwayd	96	F1
Adel	124	C6
Adelaide *Antarctic*	141	V5
Adelaide *Australia*	113	H5
Adelaide *Bahamas*	129	P8
Adelaide Island	141	V5
Adelaide Peninsula	120	G4
Aden	96	G10
Aden, Gulf of	103	J5
Adh Dhayd	97	M4
Adi	114	A2
Adi Ark'ay	96	C10
Adi Dairo	96	D9
Adige	68	C3
Adigrat	96	D9
Adiguzel Baraji	76	C3
Adi Keyah	96	D9
Adilabad	92	E5
Adilcevaz	77	K3
Adin	122	D7
Adirondack Mountains	125	N4
Adis Abeba	103	G6
Adi Ugri	96	D9
Adiyaman	77	H4
Adjud	73	J2
Adjuntas, Presa de las	131	K6
Adka	118	Aa9
Adlington	55	G3
Admello	68	C2
Admiralty Gulf	112	F1
Admiralty Inlet	120	J3
Admiralty Island *Canada*	119	Q2
Admiralty Island *U.S.A.*	118	J4
Admiralty Islands	114	D2
Admund Ringnes Island	120	G2
Ado-Ekiti	105	G4
Adonara	91	G7
Adoni	92	E5
Adorf	70	E3
Adoumaoua, Massif de l'	105	H4
Adour	65	C7
Adra	66	E4
Adrano	69	E7
Adrar	100	E3
Adre	102	D5
Adria	68	D3
Adrian *Michigan*	124	J6
Adrian *Texas*	127	L3
Adriatic Sea	68	E4
Adwa	96	D9
Adwick le Street	55	H3
Adycha	85	P3
Adzhima	88	G1
Adzvavom	78	K2
Aegean Sea	75	H3
Afafura, Laut	91	K7
Afanasevo	78	J4
Affobakka	137	F3
Affric	56	C3
Afghanistan	92	B2
Afgooye	107	J2
Afif	96	F5
Afikpo	105	G4
Afmadow	107	H2
Afognak Island	118	E4
Afon Efyrnwy	52	D2
Afrin	77	G4
Afsin	77	G3
Afyon	76	D3
Agadez	101	G5
Agadir	100	D2
Agadyr	86	C2
Agaie	105	G4
Agalta, Sierra de	132	E7
Agano	89	G7
Agapa *Russia*	84	D2
Agapa *Russia*	84	D2
Agapitovo	84	D3
Agartala	93	H4
Agaruut	87	K3
Agats	114	B3
Agatti	92	D6
Agattu Island	118	Aa9
Agbaja	105	G4
Agboville	104	E4
Agdam	94	H2
Agde	65	E7
Agematsu	89	F8
Agen	65	D6
Aghada	59	F9
Agha Jari	95	J6
Agiabampo, Estero de	130	E4
Agin	77	H3
Agira	69	E7
Aglasun	76	D4
Agnanda	75	F4
Agno	68	C3
Agnone	69	E5
Agout	65	D7
Agra	92	E3
Agram	72	C3
Agreda	67	F2
Agri	69	F5
Agri	77	K3
Agrigento	69	D7
Agrinion	75	F3
Agropoli	69	E5
Agua Clara	138	F4
Aguadas	136	B2
Aguadilla	133	P5
Aguanaval	130	H5
Agua Prieta	127	H5
Aguascalientes	130	H7
Agua, Volcan de	132	B7
Aguelhok	100	F5
Aguemour	101	F3
Aguilar de Campoo	66	D1
Aguilas	67	F4
Aguja, Cabo de la	133	K9
Aguja, Punta	136	A5
Agulhas, Kaap	108	D6
Agusan	91	H4
Ahar	94	H2
Aheim	62	A5
Ahimahasoa	109	J4
Ahipara Bay	115	D1
Ahititi	115	E3
Ahlat	77	K3
Ahmadabad	92	D4
Ahmadi	95	N8
Ahmadnagar	92	D5
Ahmadpur	92	D3
Ahmar Mountains	103	H6
Ahoskie	129	P2
Ahram	95	K7
Ahtari	62	L5
Ahtarinjarvi	62	L5
Ahuachapan	132	C8
Ahvaz	94	J6
Ahvenanmaa	63	H6
Ahwar	96	H10
Aiddejavrre	62	K2
Aidhipsos	75	G3
Aigen	68	D1
Aigues	65	F6
Aiken	129	M4
Ailao Shan	93	K4
Ailsa Craig	57	C5
Aim	85	N5
Aimores, Serra dos	138	H3
Ain	65	F5
Ain Beida	101	G1
Ain Bessem	67	H4
Ain Defla	67	G4
Ain El Hadjel	67	H5
Ain Oulmene	67	J5
Ain Sefra	100	E2
Ainsworth	123	Q6
Aioun el Atrouss	100	D5
Aiquile	138	C3
Air	101	G5
Airbangis	90	B5
Airdrie	57	E5
Aire *France*	64	F4
Aire *U.K.*	55	J3
Airedale	55	H3
Aire-sur-l'Adour	65	C7
Air Force Island	120	M4
Airgin Sum	87	L3
Airi-selka	62	L3
Aisne	64	E4
Aitape	114	C2
Aith	56	F1
Aix-en-Provence	65	F7
Aix-les-Bains	65	F6
Aiyina	75	G4
Aiyinion	75	G2
Aiyion	75	G3
Aizawl	93	H4
Aizpute	63	J8
Aizu-Wakamatsu	89	G7
Ajaccio	69	B5
Ajana	112	C4
Ajanta Range	92	E4
Ajdabiya	101	K2
Ajlun	94	B5
Ajman	97	M4
Ajmer	92	D3
Akaishi-sanchi	89	G8
Akalkot	92	E5
Akamkpa	105	G4
Akaroa Head	115	D5
Akbou	67	J4
Akbulak	79	K5
Akcaabat	77	H2
Akcakale	77	H4
Akcadag	77	G3
Akcakoca	76	D2
Akcaova	76	C4
Akcay	76	C4
Akchatau	86	C2
Ak Daglari	76	C4
Akdagmadeni	77	F3
Ak Dovurak	84	E6
Akershus	63	D6
Akeshir Golu	76	D3
Aketi	106	D2
Akgevir	77	J4
Akhalkalaki	77	K2
Akhaltsikhe	77	K2
Akhdar, Al Jabal al	101	K2
Akhdar, Jabal	97	N5
Akhdar, Wadi	96	C3
Akheloos	75	F3
Akhiok	118	E4
Akhisar	76	B3
Akhmim	103	F2
Akhtubinsk	79	H6
Akhtyrka	79	E5
Aki	89	D9
Akimiski Island	121	K7
Akincilar	77	H2
Akinkeen	59	D9
Akinli	77	J4
Akita	88	H6
Akjoujt	100	C5
Akkavare	62	J3
Akkeshi	88	K4
Akko	94	B5
Akkoy	76	B4
Akkus	77	G2
Aklavik	118	H2
Akmola	84	A6
Akniste	63	L8
Akola	92	E4
Akonolinga	105	H5
Akordat	96	C9
Akoren	76	E4
Akosombo Dam	104	E4
Akot	92	E4
Akpatok Island	121	N5
Akpinar	76	E3
Akqi	86	D3
Akranes	62	T12
Akron	125	K6
Aksar	77	K2
Aksaray	76	E3
Aksay *China*	86	G4
Aksay *Kazakhstan*	79	J5
Aksehir	76	D3
Akseki	76	D4
Aksenovo-Zilovskoye	85	K6
Aks-e Rostam	95	M7
Aksha	85	J6
Akshimrau	79	J7
Aksu *China*	86	E3
Aksu *Turkey*	76	D4
Aksu *Kazakhstan*	79	J5
Aksu-Ayuly	86	C2
Aksu Cayi	76	D4
Aksum	96	D9
Aksumbe	86	B3
Aktau *Kazakhstan*	84	A6
Aktau *Kazakhstan*	79	J7
Akti	75	H2
Aktogay	86	D2
Akulivik	120	L5
Akun Island	118	Ae9
Akune	89	C9
Akure	105	G4
Akureyri	62	V12
Akuse	104	F4
Akutan Island	118	Ae9
Akwanga	105	G4
Akyab	93	H4
Akyatan Golu	76	F4
Akyazi	76	D2
Akyurt	76	E2
Akzhar	86	C3
Al Aaiun	100	C3
Alabama *U.S.A*	129	J4
Alabama *U.S.A.*	129	J4
Alaca	76	F2
Alacahan	77	G3
Alacam	77	F2
Alacam Daglari	76	C3
Alacran, Arrecife	131	Q6
Alagoas	137	K5
Alagoinhas	137	K6
Alagon *Spain*	66	C2
Alagon *Spain*	67	F2
Al Ahmadi	97	J2
Al Ajaiz	97	N7
Alajarvi	62	K5
Alajuela	132	E9
Alakanuk	118	C3
Alakol, Ozero	86	E2
Alakyla	62	L3
Al Amarah	94	H6
Alameda *California*	126	A2
Alameda *New Mexico*	127	J3
Alamicamba	132	E8
Alamo	126	E2
Alamogordo	127	K4
Ala, Monti di	69	B5
Alamos	127	H7
Alamosa	127	K2
Aland	63	H6
Alands hav	63	M6
Alanya	76	E4
Alaotra, Lake	109	J3
Alapayevsk	84	Ad5
Al Aqulah	97	J5
Alarcon, Embalse de	66	E3
Al Artawiyah	96	G3
Alasehir	76	C3
Al Ashkhirah	97	P6
Alaska	118	E3
Alaska, Gulf of	118	F4
Alaska Peninsula	118	Af8
Alaska Range	118	E3
Alassio	68	B4
Alatna	118	E2
Alatyr	78	H5
Alausi	136	B4
Alaverdi	77	L2
Alavus	62	K5
Al Ayn	97	M4
Alayor	67	J3
Alayskiy Khrebet	86	C4
Al Azamiyah	77	L6
Alazeya	85	S2
Alba	68	B3
Al Bab	77	G4
Albacete	67	F3
Alba de Tormes	66	D2
Al Badi	96	H5
Al Badi	77	J5
Alba Iulia	73	G2
Albak	63	D8
Alba, Mount	115	B6
Albanel, Lake	121	M7
Albania	74	E2
Albano	137	F4
Albany *Australia*	112	D5
Albany *Canada*	121	K7
Albany *Georgia*	129	K5
Albany *Kentucky*	124	H8
Albany *New York*	125	P5
Albany *Oregon*	122	C5
Albarracin	67	F2
Al Basrah	94	H6
Albatross Bay	113	J1
Albatross Point	115	E3
Al Bayda	96	G10
Albayrak	77	L3
Albemarle	129	M3
Albemarle Island	136	A7
Albemarle Sound	129	P2
Albenga	68	B3
Albentosa	67	F2
Alberche	66	D2
Alberga	113	G4
Albergaria-a-Velha	66	B2
Alberique	67	F3
Albert	64	E3
Alberta	119	M5
Albert Edward, Mount	114	D3
Albert Kanaal	64	F3
Albert, Lake	107	F2
Albert Lea	124	D5
Albert Nile	107	F2
Albertville *France*	65	G6
Albertville *Zaire*	107	E4
Albi	65	E7
Albina	137	G2
Al Bir	96	C2
Al Birk	96	E7
Albocacer	67	G2
Albo, Monti	69	B5
Alboran, Isla de	66	E5
Alborg	63	D8
Alborg Bugt	63	D8
Alborz, Reshteh-ye Kuhta ye	95	K3
Albro	113	K3
Albufeira	66	B4
Albu Gharz, Sabkhat	77	J5
Albuquerque	127	J3
Al Buraymi	97	M4
Albury	113	K6
Al Busayyah	94	H6
Al Buzun	97	K9
Alcacer do Sal	66	B3
Alcala de Henares	66	E2
Alcamo	69	D7
Alcanices	66	C2
Alcaniz	67	F2
Alcantara	66	C3
Alcantara	137	J4
Alcantara, Embalse de	66	C3
Alcaraz	66	E3
Alcaraz, Sierra de	66	E3
Alcaudete	66	D4
Alcazar de San Juan	66	E3
Alcester	53	F2
Alchevsk	79	F6
Alcolea del Pinar	66	E2
Alcoutim	66	C4
Alcoy	67	F3
Alcubierre, Sierra de	67	F2
Alcublas	67	F3
Alcudia	67	H3
Aldabra Islands	82	C7
Aldama	131	K6
Aldan *Russia*	85	M5
Aldan *Russia*	85	N4
Aldanskoye Nagorye	85	M5
Alde	53	J2
Aldeburgh	53	J2
Aldeia Nova	66	C4
Alderley Edge	55	G3
Alderney	53	M6
Aldershot	53	G3
Aldridge	53	F2
Aleg	100	C5
Alegrete	138	E5
Aleksandra, Mys	85	P6
Aleksandriya	79	E6
Aleksandrov	78	F4
Aleksandrovac	73	H4
Aleksandrov Gay	79	H5
Aleksandrovsk	78	K4
Aleksandrovskoye	79	G2
Aleksandrovsk-Sakhalinskiy	85	Q6
Aleksandry, Ostrov	80	F1
Alekseyevka *Kazakhstan*	84	A6
Alekseyevka *Russia*	79	F5
Aleksin	78	F5
Alem Paraiba	138	H4
Alencon	64	D4
Alenquer	137	G4
Alentejo	66	C3
Alenuihaha Channel	126	S10
Aleppo	77	G4

Areia Branca	137	K4	Arneiroz	137	J5	Asap	77	H2
Arena de las Ventas, Punta	130	E5	Arnhem	64	F2	Asarna	62	F5
Arena, Point	122	B8	Arnhem, Cape	113	H1	Asbestos Mountains	108	D5
Arena, Punta	130	E6	Arnhem Land	113	G1	Asbury Park	125	P6
Arenas de San Pedro	66	D2	Arno	68	C4	Ascension	138	D3
Arenas, Punta de	139	C10	Arnold	53	F2	Ascension	99	B7
Arendal	63	C7	Arnon	65	E5	Ascension, Bahia de la	131	R8
Areopolis	75	G4	Arnoy	62	J1	Aschaffenburg	70	C4
Arequipa	138	A3	Arnprior	125	M4	Aschersleben	70	D3
Arevalo	66	D2	Aro	70	D1	Asco	69	B4
Arezzo	68	C4	Aroab	108	C5	Ascoli Piceno	69	D4
Arfersiorfik	120	R4	Aroeira	138	F4	Ascot	53	G3
Arga	67	F1	Arona	68	B3	Aseb	103	H5
Argan	86	F3	Aroostook	125	R3	Aseda	63	F8
Arganil	66	B2	Arorae	111	S2	Asele	62	G4
Argeles-Gazost	65	C7	Aroroy	91	G3	Asenovgrad	73	H5
Argens	65	G7	Arosa	68	B2	Asha	78	K4
Argent	65	E5	Arpa	77	K2	Ashbourne Ireland	59	K5
Argenta	68	C3	Arpacay	77	K2	Ashbourne U.K.	55	H3
Argentan	64	C4	Arpavla	84	Ad4	Ashburton Australia	112	D3
Argentat	65	D6	Arraias	137	H6	Ashburton New Zealand	115	C5
Argentera	68	A3	Ar Ramadi	94	F5	Ashburton U.K.	52	D4
Argenteuil	64	E4	Arran	57	C5	Ashbury	53	F3
Argentina	139	C7	Ar Raqqah	77	H5	Ashby-de-la-Zouch	53	F2
Argentino, Lago	139	B10	Arras	64	E3	Ashcroft	122	D2
Argenton-sur-Creuse	65	D5	Ar Rass	96	F4	Ashdod	94	B6
Arges	73	H3	Ar Rawdah	96	F6	Ashdown	128	E4
Argo	102	F4	Ar Rawuk	97	J9	Asheboro	129	N3
Argolikos Kolpos	75	G4	Arrecife	100	C3	Ashern	119	R5
Argonne, Foret d'	64	F4	Arree, Monts d'	64	B4	Asheville	129	L3
Argopuro, Gunung	90	E7	Arriaga	131	N9	Ashford Ireland	59	K6
Argo Reefs	114	S9	Ar Rifai	94	H6	Ashford U.K.	53	H3
Argos	75	G4	Arrino	112	D4	Ashgabat	95	P3
Argostolion	75	F3	Ar Riyad	96	H4	Ashikaga	89	G7
Arguello, Point	126	B3	Arromanches	64	C4	Ashington	55	H1
Argun	85	K6	Arroux	65	F5	Ashizuri-misaki	89	D9
Argungu	105	F3	Arrow	52	E2	Ashkazar	95	M6
Argunsk	85	L6	Arrow, Lough	58	F4	Ashkinak	95	R6
Arguvan	77	H3	Arrowtown	115	B6	Ashland California	122	C6
Argyle, Lake	112	F2	Arroyo Verde	139	C8	Ashland Kentucky	124	J7
Argyll	57	C4	Ar Ruays	97	L4	Ashland Montana	123	L5
Arhavi	77	J2	Ar Rub al Khali	97	L6	Ashland Nebraska	123	R7
Ar Horqin Qi	87	M3	Ar Rumaytha	97	K4	Ashland Ohio	124	J6
Arhus	63	D8	Ar Rumaythah	94	G6	Ashland Wisconsin	124	E3
Ariano Irpino	69	E5	Ar Rusafah	77	H5	Ashmore Reef	112	E1
Arica	138	B3	Ar Rustaq	97	N5	Ashqelon	94	B6
Ariege	65	D7	Ar Rutbah	94	E5	Ash Shabakah	94	F6
Ariha	77	G5	Ars	63	C8	Ash Shadadah	77	J4
Arilje	72	F4	Ars	94	H3	Ash Shamiyah	94	G6
Arima	136	E1	Arsaynshand	87	L3	Ash Shariqah	97	M4
Arinagour	57	B4	Arsenajan	95	L7	Ash Sharqat	77	K5
Arinos	137	F6	Arsenyev	88	D3	Ash Shatrah	94	H6
Aripuana	136	E5	Arsin	77	H2	Ash Shaykh Uthman	96	G10
Arisaig, Sound of	57	C4	Arsk	78	H4	Ash Shihr	97	J9
Aristazabal Island	118	K5	Arslankoy	76	F4	Ash Shisar	97	L7
Arivonimamo	109	J3	Art	114	V15	Ash Shuaybah	97	J2
Arivruaich	56	B2	Arta	75	F3	Ash Shubah	96	G2
Ariza	67	E2	Arta	67	H3	Ash Shumlul	96	H3
Arizaro, Salar de	138	C4	Artashat	94	G2	Ash Shuqayq	96	F8
Arizona Argentina	139	C7	Arteaga	130	H8	Ash Shurayf	96	D4
Arizona U.S.A.	126	F3	Artem	88	D4	Ashta	92	E4
Arjang	63	E7	Artemisa	132	F3	Ashtabula	125	K6
Arjeplog	62	H3	Artem-Ostrov	79	J7	Ashton-under-Lyne	55	G3
Arjona	136	B1	Artemovsk	79	F6	Ashuanipi Lake	121	N7
Arkadak	79	G5	Artemovskiy	84	Ad5	Asi	94	C4
Arkadelphia	128	F3	Artenay	65	D4	Asika	92	F5
Arkaig, Loch	57	B4	Artesia	127	K4	Asilah	100	D1
Arkalyk	84	Ae6	Arthur's Pass	115	C5	Asinara, Golfo dell	69	B5
Arkansas U.S.A.	128	E3	Arthur's Town	133	K2	Asinara, Isola	69	B5
Arkansas U.S.A.	128	F3	Arti	78	K4	Askale	77	J3
Arkansas City	128	D2	Artigas	138	E6	Askeaton	59	E7
Arkhangelos	75	K4	Artillery Lake	119	P3	Asker	63	H7
Arkhangelsk	78	G3	Artois	64	E3	Askersund	63	F7
Arkhipovka	88	D4	Artova	77	G2	Askilje	62	G4
Arklow	59	K7	Artrutx, Cabo 'd	67	H3	Askim	63	D7
Arkoi	75	J4	Artsiz	79	D6	Askiz	84	E6
Arkona, Kap	70	E1	Artux	86	D4	Askja	62	W12
Arkticheskogo Instituta, Ostrova	84	C1	Artvin	77	J2	Askola	63	L6
Arlagnuk Point	120	K4	Artyk	85	R4	Aslantas Baraji	77	G4
Arlanza	66	E1	Arua	107	F2	Asmera	96	D9
Arlberg Pass	68	C2	Aruana	137	G6	Asmera	103	G4
Arles France	65	E7	Aruba	133	N8	Asnen	63	F8
Arles France	65	F7	Aru, Kepulauan	114	A3	Asoteriba, Jebel	96	C6
Arlington Oregon	122	D5	Aruma	136	E4	Aspatria	55	F2
Arlington S. Dakota	123	R5	Arun	53	G4	Aspermont	127	M4
Arlington Virginia	125	M7	Arunachal Pradesh	93	H3	Aspres-sur-Buech	65	F6
Arlon	64	F4	Arundel	53	G4	As Saan	77	G5
Armadale	57	E5	Arun Qi	87	N2	As Sadiyah	94	G4
Armagh U.K.	58	J4	Aruppukkottai	92	E7	As Salif	96	F9
Armagh U.K.	58	J4	Arusha	107	G3	As Sallum	101	L2
Armagnac	65	D7	Arus, Tanjung	91	G5	As Salman	94	G6
Armah, Wadi	97	K8	Aru, Tanjung	90	F6	Assam	93	H3
Arman	85	S4	Aruwimi	106	E2	As Samawah	94	G6
Armancon	65	E5	Arvayheer	87	J2	As Saquia al Hamra	100	C3
Armathia	75	J5	Arvidsjaur	62	M4	As Sawda	97	M8
Armavir	79	G6	Arvika	63	E7	Assen	64	G2
Armenia	79	G7	Arviksand	62	J1	Assens	63	C9
Armenia Colombia	136	B3	Arxang	86	F3	Assers	63	D8
Armenis	73	G3	Arys	86	B3	Assiniboia	123	A3
Armidale	113	L5	Arzamas	78	G4	Assiniboine	123	Q3
Armori	92	E4	Arzanah	97	L4	Assiniboine, Mount	122	G2
Armoy	58	K2	Arzew	100	E1	Assis	138	F4
Armstrong	124	F1	Arzew, Golfe 'd	67	F5	Assisi	69	D4
Armthorpe	55	H3	Arzua	66	B1	As Sukhnah	77	H5
Armu	88	F2	As	63	D7	As Sulaymaniyah	96	H4
Armutlu	76	C2	Asadabad	94	J4	As Sulaymi	96	E3
Armutova	76	B3	Asad, Buhayrat al	77	H5	As Sulayyil	96	G6
Armyansk	79	E6	Asagipinar	76	E3	As Suq	96	F8
Arnaia	75	G2	Asahi-Dake	88	J4	As Suwayda	94	C5
Arnarfjordur	62	S12	Asahi Kawa	88	J4	As Suwayh	97	P5
Arnaud	121	M5	Asalem	94	J3	As Suwayrah	94	G5
Arnauti, Akra	76	E5	Asamankese	104	E4	Astakidha	75	J5
Arnedo	67	E1	Asansk	84	F5	Astara	94	J2
			Asansol	92	G4			

Name	Page	Grid
Aube	64	F4
Aubenas	65	F6
Aubigny-sur-Nere	65	E5
Aubry Lake	118	K2
Auburn *Australia*	113	L4
Auburn *Alabama*	129	K4
Auburn *California*	126	B1
Auburn *Indiana*	124	H6
Auburn *Maine*	125	Q4
Auburn *Nebraska*	124	C6
Auburn *New York*	125	M5
Aubusson	65	E6
Auca Mahuida	139	C7
Auce	63	K8
Auch	65	D7
Auchavan	57	E4
Auchengray	57	E5
Auchterarder	57	E4
Auckland	115	E2
Auckland Islands	141	M8
Aude	65	E7
Auderville	64	C4
Audierne, Baie 'd	65	A5
Aue	70	E3
Augher	58	H4
Aughnacloy	58	J4
Aughrim *Galway, Ireland*	59	F6
Aughrim *Wicklow, Ireland*	59	K7
Aughton	55	H3
Augsburg	70	D4
Augusta *Australia*	112	D5
Augusta *Georgia*	129	M4
Augusta *Italy*	69	E7
Augusta *Kansas*	128	D2
Augusta *Maine*	125	R4
Augusta *Montana*	122	H4
Augustine Island	118	E4
Augustow	71	K2
Augustus, Mount	112	D3
Auletta	69	E5
Aulia	103	F4
Auliting Island	120	N4
Aulne	64	B4
Aultbea	56	C3
Aumont	65	E6
Aupalak	121	N6
Aurangabad	92	E5
Auray	65	B5
Aurdal	63	C6
Aure *Norway*	62	B5
Aure *Norway*	62	C5
Aurich	70	B2
Aurillac	65	E6
Aurkuning	90	E6
Aurora *Colorado*	123	M8
Aurora *Illinois*	124	F6
Aurora *Missouri*	124	D8
Aurora *Nebraska*	123	R7
Au Sable	124	J4
Auskerry Sound	56	F1
Aust-Agder	63	D7
Austin *Minnesota*	124	D5
Austin *Nevada*	126	D1
Austin *Texas*	128	D5
Austin, Lake	112	D4
Australia	110	F6
Australian Capital Territory	113	K6
Austria	68	D2
Austurhorn	62	X12
Autazes	136	F4
Authie	64	D3
Autlan	130	G8
Autun	65	F5
Auvergne *Australia*	112	G2
Auvergne *France*	65	E6
Auxerre	65	E5
Avallon	65	E5
Avanos	76	F3
Avare	138	G4
Avas	75	H2
Avcilar	76	C2
Avebury	53	F3
Aveiro *Portugal*	66	B2
Aveiro *Portugal*	66	B2
Avellino	69	E5
Avelon Peninsula	121	R8
Aversa	69	E5
Aves, Isla de	133	R7
Avesnes	64	E3
Avesta	63	G6
Aveyron	65	E6
Avezzano	69	D4
Avgo	75	H5
Aviemore	57	E3
Aviemore, Lake	115	C6
Avigliano	69	E5
Avignon	65	F7
Avila	66	D2
Avila, Sierra de	66	D2
Aviles	66	D1
Avisio	68	C2
Aviz	66	C3
Avlum	63	C8
Avoca *Australia*	113	J6
Avoca *Iowa*	124	C6
Avola	69	E7
Avon *Devon, U.K.*	52	D4
Avon *Hampshire, U.K.*	53	F4
Avon *U.K.*	52	E3
Avon *U.K.*	52	E3
Avonmouth	52	E3
Avon Park	129	M7
Avon Water	57	D5
Avranches	64	C4
Avrig	73	H3
Avuavu	114	K6
Awaji-shima	89	E8
Awali	97	K3
Awanui	115	D1
Awarik, Uruq al	96	H7
Awarua Point	115	A6
Awa-shima	89	G6
Awash Wenz	103	H5
Awaso	104	E4
Awatere	115	D4
Awbari	101	H3
Aweil	102	E6
Awe, Loch	57	C4
Awful, Mount	115	B6
Awgu	105	G4
Awjilah	101	K2
Axbridge	52	E3
Axe *Dorset, U.K.*	52	E4
Axe *Somerset, U.K.*	52	E3
Axel-Heiberg Island	120	H2
Axim	104	E5
Axios	75	G2
Ax-les-Thermes	65	D7
Axminster	52	D4
Ayabe	89	E8
Ayacucho *Argentina*	139	E7
Ayacucho *Peru*	136	C6
Ayaguz	86	F2
Ayamonte	66	C4
Ayan *Russia*	84	H5
Ayan *Russia*	85	P5
Ayancik	76	F2
Ayas	76	E3
Ayaviri	136	C6
Ayayei	96	C10
Aya-Yenahin	104	E4
Aybasti	77	G2
Aydarkul, Ozero	86	B3
Aydere	95	N2
Aydin	76	B4
Aydinca	77	G2
Aydincik	76	E4
Aydin Daglari	76	C3
Ayerbe	67	F1
Ayers Rock	112	G4
Ayeshka	84	E6
Ayia Anna	75	G3
Ayia Marina	75	J5
Ayios	75	G4
Ayios Andreas	75	G4
Ayios Evstratios	75	H3
Ayios Kirikos	75	J4
Ayios Nikolaos *Greece*	75	F3
Ayios Nikolaos *Greece*	75	H5
Ayios Petros	75	F3
Aykathonisi	75	J4
Aykhal	84	J3
Aylesbury	53	G3
Ayllon	66	E2
Aylmer, Lake	119	P3
Aylsham	53	J2
Ayn al Bayda	77	G5
Ayni	86	B4
Ayn Tarfawi	77	K5
Ayn. Wadi al	97	M5
Ayod	102	F6
Ayon	85	V3
Ayon, Ostrov	85	V3
Ayora	67	F3
Ayr *U.K.*	57	D5
Ayr *U.K.*	57	D5
Ayranci	76	E4
Ayre, Point of	54	E2
Aysgarth	55	H2
Aysharak	86	C2
Aytos	73	J4
Ayun	97	L8
Ayutthaya	93	K6
Ayvacik	76	B3
Ayvali	76	D4
Azambuja	66	B3
Azamgarh	92	F3
Azaran	94	H3
Azaz	77	G4
Azazga	67	J4
Azbine	101	G5
Azerbaijan	79	H7
Azezo	96	C10
Azogues	136	B4
Azoum	102	D5
Azov, Sea of	79	F6
Azovskoye More	79	F6
Azpeitia	66	E1
Azrac, Bahr el	103	F5
Azrou	100	D2
Aztec	127	H2
Azuaga	66	D3
Azuari	137	G3
Azuero, Peninsula de	132	G11
Azul *Argentina*	139	E7
Azul *Mexico*	131	Q9
Azul, Cordillera	136	B5
Azur, Cote d'	65	G7
Azvacay	76	E2
Az Zabadani	77	G6
Az Zair	96	E7
Az Zahran	97	K3
Az Zarqa	97	L4
Az Zawiyah	101	H2
Az Zaydiyah	96	F9
Az Zilfi	96	G3
Az Zubaydiyah	94	G5
Az Zubayr	94	H6
Az Zuhrah	96	F9
Az Zuqur	96	F9

B

Name	Page	Grid
Baaba	114	W16
Baalbek	77	G5
Baamonde	66	C1
Baardheere	107	H2
Babadag	73	K3
Babaeski	76	B2
Babahoyo	136	B4
Babai Gaxun	87	J3
Baba, Koh-i-	92	C2
Babar	91	H7
Babar, Kepulauan	91	H7
Babayevo	78	F4
Babbacombe Bay	52	D4
Babelthuap	91	J4
Babine Lake	118	K5
Babo	114	A2
Babol	95	L3
Babol Sar	95	L3
Baboua	102	B6
Babruysk	79	D5
Babstovo	88	D1
Babushkin	84	H6
Babuyan *Philippines*	91	F4
Babuyan *Philippines*	91	G2
Babuyan Channel	91	G2
Babuyan Islands	91	G2
Bacabal	137	J4
Bacan	91	H6
Bacau	73	J2
Baccegalhaldde	62	J2
Back	119	R2
Backa	63	E6
Backaland	56	F1
Backa Topola	72	E3
Backe	62	G5
Bac Ninh	93	L4
Bacolod	91	G3
Bacup	55	G3
Badagara	92	E6
Badajoz	66	C3
Badalona	67	H2
Badanah	94	E6
Bad Aussee	68	D2
Badby	53	F2
Bad Doberan	70	D1
Bad Ems	70	B3
Baden	68	B2
Baden-Baden	70	C4
Badenoch	57	D4
Badgastein	68	D2
Bad Homburg	70	C3
Badiet esh Sham	94	D5
Bad Ischl	68	D2
Bad Kissingen	70	D3
Bad Kreuznach	70	B4
Bad Lands	123	N4
Bad Mergentheim	70	C4
Badminton	52	E3
Bad Neustadt	70	D3
Bad Oldesloe	70	D2
Ba Don	93	L5
Badong	93	M2
Badrah	94	G5
Badr Hunayn	96	D5
Bad Segeberg	70	D2
Bad Tolz	70	D5
Badulla	92	F7
Bad Wildungen	70	C3
Badzhal	85	N6
Badzhalskiy Khrebet	85	N6
Bae Can	93	L4
Baena	66	D4
Baeza	136	B4
Bafa Golu	76	B4
Bafang	105	H4
Bafata	104	C3
Baffin	120	H3
Baffin Bay *Canada*	120	N3
Baffin Bay *U.S.A.*	128	D7
Baffin Island	120	L3
Bafia	105	H5
Bafing Makana	100	C6
Bafoulabe	100	C6
Bafoussam	105	H4
Bafq	95	M6
Bafra	77	F2
Bafra Burun	77	F2
Baft	95	N7
Bafwasende	106	E2
Bagamoya	107	G4
Bagan Datuk	90	C5
Bagansiapiapi	90	C5
Baganuvam	78	K2
Bagaryak	84	Ad5
Bagdad	126	F3
Bagdere	77	J3
Bage	138	F6
Bagenalstown	59	J7
Baggs	123	L7
Baghdad	77	L6
Bagherhat	93	G4
Bagheria	69	D6
Baghlan	92	C1
Bagh nam Faoileann	56	A3
Bagisli	77	L4
Bagneres-de-Bigorre	65	D7
Bagneres-de-Luchon	65	D7
Bagnoles-de-l'Orne	64	C4
Bagnolo Mella	68	C3
Bagoe	104	D3
Bagrationovsk	71	J1
Bagshot	53	G3
Baguio	91	G2
Bagusa	114	B2
Bahamas	132	J2
Baharampur	93	G4
Bahau	90	C5
Bahaur	90	E6
Bahawalpur	92	D3
Bahce	77	G4
Bahia	137	J6
Bahia Blanca	139	D7
Bahia Bustamante	139	C9
Bahia, Islas de la	132	D6
Bahia Kino	126	G6
Bahia Laura	139	C9
Bahia Negra	138	E4
Bahias, Cabo dos	139	C8
Bahr	96	E7
Bahr, Abu	97	J6
Bahraich	92	F3
Bahrain	97	K3
Bahrain, Gulf of	97	K4
Bahr Sayqal	77	G6
Bahu Kalat	95	Q9
Baia de Maputo	109	F5
Baia Mare	73	G2
Baian, Band-i-	92	C2
Baiao	137	H4
Baiazeh	95	M5
Baibokoum	102	C6
Baicheng *Jilin, China*	87	N2
Baicheng *Xinjiang Uygur Zizhiqu, China*	86	E3
Baie Comeau	125	R2
Baie-du-Poste	121	M7
Baiji	77	K5
Baiju	87	N5
Baikal, Lake	84	H6
Baile Atha Cliath	59	K6
Baile Herculane	73	G3
Bailieborough	58	J5
Baillie Hamilton Island	120	H2
Baillie Island	113	K1
Bailundo	106	C5
Baimuru	114	C3
Bainbridge	129	K5
Bain-de-Bretagne	65	C5
Baing	91	G8
Bains-les-Bains	65	G4
Baird Inlet	118	C3
Baird Mountains	118	C2
Baird Peninsula	120	L4
Bairin Youqi	87	M3
Bairin Zuoqi	87	M3
Bairnsdale	113	K6
Baise	65	D7
Baixingt	87	N3
Baiyanghe	86	F3
Baja	72	E2
Baja, Punta	126	E6
Bajgiran	95	P3
Bajil	96	F9
Bajmok	72	E3
Bakchar	84	C5
Bakel	104	C3
Baker *Chile*	139	B9
Baker *California*	126	E3
Baker *Montana*	123	M4
Baker *Oregon*	122	F5
Baker Foreland	119	S3
Baker Island	111	T1
Baker Lake	119	R3
Baker, Mount	122	D3
Bakersfield	126	C3
Bakewell	55	H3
Bakharden	95	N2
Bakhardok	95	P2
Bakharz	95	P4
Bakhchisaray	79	E7
Bakhmach	79	E5
Bakhta	84	D4
Bakhtaran	94	H4
Bakhtegan, Daryacheh-ye	95	L7
Bakhty	86	F2
Bakinskikh Komissarov	95	M2
Bakir	76	B3
Bakkafjordur	62	X11
Bakkafloi	62	X11
Bakkagerdi	62	Y12
Baklan	76	C4
Bako	103	G6
Bakongan	90	B5
Bakony	72	D2
Bakouma	102	D6
Baku	79	H7
Bakwanga	106	D4
Bala	52	D2
Bala	76	E3
Balabac	91	F4
Balabac Strait	90	F4
Balabio	114	W16
Bala, Cerros de	136	D6
Balacita	73	G3
Balad	77	L6
Baladch	95	K3
Balagannoye	85	R5
Balaghat	92	F4
Balaghat Range	92	E5
Balaguer	67	G2
Balaikarangan	90	E5
Balaka	107	F5

Baruun Urt	87 L2	Baukau	91 H7	Beaumaris	54 E3	Belford	57 G5
Barvas	56 B2	Baulc, Cape	121 Q7	Beaumont *France*	64 E4	Belfort	65 G5
Barwani	92 D4	Baumann Fjord	120 J2	Beaumont *California*	126 D4	Belgaum	92 D5
Barwon	113 K4	Baume	113 L4	Beaumont *Texas*	128 E5	Belgium	64 E3
Barysaw	63 Q9	Baumtregaum	59 C8	Beaune	65 F5	Belgorod	79 F5
Barysh	79 H5	Bauru	138 G4	Beaurepaire	65 F6	Belgorod-Dnestrovskiy	79 E6
Basaidu	95 M8	Baus	138 F3	Beauvais	64 E4	Belgrade	72 F3
Basankusu	106 C2	Bautzen	70 F3	Beauvoir-sur-Mer	65 B5	Belgrano	141 X3
Basco	91 G1	Bawceswell	53 J2	Beaver *Saskatchewan, Canada*	119 P5	Belica	71 L2
Bascunan, Cabo	138 B5	Bawcsey	53 J2	Beaver *Yukon, Canada*	118 K3	Beli Lom	73 J4
Basel	68 A2	Bawean	90 E7	Beaver Dam *Kentucky*	124 G8	Beli Manastir	72 E3
Basento	69 P5	Bawiti	102 E2	Beaver Dam *Wisconsin*	124 F5	Belimbing	90 C7
Bashakerd, Kuhha-ye	95 P8	Bawku	104 E3	Beaverhill Lake	119 N5	Belin	65 C6
Bashi Haixia	87 N7	Bawtry	55 H3	Beawar	92 D3	Belinskiy	79 G5
Basht	95 K6	Baxley	129 L5	Beazley	139 C6	Belinyu	90 D6
Basilan *Philippines*	91 G4	Bayamo	132 J4	Bebedouro	138 G4	Belitsa	73 G5
Basilan *Philippines*	91 G4	Bayamon	133 P5	Bebington	55 F3	Belitung	90 D6
Basildon	53 H3	Bayan	38 A2	Beccles	53 J2	Belize	132 C6
Basingstoke	53 F3	Bayan-Aul	84 B6	Becej	72 F3	Belkina, Mys	88 F3
Baskale	77 L3	Bayandalay	87 J3	Becerrea	66 C1	Belknap, Moun	122 H8
Baskatong, Reservoir	125 N3	Bayanday	84 H6	Bechar	100 E2	Belkovskiy, Ostrov	85 P1
Baskil	77 H3	Bayan Harshan	93 J2	Becharof Lake	118 D4	Bella Bella	118 K5
Baskoy	77 K2	Bayanhongor	86 J2	Bechet	73 G4	Bellac	65 D5
Basle	68 A2	Bayan Mod	87 J3	Beckingham	55 J3	Bella Coola	118 K5
Basoko	106 D2	Bayan Obo	87 K3	Beckley	125 K8	Bellaire	128 E6
Bassano del Grappa	68 C3	Bayano, Laguna	132 H10	Beclean	73 H2	Bellary	92 E5
Bassar	104 F4	Bayan-Ondor	86 H3	Bedale	55 H2	Bella Vista *Argentina*	138 C5
Bassas da India	109 G4	Bayantsagaan	86 H3	Bedarieux	65 E7	Bella Vista *Argentina*	138 E5
Bassein	93 H5	Bayantsogt	87 K2	Bede, Point	118 E4	Belleek	58 F4
Bassenthwaite	55 F2	Bayan-Uul	87 L2	Bedford *U.K.*	53 G2	Bellefontaine	124 J6
Bassenthwaite Lake	55 F2	Bayard *Nebraska*	123 N7	Bedford *U.S.A.*	124 G7	Belle Fourche *South Dakota*	123 N5
Basse Santa Su	104 C3	Bayard *New Mexico*	127 H4	Bedford Level	53 H2	Belle Fourche *Wyoming*	123 M5
Basseterre	133 R6	Bayat *Turkey*	76 D3	Bedfordshire	53 G2	Belle Glade	129 M7
Basse Terre	133 S6	Bayat *Turkey*	76 F2	Bedlington	55 H1	Belle Ile	65 B5
Bassett	123 Q6	Bayburt	77 J2	Bedwas	52 D3	Belle Isle	121 Q7
Bassila	105 F4	Bay City *Michigan*	124 J5	Bedworth	53 F2	Belleme	64 D4
Bass Strait	113 K6	Bay City *Texas*	128 E6	Beer Sheva	94 B6	Belleville *Canada*	125 M4
Bastad	63 E8	Baydaratskaya Guba	84 Ae3	Beeston	53 F2	Belleville *Illinois*	124 F7
Bastak	95 M8	Baydhabo	107 H2	Beeswing	57 E5	Belleville *Kansas*	123 R8
Bastam	95 M3	Baydon	53 F3	Beeville	128 D6	Bellevue *Idaho*	122 G6
Basti	92 F3	Bayerischer Wald	70 E4	Befale	106 D2	Bellevue *Washington*	122 C4
Bastia	69 B4	Bayeux	64 C4	Befandriana	109 J3	Belley	65 F6
Bastogne	64 F4	Bayfield	124 E3	Begejska Kanal	72 F3	Bellingham *U.K.*	57 F5
Bastrop *Louisiana*	128 G4	Bayhan al Qasab	96 G9	Begoml	63 N10	Bellingham *U.S.A.*	122 C3
Bastrop *Texas*	128 D5	Bayindir	76 B3	Behbehan	95 K6	Bellinghaussen Sea	141 U5
Basyurt	77 J3	Bayir	94 C6	Behraamkale	76 B3	Bellingshausse	141 W6
Bata	105 G5	Baykadam	86 B3	Behshahr	95 L3	Bellinzona	68 B2
Batabano, Golfo de	132 F3	Baykal	84 G6	Beian	87 P2	Bello	136 B2
Batagay	85 N3	Baykalovo	84 Ae5	Beibu Wan	93 L4	Bellona Island	114 J7
Batagay-Alyta	85 N3	Baykal, Ozero	84 H6	Beihai	93 L4	Bellona Reefs	111 N6
Batakan	90 E6	Baykan	77 J3	Beijing	87 M4	Bellpuig	67 G2
Bataklik Golu	76 E4	Bay-Khak	84 E6	Beila	100 B5	Bellshill	57 D5
Batala	92 E2	Baykit	84 F4	Beinn a' Ghlo	57 E4	Belluno	68 D2
Batalha	66 B3	Baynunah	97 L5	Beinn Bheigier	57 B5	Bell Ville	133 D6
Batamay	85 M4	Bayombong	91 G2	Beinn Dearg *Highland, U.K.*	56 D3	Belly	122 H3
Batan	91 G1	Bayona	66 B1	Beinn Dearg *Tayside, U.K.*	57 E4	Belmont	56 A1
Batang	93 J2	Bayonne	65 C7	Beinn Dorain	57 D4	Belmonte *Portugal*	66 C2
Batangafo	102 C6	Bayo Point	91 G3	Beinn Eighe	56 C3	Belmonte *Spain*	66 E3
Batangas	91 G3	Bayram-Ali	95 R3	Beinn Fhada	56 C3	Belmopan	132 C6
Batanghari	90 C6	Bayramic	76 B3	Beinn Ime	57 D4	Belmullet	58 B4
Batan Islands	91 G1	Bayramiy	94 J2	Beinn Mhor	56 A3	Belogorsk	79 E6
Batatais	138 G4	Bayramtepe	76 C2	Beinn na Caillich	57 C3	Belogorye	71 M4
Batavia	125 L5	Bayreuth	70 D4	Beinn Resipol	57 C4	Belogradchik	73 G4
Bataysk	79 F6	Bayrut	76 F6	Beinn Sgritheall	57 C3	Belo Horizonte	138 K4
Batchelor	112 G1	Bay Saint Louis	128 H5	Beipiao	87 N3	Beloit	124 F5
Batesville	128 G3	Bayt al Faqih	96 F9	Beira	109 F3	Belokorovichi	79 D5
Bath *U.K.*	52 E3	Baytown	128 E6	Beirut	76 F6	Belomorsk	78 E3
Bath *U.S.A.*	125 M5	Bayy al Kabir, Wadi	101 H2	Bei Shan	86 H3	Belorado	66 E1
Batha	102 C5	Baza	66 E4	Beit Lahm	94 B6	Belorechensk	79 F7
Bathgate	57 E5	Bazaliya	71 M4	Beius	73 G2	Beloren	76 E4
Bathurst *Australia*	113 K5	Bazar-Dyuzi	79 H7	Beja	66 C3	Belorusskaya Gryada	71 L2
Bathurst *Canada*	125 T3	Bazaruto, Ilha do	109 G4	Beja	101 G1	Belot, Lac	118 K2
Bathurst *Gambia*	104 B3	Bazas	65 C6	Bejaia	101 G1	Belo-Tsiribihina	109 H3
Bathurst Inlet	119 P2	Bazman	95 Q8	Bejaia, Golfe de	67 J4	Belousovka	84 C6
Bathurst Island	112 G1	Bazman, Kuh-e	95 Q7	Bejar	66 D2	Belovo	84 D6
Bathurst Islands	120 F2	Bcharre	77 F5	Bejestan	95 P4	Beloye More	78 F2
Batie	104 E4	Beach	123 N4	Beji	92 C3	Beloye Ozero	78 F3
Batiki	114 R8	Beachy Head	53 H4	Bekdast	79 J7	Belozersk	78 F4
Batinah, Al	97 N4	Beaconsfield	53 G3	Bekescsaba	73 F2	Belozerskoye	84 Ae5
Batin, Wadi al	96 H2	Beadnell Bay	55 H1	Bekily	109 J4	Belper	55 H3
Batiscan	125 P3	Beagh, Lough	58 G2	Bekopaka	109 H3	Belsay	57 G5
Batitoroslar	76 D4	Beagle Gulf	112 G1	Bekwai	104 E4	Belterra	137 F4
Batlaq-e Gavkhuni	95 L5	Beagle Reef	112 E2	Bela *India*	92 F3	Belton	55 J3
Batley	55 H3	Beal	57 G5	Bela *Pakistan*	92 C3	Belturbet	58 H4
Batman *Turkey*	77 J4	Bealanana	109 J2	Belabo	105 H5	Belukha, Gora	86 F2
Batman *Turkey*	77 J4	Beaminster	52 E4	Belaga	90 E5	Belvedere Marittimo	69 E6
Batna	101 G1	Beampingaratra	109 J4	Belang	91 G5	Belvidere	124 F5
Baton Rouge	128 G5	Bear	122 J6	Bela Palanka	73 G4	Belvoir, Vale of	53 G2
Batouri	105 H5	Beara Peninsula	59 C9	Belarus	71 L2	Belyando, River	113 K3
Batroun	77 F5	Beardmore	124 G2	Bela Vista	109 F5	Belyayevka	73 L2
Batsfjord	62 N1	Beardstown	124 E6	Belawan	90 B5	Belyy, Ostrov	85 A2
Battambang	93 K6	Bear Island *Canada*	121 K7	Belaya *Russia*	78 K4	Belyy Yar	84 D5
Batticaloa	92 F7	Bear Island *Ireland*	59 C9	Belaya *Russia*	85 W3	Belzyce	71 K3
Battle *Canada*	119 N5	Bear Lake	122 J7	Belaya-Kalitva	79 G6	Bemaraha, Plateau du	109 J3
Battle *U.K.*	53 H4	Bearley	53 F2	Belaya Kholunitsa	78 J4	Bembridge	53 F4
Battle Creek	124 H5	Bearn	65 C7	Belayan	90 F5	Bemidji	124 C3
Battle Harbour	121 Q7	Bear Paw Mount	122 K3	Belcher Channel	120 G2	Benabarre	67 G1
Battle Mountain	122 F7	Bearsden	57 D5	Belcher Islands	121 L6	Ben Alder	57 D4
Batu	103 G6	Beartooth Range	123 K5	Belchiragh	94 S4	Benalla	113 K6
Batubetumbang	90 D6	Beata, Cabo	133 M6	Belchite	67 F2	Benares	92 F3
Batum	77 J2	Beata, Isla	133 M6	Belcoo	58 G4	Benavente	66 D2
Batumi	77 J2	Beatrice	123 R7	Belderg	58 C4	Ben Avon	57 E3
Batu Pahat	90 C5	Beatty	126 D2	Belebey	78 J5	Benbaun	59 C5
Batuputih	91 F5	Beattyville	125 M2	Beledweyne	103 J7	Ben Chonzie	57 E4
Baturaja	90 D6	Beau Basin	109 L7	Belem	137 H4	Bencorr	59 C5
Baturite	137 K4	Beaucaire	65 F7	Belen *Turkey*	76 E4	Ben Cruachan	57 C4
Baubau	91 G7	Beaufort *Malaysia*	90 F4	Belen *U.S.A.*	127 J3	Bend	122 D5
Bauchi	105 G3	Beaufort *U.S.A.*	129 M4	Belep, Iles	114 V15	Bende	105 G4
Bauda	92 F4	Beaufort Sea	118 H1	Belesar, Embalse de	66 C1	Bender Qaasim	103 J5
Baudette	124 C2	Beaufort West	108 D6	Belev	79 F5	Bendigo	113 J6
Baudo	136 B2	Beaugency	65 D5	Belfast *New Zealand*	115 D5	Benesov	70 F4
Baudouinville	107 E4	Beauly *U.K.*	56 D3	Belfast *U.K.*	58 L3	Benevento	69 E5
Bauge	65 C5	Beauly *U.K.*	56 D3	Belfast Lough	58 L3	Bengbu	87 M5
Bauhinia Downs	113 K3	Beauly Firth	56 D3	Belfield	123 N4	Benghazi	101 K2

Bengkalis 90 C5
Bengkulu 90 C6
Bengo, Baia do 106 B4
Bengoi 91 J6
Bengtsfors 63 E7
Benguela 106 B5
Benguerua, Ilha 109 G4
Benha 102 F1
Ben Hope 56 D2
Beni *Bolivia* 136 D6
Beni *Zaire* 107 E2
Beni Abbes 100 E2
Benicarlo 67 G2
Benidorm 67 F3
Beni Mazar 102 F2
Beni Mellal 100 D2
Benin 105 F4
Benin, Bight of 105 F4
Benin City 105 G4
Beni Saf 100 E1
Beni Suef 102 F2
Ben Klibreck 56 D2
Ben Lawers 57 D4
Ben Ledi 57 D4
Ben Lomond 57 D4
Ben Loyal 56 D2
Ben Lui 57 D4
Ben Macdui 57 E3
Ben MorCoigach 56 C3
Ben More *Central, U.K.* 57 D4
Ben More *Strathclyde, U.K.* 56 B4
Ben More Assynt 56 D2
Benmore, Lake 115 C6
Bennachie 56 F3
Benn Cleuch 57 E4
Bennetta, Ostrov 85 R1
Ben Nevis 57 C4
Bennington 125 P5
Benoni 108 E5
Be, Nosy 109 J2
Ben Rinnes 56 E3
Bensheim 70 C4
Benson *U.K.* 53 F3
Benson *U.K.* 126 G5
Ben Starav 57 C4
Bent 95 P8
Bentinck Island 93 J6
Bent Jbail 94 B5
Bentley 55 H3
Benton 128 F3
Benton Harbor 124 G5
Bentung 90 C5
Benue 105 G4
Ben Venue 57 D4
Ben Vorlich 57 D4
Benwee 58 C5
Benwee Head 58 C4
Ben Wyvis 56 D3
Benxi 87 N3
Beo 91 H5
Beograd 72 F3
Beppu 89 C9
Beqa 114 R9
Berat 74 E2
Berau, Teluk 114 A2
Berber 103 F4
Berbera 103 J5
Berberati 102 C7
Berck 64 D3
Berdichev 79 D6
Berdigestyakh 85 M4
Berdyansk 79 F6
Berea 124 H8
Bereeda 103 K5
Beregovo 79 C6
Berens 119 R5
Berens River 119 R5
Bere Regis 52 E4
Berettyo 73 F2
Berettyoujfalu 73 F2
Bereza 71 L2
Berezhany 71 L4
Berezhnykh, Mys 85 Q1
Berezina 78 D5
Berezino 78 D5
Berezna 79 E5
Berezniki 78 K4
Berezno 71 M3
Berezovka *Russia* 78 K3
Berezovka *Russia* 85 K5
Berezovka *Russia* 85 T3
Berezovka *Ukraine* 79 E6
Berezovo *Russia* 84 Ae4
Berezovo *Russia* 85 W4
Berezovskaya 85 K5
Berg 108 C6
Berga 67 G1
Bergama 76 B3
Bergamo 68 B3
Bergeforsen 62 G5
Bergen *Germany* 70 E1
Bergen *Norway* 63 J6
Bergen op Zoom 64 F3
Bergerac 65 D6
Bergfors 62 H2
Bergisch-Gladbach 70 B3
Bergsviken 62 J4
Berhala, Selat 90 C6
Beringa, Ostrov 81 T4
Bering Glacier 118 G3
Beringovskiy 85 X4
Bering Sea 143 H3
Bering Strait 118 B2
Berislav 79 E6
Beris, Ra's 95 Q9
Berja 66 E4
Berkak 62 C5
Berkakit 85 L5
Berkeley *U.K.* 52 E3
Berkeley *U.S.A.* 126 A2
Berkhamsted 53 G3
Berkner Island 141 W3
Berkovitsa 73 G4
Berkshire 53 F3
Berkshire Downs 53 F3
Berkshire Mountains 125 P5
Berlevag 62 N2
Berlin *Germany* 70 E2
Berlin *U.S.A.* 125 Q4
Bermeja, Sierra 66 D4
Bermejo *Argentina* 138 C6
Bermejo *Argentina* 138 D4
Bermeo 66 E1
Bermillo de Sayago 66 C2
Bermuda 117 N5
Bern 68 A2
Bernau 70 E2
Bernay 64 D4
Bernburg 70 D3
Berne 68 A2
Berner Alpen 68 A2
Berneray *U.K.* 57 A4
Berneray *U.K.* 56 A3
Bernina, Piz 68 B2
Beroroha 109 J4
Berounka 70 E4
Berre, Etang de 65 F7
Berriedale 56 E2
Berriedale Water 56 E2
Berrigan 113 K6
Berringarra 112 D4
Berrouaghia 67 H4
Berry *Australia* 113 L5
Berry *France* 65 E5
Berryessa, Lake 122 C8
Berry Head 52 D4
Berry Islands 132 J1
Bershad 73 K1
Berthoud Pass 123 L8
Bertoua 105 H5
Beru 111 S2
Beruri 136 E4
Berwick 125 M6
Berwick-upon-Tweed 57 F5
Berwyn Mountains 52 D2
Berzence 72 D2
Besalampy 109 H3
Besancon 65 G5
Besar, Kai 91 J7
Besbre 65 E5
Beshneh 95 M7
Besiri 77 J4
Beskidy Zachodnie 71 H4
Beslan 79 G7
Besni 77 G4
Bessarabia 73 K2
Bessarabka 73 K2
Bessbrook 58 K4
Bessemer *Alabama* 129 J4
Bessemer *Winconsin* 124 F3
Bestamak *Kazakhstan* 86 D2
Bestamak *Kazakhstan* 79 K6
Bestobe 84 A6
Bestuzhevo 78 G3
Betafo 109 J3
Betanzos 66 B1
Betare Oya 105 H4
Bethal 108 E5
Bethanie 108 C5
Bethany 124 C6
Bethel 118 C3
Bethel Park 125 L6
Bethesda *U.K.* 54 E3
Bethesda *U.S.A.* 125 M7
Bethlehem *Israel* 94 B6
Bethlehem *South Africa* 108 E5
Bethulie 108 E6
Bethune *France* 64 D4
Bethune *France* 64 E3
Betioky 109 H4
Betpak-Dala 86 B2
Bet-Pak-Data 86 B2
Betroka 109 J4
Betsiamites 125 R2
Betsiboka 109 J3
Bettiah 92 F3
Bettyhill 56 D2
Betul 92 E4
Betwa 92 E4
Betws-y-coed 54 F3
Beuvron 65 D5
Beverley *Australia* 112 D5
Beverley *U.K.* 55 J3
Beverly Hills 126 C3
Bexhill 53 H4
Beykoz 76 C2
Beyla 104 D4
Beylul 96 F10
Beyneu 79 K6
Beypazari 76 D2
Beypinar 77 G3
Beysehir 76 D4
Beysehir Golu 76 D4
Beyton 53 H2
Beytussebap 77 K4
Bezhetsk 78 F4
Beziers 65 E7
Bezmein 95 P2
Bhadgaon 92 G3
Bhadrachalam 92 F5
Bhadrakh 92 G4
Bhadravati 92 E6
Bhagalpur 92 G3
Bhakkar 92 D2
Bhamo 93 J4
Bhandara 92 E4
Bhanrer Range 92 F4
Bharatpur *Pradesh, India* 92 F4
Bharatpur *Rajasthan, India* 92 E3
Bharuch 92 D4
Bhatinda 92 D2
Bhatpara 93 G4
Bhavnagar 92 D4
Bhawanipatna 92 F5
Bhilwara 92 D3
Bhima 92 E5
Bhiwani 92 E3
Bhopal 92 E4
Bhopalpatnam 92 F5
Bhor 92 D5
Bhubaneshwar 92 G4
Bhuj 92 C4
Bhumiphol Dam 93 J5
Bhusawal 92 E4
Bhutan 93 G3
Bia 136 D4
Biaban 95 N8
Biabanak 95 S5
Biak 114 B2
Biala Podlaska 71 K2
Bialobrzegi 71 J3
Bialowieza 71 K2
Bialystok 71 K2
Bianco 69 F6
Biankouma 104 D4
Biaro 91 H5
Biarritz 65 C7
Biasca 68 B2
Biba 102 F2
Bibai 88 H4
Bibala 106 B5
Bibby Island 119 S3
Biberach 70 C4
Bibury 53 F3
Bicester 53 F3
Bicheno 113 K7
Bickle Knob 125 L7
Bida 105 G4
Bidar 92 E5
Biddeford 125 Q5
Biddulph 55 G3
Bidean Nam Bian 57 C4
Bideford 52 C3
Bideford Bay 52 C3
Bidford-on-Avon 53 F2
Bidokht 95 P4
Bidzhan *Russia* 88 C1
Bidzhan *Russia* 88 C2
Biebrza 71 K2
Biel 68 A2
Bielefeld 70 C2
Biella 68 B3
Bielsko-Biala 71 H4
Bielsk Podlaski 71 K2
Bien Hoa 93 L6
Bienne 68 A2
Bienveneu 137 G3
Bienville, Lac 121 M6
Biferno 69 E5
Biga 76 B2
Bigadic 76 C3
Big Bay 114 T11
Big Belt Mountains 122 J4
Big Blue 123 R7
Bigbury Bay 52 D4
Biggar *Canada* 123 K1
Biggar *U.K.* 57 E5
Biggleswade 53 G2
Big Horn 123 K5
Big Horn Mountains 123 L5
Big Island 120 M5
Big Pine 126 C2
Big Piney 123 J6
Big Sheep Mountains 123 L4
Big Sioux 123 R5
Big Snowy Mount 122 K4
Big Spring 127 M4
Big Stone Gap 124 J8
Big Timber 123 J5
Big Trout Lake 119 T4
Bihac 72 C3
Bihar 92 G4
Bihar 92 G3
Biharamulo 107 F3
Bihoro 88 K4
Bihu 87 M6
Bijagos, Arquipelago dos 104 B3
Bijapur 92 E5
Bijar 94 H4
Bijeljina 72 E3
Bijelo Polje 72 E4
Bijie 93 L3
Bijnor 92 E3
Bikaner 92 D3
Bikin *Russia* 88 E2
Bikin *Russia* 88 F2
Bikoro 106 C3
Bilad Bani Bu Ali 97 P5
Bilad Ghamid 96 E6
Bilad Zahran 96 E6
Bilaspur 92 F4
Bila Tserkva 79 E6
Bilauktaung Range 93 J6
Bilbao 66 E1
Bilchir 85 J6
Bilecik 76 C2
Biled 73 F3
Bile Karpaty 71 G4
Bilesha Plain 107 H2
Bilgoraj 71 K3
Bili 106 E2
Bilin 93 J5
Billabalong 112 D4
Billericay 53 H3
Billingham 55 H2
Billings 123 K5
Billingshurst 53 G3
Bilma 101 H5
Bilma, Grand Erg de 101 H5
Biloela 113 L3
Bilo Gora 72 D3
Biloxi 128 H5
Biltine 102 D5
Bilugyun 93 J5
Binalud, Kuh-e 95 P3
Binatang 90 E5
Binder 87 L2
Bindloe Island 136 A7
Bindura 108 F3
Binefar 67 G2
Binga 108 E3
Bingara 113 L4
Bingerville 104 E4
Bingham 125 R4
Binghamton 125 N5
Bingley 55 H3
Bingol 77 J3
Bingol Daglari 77 J3
Binjai *Indonesia* 90 B5
Binjai *Indonesia* 90 D5
Binongko 91 G7
Bintan 90 C5
Bintuhan 90 C6
Bintulu 90 E5
Bin Xian *Heilongjiang, China* 88 A3
Bin Xian *Shaanxi, China* 93 L2
Binyang 93 L4
Bio 114 K7
Biobio 139 B7
Biograd 72 C4
Bioko 105 G5
Bir 92 E5
Bira *Russia* 88 D1
Bira *Russia* 88 D1
Bira *Russia* 85 P7
Birag, Kuh-e 95 Q8
Birak 101 H3
Bir al Hisw 96 E4
Bir al War 101 H4
Birao 102 D5
Biratnagar 93 G3
Bir Butayman 77 H4
Birca 73 G4
Birch Island 122 D2
Birch Mountains 119 N4
Bird 119 S4
Bird Island 133 R7
Birdlip 53 E3
Birdum 113 G2
Birecik 77 G4
Bireun 90 B4
Bir Fardan 97 J5
Bir Ghabalou 67 H4
Bir Hadi 97 K7
Birhan 103 G5
Birikchul 84 D6
Birjand 95 P5
Birkenhead *New Zealand* 115 E2
Birkenhead *U.K.* 55 F3
Birksgate Range 112 F4
Birlad *Romania* 73 J2
Birlad *Romania* 73 J2
Birlestik 86 B2
Birmingham *U.K.* 53 F2
Birmingham *U.S.A.* 129 J4
Bir Moghrein 100 C3
Birnie Island 111 U2
Birnin Kebbi 105 F3
Birni nKonni 101 G6
Birobidzhan 88 D1
Birofeld 88 D1
Birr 59 G6
Bir, Ras el 103 H5
Birreencorragh 58 C5
Birrimbah 112 G2
Birsk 78 K4
Birtle 123 P2
Birtley 55 H2
Biryusa 84 F5
Birzai 63 L8
Biscay, Bay of 65 B6
Bischofshofen 68 D2
Biscotasi Lake 124 J3
Bisert 78 K4
Bisevo 72 D4
Bisha 96 C9
Bishah, Wadi 96 F6
Bishkek 86 C3
Bishnupur 93 G4
Bishop 126 C2
Bishop Auckland 55 H2
Bishop Burton 55 J3
Bishop's Castle 52 D2
Bishops Falls 121 Q8
Bishop's Stortford 53 H3
Bishri, Jbel 77 H5

Biskra	101	G2	Blanc, Cap	69	B7	Bogazkaya	77	F2	Bolvadin	76	D3

Biskra 101 G2
Biskupiec 71 J2
Bislig 91 H4
Bismarck Archipelago 114 D2
Bismarck Range 114 D3
Bismark 123 P4
Bismil 77 J4
Bismo 63 C6
Bisotun 94 H4
Bispfors 62 G5
Bissau 104 B3
Bissett 123 S2
Bistcho Lake 119 M4
Bistretu 73 G4
Bistrita *Romania* 73 H2
Bistrita *Romania* 73 J2
Bistritei, Muntii 73 H2
Bitburg 70 B3
Bitche 64 G4
Bitik 79 J5
Bitkine 102 C5
Bitlis 77 K3
Bitola 73 F5
Bitonto 69 F5
Bitterfontein 108 C6
Bitterroot 122 G4
Bitterroot Range 122 G4
Bitti 69 B5
Biu 105 H3
Bivolu 73 H2
Biwa-ko 89 E8
Biyad, Al 96 H5
Biyagundi 96 C9
Biysk 84 D6
Bizerta 69 B7
Bizerte 101 G1
Bjargtangar 62 S12
Bjelovar 72 D3
Bjerkvik 62 L2
Bjorklinge 63 G6
Bjorksele 62 H4
Bjorna 62 H5
Bjorneborg *Finland* 63 J6
Bjorneborg *Sweden* 63 F7
Bjornevatn 62 N2
Bjornoya 80 C2
Bjurholm 62 H5
Bjursas 63 F6
Bla Bheinn 56 B3
Black *Alaska* 118 G2
Black *Arizona* 127 H4
Black *Arkansas* 128 G3
Black *New York* 125 N5
Blackadder Water 57 F5
Blackall 113 K3
Black Bay 124 F2
Black Belt 129 J4
Blackburn 55 G3
Black Canyon City 126 F3
Blackdown Hills 52 D4
Blackfoot 122 H6
Blackford 57 E4
Black Head 59 D6
Blackhead Bay 59 D6
Blackhill 55 H3
Black Hills 123 N5
Black Isle 56 D3
Black Mesa 126 G2
Blackmill 52 D3
Black Mountain 52 D3
Black Mountains 52 D3
Blackpool 55 F3
Black Range 127 J4
Black River Falls 124 E4
Blackrock 58 K5
Black Rock Desert 122 E7
Black Sea 51 P7
Blacksod Bay 58 B4
Blackstairs Mount 59 J7
Blackstairs Mountains 59 J7
Blackthorn 53 F3
Black Volta 104 E4
Black Water 57 E4
Blackwater *Australia* 113 K3
Blackwater *Meath, Ireland* 58 J5
Blackwater *Waterford, Ireland* 59 F8
Blackwater *Essex, U.K.* 53 H3
Blackwater *Hampshire, U.K.* 53 G3
Blackwaterfoot 57 C5
Blackwater Lake 119 L3
Blackwater Reservoir *Highland, U.K.* 57 D4
Blackwater Reservoir *Tayside, U.K.* 57 E4
Blackwell 128 D2
Blackwood 112 D5
Blaenavon 52 D3
Blafjall 62 W12
Blagodarnyy 79 G6
Blagoevgrad 73 G4
Blagoveshchensk *Russia* 78 K4
Blagoveshchensk *Russia* 85 M6
Blagoyevo 78 H3
Blair Atholl 57 E4
Blairgowrie 57 E4
Blaka 101 H4
Blakely 129 K5
Blakeney 53 J2
Blakesley 53 F2
Blanca, Bahia 139 D7
Blanca, Costa 67 F3
Blanca Peak 127 K2
Blanca, Punta 126 E6
Blanca, Sierra 127 K4

Blanc, Cap 69 B7
Blanche Channel 114 H6
Blanche, Lake 113 H4
Blanchland 55 G2
Blanc, Mont 65 G6
Blanco 136 E7
Blanco, Cabo 139 C9
Blanco, Cape 122 B6
Blanda 62 V12
Blandford Forum 53 E4
Blanes 67 H2
Blangy 64 D4
Blankenberge 64 E3
Blanquilla, Isla 136 E1
Blantyre 107 G6
Blarney 59 E9
Blasket Islands 59 A8
Blavet 65 B5
Blaydon 55 H2
Blaye 65 C6
Bleadon 52 E3
Bleaklow Hill 55 H3
Bled 72 C2
Blekinge 63 F8
Bletchley 53 G3
Bleus, Monts 107 F2
Blida 101 F1
Bligh Water 114 R8
Blind River 124 J3
Blisworth 53 G2
Block Island 125 Q6
Bloemfontein 108 E5
Blois 65 D5
Blonduos 62 U12
Bloodvein 123 R2
Bloody Foreland 58 F2
Bloomfield 124 D6
Bloomington *Illinois* 124 F6
Bloomington *Indiana* 124 G7
Bloomington *Minnesota* 124 D4
Bloomsbury 113 K3
Blouberg 108 E4
Blubberhouses 55 H3
Bludenz 68 B2
Bluefield 125 K8
Bluefields 132 F9
Blue Mountain Lake 125 N5
Blue Mountain Peak 132 J5
Blue Mountains 122 E5
Bluemull Sound 56 A1
Bluenose Lake 119 M2
Blue Ridge 129 K3
Blue Ridge Mountains 129 L3
Blue Stack 58 F3
Blue Stack Mountains 58 F3
Bluff *New Zealand* 115 B7
Bluff *U.S.A.* 127 H2
Bluff Knoll 112 D5
Bluff Point 112 C4
Bluff, Punta 126 F6
Blumenau 138 G5
Blunt 123 Q5
Blyth *Northumberland, U.K.* 55 H1
Blyth *Nottinghamshire, U.K.* 55 H3
Blyth *Suffolk, U.K.* 53 J2
Blythe 126 E4
Blythe Bridge 53 E2
Blytheville 128 H3
Bo 104 C4
Boac 91 G3
Boa Fe 136 C5
Boa Vista *Cape Verde* 104 L7
Boa Vista *Amazonas, Brazil* 136 D4
Boa Vista *Roraima, Brazil* 136 E3
Bobai 93 M4
Bobaomby, Tanjoni 109 J2
Bobbili 92 F5
Bobbio 68 B3
Bobo Dioulasso 104 E3
Bobolice 71 G2
Bobr 70 F3
Bobrients 79 E6
Bobrka 71 L4
Bobrov 79 G5
Bobures 133 M10
Boca del Pao 136 E2
Boca do Acre 136 D5
Boca Grande 136 E2
Bocaiuva 138 H3
Boca Mavaca 136 D3
Bocaranga 102 C6
Boca Raton 129 M7
Bochnia 71 J4
Bocholt 70 B3
Bochum 70 B3
Bodalla 113 L6
Bodaybo 85 J5
Boddam 56 A2
Boden 62 J4
Bodensee 70 C5
Bodhan 92 E5
Bodmin 52 C4
Bodmin Moor 52 C4
Bodo 62 F3
Bodrum 76 B4
Bodva 71 J4
Bodza, Pasul 73 J3
Boen 65 F6
Boende 106 D3
Boffa 104 C3
Bogalusa 128 H5
Bogan 113 K5
Bogaz 76 E2
Bogazkale 76 F2

Bogazkaya 77 F2
Bogazkopru 76 F3
Bogazliyan 76 F3
Bogbonga 106 C2
Bogen 62 L2
Boggeragh Mountains 59 E8
Boghar 67 H5
Bogia 114 D2
Bognes 62 G2
Bognor Regis 53 G4
Bogo 91 G3
Bogodukhov 79 F5
Bogong, Mount 113 K6
Bogor 90 D7
Bogorodchany 71 L4
Bogorodskoye *Russia* 78 J4
Bogorodskoye *Russia* 85 Q6
Bogota 136 C3
Bogotol 84 D5
Bogra 93 G4
Boguchany 84 F5
Boguchar 79 G6
Bogue 100 C5
Bogue Chitto 128 G5
Boguslav 79 E6
Bo Hai 87 K4
Bohemia 70 E4
Bohmer Wald 70 E4
Bohol 91 G4
Bohol Sea 91 G4
Boiano 69 E5
Boigul 114 C3
Boipeba, Ilha 137 K6
Bois Blanc Island 124 H4
Boisdale, Loch 57 A3
Boise *U.S.A.* 122 F6
Boise *U.S.A.* 122 F6
Boise City 127 L2
Bois, Lac des 118 K2
Boissevain 123 P3
Boizenburg 70 D2
Bojana 74 E2
Bojnurd 95 N3
Boka 73 F3
Boka Kotorska 72 E4
Bokhara 113 K4
Boknafjord 63 A7
Bokol 107 G2
Bokoro 102 C5
Boksitogorsk 78 E4
Boktor 85 P6
Bokungu 106 D3
Bolama 104 B3
Bolanos 130 H7
Bolan Pass 92 C3
Bolbec 64 D4
Bolchary 84 Ae5
Bole 104 E4
Boleslawiec 70 F3
Bolgatanga 104 E3
Bolgrad 79 D6
Boli 88 C3
Bolia 106 C3
Boliden 62 J4
Bolinao 91 F2
Bol Irgiz 79 H5
Bolivar 139 D7
Bolivar *Missouri* 124 D8
Bolivar *Tennessee* 128 H3
Bolivar, Cerro 133 R11
Bolivar, Pico 133 M10
Bolivia 138 C3
Boljevac 73 F4
Bolkhov 79 F5
Bollington 55 G3
Bollnas 63 G6
Bollon 113 K4
Bollstabruk 62 G5
Bolmen 63 E8
Bolobo 106 C3
Bologna 68 C3
Bologoye 78 E4
Bolotnoye 84 C5
Boloven, Cao Nguyen 93 L5
Bolsena, Lago di 69 C4
Bolsherechye 84 A5
Bolsheretsk 85 T6
Bolshevik 85 R4
Bolshevik, Ostrov 81 M2
Bolshezemelskaya Tundra 78 K2
Bolshoy Anyuy 85 U3
Bolshoy Atlym 84 Ae4
Bolshoy Balkhan, Khrebet 95 M2
Bolshoy Begichev, Ostrov 84 J2
Bolshoy Chernigovka 79 J5
Bolshoy Kunyak 84 A5
Bolshoy Lyakhovskiy, Ostrov 85 Q2
Bolshoy Murta 84 E5
Bolshoy Pit 84 E5
Bolshoy Porog 84 E3
Bolshoy Shantar, Ostrov 85 P5
Bolshoy Usa 78 K4
Bolshoy Yenisey 84 E6
Bolshoy Yugan 84 A5
Bolsover 55 H3
Boltana 67 G1
Bolt Head 52 D4
Bolton *Greater Manchester, U.K.* 55 G3
Bolton *Northumberland, U.K.* 57 G5
Bolu 76 D2
Bolucan 77 G3
Bolus Head 59 B9

Bolvadin 76 D3
Bolyarovo 73 J4
Bolzano 68 C2
Bom 114 D3
Boma 106 B4
Bombala 113 K6
Bombay 92 D5
Bomili 106 E2
Bom Jesus 137 J5
Bom Jesus da Lapa 137 J6
Bomlafjord 63 A7
Bomlo 63 A7
Bomongo 106 C2
Bonab 94 H3
Bonaire 133 N8
Bonaire Trench 133 N9
Bona, Mount 118 G3
Bonar Bridge 56 D3
Bonavista 121 R8
Bonavista Bay 121 R8
Bon, Cap 101 H1
Bondo 106 D2
Bondokodi 91 F7
Bondoukou 104 E4
Bone 69 A7
Bo'ness 57 E4
Bonete, Cerro 138 C5
Bone, Teluk 91 G6
Bongabong 91 G3
Bongor 102 C5
Bonham 128 D4
Bonifacio 69 B5
Bonifacio, Strait of 69 B5
Bonn 70 B3
Bonners Ferry 122 F3
Bonnetable 64 D4
Bonneval 64 D4
Bonneville 65 G5
Bonneville Salt Flats 122 H7
Bonnie Rock 112 D5
Bonny *France* 65 E5
Bonny *Nigeria* 105 G5
Bonnyrigg 57 E5
Bono 69 B5
Bonobono 91 F4
Bonorva 69 B5
Bonthe 104 C4
Bontoc 91 G2
Booligal 113 J5
Boologooro 112 C3
Boone *Iowa* 124 D5
Boone *N. Carolina* 129 M2
Booneville *Mississippi* 128 H3
Booneville *New York* 125 N5
Booroorban 113 J5
Boosaaso 103 J5
Boothia, Gulf of 120 J4
Boothia Peninsula 120 H3
Bootle 55 F3
Boot Reefs 114 C3
Bopeechee 113 H4
Boquilla, Presa de la 127 K7
Boquillas del Carmen 127 L6
Bor *Sudan* 102 F6
Bor *Turkey* 76 F4
Bor *Yugoslavia* 73 G3
Boraha, Nosy 109 J3
Borah Peak 122 H5
Boras 63 E8
Borasambar 92 F4
Borazjan 95 K7
Borba 136 F4
Borborema, Planalto da 137 K5
Borca 73 H2
Borcka 77 J2
Bordeaux 65 C6
Borden Island 120 D2
Borden Peninsula 120 K3
Borders 57 F5
Bordertown 113 J6
Bordeyri 62 U12
Bordj-Bou-Arreridj 67 J4
Bordj Bounaama 67 G5
Bordj Omar Driss 101 G3
Borensberg 63 F7
Boreray 56 A3
Borga 63 L6
Borgarnes 62 U12
Borgefjellet 62 E4
Borger 127 M3
Borgholm 63 G8
Borgo San Lorenzo 68 C4
Borgosesia 68 B3
Borgo Val di Taro 68 B3
Borgo Valsugana 68 C2
Borislav 71 K4
Borisoglebsk 79 G5
Borispol 79 E5
Borja 67 F2
Borkovskaya 78 H2
Borkum 70 B2
Borlange 63 F6
Borlu 76 C3
Bormida 68 B3
Bormio 68 C2
Borneo 90 E5
Bornholm 70 F1
Bornholmsgattet 63 F9
Bornova 76 B3
Borohoro Shan 86 E3
Boroko 91 G5
Boromo 104 E3
Boronga Islands 93 H5
Borongan 91 H3

Borovichi	78	E4	Bovey	52	D4	Brantley	129	J5	Bridgetown *Barbados*	133	T8
Borovlyanka	84	C6	Bovey Tracy	52	D4	Brantome	65	D6	Bridgetown *Canada*	121	N9
Borovsk	78	K4	Bovingdon	53	G3	Brasileia	136	D6	Bridgewater	121	P9
Borovskoye	84	Ad6	Bovino	69	E5	Brasilia *Distrito Federal, Brazil*	138	F3	Bridgnorth	52	E2
Borrika	113	J6	Bow	122	H2	Brasilia *Minas Gerais, Brazil*	138	H3	Bridgwater	52	D3
Borris	59	J7	Bowbells	123	N3	Braslav	63	M9	Bridgwater Bay	52	D3
Borrisokane	59	F7	Bowen	113	K3	Brasov	73	H3	Bridlington	55	J2
Borrisoleigh	59	G7	Bowers Bank	118	Ab9	Brassey Range	91	F5	Bridlington Bay	55	J2
Borroloola	113	H2	Bowes	55	G2	Brates, Lacul	73	K3	Bridport	52	E4
Borrowdale	55	F2	Bowfell	55	F2	Bratislava	71	G4	Brieg	71	G3
Borshchev	73	J1	Bowie	128	D4	Bratsk	84	G5	Brienne-le-Chateau	64	F4
Borshchovochnyy Khrebet	85	J6	Bow Island	122	J3	Bratslav	73	K1	Brier Island	125	S4
Borth	52	C2	Bowkan	94	H3	Braunau	68	D1	Briey	64	F4
Borujen	95	K6	Bowland, Forest of	55	G2	Braunsberg	71	H1	Brig	68	A2
Borujerd	94	J5	Bowling Green *Kentucky*	124	G8	Braunschweig	70	D2	Brigg	55	J3
Borve	57	A4	Bowling Green *Ohio*	124	J6	Braunton	52	C3	Brighouse	55	H3
Borzhomi	77	K2	Bowman	123	N4	Brava	104	L7	Brightlingsea	53	J3
Borzya	85	K7	Bowman Bay	120	M4	Brava, Costa	67	H2	Brighton	53	G4
Bosa	69	B5	Bowness	55	G2	Bravo del Norte, Rio	127	L6	Brignoles	65	G7
Bosanski Brod	72	E3	Bowness-on-Solway	55	F2	Brawley	126	E4	Brihuega	66	E2
Bosanski Novi	72	D3	Bowraville	113	L5	Bray	59	K6	Brikama	104	B3
Bosanski Petrovac	72	D3	Boxford	53	H2	Bray Head	59	B9	Brindakit	85	P4
Boscastle	52	C4	Bo Xian	93	N2	Bray Island	120	L4	Brindisi	69	F5
Bose	93	L4	Boxing	87	M4	Brazil	137	G5	Brinian	56	F1
Bos Gradiska	72	D3	Box Tank	113	J5	Brazos	128	D5	Brinkley	128	G3
Boshruyeh	95	N5	Boyabat	76	F2	Brazzaville	106	C3	Brioude	65	E6
Bosilegrad	73	G4	Boyang	87	M6	Brcko	72	E3	Brisbane	113	L4
Boskovice	71	G4	Boyarka	84	F2	Brda	71	G2	Bristol *U.K.*	52	E3
Bosna	72	E3	Boyd Lake	119	Q3	Breadalbane	57	D4	Bristol *U.S.A*	125	P6
Bosnia-Herzegovina	72	D3	Boyer	124	C6	Breaksea Sound	115	A6	Bristol Bay	118	D4
Bosnik	114	B2	Boyle	58	F5	Brean	52	D3	Bristol Channel	52	D2
Bosobolo	106	C2	Boyne	58	K5	Brebes	90	D7	Bristol Lake	126	E3
Boso-hanto	89	H8	Boynton Beach	129	M7	Brechfa	52	C3	Bristow	128	D3
Bosphorus	76	C2	Boyuibe	138	D4	Brechin	57	F4	British Columbia	118	L4
Bossambele	102	C6	Bozburun	76	C4	Breckenridge *Texas*	128	C4	Brits	108	E5
Bossangoa	102	C6	Bozcaada	75	H3	Breckenridge *Minnesota*	124	B3	Britstown	108	D6
Bossier City	128	F4	Boz Daglari	76	B3	Breckland	53	H2	Brittle, Lake	57	B3
Bostan *Iran*	94	H6	Bozdogan	76	C4	Brecknock, Peninsula	139	B10	Brive-la-Gaillarde	65	D6
Bostan *Pakistan*	92	C2	Bozeman	122	J5	Breclav	71	G4	Briviesca	66	E1
Bostanabad	94	H3	Bozen	68	C2	Brecon	52	D3	Brixham	52	D4
Bosten Bagrax Hu	86	F3	Boze Pole	71	G1	Brecon Beacons	52	D3	Brlik	86	C3
Boston *U.K.*	53	G2	Bozkir	76	E4	Breda	64	F3	Brno	71	G4
Boston *U.S.A.*	125	Q5	Bozkurt	76	E2	Bredon Hill	53	F3	Broad	129	M3
Boston Mountains	128	E3	Bozoum	102	C6	Bredstedt	70	C1	Broadback	121	L7
Botesdale	53	J2	Bozova	77	H4	Breezewood	125	L7	Broad Bay	56	B2
Botev	73	H4	Bozqush, Kuh-e	94	H3	Bregenz	68	B2	Broad Cairn	57	E4
Botevgrad	73	G4	Bozuyuk	76	D3	Bregovo	73	G3	Broad Haven	58	C4
Bothel	55	F2	Bra	68	A3	Breidafjordur	62	T12	Broad Hinton	53	F3
Bothnia, Gulf of	62	J5	Brabant Island	141	V6	Brejo	137	J4	Broadhurst Range	112	E3
Botna	73	K2	Brabourne	53	H3	Brekken	62	D5	Broad Sound *Australia*	113	K3
Botosani	73	J2	Brac	72	D4	Brekstad	62	C5	Broad Sound *U.K.*	52	B3
Botsmark	62	J4	Bracadale	56	B3	Bremen *U.S.A.*	129	K4	Broadstairs	53	J3
Botswana	108	D4	Bracadale, Loch	56	B3	Bremen *Germany*	70	C2	Broads, The	53	J2
Botte Donato	69	F6	Bracciano	69	D4	Bremerhaven	70	C2	Broadus	123	M5
Bottenhavet	63	H6	Bracke	62	F5	Bremer Range	112	E5	Broadway	53	F2
Bottenviken	62	K4	Brackley	53	F2	Bremerton	122	C4	Brochel	56	B3
Bottesford	53	G2	Bracknell	53	G3	Bremervorde	70	C2	Brocken	70	D3
Bottineau	123	P3	Brad	73	G2	Brendon Hills	52	D3	Brockenhurst	53	F4
Bottisham	53	H2	Bradano	69	F5	Brenham	128	D5	Brock Island	120	D2
Bottrop	70	B3	Bradda Head	54	E2	Brenig, Llyn	55	F3	Brockman, Mount	112	D3
Botucatu	138	G4	Bradenton	129	L7	Brenish	56	A2	Brockton	125	Q5
Bouafle	104	D4	Bradford *U.K.*	55	H3	Brenner Pass	68	C2	Brod	73	F5
Bouake	104	D4	Bradford *U.S.A.*	125	L6	Breno	68	C3	Broddanes	62	U12
Bouar	102	C6	Bradford-on-Avon	52	E3	Brenta	68	C3	Brodeur Peninsula	120	J3
Bouarfa	100	E2	Bradwell Waterside	53	H3	Brentford	53	G2	Brodick	57	C5
Boucant Bay	113	G1	Brady	127	N5	Brentwood *U.K.*	53	H3	Brodick Bay	57	C5
Bouchegouf	69	A7	Brady Mountains	127	N5	Brentwood *U.S.A.*	125	P6	Brodnica	71	H2
Bougainville	114	E3	Brae	56	A1	Brescia	68	C3	Brodokalmak	84	Ad5
Bougainville, Cape	112	F1	Braemar	57	E3	Breskens	64	E3	Brody	79	D5
Bougainville Reef	113	K2	Braemore	56	E2	Breslau	71	G3	Brok	71	J2
Bougainville Strait	114	J5	Braeswick	56	F1	Bressanone	68	C2	Broken Bay	113	L5
Bougaroun, Cap	101	G1	Braga	66	B2	Bressay	56	A2	Broken Bow *Nebraska*	123	Q7
Bougie	67	J4	Bragado	139	D7	Bressay Sound	56	A2	Broken Bow *Oklahoma*	128	E3
Bougouni	100	D6	Braganca	66	C2	Bressuire	65	C5	Broken Bow Lake	128	E3
Bougzdul	67	H5	Braganca Paulista	138	G4	Brest *France*	64	A4	Broken Hill *Australia*	113	J5
Bouhalloufa	67	G4	Bragar	56	B2	Brest *Belorussia*	71	K2	Broken Hill *Zambia*	107	E5
Bouillon	64	F4	Brahman Baria	93	H4	Brestlitovsk	79	E5	Bromberg	71	G2
Bouira	67	H4	Brahmani	92	G4	Brest Litovsk	71	K2	Bromley	53	H3
Bou Ismail	67	H4	Brahmapur	92	F5	Bretagne	64	B4	Bromsgrove	53	E2
Boujdour	100	C3	Brahmaputra	93	H3	Bretcu	73	J2	Bromyard	52	E2
Bou Kadir	67	G4	Braidwood	113	K6	Breteuil *France*	64	D4	Bronderslev	63	C8
Boulay	64	G4	Braila	73	J3	Breteuil *France*	64	E4	Bronnoysund	62	E4
Boulder	123	M8	Brailsford	53	F2	Breton, Cape	121	Q8	Bronte	69	E7
Boulder City	126	E3	Brainerd	124	C3	Breton Sound	128	H6	Brookfield	124	D7
Boulogne-sur-Mer	64	D3	Braintree	53	H3	Brett	53	H2	Brookhaven	128	G5
Boumbe I	102	C7	Braishfield	53	F3	Brett, Cape	115	E1	Brookings *Oregon*	122	B6
Boumbe II	102	C7	Brake	70	C2	Breueh	90	B4	Brookings *S. Dakota*	123	R5
Boumo	102	C6	Brakel	70	C3	Brevoort Island	120	P5	Brookneal	125	L8
Bouna	104	E4	Brallos	75	G3	Brewer	125	R4	Brooks	122	H2
Boundiali	104	D4	Bramdean	53	F3	Brewster	122	E3	Brooks Range	118	D2
Boung Long	93	L6	Bramham	55	H3	Brewton	129	J5	Brooksville	129	L6
Boun Tai	93	K4	Bramming	63	C9	Breznice	70	E4	Broome	112	E2
Bountiful	122	J7	Brampton *Canada*	125	L5	Brezo, Sierra del	66	D1	Broom, Loch	56	C3
Bounty Islands	111	S11	Brampton *U.K.*	55	G2	Bria	102	D6	Brora	56	D2
Bourail	114	W16	Bramsche	70	B2	Briancon	65	G6	Brora *U.K.*	56	E2
Bourbon-l'Archambault	65	E5	Brancaster	53	H2	Brianne, Llyn	52	D2	Brosteni	73	G3
Bourbonnais *France*	65	E5	Brancaster Bay	53	H2	Briare	65	E5	Broto	67	F1
Bourbonnais *U.S.A.*	124	G6	Branco	136	E3	Bribie Island	113	L4	Brotton	55	J2
Bourbonne-les-Bains	65	F5	Branco, Cabo	137	L5	Brichany	73	J1	Brou	64	D4
Bourem	100	E5	Brandberg	108	B4	Bricquebe	53	N7	Brough	55	G2
Bourganeuf	65	D6	Brandbu	63	D6	Bride	54	E2	Brough Head	56	E1
Bourg-en-Bresse	65	F5	Brande	63	C9	Bridestowe	52	C4	Brough Ness	56	F2
Bourges	65	E5	Brandenburg	70	E2	Bridgend *Mid Glamorgan, U.K.*	52	D3	Broughshane	58	K3
Bourgogne	65	F5	Brandesburton	55	J3	Bridgend *Strathclyde, U.K.*	57	B5	Broughton	57	E5
Bourgogne, Canal de	65	E5	Brandon *Canada*	123	Q3	Bridge of Allan	57	E4	Broughton in Furness	55	F2
Bourg-Saint-Andeol	65	F6	Brandon *U.S.A.*	125	P5	Bridge of Gaur	57	D4	Broughton Island	120	P4
Bourke	113	K5	Brandon Bay	59	B8	Bridge of Orchy	57	D4	Broughton Poggs	53	F3
Bourne	53	G2	Brandon Mount	59	B8	Bridge of Weir	57	D5	Browerville	124	C3
Bournemouth	53	F4	Brandon Point	59	B8	Bridgeport *Alabama*	129	K3	Brow Head	59	C10
Bou Saada	101	F1	Brandval	63	E6	Bridgeport *California*	126	C1	Brownfield	127	L4
Boussac	65	E5	Branesti	73	J3	Bridgeport *Connecticut*	125	P6	Brownhills	53	F2
Bousso	102	C5	Braniewo	71	H1	Bridgeport *Nebraska*	123	N7	Browning	122	H3
Boutilimit	100	C5	Bran, Pasul	73	H3	Bridgeton	125	N7	Brownsville	128	D8
Boves	68	A3	Brantford	125	K5	Bridgetown *Australia*	112	D5	Brownwood	128	C5

Name	Page	Ref.
Brownwood, Lake	127	N5
Bru	62	Y12
Bruar, The Falls of	57	E4
Bruay-en-Artois	64	E3
Bruce Bay	115	B5
Bruce, Mount	112	D3
Bruce Mountains	120	M3
Bruchsal	70	C4
Bruck	68	F1
Bruck an der Mur	68	E2
Brue	52	E3
Bruernish Point	57	A4
Bruges	64	E3
Brugg	68	B2
Brugge	64	E3
Brühl	70	B3
Bruichladdich	57	B5
Brumado	137	J6
Brumunddal	63	D6
Brunei	90	E4
Brunette Downs	113	H2
Brunflo	62	F5
Brunico	68	C2
Brunkeberg	63	C7
Brunn	71	G4
Brunsbuttel	70	C2
Brunswick *Georgia*	129	M5
Brunswick *Maine*	121	N9
Brunswick *Maryland*	125	M7
Brunswick *Germany*	70	D2
Brunswick Bay	112	E2
Brunswick, Peninsula	139	B10
Bruny Island	111	L10
Brusa	76	C2
Brush	123	N7
Brusilovka	79	J5
Brusovo	84	D4
Brussel	64	F3
Bruthen	113	K6
Bruton	52	E3
Bruxelles	64	F3
Bryan *Ohio*	124	H6
Bryan *Texas*	128	D5
Bryan, Mount	113	H5
Bryansk	79	E5
Bryanskoye	79	H7
Bryher	52	K5
Bryne	63	D6
Brynmawr	52	D3
Brynzeny	73	J1
Brza Palanka	73	G3
Brzava	73	F3
Brzeg	71	G3
Bua *Fiji*	114	R8
Bua *Sweden*	63	E8
Buala	114	J6
Bubanza	107	E3
Bubiyan	97	J2
Buca *Fiji*	114	R8
Buca *Turkey*	76	B3
Bucak	76	D4
Bucaramanga	136	C2
Buchach	79	D6
Buchan	56	F3
Buchanan	104	C4
Buchanan, Lake	127	N5
Buchan Gulf	120	M3
Buchannan Bay	120	L2
Bucharest	73	J3
Buchholz	70	C2
Buchlgvie	57	D4
Buchloe	70	D4
Buchon, Point	126	B3
Buchs	68	B2
Buckeye	126	F4
Buckfastleigh	52	D4
Buckhannon	125	K7
Buckhaven	57	E4
Buckie	56	F3
Buckingham	53	G3
Buckingham Bay	113	H1
Buckinghamshire	53	G3
Buckkisla	76	E4
Buckley	55	F3
Bucksburn	57	F3
Buck, The	56	F3
Bucuresti	73	J3
Bud	62	B5
Budapest	72	E2
Budardalur	62	U12
Budareyri	62	X12
Budaun	92	E3
Budduso	69	B5
Bude *U.K.*	52	C4
Bude *U.S.A.*	128	G5
Bude Bay	52	B4
Budennovsk	79	G7
Budingen	70	C3
Budir	62	Y12
Budjala	106	C2
Budleigh Salterton	52	D4
Budogoshch	78	E4
Budun	87	K1
Budungbudung	91	F6
Budu, Sabkhat al	97	J5
Buea	105	G5
Buenaventura *Colombia*	136	C2
Buenaventura *Mexico*	127	J6
Buenaventura, Bahia	136	B3
Buena Vista	125	L8
Buena Vista Lake Bed	126	C3
Buenos Aires	139	D6
Buenos Aires, Lago	139	B9
Buffalo *New York*	125	L5
Buffalo *S. Dakota*	123	N5
Buffalo *Texas*	128	D5
Buffalo *Wyoming*	123	L5
Buffalo Lake	119	M3
Buffalo Narrows	119	P4
Buftea	73	H3
Bug	71	K2
Buga	136	B3
Bugdayli	95	M2
Bugel, Tanjung	90	E7
Bugoynes	62	N2
Bugrino	78	H2
Bugsuk	91	F4
Bugulma	78	J5
Buguruslan	78	J5
Buhl	122	G6
Buhusi	73	J2
Buie, Loch	57	B4
Builth Wells	52	D2
Buin	114	G5
Buinsk	78	H5
Buin Zahra	95	K4
Buitrago del Lozoye	66	E2
Bujaraloz	67	F2
Buje	72	B3
Bujumbura	107	E3
Buk	72	D2
Buka	114	E3
Bukama	106	E4
Bukavu	107	E3
Bukhara	80	H6
Bukittinggi	90	D6
Bukk	72	F1
Bukoba	107	F3
Bukoloto	107	F2
Bula	114	A2
Bulanash	84	Ad5
Bulancak	77	H2
Bulandshahr	92	E3
Bulanik	77	K3
Bulanovo	79	K5
Bulawayo	103	E4
Buldan	76	C3
Buldana	92	E4
Buldir Island	113	Ab9
Buldurty	79	J6
Bulgan *Mongolia*	85	G2
Bulgan *Mongolia*	87	J2
Bulgaria	73	G4
Buliluyan, Cape	91	F4
Bulkeley	55	G3
Bulle	68	A2
Buller	115	C4
Bullhead City	125	E3
Bull Shoals Lake	128	F2
Bulolo	114	D3
Bulum	85	M2
Buma	114	K6
Bumba	105	D2
Buna	74	E2
Bunbeg	58	F2
Bunbury	112	D5
Bunclody	59	J7
Buncrana	58	H2
Bundaberg	113	L3
Bundoran	58	F4
Bungalaut, Selat	90	B6
Bungay	53	J2
Bungo-suido	89	D9
Bunguran Utara, Kepulauan	90	D5
Bunia	107	F2
Bunkie	128	F5
Bunratty	59	E7
Buntingford	53	G3
Buntok	90	E6
Bunyan	77	F3
Buolkalakh	85	K2
Buol Kheyr	95	K7
Buorkhaya, Guba	85	N2
Buorkhaya, Mys	85	N2
Buqayq	97	J4
Buqum, Harrat al	96	F6
Buram	102	E5
Buran	86	F2
Buraydah	96	F3
Burbage	53	F3
Burbank	126	C3
Burco	103	J6
Burdalyk	95	S2
Burdekin	113	K3
Burdur	76	D4
Burdur Golu	76	D4
Bure	53	J2
Burea	62	J4
Burentsogt	87	L2
Bureya *Russia*	85	M7
Bureya *Russia*	85	N6
Burg	70	D2
Burgas	73	J4
Burgdorf	68	A2
Burgeo	121	Q8
Burgersdorp	108	E6
Burgess Hill	53	G4
Burghead	56	E3
Burghead Bay	56	E3
Burgh-le-Marsh	55	K3
Burgos	56	E1
Burgsteinfurt	70	B2
Burgsvik	63	H8
Burguete	57	F1
Burhan Budai Shan	93	J1
Burhaniye	76	B3
Burhanpur	92	E4
Burias	91	G3
Burica, Punta	132	F10
Burin Peninsula	121	Q8
Buri Peninsula	96	D9
Buriram	93	K5
Burj Safita	77	G5
Burke Island	141	S4
Burketown	113	H2
Burkhala	85	R4
Burkina Faso	104	E3
Burley	122	H6
Burli	79	J5
Burlington *Canada*	125	L5
Burlington *Colorado*	123	N8
Burlington *Iowa*	124	E6
Burlington *N. Carolina*	129	N2
Burlington *Vermont*	125	P4
Burlington *Washington*	122	C3
Burlton	52	E2
Burlyu-Tobe	86	D2
Burma (see Myanmar)	93	J4
Burmantovo	78	L3
Burnaby	122	C3
Burneston	55	H2
Burnet	128	C5
Burnham-on-Crouch	53	H3
Burnham-on-Sea	52	E3
Burnie	113	K7
Burnley	55	G3
Burns	122	E6
Burntwood	119	R4
Burqan	97	H2
Burqin	86	F2
Burra	113	H5
Burravoe	56	A1
Burray	56	F2
Burren, The	59	D6
Burriana	67	F3
Burrow Head	54	E2
Burrs Junction	122	F6
Burrundie	112	G1
Burry Port	52	C3
Bursa	76	C2
Bur Safaga	103	F2
Bur Said	103	F1
Bur Sudan	96	C7
Burt, Mount	112	F4
Burton Joyce	53	F2
Burton Lake	121	L7
Burton Latimer	53	G2
Burton upon Stather	55	J3
Burton-upon-Trent	53	F2
Burtrask	62	J4
Buru	91	H6
Burum	97	J9
Burundi	107	E3
Burunnoye	79	J5
Bururi	107	E3
Burwick	56	F2
Bury	55	G3
Burylbaytal	86	C2
Burynshik	79	J6
Bury Saint Edmunds	53	H2
Busayta, Al	96	D1
Bushat	74	E2
Bushehr	95	K7
Bushimaie	106	D4
Bushmills	58	J2
Businga	106	D2
Busira	106	C3
Busk	71	L4
Buskerud	63	C6
Busko	71	J3
Busselton	112	D5
Bussol, Proliv	85	S7
Bustakh, Ozero	85	Q2
Busto Arsizio	68	B3
Busuanga	91	G3
Buta	106	D2
Butare	107	E3
Bute	57	C5
Bute, Sound of	57	C5
Butiaba	107	F2
Butler	125	L6
Butmah	77	K4
Butte	122	H5
Buttermere	55	F2
Butterworth *Malaysia*	90	C4
Butterworth *South Africa*	108	E6
Buttevant	59	E8
Button Islands	121	P5
Butuan	91	H4
Butung	91	G7
Buturlinovka	79	G5
Buulobarde	103	J7
Buurhakaba	107	H2
Buwatah	96	D4
Buxton	55	H3
Buy	78	G4
Buyba	84	E6
Buynaksk	79	H7
Buyr Nuur	87	M2
Buyuk Agri Dagi	77	L3
Buyuklacin	76	F2
Buyuk Menderes	76	C4
Buzancais	65	D5
Buzau *Romania*	73	J3
Buzau *Romania*	73	J3
Buzi	109	F3
Buzovyazy	78	K5
Buzuluk	84	Ae6
Buzuluk	79	J5
Byam Martin, Cape	120	L3
Byam Martin Island	120	F2
Byczyna	71	H3
Bydgoszcz	71	G2
Byers	123	M8
Byfleet	53	G3
Byglandsfjord	63	B7
Bykhov	79	E5
Bykovo *Russia*	79	H6
Bykovo *Russia*	78	H3
Byla Slatina	73	G4
Bylot Island	120	L3
Byrock	113	K5
Byron, Cape	113	L4
Byron, Isla	139	A9
Byrranga, Gory	84	E2
Byrum	63	D8
Byserovo	78	J4
Byske	62	J4
Byskealven	62	J4
Bystra	71	H4
Bystraya	85	T6
Bystrzyca Klodzka	71	G3
Bytantay	85	N3
Bytca	71	H4
Byten	71	L2
Bytom	71	H3
Bytow	71	G1
Byxelkrok	63	G8

C

Name	Page	Ref.
Caala	106	C5
Caatingas	137	H5
Caballos Mestenos, Llano de los	127	K6
Caballeria, Cabo	67	J2
Cabanatuan	91	G2
Cabano	125	R3
Cabeza de Buey	66	D3
Cabeza Lagarto, Punta	136	B6
Cabezas	138	D3
Cabimas	136	C1
Cabinda *Angola*	106	B4
Cabinda *Angola*	106	B4
Cabo	137	L5
Cabo Colnet	126	D5
Cabo Gracias a Dios, Punta	132	F7
Cabonga, Reservoir	125	M3
Cabo Raso	139	C8
Caborca	126	F5
Cabot Strait	121	P8
Cabourg	64	C4
Cabourne	55	J3
Cabrach	56	E3
Cabra del Santo Cristo	66	E4
Cabrera	67	H3
Cabrera, Sierra	66	C1
Cabriel	67	F3
Cabrobo	137	K5
Cabruta	136	D2
Cacak	72	F4
Caceres *Spain*	66	C3
Caceres *Brazil*	138	E3
Caceres *Colombia*	136	B2
Cache Creek	122	C8
Cache Peak	122	H6
Cachimbo	137	G5
Cachimbo, Serra do	137	G5
Cachi, Nevado de	138	C4
Cachoeira	138	K6
Cachoeiro de Itapemirim	138	H4
Cachos, Punta de	138	B5
Cacinci	72	D3
Cacipore, Cabo	137	G3
Cacolo	106	C5
Caconda	106	C5
Cacula	106	B5
Cadadley	103	H6
Cadale	107	J2
Cadaques	67	H1
Cadereyta	128	C8
Cader Idris	52	D2
Cadibarrawirracanna, Lake	113	H4
Cadillac *Canada*	123	L3
Cadillac *U.S.A.*	124	H4
Cadi, Sierra del	67	G1
Cadiz	66	C4
Cadiz	91	G3
Cadiz, Baia de	66	C4
Cadiz, Golfo de	66	C4
Caen	64	C4
Caerdydd	52	D3
Caerfyrddin	52	C3
Caergybi	54	E3
Caernarfon	54	E3
Caernarfon Bay	54	E3
Caerphilly	52	D3
Caersws	52	D2
Caetite	137	J6
Cafayate	138	C5
Cagayan	91	G2
Cagayan de Oro	91	G4
Cagayan Islands	91	G4
Cagayan Sulu	91	F4
Cagliari	69	B6
Cagliari, Golfo d.	69	B6
Caguan	136	C3
Caguas	133	P5
Cahama	106	B6
Caha Mountains	59	C9
Caherbarnagh	59	D8

Caherciveen	**59**	B9
Caherconlish	**59**	F7
Cahir	**59**	G8
Cahore Point	**59**	K7
Cahors	**65**	D6
Caia	**109**	G3
Caiaponia	**138**	F3
Caibarien	**132**	H3
Cai Be	**93**	L6
Caicos Islands	**133**	M4
Caicos Passage	**133**	L3
Cairndow	**57**	D4
Cairn Gorm	**57**	E3
Cairngorm Mountains	**57**	E3
Cairnryan	**54**	D2
Cairns	**113**	K2
Cairn Water	**57**	E5
Cairo *Egypt*	**102**	F1
Cairo *U.S.A.*	**124**	F8
Caiundo	**106**	C6
Caiwarro	**113**	J4
Cajamarca	**136**	B5
Cajapio	**137**	J4
Cajatambo	**136**	B6
Cajati	**138**	G4
Cajazeiras	**137**	K5
Cakiralan	**77**	F2
Cakirgol Dagi	**77**	H2
Cal	**76**	C3
Cal	**103**	J5
Cala	**73**	G2
Calabar	**105**	G5
Calabozo	**136**	D2
Calafat	**73**	G4
Calafate	**139**	B10
Calafell	**67**	G2
Calagua Islands	**91**	G3
Calahorra	**67**	F1
Calais *France*	**64**	D3
Calais *U.S.A.*	**125**	S4
Calama	**138**	C4
Calamar *Colombia*	**136**	C1
Calamar *Colombia*	**136**	C3
Calamian Group	**91**	G3
Calamocha	**67**	F2
Calandula	**106**	C4
Calang	**90**	B5
Calapan	**91**	G3
Calarasi	**73**	J3
Calatayud	**67**	F2
Calatele	**73**	G2
Calatrava, Campo de	**66**	E3
Calau	**70**	F3
Calavite, Cape	**91**	G3
Calayan	**91**	G2
Calbayog	**91**	G3
Calcanhar, Ponta do	**137**	K5
Calcasieu	**128**	F5
Calcasieu Lake	**128**	F6
Calcutta	**93**	G4
Caldararu	**73**	H3
Caldas da Rainha	**66**	B3
Caldbeck	**55**	F2
Caldeirao, Sierra do	**66**	B4
Calder	**55**	H3
Caldera	**138**	B5
Caldew	**55**	G2
Caldicot	**52**	E3
Caldiran	**77**	K3
Caldwell	**122**	F6
Caledon	**108**	E6
Calella de la Costa	**67**	H2
Caleta Lobos	**138**	C4
Caleta Olivia	**139**	C9
Calexico	**126**	E4
Calf of Man	**54**	E2
Calfsound	**56**	F1
Calgary	**122**	G2
Cali	**136**	B3
Caliach Point	**57**	B4
Calicut	**92**	E6
Calienta	**126**	E2
California	**126**	B1
California, Golfo de	**126**	G7
Calimani, Muntii	**73**	H2
Calimere, Point	**92**	E6
Calingasta	**139**	C6
Calino	**75**	J4
Calitri	**69**	E5
Callabonna, Lake	**113**	J4
Callan	**59**	H7
Callander	**57**	D4
Callao	**136**	B6
Callington	**52**	C4
Calne	**53**	E3
Caloosahatchee	**129**	M7
Calpe	**67**	G3
Calpulalpan	**131**	K8
Caltagirone	**69**	E7
Caltanissetta	**69**	E7
Caltilbuk	**76**	C3
Calulo	**106**	B5
Caluula	**103**	K5
Caluula, Raas	**103**	K5
Calvados Chain, The	**114**	T10
Calvert	**113**	H2
Calvert Hills	**113**	H2
Calvert Island	**118**	K5
Calvi	**69**	B4
Calvinia	**108**	C6
Calvo, Monte	**69**	E6
Cam	**53**	G2
Camabatela	**106**	C4
Camacupa	**106**	C5
Camaguey	**132**	J4
Camaguey, Archipielago de	**132**	H3
Camalan	**76**	F4
Camana	**138**	B3
Camaqua	**138**	F6
Camardi	**76**	F4
Camaron, Cabo	**132**	E7
Camarones	**139**	C8
Camaross	**59**	J8
Camas	**122**	C5
Camatindi	**138**	D4
Cambados	**66**	B1
Camberley	**53**	G3
Cambodia	**93**	K6
Cambo-les-Bains	**65**	C7
Camborne	**52**	B4
Cambrai	**64**	E3
Cambrian Mountains	**52**	D2
Cambridge *New Zealand*	**115**	E2
Cambridge *U.K.*	**52**	H2
Cambridge *Maryland*	**125**	M7
Cambridge *Massachusetts*	**125**	Q5
Cambridge *Minnesota*	**124**	D4
Cambridge *Ohio*	**125**	K6
Cambridge Bay	**119**	Q2
Cambridge Gulf	**112**	F1
Cambridgeshire	**53**	G2
Cambrils	**67**	G2
Cambundi-Catembo	**106**	C5
Camden *Arkansas*	**128**	F4
Camden *New Jersey*	**125**	N7
Camden *S. Carolina*	**129**	M3
Cameia	**106**	D5
Camelford	**52**	C4
Cameli	**76**	C4
Camerino	**68**	D4
Cameron *Arizona*	**126**	G3
Cameron *Missouri*	**124**	C7
Cameron *Texas*	**128**	D5
Cameron Hills	**119**	M4
Cameron Island	**120**	F2
Cameron Mountains	**115**	A7
Cameroon	**105**	H4
Cameroun, Mont	**105**	G5
Cameta	**137**	H4
Camiguin *Philippines*	**91**	G2
Camiguin *Philippines*	**91**	G4
Camilla	**129**	K5
Caminha	**66**	B2
Camiri	**138**	D4
Camissombo	**106**	D4
Camlidere	**76**	E2
Camlidere	**77**	H4
Camlihemsin	**77**	J2
Camliyayla	**76**	F4
Camocim	**137**	J4
Camooweal	**113**	H2
Camorta	**93**	H7
Campana	**139**	E6
Campana, Isla	**139**	A9
Campanario	**138**	H3
Campanario *Argentina*	**139**	B7
Campanario *Spain*	**66**	D3
Campbell	**108**	D5
Campbell, Cape	**115**	E4
Campbell Island	**141**	M8
Campbellpore	**92**	D2
Campbell River	**122**	B2
Campbellsville	**124**	H8
Campbellton	**125**	S3
Campbelltown	**113**	L5
Campbeltown	**57**	C5
Campeche	**131**	P8
Campeche, Bahia de	**131**	N8
Camperdown	**113**	J6
Campillo de Arenas	**66**	E4
Campillos	**66**	D4
Campina Grande	**137**	K5
Campinas	**138**	G4
Campo	**105**	G5
Campoalegre	**136**	B3
Campobasso	**69**	E5
Campo de Diauarum	**137**	G6
Campo Grande	**138**	F4
Campo Maior *Brazil*	**137**	J4
Campo Maior *Portugal*	**66**	C3
Campo Mourao	**138**	F4
Campos *Bahia, Brazil*	**137**	J6
Campos *Rio de Janeiro, Brazil*	**138**	H4
Campos del Puerto	**67**	H3
Campos Sales	**137**	J5
Campos, Tierra de	**66**	D1
Campsie Fells	**57**	D4
Camrose	**119**	N5
Can	**76**	B2
Canada	**116**	F5
Canada de Gomez	**138**	D6
Canadian	**127**	M3
Canadian Shield	**116**	K3
Canakkale	**76**	B2
Canakkale Bogazi	**76**	B2
Canala	**114**	W16
Canal Casiquiare	**136**	D3
Canal Cockburn	**139**	B10
Cananea	**126**	G5
Canarias, Islas	**100**	B3
Canarreos, Archipielago de los	**132**	G4
Canary Islands	**100**	B3
Canastota	**125**	N5
Canaveral, Cape	**129**	M6
Canaveras	**66**	E2
Canberra	**113**	K6
Cancarli	**76**	B3
Candarli Korfezi	**75**	J3
Cande	**65**	C5
Candelaria	**131**	P8
Candia	**75**	H5
Candir	**76**	E2
Cando	**123**	Q3
Canea	**75**	H5
Canelones	**139**	E6
Canete	**67**	F2
Caney	**128**	E2
Cangallo	**136**	C6
Cangamba	**106**	C5
Cangas de Narcea	**66**	C1
Cangas de Onis	**66**	D1
Canguaretama	**137**	K5
Cangucu	**138**	F6
Cangzhou	**87**	M4
Caniapiscau *Canada*	**121**	N7
Caniapiscau *Canada*	**121**	N6
Caniapiscau, Lac	**121**	N7
Canicatti	**69**	D7
Canik Daglari	**77**	G2
Canisp	**56**	C2
Canjayar	**66**	E4
Cankaya	**76**	E3
Cankiri	**76**	E2
Canna	**57**	B3
Cannanore	**92**	E6
Canna, Sound of	**57**	B3
Cannes	**65**	G7
Cannich *U.K.*	**56**	D3
Cannich *U.K.*	**56**	D3
Canning	**118**	F2
Canning Basin	**112**	E2
Cannington	**52**	D3
Cannock	**53**	E2
Cann River	**113**	K6
Canoas	**138**	F5
Canoas	**138**	F5
Canoeiros	**138**	G3
Canoe Lake	**119**	P4
Canon City	**127**	K1
Canosa di Puglia	**69**	F5
Canta	**136**	B6
Cantabrica, Cordillera	**66**	D1
Cantabrico, Mar	**66**	D1
Cantanhede	**66**	B2
Canterbury	**53**	J3
Canterbury Bight	**115**	D6
Canterbury Plains	**115**	C6
Can Tho	**93**	L6
Canton *China*	**93**	M4
Canton *Illinois*	**124**	E6
Canton *Mississippi*	**128**	H4
Canton *New York*	**125**	N4
Canton *Ohio*	**125**	K6
Canton *S. Dakota*	**123**	R6
Canudos *Amazonas, Brazil*	**136**	F5
Canudos *Bahia, Brazil*	**137**	K5
Canuma	**136**	F4
Canutama	**136**	E5
Canvey Island	**53**	H3
Canyon	**127**	M3
Cao Bang	**93**	L4
Caombo	**106**	C4
Capanaparo	**136**	D2
Capanema	**137**	H4
Capao Bonito	**138**	G4
Capatarida	**136**	C1
Cap de la Madeleine	**125**	P3
Cape Breton Island	**121**	P8
Cape Coast	**104**	E4
Cape Coral	**129**	M7
Cape Dorset	**120**	L5
Cape Dyer	**120**	P4
Cape Egmont	**115**	D3
Cape Girardeau	**124**	F8
Capel	**53**	G3
Capelinha	**138**	H3
Capella	**114**	C2
Cape Town	**108**	C6
Cape Verde	**104**	L7
Cape York Peninsula	**113**	J1
Cap-Haitien	**133**	L5
Capim	**137**	H4
Capitan Arturo Prat	**141**	V6
Capixaba	**138**	J6
Cappoquin	**59**	G8
Capraia, Isola di	**68**	B4
Caprera, Isola	**69**	B5
Capricorn Channel	**113**	L3
Capri, Isola di	**69**	E5
Caprivi Strip	**108**	D3
Captieux	**65**	C6
Capua	**69**	E5
Caqueta	**136**	C4
Carabinani	**136**	E4
Caracal	**73**	H3
Caracarai	**136**	E3
Caracas	**136**	D1
Carajari	**137**	G4
Carajas, Serra dos	**137**	G5
Carangola	**138**	H4
Caratasca	**132**	F7
Caratasca, Laguna	**132**	F7
Caratinga	**138**	H3
Carauari	**136**	D4
Caravaca de la Cruz	**67**	F3
Caravelas	**137**	K7
Carballo	**66**	B1
Carbonara, Capo	**69**	B6
Carbondale	**125**	N6
Carbonear	**121**	R8
Carboneras de Guadazaori	**67**	F3
Carbonia	**69**	B6
Carcans, Etang de	**65**	C6
Carcans-Plage	**65**	C6
Carcarana	**138**	D6
Carcassonne	**65**	E7
Carcross	**118**	J3
Cardak	**76**	C4
Cardamon Hills	**92**	E7
Cardenas	**131**	N9
Cardiel, Lago	**139**	B9
Cardiff	**52**	D3
Cardigan	**52**	C2
Cardigan Bay	**52**	C2
Cardona	**67**	G2
Cardston	**122**	H3
Carei	**73**	G2
Carentan	**64**	C4
Carey, Lake	**112**	E4
Carhaix-Plougeur	**64**	B4
Carhue	**139**	D7
Cariacica	**138**	H4
Caribbean Sea	**132**	H7
Cariboa Lake	**124**	F1
Cariboo Mountains	**119**	L5
Caribou *Canada*	**119**	R4
Caribou *U.S.A.*	**125**	S3
Caribou Mountains	**119**	M4
Carinena	**67**	F2
Carinhanha	**137**	J6
Carinish	**56**	A3
Caripito	**133**	R9
Carleton, Mount	**125**	S3
Carlingford	**58**	K4
Carlingford Lough	**58**	K4
Carlisle *U.K.*	**55**	G2
Carlisle *U.S.A.*	**125**	M6
Carlos Chagas	**138**	H3
Carlow *Ireland*	**59**	J7
Carlow *Ireland*	**59**	J7
Carloway	**56**	C2
Carlsbad *Czech Rep.*	**70**	E3
Carlsbad *California*	**126**	D4
Carlsbad *New Mexico*	**127**	K4
Carlton *Nottinghamshire, U.K.*	**53**	F2
Carlton *N. Yorkshire, U.K.*	**55**	H2
Carlyle	**123**	N3
Carmacks	**118**	H3
Carmagnola	**68**	A3
Carmarthen	**52**	C3
Carmarthen Bay	**52**	C3
Carmaux	**65**	E6
Carmel Head	**54**	E3
Carmelo	**139**	E6
Carmen	**136**	B2
Carmen Alto	**138**	C4
Carmen de Patagones	**139**	D8
Carmen, Isla	**126**	G8
Carmen, Sierra del	**127**	L6
Carmi	**124**	F7
Carmona	**66**	D4
Carnarvon *Australia*	**112**	C3
Carnarvon *South Africa*	**108**	D6
Carn Ban	**57**	D3
Carnedd Llewelyn	**54**	F3
Carnegie, Lake	**112**	E4
Carnew	**59**	K7
Carney Island	**141**	R4
Carnforth	**55**	G2
Carn Glas-choire	**56**	E3
Carniche, Alpi	**68**	D2
Car Nicobar	**93**	H7
Carnlough	**58**	L3
Carnlough Bay	**58**	L3
Carnot	**102**	C7
Carnsore Point	**59**	K8
Carnwath	**118**	K2
Carolina	**137**	H5
Caroline Islands	**91**	K4
Carondelet Reef	**111**	U3
Caroni	**136**	E2
Carora	**133**	M9
Carpathians	**73**	F1
Carpatii Meridionali	**73**	G3
Carpentaria, Gulf of	**113**	H1
Carpentras	**65**	F6
Carpi	**68**	C3
Carpina	**137**	K5
Carra, Lough	**58**	D5
Carranza, Cabo	**139**	B7
Carranza, Presa V.	**127**	M7
Carrara	**68**	C3
Carrauntoohil	**59**	C9
Carriacou	**133**	S8
Carrick	**57**	D5
Carrickfergus	**58**	L3
Carrickmacross	**58**	J5
Carrick-on-Shannon	**58**	F5
Carrick-on-Suir	**59**	H8
Carrigallen	**58**	G5
Carrigtwohill	**59**	F9
Carrington	**123**	Q4
Carrion	**66**	D1
Carrizal	**136**	C1
Carrizal Bajo	**138**	B5
Carrizo Springs	**127**	N6
Carrizozo	**127**	K4
Carroll	**124**	C5
Carrollton *Georgia*	**129**	K4
Carrollton *Kentucky*	**124**	H7
Carron	**56**	D3
Carron, Loch	**56**	C3
Carrot	**119**	Q5
Carrowkeel	**58**	H2
Carrowmore Lough	**58**	C4

Name	Page	Grid
Carryduff	58	L3
Carsamba	76	E4
Carsamba	77	G2
Carsibasi	77	H2
Carson City	126	C1
Carson Sink	122	E8
Carsphairn	57	D5
Cartagena *Colombia*	136	B1
Cartagena *Spain*	67	F4
Cartago *Colombia*	136	B3
Cartago *Costa Rica*	132	F10
Cartaret	53	N7
Cartaxo	66	B3
Cartaya	66	C4
Carteret	64	C4
Carterton	115	E4
Carthage *Missouri*	124	C8
Carthage *Texas*	128	E4
Cartier Island	110	F4
Cartwright	121	Q7
Caruara	137	K5
Carumbo	106	C4
Carupano	136	E1
Caruthersville	128	H2
Carvoeiro, Cabo	66	B3
Cary	52	E3
Casablanca	100	D2
Casa Grande	126	G4
Casale Monferrato	68	B3
Casalmaggiore	68	C3
Casamance	104	B3
Casanare	136	C2
Casas Ibanez	67	F3
Cascade	122	F5
Cascade Mountains	122	D3
Cascade Point	115	B5
Cascade Range	122	C6
Cascais	66	B3
Cascapedia	125	S2
Cascavel *Ceara, Brazil*	137	K4
Cascavel *Parane, Brazil*	138	F4
Caschuil	138	C5
Caserta	69	E5
Casey	141	H5
Cashel	59	G7
Casiguran	91	G2
Casilda	138	D6
Casma	136	B5
Casnewydd	52	E3
Caspe	67	F2
Casper	123	L6
Caspian Sea	51	S7
Cass	124	J5
Cassamba	106	D5
Casse, Grande	65	G6
Cassiar Mountains	118	J3
Cassinga	106	C6
Cassino	69	D5
Cass Lake *U.S.A*	124	C3
Cass Lake *U.S.A*	124	C3
Cassongue	106	B5
Casteljaloux	65	D6
Castellammare del Golfo	69	D6
Castellammare, Golfo di	69	D6
Castellane	65	G7
Castellar de Santiago	66	E3
Castellar de Santisteban	66	E3
Castelli	139	E7
Castellnedd	52	D3
Castellon de la Plana	67	F3
Castellote	67	F2
Castelnaudary	65	D7
Castelo Branco	66	C3
Castelsarrasin	65	D6
Casteltermini	69	D7
Castelvetrano	69	D7
Castets	65	C7
Castilla la Nueva	66	E3
Castilla la Vieja	66	D2
Castilletes	136	C1
Castillo, Pampa del	139	C9
Castillos	139	F6
Castlebar	58	D5
Castlebay	57	A4
Castlebellingham	58	K5
Castleblayney	58	J4
Castle Bolton	55	H2
Castle Carrock	55	G2
Castleconnel	59	F7
Castledawson	58	J3
Castlederg	58	G3
Castledermot	59	J7
Castle Douglas	54	F2
Castleellis	59	K8
Castleford	55	H3
Castleisland	59	D8
Castlemaine	113	J6
Castlemartyr	59	F9
Castlepollard	58	H5
Castlerea	58	E5
Castle Rock	123	M8
Castleside	55	H2
Castleton	55	H3
Castletown *Highland, U.K.*	56	E2
Castletown *Isle of Man, U.K.*	54	E2
Castletownbere	59	C9
Castletownshend	59	D9
Castlewellan	58	L4
Castonos	127	M7
Castor	122	J1
Castres	65	E7
Castries	133	S7
Castro	139	B8
Castro Alves	137	K6
Castro del Rio	66	D4
Castropol	66	C1
Castro Urdiales	66	E1
Castro Verde	66	B4
Castrovillari	69	F6
Castuera	66	D3
Caswell Sound	115	A6
Cat	77	J3
Catacamas	132	E7
Catacaos	136	A5
Cataingan	91	G3
Catak	77	K3
Catakkopru	77	J3
Catalca	76	C2
Cataluna	67	G2
Catalzeytin	76	F2
Catamarca	138	C5
Catanduanes	91	G3
Catanduva	138	G4
Catania	69	E7
Catanzaro	69	F6
Cataqueama	136	E6
Catastrophie, Cape	113	H5
Catatumbo	133	L10
Catbalogan	91	G3
Caterham	53	G3
Catete	106	B4
Cathcart	108	E6
Cat Island	133	K2
Cato	111	N6
Catoche, Cabo	131	R7
Catria, Monte	68	D4
Catrimani *Brazil*	136	E3
Catrimani *Brazil*	136	E3
Catskill	125	P5
Catskill Mountains	125	N5
Catwick Islands	93	L6
Cauca	133	K11
Caucaia	137	K4
Caucasia	133	K11
Caucasus	77	L1
Cauit Point	91	H4
Caulkerbush	55	F1
Caungula	106	C4
Cauquenes	139	B7
Caura	133	Q11
Causapscal	125	S2
Caussade	65	D6
Cauterets	65	C7
Cauto	132	J4
Cauvery	92	E6
Cavado	66	B2
Cavaillon	65	F7
Cavalcante	138	H6
Cavally	104	D4
Cavan *Ireland*	58	H5
Cavan *Ireland*	58	H5
Cavdir	76	C4
Cavendish	53	H2
Cavite	91	G3
Caxias	136	C4
Caxias	137	J4
Caxias do Sul	138	E5
Caxito	106	B4
Cay	76	D3
Cayagzi	76	F2
Caycuma	76	E2
Cayeli	77	J2
Cayenne	137	G3
Cayeux	64	D3
Caygoren Baraji	76	C3
Cayiralan	77	F3
Cayirli	77	H3
Caykara	77	J2
Caylarbasi	77	H4
Cayman Brac	132	H5
Cayman Trench	132	F5
Caynabo	103	J6
Cayuga Lake	125	M5
Cazalla de la Sierra	66	D4
Cazma *Croatia*	72	D3
Cazma *Croatia*	72	D3
Cazombo	105	D5
Cazorla	66	E4
Cea	66	D1
Ceahlau	73	H2
Ceanannus Mor	58	J5
Ceara	137	K5
Ceara-Mirim	137	K5
Ceballos	127	K7
Cebollera	66	E1
Cebu *Philippines*	91	G3
Cebu *Philippines*	91	G3
Cecina	68	C4
Cedar	124	D5
Cedar City	126	F2
Cedar Creek Lake	128	D4
Cedar Falls	124	D5
Cedar Lake	119	Q5
Cedar Rapids	124	E6
Cedartown	129	K3
Cedros, Isla de	126	E6
Ceduna	113	G5
Ceelbuur	103	J7
Ceeldheer	103	J7
Ceerigaabo	103	J5
Cefalu	69	E6
Cega	66	D2
Cegled	72	G2
Ceica	73	G2
Cekerek *Turkey*	77	F2
Cekerek *Turkey*	76	F2
Celalli	77	G3
Celano	69	D4
Celaya	131	J7
Celebes	91	G6
Celebi	76	E3
Celestun	131	P7
Celikhan	77	H3
Celina	124	H6
Celje	72	C2
Celle	70	D2
Celtik	76	D3
Celyn, Llyn	52	D2
Cemaes Head	52	C2
Cemilbey	76	F2
Cemisgezek	77	H3
Cendrawasih, Teluk	91	K6
Cenga	91	H6
Cenrana	91	F6
Center	128	E5
Centinela, Picacho Del	127	L6
Cento	68	C3
Central	57	D4
Central African Republic	102	D6
Central Brahui Range	92	C3
Central, Cordillera *Colombia*	136	B3
Central, Cordillera *Dominican Republic*	133	M5
Central, Cordillera *Peru*	136	B5
Central, Cordillera *Philippines*	91	G2
Central Heights	126	G4
Centralia	122	C4
Central Makran Range	92	B3
Central, Massif	65	E6
Central Range	114	C2
Central Siberian Plateau	84	H3
Cephalonia	75	F3
Cepu	90	E7
Ceram	91	H6
Cercal	66	B4
Cerchov	70	E4
Ceres	138	G3
Ceret	65	E7
Cerignola	69	E5
Cerigo	75	G4
Cerkes	76	E2
Cerkeskoy	76	B2
Cermei	73	F2
Cermik	77	H3
Cerna *Romania*	73	G3
Cerna *Romania*	73	K3
Cerne Abbas	52	E4
Cerralvo	128	C7
Cerralvo, Isla	130	E5
Cerreto Sannita	69	E5
Cerro Azul	136	B6
Cerro de Pasco	136	B6
Cerro Machin	131	L9
Cerro Marantiales	139	C10
Cerros Colorados, Embalse	139	C7
Cervaro	69	E5
Cervati, Monte	69	E6
Cervera	67	G2
Cervera de Pisuerga	66	D1
Cervia	68	D3
Cervione	69	B4
Cesar	133	L9
Cesena	68	D3
Cesenatico	68	D3
Cesis	63	L8
Ceske Budejovice	70	F4
Cesky Broc	70	F3
Cesme	76	B3
Cessnock	113	L5
Cetate	73	G3
Cetinje	72	E4
Cetinkaya	77	G3
Cetraro	69	E6
Ceuta	66	D4
Ceva-i-Ra	111	R6
Cevennes	65	F6
Cevherli	76	F4
Cevio	68	B2
Cevizli	76	D4
Ceyhan *Turkey*	76	F4
Ceyhan *Turkey*	77	F4
Ceylanpinar	77	J4
Chaadayevka	79	H5
Chablis	65	E5
Chacabuco	139	D6
Chachani, Nevado de	138	B3
Chachapoyas	136	B5
Chachoengsao	93	K6
Chaco Austral	138	D5
Chaco Boreal	138	E4
Chaco Central	138	D4
Chad	102	C5
Chad *Russia*	78	K4
Chadan	84	E6
Chadderton	55	G3
Chaddesley Corbett	53	E2
Chadileovu	139	C7
Chad, Lake	102	B5
Chadobets	84	F5
Chadron	123	N6
Chagai Hills	92	B3
Chagda	85	N5
Chaghcharan	95	S4
Chagny	65	F5
Chagoda	78	F4
Chagos Archipelago	82	F7
Chah Burjan	95	R6
Chah Bahar	95	Q9
Chahbounia	67	H5
Chaho	88	B5
Chahuites	131	M9
Chaibasa	92	G4
Chai Buri	93	K5
Chaiya	93	J7
Chaiyaphum	93	K5
Chajari	138	E6
Chala	136	C7
Chalais	65	D6
Chalap Dalan	92	B2
Chala, Punta	135	B7
Chalatenango	132	C7
Chaldonka	85	K6
Chale	53	F4
Chaleur, Baie de	121	N8
Chaleur Bay	125	T3
Chalhuanca	136	C6
Chalisgaon	92	E4
Challaco	139	C7
Challacombe	52	D3
Challans	65	C5
Challis	122	G5
Chalmny Varre	78	F2
Chalna	93	G4
Chalon-sur-Marne	64	F4
Chalon-sur-Saone	65	F5
Chalus	65	D6
Chalus	95	K3
Cham	70	E4
Chama	127	J2
Chaman	92	C2
Chamba *India*	92	E2
Chamba *Russia*	84	G4
Chambal	92	E3
Chamberlain *Australia*	112	F2
Chamberlain *U.S.A.*	123	Q6
Chambersburg	125	M7
Chambery	65	F6
Chamela	130	G8
Chamical	138	C6
Chamonix	65	G6
Chamouchouane	125	P2
Champagne	64	F4
Champagnole	65	F5
Champaign	124	F6
Champflower	52	D3
Champlaine, Lake	125	P4
Champlitte	65	F5
Champoton	131	P8
Chamrajnagar	92	E6
Chamusca	66	B3
Chanaral	138	B5
Chanaran	95	P3
Chanca	66	C4
Chandalar	118	F2
Chandausi	92	E3
Chandeleur Islands	128	H6
Chandigarh	92	E2
Chandler	121	P8
Chandmani *Mongolia*	86	G2
Chandmani *Mongolia*	86	H2
Chandpur	93	H4
Chandrapur	92	E5
Chandvad	92	D4
Chanf	95	Q8
Changan	93	L2
Changane	88	B5
Changbai	88	E4
Changbai Shan	87	F3
Changchun	87	F3
Changde	93	M3
Chang-hua	87	N7
Chang Jiang	87	M5
Chang, Ko	93	K6
Changle	87	M4
Changling	87	N3
Changma	86	H4
Changnyon	87	P4
Changsan-got	87	N4
Changsha	93	M3
Changshan	87	M6
Changtai	87	M7
Changting	87	M6
Changwu	93	L2
Changxing	87	M5
Changyi	87	M4
Changzhi	87	L4
Changzhou	87	M5
Channel Islands	53	M7
Channel-Port-aux-Basques	121	Q8
Chantada	66	C1
Chanthaburi	93	K6
Chantilly	64	E4
Chantonnay	65	C5
Chantrey Inlet	120	G4
Chanute	128	E2
Chany, Ozero	84	B6
Chao	136	B5
Chao Hu	87	M5
Chao Phraya	93	K5
Chaor He	87	N2
Chaouen	100	D1
Chaoyang *China*	87	N3
Chaoyang *China*	87	N3
Chaozhou	87	M7
Chapadinha	137	J4
Chapala, Laguna de	130	H7
Chapanda	85	N5
Chapayevo	79	J5
Chapayevsk	79	H5
Chapayev-Zheday	85	K4
Chapchachi	79	H6
Chapeco	138	F5
Chapel-en-le-Frith	55	H3
Chapel Hill	129	N3
Chapeltown *Grampian, U.K.*	56	E3

Name	Pg	Ref
Chapeltown *S. Yorkshire, U.K.*	55	H3
Chapleau	124	J3
Chaplygin	79	F5
Chapman	112	F2
Chapman, Cape	120	J4
Chapman Islands	119	P2
Chaqui	138	C3
Chara *Russia*	85	K5
Chara *Russia*	85	K5
Charagua	138	D3
Charak	95	M8
Charambira, Punta	136	B3
Charcot Island	141	U5
Chard	52	E4
Chardzhev	80	H6
Charente	65	C6
Chari	102	C5
Charikar	92	C1
Chariton *U.S.A.*	124	D6
Chariton *U.S.A.*	124	D6
Charkhari	92	E3
Charlemount	58	J4
Charleroi	64	F3
Charlesbourg	125	Q3
Charles, Cape	125	N8
Charles City	124	D5
Charles Island *Canada*	120	M5
Charles Island *Ecuador*	136	A7
Charleston *Illinois*	124	F7
Charleston *Missouri*	124	F8
Charleston *S. Carolina*	129	N4
Charleston *W. Virginia*	125	K7
Charlestown	58	E5
Charlestown of Aberlour	56	E3
Charleville	113	K4
Charleville-Mezieres	64	F4
Charlotte	129	M3
Charlotte Amalie	133	Q5
Charlotte, Cape	139	J10
Charlotte Harbour	129	L7
Charlottesville	125	L7
Charlottetown	121	P8
Charlton	113	J6
Charlton Island	121	L7
Charmes	64	G4
Charnley	112	F2
Charolles	65	F5
Charters Towers	113	K3
Chartres	64	D4
Charwelton	53	F2
Charybdis Reef	114	Q8
Charyn	86	D3
Chascomus	139	E7
Chaselka	84	C3
Chaslands Mistake	115	B7
Chasong	87	P3
Chasovo	78	J3
Chasseeneuil	65	D6
Chat	95	M3
Chateaubriant	65	C5
Chateau Chinon	65	E5
Chateaudun	65	D4
Chateau-Gontier	65	C5
Chateau-la-Valliere	65	D5
Chateaulin	64	A4
Chateauneuf-en-Thimerais	64	D4
Chateauneuf-sur-Loire	65	E5
Chateaurenault	65	D5
Chateauroux	65	D5
Chateau-Salins	64	G4
Chateau-Thierry	64	E4
Chatellerault	65	D5
Chatham *New Brunswick, Canada*	125	T3
Chatham *Ontario, Canada*	124	J5
Chatham *U.K.*	53	H3
Chatham, Isla	139	B10
Chatham Island *Ecuador*	136	A7
Chatham Island *New Zealand*	115	F7
Chatham Islands	115	G7
Chatillon	68	A3
Chatillon-sur-Indre	65	D5
Chatillon-sur-Seine	65	F5
Chato, Cerro	139	B8
Chattahoochee	129	K5
Chattanooga	129	K3
Chatteris	53	H2
Chatyrtash	86	D3
Chaudiere	125	Q3
Chaumont	64	F4
Chaunskaya Guba	85	V3
Chauny	64	E4
Chautauqua Lake	125	L5
Chavantina	138	G6
Chaves *Brazil*	137	H4
Chaves *Portugal*	66	C2
Chaviva	136	C3
Chay Khanh	77	L5
Chaykovskiy	78	J4
Chazhegovo	78	J3
Cheadle	55	G3
Cheb	70	E3
Cheboksary	78	H4
Cheboygan	124	H4
Chechen , Ostrov	79	H7
Chech, Erg	100	E3
Chechuysk	84	H5
Checiny	71	J3
Chedabucto Bay	121	P8
Cheddar	52	E3
Cheduba	93	H5
Cheetham, Cape	141	L4
Chef-Boutonne	65	C5
Chehalis	122	C4
Chehel Dokhtaran	95	R4
Cheju	87	P5
Cheju do	87	P5
Chekhov	88	H2
Chekunda	85	N6
Chekurovka	85	M2
Chekuyevo	78	F3
Chelan	122	D4
Chelan, Lake	122	D3
Chela, Serra da	106	B6
Cheleken	95	L2
Chelforo	139	C7
Cheliff, Oued	100	F1
Chelkar	51	U6
Chelm	71	K3
Chelmsford	53	H3
Chelmuzhi	78	F3
Chelosh	84	D6
Cheltenham	53	E3
Chelva	67	F3
Chelyabinsk	84	Ad5
Chelyuskin	84	G1
Chelyuskin, Mys	81	M2
Chemba	109	F3
Chemille	65	C5
Chemnitz	70	E3
Chenab	92	D2
Cheney	122	F4
Chengde	87	M3
Chengdu	93	K2
Chenghai	87	M7
Chengjiang	93	K4
Chengshan Jiao	87	N4
Chenonceaux	65	D5
Chen Xian	93	M3
Chepen	136	B5
Chepes	139	C6
Chepstow	52	E3
Chequamegon Bay	124	E3
Cher	65	E5
Cherangany Hills	107	G2
Cheraw	129	N3
Cherbourg	64	C4
Cherchell	101	F1
Cherdyn	78	K3
Cheremkhovo	84	G6
Cheremosh	71	L4
Cherepovets	78	F4
Cherevkovo	78	H3
Cherkashina	84	H5
Cherkasy	79	E6
Cherkessk	79	G7
Cherlak	84	A6
Cherlakskiy	84	A6
Cherlmno	71	H2
Chermoz	78	K4
Chernaya *Russia*	78	K2
Chernaya *Russia*	78	K2
Cherni	73	G4
Chernigovka *Russia*	88	D3
Chernigovka *Ukraine*	79	F6
Chernihiv	79	E5
Chernikovsk	78	K5
Cherni Lom	73	J4
Chernivitsi	73	H1
Chernobyl	79	E5
Chernoostrovskoye	84	D4
Chernousovka	84	A6
Chernushka	78	K4
Chernutyevo	78	H3
Chernyakhovsk	71	J1
Chernyshevskiy	85	J4
Chernyy Zemli	79	H6
Chernyy Mys	84	C5
Chernyy Otrog	79	K5
Cherokee	124	C5
Cherokee Sound	129	P7
Cherry	111	Q4
Cherskiy	85	U3
Cherskogo, Khrebet	85	Q3
Chertkovo	79	G6
Chertsey *New Zealand*	115	C5
Chertsey *U.K.*	53	G3
Chervonograd	79	C5
Chervonoznamenka	73	L2
Cherwell	53	F3
Chesapeake	125	M8
Chesapeake Bay	125	M8
Chesham	53	G3
Cheshire	55	G3
Cheshkaya Guba	78	H2
Cheshunt	53	G3
Chesil Beach	52	E4
Chester *U.K.*	55	G3
Chester *Illinois*	124	F8
Chester *Montana*	122	J3
Chester *S. Carolina*	129	M3
Chesterfield	55	H3
Chesterfield, Iles	113	M2
Chesterfield Inlet	119	S3
Chester-le-Street	55	H2
Chesters	57	F5
Chesterton Range	113	K4
Chesuncook Lake	125	R3
Chetlat	92	D6
Chetumal	131	Q8
Chetvertyy Kurilskiy Proliv	85	S7
Chetwynd	119	L4
Cheviot Hills	57	F5
Cheviot, The	57	F5
Chew	52	E3
Chew Valley Lake	52	E3
Cheyenne *S. Dakota*	123	P5
Cheyenne *Wyoming*	123	M7
Cheyenne Wells	127	L1
Chhapra	92	F3
Chhatarpur	92	E4
Chhindwara	92	E4
Chia-i	87	N7
Chiange	106	B6
Chiani	69	D4
Chiari	68	B3
Chiatura	77	K1
Chiautla	131	K8
Chiavari	68	B3
Chiavenna	68	B2
Chiba	89	H8
Chibia	106	B6
Chibit	84	D6
Chibizhek	84	E6
Chibougamau	125	N2
Chibougamau Lake	125	N2
Chibuto	109	F4
Chicago	124	G6
Chicama	136	B5
Chicapa	106	D4
Chichagof Island	118	H4
Chichester	53	G4
Chichester Range	112	D3
Chichibu	89	G8
Chichigalpa	132	D8
Chickasha	128	D3
Chicko	119	L5
Chiclayo	136	B5
Chico *Argentina*	139	C10
Chico *Argentina*	139	C8
Chico *U.S.A.*	122	D8
Chicoutimi	125	Q2
Chicualacuala	109	F4
Chidambaram	92	E6
Chiddingfold	53	G3
Chidley, Cape	121	P5
Chiefland	129	L6
Chiemsee	70	E5
Chieng-Mai	93	J5
Chienti	68	D4
Chieti	69	E4
Chifeng	87	M3
Chifre, Serra do	138	H3
Chiguana	138	C4
Chigubo	109	F4
Chigwell	53	H3
Chihli, Gulf of	87	K4
Chihuahua	127	J6
Chihuatlan	130	G8
Chiili	86	B3
Chijinpu	86	H3
Chik Ballapur	92	E6
Chikishlyer	95	L3
Chikmagalur	92	E6
Chikura	89	G8
Chi, Lam	93	K5
Chilamate	132	E8
Chilapa	131	K9
Chilas	92	D1
Chilca	136	B6
Chilca, Punta	136	B6
Childers	113	L4
Childress	127	M3
Chile	139	B7
Chile Chico	139	B9
Chilete	136	B5
Chilham	53	H3
Chilia, Bratul	73	K3
Chilik *Kazakhstan*	86	D3
Chilik *Kazakhstan*	79	J5
Chililabombwe	107	E5
Chillagoe	113	J2
Chillan	139	B7
Chillicothe *Missouri*	124	D7
Chillicothe *Ohio*	124	J7
Chilliculco	138	C3
Chiloe, Isla de	139	B8
Chilpancingo	131	K9
Chiltern Hills	53	G3
Chilumba	107	F5
Chi-lung	87	N6
Chilwa, Lake	107	G6
Chimanimani	109	F3
Chimay	64	F3
Chimborazo, Volcan	136	B4
Chimbote	136	B5
Chimishliya	73	K2
Chimkent	86	B3
Chimoio	109	F3
China	128	C8
Chinandega	132	D8
Chinati Peak	127	K6
Chinchilla	113	L4
Chinchilla de Monte Aragon	67	F3
Chinchon	66	E2
Chinchorro, Banco	131	R8
Chindagatuy	86	F2
Chinde	109	G3
Chindwin	93	H4
Chingola	107	E5
Chinguetti	100	C4
Chin Hills	93	H4
Chiniot	92	D2
Chinju	87	P4
Chinon	65	D5
Chinsali	107	F5
Chintalnar	92	F5
Chioggia	68	D3
Chios	75	H3
Chipata	107	F5
Chiperone	109	G3
Chipinge	109	F4
Chiplun	92	D5
Chipoka	107	F5
Chi Pou	93	L6
Chippenham	53	E3
Chippewa	124	E4
Chippewa Falls	124	E4
Chipping	55	G3
Chipping Norton	53	F3
Chipping Ongar	53	H3
Chipping Sodbury	52	E3
Chiputneticook Lakes	125	S4
Chiquinquira	136	C2
Chirchik	86	B3
Chiredzi	109	F4
Chirikof Island	118	D4
Chirimba	84	E5
Chirinda	84	G3
Chirique, Golfo de	132	F11
Chirk	52	D2
Chiromo	107	G6
Chirovanga	114	H5
Chirpan	73	H4
Chirripo	132	F10
Chishmy	78	K5
Chisinau	79	D6
Chisinau	73	K2
Chiskovo	84	F4
Chisone	68	A3
Chisos Mountains	127	L6
Chistopol	78	J4
Chita	85	J6
Chitato	106	D4
Chitembo	106	C5
Chitina	118	G3
Chitinskaya Oblast	85	K6
Chitradurga	92	E6
Chitral	92	D1
Chittagong	93	H4
Chittaurgarh	92	D4
Chittoor	92	E6
Chitungwiza	108	F3
Chiume	106	D6
Chiusi	69	C4
Chiva	67	F3
Chivasso	68	A3
Chivato, Punta	126	G7
Chive	136	D6
Chivhu	108	F3
Chivilcoy	139	D6
Chizha	78	G2
Chizha Vtoraya	79	H5
Chizu	89	E8
Chkalovskoye	88	D3
Chmielnik	71	J3
Choctawhatchee	129	K5
Chodziez	71	G2
Choele-Choel	139	C7
Choire, Loch	56	D2
Choiseul	114	H5
Choix	127	H7
Chojnice	71	G2
Chokai-san	88	H6
Chokurdakh	85	R2
Chokwe	109	F4
Cholderton	53	F3
Cholet	65	C5
Chollerton	57	F5
Choluteca	132	D8
Choma	106	E6
Chomutov	70	E3
Chona	84	H4
Chon Buri	93	K6
Chongan	87	M6
Chongjin	88	B5
Chongju	87	P4
Chongli	87	M3
Chongming Dao	87	M5
Chongqing	93	L3
Chongren	87	M6
Chongson	89	B7
Chongyang	93	M3
Chonos, Archipielago de los	139	B8
Chon Thanh	93	L6
Chop	79	C6
Chorley	55	G3
Chorolque	138	C4
Chortkov	79	D6
Chorzele	71	J2
Choshi	89	H8
Chosica	136	B6
Chos-Malal	139	B7
Choson-Man	87	P4
Choszczno	70	F2
Choteau	122	H4
Choybalsan	87	L2
Christchurch *New Zealand*	115	D5
Christchurch *U.K.*	53	F4
Christiansfeld	63	C9
Christianshab	120	R4
Christie Bay	119	N3
Christmas Creekq	112	F2
Christmas Island *Australia*	83	J8
Christmas Island *Kiribati*	143	H4
Chrzanow	71	H3
Chu	86	C3
Chubartau	86	D2
Chubut	139	C8
Chudleigh	52	D4
Chudovo	78	E4
Chudskoye Ozero	63	M7
Chugach Mountains	118	G3
Chugoku-sanchi	89	D8

D

Name	Map	Grid
Doganhisar	76	D3
Dogankent	76	F4
Dogansehir	77	G3
Doganyol	77	H3
Doganyurt	76	E2
Dog Creek	122	C2
Dogen Co	93	H2
Dog Lake	124	F2
Dogo	89	D7
Dogondoutchi	101	F6
Dogubeyazit	77	L3
Dogukardeniz Daglari	77	J2
Doha	97	K4
Doi Luang	93	K5
Dojran	73	G5
Dojransko Jezero	73	G5
Doka *Indonesia*	114	A3
Doka *Sudan*	96	B10
Dokkum	64	G2
Dokshitsy	63	M9
Dokurcun	76	D2
Dolak	114	B3
Dolak, Tanjung	91	K7
Dolanog	52	D2
Dolbeau	125	P2
Dol-de-Bretagne	64	C4
Dole	65	F5
Dolgellau	52	D2
Dolginovo	71	M1
Dolgiy, Ostrov	84	Ac3
Dolgoye	71	K4
Dolina	79	C6
Dolinsk	88	J2
Dolinskaya	79	E6
Dollar	57	E4
Dollar Law	57	E5
Dolni Kralovice	70	F4
Dolok, Tanjung	114	A3
Dolomitiche, Alpi	68	C2
Dolo Odo	103	H7
Dolores *Argentina*	139	E7
Dolores *Uruguay*	139	E6
Dolores *U.S.A.*	122	K8
Dolphin and Union Strait	119	N1
Dolphin, Cape	139	E10
Dolsk	71	G3
Domanic	76	C3
Dombas	63	C5
Dombe	109	F3
Dombe Grande	106	B5
Dombovar	72	E2
Dombrad	73	F1
Dome, Puy de	65	E6
Domett	115	D5
Domfront	64	C4
Dominica	133	S7
Dominical	132	F10
Dominican Republic	133	M5
Dominion, Cape	120	M4
Domo	103	J6
Domodossola	68	B2
Domuya, Cerro	139	B7
Don *Grampian, U.K.*	56	F3
Don *S. Yorkshire, U.K.*	55	H3
Don *Russia*	79	G6
Donaghadee	58	L3
Donaldsville	128	G5
Donau	68	E1
Donauworth	70	D4
Don Benito	66	D3
Doncaster	55	H3
Dondo	106	B4
Dondra Head	92	F7
Donegal *Ireland*	58	F3
Donegal *Ireland*	58	G3
Donegal Bay	58	F3
Donegal Point	59	C7
Donenbay	86	D2
Doneraile	59	E8
Donetsk	79	F6
Dongan *Heilongjiang, China*	88	E2
Dongan *Hunan, China*	93	M3
Dongara	112	C4
Dongbolhai Shan	93	G2
Dongchuan	93	K3
Dongfang	93	L5
Dongfanghong	88	D2
Donggala	91	F6
Dong Hoi	93	L5
Dongjingcheng	88	B3
Dongliu	87	M5
Dongluk	86	F4
Dongning	88	C3
Dongola	102	F4
Dongping	87	M4
Dongshan	87	N5
Dongsheng	87	K4
Dongtai	87	N5
Donguena	106	B6
Dong Ujimqin Qi	87	M2
Dongxi Lian Dao	87	M5
Donington	53	G2
Doniphan	124	E8
Donji Vakuf	72	D3
Donna	62	E3
Donner Pass	122	D8
Donnington	52	E2
Dooagh	58	B5
Doon	57	D5
Doonbeg	59	C7
Doonerak, Mount	118	E2
Doon, Loch	57	D5
Doorin Point	58	F3
Dor	95	R6
Dorada, Costa	67	G2
Dora, Lake	112	E3
Dora Riparia	68	A3
Dorbiljin	86	E2
Dorchester	52	E4
Dorchester, Cape	120	L4
Dordogne	65	C6
Dordrecht	64	F3
Dore	65	E6
Dore Lake	119	P5
Dore, Mont	65	E6
Dorgali	69	B5
Dori	104	E3
Dorking	53	G3
Dormo, Ras	96	F10
Dornbirn	68	B2
Dornie	56	C3
Dornoch	56	D3
Dornoch Firth	56	D3
Dorofeyevskaya	84	C2
Dorohoi	73	J2
Dorotea	62	G4
Dorovitsa	78	H4
Dorset	52	E4
Dortdivan	76	E2
Dortmund	70	B3
Dortyol	77	G4
Doruokha	84	J2
Dorutay	77	L3
Dosatuy	85	K7
Dosso	101	F6
Dossor	79	J6
Dothan	129	K5
Douai	64	E3
Douala	105	G5
Douarnenez	64	A4
Double Mountain Fork	127	M4
Doubs	65	F5
Doubtful Sound	115	A6
Doubtless Bay	115	D1
Doue-la-Fontaine	65	C5
Douentza	100	E5
Douglas *South Africa*	108	D5
Douglas *Isle of Man, U.K.*	54	D2
Douglas *Strathclyde, U.K.*	57	E5
Douglas *Arizona*	127	H5
Douglas *Georgia*	129	L5
Douglas *Wyoming*	123	M6
Doullens	64	E3
Doulus Head	59	B9
Doume	105	H5
Doune	57	D4
Dourada, Serra	137	H6
Dourados *Brazil*	138	E3
Dourados *Brazil*	138	F4
Dourados, Serra dos	138	F4
Douro	66	B2
Dove	55	H3
Dove Dale	55	H3
Dover *U.K.*	53	J3
Dover *Delaware*	125	N7
Dover *New Hampshire*	125	Q5
Dover *Ohio*	125	K6
Dover-Foxcroft	125	R4
Dover, Strait of	53	J4
Dovrefjell	62	C5
Dowa	107	F5
Dowlatabad *Afghanistan*	95	R5
Dowlatabad *Afghanistan*	95	S3
Dowlatabad *Iran*	95	N7
Dowlat Yar	92	C2
Down	58	L4
Downham Market	53	H2
Downpatrick	58	L4
Downpatrick Head	58	D4
Downs, The	53	J3
Downton	53	F4
Dow Rud	94	J5
Dowshi	92	C1
Dozen	89	D7
Draa, Oued	100	D3
Drac	65	F6
Dracevo	73	F5
Drachten	64	G2
Dragalina	73	J3
Dragasani	73	H3
Dragoman	73	G4
Dragonera, Isla	67	H3
Dragon's Mouth	133	S9
Dragsfjard	63	K6
Draguignan	65	G7
Dra, Hamada du	100	D3
Drake	123	P4
Drakensberg	108	E6
Drake Passage	141	V7
Drama	75	H2
Drammen	63	H7
Drangedal	63	C7
Draperstown	58	J3
Dras	92	E2
Drau	68	E2
Drava	72	E3
Dravograd	72	C2
Drawa	70	F2
Drawsko, Jezioro	71	G2
Drayton Valley	119	N5
Dren	73	G4
Drenewydd	52	D2
Dresden	70	E3
Dresvyanka	78	K2
Dreux	64	D4
Drin	75	F2
Drina	72	E3
Drin i zi	74	E1
Drobak	63	H7
Drobin	71	H2
Drogheda	58	K5
Drogichin	71	L2
Drogobych	79	C6
Drohiczyn	71	K2
Droichead Atha	58	K5
Droichead Nua	59	J6
Droitwich	53	E2
Drokiya	73	J1
Drome	65	F6
Dromedary, Cape	113	L6
Dromore	58	K4
Dronfield	55	H3
Dronne	65	D6
Dronning Maud Land	141	Z5
Dropt	65	D6
Drovyanaya	84	A2
Drumcollogher	59	E8
Drumheller	122	H2
Drummond	122	H4
Drummond Islands	124	J3
Drummond Range	113	K3
Drummondville	125	P4
Drummore	54	E2
Drumochter, Pass of	57	D4
Drumshanbo	58	F4
Druridge Bay	55	H1
Druskininkai	71	K1
Druzhba *Kazakhstan*	86	E2
Druzhba *Russia*	71	J1
Druzhina	85	R3
Drvar	72	D3
Drweca	71	H2
Dry	112	G2
Dry Bay *Canada*	121	N6
Dry Bay *U.S.A.*	118	H4
Dryden	124	D2
Drysdale, River	112	F2
Dschang	105	H4
Duab	94	J4
Dualo	91	G6
Duarte, Pico	133	M5
Duba	96	B3
Dubai	97	M4
Dubawnt Lake	119	Q3
Dubayy	97	M4
Dubbagh, Jabal Ad	96	B3
Dubbo	113	K5
Dubenskiy	79	K5
Dublin *Ireland*	59	K6
Dublin *Ireland*	59	K6
Dublin *U.S.A.*	129	L4
Dublin Bay	59	K6
Dubna	78	F4
Dubno	79	D5
Du Bois	125	L6
Dubois *Idaho*	122	H5
Dubois *Wyoming*	123	K6
Dubossary	79	D6
Dubreka	104	C4
Dubrovitsa	71	M3
Dubrovka *Russia*	79	E5
Dubrovka *Russia*	79	G6
Dubrovnik	72	E4
Dubrovskoye	84	J5
Dubuque	124	E5
Duchang	87	M6
Duchesne *U.S.A.*	123	S3
Duchesne *U.S.A.*	123	J7
Duchess	113	H3
Ducie Island	143	J5
Duck	129	J3
Ducklington	53	F3
Duck Mountain	119	Q5
Duddington	53	G2
Dudinka	84	D3
Dudley	53	E2
Duenas	66	D2
Duero	66	D2
Duffield	53	F2
Duff Islands	114	N6
Dufftown	56	E3
Dufton	55	G2
Duga Zapadnaya, Mys	85	R5
Dughaill, Loch	56	C3
Dugi Otok	72	C3
Duisburg	70	B3
Dukambiya	96	C9
Dukat	73	G4
Dukou	93	K3
Duk Fadiat	102	F6
Duk Faiwil	102	F6
Dukhan	97	K4
Duki Bolen	85	P6
Dukla	71	J4
Dukou	93	K3
Dulan	93	J1
Duldurga	85	J6
Duleek	58	K5
Dulga-Kyuyel	84	J4
Dulgalakh	85	N3
Dullingham	53	H2
Dull Lake	118	C3
Dulnain	56	E3
Dulovo	73	J4
Duluth	124	D3
Duma	77	G6
Dumaguete	91	G4
Dumai	90	C5
Dumaran	91	F3
Dumas *Arkansas*	128	G4
Dumas *Texas*	127	M3
Dumbarton	57	D5
Dumbea	114	X17
Dumbier	71	H4
Dumfries	55	F1
Dumfries and Galloway	57	E5
Dumitresti	73	J3
Dumka	93	G4
Dumlu	77	J2
Dumlupinar	76	C3
Dumoine	125	M3
Dumont d'Urville	141	K5
Dumont d'Urville Sea	141	J6
Dumyat	103	F1
Duna	72	E2
Dunaj	71	H5
Dunajec	71	J3
Dunany Point	58	K5
Dunarea	73	J3
Dunaujvaros	72	E2
Dunav	73	H4
Dunay *Moldova*	73	K3
Dunay *Russia*	88	D4
Dunayevtsy	73	J1
Dunay, Ostrov	85	L2
Dunbar *Australia*	113	J2
Dunbar *U.K.*	57	F4
Dunblane	57	E4
Dunboyne	59	K6
Duncan *Canada*	122	C3
Duncan *U.S.A.*	128	D3
Duncan Passage	93	H6
Duncansby Head	56	E2
Dunchurch	53	F2
Dundaga	63	K8
Dundalk *Ireland*	58	K4
Dundalk *U.S.A.*	125	M7
Dundalk Bay	58	K5
Dundas	120	M2
Dundas, Lake	112	E5
Dundas Peninsula	120	D3
Dundas Strait	112	G1
Dun Dealgan	58	K4
Dundee *South Africa*	108	F5
Dundee *U.K.*	57	F4
Dundonald	57	D5
Dundonnell	56	C3
Dundrennan	54	F2
Dundrod	58	K3
Dundrum	58	L4
Dundrum Bay	58	L4
Dundwa Range	92	F3
Dunecht	57	F3
Dunedin *New Zealand*	115	C6
Dunedin *U.S.A*	129	L6
Dunfanaghy	58	G2
Dunfermline	57	E4
Dungannon	58	J3
Dungarpur	92	D4
Dungarvan	59	G8
Dungarvan Harbour	59	G8
Dungeness	53	H4
Dungiven	58	J3
Dungloe	58	F3
Dungu	107	E2
Dungun	90	C5
Dunholme	55	J3
Dunhua	88	B4
Dunhuang	86	F3
Dunkeld	113	J6
Dunkerque	64	E3
Dunkirk	125	L5
Dunkur	103	G5
Dunkwa	104	E4
Dun Laoghaire	59	K6
Dunlavin	59	J6
Dunleer	58	K5
Dunmanus Bay	59	C9
Dunmanway	59	D9
Dunmore Town	132	J2
Dunmurry	58	K3
Dunnet Bay	56	E2
Dunnet Head	56	E2
Dunoon	57	D5
Dunragit	54	E2
Duns	57	F4
Dunseith	123	P3
Dunsford	52	D4
Dunstable	53	G3
Dunstan Mountains	115	B6
Dunster	52	D3
Duntelchaig, Loch	56	D3
Duntroon	115	C6
Dunvegan	56	B3
Dunvegan Head	56	B3
Dupang Ling	93	M3
Dupree	123	P5
Duque de York, Isla	139	A10
Du Quoin	124	F7
Duragan	76	F2
Durance	65	F7
Durand, Recif	114	Y17
Durango *Mexico*	130	G5
Durango *U.S.A.*	127	J2
Durankulak	73	K4
Durant	128	D3
Durazno	138	E6
Durazzo	74	E2
Durban	108	F6
Durcal	66	E4
Durdevac	72	D2
Durelj	87	J4
Duren	70	B3
Durg	92	F4
Durgapur *Bangladesh*	93	H3
Durgapur *India*	93	G4
Durham *U.K.*	55	H2

Name	Pg	Grid
Durham *U.K.*	55	H2
Durham *U.S.A.*	129	N2
Durisdeer	57	E5
Durma	96	H4
Durmitor	72	E4
Durness	56	D2
Durness, Kyle of	56	D2
Durres	74	E2
Dursey Head	59	B9
Dursey Island	59	B9
Dursley	52	E3
Dursunbey	76	C3
D'Urville Island	115	D4
Dury Voe	56	B1
Dushak	95	Q3
Dushan	93	L3
Dushanbe	86	B4
Dushanzi	86	G4
Duskotna	73	J4
Dusseldorf	70	B3
Dutch Harbor	118	Ae9
Dutovo	78	K3
Duvan	78	K4
Duyun	93	L3
Duzce	76	D2
Duzkoy	77	H2
Dvinskaya Guba	78	F3
Dvorets	84	F5
Dwarka	92	C4
Dyadino	84	H5
Dyatkovo	79	E5
Dyatlovo	71	L2
Dybvad	63	D8
Dyce	56	F3
Dyer, Cape	120	P4
Dyersburg	128	H2
Dyfed	52	C3
Dyfi	52	D2
Dyje	71	G4
Dykh Tau	79	G7
Dynow	71	K4
Dyrnesvagen	62	B5
Dyulino	73	J4
Dyulovo	87	L3
Dzaoudzi	109	J2
Dzavhan Gol	86	G2
Dzaygil Hid	86	H2
Dzerzhinsk *Belarus*	78	D5
Dzerzhinsk *Russia*	78	G4
Dzhalal-Abad	86	C3
Dzhalinda	85	L6
Dzhambeyty	79	J5
Dzhambul *Kazakhstan*	86	C2
Dzhambul *Kazakhstan*	86	C3
Dzhambul *Kazakhstan*	79	J6
Dzhamm	85	N2
Dzhankoy	79	E6
Dzhebel *Bulgaria*	73	H5
Dzhebel *Turkmenistan*	95	M2
Dzhelinde	84	J2
Dzhezkazgan	80	H5
Dzhirgatal	86	C4
Dzhizak	86	B3
Dzhugdzhur, Khrebet	85	P5
Dzhulfa	94	G2
Dzhungarskiy Alatau, Khrebet	86	E2
Dzhurin	79	D6
Dzhusaly	86	A2
Dzialdowo	71	J2
Dzialoszyn	71	H3
Dzilam de Bravo	131	Q7
Dzungarian Basin	86	F2
Dzuunbayan	87	L3
Dzuunbulag	87	M2

E

Name	Pg	Grid
Eagle *Newfoundland, Canada*	121	Q7
Eagle *Yukon, Canada*	118	H2
Eagle *U.S.A.*	118	G3
Eagle Lake *Canada*	124	D2
Eagle Lake *U.S.A.*	122	D7
Eagle, Mount	59	B8
Eagle Pass	127	M6
Eagle Point	114	D4
Eaglesham	57	D5
Eagles Hill	59	B9
Eaglestone Reef	111	S4
Ealing	53	G3
Earby	55	G3
Earlsferry	57	F4
Earl Shilton	53	F2
Earlston	57	F4
Earl Stonham	53	J2
Earn	57	E4
Earn, Loch	57	D4
Earp	126	E3
Easingwold	55	H2
East Anglian Heights	53	H2
Eastbourne	53	H4
East Brent	52	E3
East Bridgford	53	G2
East Cape	115	G2
East China Sea	87	P6
East Cleddau	52	C3
East Dean	53	H4
East Dereham	53	H2
Easter Island	143	K5
Eastern Ghats	92	E6
Eastern Ross	56	D3
East Falkland	139	E10
East Grinstead	53	G3
East Haddon	53	F2

Name	Pg	Grid
East Hoathly	53	H4
East Ilsley	53	F3
East Indies	142	E5
East Kilbride	57	D5
East Lake Tarbert	56	B3
Eastleigh	53	F4
East Linton	57	F4
East Loch Roag	56	B2
East London	108	E6
Eastmain *Canada*	121	L7
Eastmain *Canada*	121	M7
Eastmain-Opinaca, Reservoir	121	L7
Eastman	129	L4
East Midlands Airport	53	F2
East Millnocket	125	R4
Eastoft	55	J3
Easton *U.K.*	52	E4
Easton *U.S.A.*	125	N6
East Point *Prince Edward Island, Canada*	121	P8
East Point *Quebec, Canada*	121	P8
Eastport	125	S4
East Retford	55	J3
Eastry	53	J3
East Saint Louis	124	E7
East Siberian Sea	85	T2
East Sussex	53	H3
East Tavaputs Plateau	123	K8
Eastville	55	K3
East Wittering	53	G4
Eastwood	55	H3
Eatonton	129	L4
Eau Claire	124	E4
Ebbw Vale	52	D3
Ebe-Basa	85	M4
Ebebiyin	105	H5
Ebeltoft	63	D8
Eber Golu	76	D3
Ebersberg	70	D4
Eberswalde	70	E2
Ebinur Hu	86	E3
Eboli	69	E5
Ebolowa	105	H5
Ebrach	70	D4
Ebro	66	G2
Ecclefechan	57	E5
Eccles	55	G3
Eccleshall	52	E2
Eccleston	55	G3
Eceabat	76	B2
Ech Cheliff	100	F1
Echeng	93	M2
Echigo-sammyaku	89	G7
Echo Bay *Ontario, Canada*	124	H3
Echo Bay *NW. Territories, Canada*	119	M2
Echternach	64	G4
Echuca	113	J6
Ecija	66	D4
Eckernforde	70	C1
Eclipse Sound	120	L3
Ecmiadzin	77	L2
Ecuador	136	B4
Ed	103	H5
Ed	63	H7
Edah Wagga	112	D4
Edam	64	F2
Eday	56	F1
Ed Damazin	103	F5
Ed Damer	96	A8
Ed Debba	102	F4
Ed-Deffa	102	E1
Edderton	56	D3
Eddrachillis Bay	56	C2
Ed Dueim	103	F5
Ede *Netherlands*	64	F2
Ede *Nigeria*	105	F4
Edea	105	H5
Edehon Lake	119	R3
Edel Land	112	C4
Eden *Australia*	113	K6
Eden *Cumbria, U.K.*	55	G2
Eden *Kent, U.K.*	53	H3
Eden *U.S.A.*	123	K6
Edenderry	59	H6
Edgecumbe	115	F2
Edgeley	123	Q4
Edgell Island	121	P5
Edgemont	123	N6
Edgeoya	80	D2
Edgeworthstown	58	G5
Edhessa	75	G2
Edievale	115	B6
Edinburg	128	D7
Edinburgh	57	E5
Edirne	76	B2
Edisto	129	M4
Edith River	112	G1
Edjeleh	101	G3
Edland	63	B7
Edmond	128	D3
Edmonds	122	C4
Edmonton	119	N5
Edmunston	125	R3
Edolo	68	C2
Edremit	76	B3
Edremit Korfezi	76	B3
Edson	119	M5
Edward, Lake	107	E3
Edwardson, Cape	115	B7
Edwards Plateau	127	M5
Edzhen	85	P4
Eeklo	64	E3
Eel	122	B7

Name	Pg	Grid
Efate	114	U12
Eferding	68	E1
Eflani	76	E2
Efyrnwy, Llyn	52	D2
Ega	63	D8
Egadi, Isole	69	D7
Egersund	63	B7
Egerton, Mount	112	D3
Eggan	105	G4
Egg Lagoon	113	J6
Egglescliffe	55	H2
Eggum	62	E2
Egham	53	G3
Eghol	114	H6
Egilsstadir	62	X12
Egiyn Gol	86	J1
Eglinton	58	H2
Eglinton Island	120	C2
Egmont, Mount	115	E3
Egremont	55	F2
Egridir	76	D4
Egridir Golu	76	D3
Egvekinot	85	Y3
Egypt	102	E2
Ehingen	70	C4
Eibar	66	E1
Eidem	62	D4
Eidfjord	63	B6
Eidi	62	Z14
Eidsvold	113	L4
Eidsvoll	63	D6
Eifel	70	B3
Eigg	57	C4
Eigg, Sound of	57	B4
Eight Degree Channel	92	D7
Eighty Mile Beach	112	E2
Eilerts de Haan Geb	137	F3
Eil, Loch	57	C4
Eilsleben	70	D2
Einbeck	70	C3
Eindhoven	64	F3
Eiriksjokull	62	U12
Eirunepe	136	D5
Eisenach	70	D3
Eisenhuttenstadt	70	F2
Eisenkappel	68	E2
Eishort, Lake	57	C3
Eisleben	70	D3
Eitorf	70	B3
Ejea de los Caballeros	67	F1
Ejido Insurgentes	130	D5
Ejin Horo Qi	87	K4
Ejin Qi	86	J3
Ejutla	131	L9
Ekenas	63	K6
Eket	105	G5
Eketahuna	115	E4
Ekhinadhes	75	F3
Ekhinos	75	H2
Ekibastuz	84	B6
Ekimchan	85	N6
Ekonda	84	G3
Eksjo	63	F8
Ekwan	121	K7
El Affroun	67	H4
El Araiche	100	D1
El Arco	126	F7
El Arish	103	F1
Elasson	75	G3
Elat	94	B7
Elazig	77	H3
El Azraq	94	C6
El Bahri, Borg	67	H4
El Balyana	103	F2
Elban	85	P6
El Banco	136	C2
El Barco de Avila	66	D2
El Barco de Valdeorras	66	C1
Elbasan	74	F2
El Bayadh	100	F2
Elbe	70	C2
Elbert, Mount	123	L8
Elberton	129	L3
Elbeuf	64	D4
Elbeyli	77	G4
Elbing	71	H1
Elbistan	77	G3
Elblag	71	H1
Elbrus	79	G7
El Burgo de Osma	66	E2
El Cajon	126	D4
El Callao	136	E2
El Campo	128	D6
El Carmen *Bolivia*	138	E3
El Carmen *Bolivia*	136	E6
El Centro	126	E4
El Cerro	138	D3
El Chaparro	136	D2
Elche	67	F3
Elche de la Sierra	67	F3
Eldikan	85	P4
Eldivan	76	E2
El Djazair	101	F1
El Djouf	100	D4
Eldon	124	D7
El Dorado *Arkansas*	128	F4
El Dorado *Kansas*	128	D3
El Dorado *Venezuela*	133	S11
Eldoret	107	G2
Elektrostal	78	H4
Elephant Butte Reservoir	127	J4
Elephant Island	141	W6

Name	Pg	Grid
Eleskirt	77	K3
El Eulma	101	G1
Eleuthera	132	J2
Elevsis	75	G3
El Faiyum	102	F2
El Fasher	102	E5
El Fashn	102	F2
El Ferrol	66	B1
El Fuerte	127	H7
Elgepiggen	63	D5
El Geteina	103	F5
Elgin *U.K.*	56	E3
Elgin *Illinois*	124	F5
Elgin *N. Dakota*	123	P4
El Giza	102	F1
Elgol	57	B3
El Golea	101	F2
El Golfo de Santa Clara	126	E5
Elgon, Mont	107	F2
El Hawata	96	B10
El Hodna, Chott	67	J5
El Homra	102	F5
El Hosh	103	F5
El Huecu	139	B7
Elikon	75	G3
Elisabethville	107	E5
Eliseu Martins	137	J5
Elista	79	G6
Elizabeth *Australia*	113	H5
Elizabeth *U.S.A.*	125	N6
Elizabeth City	129	P2
Elizabeth Reef	113	M4
Elizabethton	129	L2
Elizabethtown	124	H8
Elizondo	67	F1
El Jadida	100	D2
El Jafr	94	C6
El Jebelein	103	F5
El Jerid, Chott	101	G2
Elk	71	K2
El Kala	69	B7
El Kamlin	103	F5
Elk City	128	C3
El Khalil	94	B6
El Kharga	102	F2
Elkhart	124	H6
El Khartum	103	F4
Elkhorn	123	Q6
Elkhotovo	79	G7
Elkhovo	73	J4
Elkin	129	M2
Elkins	125	L7
Elko	122	G2
El Koran	103	H6
El Korima, Oued	100	E2
El Lagowa	102	E5
Elland	55	H3
Ellef Ringnes Island	120	F2
Ellen	55	F2
Ellendale *Australia*	112	E2
Ellendale *U.S.A.*	123	Q5
Ellen, Mount	122	J8
Ellensburg	122	D4
Ellesmere	52	E2
Ellesmere Island	120	K2
Ellesmere, Lake	115	D5
Ellesmere Port	55	G3
Ellice	119	Q2
Ellington	114	R8
Elliot	108	E6
Elliot Lake	124	J3
Elliot, Mount	113	K2
Elliston	113	H5
El Llano	132	H10
Ellon	56	F3
Ellsworth	125	R4
Ellsworth Land	141	U4
Ellwangen	70	D4
Elmadag	76	E3
Elma Dagi	76	E3
El Mahalla El Kubra	102	F1
El Manaqil	103	F5
El Mansura	102	F1
El Mesellemiya	103	F5
El Milk	102	E4
El Minya	102	F2
Elmira	125	M5
Elmore	113	J6
Elmshorn	70	C2
El Muglad	102	E5
El Nido	91	F3
El Obeid	102	F5
El Odaiya	102	E5
Elorza	136	D2
El Oued	101	G2
Eloy	126	G4
El Palmito	127	K8
El Pardo	66	E2
El Paso *Illinois*	124	F6
El Paso *Texas*	127	J5
Elphin	56	C2
El Porvenir	127	K5
El Potosi	128	B8
El Progreso	132	D7
El Puente del Arzobispo	66	D3
El Qahira	102	F1
El Qasr	102	E2
El Qunaytirah	94	B5
El Real	132	J10
El Reno	128	D3
El Ronquillo	66	C4
El Rosario	126	E5

El Sahuaro 126 F5
El Salado 139 C9
El Salto 130 G6
El Salvador 132 C8
El Sam'an de Apure 133 N11
El Sauzal 126 D5
Elsham 55 J3
El Socorro 126 F5
Elster 70 E3
Elsterwerda 70 E3
El Sueco 127 J6
El Suweis 103 F2
El Tambo 136 B4
Eltham 115 E3
El Thamad 96 B2
El Tigre 133 Q10
El Tih 96 A2
Eltisley 53 G2
El Tocuyo 133 N10
Elton *U.K.* 53 G2
Elton *Russia* 79 H6
El Tule 131 L9
El Tur 96 A2
Eluru 92 F5
Elvanfoot 57 E5
Elvas 66 C3
Elveden 53 H2
Elverum 63 D6
El Viejo 133 L11
El Vigia 136 C2
Elwy 55 F3
Ely *Cambridgeshire, U.K.* 53 H2
Ely *Mid Glamorgan, U.K.* 52 D3
Ely *Minnesota* 124 E3
Ely *Nevada* 126 E1
Elze 70 C2
Ema 63 M7
Emae 114 U12
Emamrud 95 M3
Emam Taqi 95 P4
Eman 63 G8
Emao 114 U12
Emba 79 K6
Embarcacion 138 D4
Embleton 55 H1
Embona 75 J4
Embrun 65 G6
Embu 107 G3
Emden 70 B2
Emerald 113 K3
Emerald Island 120 D2
Emerson 123 R3
Emet 76 C3
Emeti 114 C3
Emi 84 F6
Emigrant Pass 122 F7
Emin 86 E2
Emine, Nos 73 J4
Emirdag 76 D3
Emir Dagi 76 D3
Emita 113 K7
Emmaboda 63 F8
Emmaste 63 K7
Emmen 64 G2
Emory Peak 127 L6
Empalme 126 G7
Empangeni 109 F5
Empedrado 138 E5
Empingham 53 G2
Empoli 68 C4
Emporia *Kansas* 128 D1
Emporia *Virginia* 125 M8
Ems 70 B2
Emu 88 B4
Enard Bay 56 C2
Encantada, Cerro Del La 126 E5
Encarnacion 138 E5
Enchi 104 E4
Encinal 128 C6
Encontrados 136 C2
Encounter Bay 113 H6
Endau 90 C5
Ende 91 G7
Endeavour Strait 113 J1
Enderbury Island 111 U2
Enderby Land 141 D5
Endicott Mountains 118 C2
Ene 136 C6
Enez 76 B2
Enfield *Ireland* 59 J6
Enfield *U.K.* 53 G3
Engano, Cabo 133 N5
Engano, Cape 91 G2
Engaru 88 J3
Engels 79 H5
Enggano 90 C7
Engger Us 87 J3
Engineer Group 114 E4
Englehart 125 L3
Englewood 123 M8
English Channel 50 G5
Enguera 67 F3
Enguera, Sierra de 67 F3
Enid 128 D2
Enkhuizen 64 F2
Enkoping 63 G7
Enna 69 E7
Ennadai Lake 119 Q3
En Nahud 102 E5
Ennedi 102 D4
Ennell, Lough 59 H6
Ennerdale Water 55 F2
Enning 123 N5
Ennis *Ireland* 59 E7

Ennis *U.S.A.* 128 D4
Enniscorthy 59 J7
Enniskillen 58 G4
Ennistymon 59 D7
Enns 68 E1
Enonkoski 62 N5
Enontekio 62 K2
Enrekang 91 F6
Enschede 64 G2
Ensenada 126 D5
Enshi 93 L2
Enstone 53 F3
Entebbe 107 F2
Enterprise 129 K5
Entinas, Punta de las 66 E4
Entraygues 65 E6
Entrecasteaux, Recifs d' 111 N5
Enugu 105 G4
Enurmino 118 A2
Enz 70 C4
Eo 66 C1
Eolie 69 E6
Epano Fellos 75 H4
Epanomi 75 G2
Epernay 64 E4
Ephrata 122 E4
Epi 114 U12
Epinal 64 G4
Epping 53 H3
Eppynt, Mynydd 52 D2
Epsi 77 J4
Epsom 53 G3
Eqlid 95 L6
Equatorial Guinea 105 G5
Equeipa 136 E2
Erap 114 D3
Erbaa 77 G2
Erba, Jebel 96 C6
Ercek 77 K3
Ercis 77 K3
Ercsi 72 E2
Erdek 76 B2
Erdemli 76 F4
Erdenet 87 J2
Erdre 65 C5
Erechim 138 F5
Ereenstav 87 M2
Eregli *Turkey* 76 D2
Eregli *Turkey* 76 F4
Erek Dagi 77 K3
Erenhot 87 L3
Erentepe 77 K3
Eresma 66 D2
Eressos 75 H3
Erfelek 76 F2
Erfurt 70 D3
Ergani 77 H3
Ergene 76 B2
Ergli 63 L8
Ergun He 85 K6
Ergun Zuoqi 87 N1
Eriboll, Loch 56 D2
Ericht, Loch 57 D4
Ericiyas Dagi 76 F3
Erie 125 K5
Erie, Lake 125 K5
Erikousa 74 E3
Erimanthos 75 F4
Erimo-misaki 88 J5
Eriskay 57 A3
Erkelenz 70 B3
Erkilet 76 F3
Erkowit 96 C7
Erlandson Lake 121 N6
Erlangen 70 D4
Erldunda 113 G4
Erme 52 D4
Ermelo 109 F5
Ermenak 76 E4
Ernakulam 92 E7
Erne 58 H5
Erne, Lower Lough 58 G4
Erne, Upper Lough 58 G4
Erode 92 E6
Eromanga 113 J4
Er Rachidia 100 E2
Er Rahad 102 F5
Errego 109 G3
Errigal 58 F2
Erris Head 58 B4
Errochty, Loch 57 D4
Errogie 56 D3
Erromango 114 U13
Erseke 75 F2
Erskine 124 C3
Ertai 86 G2
Eruh 77 K4
Erwigol 86 F3
Eryuan 93 J3
Erzen 74 E2
Erzgebirge 70 E3
Erzin 84 F6
Erzincan 77 H3
Erzurum 77 J3
Esa-Ala 114 E3
Esan-misaki 88 H5
Esashi *Japan* 88 H5
Esashi *Japan* 88 J3
Esbjerg 63 C9
Esbo 63 N6
Escalona 66 D2
Escambia 129 J5
Escanaba 124 G4
Escarpe, Cape 114 X16

Escocesa, Bahia de 133 N5
Escondido *Brazil* 138 J3
Escondido *U.S.A.* 126 D4
Escrick 55 H3
Escuintla 132 B7
Ese-Khayya 85 N3
Esemer 77 K3
Esen 76 C4
Esendere 77 L4
Esfahan 95 K5
Esfarayen, Reshteh ye 95 N3
Eshan 93 K4
Esha Ness 56 A1
Esh Sheikh, Jbel 77 G6
Esino 68 D4
Esk 57 E5
Eskdale 57 E5
Eske, Lough 58 F3
Eskifjordur 62 Y12
Eskilstuna 63 G7
Eskimalatya 77 H3
Eskimo Lakes 118 J2
Eskimo Point 119 S3
Eskipazar 76 E2
Eskishir 76 D3
Esla 66 D1
Eslamabad-e Gharb 94 H4
Eslam Qaleh 95 Q4
Esme 76 C3
Esmeralda, Isla 139 A9
Esmeraldas 136 B3
Espalion 65 E6
Espana *Canada* 125 K3
Espanola *U.S.A.* 127 J3
Espanola, Isla 136 A7
Espenberg, Cape 118 C2
Esperance 112 E5
Esperance Bay 112 E5
Esperanza *Antarctic* 141 W6
Esperanza *Argentina* 139 B10
Esperanza *Argentina* 138 D6
Espiel 66 D3
Espinhaco, Serra da 138 H3
Espinho 66 B2
Espinosa de los Monteros 66 E1
Espirito Santo 138 H3
Espiritu Santo 114 T11
Espiritu Santo, Cape 91 H3
Espiritu Santo, Isla 130 D5
Espiye 77 H2
Espoo 63 N6
Esposende 66 B2
Espot 67 G1
Espungabera 109 F4
Esquel 139 B8
Es Sahra en Nubiya 96 B6
Essaouira 100 D2
Es Semara 100 C3
Essen 70 B3
Essex 53 H3
Essex, Punta 136 A7
Esslingen 70 C4
Esso 85 T5
Estacado, Llanos 127 L4
Estados, Isla de los 139 D10
Estahbanat 95 M7
Estancia 138 K6
Estcourt 108 E5
Este 68 C3
Esteli 132 D8
Estella 67 E1
Estepona 66 D4
Este, Punta del 139 F6
Esterhazy 123 N2
Esternay 64 E4
Estes Park 123 M7
Estevan 123 N3
Estherville 124 C5
Eston 55 H2
Estonia 63 L7
Estrela, Sierra da 66 C2
Estrella, Punta 126 E5
Estremadura 66 B3
Estremoz 66 C3
Estrondo, Serra do 137 H5
Esztergom 72 E2
Etah 92 E3
Etain 64 F4
Etampes 64 E4
Etaples 64 D3
Etawah 92 E3
Ethiopia 103 G6
Etive, Loch 57 C4
Etna, Monte 69 E7
Eton 53 G3
Etosha Pan 108 C3
Etretat 64 D4
Ettington 53 F2
Ettlingen 70 C4
Ettrick 57 E5
Ettrick Forest 57 E5
Etwall 53 F2
Eu 64 D3
Eua 111 U6
Euboea 75 H3
Euclid 125 K6
Euclides da Cunha 137 K6
Eufaula 129 K5
Eufaula Lake 128 E3
Eugene 122 C5
Eugenia, Punta 126 E7
Eunice 128 F5
Euphrates 94 G6
Eupora 128 H4

Eure 64 D4
Eureka *California* 122 B7
Eureka *Montana* 122 G3
Eureka *Nevada* 126 D1
Eureka Sound 120 J2
Europa, Ile de l 109 H4
Europa, Picos de 66 D1
Europa Point 66 D4
Eutaw 129 J4
Evans, Lake 121 L7
Evans, Mount 123 M8
Evans Strait 120 K5
Evanston *Illinois* 124 G5
Evanston *Wyoming* 122 J7
Evansville 124 G7
Evaux-les-Bains 65 E5
Evaz 95 L8
Evenlode 53 F3
Everard, Cape 113 K6
Everard, Lake 113 G5
Everest, Mount 92 G3
Everett 122 C4
Everett Mountains 120 N5
Everglades, The 129 M7
Evesham 53 F2
Evesham, Vale of 53 F2
Evigheds Fjord 120 R4
Evisa 69 B4
Evje 63 B7
Evora 66 C3
Evreux 64 D4
Evropos 75 G2
Evros 75 J2
Evrotas 75 G4
Evvoia 75 H3
Evvoikos Kolpos 75 G3
Ewasse 114 E3
Ewe, Loch 56 C3
Ewes 57 E5
Exbourne 52 D4
Exe 52 D4
Exeter 52 D4
Exford 52 D3
Exmoor 52 D3
Exmouth 52 D4
Exmouth Gulf 112 C3
Exo Hora 75 F4
Expedition Range 113 K3
Exploits 121 Q8
Exton 52 D3
Extremadura 66 C3
Exuma Sound 132 J2
Eyakit-Terde 85 J3
Eyam 55 H3
Eyasi, Lake 107 F3
Eyemouth 57 F4
Eye Peninsula 56 B2
Eyjafjallajokull 62 U13
Eyjafjordur 62 V11
Eyl 103 J6
Eynesil 77 H2
Eynsham 53 F3
Eyre 112 F5
Eyre Creek 113 H4
Eyre Mountains 115 B6
Eyre North, Lake 113 H4
Eyre Peninsula 113 H5
Eyre South, Lake 113 H4
Eysturoy 62 Z14
Eyvanaki 95 L4
Ezequil Ramos Mexia, Embalse 139 C7
Ezine 76 B3

F

Faber Lake 119 M3
Faborg 63 D9
Fabriano 68 D4
Facatativa 136 C3
Facundo 139 C9
Fada 102 D3
Fada NGourma 104 F3
Faddeya, Zaliv 84 H2
Faddeyevskiy, Ostrov 85 Q1
Faenza 68 C3
Faeros 62 Z14
Fafen Shet 103 H6
Fagaras 73 H3
Fagersta 63 F6
Faget 73 G3
Fagnano, Lago 139 C10
Fagnes 64 F3
Faguibine, Lac 100 E5
Fagurholsmyri 62 W13
Fahraj 95 P7
Fairbanks 118 F3
Fairborn 124 J7
Fairfield 126 A1
Fair Isle 56 A2
Fairlie 115 C6
Fairlight *Australia* 113 J2
Fairlight *U.K.* 53 H4
Fairmont *Minnesota* 124 C5
Fairmont *W. Virginia* 125 K7
Fair Ness 120 M5
Fairview 128 C2
Fairweather, Mount 118 H4
Faisalabad 92 D2
Faith 123 N5
Faither, The 56 A1
Faizabad 92 F3
Fajr, Wadi 96 D2

Name	Page	Ref
Fakaofo	111	U3
Fakenham	53	H2
Fåkfak	91	J6
Fakse Bugt	63	E9
Faku	87	N3
Fal	52	C4
Falaise	64	C4
Falam	93	H4
Falavarjan	95	K5
Falcarragh	58	F2
Falcone, Capo del	69	B5
Falcon Lake	128	C7
Falfurrias	128	C7
Falkenberg	63	E8
Falkenburg	70	E3
Falkensee	70	E2
Falkirk	57	E4
Falkland	57	E4
Falkland Islands	139	E10
Falkonera	75	G4
Falkoping	63	E7
Fall Line Hills	129	J4
Fallon	126	C1
Fall River	125	Q6
Fall River Pass	123	M7
Falls City	124	C6
Falmouth	52	B4
Falmouth Bay	52	B4
Falsa Chipana, Punta	139	B4
False Bay	108	C6
False Pass	118	Af9
False Pera Head	113	J1
Falset	67	G2
Falster	63	E9
Falsterbo	63	E9
Falterona, Monte	68	C4
Falticeni	73	J2
Falun	63	F6
Famatina, Sierra de	138	C5
Fanad Head	58	G2
Fandriana	109	J4
Fangak	102	F6
Fangcheng	93	M2
Fangdou Shan	93	L2
Fangshan	87	M4
Fang Xian	93	M2
Fangzheng	88	B3
Fannich, Loch	56	D3
Fannuj	95	P8
Fano	63	C9
Fano	68	D4
Fanquier	122	E3
Fan Si Pan	93	K4
Faraday	141	V5
Faraday, Cape	120	L2
Faradje	107	E2
Farafangana	109	J4
Farah	95	R5
Farah Rud	95	R5
Faraid Head	56	D2
Farallon, Punta	130	G8
Faranah	104	C3
Farasan, Jazair	96	E8
Farcau	71	L5
Fareham	53	F4
Farewell, Cape	115	D4
Farewell Spit	115	D4
Far Falls	123	T2
Fargo	123	R4
Faridpur	93	G4
Farigh, Wadi al	101	K2
Farila	63	F6
Fariman	95	P4
Faringdon	53	F3
Farjestaden	63	G8
Farmington *Maine*	125	Q4
Farmington *Missouri*	124	E8
Farmington *New Mexico*	127	H2
Farnborough	53	G3
Farnham	53	G3
Farnworth	55	G3
Faro	63	H8
Faro *Brazil*	137	F4
Faro *Portugal*	66	C4
Farosund	63	H8
Farquhar Islands	82	D8
Farrai	75	F3
Farranfore	59	C8
Farrar	56	D3
Farrashband	95	L7
Farsala	75	G3
Farsi	95	R5
Farsund	63	B7
Fartak, Ra's	97	L9
Farvel, Kap	116	Q3
Fasa	95	L7
Fasad	97	L7
Fasano	69	F5
Faske Bugt	70	E1
Fastov	79	D5
Fatehabad	92	E3
Fatehgarh	92	E3
Fatehpur *Rajasthan, India*	92	D3
Fatehpur *Uttar Pradesh, India*	92	F3
Fatezh	79	F5
Fatick	104	B3
Fatima	66	B3
Fatmomakke	62	F4
Fatsa	77	G2
Fatuna	111	T4
Faurei	73	J3
Fauro Vaghena	114	H5
Fausing	63	D8
Fauske	62	F3
Faux Cap	109	J5
Faversham	53	H3
Fawley	53	F4
Fawr, Fforest	52	D3
Faxafloi	62	T12
Faxalven	62	G5
Faya-Largeau	102	C4
Fayetteville *Arkansas*	128	E2
Fayetteville *N. Carolina*	129	N3
Fayetteville *Tennessee*	129	J3
Faylaka	97	J2
Fazilka	92	D2
Fderik	100	C4
Feale	59	D8
Fear, Cape	129	P4
Feather	122	D8
Featherston	115	E4
Fecamp	64	D4
Fedorovka	84	Ad6
Fedulki	84	Ae4
Feeagh, Lough	58	C5
Fegu	87	L4
Fehmarn	70	D1
Fehmer Boelt	70	D1
Feijo	136	C5
Feilding	115	E4
Feira de Santana	137	K6
Feistritz	68	E2
Fei Xian	87	M4
Feke	77	F4
Feklistova, Ostrov	85	P5
Felahiye	77	F3
Felanitx	67	H3
Feldbach	68	E2
Feldberg	68	A2
Feldkirch	68	B2
Feldkirchen	68	E2
Felipe Carillo Puerto	131	Q8
Felix, Cape	120	G4
Felixstowe	53	J3
Felling	55	H2
Feltre	68	C2
Femer Balt	63	D9
Femund	63	D5
Fener Burun	77	H2
Fengcheng	87	M6
Fengdu	93	L3
Fenggang	93	L3
Fengjie	93	L2
Fengning	87	M3
Fengshan	93	L4
Fengtai	93	N2
Fengxian	93	N3
Fengzhen	87	L3
Fen He	87	L4
Feni Island	114	E2
Fenoarivo Atsinanana	109	J3
Fens, The	53	H2
Fenxi	87	L4
Fenyang	87	L4
Fenyi	93	M3
Feodosiya	79	F6
Feolin Ferry	57	B5
Ferbane	59	G6
Ferdows	95	P4
Fergana	86	B3
Fergus Falls	124	B3
Fergusson Island	114	E3
Ferkessedougou	104	D4
Fermanagh	58	G4
Fermo	68	D4
Fermoy	59	F8
Fernandina Beach	129	M5
Fernandina, Isla	136	A7
Fernando de Noronha, Isla	48	E5
Ferness	56	E3
Fernie	122	G3
Ferns	59	K7
Ferrai	75	J2
Ferrans	59	J6
Ferrara	68	C3
Ferrat, Cap	67	F5
Ferreira do Alentejo	66	B3
Ferrenafe	136	B5
Ferriday	128	G5
Ferrol, Peninsula de	136	B5
Ferto	68	F2
Fes	100	D2
Fessenden	123	Q4
Fetesti	73	J3
Fethaland, Point of	56	A1
Fethiye	76	C4
Fethiye Korfezi	76	C4
Fetisovo	79	J7
Fetlar	56	B1
Fetsund	63	D7
Fetzara El Hadjar	69	A7
Feurs	65	F6
Fevralskoye	85	N6
Feyzabad	92	D1
Ffestiniog	52	D2
Fianarantsoa	109	J4
Fiandberg	62	G4
Fichtel-gebirge	70	D3
Ficksburg	108	E5
Fidenza	68	C3
Fier	74	E2
Fife Ness	57	F4
Figeac	65	E6
Figline Valdarno	68	C4
Figueira da Foz	66	B2
Figueira de Castelo Rodrigo	66	C2
Figueres	67	H1
Figuig	100	E2
Figuiro dos Vinhos	66	B3
Fiji	114	Q8
Filadelfia	138	D4
Filby	53	J2
Filchner Ice Shelf	141	X3
Filey	55	J2
Filey Bay	55	J2
Filiasi	73	G3
Filiatra	75	F4
Filipow	71	K1
Filipstad	63	F7
Fillmore *California*	126	C3
Fillmore *Utah*	126	F1
Fimi	106	C3
Finale Emilia	68	C3
Final, Punta	126	E6
Findhorn	56	E3
Findik	77	G3
Findikli	77	J2
Findikpinari	76	F4
Findlay	124	J6
Fingoe	109	F3
Finike	76	D4
Finisterre, Cabo	66	B1
Finke *Australia*	113	G4
Finke *Australia*	113	H4
Finland	63	L6
Finland, Gulf of	63	L7
Finnmark	62	L1
Finnmarksvidda	62	K2
Finnsnes	62	M2
Finschhafen	114	D3
Finsteraarhorn	68	B2
Finstown	56	E1
Fintona	58	H4
Fionn Loch	56	C3
Fionnphort	57	B4
Firat	77	H3
Firedrake Lake	119	Q3
Firenze	68	C4
Firle Beacon	53	H4
Firozabad	92	E3
Firozpur	92	D2
Firsovo	88	J2
Firuzabad	95	L7
Firuzkuh	95	L4
Fish	108	C4
Fisher, Cape	120	K5
Fishguard	52	C3
Fismes	64	E4
Fitchburg	125	Q5
Fitful Head	56	A2
Fitsitika	109	H4
Fitzgerald	129	L5
Fitz Roy	139	C9
Fitzroy	112	F2
Fitz Roy, Cerro	139	B9
Fitzroy Crossing	112	F2
Fitzwilliam Strait	120	C2
Fiuggi	69	D5
Fiume	72	C3
Fiumicino	69	D5
Fivemiletown	58	H4
Fizi	107	E3
Fjallasen	62	J3
Fladdabister	56	A2
Flagstaff	126	G3
Flakatrask	62	H4
Flamborough	55	J2
Flamborough Head	55	J2
Flaming	70	E3
Flaming Gorge Reservoir	123	K7
Flamingo	129	M8
Flash	55	H3
Flasjon	62	F4
Flathead	122	G3
Flathead Lake	122	G4
Flathead Range	122	G3
Flattery, Cape	122	B3
Fleet	53	G3
Fleetwood	55	F3
Flekkefjord	63	B7
Flen	63	G7
Flensburg	70	C1
Flers	64	C4
Flesberg	63	C7
Fleurance	65	D7
Flims	68	B2
Flinders Island	113	K6
Flinders Reefs	113	K2
Flin Flon	119	Q5
Flint *U.K.*	55	F3
Flint *Georgia*	129	K5
Flint *Michigan*	124	J5
Flintham	53	G2
Flisa	63	E6
Flix	67	G2
Fliyos	76	E2
Floka	75	F4
Florac	65	E6
Florence *Italy*	68	C4
Florence *Alabama*	129	J3
Florence *Arizona*	126	G4
Florence *Colorado*	127	K1
Florence *Oregon*	122	B6
Florence *S. Carolina*	129	N3
Florencia	136	B3
Florentino Ameghino, Embalse	139	C8
Flores *Brazil*	137	J5
Flores *Guatemala*	132	C6
Flores *Indonesia*	91	G7
Floreshty	79	D6
Flores, Laut	91	F7
Floresta	137	K5
Floriano	137	J5
Florianopolis	138	G5
Florida *Uruguay*	139	E6
Florida *U.S.A.*	129	L6
Florida Islands	114	K6
Florida Keys	129	M8
Florida, Straits of	129	N8
Floridia	69	E7
Florina	75	F2
Floro	63	A6
Flotta	56	E2
Flumen	67	F2
Fly	114	C3
Foca	76	B3
Foca	72	E4
Fochabers	56	E3
Focsani	73	J3
Foggia	69	E5
Fogi	91	H6
Fogo	104	L7
Fogo Island	121	R8
Fohr	70	C1
Foinaven	56	D2
Foix	65	D7
Folda	62	F3
Folegandros	75	H4
Foligno	69	D4
Folkestone	53	J3
Folkingham	53	G2
Folkston	129	L5
Follonica	69	C4
Foltesti	73	K3
Fond-du-Lac *Canada*	119	Q4
Fond du Lac *U.S.A.*	124	F5
Fonni	69	B5
Fonsagrada	66	C1
Fonseca, Golfo de	132	D8
Fontainebleau	64	E4
Fonte Boa	136	D4
Fonte do Pau-d'Agua	136	F6
Fontenay-le-Comte	65	C5
Font-Romeu	65	E7
Fontur	62	X11
Fonualei	111	U5
Fonyod	72	D2
Foraker, Mount	118	E3
Forbes	113	K5
Forcados	105	G4
Forcalquier	65	F7
Forde	63	A6
Fordham	53	H2
Fordon	71	H2
Ford Ranges	141	Q3
Fordyce	128	F4
Forecariah	104	C4
Foreland Point	52	D3
Forel, Mount	116	R2
Forest *Canada*	124	K5
Forest *U.S.A.*	128	H4
Forestier Peninsula	113	K7
Forest Park	129	K4
Forestville	125	R2
Forez, Monts du	65	E6
Forfar	57	F4
Forgandenny	57	E4
Fork	123	K5
Forks	122	B4
Forli	68	D3
Formartin	56	F3
Formby	55	F3
Formby Point	55	F3
Formentera	67	G3
Formentor, Cabo de	67	H3
Formia	69	D5
Formiga	138	G4
Formosa	87	N7
Formosa *Argentina*	138	E5
Formosa *Brazil*	138	G3
Formosa do Rio Preto	137	H6
Foroyar	62	Z14
Forres	56	E3
Forrest	112	F5
Forrest City	128	G3
Forsayth	113	J2
Forsnas	62	H3
Forsnes	62	C5
Forssa	63	K6
Forsyth *Missouri*	124	D8
Forsyth *Montana*	123	L4
Fort Albany	121	K7
Fortaleza *Bolivia*	136	D5
Fortaleza *Brazil*	137	K4
Fort Archambault	102	C6
Fort Beaufort	108	E6
Fort Benton	123	J4
Fort Bragg	122	C8
Fort Charlet	101	G4
Fort Chipewyan	119	N4
Fort Collins	123	M7
Fort Coulonge	125	M4
Fort-Dauphin	109	J5
Fort-de-France	133	S7
Fort de Polignac	101	G3
Fort Dodge	124	C5
Fortescue	112	D3
Fort Flatters	101	G3
Fort Foureau	105	J3
Fort Frances	124	D2
Fort Franklin	118	L2
Fort Good Hope	118	K2
Forth	57	D4
Fort Hall	107	G3
Fort Hancock	127	K5

G

Name	Page	Ref.
Garachine, Punta	132	H10
Gara, Lough	58	F5
Garanhuns	137	K5
Garara	114	D3
Garberville	122	C7
Garboldisham	53	H2
Garbosh, Kuh-e	95	K5
Garcas	138	F3
Gard	65	F7
Garda, Lago di	68	C3
Gardelegen	70	D2
Garden City	127	M2
Garden Grove	126	C4
Gardez	92	C2
Gardhiki	75	F3
Gardiner	123	J5
Gardnerville	126	C1
Gardno, Jezioro	71	G1
Garelochhead	57	D4
Gareloi Island	118	Ac9
Garessio	68	B3
Garforth	55	H3
Gargalianoi	75	F4
Gargunnock	57	D4
Garies	108	C6
Garissa	107	G3
Garland	128	D4
Garmish-Partenkirchen	70	D5
Garmsar	95	L4
Garnet Bay	120	L4
Garnett	128	E1
Garonne	65	C6
Garoua	105	H4
Garrison Dam	123	P4
Garron Point	58	L2
Garrovillas	66	C3
Garry Lake	119	R2
Garry, Loch	57	D3
Garstang	55	G3
Gartempe	65	D5
Gartocharn	57	D4
Garton Lough	58	G3
Garton-on-the-Wolds	55	J2
Garut	90	D7
Garvagh	58	J3
Garve	56	D3
Garvie Mountains	115	B6
Garwa	92	F4
Garwolin	71	J3
Gary	124	G6
Gar Zangbo	92	F2
Garze	93	J2
Garzon	136	B3
Gasan Kuli	95	L3
Gascogne	65	D7
Gascogne, Golfe de	65	C7
Gasconade	124	D8
Gascoyne	112	C3
Gascuna, Golfo de	67	F1
Gasht	95	Q8
Gashua	105	H3
Gask	95	P5
Gasmata	114	E3
Gaspar, Selat	90	D6
Gaspe	121	P8
Gaspe, Cape	121	P8
Gaspe Peninsula	121	N8
Gastonia	129	M3
Gaston, Lake	129	N2
Gastouni	75	F4
Gastre	139	C8
Gata, Cabo de	66	E4
Gatas, Akra	76	E5
Gata, Sierra de	66	C2
Gatchina	63	P7
Gatehouse of Fleet	54	E2
Gateshead	55	H2
Gateshead Island	119	Q1
Gatineau	125	N3
Gatooma	108	E3
Gatruyeh	95	M7
Gatun Lake	132	H10
Gatvand	94	J5
Gatwick	53	G3
Gaud-i-Zureh	95	R7
Gauer Lake	119	R4
Gauhati	93	H3
Gauja	63	L8
Gauldalen	62	D5
Gausta	63	C7
Gavater	95	Q9
Gavbus, Kuh-e	95	L8
Gavdhopoula	75	G5
Gavdhos	75	H5
Gaviao	66	C3
Gav Koshi	95	N7
Gavle	63	G6
Gavleborg	63	G6
Gavrilov-Yam	78	F4
Gawler	113	H5
Gawler Ranges	113	H5
Gaxun Nur	86	J3
Gaya	92	G4
Gaya La	92	F3
Gaydon	53	F2
Gayndah	113	L4
Gaysin	73	K1
Gayvoron	79	D6
Gaza	94	B6
Gazelle Peninsula	114	E2
Gazelle, Recif de la	114	W16
Gaziantep	77	G4
Gazimur	85	K6
Gazimurskiy Zavod	85	K6
Gazipasa	76	E4
Gbarnga	104	D4
Gboko	105	G4
Gdansk	71	H1
Gdov	63	M7
Geary	56	B3
Gebeit	96	C7
Gebze	76	C2
Gecitli	77	K4
Gedaref	103	G5
Gediz *Turkey*	76	B3
Gediz *Turkey*	76	C3
Gedney Hill	53	G2
Gedser	70	D1
Gee	64	F3
Geelong	113	J6
Geelvink Channel	112	C4
Geeveston	113	K7
Gegyai	92	F2
Geikie	119	Q4
Geilo	63	C6
Geita	107	F3
Geitlandsjokull	62	U12
Gejiu	93	K4
Geka, Mys	85	X4
Gela	69	E7
Geladi	103	J6
Gelendost	76	D3
Gelendzhik	79	F7
Gelibolu	76	B2
Gelibolu Yarimadasi	75	J2
Gelligaer	52	D3
Gelnhausen	70	C3
Gelsenkirchen	70	B3
Gemena	106	C2
Gemerek	77	G3
Gemlik	76	C2
Gemlik Korfezi	75	K2
Gemona del Friuli	68	D2
Gemund	70	B3
Genale Wenz	103	H6
Genc	77	J3
Geneina	102	D5
General Acha	139	D7
General Alvear	139	C7
General Bernardo O'Higgins	141	W6
General Conesa	139	D8
General La Madrid	139	D7
General Lavalle	139	E7
General Madariaga	139	E7
General Paz	139	E7
General Paz, Lago	139	B8
General Pico	139	D7
General Roca	139	C7
General Sam Martin	141	V5
General Santos	91	H4
General Villegas	139	D7
Geneseo	125	M5
Genessee	125	L5
Geneva *Switzerland*	68	A2
Geneva *U.S.A.*	125	M5
Geneva, Lake of	68	A2
Geneve	68	A2
Gen He	87	N1
Genichesk	79	E6
Genil	66	D4
Gennargentu, Monti del	69	B6
Genoa *Australia*	113	K6
Genoa *Italy*	68	B3
Genova	68	B3
Genova, Golfo di	68	B3
Genovesa, Isla	136	B7
Genriyetty, Ostrov	81	S2
Gent	64	E3
Genteng	90	D7
Genyem	91	L6
Geographe Bay	112	D5
Geographe Channel	112	C3
Geokchay	79	H7
George *Canada*	121	N6
George *South Africa*	108	D6
Georgeham	52	C3
George Island	139	E10
George, Lake	129	M6
George Sound	115	A6
Georgetown *Australia*	113	H5
George Town *Australia*	113	K7
Georgetown *Gambia*	104	C3
Georgetown *Grand Cayman, U.K.*	132	G5
Georgetown *Guyana*	136	F2
George Town *Malaysia*	90	C4
Georgetown *U.S.A.*	129	N4
George V Land	141	K4
George VI Sound	141	V4
Georgia	77	K1
Georgia	129	K4
Georgian Bay	125	K4
Georgia, Strait of	122	C3
Georgina	113	H3
Georgina Bay	121	K8
Georgiyevka	86	E2
Georgiyevsk	79	G7
Georg von Neumayer	141	Z4
Gera	70	D3
Geral de Goias, Serra	137	H6
Geraldine	115	C6
Geraldton *Australia*	112	C4
Geraldton *U.S.A.*	124	G2
Gerardmer	64	G4
Gerasimovka	84	A5
Gercus	77	J4
Gerede *Turkey*	76	E2
Gerede *Turkey*	76	E2
Gereshk	92	B2
Gergal	66	E4
Gerger	77	H4
Gerik	90	C4
Geris	76	D4
Gerlachovsky	71	J4
Germany	70	C3
Germencik	76	B4
Germi	94	J2
Germiston	108	E5
Gerona	67	H2
Gerrards Cross	53	G3
Gerze	76	F2
Geseke	70	C3
Geta	63	G6
Getafe	66	E2
Gettysburg *Pennsylvania*	125	M7
Gettysburg *S. Dakota*	123	Q5
Geumapang	90	B5
Gevan	95	N8
Gevas	77	K3
Geyik Dagi	76	E4
Geyik Daglari	76	E4
Geyve	76	D2
Gezi	77	F3
Ghadamis	101	G2
Ghaghara	92	F3
Ghana	104	E4
Ghanzi	108	D4
Gharah, Wadi	97	L8
Gharbi, Al Hajar al	97	N4
Gharbiya, Es Sahra el	103	E2
Ghardaia	101	F2
Ghardimaou	69	B7
Gharrat, Shatt al	94	H6
Gharyan	101	H2
Ghat	101	H3
Ghatampur	92	F3
Ghatere	114	J5
Ghayl Ba Wazir	97	J9
Ghayl Bin Yumayn	97	J9
Ghazaouet	100	E1
Ghaziabad	92	E3
Ghazipur	92	F3
Ghazni	92	C2
Gheorgheni	73	H2
Ghimes-Faget	73	J2
Ghisonaccia	69	B4
Ghisoni	69	B4
Ghubbah	97	P10
Ghubeish	102	E5
Ghudaf, Wadi al	94	E5
Ghurian	95	Q4
Giant's Causeway Head	58	J2
Giarre	69	E7
Gibostad	62	H2
Gibraltar	66	D4
Gibraltar Point	55	K3
Gibraltar, Strait of	66	D5
Gibson Desert	112	E3
Gichgeniy Nuruu	86	H2
Gidole	103	G6
Gien	65	E5
Giesecke Isfjord	120	Q3
Giessen	70	C3
Gifatin	96	A3
Gifford Creek	112	D3
Gifhorn	70	D2
Gifu	89	F8
Giganta, Sierra de la	130	D5
Gigha Island	57	C5
Gigha, Sound of	57	C5
Giglio, Isola di	69	C4
Gijon	66	D1
Gijunabena Islands	114	J5
Gila	126	F4
Gila Bend	126	F4
Gilan Garb	94	G4
Gilbert	113	J2
Gilbert Islands	111	R2
Gilbert, Mount	122	B2
Gilbues	137	H5
Gile	109	G3
Gilford	58	K4
Gilgandra	113	K5
Gilgit	92	D1
Gillam	119	S4
Gillen, Mount	113	G3
Gillesnuole	62	G4
Gillespie Point	115	B5
Gillette	123	M5
Gillian Lake	120	L4
Gillingham	53	H3
Gill, Lough	58	F4
Gilroy	126	B2
Giluwe, Mount	114	C3
Gimli	123	R2
Gimo	63	H6
Gimone	65	D7
Ginda	96	D9
Gingin	112	D5
Ginir	103	H6
Gioia del Colle	69	F5
Gioia, Golfo di	69	E6
Giona	75	G3
Girardot	136	C3
Girdle Ness	57	F3
Giresun	77	H2
Girga	103	F2
Girgir, Cape	114	C2
Giridih	92	G4
Girifalco	69	F6
Gironde	65	C6
Girvan	57	D5
Gisborne	115	G3
Gisenye	107	E3
Gislaved	63	E8
Gisors	64	D4
Gitega	107	E3
Giurgeni	73	J3
Giurgiu	73	H4
Givet	64	F3
Givors	65	F6
Gizhiginskaya Guba	85	T4
Gizol	114	H6
Gizycko	71	J1
Gjesvar	62	L1
Gjirokaster	75	F2
Gjoa Haven	120	G4
Gjovik	63	D6
Gjuhezes, Kep i	74	E2
Glace Bay	121	Q8
Glacier Bay	118	H4
Glacier Peak	122	D3
Gladstone *Australia*	113	L3
Gladstone *U.S.A.*	124	G4
Glama	63	D6
Glamis	57	E4
Glamoc	72	D3
Glarus	68	B2
Glasdrumman	58	L4
Glasgow *U.K.*	57	D5
Glasgow *Kentucky*	124	H8
Glasgow *Montana*	123	L3
Glas Maol	57	E4
Glass	56	D3
Glass, Loch	56	D3
Glastonbury	52	E3
Glatz	71	G3
Glauchau	70	E3
Glazov	78	J4
Glda	71	G2
Gleiwitz	71	H3
Glen Affric	56	D3
Glenan, Iles de	65	B5
Glenavy	115	C6
Glen Cannich	56	D3
Glen Canyon	126	G2
Glen Canyon Dam	126	G2
Glencarse	57	E4
Glen Coe	57	D4
Glencoe	108	F5
Glen Cove	125	P6
Glendale *Arizona*	126	F4
Glendale *California*	126	C3
Glendive	123	M4
Glenelg *Australia*	113	J6
Glenelg *U.K.*	56	C3
Glen Esk	57	F4
Glenfinnan	57	C4
Glengad Head	58	H2
Glen Garry *Highland, U.K.*	57	C3
Glen Garry *Tayside, U.K.*	57	D4
Glen Innes	113	L4
Glen Mor	57	D3
Glen Moriston	57	D3
Glennallen	118	F3
Glen Orrin	56	D3
Glenrothes	57	E4
Glens Falls	125	P5
Glenshee	57	E4
Glentham	55	J3
Glenwood	128	F3
Glenwood Springs	123	L8
Glin	59	D7
Glina	72	D3
Glittertind	63	C6
Gliwice	71	H3
Gllave	74	E2
Globe	126	G4
Glockner, Gross	68	D2
Glogau	70	G3
Glogow	70	G3
Glomach, Falls of	56	C3
Glomfjord	62	E3
Glommerstrask	62	H4
Glossop	55	H3
Glottof, Mount	118	E4
Gloucester *Australia*	113	L5
Gloucester *Papua New Guinea*	114	D3
Gloucester *U.K.*	52	E3
Gloucester *U.S.A.*	125	Q5
Gloucestershire	52	E3
Gloup	56	A1
Glover Reef	132	D6
Glowno	71	H3
Glubczyce	71	G3
Glubinnoye	88	E2
Glubokoye *Belarus*	63	M9
Glubokoye *Kazakhstan*	84	C6
Gluckstadt	70	C2
Glukhov	79	E5
Glyadyanskoye	84	Ae6
Glybokaya	73	H1
Glyder Fawr	54	E3
Gmelinka	79	H5
Gmund	68	D2
Gmunden	68	D2
Gnalta	113	J5
Gnarp	63	G5
Gniezno	71	G2
Gnoien	70	E2
Gnosall	52	E2
Goa	92	D5
Goalpara	93	H3
Goatfell	57	C5
Goba	103	H6

Gobabis 108 C4
Gobi 87 K3
Gobo 89 E9
Gochas 108 C4
Godafoss 62 W12
Godalming 53 G3
Godavari 92 F5
Godbout 125 S2
Goderich 125 K5
Godhavn 120 R4
Godhra 92 D4
Godollo 72 E2
Gods 119 S4
Godshill 53 F4
Gods Lake 119 S5
Godthab 120 R5
Godwin Austen 92 E1
Goeland, Lac au 121 L8
Goes 64 E3
Gogama 125 K3
Goginan 52 D2
Gogland, Ostrov 63 M6
Gogolin 71 H3
Goiana 137 L5
Goiania 138 G3
Goias *Brazil* 138 F3
Goias *Brazil* 137 H6
Gojome 88 H6
Gokceada 76 A2
Gokcekaya Baraji 76 D2
Gokdere 77 G2
Gokirmak 76 F2
Gokova Korfezi 76 B4
Goksu *Turkey* 76 E4
Goksu *Turkey* 77 F4
Goksun 77 G3
Goktas 77 J2
Goktepe 76 E4
Gol 63 C6
Golaghat 93 H3
Golam Head 59 C6
Golashkerd 95 N8
Golbasi *Turkey* 76 E3
Golbasi *Turkey* 77 G4
Golcar 55 H3
Golchikha 84 C2
Golconda 122 F7
Golcuk 76 C2
Golcuk Daglari 76 B3
Goldap 71 K1
Gold Coast 113 L4
Golden 122 F2
Golden Bay 115 D4
Goldendale 122 D5
Golden Hinde 122 B3
Goldsboro 129 P3
Goldsworthy 112 D3
Gole 77 K2
Golebert 77 K2
Goleniow 70 F2
Golfito 132 F10
Golfo Aranci 69 B5
Golgeli Daglari 76 C4
Golhisar 76 C4
Golija Planina 72 F4
Golkoy 77 G2
Golmarmara 76 B3
Golmud 93 H1
Golo 69 B4
Golova 76 D4
Golovanevsk 73 L1
Golovnino 88 K4
Golpayegan 95 K5
Golpazari 76 D2
Goma 107 E3
Gombe 105 H3
Gombi 105 H3
Gomera 100 B3
Gomez Palacio 127 L8
Gomishan 95 M3
Gonaives 133 L5
Gonam *Russia* 85 M5
Gonam *Russia* 85 N5
Gonave, Golfe de la 133 L5
Gonave, Ile de la 133 L5
Gonbad-e Kavus 95 M3
Gonda 92 F3
Gondal 92 D4
Gonder 103 G5
Gondia 92 F4
Gonen *Turkey* 76 B2
Gonen *Turkey* 76 B3
Gongbogyamda 93 H3
Gongolo 105 H3
Gongpoquan 86 H3
Goniadz 71 K2
Gonumillo 139 C8
Gonzales *California* 126 B2
Gonzales *Texas* 128 D6
Gonzales Chaves 139 D7
Goob Weyn 107 H3
Goodenough, Cape 141 J5
Goodenough Island 114 E3
Good Hope, Cape of 108 C6
Gooding 122 G6
Goodland 123 P8
Goole 55 J3
Goolgowi 113 K5
Goomen 113 L4
Goondiwindi 113 L4
Goose Bay 121 P7
Goose Creek 129 M4
Goose Lake 122 D7
Goplo, Jezioro 71 H2
Goppingen 70 C4
Gora Kalwaria 71 J3
Gorakhpur 92 F3
Gorazde 72 E4
Gorda, Punta 138 B3
Gordes 76 C3
Gordonsville 125 L7
Gore 115 B7
Gore 103 G6
Gorele 77 H2
Goresbridge 59 J7
Gorey *Ireland* 59 K7
Gorey *U.K.* 53 M7
Gorgan 95 M3
Gorgan, Rud-e 95 M3
Gorgona, Isola di 68 B4
Gorgoram 105 H3
Gori 77 L1
Gorice 75 F2
Gorinchem 64 F3
Goris 94 H2
Gorizia 68 D3
Gorka 78 H3
Gorkha 92 F3
Gorki *Belarus* 78 E5
Gorki *Russia* 84 Ae3
Gorki *Russia* 78 H4
Gorkovskoye Vodokhranilishche 78 G4
Gorlev 63 D9
Gorlice 71 J4
Gorlitz 70 F3
Gornji Milanovac 72 F3
Gornji Vakuf 72 D4
Gorno-Altaysk 84 D6
Gornozavodsk 88 H2
Gornyak 84 C6
Gornyy *Russia* 79 H5
Gornyy *Russia* 85 P6
Gorodenka 73 H1
Gorodets 78 G4
Gorodok 71 K4
Gorodovikovsk 79 G6
Goroka 114 D3
Gorokhov 71 L3
Gorong, Kepulauan 91 J6
Gorongoza 109 F3
Gorontalo 91 G5
Goroshikha 84 D3
Gorran Haven 52 C4
Gorseinon 52 C3
Gort 59 E6
Gortaclare 58 H3
Gortahork 58 F2
Gorumna Island 59 C6
Goryn 79 D5
Gorzow Wielkopolski 70 F2
Goschen Strait 114 E4
Gosforth 55 H1
Goshogawara 88 H5
Gospic 72 C3
Gosport 53 F4
Gostivar 73 F5
Gota 62 Z14
Gota Kanal 63 G7
Gotaland 63 E8
Goteborg 63 H8
Goteborg Och Bohus 63 D7
Gotene 63 E7
Gotha 70 D3
Gothenburg 63 D8
Gotland 63 H8
Goto-retto 89 B9
Gotse Delchev 73 G5
Gotska Sandon 63 H7
Gotsu 89 D8
Gottingen 70 C3
Gottwaldov 71 G4
Gouda 64 F2
Goudhurst 53 H3
Gough Island 48 F6
Gouin, Reservoir 125 N2
Goulais 124 J3
Goulburn 113 K5
Goulburn Islands 113 G1
Goundam 100 E5
Gourdon 65 D6
Goure 101 H6
Gourma-Rharous 100 E5
Gournay 64 D4
Gourock 57 D5
Govena, Mys 85 V5
Goverla 71 L4
Governador Valadares 138 H3
Governor's Harbour 132 J2
Govind Pant Sagar 92 F4
Govorovo 85 M2
Gowanbridge 115 D4
Gowanda 125 L5
Gower 52 C3
Gowna, Lough 58 G5
Goya 138 E5
Goynucek 77 F2
Goynuk *Turkey* 76 D2
Goynuk *Turkey* 77 J3
Goz Beida 102 D5
Gozne 76 F4
Gozo 74 C4
Goz Regeb 96 B8
Graaff Reinet 108 D6
Gracac 72 C3
Gradaus, Serra dos 137 G5
Grado *Italy* 68 D3
Grado *Spain* 66 C1
Gradoli 69 C4
Gradsko 73 F5
Grafham Water 53 G2
Grafton *Australia* 113 L4
Grafton *N. Dakota* 123 R3
Grafton *W. Virginia* 125 K7
Grafton, Islas 139 B10
Graham 128 C4
Graham Island *British Columbia, Canada* 118 J5
Graham Island *NW. Territories, Canada* 120 H2
Graham Land 141 V5
Grahamstown 108 E6
Graie, Alpi 68 A3
Graiguenamanagh 59 J7
Grain 53 H3
Grajau 137 H4
Grajewo 71 K2
Grampian 56 E3
Grampian Mountains 57 D4
Grampound 52 C4
Gramsh 75 F2
Gran 137 F3
Granada *Nicaragua* 132 E9
Granada *Spain* 66 E4
Granard 58 H5
Gran Bajo 139 C9
Granby *Canada* 125 P4
Granby *U.S.A.* 123 L7
Gran Canaria 100 B3
Gran Chaco 138 D4
Grand *Canada* 125 K5
Grand *Michigan* 124 H5
Grand *Missouri* 124 C6
Grand *S. Dakota* 123 P5
Grand Bahama 132 H1
Grand Bois, Coteau de 124 C3
Grand Canal *China* 87 M5
Grand Canal *Ireland* 59 H6
Grand Canyon *U.S.A.* 126 F2
Grand Canyon *U.S.A.* 126 F2
Grand Cayman 132 G5
Grand Coulee 122 E4
Grand Coulee Dam 122 E4
Grande *Brazil* 138 G4
Grande *Mexico* 131 L9
Grande *Nicaragua* 132 E8
Grande, Bahia 139 C10
Grande Cache 119 M5
Grande, Cienaga 133 K10
Grande Comore 109 H2
Grande Miquelon 121 Q8
Grande O'Guapay 138 D3
Grande Prairie 119 M4
Grande, Punta 137 G3
Grande, Rio 127 M6
Grande Ronde 122 F5
Gran Desierto 126 E5
Grandes Rocques 53 M7
Grand Falls *New Brunswick, Canada* 125 S3
Grand Falls *Newfoundland, Canada* 121 Q8
Grand Forks 123 R4
Grand Island 123 Q7
Grand Isle 128 H6
Grand Junction 127 H1
Grand Lahou 104 E4
Grand Lake *New Brunswick, Canada* 128 G6
Grand Lake *Newfoundland, Canada* 121 Q8
Grand Lake *U.S.A.* 125 S3
Grand Lake O' the Cherokees 128 E2
Grand-Lieu, Lac de 65 C5
Grand Manan Island 125 S4
Grand Marais *Michigan* 124 H3
Grand Marais *Minnesota* 124 E3
Grand-Mere 125 P3
Grandola 66 B3
Grand Popo 105 F4
Grand Prairie 128 D4
Grand Rapids *Canada* 119 R5
Grand Rapids *Michigan* 124 H5
Grand Rapids *Minnesota* 124 D3
Grandrieu 65 E6
Grand Saint Bernard, Col du 68 A3
Grand Santi 137 G3
Graney, Lough 59 E7
Grangemouth 57 E4
Grange-over-Sands 55 G2
Grangesberg 63 F6
Grangeville 122 F5
Granite Peak 123 K5
Granitola, Capo 69 D7
Granna 63 F7
Granollers 67 H2
Gran Pajonal 136 C6
Gran Paradiso 68 A3
Grantham 53 G2
Grant Island 141 R4
Grant, Mount 122 E8
Grantown-on-Spey 56 E3
Grants 127 J3
Grantshouse 57 F4
Grants Pass 122 C6
Granville 64 C4
Granville Lake 119 Q4
Grasby 55 J3
Gras, Lac de 119 N3
Grasmere 55 F2
Graso 63 H6
Grasse 65 G7
Grassrange 123 K4
Grass Valley 122 D8
Grassy 113 J7
Grassy Knob 125 K7
Gratens 65 D7
Graus 67 G1
Gravatai 138 F5
Gravdal 62 E2
Gravelines 64 E3
Grave, Pointe de 65 C6
Gravesend 53 H3
Gravois, Pointe-a- 133 L5
Gray 65 F5
Grayling 124 H4
Grays 53 H3
Grays Harbor 122 B4
Graz 68 E2
Great Abaco 132 J1
Great Artesian Basin 113 J4
Great Astrolabe Reef 114 R9
Great Australian Bight 112 F5
Great Ayton 55 H2
Great Baddow 53 H3
Great Bahama Bank 132 H2
Great Bardfield 53 H3
Great Barrier Island 115 E2
Great Barrier Reef 113 K2
Great Basin 122 F7
Great Bear Lake 119 L2
Great Bend 127 N1
Great Blasket Island 59 A8
Great Budworth 55 G3
Great Cumbrae 57 D5
Great Dividing Range 113 K3
Great Driffield 55 J2
Great Dunmow 53 H3
Greater Antarctica 141 D2
Greater Antilles 132 G4
Greater Khingan Range 87 N2
Greater London 53 G3
Greater Manchester 55 G3
Great Exuma Island 132 K3
Great Falls 122 J4
Great Fish 108 E6
Great Gable 55 F2
Great Guana Cay 132 J2
Great Harwood 55 G3
Great Inagua 133 L4
Great Indian Desert 92 D3
Great Island 59 F9
Great Karas Berg 108 C5
Great Karoo 108 D6
Great Lakes 143 L3
Great Longton 55 H2
Great Malvern 52 E2
Great Mercury Island 115 E2
Great Nicobar 93 H7
Great North East Channel 114 C3
Great Ormes Head 54 F3
Great Ouse 53 H2
Great Papuan Plateau 114 C3
Great Plains 123 J2
Great Ruaha 107 G4
Great Sacandaga Lake 125 N5
Great Salt Lake 122 H7
Great Salt Lake Desert 122 H7
Great Sand Hills 123 K2
Great Sandy Desert 112 E3
Great Sankey 55 G3
Great Sea Reef 114 R8
Great Sitkin Island 118 Ac9
Great Slave Lake 119 N2
Great Smeaton 55 H2
Great Stour 53 J3
Great Sugar Loaf 59 K6
Great Torrington 52 C4
Great Victoria Desert 112 F4
Great Wall of China, The 87 L4
Great Whernside 55 H2
Great Witley 52 E2
Great Yarmouth 53 J2
Great Yeldham 53 H2
Great Zab 94 F3
Gredos, Sierra de 66 D2
Greece 75 F3
Greeley 123 M7
Greely Fjord 120 K1
Green *Kentucky* 124 G8
Green *Wyoming* 123 J6
Green Bay *U.S.A.* 124 G4
Green Bay *U.S.A.* 124 G4
Green Bell, Ostrov 80 H1
Greenbrier 125 K8
Greencastle 58 K4
Greeneville 129 L2
Greenfield 125 P5
Green Hammerton 55 H2
Greenhead 55 G2
Green Island 115 C6
Greenisland 58 L3
Green Islands 114 E2
Greenland 116 Q1
Greenlaw 57 F4
Greenlough 112 D4
Greenlowther 57 D5
Green Mountains 125 P5
Greenock 57 D5
Green River *Papua New Guinea* 114 C2
Green River *Utah* 127 G1
Green River *Wyoming* 123 K7
Greensboro 129 N2
Greensburg 125 L6
Greenstone Point 56 C3
Green Valley 126 G5

Greenville *Alabama* 129 J5
Greenville *Liberia* 104 D4
Greenville *Mississippi* 128 G4
Greenville *N. Carolina* 129 P3
Greenville *S. Carolina* 129 L3
Greenville *Texas* 128 D4
Greenwood *Mississippi* 128 G4
Greenwood *S. Carolina* 129 L3
Greers Ferry Lake 128 F3
Gregorio 136 C5
Gregory, Lake 113 H4
Gregory Range 113 J2
Greian Head 57 A3
Greifswald 70 E1
Grein 68 E1
Greipstad 62 H2
Greiz 70 E3
Gremikha 78 F2
Gremyachinsk 78 K4
Grena 63 D8
Grenada 133 S8
Grenada *U.S.A.* 128 H4
Grenadines, The 133 S8
Grenen 63 D8
Grenfell 123 N2
Grenivik 62 V12
Grenoble 65 F6
Grenville, Cape 113 J1
Gresford 55 G3
Gresham 122 C5
Gresik 90 E7
Greta 55 H1
Gretna 55 F2
Grevena 75 F2
Greybull 123 K5
Grey Island 121 Q7
Grey Mare's Tail 57 E5
Greymouth 115 C5
Grey Range 113 J4
Greysteel 58 H2
Greystones 59 K6
Greytown 115 E4
Griefswald Bodden 70 E1
Griffin 129 K4
Griffith 113 K5
Griffith Island 120 G3
Grigoriopol 73 K2
Grimailov 71 M4
Grim, Cape 113 J7
Grimsby 55 J3
Grimsey 62 W11
Grimshaw 119 M4
Grimstad 63 C7
Grindavik 62 T13
Grindsted 63 C9
Gringley on the Hill 55 J3
Grinnell 124 D6
Grinnell Peninsula 120 G2
Grintavec 68 E2
Gris-Nez, Cap 64 D3
Griva 78 J3
Grmec Planina 72 D3
Grobming 68 D2
Grodekovo 88 C3
Grombalia 69 C2
Grong 62 E4
Groningen *Netherlands* 64 G2
Groningen *Suriname* 137 F2
Groot 108 D6
Groote Eylandt 113 H1
Grootfontein 108 C3
Grossa, Ponta 137 H3
Grosseto 69 C4
Grossevichi 88 G1
Gros Ventre Mountains 123 J6
Grottaglie 69 F5
Groundhog 124 J2
Grove 53 J3
Grove City 125 K6
Grove Hill 129 J5
Grover City 126 B3
Groznyy 79 H7
Grudovo 73 J4
Grudziadz 71 H2
Gruinard Bay 56 C3
Gruinart, Loch 57 B5
Grums 63 E7
Grunaw 108 C5
Grunberg 70 F3
Grund 62 U12
Grundarfjordur 62 T12
Grundy 124 J8
Gruznovka 84 H5
Gryazi 79 F5
Gryazovets 78 G4
Gryfice 70 F2
Gryfino 70 F2
Guabito 136 A2
Guacanayabo, Golfo de 132 J4
Guadajoz 66 D4
Guadalajara *Mexico* 130 H7
Guadalajara *Spain* 66 E2
Guadalcanal *Solomon Is.* 114 J6
Guadalcanal *Spain* 66 D3
Guadalete 66 D4
Guadalimar 66 E3
Guadalmez 66 D3
Guadalope 67 F2
Guadalquivir 66 D4
Guadalupe *Mexico* 128 B8
Guadalupe *Mexico* 127 J5
Guadalupe *Spain* 66 D3
Guadalupe *Texas* 128 D6

Guadalupe Mountains 127 K5
Guadalupe, Sierra de 66 D3
Guadalupe Victoria 130 G5
Guadarrama *Spain* 66 D2
Guadarrama *Spain* 66 D2
Guadarrama, Sierra de 66 E2
Guadeloupe 133 S6
Guadeloupe Passage 133 S6
Guadelupe 126 D4
Guadiana 66 C4
Guadiana, Bahia de 132 E3
Guadiana Menor 66 E4
Guadix 66 E4
Guafo, Isla 139 B8
Guainia 136 D3
Guaiquinima, Cerro 136 E2
Guajira, Peninsula de 136 C1
Gualachulian 57 C4
Gualaquiza 136 B4
Gualeguay *Argentina* 138 E6
Gualeguay *Argentina* 138 E6
Gualeguaychu 138 E6
Guam 83 N5
Guama 137 H4
Guamblin, Isla 139 A8
Guampi, Sierra de 136 D2
Guamuchil 130 E5
Gua Musang 90 C5
Guanare *Venezuela* 136 D2
Guanare *Venezuela* 136 D2
Guanay, Sierra 136 D2
Guandi 88 B4
Guangan 93 L2
Guangdong 93 M4
Guanghua 93 M2
Guangnan 93 L4
Guangning 93 M4
Guangping 87 M4
Guangxi 93 L4
Guangyuan 93 L2
Guangze 87 M6
Guangzhou 93 M4
Guanhaes 138 H3
Guanipa 133 R10
Guanoca 136 E1
Guantanamo 133 K4
Guan Xian 93 K2
Guapi 136 B3
Guapiles 132 F9
Guapore 136 E6
Guaqui 138 C3
Guarabira 137 K5
Guarapuava 138 F5
Guara, Sierra de 67 F1
Guarda *Portugal* 66 C2
Guarda *Portugal* 66 C2
Guardo 66 D1
Guarenas 136 D1
Guaribas, Cachoeira 137 G4
Guarico 136 D2
Guasave 130 E5
Guasdualito 136 C2
Guasipati 136 E2
Guastalla 68 C3
Guatemala 132 B7
Guatemala 132 B7
Guaviare 136 D3
Guaxupe 138 G4
Guayaquil 136 B4
Guayaquil, Golfo de 136 A4
Guaymas 126 G7
Guazacapan 132 B7
Guba 103 G5
Guba Dolgaya 84 Ac2
Gubakha 78 K4
Gubbio 68 D4
Gubdor 78 K3
Guben 70 F3
Gucuk 77 G3
Gudar, Sierra de 67 F2
Gudbrandsdalen 63 D6
Gudena 63 C8
Gudur 92 E6
Gudvangen 62 B6
Guekedou 104 C4
Guelma 101 G1
Guelph 125 K5
Guereda 102 D5
Gueret 65 D5
Guernsey *U.K.* 53 M7
Guernsey *U.S.A.* 123 M6
Guerrero Negro 126 E6
Gugu 73 G3
Guhakolak, Tanjung 90 D7
Guia 138 E3
Guide 93 K1
Guider 105 H4
Guidong 93 M3
Guiglo 104 D4
Gui Jiang 93 M4
Guildford 53 G3
Guildtown 57 E4
Guilin 93 M3
Guillestre 65 G6
Guimaraes 66 B2
Guinea 104 C3
Guinea Bissau 104 C3
Guinea, Gulf of 105 F5
Guines 132 F3
Guingamp 64 B4
Guiratinga 138 F3
Guiria 136 E1
Guisanbourg 137 G3
Guisborough 55 H2

Guise 64 E4
Guiseley 55 H3
Guiting Power 53 F3
Guiuan 91 H3
Guixi 87 M6
Gui Xian 93 L4
Guiyang 93 L3
Guizhou 93 L3
Gujarat 92 D4
Gujranwala 92 D2
Gujrat 92 D2
Gulbarga 92 E5
Gulbene 63 M8
Gulcayir 76 D3
Gulcha 86 C3
Gulfport 128 H5
Gulian 87 N1
Gullane 57 F4
Gullfoss 62 V12
Gull Lake 123 K2
Gullspang 63 F7
Gulluk 76 B4
Gulnar 76 E4
Gulpinar 76 B3
Gulsehir 76 F3
Gulyantsi 73 H4
Gumbaz 95 R6
Gummi 105 G3
Gumushacikoy 76 F2
Gumushane 77 H2
Guna 92 E4
Gundagai 113 K6
Gundogmus 76 E4
Gunedidalem 91 H6
Guney 76 C3
Guneydogutoroslar 77 H3
Gungu 106 C4
Gunnedah 113 L5
Gunning 113 K5
Gunnison *Colorado* 127 J1
Gunnison *Colorado* 123 K8
Gunnison *Utah* 126 G1
Guntakal 92 E5
Guntersville 129 J3
Guntersville Lake 129 J3
Guntur 92 F5
Gunungsitoli 90 B5
Gunungsugih 90 D6
Gunzenhausen 70 D4
Gurban Obo 87 L3
Gurbulak 77 L3
Gurdim 95 Q9
Gurdzhaani 79 H7
Gure 76 C3
Gurgaon 92 E3
Gurgei, Jebel 102 D5
Gurghiului, Muntii 73 H2
Gurgueia 137 J5
Gur I Topit 75 F2
Gurpinar 77 K3
Gurue 109 G3
Gurun 77 G3
Gurupa 137 G4
Gurupa, Ilha Grande do 137 G4
Gurupi 137 H4
Gurupi, Serra do 137 H4
Guruzala 92 E5
Gusau 105 G3
Gusev 71 K1
Gushgy 95 R4
Gusinoozersk 84 H6
Gus-Khrustalnyy 78 G4
Gustrow 70 E2
Gusyatin 73 J1
Gutcher 56 A1
Guthrie *Oklahoma* 128 D3
Guthrie *Texas* 127 M4
Gutian 87 M6
Guttenberg 124 E5
Guvem 76 E2
Guyana 136 F2
Guyenne 65 D6
Guymon 127 M2
Guyuan 93 L1
Guzelbag 76 D4
Guzeloluk 76 F4
Guzelsu 77 K3
Guzelyurt 76 F3
Guzman, Laguna de 127 J5
Gvardeysk 71 J1
Gvardeyskoye 73 J1
Gwa 93 H5
Gwabegar 113 K5
Gwadar 92 B3
Gwalior 92 E3
Gwanda 108 E4
Gweebarra Bay 58 F3
Gwelo 108 E3
Gwent 52 E3
Gweru 108 E3
Gwoza 105 H3
Gwydir, 113 K4
Gwynedd 52 D2
Gyandzha 79 H7
Gyangze 93 G3
Gyaring Hu 93 J2
Gydanskaya Guba 84 B2
Gydanskiy Poluostrov 84 B2
Gydnia 71 H1
Gympie 113 L4
Gynymskaya 85 N5
Gyongyos 72 E2
Gyonk 72 E2
Gyor 72 D2

Gypsumville 123 Q2
Gyueshevo 73 G4
Gyula 73 F2
Gyumri 77 K2

H

Haabunga 62 W12
Haapai Group 111 U5
Haapajarvi 62 L5
Haapamaki 63 L5
Haapsalu 63 K7
Haardt 70 B4
Haarlem 64 F2
Haast *New Zealand* 115 B5
Haast *New Zealand* 115 B5
Haast Passage 115 B6
Hab 92 C3
Habawnah, Wadi 96 G8
Habban 96 H9
Habbaniyah 94 F5
Habbaniyah, Hawr al 94 F5
Haberli 77 J4
Habirag 87 M3
Haboro 88 H3
Hachenburg 70 B3
Hachijo-jima 89 G9
Hachiman 89 F8
Hachinohe 88 H5
Hachioji 89 G8
Hacibektas 76 F3
Hacihalil Dagi 77 K2
Haciomer 77 J3
Hackas 62 F5
Hadan, Harrat 96 E6
Hadarah 96 E7
Hadarba, Ras 96 C5
Haddenham 53 H2
Haddington 57 F5
Hadd, Ra's al 97 P5
Hadejia 105 G3
Hadera 94 B5
Haderslev 63 E9
Hadhalil, Al 96 G2
Hadhramawt 97 J9
Hadiboh 97 P10
Hadim 76 E4
Hadleigh 53 H2
Hadley Bay 119 P1
Hadong 93 L4
Hadrian's Wall 57 F5
Hadsund 63 D8
Haeju 87 P4
Hafar al Batin 96 H2
Hafik 77 G3
Hafit 97 M5
Hafnarfjordur 62 U12
Hafratindur 62 U12
Haft Gel 94 J6
Haftqala 95 R4
Hag Abdullah 103 F5
Hagemeister Island 118 A3
Hagen 70 B3
Hagen, Mount 114 C3
Hagerstown 125 M7
Hagfors 63 E6
Haggenas 62 F5
Hagi 89 C9
Ha Giang 93 K4
Hagimas 73 H2
Hagley 53 E2
Hagondange 64 G4
Hags Head 59 D7
Hague, Cap de la 64 C4
Haguenau 64 G4
Haian 93 M4
Haibei 88 A2
Haicheng 87 N3
Hai Duong 93 L4
Haifa 94 B5
Haifeng 87 M7
Haikang 93 M4
Haikou 93 M5
Hail 96 E3
Hailar 87 M2
Hailar He 87 M2
Hailsham 53 H4
Hailun 88 A2
Hailuoto *Finland* 62 L4
Hailuoto *Finland* 63 L2
Hainan Dao 93 M5
Haines 118 H4
Haines City 129 M6
Haiphong 93 L4
Haiti 133 L5
Haivare 114 C3
Haiya 96 C7
Hajarah, Al 96 F2
Hajduboszormeny 73 F2
Hajdunanas 73 F2
Hajiki-saki 89 G6
Hajipur 92 G3
Hajjah 96 F9
Hajjiabad 95 M7
Hajmah 97 N7
Hajr, Wadi 97 J9
Hakataramea 115 C6
Hakkari 77 K4
Hakkas 62 J3
Hakkibey 76 F4
Hakodate 88 H5
Haku-san 89 F7
Hala 92 C3

Name	Page	Grid
Halab	94	C3
Halaban	96	G5
Halabja	94	G4
Halaib	103	G3
Halat Ammar	96	C2
Halaveden	63	F7
Halawa *Hawaii*	126	S10
Halawa *Hawaii*	126	T10
Halba	77	G5
Halberstadt	70	D3
Halcon, Mount	91	G3
Halden	63	D7
Haldensleben	70	D2
Halesowen	53	E2
Halesworth	53	J2
Halfeti	77	G4
Halfin, Wadi	97	N6
Halfmoon Bay	115	B7
Halfway	119	L4
Hali	96	E7
Haliburton Highlands	125	L4
Halifax *Canada*	121	P9
Halifax *U.K.*	55	H3
Halifax Bay	113	K2
Halikarnassos	76	B4
Halileh, Ra's-e	95	K7
Halin	88	B3
Halisah	77	G4
Halitpasa	76	B3
Halkapinar	76	F4
Halkett, Cape	118	E1
Halla	62	G5
Halladale	56	E2
Hallanca	136	B5
Halland	63	E8
Hallandsas	63	E8
Halle	70	C3
Hallefors	63	F7
Hallen	62	F5
Halley	141	Y3
Hallingdal	63	C6
Hallingskarvet	63	B6
Hall Peninsula	120	N5
Halls Creek	112	F2
Hallstavik	63	H6
Hallum	64	F2
Halmahera	91	H5
Halmahera, Laut	91	H6
Halmstad	63	E8
Hals	63	D8
Halsinge-skogen	63	F6
Halsingland	63	G6
Halstead	53	H3
Halton Lea Gate	55	G2
Halul	97	L4
Ham *France*	64	E4
Ham *U.K.*	56	A2
Hamada	89	D8
Hamad, Al	94	D6
Hamadan	94	J4
Hamah	94	C4
Hamam	77	G4
Hamamatsu	89	F8
Hamar	63	D6
Hamata, Gebel	96	B4
Hama-Tombetsu	88	J3
Hambantota	92	F7
Hambleton	55	G3
Hamburg *U.S.A.*	124	C6
Hamburg *Germany*	70	D2
Hamdaman, Dasht-i	95	Q4
Hamd, Wadi al	96	C4
Hame	63	L6
Hameln	70	C2
Hamhung	87	P4
Hami	86	F3
Hamilton	113	H3
Hamilton *Bermuda*	117	N5
Hamilton *Canada*	125	L5
Hamilton *New Zealand*	115	E2
Hamilton *U.K.*	57	D5
Hamilton *Alabama*	129	J3
Hamilton *Montana*	122	G4
Hamilton *Ohio*	124	H7
Hamilton Inlet	121	Q7
Hamim, Wadi al	101	K2
Hamina	63	M6
Hamitabat	76	D4
Hamm	70	B2
Hammar, Hawr al	94	H6
Hammarstrand	62	G5
Hammeenlinna	63	L6
Hammerdal	62	F5
Hammerfest	62	K1
Hammersley Range	112	D3
Hammond *Indiana*	124	G6
Hammond *Louisiana*	128	G5
Hammond *Montana*	123	M5
Hamnavoe	56	A1
Hampden	115	C6
Hampshire	53	F3
Hampshire Downs	53	F3
Hampton *Arkansas*	128	F4
Hampton *S. Carolina*	129	M4
Hampton *Virginia*	125	M8
Hamra , Al Hammadah al	101	H3
Hamrange	63	G6
Hamrin, Jebel	77	L5
Hamun-i Mashkel	92	B3
Hamur	77	K3
Hanahan	114	E3
Hanak	77	K2
Hanalei	126	R9
Hanamaki	88	H6
Hancheng	93	M1
Hancock	125	L7
Handa	89	F8
Handan	87	L4
Handeni	107	G4
Handlova	71	H4
Hanford	126	C2
Hangang	87	P4
Hangayn Nuruu	86	H2
Hanggin Houqi	87	K3
Hanggin Qi	87	K4
Hango	63	K7
Hangzhou	87	N5
Hangzhou Wan	87	N5
Hanhongor	87	J3
Hani	77	J3
Hanifah, Wadi	96	H4
Hanish al Kabir	96	F10
Haniyah, Al	94	H7
Han Jiang	87	M7
Hanko	63	K7
Hanksville	126	G1
Hanna	122	H2
Hannah Bay	121	L7
Hannibal	124	E7
Hann, Mount	112	F2
Hannover	70	C2
Hano-bukten	63	F9
Hanoi	93	L4
Hanover *Canada*	125	K4
Hanover *South Africa*	108	D6
Hanover *U.S.A.*	125	P5
Hanover, Isla	139	B10
Hanpan, Cape	114	E2
Han Pijesak	72	E3
Han Shui	93	M2
Hanson Bay	115	F6
Hanstholm	63	C8
Hantay	86	J2
Hanyuan	93	K3
Hanzhong	93	L2
Haparanda	62	L4
Happisburgh	53	J2
Hapsu	88	B5
Hapur	92	E3
Haql	96	B2
Hara	87	K2
Harad *Saudi Arabia*	97	J4
Harad *Yemen*	96	F8
Harads	62	J3
Haramachi	89	H7
Harare	103	F3
Harasis, Jiddat al	97	N7
Harbin	87	P2
Harbiye	77	G4
Harbour Breton	121	Q8
Harby	53	G2
Hardangerfjord	63	B6
Hardanger-Jokulen	63	B6
Hardangervidda	63	B6
Hardin	123	L5
Hardoi	92	F3
Hardy	128	G2
Hare Bay	121	Q7
Harer	103	H6
Harewood	55	H3
Hargeysa	103	H6
Hargigo	96	D9
Har Hu	93	J1
Harib	96	G9
Haridwar	92	E3
Harihari	115	C5
Harima-nada	89	E8
Harim, Jambal Al	97	N4
Hari-Rud	95	S4
Harjedalen	62	E5
Harlan	124	C6
Harlem	123	K3
Harleston	53	J2
Harlingen	64	F2
Harlow	53	H3
Harlowton	123	K4
Harmancik	76	C3
Harmil	96	E8
Harney Basin	122	D6
Harney Lake	122	E6
Harnosand	62	G5
Haro	66	E1
Haro, Cabo	126	G7
Haroldswick	56	A1
Harpanahalli	92	E6
Harpenden	53	G3
Harper	104	D5
Harper Passage	115	C5
Harpstedt	70	C2
Harrah, Ad	94	D6
Harran	77	H4
Harray, Loch of	56	E1
Harricanaw	125	M2
Harrietsham	53	H3
Harrington	55	F2
Harris	56	B3
Harrisburg *Illinois*	124	F8
Harrisburg *Pennsylvania*	125	M6
Harrismith	108	E5
Harrison	128	F2
Harrison Bay	118	E1
Harrisonburg	125	L7
Harrison, Cape	121	Q7
Harrison Lake	122	D3
Harrisonville	124	C7
Harris Ridge	140	A1
Harris, Sound of	56	A3
Harrogate	55	H3
Harrow	53	G3
Harsit	77	H2
Harstad	62	G2
Harsvik	62	D4
Hart	118	H2
Hartbees	108	D5
Hartberg	68	E2
Harteigen	63	B6
Hartford	125	P6
Harthill	57	E5
Hartkjolen	62	E4
Hartland	52	C4
Hartland Point	52	C3
Hartlepool	55	H2
Hartley	127	L3
Hartola	63	M6
Hartsville	129	M3
Hartwell Reservoir	129	L3
Hartz	108	E5
Harut	97	L8
Harvey *Australia*	112	D5
Harvey *U.S.A.*	124	G6
Harwich	53	J3
Haryana	92	E3
Harz	70	D3
Hasan Dagi	76	F3
Hashish, Ghubbat	97	P6
Haskoy	77	K2
Haslemere	53	G3
Haslingden	55	G3
Hassa	77	G4
Hassan	92	E6
Hassankeyf	77	J4
Hassela	63	L5
Hassi Habadra	101	F3
Hassleholm	63	E8
Hastings *Australia*	113	K7
Hastings *New Zealand*	115	F3
Hastings *U.K.*	53	H4
Hastings *Michigan*	124	H5
Hastings *Nebraska*	123	Q7
Hastveda	63	E8
Hasvik	62	K1
Haswell	55	H2
Hatanbulag	87	K3
Hatchie	128	H3
Hatfield *Hertfordshire, U.K.*	53	G3
Hatfield *S. Yorkshire, U.K.*	55	H3
Hatfield Peverel	53	H3
Hatgal	86	J1
Hathras	92	E3
Hatibah, Ra's	96	D6
Ha Tien	93	K6
Ha Tinh	93	L5
Hatip	76	E4
Hat Island	120	G4
Hato	136	A2
Hatohudo	91	H7
Hatskiy	84	D5
Hatteras, Cape	129	Q3
Hattiesburg	128	H5
Hatton	56	G3
Hattras Passage	93	J6
Hatunsaray	76	E4
Hatuoto	91	H6
Haugesund	63	A7
Haughton	53	E2
Hauhui	114	K6
Haukivesi	62	N5
Haukivuori	63	M5
Hauraha	114	K7
Hauraki Gulf	115	E2
Haut Atlas	100	D2
Hauts Plateaux	100	E2
Havana	124	E6
Havant	53	F4
Havasu	126	F3
Havasu, Lake	126	E3
Havel	70	E2
Havelock North	115	F3
Haverfordwest	52	C2
Haverhill *U.K.*	53	H2
Haverhill *U.S.A.*	125	Q5
Havoysund	62	L1
Havran	76	B3
Havre	123	K3
Havre-Saint-Pierre	121	P7
Havsa	76	B2
Havza	77	F2
Hawaii *U.S.A.*	126	R10
Hawaii *U.S.A.*	126	T11
Hawaya, Al	97	J6
Hawea, Lake	115	B6
Hawera	115	E3
Hawes	55	G2
Haweswater Reservoir	55	G2
Hawick	57	F5
Hawke	121	Q7
Hawke Bay	115	F3
Hawke, Cape	113	L5
Hawkesbury	125	N4
Hawkhurst	53	H3
Hawkinge	53	J3
Hawknest Point	133	K2
Hawnby	55	H2
Hawng Luk	93	J4
Hawra	97	J9
Hawran, Wadi	94	E5
Hawser	55	J2
Hawthorne	126	C1
Haxby	55	H2
Hay *New South Wales, Australia*	113	J5
Hay *Northern Territory, Australia*	113	H3
Hay *Canada*	119	M3
Hayden	123	L7
Hayes	119	R4
Hayes Halvo	120	N2
Hayes, Mount	118	F3
Hayjan	96	G8
Hayl	97	N4
Hayl, Wadi al	77	H5
Haymana	76	E3
Hayrabolu	76	B2
Hay River	119	M3
Hays	96	F10
Hays	123	Q8
Haywards Heath	53	G4
Hazaran, Kuh-e	95	N7
Hazard	124	J8
Hazar Golu	77	H3
Hazaribag	92	G4
Hazaribagh Range	92	F4
Hazar Masjed, Kuh-e	95	P3
Hazel Grove	55	G3
Hazelton *Canada*	118	K4
Hazelton *U.S.A.*	125	N6
Hazen Bay	118	B3
Hazlehurst	128	G5
Hazro	77	J3
Headcorn	53	H3
Head of Bight	112	G5
Healdsburg	126	A1
Healesville	113	K6
Heanor	55	H3
Heard Islands	142	D6
Hearst	124	J2
Hearst Island	141	V5
Heart	123	P4
Heathfield	53	H4
Heathrow	53	G3
Hebbronville	128	C7
Hebden Bridge	55	G3
Hebei	87	M4
Hebel	113	K4
Heber City	122	J7
Hebi	87	L4
Hebrides, Sea of the	57	A4
Hebron *Canada*	121	P6
Hebron *Israel*	94	B6
Hebron *N. Dakota*	123	N4
Hebron *Nebraska*	123	R7
Hecate Strait	118	J5
Hechi	93	L4
Hechuan	93	L2
Heckington	53	G2
Hecla and Griper Bay	120	D2
Hector, Mount	115	E4
Hede	62	E5
Hedland, Port	112	D3
Hedmark	63	D6
Heerenveen	64	F2
Heerlen	64	F3
Hefa	94	B5
Hefei	87	M5
Hefeng	93	M3
Hegang	87	Q2
Hegura-jima	89	F7
Heiban	102	F5
Heide	70	C1
Heidelberg	70	C4
Heidharhorn	62	U12
Heighington	55	H2
Heilbron	108	E5
Heilbronn	70	C4
Heiligenhafen	70	D1
Heiligenstadt	70	D3
Heilong Jiang *China*	88	B2
Heilongjiang *China*	88	D1
Heimaey	62	U13
Heimdal	62	D5
Heinavesi	62	N5
Heinola	63	M6
Heinze Islands	93	J6
Hejing	86	F3
Hekimhan	77	G3
Hel	71	H1
Helagsfjallet	62	E5
Helena *Arkansas*	128	G3
Helena *Montana*	122	J4
Helen Island	91	J5
Helensburgh	57	D4
Helensville	115	E2
Helgoland	70	B1
Helgolander Bucht	70	B1
Heli	88	C2
Heligenblut	68	D2
Helleh	95	K7
Hellin	67	F3
Hell's Mouth	52	C2
Hell-Ville	109	J2
Helmand	95	R6
Helmond	64	F3
Helmsdale *U.K.*	56	E2
Helmsdale *U.K.*	56	E2
Helong	88	B4
Hel, Polwysep	71	H1
Helsingborg	63	E8
Helsingfors	63	L6
Helsingor	63	E8
Helsinki	63	K6
Helston	52	B4
Helvecia	137	K7
Helvellyn	55	F2
Hemel Hempstead	53	G3
Hemsworth	55	H3

I

J

Jague	138 C5
Jahmah	94 G7
Jahrom	95 L7
Jaicos	137 J5
Jailolo	91 H5
Jailolo, Selat	91 H5
Jaipur	92 E3
Jaisalmer	92 D3
Jajarm	95 N3
Jajce	72 D3
Jajpur	92 G4
Jakarta	90 D7
Jakhau	92 C4
Jakobstad	62 K5
Jakupica	73 F5
Jalaid Qi	87 N2
Jalalabad	92 D2
Jalalpur Pirwala	92 D3
Jalapa Mexico	131 L8
Jalapa Mexico	131 N9
Jalasjarvi	62 K5
Jalgaon	92 E4
Jalingo	105 H4
Jalna	92 E5
Jalon	67 F2
Jalor	92 D3
Jalostotitlan	130 H7
Jalpa	130 H7
Jalpaiguri	93 G3
Jalpan	131 K7
Jalu	101 K2
Jam	95 Q4
Jamaica	132 J5
Jamaica Channe	133 K5
Jamalpur Bangladesh	93 G4
Jamalpur India	92 G3
Jamanxim	137 F5
Jamari	136 E5
Jambi	90 C6
James	123 R6
James Bay	121 K7
James Island	136 A7
James Ross, Cape	120 D3
James Ross Island	141 W6
James Ross Strait	120 G4
Jamestown South Africa	108 E6
Jamestown N. Dakota	123 Q4
Jamestown New York	125 L5
Jamjo	63 F8
Jamkhandi	92 E5
Jamkhed	92 E5
Jammerbugten	63 C8
Jammu	92 D2
Jammu and Kashmir	92 E2
Jamnagar	92 D4
Jampur	92 D3
Jamsa	63 L6
Jamshedpur	92 G4
Jamtland	62 F5
Jamuna	93 G3
Janda, Laguna de la	66 D4
Jandaq	95 M4
Jandiatuba	136 D4
Janesville	124 F5
Janjira	92 D5
Jan Mayen	48 F2
Jannatabad	95 Q4
Janos	127 H5
Januaria	138 H3
Janubiyah, Al Badiyah al	94 H6
Jaora	92 E4
Japan	89 G7
Japan, Sea of	88 D6
Japan Trench	142 F3
Japaratuba	137 K6
Japura	136 D4
Jarabulus	94 D3
Jaragua	138 G3
Jaraguari	138 F4
Jarama	66 E2
Jarandilla	66 D2
Jarash	94 B5
Jardee	112 D5
Jardines de la Reina	132 H4
Jari	137 G3
Jarir, Wadi al	96 F4
Jarna	63 G7
Jarnac	65 C6
Jaromer	70 F3
Jaroslaw	71 K3
Jarpen	62 E5
Jarrow	55 H2
Jarruhi	94 J6
Jartai	87 K4
Jarvso	63 G6
Jashpurnagar	92 F4
Jask	95 N9
Jasper Canada	119 M5
Jasper Alabama	129 J4
Jasper Florida	129 L5
Jasper Texas	128 F5
Jassy	73 J2
Jastrebarsko	72 C3
Jastrowie	71 G2
Jastrzebie-Zdroj	71 H4
Jaszbereny	72 E2
Jatai	138 F3
Jatapu	136 F4
Jath	92 E5
Jativa	67 F3
Jatoba	137 G6
Jau	136 E4
Jau	138 G4
Jauaperi	136 E4

Jauja	136 B6
Jaumpur	92 F3
Java	90 E7
Java Trench	142 E5
Javier, Isla	139 B9
Javor	72 E3
Javorniky	71 H4
Jawa	90 D7
Jawa, Laut	90 E7
Jawb, Al	97 K5
Jawhar	107 J2
Jawor	71 G3
Jayanca	136 B5
Java, Puncak	91 K6
Jayapura	91 L6
Jayena	66 E4
Jaypur	92 F5
Jayrud	94 C5
Jaziran, Al	94 E4
Jaz Murian, Hamun-e	95 P8
Jebal Barez, Kuh-e	95 P7
Jebba	105 F4
Jebel, Bahr el	102 F6
Jech Doab	92 D2
Jedburgh	57 F5
Jedeida	69 B7
Jefferson	122 H5
Jefferson City Missouri	124 D7
Jefferson City Tennessee	129 L2
Jefferson, Mount Nevada	122 F8
Jefferson, Mount Oregon	122 D5
Jef Jef el Kebir	102 D3
Jehile Puzak	95 Q6
Jekabp ls	63 L8
Jeldesa	103 H6
Jelenia Gora	70 F3
Jelgava	63 K8
Jelow Gir	94 H5
Jemaja	90 D5
Jember	90 E7
Jeminay	86 F2
Jemnice	70 F4
Jena	70 D3
Jendouba	69 B7
Jenin	94 B5
Jenkins	124 J8
Jennings	128 F5
Jenny Lind Island	119 Q2
Jens Munk Island	120 L4
Jequie	137 J6
Jequitinhonha Brazil	138 H3
Jequitinhonha Brazil	138 H3
Jerada	100 E2
Jerba, Ile de	101 H2
Jeremie	133 K5
Jeremoabo	137 K6
Jerevan	77 L2
Jerez	130 H6
Jerez de la Frontera	66 C4
Jericho Australia	113 K3
Jericho Israel	94 B6
Jerome	122 G6
Jersey	53 M7
Jersey City	125 N6
Jerseyville	124 E7
Jerusalem	94 B6
Jervis Inlet	122 C2
Jeseniky	71 G3
Jessheim	63 D6
Jessore	92 G4
Jesup	129 M5
Jevnaker	63 D6
Jezerce	74 E1
Jeziorak, Jezioro	71 H2
Jeznas	71 L1
Jezzine	94 B5
Jhang Maghiana	92 D2
Jhansi	92 E3
Jhelum Pakistan	92 D2
Jhelum Pakistan	92 D2
Jialing Jiang	93 L2
Jiamusi	88 C2
Jian	93 N3
Jianchuan	93 J3
Jiande	87 M6
Jiange	93 L2
Jiangjin	93 L3
Jiangjunmiao	86 F3
Jiangmen	93 M4
Jiangsu	87 M5
Jiangxi	93 M3
Jianning	87 M6
Jianou	87 M6
Jianquanzi	86 H3
Jianshi	93 L2
Jiaohe	87 P3
Jiaoling	87 M7
Jiaozuo	93 M1
Jia Xian	87 L4
Jiaxing	87 N5
Jiayin	88 C1
Jiayuguan	86 H4
Jiboia	136 D3
Jibou	73 C2
Jibsh, Ra's	97 P5
Jicatuyo	132 C7
Jiddah	96 D6
Jidong	88 C3
Jiekkevarre	62 H2
Jieknaffo	62 G3
Jiesavrre	62 L2
Jihlava Czech Rep.	70 F4
Jihlava Czech Rep.	71 G4

Jijel	101 G1
Jijia	73 J2
Jijiga	103 H6
Jijihu	86 F3
Jilava	73 J3
Jilin China	87 P3
Jilin China	87 P3
Jiloca	67 F2
Jilove	70 F4
Jima	103 G6
Jimba Jimba	112 D4
Jimena de la Frontera	66 D4
Jimenez	127 M6
Jimenez Mexico	128 C8
Jimenez Mexico	127 K7
Jimo	87 N4
Jinan	87 M4
Jincheng	93 M1
Jingbian	87 K4
Jingchuan	93 L1
Jingdezhen	87 M6
Jinghai	87 M4
Jinghe	86 E3
Jinghong	93 K4
Jingle	87 L4
Jingmen	93 M2
Jingpo	88 B3
Jingpo Hu	88 B4
Jingtai	93 K1
Jingxi	93 L4
Jing Xian	93 L3
Jinhua	87 M6
Jining Nei Mongol Zizhiqu, China	87 L3
Jining Shandong, China	87 M4
Jinja	107 F2
Jinkou	87 N4
Jinning	93 K4
Jinotepe	132 D9
Jinsha Jiang	93 J3
Jinta	86 H4
Jinxi	87 N3
Jin Xian	87 N4
Jinzhou	87 N3
Jinzhou Wan	87 N4
Jiparana	136 E5
Jipijapa	136 A4
Jiquilpan	130 H8
Jirriiban	103 J6
Jirueque	66 E2
Jirwan	97 K5
Jishou	93 L3
Jisr ash Shughur	94 C4
Jiu	73 G3
Jiujiang	93 N3
Jiuling Shan	93 M3
Jiutai	87 P3
Jiwa, Al	97 M5
Jiwani	92 B3
Jiwani, Ras	92 B4
Jixi Anhui, China	87 M5
Jixi Heilongjiang, China	87 Q2
Jixian	88 C2
Jizan	96 F8
Jizl, Wadi	96 C3
Jiz, Wadi al	97 K8
Joao Pessoa	137 L5
Joaquin V. Gonzalez	138 D5
Joban	89 H7
Jodar	66 E4
Jodhpur	92 D3
Joensuu	62 N5
Joetsu	89 G7
Jofane	109 F4
Joffre, Mount	122 G2
Jogeva	63 M7
Joghatay	95 N3
Johannesburg	108 E5
John Day U.S.A.	122 D5
John Day U.S.A.	122 E5
John H. Kerr Reservoir	129 N2
John O'Groats	56 E2
Johnshaven	57 F4
Johnson City	129 L2
Johnston U.K.	52 E1
Johnston U.S.A.	129 M4
Johnstone	57 D5
Johnston Lakes, The	112 E5
Johnstown	125 L6
Johor Baharu	90 C5
Joigny	65 E5
Joinville Brazil	138 G5
Joinville France	64 F4
Joinville Island	141 W6
Jokkmokk	62 H3
Jokulbunga	62 T11
Jokulsa a Bru	62 X12
Jokulsa-a Fjollum	62 W12
Jolfa	94 G2
Joliet	124 G6
Joliette	125 P3
Jolo Philippines	91 G4
Jolo Philippines	91 G4
Jonava	63 N9
Jonesboro	128 G3
Jones Sound	120 J2
Jonglei Canal	102 F6
Joniskis	63 K8
Jonkoping Sweden	63 F8
Jonkoping Sweden	63 F8
Jonquiere	125 P3
Jonzac	65 C6
Joplin	124 C8
Jordan	94 B6

Jordan	94 B5
Jordan U.S.A.	123 L4
Jordanow	71 H4
Jordan Valley	122 F6
Jorhat	93 H3
Jorn	62 J4
Jorong	90 E6
Jorpeland	63 B7
Jos	105 G3
Jose de San Martin	139 B8
Joseph Bonaparte Gulf	112 F1
Joseph, Lac	121 N7
Josselin	65 B5
Jos Sodarso, Pulau	91 K7
Jostedalsbreen	63 B6
Jotunheimen	63 C6
Jounie	94 B5
Joutsa	63 M6
Joyces Country	59 C5
J. Percy Priest Lake	129 J2
Juan Aldama	130 H5
Juan de Fuca Strait	122 B3
Juan de Nova	109 H3
Juan Fernandez, Islas de	135 A6
Juanjui	136 B5
Juarez, Sierra	126 D4
Juazeiro	137 J5
Juazeiro do Norte	137 K5
Juba	103 F7
Jubany	141 W6
Jubba	107 H2
Juby, Cap	100 C3
Jucar	67 F3
Juchitan	131 M9
Judenburg	68 E2
Juigalpa	132 E8
Juist	70 B2
Juiz de Fora	138 H4
Juklegga	63 E6
Julia	136 D4
Juliaca	138 B3
Julia Creek	113 J3
Julianhab	116 Q2
Julijske Alpe	72 B2
Julio de Castilhos	138 F5
Jullundur	92 E2
Jumilla	67 F3
Jumla	92 F3
Junagadh	92 D4
Junction	127 N5
Junction City	123 R8
Jundiai	138 G4
Juneau	118 J4
Junee	113 K5
Jungfrau	68 A2
Junggar Pendi	86 F2
Junin	139 D6
Junin de los Andes	139 B7
Junosuando	62 K3
Junsele	62 G5
Jun Xian	93 M2
Jura France	65 G5
Jura U.K.	57 C5
Jura, Sound of	57 C5
Juratishki	71 L1
Juriti	137 F4
Jurua Brazil	136 D4
Jurua Brazil	136 D4
Juruena	136 F6
Jussey	65 F5
Jutai Brazil	136 D4
Jutai Brazil	136 D5
Juterbog	70 E3
Juticalpa	132 D7
Jutland	63 C8
Juuka	62 N5
Juva	63 M6
Juventud, Isla de la	132 F4
Ju Xian	87 M4
Juymand	95 P4
Juyom	95 M7
Juzna Morava	73 F4
Jylland	63 C8
Jyvaskyla	62 L5

K

Kaala-Gomen	114 W16
Kaamanen	62 M2
Kaavi	62 N5
Kaba	104 C4
Kabaena	91 G7
Kabala	104 C4
Kabale	107 E3
Kabalega Falls	107 F2
Kabalo	106 E4
Kabambare	107 E3
Kabara	114 S9
Kabba	105 G4
Kabinatagami	124 H1
Kabinda	106 D4
Kabirkuh	94 H5
Kabompo	106 D5
Kabongo	106 E4
Kabud Gonbad	95 P3
Kabul Afghanistan	92 C2
Kabuli	114 D2
Kaburuang	91 H5
Kabwe	107 E5
Kabyrdak	84 A5
Kachchh, Gulf of	92 C4
Kachchh, Rann of	92 C4
Kachemak Bay	118 E4

Name	Pg	Ref
Kachikattsy	85	M4
Kachug	84	H6
Kackar Dagi	77	J2
Kadali	85	J5
Kadan Kyun	93	J6
Kadavu	114	R9
Kadavu Passage	114	R9
Kadena	89	H10
Kadhimain	94	G5
Kadikoy	76	B2
Kadina	113	H5
Kadinhani	76	E3
Kadiri	92	E6
Kadirli	77	G4
Kadoma	108	E3
Kadrifakovo	73	G5
Kadugli	102	E5
Kaduna *Nigeria*	105	G3
Kaduna *Nigeria*	105	G4
Kadzherom	78	K3
Kaedi	100	C5
Kaena Point	126	R10
Kaeo	115	D1
Kaesong	87	P4
Kafan	94	H2
Kafanchan	105	G4
Kaffrine	104	B3
Kafirevs, Akra	75	H3
Kafue *Zambia*	106	E6
Kafue *Zambia*	107	E6
Kafue Dam	108	E3
Kaga Bandoro	102	C6
Kagizman	77	K2
Kagmar	102	F5
Kagoshima	89	C10
Kagoshima-wan	89	C10
Kagul	79	D6
Kahama	107	F3
Kahan	92	C3
Kahayan	90	E6
Kahnuj	95	N8
Kahoku	89	H6
Kahoolawe	126	S10
Kahramanmaras	77	G4
Kahta	77	H4
Kahuku	126	R10
Kahurak	95	P7
Kahurangi Point	115	D4
Kaiama	105	F4
Kaiapoi	115	D5
Kaibab Plateau	126	F2
Kai Besar	114	A3
Kaifeng	93	M2
Kaihu	115	D1
Kai Kecil	114	A3
Kai, Kepulauan	91	J7
Kaikohe	115	D1
Kaikoura	115	D5
Kaikoura Range	115	D5
Kailahun	104	C4
Kailu	87	N3
Kailua *U.S.A.*	126	S10
Kaimana	91	J6
Kaimanawa Mountains	115	F3
Kaimur Range	92	F4
Kainantu	114	D3
Kainji Reservoir	105	F3
Kaipara Harbour	115	E2
Kaiping	93	M4
Kairouan	101	H1
Kairuku	114	D3
Kaiserslautern	70	B4
Kaisiadorys	71	L1
Kaitaia	115	D1
Kaitangata	115	B7
Kaiteur Falls	136	F3
Kaitumalven	62	J3
Kaiwaka	115	E2
Kaiwi Channel	126	S10
Kaiyuan *Liaoning, China*	87	N3
Kaiyuan *Yunnan, China*	93	K4
Kaiyuh Mountains	118	D3
Kajaani	62	M4
Kajo Kaji	102	F7
Kaka	103	F5
Kakabeka Falls	124	F2
Kakamari	107	F2
Kakamas	108	D5
Kakamega	107	F2
Kakapotahi	115	C5
Kake	89	D8
Kakhovskoye Vodokhranilishche	79	E6
Kaki	95	K7
Kakinada	92	F5
Kakisa Lake	119	M3
Kakogawa	89	E8
Kaktovik	118	G1
Kalabagh	92	D2
Kalabahi	91	G7
Kalabaka	75	F3
Kalabakan	91	F5
Kalabo	106	D6
Kalach	79	G5
Kalachinsk	84	A5
Kalach-Na-Donu	79	G6
Kaladar	125	M4
Ka Lae	126	T11
Kalahari	108	D4
Kalai-Khumb	86	C4
Kalajoki *Finland*	62	K4
Kalajoki *Finland*	62	L5
Kalakan	85	K5
Kalamai	75	G4
Kalamata	75	G4
Kalamazoo *U.S.A.*	124	H5
Kalamazoo *U.S.A.*	124	H5
Kalao	91	G7
Kalaotoa	91	G7
Kalapana	126	T11
Kalar	85	K5
Kalarash	73	K2
Kalarne	62	G5
Kalat	92	C3
Kalaupapa	126	S10
Kalavardha	75	J4
Kalavrita	75	G3
Kalb, Ra's	97	J9
Kalce	72	C3
Kaldakvisl	62	V12
Kaldungborg	63	D9
Kale *Turkey*	76	C4
Kale *Turkey*	76	C4
Kale *Turkey*	77	H2
Kalecik	76	E2
Kalemie	107	E4
Kalety	71	H3
Kalevala	62	P4
Kalewa	93	H4
Kaleybar	94	H2
Kalfafell	62	W13
Kalgoorlie	112	E5
Kaliakra, Nos	73	K4
Kalianda	90	D7
Kalima	106	E3
Kalimantan	90	E5
Kalimnos *Greece*	75	J4
Kalimnos *Greece*	75	J4
Kalininabad	86	B4
Kaliningrad	71	J1
Kalinino	78	K4
Kalininsk	79	G5
Kalinkovichi	79	D5
Kalinovka	79	D6
Kalis	103	J6
Kali Sindh	92	E4
Kalispell	122	G3
Kalisz *Poland*	70	F2
Kalisz *Poland*	71	H3
Kaliua	107	F4
Kalix	62	K4
Kalixalven	62	K3
Kalkan	76	C4
Kalkandere	77	J2
Kall	62	E5
Kallavesi	62	M5
Kalloni	75	J3
Kallsjon	62	E5
Kalmar *Sweden*	63	G8
Kalmar *Sweden*	63	G8
Kalmarsund	63	G8
Kalmykovo	79	J6
Kalni	93	H4
Kalomo	106	E6
Kalon	75	G2
Kalpeni	92	D6
Kalpi	92	E3
Kalpin	86	D3
Kal-Shur, Rud-e	95	P3
Kaluga	78	F5
Kaluku	91	F6
Kalush	79	C6
Kalutara	92	E7
Kalvarija	71	K1
Kalya	78	K3
Kalyan	92	D5
Kalyazin	78	F4
Kama	84	Ad4
Kamaishi	88	H6
Kamalia	92	D2
Kaman	76	E3
Kamaran	96	F9
Kamaria Falls	136	F2
Kamativi	108	E3
Kambalda	112	E5
Kambarka	78	J4
Kambia	104	C4
Kamchatka *Russia*	85	T5
Kamchatka Oblast	85	U5
Kamchiya	73	J4
Kamen	63	N9
Kamen, Gora	84	F3
Kamenjak, Rt	72	B3
Kamenka *Kazakhstan*	79	J5
Kamenka *Moldova*	73	K1
Kamenka *Russia*	84	F5
Kamenka *Russia*	79	G5
Kamenka *Russia*	78	G2
Kamen Kashirskiy	79	D5
Kamen-na-Obi	84	C6
Kamennyy, Mys	85	S1
Kamen Rybolov	88	C3
Kamensk-Shakhtinskiy	79	G6
Kamensk-Uralskiy	84	Ad5
Kamenyuki	71	K2
Kamenz	70	F3
Kames	57	C5
Kameshkovo	78	G4
Kamienna Gora	70	F3
Kamien Pombrski	70	F2
Kamiensk	71	H3
Kamilukuak Lake	119	Q3
Kamina	106	E4
Kaminak Lake	119	R3
Kaminuriak Lake	119	R3
Kamishak Bay	118	E4
Kamisli	76	F4
Kamkaly	86	C3
Kamla	93	G3
Kamloops	122	D2
Kamloops Lake	122	D2
Kammenoye, Ozero	62	P4
Kamnik	72	C2
Kamo *Japan*	88	G6
Kamo *Armenia*	77	L2
Kamp	68	E1
Kampala	107	F2
Kampar	90	C5
Kampen	64	F2
Kamphaeng Phet	93	J5
Kampot	93	K6
Kamsack	123	P2
Kamskiy	78	J3
Kamskoye Vodokhranilishche	78	K4
Kamyanets Podilskyy	73	J1
Kamyaran	94	H4
Kamyshin	79	H5
Kamzar	97	N3
Kan	84	E5
Kana	84	H4
Kanab	126	F2
Kanab Creek	126	F2
Kanab Plateau	126	F2
Kanaga Island	118	Ac9
Kanairiktok	121	P7
Kananda	84	G4
Kananga	106	D4
Kanash	78	H4
Kanastraion, Akra	75	G3
Kanawha	124	K7
Kanazawa	89	F7
Kanchanaburi	93	J6
Kanchenjunga	93	G3
Kanchipuram	92	E6
Kandahar	92	C2
Kandalaksha	62	Q3
Kandalakshskaya Guba	78	E2
Kandang	90	B5
Kandangan	90	F6
Kandanos	75	G5
Kandat	84	D5
Kandi	105	F3
Kandira	76	D2
Kandrian	114	D3
Kandukur	92	E5
Kandy	92	F7
Kane	125	L6
Kane Basin	120	M2
Kaneohe	126	S10
Kanevskaya	79	F6
Kangal	77	G3
Kangalassy	85	M4
Kangan	95	L8
Kangar	90	C4
Kangaroo Island	113	H6
Kangavar	94	H4
Kangaz	73	K2
Kangding	93	K2
Kangean	90	F7
Kangerdtuk	120	R3
Kanggye	87	P3
Kangiqsualujjuaq	121	N6
Kangiqsujuaq	121	M5
Kangirsuk	121	N5
Kangnung	89	B7
Kangping	87	N3
Kangri Karpo Pass	93	J3
Kani	93	H4
Kaniama	106	D4
Kanibadam	86	B3
Kaniet Islands	114	D2
Kanigigsualujak	121	L7
Kanin Nos	78	G2
Kanin Nos, Mys	78	G2
Kanin, Poluostrov	78	G2
Kanjiza	72	F2
Kankaanpaa	63	K6
Kankakee	124	G6
Kankan	104	D3
Kanker	92	F4
Kanmaw Kyun	93	J6
Kannapolis	129	M3
Kannonkoski	62	L5
Kannoura	89	E9
Kannus	62	N4
Kano	105	G3
Kanoya	89	C10
Kanpur	92	F3
Kansas	123	P8
Kansas City *Kansas*	124	C7
Kansas City *Missouri*	124	C7
Kansk	84	F5
Kansong	88	B6
Kant	86	D3
Kantemirovka	79	F6
Kanthi	93	G4
Kanton Island	111	U2
Kanturk	59	E8
Kanuku Mountains	136	F3
Kanye	108	E5
Kao	111	T5
Kao-hsiung	87	N7
Kaokoveld	108	B3
Kaolack	104	B3
Kaoma	106	D5
Kapanga	106	D4
Kapchagayskoye Vodokhranilishche	86	D3
Kapellskar	63	H7
Kapidagi Yarimadasi	76	B2
Kapiri Mposhi	107	E5
Kapit	90	E5
Kapiti Island	115	E4
Kapiting	137	F3
Kaplan	128	F5
Kaplice	70	F4
Kapoeta	103	F7
Kaposvar	72	D2
Kapsan	88	B5
Kaptanpasa	77	J2
Kapuae	90	E6
Kapuas	90	D6
Kapuas Hulu, Pegunungan	90	E5
Kapudzhukh	94	H2
Kapuskasing *Canada*	124	J2
Kapuskasing *Canada*	124	J2
Kapustin Yar	79	H6
Kara *Togo*	104	F4
Kara *Turkey*	77	J3
Kara *Russia*	84	Ae3
Kara Balta	86	C3
Karabas *Kazakhstan*	86	C2
Karabas *Kazakhstan*	86	D2
Karabekaul	95	S2
Karabiga	76	B2
Kara-Bogaz-Gol	79	J7
Kara-Bogaz-Gol, Proliv	79	J2
Kara-Bogaz-Gol, Zaliv	79	J2
Karabuk	76	E2
Karabulak *China*	86	D3
Karabulak *Kazakhstan*	86	E2
Karaburun	76	B3
Karacabey	76	C2
Karacadag	77	H4
Karacakoy	76	C2
Karacali Dagi	77	H4
Karacasu	76	C4
Karacay	77	G4
Karachev	79	E5
Karacheyevsk	79	G7
Karachi	92	C4
Karad	92	D5
Karadeniz Bogazi	76	C2
Karadilli	76	D3
Karagach	84	A5
Karaganda	86	C2
Karagayly	86	D2
Karagel	95	L2
Karaginskiy, Ostrov	85	U5
Karagiye, Vpadina	79	J7
Karahalli	76	C3
Karaidel	78	K4
Karaikal	92	E6
Karaikkudi	92	E6
Karaisali	76	F4
Karaj	95	K4
Karak	94	B6
Kara Kala	95	N2
Karakax He	92	E1
Karakecili	76	E3
Karakelong	91	H5
Karakocan	77	J3
Karakoram	92	E1
Karakuduk	84	B6
Karakul	86	C4
Kara Kul	86	C3
Kara-Kul , Ozero	86	C4
Karakumskiy Kanal	95	R3
Karakurt	77	K2
Karaman	76	E4
Karamay	86	E2
Karamea	115	D4
Karamea Bight	115	C4
Karamursel	76	C2
Karand	94	H4
Karanja	92	E4
Karanlik	76	F3
Karanlik Burun	76	B3
Karapelit	73	J4
Karapinar	76	E4
Karasburg	108	C5
Kara Sea	84	A2
Karashoky	84	A6
Karasjok	62	L2
Karasu *Turkey*	76	D2
Karasu *Kazakhstan*	84	A6
Karasu *Kazakhstan*	86	E2
Karasuk	84	B6
Karatal	86	D2
Karatas	76	F4
Kara Tau	86	C3
Karatau, Khrebet *Kazakhstan*	86	B3
Karatau, Khrebet *Kazakhstan*	79	J7
Karatobe	79	J6
Karaton	79	J6
Karatsu	89	B9
Karaudanawa	136	F3
Karauli	92	E3
Karaulkeldy	79	K6
Karavas	75	G4
Karawang	90	D7
Karayazi	77	K3
Karbala	94	G5
Karbole	63	F6
Karcag	73	F2
Kardhamila	75	J3
Kardhitsa	75	F3
Kardla	63	K7
Karesuando	62	K2
Kargasok	84	C5
Kargat	84	C5
Kargi *Turkey*	76	D4
Kargi *Turkey*	76	F2
Kargopol	78	F3
Kariba	108	E3

Name	Page	Grid
Kariba, Lake	108	E3
Karibib	108	C4
Kaributo	88	H4
Karigasniemi	62	L2
Karikari, Cape	115	D1
Karima	103	F4
Karimata, Kepulauan	90	D6
Karimata, Selat	90	D6
Karimganj	93	H4
Karimnagar	92	E5
Karimunjawa, Kepulauan	90	E7
Karin	103	J5
Karistos	75	H3
Kariz	95	Q4
Karkaralinsk	86	D2
Karkaralong, Kepulauan	91	H5
Karkar Island	114	D2
Karkas, Kuh-e	95	L5
Karkkila	63	L6
Karlino	70	F1
Karliova	77	J3
Karl-Marx-Stadt	70	E3
Karlobag	72	C3
Karlovac	72	C3
Karlovo	73	H4
Karlovy Vary	70	E3
Karlsborg	63	F7
Karlskoga	63	F7
Karlskrona	63	F8
Karlsruhe	70	C4
Karlstad *Sweden*	63	E7
Karlstad *U.S.A.*	124	B2
Karlstadt	70	C4
Karmanovka	79	J6
Karmoy	63	A7
Karnafuli Reservoir	93	H4
Karnal	92	E3
Karnali	92	F3
Karnataka	92	E6
Karnobat	73	J4
Karonie	112	E5
Karora	103	G4
Karossa, Tanjung	91	F7
Karousadhes	74	E3
Karoy	86	D2
Karpathos *Greece*	75	J5
Karpathos *Greece*	75	J5
Karpathos Straits	75	J5
Karpathou, Stenon	75	J5
Karpenision	75	F3
Karpinsk	84	Ad5
Karpogory	78	G3
Karratha	112	D3
Karrats Fjord	120	R3
Karree Berge	108	D6
Kars *Turkey*	77	K2
Kars *Turkey*	77	K2
Karsakpay	86	B2
Karsamaki	62	L5
Karsanti	76	F4
Karshi *Kazakhstan*	79	J7
Karshi *Uzbekistan*	80	H6
Karsiyaka	76	B3
Karskoye More	84	A2
Karsun	78	H5
Kartal	76	C2
Kartayel	78	J3
Kartuni	133	T11
Kartuzy	71	H1
Karufa	91	J6
Karun	94	J6
Karvina	71	H4
Karwar	92	D6
Karym	84	Ae4
Karymskoye	85	J6
Kas	76	C4
Kasai	106	C3
Kasaji	106	D5
Kasama	107	F5
Kasane	108	E3
Kasanga	107	F4
Kasangulu	106	C3
Kasaragod	92	D6
Kasar, Ras	96	D7
Kasba Lake	119	Q3
Kasba Tadla	100	D2
Kasempa	106	E5
Kasese	107	F2
Kashaf	95	Q3
Kashan	95	K5
Kashary	79	G6
Kashgar	86	D4
Kashi	86	D4
Kashima	89	C9
Kashin	78	F4
Kashipur	92	E3
Kashira	78	F5
Kashiwazaki	89	G7
Kashkanteniz	86	C2
Kashkarantsy	78	F2
Kashmar	95	P4
Kasimov	78	G5
Kasin	92	D2
Kasiruta	91	H6
Kaskinen	62	J5
Kasko	62	J5
Kas Kong	93	K6
Kasli	84	Ad5
Kasmere Lake	119	Q4
Kasongo	106	E3
Kasongo-Lunda	106	C4
Kasos	75	J5
Kasos, Stenon	75	J5
Kaspiyskiy	79	H6
Kassala	103	G4
Kassandra	75	G2
Kassel	70	C3
Kasserine	101	G1
Kastamonu	76	E2
Kastaneai	75	J2
Kastelli	75	G5
Kastellorizon	76	C4
Kastoria	75	F2
Kastorias, Limni	75	F2
Kastornoye	79	F5
Kastron	75	H3
Kasulu	107	F3
Kasumi	89	E8
Kasumiga-ura	89	H7
Kasungu	107	F5
Kata	84	G5
Kataba	106	E6
Katagum	105	H3
Katahdin, Mount	125	R4
Katako Kombe	106	D3
Katanning	112	D5
Katastari	75	F4
Katav Ivanovsk	78	K5
Katchall	93	H7
Katen	88	F2
Katerini	75	G2
Katha	93	J4
Katherina, Gebel	103	F2
Katherine	112	G1
Kathmandu	92	G3
Kati	100	D6
Katihar	93	G3
Katikati	115	E2
Katiola	104	D4
Katla	62	V13
Katlabukh, Ozero	73	K3
Katmai Volcano	118	E4
Kato Nevrokopion	75	G2
Katoomba	113	L5
Kato Stavros	75	G2
Katowice	71	H3
Katrineholm	63	G7
Katrine, Loch	57	D4
Katsina	105	G3
Katsina Ala	105	G4
Katsuura	89	H8
Katsuyama	89	F7
Kattavia	75	J5
Kattegat	63	D8
Kauai	126	R9
Kauai Channel	126	R10
Kauhajoki	62	K5
Kauiki Head	126	S10
Kaujuitok	120	H3
Kaulakahi Channel	126	Q9
Kaunakakai	126	S10
Kaunas	71	K1
Kaura Namoda	105	G3
Kaushany	73	K2
Kautokeino	62	K2
Kavacha	85	V4
Kavaje	74	E2
Kavak	77	G2
Kavaklidere	76	C4
Kavalerovo	88	E3
Kavali	92	E6
Kavalla	75	H2
Kavar	95	L7
Kavarna	73	K4
Kavgamis	77	H4
Kavieng	114	E2
Kavir, Dasht-e	95	M4
Kavir-e Namak	95	N4
Kavungo	106	D5
Kavusshap Daglari	77	K3
Kaw	137	G3
Kawagoe	89	G8
Kawaguchi	89	G8
Kawaihae	126	T10
Kawakawa	115	E1
Kawambwa	107	E4
Kawardha	92	F4
Kawasaki	89	G8
Kawerau	115	F3
Kawhia	115	E3
Kawhia Harbour	115	E3
Kawimbe	107	F4
Kawkareik	93	J5
Kawthaung	93	J7
Kayak Island	118	G4
Kayan	91	F5
Kaydak, Sor	79	J7
Kaye, Cape	120	H3
Kayenta	127	G2
Kayes	100	C6
Kaymaz	76	D3
Kaynar	86	D2
Kaynarca	76	D2
Kayseri	76	F3
Kayuagung	90	C6
Kazachinskoye	84	H5
Kazachye	85	P2
Kazakh	77	L2
Kazakhskiy Melkosopochnik	86	C2
Kazakhskiy Zaliv	79	J2
Kazakhstan	79	J6
Kazan	78	H4
Kazan *Turkey*	76	E2
Kazan	119	R3
Kazandzhik	95	M2
Kazan Lake	119	R3
Kazanluk	73	H4
Kazan-retto	83	N4
Kazatin	79	D6
Kazbek	77	L1
Kazerun	95	K7
Kazgorodok	84	Ae6
Kazhim	78	J3
Kazi Magomed	94	J1
Kazim Karabekir	76	E4
Kaztalovka	79	H6
Kazumba	106	D4
Kazy	95	N2
Kazym	84	Ae4
Kazymskaya	84	Ae4
Kazymskiy Mys	84	Ae4
Kea *Greece*	75	H4
Kea *Greece*	75	H4
Keady	58	J4
Keal, Loch na	57	B4
Kearny	126	G4
Keaukaha	126	T11
Keban	77	H3
Keban Baraji	77	H3
Kebemer	104	B2
Kebezen	84	D6
Kebnekaise	62	H3
Kebock Head	56	B2
Kebri Dehar	103	H6
Kech a Terara	103	G6
Kechika	118	K4
Keciborlu	76	D4
Kecil, Kai	91	J7
Kecskemet	72	E2
Kedainiai	63	K9
Kedgwick	125	S3
Kediri	90	E7
Kedong	87	P2
Kedougou	104	C3
Kedva	78	J3
Keel	58	B5
Keelby	55	J3
Keele	118	K3
Keele Peak	118	J3
Keeler	126	D2
Keene	125	P5
Keeper Hill	59	F7
Keetmanshoop	108	C5
Keewatin *N.W. Territories, Canada*	119	R3
Keewatin *Ontario, Canada*	124	C2
Kefallinia	75	F3
Kefamenanu	91	G7
Kefken	76	D2
Keflavik	62	T12
Keglo Bay	121	N6
Kegulta	79	G6
Kehsi Mansam	93	J4
Keighley	55	H3
Keitele *Kaskisuomi, Finland*	62	L5
Keitele *Kuopio, Finland*	62	M5
Keith	56	F3
Keith Arm	119	L2
Keiyasi	114	Q8
Kekertaluk Island	120	N4
Keketa	114	C3
Kel	85	M3
Kelang	90	C5
Keld	55	G2
Keles	76	C3
Kelibia	101	H1
Kelkit *Turkey*	77	G2
Kelkit *Turkey*	77	H2
Keller Lake	119	L3
Kellett, Cape	118	K1
Kellog	84	D4
Kellogg	122	F4
Kelloselka	62	N3
Kells	58	J5
Kelme	63	K9
Kelmentsy	73	J1
Kelo	102	C6
Kelolokan	91	F5
Kelowna	122	E3
Kelsey Bay	122	B2
Kelso *New Zealand*	115	B6
Kelso *U.K.*	57	F5
Keluang	90	C5
Kelvedon	53	H3
Kem	78	E3
Kemah	77	H3
Kemaliye	77	H3
Kemalpasa	77	J2
Kemalpasar	76	B3
Kemano	118	K5
Kemer *Turkey*	76	C4
Kemer *Turkey*	76	C4
Kemer *Turkey*	76	D4
Kemerovo	84	D5
Kemi	62	L4
Kemijarvi *Finland*	62	L3
Kemijarvi *Finland*	62	M3
Kemijoki	62	L3
Kemmerer	123	J7
Kempen	64	F3
Kempendyayi	85	K4
Kemp, Lake	127	N4
Kemps Bay	132	H2
Kempsey	113	L5
Kempten	70	D5
Kempt, Lac	125	N3
Kempton	113	K7
Ken	92	F3
Kenadsa	100	E2
Kenai	118	E3
Kenai Mountains	118	E4
Kenai Peninsula	118	F3
Kendal	55	G2
Kendall, Cape	120	J5
Kendari	91	G6
Kendawangan	90	E6
Kendraparha	92	G4
Kendyrliki	86	F2
Kenema	104	C4
Kenete Karavastas	74	E2
Kenge	106	C3
Kengtung	93	J4
Kenhardt	108	D5
Kenilworth	53	F2
Kenitra	100	D2
Keniut	85	X4
Kenli	87	M4
Kenmare *Ireland*	59	C9
Kenmare *Ireland*	59	C9
Kenmore	57	D4
Kennacraig	57	C5
Kennebec	125	R4
Kenner	128	C5
Kennet	53	F3
Kennewick	122	E4
Kenninghall	53	J2
Kenn Reef	113	M3
Kenogami	121	K7
Keno Hill	118	H3
Kenora	124	C2
Kenosha	124	G5
Kent *U.K.*	53	H3
Kent *U.S.A.*	127	K5
Kentau	86	B3
Kentford	53	H2
Kentmere	55	G2
Kent Peninsula	119	P2
Kentucky *U.S.A.*	124	C8
Kentucky *U.S.A.*	124	H8
Kentucky Lake	124	F8
Kentwood	128	C5
Kenya	107	G2
Keokea	126	S10
Keokuk	124	E6
Keos	75	H4
Kepi	91	K7
Kepno	71	C3
Keppel Bay	113	L3
Kepsut	76	C3
Kerala	92	E6
Kerama-retto	89	H10
Keravat	114	E2
Kerch	79	F5
Kerchenskiy Proliv	79	F5
Kerema	114	D3
Keremeos	122	E3
Keren	103	C4
Kerguelen, Ile	142	D6
Keri	75	F4
Kericho	107	C3
Kerinci, Gunung	90	C6
Keriya He	92	F1
Kerki	95	S3
Kerkinitis, Limni	75	G2
Kerkira *Greece*	74	E3
Kerkira *Greece*	74	E3
Kerma	102	F4
Kermadec Islands	111	T8
Kermadec Trench	143	H6
Kerman	95	N6
Kerman Desert	95	P7
Kermen	73	J4
Kermit	127	L5
Kern	126	C2
Keros	78	J3
Kerpineny	73	K2
Kerrera	57	C4
Kerrville	127	N5
Kerry	59	C8
Kerry Head	59	C8
Kerrykeel	58	G2
Keruh	90	C4
Kerulen	87	L2
Kesalahti	63	N6
Kesan	76	B2
Kesap	77	H2
Kesennuma	88	H6
Keshvar	94	J5
Keskin	76	E3
Keski-Suomi	62	K5
Keskozero	78	E3
Keswick	55	F2
Keszthely	72	D2
Ket	84	D5
Keta	104	F4
Keta, Ozero	84	E3
Ketapang	90	D6
Ketchikan	118	J4
Kete	104	E4
Ketmen, Khrebet	86	E3
Ketoy, Ostrov	85	S7
Ketrzyn	71	J1
Kettering	53	G2
Kettle Ness	55	J2
Kettle River Range	122	E3
Kettlewell	55	G2
Kettusoja	62	N3
Keurus-selka	63	L5
Keushki	84	Ae4
Kew	133	M4
Kewanee	124	F5
Keweenaw	124	C3
Keweenaw Bay	124	C3
Keweenaw Point	124	C3
Keyano	121	M7
Keyaygyr	86	D3

Name	Page	Grid
Keyi	86	E3
Key Largo	129	M8
Key, Lough	58	F4
Keynsham	52	E3
Key West	129	M8
Keyworth	53	F2
Kez	78	J4
Kezhma	84	G5
Khabarovo	84	Ad3
Khabarovsk	88	E1
Khabarovsk Kray	85	P6
Khabur	94	E4
Khadki	92	D5
Khairagarh	92	F4
Khairpur *Pakistan*	92	C3
Khairpur *Pakistan*	92	D3
Khakhar	85	P5
Khalafabad	94	J6
Khalili	95	L8
Khalkhal	94	J3
Khalki	75	J4
Khalkis	75	G3
Khalmer-Yu	84	Ad3
Khalturin	78	H4
Khamar Daban, Khrebet	84	G6
Khambhat	92	D4
Khambhat, Gulf of	92	D4
Khamili	75	J5
Khamir	96	F8
Khamis Mushayt	96	F7
Kham Keut	93	K5
Khammam	92	F5
Khamra	85	J4
Khanabad	92	C1
Khan al Baghdadi	94	F5
Khanaqin	94	G4
Khanda	84	H6
Khandela	92	E3
Khandra	75	J5
Khandwa	92	E4
Khandyga	85	P4
Khangokurt	84	Ad4
Khanh Hoa	93	L6
Khanh Hung	93	L7
Khani	85	L5
Khania	75	H5
Khaniadhana	92	E4
Khanion Kolpos	75	G5
Khanka, Ozero	88	D3
Khankendi	92	H2
Khanpur	92	D3
Khan Shaykhun	94	C4
Khantau	86	C3
Khantayka	84	D3
Khantayskoye, Ozero	84	E3
Khanty-Mansiysk	84	Ae4
Khan Yunis	94	B6
Kharabali	79	H6
Kharagpur	93	G4
Kharalakh	85	L3
Kharan	95	N7
Kharanaq	95	M5
Kharaulakhskiy Khrebet	85	M2
Kharbur	77	J5
Kharga, El Wahat el	102	F3
Kharg Island	97	K2
Kharitah, Shiqqat al	96	H8
Khark	97	K2
Kharkiv	79	F6
Kharku	97	K2
Khar Kuh	95	L6
Kharlovka	78	F2
Kharsawan	92	G4
Kharstan	85	Q2
Khartoum	103	F4
Khartoum North	103	F4
Kharutayuvam	78	K2
Khasalakh	85	M2
Khasan	88	C4
Khasavyurt	79	H7
Khash	95	Q7
Khash	95	R6
Khash, Dasht-i-	92	B2
Khashm el Girba	96	B9
Khash Rud	95	R6
Khashuri	77	K2
Khasi Hills	93	H3
Khaskovo	73	H5
Khatanga *Russia*	84	G2
Khatanga *Russia*	84	G2
Khatangskiy Zaliv	84	H2
Khatayakha	78	K2
Khatyrka	85	X4
Khaybar, Harrat	96	E4
Khaypudyrskaya Guba	78	K2
Khayran, Ra's al	97	P5
Khaysardakh	85	M4
Khe Bo	93	K5
Kheisia	77	J5
Khemis Miliana	67	H4
Khemisset	100	D2
Khenchela	101	G1
Khenifra	100	D2
Kherrata	67	J4
Khersan	95	K6
Kherson	79	E6
Khe Sanh	93	L5
Kheta	84	G2
Khiitola	63	N6
Khilok	85	J6
Khios *Greece*	75	H3
Khios *Greece*	75	J3
Khirbat Isriyah	77	G5
Khiva	80	H5
Khlebarovo	73	J4
Khmelnik	79	D6
Khmelnytskyy	79	D6
Khodzhakala	95	N2
Kholm *Afghanistan*	92	C1
Kholm *Russia*	78	E4
Kholmogory	78	G3
Kholmsk	88	J2
Khomas Highland	108	C4
Khomeyn	95	K5
Khomeynishahr	95	K5
Khong	93	L6
Khongkhoyuku	85	N4
Khonj	95	L8
Khoper	79	G5
Khor *Russia*	88	E2
Khor *Russia*	88	E2
Khora Sfakion	75	H5
Khorat, Cao Nguyen	93	K5
Khordha	92	G4
Khordogoy	85	K4
Khoreyver	78	K2
Khorgo	84	J2
Khorinsk	84	H6
Khorod	79	E6
Khorol	88	C3
Khorovaya	84	A3
Khorramabad *Iran*	94	J5
Khorramabad *Iran*	95	N4
Khorramshahr	94	J6
Khosf	95	P5
Khosheutovo	79	H6
Khosk	95	R4
Khosrowabad	94	J6
Khotin	73	J1
Khouribga	100	D2
Khoyniki	79	D5
Khristiana	75	H4
Khroma	85	Q2
Khudzhand	86	B3
Khuff	96	G4
Khulna	93	G4
Khulo	77	K2
Khunjerab Pass	92	E1
Khunsar	95	K5
Khunti	92	G4
Khur	95	P4
Khurays	97	J4
Khurja	92	E3
Khuryan Munjan, Jazair	97	N8
Khust	79	C6
Khutu Datta	85	Q7
Khuzdar	92	C3
Khvaf	95	Q4
Khvalynsk	79	H5
Khvor	95	M5
Khvormuj	95	K7
Khvoy	94	G2
Khvoynaya	78	E4
Khwaja Muhammad, Koh-i-	92	D1
Khyber Pass	92	D2
Khyrov	71	K4
Kiamba	91	G4
Kiantajarvi	62	N4
Kiaton	75	G3
Kiberg	62	P1
Kibombo	106	E3
Kibondo	107	F3
Kibwezi	107	G3
Kibworth Harcourt	53	G2
Kicevo	73	F5
Kicking Horse Pass	119	M5
Kidal	100	F5
Kidan, Al	97	M5
Kidderminster	52	E2
Kidnappers, Cape	115	F3
Kidsgrove	55	G3
Kidwelly	52	C3
Kidyut, Wadi	97	K8
Kiel	70	D1
Kielce	71	J3
Kielder	57	F5
Kielder Forest	57	F5
Kielder Water	57	F5
Kieler Bucht	70	D1
Kieta	114	F3
Kiev	79	E5
Kiffa	100	C5
Kifissos	75	G3
Kifri	94	G4
Kigali	107	F3
Kigi	77	J3
Kiglapait, Cape	121	P6
Kigoma	107	E3
Kiholo	126	T11
Kii-sanchi	89	E9
Kii-suido	89	E9
Kikai-jima	89	B11
Kikiakki	84	C4
Kikinda	72	F3
Kikladhes	75	H4
Kikonai	88	H5
Kikori	114	C3
Kikwit	106	C3
Kil	63	E7
Kilafors	63	G6
Kilakh	97	K5
Kilauea	126	R9
Kilauea Crater	126	T11
Kilbasan	76	E4
Kilbeggan	59	H6
Kilberry	58	J5
Kilbirnie	57	D5
Kilbrannan Sound	57	C5
Kilbride *Ireland*	59	K7
Kilbride *U.K.*	57	A3
Kilbuck Mountains	118	D3
Kilchu	88	B5
Kilcock	59	J6
Kilcolgan	59	E6
Kilcormac	59	G6
Kilcoy	113	L4
Kilcullen	59	J6
Kildare *Ireland*	59	J6
Kildare *Ireland*	59	J6
Kildin, Ostrov	62	R2
Kildinstroy	62	Q2
Kilfinnane	59	F8
Kilgore	128	E4
Kilham	57	F5
Kilickaya	77	J2
Kilifi	107	G3
Kilimanjaro	107	G3
Kilinailau Islands	114	F2
Kilis	77	G4
Kiliya	79	D6
Kilkee	59	C7
Kilkeel	58	L4
Kilkelly	58	E5
Kilkenny *Ireland*	59	H7
Kilkenny *Ireland*	59	H7
Kilkhampton	52	C4
Kilkieran Bay	59	C6
Killadysert	59	D7
Killala	58	D4
Killala Bay	58	D4
Killaloe	59	F7
Killarney	59	C8
Killashandra	58	G4
Killeen	128	D5
Killenaule	59	G7
Killiecrankie	57	E4
Killiecrankie, Pass of	57	E4
Killin	57	D4
Killinek Island	121	P5
Killini	75	G4
Killorglin	59	C8
Killybegs	58	F3
Killylea	58	J4
Kilmacthomas	59	H8
Kilmallock	59	E8
Kilmaluag	56	B3
Kilmarnock	57	D5
Kilmaurs	57	D5
Kilmelford	57	C4
Kilmez	78	J4
Kilmurry	59	D7
Kilnsea	55	K3
Kiloran	57	B4
Kilosa	107	G4
Kilpisjarvi	62	J2
Kilrea	58	J3
Kilrush	59	D7
Kilsyth	57	D5
Kiltan	92	D6
Kilwa Masoko	107	G4
Kilwinning	57	F4
Kilyos	76	C2
Kimbal, Mount	118	G3
Kimbe Bay	114	E3
Kimberley *Canada*	122	G3
Kimberley *South Africa*	108	D5
Kimberley Plateau	112	F2
Kimi	75	H3
Kimito	63	K6
Kimmeridge	53	E4
Kimolos	75	H4
Kimry	78	F4
Kimvula	106	C4
Kimzha	78	G2
Kinabalu, Gunung	90	F4
Kinbasket Lake	122	F2
Kinbrace	56	E2
Kincardine *Canada*	125	K4
Kincardine *U.K.*	57	E4
Kindat	93	H4
Kinder	128	F5
Kinder Scout	55	H3
Kindersley	123	K2
Kindia	104	C3
Kindu	106	E3
Kinel	79	J5
Kinel-Cherkasy	78	J5
Kineshma	78	G4
Kingaroy	113	L4
Kingarth	57	C5
King Christian Island	120	F2
King City	126	B2
King George Island	141	W6
King George Sound	112	D5
Kinghorn	57	E4
Kingisepps	63	K7
King Island	113	J6
King, Lake	112	D5
King Leopold Ranges	112	F2
Kingman	126	E3
Kingoonya	113	H5
Kings	126	B2
King Salmon	118	D4
Kingsbarns	57	F4
Kingsbridge	52	D4
King's Bromley	53	F2
Kingsclere	53	F3
Kingscote	113	H6
Kingscourt	58	J5
Kingsford	124	F4
Kingsley	55	H3
King's Lynn	53	H2
Kingsmill Group	111	R2
King Sound	112	E2
Kings Peak	123	J7
Kingsport	129	L2
Kingston *Australia*	113	H6
Kingston *Canada*	125	M4
Kingston *Jamaica*	132	J5
Kingston *New Zealand*	115	B6
Kingston *U.S.A.*	125	P6
Kingston Bagpuize	53	F3
Kingston-upon-Hull	55	J3
Kingston-upon-Thames	53	G3
Kingstown	133	S8
Kingsville	128	D7
Kingswood	52	E3
Kington	52	D2
Kingussie	57	D3
King William Island	120	G3
King William's Town	108	E6
Kiniama	107	F4
Kinik	76	B3
Kinloch	57	B3
Kinlochewe	56	C3
Kinloch Hourn	57	C3
Kinna	63	E8
Kinnaird Head	56	F3
Kinnegad	59	H6
Kinnerley	52	E2
Kinnert, Yam	94	B5
Kinoosao	119	Q4
Kinross	57	E4
Kinsale	59	E9
Kinsalebeg	59	G9
Kinsarvik	63	B6
Kinshasa	106	C3
Kinsley	127	N2
Kinston	129	P3
Kintampo	104	E4
Kintore	56	F3
Kintyre	57	C5
Kintyre, Mull of	57	C5
Kinuachdrachd	57	C4
Kiparissia	75	F4
Kiparissiakos Kolpos	75	F4
Kipawa, Lac	125	L3
Kipengere Range	107	F4
Kipili	107	F4
Kipini	107	H3
Kipnuk	118	C4
Kipseli	75	G3
Kirakira	114	K7
Kiraz	76	B3
Kirazli	76	B2
Kirbasi	76	D2
Kirbey	84	H3
Kircubbin	58	L4
Kirec	76	C3
Kirenga	84	H5
Kirenis	76	C4
Kirensk	84	H5
Kirgizskiy Khrebet	86	C3
Kirgiz Step	79	J6
Kiri	106	C3
Kiribati	111	S2
Kirik	77	J2
Kirikhan	77	G4
Kirikkale	76	E3
Kirillo	78	F4
Kirin	87	P3
Kirinyaga	107	G3
Kirka	76	D3
Kirkagac	76	B3
Kirk Bulag Dag	94	H3
Kirkburton	55	H3
Kirkby	55	G3
Kirkby in Ashfield	55	H3
Kirkby Lonsdale	55	G2
Kirkby Stephen	55	G2
Kirkcaldy	57	E4
Kirkcambeck	57	F4
Kirkcolm	54	D2
Kirkcudbright	54	E2
Kirkcudbright Bay	54	E2
Kirkenes	62	P2
Kirkestinden	62	H2
Kirkheaton	57	G5
Kirkintilloch	57	D5
Kirkland Lake	125	K2
Kirk Langley	53	F2
Kirklareli	76	B2
Kirklington	55	J3
Kirk Michael	54	E2
Kirkoswald	55	G2
Kirk Smeaton	55	H3
Kirksville	124	D6
Kirkton	57	F4
Kirkton of Culsalmond	56	F3
Kirkton of Largo	57	F4
Kirkuk	94	G4
Kirkwall	56	F2
Kirkwhelpington	57	F5
Kirkwood	108	E6
Kirlangic Burun	76	D4
Kirmir	76	E2
Kirov *Russia*	78	E5
Kirov *Russia*	78	H4
Kirova	86	D2
Kirovhrad	79	E6
Kirovo-Chepetsk	78	H4
Kirovsk *Russia*	62	Q3
Kirovsk *Turkmenistan*	95	Q3
Kirovskiy	88	D3
Kirriemuir	57	F4
Kirs	78	J4

Name	Page	Ref
Kirsanov	79	G5
Kirsehir	76	F3
Kirtgecit	77	K3
Kirthar Range	92	C3
Kirtlington	53	F3
Kirton	55	J3
Kiruna	62	J3
Kiryu	89	G7
Kisa	63	F8
Kisamou, Kolpos	75	G5
Kisangani	106	E2
Kisar	91	H7
Kisarazu	89	G8
Kiselevsk	84	D6
Kishanganj	93	G3
Kishangarh	92	D3
Kishb, Harrat	96	E5
Kishika-zaki	89	C10
Kishiwada	89	E8
Kishorganj	93	H4
Kishorn, Loch	56	C3
Kisii	107	F3
Kiska Island	118	Ab9
Kiskunfelegyhaza	72	E2
Kiskunhalas	72	E2
Kislovodsk	79	G7
Kismaayo	107	H3
Kiso-Fukushima	89	F8
Kiso-sammyaku	89	F8
Kispest	72	E2
Kissidougou	104	C4
Kissimmee	129	M7
Kisumu	107	F3
Kita	100	D6
Kitajaur	62	J3
Kitakami *Japan*	88	H6
Kitakami *Japan*	88	H6
Kitakami-sanmyaku	88	J3
Kita-kyushu	89	C9
Kitale	107	G2
Kitami	88	J4
Kitami-sammyaku	88	H6
Kitangari	107	G5
Kitay, Ozero	73	K3
Kit Carson	127	L1
Kitchener	125	K5
Kitee	62	P5
Kitgum	107	F2
Kithira *Greece*	75	G4
Kithira *Greece*	75	G4
Kithnos *Greece*	75	H4
Kithnos *Greece*	75	H4
Kitikmeot	119	N1
Kitimat	118	K5
Kitinen	62	M3
Kitkiojoki	62	K3
Kitsuki	89	C9
Kittanning	125	L6
Kittila	62	L3
Kitui	107	G3
Kitunda	107	F4
Kitwe	107	E5
Kitzbuhel	68	D2
Kitzbuheler Alpen	68	D2
Kitzingen	70	D4
Kivalo	62	L3
Kivijarvi	62	L5
Kivu, Lake	107	E3
Kiyevka	83	D4
Kiyevskoye Vodokhranilishche	79	E5
Kiyikoy	76	C2
Kizel	78	K4
Kizema	78	H3
Kizilagac	77	J3
Kizilcaboluk	76	C4
Kizilcadag	76	C4
Kizilhisar	76	C4
Kizilirmak	76	E2
Kizil Irmak	77	F2
Kizilkaya	76	D4
Kiziloren	76	E4
Kiziltepe	77	J4
Kizlyar	79	H7
Kizyl-Arvat	95	N2
Kizyl-Atrek	95	M3
Kizyl Ayak	95	S3
Kizyl-Su	95	L2
Kjollefjord	62	M1
Kjopsvick	62	L2
Kladanj	72	E3
Kladno	70	F3
Kladovo	73	G3
Klagenfurt	68	E2
Klaipeda	63	L9
Klamath *U.S.A.*	122	B7
Klamath *U.S.A.*	122	C7
Klamath Falls	122	D6
Klamath Mountains	122	C6
Klamono	91	J6
Klaralven	63	J6
Klatovy	70	E4
Klekovaca	72	D3
Klenak	72	E3
Klerksdorp	108	E5
Klichka	85	K7
Klimovichi	79	E5
Klin	78	F4
Klinovec	70	E3
Klintsovka	79	H5
Klintsy	79	E5
Klisura	73	H4
Kljuc	72	D3
Klobuck	71	H3
Klodzka *Poland*	71	G3
Klodzko *Poland*	71	G3
Klos	75	F2
Klosterneuberg	68	F1
Klosters	68	B2
Klrovskiy	79	H6
Kluane	118	H3
Kluane Lake	118	H3
Kluczbork	71	H3
Klyevka	84	A6
Klyuchevskaya Sopka	85	U5
Klyuchi	85	U5
Klyukvinka	84	C5
Kmagta	114	J6
Kmanjab	103	B3
K2, Mount	92	E1
Knapdale	57	C5
Knaresborough	55	F2
Knife	123	N4
Knight Island	118	F3
Knighton	52	D2
Knin	72	D3
Knjazevac	73	G4
Knockadoon Head	59	G9
Knockalla Mount	58	G2
Knockanaffrin	59	G8
Knockaunapeebra	59	G8
Knocklayd	58	K2
Knockmealdown Mountains	59	G8
Knocknaskagh	59	F8
Knottingley	55	H3
Knox, Cape	118	J5
Knoxville *Iowa*	124	D6
Knoxville *Tennessee*	129	L3
Knoydart	57	C3
Knud Rasmussen Land	120	F2
Knutholstind	63	C6
Knutsford	55	G3
Knyazhaya Guba	62	Q3
Knyazhevo	78	G4
Knysna	108	D6
Knyszyn	71	K2
Koba	90	D6
Kobarid	72	B2
Kobayashi	89	C10
Kobberminebugt	120	R5
Kobelyaki	79	E6
Kobenhavn	63	E9
Koblenz	70	B3
Kobowre, Pegunungan	91	K6
Kobrin	71	L2
Kobroor	91	J7
Kobuk	118	D2
Kobya	85	M4
Koca *Turkey*	76	B3
Koca *Turkey*	76	C3
Koca *Turkey*	76	E2
Kocapinar	77	K3
Kocarli	76	B4
Koceljevo	72	E3
Koch Bihar	93	G3
Kochechum	84	G3
Kochegarovo	85	K5
Kocher	70	C4
Kochi	89	D9
Koch Island	120	L4
Kochkorka	86	D3
Koch Peak	122	I5
Kochumdek	84	I4
Koden	71	K3
Kodiak	118	E4
Kodiak Island	118	E4
Kodima	78	G3
Kodinar	92	D4
Kodok	103	F6
Kodomari	88	H5
Kodyma	73	L2
Kofcaz	76	B2
Koffiefontein	108	D5
Koflach	68	E2
Koforidua	104	E4
Kofu	89	G8
Koge	63	E9
Kogilnik	73	K2
Ko, Gora	88	F2
Kohat	92	D2
Kohima	93	H3
Koh-i Qaisar	95	S5
Kohtla-Jarve	63	M7
Koide	89	G7
Koi Sanjaq	94	G3
Koitere	62	P5
Koivu	62	L3
Koje	89	B8
Kojonup	112	D5
Kokand	86	B3
Kokas	91	J6
Kokchetav	84	Ae6
Kokemaenjoki	63	K6
Kokenau	91	K6
Kokkola	62	K5
Koko	105	G4
Kokoda	114	D3
Kokomo	124	G6
Kokpekty	85	E2
Koksoak	121	N6
Kokstad	108	E6
Koktas	85	C2
Kokubu	89	C10
Kokuora	85	R2
Kokura	89	C9
Kokuy	85	K6
Kok-Yangak	86	C3
Kola	62	Q2
Kolaka	91	G6
Kolar	92	E6
Kolari	62	K3
Kolarovgrad	73	J4
Kolasin	72	E4
Kolay	77	F2
Kolberg	70	F1
Kolbuszowa	71	J3
Kolchugino	78	F4
Kolda	104	C3
Kolding	63	C9
Kole	106	D3
Kolguyev, Ostrov	78	H2
Kolhapur	92	D5
Kolin	70	F3
Kolki	71	L3
Kolkuskull	62	V12
Kollabudur	62	T12
Koln	70	B3
Kolno	71	J2
Koloa	126	R10
Kolobrzeg	70	F1
Kologriv	78	G4
Kolombangara	114	H5
Kolomna	78	F4
Kolono	91	G6
Koloubara	72	F3
Kolozsvar	73	G2
Kolpashevo	84	C5
Kolpino	78	E4
Kolskiy Poluostrov	78	F2
Koltubanovskiy	79	J5
Kolva *Russia*	78	K3
Kolva *Russia*	78	K2
Kolwezi	106	E5
Kolyma	85	U3
Kolymskaya Nizmennost	85	T3
Kolymskiy, Khrebet	85	T4
Komadugu Gana	105	H3
Komandorskiye Ostrova	81	T4
Komarno	71	H5
Komarom	72	E2
Komatsu	89	F7
Komering	90	C6
Komodo	91	F7
Komoe	104	E4
Kom Ombo	103	F3
Komoran	91	K7
Komosomolets, Ostrov	81	L1
Komotini	75	H2
Komovi	74	E1
Kompong Cham	93	L6
Kompong Chhnang	93	K6
Kompong Som	93	K6
Kompong Speu	93	K6
Kompong Sralao	93	L6
Kompong Thom	93	K6
Komrat	79	D6
Komsomolets, Zaliv	79	J6
Komsomolsk	79	E6
Komsomolskiy	79	J6
Komsomolsk-na-Amure	85	P6
Konakovo	78	F4
Koncanica	72	D3
Konch	92	E3
Konda *Indonesia*	91	J6
Konda *Russia*	84	Ae4
Kondagaon	92	F5
Kondinin	112	D5
Kondinskoye	84	Ae5
Kondoa	107	G3
Kondon	85	P6
Kondoponga	78	E3
Konduz	92	C1
Kone	114	W16
Konevo	78	F3
Kong	104	E4
Kongan	89	J10
Kong Christian den X Land	120	W3
Kong Karls Land	80	D2
Kongolo	106	E4
Kongsberg	63	C7
Kongsvinger	63	E6
Kong Wilhelms Land	120	X2
Koniecpol	71	H3
Konigsberg	71	J4
Konigs Wusterhausen	70	E2
Konin	71	H2
Konitsa	75	F2
Koniya	89	B11
Konkamaalv	62	J2
Konkoure	104	C3
Konnern	70	D3
Konnevesi	62	M5
Konosha	78	G3
Konotop	79	E5
Konqi He	86	F3
Konskie	71	J3
Konstantinovsk	79	G6
Konstanz	68	B2
Konstyantynivka	79	F6
Kontagora	105	G3
Kontcha	105	H4
Kontiomaki	62	N4
Kontum	93	L6
Kontum, Plateau du	93	L6
Konya	76	E4
Konya Ovasi	76	E3
Konzhakovskiy Kamen, Gora	78	K4
Kootenai	122	G3
Kootenay	122	F3
Kootenay Lake	122	F3
Kopaonik	73	F4
Kopasker	62	W11
Kopavogur	62	U12
Koper	72	B3
Kopervik	63	A7
Kopet Dag, Khrebet	95	N2
Kopeysk	84	Ad5
Koping	63	F7
Kopka	124	F1
Kopmanholmen	62	H5
Koppang	63	D6
Kopparberg *Sweden*	63	F7
Kopparberg *Sweden*	63	F6
Koppi *Russia*	88	G1
Koppi *Russia*	88	H1
Kopru	76	D4
Koprubasi	76	C3
Koprulu	76	E4
Kopruoren	76	C3
Kopychintsy	73	H1
Kor	95	L6
Kora	77	K2
Korab	72	F5
Korahe	103	H6
Koraluk	121	P6
Korana	72	C3
Korba	69	C7
Korbach	70	C3
Korbu, Gunung	90	C5
Korce	75	F2
Korcula	72	D4
Korda	84	F4
Kord Kuv	95	M3
Korea Bay	87	N4
Korea, North	87	P4
Korea, South	87	P4
Korea Strait	89	B8
Korennoye	84	H2
Korenovsk	79	F6
Korf	85	V4
Korforskiy	88	E1
Korgan	77	G2
Korgen	62	E3
Korhogo	104	D4
Korido	91	K6
Korim	91	K6
Korinthiakos Kolpos	75	G3
Korinthos	75	G4
Koriyama	89	H7
Korkinitskiy Zaliv	79	E6
Korkodon	85	T4
Korkuteli	76	D4
Korla	86	F3
Kormakiti, Akra	76	E5
Kornat	72	C4
Koro	114	R8
Korocha	79	F5
Koroglu Daglari	76	E2
Koronia, Limni	75	G2
Koronowo	71	G2
Koros	72	F2
Korosten	79	D5
Korostyshev	79	D5
Korotaikha	78	L2
Korovin Volcano	118	Ad9
Korpilombolo	62	K3
Korsakov	88	J2
Korsnas	62	J5
Korsor	63	D9
Korti	103	F4
Kortrijk	64	E3
Korucu	76	B3
Koryakskaya Sopka	85	U6
Koryanskiy Khrebet	85	Z5
Koryazhma	78	H3
Korzybie	71	G1
Kos *Greece*	75	J4
Kos *Greece*	75	J4
Koschagyl	79	J6
Koscian	71	G2
Koscierzyna	71	G1
Kosciusco, Mount	113	K6
Kosciusko	128	H4
Kose	77	H2
Kos Golu	76	B2
Koshiki-retto	89	B10
Kosice	71	J4
Koski	63	K6
Koslan	78	H3
Koslin	71	G1
Kosma	78	H2
Kosong	88	B6
Kosong-ni	88	B5
Kossou, Lac de	104	D4
Kossovo	71	L2
Kostajnica	72	D3
Kosti	103	F5
Kostino	84	D3
Kostomuksha	62	P4
Kostopol	71	M3
Kostroma *Russia*	78	G4
Kostroma *Russia*	78	G4
Kostrzyn	70	F2
Kosu-dong	89	B8
Kosva	78	K4
Kosyu	78	K2
Kosyuvom	78	K2
Koszalin	71	G1
Kota	92	E3
Kotaagung	90	C7
Kota Baharu	90	C4
Kotabaru *Indonesia*	90	E6
Kotabaru *Indonesia*	90	F6
Kota Belud	90	F4
Kotabumi	90	C5

Kota Kinabalu 90 F4
Kotala 62 N3
Kotamubagu 91 G5
Kota Tinggi 90 C5
Kotel 73 J4
Kotelnich 78 H4
Kotelnikovo 79 G6
Kotelnyy, Ostrov 85 P1
Kotikovo 88 E2
Kotka 63 M6
Kot Kapura 92 D2
Kotlas 78 H3
Kotli 92 D2
Kotlik 118 C3
Koto 85 P7
Kotor 72 E4
Kotovo 79 G5
Kotovsk *Russia* 79 G5
Kotovsk *Ukraine* 79 D6
Kotri 92 C3
Kottagudem 92 F5
Kottayam 92 E7
Kotto 102 D6
Kotuy 84 G2
Kotyuzhany 73 K2
Kotzebue 118 C2
Kotzebue Sound 118 C2
Kouango 102 C6
Koudougou 104 E3
Koufonisi 75 J5
Koukajuak, Great Plain
  of the 120 M4
Kouki 102 C6
Koumac 114 W16
Koumenzi 86 F3
Koumra 102 C6
Koundara 104 C3
Koungou Mountains 106 B3
Kounradskiy 86 D2
Kourou 137 G2
Kouroussa 104 D3
Kousseri 105 J3
Koutiala 100 D6
Kouvola 63 M6
Kova 84 G5
Kovachevo 73 J4
Kovanlik 77 H2
Kovdor 62 P3
Kovdozero, Ozero 62 Q3
Kovel 71 L3
Kovernino 78 G4
Kovero 62 P5
Kovik Bay 121 L5
Kovno 71 K1
Kovrov 78 G4
Kovylkino 78 G5
Kowalewo 71 H2
Kowloon 87 L7
Koycegiz 76 C4
Koyda 78 G2
Koyuk 118 C3
Koyukuk 118 D3
Koyulhisar 77 G2
Koza 89 E9
Kozakli 76 F3
Kozan 77 F4
Kozani 75 F2
Kozekovo 71 M1
Kozelsk 78 F5
Kozhevnikovo 84 B5
Kozhikode 92 E6
Kozhim 78 K2
Kozhposelok 78 F3
Kozhva 78 K2
Kozlu 76 D2
Kozludere 77 G4
Kozluk 77 J3
Kozmodemyansk 78 H4
Kozu-shima 89 G8
Kpalime 104 F4
Krabi 93 J7
Kragero 63 C7
Kragujevac 73 F3
Krakow 71 H3
Krakowska, Jura 71 H3
Kral Chlmec 71 K4
Kralendijk 133 N8
Kraljevo 72 F4
Kralovvany 71 H4
Kralupy 70 F3
Kramatorsk 79 F6
Kramfors 62 G5
Krania 75 F3
Kranidhion 75 G4
Kranj 72 C2
Kranskop 108 F5
Krasavino 78 H3
Krasino 84 Ab2
Kraskino 88 C4
Krasneno 85 X4
Krasnoarmeyesk 84 Ae6
Krasnoarmeyskiy 85 W3
Krasnoborsk 78 H3
Krasnodar 79 F6
Krasnogorsk 88 J1
Krasnograd 79 F6
Krasnokamsk 78 K4
Krasnokutskoye 84 B6
Krasnolesnyy 79 F5
Krasnorechenskiy 88 E3
Krasnoselkup 84 C3
Krasnoslobodsk 78 G5
Krasnoturinsk 84 Ad5
Krasnoufimsk 78 K4

Krasnousolskiy 78 K5
Krasnovishersk 78 K3
Krasnovodsk 95 L2
Krasnovodskiy Poluostrov 79 J7
Krasnoyarsk 84 E5
Krasnoyarskiy Kray 84 E3
Krasnoye 78 G4
Krasnstaw 71 K3
Krasnyy Chikoy 84 H6
Krasnyye Okny 73 K2
Krasnyy Kholm 79 J5
Krasnyy Kut 79 H5
Krasnyy Luch 79 F6
Krasnyy Yar *Russia* 79 G5
Krasnyy Yar *Russia* 79 H6
Kratie 93 L6
Kraulshavn 120 Q3
Kravanh, Chuor Phnum 93 K6
Krefeld 70 B3
Kremenchugskoye
  Vodokhranilishche 79 E6
Kremenchuk 79 E6
Kremnets 79 D5
Krems 68 E1
Krenitzin Islands 118 Ae9
Kresevo 72 E4
Kresttsy 78 E4
Kresty 84 D2
Krestyakh 85 K4
Krestyanka 84 C2
Kretinga 63 J9
Kribi 105 G5
Krichev 79 E5
Krichim 73 H4
Krieza 75 H3
Krifovon 75 F3
Krilon, Mys 88 J3
Krios, Akra 75 G5
Krishna 92 E5
Krishnagiri 92 E6
Krishnanagar 93 G4
Kristdala 63 G8
Kristel 67 F5
Kristiansand 63 B7
Kristianstad *Sweden* 63 E8
Kristianstad *Sweden* 63 E8
Kristiansund 62 B5
Kristiinankaupunki 63 J5
Kristinestad 63 J5
Kristinovka 73 K1
Kriti 75 H5
Kritikon Pelagos 75 H5
Kriulyany 73 K2
Kriva Palanka 73 G4
Krivoye Ozero 73 L2
Krk 72 C3
Krnov 71 G3
Krokodil 108 E4
Krokom 62 F5
Krokong 90 E5
Krokowa 71 H1
Krolevets 79 E5
Kromy 79 F5
Kronach 70 D3
Krononberg 63 F8
Kronshtadt 63 N7
Kroonstad 108 E5
Kropotkin 79 G6
Krosno 71 J4
Krotoszyn 71 G3
Krsko 72 C3
Krugersdorp 108 E5
Krui 90 C7
Kruje 74 E2
Krumbach 70 D4
Krumovgrad 73 H5
Krung Thep 93 K6
Krusenstern, Cape 118 C2
Krusevac 73 F4
Krusevo 73 F5
Krustpils 63 M8
Kruzenshterna, Proliv 85 S7
Kruzof Island 118 H4
Krym 79 E6
Krymsk 79 F7
Krynki 71 K2
Kryry 70 E3
Kryvyy Rih 79 E6
Krzeszowice 71 H3
Ksabi 100 E3
Ksar El Boukhari 101 F1
Ksarel Kebir 100 D2
Ksar es Souk 100 E2
Ksenofontova 78 K3
Ksour Essaf 101 H1
Kstovo 78 G4
Kualakapuas 90 E6
Kuala Kerai 90 C4
Kuala Lipis 90 C5
Kuala Lumpur 90 C5
Kualapembuang 90 E6
Kuala Penyu 90 F4
Kuala Terengganu 90 C4
Kuandian 87 N3
Kuantan 90 C5
Kuba 89 D8
Kuban 79 G6
Kubenskoye Ozero 78 F4
Kubkain 114 C2
Kubokawa 89 D9
Kubonitu, Mount 114 J6
Kubor, Mount 114 C3
Kubrat 73 J4
Kubuang 90 F5

Kucevo 73 F3
Kuching 90 E5
Kuchinoerabu-jima 89 C10
Kuchinotsu 89 C9
Kuchurgan 73 K2
Kucuk 76 B3
Kucukcekmece 76 C2
Kucuk Kuyu 76 B3
Kudat 90 F4
Kudirkos-Naumiestis 71 K1
Kudus 90 E7
Kudymkar 78 J4
Kufi 76 C3
Kufstein 68 D2
Kugaly 86 D3
Kugi 84 Ad4
Kugmallit Bay 118 J2
Kuhdasht 94 H5
Kuh-e Bul 95 L6
Kuh-e Garbosh 95 K5
Kuh Lab, Ra's 95 Q9
Kuhmo 62 N4
Kuhpayeh *Iran* 95 L5
Kuhpayeh *Iran* 95 N6
Kuhran, Kuh-e 95 P8
Kuh, Ra's-al- 95 N9
Kuito 106 C5
Kuji 88 H5
Kuju-san 89 C9
Kukalar, Kuh-e 95 K6
Kukes 75 F1
Kukhomskaya Volya 71 L3
Kukmor 78 J4
Kukpowruk 118 C2
Kukudu 114 H6
Kukup 90 C5
Kukushka 85 M6
Kula *Turkey* 76 C3
Kula *Yugoslavia* 72 E3
Kulagino 79 J6
Kulakshi 79 K6
Kulal, Mont 107 G2
Kulata 73 G5
Kuldiga 63 N8
Kule 108 D4
Kulebaki 78 G4
Kulgera 113 G4
Kulikov 71 L4
Kulinda *Russia* 84 G4
Kulinda *Russia* 84 H4
Kulmac Daglari 77 G3
Kulmbach 70 D3
Kuloy *Russia* 78 G3
Kuloy *Russia* 78 G2
Kulp 77 J3
Kulsary 79 J6
Kultay 79 J6
Kultuk 84 G6
Kulu 76 E3
Kulu Island 118 J4
Kulul 96 E9
Kulunda 84 B6
Kulundinskoye, Ozero 84 B6
Kulyab 86 B4
Kuma 79 H7
Kumagaya 89 G7
Kumakh-Surt 85 M2
Kumamoto 89 C9
Kumano 89 F9
Kumanovo 73 F4
Kumara 115 C5
Kumasi 104 E4
Kumba 105 G5
Kumbakonam 92 E6
Kum-Dag 95 M2
Kumertau 79 K5
Kuminki 62 L4
Kuminskiy 84 Ae5
Kumkuduk 86 F3
Kumluca 76 D4
Kummerower See 70 E2
Kumnyong 87 P5
Kumon Bum 93 J3
Kumru 77 G2
Kumsong 87 P4
Kumta 92 D6
Kumyr 86 C3
Kunas 86 E3
Kunas Chang 86 E3
Kunashir, Ostrov 88 L3
Kundelungu Mountains 107 E5
Kunduz 92 C1
Kungalv 63 H8
Kungar 78 K4
Kunghit Island 118 J5
Kungrad 51 U7
Kungsor 63 G7
Kungu 106 C2
Kunlun Shan 92 F1
Kunmadaras 72 F2
Kunming 93 K4
Kunsan 87 P4
Kununurra 112 F2
Kunu-ri 87 P4
Kuolayarvi 62 N3
Kuopio *Sweden* 62 M5
Kuopio *Sweden* 62 M5
Kupa 72 C3
Kupang 91 G7
Kuparuk 118 E2
Kupino 84 B6
Kupreanof Island 118 J4
Kupreanof Point 118 Ag8
Kupyansk 79 F6

Kuqa 86 E3
Kura 77 L2
Kurashasayskiy 79 K5
Kurashiki 89 D8
Kurayoshi 89 D8
Kurday 86 D3
Kurdzhali 73 H5
Kure 89 D8
Kure 76 E2
Kurecik 77 G3
Kure Daglari 76 F2
Kuresaare 63 M7
Kureyka 84 D3
Kurgan 84 Ae5
Kurganinsk 79 G7
Kurgan-Tyube 86 B4
Kurikka 62 N4
Kurilskiye Ostrova 85 S7
Kuril Trench 142 G3
Kurkcu 76 E4
Kurlek 84 C5
Kurmuk 103 F5
Kurnool 92 E5
Kuroi 89 E8
Kuroiso 89 G7
Kurow 71 K3
Kursk 79 F5
Kursumlija 73 F4
Kursunlu 76 E2
Kurtalan 77 J4
Kurtamysh 84 Ad6
Kurtun 77 H2
Kuru 63 K6
Kurucasile 76 E2
Kuruman *South Africa* 108 D5
Kuruman *South Africa* 108 D5
Kurume 89 C9
Kurunegala 92 F7
Kurzeme 63 K8
Kusadasi 76 B4
Kusadasi Korfezi 76 B4
Kusel 70 B4
Kusey Andolu Daglari 77 H2
Kushchevskaya 79 F6
Kushima 89 C10
Kushimoto 89 E9
Kushiro 88 K4
Kushka *Russia* 85 U4
Kushmurun 84 Ad6
Kushtia 93 G4
Kushva 78 K4
Kuskokwim 118 C3
Kuskokwim Bay 118 C4
Kuskokwim Mountains 118 D3
Kusma 92 F3
Kussharo-ko 88 K4
Kustanay 84 Ad6
Kustrin 70 F2
Kuta 105 G4
Kutahya 76 C3
Kutaisi 77 K1
Kutchan 88 H4
Kutima 84 H5
Kut, Ko 93 K6
Kutna Hora 70 F4
Kutno 71 H2
Kutu 106 C3
Kutubdia 93 H4
Kutum 102 D5
Kuujjuaq 121 N6
Kuujjuarapik 121 L6
Kuuli-Mayak 79 J7
Kuusamo 62 N4
Kuvango 106 C5
Kuvet 85 X3
Kuwait 94 H7
Kuwait 97 J2
Kuwana 89 F8
Kuya 78 G2
Kuybyshev *Russia* 84 B5
Kuybyshevskoye
  Vodokhranilishche 78 H4
Kuyeda 78 K4
Kuygan 86 C2
Kuytun 86 F3
Kuyucak 76 C4
Kuyumba 84 F4
Kuyus 84 D6
Kuzino 78 K4
Kuzitrin 118 C2
Kuzmovka 84 E4
Kuznetsk 79 H5
Kuznetsovo 88 G2
Kuzomen 78 F2
Kuzucubelen 76 E4
Kvaloy 62 H2
Kvaloya 62 K1
Kvalsund 62 L1
Kvarner 72 C3
Kvarneric 72 C3
Kvichak Bay 118 D4
Kvidinge 63 E8
Kvigtind 62 E4
Kvikkjokk 62 G3
Kvina 63 B7
Kvorning 63 C8
Kwa 106 C3
Kwale 105 G4
Kwamouth 106 C3
Kwangju 87 P4
Kwango 106 C3
Kwanso-ri 88 B5
Kwatisore 91 J6
Kwekwe 108 E3

Name	Page	Ref
Kwidzyn	71	H2
Kwilu	106	C3
Kwoka	91	J6
Kyabe	102	C6
Kyaikto	93	J5
Kyakhta	84	H6
Kyaukpyu	93	H5
Kyaukse	93	J4
Kybartai	71	K1
Kychema	78	G2
Kyeburn	115	C6
Kyelang	92	E2
Kyle	57	D5
Kyleakin	56	C3
Kyle of Lochalsh	56	C3
Kylestrome	56	C2
Kymi	63	M6
Kymijoki	63	M6
Kynuna	113	J3
Kyoga, Lake	107	F2
Kyongju	89	B8
Kyoto	89	E8
Kyrdanyy	85	M3
Kyrgyzstan	86	C3
Kyritz	70	E2
Kyrkheden	63	E6
Kyronjoki	62	K5
Kyrosjarvi	63	K6
Kyrta	78	K3
Kyssa	78	H3
Kystyk, Plato	85	L2
Kyuekh-Bulung	84	J3
Kyurdamir	79	H7
Kyushu	89	C9
Kyushu-sanchi	89	C9
Kyustendil	73	G4
Kyyiv	79	E5
Kyyjarvi	62	L5
Kyyvesi	63	M6
Kyzyk	79	J7
Kyzyl	84	E6
Kyzyldyykan	86	B2
Kyzylkoga	79	J6
Kyzyl-Kommuna	86	B2
Kyzylkum	80	H5
Kzyl-Dzhar	86	B2
Kzyl-Orda	86	B3
Kzyltu	84	A6

L

Name	Page	Ref
La Almunia de Dona Godina	67	F2
Laascaanood	103	J6
Laas Dhuure	103	J5
La Asuncion	136	E1
Laayoune	100	C3
La Baie	125	Q2
La Banda	138	D5
La Baneza	66	D1
La Barca	130	H7
Labasa	114	R8
La Baule	65	B5
Labaz, Ozero	84	F2
Labbah, Al	96	E2
Labe	104	C3
Labe	70	F3
Labelle	125	N3
Laberge, Lake	118	H3
Labi	90	E5
Labin	72	C3
Labinsk	79	G7
Labis	90	C5
La Bisbal	67	H2
Labouheyre	65	C6
Laboulaye	139	D6
La Bourboule	65	E6
Labrador	121	P7
Labrador City	121	N7
Labrador Sea	121	Q6
Labrea	136	E5
Labrit	65	C6
Labuha	91	H6
Labuhan	90	D7
Labuhanbajo	91	F7
Labuhanbilik	90	C5
Labytnangi	84	Ae3
Lac	74	E2
La Calzada de Calatrava	66	E3
Lacanau	65	C6
La Carlota	139	D6
La Carolina	66	E3
La Cava	67	G2
Laccadive Islands	92	D6
Laccadive Sea	92	E7
La Ceiba	132	D7
Lacepede Bay	113	H6
La Chaise-Dieu	65	E6
Lacha, Ozero	78	F3
La Charite	65	E5
La Chartre-sur-le-Loir	65	D5
La Chatre	65	D5
La Chaux-de-Fonds	68	A2
Lachin	94	H2
Lachlan	113	K5
La Chorrera	132	H10
Lachute	125	N4
La Cieneguita	126	G6
La Ciotat	65	F7
Lac la Biche	119	N5
Lac Megantic	125	Q4
La Colorada	126	G6
Laconi	69	B6
Laconia	125	Q5
La Coruna	66	B1
La Croix, Lac	124	D2
La Crosse	124	E5
La Cruz Costa Rica	132	E9
La Cruz Mexico	130	F6
Lacul Razelm	73	K3
Ladakh Range	92	E2
Ladder Hills	56	E3
La Desirade	133	S6
Ladik	77	F2
Ladismith	108	D6
Ladiz	95	Q7
Ladozhskoye Ozero	63	P6
Ladybank	57	E4
Ladybower Reservoir	55	H3
Ladybrand	108	E5
Ladysmith Canada	122	C3
Ladysmith South Africa	108	E5
Ladysmith U.S.A.	124	E4
Ladyzhenka	84	Ae6
Ladyzhinka	79	D6
Lae	93	K5
Laem Ngop	93	K6
La Esmeralda Paraguay	138	D4
La Esmeralda Venezuela	136	D3
La Fayette	129	K3
Lafayette Colorado	123	M8
Lafayette Indiana	124	G6
Lafayette Louisiana	128	F5
La Fe	132	E3
La Ferte-Bernard	64	D4
La-Ferte-Saint-Aubin	65	D5
Laffan, Ra's	97	K4
Lafia	105	G4
Lafiagi	105	G4
La Fleche	65	C5
La Follette	129	K2
La Fria	136	C2
Laft	95	M8
La Fuente de San Esteban	66	C2
La Galite	69	B7
Lagan	63	E8
Lagarfljot	62	X12
Lagen Norway	63	C6
Lagen Norway	63	D6
Laggan	57	D3
Laggan Bay	57	B5
Laggan, Loch	57	D4
Laghouat	101	F2
Lagny	64	E4
Lagonegro	69	E5
Lago Posadas	139	B9
Lagos Nigeria	105	F4
Lagos Portugal	66	B4
Lagos de Moreno	130	J7
La Grande Canada	121	M7
La Grande U.S.A.	122	E5
La Grande 2, Reservoir	121	L7
La Grande 3, Reservoir	121	L7
La Grande 4, Reservoir	121	M7
La Grange Georgia	129	K4
La Grange Kentucky	124	H7
La Grange Texas	128	D6
La Granja	66	D2
La Gran Sabana	136	E2
La Guardia	66	B2
Laguardia	66	E1
La Gudina	66	C1
La Guerche-de-Bretagne	65	C5
Laguna	138	G5
Laguna Grande	139	C9
Lagunillas Bolivia	138	D3
Lagunillas Venezuela	133	M9
Laha	87	N2
La Habana	132	F3
Lahad Datu	91	F4
Lahave	121	P9
Lahij	96	G10
Lahijan	95	J3
Lahn Germany	70	C3
Lahn Germany	70	C3
Lahore	92	D2
Lahr	70	B4
Lahti	63	L6
Laibach	72	C2
Laibin	93	L4
Lai Chau	93	K4
L'Aigle	64	D4
Laihia	62	J5
Laimbele, Mount	114	T12
Laina	75	J2
Laingsburg	108	D6
Lainioalven	62	K3
Lair	56	C3
Lairg	56	D2
Lais	90	C6
Laitila	63	J6
Laiwui	91	H6
Laixi	87	N4
Laiyang	87	N4
Laiyuan	87	L4
Laizhou Wan	87	M4
Lajes	138	F5
La Junta	127	L2
Lakatrask	62	J3
Lake Andes	123	Q6
Lakeba	114	S9
Lakeba Passage	114	S9
Lake Cargelligo	113	K5
Lake Charles	128	F5
Lake City Florida	129	L5
Lake City S. Carolina	129	N4
Lake District	55	F2
Lake Grace	112	D5
Lake Harbour	120	N5
Lake Havasu City	126	E3
Lake Jackson	128	E6
Lake King	112	D5
Lake Kopiago	114	C3
Lakeland	129	M6
Lake Louise	122	F2
Lake Murray	114	C3
Lakeport	122	C8
Lake Providence	128	G4
Lakeview	122	D6
Lake Wales	129	M7
Lakewood	124	K6
Lakhdaria	67	H4
Lakhpat	92	C4
Lakki	75	G4
Lakonikos Kolpos	75	G4
Laksefjorden	62	M1
Lakselv	62	L1
Lakshadweep	92	D6
Lakuramau	114	E2
Lala Musa	92	D2
Lalaua	109	G2
Laleh Zar, Kuh-e	95	N7
Lalibela	103	G5
La Libertad	132	B6
La Ligua	139	B6
Lalin	66	B1
Lalin	87	P2
La Linea	66	D4
Lalin He	88	A3
Lalitpur	92	E4
Lalla Khedidja	67	J4
La Loche	119	P4
La Loupe	64	D4
La Louviere	64	F3
La Luz	132	E8
Lalyo	102	F7
Lamag	91	F4
La Mancha	66	E3
La Manza	136	D6
Lama, Ozero	84	D3
Lamar Colorado	127	L1
Lamar Missouri	124	C8
Lamas	136	B5
Lamastre	65	F6
Lamballe	64	B4
Lambarene	106	B3
Lambas	114	R8
Lambay Island	59	K6
Lamberhurst	53	H3
Lambert, Cape	114	E2
Lambert Glacier	141	E4
Lamberts Bay	108	C6
Lamb Head	56	F1
Lambia	75	F4
Lambon	114	E2
Lambourn	53	F3
Lamb's Head	59	B9
Lambton, Cape	118	L1
Lame	102	B6
Lamego	66	C2
Lamenu	114	U12
Lameroo	113	J6
Lamia	75	G3
Lammermuir	57	F5
Lammermuir Hills	57	F5
Lammhult	63	F8
Lammi	63	L6
Lamon Bay	91	G3
Lamont California	126	C3
Lamont Wyoming	123	L6
La Morita	127	K6
La Moure	123	Q4
Lam Pao Reservoir	93	K5
Lampasas	128	C5
Lampazos de Naranjo	128	B7
Lampedusa	74	B5
Lampeter	52	C2
Lampinou	75	G3
Lampione	74	B5
Lamport	53	G2
Lampsa	62	P4
Lamu	107	H3
Lan	71	M2
Lanai	126	S10
Lanai City	126	S10
Lanark	57	D5
La Nava de Ricomalillo	66	D3
Lanbi Kyun	93	J6
Lancang	93	K4
Lancashire	55	G3
Lancaster U.K.	55	G2
Lancaster Ohio	124	J7
Lancaster Pennsylvania	125	M6
Lancaster S. Carolina	129	M3
Lancaster Sound	120	J3
Lanciano	69	E4
Lancut	71	K3
Landau	70	C4
Landeck	68	C2
Lander	123	K6
Landerneau	64	A4
Landes	65	C6
Landi	95	R6
Landor	112	D4
Landrum	129	L3
Landsberg Poland	70	F2
Landsberg Germany	70	D4
Landsborough	113	J3
Land's End	52	B4
Lands End	120	B2
Landshut	70	E4
Landskrona	63	E9
Lanesborough	58	G5
Lanett	129	K4
Langa Co	92	F2
Langadhia	75	F4
Langavat, Loch	56	B2
Langdon	123	Q3
Lange Berg	108	C6
Langebergen	108	D5
Langeland	63	D9
Langelmavesi	63	L6
Langeoog	70	B2
Langesund	63	C7
Langevag	62	B5
Langfang	87	M4
Langhirano	68	C3
Langholm	57	E5
Langjokull	62	U12
Langkawi	93	J7
Langnau	68	A2
Langness Point	54	E2
Langogne	65	E6
Langon	65	C6
Langoya	62	F2
Langport	52	E3
Langres	65	F5
Langsa	90	B5
Langsele	62	G5
Langsett	55	H3
Lang Son	93	L4
Langtoft	55	J2
Langtrask	62	J4
Languedoc	65	E7
Langwathby	55	G2
Langzhong	93	L2
Lannemezan	65	D7
Lannion	64	B4
Lansing	124	H5
Lansjarv	62	K3
Lanslebourg	65	G6
Lanta, Ko	93	J7
Lanusei	69	B6
Lanvaux, Landes de	65	B5
Lanxi	87	P2
Lanzarote	100	C3
Lanzhou	93	K1
Laoag	91	G2
Laoang	91	H3
Lao Cai	93	K4
Laois	59	H7
Laon	64	E4
La Oroya	136	B6
Laos	90	C2
Laoye Ling	88	B3
Laoyemiao	86	F3
Lapa	138	G5
Lapalisse	65	E5
La Palma Panama	132	H10
La Palma Spain	100	B3
La Palma del Condado	66	C4
La Paragua	136	E2
La Paz Argentina	139	C6
La Paz Argentina	138	E6
La Paz Bolivia	138	C3
La Paz Mexico	130	D5
La Pedrera	136	D4
La Piedad	130	H7
La Place	128	G5
La Plant	123	P5
La Plata	139	E6
La Pocatiere	125	R3
La Pola de Gordon	66	D1
La Porte	124	G6
Lapovo	73	F3
Lappajarvi	62	K5
Lappeenranta	63	N6
Lappi	62	M3
Lapseki	76	B2
Laptev Sea	85	M1
Laptevykh, More	85	M1
Lapua	62	K5
La Puebla	67	H3
La Puntilla	136	A4
La Quiaca	138	C4
L'Aquila	69	D4
Lar	95	M8
Larache	100	D1
Larak	95	N8
La Rambla	66	D4
Laramie	123	M7
Laramie Mountains	123	M6
Laranjal	137	F4
Larantuka	91	G7
Larat Indonesia	114	A3
Larat Indonesia	114	A3
Larba	67	H4
Laredo Spain	66	E1
Laredo U.S.A.	128	C7
La Reole	65	C6
Largo U.S.A.	129	L7
Largo Venezuela	133	R10
Largoward	57	F4
Largs	57	D5
Lari	94	H2
Larino	69	E5
La Rioja	138	C5
Larisa	75	G3
Lark	53	H2
Larkana	92	C3
Larkhall	57	F4
Larlomkiny	84	A5
Larne	58	L3
La Robla	66	D1

Liddesdale	57	F5
Liden	62	G5
Lidingo	63	H7
Lidkoping	63	E7
Lidzbark Warminski	71	J1
Liebling	73	F3
Liechtenstein	70	C5
Liege	64	F3
Liegnitz	71	G3
Lielope	63	L8
Lienz	68	D2
Liepaja	63	L8
Lier	64	F3
Liestal	68	A2
Liezen	68	E2
Liffey	59	J6
Lifford	58	H3
Lifi Mahuida	139	C8
Lifou	114	X16
Ligger Bay	52	B4
Lighthouse Reef	132	D6
Ligonha	109	G3
Ligui	126	G8
Ligure, Appennino	68	B3
Ligurian Sea	68	B4
Lihir Group	114	E2
Lihou Reefs	113	L2
Lihue	126	R10
Lihula	63	K7
Lijiang	93	K3
Likasi	106	E5
Likhoslavl	78	F4
Liku	90	D5
Likupang	91	H5
L'Ile-Rousse	69	B4
Lille	64	E3
Lille Balt	63	C8
Lillebonne	64	D4
Lillehammer	63	D6
Lillesand	63	C7
Lillestrom	63	H7
Lillhamra	63	F6
Lillhardal	63	F6
Lillholmsjon	62	F5
Lillo	66	E3
Lillviken	62	G3
Lilongwe	107	F5
Liloy	91	G4
Lima *Paraguay*	138	E4
Lima *Peru*	136	B6
Lima *Portugal*	66	B2
Lima *Montana*	122	H5
Lima *Ohio*	124	H6
Limah	97	N4
Limankoy	76	C2
Limavady	58	J2
Limay	139	C7
Limbang	90	E5
Limbani	136	D6
Limbe *Cameroon*	105	G5
Limbe *Malawi*	107	G6
Limburg	70	C3
Limeira	138	G4
Limenaria	75	H2
Limen Vatheos	75	J4
Limerick *Ireland*	59	E8
Limerick *Ireland*	59	E7
Limfjorden	63	C8
Limin	75	H2
Limmen Bight	113	H1
Limni	75	G3
Limnos	75	H3
Limoeiro *Ceara, Brazil*	137	K5
Limoeiro *Pernambuco, Brazil*	137	K5
Limoges	65	D6
Limon	132	F9
Limon	123	N8
Limousin	65	D6
Limoux	65	E7
Limpopo	109	F4
Linaalv	62	J3
Linah	96	F2
Linapacan Strait	91	F3
Linares *Chile*	139	B7
Linares *Mexico*	128	C8
Linares *Spain*	66	E3
Lincang	93	K4
Lincoln *New Zealand*	115	D5
Lincoln *U.K.*	55	J3
Lincoln *Illinois*	124	F6
Lincoln *Maine*	125	R4
Lincoln *Nebraska*	123	R7
Lincoln City	122	B5
Lincoln Sea	140	R2
Lincolnshire	55	J3
Lincolnton	129	M3
Lindau	70	C5
Linde	85	L3
Linden *Guyana*	136	F2
Linden *U.S.A.*	129	J3
Linderodsasen	63	E9
Lindesberg	63	F7
Lindi	107	G4
Lindley	108	E5
Lindos	75	K4
Lindsay *Canada*	125	L4
Lindsay *California*	126	C2
Lindsay *Montana*	123	M4
Lindu Point	114	S8
Linfen	93	M1
Lingao	93	L5
Lingayen	91	G2
Lingen	70	B2
Lingfield	53	G3

Lingga	90	C6
Lingga, Kepulauan	90	C6
Lingle	123	M6
Lingling	93	M3
Lingshi	37	L4
Lingshui	93	M5
Lingsugur	92	E5
Linguere	104	B2
Ling Xian	93	M3
Lingyuan	37	M3
Lingyun	93	L4
Linhai	37	N6
Linhares	138	H3
Linhe	37	K3
Linh, Ngoc	93	L5
Linkoping	53	F7
Linkou	38	C3
Linlithgow	57	E5
Linnhe, Loch	57	C4
Linosa	74	B5
Linru	93	M2
Lins	138	G4
Linsell	53	E5
Linslade	53	G3
Lintao	93	K1
Linton *U.K.*	53	H2
Linton *U.S.A.*	123	P4
Linwu	93	M3
Linxi	37	M3
Linxia	93	K1
Linyi *China*	37	M4
Linyi *China*	37	M4
Linz *Austria*	68	E1
Linz *Germany*	70	B3
Linze	86	J4
Lion, Golfe du	65	F7
Liouesso	106	C2
Lipa *Philippines*	91	G3
Lipa *Bos.*	72	D3
Lipari, Isola	69	E6
Lipari, Isole	69	E6
Lipenska nadrz	70	F4
Lipetsk	79	F5
Lipiany	70	F2
Lipin Bor	78	F3
Liping	93	L3
Lipkany	79	D6
Lipljan	73	F4
Liprishki	71	L2
Lipno	71	H2
Lippe	70	C3
Lipsoi	75	J4
Lipson	75	F3
Lipu	93	M4
Lipusz	71	G1
Lira	107	F2
Lircay	136	C6
Liri	69	D5
Lisabata	91	H6
Lisala	106	D2
Lisboa	66	B3
Lisbon *Portugal*	66	B3
Lisbon *U.S.A.*	123	R4
Lisburn	58	K3
Lisburne, Cape	118	B2
Liscannor Bay	59	D7
Lisdoonvarna	59	D6
Lishi	87	L4
Lishui	87	M6
Lisieux	64	D4
Liskeard	52	C4
Liski	79	F5
L'Isle-Jourdain	65	D7
Lismore *Australia*	113	L4
Lismore *Ireland*	59	G8
Lismore *U.K.*	57	C4
Liss	53	G3
Listowel	59	D8
Lit	62	F5
Litang	93	K3
Litani	137	G3
Litchfield	124	F7
Litherland	55	G3
Lithgow	113	L5
Lithinon, Akra	75	H5
Litos	66	C2
Lithuania	63	K9
Litovko	85	P7
Little	128	E4
Little Abaco	132	J1
Little Aden	96	G10
Little Andaman	93	H6
Little Bahama Bank	132	H1
Little Barrier Island	115	E2
Little Belt Mountains	122	J4
Littleborough	55	G3
Little Bow	122	H2
Little Cayman	132	G5
Little Colorado	126	G3
Little Falls *Minnesota*	124	C3
Little Falls *New York*	125	N5
Littlefield	127	L4
Littlehampton	53	G4
Little Inagua Island	133	L4
Little Karoo	108	D6
Little Minch, The	56	B3
Little Missouri	123	M5
Little Nicobar	93	H7
Little Ouse	53	H2
Little Pamir	92	D1
Littleport	53	H2
Little Red	128	G3
Little Rock	128	F3
Little Rocky Mountains	123	K3

Little Scarcies	104	C4
Little Sitkin Island	118	Ab9
Little Smoky	119	M5
Little Snake	123	K7
Little South-west Miramichi	125	S3
Little Strickland	55	G2
Littleton *Colorado*	123	M8
Littleton *New Hampshire*	125	Q4
Little Wabash	124	F7
Little Waltham	53	H3
Liulin	87	L4
Liupan Shan	93	L1
Liuyang	93	M3
Liuzhou	93	L4
Livani	63	M8
Live Oak	129	L5
Livermore	126	B2
Livermore, Mount	127	K5
Liverpool *Australia*	113	L5
Liverpool *U.K.*	55	G3
Liverpool Bay *Canada*	118	K1
Liverpool Bay *U.K.*	55	F3
Livingston *Canada*	121	N7
Livingston *U.K.*	57	E5
Livingston *Montana*	123	J5
Livingston *Texas*	128	E5
Livingstone	106	E6
Livingstone, Chutes de	106	B4
Livingstone Falls	106	B4
Livingstone Mountains	107	F4
Livingston Island	141	V6
Livingston, Lake	128	E5
Livno	72	D4
Livny	79	F5
Livojoki	62	M4
Livonia	124	J5
Livorno	68	C4
Liwiec	71	J2
Liwonde	107	G6
Li Xian	93	M3
Liyang	87	M5
Lizard	52	B4
Lizardo	137	H5
Lizard Point	52	B4
Ljosavatn	62	W12
Ljubinje	72	E4
Ljubisnja	72	E4
Ljubljana	72	C2
Ljungan	62	G5
Ljungby	63	E8
Ljusdal	63	G6
Ljusnan	63	F5
Llanarmon Dyffryn Ceiriog	52	D2
Llanbadarn Fynydd	52	D2
Llanbedr	52	C2
Llanberis	54	E3
Llanbrynmair	52	D2
Llandeilo	52	D3
Llandovery	52	D3
Llandrindod Wells	52	D2
Llandudno	54	F3
Llanelli	52	C3
Llanerchymedd	54	E3
Llanes	66	D1
Llanfaethlu	54	E3
Llanfair Caereinion	52	D2
Llanfairfechan	54	F3
Llanfair Talhaiarn	55	F3
Llanfyllin	52	D2
Llangefni	55	E3
Llanglydwen	52	C3
Llangollen	52	D2
Llangranog	52	C2
Llangurig	52	D2
Llanidloes	52	D2
Llanilar	52	C2
Llanos	136	D2
Llanquihue, Lago	139	B8
Llanrhystud	52	C2
Llanrwst	54	F3
Llantrisant	52	D3
Llanwenog	52	C2
Llanwrtyd Wells	52	D2
Llawhaden	52	C3
Llerena	66	C3
Lleyn Peninsula	52	C2
Lliria	67	F3
Llivia	67	G1
Llobregat	67	G2
Lloydminster	119	P5
Lluchmayor	67	H3
Llyswen	52	D2
Loa	138	C4
Loanhead	57	E5
Lobatse	108	E5
Lobau	70	F3
Loberia	139	E7
Lobez	70	F2
Lobito	106	B5
Lobos	139	E7
Lobos, Island	126	G7
Locarno	68	B2
Lochaber	57	D4
Lochailort	57	C4
Lochan Fada	56	C3
Loch Ard Forest	57	D4
Lochboisdale	57	A3
Lochearnhead	57	D4
Loches	65	D5
Lochgelly	57	E4
Lochgilphead	57	C4
Lochinver	56	C2
Lochmaben	57	E5
Lochmaddy	56	A3

Lochnagar	57	E4
Lochranza	57	C5
Loch Shin	56	D2
Lochy, Loch	57	D4
Lock	113	H5
Lockerbie	57	E5
Lockhart	128	D6
Lock Haven	125	M6
Lockport	125	L5
Locri	69	F6
Loddekopinge	63	E9
Loddon *Australia*	113	J6
Loddon *U.K.*	53	J2
Lodeve	65	E7
Lodeynoye Pole	78	E3
Lodge Grass	123	L5
Lodgepole	123	M7
Lodi *Italy*	68	B3
Lodi *U.S.A.*	126	B1
Lodingen	62	F2
Lodja	106	D3
Lodwar	107	G2
Lodz	71	H3
Loeriesfontein	108	C6
Lofoten	62	E2
Loftus	55	J2
Logan	122	J7
Logan, Mount	118	G3
Logansport *Indiana*	124	G6
Logansport *Louisiana*	128	F5
Loge	106	B4
Logishin	71	M2
Logone	102	C5
Logrono	66	E1
Logrosan	66	D3
Loh	114	T10
Lohardaga	92	F4
Loharu	92	E3
Lohit	93	J3
Lohja	63	L6
Lohtaja	62	K4
Loikaw	93	J5
Loimaa	63	K6
Loimijoki	63	K6
Loing	65	E5
Loi, Phu	93	K4
Loir	65	C5
Loire	65	B5
Loja *Ecuador*	136	B4
Loja *Spain*	66	D4
Lokantekojarvi	62	M3
Lokhpodgort	78	M2
Lokhvitsa	79	E5
Lokichokio	107	F2
Lokilalaki, Gunung	91	G6
Lokka	62	M3
Loknya	78	E4
Lokoja	105	G4
Lokshak	85	N6
Lokuru	114	H6
Lol	102	E6
Lola	104	D4
Lolland	63	D9
Lolo	122	G4
Loloda	91	H5
Lolo Pass	122	G4
Lolvavana, Passage	114	U11
Lom *Bulgaria*	73	G4
Lom *Norway*	63	C6
Lomami	106	D3
Lomas Coloradas	139	C8
Lomazy	71	K3
Lombarda, Serra	137	G3
Lombe	107	G4
Lombez	65	D7
Lomblen	91	G7
Lombok	90	F7
Lome	104	F4
Lomela	106	D3
Lomir	94	J2
Lomond Hills	57	E4
Lomond, Loch	57	D4
Lomonosov Ridge	140	A1
Lompobattang, Gunung	91	F7
Lompoc	126	B3
Lomza	71	K2
London *Canada*	125	K5
London *U.K.*	53	G3
Londonderry *U.K.*	58	H2
Londonderry *U.K.*	58	J3
Londonderry, Cape	112	F1
Londonderry, Isla	139	B11
Londoni	114	R8
Londrina	138	F4
Lone Pine	126	C2
Longa *Angola*	106	C5
Longa *Angola*	106	C6
Longa Island	56	C3
Long Akah	90	E5
Longa, Ostrova de	81	S2
Long Bay	129	N4
Long Beach *California*	126	C4
Long Beach *New York*	125	P6
Long Branch	125	P6
Longchang	93	L3
Longchuan	87	M7
Longde	93	L1
Long Eaton	53	F2
Longford *Ireland*	58	G5
Longford *Ireland*	58	G5
Longformacus	57	F5
Longframlington	57	G5
Longhoughton	55	H1
Longhua	87	M3

M

Name		
Mashkid	95	R8
Masi	62	K2
Masilah, Wadi al	97	J9
Masi-Manimba	106	C3
Masindi	107	F2
Masirah	97	P6
Masirah, Khalij	97	N7
Masirah, Khawr al	97	P6
Masiri	95	K6
Masisi	107	E3
Masjed Soleyman	94	J6
Mask, Lough	58	D5
Maskutan	95	P8
Maslen Nos	73	J4
Masoala, Cap	109	K3
Mason Bay	115	A7
Mason City	124	D5
Ma, Song	93	K4
Masqat	97	P5
Massa	68	C3
Massachusetts	125	P5
Massachusetts Bay	125	Q5
Massakori	102	C5
Massa Marittima	68	C4
Massangena	109	F4
Massape	137	J4
Massava	84	Ad4
Massenya	102	C5
Massigui	100	D6
Massillon	124	K6
Massinga	109	G4
Massingir	109	F4
Masteksay	79	H6
Masterton	115	E4
Mastikho, Akra	75	J3
Mastuj	92	D1
Masturah	96	D5
Masuda	89	C8
Masulch	94	J3
Masurai, Bukit	90	C6
Masvingo	108	F4
Masyaf	94	C4
Mat	74	F2
Mataboor	91	K6
Mataca	109	G2
Matachel	66	C3
Matad	87	M2
Matadi	106	B4
Matafome	66	B3
Matagalpa	132	E8
Matagami *Ontario, Canada*	125	M2
Matagami *Quebec, Canada*	125	M2
Matagami, Lac	125	M1
Matagorda Bay	128	D6
Matagorda Island	128	D6
Matakana Island	115	F2
Matakaoa Point	115	G2
Matala	106	C5
Matale	92	F7
Matam	104	C2
Matamata	115	E2
Matamoros *Mexico*	128	D8
Matamoros *Mexico*	127	L8
Matane	125	S2
Mata Negra	136	E2
Matanzas	132	G3
Matapan, Cape	75	G4
Matapedia	125	S2
Matara	92	F7
Mataram	90	F7
Matarani	138	B3
Mataranka	112	G1
Mataro	67	H2
Matata	115	F2
Matatiele	108	E6
Mataura *New Zealand*	115	B6
Mataura *New Zealand*	115	B7
Matawai	115	F3
Matay	86	D2
Matcha	86	B4
Matehuala	131	J6
Matera	69	F5
Mateszalka	73	G2
Mateur	101	G1
Matfors	62	G5
Matheson	125	K2
Mathis	128	D6
Mathry	52	B3
Mathura	92	E3
Mati	91	H4
Matlock	55	H3
Mato, Cerro	133	Q11
Mato Grosso	136	F6
Mato Grosso do Sul	138	E3
Mato Grosso, Planalto do	138	E3
Matra	72	E2
Matrah	97	P5
Matrosovo	71	J1
Matruh	102	E1
Matsubara	89	J10
Matsue	89	D8
Ma-tsu Lieh-tao	87	M6
Matsumae	88	H5
Matsumoto	89	F7
Matsusaka	89	F8
Matsuyama	89	D9
Mattagami	121	K8
Mattancheri	92	E7
Mattawa	125	L3
Matterhorn *Switzerland*	68	A3
Matterhorn *U.S.A.*	122	G7
Matthews Peak	107	G2
Matthew Town	133	L4
Matti, Sabkhat	97	K10

Name		
Mattoon	124	F7
Matty Island	120	G3
Matua, Ostrov	85	S7
Matuku	115	R9
Maturin	136	E2
Matyushkinskaya	84	B5
Mau	92	F3
Maua	109	G2
Maubara	91	H7
Maubeuge	64	E3
Maubin	93	J5
Maubourguet	65	D7
Mauchline	57	D5
Maud	56	F3
Maues	136	F4
Mauganj	92	F4
Maui	125	S10
Maula	62	L4
Maule	139	B7
Mauleon-Licharre	65	C7
Maumere	91	G7
Maumtrasna	58	C5
Maumturk Mountains	59	C5
Maun	108	D4
Mauna Kea	125	T11
Mauna Loa	125	T11
Maungmagan Islands	93	J6
Maunoir, Lac	118	L2
Maures	65	G7
Mauriac	65	E6
Maurice, Lake	112	G4
Mauritania	100	C5
Mauritius	109	L7
Mauron	64	B4
Mauston	124	E5
Mautern	68	E2
Mavinga	106	D6
Mawbray	55	F2
Mawhai Point	115	G3
Mawlaik	93	H4
Mawson	141	E5
Maxaila	109	H4
Maxmo	62	K5
Maya	55	N5
Mayaguana Island	133	L3
Mayaguana Passage	133	L3
Mayaguez	133	P5
Mayak *China*	86	F2
Mayak *Russia*	71	H1
Mayak *Russia*	79	K5
Mayamey	95	M3
Mayas, Montanas	132	C6
Maybole	57	D5
May, Cape	125	N7
Maychew	96	D10
Maydh	103	J5
Mayenne *France*	64	C4
Mayenne *France*	65	C5
Mayero	84	G3
Mayfaah	97	H9
Mayfield *U.K.*	53	H3
Mayfield *U.S.A.*	124	F8
May, Isle of	57	F4
Maykop	79	G7
Maykor	78	K4
Maymakan *Russia*	85	M3
Maymakan *Russia*	85	P5
Maymyo	93	J4
Mayn	85	W4
Maynooth	59	J6
Mayo *Argentina*	139	B9
Mayo *Canada*	118	H3
Mayo *Ireland*	58	D5
Mayo *Mexico*	130	E4
Mayor Island	115	F2
Mayor, Pic	67	H3
Mayotte	109	J2
May Pen	132	J6
Mayraira Point	91	G2
Mayrata	75	F3
Maysville	124	J7
Mayumba	106	A3
Mayuram	92	E6
Mayville	123	R4
Mayyun Island	96	F10
Mazalat	73	H4
Mazamari	136	C6
Mazamet	65	E7
Mazar	92	E1
Mazar-e Sharif	92	C1
Mazarete	67	E2
Mazarredo	139	C9
Mazarron	67	F4
Mazarsu	86	C3
Mazaruni	136	F2
Mazatenango	132	B7
Mazatlan	130	F6
Mazdaj	95	K5
Mazeikiai	63	K8
Mazgirt	77	H3
Mazinan	95	N3
Mazirbe	63	K8
Mazury	71	J2
Mbabane	108	F5
Mbaiki	102	C7
Mbala	107	F4
Mbalavu	114	S8
Mbale	107	F2
Mbalmayo	105	H5
Mbalo	114	K6
Mbandaka	106	C2
MBanza Congo	106	B4

Name		
Mbanza-Ngungu	106	B4
Mbarara	107	F3
Mbengwi	105	G4
Mbeya	107	F4
Mbouda	105	H4
Mbour	104	B3
Mbout	100	C5
Mbuji-Mayi	106	D4
Mchinji	107	F5
MClintock	119	S4
Meade *Alaska*	118	D1
Meade *Kansas*	127	M2
Meadie, Loch	56	D2
Mead, Lake	126	E2
Meadow Lake	119	P5
Meadville	125	K6
Mealhada	66	B2
Meana	95	Q3
Meath	58	J5
Meaux	64	E4
Mebula	91	G7
Mecca	96	D6
Mechelen	64	F3
Mecheria	100	E2
Mechigmen	118	A2
Mechigmen Zaliv	118	A2
Mecidie	76	B2
Mecitozu	76	F2
Mecklenburger Bucht	70	D1
Mecsek	72	E2
Mecufi	109	H2
Mecula	109	G2
Medak	92	E5
Medan	90	B5
Medanos	139	D7
Medanosa, Punta	139	C9
Medea	101	F1
Medellin	136	B2
Medelpad	62	G5
Medenine	101	H2
Mederdra	100	B5
Medford	122	C6
Medgidia	73	K3
Medicine Bow Mountains	123	L7
Medicine Bow Peak	123	L7
Medicine Hat	123	J3
Medicine Lodge	127	N2
Medina *Saudi Arabia*	96	D4
Medina *N. Dakota*	123	Q4
Medina *New York*	125	L5
Medinaceli	66	E2
Medina del Campo	66	D2
Medina de Rioseco	66	D2
Medina Sidonia	66	D4
Medina Terminal Canal	125	L5
Medinipur	93	G4
Mediterranean Sea	98	C3
Medjerda, Monts de la	69	B7
Medkovets	73	G4
Mednyy, Ostrov	81	T4
Medoc	65	C6
Medole	68	C3
Medvezhl, Ostrova	85	U2
Medvezhyegorsk	78	E3
Medvyeditsa	78	F4
Medway	53	H3
Medyn	78	F5
Medynskiy Zavorot, Poluostrov	78	K2
Meeberrie	112	D4
Meechkyn, Kosa	85	Y3
Meekatharra	112	D4
Meeker	123	L7
Meerut	92	E3
Meeteetse	123	K5
Mega	91	J6
Megalo Khorio	75	J4
Megalopolis	75	G4
Megara	75	G3
Megeve	65	G6
Megget Reservoir	57	E5
Meghalaya	93	H3
Megion	84	B4
Megisti	76	C4
Megra *Russia*	78	F3
Megra *Russia*	78	G2
Mehamn	62	M1
Mehndawal	92	F3
Mehran	94	H5
Meig	56	D3
Meighen Island	120	G2
Meiktila	93	J4
Meiningen	70	D3
Meira	66	C1
Meissen	70	E3
Mei Xian	87	M7
Mejez El Bab	69	B7
Mejillones	138	B4
Mekambo	106	B2
Mekele	103	G5
Meknes	100	D2
Mekong	93	L6
Mekong, Mouths of the	93	L7
Mela	62	U12
Melaka	90	C5
Melambes	75	H5
Melanesia	142	F4
Melawi	90	E6
Melbourne *Australia*	113	J6
Melbourne *U.S.A.*	129	M6
Melbourne Island	119	Q2
Melbu	62	F2
Melchor Muzquiz	127	M7
Melenki	78	G4

Name		
Meleuz	78	K5
Melfi *Chad*	102	C5
Melfi *Italy*	69	E5
Melfort	119	Q5
Melgaco	137	G4
Melhus	62	D4
Melilla	100	E1
Melipilla	139	B6
Melita	123	P3
Melito di Porto Salvo	69	E7
Melitopol	79	F6
Melk	68	E1
Melksham	53	E3
Mellegue, Oued	101	G1
Mellerud	63	E7
Melle-sur-Bretonne	65	C5
Melling	55	G2
Mellish Reef	113	M2
Mellte	52	D3
Melnik	70	F3
Melo	138	F6
Mololo	91	G7
Melozitna	118	E2
Melrhir, Chott	101	G2
Melrose	124	C4
Melsungen	70	C3
Meltaus	62	L3
Melton Mowbray	53	G2
Melun	64	E4
Melut	103	F5
Melvern Lake	124	C7
Melville	123	N2
Melville Bugt	120	P2
Melville, Cape	113	J1
Melville Hills	118	L2
Melville Island *Australia*	112	G1
Melville Island *Canada*	120	D2
Melville, Kap	120	P2
Melville, Lake	121	Q7
Melville Peninsula	120	K4
Melvin, Lough	58	F4
Melykut	72	E2
Melyuveyem	85	W4
Memba	109	H2
Memberamo	91	K6
Memboro	91	F7
Memel	63	L9
Memmingen	70	D4
Mempawah	90	D5
Memphis *Tennessee*	128	H3
Memphis *Texas*	127	M3
Mena	128	E3
Menai Bridge	55	E3
Menaka	101	F5
Mendawai	90	E6
Mende	65	E6
Mendi	114	C3
Mendip Hills	52	E3
Mendocino, Cape	122	B7
Mendoza	138	C6
Menemen	76	B3
Menen	64	E3
Menfi	69	D7
Mengcheng	93	N2
Mengcun	87	M4
Mengen	76	E2
Mengene Dagi	77	L3
Menggala	90	D6
Menghai	93	K4
Mengjiagang	88	C2
Mengjiawan	87	K4
Mengla	93	K4
Mengshan	93	M4
Mengyin	87	M4
Meniet	101	F3
Menihek, Lac	121	N7
Meningie	113	H6
Menkya	78	L3
Menominee *U.S.A.*	124	G4
Menominee *U.S.A.*	124	G4
Menomonee Falls	124	F5
Menongue	106	C5
Menorca	67	J3
Mentawai, Kepulauan	90	B6
Mentawai, Selat	90	B6
Mentok	90	D6
Menton	68	A4
Mentor	125	K6
Menyamya	114	D3
Menzel Bourguiba	69	B7
Meon	53	F4
Meppel	64	G2
Meppen	70	B2
Mequinenza	67	G2
Merabellou, Kolpos	75	H5
Merak	90	D7
Merano	68	C2
Merauke	91	L7
Mercan Dagi	77	H3
Mercato Saraceno	68	D4
Merced	126	B2
Mercedario, Cerro	138	B6
Mercedes *Argentina*	139	C6
Mercedes *Argentina*	139	E6
Mercedes *Argentina*	138	E5
Mercedes *Uruguay*	138	E6
Mercimek	77	F4
Mercimekkale	77	J3
Mercurea	73	G3
Mercury Bay	115	E2
Mercy, Cape	120	P5
Mere	52	E3
Meredith, Cape	139	D10
Meredoua	100	F3

Name	Page	Grid	Name	Page	Grid	Name	Page	Grid	Name	Page	Grid	Name	Page	Grid
Mocamedes	106	B6	Monahans	127	L5	Monterey	126	B2	Mores Island	132	J1
Mocha, Isla	139	B7	Mona, Isla	133	P5	Monterey Bay	126	B2	Moreton Bay	113	L4
Mochudi	108	E4	Mona Passage	133	N5	Monteria	136	B2	Moreton-in-Marsh	53	F3
Mocimboa da Praia	109	H2	Monarch Mount	118	K5	Montero	138	D3	Moreton Island	113	L4
Moctexuma	127	H6	Monarch Pass	123	L8	Monterotondo	69	D4	Morez	65	G5
Moctezuma	131	K7	Monar, Loch	56	C3	Monterrey	128	B8	Morgan City	128	G6
Mocuba	109	G3	Monashe Mountains	122	E2	Monte Santu, Capo di	69	B5	Morganton	129	M3
Modder	108	E5	Monasterevin	59	H6	Montes Claros	138	E3	Morgantown	125	L7
Modena Italy	68	C3	Monastir Albania	73	F5	Montevideo Uruguay	139	E6	Morgongava	63	G7
Modena U.S.A.	126	F2	Monastir Italy	69	B6	Montevideo U.S.A.	124	C4	Mori China	86	F3
Modesto	126	B2	Monastir Tunisia	101	H1	Monte Vista	127	J2	Mori Japan	88	H4
Modica	69	E7	Monastyriska	73	H1	Montezuma Peak	127	J2	Moriarty	127	K3
Modigliana	68	C3	Monatele	105	H5	Montfort-sur-Meu	64	B4	Morioka	88	H6
Modling	68	F1	Moncalieri	68	A3	Montgomery U.K.	52	D2	Morlaix	64	B4
Modowi	91	J6	Moncao	66	B1	Montgomery U.S.A.	129	J4	Morley	55	H3
Moe	113	K6	Monchdorf	68	E1	Montguyon	65	C6	Morlunda	63	F8
Moelv	63	D6	Monchegorsk	62	Q3	Monti	69	B5	Mormanno	69	F6
Moengo	137	G2	Monchique	66	B4	Monticello Arkansas	128	G4	Mornington, Isla	139	A9
Moffat	57	E5	Monclova	127	M7	Monticello Florida	129	L5	Mornington Island	113	H2
Moffat Peak	115	B6	Moncontour	64	B4	Monticello New York	125	N6	Morobe	114	D3
Mogadishu	107	J2	Moncton	121	P8	Monticello Utah	127	H2	Morocco	100	D2
Mogadouro	66	C2	Mondego	65	C2	Montiel, Campo de	66	E3	Morogoro	107	G4
Mogdy	85	N6	Mondonedo	65	C1	Montignac	65	D6	Moro Gulf	91	G4
Mogilev-Podolskiy	79	D6	Mondovi	68	A3	Montilla	66	D4	Morokovo	85	W3
Mogi-Mirim	138	G4	Mondragone	69	D5	Mont-Joli	125	R2	Moroleon	131	J7
Mogincual	109	H3	Mondsee	68	D2	Mont Laurier	125	N3	Morombe	109	H4
Moglice	75	F2	Monemvasia	75	G4	Montlucon	65	E5	Moron	132	H3
Mogocha	85	L6	Moneron, Ostrov	88	H2	Montmagny	125	Q3	Moron Mongolia	86	J2
Mogoi	91	J6	Monesterio	66	C3	Montmedy	64	F4	Moron Mongolia	87	L2
Mogok	93	J4	Moneymore	58	J3	Montmirail	64	E4	Moronade, Cerro des	130	G7
Mogollon Plateau	126	G3	Monfalcone	68	D3	Montmorillon	65	D5	Morondava	109	H4
Mogotoyevo, Ozero	85	R2	Monforte	66	C3	Monto	113	L3	Moron de la Frontera	66	D4
Mogoyn	86	H2	Monforte de Lemos	66	C1	Montoro	66	D4	Moroni	109	H2
Mogoytuy	85	J6	Monga	106	D2	Montpelier	122	J6	Moron Us He	93	H2
Moguer	66	C4	Mongala	106	D2	Montpellier France	65	E7	Morotai	91	H5
Mohacs	72	E2	Mongalla	103	F6	Montpellier U.S.A.	125	P4	Moroto	107	F2
Mohaka	115	F3	Mong Cai	93	L4	Montraux	68	A2	Morozovsk	79	G6
Mohall	123	P3	Mongga	114	H5	Montreal	124	H3	Morpara	137	J6
Mohammadabad	95	Q6	Mongge	91	J6	Montreal	125	P4	Morpeth	55	H1
Mohammadia	100	F1	Mong Hang	93	J4	Montreal Lake	119	P5	Morrilton	128	F3
Mohawk	125	N5	Monghyr	92	G3	Montreal River Harbour	124	H3	Morrinhos	138	G3
Moheli	109	H2	Mong Lin	93	K4	Montrose U.K.	57	F4	Morrinsville	115	E2
Mohill	58	G5	Mongo	102	C5	Montrose U.S.A.	127	J1	Morris Canada	123	R3
Mohoro	107	G4	Mongolia	86	G2	Mont Saint-Michel	64	C4	Morris U.S.A.	124	C4
Moi	63	B7	Mongororo	102	D5	Montseny	67	H2	Morris Jesup, Kap	140	Q2
Moidart	57	C4	Mongu	106	D6	Montserrat	133	R6	Morris, Mount	112	G4
Moimenta da Beira	66	C2	Monhhaan	87	L2	Mont Wright	121	N7	Morristown	129	L2
Moindou	114	W16	Moniaive	57	E5	Monywa	93	J4	Morro Bay	126	B3
Mointy	86	C2	Monifieth	57	F4	Monza	68	B3	Morro do Chapeu	137	J6
Mo i Rana	62	F3	Moniquira	136	C2	Monzon	67	G2	Morro, Punta	139	B5
Moisie	121	N7	Monitor Range	122	F8	Moonie	113	K4	Morros, Punta	131	P8
Moissac	65	D6	Monkira	113	J3	Moopna	112	F5	Morrosquillo, Golfo de	133	K10
Moissala	102	C6	Monkland	52	E2	Moora	112	D5	Mors	63	C8
Mojave	126	C3	Monkoto	106	D3	Mooraberree	113	J4	Morshansk	79	G5
Mojave Desert	126	D3	Monmouth U.K.	52	E3	Moorcroft	123	M5	Mortagne	64	D4
Moji	89	C9	Monmouth U.S.A.	124	E6	Moore, Lake	112	D4	Mortain	64	C4
Mojones, Cerro	138	C5	Monnow	52	E3	Moorfoot Hills	57	E5	Mortara	68	B3
Moju	137	H4	Mono	105	F4	Moorhead	124	B3	Morteau	65	G5
Mokai	115	E3	Mono Lake	126	C2	Moorlands	113	H6	Morte Bay	52	C3
Mokelumne	122	D8	Monolithos	75	J4	Moorlinch	52	E3	Mortes	137	G6
Moknine	101	H1	Monopoli	69	F5	Moose	121	K7	Morton U.K.	53	G2
Mokohinau Island	115	E1	Monovar	67	F3	Moosehead Lake	125	R4	Morton U.S.A.	122	C4
Mokokchung	93	H3	Monreal del Campo	67	F2	Moose Jaw	123	M2	Morundah	113	K5
Mokolo	105	H3	Monreale	69	D6	Moose Lake Canada	119	Q5	Morven Australia	113	K4
Mokpo	87	P5	Monroe Georgia	129	L4	Moose Lake U.S.A.	124	D3	Morven U.K.	57	E3
Mokra Gora	72	F4	Monroe Louisiana	128	F4	Moose Mountain Creek	123	N2	Morvern	57	C4
Molaoi	75	G4	Monroe Michigan	124	J6	Moosonee	121	K7	Morwell	113	K6
Molat	72	C3	Monroe N. Carolina	129	M3	Mopeia Velha	109	G3	Mosakula	63	L7
Mold	55	F3	Monroe Wisconsin	124	F5	Mopti	100	E6	Mosby	63	B7
Moldavia	73	J2	Monrovia	104	C4	Moqor	92	C2	Moscow U.S.A.	122	F4
Molde	62	B5	Mons	64	E3	Moquequa	138	B3	Moscow Russia	78	F4
Moldova	73	J2	Monsaras, Ponta da	138	J3	Mora Cameroon	105	H3	Mosedale	55	F2
Moldova Noua	73	F3	Monselice	68	C3	Mora Portugal	66	B3	Mosel	70	B4
Moldoveanu	73	H3	Monserrat	67	F3	Mora Sweden	63	F6	Moselle	64	G4
Moldovita	73	H2	Montaigu	65	C5	Moradabad	92	E3	Moses Lake	122	E4
Mole Devon, U.K.	52	D4	Montalban	67	F2	Moradal, Sierra do	66	C3	Moseyevo	78	H2
Mole Surrey, U.K	53	G3	Montalbo	66	E3	Mora de Rubielos	67	F2	Mosgiel	115	C6
Molepolole	108	E4	Montalcino	68	C4	Morafenobe	109	H3	Mosha	78	G3
Molfetta	69	F5	Montalto	69	E6	Morag	71	H2	Moshchnyy, Ostrov	63	M6
Molina de Aragon	67	F2	Montalvo	136	B4	Morales	132	C7	Moshi	107	G3
Molina de Segura	67	F3	Montamarta	66	D2	Moramanga	109	J3	Mosjoen	62	E4
Moline	124	E6	Montana	122	K4	Moran	123	J6	Moskenesoya	62	E3
Molkom	63	E7	Montanchez	66	C3	Morant Cays	132	K6	Moskosel	62	H4
Mollakendi	77	H3	Montanita	136	B3	Morant Point	132	J6	Moskva	78	F4
Mollaosman	77	K3	Montargis	65	E5	Moratuwa	92	E7	Mosonmagyarovar	72	D2
Mollendo	138	B3	Montauban	65	D6	Morava Czech Rep.	71	G4	Mosquera	136	B3
Molln	70	D2	Montauk Point	125	Q6	Morava	73	F3	Mosquitia	132	E7
Molnlycke	63	E8	Montbard	65	F5	Moraveh Tappeh	95	M3	Mosquito Lake	119	Q3
Molodechno	71	M1	Montbeliard	65	G5	Morawa	112	D4	Mosquitos, Costa de	132	F8
Molodezhnaya	141	D5	Montblanch	67	G2	Moray Firth	56	E3	Mosquitos, Golfo de los	132	G10
Molodo Russia	85	L3	Montbrison	65	F6	Morbi	92	D4	Moss	63	D7
Molodo Russia	85	L3	Monteau-les-Mines	55	F5	Mor Budejovice	70	F4	Mossaka	106	C3
Mologa	78	F4	Mont-de-Marsan	55	C7	Morbylanga	63	G8	Mossburn	115	B6
Molokai	126	S10	Montdidier	54	E4	Morden	123	Q3	Mosselbaai	108	D6
Moloma	78	H4	Monte Alegre	137	G4	Mordogan	76	B3	Mossley	58	L3
Molotov	78	K4	Monte Azul	138	H3	Mordovo	79	G5	Mossman	113	K2
Moloundou	105	J5	Monte Bello	136	B5	Moreau	122	N5	Mossoro	137	K5
Molsheim	64	G4	Montebello	125	N4	Morebattle	57	F5	Most	70	E3
Molson Lake	119	R5	Monte Carlo	68	A4	Morecambe	55	G2	Mosta	74	C5
Moluccas	91	H6	Monte Caseros	139	E6	Morecambe Bay	55	G2	Mostaganem	100	F1
Moma Mozambique	109	R3	Montecatini Terme	68	C4	Moreda	66	E4	Mostar	72	D4
Moma Russia	85	Q3	Monte Cristi	133	M5	Moree	113	K4	Mostiska	71	K4
Mombasa	107	R3	Montecristo, Isola di	69	C4	Morehead Papua New Guinea	114	C3	Mosty	71	L2
Mombetsu	88	J3	Montego Bay	132	J5	Morehead U.S.A.	124	J7	Mostyn	55	F3
Momboyo	106	C3	Montelimar	65	F6	Morehead City	129	P3	Mosul	77	K4
Momi, Ra's	97	P9	Montemaggiore Belsito	69	D7	Morelia	131	J8	Mosulpo	87	P5
Momol	71	L2	Montemorelos	128	C8	Morella	67	F2	Mota	103	G5
Mompos	136	C2	Montemor-o-Novo	66	B3	More, Loch U.K.	56	D2	Mota	114	T10
Mon	63	E9	Montenegro	72	E4	More, Loch U.K.	56	E2	Mota del Cuervo	66	E3
Monach Islands	56	A3	Montepuez	109	G2	Morena, Sierra	66	D3	Motala	63	F7
Monach, Sound of	56	A3	Montepulciano	68	C4	Moreno	126	G6	Mota Lava	114	T10
Monaco	65	G7	Monte Quemado	138	D5	Moreno, Bahia	138	B4	Motegi	89	H7
Monadhliath Mountains	57	D3	More og Romsdal	62	C5	Motherwell	57	E5
Monaghan	58	J4	Montereau-faut-Yonne	64	E4	Moresby Island	118	J5	Motihari	92	F3

Name	Pg	Ref
Motilla del Palancar	67	F3
Motovskiy Zaliv	62	G2
Motril	66	E4
Motueka *New Zealand*	115	D4
Motueka *New Zealand*	115	D4
Motupiko Blenheim	115	D4
Motykleyka	85	R5
Moudhros	75	H3
Moudjeria	100	C5
Mouka	102	D6
Mould Bay	120	C2
Moulins	65	E5
Moulmein	93	J5
Moulouya, Oued	100	E2
Moulton	55	H2
Moultrie	129	L5
Moultrie, Lake	129	M4
Mounda, Akra	75	F3
Mound City	124	C6
Moundou	102	C6
Moung	93	K6
Mountain	118	K2
Mountain Ash	52	D3
Mountain Home *Arkansas*	128	F2
Mountain Home *Idaho*	122	G6
Mountain Village	118	C3
Mount Airy	129	M2
Mount Ararat	77	L3
Mount Bellew	59	E6
Mount Desert Island	125	R4
Mount Doreen	112	G3
Mount Douglas	113	K3
Mount Elba	113	H5
Mount Gambier	113	J6
Mount Hagen	114	C3
Mount Isa	113	H3
Mount Magnet	112	D4
Mountmellick	59	H6
Mount Pleasant *Iowa*	124	E6
Mount Pleasant *Michigan*	124	H5
Mount Pleasant *Texas*	128	E4
Mount Pleasant *Utah*	126	G1
Mountrath	59	H6
Mount's Bay	52	B4
Mount Shasta	122	C7
Mount Thule	120	L3
Mount Vernon *Alabama*	129	H5
Mount Vernon *Illinois*	124	F7
Mount Vernon *Indiana*	124	G8
Mount Vernon *Ohio*	124	J6
Mount Vernon *Washington*	122	C3
Moura *Brazil*	136	E4
Moura *Portugal*	66	C3
Mourdi, Depression du	102	D4
Mourne Mountains	58	K4
Moussoro	102	C5
Moutong	91	G5
Movas	127	H6
Moville	58	H2
Moy	58	D4
Moyale	107	G2
Moyamba	104	C4
Moyen Atlas	100	E2
Moygashel	58	J4
Moyo *Indonesia*	91	F7
Moyo *Uganda*	106	F2
Moyobamba	136	B5
Moyu	92	E1
Mozambique	109	G3
Mozambique Channel	109	H3
Mozhaysk	78	F4
Mozhga	78	J4
Mozyr	79	D5
Mpanda	107	F4
Mpe	106	B3
Mpika	107	F5
Mporokoso	107	F4
Mpraeso	104	E4
Mrakovo	79	K5
M.R. Gomez, Presa	127	N7
Mrkonjic Grad	72	D3
Msaken	101	H1
MSila	67	J5
Msta	78	E4
Mstislav	78	E5
Mtsensk	79	F5
Mtwara	107	G5
Mualo	109	G2
Muang Chiang Rai	93	J5
Muang Khon Kaen	93	K5
Muang Lampang	93	J5
Muang Lamphun	93	J5
Muang Loei	93	K5
Muang Nan	93	K5
Muang Phayao	93	J5
Muang Phetchabun	93	K5
Muang Phichit	93	K5
Muang Phitsanulok	93	K5
Muang Phrae	93	K5
Muanza	109	F3
Muar	90	C5
Muara	90	E4
Muarabungo	90	D6
Muaraenim	90	D6
Muaralesan	91	F5
Muarasiberut	90	B6
Muarasigep	90	B6
Muarasipongi	90	B5
Muaratebo	90	D6
Muarateweh	90	E6
Mubende	107	F2
Mubi	105	H3
Mubrani	91	J6
Mucajai	136	E3
Muchinga Escarpment	107	F5
Much Wenlock	52	E2
Muck	57	B4
Muckanagh Lough	59	E7
Muckish Mount	58	G2
Muckle Roe	56	A1
Muckross Head	58	E3
Muconda	106	D5
Mucuim	136	E5
Mucur	76	F3
Mudanjiang	88	B3
Mudan Jiang	88	B3
Mudanya	76	C2
Mudayy	97	L8
Muddy Gap Pass	123	L6
Mudgee	113	K5
Mudurnu	76	D2
Mueda	109	G2
Muelas	66	D2
Mueo	114	W16
Mufulira	107	E5
Mufu Shan	93	M3
Muganskaya Step	94	J2
Mughar	95	L5
Mughshin	97	M7
Mugi	89	E9
Mugia	66	B1
Mugia, Monts	107	E4
Mugla	76	C4
Muhammad Qol	103	G3
Muhammad, Ras	103	F2
Muhaywir	77	J6
Muhldorf	70	E4
Muhlhausen	70	D3
Muhu	63	K7
Mui Bai Bung	93	K7
Muick	57	E3
Muirkirk	57	D5
Muite	109	G2
Mukachevo	79	C6
Mukah	90	E5
Mukawa	88	H4
Mukawwar	96	C6
Mukdahan	93	K5
Mukden	87	N3
Mukhen	88	F1
Mukhor-Konduy	85	J6
Mukomuko	90	D6
Mukur	79	J6
Mula	67	F3
Mulaly	86	D2
Mulan	88	B3
Mulanay	91	G3
Mulayit Taung	93	J5
Mulchatna	118	D3
Mulchen	139	B7
Mulde	70	E3
Muleshoe	127	L3
Mulga Downs	112	D3
Mulgrave	121	P8
Mulgrave Island	114	C4
Mulhacen	66	E4
Mulheim	70	B3
Mulhouse	65	G5
Muligort	84	Ad4
Muling *China*	88	C3
Muling *China*	88	C3
Muling He	88	D3
Mull	57	C4
Mullaghanattin	59	C9
Mullaghanish	59	D9
Mullaghareirk Mountains	59	D8
Mullaghcleevaun	59	K6
Mullaghmore	58	J3
Muller, Pegunungan	90	E5
Mullet, The	58	B4
Mullewa	112	D4
Mull Head *U.K.*	56	F2
Mull Head *U.K.*	56	F1
Mullinavat	59	H8
Mullingar	59	H5
Mullsjo	63	E8
Mull, Sound of	57	C4
Mulobezi	106	E6
Mulrany	58	C5
Multan	92	D2
Multanovy	84	A4
Multia	62	L5
Mulymya	84	Ad4
Mumbles, The	52	C3
Mumbwa	106	E6
Mumra	79	H6
Muna *Indonesia*	91	G7
Muna *Russia*	85	L3
Munayly	79	J6
Munchberg	70	D3
Munchen	70	D4
Munchengladbach	70	B3
Muncie	124	H6
Munda	114	H6
Mundesley	53	J2
Mundford	53	H2
Mundo	67	F3
Mundo Novo	138	J6
Mungbere	107	E2
Munich	70	D4
Muniesa	67	F2
Munkfors	63	E7
Mun, Mae Nam	93	K5
Munoz Gamero, Peninsula de	139	B10
Munster	70	B3
Munster	59	D8
Munsterland	70	B3
Muntenia	73	J3
Muntinlupa	91	G3
Munzur Daglari	77	H3
Muong Khoua	93	K4
Muong Ou Tay	93	K4
Muong Sing	93	K4
Muonio	62	K3
Muoniojoki	62	K3
Muqdisho	107	J2
Muqshin, Wadi	97	M7
Mur	68	E2
Mura	72	D2
Muradiye *Turkey*	76	B3
Muradiye *Turkey*	77	K3
Murallon, Cerro	139	B9
Muranga	107	G3
Murashi	78	H4
Murat *France*	65	E6
Murat *Turkey*	77	J3
Muratbasi	77	K3
Murat Dagi	76	C3
Muratli	76	B2
Muraysah, Ras al	101	K2
Murban	97	L5
Murcheh Khvort	95	K5
Murchison *Australia*	112	C4
Murchison *Canada*	120	H4
Murchison *New Zealand*	115	D4
Murchison Sund	120	M2
Murcia *Spain*	67	F4
Murcia *Spain*	67	F3
Murdo	123	P6
Murdochville	125	T2
Murefte	76	B2
Mures	73	F2
Muret	65	D7
Murfreesboro *N. Carolina*	129	P2
Murfreesboro *Tennessee,*	129	J3
Murgab *Tajikistan*	86	C4
Murgab *Turkmenistan*	95	R3
Muri	95	N3
Muriae	138	H4
Muriege	106	D4
Muritz See	70	E2
Murmansk	78	E2
Murmanskaya Oblast	62	P2
Murmansk Bereg	78	F2
Murmashi	62	Q2
Murnau	70	D5
Murom	78	G4
Muromtsevo	84	B5
Muroran	88	H4
Muros	66	B1
Muroto-zaki	89	E9
Murphy	129	L3
Murra Murra	113	K4
Murray *Australia*	113	H5
Murray *Kentucky*	124	F8
Murray *Utah*	122	J7
Murray Bridge	110	J9
Murray Harbour	121	P8
Murray, Lake *Papua New Guinea*	114	C3
Murray, Lake *U.S.A.*	129	M3
Murraysburg	108	D6
Murree	92	D2
Murrumbidgee	113	K5
Mursal	77	H3
Mursala	90	B5
Murud	90	F5
Murukta	84	G3
Murupara	115	F3
Murwara	92	F4
Murwillumbah	113	L4
Murz	68	E2
Murzuq	101	H3
Murzuq, Idhan	101	H4
Murzzuschlag	68	E2
Mus	77	J3
Musala	73	G4
Musallam, Wadi	97	N5
Musan	88	B4
Musandam Peninsula	97	N3
Musayid	97	K4
Muscat	97	P5
Musgrave Ranges	112	G4
Mushash al Hadi	97	J3
Musheramore	59	D8
Mushie	106	C3
Musi	90	C6
Musian	94	H5
Muskegon *U.S.A.*	124	G5
Muskegon *U.S.A.*	124	H5
Muskingum	124	K7
Muskogee	128	E3
Musmar	103	G4
Musoma	107	F3
Mussau	114	D2
Musselburgh	57	E5
Musselshell	123	K4
Mussende	106	C5
Musserra	106	B4
Mussidan	65	D6
Mussuma	106	D5
Mussy	65	F5
Mustafakemalpasa	76	C2
Mustang	92	F3
Mustang Draw	127	L4
Musters, Lago	139	C9
Mustvee	63	M7
Musu-dan	88	B5
Muswellbrook	113	L5
Mut *Egypt*	102	E2
Mut *Turkey*	76	E4
Muta Ponta do	137	K6
Mutarara	109	G3
Mutare	109	F3
Mutki	77	J3
Mutnyy Materik	78	K2
Mutoko	109	F3
Mutoray	84	G4
Mutsu-wan	88	H5
Muurame	63	L5
Muurola	62	L3
Muwaffaq	97	M7
Muxima	106	B4
Muya	85	J5
Muyunkum, Peski	86	C3
Muzaffarabad	92	D2
Muzaffargarh	92	D2
Muzaffarnagar	92	E3
Muzaffarpur	92	G3
Muzon, Cape	118	J5
Muz Tagh Ata Range	92	E1
Mvuma	108	F3
Mwaniwowo	114	L7
Mwanza	107	F3
Mwaya	107	F4
Mweelrea	58	C5
Mwene Ditu	106	D4
Mwenezi *Zimbabwe*	108	F4
Mwenezi *Zimbabwe*	108	F4
Mwenga	107	E3
Mweru, Lake	107	E4
Mweru Wantipa, Lake	107	E4
Mwinilunga	106	D6
Myakit	85	S4
Myanaung	93	J5
Myanmar	93	J4
Myaundzha	85	R4
Myaungmya	93	H5
Myeik Kyunzu	93	J6
Myingyan	93	J4
Myinmu	93	J4
Myitkyina	93	J3
Myitnge	93	J4
Myittha	93	J4
Mykolayiv	79	E6
Myla	78	J2
Mymensingh	93	H4
Myre	62	F2
Myri	62	W12
Myrtle Beach	129	N4
Myrviken	62	F5
Mysen	63	H7
Mysliborz	70	F2
Mysore	92	E6
Mys Shmidta	85	Y3
My Tho	93	L6
Mytishchi	78	F4
Mzab	101	F2
Mze	70	E4
Mzuzu	107	F5

N

Name	Pg	Ref
Naalehu	126	T11
Naantali	63	K6
Naas	59	J6
Nabao	66	B3
Nabavatu	114	R8
Naberezhnyye Chelny	78	J4
Nabeul	101	H1
Nabire	91	K6
Nablus	94	B5
Nabouwalu	114	R8
Naburn	55	H3
Nacala-a-Velha	109	H2
Nacaome	132	D8
Nachiki	85	T6
Nachvak Fjord	121	P6
Nacogdoches	128	E5
Nacozari de Garcia	127	H5
Nadachi	89	G7
Nadezhdinskoye	88	D1
Nadezhnyy, Mys	85	S2
Nadi	114	Q8
Nadiad	92	D4
Nadlac	72	F2
Nador	100	E1
Naduri	114	R8
Nadvornaya	71	L4
Nadym	84	A3
Naft-e Safid	94	J6
Nafud, An	96	E2
Nafy	96	F4
Naga	91	G3
Nagagami	124	H2
Nagahama	89	D9
Naga Hills	93	H3
Nagai	89	G6
Nagaland	93	H3
Nagano	89	G7
Nagaoka	89	G7
Nagappattinam	92	E6
Nagarjuna Sagar	92	E5
Nagasaki	89	B9
Nagashima	89	F8
Nagato	89	C8
Nagaur	92	D3
Nagercoil	92	E7
Nagishot	103	F7
Nagles Mountains	59	F8
Nagornyy	85	L5
Nagoya	89	F8
Nagpur	92	E4
Nagqu	93	H2

Name	Pg	Grid
Nags Head	129	Q3
Nagykanizsa	72	D2
Nagykata	72	E2
Nagykoros	72	E2
Naha	89	H10
Nahariya	94	B5
Nahavand	94	J4
Nahe	70	B4
Nahoi, Cap	114	T11
Nahuel Huapi, Lago	139	B8
Naikliu	91	G7
Nailsea	52	E3
Nailsworth	52	E3
Naiman Qi	87	N3
Nain	95	L5
Nain	121	P6
Naini Tal	92	E3
Nairai	114	R8
Nairn	56	E3
Nairobi	107	G3
Najafabad	95	K5
Najd	96	E4
Najibabad	92	E3
Najin	88	C4
N Ajjer, Tassili	101	G3
Najran	96	G8
Najran, Wadi	96	G8
Nakadori-shima	89	B9
Nakajo	89	G6
Nakamura	89	D9
Nakano	89	G7
Nakano-shima	89	B11
Nakatay	84	Ad5
Nakatsu	89	C9
Nakatsugawa	89	F8
Nakfa	103	G4
Nakhichevan	77	L3
Nakhl Eygpt	96	A2
Nakhl Oman	97	N5
Nakhodka Russia	84	B3
Nakhodka Russia	88	D4
Nakhon Pathom	93	J6
Nakhon Phanom	93	K5
Nakhon Ratchasima	93	K6
Nakhon Sawan	93	K5
Nakhon Si Thammarat	93	J7
Nakina	121	J7
Nakiri	89	F8
Naknek Lake	118	D4
Nakskov	63	F9
Naktong	87	P4
Nakuru	107	G3
Nakusp	122	F2
Nalchik	79	G7
Nalgonda	92	E5
Nallamala Hills	92	E5
Nallihan	76	D2
Nalut	101	H2
Namaa, Tanjung	91	H6
Namacunde	106	C6
Namacurra	109	G3
Namak, Daryacheh-ye	95	K4
Namaki	95	M6
Namakzar	95	Q5
Namakzar, Daryacheh-ye	95	Q5
Namangan	86	C3
Namapa	109	G2
Namaponda	109	G3
Namarroi	109	G3
Namasagali	107	F2
Namatanai	114	E2
Nambour	113	L4
Nam Can	93	K7
Nam Co	93	H2
Nam Dinh	93	L4
Nametil	109	G3
Namib Desert	108	B4
Namibe	106	B6
Namibia	108	C4
Namlea	91	H6
Namoi	113	L5
Namosi Peak	114	R8
Nampa	122	F6
Nampula	109	G3
Namse La	92	F3
Namsen	62	E4
Namsos	62	D4
Namti	93	J3
Namtok	93	J5
Namuka-i-Lau	114	S9
Namuli	109	G3
Namur	64	F3
Namutoni	108	C3
Namwala	106	E6
Nana Barya	102	C6
Nanaimo	122	C3
Nanam	88	B5
Nanao	89	F7
Nancha	88	B2
Nanchang	87	M6
Nanchong	93	L2
Nancowry	93	H7
Nancy	64	G4
Nanda Devi	92	E2
Nandan	93	L3
Nanded	92	E5
Nandurbar	92	D4
Nandyal	92	E5
Nanfeng	87	M6
Nanga Eboko	105	H5
Nangahpinoh	90	E6
Nanga Parbat	92	D1
Nangatayap	90	E6
Nangong	87	M4
Nan Hai	83	K5
Nanjing	87	M5
Nanking	87	M5
Nan, Mae Nam	93	K5
Nanning	93	L4
Nanortalik	116	Q2
Nanpan Jiang	93	K4
Nanpara	92	F3
Nanpi	87	M4
Nanping	87	M6
Nansei-shoto	89	H10
Nansen Sound	120	H1
Nanshan Islands	90	E4
Nansha Qundao	90	E4
Nantais, Lac	121	M5
Nantes	65	C5
Nantong	87	N5
Nantua	65	F5
Nantucket Island	125	Q6
Nantucket Sound	125	Q6
Nantwich	55	G3
Nant-y-moch Reservoir	52	D2
Nanuku Passage	114	S8
Nanuku Reef	114	S8
Nanumanga	111	S3
Nanumea	111	S3
Nanusa, Kepulauan	91	H5
Nanyang	93	M2
Nanyuki	107	G2
Nao, Cabo de la	67	G3
Naococane, Lake	121	M7
Naousa	75	G2
Napa	126	A1
Napabalana	91	G6
Napalkovo	84	A2
Napas	84	C5
Nape	93	L5
Napier	115	F3
Naples Italy	69	E5
Naples U.S.A.	129	M7
Napo	136	C4
Napoleon	124	H6
Napoletano, Appennino	69	E5
Napoli	69	E5
Napoli, Golfo di	69	E5
Naqadeh	94	G3
Nar	55	H2
Nara Japan	89	E8
Nara Mali	100	D5
Nara Pakistan	92	C4
Naracoorte	113	J6
Naran	87	L2
Narasapur	92	F5
Narat	86	E3
Narathiwat	93	K7
Narayanganj	93	H4
Narberth	52	C3
Narbonne	65	E7
Narborough Island	136	A7
Narcea	66	C1
Nardin	95	M3
Narew Poland	71	J2
Narew Poland	71	K2
Narince	77	H4
Narken	62	K3
Narkher	92	E4
Narli	77	G4
Narmada	92	E4
Narman	77	J2
Narnaul	92	E3
Narodnaya, Gora	84	Ad3
Naro-Fominsk	78	F4
Narowal	92	D2
Narpes	62	J5
Narrabi	113	K5
Narrandera	113	K5
Narrogin	112	D5
Narromine	113	K5
Narsimhapur	92	E4
Narsinghgarh	92	E4
Nart	87	M3
Nartabu	91	J6
Naruko	89	H6
Narva	63	N7
Narvik	62	G2
Naryan Mar	73	J2
Narymskiy Khrebet	85	E2
Naryn Russia	85	C3
Naryn Kyrgyzstan	86	D3
Nasarawa	105	G4
Naseby	115	C6
Nashua	125	Q5
Nashville	129	J2
Nasice	72	E3
Nasielsk	71	J2
Nasijarvi	63	K6
Nasik	92	D5
Nasir	103	F6
Nasir, Buhayrat	103	F3
Nasorolevu	114	R8
Nasrabad	95	K4
Nass	118	K4
Nassau	129	P8
Nasser, Lake	103	F3
Nassjo	63	F8
Nastapoka Islands	121	L6
Nastved	63	D9
Nata	108	E4
Natagaima	136	B3
Natal Brazil	137	K5
Natal Indonesia	90	B5
Natanz	95	K5
Natara	85	L3
Natashquan	121	P7
Natchez	128	G5
Natchitoches	128	F5
Natewa Bay	114	R8
National City	126	D4
Natitingou	105	F3
Natividade	137	H6
Natori	89	H6
Natron, Lake	107	G3
Nattavaara	62	J3
Natuna Besar	89	H10
Natuna, Kepulauan	90	D5
Naturaliste, Cape	112	D5
Naturaliste Channel	112	C4
Nauen	70	E2
Nauevi Akmyane	63	K8
Naujoji Vilnia	71	L1
Naul	58	K5
Naumburg	70	D3
Naungpale	93	J5
Nauru	111	Q2
Naurzum	84	Ad6
Nausori	114	R9
Nautanwa	92	F3
Nautla	131	L7
Nauzad	95	S5
Navadwip	93	G4
Navahermosa	66	D3
Naval	91	G3
Navalcarnero	66	D2
Navalmoral de la Mata	66	D3
Navalpino	66	D3
Navan	58	J5
Navarin, Mys	85	X4
Navarino, Isla	139	C11
Navarra	67	F1
Navars	67	G2
Navasota	128	D5
Navassa Island	133	K5
Navax Point	52	B4
Navenby	55	J3
Naver, Loch	56	D2
Navia Spain	66	C1
Navia Spain	66	C1
Naviti	114	Q8
Navlya	79	E5
Navojoa	130	F5
Navolato	130	F5
Navpaktos	75	F3
Navplion	75	G4
Navrongo	104	E3
Navsari	92	D4
Navua	114	R9
Nawabshah	92	C3
Nawada	92	G4
Nawah	92	C2
Nawasif, Harrat	96	F6
Naws, Ra's	97	M8
Nawton	55	J2
Naxos Greece	75	H4
Naxos Greece	75	H4
Nayagarh	92	G4
Nayau	114	S8
Nay Band	95	L8
Nay Band	95	N5
Nayoro	88	J3
Nazare	137	K6
Nazareth Israel	94	B5
Nazareth Peru	136	B5
Nazarovo	84	E5
Nazas	130	G5
Nazca	136	C6
Naze	89	B11
Nazerat	94	B5
Naze, The	53	J3
Nazik	94	G2
Nazik Golu	77	K3
Nazilli	76	C4
Nazmiye	77	H3
Nazwa	97	N5
Nazyvayevsk	84	A5
Ncheu	107	F5
Ndalatando	106	B4
Ndele	102	D6
Ndeni	114	N7
Ndjamena	102	C5
Ndjote	106	B3
Ndola	107	E5
Nea	62	D5
Nea Filippias	75	F3
Neagh, Lough	58	K3
Neah Bay	122	B3
Neale, Lake	112	G3
Nea Moudhania	75	G2
Neapolis Greece	75	F2
Neapolis Greece	75	H5
Nea Psara	75	G3
Near Islands	118	Aa9
Neath	52	D3
Nebine	113	K4
Nebit Dag	95	M2
Neblina, Pico da	136	D3
Nebraska	123	N7
Nebraska City	124	C6
Nebrodi, Monti	69	E7
Nechako	118	L5
Nechi	133	K11
Neckar	70	C4
Necochea	139	E7
Nedong	93	H3
Nedstrand	63	A7
Needles Canada	122	E3
Needles U.S.A.	126	E3
Needles Point	115	E2
Needles, The	53	F4
Neepawa	123	Q2
Neergaard Lake	120	L3
Nefedovo	84	A5
Nefta	101	G2
Neftechala	94	J2
Neftegorsk	79	J5
Neftekamsk	78	J4
Nefyn	52	C2
Nefza	69	B7
Negele	103	G6
Negev	94	B6
Negoiu	73	H3
Negombo	92	E7
Negotin	73	G3
Negrais, Cape	93	H5
Negra, Punta	136	A5
Negritos	136	A4
Negro Argentina	139	C7
Negro Amazonas, Brazil	136	E4
Negro Santa Catarina, Brazil	138	F5
Negro Uruguay	138	F6
Negros	91	G3
Negru Voda	73	K4
Nehavand	94	J4
Nehbandan	95	Q6
Nehe	87	N2
Nehoiasu	73	J3
Neijiang	93	K3
Nei Mongol Zizhiqu	87	L3
Neisse Poland	70	F3
Neisse Poland	71	G3
Neiteyugansk	84	A4
Neiva	136	B3
Neixiang	93	M2
Nekemte	103	G6
Neksikan	85	R4
Nekso	63	H9
Nelidovo	78	E4
Neligh	123	Q6
Nelkan	85	P5
Nellore	92	E6
Nelma	88	G2
Nelson Canada	122	F3
Nelson New Zealand	115	D4
Nelson U.K.	55	G3
Nelson, Cape Australia	113	J6
Nelson, Cape Papua New Guinea	114	D3
Nelson Lagoon	118	Af8
Nelspruit	108	F5
Nema	100	D5
Neman	78	C4
Neman	71	K1
Nemira	73	J2
Nemirov	73	K1
Nemiscau	121	L7
Nemours	64	E4
Nemun	63	J9
Nemuro	88	K4
Nemuro-kaikyo	88	K4
Nemuy	85	P5
Nenagh	59	F7
Nenana	118	F3
Nene	53	G2
Nen Jiang	87	P1
Nenjiang	87	P2
Nenthead	55	G2
Neokhorion	75	F3
Neon Karlovasi	75	J4
Neosho Kansas	124	C7
Neosho Missouri	124	C8
Nepa Russia	84	H5
Nepa Russia	84	H5
Nepal	92	F3
Nephi	126	G1
Nephin Beg Range	58	C4
Nera	69	D4
Nerac	65	D6
Nerchinsk	85	K6
Neretva	72	D4
Neriquinha	106	D6
Neris	63	L9
Nermete, Punta	136	A5
Neryuktey-l-y	85	K4
Neryuvom	84	Ad3
Nes	63	C6
Nesbyen	63	C6
Neskaupstadur	62	Y12
Nesna	62	E3
Nesscliffe	52	E2
Ness, Loch	56	D3
Nesterov Russia	71	K3
Nesterov Ukraine	71	K1
Nesterovo	84	H6
Neston	55	F3
Nestos	75	H2
Nesvizh	71	M2
Netanya	94	B5
Netherlands	64	F2
Neto	69	F6
Nettilling Lake	120	M4
Nettleham	55	J3
Netzahualcoyotl, Presa	131	N9
Neubrandenburg	70	E2
Neuchatel	68	A2
Neuchatel, Lac de	68	A2
Neufchateau Belgian	64	F4
Neufchateau France	64	F4
Neufchatel	64	D4
Neufelden	68	D1
Neumunster	70	C1
Neunkirchen Austria	68	F2
Neunkirchen Germany	70	B4

Norresundby 63 C8
Norrfjarden 62 J4
Norristown 125 N6
Norrkoping 63 L7
Norrland 62 F5
Norrtalje 63 H7
Norseman 112 E5
Norsjo 62 M4
Norsk 85 N6
Norsup 114 T12
Norte, Punta *Argentina* 139 D8
Norte, Punta *Argentina* 139 E7
Norte, Serra do 136 F6
Northallerton 55 H2
Northam 112 D5
Northampton *U.K.* 53 G2
Northampton *U.S.A.* 125 P5
Northamptonshire 53 G2
North Andaman 93 H6
North Arm 119 N3
North Astrolabe Reef 114 R9
North Battleford 119 P5
North Bay *Canada* 125 L3
North Bay *Ireland* 59 K8
North Bend 122 B6
North Berwick 57 F4
North Canadian 128 C3
North, Cape 121 P8
North Cape *New Zealand* 115 D1
North Cape *Norway* 62 L1
North Cape *U.S.A.* 118 A3
North Carolina 129 M3
North Cave 55 J3
North Channel *Canada* 124 J3
North Channel *U.K.* 58 L2
Northchapel 53 G3
North Charlton 55 H1
Northcliffe 112 D5
North Dakota 123 P4
North Dorset Downs 52 E4
North Downs 53 H3
Northeast Cape 118 B3
Northeast Providence Channel 132 J2
North Elmham 53 H2
Northern Ireland 58 H3
Northern Sporades 75 H3
Northern Territory 112 G3
North Esk 57 F4
Northfield 124 D4
North Flinders Range 113 H5
North Foreland 53 J3
North Geomagnetic Pole 140 S3
North Henik Lake 119 R3
North Korea 87 P4
North Kyme 55 J3
North Lakhimpur 93 H3
Northleach 53 F3
North Magnetic Pole 140 U3
North Miami Beach 129 M8
North Platte *U.S.A.* 123 N7
North Platte *U.S.A.* 123 P7
North Point *Canada* 121 P8
North Point *U.S.A.* 124 J4
North Pole 140 A1
North River 119 S4
North Roe 56 A1
North Ronaldsay 56 F1
North Ronaldsay Firth 56 F1
North Saskatchewan 119 P5
North Sea 50 H4
North Sentinel 93 H6
North Shields 55 H1
North Shoshone Peak 122 F8
North Sound 59 C6
North Sound, The 56 F1
North Stradbroke Island 113 L4
North Taranaki Bight 115 E3
North Tawton 52 D4
North Thoresby 55 J3
North Tolsta 56 B2
North Tonawanda 125 L5
North Twin Island 121 K7
North Tyne 57 F5
North Uist 56 A3
Northumberland 57 F5
Northumberland Islands 113 L3
Northumberland C 120 M2
Northumberland Strait 121 P8
Northwall 56 F1
North Walsham 53 J2
Northway Junction 118 G3
Northwest Cape 118 A3
North West Cape 112 C3
North West Highlands 56 C3
Northwest Providence Channel 132 H1
Northwest Territories 119 Q2
Northwich 55 G3
North York 125 L5
North Yorkshire 55 H2
Norton *U.K.* 55 J2
Norton *U.S.A.* 123 Q8
Norton Bay 118 C3
Norton Sound 118 C3
Norvegia, Cape 141 Z4
Norwalk 124 J6
Norway 63 C6
Norway House 119 R5
Norwegian Bay 120 H2
Norwegian Sea 62 A3
Norwich *U.K.* 53 J2
Norwich *U.S.A.* 125 Q6
Noshiro 88 G5
Noshul 78 H3
Nosok 84 C2
Nosop 108 D5
Nosovshchina 78 F3
Nosratabad 95 P7
Nossen 70 E3
Noss Head 56 E2
Noss, Island of 56 A2
Nosy-Varika 109 J4
Notec 71 G2
Noto 69 E7
Notodden 63 C7
Noto-hanto 89 F7
Notre Dame Bay 121 Q8
Notre Dame Mountains 121 N8
Nottingham 53 F2
Nottingham Island 120 L5
Nottinghamshire 55 H3
Notukeu Creek 123 L3
Nouadhibou 100 B4
Nouadhibou, Ras 100 B4
Nouakchott 100 B5
Noukloof Mountains 108 C4
Noumea 114 X17
Noup Head 56 E1
Noupoort 108 D6
Nouvelle-Caledonie 114 W16
Nouvelle Caledonie 114 W16
Nouvelle-France, Cap de 120 M5
Novabad 86 C4
Nova Bana 71 H4
Nova Cruz 137 K5
Nova Era 138 H3
Nova Friburgo 138 H4
Nova Iguacu 138 H4
Nova Lima 138 H4
Nova Mambone 109 G4
Novara 68 B3
Nova Remanso 137 J5
Nova Scotia 121 P8
Nova Sento Se 137 J5
Nova Sofala 109 F4
Nova Vanduzi 109 F3
Nova Varos 72 E4
Novaya Kakhovka 79 E6
Novaya Katysh 84 Ae5
Novaya Kazanka 79 H6
Novaya Novatka 84 G5
Novaya Odessa 79 E6
Novaya Sibir, Ostrov 85 R1
Novaya Tevriz 84 B5
Novaya Vodolaga 79 F6
Novaya Zemlya 84 Ab2
Novayo Ushitsa 73 J1
Nove Mesto 70 G4
Nove Zamky 71 H4
Novgorod 78 E4
Novgorod Serverskiy 79 E5
Novigrad 72 C3
Novikovo 88 J2
Novi Ligure 68 B3
Novi Pazar 72 F4
Novi Sad 72 E3
Novo Acre 137 J6
Novoaleksandrovsk 79 G6
Novoalekseyevka 79 K5
Novoanninskiy 79 G5
Novoarchangelsk 73 L1
Novo Aripuana 136 E5
Novobogatinskoye 79 J6
Novocheboksarsh 78 H4
Novocherkassk 79 G6
Novodolinka 84 A6
Novodvinsk 78 G3
Novograd-Volynskiy 79 D5
Novogrudok 71 L2
Novo Hamburgo 138 F5
Novoilinovka 85 P6
Novokazalinsk 86 A2
Novokhopersk 79 G5
Novokiyevskiy Uval 85 M6
Novokocherdyk 84 Ad6
Novokuybyshevsk 79 H5
Novokuznetsk 84 D6
Novolazareyskaya 141 A4
Novoletovye 84 G2
Novo Milosevo 72 F3
Novomitino 84 Ae5
Novomoskovsk *Russia* 78 F5
Novomoskovsk *Ukraine* 79 F6
Novopavlovka 84 H6
Novopokrovskaya 79 G6
Novopolotsk 63 N9
Novo Redondo 106 B5
Novo-Rokrovka 83 E3
Novoromanovo 84 C6
Novorossiysk 79 F7
Novorzhev 63 N8
Novo Sagres 91 H7
Novo Sergeyevka 79 J5
Novoshakhtinsk 79 F6
Novosibirsk 84 C4
Novosibirskiye Ostrova 85 Q1
Novospasskoye 79 H5
Novoukrainka 79 E6
Novo Uzensk 79 H5
Novo-Vyatsk 78 H4
Novoyeniseysk 84 E5
Novozhilovskaya 78 J3
Novozybkov 79 E5
Novska 72 D3
Novy Jicin 71 G4
Novyy 84 H2
Novyy Bor 78 J2
Novyy Bug 79 E6
Novyy Oskol 79 F5
Novyy Port 84 A3
Novyy Uzen 79 J7
Nowbaran 95 J4
Nowe 71 H2
Nowen Hill 59 D9
Nowgong 93 H3
Nowitna 118 E3
Nowograd 70 F2
Nowogrod 71 J2
Nowra 113 L5
Now Shahr 95 K3
Nowshera 92 D2
Nowy Sacz 71 J4
Nowy Targ 71 J4
Noyon *France* 64 E4
Noyon *Mongolia* 86 J3
Nozay 65 C5
Nsanje 107 G6
Nsukka 105 G4
Nsuta 104 E4
Ntem 105 H5
Ntwetwe Pan 108 E4
Nuba, Lake 102 F3
Nuba Mountains 102 F5
Nubian Desert 103 F3
Nubiya 102 E4
Nubiya, Es Sahra en 103 F3
Nudo Coropuna 136 C7
Nueces 128 C6
Nueltin Lake 119 R3
Nueva Florida 133 N10
Nueva Rosita 127 M7
Nueva San Salvador 132 C8
Nueve de Julio 139 D7
Nuevitas 132 J4
Nuevo, Bajo 132 H7
Nuevo Casas Grandes 127 J5
Nuevo Churumuco 130 J8
Nuevo Laredo 128 C7
Nugaruba Islands 114 E2
Nugget Point 115 B7
Nugrus, Gebel 96 B4
Nuhaka 115 F3
Nuh, Ra's 95 R9
Nui 111 S3
Nuits-Saint-Georges 65 F5
Nu Jiang 93 J3
Nukhayb 94 F5
Nukiki 114 H5
Nukualofa 111 T6
Nukufetau 111 S3
Nukuhu 114 D3
Nukulaelae 111 S3
Nukumanu Islands 111 N2
Nukunau 111 S2
Nukunono 111 U3
Nukus 51 U7
Nullarbor 112 G5
Nullarbor Plain 112 F5
Numan 105 H4
Numata 89 G7
Numazu 89 G8
Numedal 63 C6
Numfor 114 B2
Numto 84 A4
Nuneaton 53 F2
Nunivak Islands 116 C2
Nunligran 85 Y4
Nunney 52 E3
Nuomin He 87 N2
Nuoro 69 B5
Nupani 114 M7
Nuqdah, Ra's an 97 P6
Nuqrah 96 E4
Nur 95 K3
Nura 86 C2
Nurabad 95 K6
Nur Daglari 77 G4
Nure 68 B3
Nurek 86 B4
Nurhak 77 G4
Nurhak Dagi 77 G3
Nuristan 92 D1
Nurmes 62 N5
Nurnberg 70 D4
Nurri 69 B6
Nurzec 71 K2
Nusaybin 77 J4
Nusayriyah, Jebel al 77 G5
Nushagak Bay 118 D4
Nu Shan 93 J3
Nushki 92 C3
Nutak 121 P6
Nuugaatsiaq 120 R3
Nuuk 120 R5
Nuupas 62 M3
Nuwara 92 F7
Nuweveldreeks 108 D6
Nuyakuk, Lake 118 D4
Nuyts, Point 112 D6
Nuzayzah 77 H5
Nyahururu 107 G2
Nyainqentanglha Shan 92 G3
Nyaksimvol 84 Ad4
Nyala 102 D5
Nyamboyto 84 C3
Nyandoma 78 G3
Nyang 93 H3
Nyanza 107 E3
Nyasa, Lake 107 F5
Nyashabozh 78 J2
Nyaungu 93 H4
Nyayba 85 N2
Nyborg 63 D9
Nybster 56 E2
Nyeri 107 G3
Nyerol 103 F6
Nyima 93 G2
Nyirbator 73 G2
Nyiregyhaza 73 F2
Nyiru, Mont 107 G2
Nykarleby 62 N4
Nykobing *Denmark* 63 C8
Nykobing *Denmark* 63 D9
Nykoping 63 G7
Nylstroom 108 E4
Nymagee 113 K5
Nymburk 70 F3
Nynashamn 63 G7
Nyngan 113 K5
Nyong 105 H5
Nyons 65 F6
Nyrany 70 E4
Nyrud 62 N2
Nysa 71 G3
Nysh 85 Q6
Nyshott 63 N6
Nystad 63 J6
Nytva 78 K4
Nyuk, Ozero 62 P4
Nyuksenitsa 78 G3
Nyunzu 107 E4
Nyurba 85 K4
Nyurolskiy 84 B5
Nyuya 85 J4
Nyvrovo 85 Q6
Nzambi 106 B3
Nzega 107 F3
Nzerekore 104 D4
Nzeto 106 B4
Nzo 104 D4

O

Oadby 53 F2
Oahe Dam 123 P5
Oahe, Lake 123 P5
Oahu 126 S10
Oakdale 126 B2
Oakengates 52 E2
Oakes 123 Q4
Oakford 52 D4
Oakham 53 G2
Oak Hill 125 K8
Oakington 53 H2
Oakland *California* 126 A2
Oakland *Nebraska* 123 R7
Oak Lawn 124 G6
Oakley 123 P8
Oakover 112 E3
Oakridge 122 C6
Oak Ridge 129 K2
Oak Valley 125 N7
Oamaru 115 C6
Oa, Mull of 57 B5
Oates Land 141 L4
Oa, The 57 B5
Oatlands 113 K7
Oaxaca 131 L9
Ob 84 Ae3
Oban 57 D4
Oberammergau 70 D5
Oberhausen 70 B3
Oberlin 123 P8
Obidos *Brazil* 137 F4
Obidos *Portugal* 66 B3
Obihiro 88 J4
Obi, Kepulauan 91 H6
Obilnoye 79 G6
Obion 128 H2
Obninsk 78 F4
Obo 102 E6
Obock 103 H5
Obok-tong 88 B5
Oborniki 71 G2
Oboyan 79 F5
Obozerskiy 78 G3
Obregon, Presa 127 H6
Obruk 76 E3
Obryvistoye 85 Q7
Observatoire, Caye de l' 111 N6
Obskaya Guba 84 A3
Obuasi 104 E4
Ocala 129 L6
Ocana *Colombia* 136 C2
Ocana *Spain* 66 E3
Occidental, Cordillera *Colombia* 136 B3
Occidental, Cordillera *Peru* 136 B6
Occidental, Grand Erg 100 F2
Oceanside 126 D4
Ocejon, Pic 66 E2
Ochamchire 77 J1
Ochil Hills 57 E4
Ochiltree 57 D5
Ock 53 F3
Ockelbo 63 G6
Ocmulgee 129 L5
Ocna Mures 73 G2
Oconee 129 L4
Ocotlan 130 H7
Ocracoke Island 129 Q3
Ocreza 66 C3
Ocsa 72 E2
Oda 89 D8

Name	Page	Grid
Ormos	75	H4
Ormskirk	55	G3
Ornain	64	F4
Orne	64	C4
Ornskoldsvik	62	H5
Oro	130	G4
Orobi, Alpi	68	B3
Orocue	136	C3
Orofino	122	F4
Oromocto	125	S4
Oron	85	K5
Orona	111	U2
Oronsay	57	B5
Oronsay, Passage of	57	B5
Orontes	77	G5
Oropesa	66	D3
Oroqen Zizhiqi	87	N1
Oroquieta	91	G4
Orosei, Golfo di	69	B5
Oroshaza	72	F2
Orotukan	85	S4
Oroville *California*	122	D8
Oroville *Washington*	122	E3
Oroville, Lake	122	D8
Orrin Reservoir	56	D3
Orsa	63	F6
Orsa Finnmark	63	F6
Orsaro, Monte	68	C3
Orsha	78	E5
Orsta	62	B5
Orta	76	E2
Ortabag	77	K4
Ortaca	76	C4
Ortakoy *Turkey*	76	F2
Ortakoy *Turkey*	76	F3
Ortatoroslar	76	F4
Ortega	136	B3
Ortegal, Cabo	66	C1
Ortelsburg	71	J2
Orthez	65	C7
Ortigueira	66	C1
Ortiz	133	P10
Ortles	68	C2
Ortona	69	E4
Orto-Tokoy	86	D3
Orumiyeh	77	L4
Orumiyeh, Daryacheh-ye	94	G3
Oruro	138	C3
Orvieto	69	D4
Orwell	53	J3
Oryakhovo	73	G4
Os	62	D5
Osa	78	K4
Osage	124	D7
Osaka *Japan*	39	E8
Osaka *Japan*	39	F8
Osaka-wan	89	E8
Osa, Peninsula de	132	F10
Osceola *Arkansas*	128	H3
Osceola *Iowa*	124	D6
Osh	86	B3
Oshamambe	88	H4
Oshawa	125	L5
O-shima	89	G8
Oshkosh	124	F4
Oshkurya	84	Ac3
Oshmarino	84	C2
Oshmyanskaya Vozvyshennost	71	M1
Oshmyany	71	L1
Oshnoviyeh	94	G3
Oshogbo	105	F4
Oshtoran Kuh	94	J5
Oshtorinan	94	J4
Oshwe	106	C3
Osijek	72	E3
Osimo	68	D4
Osinniki	84	D6
Osipovichi	79	D5
Oskaloosa	124	D6
Oskamull	57	B4
Oskara, Mys	84	F1
Oskarshamn	63	G8
Oskarstrom	63	E8
Oskoba	84	G4
Oskol	79	F5
Oslo *Norway*	63	D7
Oslo *Norway*	63	D7
Oslob	91	G4
Oslofjorden	63	H7
Osmanabad	92	E5
Osmancik	76	F2
Osmaneli	76	C2
Osmaniye	77	G4
Osmington	52	E4
Osmino	63	N7
Osmo	63	G7
Osnabruck	70	C2
Osogovska Planina	73	G4
Osorno *Chile*	139	B8
Osorno *Spain*	66	D1
Osoyro	63	A6
Osprey Reef	113	K1
Oss	64	F3
Ossa	75	G3
Ossa, Mount	110	L10
Ossett	55	H3
Ossian, Loch	57	D4
Ossokmanuan Lake	121	P7
Ostashkov	78	E4
Ostavall	62	F5
Ostby	63	E6
Oste	70	C2
Osterburken	70	C4
Osterdalalven	63	E6
Osterdalen	63	D5
Ostergotland	63	F7
Osterode	71	H2
Ostersund	62	F5
Ostfold	63	D7
Ost Friesische Inseln	70	B2
Ostfriesland	70	B2
Osthammar	63	H6
Ostiglia	68	C3
Ostra	68	D4
Ostrava	71	H4
Ostroda	71	H2
Ostrog	79	D5
Ostrogozhsk	79	F5
Ostroleka	71	J2
Ostrov	63	N8
Ostrovnoy, Mys	38	D4
Ostrow	71	G3
Ostrowiec	71	J3
Ostrow Mazowiecki	71	J2
Ostuni	69	F5
Osum	75	F2
Osum	75	H4
Osumi-kaikyo	89	C10
Osumi-shoto	89	C10
Osuna	66	D4
OsVan	78	K2
Oswaldtwistle	55	G3
Oswego	125	M5
Oswestry	52	D2
Otaki	115	E4
Otaru	83	H4
Otava	71	E4
Otavi	108	C3
Otawara	89	G7
Otchinjau	108	B6
Otelec	73	F3
Otelu Rosu	73	G3
Otematata	115	C6
Othe, Foret d'	65	E4
Othonoi	74	E3
Othris	75	G3
Oti	104	F4
Otira	115	C5
Otis	123	N7
Otish, Monts	121	M7
Otjiwarongo	108	C4
Otley	55	H3
Otlukbeli Daglari	77	J2
Otnes	63	D6
Otocac	72	C3
Otorohanga	115	E3
Otoskwin	121	H7
Otra	63	B7
Otranto	69	G5
Otranto, Capo d	69	G5
Otranto, Strait of	74	E2
Otsu	39	E8
Otsu	39	H7
Otta *Norway*	63	C6
Otta *Norway*	63	C6
Ottawa *Canada*	125	L3
Ottawa *Canada*	125	N4
Ottawa Islands	121	K6
Otter	52	D4
Otterburn	57	F5
Otter Rapids	125	K1
Otterup	63	D9
Ottery	52	C4
Ottery Saint Mary	52	D4
Ottumwa	124	D6
Oturkpo	105	G4
Otway, Bahia	139	B10
Otway, Cape	113	J6
Otway, Seno	139	B10
Otwock	71	J2
Otynya	71	L4
Otztaler Alpen	68	C2
Ouachita	128	F4
Ouachita, Lake	128	F3
Ouachita Mountains	128	E3
Ouadda	102	D6
Ouagadougou	104	E3
Ouahigouya	104	E3
Oualata	100	D5
Oua-n Ahagar, Tassili	101	G4
Ouanda Djaile	102	D6
Ouarane	100	D4
Ouargla	101	G2
Ouarra	102	E6
Ouarsenis, Massif de l'	67	G5
Ouarzazate	100	D2
Ouatoais	125	M4
Oubangui	106	C3
Oudenaarde	64	E3
Oude Rijn	64	F2
Oudtshoorn	108	D6
Oued Zem	100	D2
Oueme	105	F4
Ouen	114	X17
Ouessant, Ile d'	64	A4
Ouesso	106	C2
Ouezzane	100	D2
Oughterard	59	D6
Oughter, Lough	58	H4
Ouidah	105	F4
Oujda	100	E2
Oulainen	62	L4
Oulmes	100	D2
Oulu *Finland*	62	L4
Oulu *Finland*	62	M4
Oulujarvi	62	M4
Oulujoki	62	M4
Oulx	68	A3
Oum Chalouba	102	D4
Oum El Bouaghi	101	G1
Oum er Rbia, Oued	100	D2
Ou, Nam	93	K4
Ounasjoki	62	L3
Oundle	53	G2
Ounianga Kebir	102	D4
Oupu	87	P1
Ouricuri	137	J5
Ourinhos	138	G4
Ouro Preto	138	H4
Ourthe	64	F3
Ouse *Australia*	113	K7
Ouse *U.K.*	55	H3
Oust	65	B5
Outardes, Reservoir	121	N7
Outer Hebrides	56	A3
Outokumpu	62	N5
Out Skerries	56	B1
Outwell	53	H2
Ouvea	114	X16
Ouyen	113	J6
Ovacik *Turkey*	77	H4
Ovacik *Turkey*	77	J2
Ovada	68	B3
Ovalau Batiki	114	R8
Ovalle	138	B6
Ovau	114	H5
Ovejo	66	D3
Oven *Croatia*	115	X17
Overbister	56	F1
Overbygd	62	H2
Overkalix	62	K3
Overnas	62	G3
Overtornea	62	K3
Oviedo	66	D1
Ovinishche	78	F4
Ovre Ardal	63	B6
Ovruch	79	D5
Owahanga	115	F4
Owaka	115	B7
Owando	106	C3
Owase	89	F8
Owatonna	124	D4
Owbeh	95	R4
Owel, Lough	58	H5
Owenbeg	58	E4
Owenkillew	58	H3
Owenmore	58	C4
Owens	126	C2
Owensboro	124	G8
Owens Lake	126	D2
Owen Sound	125	K4
Owen Stanley Range	114	D3
Owerri	105	G4
Owo	105	G4
Owosso	124	H5
Owyhee *Nevada*	122	F7
Owyhee *Oregon*	122	F6
Oxbow	123	N3
Oxelosund	63	G7
Oxenholme	55	G2
Oxenhope	55	H3
Oxford *New Zealand*	115	D5
Oxford *U.K.*	53	F3
Oxford *U.S.A.*	128	H3
Oxfordshire	53	F3
Ox Mountains	58	E4
Oxnard	126	C3
Oxton	55	H3
Oyaca	76	E3
Oyali	77	J4
Oyapock	137	G3
Oyem	106	B2
Oykel	56	D3
Oykel Bridge	56	D3
Oymyakon	85	Q4
Oyo	105	F4
Ozalp	77	L3
Ozamiz	91	G4
Ozark Plateau	124	D8
Ozarks, Lake of the	124	D7
Ozd	72	F1
Ozernovskiy	85	T6
Ozernoye	84	A5
Ozersk	71	K1
Ozhogina	85	R3
Ozieri	69	B5
Ozinki	79	H5
Ozona	127	M5
Ozora	72	E2
Ozyurt	76	F3

P

Name	Page	Grid
Paama	114	U12
Paarl	108	C6
Pabbay *U.K.*	56	A3
Pabbay *U.K.*	57	A4
Pabellon de Arteaga	130	H6
Pabjanice	71	H3
Pabna	92	G4
Pabrade	63	L9
Pacaas Novos, Serra dos	136	E6
Pacaraima, Sierra	136	E3
Pacasmayo	136	B5
Pachino	69	E7
Pachora	92	E4
Pachuca	131	K7
Pacifica	126	A2
Pacific Ocean	87	P7
Pacific Ocean, North	143	H3
Pacific Ocean, South	143	J5
Pacitan	90	E7
Packwood	122	D4
Padang *Indonesia*	90	C6
Padang *Indonesia*	90	C5
Padangpanjang	90	D6
Padangsidimpuan	90	B5
Padasjoki	63	L6
Padauiri	136	E3
Paderborn	70	C3
Pades	73	G3
Padiham	55	G3
Padilla *Bolivia*	138	D3
Padilla *Mexico*	131	K5
Padina	73	J3
Padje-Ianta	62	G3
Padloping Island	120	P4
Padova	68	C3
Padrao, Ponta do	106	B4
Padron	66	B1
Padstow	52	C4
Padstow Bay	52	C4
Padua	68	C3
Paducah *Kentucky*	124	F8
Paducah *Texas*	127	M4
Padunskoye More	62	P2
Paekariki	115	E4
Paengnyong-do	87	N4
Paeroa	115	E2
Pag *Croatia*	72	C3
Pag *Croatia*	72	C3
Pagadian	91	G4
Pagasitikos Kolpos	75	G3
Pagatan	90	F6
Page	126	G2
Pagosa Springs	127	J2
Pagwa River	124	H2
Pagwi	114	C2
Pahala	126	T11
Pahang	90	C5
Pahia Point	115	A7
Pahiatua	115	E4
Pahlavi Dezh	95	M3
Pahoa	126	T11
Pahokee	129	M7
Pahra Kariz	95	Q4
Paia	126	S10
Paide	63	L7
Paignton	52	D4
Paijanne	63	L6
Pailolo Chan	126	S10
Paimpol	64	B4
Painswick	53	E3
Painted Desert	126	G2
Paisley	57	D5
Paita	136	A5
Paita	114	X17
Paittasjarvi	62	K2
Pajala	62	K3
Pakaraima Mountains	136	E2
Pakistan	92	C3
Pak Lay	93	K5
Pakokku	93	H4
Pakpattan	92	D2
Pakrac	72	D3
Paks	72	E2
Pakse	93	L5
Pala	102	B6
Palabuhanratu	90	D7
Palafrugell	67	H2
Palagruza	72	D4
Palaiokastron	75	J5
Palaiokhora	75	G5
Pala Laharha	92	G4
Palamos	67	H2
Palana	85	T5
Palanan Point	91	G2
Palanga	63	J9
Palangan, Kuh-e-	95	Q6
Palangkaraya	90	E6
Palanpur	92	D4
Palapye	108	E4
Palar	92	E6
Palata	69	E5
Palatka *U.S.A.*	129	M6
Palatka *Russia*	85	S4
Palau	69	B5
Palau Islands	91	J4
Palawan	91	F4
Palawan Passage	91	F4
Palayankottai	92	E7
Palazzola Acreide	69	E7
Paldiski	63	L7
Palembang	90	C6
Palena, Lago	139	B8
Palencia	66	D1
Palermo	69	D6
Palestine	128	E5
Paletwa	93	H4
Palghat	92	E6
Palgrave Point	108	B4
Palhoca	138	G5
Pali	92	D3
Palisade	127	H1
Palit, Kep i	74	E2
Palkane	63	L6
Palk Strait	92	E7
Pallaresa	67	G1
Pallas Grean	59	F7
Pallasovka	79	H5
Pallastunturi	62	K2
Palliser Bay	115	E4
Palliser, Cape	115	E4
Palma *Mozambique*	109	H2

Name	Map	Ref
Palma *Spain*	67	H3
Palma, Baia de	67	H3
Palma del Rio	66	D4
Pal Malmal	114	E3
Palmanova	68	D3
Palmares	137	K5
Palmar, Punta del	139	F6
Palmas	138	G5
Palmas, Cape	104	D5
Palmas, Golfo di	69	B6
Palma Soriano	132	J4
Palmatkina	85	V4
Palmeira	138	F5
Palmeiras	137	J6
Palmer *Antarctic*	141	V6
Palmer *U.S.A.*	118	F3
Palmer Land	141	V4
Palmerston	115	C6
Palmerston Island	111	W5
Palmerston North	115	E4
Palm Harbor	129	L6
Palmi	69	E6
Palmira	136	B3
Palm Springs	126	D4
Palmyra	94	D4
Palmyras Point	92	G4
Palo de las Letras	136	B2
Palomar, Mount	126	D4
Palopo	91	G6
Palos, Cabo de	67	F4
Palpetu, Tanjung	91	H6
Palu *Indonesia*	91	F6
Palu *Indonesia*	91	F6
Palu *Turkey*	77	H3
Palyavaam	85	W3
Pama	104	F3
Pamban	92	E7
Pamekasan	90	E7
Pameungpeuk	90	D7
Pamiers	65	D7
Pamisos	75	F4
Pamlico Sound	129	P3
Pampa	127	M3
Pampachiri	136	C6
Pampas *Argentina*	139	D7
Pampas *Peru*	136	C6
Pampilhosa da Serra	66	C2
Pamplona *Colombia*	136	C2
Pamplona *Spain*	67	F1
Pana	124	F7
Panaca	126	E2
Panagyurishte	73	H4
Panaji	92	D5
Panama	132	G10
Panama	132	H10
Panama, Bahia de	132	H10
Panama Canal	136	B2
Panama City	129	K5
Panama, Golfo de	136	B2
Panandak	95	K4
Panaro	68	C3
Panay	91	G3
Pancevo	72	F3
Panda	109	F4
Pandan *Philippines*	91	G3
Pandan *Philippines*	91	G3
Pandany	78	E3
Pandharpur	92	E5
Pando	139	E6
Pandunskoye More	78	E2
Panevezys	63	N9
Panfilov	86	E3
Pangalanes, Canal des	109	J4
Pangani	107	G4
Panggoe	114	H5
Pangi	106	E3
Pangkalanbuun	90	E6
Pangkalpinang	90	D6
Pangnirtung	120	N4
Pangong Tso	92	E2
Pangrango, Gunung	90	D7
Pangtara	93	J4
Pangururur	90	B5
Pangutaran Group	91	G4
Panhandle	127	M3
Paniai, Danau	114	B2
Panie, Mount	114	W16
Panipat	92	E3
Panjim	92	D5
Panna	92	F4
Panovo	84	G5
Pant *Essex, U.K.*	53	H3
Pant *Shropshire, U.K.*	52	D2
Pantar	91	G7
Pantelleria, Isola di	69	D7
Pantones	66	E3
Panuco *Mexico*	131	K6
Panuco *Mexico*	131	K6
Pan Xian	93	K3
Panyam	105	G4
Pao-de-Acucar	137	K5
Paola	69	F6
Paoua	102	C6
Papa	72	D2
Papakura	115	E2
Papantla	131	L7
Paparoa	115	E2
Paparoa Range	115	C5
Papa Stour	56	A1
Papatoetoe	115	E2
Papa Westray	56	F1
Papenburg	70	B2
Papigochic	127	J6
Papisoi, Tanjung	114	A2
Paps of Jura	57	B5
Paps, The	59	D8
Papua, Gulf of	114	C3
Papua New Guinea	114	C2
Papuk	72	D3
Papun	93	J5
Para	137	G4
Paracas, Peninsula	136	B6
Paracatu *Brazil*	138	G3
Paracatu *Brazil*	138	G3
Paracin	73	F4
Paradubice	70	F3
Paragould	128	G2
Paragua	136	E6
Paragua	136	E2
Paraguacu	137	J6
Paraguai	136	F7
Paraguana, Peninsula de	133	M8
Paraguari	138	E5
Paraguay	138	E4
Paraguay	138	E4
Paraiba	138	H4
Paraiba	137	K5
Parajuru	137	K4
Parakou	105	F4
Paralakhemundi	92	F5
Paralkot	92	F5
Paramaribo	137	F2
Paramillo	136	B2
Paramirim	137	J6
Paramonga	136	B6
Paramushir, Ostrov	85	T6
Parana	138	D6
Parana	137	H6
Paranagua	138	G5
Paranaiba *Maranhao, Brazil*	137	J4
Paranaiba *Mato Grosso do Sul, Brazil*	138	F3
Paranaiba *Minas Gerais, Brazil*	138	G3
Paranaidji	137	H5
Paranapanema	138	F4
Paranapiacaba, Serra	138	G4
Paranatinga	137	F6
Parangipettai	92	E6
Paraparaum	115	E4
Parapola	75	G4
Parauna	138	F3
Parbati	92	E4
Parbhani	92	E5
Parcel Islands	93	M5
Parchim	70	D2
Pardo	138	F4
Parecis, Serra dos	136	F6
Pareditas	139	C6
Pare Mountains	107	G3
Parengarenga Harbour	115	D1
Parepare	91	F6
Paria, Golfo de	133	R9
Pariaguan	136	E2
Paria, Peninsula de	133	R9
Paricutin, Volcan el	130	H8
Parigi	91	G6
Parikkala	63	N6
Parima, Serra	136	E3
Parintins	137	F4
Paris *France*	64	E4
Paris *Kentucky*	124	H7
Paris *Tennessee*	129	H2
Paris *Texas*	128	E4
Parkano	63	K5
Parker	126	E3
Parkersburg	125	K7
Parkes	113	K5
Parkgate	57	E5
Park Range	123	L7
Parksville	122	B3
Parma *Italy*	68	C3
Parma *U.S.A.*	125	K6
Parnaiba	137	J4
Parnamirim	137	K5
Parnassos	75	G3
Parnassus	115	D5
Parnis	75	G3
Parnon Oros	75	G4
Parnu	63	L7
Parnu	63	L7
Paro	93	G3
Paropamisus	95	R4
Paros *Greece*	75	H4
Paros *Greece*	75	H4
Parowan	126	F2
Parral	139	B7
Parras	127	L8
Parrett	52	E3
Parrsboro	121	P8
Parry Bay	120	K4
Parry Islands	120	C2
Parry, Kap	120	M2
Parry Peninsula	118	L2
Parry Sound	125	L4
Parseta	71	G2
Parshino	85	J5
Parsons	128	E2
Partabpur	92	F4
Parthenay	65	C5
Partizansk	88	D4
Parton	57	D5
Partry Mountains	58	C5
Paru	137	G4
Parys	108	E5
Pasa Barris	137	K6
Pasadena *California*	126	C3
Pasadena *Texas*	128	E6
Pasado, Cabo	136	A4
Pa Sak, Mae Nam	93	K5
Pasarwajo	91	G7
Pascagoula *U.S.A.*	128	H5
Pascagoula *U.S.A.*	128	H5
Pascani	73	J2
Pasco	122	E4
Pascua, Isla de	143	K5
Pasewalk	70	F2
Pashiya	78	K4
Pashkovo	88	C1
Pasig	91	G3
Pasinler	77	J3
Pasirpangarayan	90	C5
Paslek	71	H1
Pasley, Cape	112	E5
Pasmajarvi	62	L3
Pasman	72	C4
Pasni	92	B3
Paso de los Indios	139	C8
Paso de los Libres	138	E5
Paso de los Toros	138	E6
Paso Real	131	M9
Paso Rio Mayo	139	B9
Paso Robles	126	B3
Pasquia Hills	119	Q5
Passage East	59	J8
Passage West	59	F9
Passamaquoddy Bay	125	S4
Passau	70	E4
Passero, Capo	69	E7
Passo Fundo	138	F5
Passos	138	G4
Pastaza	136	B4
Pas, The	119	Q5
Pasto	136	B3
Pastol Bay	118	C3
Pastos Bons	137	J5
Pastrana	66	E2
Pasuruan	90	E7
Patache, Punta de	138	B4
Patagonia	139	C9
Patan *India*	92	D4
Patan *Nepal*	92	G3
Patani	91	H5
Patea	115	E3
Pateley Bridge	55	H2
Paterno	69	E7
Paterson	125	N6
Pathankot	92	E2
Pathfinder Reservoir	123	L6
Pathhead	57	F4
Patiala	92	E2
Patkai Bum	93	J3
Patman, Lake	128	E4
Patmos	75	J4
Patna	92	G3
Patnagarh	92	F4
Patnos	77	K3
Patomskoye Nagorye	85	J4
Patos	137	K5
Patos de Minas	138	G3
Patos, Lagoa dos	138	F6
Patquia	138	C6
Patrai	75	F3
Patras	75	F3
Patrasuy	78	L3
Patricio Lynch, Isla	139	A9
Patrington	55	J3
Patrocinio	138	G3
Pattani	93	K7
Patterdale	55	G2
Patti	69	E6
Patu	137	K5
Patuca	132	E7
Patuca, Punta	132	E7
Patzcuaro	130	J8
Patzcuaro, Laguna	130	J8
Pau	65	C7
Pau d'Arco	137	H5
Pau dos Ferros	137	K5
Pau, Gave de	65	C7
Pauini *Brazil*	136	D5
Pauini *Brazil*	136	D5
Paulilatino	69	B5
Paulista	137	K5
Paulistana	137	J5
Pauls Valley	128	D3
Paungde	93	J5
Pauni	92	E4
Pauri	92	E2
Pauto	136	C2
Pavarandocito	136	B2
Paveh	94	H4
Pavia	68	B3
Pavilosta	63	J8
Pavlikeni	73	H4
Pavlodar	84	B6
Pavlof Volcano	118	Af8
Pavlohrad	79	F6
Pavlovo	78	G4
Pavlovsk	79	G5
Pavlovskaya	79	F6
Pavullo nel Frignano	68	C3
Pavuvu	114	J6
Pawan	90	E6
Paxoi	75	F3
Paxton	57	F4
Payakumbuh	90	D6
Payette *U.S.A.*	122	F5
Payne, Lake	121	M6
Paynes Find	112	D4
Paysandu	138	E6
Payun, Volcan	139	C7
Pazanan	95	J6
Pazar	77	J2
Pazarbasi Burun	76	D2
Pazarcik	77	G4
Pazardzhik	73	H4
Pazaroren	77	G3
Pazaryeri	76	C2
Paz, Bahia de la	130	D5
Pazin	72	B3
Pcim	71	H4
Peabody Bugt	120	N2
Peace *Canada*	119	N4
Peace *U.S.A.*	129	M7
Peacehaven	53	H4
Peace River	119	M4
Peaima Falls	136	E2
Pea Island	129	Q3
Peak Hill	112	D4
Peale, Mount	123	K8
Pearl	128	H5
Pearl City	126	R10
Pearl Harbor	126	R10
Pearsall	128	C6
Peary Channel	120	F2
Pease	127	N3
Pebane	109	G3
Pec	72	F4
Pechenezhin	71	L4
Pechenga	62	P2
Pechora	78	J2
Pechorskaya Guba	78	J2
Pechorskoye More	78	J2
Pechory	63	M8
Pecos *U.S.A.*	127	L5
Pecos Plains	127	K4
Pecs	72	E2
Pedasi	132	G11
Pededze	63	M8
Pedernales	133	M5
Pedo La	92	F3
Pedorovka	79	J5
Pedra Azul	138	H3
Pedregal	132	F10
Pedreiras	137	J4
Pedro Afonso	137	H5
Pedro Cays	132	J6
Pedro Juan Caballero	138	E4
Pedro Luro	139	D7
Peebles	57	E5
Pee Dee	129	N3
Peel *Canada*	118	J2
Peel *U.K.*	54	E2
Peel Sound	120	G3
Peene	70	E2
Pegasus Bay	115	D5
Pegnitz *Germany*	70	D4
Pegnitz *Germany*	70	D4
Pegu	93	J5
Pegu Yoma	93	J5
Pegwell Bay	53	J3
Pegysh	78	J3
Pehlivankoy	76	B2
Pehuajo	139	D7
Peine	70	D2
Peipus, Lake	63	M7
Peixe	137	H6
Pei Xian	93	N2
Pekalongan	90	D7
Pekan	90	C5
Pekanbaru	90	C5
Pekin	124	F6
Peking	87	M4
Pekkala	62	M3
Pelabuanratu, Teluk	90	D7
Pelabuhan Kelang	90	C5
Pelagie, Isole	74	B5
Pelagos	75	H3
Pelat, Mont	65	G6
Peleaga	73	G3
Peleduy	85	J3
Pelee Island	124	J6
Peleng	91	G6
Peljesac	72	D4
Pelkosenniemi	62	M3
Pella	124	D6
Pellegrini	139	D7
Pello	62	L3
Pellworm	70	C1
Pelly	118	J3
Pelly Bay	120	J4
Pelly Mountains	118	J3
Peloponnisos	75	G4
Pelotas	138	F5
Pelplin	71	H2
Pelym	78	L3
Pemali, Tanjung	91	G6
Pematangsiantar	90	B5
Pemba	109	H4
Pemba Island	107	G4
Pemberton	122	C2
Pembina	119	M5
Pembroke *Canada*	125	M4
Pembroke *U.K.*	52	C3
Pembroke Dock	52	C3
Pena de Francia, Sierra da	66	C2
Penafiel	66	B2
Penafiel	66	D2
Penala	113	J6
Penalara, Pic de	66	E2
Penamacor	66	C2
Penapolis	138	F4
Penaranda de Bracamonte	66	D2
Penarroya	67	C2
Penarroya-Pueblonuevo	66	D3
Penarth	52	D3

Name			Name		
Prasto	63	E9	Prinzapolca	132	E8
Prata	138	G3	Priozersk	53	P6
Prato	68	C4	Pripet Marshes	79	D5
Pratt	127	N2	Pripyat	71	M2
Pravets	73	G4	Pristina	73	F4
Pravia	66	C1	Pritzwalk	70	E2
Predazzo	68	C2	Privas	65	F6
Predcal	73	H3	Privolzhskaya Vozvyshennost	79	H5
Predeal, Pasul	73	H3	Prizzi	69	D7
Predivinsk	84	E5	Probolinggo	90	E7
Predlitz	68	D2	Proddatur	92	E6
Premer	113	K5	Progreso	131	Q7
Premuda	72	C3	Prokhladnyy	79	G7
Prenai	71	K1	Prokletije	74	E1
Prentice	124	E4	Prokopyevsk	84	D6
Prenzlau	70	E2	Prokuplje	73	F4
Preobrazhenka	84	H5	Proletarsk	79	G6
Preparis	93	H6	Prome	93	J5
Preparis North Channel	93	H5	Proprad	71	J4
Preparis South Channel	93	H6	Propria	137	K6
Prerov	71	G4	Propriano	69	B5
Prescot	55	G3	Prorva	79	J6
Prescott *Arizona*	126	F5	Prosna	71	G3
Prescott *Arkansas*	128	F4	Prospect	122	C6
Prescott Island	120	G3	Prosperous	59	J6
Preseli, Mynydd	52	C3	Prostejov	71	G4
Preservation Inlet	115	A7	Provence	65	G7
Presevo	73	F4	Providence *Seychelles*	82	D7
Presho	123	Q6	Providence *U.S.A.*	125	Q6
Presidencia Roque Saenz Pena	138	D5	Providence, Cape *Canada*	120	D3
Presidente Dutra	137	J4	Providence, Cape *New Zealand*	115	A7
Presidente Epitacio	138	F4	Providencia	136	B4
Presidente Prudente	138	E4	Providencia, Isla de	132	G8
Presidio	127	K6	Provideniya	81	V3
Preslav	73	J4	Provincetown	125	Q5
Presnovka	84	Ae6	Provins	64	E4
Presov	71	J4	Provo	122	J7
Prespansko Jezero	75	F2	Prudhoe	55	H2
Presque Isle	125	S3	Prudhoe Bay	118	F1
Pressburg	71	G4	Prum	70	B3
Prestatyn	55	F3	Pruszkow	71	J2
Presteigne	52	D2	Prut	73	K2
Preston *U.K.*	55	G3	Prutul	73	J2
Preston *Minnesota*	124	D5	Pruzhany	71	L2
Preston *Missouri*	124	D8	Pryazha	78	E3
Prestonburg	124	J8	Prydz Bay	141	F5
Prestonpans	57	F5	Pryor	128	E2
Prestwick	57	F4	Przechlewo	71	G2
Pretoria	108	E5	Przemysl	71	K4
Preveza	75	F3	Przeworsk	71	K3
Prey Veng	93	L6	Przhevalsk	86	D3
Pribilof Islands	118	Ad8	Przysucha	71	J3
Pribinic	72	D3	Psakhna	75	G3
Pribram	70	F4	Psara	75	H3
Price	126	G1	Pskov	63	Q8
Price, Cape	93	H6	Pskovskoye, Ozero	63	M7
Prichard	129	H5	Ptolemais	75	F2
Priego	66	E2	Ptuj	72	C2
Priego de Cordoba	66	D4	Puan	87	P4
Prieska	108	D5	Pucallpa	136	C5
Priest Lake	122	F3	Pucarani	138	C3
Priest River	122	F3	Pudai	95	R6
Prievidza	71	H4	Pudasjarvi	62	M4
Prignitz	70	D2	Puddletown	52	E4
Prijedor	72	D3	Pudnya	63	N8
Prikaspiyskaya Nizmennost	79	J6	Pudozh	78	F3
Prilep	73	F5	Pudsey	55	H3
Priluki *Russia*	78	G3	Puduchcheri	92	E6
Priluki *Ukraine*	79	E5	Pudukkottai	92	E6
Primavera	141	V6	Puebla	131	K8
Primorsk *Azerbaijan*	79	H7	Puebla de Don Rodrigo	66	D3
Primorsk *Ukraine*	79	F6	Puebla de Sanabria	66	C1
Primorsk *Russia*	79	H6	Puebla de Trives	66	C1
Primorsk *Russia*	63	N6	Pueblo	127	K1
Primorskiy Kray	88	E3	Pueblo Hundido	138	B5
Primorsko	73	J4	Pueblo Nuevo	136	D1
Primorsko-Akhtarsk	79	F6	Puelen	139	C7
Primrose Lake	119	P5	Puente Alto	139	C6
Prince Albert *Canada*	119	P5	Puerto Acosta	138	C3
Prince Albert *South Africa*	108	D6	Puerto Aisen	139	B9
Prince Albert Peninsula	119	N1	Puerto Asis	136	B3
Prince Albert Road	108	D6	Puerto Ayacucho	136	D2
Prince Albert Sound	119	N1	Puerto Ayora	136	A7
Prince Alfred, Cape	120	B3	Puerto Barrios	132	C7
Prince Charles Island	120	L4	Puerto Cabello	136	D1
Prince Charles Mountains	141	E4	Puerto Cabezas	132	F7
Prince Edward Island	121	P8	Puerto Carreno	136	D2
Prince Edward Islands	142	C6	Puerto Casado	138	E4
Prince George	119	L5	Puerto Coig	139	C10
Prince Gustav Adolph Sea	120	E2	Puerto Cortes *Costa Rica*	132	F10
Prince of Wales, Cape *Canada*	121	M5	Puerto Cortes *Honduras*	132	D7
Prince of Wales, Cape *U.S.A.*	118	B2	Puerto Cumarebo	136	D1
Prince of Wales Island *Australia*	114	C4	Puerto del Rosario	100	C3
Prince of Wales Island *Canada*	120	G3	Puerto de Pollensa	67	H3
Prince of Wales Island *U.S.A.*	118	J4	Puerto Deseado	139	C9
Prince of Wales Strait	119	M1	Puerto Escondido	131	L10
Prince Patrick Island	120	B2	Puerto Estrella	136	C1
Prince Regent Inlet	120	H3	Puerto Eten	136	B5
Prince Rupert	118	J5	Puerto Guarani	138	E4
Princes Risborough	53	G3	Puerto Juarez	131	R7
Princess Astrid Coast	141	A4	Puerto La Cruz	136	E1
Princess Charlotte Bay	113	J1	Puerto-Lapice	66	E3
Princess Elizabeth Land	141	F4	Puerto Leguizamo	136	C4
Princess Marie Bay	120	L2	Puerto Libertad	126	F6
Princethorpe	53	F2	Puerto Lobos	139	C8
Princeton *Canada*	122	D3	Puerto Madryn	139	C8
Princeton *Illinois*	124	F6	Puerto Maldonado	136	D6
Princeton *Kentucky*	124	G8	Puerto Merazan	132	D8
Princeton *Missouri*	124	D6	Puerto Montt	139	B8
Princeton *W. Virginia*	125	K8	Puerto Natales	139	B10
Prince William Sound	118	F3	Puerto Ordaz	133	R10
Principe	105	G5	Puerto Paez	136	D2
Prineville	122	D5			
Prins Karls Forland	80	C2			

Name			Name		
Puerto Penasco	126	F5	Puzla	78	J3
Puerto Pico	138	E5	Pweto	107	E4
Puerto Plata	133	M5	Pwllheli	52	C2
Puerto Portillo	136	C5	Pyaozero, Ozero	62	P3
Puerto Princesa	91	F4	Pyapon	93	J5
Puerto Rey	132	J10	Pyasina	84	D2
Puerto Rico *Bolivia*	136	D6	Pyasinado	84	B3
Puerto Rico *U.S.A.*	133	P5	Pyasino, Ozero	84	D3
Puerto Rico Trench	133	P5	Pyatigorsk	79	G7
Puerto San Antonio Oeste	139	C8	Pygmalion Point	93	H7
Puerto Santa Cruz	139	C10	Pyhajarvi *Finland*	62	L5
Puerto Sastre	138	E4	Pyhajarvi *Finland*	62	L5
Puerto Siles	136	D6	Pyhajarvi *Turku-Pori, Finland*	63	K6
Puerto Suarez	138	E3	Pyhajoki	62	L4
Puerto Tejado	136	B3	Pyhaselka	62	N5
Puerto Vallarta	130	G7	Pyinmana	93	J5
Puerto Varas	139	B8	Pylkaram	84	C4
Puerto Villazon	136	E6	Pyonggok-tong	89	B7
Puesto Arturo	136	C4	Pyonghae-ri	89	B7
Pueyrredan, Lago	139	B9	Pyongyang	87	P4
Pugachev	79	H5	Pyramid Lake	122	E7
Pugachevo	88	J1	Pyrenees	65	D7
Pugal	92	D3	Pyrzyce	70	F2
Puger	90	E7	Pytalovo	63	M8
Puget-Theniers	65	G7			
Pui	73	G3			
Puigcerda	67	G1			
Pujehun	104	C4			

Q

Name			Name		
Pukaki, Lake	115	C6	Qaamiyat, Al	97	J7
Pukchong	88	B5	Qabr Hud	97	J8
Puke	74	E1	Qadimah	96	D5
Pukekohe	115	E2	Qadub	97	P10
Pukeuri	115	C6	Qaemshahr	95	L3
Puksa	78	F3	Qagan Tolgoi	87	K4
Pula	72	B3	Qaidam Pendi	93	H1
Pular, Cerro	138	C4	Qaidam Shan	93	J1
Pulaski *New York*	125	M5	Qaisar	94	S4
Pulaski *Tennessee*	129	J3	Qala Adras Kand	95	R5
Pulaski *Virginia*	125	K8	Qalaen Nahl	96	B10
Pulau Jos Sodarso	114	B3	Qalamat ar Rakabah	97	L6
Pulaupunjung	90	D6	Qalamat Faris	97	K6
Pulborough	53	G4	Qalansiyah	97	P10
Pulicat Lake	92	F6	Qalat	92	C2
Pulkkila	62	L4	Qalat Bishah	96	F6
Pullman	122	F4	Qalat Salih	94	H6
Pulo Anna	91	J5	Qalat Sukkar	94	H6
Pulog, Mount	91	G2	Qala Vali	95	R4
Pulonga	78	G2	Qaleh-ye Now	95	R4
Pulpito, Punta	126	G7	Qamar, Ghubbat al	97	L8
Pultusk	71	J2	Qamar, Jabal al	97	L8
Pulumur	77	H3	Qaminis	101	K2
Pumasillo, Cerro	136	C6	Qamsar	95	K5
Pumsaint	52	D2	Qandala	103	J5
Puna, Isla	136	A4	Qapqal	95	Q4
Punakha	93	G3	Qarabagh	97	M8
Pune	92	D5	Qara, Jabal al	97	M8
Pungsan	88	B5	Qaratshuk	94	F3
Punjab	92	E2	Qardho	103	J6
Puno	138	B3	Qareh Aqaj	94	H3
Punta Alta	139	D7	Qareh Su	94	H2
Punta Arenas	139	B10	Qareh Su	94	H5
Punta, Cerro de	133	P5	Qarqan He	86	F4
Punta de Diaz	138	B5	Qarqi	86	F3
Punta Delgada	139	D8	Qaryat al Ulya	97	H3
Punta Delgada	139	C10	Qasab	77	K4
Punta Gorda	132	C6	Qasa Murg	95	S4
Punta Prieta	126	E6	Qasr Amij	77	J6
Puntarenas	132	E9	Qasr-e-Qand	95	Q8
Punta Saavedra	139	B7	Qasr-e-Shirin	94	G4
Punto Fijo	136	C1	Qatabah	96	G10
Puolanka	62	M4	Qatah	77	J5
Puquio	136	C6	Qatana	94	C5
Puquios	138	C5	Qatar	97	K4
Pur	84	B3	Qatrana	94	C6
Pura	84	D2	Qattara Depression	102	E2
Purari	114	D3	Qattara, Munkhafed el	102	E2
Purbeck, Isle of	53	E4	Qayen	95	P5
Purchena	66	E4	Qazvin	95	K3
Purdy Islands	114	D2	Qeisum	96	A3
Purepero	130	J8	Qena	103	F2
Puri	92	G5	Qeshm *Iran*	95	N8
Purnia	93	G3	Qeshm *Iran*	95	N8
Pursat	93	K6	Qeydar	94	J3
Purtuniq	120	M5	Qeys	95	L8
Puruliya	92	G4	Qezel Owzan	94	J3
Purus	136	E4	Qeziot	94	B6
Puruvesi	63	N6	Qianan	87	N2
Purwakarta	90	D7	Qianjiang	93	L3
Purwokert	90	D7	Qianwei	87	N3
Puryong	88	B4	Qianxi	93	L3
Pusa	63	M8	Qianxinan	93	K3
Pusan	89	B8	Qiaowar	86	H3
Pushkino	94	J2	Qidong *Hunan, China*	93	M3
Pushkin	78	F3	Qidong *Jiangsu, China*	87	N5
Pusht-i-Rud	95	R6	Qiemo	92	G1
Pustoshka	63	N8	Qihe	87	M4
Putao	93	J3	Qihreg	87	L3
Putaruru	115	E3	Qijiaojing	86	F3
Putian	87	M6	Qikou	87	M4
Putila	71	L5	Qila Ladgasht	92	B3
Puting, Tanjung	90	E6	Qila Saifullah	92	C2
Putnok	72	F1	Qilian Shan	86	H4
Putorana, Gory	84	F3	Qinab, Wadi	97	J8
Putorino	115	F3	Qingan	88	A2
Puttalam	92	E7	Qingdao	87	N4
Puttgarden	70	D1	Qinggang	87	P2
Putumayo	136	C4	Qinghai	93	J2
Putusibau	90	E5	Qinghai Hu	93	K1
Puulavesi	63	M6	Qinghai Nanshan	93	J1
Puuwai	126	Q10	Qinghe	88	B2
Pu Xian	93	M1	Qing Xian	87	M4
Puyko	84	Ae3	Qingyuan	93	L1
Puyo	136	B4	Qingyuan *Liaoning, China*	87	N3
			Qingyuan *Zhejiang, China*	87	M6

Name	Map	Grid
Qinhuangdao	87	M4
Qin Ling	93	L2
Qinshui	93	M1
Qin Xian	87	L4
Qinyuan	87	L4
Qinzhou	93	L4
Qionglai	93	K2
Qionglai Shan	93	K2
Qiongzhong	93	L5
Qiongzhou Haixia	93	L4
Qiqihar	87	N2
Qir	95	L7
Qishn	97	K9
Qishran	96	E6
Qitai	86	F3
Qitaihe	87	Q2
Qitbit, Wadi	97	M7
Qixing He	88	D2
Qixingpao	88	C2
Qiyang	93	M3
Qizil Bulak	95	Q4
Qojur	94	H3
Qolleh-ye Damavand	95	L4
Qom	95	K4
Qomisheh	95	K5
Qomolangma Feng	92	G3
Qornetes Saouda	94	B4
Qorveh	94	H4
Qotbabad	95	N8
Qotur *Iran*	77	L3
Qotur *Iran*	77	L3
Quaidabad	92	D2
Quairading	112	D5
Quakenbruck	70	B2
Quanah	127	N3
Quang Ngai	93	L5
Quang Tri	93	L5
Quang Yen	93	L4
Quan Long	93	L7
Quannan	87	L7
Quan Phu Quoc	93	K6
Quantock Hills	52	D3
Quanzhou *Fujian, China*	87	M7
Quanzhou *Guangxi, China*	93	M3
Qu'Appelle	123	N2
Quaqtaq	121	N5
Quarai *Brazil*	138	E6
Quarai *Brazil*	138	E6
Quartu San Elena	69	B6
Quartzsite	126	E4
Quatsino Sound	122	A2
Quayti	97	J9
Quchan	95	P3
Qudaym	77	H5
Queanbeyan	113	K6
Quebec *Canada*	121	L7
Quebec *Canada*	125	Q3
Quedal, Cabo de	139	B8
Queen Bess, Mount	122	B2
Queen, Cape	120	L5
Queen Charlotte Islands	118	J5
Queen Charlotte Sound	118	K5
Queen Charlotte Strait	118	K5
Queen Elizabeth Islands	120	G2
Queen Mary Land	141	G4
Queen Maud Gulf	119	Q2
Queen Maud Land	141	A4
Queen Maud Mountains	141	N1
Queensbury	55	H3
Queens Channel	112	F1
Queensferry *Clwyd, U.K.*	55	F3
Queensferry *Lothian, U.K.*	57	E5
Queensland	113	J3
Queenstown *Australia*	113	K7
Queenstown *New Zealand*	115	B6
Queenstown *South Africa*	108	E6
Queija, Sierra de	66	C1
Queimadas	137	K6
Quela	106	C4
Quelimane	109	G3
Quelpart Island	87	P5
Quemado	127	H3
Quembo	106	C5
Quepos	132	E10
Que Que	108	E3
Queretaro	131	J7
Queshan	93	M2
Quesnel	119	L5
Quesnel Lake	119	L5
Quetena	138	C4
Quetta	92	C2
Quettehou	64	C4
Quevedo	136	B4
Quezaltenango	132	B7
Quezon City	91	G3
Quibala	106	B5
Quibaxi	106	B4
Quibdo	136	B2
Quiberon	65	B5
Quiberon, Baie de	65	B5
Quilengues	106	B5
Quillabamba	136	C6
Quillacollo	138	C3
Quillagua	138	C4
Quillan	65	E7
Quill Lakes	123	M2
Quillota	139	B6
Quilon	92	E7
Quilpie	113	J4
Quimbele	106	C4
Quimper	64	A4
Quimperle	65	B5
Quinag	56	C2
Quince Mil	136	C6
Quincy *California*	122	D8
Quincy *Illinois*	124	E7
Quincy *Massachusetts*	125	Q5
Quines	139	C6
Qui Nhon	93	L6
Quintanar de la Orden	66	E3
Quintero	139	B6
Quipungo	106	B5
Quiroga	66	C1
Quissanga	109	H2
Quita Sueno Bank	132	G2
Quito	136	B4
Quixada	137	K4
Qu Jiang	93	L2
Qujing	93	K3
Qulban Layyah	94	H7
Qumarleb	93	J2
Qumbu	108	E6
Qunayfidhah, Nafud	96	G4
Quoin Point	108	C6
Quorn	113	H5
Quorndon	53	F2
Quru Gol Pass	94	G2
Qus	103	F2
Quseir	103	F2
Qutiabad	94	J4
Qutu	96	E7
Quzhou	87	M6

R

Name	Map	Grid
Raab *Austria*	68	E2
Raab *Hungary*	72	D2
Raahe	62	L4
Raakkyla	62	N5
Raanes Peninsula	120	J2
Raanujarvi	62	L3
Raasay	56	B3
Raasay, Sound of	56	B3
Rab	72	C3
Raba	72	D2
Raba *Indonesia*	91	F7
Raba *Poland*	71	H4
Rabastens	65	D7
Rabat *Morocco*	100	D2
Rabat *Turkey*	77	J2
Rabaul	114	E2
Rabi	114	S8
Rabigh	96	D5
Rabor	95	N7
Rabyanah, Ramlat	101	K4
Race, Cape	121	R8
Rach Gia	93	L6
Raciborz	71	H3
Racine	124	G5
Rackwick	56	E2
Racoon	124	C5
Racoon Mountains	129	J3
Rada	96	G9
Radauti	73	H2
Radcliff	124	H8
Radde	88	C1
Radekhov	71	L3
Radford	125	K8
Radisson	121	L7
Radna	73	F2
Radnice	70	E4
Radnor Forest	52	D2
Radom	71	J3
Radomsko	71	H3
Radomyshl	79	D5
Radovis	73	G5
Radstadt	68	D2
Radstock	52	E3
Radstock, Cape	113	G5
Radzyn Podlaski	71	K3
Rae	119	M2
Rae Bareli	92	F3
Rae Isthmus	120	J4
Raetihi	115	E3
Rafaela	138	D6
Rafai	102	D6
Rafalovka	71	L3
Rafha	96	F2
Rafsanjan	95	M6
Raga	102	E6
Ragged Cays	133	K3
Raghtin More	58	H2
Raglan Harbour	115	E2
Ragusa *Croatia*	72	E4
Ragusa *Italy*	69	E7
Rahad	96	B10
Rahat, Harrat	96	E5
Rahimyar Khan	92	D3
Rahuri	92	D5
Raichur	92	E5
Raigarh *Madhya Pradesh, India*	92	F4
Raigarh *Orissa, India*	92	F5
Rainbow City	129	J4
Rainham	53	H3
Rainier, Mount	122	D4
Rainy	124	C2
Rainy Lake	124	D2
Raippaluoto	62	J5
Raipur	92	F4
Raisduoddarhaldde	62	J2
Raistakka	62	N3
Rajada	137	J5
Rajahmundry	92	F5
Rajang	90	E5
Rajanpur	92	D3
Rajapalaiyam	92	E7
Rajapur	92	D5
Rajasthan	92	D3
Rajasthan Canal	92	D3
Rajgarh	92	E4
Rajgrod	71	K2
Rajkot	92	D4
Rajmahal Hills	93	G4
Raj Nandgaon	92	F4
Rajpipla	92	D4
Rajshahi	92	G4
Rakaia	115	C5
Rakan, Ra's	97	K3
Rakbah, Sahl	96	E5
Raketskjutfalt	62	J2
Rakhes	75	G3
Rakhov	79	C6
Rakhovo	71	L4
Rakitnoye	88	E3
Rakkestad	63	D7
Rakops	108	D4
Rakov	71	M2
Rakusha	79	J6
Rakvere	63	M7
Raleigh	129	N3
Rama	132	E8
Ramallah	94	B6
Ramasaig	56	B3
Rambi	114	S8
Rambouillet	64	D4
Rambutyo Island	114	D2
Ramdurg	92	E5
Rameco	139	D7
Rame Head	52	C4
Rameswaram	92	E7
Ramgarh	92	F4
Ramhormoz	95	J6
Ram, Jambal	96	B2
Ramor, Lough	58	H5
Ramos	130	G5
Ramos Island	114	K6
Rampart	118	E2
Rampur	92	E3
Ramree	93	H5
Ramsbottom	55	G3
Ramsele	62	G5
Ramsey *Cambridgeshire, U.K.*	53	G2
Ramsey *Essex, U.K.*	53	J3
Ramsey *Isle of Man, U.K.*	54	E2
Ramsey Bay	54	E2
Ramsey Island	52	B3
Ramsgate	53	J3
Ramsjo	63	F5
Ramtha	94	C5
Ramu	114	C3
Ramvik	62	G5
Ranau	90	F4
Rancagua	139	J6
Rance	64	B4
Rancha Cordova	126	B1
Ranchi	92	G4
Rancho California	126	D4
Randalstown	58	K3
Randazzo	69	E7
Randers	63	D8
Randolph	123	R6
Randsfjord	63	D6
Ranea	62	K4
Ranfurly	115	C6
Rangas, Tanjung	91	F6
Rangiora	115	D5
Rangitaiki	115	F3
Rangitata	115	C5
Rangkasbitung	90	D7
Rangkul	86	C4
Rangoon (Yangon)	93	J5
Rangpur	93	G3
Rangsang	90	C5
Ranibennur	92	E6
Raniganj	93	G4
Ranken	113	H3
Rankin Inlet *Canada*	119	S3
Rankin Inlet *Canada*	119	S3
Rankins Springs	113	K5
Rannoch Moor	57	D4
Rannoch, Loch	57	D4
Ranon	114	U12
Ranongga	114	H5
Ransiki	91	J6
Ranskill	55	H3
Rantau *Kalimantan, Indonesia*	90	F6
Rantau *Sumatera, Indonesia*	90	C5
Rantauprapat	90	B5
Rantoul	124	F6
Ranya	94	G3
Raohe	88	D2
Raon-l'Etape	64	G4
Raoul	111	T7
Rapallo	68	B3
Raper, Cape	120	N4
Rapid City	123	N5
Rapla	63	L7
Rapli	92	F3
Rapness	56	F1
Rappahannock	125	M7
Rapperswil	68	B2
Rapsani	75	G3
Rapulo	136	D6
Rapur	92	E6
Ras al Ayn	77	J4
Ras al Khafji	97	J2
Ra's al Khaymah	97	M4
Rasa, Punta	139	D8
Ras Dashen	96	D10
Ras el Ma	100	E5
Ras en Naqb	94	B6
Rashad	102	F5
Rasharkin	58	K3
Rashid	102	F1
Rasht	95	J3
Rask	95	Q8
Raska	72	F4
Raso, Cabo	139	C8
Rason, Lake	112	E4
Rasshua, Ostrov	85	S7
Rasskazovo	79	G5
Rassokha	84	H2
Rastenburg	71	J1
Rastigaissa	62	M1
Rasul	95	M8
Ratangarh	92	D3
Rat Buri	93	J6
Rathangan	59	J6
Rathcoole	59	K6
Rathdowney	59	G7
Rathdrum	59	K7
Rathen	56	F3
Rathenow	70	E2
Rathfriland	58	K4
Rathkeale	59	E7
Rathlin Island	58	K2
Rathlin Sound	58	K2
Rathluirc	59	E8
Rathmore	59	D8
Rathnew	59	K7
Rathoath	59	K5
Ratibor	71	H3
Ratisbon	70	E4
Rat Islands	118	Ab9
Ratlam	92	E4
Ratnagiri	92	D5
Ratnapura	92	F7
Ratno	79	C5
Raton	127	K2
Ratta	84	C4
Rattray	57	E4
Rattray Head	56	G3
Rattvik	63	F6
Ratzeburg	70	D2
Ratz, Mount	118	J4
Rauch	139	E7
Rauchua	85	V3
Raudales	131	N9
Raudhatain	97	H2
Raufarhofn	62	X11
Raufoss	63	D6
Raukumara Range	115	F3
Raul Leoni, Represa	133	R11
Rauma	63	J6
Raung, Gunung	90	F7
Raurkela	92	F4
Rausu	88	K3
Ravansar	94	H4
Ravar	95	N6
Rava Russkaya	79	C5
Ravenglass	55	F2
Ravenna	68	D3
Ravenscar	55	J2
Ravensthorpe	112	E5
Ravenstonedale	55	G2
Ravenswood	125	K7
Ravensworth	55	H2
Ravi	92	D2
Ravno	72	E3
Rawa	93	J3
Rawah	77	J5
Rawaki	111	U2
Rawalpindi	92	D2
Rawandiz	94	G3
Rawcliffe	55	J3
Rawdah	77	J5
Rawicz	71	G3
Rawlinna	112	F5
Rawlins	123	L7
Rawmarsh	55	H3
Rawson	139	C8
Rawtenstall	55	G3
Ray	53	F3
Rayachoti	92	E6
Rayadurg	92	E6
Rayagarha	92	F5
Rayakoski	62	N2
Ray, Cape	121	Q8
Raychikhinsk	85	M7
Rayen	95	N7
Rayeskiy	78	J5
Rayleigh	53	H3
Raymondville	128	D7
Ray Mountains	118	E2
Raysut	97	L8
Razan	94	J5
Razan	94	J4
Razdelnaya	79	E6
Razdolnoye	88	C4
Razgrad	73	J4
Razmak	92	C2
Raznas Ezers	63	M8
Raz, Pointe du	64	A4
Reading *U.K.*	53	G3
Reading *U.S.A.*	125	N6
Realico	139	D7
Rea, Lough	59	E6
Rearsby	53	F2
Reawick	56	A2
Reay	56	E2
Rebecca, Lake	112	E5
Rebi	91	J7
Reboly	62	P5
Rebrikha	84	C6

Rebrovo 73 G4
Rebun-to 88 H3
Recanati 68 D4
Recea 73 G3
Recherche, Archipelago of the 112 E5
Rechitsa 79 E5
Rechna Doab 92 D2
Recife 137 L5
Recklinghausen 70 B3
Recknitz 70 E2
Reconquista 138 E5
Recreio 136 F5
Red *Canada* 123 R2
Red *U.S.A.* 128 F5
Redalen 63 D6
Red Bay 121 Q7
Redbird 123 M6
Red Bluff 122 C7
Red Bluff Lake 127 L5
Redcar 55 H2
Redcliffe 113 L4
Red Cloud 123 Q7
Red Deer *Canada* 122 G2
Red Deer *Canada* 122 H1
Red Deer *Canada* 123 J2
Red Deer *Saskatchewan, Canada* 119 Q5
Redding 122 C7
Redditch 53 F2
Redencao 137 J5
Redfield 123 Q5
Redhakhol 92 F4
Redhill 53 G3
Red Hills 127 N2
Red Lake *Canada* 123 S2
Red Lake *Canada* 123 T2
Red Lake *U.S.A.* 124 C3
Red Lake *U.S.A.* 123 R4
Red Lodge 123 K5
Redmond 122 D5
Redon 65 B5
Redondela 66 B1
Redondo 66 C3
Red Rock 124 F2
Redruth 52 B4
Red Sea 103 G3
Red Tank 113 K5
Red Wharf Bay 54 E3
Red Wing 124 D4
Redwood City 126 A2
Reed City 124 H5
Reedsport 122 B6
Ree, Lough 58 G5
Reeton 115 C5
Refahiye 77 H3
Refresco 138 C5
Rega 70 F2
Regen 70 E4
Regensburg 70 E4
Reggane 100 F3
Reggio di Calabria 69 E6
Reggio nell Amelia 68 C3
Regina *Brazil* 137 G3
Regina *Canada* 123 M2
Reguengos de Monsaraz 66 C3
Rehna 70 D2
Rehoboth 108 C4
Rehoboth Beach 125 N7
Rehovot 94 B6
Reidh, Rubha 56 C3
Reidsville 129 N2
Reiff 56 C2
Reigate 53 G3
Reighton 55 J2
Re, Ile de 65 C5
Reims 64 F4
Reina Adelaida, Archipielago de la 139 B10
Reindeer Lake 119 Q4
Reine 62 E3
Reinga, Cape 115 D1
Reinheimen 62 B5
Reinosa 66 D1
Reitz 108 E5
Relizane 100 F1
Remada 101 H2
Rembang 90 E7
Remeshk 95 P8
Remiremont 65 G4
Remontnoye 79 G6
Remoulins 65 F7
Remscheid 70 B3
Rena *Norway* 63 D6
Rena *Norway* 63 D6
Renaix 64 E3
Renard Islands 114 E4
Rendova Island 114 H6
Rendsburg 70 C1
Renfrew *Canada* 125 M4
Renfrew *U.K.* 57 D5
Rengat 90 D6
Rengo 139 B6
Renish Point 56 B3
Renk 103 F5
Renmark 113 J5
Renmin 87 P2
Rennell Island 114 K7
Rennes 64 C4
Reno *Italy* 68 C3
Reno *U.S.A.* 122 E8
Reo 91 G7
Repetek 95 R2
Repolovo 84 Ae4
Republican 123 R7
Repulse Bay *Australia* 113 K3
Repulse Bay *Canada* 120 J4
Requena *Peru* 136 C5
Requena *Spain* 67 F3
Rere 114 K6
Resadiye *Turkey* 76 B4
Resadiye *Turkey* 77 G2
Resen 73 F5
Resia, Passo de 68 C2
Resistencia 138 E5
Resita 73 F3
Resolution Island *Canada* 121 P5
Resolution Island *New Zealand* 115 A6
Resolution Lake 121 P6
Restigouche 125 S3
Retalhuleu 132 B7
Rethel 64 F4
Rethimnon 75 H5
Retiche, Alpi 68 C2
Retsag 72 E2
Retuerta de Bullaque 66 D3
Reunion 109 L7
Reus 67 G2
Reuss 68 B2
Reut 73 J2
Reutlingen 70 C4
Revel 65 D7
Revelstoke 122 E2
Reventador, Volcan 136 B4
Revillagigedo Island 118 J5
Revillagigedo, Islas 130 D8
Rewa 92 F4
Rewari 92 E3
Rexburg 122 J6
Reyes, Point 122 C9
Reyhanli 77 G4
Rey, Isla del 132 H10
Reykjaheidi 62 W12
Reykjahhd 62 W12
Reykjanesta 62 T13
Reykjavik 62 U12
Reynivellir *Iceland* 62 U12
Reynivellir *Iceland* 62 W12
Reynosa 128 C7
Rezekne 63 M8
Rhatikon Pratigau 68 B2
Rhayader 52 D2
Rheda-Wiedenbruck 70 C3
Rhee 53 G2
Rhein 70 B3
Rheine 70 B2
Rhewl 55 F3
Rhiconich 56 D2
Rhine 64 G4
Rhinelander 124 F4
Rhino Camp 107 F2
Rhir, Cap 100 D2
Rho 68 B3
Rhode Island 125 Q6
Rhodes 75 J4
Rhodopi Planina 73 G4
Rhondda 52 D3
Rhone 65 F7
Rhoose 52 D3
Rhosneigr 55 E3
Rhuddlan 55 F3
Rhum 57 B3
Rhum, Sound of 57 B4
Rhydaman 52 C3
Rhyl 55 F3
Rhynie 56 F3
Riachao do Jacuipe 138 K6
Riacho de Santana 138 J6
Riano 66 D1
Riansares 66 E3
Riau, Kepulauan 90 C5
Riaza 66 E2
Ribadeo 66 C1
Ribadesella 66 D1
Ribas do Rio Pardo 138 F4
Ribat 95 R5
Ribatejo 66 B3
Ribble 55 G2
Ribe 63 C9
Ribeirao Preto 138 G4
Ribeiro do Pombal 137 K6
Riberac 65 D6
Riberalta 136 D6
Ribnica 72 C3
Ribnitz-Damgarten 70 E1
Riccall 55 H3
Rice Lake *Canada* 125 L4
Rice Lake *U.S.A.* 124 E4
Richard Collinson Inlet 119 N1
Richards Island 118 H2
Richardson 128 D4
Richardson Mountains 118 H2
Richelieu 125 P4
Richfield 126 F1
Richland 122 E4
Richlands 125 K8
Richmond *Australia* 113 J3
Richmond *New Zealand* 115 D4
Richmond *South Africa* 108 D6
Richmond *Greater London, U.K.* 53 G3
Richmond *North Yorkshire, U.K.* 55 H2
Richmond *Indiana* 124 H7
Richmond *Kentucky* 124 H8
Richmond *Virginia* 125 M8
Richmond Range 115 D4
Rickmansworth 53 G3
Ricla 67 F2
Ricobayo, Embalse de 66 D2
Ridgecrest 126 D3
Ridgeland 129 M4
Ridgway 125 L6
Riding Mountain 123 P2
Ridsdale 57 F5
Ried 68 D1
Rienza 68 C2
Riesa 70 E3
Riesco, Isla 139 B10
Rietfontein 108 D4
Rieti 69 D4
Rifle 123 L8
Rifstangi 62 W11
Riga 63 L8
Riga, Gulf of 63 K8
Rigan 95 P7
Rigistan 92 B2
Rigolet 121 Q7
Rihab, Ar 94 G6
Rihand 92 F4
Riiser-Larsen Sea 141 B5
Rijeka 72 C3
Rika 71 K4
Rika, Wadi al 96 G5
Rimah, Wadi al 96 E3
Rimal, Ar 97 L6
Rimavska Sobota 71 J4
Rimbo 63 H7
Rimini 68 D3
Rimna 73 J3
Rimnicu Sarat 73 J3
Rimnicu Vilcea 73 H3
Rimouski 125 R2
Rinca 91 F7
Rinchinlhumbe 86 H1
Ringe 63 D9
Ringebu 63 D6
Ringgold Isles 114 S8
Ringkobing 63 C8
Ringkobing Fjord 63 C9
Ringmer 53 H4
Ringselet 62 L3
Ringvassoy 62 H2
Ringwood 53 F4
Rinia 75 H4
Rinjani, Gunung 90 F7
Rinns Point 57 B5
Riobamba 136 B4
Rio Branco *Brazil* 136 D5
Rio Branco *Uruguay* 138 F6
Rio Bravo 128 D8
Rio Bueno 139 B8
Rio Caribe 136 E1
Rio Claro 136 E1
Rio Colorado 139 D7
Rio Cuarto 138 D6
Rio de Janeiro *Brazil* 138 H4
Rio de Janeiro *Brazil* 138 H4
Rio de Oro, Baie de 100 B4
Rio Gallegos 139 C10
Rio Grande *Argentina* 139 C10
Rio Grande *Brazil* 138 F6
Rio Grande *U.S.A.* 130 H6
Rio Grande City 128 C7
Rio Grande de Santiago 130 G7
Rio Grande do Norte 137 K5
Rio Grande do Sul 138 F5
Riohacha 136 C1
Rio Hato 132 G10
Rio Lagartos 131 Q7
Riom 65 E6
Riom-es-Montagnes 65 E6
Rio Mulatos 138 C3
Rionegro 136 C2
Rio Negro *Brazil* 138 G5
Rio Negro *Spain* 66 C1
Rio Negro, Embalse del 138 E6
Rio Negro, Pantanal do 138 E3
Rioni 77 J1
Rio Pardo de Minas 138 H3
Rio Primero 138 D6
Rio Sao Goncalo 138 H4
Riosucio *Colombia* 136 B2
Riosucio *Colombia* 136 B2
Rio Verde 138 F3
Ripley *Ohio* 124 J7
Ripley *Tennessee* 128 H3
Ripley *W. Virginia* 125 K7
Ripoll 67 H1
Ripon 55 H2
Ripponden 55 H3
Risca 52 D3
Rishiri-to 88 H3
Rishon le Zion 94 B6
Risle 64 D4
Risor 63 C7
Risoyhamn 62 F2
Ritchie's Archipelago 93 H6
Ritter, Mount 122 E9
Ritzville 122 E4
Riva 68 C3
Rivas 132 E9
Rivera 138 E6
River Falls 124 D4
Riverina 113 K5
Riversdale 108 D6
Riverside 126 D4
Riverton *Australia* 113 H5
Riverton *Canada* 123 R2
Riverton *New Zealand* 115 B7
Riverton *U.S.A.* 123 K6
Riviere-du-Loup 125 R3
Rivne 79 D5
Rivoli 68 A3
Riwaka 115 D4
Riwoqe 93 J2
Riyan 97 J9
Rize 77 J2
Rizhskiy Zaliv 63 K8
Rizokarpaso 76 F5
Rjukan 63 C7
Rjuven 63 B7
Roa 66 E2
Road Town 133 Q5
Roan Fell 57 F5
Roanne 65 F5
Roanoke *N. Carolina* 129 P2
Roanoke *Virginia* 125 L8
Roanoke Rapids 129 P2
Roan Plateau 123 K8
Robat 95 R6
Robat Karim 95 K4
Robat Thand 95 Q7
Robel 70 E2
Robert Brown, Cape 120 K4
Roberton 57 E5
Robertsbridge 53 H4
Robertsfors 62 J4
Robert S. Kerr Reservoir 128 E3
Robertson Range 112 E3
Robertsport 104 C4
Roberval 125 P2
Robinson 124 G7
Robinson Ranges 112 D4
Robleda 66 C2
Robledollano 66 D3
Robles La Paz 136 C1
Roblin 123 P2
Robore 138 E3
Rob Roy Island 114 H5
Robson, Mount 119 M5
Roca, Cabo da 66 B3
Roca Partida, Isla 130 C8
Roca Partida, Punta 131 M8
Roccella Ionica 69 F6
Rocha 139 F6
Rocha da Gale, Barragem 66 C4
Rochdale 55 G3
Rochechouart 65 D6
Rochefort 65 C6
Rochelle 124 F6
Rochester *Kent. U.K.* 53 H3
Rochester *Northumberland, U.K.* 57 F5
Rochester *New Hamshire* 125 Q5
Rochester *New York* 125 M5
Rochester *Winconsin* 124 D4
Rochford 53 H3
Rochfortbridge 59 H6
Rock 124 F5
Rockefeller Plateau 141 R3
Rock Falls 124 F6
Rockford 124 F5
Rockglen 123 L3
Rockhampton 113 L3
Rockingham *Australia* 112 D5
Rockingham *U.S.A.* 129 N3
Rockingham Bay 113 K2
Rock Island 124 E6
Rockland *Maine* 125 R4
Rockland *Michigan* 124 F3
Rock Springs *Montana* 123 L4
Rock Springs *Wyoming* 123 K7
Rockwood 125 R4
Rocky Ford 127 L1
Rocky Mount 129 P3
Rocky Mountain House 119 N5
Rocky Mountains 116 G3
Rocroi 64 F4
Rodberg 63 C6
Rodby 63 D9
Rodeby 63 F8
Rodel 56 B3
Roden 52 E2
Rodez 65 E6
Rodhos *Greece* 75 J4
Rodhos *Greece* 75 K4
Rodi Garganico 69 E5
Roding 53 H3
Rodinga 113 G3
Rodna 73 H2
Rodnei, Muntii 73 H2
Rodney, Cape *New Zealand* 115 E2
Rodney, Cape *U.S.A.* 118 B3
Rodonit, Kep i 74 E2
Rodosto 76 B2
Roebuck Bay 112 E2
Roermond 64 F3
Roeselare 64 E3
Roes Welcome Sound 120 J5
Rogachev 79 E5
Rogaland 63 B7
Rogatin 71 L4
Rogers 128 E2
Rogers, Mount 125 K8
Roggeveld Berge 108 D6
Rogliano 68 B4
Rognan 62 F3
Rogozno 71 G2
Rohri 92 C3
Rohtak 92 E3
Rois Bheinn 57 C3
Rojas 139 D6
Rojo, Cabo *Mexico* 131 L7
Rojo, Cabo *U.S.A.* 133 P6
Rokan 90 C5

S

Name	Page	Grid
Santo Antao	104	L7
Santo Antonio do Ica	136	D4
Santo Domingo *Dominican Republic*	133	N5
Santo Domingo *Mexico*	126	E5
Santo Domingo de la Calzada	66	E1
Santo Domingo de los Colorados	136	B4
Santorini	75	H4
Santos	138	G4
Santos Dumont *Amazonas, Brazil*	136	D5
Santos Dumont *Minas Gerais, Brazil*	138	H4
Santo Tomas	126	D5
Santo Tome	138	E5
San Valentin, Cerro	139	B9
San Vicente de la Barquera	66	D1
San Vicente del Caguan	136	C3
San Vincent	132	C8
San Vincente	91	G2
San Vito, Capo	59	D6
Sanyati	108	E3
Sanyshand	87	L3
Sao Borja	138	E5
Sao Bras de Alportel	66	C4
Sao Carlos *Rondonia, Brazil*	136	E5
Sao Carlos *Sao Paulo, Brazil*	138	G4
Sao Domingos	137	H6
Sao Felix	137	G5
Sao Francisco *Acre, Brazil*	136	D6
Sao Francisco *Bahia, Brazil*	137	K5
Sao Francisco do Sul	138	G5
Sao Francisco, Ilha de	138	G5
Sao Joao del Rei	138	H4
Sao Joao do Araguaia	137	H5
Sao Joao do Piaui	137	J5
Sao Joao, Ilhas de	137	H4
Sao Jose	136	D4
Sao Jose do Gurupi	137	H4
Sao Jose do Rio Preto	138	G4
Sao Jose dos Campos	138	G4
Sao Leopoldo	138	F5
Sao Lourenco	138	E3
Sao Luis	137	J4
Sao Manuel	136	F5
Sao Marcos	138	G3
Sao Marcos, Baia de	137	J4
Sao Maria da Boa Vista	137	K5
Sao Mateus	138	K7
Sao Miguel dos Campos	137	K5
Sao Miguel do Tapuio	137	J5
Saona, Isla	133	N5
Saone	65	F5
Sao Nicolau	104	L7
Sao Paulo *Brazil*	138	G4
Sao Paulo *Brazil*	138	G4
Sao Paulo de Olivenca	136	D4
Sao Pedro do Sul	66	B2
Sao Raimundo Nonato	137	J5
Sao Romao	138	G3
Sao Roque, Cabo de	137	K5
Sao Sebastiao do Paraiso	138	G4
Sao Tiago	104	L7
Sao Tome	105	G5
Sao Tome	105	G5
Sao Tome and Principe	105	G5
Sao Tome, Cabo de	138	H4
Saouda, Qornet es	77	G5
Saoura, Oued	100	E2
Sao Vicente	138	G4
Sao Vicente, Cabo de	66	B4
Sao Vincente	104	L7
Sapai	75	H2
Sapanca	76	D2
Sapanca Golu	76	D2
Sape	91	F7
Sapele	105	G4
Sapientza	75	F4
Saposoa	136	B5
Sapporo	88	H4
Sapri	69	E5
Sapulut	90	F5
Saqqez	94	H3
Sarab	94	H3
Sara Buri	93	K6
Saragossa	67	F2
Saraguro	136	B4
Sarajevo	72	E4
Sarakhs	95	Q3
Sarakli	75	G2
Saraktash	79	K5
Saralzhin	79	J6
Saranac Lake	125	P4
Sarande	74	E3
Saran, Gunung	90	E6
Saranpaul	84	Ad4
Saransk	78	H5
Sarapul	78	J4
Sarapul'skoye	88	F1
Sarasota	129	L7
Sarata	73	K2
Saratoga	126	A2
Saratoga Springs	125	P5
Saratov	79	H5
Saravan	95	R8
Saravane	93	L5
Sarawak	90	E5
Saray *Turkey*	76	B2
Saray *Turkey*	77	L3
Saraychik	79	J6
Saraykent	76	F3
Saraykoy *Turkey*	76	C4
Saraykoy *Turkey*	76	F3
Sarayonu	76	E3
Sarbaz	95	Q8
Sarbisheh	95	P5
Sarcham	94	J3
Sarda	92	F3
Sardarshahr	92	D3
Sardegna	69	B5
Sardinia	69	B5
Sardis Lake	123	H3
Sareks	62	G3
Sar-e Pol	92	C1
Sar-e Yazd	95	M6
Sargans	68	B2
Sargodha	92	D2
Sarh	102	C6
Sari	95	L3
Saria	75	J5
Sarickaya	76	D2
Sarigol	76	C3
Sarikamis	77	K2
Sarikaya	76	F3
Sarinay	86	C4
Sarine	68	A2
Sarioglan	77	F3
Sarisu	77	K3
Sariwon	87	P4
Sariyar Baraji	76	D2
Sariz	77	G3
Sark	53	M7
Sarkikaraagac	76	D3
Sarkisla	77	G3
Sarkoy	76	B2
Sarmi	91	K6
Sarmiento	139	C9
Sarna	53	E6
Sarneh	94	H5
Sarnen	58	B2
Sarnia	124	J5
Sarny	79	D5
Saronikos Kolpos	75	G4
Saronno	68	B3
Saros Korfezi	76	B2
Sarowbi	92	C2
Sar Planina	72	F5
Sarpsborg	63	H7
Sarralbe	64	G4
Sarre	64	G4
Sarrebourg	64	G4
Sarria	66	C1
Sarshive	94	H4
Sartang	85	N3
Sartatovskoye Vodokhranilishche	79	H5
Sartene	69	B5
Sarthe	65	C5
Sartu	87	N2
Saruhanli	76	B3
Sarvabad	94	H4
Sarvar	72	D2
Sarvestan	95	L7
Sarviz	72	E2
Sarych, Mys	79	E7
Sary-Ishikotrau, Peski	86	D2
Sary Ozek	86	D3
Sary-Shagan	86	C2
Sary-Tash	86	C4
Sarzana	68	B3
Sasamungga	114	H5
Sasaram	92	F4
Sasd	72	E2
Sasebo	89	B9
Saskatchewan *Canada*	119	P5
Saskatchewan *Canada*	119	Q5
Saskatoon	123	L1
Saskylakh	84	J2
Sasovo	78	G5
Sassandra *Ivory Coast*	104	D4
Sassandra *Ivory Coast*	104	D5
Sassari	69	B5
Sassnitz	70	E1
Sasstown	104	D5
Sassuolo	68	C3
Sas-Tobe	86	C3
Sasyk, Ozero	73	K3
Satadougou	100	C6
Satara	92	D5
Sater	63	F6
Satley	55	H2
Satmala Range	92	E5
Satna	92	F4
Satoraljaujhely	71	J4
Satpura Range	92	E4
Sattahip	93	K6
Satu Mare	73	G2
Satun	93	K7
Satyga	84	Ad5
Sauceda	127	M8
Saucillo	127	K6
Sauda	63	B7
Saudarkrokur	62	V12
Saudi Arabia	96	F3
Sauerland	70	B3
Saugeen	124	K4
Sauk City	124	F5
Saulieu	65	E5
Sault Sainte Marie *Canada*	124	H3
Sault Sainte Marie *U.S.A.*	124	H3
Saumarez Reef	113	L3
Saumlakki	91	J7
Saumur	65	C5
Saunders, Cape	115	C6
Saundersfoot	52	C3
Saurimo	106	D4
Sava	72	E3
Savaii	111	U4
Savalou	105	F4
Savannah *Georgia*	129	M4
Savannah *Tennessee*	129	H3
Savannakhet	93	K5
Savant Lake	124	E1
Savantvadi	92	D5
Savanur	92	E6
Savar	62	J5
Savastepe	76	B3
Save	105	F4
Save *France*	65	D7
Save *Mozambique*	109	F4
Saveh	95	K4
Saveni	73	J2
Saverne	64	G4
Savinja	72	C2
Savirsin	73	G2
Savitaipale	63	M6
Savnik	72	E4
Savoie	65	G6
Savona	68	B3
Savo Nggatokae	114	J6
Savonlinna	63	N6
Savsat	77	K2
Savsjo	63	F8
Savukoski	62	N3
Savur	77	J4
Savusavu	114	R8
Savusavu Bay	114	R8
Sawab, Wasi as	77	J5
Sawadah, As	96	G5
Sawara	88	H4
Sawatch Mountains	123	L8
Sawbridgeworth	53	H3
Sawel	58	H3
Sawqirah, Ghubbat	97	N7
Sawqirah, Ra's	97	N7
Sawston	53	H2
Sawtooth Mountains *Idaho*	122	G5
Sawtooth Mountains *Minnesota*	124	E3
Sawtry	53	G2
Sawu	91	G8
Sawu, Laut	91	G7
Saxby Downs	113	J3
Saxmundham	53	J2
Saxthorpe	53	J2
Sayak	86	D2
Saydy	85	N3
Sayhan-Ovoo	87	J2
Sayhut	97	K9
Saylac	103	H5
Sayula	130	H8
Sayulita	130	G7
Sayun	97	J9
Say-Utes	79	J7
Sazan	74	E2
Sazava	70	F4
Sazin	92	D1
Scafell Pikes	55	G2
Scalasaig	57	B4
Scalby	55	J2
Scalea	69	E6
Scalloway	56	A2
Scalpay	56	C3
Scamblesby	55	J3
Scammon Bay	118	B3
Scapa Flow	56	E2
Scaraben	56	E2
Scaramia, Capo	69	E7
Scarba	57	C4
Scarborough *Canada*	125	L5
Scarborough *Trinidad and Tobago*	133	S9
Scarborough *U.K.*	55	J2
Scarinish	57	B4
Scarp	56	A2
Scarpanto	75	J5
Scarpe	64	E3
Scarriff	59	E7
Schaal See	70	D2
Schaffhausen	68	B2
Scharhorn	70	C2
Schefferville	121	N7
Scheibbs	68	E1
Scheitling	68	E2
Schelde	64	E3
Schenectady	125	P5
Schiedam	64	F3
Schiehallion	57	D4
Schiermonnikoog	64	G2
Schio	68	C3
Schitu Duca	73	J2
Schlei	70	C1
Schleiz	70	D3
Schleswig	70	C1
Schneidemuhl	71	G2
Schoningen	70	D2
Schonsee	70	E4
Schouten Islands	114	C2
Schouwen	64	E3
Schreiber	124	G2
Schwabische Alb	70	C4
Schwandorf	70	H3
Schwaner, Pegunungan	90	E6
Schwarmstedt	70	C2
Schwarze Elser	70	E3
Schwarzwald	70	C5
Schwaz	68	C2
Schwedt	70	F2
Schweinfurt	70	D3
Schwerin	70	D2
Schweriner See	70	D2
Schwieloch See	70	F2
Schwyz	68	B2
Sciacca	69	D7
Scilly, Isles of	52	L5
Scioto	124	J7
Sckuls	68	C2
Scobey	123	M3
Sconser	56	B3
Score Head	56	A1
Scoresby, Cape	120	H3
Scotia Ridge	139	F10
Scotia Sea	139	F1
Scott Base	141	M3
Scottburgh	108	F6
Scott, Cape	118	K5
Scott City	127	M1
Scott Glacier	141	P1
Scott Lake	119	P4
Scott Reef	112	E1
Scottsbluff	123	N7
Scottsboro	129	J3
Scottsdale	126	G4
Scourie	56	C2
Scrabster	56	E2
Scranton	125	N6
Screeb	59	C6
Scridain, Loch	57	B4
Scunthorpe	55	J3
Scuol	68	C2
Scurrival Point	57	A3
Scutari	74	E1
Seaford *U.K.*	53	H4
Seaford *U.S.A.*	125	N7
Seaforth, Loch	56	B3
Seaham	55	H2
Seahorse Point	120	K5
Seahouses	55	H1
Seal	119	R4
Sea Lake	113	J6
Seal, Cape	108	D6
Seal Cape	118	D4
Seamer	55	J2
Searcy	128	G3
Searles Lake	126	D3
Seascale	55	F2
Seaside	122	C5
Seathwaite	55	F2
Seaton	52	D4
Seaton Sluice	55	H1
Seattle	122	C4
Sebago Lake	125	Q5
Sebangka	90	C5
Sebastian Vizcaino, Bahia de	126	E6
Sebderat	103	G4
Seben	76	D2
Sebenico	72	C4
Sebes	73	G3
Sebesului, Muntii	73	G3
Sebezh	63	N8
Sebinkarahisar	77	H2
Sebring	129	M7
Sebta	66	D5
Sebuku	90	F6
Secchia	68	C3
Sechura, Bahia de	136	A5
Sechura, Desierto de	136	A5
Secretary Island	115	A6
Secunderabad	92	E5
Seda	66	C3
Sedalia	124	D7
Sedan	64	F4
Sedano	66	E1
Sedbergh	55	G2
Sedden, Kap	120	Q2
Seddonville	115	C4
Sedeh	95	P5
Sedgefield	55	H2
Sedona	126	G3
Seduva	68	C2
Seefeld	68	C2
Seefin	59	E8
Sees	64	D4
Sefaatli	76	F3
Sefadu	104	C4
Seferihisar	76	B3
Sefrou	100	E2
Sefton, Mount	115	C5
Segamat	90	C5
Segbwema	104	C4
Segea	91	H5
Segendy	79	J7
Segeneyti	96	D9
Seget	91	J6
Segezha	78	E3
Seghe	114	H6
Segid	96	F8
Segorbe	67	F3
Segou	100	D6
Segovia *Honduras*	132	E7
Segovia *Spain*	66	D3
Segozero, Ozero	78	E3
Segre	65	C5
Segre	67	G2
Seguam Island	118	Ad9
Seguela	104	D4
Segula Island	118	Ab9
Segura *Portugal*	66	C3
Segura *Spain*	67	F3
Segurra, Sierra de	66	E4
Sehwan	92	C3
Seia	66	C2
Seil	57	D4
Seiland	62	K1

South Haven 124 G5
South Hayling 53 G4
South Henik Lake 119 R3
South Hill 125 L8
South Korea 87 P4
South Lake Tahoe 126 C1
South Magnetic Pole 141 K5
Southminster 53 H3
South Molton 52 D3
South Morar 57 C4
South Nahanni 118 K3
South Negril Point 132 H5
South Orkney Islands 141 W4
South Platte 123 N7
South Point 133 K3
South Pole 141 A1
Southport 55 F3
South River 125 L4
South Ronaldsay 56 F2
South Sandwich Islands 141 Y7
South Saskatchewan 123 L2
South Seal 119 R4
South Shields 55 H2
South Sister 122 D5
South Skirlaugh 55 J3
South Sound 59 C6
South Taranaki Bight 115 E3
South Twin Island 121 K7
South Tyne 55 G2
South Uist 56 A3
Southwell 55 J3
Southwest Bay 139 J10
Southwest Cape 115 A7
South West Cape 113 K7
South-west Miramichi 121 N8
Southwold 53 J2
South Woodham Ferrers 53 H3
South Yemen 97 J8
South Yorkshire 55 H3
South Zeal 52 D4
Sovata 73 H2
Sovets 78 H4
Sovetsk 71 J1
Sovetskaya Gavan 88 H1
Soya-Kaikyo 88 J3
Soya-misaki 88 H3
Soyana 78 G2
Soylemez 77 J3
Soyo 106 B4
Sozopol 73 J4
Spa 64 F3
Spain 66 D2
Spalato 72 D4
Spalding 53 G2
Spaldwick 53 G2
Spanish Town 132 J5
Sparkford 52 E3
Sparks 122 E8
Sparta 75 G4
Spartanburg 129 M3
Spartel, Cap 100 D1
Sparti 75 G4
Spartivento, Capo *Italy* 69 B6
Spartivento, Capo *Italy* 69 F7
Sparwood 122 G3
Spas Demensk 78 E5
Spasskaya Guba 78 E3
Spassk Dalniy 88 D3
Spatha, Akra 75 G5
Spean Bridge 57 D4
Spearfish 123 N5
Spence Bay 120 H4
Spencer *Indiana* 124 G7
Spencer *Iowa* 124 C5
Spencer *W. Virginia* 125 K7
Spencer, Cape 113 H6
Spencer Gulf 113 H5
Spences Bridge 122 D2
Spennymoor 55 H2
Spenser Mountains 115 D5
Sperrin Mountains 58 H3
Spessart 70 C3
Spetsai 75 G4
Spey 56 E3
Spey Bay 56 E3
Speyer 70 C4
Spicer Islands 120 L4
Spiddle 59 D6
Spiekeroog 70 B2
Spiez 68 A2
Spili 75 H5
Spilsby 55 K3
Spinazzola 69 F5
Spithead 53 F4
Spitsbergen 80 C2
Spittal 68 D2
Spittal of Glenshee 57 E4
Spjelkavik 62 B5
Split 72 D4
Spokane *U.S.A.* 122 E4
Spokane *U.S.A.* 122 F4
Spoleto 69 D4
Spooner 124 E4
Spornoye 85 S4
Spremberg 70 F3
Spring 124 C8
Springbok 108 C5
Springdale *Canada* 121 Q8
Springdale *U.S.A.* 128 E2
Springer 127 K2
Springerville 127 H3
Springfield *New Zealand* 115 C5
Springfield *Colorado* 127 L2
Springfield *Illinois* 124 F7
Springfield *Massachusetts* 125 P5
Springfield *Missouri* 124 D8
Springfield *Ohio* 124 J7
Springfield *Oregon* 122 C5
Springfield *Tennessee* 129 J2
Springfield *Vermont* 125 P5
Springfontein 108 E6
Spring Garden 136 F2
Spring Mountains 126 E2
Springs 108 E5
Springs Junction 115 D5
Spruce Knob 125 L7
Spurn Head 55 K3
Squamish 122 C3
Squillace, Golfo di 69 F6
Srbica 72 F4
Srebrnica 72 E3
Sredhiy 85 S5
Sredinnyy Khrebet 85 U5
Sredna Gora 73 H4
Srednekolymsk 85 S3
Sredne Olekma 85 L5
Sredne Russkaya Vozvyshennost 79 F5
Sredne-Sibirskoye Ploskogorye 84 H3
Sredneye Kuyto, Ozero 62 P4
Sredni Rodopi 73 H5
Sredniy Kalar 85 K5
Sremska Mitrovica 72 E3
Sretensk 85 K6
Sre Umbell 93 K6
Srikakulam 92 F5
Sri Lanka 92 F7
Srinagar 92 D2
Sroda 71 G2
Sroda Slaska 71 G3
Stack, Loch 56 D2
Stade 70 C2
Stadhampton 53 F3
Stadthagen 70 C2
Staffin 56 B3
Stafford 53 E2
Staffordshire 53 F2
Staines 53 G3
Staintondale 55 J2
Stakhanov 79 F6
Stalac 73 F4
Stalham 53 J2
Stalingrad 79 G6
Stalybridge 55 G3
Stamford *Australia* 113 J3
Stamford *U.K.* 53 G2
Stamford *Connecticut* 125 P6
Stamford *New York* 125 N5
Stamford *Texas* 127 N4
Stamford Bridge 55 J3
Stamfordham 57 G5
Stampiky 109 J3
Stamsund 62 E2
Standerton 108 E5
Standish *U.K.* 55 G3
Standish *U.S.A.* 124 J4
Stanford 123 J4
Stanford-le-Hope 53 H3
Stanger 108 F5
Stanhope 55 G2
Stanislav 71 L4
Stanke Dimitrov 73 G4
Stanley *Durham, U.K.* 55 H2
Stanley *Falkland Islands, U.K.* 139 E10
Stanley *U.S.A.* 123 N3
Stanley *Zaire* 107 E2
Stanley Mission 119 Q4
Stanleyville 106 E2
Stann Creek 132 C6
Stanos 75 F3
Stanovoye Nagorye 85 J5
Stanovoy Khrebet 85 L5
Stansted 53 H3
Stanthorpe 113 L4
Stanton 53 H2
Stapleford 53 F3
Stara Planina 73 G4
Staraya Russa 78 E4
Staraya Vorpavla 84 Ae4
Stara Zagora 73 H4
Starcross 52 D4
Stargard 70 F2
Starikovo 85 R2
Starke 129 L6
Starkville 128 H4
Starmyri 62 X12
Starnberg 70 D5
Starnberger See 70 D5
Staroaleyskoye 84 C6
Starobelsk 79 F6
Starodub 79 E5
Starodubskoye 88 J2
Starogard 71 H2
Starokazachye 73 K2
Starokonstantinov 79 D6
Starominskaya 79 F6
Starosielce 71 K2
Start Bay 52 D4
Start Point *Devon, U.K.* 52 D4
Start Point *Orkney Islands, U.K.* 56 F1
Stary Sacz 71 J4
Staryy Oskol 79 F5
Staryy Sambor 71 K4
State College 125 M6
Staten Island 139 D10
Statesboro 129 M4
Statesville 129 M3
Staunton *U.K.* 52 E3
Staunton *U.K.* 52 E3
Staunton *U.S.A.* 125 L7
Staunton on Wye 52 E2
Stavanger 63 A7
Staveley *Cumbria, U.K.* 55 G2
Staveley *Derbyshire, U.K.* 55 H3
Staveley *N Yorkshire, U.K.* 55 H2
Stavelot 64 F3
Stavropol 79 G6
Stavropolskaya Vozvyshennost 79 G6
Stawiski 71 K2
Staxton 55 J2
Steensby Inlet 120 L3
Steensby Peninsula 120 J3
Steens Mountain 122 E6
Steenstrups Glacier 120 Q2
Steeping 55 K3
Steere, Mount 112 D3
Stefanesti 73 J2
Stefansson Island 120 E3
Stege 63 E9
Steigerwald 70 D4
Steinbach 123 R3
Steinhuder Meer 70 C2
Steinkjer 62 D4
Stellenbosch 108 C6
Steller, Mount 118 G3
Stenay 64 F4
Stendal 70 D2
Stenhousemuir 57 E4
Stenness 56 A1
Stenness, Loch of 56 E2
Stentrask 62 H3
Stepan 71 M3
Stephens, Cape 115 D4
Stephenville *Canada* 121 Q8
Stephenville *U.S.A.* 128 C4
Stepnogorsk 84 A6
Stepnyak 84 A6
Sterkstroom 108 E6
Sterlibashevo 78 K5
Sterling *Colorado* 123 N7
Sterling *Illinois* 124 F6
Sterling Heights 124 J5
Sterlitamak 78 K5
Steshevskaya 78 F3
Stettin 70 F2
Steubenville 125 K6
Stevenage 53 G3
Stevens Point 124 F4
Stevenston 57 D5
Stewart 118 H3
Stewart Island 115 A7
Stewart Islands 111 P3
Stewarton 57 D5
Stewartstown 58 J3
Steynsburg 108 E6
Steyr 68 E1
St-Gildas, Pointe de 65 B5
Stibb Cross 52 C4
Stickford 55 K3
Stikine 118 J4
Stikine Mountains 118 K4
Stilis 75 G3
Stillwater *Minnesota* 124 D4
Stillwater *Oklahoma* 128 D2
Stilo, Punta 69 F6
Stinchar 57 D5
Stip 73 G5
Stirling *Australia* 113 G3
Stirling *U.K.* 57 E4
Stirling Range 112 D5
Stjernoya 62 K1
Stjordal 62 D5
Stockach 70 C5
Stockbridge 53 F3
Stockerau 68 F1
Stockholm *Sweden* 63 H7
Stockholm *Sweden* 63 H7
Stockport 55 G3
Stocksbridge 55 H3
Stockton *California* 126 B2
Stockton *Kansas* 123 Q8
Stockton Heath 55 G3
Stockton-on-Tees 55 H2
Stockton Plateau 127 L5
Stode 62 G5
Stoer, Point of 56 C2
Stoke Ferry 53 H2
Stoke-on-Trent 55 G3
Stokesley 55 H2
Stokes Point 113 J7
Stokhod 71 L3
Stokkseyri 62 U13
Stokmarknes 62 F2
Stolbovoy, Ostrov 85 P2
Stolbtsy 71 M2
Stolica 71 J4
Stolin 79 D5
Stolp 71 G1
Stolsheimen 63 B6
Stone 53 E2
Stonehaven 57 F4
Stonehouse *Gloucestershire, U.K.* 52 E3
Stonehouse *Strathclyde, U.K.* 57 E5
Stony 118 D3
Stora 63 C8
Stora Lulevatten 62 H3
Storavan 62 H4
Storby 63 H6
Stord 63 A7
Store Balt 63 D9
Store Heddinge 63 E9
Storen 62 D5
Storjord 62 F3
Storlien 62 E5
Storm Bay 113 K7
Storm Lake 124 C5
Stornoway 56 B2
Storozhevsk 78 J3
Storozhinets 73 H1
Storr, The 56 B3
Storsjon 62 F5
Storslett 62 J2
Storsteinfjellet 62 G2
Stort 53 H3
Storuman *Sweden* 62 G4
Storuman *Sweden* 62 G4
Stosch, Isla 139 A9
Stour *Dorset, U.K.* 53 E4
Stour *Suffolk, U.K.* 53 H3
Stourbridge 53 E2
Stourport-on-Severn 52 E2
Stowmarket 53 J2
Stow-on-the-Wold 53 F3
Stoyba 85 N6
Stozac 72 E4
Strabane 58 H3
Strachur 57 C4
Stradbroke 53 J2
Strait of Belle Isle 121 Q7
Strakonice 70 E4
Stralsund 70 E1
Strand 108 C6
Stranda 62 B5
Strandhill 58 E4
Strangford 58 L4
Strangford Lough 58 L4
Strangnas 63 G7
Stranorlar 58 G3
Stranraer 54 D2
Strasbourg 64 G4
Strasheny 73 K2
Strasswalchen 68 D2
Stratfield Mortimer 53 F3
Stratford *Canada* 125 K5
Stratford *New Zealand* 115 E3
Stratford *U.S.A.* 127 L2
Stratford-upon-Avon 53 F2
Strathaven 57 D5
Strathblane 57 D5
Strathbogie 56 F3
Strath Carron 56 D3
Strathclyde 57 D5
Strath Dearn 56 E3
Strath Earn 57 E4
Strath Halladale 56 E2
Strathmore *Canada* 122 H2
Strathmore *Highland, U.K.* 56 D2
Strathmore *Tayside, U.K.* 57 F4
Strath Naver 56 D2
Strath of Kildonan 56 E2
Strath Oykel 56 D2
Strath Spey 56 E3
Strathy Point 56 D2
Stratos 75 F3
Stratton *U.K.* 52 C4
Stratton *U.S.A.* 125 Q4
Straubing 70 E4
Straumnes 62 T11
Straumsjoen 62 F2
Strausberg 70 E2
Strawberry Mountains 122 E5
Strawberry Reservoir 122 J7
Streaky Bay *Australia* 113 G5
Streaky Bay *Australia* 113 G5
Streator 124 F6
Strehaia 73 G3
Strela 70 E4
Strelka-Chunya 84 G4
Stretford 55 G3
Stretton 53 G2
Streymoy 62 Z14
Strezhevoy 84 B4
Strimasund 62 F3
Strimon 75 G2
Strimonikos, Kolpos 75 G2
Strokestown 58 F5
Strolka 84 E5
Stroma 56 E2
Stromboli, Isola 69 E6
Stromness 56 E2
Stromsburg 123 R7
Stromstad 63 D7
Stromsund 62 F5
Stroms Vattudal 62 F4
Strongoli 69 F6
Stronsay 56 F1
Stronsay Firth 56 F1
Strontian 57 C4
Strood 53 H3
Stropkov 71 J4
Stroud 52 E3
Struer 63 C8
Struga 72 F5
Strugi Krasnye 63 N7
Struma 73 G4
Strumble Head 52 B2
Strumica 73 G5
Stryama 73 H4
Stryn 63 B6
Stryy 79 C6
Strzyzow 71 J4
Stuart *Florida* 129 M7

Stuart *Nebraska* 123 Q6
Stuart Island 118 C3
Stuart Lake 118 L5
Stuart, Mount 122 D4
Stung Treng 93 L6
Stura 68 A3
Sturgeon 125 K3
Sturgeon Bay 124 G4
Sturgeon Falls 125 L3
Sturgeon Lake 124 E1
Sturgis 123 N5
Sturovo 71 H5
Sturry 53 J3
Sturt Desert 113 J4
Sturton by Stow 55 J3
Stutterheim 108 E6
Stuttgart *U.S.A.* 128 G3
Stuttgart *Germany* 70 C4
Stykkisholmur 62 T12
Styr 71 L3
Suakin 103 G4
Suakin Archipelago 96 D7
Suavanao 114 J5
Subashi 94 J4
Subay, Irq 96 F6
Subei 86 H4
Subi 90 D5
Subiaco 69 D5
Sublette 127 M2
Subotica 72 E2
Suceava 73 J2
Sucha 71 H4
Suchedniow 71 J3
Suck 59 F6
Sucre 138 C3
Suda 78 F4
Sudan 102 E5
Sudbury *Canada* 125 K3
Sudbury *Derbyshire, U.K.* 53 F2
Sudbury *Suffolk, U.K.* 53 H2
Sudety 70 F3
Sudirman, Pegunungan 91 K6
Sudr 96 A2
Sud, Recif du 114 X17
Suduroy 62 Z14
Sudzha 79 F5
Sue 102 E6
Suess Land 120 W3
Suez 103 F2
Suez Canal 103 F1
Suez, Gulf of 103 F2
Suffolk 53 H2
Sufian 94 G2
Sugarloaf Mount 125 Q4
Sugla Golu 76 D4
Sugoy 85 T4
Suhait 87 J4
Suhar 97 N4
Suhbaatar 87 K1
Suhut 76 D3
Suibin 88 C2
Suichuan 93 M3
Suide 87 L4
Suidong 88 D2
Suifenhe 88 C3
Suifen He 88 C4
Suihua 88 A2
Suileng 88 A2
Suining 93 L2
Suiping 93 M2
Suir 59 G8
Suixi 93 M4
Sui Xian 93 M2
Suizhong 87 N3
Suj 87 K3
Sukabumi 90 D7
Sukhinichi 78 F5
Sukhona 78 G3
Sukkertoppen 120 R5
Sukkertoppen Iskappe 120 R4
Sukkur 92 C3
Sukma 92 F5
Sukon 91 G6
Sukpay 88 F2
Sukpay Datani 88 F2
Suksun 78 K4
Sukumo 89 D9
Sulaiman Range 92 C3
Sula, Kepulauan 91 H6
Sulakyurt 76 E2
Sulawesi 91 G6
Sulawesi, Laut 91 G5
Sulaymaniyah 94 G4
Sulby 54 E2
Sulejow 71 H3
Sulina 73 K3
Sulina, Bratul 73 K3
Sulingen 70 C2
Sulitjelma 62 G3
Sullana 136 A4
Sullivan 124 E7
Sullivan Lake 122 J2
Sullom Voe 56 A1
Sullorsuaq 120 R3
Sully 65 E5
Sulmona 69 D4
Sulphur *Oklahoma* 128 D3
Sulphur *Texas* 128 E4
Sulphur Springs 128 E4
Sultandagi 76 D3
Sultanhani *Turkey* 76 E3
Sultanhani *Turkey* 77 H2
Sultanhisar 76 C4
Sultanpur 92 F3

Sulu Archipelago 91 G4
Suluklu 76 E3
Sulu Sea 91 F4
Suly 84 Ae6
Sulz 70 C4
Sulzberger Bay 141 P3
Sumar 94 G5
Sumarokovo 84 D4
Sumatera 90 C6
Sumba 91 F7
Sumbar 95 H2
Sumbawa 91 F7
Sumbawabesar 91 F7
Sumbawanga 107 F4
Sumbe 106 B5
Sumburgh 56 A2
Sumburgh Head 56 A2
Sumedang 90 D7
Sumenep 90 E7
Sumgayyt 79 H7
Summan, As *Saudi Arabia* 96 H3
Summan, As *Saudi Arabia* 97 J5
Summer Isles 56 C2
Summer Lake 122 D6
Summerside 121 P8
Summit Lake 118 L4
Sumner Lake 127 K3
Sumperk 71 G4
Sumprabum 93 J3
Sumter 129 M4
Sumy 79 E5
Sunamganj 93 H3
Sunart, Loch 57 C4
Sunaynah 97 M5
Sunaysilah 77 J5
Sunbury 125 M6
Sunchon 87 P5
Sun City 126 F4
Sundance 123 M5
Sundargarh 92 F4
Sunda, Selat 90 D7
Sunday Strait 112 E2
Sunde 63 D6
Sunderland 55 H2
Sundiken Daglari 76 D3
Sundsvall 62 G5
Sungaipenuh 90 D6
Sungikai 102 E5
Sungurlu 76 F2
Suning 87 M4
Sunland Park 127 J5
Sunlight Peak 127 J2
Sunndalsora 62 C5
Sunne 63 E7
Sunnyside 122 D4
Sunnyvale 126 A2
Suntar 85 K4
Sun Valley 122 G6
Sunwu 87 P2
Sunyani 104 E4
Suoirman, Pegunungan 114 B2
Suomenlahti Finskij Zaliv 63 L7
Suomussalmi 62 N4
Suo-nada 89 C9
Suonenjoki 62 M5
Suoyarvi 78 E3
Supaul 92 G3
Superior *Arizona* 126 G4
Superior *Nebraska* 123 Q7
Superior *Wisconsin* 124 D3
Superior, Lake 124 G3
Suphan Dagi 77 K3
Supiori 91 K6
Supsa 77 J1
Suq ash Shuyukh 94 H6
Suqian 87 M5
Suqutra 97 P10
Sur 97 P5
Sura 78 H4
Surab 92 C3
Surabaya 90 E7
Surahammar 63 G7
Surak 95 P9
Surakarta 90 E7
Suran 95 Q8
Surat *Australia* 113 K4
Surat *India* 92 D4
Suratgarh 92 D3
Surat Thani 93 J7
Surduc, Pasul 73 G3
Surendranagar 92 D4
Surgeres 65 C5
Surgut 84 A4
Surigao 91 H4
Surigao Strait 91 H3
Surin 93 K6
Suriname 137 F3
Surmene 77 J2
Surnadalsora 62 C5
Surovikino 79 G6
Surrah, Nafud as 96 G5
Surrey 53 G3
Sur Sari 63 M6
Surt 101 J2
Surt, Khalij 101 J2
Surtsey 62 U13
Suruc 77 H4
Suruga-wan 89 G8
Surulangun 90 D6
Susa *Italy* 68 A3
Susa *Japan* 89 C8
Susac 72 D4
Susak 72 C3
Susaki 89 D9

Susami 89 E9
Susangerd 94 J6
Susanville 122 D7
Susehri 77 H2
Susitna 118 E3
Suso 93 J7
Susquehanna 125 M6
Susuka 114 H5
Susurluk 76 C3
Susuz 77 K2
Sutculer 76 D4
Sutherland 108 D6
Sutherlin 122 C6
Sutlej 92 D2
Sutterton 53 G2
Sutton 53 G3
Sutton Bridge 53 H2
Sutton Coldfield 53 F2
Sutton in Ashfield 55 H3
Sutton-on-the-Forest 55 H2
Sutton Scotney 53 F3
Suttor 113 K3
Suttsu 88 H4
Sutwik Island 118 D4
Suva 114 R9
Suvasvesi 62 N5
Suverovo 88 E3
Suvorov Island 111 W4
Suwalki 71 K1
Suwannee 129 L6
Suwanose-jima 89 B11
Suwar 77 J5
Suwayqiyah, Hawr as 94 G5
Suweis, Khalij-as- 103 F2
Suwon 87 P4
Suyevatpaul 78 L3
Suyfun 88 C4
Suzaka 89 G7
Suzhou *Anhui, China* 93 N2
Suzhou *Jiangsu, China* 87 N5
Suzu 89 F7
Suzu-misaki 89 F7
Suzun 84 C6
Svalbard 80 C2
Svalyava 71 K4
Svappavaara 62 J3
Svarta 63 F7
Svartisen 62 E3
Svartvik 63 G5
Svarvolthalvoya 62 M1
Svatovo 79 F6
Svatoy Nos, Mys 85 Q2
Svay Rieng 93 L6
Sveg 63 F5
Svelvik 63 D7
Svencioneliai 63 M9
Svendborg 63 D9
Svenstavik 62 F5
Sventoji 63 N8
Sverdrup Islands 120 G2
Sverdrup, Ostrov 84 B2
Svetlaya 88 G2
Svetlogorsk 79 D5
Svetlograd 79 G6
Svetlyy 85 K5
Svetogorsk 63 N6
Svilajnac 73 F3
Svilengrad 73 J5
Svir 63 M9
Svirtsa 78 E3
Svishtov 73 H4
Svisloc 71 L2
Svitavy 71 G4
Svobodnyy 85 M6
Svolvar 62 F2
Svrljig 73 G4
Svyatoy Nos, Mys 78 H2
Svyatoy Nos, Mys 85 R2
Swadlincote 53 F2
Swaffham 53 H2
Swainby 55 H2
Swain Reefs 113 L3
Swainsboro 129 L4
Swains Island 111 U4
Swakop 108 C4
Swakopmund 108 B4
Swale 55 H2
Swaledale 55 H2
Swale, The 53 H3
Swallow Falls 54 F3
Swallow Island 114 N7
Swanage 53 F4
Swan Hill 113 J6
Swan Islands 132 F6
Swankhalok 93 J5
Swanley 53 H3
Swan Reach 113 H5
Swan River 119 Q5
Swansea 52 D3
Swansea Bay 52 D3
Swanton 125 P4
Swatragh 58 J3
Swaziland 109 F5
Sweden 63 F8
Sweet Home 122 C5
Sweetwater *Texas* 127 M4
Sweetwater *Wyoming* 123 K6
Swellendam 108 D6
Swidnica 71 G3
Swiebodzin 70 F2
Swietokrzyskie, Gory 71 J3
Swift Current 123 L2
Swinburne, Cape 120 G3
Swindon 53 F3
Swinemunde 70 F2

Swineshead 53 G2
Swinoujscie 70 F2
Swinton *Borders, U.K.* 57 F5
Swinton *S. Yorkshire, U.K.* 55 H3
Switzerland 68 A2
Swona 56 E2
Swords 59 K6
Syalakh 85 L3
Syamzha 78 G3
Sybil Point 59 B8
Sychevka 78 E4
Sydney *Australia* 113 L5
Sydney *Canada* 121 P8
Sydney Lake 123 S2
Syeverodonetsk 79 F6
Sykehouse 55 H3
Syktyvkar 78 J3
Sylacauga 129 J4
Sylene 63 E5
Sylhet 93 H4
Sylt 70 C1
Sylva 78 K4
Sylvania 129 M4
Sym 84 D4
Synya 78 K2
Synzhera 73 K2
Syracuse *Italy* 69 E7
Syracuse *Kansas* 127 M2
Syracuse *New York* 125 M5
Syr-Darya 86 C3
Syrdar-ya 80 H5
Syrdaryn 86 B3
Syria 94 C4
Syriam 93 J5
Sysola 78 J3
Syston 53 F2
Sytomino 84 A4
Syumsi 78 J4
Syutkya 73 G5
Syzran 79 H5
Szarvas 72 F2
Szczecin 70 F2
Szczecinek 71 G2
Szczecinski, Zalew 70 F2
Szczekociny 71 H3
Szczucin 71 J3
Szczuczyn 71 K2
Szczytno 71 J2
Szeged 72 F2
Szeghalom 73 F2
Szekesfehervar 72 E2
Szekszard 72 E2
Szentes 72 F2
Szentgotthard 72 D2
Szolnok 72 F2
Szombathely 72 D2
Szprotawa 70 F3

T

Taal, Lake 91 G3
Tabaqah 94 D4
Tabar Islands 114 E2
Tabarka 69 B7
Tabas *Iran* 95 N5
Tabas *Iran* 95 Q5
Tabasara, Serrania de 132 G10
Tabashimo 78 H4
Tabatinga, Serra da 137 J6
Tabiteuea 111 R2
Tablas 91 G3
Tablas, Cabo 138 B6
Table Cape 115 G3
Taboleiro 137 K5
Tabor 70 F4
Tabora 107 F4
Tabou 104 D5
Tabriz 94 H2
Tabuk 96 C2
Tabuka 89 C9
Tabut 97 L9
Tabwemasana 114 T11
Taby 63 H7
Tacheng 86 F2
Tacloban 91 G3
Tacna *Peru* 138 B3
Tacna *U.S.A.* 126 F4
Tacoma 122 C4
Tacora, Cerro de 138 C3
Tacuarembo 138 E6
Tadcaster 55 H3
Tademait, Plateau du 101 F3
Tadjoura 103 H5
Tadmur 77 H5
Tadoule Lake 119 R4
Tadoussac 125 R2
Tadpatri 92 E6
Tadworth 53 G3
Taegu 89 B8
Taehuksan 87 P5
Taejon 87 P4
Taf 52 C3
Tafahi 111 U5
Tafalla 67 F1
Tafassasset 101 G4
Tafassasset, Tenere du 101 H4
Taff 52 D3
Taff, At 97 M4
Tafila 94 B6
Tafi Viejo 138 C5
Tafresh 95 K4
Taft 95 M6
Taftan, Kuh-e- 95 Q7

Taganrog 79 F6
Taganrogskiy Zaliv 79 F6
Tagbilaran 91 G4
Taghmon 59 J8
Tagliamento 68 D3
Tagolo Point 91 G4
Tagounite 100 D3
Tagu 73 H2
Taguatinga 138 H6
Tagudin 91 G2
Tagula 114 E4
Tagula Island 114 E4
Tagum 91 H4
Tagus 66 C3
Tahan, Gunung 90 C5
Tahat, Mont 101 G4
Ta He 87 N1
Tahe 87 N1
Taheri 95 L8
Tahiryuak Lake 119 N1
Tahiti 143 J5
Tahlab, Dasht-i- 92 B3
Tahlequah 128 E3
Tahoe Lake *Canada* 119 P1
Tahoe, Lake *U.S.A.* 122 E8
Tahoka 127 M4
Tahoua 101 G6
Tahrud 95 N7
Tahta 102 F2
Tahtali Daglari 77 G3
Tahuamanu 136 D6
Tahulandang 91 H5
Taian 87 M4
Taibai Shan 93 L2
Taibus Qi 87 M3
Tai-chung 87 N7
Taier 115 C6
Taieri 115 C6
Taigu 87 L4
Taihape 115 E3
Taihe *Anhui, China* 93 N2
Taihe *Jiangxi, China* 93 M3
Tai Hu 87 N5
Taimba 84 F4
Tain 56 D3
Tai-nan 87 N7
Tainaron, Akra 75 G4
Taining 87 M6
Taipale 62 N5
Tai-pei 87 N6
Taiping 90 C5
Taipingbao 86 J4
Taipinggou 88 C1
Taira 89 H7
Taisei 88 G4
Taisha 89 D8
Taitao, Peninsula de 139 B9
Tai-tung 87 N7
Taivalkoski 62 N4
Taiwan 87 N7
Taiwan Haixia 87 M7
Taiyetos Oros 75 G4
Taiyuan 87 L4
Taiza 89 E8
Taizhou 87 M5
Taizz 96 G10
Tajabad 95 M6
Tajikistan 86 B4
Tajima 89 G7
Tajin-dong 88 B5
Tajito 126 F5
Tajo 66 D3
Tajrish 95 K4
Tajumuclo, Volcan de 132 B7
Tajuna 66 E2
Tak 93 J5
Takab 94 H3
Takada 89 G7
Takaka 115 D4
Takamatsu 89 E8
Takanabe 89 C9
Takaoka 89 F7
Takapuna 115 E2
Takasaki 89 G7
Takatshwane 108 D4
Takaungu 107 G3
Takayama 89 F7
Takefu 89 F8
Takengon 90 B5
Takeo 93 K6
Takestan 95 J3
Takhadid 94 G7
Takhi-i-Suleiman 95 K3
Takhta Bazar 95 R4
Takhtabrod 84 Ae6
Takikawa 88 H4
Takinoue 88 J3
Taklimakan Shamo 92 F1
Taku 118 J4
Takum 105 G4
Takwa 114 K6
Talagang 92 D2
Talamanca, Cordillera de 132 F10
Talangbetutu 90 C6
Talara 136 A4
Talar-i-Band 92 B3
Talas 86 C3
Talasea 114 E3
Talaton 52 D4
Talaud, Kepulauan 91 H5
Talavera de la Reina 66 D3
Talavuelas 67 F3
Talbot Inlet 120 L2
Talca 139 B7

Talcahuano 139 B7
Talcher 92 G4
Taldy-Kurgan 36 D2
Talgarth 52 D3
Taliabu 91 G6
Talihira 128 E3
Tali Post 102 F6
Talisay 91 G3
Talitsa 84 Ad5
Taliwang 91 F7
Talkeetna 118 E3
Talkeetna Mountains 118 F3
Talladega 129 J4
Tall Afar 77 K4
Tallahassee 129 K5
Tallinn 63 L7
Tall Kalakh 77 G5
Tall Kayf 77 K4
Tall Kujik 77 K4
Tallow 59 F8
Tall Tamir 77 J4
Talmenka 84 C6
Talnoye 79 E6
Taloda 92 D4
Talodi 102 F5
Talok 91 F5
Talovka 84 E5
Talove 85 M4
Talsi 63 K8
Taltal 138 B5
Taltson 119 N3
Talu 114 F3
Taluma 85 L5
Talvik 62 K1
Tama 124 D6
Tamabo Range 90 F5
Tamale 104 E4
Tamames 66 C2
Tamana 111 S2
Tamano 89 D8
Tamanrasset *Algeria* 100 F4
Tamanrasset *Algeria* 101 G4
Tamar *Australia* 113 K7
Tamar *U.K.* 52 C4
Tamar, Alto de 133 K11
Tamarite de Litera 67 G2
Tamatave 109 J3
Tamaulipas, Llanos de 128 C8
Tamazunchale 131 K7
Tambacounda 104 C3
Tambangsawah 90 C6
Tambelan, Kepulauan 90 D5
Tambey 84 A2
Tambo 113 K3
Tambora, Gunung 91 F7
Tamboril 137 J4
Tambov 79 G5
Tambre 66 B1
Tambura 102 E6
Tamchaket 100 C5
Tame 136 C2
Tamega 66 C2
Tamiahua, Laguna de 131 L7
Tamil Nadu 92 E6
Tamis 72 F3
Tamit, Wadi 101 J2
Tammerfors 63 M6
Tammisaari 63 K6
Tampa 129 L7
Tampa Bay 129 L7
Tampere 63 M6
Tampico 131 L6
Tamsagbulag 87 M2
Tamuin 131 K7
Tamworth *Australia* 113 L5
Tamworth *U.K.* 53 F2
Tana *Chile* 138 C3
Tana *Kenya* 107 H3
Tana *Norway* 62 M1
Tanabe 89 E9
Tana bru 62 N2
Tanafjorden 62 N1
Tana Hayk 103 G5
Tanahbala 90 B6
Tanahgrogot 90 F6
Tanahjampea 91 G7
Tanahmasa 90 B6
Tanahmerah 114 C3
Tanah Merah 90 C4
Tanami 112 F3
Tanana 118 E2
Tananarive 109 J3
Tanchon 88 B5
Tandag 91 H4
Tandek 91 F4
Tandil 139 E7
Tando Adam 92 C3
Tandragee 58 K4
Taneatua 115 F3
Tanega-shima 89 C10
Tan Emellel 101 G3
Tanen Tong Dan 93 J5
Tanew 71 K3
Tanezrouft 100 E4
Tanf, Jbel al 77 H6
Tanga *Tanzania* 107 G4
Tanga *Russia* 85 J6
Tanga Islands 114 E2
Tanganyika, Lake 107 F4
Tangarare 114 J6
Tanger 100 D1
Tanggula Shan 93 G2
Tanggula Shankou 93 H2
Tangra Yumco 92 G2

Tangshan 87 M4
Tangwang He 88 B2
Tangwanghe 88 B1
Tangyuan 88 B2
Tan Hill 53 F3
Tanhua 62 M3
Taniantaweng Shan 93 J2
Tanimbar, Kepulauan 114 A3
Tanjung 90 F6
Tanjungbalai 90 B5
Tanjungkarang Telukbetung 90 D7
Tanjungpandan 90 D6
Tanjungpura 90 B5
Tanjungredeb 91 F5
Tanjungselor 91 F5
Tankapirtti 62 M2
Tankovo 84 D4
Tankse 92 E2
Tanlovo 84 A3
Tanna 114 U13
Tannu Ola 84 E6
Tannurah, Ra's 97 K3
Tanout 101 G6
Tan-shui 87 N6
Tanta 102 F1
Tan-Tan 100 C3
Tantoyuca 131 K7
Tanumshede 63 D7
Tanzania 107 G4
Taoan 87 N2
Tao He 93 K2
Tao, Ko 93 J6
Taolanaro 109 J5
Taormina 69 E7
Taos 127 K2
Taoudenni 100 E4
Taourirt 100 E2
Tapa 63 L7
Tapachula 131 N10
Tapah 90 C5
Tapajos 137 F4
Tapaktuan 90 B5
Tapan 90 D6
Tapanahoni 137 F3
Tapaua 136 D5
Taperoa 137 K6
Tappahannock 125 M8
Tappi-saki 88 H5
Tapsuy 78 L3
Tapti 92 D4
Tapuaenuku 115 D4
Tapul Group 91 G4
Taqah 97 M8
Taqtaq 94 G4
Taquari 138 E3
Taquari, Pantanal do 138 E3
Tara 84 A5
Tarabulus 101 H2
Taradale 115 F3
Tara, Hill of 58 J5
Tarakan 91 F5
Tarakli 76 D2
Tarakliya 73 K3
Taramana 91 G7
Taramo-jima 89 G11
Taran 84 A2
Tarancon 66 E2
Taransay 56 A3
Taransay, Sound of 56 A3
Taranto 69 F5
Taranto, Golfo di 69 F5
Tarapoto 136 B5
Tararua Range 115 E4
Tarascon 65 F7
Tarasovo 78 H2
Tarauaca *Brazil* 136 C5
Tarauaca *Brazil* 136 C5
Taravo 69 B5
Tarazona 67 F2
Tarazona de la Mancha 67 F3
Tarbagatay, Khrebet 86 E2
Tarbert *Ireland* 59 D7
Tarbert *Strathclyde, U.K.* 57 C5
Tarbert *Western Isles, U.K.* 56 B3
Tarbes 65 D7
Tarbet 57 D4
Tarbolton 57 D5
Tarboro 129 P3
Tarcaului, Muntii 73 J2
Tarcoola 113 G5
Tardienta 67 F2
Tardoki-yani, Gora 88 F1
Taree 113 L5
Tarendo 62 K3
Tareya 84 E2
Tarfa, Ra's at 96 F8
Tarfa, Wadi el 103 F2
Tarfaya 100 C3
Tarfside 57 F4
Targhee Pass 122 J5
Tarhunah 101 H2
Tarif 97 L4
Tarifa 66 D4
Tarija 138 D4
Tariku 114 B2
Tarim 97 J8
Tarim Basin 86 E3
Tarim He 86 E3
Tarim Pendi 86 E3
Taritatu 114 B2
Tarkasale 84 A3
Tarkastad 108 E6
Tarkhankut, Mys 79 E6
Tarkio 124 C6

Tarkwa 104 E4
Tarlac 91 G2
Tarlak 86 E3
Tarleton 55 G3
Tarma 136 B6
Tarn 65 D7
Tarna 72 F2
Tarnaby 62 F4
Tarnobrzeg 71 J3
Tarnow 71 J4
Tarnsjo 63 G6
Taro 68 B3
Taron 114 E2
Taroom 113 K4
Taroudannt 100 D2
Tarporley 55 G3
Tarragona 67 G2
Tarrasa 67 H2
Tarrega 67 G2
Tarsus 76 F4
Tartagal 138 D4
Tartas 65 C7
Tartu 63 P7
Tartung 90 B5
Tartus 94 B4
Tartus 77 F5
Tarutino 73 K2
Tarzout 67 G4
Tasci 77 F3
Tashakta 86 F2
Tashigang 93 H3
Tashk, Daryacheh-ye 95 L7
Tashkent 36 B3
Tashkepri 95 R3
Tashla 79 J5
Tashtagol 84 D6
Tasikmalaya 90 D7
Tasiujaq 121 N6
Taskesken 86 E2
Taskopru 76 F2
Tas-Kumsa 85 N3
Taslicay 77 K3
Tasman Bay 115 D4
Tasmania 113 K7
Tasman Mountains 115 D4
Tasnad 73 G2
Tasova 77 G2
Tas-Tumus 85 N2
Tasty 86 B3
Tasucu 76 E4
Tasuj 77 L3
Tataba 91 G6
Tatabanya 72 E2
Tatarbunary 73 K3
Tatarka 84 B6
Tatarsk 84 B5
Tataurovo 85 J6
Tateyama 89 G8
Tathlina Lake 119 M3
Tathlith 96 F7
Tathlith, Wadi 96 F6
Tatnam, Cape 119 S4
Tatry 71 H4
Tatsinskiy 79 G6
Tatsuno 89 E8
Tatta 92 C4
Tatum 127 L4
Tatvan 77 K3
Tau 111 V4
Tauari 137 F2
Taubate 138 G4
Tauchik 79 J7
Taumarunui 115 E3
Taung-gyi 93 J4
Taungnyo Range 93 J5
Taunton *U.K.* 52 D3
Taunton *U.S.A.* 125 Q6
Taunus 70 C3
Taupo 115 F3
Taupo, Lake 115 E3
Tauq 94 G4
Tauq 77 L5
Taurage 63 K9
Tauranga 115 F2
Tauroa Point 115 D1
Taurus 76 E4
Tauste 67 F2
Tauu Islands 114 F2
Tavalesh, Kuhha-ye 94 J3
Tavara-i-Tholo 111 T6
Tavas 76 C4
Tavda *Russia* 84 Ad5
Tavda *Russia* 84 Ae5
Taverner Bay 120 M4
Taveuni 114 S8
Tavira 66 C4
Tavistock 52 C4
Tavolara, Isola di 69 B5
Tavoy 93 J6
Tavrichanka 88 C4
Tavsanli 76 C3
Tavua 114 Q8
Tavuna-i-Ra 111 T6
Tavy 52 C4
Taw 52 D4
Tawakoni, Lake 128 E4
Tawau 91 F5
Tawe 52 D3
Taweisha 102 E5
Tawila 96 A3
Tawil, Al 96 D2
Tawitawi Group 91 G4
Ta-wu 87 N7
Tawurgha, Sabkhat 101 J2

Name	Pg	Ref
Till	57	F5
Tillaberi	100	F6
Tillanchang	93	H7
Tillicoultry	57	E4
Tilomar	91	H7
Tilos	75	J4
Tilsit	71	J1
Tilt	57	E4
Timanskiy Kryazh	78	H3
Timar	77	K3
Timaru	115	C6
Timashevsk	79	F6
Timbakion	75	H5
Timbedra	100	D5
Timbo *Guinea*	104	C3
Timbo *Liberia*	104	D4
Timbuktu	100	E5
Timfristos	75	F3
Timimoun	100	F3
Timiris, Cap	100	B5
Timis	73	G3
Timisoara	73	F3
Timkapaul	84	Ad4
Timmernabben	63	G8
Timmins	125	K2
Timok	73	G3
Timolin	59	J7
Timor	91	H7
Timor, Laut	91	H7
Timoshino	78	F3
Timsher	78	J3
Tinaca Point	91	H4
Tinaco	133	N10
Tinahely	59	K7
Tinakula	114	M7
Tindivanam	92	E6
Tindouf	100	D3
Tineo	66	C1
Tinglev	63	C9
Tingo Maria	136	B5
Tingsryd	63	F8
Tingvoll	62	C5
Tinhare, Ilha de	137	K6
Tinogasta	138	C5
Tinompo	91	G5
Tinos *Greece*	75	H4
Tinos *Greece*	75	H4
Tintinara	113	J6
Tinto *Spain*	66	C4
Tinto *U.K.*	57	E5
Tinto Hills	57	E5
Tinwald	115	C5
Tiomilaskogen	63	E6
Tipaza	67	H4
Tipitapa	132	D8
Tippecanoe	124	G6
Tipperary *Ireland*	59	F8
Tipperary *Ireland*	59	G7
Tipton	124	H6
Tiptree	53	H3
Tiquicheo	131	J8
Tiracambu, Serra do	137	H4
Tiran	96	B3
Tirana	74	E2
Tirane	74	E2
Tirano	68	C2
Tiraspol	79	D6
Tire	76	B3
Tirebolu	77	H2
Tiree	57	C4
Tirga Mor	56	B3
Tirgoviste	73	H3
Tirgu Bujor	73	J3
Tirgu Carbunesti	73	G3
Tirgu Frumos	73	J2
Tirgu Jiu	73	G3
Tirgu Mures	73	H2
Tirgu Neamt	73	J2
Tirgu Ocna	73	J2
Tirich Mir	92	D1
Tirnava Mare	73	H2
Tirnava Mica	73	H2
Tirnavos	75	G3
Tirol	68	C2
Tirpul	95	Q4
Tirso	69	B6
Tirua Point	115	E3
Tiruchchirappalli	92	E6
Tirumangalam	92	E7
Tirunelveli	92	E7
Tirupati	92	E6
Tiruppur	92	E6
Tiruvannamalai	92	E6
Tisa	72	F3
Tisisat Falls	103	G5
Tissa	71	K4
Tissington	55	H3
Tista	93	G3
Tisza	72	F2
Tit-Ary	85	M2
Titchfield	53	F4
Titicaca, Lago	138	C3
Titograd	72	E4
Titova Mitrovica	73	F4
Titovo Uzice	72	E4
Titovo Velenje	72	C2
Titov Veles	73	F5
Titran	62	C5
Tittmoning	70	E4
Titu	73	H3
Titusville	129	M6
Tiumpan Head	56	B2
Tivaouane	104	B2
Tiveden	63	F7
Tiverton	52	D4
Tivoli	69	D5
Tiwi	97	P5
Tiyas	77	G5
Tizimin	131	Q7
Tizi Ouzou	101	F1
Tiznit	100	D3
Tjamotis	62	H3
Tjornuvik	62	Z14
Tjotta	62	E4
Tlaltenango	130	H7
Tlapa	131	K9
Tlapehuala	131	J8
Tlaxiaco	131	L9
Tlemcen	100	E2
Toad River	118	K4
Toamasina	109	J3
Tobago	133	S9
Toba Kakar Ranges	92	C2
Tobercurry	58	E4
Tobermory *Canada*	125	K4
Tobermory *U.K.*	57	B4
Toberonochy	57	C4
Tobi	91	J5
Tobin Lake	112	F3
Tobi-shima	88	G6
Toboali	90	D6
Tobol	84	Ae5
Tobolsk	84	Ae5
Tobseda	78	J2
Tobysh	78	J3
Tocache Nuevo	136	B5
Tocartins	137	H4
Toccoa	129	L3
Toco	133	S9
Toconao	138	C4
Tocopilla	138	B4
Tocuyo	133	N9
Todeli	91	G6
Todi	68	B2
Todi	69	D4
Todmorden	55	G3
Todog	86	E3
Todos os Santos, Baia de	137	K6
Todos Santos *Bolivia*	138	C3
Todos Santos *Mexico*	130	D6
Todos Santos, Bahia de	126	D5
Toe Head *Ireland*	59	D10
Toe Head *U.K.*	56	A3
Toetoes Bay	115	B7
Tofino	122	B3
Toft	56	A1
Tofte	63	D7
Tofua	111	T5
Toga	114	T10
Togi	89	F7
Togiak	118	C4
Togian, Kepulauan	91	G6
Togni	96	B7
Togo	104	F4
Togtoh	87	L3
Toguchi	89	H10
Togur	84	C5
Tohamiyam	103	G4
Tohatchi	127	H3
Tohma	77	G3
Toi-misaki	89	C10
Tojo	89	D8
Tok	118	G3
Tokachi	88	J4
Tokachi-Dake	88	J4
Tokaj	73	F1
Tokanui	115	B7
Tokar	103	G4
Tokara-kaikyo	89	C10
Tokara-retto	89	B11
Tokat	77	G2
Tokelau	111	U3
Tokiwa	88	J3
Tokke	63	C7
Toklar	77	G3
Tokmak	86	D3
Tokolon	84	H5
Tokoro	88	K3
Tokoroa	115	E3
Toksun	86	F3
Tok-to	89	C7
Toktogul	86	C3
Tokuno-shima	89	J10
Tokushima	89	E8
Tokuyama	89	C8
Tokyo	89	G8
Tolar, Cerro	138	C5
Tolbonuur	86	G2
Tolbukhin	73	J4
Toledo *Spain*	66	D3
Toledo *U.S.A.*	124	J6
Toledo Bend Reservoir	128	F5
Toledo, Montes de	66	D3
Tolentino	68	D4
Toliara	109	H4
Tolitoli	91	G5
Tolka	84	C4
Tolmezzo	68	D2
Tolmin	72	B2
Tolochin	78	D5
Tolosa	67	E1
Tolo, Teluk	91	G6
Tolsta Head	56	B2
Tolstoye	73	H1
Tolstoy, Mys	85	T5
Toluca	131	K8
Toluca, Nevado de	131	K8
Tolyatti	79	H5
Tomah	124	E4
Tomahawk	124	F4
Tomakomai	88	H4
Tomani	90	F5
Tomaniivi	114	R8
Tomar *Portugal*	66	B3
Tomar *Kazakhstan*	86	D2
Tomari	88	J2
Tomarza	77	F3
Tomasevo	72	E4
Tomashevka	71	K3
Tomaszow Lubelski	71	K3
Tomaszow Mazowiecka	71	J3
Tombador, Serra do	136	F6
Tombe	103	F6
Tombigbee	129	H5
Tomboco	106	B4
Tombouctou	100	E5
Tombua	106	B6
Tomelilla	63	E9
Tomelloso	66	E3
Tomini, Teluk	91	G6
Tomioka	89	H7
Tomkinson Ranges	112	F4
Tomma	62	E3
Tommot	85	M5
Tomo	136	D2
Tomochic	127	J6
Tompa	84	H5
Tompo	85	P4
Tomsk	84	D5
Tonbridge	53	H3
Tondano	91	G5
Tonder	70	C1
Tone	52	E3
Tonelagee	59	K6
Tonga	111	U6
Tonga *Sudan*	102	F6
Tongariro	115	E3
Tongatapu	111	U6
Tongatapu Group	111	T6
Tonga Trench	143	H5
Tongcheng	93	M3
Tongchuan	93	L1
Tongdao	93	L3
Tonggu	93	M3
Tongguan	93	M2
Tonghai	93	K4
Tonghe	88	B2
Tonghua	87	P3
Tongjiang	88	D2
Tongking, Gulf of	93	L5
Tongliao	87	N3
Tongling	87	M5
Tonglu	87	M6
Tongnae	89	B8
Tongoa	114	U12
Tongren	93	L3
Tongtianheyan	93	H2
Tongue *U.K.*	56	D2
Tongue *U.S.A.*	123	L5
Tongue, Kyle of	56	D2
Tongue of the Ocean	132	J2
Tong Xian	87	M4
Tongxin	93	L1
Tongyu	87	N3
Tongzi	93	L3
Tonichi	127	H6
Tonk	92	E3
Tonkabon	95	K3
Tonle Sap	93	K6
Tonneins	65	D6
Tonnerre	65	E5
Tono	88	H6
Tonopah	126	D2
Tonosi	132	G11
Tonsberg	63	D7
Tonstad	63	B7
Tonya	77	H2
Tooele	122	H7
Toowoomba	113	L4
Topeka	124	C7
Toplane	74	E1
Toplica	73	F4
Toplita	73	H2
Topocalma, Punta	138	B6
Topola	72	F3
Topolcani	73	F5
Topoli	79	J6
Topolkki	63	N6
Topolovgrad	73	J4
Topozero, Ozero	62	P4
Toppenish	122	D4
Toprakli	76	F3
Toraka Vestale	109	H3
Tora-Khem	84	F6
Torbali	76	B3
Torbat-e-Heydariyeh	95	P4
Torbat-e Jam	95	Q4
Tor Bay *Australia*	112	D5
Tor Bay *U.K.*	52	D4
Tordesillas	66	D2
Tore	56	D3
Tore	62	K4
Torfastadir	62	U12
Torgau	70	E3
Torgo	85	K5
Torhout	64	E3
Torino	68	A3
Torkaman	94	H3
Tormes	66	D2
Tornealven	62	K3
Tor Ness	56	E2
Torne-trask	62	H2
Torngat Mountains	121	P6
Tornio	62	L4
Toro, Cerro de	138	C5
Torciaga	73	H2
Torokina	114	F3
Torokszentmiklos	72	F2
Toronaios, Kolpos	75	G2
Toronto	125	L5
Toropets	78	E4
Tororo	107	F2
Toros Dagi	76	F4
Toros Daglari	76	E4
Torpoint	52	C4
Torquay	52	D4
Torrance	126	C4
Torrao	66	B3
Torre Annunziata	69	E5
Torre Baja	67	F2
Torreblanca	67	G2
Torrecilla en Cameros	66	E1
Torre del Greco	69	E5
Torrelaguna	66	E2
Torrelavega	66	D1
Torremolinos	66	D4
Torrens Creek	113	K3
Torrens, Lake	113	H5
Torrente	67	F3
Torreon	127	L8
Torres Island	114	T10
Torres Novas	66	B3
Torres Strait	114	C4
Torres Vedras	66	B3
Torrevieja	67	F4
Torr Head	58	K2
Torridge	52	C4
Torridon, Loch	56	C3
Torrijos	66	D3
Torrington *Connecticut*	125	P6
Torrington *Wyoming*	123	M6
Torrox	66	E4
Torsas	63	F8
Torsby	63	E6
Torshavn	62	Z14
Torsken	62	L2
Tortkuduk	84	A6
Tortola	133	Q5
Tortona	58	B3
Tortosa	67	G2
Tortosa, Cabo de	67	G2
Tortue, Ile de la	133	L4
Tortuga, Isla	126	G7
Tortuga, Isla la	136	D1
Tortum	77	J2
Torul	77	H2
Torun	71	H2
Tory Island	58	F2
Torysa	71	J4
Tory Sound	58	F2
Torzhok	78	F4
Torzym	70	F2
Tosa-shimizu	89	D9
Tosa-wan	89	D9
Toscaig	56	C3
Tosco-Emiliano, Appennino	68	C3
Tostado	138	D5
Tosya	76	F2
Totana	67	F4
Totes	64	D4
Totma	78	G4
Totnes	52	D4
Totness	137	F2
Totora	138	C3
Totota	104	C4
Totoya	114	S9
Totton	53	F4
Tottori	89	E8
Touba	104	D4
Toubkal, Jebel	100	D2
Tougan	104	E3
Touggourt	101	G2
Touho Ouegoa	114	W16
Toul	64	F4
Toulon	65	F7
Toulouse	65	D7
Toummo	101	H4
Toumodi	104	D4
Toungoo	93	J5
Touraine	65	D5
Tourcoing	64	E3
Tournai	64	E3
Tournon *France*	65	D5
Tournon *France*	65	F6
Tournus	65	F5
Touros	137	K5
Tours	65	D5
Tousside, Pic	102	C3
Touws River	108	D6
Tovarkovskiy	79	F5
Towada	88	H5
Towanda	125	M6
Towcester	53	G2
Tower Island	136	B7
Towie	56	F3
Townsend	122	J4
Townshend Island	113	L3
Townsville	113	K2
Towson	125	M7
Toxkan He	86	D3
Toya-ko	88	H4
Toyama	89	F7
Toyama-wan	89	F7
Toyohashi	89	F8
Toyooka	89	E8
Toyooka	89	E8

Tyanya	35 K5	Ujung Pandang	51 F7	Union City	128 H2	Ust-Chara	85 L4
Tychany	84 F4	Uka	85 U5	Uniondale	108 D6	UstChizhapka	84 B5
Tychy	71 H3	Ukholovo	79 G5	Union Springs	129 K4	Ustica, Isola di	69 D6
Tygda	85 M6	Ukhta	78 J3	Uniontown	125 L7	Ustlimsk	84 G5
Tyler	128 E4	Ukhunku	85 L3	United Arab Emirates	97 L5	Ust-Ilimskiy	
Tyloskog	63 F7	Uki	114 K7	United States of America	116 H4	Vodokhranilishche	84 J4
Tym	34 C5	Ukiah	122 C8	Unity	122 E5	Ust-Ilych	84 Ac4
Tymovskoye	85 Q6	Ukmerge	53 L9	Universales, Montes	67 F2	Usti nad Labem	70 F3
Tynda	85 L5	Ukraine	79 D6	University Park	127 J4	Ustka	71 G1
Tyndall, Mount	115 C5	Ukta	71 J2	Unnao	92 F3	UstKamchatsk	85 U5
Tyndrum	57 D4	Uku	106 B5	Unst	56 B1	Ust-Kamenogorsk	86 E2
Tyne	55 H2	Uku-jima	89 B9	Untaek	88 A5	Ust-Kamo	84 F4
Tyne and Wear	55 H2	Ukuma	106 C5	Unye	77 G2	Ust-Kan	84 E5
Tynemouth	55 H1	Ula	76 C4	Unzha	78 G4	Ust-Kara	84 Ad3
Tynset	62 D5	Ulaangom	86 G2	Uodgan	96 D8	Ust-Karenga	85 K6
Tyr	85 P6	Ulan Bator	87 K2	Uoyan	85 J5	UstKatav	78 K5
Tyre	94 B5	Ulan-Erge	79 G6	Upata	133 R10	Ust-Kulom	78 J3
Tyret	84 G6	Ulanhad	87 M3	Upavon	53 F3	Ust-Kut	84 H5
Tyrma	85 N6	Ulan-Khol	79 H6	Upemba, Lake	106 E4	Ust-Kuyga	85 P3
Tyrone U.K.	58 H3	Ulan Tohoi	86 J3	Upernavik	120 Q3	Ust-Labinsk	79 F6
Tyrone U.S.A.	125 L6	Ulan-Ude	84 H6	Upernavik Isfjord	120 R3	UstLuga	63 N7
Tyrrhenian Sea	69 D5	Ulan Ula	93 H2	Upington	108 D5	UstMaya	85 N4
Tysnesoy	63 A7	Ulas	77 G3	Upolu	111 U4	Ust-Mayn	85 W3
Tyukalinsk	84 A5	Ulawa	114 K6	Upolu Point	126 T10	Ust-Mil	85 N5
Tyulgan	79 K5	Ulchin	89 B7	Upper Arrow Lake	122 F2	Ust-Muya	85 K5
Tyuli	84 Ae4	Ulcinj	74 E2	Upper Broughton	53 G2	UstNem	78 J3
Tyung	85 L4	Uled Saidan	101 J3	Upper Hutt	115 E4	Ust-Nera	85 Q4
Tywi	52 C3	Ulfborg	63 C8	Upper Klamath Lake	122 D6	UstNiman	85 N6
Tywyn	52 C2	Ulgumdzha	85 K4	Upper Seal Lake	121 M6	UstOmchug	85 R4
Tzaneen	108 F4	Ulhasnagar	92 D5	Uppingham	53 G2	Ust-Ordynskiy	84 G6
Tzoumerka	75 F3	Uliastay	86 H2	Uppsala *Sweden*	63 G6	Ustovo	73 H5
		Ulithi Atoll	91 K4	Uppsala *Sweden*	63 L7	Ust-Ozernoye	84 D5

U

		Uljan	72 C3	Upsala	124 E2	UstPenzhino	85 V4
		Uljma	73 F3	Upstart Bay	113 K2	Ust-Pit	84 E5
		Ulla	66 B1	Uqla Sawab	77 J6	Ust-Port	84 C3
Uainambi	136 C3	Ullaanbaatar	87 K2	Urad Qianqi	87 K3	UstReka	78 H3
Uapao, Cape	114 X16	Ullanger	62 H5	Urad Zhongqi	87 K3	UstSara	78 E3
Uapes	136 D4	Ullapool	56 C3	Urak	85 Q5	UstTapsuy	78 L3
Uatuma	136 F4	Ullock	55 F2	Urakan	84 H5	Ust-Tatta	85 N4
Uaupes	136 D3	Ullswater	55 G2	Urakawa	88 J4	Ust-Tsilma	78 J2
Uava	137 K5	Ullung-do	89 C7	Ural	79 J6	Ust-Tym	34 C5
Uba	138 H4	Ulm	70 C4	Ural Mountains	78 K3	UstTyrma	85 N6
Ubaitaba	137 K6	Ulog	72 E4	Uralsk	79 J5	UstUra	78 G3
Ube	89 C9	Ulongue	109 F2	Uralskiy Khrebet	78 K3	UstUsa	78 K2
Ubeda	66 E3	Ulricehamn	63 E8	Urandangi	113 H3	UstVaga	78 G3
Ubekendt O	120 R3	Ulsan	89 B8	Urandi	137 J6	UstVyyskaya	78 H3
Uberaba	138 J3	Ulsta	56 A1	Uranium City	119 P4	UstYuribey	84 Ae3
Uberaba, Laguna	138 E3	Ulsteinvik	62 A5	Uraricoera	136 E3	Ustyurt, Plato	51 T7
Uberlandia	138 G3	Ulster	58 H3	Urawa	89 G8	Usuki	89 C9
Ubinskoye	84 B5	Ulster Canal	58 H4	Urayirah	97 J4	Usulatan	132 C8
Ubolratna Reservoir	93 K5	Ulubat Golu	76 C2	Urayq, Al	96 D2	Usumacinta	131 P9
Ubombo	109 F5	Ulubey *Turkey*	76 C3	Urayq, Nafud al	96 F4	Utah	122 H8
Ubon Ratchathani	93 K5	Ulubey *Turkey*	77 G2	Urbana	124 J6	Utah Lake	122 J7
Ubundu	106 E3	Uluborlu	76 D3	Urbino	68 D4	Utajarvi	62 M4
Ucayali	136 C4	Ulucinar	77 F4	Urda	79 H6	Utara	90 C6
Ucdam	77 J3	Uludag	76 C2	Urdzhar	86 E2	Ute Creek	127 L2
Uch Adzhi	95 R2	Ulu Dagi	76 C2	Uren	78 H4	Utena	63 N9
Uchami	84 F4	Uludere	77 K4	Urengoy	84 B3	Uthal	92 C3
Ucharal	86 F2	Uluguru Mountains	107 G4	Ureparapara	114 T10	Utiariti	136 F6
Uchiura-wan	88 H4	Ulukisla	76 F4	Ures	126 G6	Utica	125 N5
Uchte	70 C2	Ulunkhan	85 J6	Urfa	77 H4	Utiel	67 F3
Uchur	85 N5	Ulus	76 E2	Urgal	85 N6	Utikuma Lake	119 M4
Uckermark	70 E2	Ulva	57 B4	Urgel, Llanos de	67 G2	Utkholok	85 T5
Uckfield	53 H4	Ulverston	55 F2	Urgench	80 G5	Utrecht	64 F2
Ucluelet	122 B3	Ulyanovsk	78 H5	Urgup	76 F3	Utrera	66 D4
Uda	85 N6	Ulysses	127 M2	Urho	86 F2	Utsera	77 K1
Udachnyy	84 J3	Ulzburg	70 C2	Uritskiy	84 Ae6	Utsjoki	62 M2
Udaipur	92 D4	Umala	138 C3	Urkan	85 M6	Utsonomiya	89 G7
Udayd, Ra's al	97 K4	Uman	79 E6	Urla	76 B3	Utta	79 H6
Udbina	72 C3	Uman	131 Q7	Urlingford	59 G7	Uttaradit	93 K5
Uddevalla	63 D7	Umanak Fjord	120 R3	Urmi	88 D1	Uttar Pradesh	92 F3
Uddjaur	62 G4	Umari	114 B2	Urosevac	73 F4	Uttoxeter	53 F2
Udine	68 D2	Umarkot	92 C3	Urr Water	57 E5	Uttyakh	85 N3
Udon Thani	93 K5	Umba	78 E2	Ursatyevskaya	86 B3	Utubulak	86 F2
Udskoye	85 N6	Umbertide	68 D4	Uruacu	137 H6	Utukok	118 C2
Udupi	92 D6	Umboi Island	114 D3	Uruapan	130 H8	Utupua	114 N7
Ueckermunde	70 F2	Umbro-Marchigiano,		Urubamba	136 C6	Uuldza	87 L2
Ueda	89 G7	Appennino	68 D4	Urubu	136 F4	Uummannaq	120 R3
Uele *Russia*	84 J2	Umea	62 J5	Urucui	137 J5	Uusikaarlepyy	62 K5
Uele *Zaire*	106 D2	Umealven	62 H4	Urucuia	138 G3	Uusikaupunki	63 J6
Uelen	81 V3	Umm al Qaywayn	97 M4	Urucui, Serra do	137 J5	Uusimaa	63 L6
Uelkal	85 Y3	Umm as Samim	97 M6	Uruguaiana	138 E5	Uvac	72 E4
Uelzen	70 D2	Umm Bel	102 E5	Uruguay	138 E6	Uvalde	127 N6
Ufa *Russia*	78 K4	Umm Keddada	102 E5	Urumchi	86 F3	Uvarovo	79 G5
Ufa *Russia*	78 K5	Umm Lajj	96 C4	Urumqi	86 F3	Uvea	111 T4
Ugab	108 B4	Umm Ruwaba	102 F5	Urupadi	137 F4	Uvinza	107 F4
Uganda	107 F2	Umm Said	97 K4	Urup, Ostrov	85 S7	Uvira	107 E3
Ugashik Bay	118 D4	Umm Urumah	96 C4	Uruti Point	115 F4	Uvol	114 E3
Ugashik Lakes	118 D4	Umnak Island	118 Ae9	Urville, Tanjung d'	114 B2	Uvs Nuur	86 G1
Ughelli	105 G4	Umred	92 E4	Uryupinsk	79 G5	Uwajima	89 D9
Ugijar	66 E4	Umtali	109 F3	Urzhum	78 H4	Uwayrid, Harrat al	96 C3
Uglich	78 F4	Umtata	108 E6	Urziceni	73 J3	Uy	84 Ad6
Ugljane	72 D4	Umzingwani	108 E4	Usa	78 K2	Uyak	118 E4
Ugra	78 E5	Una *Brazil*	137 K7	Usak	76 C3	Uyandina	85 Q3
Ugun	85 M5	Una *Bosnia-Herzegovina*	72 C3	Usambara Mountains	107 G3	Uyeg	78 J2
Ugurlu	77 J2	Unalaska Island	118 Ae9	Usedom	70 F1	Uyuni	138 C4
Ugurludag	76 F2	Unare	133 Q10	Ushant	64 A4	Uyuni, Salar de	138 C4
Ugut	84 A4	Unayzah	96 F3	Ushitsa	73 J1	Uz	71 K4
Uherske Hradiste	71 G4	Uncia	138 C3	Ushtobe	86 D2	Uzaym, Nahr al	94 G4
Uhlava	70 E4	Uncompahgre Peak	123 L8	Ushuaia	139 C10	Uzbekistan	86 B3
Uhrusk	71 K3	Uncompahgre Plateau	122 K8	Usk *Gwent, U.K.*	52 E3	Uzda	71 M2
Uig	56 B3	Underwood	123 P4	Usk *Powys, U.K.*	52 D3	Uzen	79 J7
Uige	106 C4	Unecha	79 E5	Usk Reservoir	52 D3	Uzerche	65 D6
Uil *Kazakhstan*	79 J6	Uneiuxi	136 D4	Uskudar	76 C2	Uzes	65 F6
Uil *Kazakhstan*	79 J6	Ungava Bay	121 N6	Uslar	70 C3	Uzhgorod	79 C6
Uinskoye	78 K4	Ungave, Peninsule d'	121 L5	Usman	79 F5	Uzhok	71 K4
Uinta Mountains	122 J7	Unggi	88 C4	Usolye	78 K4	Uzlovaya	78 F5
Uisong	89 B7	Uniao dos Palmares	137 K5	Usolye-Sibirskoye	84 G6	Uzumlu	76 D4
Uitenhage	108 E6	Uniao do Vitoria	138 E5	Uspenka	84 B6	Uzur	84 D6
Ujiji	107 E3	Unije	72 C3	Ussel	65 E6	Uzur dere	77 J2
Uji-shoto	89 B10	Unimak Island	118 Af9	Ussuri	88 E2	Uzurgol	77 J2
Ujjain	92 E4	Unimak Pass	118 Ae9	Ussuriysk	88 C4	Uzurisa	77 G2
Ujpest	72 E2	Unini	136 E4	Ust-Barguzin	84 H6	Uzunkopru	76 B2
Ujscie	71 G2	Union	129 M3	Ust-Belaya	85 W3	Uzunkuyu	76 B3

V

Vaajakoski	62	L5
Vaal	108	E5
Vaala	62	M4
Vaal Dam	108	E5
Vaasa *Finland*	62	J5
Vaasa *Finland*	62	K5
Vacaria	138	F5
Vacha	70	D3
Vache, Ile-a-	133	L5
Vadodara	92	D4
Vadso	62	N1
Vadu	73	K3
Vaduz	68	B2
Vaga	78	G3
Vagar	62	Z14
Vagay *Russia*	84	Ae5
Vagay *Russia*	84	Ae5
Vage	63	A6
Vaghena	114	H5
Vagnharad	63	G7
Vah	71	G5
Vaich, Loch	56	D3
Vainikkala	63	N6
Vaitupu	111	S3
Vakarel	73	G4
Vakfikebir	77	H2
Valaam, Ostrov	63	P6
Valandovo	73	G5
Valcheta	139	C8
Valday *Russia*	78	E4
Valday *Russia*	78	F3
Valdayskaya Vozvyshennost	78	E4
Valdemarsvik	63	G7
Valdepenas	66	E3
Valderaduey	66	D2
Valderrobres	67	G2
Valdes, Peninsula	139	D8
Valdez	118	F3
Valdivia	139	B7
Val-d'Or	125	M2
Valdosta	129	L5
Valdres	63	C6
Valea Lui Mihai	73	G2
Valenca	66	B2
Valenca	138	K6
Valenca do Piaui	137	J5
Valencay	65	D5
Valence	65	F6
Valencia *Spain*	67	F3
Valencia *Venezuela*	136	D1
Valencia de Alcantara	66	C3
Valencia de Don Juan	66	D1
Valencia, Golfo de	67	G3
Valencia Island	59	B9
Valencia, Lago de	133	P9
Valenciennes	64	E3
Valentim, Serra do	137	J5
Valentin	88	E4
Valentine	123	P6
Valenzuela	91	G3
Valera	136	C2
Valga	63	M8
Valiente, Peninsula	132	G10
Valjevo	72	E3
Valkininkay	71	L1
Valladolid *Mexico*	131	Q7
Valladolid *Spain*	66	D2
Vallasana de Mena	66	E1
Vallay	56	A3
Valle de la Pascua	136	D2
Valle de Santiago	131	J7
Valledupar	136	C1
Valle Grande	138	D3
Valle Hermosa	128	D8
Vallejo	126	A1
Vallenar	138	B5
Valletta	74	C5
Valley Falls	122	D6
Valleyview	119	M4
Vallgrund	62	J5
Vallimanca	139	D7
Vallo di Lucania	69	E5
Valls	67	G2
Valmiera	63	L8
Valognes	64	C4
Val-Paradis	125	L2
Valparaiso	129	J5
Valparaiso *Chile*	139	B6
Valparaiso *Mexico*	130	H6
Valpovo	72	E3
Valsjobyn	62	F4
Vals, Tanjung	114	B3
Valtos	56	B2
Valurfossen	63	B6
Valuyki	79	F5
Valverde	100	B3
Valverde de Jucar	66	E3
Valverde del Camino	66	C4
Van	77	K3
Vanadzor	77	L2
Vanajanselka	63	L6
Vanavona	114	H6
Van Buren *Arkansas*	128	E3
Van Buren *Maine*	125	S3
Van Canh	93	L6
Vancouver *Canada*	122	C3
Vancouver *U.S.A.*	122	C5
Vancouver Island	122	A2
Vanda	63	N6
Vandalia	124	F7
Vanderhoof	118	L5
Van Diemen, Cape	112	G1
Van Diemen Gulf	112	G1
Vanern	63	E7
Vanersborg	63	E7
Vanga	107	G3
Vangaindrano	109	J4
Van Golu	77	K3
Vangou	88	D4
Vangunu	114	J6
Van Horn	127	K5
Vanikoro Islands	114	N7
Vanimo	114	C2
Vanna	62	H1
Vannas	62	H5
Vannes	65	B5
Van Rees, Pegunungan	114	B2
Vanrhynsdorp	108	C6
Vanrock	113	J2
Vansbro	63	F6
Vanset	77	K4
Vansittart Island	120	K4
Vantaa	63	N6
Vanua Balavu	114	S8
Vanua Lava	114	T10
Vanua Levu	114	R8
Vanua Levu Barrier Reef	114	R8
Vanuatu	114	T12
Vanwyksvlei	108	D6
Vanzevat	84	Ae4
Vapnyarka	73	K1
Varallo	68	B3
Varamin	95	K4
Varanasi	92	F3
Varandey	78	K2
Varangerfjorden	62	P1
Varangerhalvoya	62	N1
Varazdin	72	D2
Varazze	68	B3
Varberg	63	E8
Vardar	73	F5
Varde	63	C9
Vardo	62	P1
Varena	71	L1
Varennes	65	E5
Varese	68	B3
Varfolomeyevka	88	D3
Vargarda	63	E7
Vargas Guerra	136	B4
Varginha	138	G4
Varilla	138	B4
Varkaus	63	L5
Varmland	63	E7
Varmlands-nas	63	E7
Varna	73	J4
Varnamo	63	F8
Varnek	84	Ad3
Varnya	84	A3
Varoy	62	E3
Varto	77	J3
Vartry Reservoir	59	K6
Varzea Grande	137	J5
Varzino	78	F2
Varzuga	78	F2
Varzy	65	E5
Vasa	62	J5
Vascao	66	C4
Vascongadas	66	E1
Vashkovtsy	73	H1
Vasilishki	71	L2
Vasilkov	79	E5
Vasilyevka	79	F6
Vaskha	78	H3
Vaslui	73	J2
Vassdalssegga	63	B7
Vasteras	63	G7
Vasterbotten	62	G4
Vasterdalalven	63	E6
Vastergotland	63	E7
Vasterhaninge	63	H7
Vasternorrland	62	G5
Vastervik	63	G8
Vastmanland	63	G7
Vasto	69	E4
Vasyugan	84	B5
Vatersay	57	A4
Vathi *Greece*	75	F3
Vathi *Greece*	75	J4
Vaticano, Capo	69	E6
Vatilau	114	J6
Vatnajokull	62	W12
Vatneyri	62	A2
Vatoa	111	T5
Vatomandry	109	J3
Vatra Dornei	73	H2
Vattern	63	F7
Vatu-i-Ra Channel	114	R8
Vatulele	114	Q9
Vaughn	127	K3
Vaupes	136	C3
Vavatenina	109	J3
Vavau Group	111	U5
Vavuniya	92	F7
Vaxholm	63	H7
Vaxjo	63	F8
Vayalpad	92	E6
Vaygach	84	Ac2
Vaygach, Ostrov	84	Ac2
Veberod	63	E9
Vebomark	62	J4
Vecht	64	G2
Vechta	70	C2
Vechte	70	B2
Veddige	63	E8
Vega *Norway*	62	D4
Vega *U.S.A.*	127	L3
Vegorritis, Limni	75	F2
Vegreville	119	N5
Veidholmen	62	B5
Veinge	63	E8
Vejen	63	C9
Vejer de la Frontera	66	D4
Vejle	63	C9
Velanidhia	75	G4
Velas, Cabo	132	E9
Velasco, Sierra de	138	C5
Velay, Monts du	65	E6
Velebit Planina	72	C3
Velestinon	75	G3
Velez Malaga	66	D4
Velez Rubio	67	E4
Velhas	138	H3
Velichayevskoye	79	H7
Velika Gorica	72	D3
Velika Kapela	72	C3
Velikaya *Russia*	78	H2
Velikaya *Russia*	85	W4
Velikaya Kema	88	F3
Veliki Kanal	72	E3
Velikiy Bereznyy	71	K4
Velikiye Luki	78	E4
Velikonda Range	92	E6
Veliko Turnovo	73	H4
Veliky Ustyug	78	H3
Velingara	104	C3
Velingrad	73	H4
Velizh	78	E4
Vella Gulf	114	H5
Vella Lavella	114	H5
Velletri	69	D5
Vellore	92	E6
Velsk	78	G3
Velt	78	J2
Velvestad	62	E4
Venado Tuerto	139	D6
Venafro	69	E5
Venaria	68	A3
Venda Nova	66	C2
Vendas Novas	66	B3
Vendome	65	D5
Vendsyssel	63	D8
Venecia	136	D6
Venezia	68	D3
Venezia, Golfo di	68	D3
Venezuela	136	D2
Venezuela Basin	134	C1
Venezuela, Golfo de	136	C1
Vengurla	92	D5
Veniaminof Volcano	118	Ag8
Venice *Italy*	68	D3
Venice *U.S.A.*	128	H6
Venkatapuram	92	F5
Venlo	64	G3
Vennesla	63	C7
Venta	63	J8
Ventimiglia	68	A4
Ventnor	53	F4
Ventry	59	B8
Ventspils	63	N8
Ventuari	136	D3
Ventura	126	C3
Venus Bay	113	K6
Venustiano Carranza *Mexico*	130	G5
Venustiano Carranza *Mexico*	131	N9
Vera *Argentina*	138	D5
Vera *Spain*	67	F4
Veracruz	131	L8
Veranopolis	138	F5
Veraval	92	D4
Verbania	68	B3
Vercelli	68	B3
Verdalsora	62	D5
Verde *Mexico*	131	L9
Verde *U.S.A.*	126	G3
Verden	70	C2
Verdigris	124	C8
Verdinho, Serra do	138	F3
Verdon	65	G7
Verdun	64	F4
Vereeniging	108	E5
Vereshchagino	78	J4
Verga, Cap	104	C3
Verin	66	C2
Verin Talin	77	K2
Verkhne-Avzyar	78	K5
Verkhnedvinsk	63	M9
Verkhne-Imanskiy	88	E3
Verkhneimbatskoye	84	D4
Verkhne Matur	84	D6
Verkhne Nildino	84	Ad4
Verkhne Skoblino	84	D5
Verkhnetulomskiy	62	P2
Verkhne Tura	78	K4
Verkhnevilyuysk	85	L4
Verkhniy Baskunchak	79	H6
Verkhniy Shar	78	J2
Verkhnyaya Amga	85	M5
Verkhnyaya Inta	78	L2
Verkhnyaya Toyma	78	H3
Verkhoturye	84	Ad5
Verkhovye	79	F5
Verkhoyansk	85	N3
Verkhoyanskiy Khrebet	85	M3
Verkhyaya Nildino	78	L3
Vermilion	119	N5
Vermilion Bay	128	G6
Vermilion Lake	124	D3
Vermillion	123	R6
Vermillion Bay	124	D2
Vermont	125	P5
Vernal	123	K7
Verneuil	64	D4
Vernon *Canada*	122	E2
Vernon *France*	64	D4
Vernon *U.S.A.*	127	N3
Veroia	75	G2
Verona	68	C3
Versailles	64	E4
Vert, Cape	104	B3
Verviers	64	F3
Vervins	64	E4
Veryan Bay	52	C4
Veryuvom	78	L2
Veshenskaya	79	G6
Veslos	63	C8
Veslyana	78	J3
Vesoul	65	G5
Vest-Agder	63	B7
Vesteralen	62	F2
Vestfjorden	62	F2
Vest-Fold	63	D7
Vestre Jakobselv	62	N1
Vestvagoy	62	E2
Vesuvio	69	E5
Vesyegonsk	78	F4
Veszprem	72	D2
Vetekhtina	85	K5
Vetlanda	63	F8
Vetluga *Russia*	78	H4
Vetluga *Russia*	78	H4
Vetluzskiy	78	H4
Vettore, Monte	69	D4
Veun Kham	93	L6
Veurne	64	E3
Vevey	68	A2
Veyatie, Loch	56	C2
Veyzelay	65	E5
Vezere	65	D6
Vezirkopru	76	F2
Viacha	138	C3
Viamao	138	F6
Viana	137	J4
Viana do Castelo	66	B2
Viangchan	93	K5
Viareggio	68	C4
Viaur	65	E6
Viborg	63	C8
Vibo Valentia	69	F6
Vicecomodoro Marambio	141	W6
Vicente Guerrero	130	H6
Vicenza	68	C3
Vich	67	H2
Vichada	136	D3
Vichuga	78	G4
Vichy	65	E5
Vicksburg	128	G4
Vico	69	B4
Vicosa	137	K5
Victor Emanuel Range	114	C3
Victor Harbor	113	H6
Victoria *Argentina*	138	D6
Victoria *Northern Territory, Australia*	112	G2
Victoria *Victoria, Australia*	113	J6
Victoria *Cameroon*	105	G5
Victoria *Canada*	122	C3
Victoria *Chile*	139	B7
Victoria *Hong Kong*	90	E1
Victoria *Malaysia*	90	F4
Victoria *Seychelles*	82	D7
Victoria *U.S.A.*	128	D6
Victoria de las Tunas	132	J4
Victoria Falls	108	E3
Victoria Island	119	P1
Victoria, Lake	107	F3
Victoria Land	141	L4
Victoria, Mount *Myanmar*	93	H4
Victoria, Mount *Papua New Guinea*	114	D3
Victoria Nile	107	F2
Victoria Peak	118	K5
Victoria Strait	119	Q2
Victoriaville	125	Q3
Victoria West	108	D6
Victorica	139	C7
Victorville	126	D3
Vidago	138	B6
Vidalia	129	L4
Vidareidi	62	Z14
Vididalur	62	X12
Vidim	84	G5
Vidimyri	62	V12
Vidin	73	G4
Vidisha	92	E4
Vidivellir	62	X12
Vidomlya	71	K2
Vidsel	62	J4
Viedma	139	D8
Viedma, Lago	139	B9
Viella	67	G1
Vienna *Austria*	68	F1
Vienna *Illinois*	124	F8
Vienna *Ohio*	125	K7
Vienne *France*	65	D5
Vienne *France*	65	F6
Vientiane	93	K5
Vieques	133	Q5
Vierwaldstatter See	68	B2
Vierzon	65	E5
Vieste	69	F5
Vietnam	93	L5
Vif	65	F6

Vigan 91 G2
Vigevano 68 B3
Viggiano 69 E5
Vigia 137 G4
Viglio, Monte 69 D5
Vigo 66 B1
Vigrestad 63 A7
Viiala 63 K6
Vijayawada 92 F5
Vijose 74 E2
Vik 62 E4
Vik 62 V13
Vikajarvi 62 M3
Vikersund 63 D7
Vikhorevka 84 G5
Vikna 62 D4
Viksoyri 63 B6
Vila 114 U12
Viladikars 77 K2
Vila Franca 66 B3
Vilaine 65 C5
Vilaller 67 G1
Vilanculos 109 G4
Vila Nova 137 F4
Vila Nova de Famalicao 66 B2
Vila Pouca de Aguiar 66 C2
Vila Real 66 C2
Vila Real de Santo Antonio 66 C4
Vila Velha 138 H4
Vila Velha de Rodao 66 C3
Vila Vicosa 66 C3
Vilcheka, Zemlya 80 H1
Viled 78 H3
Vileyka 71 M1
Vilhelmina 62 G4
Vilhena 136 E6
Viliga-Kushka 85 T4
Viljandi 63 L7
Vilkitskogo, Proliv 81 M2
Vilkovo 73 K3
Villa Abecia 138 C4
Villa Angela 138 D5
Villa Aroma 138 C3
Villa Bella 136 D6
Villa Bens 100 C3
Villablino 66 C1
Villacarrillo 66 E3
Villacastin 66 D2
Villach 68 D2
Villa Cisneros 100 B4
Villa Constitucion 138 D6
Villa de Cura 136 D2
Villadiego 66 D1
Villa Dolores 139 C6
Villafranca del Bierzo 66 C1
Villafranca de los Barros 66 C3
Villafranca del Penedes 67 G2
Villafranca di Verona 68 C3
Villaguay 138 E6
Villa Hayes 138 E5
Villahermosa 131 N9
Villa Huidobro 139 D6
Villa Iris 139 D7
Villajoyosa 67 F3
Villalba 66 C1
Villalon de Campos 66 D1
Villalpando 66 D2
Villa Maria 138 D6
Villamayor de Santiago 66 E3
Villa Montes 138 D4
Villanueva 130 H6
Villanueva de Cordoba 66 D3
Villanueva del Fresno 66 C3
Villanueva de los Castillejos 66 C4
Villanueva de los Infantes 66 E3
Villanueva y Geltru 67 G2
Villaputzu 69 B6
Villarcayo 66 E1
Villarejo 66 E2
Villarrica 138 E5
Villarrobledo 66 E3
Villasandino 66 D1
Villa Union *Argentina* 138 C5
Villa Union *Mexico* 127 M6
Villavicencio 136 C3
Villaviciosa 66 D1
Villazon 138 C4
Villedieu 64 C4
Villefort 65 E6
Villefranche-de-Rouergue 65 E6
Villefranche-sur-Saone 65 F6
Villena 67 F3
Villeneuve-sur-Lot 65 D6
Villeneuve-sur-Yonne 65 E4
Ville Platte 128 F5
Villers-Bocage 64 C4
Villers-Cotterets 64 E4
Villeurbanne 65 F6
Villodrigo 66 D1
Vilna 71 L1
Vilnius 71 L1
Vilnya 71 L1
Vilshofen 70 E4
Vilyuy 85 M4
Vilyuysk 85 L4
Vilyuyskoye Plato 84 H3
Vimmerby 63 F8
Vimperk 70 E4
Vina del Mar 139 B6
Vinaroz 67 G2
Vinas 63 F6
Vincennes 124 G7
Vincennes Bay 141 H5
Vinchina 138 C5
Vindelalven 62 J4
Vindeln 62 H4
Vindhya Range 92 E4
Vineland 125 N7
Vinga 73 F3
Vinh 93 L5
Vinh Loi 93 L7
Vinh Long 93 L6
Vinh Yen 93 L4
Vinica 73 G5
Vinkovci 72 E3
Vinnytsya 79 D6
Vinogradov 71 K4
Vipiteno 68 C2
Vir 72 C3
Virac 91 G3
Viramgam 92 D4
Virandozero 78 F3
Viransehir 77 H4
Virarajendrapet 92 E6
Virden 123 P3
Vire *France* 64 C4
Vire *France* 64 C4
Virfurile 73 G2
Virgenes, Cabo 139 C10
Virgin 126 E2
Virgin Gorda 133 Q5
Virginia *Ireland* 58 H5
Virginia *Minnesota* 124 D3
Virginia *U.S.A.* 125 L8
Virginia Beach 125 N8
Virginia Falls 118 L3
Virgin Islands 133 Q5
Virmasvesi 62 M5
Virovitica 72 D3
Virrat 63 K5
Virudunagar 92 E7
Vis 72 D4
Visalia 126 C2
Visayan Sea 91 G3
Visby 63 H8
Viscount Melville Sound 120 E3
Visegrad 72 E4
Viseu *Brazil* 137 H4
Viseu *Portugal* 66 C2
Vishakhapatnam 92 F5
Vishera 78 K3
Vishnevets 71 L4
Vislanda 63 F8
Visoko 72 E4
Viso, Monte 68 A3
Vista 126 D4
Vistonis, Limni 75 H2
Vit 73 H4
Vitava 70 F4
Viterbo 69 D4
Viterog Planina 72 D3
Vitiaz Strait 114 C3
Vitichi 138 C4
Vitigudino 66 C2
Viti Levu 114 Q9
Vitim *Russia* 85 J5
Vitim *Russia* 85 J5
Vitina 75 G4
Vitoria 66 E1
Vitoria 138 H4
Vitoria da Conquista 137 J6
Vitoria de Santa Antao 137 K5
Vitre 64 C4
Vitry-le-Francois 64 F4
Vitsyebsk 78 E4
Vittangi 62 J3
Vittel 64 F4
Vittoria 69 E7
Vittorio Veneto 68 D3
Vivarais, Monts du 65 F6
Viver 67 F3
Vivero 66 C1
Vivi *Russia* 84 F4
Vivi *Russia* 84 F4
Vizcaino, Desierto de 126 F7
Vizcaino, Sierra 126 E7
Vize 76 B2
Vizhas 78 H2
Vizianagaram 92 F5
Vizinga 78 J3
Vizzavona 69 B4
Vladicin Han 73 G4
Vladikavkaz 77 L1
Vladimir 78 G4
Vladimirets 71 M3
Vladimirovka 79 J5
Vladimir Volynskiy 71 L3
Vladivostok 88 C4
Vlakherna 75 G4
Vlasenica 72 E3
Vlieland 64 F2
Vlissingen 64 E3
Vlore 74 E2
Vodice 72 C4
Vodlozero, Ozero 78 F3
Vogan 105 F4
Voghera 68 B3
Voh 114 W16
Vohemar 109 J2
Vohilava 109 J4
Vohimarina 109 J2
Vohipeno 109 J4
Voi 107 G3
Voiron 65 F6
Vojens 63 C9
Vojmsjon 62 G4
Vojnic 72 C3
Volary 70 E4
Volborg 123 M5
Volchansk 79 F5
Volda 62 B5
Volga 79 H6
Volgodonsk 79 G6
Volgograd 79 G6
Volgogradskoye
Vodokhranilishche 79 H6
Volgsele 62 G4
Volissos 75 H3
Volkhov *Russia* 78 E4
Volkhov *Russia* 78 E4
Volklinger 70 B4
Volkovysk 71 L2
Volksrust 108 E5
Volnovakha 79 F6
Volochanka 84 E2
Volochayevka 88 E1
Volochisk 71 M4
Volodskaya 78 G3
Vologda 78 F4
Volokon 84 H5
Volonga 78 H2
Volos 75 G3
Voloshka 78 F3
Volovets 71 K4
Volozhin 71 M1
Volpa 71 L2
Volsk 79 H5
Volta 104 F4
Volta, Lake 104 E4
Volta Redonda 138 H4
Volterra 68 C4
Volteva 78 G3
Volturno 69 E5
Volvi, Limni 75 G2
Volynskaya Vozvyshennost 71 L3
Volynskoje Polesje 71 L3
Volzhskiy 79 G6
Von Martius, Cachoeira 137 G6
Vopnafjordur 62 X12
Voras Oros 75 F2
Vordingborg 63 D9
Voriai Sporadhes 75 H3
Vorkuta 78 L2
Vormsi 62 K7
Voronezh 79 F5
Voronovo 71 L1
Vorontsovo 63 N8
Voronya 78 F2
Voroshno 78 H4
Vortsjarv 63 M7
Voru 63 M8
Vosges 64 G4
Voskresensk 78 F4
Voss *Norway* 63 B6
Voss *Norway* 63 B6
Vostochno-Sibirskoye More 85 T2
Vostochnyy *Russia* 88 D4
Vostochnyy *Russia* 88 J1
Vostock 141 H3
Vostretsovo 88 E3
Votice 70 F4
Votkinsk 78 J4
Votkinskoye
Vodokhranilishche 78 K4
Vot Tande 114 T10
Vouga 66 C2
Vouziers 64 F4
Vowchurch 52 E2
Voxnan *Sweden* 63 F6
Voxnan *Sweden* 63 F6
Voynitsa 62 P4
Voy Vozh 78 J3
Voyvozh 78 K3
Voza 114 H5
Vozhayel 78 H3
Vozhega 78 G3
Vozhe, Ozero 78 F3
Voznesensk 79 E6
Voznesenye 78 F3
Vozvyshennost Karabil 95 R3
Vrancei, Muntii 73 J3
Vrangelya, Mys 85 P6
Vrangelya, Ostrov 81 U2
Vranje 73 F4
Vranov 71 J4
Vratsa 73 G4
Vrbas 72 D3
Vrbovsko 72 C3
Vrede 108 E5
Vrhnika 72 C3
Vrindavan 92 E3
Vrlika 72 D4
Vrondadhes 75 J3
Vrsac 73 F3
Vrsacki Kanal 73 F3
Vryburg 108 D5
Vryheid 108 F5
Vucitrn 73 F4
Vukovar 72 E3
Vulavu 114 J6
Vulcan 73 G3
Vulcano, Isola 69 E6
Vung Tau 93 L6
Vunisea 114 R9
Vuokatti 62 N4
Vuollerim 62 J3
Vyartsilya 62 P5
Vyatka 78 J4
Vyatskiye Polyany 78 J4
Vyazemskiy 88 E2
Vyazma 78 E4
Vyazniki 78 G4
Vyborg 63 N6
Vychegda 78 H3
Vydrino 84 F5
Vygoda 73 L2
Vygozero, Ozero 78 F3
Vyhorlat 71 K4
Vyksa 78 G4
Vym 78 J3
Vyrnwy 52 D2
Vyshniy-Volochek 78 E4
Vysokoye 71 K2
Vytegra 78 F3
Vyzhva 71 L3

W

Wa 104 E3
Waal 64 F3
Waat 103 F6
Wabana 121 R8
Wabasca 119 N4
Wabash 124 G7
Wabe Gestro Wenz 103 H6
Wabe Shabele Wenz 103 H6
Wabigoon Lake 124 D2
Wabowden 119 R4
Wabush 121 N7
Waccasassa Bay 129 L6
Waco 128 D5
Wad Banda 102 E5
Waddan 101 J3
Waddeneilanden 64 F2
Waddenzee 64 F2
Waddesdon 53 G3
Waddington, Mount 118 K5
Wadebridge 52 C4
Wadena 124 C3
Wadi Gimal 96 B4
Wadi Halfa 102 F3
Wad Medani 103 F5
Wadomari 89 J10
Wad Rawa 103 F4
Wafra 97 H2
Wager Bay 120 J4
Wagga Wagga 113 K6
Wagin 112 D5
Wahai 91 H6
Waharoa 115 E2
Wahiawa 126 R10
Wahibah, Ramlat ahl 97 P6
Wahidi 96 H9
Wahoo 123 R7
Wahpeton 123 R4
Waialua 126 R10
Waianae 126 R10
Waiau *New Zealand* 115 A6
Waiau *New Zealand* 115 D5
Waiau *New Zealand* 115 D5
Waibeem 91 J6
Waidhofen *Austria* 68 E2
Waidhofen *Austria* 68 E1
Waigeo 91 J6
Waiheke Island 115 E2
Waihi 115 E2
Waikabubak 91 F7
Waikato 115 E3
Waikerie 113 H5
Waikouaiti 115 C6
Wailuku 126 S10
Waimakariri 115 D5
Waimamaku 115 D1
Waimate 115 C6
Wainganga 92 E4
Waingapu 91 G7
Waini Point 136 F2
Wainwright 118 D1
Waiotapu 115 F3
Waiouru 115 E3
Waipa 115 E2
Waipahi 115 B7
Waipara 115 D5
Waipawa 115 F3
Waipiro 115 G3
Waipu 115 E1
Waipukurau 115 F3
Wairau 115 D4
Wairau Valley 115 D4
Wairio 115 B7
Wairoa 115 F3
Waitaki 115 C6
Waitangi 115 F6
Waitara 115 E3
Waitoa 115 E2
Waiuku 115 E2
Wajima 89 F7
Wajir 107 H2
Wakasa-wan 89 E8
Waka, Tanjung 91 H6
Wakatipu, Lake 115 B6
Wakaya 114 R8
Wakayama 89 E8
Wake 89 E8
Wakeeny 123 Q8
Wakefield 55 H3
Wakkanai 88 H3
Wakool *Australia* 113 J6
Wakool *Australia* 113 J6
Waku Kungo 106 C5
Walachia 73 H3
Walade 114 K6
Walagan 87 N1
Walbrzych 71 G3
Walcha 113 L5

Walcheren **64** E3
Walcz **71** G2
Waldenburg **71** G3
Waldon **52** C4
Waldron **128** E3
Waldshut **70** C5
Wales **118** A2
Wales Island **120** J4
Walgett **113** K4
Walikale **107** E3
Walinga **114** D3
Walker **122** E8
Walkeringham **55** J3
Walker Lake **122** E8
Wallace **129** P3
Wallaceburg **124** J5
Wallal Downs **112** E2
Wallasey **55** F3
Walla Walla **122** E4
Walldurn **70** C4
Wallhallow **113** H2
Wallingford **53** F3
Wallis, Iles **111** T4
Wallowa **122** F5
Walls **56** A1
Wallsend **55** H2
Walney, Island of **55** F2
Walpole **114** Y17
Walsall **53** F2
Walsenburg **127** K2
Walsingham, Cape **120** P4
Walsrode **70** C2
Walterboro **129** M4
Walter F. George Reservoir **129** K5
Waltham Abbey **53** H3
Walton **53** G3
Walvis Bay **108** B4
Wama **106** C5
Wamba *Nigeria* **105** G4
Wamba *Zaire* **106** C4
Wami **114** A2
Wana **92** C2
Wanaaring **113** J4
Wanaka **115** B6
Wanaka, Lake **115** B6
Wanapiri **91** K6
Wanapitei **124** K3
Wanda Shan **88** C3
Wandel Sea **140** P2
Wandingzhen **93** J4
Wanganui *New Zealand* **115** E3
Wanganui *New Zealand* **115** E3
Wangaratta **113** K6
Wangary **113** H5
Wangerooge **70** B2
Wangiwangi **91** G7
Wangjiadian **88** C2
Wangkui **87** P2
Wang, Mae Nam **93** J5
Wangqing **88** B4
Wanie-Rukula **106** E2
Wankaner **92** D4
Wankie **108** E3
Wanlaweyn **107** H2
Wanquan **87** L3
Wantage **53** F3
Wanxian **93** L2
Wanyuan **93** L2
Wanzai **93** M3
Wapenamanda **114** C3
Wapsipinicon **124** E5
Warangal **92** E5
Waratah Bay **113** K6
Warboys **53** G2
Warbreccan **113** J3
Warburg **70** C3
Warburton **113** H4
Ward **115** E4
Wardha **92** E4
Ward Hunt, Cape **114** D3
Ward Hunt Strait **114** E3
Ware *Canada* **118** K4
Ware *U.K.* **53** G3
Ware *U.S.A.* **125** P5
Wareham **53** E4
Waren *Germany* **70** E2
Waren *Indonesia* **91** K6
Warka **71** J3
Wark Forest **57** F5
Warkworth **115** E2
Warlingham **53** G3
Warmbad **108** C5
Warminster **53** E3
Warm Springs **126** D1
Warner Robins **129** L4
Warnow **70** D2
Warora **92** E4
Warracknabeal **113** J6
Warrego **113** K5
Warren *Minnesota* **124** B2
Warren *Ohio* **125** K6
Warren *Pennsylvania* **125** L6
Warrenpoint **58** K4
Warrenton *South Africa* **108** D5
Warrenton *U.S.A.* **125** M7
Warri **105** G4
Warrina **113** H4
Warrington *U.K.* **55** G3
Warrington *U.S.A.* **129** J5
Warrior Reefs **114** C3
Warrnambool **113** J6
Warroad **124** C2
Warsaw **71** J2
Warshiikh **107** J2
Warsop **55** H3
Warszawa **71** J2
Warta **71** G2
Waru **91** J6
Warwick *Australia* **113** L4
Warwick *U.K.* **53** F2
Warwick *U.S.A.* **125** Q6
Warwick Channel **113** H1
Warwickshire **53** F2
Wasbister **56** E1
Wasco **126** C3
Wasdale Head **55** F2
Washburn Lake **119** P1
Washim **92** E4
Washington *U.K.* **55** H2
Washington *District of Columbia* 125 M7
Washington *Georgia* **129** L4
Washington *Indiana* **124** G7
Washington *Missouri* **124** E7
Washington *N. Carolina* **129** P3
Washington *Pennsylvania* **125** K6
Washington *U.S.A.* **122** D4
Washington Cape **141** M4
Washington Land **120** N1
Washington, Mount **125** Q4
Wash, The **53** H2
Wasian **91** J6
Wasior **91** J6
Wasisi **91** H6
Waskaganish **121** L7
Waspan **132** E7
Wast Water **55** F2
Watam **114** C2
Watampone **91** G6
Watansoppeng **91** F6
Watchet **52** D3
Waterbeach **53** H2
Waterbury **125** P6
Wateree **129** M3
Waterford *Ireland* **59** G8
Waterford *Ireland* **59** H8
Watergrasshill **59** F8
Waterloo *Belgium* **64** F3
Waterloo *U.S.A.* **124** D5
Waterlooville **53** F4
Waternish **56** B3
Waternish Point **56** B3
Waterside **57** D5
Watertown *New York* **125** N4
Watertown *S. Dakota* **123** R5
Watertown *Wisconsin* **124** F5
Waterville *Ireland* **59** B9
Waterville *U.S.A.* **125** R4
Watford **53** G3
Watford City **123** N4
Watheroo **112** D5
Watkaremoana, Lake **115** F3
Watling Island **133** K2
Watlington **53** F3
Watroa **115** F3
Watsa **107** E2
Watseka **124** G6
Watson **123** M1
Watson Lake **118** K3
Watsonville **126** B2
Watten **56** E2
Watten, Loch **56** E2
Watton **53** H2
Watubela, Kepulauan **91** J6
Wau *Papua New Guinea* **114** D3
Wau *Sudan* **102** E6
Wauchope **113** G3
Waukarlycarly, Lake **112** E3
Waukegan **124** G5
Waurika **128** D3
Wausau **124** F4
Wave Hill **112** G2
Waveney **53** J2
Waverly **125** M5
Wavre **64** F3
Wawa **124** H3
Waxahachie **128** D4
Waya **114** Q8
Wayabula **91** H5
Waycross **129** L5
Way, Lake **112** E4
Waynesboro *Georgia* **129** L4
Waynesboro *Mississippi* **128** H5
Waynesboro *Pennsylvania* **125** M7
Waynesburg **125** K7
Waynesville *Missouri* **124** D8
Waynesville *Tennessee* **129** L3
Waynoka **128** C2
Wda **71** H2
We **90** B4
Wé **114** X16
Weald, The **53** H3
Wear **55** H2
Weardale **55** H2
Weasenham **53** H2
Weatherall Bay **120** E2
Weatherford **128** C3
Weaver **55** G3
Webi Shabeelle **103** J7
Webster **123** R5
Webster City **124** D5
Weda **91** H5
Weddell Sea **141** W4
Wedel **70** C2
Weduar, Tanjung **91** J7
Weeley **53** J3
Weemelah **113** K4
Wegorzewo **71** J1
Wegorzyno **70** F2
Weichang **87** M3
Weiden **70** E4
Weifang **87** M4
Weihai **87** N4
Weihe **88** B3
Wei He **93** L2
Weilu **87** L3
Weimar **70** D3
Weinan **93** L2
Weingarten **70** C5
Weiser **122** F5
Weissenburg **70** D4
Weissenfels **70** D3
Weiss Lake **129** K3
Weitra **68** E1
Weixin **93** K3
Wejherowo **71** H1
Welch **125** K8
Welcome Kop **108** C6
Welda **70** E3
Weldiya **103** G5
Welkom **108** E5
Welland **53** G2
Wellesley Islands **113** H2
Wellingborough **53** G2
Wellington *New Zealand* **115** E4
Wellington *South Africa* **108** C6
Wellington *Shropshire, U.K.* **52** E2
Wellington *Somerset, U.K.* **52** D4
Wellington *Kansas* **128** D2
Wellington *Texas* **127** M3
Wellington Channel **120** H2
Wellington, Isla **139** B9
Wells *U.K.* **52** E3
Wells *U.S.A.* **122** G7
Wellsford **115** E2
Wells-next-the-Sea **53** H2
Welney **53** H2
Wels **68** D1
Welshpool **52** D2
Welwyn Garden City **53** G3
Wemindji **121** L7
Wenasaga **123** T2
Wenatchee **122** D4
Wenchang **93** M5
Wenchuan **93** K2
Wendover **122** G7
Wengen **68** A2
Wenling **87** N6
Wenlock Edge **52** E2
Wenshan **93** K4
Wensleydale **55** H2
Wensu **86** E3
Wen Xian **93** K2
Wenzhou **87** N6
Wepener **108** E5
Weri **91** J6
Wernigerode **70** D3
Werra **70** D3
Werris Creek **113** L5
Wertach **70** D4
Weser **70** C2
Weslaco **128** D7
Wessel Islands **113** H1
West Auckland **55** H2
West Bay **128** H6
West Bengal **93** G4
West Branch Susquehanna **125** M6
West Bromwich **53** E2
Westbrook **125** Q5
West Burra **56** A2
Westbury **53** E3
Westbury-sub-Mendip **52** E3
Westby **124** E5
West Calder **57** E5
West End **129** N7
Westerdale **55** J2
Westerham **53** H3
Westerland **70** C1
Western Australia **112** E3
Western Desert **103** E2
Western Ghats **92** D5
Western Isles **56** A3
Westernport **125** L7
Western Ross **56** C3
Western Sahara **100** C4
Western Samoa **111** U4
Westerschelde **64** E3
Westerstede **70** B2
Westerwald **70** B3
West Falkland **139** E10
Westfield *U.K.* **56** E2
Westfield *Massachusetts* **125** P5
Westfield *New York* **125** L5
West Frankfort **124** F8
Westgate **55** G2
West Gerinish **56** A3
West Glamorgan **52** D3
West Glen **53** G2
West Harptree **52** E3
West Heslerton **55** J2
West Hoathly **53** G3
West Indies **48** D4
West Kilbride **57** D5
West Kirby **55** F3
West Linton **57** E5
Westlock **119** N5
Westmeath **59** G6
West Memphis **128** G3
West Meon **53** F3
West Mersea **53** H3
West Midlands **53** F2
West Moors **53** F4
Westmoreland **113** H2
Weston **125** K7
Weston-Super-Mare **52** E3
West Palm Beach **129** M7
West Plains **124** E8
West Point *Mississippi* **128** H4
West Point *Nebraska* **123** R7
Westport *Ireland* **58** C5
Westport *New Zealand* **115** C4
Westport Quay **58** C5
Westray **56** F1
Westray Firth **56** E1
West Road **118** L5
West Sussex **53** G4
West Tavaputs Plateau **122** J8
West Virginia **125** K7
West Wellow **53** F4
West Wyalong **113** K5
West Yellowstone **122** J5
West Yorkshire **55** H3
Wetar **91** H7
Wetar, Selat **91** H7
Wetaskiwin **119** N5
Wetherby **55** H3
Wewahitchka **129** K5
Wewak **114** C2
Wexford *Ireland* **59** J8
Wexford *Ireland* **59** K8
Wexford Bay **59** K8
Wey **53** G3
Weybridge **53** G3
Weyburn **123** N3
Weyhill **53** F3
Weymouth **52** E4
Weymouth Bay *Australia* **113** J1
Weymouth Bay *U.K.* **52** E4
Whakataki **115** F4
Whakatane **115** F2
Whalsay **56** A1
Whanganui Inlet **115** D4
Whangaparaoa **115** G2
Whangarei **115** E1
Whangaruru Harbour **115** D1
Whaplode **53** G2
Wharanui **115** E4
Wharfe **55** H2
Wharfedale **55** H3
Wharton **128** D6
Whataroa **115** C5
Wheatland **123** M6
Wheatley *Nottinghamshire, U.K.* **55** J3
Wheatley *Oxfordshire, U.K.* **53** F3
Wheeler Peak **122** G8
Wheeling **125** K6
Whernside **55** G2
Whidbey, Point **113** H5
Whitburn *Lothian, U.K.* **57** E5
Whitburn *Tyne and Wear, U.K.* **55** H2
Whitby **55** J2
Whitchurch *Avon, U.K.* **52** E3
Whitchurch *Hampshire, U.K.* **53** F3
Whitchurch *Shropshire, U.K.* **52** E2
White *Canada* **118** G3
White *Arkansas* **128** G3
White *Indiana* **124** G7
White *Missouri* **124** D8
White *S. Dakota* **123** P6
White *Texas* **127** M4
Whiteadder Reservoir **57** F5
White Bay **121** Q7
Whitecourt **119** M5
Whitefish **122** G3
Whitefish Lake **119** P3
Whitefish Point **124** H3
White Gull Lake **121** P6
Whitehall **125** P5
White Handkerchief, Cape **121** P6
Whitehaven **55** F2
Whitehead **58** L3
Whitehorse **118** H3
Whitehorse Hill **53** F3
White Island **115** F2
White, Lake **112** F3
White Lake **128** F6
Whiteman Range **114** E3
White Mountains **118** F2
White Mount Peak **122** E9
Whitemouth **124** B2
Whiten Head **56** D2
Whiteparish **53** F3
White Pass **118** H4
White River **124** H2
White River Plateau **123** L8
White Salmon **122** D5
White Sea **78** F2
White Sulphur Springs **122** J4
White Volta **104** E4
Whitewater **124** F5
Whitewood **123** N2
Whitfield Moor **55** G2
Whithorn **54** E2
Whiting Bay **57** C5
Whitley Bay **55** H1
Whitmore **52** E2
Whitney, Mount **126** C2
Whitney-on-Wye **52** D2
Whitsand Bay **52** C4
Whitstable **53** J3
Whittlesey **53** G2
Whitton **55** J3
Whittonstall **55** H2
Whitworth **55** G3

X

Y

Z